GREGORY OF NYSSA:
HOMILIES ON THE SONG OF SONGS

Society of Biblical Literature

Writings from the Greco-Roman World

John T. Fitzgerald, General Editor

Editorial Board

Number 13

Gregory of Nyssa:
Homilies on the Song of Songs

Volume Editors
Brian E. Daley, S.J., and John T. Fitzgerald

GREGORY OF NYSSA:
HOMILIES ON THE SONG OF SONGS

Translated with an Introduction and Notes

by

Richard A. Norris Jr.

Society of Biblical Literature
Atlanta

GREGORY OF NYSSA:
HOMILIES ON THE SONG OF SONGS

Copyright © 2012 by the Society of Biblical Literature

Library of Congress Cataloging-in-Publication Data

Gregory, of Nyssa, Saint, ca. 335–ca. 394.
    [Commentarius in Canticum canticorum. English]
    Homilies on the Song of songs / Gregory of Nyssa ; translated with an introduction and notes by Richard A. Norris Jr.
        p. cm. — (Writings from the Greco-Roman world ; v. 13)
    Includes bibliographical references and indexes.
    ISBN-13: 978-1-58983-105-6 (paper binding : alk. paper)
    ISBN-10: 1-58983-105-5 (paper binding : alk. paper)
    ISBN-13: 978-1-58983-787-4 (hardcover binding : alk. paper)
    1. Bible. O.T. Song of Solomon—Commentaries. 2. Bible. O.T. Song of Solomon—Sermons. 3. Sermons, Greek—Translations into English. I. Norris, Richard A. (Richard Alfred), 1930–2005. II. Title. III. Series.
    BR65.G75C6513 2012
    223'.907—dc22   2006008712

Printed on acid-free, recycled paper conforming to
ANSI/NISO Z39.48-1992 (R1997) and ISO 9706:1994
standards for paper permanence.

CONTENTS

Foreword.. vii
Abbreviations ix

Introduction: Gregory of Nyssa and His Fifteen
Homilies on the Song of Songs.. xiii
    1. Gregory of Nyssa: Background, Life, and Major Writings   xiii
        Historical Context   xiii
        Career and Major Writings   xv
        The Homilies on the Song   xx
    2. The Themes, Method, and Sources of Gregory's
        Interpretation of the Song   xxiii
        The Problem of "Allegory"   xxiii
        Structures of Reality   xxiv
        The Question of Σκοπός   xxix
        The Question of Ἀκολουθία   xxxviii
        The Allegory of the Song of Songs   xliv

HOMILIES ON THE SONG OF SONGS

Preface..2
Homily 1 14
Homily 2 46
Homily 3 78
Homily 4 110
Homily 5 148
Homily 6 182
Homily 7 212
Homily 8 256
Homily 9 276
Homily 10 310
Homily 11 332
Homily 12 360
Homily 13 390
Homily 14 422

Homily 15 456

Bibliography 501
Index of Biblical References 505
Index of Modern Authors 517

FOREWORD

Richard A. Norris (1930–2005) was one of the great patristic scholars of modern times. Readers who wish to know more about Norris as a person, scholar, and theologian can gain valuable insights into him by reading the special issue of *Anglican Theological Review* (90:3) that was published in honor of his numerous contributions (2008). He was especially interested in the history of biblical interpretation, and one of the texts to which he devoted particular attention was the Song of Songs. A highly influential patristic interpreter of this text was Gregory of Nyssa (ca. 335–395 C.E.), whose fifteen homilies on the Song are translated by Norris in this volume.

Norris submitted the final portion of his manuscript approximately six weeks before his death. Preparing it for press has presented a significant number of daunting challenges, and these have resulted in a much more protracted process than we had initially envisioned. We deeply regret that Norris was not able to offer us his sagacious counsel on various matters, but we trust that he would be pleased with the final result. We are proud to have played a small part in making the fruits of his scholarship accessible to a wider reading audience.

The Greek text that Norris used for his translation is that of Hermann Langerbeck, which was published in 1960 as volume 6 of Werner Jaeger's edition of the works of Gregory of Nyssa (Gregorii Nysseni Opera). This text, minus the critical apparatus, accompanies Norris's translation. The numbers that appear to the right of the Greek text indicate the page number of Langerbeck's edition. When Norris in his footnotes refers to "Jaeger," he is referring to the GNO edition as a whole, though the specific reference is usually to Langerbeck's edition of Gregory's homilies on the Song of Songs. We wish to express our gratitude to Brill for permission to include the text in this Writings from the Greco-Roman World volume.

There are many people who have helped us prepare this volume for publication, but there are five individuals in particular to whom we wish to express our gratitude. They are Brent Nongbri and Justin Schedtler for checking the Greek text against that of Langerbeck; Margaret M. Mitchell for reading through the first proofs of this volume and supplying us with a list of errata

and helpful suggestions, especially in regard to the introduction, Gregory's preface to his homilies, and Homily 1; Hans Boersma, who called our attention to several cases of omitted words and misplaced accents; and Bob Buller, the Editorial Director of the Society of Biblical Literature, who copyedited the manuscript and alerted us to various potential problems. Although there are doubtless remaining errors that we did not detect, these five individuals helped us to reduce the number of such instances contained in this volume.

Brian E. Daley, S.J.
John T. Fitzgerald

ABBREVIATIONS

Abr.	Philo, *De Abrahamo* (*On the Life of Abraham*)
ACW	Ancient Christian Writers
Apol. Hex.	Gregory of Nyssa, *Apologia in Hexaemeron* (*In Defense of the Hexaemeron*)
Barn.	*Barnabas*
Beat.	Gregory of Nyssa, *De beatitudinibus* (*On the Beatitudes*)
C. Ar.	Athanasius, *Orationes contra Arianos* (*Orations against the Arians*)
Cael.	Aristotle, *De caelo* (*Heavens*)
Cat. Cant.	Procopius, *Catena in Canticum canticorum* (*Catena on the Song of Songs*)
CCSL	Corpus Christianorum Series latina
Cher.	Philo, *De cherubim* (*On the Cherubim*)
Comm. Cant.	Origen, *Commentarius in Canticum* (*Commentary on the Song of Songs*)
Comm. Jo.	Origen, *Commentarii in evangelium Joannis* (*Commentary on the Gospel of John*)
Conf.	Philo, *De confusione linguarum* (*On the Confusion of Tongues*)
CSEL	Corpus scriptorum ecclesiasticorum latinorum
CWS	Classics of Western Spirituality
De an.	Gregory of Nyssa, *De anima et resurrectione* (*On the Soul and the Resurrection*)
Div.	Cicero, *De divinatione* (*On Divination*)
Ebr.	Philo, *De ebrietate* (*On Drunenness*)
Enn.	Plotinus, *Enneades*
Ep.	Basil, *Epistulae* (*Letters*)
Eth. nic.	Aristotle, *Ethica nichomachea* (*Nichomachean Ethics*)
Eun.	Gregory of Nyssa, *Contra Eunomium* (*Against Eunomius*)
Exc.	Clement of Alexandria, *Excerpta ex Theodoto* (*Excerpts from Theodotus*)
Exp. Cant.	Gregory the Great, *Expositio in Canticum canticorum* (*Exposition of the Song of Songs*)

FC	Fathers of the Church
GCS	Die griechische christliche Schriftsteller der ersten [drei] Jahrhunderte
GNO	Gregorii Nysseni Opera. Edited by Werner Jaeger et al.
Her.	Philo, *Quis rerum divinarum heres sit* (*Who Is the Heir?*)
Hex.	Basil, *Homiliae in Hexaemeron* (*Homilies on the Hexaemeron = Homilies on the Six Days of Creation*)
Hist. an.	Aristotle, *Historia animalium* (*History of Animals*)
Hom. Exod.	Origen, *Homiliae in Exodum* (*Homilies on Exodus*)
Inscr. Pss.	Gregory of Nyssa, *In inscriptiones Psalmorum* (*On the Titles of the Psalms*)
Isaac	Ambrose of Milan, *De Isaac vel anima* (*Isaac, or The Soul*)
Jaeger	See GNO
JTS	*Journal of Theological Studies*
LCL	Loeb Classical Library
LXX	Septuagint
Metaph.	Aristotle, *Metaphysica* (*Metaphysics*)
Midr. Rab.	*Midrash Rabbah*
Mos.	Philo, *De vita Mosis* (*On the Life of Moses*)
Mut.	Philo, *De mutatione nominum* (*On the Change of Names*)
Nat.	Pliny the Elder, *Naturalis historia* (*Natural History*)
Nat. an.	Aelian, *De natura animalium* (*On the Nature of Animals*)
NPNF[2]	Nicene and Post-Nicene Fathers, Series 2
Opif.	Philo, *De opificio mundi* (*On the Creation of the World*)
Opif. hom.	Gregory of Nyssa, *De opificio hominis* (*On the Creation of Humanity*)
Paed.	Clement of Alexandria, *Paedagogus* (*Christ the Educator*)
PG	Patrologia graeca [= Patrologiae cursus completus: Series graeca]. Edited by J.-P. Migne. 162 vols. Paris, 1857–86.
Phaed.	Plato, *Phaedo*
Phaedr.	Plato, *Phaedrus*
Poet.	Aristotle, *Poetica* (*Poetics*)
Princ.	Origen, *De principiis* (*First Principles*)
Prot.	Plato, *Protagoras*
REAug	*Revue des Études Augustiniennes*
Reg. fus.	Basil of Caesarea, *Regulae fusius tractatae* (*Longer Rules*)
Res.	Methodius, *De resurrectione* (*On the Resurrection*)
Resp.	Plato, *Respublica* (*Republic*)
RSV	Revised Standard Version
SBLWGRW	Society of Biblical Literature Writings from the Greco-Roman World

SC	Sources chrétiennes. Paris: Cerf, 1943–.
StPatr	Studia patristica
SVF	*Stoicorum veterum fragmenta*. Hans Friedrich August von Arnim. 4 vols. Leipzig: Teubner, 1903–24.
Symp.	Methodius, *Symposium (Convivium decem virginum)*
Theaet.	Plato, *Theaetetus*
Tim.	Plato, *Timaeus*
TLZ	*Theologische Literaturzeitung*
TP	*Theologie und Philosophie*
TU	Texte und Untersuchungen
VC	*Vigiliae christianae*
Virg.	Gregory of Nyssa, *De virginitate* (*On Virginity*)
Vit. Mos.	Gregory of Nyssa, *De vita Mosis* (*Life of Moses*)

INTRODUCTION: GREGORY OF NYSSA
AND HIS FIFTEEN *HOMILIES ON THE SONG OF SONGS*

1. Gregory of Nyssa: Background, Life, and Major Writings

Historical Context

Gregory of Nyssa was the youngest among the threesome commonly referred to as "the Cappadocian Fathers." The other two were his older brother Basil (called "the Great") and Basil's friend from their student days in Athens, Gregory of Nazianzus (called "the Theologian"). Taken together, these three men—temperamentally very different from each other, to say the least—are remembered as the principal theological architects of the victory of Nicene orthodoxy over the various forms and degrees of Arianism at the "ecumenical" Council of Constantinople (381). At the same time, they were in their different manners leaders of the ascetic or "monastic" movement in Asia Minor, organizing its communities, popularizing its ideals, and evolving the "theory" that guided its practice. To be sure, they did not stand alone in these enterprises. If one is to speak of "the Cappadocians," one must think not only of these three men but also, at the very least, of the larger familial circle to which they belonged: Basil and Gregory's sister Macrina the Younger, who presided over a "double" monastery on their ancestral estate; their younger brother Peter, bishop of Sebaste; and Gregory Nazianzen's cousin Amphilochius, the bishop of Iconium.

Basil, Gregory, and Peter were the children of another Basil ("the Elder") and his wife Emmelia. Basil the Elder (d. 341) had been a prominent rhetorician in the city of Neocaesarea. His mother, Macrina the Elder, had been martyred in the persecutions of the early fourth century and had been a disciple of Gregory Thaumaturgus (d. ca. 270), himself a pupil of Origen and a native (later the bishop) of Neocaesarea. Basil the Great and Gregory of Nyssa stemmed, then, from an established, landed, and aristocratic family with roots in the region of Pontus embraced by the course of the river Iris as it flowed into the Black Sea, a region that had Neocaesarea as its urban focus. Theirs was also a family marked by deep commitment to

Christian faith and by a tradition of attachment to the calling and skills of the rhetorician.

Gregory's older brother Basil (d. 379) was the one of the three Cappadocians who had the qualities of a natural "leader." For all his ascetic style of life, he was plainly impressive, and more than just impressive, as a figure in the public sphere. He had political skills of a high order together with a dutiful grasp of the uses of power—not to mention something of a genius for organization, as revealed in his work of disseminating and ordering the ascetic movement in his region. Beyond all that, Basil exhibited a remarkable social vision combined with genuine theological acumen. He had enjoyed the best of educations for his day. He had studied rhetoric at Caesarea in Cappadocia (present-day Kayseri), at Constantinople (under the great Libanius), and, finally, in 351, at Athens. There he met his best friend and temperamental opposite, Gregory of Nazianzus, perhaps the most brilliant rhetorician of his time, a self-scrutinizing, sometimes moody poet with a marked tendency, to say the least, to find ways out of public office and the responsibilities and ambiguities that attend it. From Athens, Basil moved back to Caesarea, and there he taught rhetoric from around 355 until 357, at which time he underwent what might best be called a conversion, was baptized, and undertook a tour of the principal sites where the ascetical movement had blossomed in Egypt and Palestine/Syria. Returning to Asia Minor, he sold his possessions and retired to practice the contemplative life on a site by the Iris River near Neocaesarea. There a small community was gradually formed as he was joined by others and, for a short time, by Gregory of Nazianzus. There too he and Gregory put together a now famous anthology of the works of Origen (the *Philokalia*), a book that nicely defines the intellectual tradition in which the Cappadocians consciously, but never uncritically, stood.

Permanent withdrawal from the public realm, however, was really not in Basil's nature. In 364, at the request of the bishop of Caesarea, one Eusebius, he emerged from his retreat, became a presbyter of that church, and, indeed, not without the help of his friend Nazianzen, succeeded Eusebius on the latter's death in 370. Thus he found himself in the position of a metropolitan bishop and was thrust into the midst of the Trinitarian controversy at a time when imperial policy had set itself firmly against the Nicene cause.

It is against the background thus sketched of the life of Basil that one does best to introduce an account of the life and works of Gregory of Nyssa, for if anything is clear about Gregory, it is that he regarded Basil as his leader and teacher and that he devoted himself loyally throughout his career not merely to the defense of Basil's reputation but to the furtherance of his causes. The same, indeed, might be said of his relation to his older sister Macrina, whom he venerated; after her death he wrote a biography of her that qualifies as a

piece of highly sophisticated hagiography, and in a major work, his dialogue *De anima et resurrectione* (*On the Soul and the Resurrection*), he attributes to her many of what posterity has taken to be his own characteristic ideas. While, then, one may suspect that Gregory was being entirely too modest in his estimate of the influence of Basil and Macrina on his thought, one cannot doubt that he consciously saw himself in the role of a disciple—and creative interpreter—of his two elder siblings.

Career and Major Writings

No one is perfectly sure of the year of Gregory's birth, or, for that matter, of Basil's. If Basil was born in 329 or 330, as seems reasonably likely, then Gregory, whose reverence for his brother might plausibly be taken to indicate a significant difference in their ages, most probably came along between 335 and 340.[1] His education was undertaken at home, in local schools, unlike Basil's, and it was Basil who taught him rhetoric at Caesarea in the years 355–357. There was, of course, more to Gregory's education than this; no one can read his writings without recognizing not merely that that his mind was well stocked but also that he was endowed with a natively curious and questing intellect as well as the instincts and talents of a systematizer. His works exhibit an acquaintance with the biological, medical, and physical science of his day (which he uses for more than just illustration), with the Greek philosophical tradition (Platonic, Aristotelian, Stoic, Neo-Pythagorean) as that had been pulled together in Middle and Neo-Platonism, and, needless to say, with the theory and practice of Greek rhetoric, a discipline whose practice he seems to have enjoyed, though without the *gravitas* of his brother's style or the brilliance of that of his namesake of Nazianzus.

Little is known of the events of Gregory's life before, say, 370. It is clear that, following in Basil's footsteps, he too took up the profession of a rhetor, perhaps around 364, when the emperor Julian's decree forbidding Christians to teach the classical subjects was repealed.[2] It is also clear that he married around this time. This is evident from his remarks, in the early treatise *De virginitate* (*On Virginity*), on the relative merits of the married and the celibate conditions; the full joys—and freedom—of the virgin state can never be his, he says, for he is separated from them by the "chasm" created by his participation in "the life of this world."[3] As Daniélou observed, however, this passage, while it leaves open the question whether Gregory kept his wife after

---

1. See May 1971, 53.
2. Ibid.
3. *Virg.* 3 (in GNO 8.1:256).

his elevation to the episcopate, nevertheless suggests that he did not himself undertake the monastic life,[4] and Daniélou thought it more than likely, in the light of a letter that Gregory received from Gregory of Nazianzus on the death of one Theosebeia, that the latter was Nyssen's wife at the time of her death.[5] There are difficulties with this interpretation of the evidence,[6] but there is no doubt whatever that Gregory had refused an early invitation of Basil's to join him in the ascetical community that was taking shape in the north at Annesi and that it was in 372, when he was still following the career of a rhetor in Caesarea, that Basil summoned him to surrender that vocation and become the first bishop of the city of Nyssa, an insignificant town slightly north and west of Caesarea, which Basil created as a bishopric in order to reinforce his own authority and with it the strength of the Nicene cause. This was Basil's response to an imperial effort to diminish both by splitting the province of Cappadocia in two and assigning the southern sector of it to the metropolitical jurisdiction of the Arian bishop of Tyana. Gregory reluctantly allowed himself to be installed in this post just before Easter 372.[7]

Gregory was not a success as bishop of Nyssa, at least not from Basil's point of view. He, of course, came under theological attack at the hands of Eustathius, then the bishop of Sebaste, for his stand in favor of the deity of the Holy Spirit, classically defended by Basil in his treatise *De Spiritu Sancto* (*On the Holy Spirit*) of 375.[8] Gregory's real difficulties began, however, when, with the imperially sponsored Homœan party taking the initiative, he contrived to get himself accused in 375 both of mishandling church finances and of a violation of canon law in the process of his appointment as bishop of Nyssa. Taken ill (with a chill and a kidney complaint, as Basil insists in his *Ep.* 225), Gregory was unable to answer a summons to appear before the court of the imperial vicar of Pontus, one Demosthenes. Instead, he retired somewhere to recover and was exiled and then deposed from his see in 376.[9] It is not known where he spent his exile, but he was restored in 378—no doubt after the battle of Adrianople, which occurred in August of that year and in which Emperor Valens, the imperial supporter of the Arian cause, was killed. Basil himself died in the very next year, and Gregory was present at his brother's

---

4. Daniélou 1956, 72. Daniélou described *De virginitate* as an "encomium on Basilian monachism written by a married layperson" (ibid.).

5. PG 37:321B.

6. See the judgments of May 1971, 53; Aubineau 1966, 65–77.

7. Basil also assigned his friend Gregory of Nazianzus to the new see of Sasima, but Gregory disliked the place intensely (not without justification) and for all practical purposes declined the honor.

8. See Basil, *Ep.* 237.

9. See ibid., 231 and 237.

end, reflecting, no doubt, on the misfortune that Basil should die just as the Nicene cause was being vindicated by the appointment of Theodosius I ("the Great") as emperor in the East.

For the period between Basil's elevation to the see of Caesarea and his death (370–379), little can be known with assurance of Gregory's literary production. It is generally agreed that the treatise *De virginitate* was produced during this period, though the precise date of 371, defended by Daniélou,[10] has been questioned, and some have located the treatise *De perfectione* (*On Perfection*) in this period. Daniélou further urged that a whole series of Gregory's works be assigned to this period,[11] which included his years of exile. The principal grounds given for this judgment have to do with the presence in the writings in question of theological themes that they share not only with each other (in some cases) but also with the treatise *De virginitate* and, further, with the presence in them of Origenist ideas against which Gregory seems to have reacted after 379. May has pointed out that these conclusions cannot claim any very high degree of certainty but concedes that they are, for some of the works in question, as likely as any alternative, and Heine has located the composition of *In inscriptiones Psalmorum* (*The Titles of the Psalms*) in the year or so just prior to Gregory's return to Nyssa.[12]

It is only for the period after the death of Basil, however, that Gregory's literary output, and at the same time his new-found prominence as a leader in the Nicene cause, can be reliably documented. In 379, after Basil's death, Gregory Nazianzen was summoned to Constantinople, whose bishop was an Arian (Homœan) named Demophilus, by supporters of the Nicene cause. There, based in a private chapel called the "Anastasia," he began the labors that culminated in the delivery of his five "theological orations," an eloquent—and effective—defense of the Nicene cause. This defense led Theodosius I, on his arrival in the East, to appoint Nazianzen bishop of Constantinople in place of Demophilus. During this period Gregory of Nyssa, for his part, undertook in 379 his treatises *De opificio hominis* (*On the Creation of Humanity*) and *Apologia in Hexaemeron* (*In Defense of the Hexaemeron*)—both of which were, though in different ways, defenses and friendly supplemental amendments of Basil's *Homiliae in Hexaem-*

---

10. See Daniélou 1956, 78; 1966, 159–60.

11. Daniélou 1966, 160–62. The works in question were *De mortuis non esse dolendum* (*On the Dead*), *De beatitudinibus* (*On the Beatitudes*), *In inscriptiones Psalmorum* (*The Titles of the Psalms*), *De oratione dominica* (*The Lord's Prayer*), *In sextum psalmum* (*On Psalm 6*), and *Ad Eustathium de Sancta Trinitate* (*To Eustathius on the Trinity*).

12. See May 1971, 56–57, and Heine 1995, 8–11, where these arguments are usefully reviewed.

eron (*Homilies on the Hexaemeron*) and both of which are important for an understanding of Gregory's exegetical policies. Gregory was paying, in effect, a debt to his elder brother, while at the same time expanding the scope of Basil's commentary. In autumn of the same year he attended the council in Antioch summoned by its bishop Meletius (a former bishop of Sebaste), who now, in effect, was assuming the leadership of the Nicene cause in the East. On his return from the council, Gregory attended the deathbed of his sister Macrina and perhaps in the following year (380) or not long after composed his dialogue *De anima et resurrectione,* presented as an account of his last conversation with Macrina.

The year 380 was a busy one for Gregory. Much of it was spent in Sebaste, where he had been summoned to take charge of the election of a successor to Eustathius, the leader of the *Pneumatomachi* ("Spirit-fighters," who accepted the deity of the second person of the Trinity, the Son or Word, but rejected that of the Spirit). No doubt to his surprise, Gregory was himself elected to the post and indeed spent much of the year there in a vain attempt to reconcile Nicenes and *Pneumatomachi.* In the end, he resigned and returned to Nyssa. During this period or shortly after it, he produced his polemical treatise *Ad Eustathium de Sancta Trinitate* (*To Eustathius on the Holy Trinity*), whose content reflects the issues with which Gregory wrestled in the course of his time at Sebaste,[13] and *In Ecclesiasten homiliae* (*Homilies on Ecclesiastes*). (Some authorities assign *In inscriptiones Psalmorum* to the period between Basil's death and the opening of the Council of 381.)

It was, moreover, just after the death of Basil in 379 that Eunomius of Cyzicus, the leader of the Anomœan or Neo-Arian party, circulated a response to Basil, who in his *Adversus Eunomium* (*Against Eunomius*) had mounted an attack on Eunomius's *Apologia* (*Apology*). To this *Apologia apologiae* (*Apology for the Apology*), Gregory—ever his brother's defender—undertook to respond in his first two books *Contra Eunomium* (*Against Eunomius*). They were written in 380 and the early part of 381, respectively. In them, and in two later works with the same title,[14] Gregory further devel-

---

13. May 1971, 57–58.

14. The "work" to which this title has traditionally been applied in fact contains four distinct writings of Gregory's, the order of which has become thoroughly confused in the manuscript tradition and therefore in the standard English translation. Here, as indicated above, Gregory is taking up a task originally begun by Basil, whose treatise *Adversus Eunomium* answered the latter's *Apologia.* After Basil's death Eunomius circulated his *Apologia apologiae,* and Gregory replied to the first part of this in what is now book 1 of his own *Contra Eunomium.* Slightly later he replied to the second part of Eunomius's work by writing what has traditionally been called book 12b. But Eunomius then published a further attack on Basil, and to this Gregory also replied—after the Council of 381—in a work that was early divided

oped themes already sounded by Basil and by Gregory Nazianzen in his *Orationes theologicae (Theological Orations)*, themes having to do with the indefinabilty and incomprehensibility of the divine nature, a cornerstone of the Nicene case against Neo-Arianism. To his own somewhat radicalized version of these ideas Gregory joined, in these writings against Eunomius, a correlative theory of theological predication, and these eventually played a significant role in his construction of the meaning of the Song of Songs for the human relationship to God.

From May to July of 381, Gregory was in attendance at the Council of Constantinople, a council called by Theodosius I to reunite the churches of the East around the faith of the Council of Nicaea (325). The principal theological issue by this time was that of the Holy Spirit, and the debate over it in fact continued after the close of the Council. Thus Gregory's treatise *Adversus Macedonianos de Spiritu Sancto (Against the Macedonians [Pneumatomachians] on the Holy Spirit)* appeared immediately after the conclusion of the Council, and it was on behalf of this Council and its decisions that Gregory undertook a journey to Arabia and Jerusalem.[15] The matter of the status of the Spirit was not closed, and at the Constantinopolitan Council of 383, Gregory delivered his work *De deitate Filii et Spiritus Sancti (On the Deity of the Son and the Holy Spirit)*—and presumably heard Eunomius read out his *Expositio fidei (Confession of Faith)*, which Gregory then proceeded to confute in the final piece of his extended response to that Neo-Arian divine. It is safe to say, then, that at the Council and throughout the time of Theodosius's residence in Constantinople, which came to an end in 387, Gregory was a principal apologist and theological resource for the imperial court in its effort to establish the "new Nicene" solution to the Arian controversy. This judgment is supported by the invitation issued him in 385, at yet another Council of Constantinople, to deliver the official eulogies of the Princess Pulcheria and the Empress Flacilla. It also tends to confirm the common opinion that Gregory's *Oratio catechetica magna (Great Catechesis)* belongs to the later part of the period between 381 and 387 and was roughly contemporary with his polemical work *Antirrheticus adversus Apollinarium (Against Apollinarius)*.

---

into ten (short) books: traditionally books 3–12a of *Contra Eunomium*. Finally, in 383, Eunomius presented an *Expositio fidei (Confession of Faith)* to Emperor Theodosius I, and Gregory wrote, as a rebuttal of it, what has traditionally been counted as book 2 of his *Contra Eunomium*. Thus the correct order of Gregory's several works in reply to Eunomius, an order now reproduced in the Jaeger (GNO) edition, is as follows: (a) book 1; (b) book 12b; (c) books 3–12a; (d) book 2.

15. May 1966, 118–20; note the contrary view of Daniélou 1966, 163–64.

The Homilies on the Song

Gregory's *In Canticum canticorum* (*Homilies on the Song of Songs;* hereafter *Homilies*), however, belongs to the very last years of his life, and the same is probably true, as Daniélou argued, of *De vita Mosis* (*Life of Moses*) and the treatise *De perfectione* (*On Perfection*), which share significant themes with the *Homilies*. The occasion for the composition of the latter is—uncharacteristically, one might add—indicated by Gregory himself in the dedicatory letter that he prefixed to it. The letter contains, at its end, a brief account of how the homilies took shape, prefaced by a much longer defense of the "allegorical" method he followed in his exegesis of the Song (he preferred on the whole to call it "anagogical"). Equally important from our point of view is his dedication of the work to the lady Olympias, who, as he there observes, solicited it "both in person and by [her] letters."

Olympias, as it happens, was a person of high reputation. Thirty or more years younger than Gregory, she was of noble descent (her grandfather had been Constantine's praetorian prefect) and wealthy as befitted her rank.[16] Theodosius I, living then in Constantinople, brought about her marriage to a relative of his, Nebridius, praetor of the city, when Olympias was still in her teens. Nebridius, however, died some twenty months after the marriage, leaving her, in 386, a young widow of vast riches. Theodosius doubted whether such wealth could be administered to useful public ends by an inexperienced young woman devoted to asceticism and good works and accordingly ordered her to marry another of his relatives, Elpidius. She refused, wanting nothing to do with marriage, and the emperor reacted by impounding her possessions until she should reach the age of thirty and by forbidding her to keep the company of high-ranking ecclesiastics. He relented, however, in 391, on his return to Constantinople, well before she had achieved the required age. After that time Olympias was free to conduct her life in the service of the church, especially in care of the poor and the sick. The anonymous biography of Olympias[17] reports that she built a convent on property of her own in Constantinople (which, as it happens, adjoined the church of the Holy Wisdom), whose membership initially consisted of herself and her *familia* of maidservants.

It was entirely consonant with the character of Olympias, who was much given to study of the Scriptures, that she should request of Gregory an

---

16. For what follows, I am indebted to Kelly 1994, 112–13, and to Cahill 1981, although I have not followed either in all details.

17. See the edition of Malingrey 1968. Cahill (1981, 451 n. 1) doubts this evidence on the ground that Palladius does not mention the convent.

interpretation of the Song of Songs; the problem is to know when she might have done so. After 386, Olympias was, after all, forbidden the company of higher clergy, but it is possible that she had met, or become acquainted with the reputation of, Nyssen as early as 381, when he was attending the Council of Constantinople, for she was known to Gregory Nazianzen through her governess Theodosia, Gregory's cousin and the sister of Amphilochius of Iconium. This does not, however, seem to be a setting in which a young girl, for all practical purposes a child, might have "enjoined" (ἐπιτίθημι) upon a prominent, not to say elderly, bishop the composition of a commentary on the Song. Gregory and Olympias may have become acquainted before 386, but Olympias's request is best assigned to the year 391 or shortly thereafter, when, though still in her twenties, she had emerged as a person of significance in her own right. Daniélou believed that the homilies were delivered between 390 and 394, but 390 is too early, and for all we know the homilies might have been delivered even a bit later than 394 (the year of Gregory's last known attendance at a council in the imperial city).[18]

Daniélou took the view that Olympias's request to Gregory included an invitation to make her community of ascetic women the initial audience of his homilies, but Gregory's dedicatory letter makes it perfectly plain that this hypothesis is out of the question. The homilies, Gregory says, were initially delivered "in the presence of the assembly" (ἐπ᾽ ἐκκλησίας) and "during the days of fasting" (κατὰ τὰς ἡμέρας τῶν νηστειῶν); what this means, plainly enough, is that they were originally addressed to the regular congregation at Nyssa in the season of Lent, presumably on weekdays. Daniélou thought this unlikely, partly because he judged that during this last period of his life Gregory was doing his thinking and writing before a mental audience of ascetics and partly because he reckoned it implausible and inappropriate for such "homilies of mystical inspiration"[19] to be given before a collection of ordinary types whose prepossessions they did not, and could not, address. The difficulty with this judgment is twofold. In the first place, it is doubtful whether Gregory saw his subject matter as "mysticism" in the modern sense of that word; in the second place, he openly says, at the beginning of the dedicatory letter, that the homilies did not have Olympias (and presumably, therefore, people like her) in mind but were intended to give direction "to more fleshly folk for the sake of the spiritual and immaterial welfare of their souls." From Gregory's point of view, the "way" that his homilies discern as the theme of

---

18. Note the sensible proposal of Tillemont, quoted by Cahill 1981, 452–53.
19. Daniélou 1966, 168.

the Song of Songs is not a way reserved for the "advanced" but one that is meant to be trodden by all serious Christians.

Finally, it is clear that what has come down in the manuscript tradition is indeed a set of homilies, and in a form not too far removed from that in which they were delivered. Gregory explains[20] that certain of his "associates" had "taken down notes" (no doubt in shorthand) of "the greater part" (τὰ πολλά) of what he had said. He then, so the report says, did three things. He accepted what these associates had given him (surely rendered already into longhand) if it was in sequence; he added what he thought was lacking to make proper sense of the transcription; and he put everything into the form of homilies in which "the interpretation of the words followed the order of the text." The last of these undertakings seems to imply that as originally delivered the homilies contained some passages in which the preacher treated certain lines or verses not in the order in which they appear but perhaps in connection with other, thematically related lines or verses—and that Gregory wanted the homilies to have the form of a proper verse-by-verse commentary (like Origen's). Dünzl is quite right to point out that there is no reason to suppose that Gregory's revisions or additions were either extensive or thorough.[21] Gregory himself suggests that he had little time to work on revisions "during the days of fasting" (which, I am inclined to suspect, means that his original delivery of the sermons and his revisions were undertaken during the same—busy—Lenten season). He also comments that his commentary had only got halfway through the text of the Song, a vague, perhaps even careless, remark that nevertheless inspired Dörries to suggest that, since homilies 13–15 go beyond the (precisely calculated) first half of the Song of Songs, they must have been added to the set after Gregory's work of oral delivery was done.[22] Quite apart from the fact that this hypothesis, as Dünzl has observed, does little to clarify the way in which the homilies assumed their present form,[23] it also seems to imply, on the best interpretation of the chronology, that the manuscript Gregory originally sent to Olympias was shorter by three homilies than the one we presently possess and that Gregory did not so much hope, as positively intend, to expand it. His language however—"If the God who provides life provides us with both a long enough life and a time of quiet, we shall perhaps work our way through what remains"—does not seem to rise even to the level of hope.

---

20. Homily preface, p. 13 (Jaeger). All references to Gregory's *Homilies on the Song of Songs* are to the page numbers of the edition by Hermann Langerbeck in vol. 6 of the GNO, for which Jaeger served as the general editor.

21. Dünzl 1994b, 1:32–35.

22. Dörries 1963, 572–73.

23. Dünzl 1994b, 1:36–37.

Gregory sounds tired, and his language is not that of a person who foresees a much longer life. Indeed, he did not enjoy a much longer life. His death occurred at some time around, though probably shortly after, 395.

2. THE THEMES, METHOD, AND SOURCES OF GREGORY'S INTERPRETATION OF THE SONG

THE PROBLEM OF "ALLEGORY"

Anyone with a properly modern outlook and a properly modern taste in literary—and especially biblical—interpretation is likely, on reading Gregory's *Homilies* for the first time, to undergo something of a shock. If, moreover, such a person is asked what occasions this reaction—of dismay, incredulity, and rejection—the answer that comes is likely to specify (1) Gregory's systematic treatment of the text as allegory, and, in the particular case of the Song, (2) his use of allegory to cleanse away or purge or trivialize its marked, and cheerful, sexual eroticism. Gregory himself acknowledges that there are, in his own day, exegetes who could be said to have shared something of this aversion to allegory, teachers who "do not agree that Scripture says anything for our profit by way of enigmas and below-the-surface meanings"[24] (a phraseology that represents Gregory's carefully neutral way of saying what "allegory" means as he understands it). Nor is there much doubt that the people he has in mind here are representatives of the so-called Antiochene School, teachers such as Diodore of Tarsus or Theodore of Mopsuestia. The first of these, moreover (Diodore) he could well have met, and probably did meet, at the Council of Antioch (379) or the Council of Constantinople (381) or both.[25] In any case, Gregory's dedicatory letter to Olympias undertakes what he doubtless regarded as an obligation, namely, the defense of his exegetical policy—a policy he had already followed in his *De vita Mosis* and *In inscriptiones Psalmorum*—against just such critics. And he does so in terms that indicate his debt to Origen but, at the same time, as we shall see, depart significantly in some ways from Origen's theory and practice.

It is a temptation, then, when confronted with Gregory's exegetical policies in the *Homilies*, to turn straightway to this dedicatory letter and to set out the terms of his defense of allegory, that is, to attend deliberately and narrowly to the question of his *method* of eliciting what he takes to be the teaching of the Song. To adopt this procedure, however, would be to ignore the presupposi-

---

24. Homily preface, p. 4 (Jaeger). On the meaning of "enigma," see ibid., n. 1
25. For an excellent discussion of this issue, see Cahill 1981, 453ff.

tions of his use of allegory, that is, the extent to which his understanding of it is correlative with (1) a picture of the structures of reality, (2) a conception of the subject matter (the σκοπός, i.e., the "aim" or "purpose") of the Song, and (3) a picture of the workings of human language that goes along with these. These presuppositions are not, to be sure, original with Gregory. His phrasing and deployment of them are in every case developments of an inherited tradition that he adopts and sometimes reworks. They embody or imply both an idea of how a biblical text "works" and an understanding of the human relationship to God, and allegorical interpretation of the Scriptures as Gregory sees it plays a central role in the maturation of this relationship; in other words, it has, in practice, as Gregory sees the matter, a transformative function.

STRUCTURES OF REALITY

More than once in the course of the *Homilies* Gregory argues that the Song intimates a certain manner of envisaging the way in which reality is structured. One of the clearest of these is found in the opening section of homily 6, where Gregory is addressing Song 3:1–4.[26] In that passage the Bride of the Song,[27] alone on her bed at night, goes out in search of her Beloved: she cries out for him and, receiving no answer, steps out into *the markets and … the streets* of the city to find him. She even asks the *watchmen* of the city as they go their rounds whether they have seen him; when their response disappoints her, she leaves them behind—then and only then to find the one she seeks. What this passage conveys, Gregory says, is a kind of philosophy whose aim it is to explain how "lovers of the transcendent Beauty are to relate themselves to the Divine."[28]

The basis of this "philosophy"—which, as we shall see further on, does indeed have practical implications—is initially a division of reality into two realms or orders. The division in question appears as early as Gregory's *Apologia in Hexaemeron*, where he teaches that the creation "of heaven and earth" related by Moses in the first chapter of Genesis is, by intent, limited to an account of the coming-to-be of the *perceptible* order, the world of "things that appear," but also insists that the "third heaven" to which Paul was exalted (2 Cor 12:2), while a part—the highest, not to say noblest, part—of the

---

26. See homily 6, pp. 172–74 (Jaeger); cf. homily 5, pp. 157ff. (Jaeger).

27. Gregory follows the established tradition that the female figure of the Song, when the text is read in its literal sense, is a bride of King Solomon, commonly thought to be the daughter of Pharaoh (cf. 1 Kgs 3:1; 11:1). In the Song, she is neither bride nor soul nor church but simply a woman.

28. Homily 6, p. 173 (Jaeger).

perceptible order, is in fact the borderline beyond which there lies the "inner-most shrine of wisdom," that "paradise" (2 Cor 12:3) which is the *intelligible* cosmos. The latter, he thinks, is the realm experienced by Paul, the very realm that the apostle describes elsewhere as "unseen" and "eternal" (2 Cor 4:18) and with regard to which he says that its contents are inexpressible in human words.[29] The very same division of reality appears at various points in the *Homilies* and at first glance seems simply to reiterate the momentous distinc-tion originally made by Plato at the opening of his *Timaeus* (27D–28A). For example, Gregory writes in one place:

> The nature of things that exist is divided, at the highest level of general-ity, into two kinds. On the one hand, there is that which is perceptible and material; on the other, that which is intelligible and nonmaterial. Hence we reckon something to fall into the category of the perceptible to the extent that it is grasped by sense perception, but we reckon as intelligible that which falls beyond the observation of the senses.[30]

Yet there is a subtle divergence here between Plato and Gregory. Plato's distinction puts its primary emphasis on the difference between that-which-unchangeably-is and that-which-comes-to-be and then secondarily on the description of these two realms as intelligible and perceptible, respectively. Gregory, however, in the passage just quoted, ignores the former of these two differences—for the good enough reason that in his mind the distinc-tion between intelligible and perceptible does not coincide with that between Being and Becoming as Plato understood it. His point emerges when he goes on to explain that, in addition to this most fundamental distinction, there is a second to be made, this time within the category of the intelli-gible itself, which, Gregory asserts, "is also divided into two kinds." This, to put it bluntly, is the distinction between God the Creator ("the uncre-ated") and that segment or division of the intelligible realm that comes to be, that is created. The Divine alone is eternal in the proper sense and eter-nally self-identical; it is God alone who possesses the characteristics that Plato ascribed to the realm of Forms or Ideas—although God, as will soon become plain, is well beyond Form or Idea. The remainder of the intelli-gible realm thus consists of created beings. Indeed, Gregory insists, they "are always being created."[31] Their life is, as it were, always in process, which means that they have to be described, intelligible though they be, as always

---

29. 2 Cor 12:4; see Gregory's discussion of all this in *Apol. Hex.* (PG 44:120D–121C).
30. Homily 6, p. 173 (Jaeger).
31. Ibid., p. 174.

coming to be, and this, needless to say, would from Plato's point of view have constituted a perfect oxymoron.

Gregory's Platonism, then, is a strictly Christian Platonism in the sense that the difference between perceptible reality and intelligible reality is in practice subordinated to the further, biblical distinction between Creator and creature, and within the terms of that distinction the intelligible and perceptible realms as Plato knew them fall together into the category of the creaturely: of that-which-comes-to-be. There is, moreover, a further divergence here between Gregory and Plato that should not go unremarked, even though it does not represent a characteristically Christian development. For later Platonism, through whose eyes Gregory understood the master, the intelligible realm is also the realm of intellect; that is, what it contains is not simply Ideas or Forms but Ideas or Forms *as known,* as entertained by mind or by minds that are themselves immaterial, nonperceptible, realities. The "intelligible" realm, then, is that dimension of reality in which knower and known, intellect and intelligible, subject and object, approximate unity. It is the realm in which what-one-is and what-one-knows move toward coincidence. Naturally enough, then, for Gregory this realm is the home of the angelic host—and, at least intermittently and eschatologically, of human beings in their capacity as rational, intellectual subjects.

Hence, to return to the passage in homily 6 with which we started, the Bride, when at night she sallies forth to find her Beloved, follows a route that is determined by just this map of reality. The *night* in which she starts her search is the "darkness" that is God's "hiding-place" (Ps 17:2; cf. Exod 20:21) and that is "entered" when God is sought as an identifiable phenomenon of the *perceptible* order; for then the One she seeks is experienced simply as the invisible. But then, we are told, she goes out into the city, its streets and markets; this, Gregory tells us, represents "the intelligible and supracosmic order," the angelic realm. But even the *watchmen* who represent this incorporeal cosmos testify by their silence that the Beloved is no acquaintance of theirs. The Bride, therefore, must pass them by, must pierce beyond the intelligible order, and there she meets the One whose "existence is known only in incomprehension of what it is."

God, then, stands beyond intelligibility. Gregory—in what may be one of his most frequent and characteristic ways of referring to God—asserts dogmatically in his *Homilies* that "the blessed and eternal Nature ... transcends every intellect."[32] The same point is made in slightly different language in the course of Gregory's comments on Song 1:11. God is "that Reality ... which

---

32. Homily 5, p. 157 (Jaeger).

transcends the entire structure and order of Being, [and] is unapproachable, impalpable, and incomprehensible."[33] Gregory may seem to conceive of God in the first instance as a "sector" of the realm of the intelligible, but in the end he acknowledges that God, who contains or encompasses all things but cannot be contained,[34] is no part, aspect, or dimension of the cosmic order. In his Song commentary, this teaching—extensively developed in the writings *Contra Eunomium* as a response to Neo-Arianism—is in full bloom and is characteristically developed in the form of a doctrine of divine infinity[35] that is at least partially rooted in Gregory's belief that the divine goodness is unlimited, whether externally or internally.[36]

Into this frame of a twofold, perceptible and intelligible, created order posited and sustained by a Goodness so deep and so intense as to reach beyond the grasp of any human word or concept, Gregory inserts the human creature. And clearly, there is a certain sense in which he finds humanity baffling. On the one hand, this Adam/Eve is said to be created "after the image and likeness of God," and to Gregory this signifies that the human being participates in the divine way of being, thus imitating that way of being at the level of the creature. To be "after the image ... of God" means, then, to be possessed of self-determination (and the capacity for choice that that presupposes). It means to enjoy an immortality that is a participation in the eternity of God. It means to be characterized by love—love of the good, for God, after all, *is* the Good and is called "Love." In brief, it means to possess on a human scale the excellences—the "virtues"—that are proper to God, not excluding impassibility.[37] On the other hand, in Gregory's eyes "the piteous and wretched state of the human race" as one now sees it is not consistent with its description as "image of God."[38] The passions that are proper to the "nature" of humanity's animal dimension—that is, to the lower reaches of its life principle, soul in its nutritive and perceptive phases—can as it were "infect" the

---

33. Homily 3, p. 90 (Jaeger).

34. Homily 5, p. 157 (Jaeger); cf., e.g., homilies 11, p. 338; 13, p. 386; and 15, p. 438. This language goes back to Philo of Alexandria and was much favored by Irenaeus in his controversy with Christian Gnostics.

35. On this idea, see the essential study of Mühlenberg 1966.

36. This is an idea that Gregory intimates fairly clearly as early as his treatise *Opif. hom.* 21 (PG 44:201B). Cf. *Vit. Mos.* preface 7 (trans. Malherbe and Ferguson 1978, 33): "The Divine One is himself the Good..., whose very nature is Goodness.... and since the Divine does not admit of an opposite, we hold the divine nature to be unlimited and infinite." Above all, see *Eun.* 1.360–369 (GNO 1:133ff.).

37. For Gregory's full account of what is involved in the concept "image of God," see *Opif. hom.* 4–5 (PG 44:136B–137C).

38. See *Opif. hom.* 16 (PG 44:180B–C).

intellect in which the divine image is rooted. That happens when the intellect turns away from God and seeks its good not in God but in the realm of things perceptible. In doing so, it assumes a new identity to the extent that in turning to perceptible "goods" it takes on the likeness of what it attends to; this, for Gregory, is the meaning of "Adam's" fall. "Nature"—which here means the "logic" (λόγος), the indwelling cunning and dynamic instilled by the Creator in plant and animal forms of life—takes control of the human self and makes the human self over in its own image instead of itself being brought to participate in the divine image implanted in the intelligible self, the intellect.[39] The human project, then, is restoration of the divine image, the return of humanity, intelligible and perceptible, to its original identity.

Such imaging comes about, however, within a relationship of "mirroring," for "the intellect," says Gregory, "is decked out with the likeness of the prototypical beauty, rather like a mirror marked with the form of what is reflected in it."[40] This metaphor of the mirror is frequent, needless to say, in the *Homilies,* and when examined closely it conveys one or two essential elements in Gregory's understanding of the image idea. For one thing, of course, it indicates that the image, while a reproduction of its original, does not normally count as another instance of its original.[41] An image reproduces its original *in another medium,* such as in the form of a reflection on the surface of glass or in that of a portrait painted on wood or canvas. In the case of the ἄνθρωπος that God summoned into existence (Gen 1:26–27), the image takes form in a *created* and *mutable* nature and not that of uncreated Deity. Further, and just as important, the human mirror conveys an image of its original only as and when it is "looking to" its original. The "life-endued and choice-endowed mirror"—that is, the soul that is the Bride—asserts that she focuses "upon the face of [her] Kinsman with [her] entire being," and the result of this attentiveness to the incarnate divine Word is that "the entire beauty of his form is seen in me."[42] And in general, "Those who look upon the true Godhead take to themselves the characteristics of the divine Nature."[43] There is a close relation, therefore, between knowing God (or "seeing" God) and being like God. In

---

39. See *Opif. hom.* 17 (*PG* 44:189C–D and 192Dff.). Cf. homily 15, pp. 457–59 (Jaeger).

40. *Opif. hom.* 12 (PG 44:161C; cf. 164A).

41. The exception that proves this rule is, of course, the relations of the persons of the Trinity: the Word or Son is indeed a "reproduction" of the Father, but (so the Nicene argument ran) a reproduction that counts as "spitting image," i.e., the very same thing all over again.

42. Homily 15, p. 440 (Jaeger).

43. Homily 5, p. 147 (Jaeger). One wonders whether Gregory—or those Christians before him who shared this understanding of the relation between likeness and knowledge/vision—had noted 1 John 3:2 ("we know that when he appears we shall be like him, for we shall see him as he is"). Certainly Gregory had taken account of 2 Cor 3:18.

Gregory, indeed (and surely not in Gregory only), the two seem to be correlative. He can talk the language of Matt 5:8, according to which virtue (purity of heart) is a condition of seeing God (and therefore of actualizing the divine image): "knowledge," he says, "of the Good that transcends every intellect comes to us through the virtues."[44] He can also, however, as we have just seen, talk the language of 1 John 3:2, according to which the vision of God is a condition of bearing the likeness, for people become like what they look at.[45] The good that human nature seeks can thus be defined in two ways[46] that come to the same thing: virtue makes the vision of God possible, and the vision of God makes virtue possible. Progress in respect of either virtue or knowledge thus entails progress in the other.

THE QUESTION OF ΣΚΟΠΟΣ

Against the background of this account of the structure of reality, and of the human situation within it, one can turn to the question of Gregory's exegetical procedures, which in one way or another are informed by his world picture. In this connection, the first thing to be noted is simply that Gregory had enjoyed a standard rhetorical education in the Greek tradition and that he was familiar with the questions customarily posed by grammar-teacher and rhetor alike to a classical text and with the techniques they employed to answer their questions. In the *Homilies* as elsewhere, then, he can be observed raising issues about the syntax of a sentence or word,[47] explaining the sense of a word by reference to other occurrences of it in the Scriptures,[48] or complaining of the difficulty of turning Hebrew into idiomatic Greek.[49] Among these normal preoccupations of the exegete, however, there looms one that is of more central and critical importance, since it determines what shall be taken to be the business—the aim or purpose—of the work to be interpreted; this is the question of its σκοπός.

That question, as has often been noted, grew out of concern for the organic unity of a literary composition. Such an interest goes back at least as far as Plato himself, who in the *Phaedrus* argues that "any speech ought

---

44. Homily 3, p. 91 (Jaeger).

45. Homily 4, p. 105 (Jaeger); cf. homily 5, pp. 147, 150.

46. For another way of putting this idea, see homily 13, p. 376 (Jaeger).

47. See, e.g., his discussion of Song 4:9c and the phrase "in one" (homily 8, pp. 258–59 [Jaeger]).

48. Thus his discussion of the sense of "sweet-smelling" in homily 9, p. 266 (Jaeger), which enables him to construe "spice" as a reference to sacrifice.

49. See homily 2, pp. 53–54 (Jaeger), where Gregory is worried at the suggestion that it was "the sons of my mother" who assigned the Bride to "guard" the vineyard.

to hang together like a living organism" (ζῷον). Plato goes on to insist that someone may well be competent to create examples of the sorts of compositions proper to a tragedy without being thereby constituted the equal of a Sophocles or Euripides. The genius of the latter depends on their sense of the unity-in-difference of the concrete whole, and they understand, in practice, that "a tragedy is nothing other than a combination of ... components that harmonizes them with one another and with the whole" (*Phaedr.* 264B, 268D). Similarly Aristotle—with dramas primarily in mind—insists that,

> just as, in the other forms of mimesis,[50] a single work of mimesis has a single action as its focus, so it is also in the case of the mythos [story? plot?]: since it is mimesis of an action, it must concern a single action, and that action as a whole,[51] and the deeds or events that make it up must hang together in such a way that if any of them is relocated or removed the whole is disrupted and disturbed; for any element whose presence or absence makes no difference is no part of the whole. (*Poet.* 8 [1451a29–35])

This concern for the organic unity of a literary composition was not necessarily or universally shared by the posterity of Plato and Aristotle. Indeed, it is by now a commonplace that self-conscious interest in the σκοπός of a text as a hermeneutical key to its unity was first given articulate and systematic shape in Neoplatonist circles by Iamblichus (d. ca. 325). This pupil of Porphyry (and beneficiary of Plotinus) wrote commentaries on works of Plato and Aristotle and appears to have adopted Plato's analogy of the organism for a literary creation.[52] Iamblichus insisted that the interpreter give an account of the subject matter of an individual work, an account that, for all practical purposes, is at the same time a specification of the author's intent or purpose in producing the work: "for with the Neoplatonists it is above all the conscious intention of the artist, what they call the σκοπός, which imparts to the various elements of his work the quality of being necessary or belonging."[53] Excellence in a literary work, then, would on this hypothesis require, among other things, that its every part contribute to the sense of the whole and, at the same time, that the sense of the whole control the articulation of each of its parts. The critic

---

50. He has just praised Homer for the way in which both the *Iliad* and the *Odyssey* portray a single "action": the "wrath of Achilles" with its effects, on the one hand, and the return of Odysseus, on the other.

51. Aristotle has already explained that "whole" means having "a beginning, middle, and end" (*Poet.* 7 [1450b25–26])

52. For Iamblichus and the Neoplatonist interest in σκοπός, see Coulter 1976; Dalsgaard Larsen 1972; and the discussions in Rondeau 1974; Heine 1995; and Young 1997.

53. Coulter 1976, 77.

or exegete is thus bound, in approaching a text, to begin by indicating what he takes its "business" to be, for this consideration defines the course that its interpretation must take.

At any rate, in Christian circles there was an interest in these matters even before Iamblichus wrote his commentaries. Thus one finds Origen explaining that the primary "aim" (σκοπός) embodied in the prophetic and apostolic Scriptures is that of familiarizing human beings with "the ineffable mysteries that concern human affairs," which turn out to be in the first instance the mysteries of God the Trinity and of the incarnation, the work of Christ, and all matters concerning the creation and fall of the rational spirits.[54] To be sure, the Spirit also had a secondary aim (δεύτερος … σκοπός), which was

> to conceal the λόγος relating to the subjects just mentioned in expressions that convey a narrative containing a recital concerned with the acts by which the perceptible order was constructed, the creation of humanity, and successive offspring of the original human beings down to the point where they become many. (*Princ.* 4.2.8)

Needless to say, this definition of the Scripture's twofold "aim" is simply a more explicit way of stating Origen's earlier description of the scriptural texts as the "forms … of certain mysteries and images of divine things" (*Princ.* 1 preface 8). The picture in Origen's mind seems to be that of the scriptural text as the perceptible clothing or embodiment of a "meaning" that belongs to the intelligible or spiritual order. It is the Spirit's first σκοπός, then, that defines the real—and single—burden of the Scriptures, even though there is a partial and elementary truth conveyed by the perceptible, corporeal "letter" itself.

Ronald Heine further cites two places where Origen appears to discuss the "aim," not of the Scriptures as a whole, but of an individual work or type of work within the Scriptures.[55] One of these is the Song itself, for in the lengthy preface to his commentary on the Song of Songs Origen asserts that "love [ἔρως] … is the principal theme of this writing."[56] The other example is a brief passage in book 10 of Origen's commentary on John, where he speaks of the "mystical σκοπός" of the Gospels and explains that the Gospel writers sometimes alter their narrative (ἱστορία) in order to accommodate this aim, which is thus "higher" both in the sense that it governs the detail of the

---

54. Origen, *Princ.* 4.2.7. These, of course, constitute the core subject matter of Origen's treatise "on first principles."

55. Heine 1995, 38–39.

56. Heine 1995, 38. I insert the Greek word ἔρως here because I assume that Rufinus's *amor,* here and elsewhere in his Latin version of the commentary, is a translation of that term.

text and in the sense that it has to do with matters spiritual rather than with goings-on in the perceptible realm (*Comm. Jo.* 10.19).

To this evidence from Origen it is worth adding testimony from a later source. About a quarter of a century after the death of Iamblichus (and a good century after that of Origen), Athanasius, writing against his Arian opponents, accused them of misunderstanding the Gospels. The cure for this condition, he suggests, would consist in their "grasping the σκοπός of our Christian belief" and "using it as a norm" while they pay attention "to the reading of the God-inspired Scriptures" (1 Tim 4:13; cf. 2 Tim 3:16). What the "belief" (πίστις)—that is, the baptismal creed—thus intends to convey is the same as the purport of the Scriptures themselves, Athanasius thinks, for, as he goes on to say, the aim and distinguishing characteristic of Scripture is that it everywhere proclaims Christ and Christ as at once divine and human.[57] Athanasius may or may not have been acquainted with Iamblichus's views and hermeneutical policies; if not, then his language, like Origen's, attests an independent concern, in some Christian circles at least, for the unity of the Scriptures taken as a whole and also of individual writings among their number, understood in terms of σκοπός.

By Gregory of Nyssa's time, however, the influence of Neoplatonist ideas in Christian circles is clear. It may be most clear in the case of Antiochene exegetes. Anyone who consults, say, Theodore of Mopsuestia's commentary on the Psalms,[58] with its careful expositions of the "hypothesis" (*argumentum*) of each psalm and its insistence that a psalm's meaning be limited to its explicit aim, is bound to be impressed with the systematic way in which Theodore employs the inferred setting of a psalm to determine its aim.[59]

Gregory of Nyssa is perhaps not so "systematic" as Theodore in his use of the concept of *skopos:* he is a debtor to Origen before he is to Iamblichus.[60]

---

57. Athanasius, *C. Ar.* 3.28–29 (ed. Bright 1873, 183–84).

58. See Hill 2006.

59. Thus, to take the first example that comes to hand, Theodore rejects the view of those who say that the "subject" of Ps 1 is King Jehoash on the ground that the latter, given his acquiescence to popular frequentation of "high places" (4 Kgdms 12:3), could not have embodied the virtues of the sort of person whose "delight is in the law of the Lord." The psalm is in fact, then, a piece of paraenesis dealing with "desire for the virtues and abstinence from errors," neither of which was characteristic of Jehoash, and Theodore proceeds to develop its inherent "aim," which is the same as its *hypothesis:* to teach that correct faith and good morals are alike essential to beatitude.

60. See Heine 1995, 40: "[Gregory] has retained and expanded Origen's use of the concept of the *skopos* of Scripture and its individual books by applying to it various principles derived from Iamblichus." This is a just estimate of Gregory's method in *In inscriptiones Psalmorum*, but it might—oddly—be less plausible, I think, if taken of the *Homilies* or the *De vita Mosis*.

Nevertheless, he seems to address the question systematically in his early exegetical works. It raises its head, indeed, in one of his earliest "commentaries," of the year 379: the *Apologia in Hexaemeron*. This is, as indicated above, a work designed both to defend and to complement his brother Basil's nine sermons on the narrative of creation in Gen 1. The slightly earlier treatise, *De opificio hominis,* in fact adds to Basil's work, for Basil's explication of Gen 1 had not reached as far as the account of the creation of the ἄνθρωπος on the sixth day, but the *Apologia in Hexaemeron* is an effort to come to terms with Basil's way of reading Gen 1, regarding which Gregory asserts that it has for him an authority second only to that of Scripture itself.[61] It is clear, nevertheless, that Basil's account disappointed him in two respects—not by its content but by what it had omitted, or at any rate partially omitted. The first of these disappointments (the second we will take up in the next section) had, of course, to do with Basil's addressing the text as it stood, taking it in its "literal" sense. In this regard, Basil had departed from Origen's conviction that the narrative of "the acts by which the perceptible order was constructed" was intended by the Spirit to "conceal" teaching about the mysteries of the faith (Origen, *Princ.* 4.2.8), and this meant, of course, that the language of the narrative required an allegorical interpretation to bring out its full meaning. Gregory, however, true to his fraternal loyalty to Basil, agrees that the literal sense must in this case stand, for, he argues, it was the σκοπός of Basil's work to present the teaching of Moses' narrative in a manner adapted to the average understanding of his audience. Moreover, Basil's aim corresponded exactly to that of Moses himself:

> For … the prophet composed the book of Genesis as an introduction to the knowledge of God, and Moses' σκοπός is to take those who are enslaved to sense perception and to guide them, by way of things that appear, toward that which transcends the grasp of sense perception. Hence when he says heaven and earth, he is specifying the knowledge that comes to us by way of the eyes.[62]

To be sure, as we have seen,[63] Gregory is sure that Moses' mention of "waters that are above the firmament" is a reference to what lies beyond Paul's "third heaven," that is, the realm of intelligible reality; however, he agrees that that is not the business (σκοπός) of the narrative of the six days. Gregory, then, assigns a carefully defined σκοπός not only to Moses' treatment of the

---

61. PG 44:68B–C.

62. PG 44:69D; cf. Basil, *Hex.* 1.6 (PG 29:16C).

63. See p. xxiv above, with the reference there.

creation narrative but to Basil's explication of it—and indeed suggests how the former is related to the intent of the book of Genesis as a whole.

Similarly, in the (probably slightly earlier) treatise *In inscriptiones Psalmorum*, Gregory begins by considering the character of the Psalter as a whole; the first task that this entails, he says, is that of identifying the σκοπός of the book of Psalms. The decisive clue here is the first word of Ps 1: "blessed" (μακάριος). The "aim" or "business" of the entire Psalter is the human blessedness (i.e., likeness to God) attained through the practice of virtue.[64] Gregory then proceeds to assign to each of the five successive "books" of the Psalter a stage along the way of virtue as its subtopic. In this way he follows Iamblichus's program and interprets each of the parts of the work in and through its relation to the business of the whole.

The same, I think, cannot be said of *De vita Mosis*, the work that in its outlook most closely approximates the teaching of the *Homilies*. In the case of *De vita Mosis*, it is crucially important to distinguish between Gregory's σκοπός[65] in writing and the subject matter (ὑπόθεσις), as he saw it, of the text he was studying, which he had brought out, he says, by elaborating a bit on the (literal) text in his summary of it.[66] Gregory's personal aim was to address a particular question: the question of "the perfect life."[67] This was an issue with regard to which he entertained idiosyncratic ideas. As he saw the matter, since God is the Good, and since there is no limit to God's goodness, and since one's desire (ἐπιθυμία) for the Good will therefore stretch out beyond all possible limits, there can be no static condition of perfection. "The perfection of human nature is a disposition ever to want to possess more in the way of goodness."[68] He supported this view by reference to what was, for him, a seminal text, Phil 3:13–14, where the participle ἐπεκτεινόμενος ("stretching out") embodies his whole "picture" of the way of perfection as an unending ascent from lower to higher things. He also believed, however, that the narrative of Moses' life was relevant to the topic of spiritual perfection, both in the sense that it presents itself as an example to be imitated[69] and in the sense that it is an account of an ascent in which Moses is initiated into progressively greater

---

64. *Inscr. Pss.* 1.8 (GNO 5:23,8–10).

65. This surely is the proper way to take τὸν προκείμενον ... σκοπόν at 1.70. Cf. the version of Malherbe and Ferguson 1978, 51.

66. *Vit. Mos.* 1.77 (GNO 7.1:33,5).

67. Ibid., 1.2–3 (GNO 7.1:2).

68. Ibid., 1.7 (GNO 7.1:4,14–15); see above, n. 35.

69. Cf. ibid., 1.13 (GNO 17.1:6,5–8).

mysteries[70]—although, Gregory insists, Moses' nature was unchangeable in preserving the beauty of goodness.

In the case of the *Homilies,* the situation is much the same. Gregory is quite clear about what he himself is up to. He announces it in his dedicatory letter, where he explains to Olympias that his homilies are not intended to be "of assistance to [her] in the conduct of [her] life" but are on the contrary to give "some direction to more fleshly folk for the sake of the spiritual and immaterial welfare of their souls."[71] To be sure, he addresses his audience in homily 1 as people "who have 'taken off' the old humanity with its deeds and lusts like a filthy garment and have clothed [themselves] … in the lightsome raiment of the Lord." He says, indeed, that they have " 'put on' our Lord Jesus Christ himself, and with him have been transfigured for impassibility and the life divine."[72] Such language is bound to impress the modern reader as describing persons who are advanced in the spiritual life, and the more so since shortly thereafter Gregory suggests that Jesus addresses his disciples as folk who have "surpassed the human condition," on the ground that at Caesarea Philippi Jesus had contrasted his followers with (mere) "human beings."[73] In saying this sort of thing, however, Gregory may have been in the business—all but statutory for a rhetorician—of flattering his audience; this seems especially likely when it is noted that the language he employs belongs to the sphere of customary accounts of the meaning of baptism and therefore conveys no more (or less) than that his hearers were indeed "in Christ," if only as beginners in the exercise of this identity. Thus he speaks of the baptized as "children" who are no longer "earth-treaders" but participants in the "procession" that leads upward toward things divine.[74] His references to putting off "the old humanity" and "putting on" Christ are allusions to Col 3:9–10 and Gal 3:27, which is to say that they are not talking about spiritual attainments, or any degrees of "perfection," as such. If Jesus' disciples have "surpassed the human condition," it is because they have been given entrance into the realm of God's "new creation" in Christ, a new status that makes surpassing the human condition a possibility and a calling upon which they have now truly and properly entered. Hence Gregory in homily 1 portrays a line of progress from the elementary moral teachings of Proverbs, through the enlightenment and purification worked by Ecclesiastes, to the higher "philosophy" of the Song; while there is no doubt that he thinks his hearers have

---

70. Cf. homily 12, pp. 354–55 (Jaeger).

71. Homily, preface, p. 4 (Jaeger).

72. Homily 1, p. 14 (Jaeger).

73. Ibid., p. 29 *ad fin.* Cf. Mark 8:27 (οἱ ἄνθρωποι) and 29 (ὑμεῖς).

74. Homily 2, pp. 52–53 (Jaeger).

their feet on that path, his words imply nothing about how far along it any one of them has traveled.[75] They imply only that this way is indeed theirs and that as people who have "put on" Christ they are drawn to him. Their like are to be seen in the "maidens" of the Song, the companions of the Bride, who have the Bride as their schoolmistress, while the Bride herself represents the most "advanced" among believers, people such as "the bride Moses"[76] or Paul himself,[77] who had mounted in spirit to the third heaven.

None of this means, however, that Gregory regards the Song itself as somehow elementary in its function—far from it. He does not speak explicitly of the σκοπός of the Song, but it is clear enough that he remains firmly in the tradition of Origen in this regard. For one thing, he adopts Origen's view that the Song has love (ἔρως) as its fundamental subject matter. God, he thinks, "who wills all to be saved and to come to the knowledge of truth" (1 Tim 2:4), reveals "in this work the blessed and most perfect way of salvation … that which comes through love."[78] For in the Song, "the soul is led as a bride toward an incorporeal and spiritual and undefiled marriage with God."

It is perhaps typical of Gregory that he explicitly conceives this "way" on the model of a progressive transformation. As we have seen, it starts with the instruction of Proverbs, in which the true, the divine, Solomon appears in the persona of Wisdom to draw beginners in the way toward love and a desire for virtue. It passes through Ecclesiastes and culminates in the Song, where the same Solomon now appears in the persona of the Bridegroom, the Word of God, who, as Gregory saw the matter, brings the Bride step by step to ever greater and higher attainments. Indeed, Gregory saw the Song's successive praises and characterizations of the believing soul (i.e., the Bride) as marking a series of steps or "ascents" (ἀναβάσεις); there is nothing more characteristic of these homilies than the many passages in which the Bride's progress is

---

75. See homily 15, pp. 460–61 (Jaeger), as well as Gregory's interpretation of Song 5:3 ("I have removed my tunic, how shall I put it on? I have washed my feet, how shall I soil them?), which he takes to refer to the Bride's baptism (homily 11, pp. 328–30).

76. For this phrase, see homily 1, p. 31 (Jaeger); for Gregory's portrayal of the "maidens," see homily 1, pp. 39 *ad fin.* 46–47. Homily 1, p. 39, draws a contrast between "the more perfect soul" and "those who do not yet possess the fulness of virtue," even though the latter are souls that follow the way of love, as distinct from those who obey out of fear or out of desire for an external reward (homily 1, pp. 15–16). Gregory's compliment to his audience, then, comes to this, that in the language of the Song they are drawn in love to the sweet scent of the Bridegroom's perfumes.

77. See, e.g., homily 1, pp. 46–47 (Jaeger), where the Bride follows the example of "the great Paul."

78. Ibid., p. 15; cf. homily 4, p. 119.

rehearsed in detail,[79] invariably to make a single basic point. Commenting on Song 3:1–4, Gregory makes the point in question by observing first that, in the light of her previous ascents, the Bride ought to have attained "the hope of the very highest good." He then goes on to say that, even though she has "received the object of her desire within [herself]," she is still "perplexed and dissatisfied," and he finally explains why:

> we are taught plainly that the greatness of the divine Nature knows no limit, and that no measure of knowledge sets bounds to a seeker's looking— bounds beyond which one who is reaching to the heights must cease to move ahead. On the contrary, the intelligence that makes its course upward by searching into what lies beyond it is so constituted that every fulfillment of knowledge that human nature can attain becomes the starting point of desire for things yet more exalted.[80]

It turns out, then, that the "ascents" that lead the soul toward marriage with God and toward that "likeness to God" that is "the limit that the virtuous life approaches"[81] are successive approximations. In the *Homilies*—as earlier in the *De vita Mosis* and the *In inscriptiones Psalmorum*—Gregory is opposed to the very notion of a final, static perfection. Perfection consists in unending transformations that lead to a goal that is reached in never being fully attained. To his insistence upon the infinity of the Good (i.e., of God) Gregory thus weds his equally firm belief that it is precisely in its mutability, its capacity for infinite change for the better, that the human soul images and thus participates in the divine way of being.

It is true enough, then, to say that Gregory in the *Homilies* follows Origen in the latter's estimate of the Song's σκοπός. The aim of the Song is indeed to present the way of love—desire—as that which draws people to chase after the Word towards a "marriage" with the Divine, but Gregory introduces a distinctive qualification into this tradition. He does not share the Platonist distaste for that which is unlimited and therefore indefinable. As Plato himself at least hinted, Gregory sees the ultimate Good as that which is "beyond being" and therefore as infinite, beyond intelligibility. Hence he does not perceive mutability or finitude simply as the source of evil. He clearly sees—or wants to see—human perfection to consist in this unending change in the

---

79. For the longest of these, see homily 6, pp. 175–80 (Jaeger). See also, e.g., homilies 6, pp. 186–87; 9, pp. 279–81; and 11, pp. 319–20, 323–24.

80. Homily 6, pp. 179–180 (Jaeger); cf. homily 11, p. 320.

81. Homily 9, p. 271 (Jaeger).

direction of a Good that has no limit,[82] and this idea is one of the themes that is built into his version of the σκοπός of the Song.

The Question of Ἀκολουθία

To grasp the importance of this understanding of the σκοπός, or central theme, of the Song of Songs, as well as the way in which Gregory conceives its relation to the text of that work, it is necessary to make a short detour and take account of his exegetical use of the idea of ἀκολουθία.[83] An abstract noun formed on the stem of a verb meaning to follow, or to come or go after, the term most often means a sequence or series or succession, but with the additional implication that what follows is connected with and even consequent upon what precedes it. Thus in Stoic logic ἀκολουθία could refer to a form of logical entailment[84] and in Stoic physics to "the order and series of causes"[85] that constitute Fate. It is from Zeno himself that we learn that

> The primary Fire is like a kind of seed that contains the *logoi* and the causes of all things that have come-to-be, that are coming-to-be, and that will come-to-be; and the knitting together and ἀκολουθία of the latter are the fate and knowledge and truth and law of all things, something inevitable and inescapable.[86]

One might say, then, that ἀκολουθία connotes, in its broadest sense, a series or succession in which the members of the series do not constitute a jumble of items but are closely and intelligibly connected, like the links of a "chain": what "follows" is entailed or is caused or is at any rate consistent with what precedes.

Daniélou was no doubt correct in arguing that Gregory of Nyssa met this idea initially not in any writings of the Stoics but in those of Philo of Alexandria, in particular in the latter's exegesis of the story of creation in Gen 1. There Philo had explained:

---

82. For an excellent illustration of this, see homily 5, pp. 158–59 (Jaeger).

83. For the classical treatment of this subject, on which I have liberally drawn, see Daniélou 1970, 18–50; see also the thoughtful treatment of Gregory's exegesis in *De opificio hominis* and in *Apologia in Hexaemeron* by Alexandre 1971.

84. Of the form "If A, then B," see *SVF* 2:71,10; 2:72,7.

85. Cicero, *Div.* 1.55, where in the phrase "ordinem seriemque causarum," the terms *ordo* and *series* seem to render the Greek τάξις and ἀκολουθία, respectively.

86. *SVF* 1:27.

[Moses] says that the cosmos was formed in six days, but not because the Maker needed a length of time to do the job, for God surely accomplished all the things he did at once, not only the giving of commands but also the conception behind them. Rather was it because order was necessary for the things that came-to-be.[87]

What this means is that "even if the Maker made everything all at once, the things that came-to-be in beauty possessed an order" (Philo, *Opif.* 7.28). "Order" Philo then defines as "a sequence [ἀκολουθία] and a chain [εἱρμός] of things that precede and that follow, considered not in their finished products, but in the mental scheme [ἐπίνοιαι] of those who originated the plan." In the case of the world's creation, of course, the Originator is God, and the "plan" is the "content" of the same divine Word (λόγος) who is the agent of its actualization (*Opif.* 6.24). What is created, then, is a finite totality that is internally ordered to follow an intelligible sequence that brings things along to their intended fulfillment. It is this idea, with its fairly plain Stoic roots, that Gregory seems to have picked up on in his two amplifications of Basil's *Homiliae in Hexaemeron.*

Like Philo, then, Gregory insists that "God posited the occasions and the causes and the powers of all things taken together as a whole in a timeless moment."[88] This idea recurs in another connection, and in a slightly different form, in *De opificio hominis,* where Gregory raises with himself the difficult question why the text of Genesis says that God first created humanity (the ἄνθρωπος) after his image and likeness and only after that adds the distinction between male and female, the latter being a characteristic pertaining not to the intellectual soul that is created after the divine image but to the corporeal realm. His answer was inspired by a text he would also quote in his *Apologia in Hexaemeron,*[89] namely, Sus 42,[90] where "the Eternal God" is described as the One "who knows all things before they come-to-be." Gregory's suggestion is that, "in virtue of the divine foreknowledge and power, the whole of humanity was comprehended in the first creation.... the entire fullness of humanity was embraced as it were in a single body by the universal God through his power of foreknowledge." Understood in this way, "human

---

87. Philo, *Opif.* 3.13. It should be noted that Basil—and therefore Gregory, to be sure—followed Philo in asserting that God created everything in a single instant (see Basil, *Hex.* 1.6 [PG 29:16C–17A]; Gregory, *Apol. Hex.* [PG 44:69A–71B]).

88. Gregory, *Apol. Hex.* (PG 44:72B). He had earlier (69D) appealed to Aquila's translation of "In the beginning" as ἐν κεφαλαίῳ ("in summation," "all at once").

89. Ibid.

90. Or, alternatively, Dan 12:42.

nature as a whole,[91] extending as it does from the things that came first to the last things of all, constitutes a single image of Being." In other words, the act of creation embraces humanity's end as well as its beginning.

The reason for this unusual line of thought is Gregory's belief that as a result of Adam's sin, humanity's end—its perfection—and its beginning ceased to coincide: humanity's τέλος is real in God's foresight but not in its own present condition. Between beginning and end there comes an "interval" (διάστημα), within which there occur the steps through which this creature moves from the one to the other, and this sequence or succession of stages—which is what entails a linear, corporeal, and sexual mode of reproduction[92]—is precisely "the ... path and ... sequence [ἀκολουθία]" that "the Word follows" as he adapts "human nature to God."[93] In Gregory's view, then, God's creation of "everything" simultaneously means something slightly different in the cases of humanity and of the other creatures. For all creatures, including the ἄνθρωπος, actualization and perfection originally coincide (which is why the narrative form of Moses' account of creation must be taken with a grain of salt), but because Adam, created perfect, turned away from God and thus from his own perfection, a process of re-creation became necessary, and this does not, says Gregory, occur "in the same sequence and order" as did the original act of creation.[94] It is this picture of things—this picture of an ongoing ἀκολουθία that leads to human redemption—that no doubt influences his insistence, cited earlier, that even the members of the intelligible order are "always being created."[95]

This conception also helps to explain the second disappointment that Gregory experienced in reading Basil's exegetical treatment of the creation narrative. The first disappointment, dutifully suppressed, was, as we have seen, Basil's decision to follow and embroider the literal text—a departure from Origen's conviction that the creation narrative is anagogical throughout. This policy Gregory could explain reasonably on the double ground that Basil's aim was not to address the questions of educated persons but to adapt his exegesis to the simplicity of an audience of ordinary folk[96] and that in any case Moses' narrative concerned only the visible cosmos, the cosmos as

---

91. What Gregory means by this use of "nature" is essentially "species," humanity taken collectively.

92. For all this, see *Opif. hom.* 16 (PG 44:185B–D). Gregory thought that union with a bodily constitution made it impossible for humans to reproduce in the angelic—i.e., presumably nonsexual—fashion normal for members of the intelligible realm.

93. Homily 5, p. 144 *ad fin.* (Jaeger).

94. Homily 15, pp. 457–58 (Jaeger).

95. Homily 6, p. 174 (Jaeger).

96. *Apol. Hex.* (PG 44:65B).

perceived by the senses. Gregory's second disappointment, however, was precisely that, in pursuing this policy, Basil also ignored the sorts of questions that in Gregory's eyes were rightly being raised by "those who seek the coherent sequence [τὸ ἀκόλουθον] within the scriptural ideas." One such person was, clearly enough, Basil's—and Gregory's—younger brother Peter, who thought that the text of Gen 1 as it stood written was not self-consistent and had therefore charged Gregory with the duty of reconciling Moses' statements by bringing them together into a "chain" by way of a "coherently sequential" (ἀκόλουθον) interpretation.[97]

Gregory for his part was willing to follow Basil in holding to the ordinary sense of the scriptural words, but he was also willing to go Basil one better by reconciling investigation into the workings of nature (φυσικὴν θεωρίαν) with the scriptural letter,[98] or, as he puts it elsewhere, by following out "the chain of nature through a close look [θεωρίαν] into the [scriptural] terminology, while the text continues in its plain sense."[99]

Here there are two points to be noted. In the first place, the ἀκολουθία in question here is that which is presupposed by a narrative whose explicit σκοπός is portrayal of the coming-to-be of the perceptible—and therefore not the intelligible—cosmos. What is at stake, therefore, is Gregory's version of the cosmological ἀκολουθία of the Stoics, and such matters as the marriage of the soul to God can scarcely be in question. In the second place, it follows that Gregory is employing the term "nature" to denote what might now be called "the natural order," meaning by that, of course, what Moses meant by "heaven and earth," that is, that which is the object of sense knowledge.[100] What this "nature" amounts to is a "necessary chaining" that "is followed out in accordance with a certain order."[101] It is, in a word, the way things work as a result of God's first, summary act of creation, in and with which were posited, as we have seen, "the occasions and the causes and the powers of all things."[102]

In other words, Gregory took the divine commands—into whose sequence the Genesis narrative dissolves the divine act of creation—as λόγοι. By use of this term he no doubt intends to say that these were in some sense words, for what they conveyed was comprehensible, but what they communicated was each creature's intelligible principle, that is, the divine

97. Ibid. (PG 44:61A).
98. Ibid. (PG 44:124B); cf. 89C.
99. Ibid. (PG 44:121D).
100. Cf. ibid. (PG 44:68D).
101. Ibid. (PG 44:72C).
102. See above, n. 85.

power-and-wisdom in the particular form in which these indwell each of the things God creates.[103] Further, however, these λόγοι were "spoken" all together in the "summary act" of creation. In this way, there is established a "necessary order of nature" that "seeks the order of succession [τὸ ἀκόλουθον] within the things that have come to be," and it is this that Gregory wants to get at, by unpacking the content of the scriptural "names." The ἀκολουθία in question, then, is the rationale, as one might say, that is presupposed in, and makes sense of, the Mosaic narrative of creation. Moreover, the ἀκολουθία of the perceptible realm, the cosmic ἀκολουθία, embraces any number of particular serial, and therefore temporal, processes. Gregory can speak of the (human) "seed" in which the mature form of the human person exists potentially, and this he regards as the λόγος that determines the causal ἀκολουθία by which human nature unfolds or develops.[104]

There was, however, in Gregory's mind, a difficulty to be noted in this undertaking. The story told by Moses' narrative refers directly only to things that might in principle be seen, heard, and touched—to phenomena of the perceptible realm. To inquire after the ἀκολουθία of this narrative, its under-lying "rationale" or "logic," however, is to look beyond the perceptible realm to seek the intelligible "sense" of it, that which lends the phenomena their coherence. Yet "the poverty of our nature perceives that which comes-to-be but is unable to see or to praise the λόγος in accordance with which it comes-to-be,"[105] and Gregory tells his brother Peter that if he seeks to understand "the necessity of the order of the creation," he must follow Moses "into the darkness of investigation (θεωρίας) of the inexpressible."[106] What this pre-sumably means is that Moses in his narrative must "explain," for example, the segregation of light from darkness by attributing it to a further, discrete act of God, when in fact it comes about ἀκολούθως—that is, consequen-tially, on the basis of the nature assigned to the creatures in God's primordial, single, all-embracing originative act (ἀρχή).[107] The σκοπός of Gen 1, it seems, requires employment of the narrative form in order to convey the "order" of God's original creative act in terms of a series of "perceptible" events, but that narrative form obscures what is really going on: the temporal spelling-out (ἀκολουθία) of the innate, intelligible "codes" (λόγοι) that underlie and deter-mine what goes on. Moses' purpose or aim in telling the story of creation

---

103. *Apol. Hex.* (PG 44:113B–C; cf. 73B).
104. *Opif. hom.* 29.3 (PG 44:236B–C).
105. *Apol. Hex.* (PG 44:76B).
106. Ibid. (PG 44:65C).
107. Ibid. (PG 44:76B).

dictates one sort of discourse, but the desire for rational explanation dictates another, parallel sort of discourse.

Here, though, we have what might at first glance seem to be an illustration of allegory as Gregory understands it. "Allegory" notoriously meant saying one thing and conveying another at the same time; in the words of Trypho's *De tropis* (*On Tropes*), "*Allēgoria* is speech which makes precisely clear some one thing but which presents the conception of another by way of likeness."[108] What Trypho does not say, and Gregory would have to add to make his practice clear, is that the latter perceives the secondary reference not merely as having to do with something "other" but as having to do with something *of a different order*. The movement from one type of reference to another is, in fact, as we have seen, a movement from perceptible to intelligible reality, and the difficulty this creates is that ideas and language adapted to the description of perceptible phenomena are not well adapted to expressing truth at the level of the intelligible. Hence Gregory insists that the undertaking his brother Peter has imposed upon him can only be carried through if it is understood as, on the one hand, an academic exercise, and as, on the other, involving guesswork—all of which means that one cannot make dogmas of the conclusions one reaches but must be content with corrigible approximations.[109] What Gregory does in his "rationalization" of the Genesis creation narrative is in some ways, then, not unlike Neoplatonist exegesis of Timaeus's "likely story" in Plato's dialogue on the structures of the world order.[110]

To the extent that this comparison is reasonable, however, it becomes apparent that what is going on in Gregory's *Apologia in Hexaemeron* is not "allegorical interpretation"—as he himself insists when he says that he is respecting the plain or literal sense of Moses' language. His exegesis does indeed employ the "phenomenal" narrative description that Genesis provides (and Basil had followed) to get at something "other," namely, the natural "chain" of cause and consequence that makes sense of Moses' διήγησις. But that ἀκολουθία, however difficult to discern with certainty, is nevertheless, when articulated, an account in another form of the same phenomena that Genesis relates in the form of a narrative of perceptible events. The Genesis narrative, then, is not a "figure" of another, higher-level process, "by way of likeness." No doubt that explains why Gregory says that his exegesis proceeds by attending to the meanings of the words that Moses employs; thus he explains the various statements about "light" by reference to the relation of fire with the other elements as that was portrayed in the natural philosophy

---

108. Spengel 1853–56, 3:193.
109. *Apol. Hex.* (PG 44:68C).
110. See Plato, *Tim.* 29C–D.

of his day, and in *De opificio hominis* he develops the meaning of "image" at length and expands on the relation of intelligence and bodily "nature" in the human person by appealing to the biology of his time. He is showing, or trying to show, that the creation narrative and the ἀκολουθία of the natural order fit together.

THE ALLEGORY OF THE SONG OF SONGS

But if, in *De opificio hominis* and *Apologia in Hexaemeron*, Gregory denies that his personal program (σκοπός)—that of interpreting Gen 1 by a defensive enhancement of Basil's commentary on it—calls for the use of allegory, the same is not true of *De vita Mosis, In inscriptiones Psalmorum,* or his *Homilies,* for there, as we have seen, he feels obliged not only to employ allegorical interpretation but also, in the dedicatory letter that is his preamble to the *Homilies,* to provide an apology for this practice. It is interesting, moreover, that these three works share, no doubt in slightly differing manners and with different foci, a single concern: that of characterizing the Christian "way," the way that leads to human fulfillment in likeness to, and knowledge of, God by the pursuit of ἀρετή, "excellence."

It is this interest that undergirds Gregory's conception at once of the nature of allegory, its function, and its relation to the intent of the Scriptures. Where the last of these matters is concerned, it seems fairly clear that Gregory follows in the footsteps of Origen, whose essay on the interpretation of the Bible (book 4 of the treatise *De principiis*) was the opening item in the set of excerpts from Origen's writings assembled by Basil and Gregory Nazianzen in their *Philokalia.* There, as we have seen, Origen had asserted that the "intent [σκοπός] of the Spirit who in the providence of God illumined those ministers of Truth, the prophets and apostles, was primarily to provide instruction regarding the ineffable mysteries that have to do with human affairs, so that anyone who is capable of receiving this instruction … might become a participant in all the teachings of his counsel."[111] The "mysteries" in question, Origen goes on to say, are things like the Trinity, the incarnation, and the truths about the human condition intimated in the story of the creation and fall. This definition of the Spirit's "intent" is, of course, then, a hermeneutical principle: it specifies what there is to look for in the Scriptures, or at any rate what the church seeks in them.

As might be expected, moreover, Gregory takes essentially the same view in his *Homilies.* He does not employ the word σκοπός in his prefatory letter

---

111. *Princ.* 4.2.7 (15).

to Olympias. He does, however, emphasize, as what amounts to an unquestioned assumption, that the Scriptures say what they say "for our profit" and that what the exegete seeks in the Scriptures is "that which is profitable."[112] He further explains what he means by "profitable": it is "teaching that guides those who pay careful heed to it toward knowledge of the mysteries and toward a pure life,"[113] a characterization that dwells, as one might expect, on the correlative themes of knowledge and virtue and at the same time evokes the idea of growth, of a progressive transformation. There can be no question, then, that this is the same Gregory as the one who speaks in *In inscriptiones Psalmorum* and in *De vita Mosis*. It is important to observe, however, that it is also the Gregory who had spoken in the *Apologia in Hexaemeron,* for even there he insists that, although Moses in Gen 1 is speaking of the perceptible cosmos, the aim of his literal and corporeal discourse is "to take those who are enslaved to sense perception and to guide them, by way of things that appear, toward that which transcends the grasp of sense perception."[114] Thus Moses' intent feeds, as it were, into the overall σκοπός of the Scriptures, which is defined in a fashion that Origen could have acknowledged as equivalent to his own and in Gregory's basic formulation is verbally reminiscent of it.

Gregory further offers, as we have seen, a characterization of the aim and central theme of the Song of Songs itself. Homily 1, which in effect contains his introduction to the Song, asserts that "by what is written [in the Song], the soul is in a certain manner led as a bride toward an incorporeal and spiritual and undefiled marriage with God."[115] In more general terms, what it is up to is the "adapting of human nature to God."[116] This account of the business of the Song is, to be sure, a bit odd from the point of view of a modern exegete: it says not only that the Song in some fashion *narrates* an exemplary soul's progress in knowledge and love of God but also that readers of the Song may themselves, through their comprehension of it, be brought along as actual participants in the same progress. The text of the Song has a kind of symbolic or sacramental character, then, in that to understand it fully is to be involved with the reality it speaks of.

Here, however, there is implied a significant difference as between the text of the Song and, say, the text of the creation story in Genesis. The account of the man and woman who figure as lovers in the Song is assuredly an account of corporeal—phenomenal—realities. It is therefore, as Gregory and the

---

112. Εἰς ὠφέλειαν ἡμῶν … τὸ ὠφέλιμον (homily preface, p. 4 [Jaeger]).

113. Homily preface, p. 5 (Jaeger).

114. *Apol. Hex.* (PG 44:69D).

115. Homily 1, p. 15 (Jaeger).

116. Homily 5, pp. 144–45 (Jaeger).

whole tradition in which he stands insist, an account of an ordinary courtship and wedding, and there is no question in anyone's mind that that is its literal sense—just as there is no doubt that Gen 1 is talking about a literal heaven and earth. In the case of the Song, however, the "logic" that informs and governs its literal sense—the truth that it conveys—is not an intelligible truth about "nature" but an intelligible truth that concerns intelligible realities, that is, the life of the soul—no doubt the embodied soul but the soul nonetheless—in relation to God. And this implies (1) that the ἀκολουθία in which the interpreter of the Song is interested is not that which governs the "nature" of the perceptible cosmos but that through which the "new creation"—humanity's "re-adaptation" to God—is accomplished and (2) that to get at that truth, that redemptive ἀκολουθία, allegory—or better, perhaps, anagogy—is in order.

Gregory of course insists that he has no investment in the labels one puts on his procedures. The apostle Paul, he observes, speaks of "allegory," of "type," and even of "enigma" (see 1 Cor 13:12) or of a change in "manner of speech."[117] He also allows of "tropology" and "below-the-surface meanings" (ὑπόνοιαι).[118] As far as Gregory is concerned, however, these terms all mean roughly the same thing: "the movement from corporeal to intelligible realities" or "intellectual discernment" or "a shift to an understanding that concerns the immaterial and intelligible."[119] Language of this sort is repeated throughout the *Homilies*. Thus Gregory writes, thinking of the Song as a whole: "What is described … is the business of a wedding, but what is intellectually discerned is the human soul's mingling with the Divine,"[120] and this means that in the Song "the language of passion" is employed "to render thought that is undefiled."[121] Again, what anagogy or allegory does is to "transpose the outward meaning of the words into the key of what is pure and undefiled,"[122] or—using the Pauline distinction between "spirit" and "letter"—"transpose what is said to the level of spiritual comprehension, after distancing the mind from the literal sense."[123]

The equivalence here of the spiritual, the pure, and the intellectual is manifest. All of them, in Gregory's mind, have to do precisely with the distinction between perceptible and intelligible realities, and an exegesis involving "transposition" is seen as necessary because (1) the text at hand

---

117. Homily preface, pp. 5–6 (Jaeger).
118. Ibid., pp. 4–5.
119. Ibid., p. 6. "Intellectual discernment" renders ἡ κατὰ νοῦν θεωρία.
120. Homily 1, pp. 22–23 (Jaeger). "Intellectually discerned" renders τὸ … νοούμενον.
121. Ibid., p. 29.
122. Homily 9, p. 262 (Jaeger).
123. Homily 6, p. 190 (Jaeger).

gives an account of perceptible realities, but (2) the reality it ultimately concerns is of the intelligible order. It is the gap between these that "allegory" bridges. Thus when Gregory proposes to employ the narrative account of Moses' life in Exodus to delineate the nature of human "perfection," he must face the objection that the particular circumstances of Moses' life do not correspond with the circumstances of the person to whom *De vita Mosis* is addressed. Gregory's response is to say that the particular details of Moses' life (e.g., that his early life was led in Egypt) are not what he and his correspondent are interested in or bound to imitate. Rather, he says, they must cultivate a "more subtle" habit of mind and "keener sight," so that the narrative may teach them what kind of Egyptians *they* must escape so as "to enter upon the blessed life."[124] In other words, they must transpose the meaning of the text to a higher level by way of an analogy or "likeness," so that the Egyptians of the text may be seen to be not merely the oppressors of the literal and historical Israel but also symbols of vice, that is, of every sort of "evil" that constrains and contorts human life.[125]

Alongside this image of allegory as an "ascent" from perceptible to intelligible, from literal to spiritual, from particular to universal, there stands another, for Gregory less central, image that portrays it as involving a move from the "external" to the "internal" sense of a text. A form of this image occurs at the very opening of homily 2, where in an eloquent introduction Gregory contrasts the plainness and dullness of the exterior hangings of the tent of witness with the glories of its interior—and then explains that the Song of Songs is "the true tent of witness," its text, taken literally, being as it were an exterior clothing of the holy of holies that lies within. Again, when considering the *sixty mighty men* of Song 3:7, Gregory observes that he is certain that the number sixty there has a "mystical meaning," but being uncertain whether he is sufficiently gifted with the Spirit to seek that meaning out, he announces that in this case "all is well with those who are satisfied by the surface meanings of the text." He then justifies this statement. Alluding to Num 9:11–12, he likens the hidden sense to the "secret marrow" that is concealed within the bones of the Passover lamb, bones that Moses forbade the Israelites to break.[126] The literal sense, then, encloses and conceals—and perhaps protects—the spiritual sense of the text. This image in its way no doubt echoes Origen's description of the Scriptures as "the outward forms of certain mysteries."[127]

---

124. *Vit. Mos.* 1 (GNO 7.1:6,8ff.)
125. Ibid. 2.100–101, 112 (GNO 7.1:63,17ff.; 67,9ff.). Cf. homily 3, p. 76 *ad fin.* (Jaeger).
126. Homily 6, p. 193 (Jaeger). Cf. *Vit. Mos.* 2:111 (GNO 7.1:67,5–8.)
127. *Princ.* 1 preface 8.

There are, then, points in the biblical text at which it is not positively wrong to be content with the text taken literally. On the other hand, there are points at which, for Gregory and the whole tradition he represents, the "surface meaning" more or less demands to be transposed to a higher level. In the dedicatory letter to Olympias, he mentions or illustrates the accepted indications that this is the case. These are the traditional "faults" in the literal sense of the text that Origen himself had pointed to. If the text "contains examples of evildoing," if it says something that is logically or physically impossible (as in the case of Gen 2:9, which indicates that two trees, the tree of life and the tree of the knowledge of good and evil, both stood at the exact center of the paradise), if the text is theologically unacceptable (as in the case of the same verse, with its suggestion that God is the one who planted the tree that kills people[128]), if a text makes sense but is unprofitable for the life of virtue—in all cases of this sort anagogical or spiritual understanding is called for.[129] M. Alexandre points out that in addition to these occasions, Gregory—again not without precedent—appeals to κατάχρησις ("misuse"; i.e., use of a word to characterize something its normal connotation does not fit, hence figurative language generally—as when the heavens are said to "speak") to justify anagogy. He will also appeal to a "historical" inaccuracy to justify such a procedure: Song 1:9 refers to the Bride as *my horse among the chariots of Pharaoh,* but Gregory—taking no explicit notice of the fact that "horse" here is used figuratively—observes that the exodus narrative mentions "no cavalry force" that was "arrayed against the Egyptian army,"[130] and this circumstance induces him to look for his "horse" higher up in the orders of existence.

From all this, it should be plain that Gregory is serious when he says that he does not much care what his procedure is called: "anagogy" fits his conception of it better than does "allegory," but neither is inaccurate, any more than is "tropology." Nor is he unaware of the custom of taking events or persons or things referred to in the Law and the Prophets as "types"; he gives an account of it in homily 5[131] and again, more briskly, in homily 7, where he states that types "sketch out, in an anticipatory way, the power of the gospel."[132] Clearly, though, unlike many present-day scholars, he failed to discern any important difference between "typology" (a word for which he had no equivalent) and

---

128. Cf. homily 12, pp. 349–50 (Jaeger).

129. See Heine 1984, 360; Alexandre 1971, 103–4.

130. Homily 3, p. 73 (Jaeger). In this passage, following Song 1:9, ἵππος is employed in the feminine and might well be translated "mare." Gregory, however, seizes upon a secondary meaning, that of "a body of horse."

131. Homily 5, p. 148 (Jaeger).

132. Homily 7, p. 201 (Jaeger); cf. p. 231.

"allegory." This may be attributable to the practice of Paul as Gregory perceived it, for the apostle in Galatians clearly takes Sarah and Hagar and their two sons as types but calls the resulting exegesis a case of "allegorizing" (see Gal 4:22–24). Gregory may also have recognized that the analogy or similarity discerned in the relation of type and antitype presupposed an "ascent" by way of abstraction to the level of intelligible reality, and in any case he sees the mysteries of the gospel to represent not just the higher form but also the higher sense of the law.

Gregory's allegory, then, is meant, like Origen's, to elicit from the text a portrayal of the "mysteries" of Christian faith. In his case, however, the mysteries in question are explicitly treated as forming an ἀκολουθία—an extended, logically connected sequence that brings about the actualization of a divine plan that is somehow implicit in the very ἀρχή of things. He had sought in his descant on Basil's *Homiliae in Hexaemeron* to show that this was the case with the "nature" that governs the perceptible order referred to by Moses as "heaven and earth." In the Song, however, he understands himself to be dealing with a work that concerns the human self—"soul"—in its relation to God. Its σκοπός is precisely, as we have seen, an account of how "the soul is in a certain manner led as a bride toward an incorporeal and spiritual and undefiled marriage with God,"[133] and that σκοπός specifies the "what" of which the Song's ἀκολουθία delineates the "how."

Once that is said, however, it is necessary to observe that in Gregory's practice, ἀκολουθία is discerned in two different forms. For one thing, there is a logically connected sequence proper to the text itself: a sequential order that governs the presentation of ideas or topics and in that way serves the intelligibility of the text. Thus Gregory notes in homily 15 that when the chorus of maidens, disciples of the Bride, asks her *Where has your kinsman gone?* (Song 6:1), they are speaking ἀκολούθως, that is, in accordance with a logical order, for their first question had been *What is your kinsman?* (Song 5:9), and it makes sense that "what" should come first and "where" follow it.[134] Similarly, Gregory speaks at the beginning of homily 2 of the "thought sequence" of the opening verses of the Song, which have portrayed the "maidens" of the poem as touched by a love for the Good that the Bride for her part has already experienced in the *kiss* of Song 1:2, the kiss that is at once "the illumination of the Word" and "the firstfruits of the Spirit."[135] Thus, seeing that the Bride has already experienced what they can only chase after, they say *Let us rejoice and be glad in you,* and accordingly—"consequentially"—they come to the

---

133. Homily 1, p. 15 (Jaeger).

134. Homily 15, pp. 434–35 (Jaeger).

135. Homily 1, pp. 39–40 (Jaeger). Gregory seems to identify the "kiss" with baptism.

Bride as to their teacher, and she "starts off her account of the good by taking up matters that are requisite for souls in the status of learners."[136] Ἀκολουθία refers, then, in these two instances, to a logical—a comprehensible—course of action that is reflected in the ordering of a particular portion of the text.

A second and somewhat different use of this idea appears later on in the same homily. There the Bride is found asking the Word to speak to her. *Speak to me,* she says, *you whom my soul loves* (Song 1:7). She wants her Bridegroom to say where he pastures his flock, so that she may go to him there and "be filled with heavenly nourishment." But, Gregory observes, the Bridegroom does not answer her, for "she is not yet deemed worthy" of hearing his voice. Instead, the "friends of the Bridegroom" give her advice about the way she can safeguard "the good things that she presently possesses." Their advice (Song 1:8), as it turns out, is somewhat obscure—but not, Gregory says, because one cannot see the *point* of their words, for that, he says, "is apparent from the ἀκολουθία of the passages we have already studied." In other words, one can see in Song 1:8 a meaning that is the—or a—logical sequel of the sense of the preceding verses, and this circumstance legitimates Gregory's way of reading it. On the basis of this assurance he can proceed both to clarify the obscurity of some of the phraseology and to give his overall interpretation of the verse.[137] In this case, then, the ἀκολουθία embraces more than a particular passage in the Song, and the meaning assigned the individual verse is determined by its consistency with the course taken, the trend followed, by Gregory's interpretation of previous passages.

The same criterion is even more obviously at work in homily 11, where Gregory confronts some words of the Bridegroom: *Open to me, my sister, my close one, for my head is covered with dew and my locks with the drops of the night* (Song 5:2). Here he begins his exegesis by summarizing what he takes the general meaning of the verse to be. He opens this summary by appealing to God's successive self-manifestations to Moses as he had already treated them in his *De vita Mosis:*[138] "The revelation of God to … Moses began with light as its medium, but afterwards God spoke to him through the medium of a cloud, and when he had become more lifted up and more perfect, he saw God in darkness."[139] Moses is then—as often in the *Homilies*—taken as a pattern for the soul that is the Bride. It is suggested that the Bride's progress begins with her enlightenment, as she is liberated from "false and erroneous notions about God." Then she graduates to "apprehension of hidden realities,"

---

136. Homily 2, p. 46 (Jaeger).
137. See the whole passage: homily 2, pp. 61–63 (Jaeger).
138. See *Vit. Mos.* 2.162–163 (GNO 7.1:86).
139. Homily 11, p. 322 (Jaeger).

that is, to awareness of the "invisible realm," though in doing so she enters a "cloud that casts a shadow on everything that appears" (cf. Exod 19:9; 34:5). Then the soul passes to still "higher things" and enters the "divine darkness"—the darkness in which perception and intellection alike are left behind and where God dwells (Exod 20:21 LXX).

Having in these terms summarized the truth that he thinks Song 5:2 reflects and, taken anagogically, conveys, Gregory asks himself whether the verse under consideration really does exhibit compatibility (συγγένεια: "kinship") with his summary. He finds his answer in a reconstruction of the Bride's progress from the days when she was "dark," through her baptism and enlightenment (the "kiss" of Song 1:2) and her rest in the "shadow"—the cloud—of the Incarnate Word (Song 2:3b), to the point where, as Song 5:2 intimates, "she is already surrounded by the dark night, in which the Bridegroom draws near but is not manifest."[140]

This procedure, in which Gregory states the meaning of a line or verse as he understands it and then sets about fitting the words of the text to his exegesis, seems less arbitrary if one understands that what he is attempting to do is to fit the line or verse in question into what he takes to be the ἀκολουθία of the Song as a whole. The σκοπός of the Song is, as we have seen, the way of salvation, the way on which, by love, the Bride comes to a "marriage" with God, a marriage that is consummated in that "likeness" to God that itself involves both knowledge of God and virtue. This way of salvation lies beyond the scope of sense perception. It is grasped, therefore, only when the text is allegorized, that is, transposed to the level of intelligible reality, and this process, since it pierces beyond the literal/corporeal realm to which the language of the Song refers, is a delicate and often uncertain one. Like the search for the ἀκολουθία of "nature" in his exegesis of Gen 1, it involves "guesswork," that is, a certain divinatory skill, not to mention the assistance of the Spirit.[141] Gregory does not, however, for all the difficulty of the task, see any reason to give up on this enterprise of discernment, for he is confident that "the Word follows a certain path and a certain ἀκολουθία in adapting human nature to God."[142]

In these two passages the ἀκολουθία that Gregory has in mind is the "logic" that governs the progress of the Bride on the way to union with God, and I think there is little question that this "logic" represents the dominant theme of the Song. As one would expect, the heart of it—the truth that it

---

140. Ibid., pp. 322–24.

141. See, e.g., on this score, the introductions to homilies 10 and 12, pp. 294 and 340–42 (Jaeger).

142. Homily 5, pp. 144–45 (Jaeger).

spells out sequentially—lies in Gregory's picture of the structure of reality and of the destiny of humanity within it. That is, it presupposes both (1) the distinction between perceptible and intelligible reality and (2) the ineffable and infinite Deity that embraces and transcends both of these, and it rehearses the progress by which the human person, moving from perceptible through intelligible to their "Beyond"—from light to cloud to darkness—is transformed into the "image and likeness" of that infinite Good, in accord with God's original purpose in the creation of humanity. Ever and again Gregory summarizes this progress as the Song in his reading presents it. The progress obviously begins, for him, with baptism—the "kiss" through which the Bride is turned from addiction to "things that appear" to a preliminary awareness of the transforming grace and beauty of the true Solomon. It continues, he thinks, as she first *hears* the Bridegroom and then, eventually, *sees* him—and ultimately, comes to "that time when, since all have become one in desiring the same goal, and there is no vice in any, God may become all in all persons, in those who by their oneness are blended together with one another in the fellowship of the Good in our Lord Jesus Christ."[143] This theme of unending change, growth, and transformation moves into the background of Gregory's exegesis only in those passages where one or other of the lovers is found engaged in a passionate enumeration of the beauties of his or her consort. At these points Gregory's allegory, or anagogy, tends to dwell upon the Bride's virtues, the character of the divine Word incarnate, or the "members" of the body of Christ, the church.

There is, however, another dimension to this ἀκολουθία, this "logic" that governs (as Gregory sees it) the progressive restoration of the Bride to her paradisal state. It is necessary to remember that this "Bride" is a symbolic figure for Gregory and that what she symbolizes is not only the exemplary believer but also the collective "church," and indeed the human species as such, for as Gregory sees it, these two are in the end—that is, in the age to come—to coincide (since, as he repeatedly notes, "God our Savior ... desires all to be saved and to come to knowledge of the truth" [1 Tim 2:3–4]). Consequently, Gregory intermittently slides from tracing the logical pattern that defines the progress of the paradigmatic soul to sketching the logical pattern of the universal history of salvation—the focus of which, needless to say, is the incarnation, itself a marriage of divinity and humanity. He remarks, as we have seen, that "Members of the realm of being"—that is, beings of the intelligible and intellectual order—"are not re-created in the same order [τάξις] and sequence [ἀκολουθία] in which they were created." What this means

---

143. Homily 15, pp. 468–69 (Jaeger).

is that the human species, as a consequence of its acquired "kinship with death" and "its inclination toward evil...", does not achieve its perfect state again all at once, as at its first creation. Rather does it advance toward the better along a road of sorts, in an orderly fashion, one step after another [διά τινος ἀκολουθίας καὶ τάξεως]," for "in the process of restoration, lapses of time necessarily attend those who are retracing their way toward the original good."[144]

As to the landmarks along this road, Gregory indicates what some of them are in his exegesis of Song 2:8–9. First he explains the words *The voice of my kinsman: behold, he comes.* "These expressions," he says, "look forward to the economy of the divine Word [i.e., the incarnation], made known to us in the gospel." The word "voice" is an allusion to the prophetic announcement of what is coming. But, he continues, "the divine voice is attested by deeds, and to the word of promise its accomplishment is attached"; hence the sequel, *Behold he comes,* for as Hebrews bears witness, "In the last days he spoke to us by a Son" (Heb 1:2).[145] This pattern of promise and fulfillment, then, structures the ἀκολουθία of the process by which humanity is re-created in Christ.

Gregory reiterates this point in slightly different terms later on, when he comes to the words, *Behold, [the divine Word] stands behind our wall, looking through the windows, peeping through the lattices.* Here we see the order and the sequence by which the Word adapts humanity to God. "First of all, he shines upon it by means of the Prophets and the Law's injunctions" (for "the windows are the Prophets, who bring in the light," and "the lattices are the network of the Law's injunctions"). Gregory goes on: "After that, however, comes the Light's perfect illumination, when, by its mingling with our nature, the true Light shows itself to those who are in darkness and the shadow of death."[146] Whence it becomes fairly obvious what is being said in the oft-quoted passage of the Song celebrating the arrival of springtime (*For behold, the winter is past* [Song 2:11–13]). It means that "the Sun of Righteousness rises upon this harsh winter and brings the spring of the Spirit, which melts [the] ice [of idolatry] and ... warms everything that lies beneath." And of course in the end this ἀκολουθία that defines the route followed in humanity's re-creation is also the route followed by the Bride of the Song: she too is enlightened by the Law and the Prophets, enlivened by the Spirit, and brought to share in that "mingling" of God and humanity of which the incarnation is the original manifestation.

---

144. See ibid., pp. 457–59.
145. See homily 5, pp. 140–41 (Jaeger).
146. See ibid., pp. 144–45.

There is, then, a certain thoughtful quality about Gregory's use of allegory/anagogy; that is to say, he has attempted to think through questions about its function and use, though perhaps not with perfect self-consistency. It is requisite, he thinks, when language whose proper reference is to the perceptible realm is seen to intimate truth of the intelligible or spiritual order. Furthermore, its use is governed at once by the σκοπός of the Scriptures generally and by that of particular works within the Scriptures—a condition that is not inconsistent with Augustine's opinion that exegesis must be ruled by the church's faith (i.e., its baptismal faith, summed up in what is now called "creed") and by the double love commandment. Finally, its aim is by inquiry and discernment (θεωρία) to understand the principle or set of principles that govern human life at the spiritual level, and in the case of the Song of Songs these principles determine a coherent course of growth or transformation—an ἀκολουθία through which human persons are "re-created" and restored to their original destiny. To be sure, allegorical or anagogical interpretation does not reach far enough to speak *conceptually* about God or the divine "Nature," which transcends the intelligible order. Literal, corporeal language may be "transposed" to the level of intelligible reality—presumably because there is some stable analogy between them—but the language of the human intellect cannot be transposed in such wise as to conceptualize the things of God, who is known only indirectly, in darkness (Exod 20:21 LXX), and from behind (Exod 33:21–23), that is, through effects.[147] There are some purposes for which allegory is not useful.

---

147. See homily 7, pp. 212–14 (Jaeger).

HOMILIES ON THE SONG OF SONGS

Τῇ σεμνοπρεπεστάτῃ Ὀλυμπιάδι Γρηγόριος ἐπίσκοπος
Νύσσης ἐν κυρίῳ χαίρειν.

5   Ἀπεδεξάμην ὡς πρέπουσαν τῷ σεμνῷ σου βίῳ καὶ τῇ καθαρᾷ σου ψυχῇ
τὴν περὶ τοῦ Ἄισματος τῶν Ἀισμάτων σπουδήν, ἣν καὶ κατὰ πρόσωπον καὶ
διὰ γραμμάτων ἡμῖν ἐπέθου, ὥστε διὰ τῆς καταλλήλου θεωρίας φανερωθῆναι
τὴν ἐγκεκρυμμένην τοῖς ῥητοῖς φιλοσοφίαν τῆς προχείρου κατὰ | τὴν   4
λέξιν ἐμφάσεως ἐν ταῖς ἀκηράτοις ἐννοίαις κεκαθαρμένην. διὸ προθύμως
ἐδεξάμην τὴν περὶ τούτου φροντίδα, οὐχ ὡς σοί τι χρησιμεύσων εἰς τὸ σὸν
10 ἦθος (πέπεισμαι γάρ σου καθαρεύειν τὸν τῆς ψυχῆς ὀφθαλμὸν ἀπὸ πάσης
ἐμπαθοῦς τε καὶ ῥυπώσης ἐννοίας καὶ πρὸς τὴν ἀκήρατον χάριν διὰ τῶν θείων
τούτων ῥητῶν ἀπαραποδίστως βλέπειν), ἀλλ' ἐφ' ᾧτε τοῖς σαρκωδεστέροις
χειραγωγίαν τινὰ γενέσθαι πρὸς τὴν πνευματικήν τε καὶ ἄϋλον τῆς ψυχῆς
κατάστασιν, πρὸς ἣν ἄγει τὸ βιβλίον τοῦτο διὰ τῆς ἐγκεκρυμμένης αὐτῷ
15 σοφίας.
    ἐπειδὴ δέ τισι τῶν ἐκκλησιαστικῶν παρίστασθαι τῇ λέξει τῆς ἁγίας
γραφῆς διὰ πάντων δοκεῖ καὶ τὸ δι' αἰνιγμάτων τε καὶ ὑπονοιῶν εἰρῆσθαί τι
παρ' αὐτῆς εἰς ὠφέλειαν ἡμῶν οὐ συντίθενται, ἀναγκαῖον ἡγοῦμαι πρῶτον
περὶ τούτων τοῖς τὰ τοιαῦτα ἡμῖν ἐγκαλοῦσιν ἀπολογήσασθαι,
20   ὅτι οὐδὲν ἀπὸ τρόπου γίνεται παρ' ἡμῶν ἐν τῷ σπουδάζειν ἡμᾶς παντοίως
θηρεύειν ἐκ τῆς θεοπνεύστου γραφῆς τὸ ὠφέλιμον· ὥστε εἰ μὲν ὠφελοίη τι
καὶ ἡ λέξις ὡς εἴρηται νοουμένη, ἔχειν ἐξ ἑτοίμου τὸ σπουδαζόμενον, εἰ δέ
τι μετὰ | ἐπικρύψεως ἐν ὑπονοίαις τισὶ καὶ αἰνίγμασιν εἰρημένον ἀργὸν εἰς   5
ὠφέλειαν εἴη κατὰ τὸ πρόχειρον νόημα, τοὺς τοιούτους λόγους ἀναστρέφειν,
25 καθὼς ὑφηγεῖται ὁ διὰ τῶν Παροιμιῶν ἡμᾶς παιδεύων λόγος, εἰς τὸ νοῆσαι
ἢ ὡς παραβολὴν τὸ λεγόμενον ἢ ὡς σκοτεινὸν λόγον ἢ ὡς ῥῆσιν σοφῶν ἢ
ὥς τι τῶν αἰνιγμάτων. ὧν τὴν διὰ τῆς ἀναγωγῆς θεωρίαν εἴτε τροπολογίαν

PREFACE

Gregory the Bishop of Nyssa to the Most Holy Olympias
Greeting in the Lord!

You have enjoined upon me, both in person and by your letters, a study of the Song of Songs, and I have undertaken it because it is suited to your holy life and your pure heart. My hope is that by the right process of inquiry and discernment,[1] once | the text has been cleansed of its obvious literal sense by undefiled thoughts, the philosophy hidden in the words may be brought to light. The reason I accept your proposal with alacrity is not that I may be of assistance to you in the conduct of your life—for I am confident that the eye of your soul is clean of any passionate or indecent thought and that by means of these divine words it looks without hindrance toward the undefiled Beauty—but rather that some direction may be given to more fleshly folk for the sake of the spiritual and immaterial welfare of their souls. It is that to which this book brings us through the wisdom hidden within it.

It seems right to some church leaders, however, to stand by the letter of the Holy Scriptures in all circumstances, and they do not agree that Scripture says anything for our profit by way of enigmas[2] and below-the-surface meanings. For this reason I judge it necessary first of all to defend my practice against those who thus charge us.

In our earnest search for what is profitable in the inspired Scripture (2 Tim 3:16), there is nothing to be found that is unsuitable. Therefore, if there is profit even in the text taken for just what it says, we have what is sought right before us. On the other hand, if something is stated | in a concealed manner by way of enigmas and below-the-surface meanings, and so is void of profit in its plain sense, such passages we turn over in our minds, just as the Word teaches us in Proverbs, so that we may understand what is said either as a parable or as a dark saying or as a word of the wise or as an enigma (cf. Prov 1:6). One may wish to refer to the anagogical interpretation of such

---

1. Greek διὰ τῆς καταλλήλου θεωρίας. On the meaning of the term θεωρία for Gregory, see Daniélou 1970, 1–19.

2. Paul uses the word "enigma" (αἴνιγμα) in 1 Cor 13:12 ("now we see by way of a mirror *in an enigma*"—of which word "dimly" in the RSV is a pale and optimistic translation). It was a technical term in Greek rhetoric and meant a manner of speech that is deliberately puzzling and obscure; in Augustine's later explanation (which of course follows Quintilian), an "obscure" allegory.

εἴτε ἀλληγορίαν εἴτε τι ἄλλο τις ὀνομάζειν ἐθέλοι, οὐδὲν περὶ τοῦ ὀνόματος
διοισόμεθα, μόνον εἰ τῶν ἐπωφελῶν ἔχοιτο νοημάτων·

    καὶ γὰρ ὁ μέγας ἀπόστολος πνευματικὸν εἶναι λέγων τὸν νόμον,
ἐμπεριλαμβάνων δὲ τῷ ὀνόματι τοῦ νόμου καὶ τὰ ἱστορικὰ διηγήματα, ὡς
5 πᾶσαν τὴν θεόπνευστον γραφὴν νόμον εἶναι τοῖς ἐντυγχάνουσιν, οὐ μόνον
διὰ τῶν φανερῶν παραγγελμάτων ἀλλὰ καὶ διὰ τῶν ἱστορικῶν διηγημάτων
παιδεύουσαν πρός τε γνῶσιν τῶν μυστηρίων καὶ πρὸς καθαρὰν πολιτείαν
τοὺς ἐπιστατικῶς ἐπαΐοντας, κέχρηται μὲν τῇ ἐξηγήσει κατὰ τὸ ἀρέσκον
αὐτῷ πρὸς τὸ ὠφέλιμον βλέπων, οὐ φροντίζει δὲ τοῦ ὀνόματος, ᾧ χρὴ
10 κατονομάζεσθαι τὸ εἶδος τῆς ἐξηγήσεως· ἀλλὰ νῦν μὲν ἀλλάσσειν φησὶ τὴν
φωνήν, μέλλων μετάγειν τὴν ἱστορίαν εἰς ἔνδειξιν τῆς περὶ τῶν διαθηκῶν
οἰκονομίας, | εἶτα μνησθεὶς τῶν δύο τοῦ Ἀβραὰμ τέκνων, τῶν ἔκ τε τῆς 6
παιδίσκης καὶ τῆς ἐλευθέρας αὐτῷ γεγονότων, ἀλληγορίαν ὀνομάζει τὴν περὶ
αὐτῶν θεωρίαν, πάλιν δὲ πράγματά τινα διηγησάμενος τῆς ἱστορίας φησὶν
15 ὅτι Τυπικῶς μὲν συνέβαινεν ἐκείνοις, ἐγράφη δὲ πρὸς νουθεσίαν ἡμῶν. καὶ
πάλιν τὸ μὴ δεῖν κημοῦσθαι τὸν ἀλοῶντα βοῦν εἰπὼν προσέθηκεν ὅτι Οὐ
μέλει τῷ θεῷ περὶ τῶν βοῶν, ἀλλ᾽ ὅτι Δι᾽ ἡμᾶς πάντως ἐγράφη. ἔστι δὲ ὅπου
τὴν ἀμυδροτέραν κατανόησιν καὶ τὴν ἐκ μέρους γνῶσιν ἔσοπτρον ὀνομάζει
καὶ αἴνιγμα. καὶ πάλιν τὴν ἀπὸ τῶν σωματικῶν πρὸς τὰ νοητὰ μετάστασιν
20 πρὸς κύριον ἐπιστροφὴν λέγει καὶ καλύμματος περιαίρεσιν.

    ἐν πᾶσι δὲ τούτοις τοῖς διαφόροις τρόποις τε καὶ ὀνόμασι τῆς κατὰ
τὸν νοῦν θεωρίας ἓν ὑφηγεῖται διδασκαλίας εἶδος ἡμῖν, τὸ μὴ δεῖν πάντως
παραμένειν τῷ γράμματι ὡς βλαπτούσης ἡμᾶς ἐν πολλοῖς εἰς τὸν κατ᾽ ἀρετὴν
βίον τῆς προχείρου τῶν λεγομένων ἐμφάσεως, ἀλλὰ μεταβαίνειν πρὸς τὴν
25 ἄϋλόν τε καὶ νοητὴν θεωρίαν, ὥστε τὰς σωματικωτέρας ἐννοίας μεταβληθῆναι
πρὸς νοῦν καὶ διάνοιαν κόνεως δίκην τῆς σαρκωδεστέρας ἐμφάσεως τῶν
| λεγομένων ἐκτιναχθείσης.   7

    καὶ διὰ τοῦτό φησιν ὅτι Τὸ γράμμα ἀποκτείνει, τὸ δὲ πνεῦμα ζωοποιεῖ,
ὡς πολλαχῇ τῆς ἱστορίας, εἴπερ ἐπὶ ψιλῶν σταίημεν τῶν πραγμάτων, οὐκ
30 ἀγαθοῦ βίου παρεχομένης ἡμῖν τὰ ὑποδείγματα· τί γὰρ ὠφελεῖ πρὸς ἀρετὴν
τὸν ἀκούοντα Ὡσηὲ ὁ προφήτης ἐκ πορνείας παιδοποιούμενος καὶ Ἡσαΐας
εἰσιὼν πρὸς τὴν προφῆτιν, εἰ μέχρι τῆς λέξεώς τις στήσειε τὸ λεγόμενον; ἢ

sayings as "tropology" or "allegory" or by some other name. We shall not
quarrel about the name as long as a firm grasp is kept on thoughts that edify.

For the grand apostle, when he says that the law is spiritual (Rom 7:14),
is including the historical narratives too under the heading "law," because
the whole of the divinely inspired Scripture is law for those who read it. Not
only through its explicit commands, but also through its historical narratives, Scripture affords a teaching that guides those who pay careful heed
to it toward knowledge of the mysteries and toward a pure life. The apostle,
moreover, does the work of interpretation in accordance with what gives
him satisfaction in his search for what edifies, though he does not concern
himself with the label that is to be assigned to a type of exegesis. Rather the
contrary. At one point, when he is about to transpose the biblical narrative
so as to unfold the economy of the covenants, he says that he is changing his
manner of speech (Gal 4:20),[3] | but then, after he has mentioned the two sons
of Abraham, born to him of the maidservant and the free woman, Paul des-
ignates his way of understanding them an "allegory" (Gal 4:24). And again,
when he has been recounting certain events of the biblical history, he says:
"They happened to those people as types" but "were written for our admoni-
tion" (1 Cor 10:11). Or again, when he has said that the threshing ox should
not be muzzled, he adds: "God's concern is not for oxen," but "these things
were surely written for our sakes" (1 Cor 9:9–10). Also there is a place where
he calls dimmer understanding and partial knowledge a "mirror" and an
"enigma" (1 Cor 13:12), and again he says that the movement from corporeal
to intelligible realities is a turning toward the Lord and the removal of a veil
(2 Cor 3:16).

By all these different modes of speech and names for intellectual discernment, the apostle is pointing us to a single form of instruction: one ought
not in every instance to remain with the letter (since the obvious sense of the
words often does us harm when it comes to the virtuous life), but one ought
to shift to an understanding that concerns the immaterial and intelligible, so
that corporeal ideas may be transposed into intellect and thought when the
fleshly sense of the | words has been shaken off like dust (cf. Matt 10:14)

This moreover is why he says, "The letter kills, but the spirit gives life"
(2 Cor 3:6), for frequently the narrative, if we stop short at the mere events,
does not furnish us with models of the good life. How does it profit the cause
of a virtuous life to hear that the prophet Hosea got himself a child by sexual
malfeasance (Hos 1:2) and that Isaiah went in to the prophetess (Isa 8:3),

---

3. Ἀλλάξαι τὴν φωνήν μου (RSV "change my tone"), which Gregory understands to refer to
the allegorical interpretation of Sarah and Hagar that follows in Gal 4:21–31.

τί πρὸς τὸν ἐνάρετον συντελεῖ βίον τὰ περὶ τοῦ Δαβὶδ διηγήματα, μοιχείας
καὶ φόνου κατὰ ταὐτὸ περὶ τὸ ἓν συνδεδραμηκότων ἄγος; εἰ δέ τις εὑρεθείη
λόγος ὁ τὸ διὰ τούτων οἰκονομούμενον ἐπιδεικνύων ἀνεύθυνον, τότε
ἀληθεύων ὁ τοῦ ἀποστόλου λόγος ἐπιδειχθήσεται ὅτι Τὸ γράμμα ἀποκτείνει
5   (πονηρῶν γὰρ ἔχει πραγμάτων ἐν ἑαυτῷ ὑποδείγματα), τὸ δὲ πνεῦμα
ζωοποιεῖ· μετατίθησι γὰρ τὴν ἀπεμφαίνουσάν τε καὶ διαβεβλημένην ἔννοιαν
εἰς θειοτέρας ἐμφάσεις.

οἴδαμεν δὲ καὶ αὐτὸν τὸν λόγον τὸν παρὰ πάσης κτίσεως προσκυνούμενον,
ὅτε ἐν ὁμοιώματι ἀνθρώπου καὶ σχήματι διὰ σαρκὸς παρεδίδου τὰ θεῖα
10   μυστήρια, οὕτως | ἀνακαλύπτοντα ἡμῖν τὰ τοῦ νόμου νοήματα, ὥστε τοὺς   8
δύο ἀνθρώπους, ὧν ἀληθής ἐστιν ἡ μαρτυρία, ἑαυτὸν καὶ τὸν πατέρα λέγειν
εἶναι· καὶ τὸν χαλκοῦν ὄφιν τὸν ἐπὶ τοῦ ὕψους ἀνατεθέντα, ὃς ἦν τῷ λαῷ τῶν
θανατηφόρων δηγμάτων ἀλεξητήριος, εἰς τὴν διὰ τοῦ σταυροῦ γενομένην
ὑπὲρ ἡμῶν οἰκονομίαν μεταλαμβάνοντα· καὶ αὐτῶν δὲ τῶν ἁγίων αὐτοῦ
15   μαθητῶν τὴν ἀγχίνοιαν διὰ τῶν ἐπικεκαλυμμένων τε καὶ ἐπικεκρυμμένων
λόγων διαγυμνάζοντα ἐν παραβολαῖς, ἐν ὁμοιώμασιν, ἐν σκοτεινοῖς λόγοις,
ἐν ἀποφθέγμασι, τοῖς δι᾽ αἰνιγμάτων προφερομένοις, ὑπὲρ ὧν κατὰ μόνας
μὲν ἐποιεῖτο τὰς ἐξηγήσεις ἐπιλύων αὐτοῖς τὴν ἀσάφειαν, ἔστι δὲ ὅπου, εἰ
μὴ κατελήφθη παρ᾽ αὐτῶν ἡ τῶν λεγομένων διάνοια, διεμέμφετο αὐτῶν τὸ
20   βραδύνουν καὶ περὶ τὴν σύνεσιν ἄτονον· ὅτε γὰρ ἀπέχεσθαι τῆς Φαρισαϊκῆς
αὐτοῖς ἐνεκελεύετο ζύμης, οἱ δὲ μικροψύχως πρὸς τὰς πήρας ἀπέβλεπον,
ἐν αἷς τὸν ἐκ τῶν ἄρτων ἐπισιτισμὸν οὐκ ἐπήγοντο, τότε καθάπτεται τῶν
μὴ συνιέντων, ὅτι διδασκαλία ἦν τὸ διὰ | τῆς ζύμης δηλούμενον. καὶ πάλιν   9
τράπεζαν αὐτῷ τῶν μαθητῶν παρατιθέντων ἀποκρινόμενος ὅτι Ἐγὼ βρῶσιν
25   ἔχω φαγεῖν, ἣν ὑμεῖς οὐκ οἴδατε, ὑπονοησάντων αὐτῶν περὶ σωματικῆς αὐτὸν
λέγειν τροφῆς ὡς ἑτέρωθεν αὐτῷ προσενεχθείσης, ἑρμηνεύει τὸν ἑαυτοῦ
λόγον ὅτι βρῶσίς ἐστιν αὐτῷ πρέπουσα καὶ κατάλληλος ἡ τοῦ σωτηρίου
θελήματος ἀποπλήρωσις.

καὶ μυρία τοιαῦτα ἐκ τῶν εὐαγγελικῶν φωνῶν ἔστιν ἀναλέξασθαι, ἐφ᾽
30   ὧν ἄλλο μὲν ἔστι τὸ ἐκ τοῦ προχείρου νοούμενον, ἕτερον δὲ πρὸς ὃ βλέπει
ἡ τῶν λεγομένων διάνοια· οἷον τὸ ὕδωρ ὃ τοῖς διψῶσι κατεπηγγείλατο δι᾽
οὗ πηγαὶ ποταμῶν γίνονται οἱ πιστεύοντες, τὸν ἄρτον τὸν ἐκ τῶν οὐρανῶν

if one stops short at the literal sense? Or what do the stories about David, in which adultery and murder have agreed together in a single crime (cf. 2 Kgdms 11), contribute to the virtuous life? But if an account is found that gives an incontestable indication of how these events fit into the history of salvation, then the word of the apostle will be shown to be true: "The letter kills" (for it contains examples of evildoing), "but the Spirit gives life" (for it transposes a meaning that is incongruous and discordant into a more divine sense).

We know too that when, in the likeness and form of a human being (Phil 2:7), the Word who is worshiped by the whole creation transmitted the divine mysteries through the medium of flesh, it was in the following manner | that he unveiled for us the thoughts contained in the law. He says that he and his Father are the two witnesses whose testimony is true (John 8:18; cf. Deut 19:15), and the brazen serpent that was lifted up high and was the people's remedy against deadly stings he refers to the dispensation that took place for our sake on the cross (John 3:14). Also he exercises the wits of his own holy disciples by the veiled and hidden things he speaks in parables, in similitudes, in dark sayings, in aphorisms—things set forth in the form of enigmatic statements.[4] In private, he would give interpretations of these and explain to them what was obscure, but on occasion, when they did not grasp the meaning of his words, he would blame them for being slow to understand and slack in intelligence. For when he commanded them to beware of the leaven of the Pharisees, and they in their small-minded way looked to their food pouches, in which they had failed to bring a supply of bread, he reprimanded them for failing to grasp that | the word "leaven" is a reference to teaching (Matt 16:5–12). Again, when the disciples were setting a meal before him, he responded, "I have food to eat of which you do not know" (John 4:32), and since they supposed that he was speaking of corporeal food that had been brought him from elsewhere, he explained his statement by saying that the food that is proper and appropriate for him is to fulfill the salutary [divine] will.

There are, moreover, countless instances of this sort of thing to be gathered from the sayings in the Gospels, instances in which one thing is conveyed by the obvious sense but something else is indicated by the intelligible meaning of what is said. For example: the water that [Christ] promised to the thirsty, through which believers become springs of flowing waters (John 7:37–38); or the bread that comes down from heaven (John 6:50–51);

---

4. Here Gregory's phraseology suggests that he takes "enigma" as a general term for various specific forms of figurative speech, and this conclusion is supported by much of his usage in these homilies.

καταβαίνοντα, τὸν ναὸν τὸν λυόμενον καὶ διὰ τριῶν ἡμερῶν ἐγειρόμενον, τὴν ὁδόν, τὴν θύραν, τὸν λίθον τὸν παρὰ τῶν οἰκοδόμων ἐξουθενημένον καὶ τῇ ἐπιγωνίῳ κεφαλῇ ἁρμοζόμενον, τοὺς δύο τοὺς ἐπὶ κλίνης μιᾶς, τὸν μυλῶνα, τὰς ἀληθούσας, τὴν παραλαμβανομένην, τὴν καταλιμπανομένην, τὸ πτῶμα,

5   τοὺς ἀετούς, τὴν συκῆν τὴν ἁπαλυνομένην καὶ τοὺς κλάδους ἐκφύουσαν.

ἅπερ πάντα καὶ ὅσα τοιαῦτα γένοιτο ἂν εἰς προτροπὴν ἡμῖν τοῦ χρῆναι | διερευνᾶν τὰς θείας φωνὰς καὶ προσέχειν τῇ ἀναγνώσει καὶ κατὰ πάντα   10 τρόπον ἀνιχνεύειν, εἴ πού τις εὑρεθείη λόγος τῆς προχείρου κατανοήσεως ὑψηλότερος ἐπὶ τὰ θειότερά τε καὶ ἀσώματα χειραγωγῶν τὴν διάνοιαν.

10   τούτου χάριν τὸ ἀπηγορευμένον τῇ βρώσει ξύλον οὐχὶ συκῆν, ὥς τινες ἀπεφήναντο, οὔτε ἄλλο τι τῶν ἀκροδρύων εἶναι πειθόμεθα· εἰ γὰρ τότε θανατηφόρος ἦν ἡ συκῆ, οὐδ' ἂν νῦν πάντως ἐδώδιμος ἦν· ἅμα δὲ καὶ μεμαθήκαμεν παρὰ τῆς τοῦ δεσπότου φωνῆς, δι' ἀποφάσεως τοῦτο δογματιζούσης, ὅτι Οὐδέν ἐστι τῶν εἰσπορευομένων διὰ στόματος ὃ

15   δύναται κοινῶσαι τὸν ἄνθρωπον· ἀλλ' ἑτέραν τινὰ ζητοῦμεν διάνοιαν ἐπὶ τοῦ νόμου τούτου, ἀξίαν τῆς τοῦ νομοθέτου μεγαλειότητος· κἂν τῆς τοῦ θεοῦ φυτείας ἔργον τὸν παράδεισον εἶναι ἀκούσωμεν, κἂν ξύλον ζωῆς ἐν μέσῳ τοῦ παραδείσου πεφυτευμένον, ζητοῦμεν παρὰ τοῦ ἀποκαλύπτοντος τὰ κεκρυμμένα μυστήρια μαθεῖν, ποίων φυτῶν γίνεται ὁ πατὴρ γεωργός τε

20   καὶ φυτηκόμος, καὶ πῶς δυνατόν ἐστι κατὰ τὸ μεσαίτατον τοῦ παραδείσου τὰ δύο εἶναι ξύλα, τό τε τῆς σωτηρίας καὶ τὸ τῆς ἀπωλείας· τὸ γὰρ ἀκριβῶς μέσον καθάπερ ἐν κύκλου περιγραφῇ ἐν τῷ ἑνὶ κέντρῳ πάντως ἐστίν. εἰ δὲ παρατεθείη τῷ κέντρῳ κατά τι μέρος ἕτερον κέντρον, ἀνάγκη πᾶσα συμμετατεθῆναι τῷ κέντρῳ τὸν κύκλον, ὥστε μηκέτι μέσον εἶναι τὸ πρότερον.

25   ἐκεῖ τοίνυν ἑνὸς ὄντος τοῦ παραδείσου, | πῶς φησιν ὁ λόγος ἰδιαζόντως   11 μὲν ἑκάτερον θεωρεῖσθαι τῶν ξύλων, ἐπὶ δὲ τοῦ μέσου εἶναι καὶ τοῦτο καὶ τοῦτο, ὧν τὸ θανατηφόρον τῆς τοῦ θεοῦ φυτείας ἀλλότριον εἶναι διδάσκει ὁ πάντα καλὰ λίαν εἶναι τὰ τοῦ θεοῦ ἔργα ἀποφηνάμενος λόγος; οἷς εἰ μή τις διὰ φιλοσοφίας ἐνθεωρήσειε τὴν ἀλήθειαν, ἀσύστατον ἢ μυθῶδες εἶναι τοῖς

30   ἀνεπισκέπτοις τὸ λεγόμενον δόξει.

Καὶ μακρὸν ἂν εἴη τὰ καθ' ἕκαστον ἐκ τῶν προφητῶν ἀναλέγεσθαι· πῶς ὁ Μιχαίας ἐπ' ἐσχάτων τῶν ἡμερῶν ἐμφανὲς ὄρος λέγει γενήσεσθαι

the temple that is destroyed and raised up in three days (John 2:19); the way (John 14:6); the door (John 10:9); the stone that is rejected by the builders and is fitted in as the chief cornerstone (Mark 12:10); two persons upon a single bed (Luke 17:34); the mill, the two women grinding, one of whom is taken and the other left (Matt 24:41); the corpse and the eagles (Matt 24:28); the fig tree that becomes tender and puts forth its leaves (Matt 24:32). All these examples—and as many other expressions as are of the same sort— can serve to encourage us | to examine the divine words closely and to "give careful heed to our reading" (1 Tim 4:13) and to ascertain by every possible means whether perhaps one can discover a meaning higher than that of the surface sense, one that leads the mind upward in the direction of something more divine and incorporeal.

For this reason I am persuaded that the tree of which it was forbidden to eat (Gen 2:17) was not, as some have asserted, a fig tree or any other fruit-bearing tree. For if the fig was a death-dealer in those days, it would not be perfectly edible now. We have at the same time learned this truth, in a negative form, from the voice of the Master, as it lays down the principle that none of the things that enter through the mouth is capable of defiling a person (Matt 15:11). Where that law (Gen 2:17) is concerned, then, we look for some other meaning, and one that is worthy of the greatness of the Lawgiver. Even though we are informed that the garden is a product of divine husbandry and that the tree of life is planted in the middle of the garden, we want to learn from the Revealer of hidden mysteries what growths they are that the Father plants and tends and also how it is possible for there to be two trees right at the midpoint of the garden: the tree that saves and the tree that destroys. For the exact midpoint lies precisely at the one center, just as within the circumference of a circle. If, however, another center is set to one side of the center, it follows of necessity that the circle's position is shifted along with the center, with the result that the first center is no longer the midpoint. But if there was only a single garden in that place, | how can the Word assert that each of the trees is to be treated of separately and yet say that both of them stand at the midpoint, even while the Word, in asserting that all the works of God are "very good" (Gen 1:31), informs us that of the two trees the death-dealer has no place in the estate that God plants?[5] Unless one perceives the truth in these matters through philosophy, what is being said will appear to the inattentive to be incoherent or mythical.

It would take a long time to assemble the individual examples out of the prophetic books: how Micah says that in the last days a mountain shall

---

5. For Gregory's solution to this enigma, see homily 12 below.

ἐπὶ τὰς κορυφὰς τῶν ὀρέων, τὸ ἐπὶ καθαιρέσει τῶν ἀντικειμένων δυνάμεων
ἀναδεικνύμενον τῆς εὐσεβείας μυστήριον οὕτω κατονομάζων· πῶς δὲ
ῥάβδον ἀνατέλλειν φησὶ καὶ ἄνθος ἐκ τῆς ῥίζης, τὴν διὰ σαρκὸς τοῦ κυρίου
ἀνάδειξιν ὁ ὑψηλὸς Ἡσαΐας οὕτω μηνύων· ἢ τὸ τετυρωμένον ὄρος παρὰ τῷ
5   μεγάλῳ Δαβίδ, ποῖον ἔχει νοῦν ἐν τῇ λέξει φαινόμενον· ἢ τὸ μυριοπλάσιον
ἅρμα· ἢ τῶν ταύρων ἡ συναγωγὴ ἡ ἐπαφιεμένη ταῖς δαμάλεσι τῶν λαῶν· ἢ ὁ
βαπτόμενος τῷ αἵματι ποῦς ἢ τῶν κυνῶν αἱ γλῶσσαι· ἢ καθ' ὁμοιότητα τοῦ
μόσχου διαλεπτυνόμενος | μετὰ τῶν κέδρων ὁ Λίβανος·   12
       καὶ μυρία πρὸς τούτοις ἔστιν ἐκ τῆς λοιπῆς ἀναλεξάμενον
10   προφητείας δεῖξαι τὸ ἀναγκαῖον τῆς κατὰ διάνοιαν τῶν ῥητῶν θεωρίας, ἧς
ἀποβαλλομένης, καθὼς ἀρέσκει τισίν, ὅμοιον εἶναί μοι δοκεῖ τὸ γινόμενον,
ὡς εἴ τις ἀκατέργαστα προθείη πρὸς ἀνθρωπίνην βρῶσιν ἐπὶ τραπέζης τὰ
λήϊα, μὴ τρίψας τὴν καλάμην, μὴ τῷ λικμητῷ διακρίνας ἐκ τῶν ἀχύρων τὰ
σπέρματα, μὴ λεπτύνας τὸν σῖτον εἰς ἄλευρον, μηδὲ κατασκευάσας ἄρτον
15   τῷ καθήκοντι τρόπῳ τῆς σιτοποιΐας. ὥσπερ οὖν τὸ ἀκατέργαστον γένημα
κτηνῶν ἐστι καὶ οὐκ ἀνθρώπων τροφή, οὕτως εἴποι τις ἂν ἀλόγων μᾶλλον
ἢ λογικῶν εἶναι τροφὴν μὴ κατεργασθέντα διὰ τῆς λεπτοτέρας θεωρίας τὰ
θεόπνευστα ῥήματα οὐ μόνον τῆς παλαιᾶς διαθήκης, ἀλλὰ καὶ τὰ πολλὰ
τῆς εὐαγγελικῆς διδασκαλίας· τὸ πτύον τὸ διακαθαῖρον τὴν ἅλωνα, τὸ
20   ἀποφυσώμενον ἄχυρον, ὁ παραμένων σῖτος τοῖς ποσὶ τοῦ λικμήτορος, τὸ
ἄσβεστον πῦρ, ἡ ἀγαθὴ ἀποθήκη, τὸ τῶν κακῶν εὔφορον δένδρον, ἡ ἀπειλὴ
τῆς ἀξίνης ἡ φοβερῶς τῷ δένδρῳ τὴν ἀκμὴν προδεικνύουσα, οἱ πρὸς τὴν
ἀνθρωπίνην φύσιν μεταποιούμενοι λίθοι.
       Ταῦτά μοι διὰ τῶν πρὸς τὴν σύνεσίν σου γραμμάτων | ἀπολογία τις   13
25   γεγράφθω πρὸς τοὺς μηδὲν πλέον παρὰ τὴν πρόχειρον τῆς λέξεως ἔμφασιν
ἐκ τῶν θείων ῥημάτων ἀναζητεῖν νομοθετοῦντας.
       εἰ δὲ τοῦ Ὠριγένους φιλοπόνως περὶ τὸ βιβλίον τοῦτο σπουδάσαντος καὶ
ἡμεῖς γραφῇ παραδοῦναι τὸν πόνον ἡμῶν προεθυμήθημεν, ἐγκαλείτω μηδεὶς

become visible above the peaks of the mountains (Mic 4:1)—thus naming
what is manifested in the destruction of opposing powers the "mystery of
true religion" (1 Tim 3:16); how the sublime Isaiah says that a branch shall
spring up and a new shoot from the root (Isa 11:1) and in this way indicates
the Lord's disclosure by way of flesh; or the great David's "curdled mountain"
(Ps 67:16)—and what sort of sense does *that* make if taken literally?—or the
"chariot" that is "a thousandfold" (Ps 67:17); or the "herd of bulls" that is let
loose upon "the heifers of the peoples" (Ps 67:30); or the foot bathed in blood,
not to mention the tongues "of the dogs" (Ps 67:23); or Lebanon with its
cedars | "skipping" like a calf (Ps 28:5–6).

When, moreover, one has collected from the rest of the prophetic books
the countless additional examples of this sort of thing, it is possible to show
the necessity of interpreting the words of Scripture at the level of their higher
meaning, and should this necessity be denied, as some people wish, the result
seems to me to be like someone's setting out unprepared grain on the table for
human beings to eat, without threshing the stalk or separating the seeds from
their husks by winnowing or reducing the grain to flour or making bread in
the proper fashion. So then, just as unprepared produce is food for animals
and not for human beings, so too one may say that the divinely inspired words
are food for nonrational animals rather than for rational persons unless they
have been prepared by a properly subtle[6] and discerning inquiry. This applies
not only to the words of the Old Covenant but also to the greater part of
the Gospel teaching: the winnowing fork that clears the threshing floor, the
chaff being blown away, the wheat remaining at the feet of the winnower, the
unquenchable fire, the good granary, the fertile tree of the wicked, the threat
of the axe that terrifyingly exhibits its sharp edge to the tree beforehand, the
stones being altered to human nature (Matt 3:9–12; Luke 3:8–9).

Let this be my apologia—addressed to your understanding in this letter—
| in response to the people who lay it down as a law that one is not to seek
from the inspired words any meaning that goes beyond the obvious sense of
the text.

If, however, we are eager, even after Origen has addressed himself diligently to the study of this book,[7] to commit our own work to writing, let

---

6. It is perhaps worth noting that the Greek word λεπτός (here used as a comparative and
translated as "subtle") originally connoted something peeled or husked. Could Gregory have
been aware of this?

7. Origen's *Commentary on the Song of Songs* in ten books was composed in Athens and
Caesarea toward the end of his career. Of these ten books, we possess just three in the Latin
translation of Rufinus of Aquileia, in addition to some fragments of the original Greek. The
Latin text is edited by W. Baehrens in volume 33 of Die griechischen christlichen Schriftsteller

πρὸς τὸ θεῖον τοῦ ἀποστόλου λόγιον βλέπων, ὅς φησιν ὅτι Ἕκαστος τὸν
ἴδιον μισθὸν λήψεται κατὰ τὸν ἴδιον κόπον. ἐμοὶ δὲ οὐ πρὸς ἐπίδειξίν ἐστι
συντεταγμένος ὁ λόγος· ἀλλ᾿ ἐπειδὴ τὰ πολλὰ τῶν ἐπ᾿ ἐκκλησίας ῥηθέντων
τινὲς τῶν συνόντων ἡμῖν ὑπὸ φιλομαθείας ἐσημειώσαντο, τὰ μὲν παρ᾿
5   ἐκείνων λαβών, ὅσα δι᾿ ἀκολούθου ἔσχεν αὐτῶν ἡ σημείωσις, τὰ δὲ καὶ
ἀπ᾿ ἐμαυτοῦ προσθείς, ὧν ἀναγκαία ἦν ἡ προσθήκη, ἐν ὁμιλιῶν εἴδει τὴν
ὑπηγορίαν πεποίημαι καθεξῆς πρὸς λέξιν προαγαγὼν τὴν τῶν ῥητῶν θεωρίαν,
ἐφ᾿ ὅσον ὁ καιρός τε καὶ τὰ πράγματα τὴν περὶ τούτου μοι σχολὴν ἐνεδίδου
κατὰ τὰς ἡμέρας τῶν νηστειῶν· ἐν ταύταις γὰρ ἡμῖν πρὸς τὴν δημοσίαν
10   ἀκοὴν ὁ περὶ τούτου λόγος διεσπουδάσθη. εἰ δὲ παράσχοι καὶ ζωῆς χρόνον
ὁ τῆς ζωῆς ἡμῶν ταμίας θεὸς καὶ εἰρηνικὴν εὐκαιρίαν, καὶ τοῖς λειπομένοις
ἴσως ἐπιδραμούμεθα· νῦν γὰρ ἡμῖν μέχρι τοῦ ἡμίσεος προῆλθεν ὁ λόγος καὶ
ἡ θεωρία.

no one who has before his eyes the divine saying of the apostle to the effect that "each one will receive his own reward in proportion to his labor" (1 Cor 3:8) lay a charge against us. As far as I am concerned, this work was not put together for the sake of display. Rather, it is the case that certain of our associates had, out of their love of knowledge, taken down notes of much of what was said in the assembly of the church. Consequently, I took from them whatever their notes contained that was in proper order but also added for my own part what was necessary by way of supplement. Then I took this compilation and fashioned it in the form of homilies in which the interpretation of the words followed the order of the text, to the extent that time and circumstance afforded me the leisure for this during the days of fasting, for on these days we devoted ourselves to speaking on this subject in public. But if the God who bestows life provides us both with a long enough life and with a time of quiet, we shall perhaps work our way through what remains, for at this point our discourse and our interpretation have advanced to the halfway point in the text.

der ersten drei Jahrhunderte (Leipzig, 1925), and there is an excellent English translation by R. P. Lawson in the series Ancient Christian Writers, vol. 26.

[Ἆισμα ᾀσμάτων, ὅ ἐστιν τῷ Σαλωμων.]
Φιλησάτω με ἀπὸ φιλημάτων στόματος αὐτοῦ,
ὅτι ἀγαθοὶ μαστοί σου ὑπὲρ οἶνον,
Καὶ ὀσμὴ μύρων σου ὑπὲρ πάντα τὰ ἀρώματα,
5   μύρον ἐκκενωθὲν ὄνομά σοι.
διὰ τοῦτο νεάνιδες ἠγάπησάν σε,
Εἵλκυσάν σε,
ὀπίσω σου εἰς ὀσμὴν μύρων σου δραμούμεθα.
εἰσήγαγέ με ὁ βασιλεὺς εἰς τὸ ταμιεῖον αὐτοῦ.
10   ἀγαλλιασώμεθα καὶ εὐφρανθῶμεν ἐν σοί,
ἀγαπήσωμεν μαστούς σου ὑπὲρ οἶνον·
εὐθύτης ἠγάπησέ σε.

Ὅσοι κατὰ τὴν συμβουλὴν τοῦ Παύλου τὸν παλαιὸν ἄνθρωπον ὥσπερ τι
περιβόλαιον ῥυπαρὸν ἀπεδύσασθε σὺν ταῖς πράξεσι καὶ ταῖς ἐπιθυμίαις αὐτοῦ
15   καὶ τὰ φωτεινὰ τοῦ κυρίου ἱμάτια, οἷα ἐπὶ τῆς τοῦ ὄρους μεταμορφώσεως
ἔδειξε, διὰ τῆς καθαρότητος τοῦ βίου περιεβάλεσθε, μᾶλλον δὲ οἱ αὐτὸν τὸν
κύριον ἡμῶν Ἰησοῦν Χριστὸν μετὰ τῆς ἁγίας αὐτοῦ στολῆς ἐνδυσάμενοι
καὶ συμμεταμορφωθέντες αὐτῷ | πρὸς τὸ ἀπαθές τε καὶ θειότερον, ὑμεῖς   15
ἀκούσατε τῶν μυστηρίων τοῦ Ἄισματος τῶν Ἀισμάτων· ὑμεῖς ἐντὸς γένεσθε
20   τοῦ ἀκηράτου νυμφῶνος λευχειμονοῦντες τοῖς καθαροῖς τε καὶ ἀμολύντοις
νοήμασιν. μή τις ἐμπαθῆ καὶ σαρκώδη λογισμὸν ἐπαγόμενος καὶ μὴ ἔχων
πρέπον τῷ θείῳ γάμῳ τὸ τῆς συνειδήσεως ἔνδυμα συνδεθῇ τοῖς ἰδίοις
νοήμασι, τὰς ἀκηράτους τοῦ νυμφίου τε καὶ τῆς νύμφης φωνὰς εἰς κτηνώδη
καὶ ἄλογα καθέλκων πάθη, καὶ δι' αὐτῶν ταῖς αἰσχραῖς ἐνδεθεὶς φαντασίαις
25   ἔξω τῶν ἐν τῷ γάμῳ φαιδρυνομένων ἀπορριφῇ, τὸν βρυγμὸν καὶ τὸ δάκρυον
ἀντὶ τῆς ἐν παστάδι χαρᾶς ἀλλαξάμενος.
ταῦτα διαμαρτύρομαι μέλλων ἅπτεσθαι τῆς ἐν τῷ Ἄισματι τῶν Ἀισμάτων
μυστικῆς θεωρίας. διὰ γὰρ τῶν ἐνταῦθα γεγραμμένων νυμφοστολεῖται
τρόπον τινὰ ἡ ψυχὴ πρὸς τὴν ἀσώματόν τε καὶ πνευματικὴν καὶ ἀμόλυντον
30   τοῦ θεοῦ συζυγίαν· ὁ γὰρ πάντας θέλων σωθῆναι καὶ εἰς ἐπίγνωσιν ἀληθείας
ἐλθεῖν τὸν τελεώτατον ἐνταῦθα καὶ μακάριον τῆς σωτηρίας ὑποδείκνυσι

HOMILY 1
Song 1:1–4

[¹*The Song of Songs, which is Solomon's.*]
²*Let him kiss me with the kisses of his mouth,*
for your breasts are better than wine,
³*and the fragrance of your perfumed ointments is better than all spices,*
your name is perfumed ointment emptied out.
That is why young maidens have loved you,
⁴*they have drawn you.*
We will run after you, toward the fragrance of your perfumed ointments.
The king brought me into his treasure house.
Let us rejoice and be glad in you,
let us love your breasts more than wine:
righteousness has loved you.

You who in accordance with the counsel of Paul have "taken off" the old humanity with its deeds and lusts like a filthy garment (Col 3:9) and have clothed yourselves by purity of life in the lightsome raiment of the Lord, raiment such as he revealed in his transfiguration on the mountain (cf. Mark 9:2–3 and par.), or, rather, you who have "put on" our Lord Jesus Christ himself (Gal 3:27) together with his holy garb and with him have been transfigured for | impassibility and the life divine: hear the mysteries of the Song of Songs. Enter the inviolate bridal chamber dressed in the white robes of pure and undefiled thoughts. If any bear a passionate and carnal habit of mind and lack that garment of conscience that is proper dress for the divine wedding feast, let such persons not be imprisoned by their own thoughts and drag the undefiled words of the Bridegroom and Bride down to the level of brutish, irrational passions; let them not because of these passions be constrained by indecent imaginings[1] and get cast out of the bright cheer of the wedding chamber, exchanging gnashing of teeth and tears for the joy within the bridal chamber (Matt 22:10–13).

I testify thus as one who is about to treat the mystical vision contained in the Song of Songs. For by what is written there, the soul is in a certain manner led as a bride toward an incorporeal and spiritual and undefiled marriage with God. For he "who wills all to be saved and to come to the knowledge of truth"

---

1. See Daniélou 1954, 85–86, and esp. 86 *infra*, where this passage is cited as showing Gregory's identification of passions with "the thoughts of the flesh."

τρόπον, τὸν διὰ τῆς ἀγάπης λέγω. ἔστι μὲν γὰρ καὶ διὰ φόβου τισὶ γινομένη ἡ σωτηρία, ὅταν πρὸς τὰς ἀπειλὰς τῆς ἐν τῇ γεέννῃ κολάσεως | βλέποντες   16 τοῦ κακοῦ χωριζώμεθα. εἰσὶ δέ τινες οἱ καὶ διὰ τὴν ἀποκειμένην τοῖς εὖ βεβιωκόσι τῶν μισθῶν ἐλπίδα τὴν ἀρετὴν κατορθοῦντες, οὐκ ἀγάπῃ τοῦ 5   ἀγαθοῦ, ἀλλὰ τῇ προσδοκίᾳ τῆς ἀμοιβῆς κατακτώμενοι. ὁ μέντοι πρὸς τὸ τέλειον ἀναδραμὼν τῇ ψυχῇ ἀπωθεῖται μὲν τὸν φόβον (ἀνδραποδώδης γὰρ ἡ τοιαύτη διάθεσις, τὸ μὴ δι᾽ ἀγάπης παραμένειν τῷ κυριεύοντι, ἀλλὰ τῷ τῶν μαστίγων φόβῳ μὴ δραπετεύειν), ὑπερορᾷ δὲ καὶ αὐτῶν τῶν μισθῶν, ὡς ἂν μὴ δοκοίη τὸν μισθὸν ποιεῖσθαι προτιμότερον τοῦ δωρουμένου τὸ 10 κέρδος· ἀγαπᾷ δὲ ἐξ ὅλης καρδίας τε καὶ ψυχῆς καὶ δυνάμεως οὐκ ἄλλο τι τῶν παρ᾽ αὐτοῦ γινομένων, ἀλλ᾽ αὐτὸν ἐκεῖνον ὅς ἐστι τῶν ἀγαθῶν ἡ πηγή. ταύτην τοίνυν ὁ καλῶν ἡμᾶς πρὸς τὴν ἑαυτοῦ μετουσίαν νομοθετεῖ ταῖς τῶν ἀκουόντων ψυχαῖς τὴν διάθεσιν.

ὁ δὲ βεβαιῶν τὴν νομοθεσίαν ταύτην ἐστὶ Σολομῶν, οὗ ἡ σοφία κατὰ τὴν 15 θείαν μαρτυρίαν μέτρον οὐκ ἔχει, πᾶσιν ἐπ᾽ ἴσης τοῖς τε προγεγονόσι καὶ τοῖς ἐσομένοις ἀσύγκριτος οὖσα καὶ ἀπαράθετος, ὃν ἔλαθε τῶν ὄντων οὐδέν.

ἆρά με τοῦτον οἴει λέγειν τὸν ἐκ τῆς Βηρσαβεὲ Σολομῶντα, τὸν ἐπὶ τοῦ ὄρους ἀνενεγκόντα τὴν χιλιόμβην, τὸν ἐκ τῆς Σιδωνίας συμβόλῳ | πρὸς τὴν   17 ἁμαρτίαν χρησάμενον; ἀλλὰ Σολομῶν διὰ τούτου σημαίνεται ἄλλος· ὁ καὶ 20 αὐτὸς ἐκ τοῦ σπέρματος Δαβὶδ τὸ κατὰ σάρκα γενόμενος, ᾧ ὄνομα εἰρήνη, ὁ ἀληθινὸς τοῦ Ἰσραὴλ βασιλεύς, ὁ οἰκοδόμος τοῦ ναοῦ τοῦ θεοῦ, ὁ πάντων ἐμπεριειληφὼς τὴν γνῶσιν, οὗ ἀόριστος ἡ σοφία, μᾶλλον δὲ οὗ τὸ εἶναι σοφία ἐστὶ καὶ ἀλήθεια, καὶ πᾶν θεοπρεπές τε καὶ ὑψηλὸν ὄνομά τε καὶ νόημα.

(1 Tim 2:4) manifests in this work the blessed and most perfect way of salvation—I mean that which comes though love. It may happen that salvation
comes to some people even through fear, as we separate ourselves from evil |
in face of the threats of punishment in Gehenna. And there are some who suc-
cessfully practice virtue because of the hope for rewards that is stored up for
people who have conducted their lives well, achieving victory not out of love
for the Good but out of an expectation of recompense. The person who pursues
perfection in the soul, however, drives out fear (for a fearful disposition is servile; it does not abide with the Master for love's sake but out of fear of scourging
does not run away). Moreover, such a person despises the rewards themselves,
on the ground that to make the reward a gain more precious than the gift-giver
does not seem right. He loves, with his whole heart and soul and strength, not
something else, something that comes from the Giver, but that very One who is
the source of the good things.[2] This is the frame of mind that he who calls us to
share in himself enjoins upon the souls of those who attend to him.

Now the one who warrants this legislation for us is Solomon, whose
wisdom, as God himself bears witness, has no measure because it is in the
same degree unequaled by and incomparable to the wisdom both of his pre-
decessors and of his posterity. Nothing that is real[3] was hidden from him.

Do you suppose, then, I am speaking of the Solomon from Beersheba,
the one who sacrificed a thousand oxen on the mountain (cf. 3 Kgdms 3:4),
who made use of the idol from Sidon (cf. 3 Kgdms 11:5) | for sin's purposes?
Surely not! In this case, another Solomon is meant: the Solomon who "was
born of the seed of David according to the flesh" (Rom 1:3), whose name
is Peace,[4] the true King of Israel, the builder of God's temple, the One who
has received knowledge of all things, whose wisdom is without limit, whose
being, indeed, is Wisdom and Truth, and to whom belongs every name and
idea that is exalted and worthy of God.

---

2. For these characterizations of various motives for pursuing the way of salvation, see Basil
of Caesarea, *Reg. fus.*, preface (PG 31:896Bff.; trans. Wagner 1950, 227–28); and homily 15 below
(p. 461 [Jaeger]). Gregory here is perhaps repeating his brother's wisdom, but his statement that
it is the Song of Songs that depicts "the blessed and most perfect way" (i.e., the way of love) indicates that he has at least partly assimilated Basil's classification of motives to his own portrayal
of three stages in the soul's progress (on which see below, n. 5). Daniélou (1954, 22) notes the
fundamental difference that this passage marks between Gregory's account of the spiritual life
and that of Evagrius Ponticus, whose scheme envisages a progress from πράξις to θεωρία and
assigns love (ἀγάπη) to the order of πράξις.

3. Literally, "none of the things that are" (τῶν ὄντων οὐδέν). In Gregory's vocabulary "the
things that are" (τὰ ὄντα) is an expression that refers to intelligible reality as distinct from the
perceptible order.

4. The Hebrew form of the name "Solomon" is etymologically related to the Hebrew word
for peace (*shalom*).

οὗτος ὀργάνῳ τῷ Σολομῶντι τούτῳ χρησάμενος διὰ τῆς ἐκείνου φωνῆς
ἡμῖν διαλέγεται πρότερον μὲν ἐν Παροιμίαις, εἶτα ἐν τῷ Ἐκκλησιαστῇ καὶ
μετὰ ταῦτα ἐν τῇ προκειμένῃ τοῦ Ἄισματος τῶν Ἀισμάτων φιλοσοφίᾳ ὁδῷ
καὶ τάξει τὴν πρὸς τὸ τέλειον ἄνοδον ὑποδεικνύων τῷ λόγῳ.

5   καθάπερ γὰρ
ἐπὶ τῆς κατὰ σάρκα ζωῆς οὐ πᾶσα ἡλικία πάσας χωρεῖ τὰς φυσικὰς ἐνεργείας
οὐδὲ διὰ τῶν ὁμοίων ἡμῖν ἐν ταῖς τῶν ἡλικιῶν διαφοραῖς ὁ βίος | προέρχεται   18
(οὔτε γὰρ τὸ νήπιον τὰ τῶν τελείων ἔργα μετέρχεται οὔτε ὁ τέλειος ἐν
ταῖς ἀγκάλαις τῆς τιθήνης ἀναλαμβάνεται, ἀλλ᾿ ἑκάστῳ καιρῷ τῆς ἡλικίας
ἄλλο τι πρόσφορόν ἐστι καὶ κατάλληλον), οὕτως ἔστιν ἰδεῖν καὶ ἐν τῇ ψυχῇ
10 ἀνάλογόν τινα πρὸς τὰς σωματικὰς ἡλικίας, δι᾿ ὧν εὑρίσκεται τάξις τις καὶ
ἀκολουθία πρὸς τὸν κατ᾿ ἀρετὴν βίον χειραγωγοῦσα τὸν ἄνθρωπον. οὗ χάριν
ἄλλως ἡ Παροιμία παιδεύει καὶ ἄλλως ὁ Ἐκκλησιαστὴς διαλέγεται· καὶ ἡ
διὰ τοῦ Ἄισματος τῶν Ἀισμάτων φιλοσοφία διὰ τῶν ὑψηλοτέρων δογμάτων
ἀμφοτέρων ὑπέρκειται.

15 ἡ γὰρ διὰ τῶν παροιμιῶν διδασκαλία πρὸς τὸν ἔτι νηπιάζοντα ποιεῖται
τοὺς λόγους καταλλήλως τῇ ἡλικίᾳ τὴν νουθεσίαν ἁρμόζουσα· Ἄκουε, φησίν,
υἱέ, νόμους πατρός σου καὶ μὴ ἀπώσῃ θεσμοὺς μητρός σου. ὁρᾷς ἐκ τῶν
λεγομένων τὸ ἁπαλὸν ἔτι τῆς κατὰ ψυχὴν ἡλικίας καὶ εὔπλαστον· ἔτι μητρῴων
αὐτὸν θεσμῶν ἐπιδεᾶ βλέπει καὶ πατρικῆς νουθεσίας καί, ὡς ἂν προθυμότερον
20 προσέχοι τοῖς γονεῦσι τὸ νήπιον, τοὺς παιδικοὺς αὐτῷ κατεπαγγέλλεται
κόσμους ἐκ τῆς περὶ τὰ μαθήματα σπουδῆς προσγενήσεσθαι· παιδίῳ γάρ ἐστι
κόσμος <ὁ> | χρύσεος μανιάκης τῷ τραχήλῳ περιλαμπόμενος καὶ ὁ ἐξ ἀνθῶν   19
τινων ἐπιχαρίτων ἀναπλεκόμενος στέφανος. νοεῖν δὲ χρὴ ταῦτα πάντως
ὅπως ἂν ὁδηγήσῃ πρὸς τὸ κρεῖττον ἡ τοῦ αἰνίγματος ἔννοια.

25 καὶ οὕτως ὑπογράφειν ἄρχεται τὴν σοφίαν αὐτῷ ποικίλως τε καὶ
πολυειδῶς τοῦ ἀφράστου κάλλους διερμηνεύων τὴν ὥραν, ὥστε μὴ φόβῳ
τινὶ καὶ ἀνάγκῃ ἀλλὰ ἐπιθυμίᾳ καὶ πόθῳ πρὸς τὴν τῶν ἀγαθῶν μετουσίαν
διαναστῆναι· ἡ γὰρ τοῦ κάλλους ὑπογραφὴ ἐπισπᾶταί πως τὴν τῶν νέων
ἐπιθυμίαν πρὸς τὸ δεικνύμενον πρὸς κοινωνίαν τῆς ὥρας τὸν πόθον
30 ἀναρριπίζουσα. ὡς ἂν οὖν μᾶλλον αὐτῷ τὸ ἐπιθυμητικὸν αὐξηθείη μετατεθὲν

This Solomon used our Solomon as an instrument and by means of his voice speaks with us—first in Proverbs, then in Ecclesiastes, and after that in the philosophy of the Song of Songs, which is now before us—and by his word shows us, in systematic and orderly fashion, the way that leads upward to perfection. For where our life in the flesh is concerned, not every age makes a place for all our natural activities, nor does our life move forward by like steps in the different ages; | for the children do not attend to the business of grown-ups, nor is the grown-up taken into the embrace of a nurse, but there is something different that is profitable and appropriate for each period of growth. Correspondingly, one can see in the soul something analogous to the ages of the body, stages by means of which there is discovered a particular order and sequence that brings the human person to the life of virtue. That is why Proverbs instructs in one fashion and Ecclesiastes discourses in another, and the philosophy that comes in the Song of Songs surpasses both because of the more sublime character of its teachings.[5]

For the instruction in Proverbs is addressed to someone who is still a child and adapts its exhortation to that stage of life. It says, "Attend, my son, to the laws of your father, and do not reject the precepts of your mother" (Prov 1:8). From these words you see that at this stage of life the soul is still tender and malleable. The true Solomon has in mind someone who is still in need of a mother's precepts and a father's admonition, and in order to present the parents with a more zealous child, he promises the child that eagerness to learn will procure it adornments of a sort proper to its age. Now the finery proper to a child is | a golden necklace that gleams about the neck and a "crown" woven of charming flowers (Prov 1:9). This finery must certainly be interpreted in a manner that assures that the sense discerned in the enigma points the way to something nobler and better.

Thus he sets out to portray Wisdom for the child, interpreting, in various ways and forms, the splendor of her unspeakable beauty, so that the child may be roused to the participation of good things, not out of any fear or compulsion, but out of desire and yearning; for a description of something beautiful has a way of attracting the desire of the young for what is being shown them and fans their yearning to share in its splendor. So in

---

5. This doctrine of the three stages of spiritual growth, each of which corresponds with one of the books of Solomon (Proverbs, Ecclesiastes, Song of Songs), finds its inspiration and precedent in the preface of Origen's *Commentarius in Canticum*, where "philosophy" is said to have three (successive) parts: moral, natural, and contemplative (Baehrens 1925, 75). See further below, n. 10. For further indications of Gregory's understanding of the stages, see also below, homily 11, p. 322 (Jaeger) and n. 5.

ἀπὸ τῆς ὑλικῆς προσπαθείας πρὸς τὴν ἄϋλον σχέσιν, ὡραΐζει διὰ τῶν
ἐγκωμίων τῆς σοφίας τὸ κάλλος.

    καὶ οὐ μόνον τὸ κάλλος τῆς ὥρας διὰ τῶν λόγων προδείκνυσιν, ἀλλὰ καὶ
τὸν πλοῦτον αὐτῆς ἀπαριθμεῖται, οὗ κύριος πάντως ὁ συνοικήσας γενήσεται.
5   ὁ δὲ πλοῦτος τέως ἐν τοῖς προκοσμήμασιν αὐτῆς θεωρεῖται· κόσμος μὲν γὰρ
αὐτῇ περιδέξιος αἰῶνες ὅλοι οὕτως εἰπόντος τοῦ λόγου ὅτι Μῆκος βίου καὶ
ἔτη ζωῆς ἐν τῇ δεξιᾷ αὐτῆς, ἐν δὲ τῇ ἑτέρᾳ χειρὶ τὸν πολύτιμον τῶν ἀρετῶν
| περίκειται πλοῦτον τῇ λαμπηδόνι τῆς δόξης συνδιαλάμποντα· λέγει γὰρ ὅτι   20
Ἐν τῇ ἀριστερᾷ αὐτῆς πλοῦτος καὶ δόξα. εἶτα καὶ τοῦ στόματος αὐτῆς λέγει
10   τὴν εὔπνοιαν τοῦ καλοῦ τῆς δικαιοσύνης ἀρώματος ἀποπνέουσαν λέγων Ἐκ
τοῦ στόματος αὐτῆς ἐκπορεύεται δικαιοσύνη. τοῖς δὲ χείλεσιν αὐτῆς φησιν
ἀντὶ τοῦ φυσικοῦ ἐρυθήματος τὸν νόμον ἐπανθεῖν καὶ τὸν ἔλεον. καὶ ὡς ἂν
διὰ πάντων εὑρεθείη τῇ τοιαύτῃ νύμφῃ τὸ κάλλος ἐρανιζόμενον, ἐπαινεῖται
αὐτῆς καὶ τὸ βάδισμα· φησὶ γὰρ ὅτι Ἐν ὁδοῖς δικαιοσύνης περιπατεῖ.
15   οὐ λείπει τοῖς ἐπαίνοις τῆς ὥρας οὐδὲ τὸ μέγεθος ἴσα φυτῷ τινι τῶν
εὐερνῶν τῆς αὐξήσεως ἀναδραμούσης. τὸ δὲ φυτὸν τοῦτο ᾧ τὸ ὕψος αὐτῆς
προσεικάζεται, Αὐτό, φησί, τὸ τῆς ζωῆς ξύλον ἐστίν, ὃ τροφὴ μὲν γίνεται τοῖς
ἀντεχομένοις, στῦλος δὲ τοῖς ἐπερειδομένοις ἀσφαλής τε καὶ ἄσειστος. νοῶ
δὲ δι᾽ ἀμφοτέρων τὸν κύριον· αὐτὸς γάρ ἐστι καὶ ἡ ζωὴ καὶ τὸ ἔρεισμα. ἔχει
20   δὲ ἡ λέξις οὕτως· Ξύλον ζωῆς ἐστι πᾶσι τοῖς ἀντεχομένοις αὐτῆς καὶ τοῖς
ἐπερειδομένοις ἐπ᾽ αὐτὴν ὡς ἐπὶ κύριον ἀσφαλής.

    συμπαραλαμβάνεται δὲ μετὰ τῶν λοιπῶν ἐγκωμίων αὐτῆς καὶ ἡ δύναμις,
ὡς ἂν διὰ πάντων τῶν ἀγαθῶν πληρωθείη τοῦ κάλλους τῆς σοφίας ὁ ἔπαινος.
Ὁ θεὸς γάρ, φησί, τῇ σοφίᾳ ἐθεμελίωσε τὴν γῆν, ἡτοίμασε δὲ οὐρανοὺς ἐν
25   φρονήσει, καὶ τὰ καθ᾽ ἕκαστον | τῶν ἐν τῇ κτίσει θεωρουμένων εἰς τὴν τῆς   21
σοφίας ἀνάγει δύναμιν διαποικίλλων αὐτὴν τοῖς ὀνόμασιν· τὴν γὰρ αὐτὴν
καὶ σοφίαν λέγει καὶ φρόνησιν, αἴσθησίν τε καὶ γνῶσιν καὶ σύνεσιν καὶ τὰ
τοιαῦτα.

    μετὰ δὲ ταῦτα νυμφοστολεῖν ἄρχεται τὸν νέον πρὸς τὴν τοιαύτην
30   συνοίκησιν ἤδη πρὸς τὸν θεῖον θάλαμον βλέπειν ἐγκελευόμενος· λέγει γὰρ

order that the child's faculty of desire[6] may be improved by being withdrawn from material attachments and fixed on the immaterial state, he glorifies the beauty of Wisdom by his praises.[7]

Nor do his his words merely call attention to the splendor of Wisdom's beauty. He also recounts her riches, of which the person who dwells with her will be the entire possessor. To begin with, these riches are discerned in her outward adornments, and the adornment that graces her right arm is whole ages, since the text says, "Length of days and years of life are on her right hand" (Prov 3:16). But on her other hand she bears the precious riches of the virtues, | gleaming with the luster of glory, for it says, "On her left hand are riches and glory" (Prov 3:16). Then, too, it says that the sweet breath of her mouth gives forth the beautiful fragrance of righteousness: "Righteousness issues from her mouth" (Prov 3:16a). And on her lips, he says, the law blooms, and mercy, in place of nature's blush. Further, in order that every kind of beauty may be seen to be combined in this Bride, even her way of walking is praised, for he says, "She walks[8] in the ways of righteousness" (Prov 8:20).

Nor in its praises of her splendor does the text forget her stature, which increases even as a flourishing plant. And as for this plant to which her height is likened, it is, says our text, "the tree of life," which becomes nourishment for "those who cleave to it" and a sure and unshaken support for "those who lean" upon it. By both of these I understand the Lord, for he is at once Life and Support. The text in fact runs like this: "She is the tree of life for all those who cleave to her and surety for those who lean upon her as upon the Lord" (Prov 3:18).

Power, too, is included along with the rest of the commendations, so that the praise of Wisdom's beauty may be filled out by all good things. "For God," he says, "laid the foundation of the earth by Wisdom and prepared the heavens by understanding" (Prov 3:19), and he refers every individual thing | that is seen in the created order to Wisdom's power, adorning her with a variety of names. For he calls the same one "wisdom" and "understanding," "perception" and "knowledge," and "sagacity" and the like.

Then, after this, our Solomon begins to array the youth as a bridegroom, wanting to prepare him for this marriage with Wisdom; already he commands

---

6. This is no doubt a reminiscence of the language of Plato's allegory of the charioteer and his two horses, the "dark" one of which is styled τὸ ἐπιθυμητικόν; see *Phaedr.* 253–254.

7. On this point, see the observation of Daniélou: "Gregory defines the first way more by the manifestation of divine goods than by purification.… The first way is κάθαρσις, purification, but it is also φωτισμός, illumination" (1954, 18).

8. Gregory has slightly altered the text of Prov 8:20; the original reads, "I walk.…"

ὅτι Μὴ ἐγκαταλίπῃς αὐτὴν καὶ ἀνθέξεταί σου· ἐράσθητι αὐτῆς καὶ τηρήσει
σε, περιχαράκωσον αὐτὴν καὶ ὑψώσει σε· τίμησον αὐτὴν ἵνα σε περιλάβῃ, ἵνα
δῷ τῇ σῇ κεφαλῇ στέφανον χαρίτων, στεφάνῳ δὲ τρυφῆς ὑπερασπίσῃ σου.
ἐν τούτοις δὲ τοῖς στεφάνοις ἤδη τοῖς γαμικοῖς ὡς νυμφίον κατακοσμήσας
5   ἀχώριστον αὐτῆς εἶναι διακελεύεται λέγων Ἡνίκα ἂν περιπατῇς, ἐπάγου
αὐτὴν καὶ μετὰ σοῦ ἔστω· ὡς δ' ἂν καθεύδῃς, φυλασσέτω σε, ἵνα ἐγειρομένῳ
συλλαλήσῃ σοι.

διὰ τούτων καὶ τῶν τοιούτων τοῦ νεάζοντος ἔτι κατὰ τὸν ἔσω ἄνθρωπον
τὸ ἐπιθυμητικὸν ἀναφλέξας καὶ αὐτὴν ἐκείνην τὰ περὶ ἑαυτῆς διηγουμένην
10   ὑποδείξας τῷ λόγῳ, δι' ὧν μάλιστα τὴν ἀγαπητικὴν σχέσιν τῶν ἀκουόντων
ἐφέλκεται τοῦτο μετὰ τῶν ἄλλων εἰποῦσα ὅτι Τοὺς ἐμὲ | φιλοῦντας   22
ἀγαπῶ (ἡ γὰρ ἐλπὶς τοῦ ἀνταγαπηθῆναι σφοδρότερον εἰς ἐπιθυμίαν τὸν
ἐραστὴν διατίθησι), καὶ μετὰ τούτων τὰς λοιπὰς ἐπαγαγὼν συμβουλὰς ἐν
ἀποφαντικοῖς τισι καὶ εὐπεριγράπτοις ἀποφθέγμασι καὶ εἰς τελειοτέραν ἕξιν
15   αὐτὸν ἀγαγὼν εἶτα πρὸς τοῖς τελευταίοις τῶν Παροιμιῶν μακαρίσας ταύτην
τὴν ἀγαθὴν συζυγίαν, ἐν οἷς διεξῆλθε τὰ τῆς ἀνδρείας γυναικὸς ἐκείνης
ἐγκώμια, τότε προστίθησι τὴν ἐν τῷ Ἐκκλησιαστῇ φιλοσοφίαν τῷ ἱκανῶς
διὰ τῆς παροιμιώδους ἀγωγῆς εἰσηγμένῳ εἰς τὴν τῶν ἀρετῶν ἐπιθυμίαν.

καὶ διαβαλὼν ἐν τούτῳ τῷ λόγῳ τὴν περὶ τὰ φαινόμενα τῶν ἀνθρώπων
20   σχέσιν καὶ μάταιον εἰπὼν εἶναι πᾶν τὸ ἀστατοῦν τε καὶ παρερχόμενον, ἐν οἷς
φησιν ὅτι Πᾶν τὸ ἐρχόμενον ματαιότης, ὑπερτίθησι παντὸς τοῦ δι' αἰσθήσεως
καταλαμβανομένου τὴν ἐπιθυμητικὴν τῆς ψυχῆς ἡμῶν κίνησιν ἐπὶ τὸ ἀόρατον
κάλλος καὶ οὕτως ἐκκαθάρας τὴν καρδίαν τῆς περὶ τὰ φαινόμενα σχέσεως
τότε διὰ τοῦ Ἄισματος τῶν Ἀισμάτων ἐντὸς τῶν θείων ἀδύτων μυσταγωγεῖ
25   τὴν διάνοιαν·

him to look toward the divine bridal chamber. For he says: "Do not desert her and she will sustain you. Be in love with her,[9] and she will keep you. Fortify her, and she will exalt you. Honor her that she may embrace you, that she may give your head a crown of graces, that she may protect you with a crown of plenty" (Prov 4:6–9). Having already adorned him as a bridegroom with these wedding crowns, it commands him to be inseparable from her: "When you walk, bring her and let her be with you. Should you sleep, let her guard you, so that when you awaken she may speak with you" (Prov 6:22).

When he has again, with these and other words like them, set fire to that principle of desire that dwells in the interior self of one who is still youthful and has exhibited, in the words of the text, Wisdom herself explaining the things that belong to her—the things by which above all she attracts to herself her hearers' disposition to love—at that point she makes this statement, among others: "I love those who | love me" (Prov 8:17), for it is the hope of being loved in return that most ardently disposes the lover to desire. After this she introduces the remaining counsels in the form of a number of succinct and categorical statements and brings the youth into a more mature and perfect state of mind. Then, toward the end of Proverbs, where the praises of that "virtuous wife" are recited, she gives a blessing to this godly union and at that point, for the benefit of one who has been introduced to the desire for virtue by the guidance given in Proverbs, adds the philosophy contained in Ecclesiastes.

In the latter work, she disparages the human tendency to dwell on the appearances of things and asserts that everything unstable and passing is vanity, as, for example, in the statement, "All that comes and goes is vanity" (Eccl 11:8). Thus she points our soul's motion of desire toward the invisible Beauty that is beyond anything grasped by the senses, and having in this way purified the heart of its bent toward appearances, she then, in the Song of Songs, initiates the mind into the innermost divine sanctuary.[10]

---

9. Prov 4:6b says ἐράσθητι αὐτῆς ("be enamored of her"). For the significance of this for Gregory, see below, p. 23 (Jaeger), and n. 11.

10. The midrash on the Song of Songs (*Midr. Rab.* 1.1:10) raises the question of the order in which Solomon wrote his three books (Proverbs, Ecclesiastes, and Song of Songs). R. Jonathan argued: "When a man is young he composes songs; when he grows older he makes sententious remarks; when he becomes an old man he speaks of the vanity of things." Origen, by contrast, starts with the order of the three books in the Septuagint and associates them, in that very order, with a division of the subject matter of philosophy (into ethics, physics, theoretics) and argues that the Greeks borrowed this division from Solomon, who defined the disciplines by discussing them in three separate books: Proverbs (ethics), Ecclesiastes (physics), and the Song of Songs (theoretics). The Song of Songs, therefore, on his account, treats of the contemplation

ἐν οἷς τὸ μὲν ὑπογραφόμενον ἐπιθαλάμιός τίς ἐστι διασκευή, τὸ δὲ νοούμενον τῆς ἀνθρωπίνης ψυχῆς ἡ πρὸς τὸ θεῖόν | ἐστιν ἀνάκρασις. διὰ 23 τοῦτο νύμφη ὧδε ὁ ἐν ταῖς Παροιμίαις υἱὸς ὀνομάζεται καὶ ἡ σοφία εἰς νυμφίου τάξιν ἀντιμεθίσταται, ἵνα μνηστευθῇ τῷ θεῷ ὁ ἄνθρωπος ἁγνὴ

5 παρθένος ἐκ νυμφίου γενόμενος καὶ κολληθεὶς τῷ κυρίῳ γένηται πνεῦμα ἕν διὰ τῆς πρὸς τὸ ἀκήρατόν τε καὶ ἀπαθὲς ἀνακράσεως νόημα καθαρὸν ἀντὶ σαρκὸς βαρείας γενόμενος. ἐπειδὴ τοίνυν σοφία ἐστὶν ἡ λαλοῦσα, ἀγάπησον ὅσον δύνασαι ἐξ ὅλης καρδίας τε καὶ δυνάμεως, ἐπιθύμησον ὅσον χωρεῖς. προστίθημι δὲ θαρρῶν τοῖς ῥήμασι τούτοις καὶ τὸ ἐράσθητι· ἀνέγκλητον γὰρ

10 τοῦτο καὶ ἀπαθὲς ἐπὶ τῶν ἀσωμάτων τὸ πάθος, καθώς φησιν ἡ σοφία ἐν ταῖς Παροιμίαις τοῦ θείου κάλλους νομοθετοῦσα τὸν ἔρωτα.

ἀλλὰ καὶ ὁ νῦν προκείμενος λόγος τὰ ἴσα διακελεύεται οὐ γυμνήν σοι τὴν περὶ τούτου συμβουλὴν προσάγων, ἀλλὰ δι' ἀπορρήτων φιλοσοφεῖ τοῖς νοήμασιν εἰκόνα τινὰ τῶν κατὰ τὸν βίον ἡδέων εἰς τὴν τῶν δογμάτων

15 τούτων κατασκευὴν προστησάμενος. ἡ δὲ εἰκὼν γαμικὴ τίς ἐστι διασκευή, ἐν ᾗ κάλλους ἐπιθυμία μεσιτεύει τῷ πόθῳ, οὐ κατὰ τὴν ἀνθρωπίνην συνήθειαν τοῦ νυμφίου τῆς ἐπιθυμίας κατάρξαντος, ἀλλὰ προλαμβάνει τὸν νυμφίον ἡ παρθένος ἀνεπαισχύντως τὸν πόθον δημοσιεύουσα καὶ εὐ|χὴν ποιουμένη τοῦ 24 νυμφικοῦ ποτε κατατρυφῆσαι φιλήματος. ἐπειδὴ γὰρ οἱ ἀγαθοὶ τῆς παρθένου

20 προμνήστορες, πατριάρχαι τε καὶ προφῆται καὶ νομοθέται, προσήγαγον τῇ μεμνηστευμένῃ τὰ θεῖα χαρίσματα, ἅπερ ἔδνα καλεῖ ἡ συνήθεια τὰ πρὸ τῶν γάμων δῶρα οὕτω κατονομάζουσα (ταῦτα δὲ ἦν ἄφεσις παραπτωμάτων,

What is described there is an account of a wedding, but what is intellectually discerned is the human soul's | mingling with the Divine. That is why the one who is called "son" in Proverbs is here called "bride," and Wisdom, correspondingly, is transferred into the role of bridegroom. This is to assure that the human person, once separated from the bridegroom, might be betrothed to God as a holy virgin (cf. 2 Cor 11:2), and, once joined to the Lord, may become "one spirit" (1 Cor 6:17) through being mingled with that which is inviolate and impassible, having become purified thought rather than heavy flesh. Therefore since it is Wisdom who speaks, *love* her as much as you are able, with your whole heart and strength; *desire* her as much as you can. To these words I am bold to add, *Be in love,* for this passion,[11] when directed toward things incorporeal, is blameless and impassible, as Wisdom says in Proverbs when she bids us to be in love with the divine Beauty.

But the book now before us enjoins the same thing. To be sure, it does not bring you an explicit word of counsel on this score. Instead, it philosophizes by means of things not to be spoken, that is, by setting before our minds, with a view to establishing these teachings, a picture of the pleasurable things of this life. The picture in question is an account of a marriage, through which it mediates to our yearning a desire for Beauty—but which does not, after the human custom, take the Bridegroom's desire as its starting point. Ahead of the Bridegroom it presents the virgin, who is blamelessly giving voice to her desire and | praying that she may at some time savor the Bridegroom's kiss.[12] For the virgin's good matchmakers—the patriarchs and prophets and lawgivers—brought the divine gifts of grace to the betrothed virgin. Custom calls these "wedding gifts,"[13] meaning by this expression presents that are given

---

or discernment (θεωρία) of "things divine and heavenly" (*Comm. Cant.* praef. 3, Baehrens 1925, 75; trans. Lawson 1956, 39ff.). Nyssen's view of the relation of the three books is plainly derived from Origen's, but it is characteristic of him that it is not so much contemplation of things heavenly that he finds in the Song as it is an account of the soul's union with the Word.

11. The passion in question is that of ἔρως, for Gregory has just been "bold to add" to the scriptural injunction to love (ἀγαπήσον, says Gregory; ἀγαπήσεις, say Deut 6:5; Lev 19:18; and Matt 22:27–39) the command to "be in love" (ἐράσθητι), an imperative form of a verb that the Greek Bible apparently does not much like (and which the Song of Songs in the LXX version does not employ). Ἔρως, or a form of it, is the subject of Plato's *Symposium,* and of course Gregory has throughout this first homily enjoined and praised ἐπιθυμία ("desire," "lust"; cf. Rom 7:7–8!). For a possible stimulus of Gregory's usage, see Origen's preface to his *Commentarius in Canticum,* where there is a lengthy discussion of the various Greek words that English tends perforce to render by the single term "love."

12. This is an allusion to the opening words of the Song (1:2a): "Let him kiss me with the kisses of his mouth."

13. See Origen, *Comm. Cant.* 1.1 (Baehrens 1925, 90; trans. Lawson 1956, 59), for whom the givers of the wedding gifts are the angels who gave the Law and the Prophets. This, however,

ἀμνηστία κακῶν, ἁμαρτίας ἀναίρεσις, μεταστοιχείωσις φύσεως, τοῦ φθαρτοῦ
πρὸς τὸ ἄφθαρτον μεταποίησις, παραδείσου τρυφή, βασιλείας ἀξίωμα,
εὐφροσύνη τέλος οὐκ ἔχουσα), ταῦτα τοίνυν ἡ παρθένος δεξαμένη τὰ θεῖα
δωρήματα παρὰ τῶν καλῶν ἐδνοφόρων τῶν διὰ τῆς προφητικῆς διδασκαλίας
5   αὐτῇ προσαγαγόντων τὰ δῶρα καὶ ὁμολογεῖ τὴν ἐπιθυμίαν καὶ ἐπισπεύδει
τὴν χάριν ἤδη τῆς ὥρας τοῦ ποθουμένου κατατρυφῆσαι σπουδάζουσα.
    ἀκροῶνται δὲ αὐτῆς συνήθεις τινὲς καὶ ὁμήλικες πρὸς μείζονα τὴν
νύμφην ἐπιθυμίαν διερεθίζουσαι. παραγίνεται δὲ καὶ ὁ νυμφίος φίλων αὐτῷ
τινων καὶ καταθυμίων χορὸν ἐπαγόμενος. οὗτοι δ᾽ ἂν εἶεν ἢ τὰ λειτουργικὰ
10   πνεύματα, δι᾽ ὧν οἱ ἄνθρωποι σῴζονται, ἢ οἱ προφῆται οἱ ἅγιοι, οἳ τῆς φωνῆς
τοῦ νυμφίου ἀκούοντες χαίρουσί τε καὶ ἀγάλλονται τῆς ἀκηράτου συζυγίας
ἁρμοζομένης, δι᾽ ἧς ἡ κολλωμένη | τῷ κυρίῳ ψυχὴ ἓν πνεῦμα γίνεται, καθώς   25
φησιν ὁ ἀπόστολος.
    Πάλιν τοίνυν τὸν ἐν τοῖς προοιμίοις ἐπαναλήψομαι λόγον· μή τις
15   ἐμπαθὴς καὶ σαρκώδης ἔτι τῆς νεκρᾶς τοῦ παλαιοῦ ἀνθρώπου δυσωδίας
ἀπόζων πρὸς τὰς κτηνώδεις ἀλογίας κατασυρέτω τὰς τῶν θεοπνεύστων
νοημάτων τε καὶ ῥημάτων ἐμφάσεις, ἀλλ᾽ ἐκβὰς ἕκαστος αὐτὸς ἑαυτοῦ καὶ
ἔξω τοῦ ὑλικοῦ κόσμου γενόμενος καὶ ἐπανελθὼν τρόπον τινὰ δι᾽ ἀπαθείας
εἰς τὸν παράδεισον καὶ διὰ καθαρότητος ὁμοιωθεὶς τῷ θεῷ οὕτως ἐπὶ τὸ
20   ἄδυτον τῶν προφαινομένων ἡμῖν διὰ τοῦ βιβλίου τούτου μυστηρίων χωρείτω.
εἰ δέ τισιν ἀπαρασκεύαστός ἐστιν ἡ ψυχὴ πρὸς τὴν τοιαύτην ἀκρόασιν,
ἀκουσάτωσαν τοῦ Μωϋσέως νομοθετοῦντος μὴ κατατολμῆσαι τῆς ἐπὶ τὸ
ὄρος τὸ πνευματικὸν ἀναβάσεως, πρὶν πλῦναι τῶν καρδιῶν ἡμῶν τὰ ἱμάτια
καὶ τοῖς καθήκουσι τῶν λογισμῶν περιρραντηρίοις τὰς ψυχὰς ἀφαγνίσασθαι.
25   ὥστε νῦν ἐν ᾧ χρόνῳ προσεδρεύομεν τῇ θεωρίᾳ ταύτῃ, λήθην τῶν
γαμικῶν νοημάτων ποιήσασθαι κατὰ τὸ παράγγελμα τοῦ Μωϋσέως τοῦ
καθαρεύειν ἀπὸ τῶν γάμων τοῖς μυσταγωγουμένοις νομοθετήσαντος καὶ
διὰ πάντων ἀναλαβεῖν | οἶμαι δεῖν ἡμᾶς τὰ τοῦ νομοθέτου προστάγματα   26
μέλλοντας προσβαίνειν τῷ πνευματικῷ τῆς θεογνωσίας ὄρει, ἐν ᾧ τὸ θῆλυ

before the marriage (which are remission of transgressions, forgetfulness of misdeeds, removal of sin, transformation of nature, change of the corruptible into the incorruptible, the delight of paradise, the honor of a kingdom, joy without end). The virgin, then, when she has received these divine gifts from their good bearers, who have brought them to her through the prophetic teaching, both confesses her desire and calls upon grace to hasten, since she is already eager to savor the splendor of the One she desires.

Certain companions and contemporaries attend to her words and stimulate the Bride to greater desire. Then the Bridegroom too appears, bringing along a troop of his friends and boon companions. These would be either the ministering spirits (cf. Heb 1:14) by which human beings are rescued or the holy prophets who, hearing the voice of the Bridegroom, both rejoice and exult because the undefiled marriage is being consummated (John 3:29)—the marriage by which the soul that is joined | to the Lord becomes "one spirit," as the apostle says (1 Cor 6:17).

Again, therefore, we reiterate what we said by way of preamble. Let not any passionate and fleshly person, who still gives off the deathly smell of the old humanity, drag the meaning of the divinely inspired ideas and words down to the level of brutish irrationality. No, let each depart from himself and get beyond the material cosmos and ascend somehow, by way of impassibility, into paradise, and having by purity been made like to God,[14] let him in this fashion journey to the inner shrine of the mysteries manifested to us in this book. And if the soul of some persons is not prepared to listen in this way, let them pay attention to Moses when he decrees that no one should dare the ascent of the spiritual mountain until the garments of our hearts are washed clean and our souls are purified by the appropriate sprinklings of reasoned thoughts (cf. Exod 19:10, 14).

So now, at this time when we are addressing ourselves to this task of interpretation, we ought, I think, to forget notions about marriage, in accordance with the injunction of Moses, who commanded candidates for initiation to be purified of marital relations (cf. Exod 19:15), and we ought, as I see it, to apply | to ourselves the Lawgiver's instructions as we come to approach the spiritual mountain of the knowledge of God, where the female

---

applies when the Bride is taken to be the church; if the Bride is interpreted of the individual soul, then it is "natural law and reason" that are the wedding gifts (ibid., p. 61). Gregory's list of gifts seems to contemplate the effects of the rite of baptism.

14. See Plato, *Resp.* 613B ("be made like to God as far as that is possible for a human being") and *Theaet.* 176B–C, not to mention Gen 1:26–27 and the long tradition of Jewish and Christian commentary thereon. Gregory's exegesis of those verses is given in his treatise *Opif. hom.* 16–17 (PG 44:177Dff.).

γένος τῶν λογισμῶν μετὰ τῆς ὑλικῆς ἀποσκευῆς τῷ κάτω καταλείπεται βίῳ. πᾶν δὲ ἄλογον νόημα εἰ περὶ τὸ τοιοῦτον ὄρος ὀφθείη, τοῖς στερροτέροις λογισμοῖς οἷόν τισι λίθοις καταφονεύεται. μόγις γὰρ ἂν οὕτω χωρήσαιμεν τὴν φωνὴν τῆς σάλπιγγος ταύτης μέγα τι καὶ ἐξαίσιον καὶ ὑπὲρ τὴν δύναμιν τῶν
5   δεχομένων ἠχούσης, ἣν αὐτὸς ὁ γνόφος τῆς ἀσαφείας προΐεται, ἐν ᾧ ἐστιν ὁ θεὸς ὁ τὸ ὑλικὸν ἅπαν ἐπὶ τοῦ τοιούτου ὄρους τῷ πυρὶ καταφλέγων.
Ἤδη τοίνυν ἐντὸς τοῦ ἁγίου τῶν ἁγίων γενώμεθα, ὅπερ ἐστὶ τὸ ᾆσμα τῶν ᾀσμάτων. ὡς γὰρ ἐν τῷ ἁγίῳ τῶν ἁγίων πλεονασμόν τινα καὶ ἐπίτασιν τῆς ἁγιότητος διὰ τῆς ὑπερθετικῆς ταύτης φωνῆς διδασκόμεθα, οὕτω καὶ διὰ τοῦ
10   ᾄσματος τῶν ᾀσμάτων μυστηρίων μυστήρια διδάσκειν ἡμᾶς ὁ ὑψηλὸς λόγος κατεπαγγέλλεται. πολλῶν γὰρ ὄντων κατὰ τὴν θεόπνευστον διδασκαλίαν ᾀσμάτων, δι' ὧν τὰ μεγάλα νοήματα περὶ τοῦ θεοῦ διδασκόμεθα παρά τε τοῦ μεγάλου Δαβὶδ καὶ Ἡσαΐου καὶ Μωϋσέως καὶ ἄλλων | πολλῶν, τοῦτο παρὰ τῆς ἐπιγραφῆς ταύτης μανθάνομεν, ὅτι ὅσον ἀπέχει τῶν τῆς ἔξω σοφίας   27
15   ᾀσμάτων τὰ τῶν ἁγίων ᾄσματα, τοσοῦτον ὑπέρκειται τῶν ἁγίων ᾀσμάτων τὸ ἐν τῷ ᾄσματι τῶν ᾀσμάτων μυστήριον, οὗ τὸ πλέον εἰς κατανόησιν οὔτε εὑρεῖν οὔτε χωρῆσαι ἡ ἀνθρωπίνη δύναται φύσις. καὶ τούτου χάριν τὸ σφοδρότατον τῶν καθ' ἡδονὴν ἐνεργουμένων (λέγω δὲ τὸ ἐρωτικὸν πάθος) τῆς τῶν δογμάτων ὑφηγήσεως αἰνιγματωδῶς προεστήσατο, ἵνα διὰ τούτου
20   μάθωμεν, ὅτι χρὴ τὴν ψυχὴν πρὸς τὸ ἀπρόσιτον τῆς θείας φύσεως κάλλος ἐνατενίζουσαν τοσοῦτον ἐρᾶν ἐκείνου, ὅσον ἔχει τὸ σῶμα τὴν σχέσιν πρὸς τὸ συγγενὲς καὶ ὁμόφυλον, μετενεγκοῦσαν εἰς ἀπάθειαν τὸ πάθος, ὥστε πάσης κατασβεσθείσης σωματικῆς διαθέσεως μόνῳ τῷ πνεύματι ζέειν ἐρωτικῶς ἐν ἡμῖν τὴν διάνοιαν διὰ τοῦ πυρὸς ἐκείνου θερμαινομένην, ὃ βαλεῖν ἐπὶ τὴν γῆν
25   ἦλθεν ὁ κύριος.
Ἀλλὰ ταῦτα μέν, ὅπως χρὴ διακεῖσθαι τὴν ψυχὴν τῶν μυστικῶν ῥημάτων ἀκούοντας, ἱκανῶς ἔχειν φημί. καιρὸς δὲ ἂν εἴη καὶ αὐτὰς τὰς θείας τοῦ ᾄσματος τῶν ᾀσμάτων φωνὰς ἤδη προσθεῖναι τῇ θεωρίᾳ τοῦ λόγου. καὶ πρότερόν γε τὴν τῆς ἐπιγραφῆς κατανοήσωμεν δύναμιν· οὐ γὰρ ἀργῶς μοι
30

species of thoughts is left behind in the lower existence together with our material equipment. For every irrational idea that shows itself in the neighborhood of such a mountain will be done to death by more solid thoughts as by so many stones. Scarcely even in this way shall we be able to bear the voice of that trumpet (Exod 19:16, 19), which makes a sound that is great and portentous and above the capacity of those who hear it—a voice preceded by the very darkness of obscurity, in which there is found the God who, on such a mountain, burns up every material thing with fire.

Let us then come within the holy of holies, that is, the Song of Songs.[15] For we are taught by this superlative form of expression that there is a superabundant concentration of holiness within the holy of holies, and in the same way the exalted Word promises to teach us mysteries of mysteries by the agency of the Song of Songs. For although there are many songs within the divinely inspired teaching, through which—from the great David and Isaiah and Moses and many | others—we are instructed in noble thoughts about God, from this title we learn that the mystery contained in the Song of Songs transcends these songs of the saints by as much as they stand apart from the songs of profane wisdom.[16] Human nature can neither discover nor entertain anything greater than this for purposes of understanding. This is why, moreover, the most intense of pleasurable activities (I mean the passion of erotic love) is set as a figure at the very fore of the guidance that the teachings give: so that by this we may learn that it is necessary for the soul, fixing itself steadily on the inaccessible beauty of the divine nature, to love that beauty as much as the body has a bent for what is akin to it and to turn passion into impassibility, so that when every bodily disposition has been quelled, our mind within us may boil with love, but only in the Spirit, because it is heated by that "fire" that the Lord came to "cast upon the earth."

But of these things—how those who hear the mystic words should dispose their souls—enough has been said. It is surely time to set out, by discernment of the text, the divine sayings of the Song of Songs themselves. And first of all let us understand the force of the inscription, for it does not seem

---

15. See the midrash on the Song of Songs (*Midr. Rab.* 1.1:11), which attributes to R. Akiba the statement that "all the Writings are holy, and this is holy of holies."

16. These words represent, in effect, Gregory's interpretation of the first phrase of Song 1:1, which is the book's title. Origen in the prologue to his commentary on the Song of Songs names six other songs "that the Law and the Prophets sang … to the Bride while she … had not yet attained maturity" and that the Song of Songs surpasses. He doubts whether "the song of Isaiah" should be counted among them, since Isaiah lived after Solomon, but admits that one might include psalms (of David) whose title calls them "song" (Baehrens 1925, 80–81; trans. Lawson 1956, 47–50). See also the midrash on the Song of Songs (*Midr. Rab.* 1.1:10).

δοκεῖ τῷ Σολομῶντι τὸ βιβλίον ἐκ τῆς ἐπιγραφῆς | ἀνατεθεῖσθαι, ἀλλ᾽ ὥστε   28
γενέσθαι διάνοιαν τοῖς ἐντυγχάνουσι τοῦ μέγα τι καὶ θεῖον ἐν τοῖς λεγομένοις
προσδέχεσθαι. ἐπειδὴ γὰρ ἀνυπέρβλητόν ἐστι παρ᾽ ἑκάστῳ διὰ τῆς περὶ
αὐτοῦ μαρτυρίας ἐπὶ τῇ σοφίᾳ τὸ θαῦμα, τούτου χάριν εὐθὺς ἐκ προοιμίων ἡ
5   τοῦ ὀνόματος μνήμη παραλαμβάνεται, ὥστε τι μέγα καὶ τῆς περὶ αὐτοῦ δόξης
ἐπάξιον ἐλπισθῆναι διὰ τοῦ βιβλίου τούτου τοῖς ἐντυγχάνουσιν.
    ὥσπερ δὲ κατὰ τὴν γραφικὴν ἐπιστήμην ὕλη μέν τις πάντως ἐστὶν ἐν
διαφόροις βαφαῖς ἡ συμπληροῦσα τοῦ ζῴου τὴν μίμησιν, ὁ δὲ πρὸς τὴν
εἰκόνα βλέπων τὴν ἐκ τῆς τέχνης διὰ τῶν χρωμάτων συμπληρωθεῖσαν οὐ
10   ταῖς ἐπιχρωσθείσαις τῷ πίνακι βαφαῖς ἐμφιλοχωρεῖ τῷ θεάματι, ἀλλὰ πρὸς
τὸ εἶδος βλέπει μόνον, ὃ διὰ τῶν χρωμάτων ὁ τεχνίτης ἀνέδειξεν, οὕτω
προσήκει καὶ ἐπὶ τῆς παρούσης γραφῆς μὴ πρὸς τὴν ὕλην τῶν ἐν τοῖς ῥήμασι
χρωμάτων βλέπειν, ἀλλὰ καθάπερ τι βασιλέως εἶδος ἐν αὐτοῖς καθορᾶν
τὸ διὰ τῶν καθαρῶν νοημάτων ἀνατυπούμενον. λευκὸν γὰρ ἢ ὠχρὸν ἢ
15   μέλαν ἢ ἐρυθρὸν ἢ κυάνεον ἢ ἄλλο τι χρῶμά ἐστι τὰ ῥήματα ταῦτα κατὰ
τὰς προχείρους ἐμφάσεις, στόμα καὶ φίλημα καὶ μύρον καὶ οἶνος καὶ τὰ
τῶν μελῶν ὀνόματα καὶ κλίνη καὶ νεάνιδες καὶ τὰ τοιαῦτα· ἡ δὲ διὰ τούτων
ἀποτελουμένη μορφὴ μακαριότης ἐστὶ καὶ ἀπάθεια καὶ ἡ πρὸς τὸ θεῖον
συνάφεια καὶ ἡ τῶν κακῶν ἀλλοτρίωσις καὶ ἡ πρὸς τὸ ὄντως καλόν | τε καὶ   29
20   ἀγαθὸν ἐξομοίωσις. ταῦτά ἐστι τὰ νοήματα τὰ μαρτυροῦντα τῷ Σολομῶντι
τὴν σοφίαν ἐκείνην τὴν ὑπερβαίνουσαν τοὺς ὅρους τῆς ἀνθρωπίνης σοφίας.
τί γὰρ ἂν γένοιτο τούτου παραδοξότερον ἢ τὸ αὐτὴν ποιῆσαι τὴν φύσιν
τῶν ἰδίων παθημάτων καθάρσιον διὰ τῶν νομιζομένων ἐμπαθῶν ῥημάτων
τὴν ἀπάθειαν νομοθετοῦσάν τε καὶ παιδεύουσαν; οὐ γὰρ λέγει τὸ δεῖν ἔξω
25   τῶν τῆς σαρκὸς γίνεσθαι κινημάτων καὶ νεκροῦν τὰ μέλη τὰ ἐπὶ τῆς γῆς καὶ
καθαρεύειν ἀπὸ τῶν ἐμπαθῶν ῥημάτων τῷ στόματι, ἀλλ᾽ οὕτω διέθηκε τὴν
ψυχήν, ὡς διὰ τῶν ἀπεμφαίνειν δοκούντων πρὸς τὴν καθαρότητα βλέπειν,
διὰ τῶν ἐμπαθῶν ῥήσεων τὴν ἀκήρατον ἑρμηνεύων διάνοιαν.
    ἓν μὲν δὴ τοῦτο διὰ τῶν προοιμίων ἡμᾶς παιδευσάτω ὁ λόγος, τὸ μηκέτι
30   ἀνθρώπους εἶναι τοὺς ἐπὶ τὰ ἄδυτα τῶν τοῦ βιβλίου τούτου μυστηρίων
εἰσαγομένους ἀλλὰ μεταποιηθῆναι τῇ φύσει διὰ τῆς τοῦ κυρίου μαθητείας
πρὸς τὸ θειότερον, καθὼς μαρτυρεῖ τοῖς ἑαυτοῦ μαθηταῖς ὁ λόγος, ὅτι
κρείττους ἦσαν ἢ κατὰ ἄνθρωπον, οὓς διέκρινεν ἀπὸ τῶν ἀνθρώπων ἡ
γενομένη πρὸς αὐτοὺς παρὰ τοῦ κυρίου διαστολή, ὅτε φησί· Τίνα με

to me an idle thing that the book is attributed to Solomon starting with its very title; | rather, this attribution aims to dispose the reader's mind to take in something great and divine through the words of the text. The testimony given about Solomon fills everyone with an unequaled sense of awe before his wisdom, and for this reason mention of his name is made straightaway in the preamble, so that readers may have hope of receiving from this book something great and worthy of Solomon's repute.

In the art of portraiture, there is a piece of wood that, when touched with different colors, presents an imitation of a living thing, but the person who looks at the image that art has created with colors does not dwell upon the sight contrived by dyes painted on the tablet.[17] Rather, he looks solely upon the form that the artist has used colors to indicate. In the same way, where the writing now before us is concerned, the right thing is not to attend to the material stuff of the "colors" contained in the words but rather to discern in them as it were the royal form traced by pure thoughts. According to their obvious sense, these words mean white or yellow or black or red or blue or some other color; they mean mouth and kiss and myrrh and wine and the names of parts of the body and a bed and young men and the like. But the form that is delineated by these words is blessedness and impassibility and fellowship with the Divine and alienation from evil and assimilation to what is truly beautiful | and good. These are the thoughts that attest as Solomon's a wisdom that transcends the heights of human wisdom. For what could be more incredible than to make human nature itself the purifier of its own passions, teaching and legislating impassibility by words that are considered to be tinctured with passion? For he does not say that one must be outside the motions of the flesh and put to death one's earthly members and have one's mouth cleansed of the language of passion. On the contrary, he has so disposed the soul that she directs her gaze toward purity by means of instruments that seem inconsistent with it and by means of impassioned utterances communicates a meaning that is undefiled.

By these prefatory materials let the Word teach us this one thing: it is not any longer human beings who are brought to the shrine of the mysteries of this book. They have been changed in nature into something more divine by the Lord's instruction—just as the Word testifies to his disciples that they surpassed the human condition. He said, "Who do human beings say that I am? … Who do you say that I am?" (Matt 16:13–15)—and the distinction he thus made in their regard separated them out from human beings. For

---

17. This is a favorite analogy of Gregory's; see, for example, *Opif. hom.* 4, 5 (PG 44:137A, 136C), where it is employed to explicate the idea of Adam's creation "after the image and likeness" of God.

λέγουσιν οἱ ἄνθρωποι εἶναι; Ὑμεῖς δὲ τίνα με λέγετε εἶναι; ἀληθῶς | γὰρ ὁ διὰ   30
τῶν τοιούτων ῥημάτων, ὧν ἡ πρόχειρος ἔμφασις τὰς σαρκώδεις ἡδυπαθείας
ἐνδείκνυται, μὴ κατολισθαίνων εἰς τὴν ῥυπῶσαν διάνοιαν ἀλλὰ πρὸς τὴν
τῶν θείων φιλοσοφίαν, ἐπὶ τὰς καθαρὰς ἐννοίας διὰ τῶν ῥημάτων τούτων
5   χειραγωγούμενος δείκνυσι τὸ μηκέτι ἄνθρωπος εἶναι μηδὲ σαρκὶ καὶ αἵματι
συμμεμιγμένην τὴν φύσιν ἔχειν, ἀλλὰ τὴν ἐλπιζομένην ἐν τῇ ἀναστάσει τῶν
ἁγίων ζωὴν ἐπιδείκνυται ἰσάγγελος διὰ τῆς ἀπαθείας γενόμενος. ὡς γὰρ μετὰ
τὴν ἀνάστασιν τὸ μὲν σῶμα μεταστοιχειωθὲν πρὸς τὸ ἄφθαρτον τῇ ψυχῇ
τοῦ ἀνθρώπου συμπλέκεται, τὰ δὲ νῦν διὰ σαρκὸς ἡμῖν ἐνοχλοῦντα πάθη
10   τοῖς σώμασιν ἐκείνοις οὐ συνανίσταται ἀλλά τις εἰρηνικὴ κατάστασις τὴν
ζωὴν ἡμῶν διαδέξεται, μηκέτι τοῦ φρονήματος τῆς σαρκὸς πρὸς τὴν ψυχὴν
στασιάζοντος μηδὲ διὰ τοῦ ἐμφυλίου πολέμου τῶν ἐμπαθῶν κινημάτων
ἀντιστρατευομένου τῷ νόμῳ τοῦ νοὸς καὶ ὥσπερ αἰχμάλωτόν τινα τῇ
ἁμαρτίᾳ προσάγοντος τὴν ἡττηθεῖσαν ψυχήν, ἀλλὰ πάντων τῶν τοιούτων
15   καθαρεύσει τότε ἡ φύσις καὶ ἓν δι' ἀμφοτέρων ἔσται τὸ φρόνημα (τῆς σαρκός
φημι καὶ τοῦ πνεύματος) πάσης σωματικῆς διαθέσεως ἐξαφανισθείσης
ἀπὸ τῆς φύσεως, οὕτω παρακελεύεται καὶ διὰ τοῦ βιβλίου | τούτου ὁ   31
λόγος τοῖς ἐπαΐουσι, κἂν ἐν σαρκὶ ζῶμεν, μηδ' ἐν τοῖς νοήμασι πρὸς αὐτὴν
ἐπιστρέφεσθαι, ἀλλὰ πρὸς μόνην τὴν ψυχὴν βλέπειν καὶ τὰς ἀγαπητικὰς τῶν
20   ῥημάτων ἐμφάσεις καθαράς τε καὶ ἀμολύντους ἀνατιθέναι τῷ ὑπερέχοντι
πάντα νοῦν ἀγαθῷ, ὃ μόνον ἐστὶν ὡς ἀληθῶς γλυκύ τε καὶ ἐπιθυμητὸν καὶ
ἐράσμιον, οὗ ἡ ἀπόλαυσις ἡ ἀεὶ γινομένη ἀφορμὴ μείζονος ἐπιθυμίας γίνεται
τῇ μετουσίᾳ τῶν ἀγαθῶν τὸν πόθον συνεπιτείνουσα.

οὕτως ὁ Μωϋσῆς, ἡ νύμφη, τὸν νυμφίον ἐφίλει κατὰ τὴν ἐν τῷ Ἄισματι
25   παρθένον τὴν λέγουσαν Φιλησάτω με ἀπὸ φιλημάτων στόματος αὐτοῦ,
ὃς διὰ τῆς στόμα κατὰ στόμα γινομένης αὐτῷ παρὰ τοῦ θεοῦ ὁμιλίας,
καθὼς μαρτυρεῖ ἡ γραφή, ἔτι ἐν ἐπιθυμίᾳ μείζονι τῶν τοιούτων φιλημάτων
ἐγίνετο μετὰ τοσαύτας θεοφανείας | ὡς μήπω τεθεαμένος ἰδεῖν ἀξιῶν τὸν   32
ποθούμενον, οὕτως οἱ λοιποὶ πάντες, οἷς ὁ θεῖος πόθος διὰ βάθους ἐνέκειτο,
30   οὐδαμοῦ τῆς ἐπιθυμίας ἵσταντο πᾶν τὸ θεόθεν αὐτοῖς εἰς ἀπόλαυσιν τοῦ
ποθουμένου γινόμενον ὕλην καὶ ὑπέκκαυμα τῆς σφοδροτέρας ἐπιθυμίας
ποιούμενοι. ὥσπερ δὴ καὶ νῦν ἡ τῷ θεῷ συναπτομένη ψυχὴ ἀκορέστως ἔχει
τῆς ἀπολαύσεως, ὅσῳ δαψιλέστερον ἐμφορεῖται τοῦ κάλλους, τοσούτῳ
σφοδρότερον τοῖς πόθοις ἀκμάζουσα. ἐπειδὴ γὰρ τὰ ῥήματα τοῦ νυμφίου
35   πνεῦμά ἐστι καὶ ζωή ἐστι, πᾶς δὲ ὁ τῷ πνεύματι κολλώμενος πνεῦμα γίνεται
καὶ ὁ τῇ ζωῇ συναπτόμενος ἀπὸ θανάτου εἰς ζωὴν μεταβαίνει κατὰ τὴν τοῦ

truly | the person who employs words of the sort contained in the Song of Songs, whose obvious sense refers to fleshly pleasures, not in order to sink down into a sordid sense but by them to be led to the philosophy that concerns things divine and to pure thoughts, gives evidence that he is no longer a human being, that his nature is no longer mingled with flesh and blood (Matt 16:17). Having by impassibility become equal to the angels, he exhibits the hoped-for life of the resurrection of the saints. For after the resurrection, the body, transmuted into incorruptibility, is knit together with the person's soul, but the passions that now afflict us through the flesh do not rise up together with those bodies, and a certain peaceable state will succeed our present life. The "mind of the flesh" (Rom 8:6–7) will no longer be at variance with the soul or "fight against the law of the intellect" (Rom 7:23) by means of the internal battle of our passionate motions and lead the weakened soul a captive to sin. On the contrary, in that state our nature will be purified of all such things, and there will be one mind in both parts (I mean the flesh and the spirit), because every corporeal disposition has disappeared from our nature. In just the same way, by this book | the Word enjoins his hearers, even though we live in the flesh, not to turn toward the flesh in our thoughts but to look only to the soul and to apply the language of love, pure and undefiled, to that Good that transcends all understanding (Phil 4:7), that Good that alone is truly pleasant and desirable and lovable and whose enjoyment is the ever-available opportunity of a yet nobler desiring because by participation in good things it stretches and expands our longing.[18]

The bride Moses kissed the Bridegroom in the same way as the virgin in the Song who says *Let him kiss me with the kisses of his mouth,* and through the face-to-face converse accorded him by God (as the Scripture testifies [cf. Num 12:8]), he became more intensely desirous of such kisses after these theophanies, praying to see the Object of his yearning | as if he had never glimpsed him. In the same way, all of the others in whom the divine desire was deeply lodged never ceased from desire; everything that came to them from God for the enjoyment of the Object of yearning they made into the material and fuel for a more ardent desire. And just as now the soul that is joined to God is not satiated by her enjoyment of him, so too the more abundantly she is filled up with his beauty, the more vehemently her longings abound. For since the words of the Bridegroom are "spirit and life" (John 6:63) and everyone who is joined to the Spirit becomes spirit (1 Cor 6:17), while everyone who is attached to life "passes from death to life" (John 5:24),

---

18. See Aristotle, *Eth. nic.* 7.12 (1153a22): "the pleasures arising from contemplation and learning will make us contemplate and learn all the more."

κυρίου φωνήν, διὰ τοῦτο ποθεῖ προσεγγίσαι τῇ πηγῇ τῆς πνευματικῆς ζωῆς ἡ παρθένος ψυχή. ἡ δὲ πηγή ἐστι τοῦ νυμφίου τὸ στόμα, ὅθεν τὰ ῥήματα τῆς αἰωνίου ζωῆς ἀναβρύοντα πληροῖ τὸ στόμα τὸ ἐφελκόμενον, καθὼς ἐποίει ὁ προφήτης διὰ τοῦ στόματος ἕλκων τὸ πνεῦμα. ἐπειδὴ τοίνυν χρὴ προσθεῖναι

5   τὸ στόμα τῷ στόματι τὸν ἐκ τῆς πηγῆς ποτὸν ἐφελκόμενον, πηγὴ δὲ ὁ κύριος ὁ εἰπὼν Εἴ τις διψᾷ, ἐρχέσθω πρός με καὶ πινέτω, διὰ τοῦτο ἡ ψυχὴ ἡ διψῶσα προσαγαγεῖν τὸ ἑαυτῆς στόμα τῷ τὴν ζωὴν πηγάζοντι | στόματι βούλεται   33 λέγουσα Φιλησάτω με ἀπὸ φιλημάτων στόματος αὐτοῦ.

καὶ ὁ πᾶσι τὴν ζωὴν βρύων καὶ πάντας σωθῆναι θέλων οὐδένα βούλεται
10   τῶν σῳζομένων τοῦ τοιούτου φιλήματος εἶναι ἀμέτοχον· καθάρσιον γάρ ἐστι ῥύπου παντὸς τοῦτο τὸ φίλημα. διό μοι δοκεῖ τῷ λεπρῷ Σίμωνι τὸ τοιοῦτον ὀνειδιστικῶς προφέρειν ὁ κύριος, ὅτι Φίλημά μοι οὐκ ἔδωκας. ἦ γὰρ ἂν ἐκαθαρίσθης τοῦ πάθους τῷ στόματι σπάσας τὴν καθαρότητα. ἀλλ᾽ ἐκεῖνος μὲν εἰκότως ἀνέραστος ἦν ὑπερσαρκήσας διὰ τῆς νόσου καὶ πρὸς τὴν θείαν
15   ἐπιθυμίαν μένων ὑπὸ τοῦ πάθους ἀκίνητος, ἡ δὲ κεκαθαρμένη ψυχὴ μηδεμιᾶς σαρκώδους λέπρας ἐπιπροσθούσης βλέπει τὸν τῶν ἀγαθῶν θησαυρόν.

ὄνομα δέ ἐστι τῷ θησαυρῷ ἡ καρδία, ἀφ᾽ ἧς ἐστι τοῖς μαζοῖς ἡ χορηγία τοῦ θείου γάλακτος, ᾧ τρέφεται ἡ ψυχὴ κατὰ τὴν ἀναλογίαν τῆς πίστεως ἐφελκομένη τὴν χάριν. διὰ τοῦτό φησιν ὅτι Ἀγαθοὶ μαστοί σου ὑπὲρ οἶνον, ἐκ
20   τῆς τοπικῆς θέσεως διὰ τῶν μαζῶν τὴν καρδίαν ὑποσημαίνουσα. πάντως δὲ καρδίαν μὲν τὴν κεκρυμμένην τε καὶ ἀπόρρητον τῆς θεότητος δύναμιν νοῶν τις οὐχ ἁμαρτήσεται. μαζοὺς δὲ τὰς ἀγαθὰς τῆς θείας δυνάμεως ὑπὲρ ἡμῶν ἐνεργείας εἰκότως ἄν τις ὑπονοήσειε, δι᾽ ὧν τιθηνεῖται τὴν ἑκάστου ζωὴν ὁ θεὸς κατάλληλον ἑκάστῳ τῶν δεχομένων τὴν τροφὴν χαριζόμενος.

| Μανθάνομεν δέ τι κατὰ πάροδον καὶ ἕτερον δόγμα διὰ τῆς τοῦ βιβλίου   34 τούτου φιλοσοφίας, ὅτι διπλῆ τίς ἐστιν ἐν ἡμῖν ἡ αἴσθησις, ἡ μὲν σωματικὴ

according to the Lord's word, it follows that the virgin soul longs to approach the fount of the spiritual life. And that fount is the mouth of the Bridegroom, whence "the words of eternal life" (John 6:68) as they gush forth fill the the mouth that is drawn to it, just as the prophet does when drawing spirit through his mouth (cf. Ps 118:131). Since, then, it is necessary for the one who draws drink from the fount to fix mouth to mouth and the fount is the Lord who says, "If anyone thirst, let him come to me and drink" (John 7:37), it follows that the soul, thirsty as she is, wills to bring her own mouth | to the mouth that pours out life, saying *Let him kiss me with the kisses of his mouth.*

Moreover, he who is bursting with life for all and wills all to be saved wants none of those who are being saved to be deprived of such a kiss, for this kiss cleanses away all filth. That, it seems to me, is why the Lord reproached Simon the leper with the words, "You have not given me a kiss" (Luke 7:45). "For surely you would have been cleansed of your disease if you had drawn the purity with your mouth." But very likely that man was without love, having become grotesquely fleshy because of his disease and remaining, by reason of the affliction, without any impulse toward a desire for God. But the soul that has been cleansed, not darkened by any leprosy of the flesh, gazes upon the treasure house of good things.

Now the treasure house is named "heart," and from it the breasts acquire their abundance of the divine milk on which, "according to the proportion of faith" (Rom 12:6), the soul feeds as it draws in grace. That is why it says, *Your breasts are better than wine,* by *breasts* hinting, because of their location, at the heart. For someone who conceives of the heart as the hidden and ineffable Power of the Godhead will surely not be mistaken, and one may reasonably interpret breasts as the beneficent activities[19] of the divine Power on our behalf. Through them God suckles the life of each individual, bestowing the food that is appropriate to each of those who receive it.

| We also learn, in an incidental way, another truth through the philosophical wisdom of this book, that there is in us a dual activity of perception,

---

19. Nyssen sees in the relation of heart and breasts an analogy to the distinction, basic to his theology, between the divine nature, which is hidden, and the divine *energeia*, i.e., God's "activity" as it touches us. By contrast, Origen's exegesis of this phrase depends on the contention that "breasts" (or "bosom") here means the same as "heart," that is, the *principale cordis* (τὸ ἡγεμονικόν) considered as the bearer of truthful teachings (Baehrens 1925, 93; trans. Lawson 1956, 63–64). Gregory the Great, however, took "breasts" to allude to the incarnation and the "praedicatio" that occurs through it. For him v. 2b means: "Plus enim nos nutrivit incarnationis praedicatio quam legis doctrina" (*Exp. Cant.* 13 [CCSL 144:16]; cf. 16 [144:18]). This is not without a certain analogy to the teaching of some rabbis, who took this stichos to convey the principle that "the injunctions of the Scribes are more beloved than those of the Torah" (midrash on Song of Songs, *Midr. Rab.* 1.2:2).

ἡ δὲ θειοτέρα, καθώς φησί που τῆς Παροιμίας ὁ λόγος ὅτι αἴσθησιν θείαν
εὑρήσεις· ἀναλογία γάρ τίς ἐστιν ἐν τοῖς ψυχικοῖς ἐνεργήμασι πρὸς τὰ τοῦ
σώματος αἰσθητήρια. καὶ τοῦτο ἐκ τῶν παρόντων <ῥημάτων> μανθάνομεν·
ὁ μὲν γὰρ οἶνός τε καὶ τὸ γάλα τῇ γεύσει κρίνεται, νοητῶν δὲ ὄντων ἐκείνων
5 νοητὴ πάντως καὶ ἡ ἀντιληπτικὴ τούτων τῆς ψυχῆς ἐστι δύναμις. τὸ δὲ
φίλημα διὰ τῆς ἁπτικῆς αἰσθήσεως ἐνεργεῖται· ἐφάπτεται γὰρ ἀλλήλων τὰ
χείλη ἐν τῷ φιλήματι. ἔστι δέ τις καὶ ἁφὴ τῆς ψυχῆς ἡ ἁπτομένη τοῦ λόγου
διά τινος ἀσωμάτου καὶ νοητῆς ἐπαφήσεως ἐνεργουμένη, καθὼς εἶπεν ὁ
εἰπὼν ὅτι Αἱ χεῖρες ἡμῶν ἐψηλάφησαν περὶ τοῦ λόγου τῆς ζωῆς. ὡσαύτως δὲ
10 καὶ ἡ τῶν θείων μύρων ὀσμὴ οὐ μυκτήρων ἐστὶν ὀσμή, ἀλλά τινος νοητῆς καὶ
ἀΰλου δυνάμεως τῇ τοῦ πνεύματος ὁλκῇ τὴν τοῦ Χριστοῦ συνεφελκομένης
εὐωδίαν.

οὕτω γὰρ ἡ ἀκολουθία τῆς παρθενικῆς εὐχῆς ἐν προοιμίοις ἔχει Ὅτι
ἀγαθοὶ μαστοί σου ὑπὲρ οἶνον καὶ ὀσμὴ | μύρων σου ὑπὲρ πάντα τὰ   35
15 ἀρώματα. δηλοῦται δὲ διὰ τούτων, καθὼς ἡμεῖς ὑπειλήφαμεν, οὐ μικρόν τι
οὐδὲ εὐκαταφρόνητον νόημα· τάχα γὰρ ἐν τῷ ὑπερθεῖναι διὰ συγκρίσεως
τὸ ἐκ τῶν θείων μαστῶν γάλα τῆς ἐκ τοῦ οἴνου γινομένης ἡμῖν εὐφροσύνης
μανθάνομεν διὰ τῶν εἰρημένων, ὅτι πᾶσα ἀνθρωπίνη σοφία καὶ ἐπιστήμη τῶν
ὄντων καὶ πᾶσα δύναμις θεωρητικὴ καὶ καταληπτικὴ φαντασία ἀδυνάτως ἔχει
20 παρισωθῆναι διὰ συγκρίσεως τῇ ἁπλουστέρᾳ τῶν θείων μαθημάτων τροφῇ.
ἐκ γὰρ τῶν μαστῶν τὸ γάλα φέρεται· νηπίων δέ ἐστι τὸ γάλα τροφή. ὁ δὲ
οἶνος δι' εὐτονίαν τε καὶ θερμότητα τῶν τελειοτέρων ἀπόλαυσις γίνεται. ἀλλ'
ὅμως τὸ ἐν τῇ ἔξω σοφίᾳ τέλειον τῆς νηπιώδους τοῦ θείου λόγου διδασκαλίας
ἐστὶ μικρότερον. διὰ τοῦτο κρείττους οἱ θεῖοι μαστοὶ τοῦ ἀνθρωπίνου οἴνου.
25 ἡ δὲ ὀσμὴ τῶν θείων μύρων καλλίων ἐστὶ πάσης τῆς ἐν τοῖς ἀρώμασιν
εὐωδίας. ὅπερ τοιοῦτόν μοι δοκεῖ νοῦν ὑποδεικνύειν· ἀρώματα νοοῦμεν
τὰς ἀρετὰς οἷον σοφίαν σωφροσύνην δικαιοσύνην ἀνδρείαν φρόνησιν καὶ

the one bodily, the other more divine—just as the Word says somewhere in Proverbs, "You will find a divine mode of perception."[20] For there is a certain analogy between the sense organs of the body and the operations of the soul.[21] And it is this that we learn from the words before us. For both wine and milk are discerned by the sense of taste, but when they are intelligible things, the power of the soul that grasps them is a fully intellectual power. And a kiss comes about through the sense of touch, for in a kiss lips touch each other. There is also, though, a "touch" that belongs to the soul, one that makes contact with the Word and is actuated by an incorporeal and intelligible touching, just as someone said, "Our hands have touched concerning the Word of life" (1 John 1:1). In the same way, too, the scent of the divine perfumes is not a scent in the nostrils but pertains to a certain intelligible and immaterial faculty that inhales the sweet smell of Christ by sucking in the Spirit.

Thus the sequel of the virgin's request in the prologue says: *Your breasts are better than wine, and the fragrance | of your perfumed ointments is better than all spices.* What these words convey as we have understood them is no slight or contemptible idea. For we immediately learn by these statements—that is, from the fact that the milk of the divine breasts is superior by comparison with the wine that brings us gladness (cf. Ps 103:15)—that all human wisdom and knowledge of reality as well as every power of discernment and direct apprehension are incapable, in a comparison, of matching the simpler fare of the divine teachings.[22] For what flows from the breasts is milk, and milk is the food of babes. Wine, however, because of its vigor and warmth, becomes the enjoyment of the more mature. Nevertheless, that which is mature and perfect in the non-Christian wisdom is a slighter thing than the most childish teaching of the divine Word. Hence the divine breasts are better than human wine.

And the *fragrance* of the divine *perfumed ointments* is lovelier than any sweet scent among the *spices.* This seems to me to point to the following

---

20. There is no such text to be found in the LXX book of Proverbs.

21. For this doctrine of "internal" or spiritual "senses," see Origen, *Comm. Cant.* 1.4 (Baehrens 1925, 105; trans. Lawson 1956, 79–80). Origen develops it in an excursus on v. 3b (where he also cites Prov 2:5) and not, as here, in a general meditation on the meaning of words referring to taste, touch, and smell.

22. Origen, by contrast, interprets the "wine" of "the ordinances and teachings which the Bride had been wont to receive through the Law and the Prophets" (*Comm. Cant.* 1.2, Baehrens 1925, 94; trans. Lawson 1956, 65; cf. 68). Gregory the Great in one place (*Exp. Cant.* 13 [CCSL 144:15]) follows Origen: "Vinum fuit scientia legis, scientia prophetarum," but later (16 [144:18]) he identifies the wine as "sapientia saeculi," which I take it is roughly what Nyssen means by ἡ ἔξω σοφία ("external" or "foreign wisdom") below. (Origen does, however, allow that the "spices" of v. 3a may be taken to signify "moral and natural philosophy"; Lawson 1956, 73.)

τὰ τοιαῦτα, οἷς προσχρωννύμενος κατὰ τὴν ἑαυτοῦ δύναμιν καὶ προαίρεσιν ἕκαστος ἄλλος ἄλλως ἐν εὐωδίᾳ γινόμεθα· ὁ | μὲν ἐκ σωφροσύνης ἢ σοφίας,   36
ὁ δὲ ἐκ δικαιοσύνης ἢ ἀνδρείας ἢ ἄλλου τινὸς τῶν κατ᾽ ἀρετὴν νοουμένων,
ὁ δὲ τυχὸν καὶ ἐκ πάντων τῶν τοιούτων ἀρωμάτων συγκεκραμένην ἔχει ἐν
5   ἑαυτῷ τὴν εὐωδίαν. ἀλλ᾽ ὅμως ταῦτα πάντα οὐκ ἂν εἰς σύγκρισιν ἔλθοι τῆς
παντελοῦς ἀρετῆς ἐκείνης, ἣν τοὺς οὐρανοὺς διειληφέναι φησὶν Ἀμβακοὺμ ὁ
προφήτης εἰπὼν Ἐκάλυψεν οὐρανοὺς ἡ ἀρετὴ αὐτοῦ, ἥτις ἐστὶν αὐτοσοφία
καὶ αὐτοδικαιοσύνη καὶ αὐτοαλήθεια καὶ τὰ καθ᾽ ἕκαστον πάντα. τῶν
οὖν σῶν μύρων ἡ ὀσμή, φησίν, ἀπαράθετον ἔχει τὴν χάριν πρὸς ταῦτα τὰ
10   ἀρώματα τὰ παρ᾽ ἡμῶν γινωσκόμενα.

Πάλιν ἐν τοῖς ἐφεξῆς ὑψηλοτέρας ἅπτεται φιλοσοφίας ἡ ψυχή, ἡ νύμφη,
τὸ ἀπρόσιτόν τε καὶ ἀχώρητον λογισμοῖς ἀνθρωπίνοις τῆς θείας δυνάμεως
ἐνδεικνυμένη, ἐν οἷς φησι Μύρον ἐκκενωθὲν ὄνομά σοι· τοιοῦτον γάρ τι δοκεῖ
μοι διὰ τοῦ λόγου τούτου σημαίνεσθαι, ὅτι οὐκ ἔστιν ὀνοματικῇ σημασίᾳ
15   περιληφθῆναι δι᾽ ἀκριβείας τὴν ἀόριστον φύσιν· ἀλλὰ πᾶσα νοημάτων δύναμις
καὶ πᾶσα ῥημάτων τε καὶ ὀνομάτων ἔμφασις, κἄν τι μέγα καὶ θεοπρεπὲς ἔχειν
δόξῃ, αὐτοῦ τοῦ ὄντος ἐφάψασθαι φύσιν οὐκ ἔχει· ἀλλ᾽ ὥσπερ ἐξ | ἰχνῶν   37
τινων καὶ ἐναυσμάτων ὁ λόγος ἡμῶν τοῦ ἀδήλου καταστοχάζεται διὰ τῶν
καταλαμβανομένων εἰκάζων ἔκ τινος ἀναλογίας τὸ ἀκατάληπτον. ὅ τι γὰρ
20   ἂν ἐπινοήσωμεν, φησίν, ὄνομα γνωριστικὸν τοῦ τῆς θεότητος μύρου, οὐκ
αὐτὸ τὸ μύρον διὰ τῆς ἐμφάσεως τῶν λεγομένων σημαίνομεν, ἀλλὰ βραχύ τι
λείψανον ἀτμοῦ τῆς θείας εὐωδίας τοῖς θεολογικοῖς ὀνόμασιν ἐνδεικνύμεθα.
ὡς ἐπὶ τῶν ἀγγείων, ὧν ἂν ἐκκενωθῇ τὸ μύρον, αὐτὸ μὲν τῇ ἑαυτοῦ φύσει
ἀγνοεῖται τὸ μύρον τὸ ἐκκενωθὲν τῶν ἀγγείων, οἷόν ἐστιν· ἐξ ἀμυδρᾶς δέ

thought. The *spices* we take to be virtues, such as wisdom, temperance, justice, courage, prudence, and the like, and each different individual assumes a different scent as he is dabbed with them in accord with his own power and choice.[23] One | has within himself the fragrance that comes from temperance or wisdom; another, that which comes from justice or courage or some other quality that is reckoned among the virtues; and yet another, the scent that comes from the mingling of all these *spices*. Nevertheless, none of these can be compared with that absolute virtue of which the prophet Habakkuk asserts that it encloses the heavens when he says, "His virtue veiled the heavens" (Hab 3:3). This is Wisdom herself and Justice itself and Truth herself and all things severally. Therefore she says, "The fragrance of your perfumed ointments possesses a grace that is incomparable to the spices known to us."

Once again, in what comes next, the soul, the Bride, touches on a higher philosophy. When she says *Your name is a perfumed ointment emptied out*, she makes it manifest that the divine power is inaccessible and incapable of being contained by human thought processes, for to me it seems that by this statement there is conveyed something like the following: that the Nature that has no boundaries cannot be accurately comprehended by means of the connotations of words. On the contrary, all the power of concepts and all the significance of words and names, even if they seem to have about them something grand and worthy of the Divine, cannot attain the nature of the Real itself. On the contrary, it is as if | by certain traces and hints that our reason guesses at the Invisible; by way of some analogy based on things it has comprehended, it forms a conjecture about the Incomprehensible. For whatever name we may think up, she says, to make the scent of the Godhead known, the meaning of the things we say does not refer to the perfume itself. Rather does our theological vocabulary refer to a slight remnant of the vapor of the divine fragrance.[24] In the case of vessels from which perfumed ointment is emptied out, the ointment itself that has been emptied out is not known for what it is in its own nature. We make a guess about the perfume that has been

---

23. Contrast Gregory the Great, *Exp. Cant.* 14 (CCSL 144:16): "Unguenta domini virtutes sunt.... Odor unguentorum eius est flagrantia virtutum, quas operatus est." The "spices" are "Illa legis aromata per angelos amministrata."

24. Origen's exegesis, by contrast, turns on the word ἐκκενωθέν ("poured" or "emptied" out), which occasions him to recall Phil 2:7 and to see the stichos as referring to the incarnation of the Word (*Comm. Cant.* 1.4, Baehrens 1925, 102; trans. Lawson 1956, 75–76). Cf. Gregory the Great, *Exp. Cant.* 21 (CCSL 144:23): "Unguentem effusum est divinitas incarnata." Only Apollinarius (as reported by Procopius, *Cat. Cant.*; PG 87:1552) cites 1 Cor 6:11 and comments that "the name that has been poured out brings about the pouring out of the Spirit upon all," thus referring the words of the text to baptism.

τινος τῆς ὑπολειφθείσης ἐκ τῶν ἀτμῶν τῷ ἀγγείῳ ποιότητος στοχασμόν τινα περὶ τοῦ ἐκκενωθέντος μύρου ποιούμεθα.

τοῦτο οὖν ἐστιν ὃ διὰ τῶν εἰρημένων μανθάνομεν, ὅτι αὐτὸ μὲν τὸ τῆς θεότητος μύρον, ὅ τί ποτε κατ' οὐσίαν ἐστίν, ὑπὲρ πᾶν ἐστιν ὄνομά τε καὶ
5   νόημα· τὰ δὲ τῷ παντὶ ἐνθεωρούμενα θαύματα τῶν θεολογικῶν ὀνομάτων τὴν ὕλην δίδωσι, δι' ὧν σοφόν, δυνατόν, ἀγαθόν, ἅγιον, μακάριόν τε καὶ ἀΐδιον καὶ κριτὴν καὶ σωτῆρα καὶ τὰ τοιαῦτα κατονομάζομεν· ἅπερ πάντα ποιότητά τινα βραχεῖαν τοῦ θείου μύρου ἐνδεί|κνυται, ἣν πᾶσα ἡ κτίσις διὰ   38
τῶν ἐνθεωρουμένων θαυμάτων σκεύους τινὸς μυρεψικοῦ δίκην ἐν ἑαυτῇ
10   ἀπεμάξατο.

Διὰ τοῦτο, φησί, νεάνιδες ἠγάπησάν σε, εἵλκυσάν σε. εἶπε τὴν αἰτίαν τῆς ἐπαινετῆς ἐπιθυμίας καὶ τῆς ἀγαπητικῆς διαθέσεως. τίς γὰρ τοῦ τοιούτου κάλλους ἀνέραστος γίνεται, εἰ μόνον ὀφθαλμὸν ἔχοι τὸν ἐνατενίσαι τῇ ὥρᾳ δυνάμενον, οὗ πολὺ μὲν τὸ καταλαμβανόμενον κάλλος, ἀπειροπλάσιον δὲ
15   τὸ διὰ τοῦ φαινομένου στοχαστικῶς εἰκαζόμενον; ἀλλ' ὥσπερ ὁ ὑλικὸς ἔρως τῶν ἔτι νηπιαζόντων οὐχ ἅπτεται (οὐ γὰρ χωρεῖ τὸ πάθος ἡ νηπιότης), οὐδὲ μὴν τοὺς ἐν ἐσχάτῳ γήρᾳ πεπονηκότας ἐν τοῖς τοιούτοις ἔστιν ἰδεῖν, οὕτω καὶ ἐπὶ τοῦ θείου κάλλους ὅ τε νήπιος ἔτι καὶ κλυδωνιζόμενος καὶ περιφερόμενος παντὶ ἀνέμῳ τῆς διδασκαλίας καὶ ὁ παλαιὸς καὶ γηράσας καὶ τῷ ἀφανισμῷ
20   προσεγγίσας ἀκίνητοι πρὸς τὴν ἐπιθυμίαν ταύτην εὑρίσκονται· οὐ γὰρ ἅπτεται τῶν τοιούτων τὸ ἀόρατον κάλλος, μόνη δὲ ἡ τοιαύτη ψυχὴ ἡ διαβᾶσα μὲν τὴν νηπιώδη κατάστασιν καὶ διὰ τῆς πνευματικῆς ἡλικίας ἀκμάσασα, μὴ προσλαβοῦσα δὲ σπίλον ἢ ῥυτίδα ἤ τι τῶν τοιούτων, ἡ μήτε ὑπὸ νηπιότητος ἀναισθητοῦσα μήτε ὑπὸ παλαιότητος ἀδρανοῦσα, ἣν νεᾶνιν ὀνομάζει ὁ
25   λόγος, αὕτη πείθεται τῇ μεγάλῃ καὶ πρώτῃ ἐντολῇ τοῦ νόμου ἐξ ὅλης καρδίας τε καὶ δυνάμεως ἀγαπῶσα τὸ κάλλος ἐκεῖνο, οὗ ὑπογραφὴν καὶ ὑπόδειγμα καὶ ἑρμηνείαν οὐχ | εὑρίσκει ἡ ἀνθρωπίνη διάνοια. αἱ τοιαῦται τοίνυν   39
νεάνιδες αἱ διὰ τῶν ἀρετῶν αὐξηθεῖσαι καὶ καθ' ὥραν ἤδη τῶν μυστηρίων τοῦ θείου θαλάμου γενόμεναι ἀγαπῶσι τοῦ νυμφίου τὸ κάλλος καὶ διὰ τῆς
30   ἀγάπης πρὸς ἑαυτὰς ἐπιστρέφουσι. τοιοῦτος γὰρ ὁ νυμφίος, ὡς ἀντιδιδόναι τοῖς ἀγαπῶσι τὸν πόθον, ὁ οὕτως εἰπὼν ἐκ προσώπου τῆς σοφίας ὅτι Ἐγὼ τοὺς ἐμὲ φιλοῦντας ἀγαπῶ· καὶ ὅτι Μεριῶ τοῖς ἐμὲ ἀγαπῶσιν ὕπαρξιν (αὐτὸς

emptied out on the basis of some faint quality of the vapor that has been left behind in the vessel.

Here, then, is what we learn from the words: the perfumed ointment of the Godhead, whatever it may be in its own essence, is beyond every name and every thought, but the marvels discerned in each name and thought provide matter for our theological naming. By their help we name God wise, powerful, good, holy, blessed and eternal, and judge and savior and the like. And all these refer to some slight trace of the divine perfume | that the whole creation imitates within itself, after the manner of a jar for unguents, by the wonders that are seen in it.

That is why, she says, *young maidens have loved you, they have drawn you.* She speaks about the source of praiseworthy desire and of the disposition to love. For who is there without desire for such a Beauty, if only he has an eye capable of gazing upon its splendor? And while the beauty so discerned is great, that which such perception images and hints at is a thousandfold greater. But just as erotic love of the material order does not affect those who are still young (for childhood has no place for this passion) and one cannot see extremely old people afflicted in this way, so too in the case of the divine Beauty one still a child, "tossed to and fro and carried about by every wind of doctrine" (Eph 4:14), and the elderly person who has aged and is approaching dissolution are both unmoved by this desire. For such people are not touched by the invisible Beauty, but only a soul of the sort that has passed through the condition of childhood and has arrived at the height of spiritual maturity without receiving any "spot or wrinkle or any such thing"—the soul that is neither imperceptive by reason of youth nor weakened by old age.[25] This soul our text calls a *young maiden,* and she is faithful to "the first and great commandment" of the law. With her whole heart and strength she loves that Beauty whose description and form and explanation | the human mind fails to discover. *Young maidens* of this sort, then, who have made increase by the practice of the virtues and have already participated in the mysteries of the inner divine chamber as their youthfulness prescribes, love and delight in the beauty of the Bridegroom and through love turn to themselves. For this Bridegroom returns the love of those who love him. Speaking in the person of Wisdom he says, "I love those who love me" (Prov 8:17), and then, "With

---

25. Cf. Origen, *Comm. Cant.* 1.4 (Baehrens 1925, 101; trans. Lawson 1956, 75): "not those little old souls clothed in the old man, nor yet the spotted and wrinkled, but … the young souls growing up in years and beauty, who are always being made new and renewed from day to day." Gregory the Great, *Exp. Cant.* 22 (CCSL 144:23), identifies the "maidens" ("adulescentulae") as "electorum animas per baptismum renovatas," but he uses the same contrast between "puerilis aetas" and "senilis" as Nyssen.

δέ ἐστιν ἡ ὕπαρξις) καὶ τοὺς θησαυροὺς αὐτῶν ἐμπλήσω ἀγαθῶν. ἕλκουσι τοίνυν αἱ ψυχαὶ πρὸς ἑαυτὰς τοῦ ἀφθάρτου νυμφίου τὸν πόθον ὀπίσω, καθὼς γέγραπται, κυρίου τοῦ θεοῦ πορευόμεναι.

τῆς δὲ ἀγάπης αὐτῶν αἰτία ἡ τοῦ μύρου εὐωδία γίνεται, πρὸς ἣν ἀεὶ
5 τρέχουσαι τοῖς ἔμπροσθεν ἐπεκτείνονται τοῦ κατόπιν λήθην ποιούμεναι. Ὀπίσω γάρ σου, φησίν, εἰς ὀσμὴν μύρων σου δραμούμεθα. ἀλλὰ αἱ μὲν οὔπω τῆς ἀρετῆς τὸ τέλειον ἔχουσαι καὶ καθ' ἡλικίαν ἔτι νεάζουσαι δραμεῖσθαι πρὸς τὸν σκοπόν, ὃν ὑποδείκνυσιν ἡ ὀσμὴ τῶν μύρων, κατεπαγγέλλονται (λέγουσι γὰρ ὅτι Εἰς ὀσμὴν μύρων σου δραμούμεθα), ἡ δὲ τελειοτέρα ψυχὴ
10 σφοδρότερον ἐπεκταθεῖσα τοῖς ἔμπροσθεν ἤδη τυγχάνει τοῦ σκοποῦ, δι' ὃν ὁ δρόμος ἀνύεται, καὶ τῶν ἐν τοῖς ταμείοις θησαυρῶν | ἀξιοῦται. φησὶ γὰρ   40 ὅτι Εἰσήγαγέ με ὁ βασιλεὺς εἰς τὸ ταμεῖον αὐτοῦ. ἡ γὰρ ἄκροις χείλεσι τοῦ ἀγαθοῦ ψαῦσαι ποθήσασα καὶ τοσοῦτον μόνον ἐφαψαμένη τοῦ κάλλους, ὅσον ἡ τῆς εὐχῆς ἐνδείκνυται δύναμις (ηὔξατο δὲ οἷόν τινος φιλήματος
15 ἀξιωθῆναι διὰ τῆς τοῦ λόγου ἐλλάμψεως), αὕτη δι' ὧν ἔτυχε καὶ ἐπὶ τὸ ἐνδότερον τῶν ἀπορρήτων τῷ λογισμῷ διαδυεῖσα βοᾷ τὸ μὴ μόνον ἐν προθύροις τῶν ἀγαθῶν εἶναι τὸν δρόμον, ἀλλὰ τῇ ἀπαρχῇ τοῦ πνεύματος, οὗ διὰ τῆς πρώτης χάριτος οἷον διά τινος φιλήματος ἠξιώθη, διερευνᾶν τοῦ θεοῦ τὰ βάθη καὶ ἐν τοῖς ἀδύτοις γενομένη τοῦ παραδείσου κατὰ τὸν μέγαν
20 Παῦλον ὁρᾶν τέ φησι τὰ ἀθέατα καὶ τῶν ἀλαλήτων ἐπακροᾶσθαι ῥημάτων.

Ἡ δὲ ἐφεξῆς ῥῆσις τὴν ἐκκλησιαστικὴν οἰκονομίαν ἐκκαλύπτει τῷ λόγῳ. οἱ γὰρ πρῶτοι μαθητευθέντες τῇ χάριτι καὶ αὐτόπται τοῦ λόγου γενόμενοι οὐκ ἐν ἑαυτοῖς τὸ ἀγαθὸν περιώρισαν, ἀλλὰ καὶ τοῖς μετ' ἐκείνους ἐκ διαδόσεως τὴν αὐτὴν ἐνεποίησαν χάριν. διὰ τοῦτο πρὸς τὴν νύμφην
25 φασὶν αἱ νεάνιδες τὴν πρώτην διὰ τοῦ κατὰ στόμα γενέσθαι τοῦ λόγου τῶν

those who love me I share what I possess" (and *he* is her possession), "and I will fill their treasure houses with good things" (Prov 8:21). Hence the souls draw to themselves the longing for the incorruptible Bridegroom, "going after the Lord God," as it is written (cf. Hos 11:10).

Now what awakens their love is the sweet scent of the perfume, toward which, as they run unceasingly, they stretch themselves out for what lies ahead, forgetting what lies behind (cf. Phil 3:13). Hence it says: *We will run after you, toward the fragrance of your perfumed ointments.* But it is those who do not yet possess the fullness of virtue and are still immature who promise that they will pursue the goal toward which the fragrance of the perfumes points them (for it says, *We will run … toward the fragrance of your perfumed ointments*); the more perfect soul,[26] on the other hand, who has more eagerly "been stretched out toward what lies ahead," already attains the goal for the sake of which the course is run and is reckoned worthy of the goods that the treasure house contains | —which is why she for her part says, *The king brought me into his treasure house.* For the soul that has desired to touch the Good with the tips of her lips and has laid hold on the Beautiful just to the extent that the strength of her prayer indicates (she prayed, one might say, to be made worthy of a kiss through the illumination of the Word), this same soul, empowered by its success in slipping through to the interior of what thought cannot articulate, cries out her request that her running not be confined to the outer courts of the Good but that by the firstfruits of the Spirit (cf. Rom 8:23)—of which she was made worthy by the first gift of grace, that is, by a kiss[27]—she may come to the inner shrine of paradise and search "the depths of God" (1 Cor 2:10) and, like the great Paul, see (as he says) invisible things and hear unspeakable words[28] (cf. 2 Cor 12:2–4).

The following expression unveils in the Word the dispensation of the church. Those who were first made disciples by grace and became "eyewitnesses … of the Word" (Luke 1:2) did not keep the Good to themselves. Rather did they work the same grace, by transmission, in those who were their companions. That is why the young women say to the Bride[29]—who

---

26. See Origen, *Comm. Cant.* 1.4, for a similar distinction between the Bride, who is classed with "the perfect," and the maidens (Baehrens 1925, 108; trans. Lawson 1956, 83 and cf. 77). Origen, however, understands the "pouring out" of the ointment as the incarnation of the Word (see note 24 above); unlike Origen, Gregory is careful to describe the Bride not as "perfect" but as "more perfect."

27. It appears that Gregory here sees the "kiss" of Song 1:2 as symbolic of baptism, where the believer receives "the firstfruits of the Spirit."

28. Cf. Origen, *Comm. Cant.* 1.5 (Baehrens 1925, 109; trans. Lawson 1956, 85), where the same text is alluded to in the same connection.

29. Origen, *Comm. Cant.* 1.5 (Baehrens 1925, 110; trans. Lawson 1956, 86–87), takes

ἀγαθῶν πληρωθεῖσαν καὶ τῶν κεκρυμμένων μυστηρίων ἀξιωθεῖσαν ὅτι
Ἀγαλλιασώμεθα καὶ εὐφρανθῶμεν ἐν σοί (κοινὴ γὰρ ἡμῶν ἐστι χαρὰ | τὸ   41
σὸν ἀγαλλίαμα) καὶ ὅτι ὡς σὺ ἀγαπᾷς ὑπὲρ οἶνον τοὺς μαζοὺς τοῦ λόγου,
οὕτω καὶ ἡμεῖς σὲ μιμησώμεθα καὶ τοὺς σοὺς μαζούς, δι᾽ ὧν τοὺς νηπίους
5   ἐν Χριστῷ γάλα ποτίζεις, ὑπὲρ τὸν ἀνθρώπινον ἀγαπήσωμεν οἶνον. καί, ὡς
ἄν τις ἐπὶ τὸ σαφέστερον προαγάγοι τὸ νόημα, τοιοῦτόν ἐστι τὸ λεγόμενον·
ἠγάπησε τοὺς μαζοὺς τοῦ λόγου ὁ ἐπὶ τὸ στῆθος τοῦ κυρίου ἀναπεσὼν
Ἰωάννης καὶ οἷόν τινα σπογγιὰν τὴν ἑαυτοῦ καρδίαν παραθεὶς τῇ πηγῇ
τῆς ζωῆς καὶ πλήρης ἔκ τινος ἀρρήτου διαδόσεως τῶν ἐγκειμένων τῇ τοῦ
10   κυρίου καρδίᾳ μυστηρίων γενόμενος καὶ ἡμῖν ἐπέχει τὴν πληρωθεῖσαν ὑπὸ
τοῦ λόγου θηλὴν καὶ πλήρεις ποιεῖ τῶν ἐντεθέντων αὐτῷ παρὰ τῆς πηγῆς
ἀγαθῶν κηρύσσων ἐν μεγαλοφωνίᾳ τὸν ἀεὶ ὄντα λόγον. ὅθεν εἰκότως καὶ
ἡμεῖς πρὸς αὐτὸν ἐροῦμεν ὅτι Ἀγαπήσωμεν μαστούς σου ὑπὲρ οἶνον, εἴπερ
δὴ τοιοῦτοι γεγόναμεν, ὡς νεάνιδες εἶναι καὶ μήτε ταῖς φρεσὶ νηπιάζειν ὑπὸ
15   τῆς τῇ ματαιότητι συνεζευγμένης νεότητος μήτε ῥυτιδοῦσθαι δι᾽ ἁμαρτίας
ἐν παλαιότητι τῇ εἰς ἀφανισμὸν καταληγούσῃ· διὰ τοῦτο δὲ ἀγαπῶμεν τὴν
τῶν σῶν | διδαγμάτων ἐπιρροήν, ὅτι Σὲ ἡ εὐθύτης ἠγάπησεν. οὗτος γάρ   42
ἐστιν ὁ μαθητής, ὃν ἠγάπα ὁ Ἰησοῦς. Ἰησοῦς δέ ἐστιν ἡ εὐθύτης. κάλλιον
δὲ καὶ θεοπρεπέστερον ὁ λόγος οὗτος παρὰ τὸν προφήτην Δαβὶδ ὀνομάζει
20   τὸν κύριον· ὁ μὲν γάρ φησιν ὅτι Εὐθὺς κύριος ὁ θεός, οὗτος δὲ εὐθύτητα
ὀνομάζει, ᾧ πᾶν τὸ σκολιὸν πρὸς τὸ ὀρθὸν ἀπευθύνεται, ἀλλὰ γένοιτο καὶ
ἡμῖν πᾶν τὸ σκολιὸν εἰς εὐθεῖαν καὶ τὰ τραχέα εἰς ὁδοὺς λείας χάριτι τοῦ
κυρίου ἡμῶν Ἰησοῦ Χριστοῦ·

        ᾧ ἡ δόξα εἰς τοὺς αἰῶνας τῶν αἰώνων.
25   ἀμήν.

because she came face to face with the Word was the first to to be filled with good things and to be adjudged worthy of hidden mysteries—*Let us rejoice and be glad in you* (for we share the joy | of your exultation); and, "As you love the breasts of the Word more than wine, so too let us imitate you and love your breasts, through which you give 'babes in Christ' milk to drink, more than the wine that human beings make." And in order that we may be perfectly clear about the matter, the sense of what we are saying is this: John, who rested on the Lord's bosom, loved the breasts of the Word, and having brought his own heart, as if it were a sponge, up to the fount of life, he was filled, by an indescribable transmission, with the mysteries lodged in the Lord's heart, and he offers to us the teat that has been filled up by the Word. He fills us up with the things lodged within him by the fount of Goodness as, in a loud voice, he proclaims the eternal Word. For this reason it is fitting that we too turn to him and say *Let us love your breasts more than wine,* if indeed we have become the sort of people who are youthful, neither immature in heart and mind because of childishness yoked with vanity nor yet shriveled up and wrinkled by sin in an old age that issues in destruction. And the reason why we love the flowing milk | of your teaching is that *Righteousness has loved you.* For this is the disciple whom Jesus loved. And Jesus is righteousness.[30] This saying adorns the Lord with a name more lovely and more worthy of God than that accorded by the prophet David. For David says, "Righteous is the Lord God" (Ps 91:16), and he in turns names him "Righteousness," by which everything that is crooked is again made straight. But for us may everything "crooked be … made straight, and the rough ways … smooth" (Isa 40:4) by the grace of our Lord Jesus Christ,

To whom be glory to the ages of ages.
Amen.

---

these words as addressed to the Bridegroom by the maidens. The next stichos ("We will love your breasts…"), he asserts, is addressed to the Bride, although his interpretation does not seem consistent with that statement. Gregory's exegesis turns on his taking both stichoi as addressed to the Bride.

30. Gregory interprets this phrase in a fashion that is the exact converse of Origen's. For Origen (*Comm. Cant.* 1.5 [Baehrens 1925, 112; trans. Lawson 1956, 88–89]) it means that only the righteous soul can love the Bridegroom.

Λόγος β′

Μέλαινά εἰμι καὶ καλή, θυγατέρες Ἰερουσαλήμ,
ὡς σκηνώματα κηδάρ, ὡς δέρρεις Σολομών.
Μὴ βλέψητέ με ὅτι ἐγώ εἰμι μεμελανωμένη,
ὅτι παρέβλεψέ με ὁ ἥλιος·
5   υἱοὶ μητρός μου ἐμαχέσαντο ἐν ἐμοί,
ἔθεντό με φυλάκισσαν ἐν ἀμπελῶσιν·
ἀμπελῶνα ἐμὸν οὐκ ἐφύλαξα.

Ἀπάγγειλόν μοι, ὃν ἠγάπησεν ἡ ψυχή μου,
| ποῦ ποιμαίνεις,   43
10   ποῦ κοιτάζεις ἐν μεσημβρίᾳ,
μήποτε γένωμαι ὡς περιβαλλομένη ἐπ᾽ ἀγέλαις ἑταίρων σου.

Ἐὰν μὴ γνῷς σεαυτήν, ἡ καλὴ ἐν γυναιξίν,
ἔξελθε σὺ ἐν πτέρναις τῶν ποιμνίων
καὶ ποίμαινε τὰς ἐρίφους ἐπὶ σκηνώμασι τῶν ποιμνίων.

15   Τῆς ἱερᾶς τοῦ μαρτυρίου σκηνῆς οὐχ ὁμότιμον ἦν τῷ ἔνδοθεν κεκρυμμένῳ
κάλλει τὸ ἐκτὸς προφαινόμενον· αὐλαῖαι μὲν γὰρ ἐκ λινῶν ὑφασμάτων καὶ αἱ
διὰ τῶν τριχῶν τῶν αἰγῶν δέρρεις καὶ αἱ τῶν ἐρυθρῶν δερμάτων περιβολαὶ
τὸν ἔξωθεν τῆς σκηνῆς κόσμον ἐπλήρουν καὶ οὐδὲν ἦν μέγα καὶ τίμιον τοῖς
τὰ ἐκτὸς ὁρῶσι παρὰ ταῦτα φαινόμενον, ἔσωθεν δὲ χρυσῷ καὶ ἀργύρῳ καὶ
20   τοῖς τιμίοις τῶν λίθων πᾶσα ἡ τοῦ μαρτυρίου σκηνὴ κατελάμπετο· οἱ στῦλοι,
αἱ βάσεις, αἱ κεφαλίδες, τὸ θυμιατήριον, τὸ θυσιαστήριον, | ἡ κιβωτός, ἡ   44
λυχνία, τὸ ἱλαστήριον, οἱ λουτῆρες, τὰ τῶν εἰσόδων καταπετάσματα, οἷς τὸ
κάλλος ἐκ παντὸς εἴδους τῆς εὐχροούσης βαφῆς συνεκίρνατο, νῆμα χρύσεον
ὑακίνθῳ καὶ πορφύρᾳ καὶ βύσσῳ καὶ κόκκῳ διά τινος τεχνικῆς λεπτουργίας
25   εὐκόσμως συνυφαινόμενον, σύγκρατον ἐκ πάντων, καθάπερ ἐν ἴριδος αὐγαῖς
ἀποστίλβειν ἐποίει τὴν αὐγὴν τοῦ ὑφάσματος.
     πρὸς ὅ τι δὲ βλέπων ἐντεῦθεν προοιμιάζομαι, πρόδηλον ὑμῖν πάντως ἐκ
τῶν ῥηθησομένων γενήσεται. πάλιν πρόκειται ἡμῖν τὸ Ἄισμα τῶν Ἀισμάτων

[5]*I am dark and beautiful, O daughters of Jerusalem,*
As the tents of Kedar, as the curtains of Solomon.
[6]*Do not gaze at me, for I have been made dark,*
Because the sun has looked askance at me:
The sons of my mother fought within me,
They made me a guard in the vineyards.
I did not guard my vineyard.

[7]*Speak to me, you whom my soul loves,*
| Where do you pasture your flock?
Where do you rest them at noontide?
Lest I become as one who is veiled by the flocks of your companions.

[8]*If you do not know yourself, O beautiful one among women,*
Go forth in the footsteps of the flocks,
And tend the kids by the shepherds' tents.

The outward appearance of the sacred tent of witness[1] was not so precious as the beauty hidden within it. Hangings of linen cloth and goats-hair curtains and coverings of red skins made up the external adornment of the tent, and those who looked on its exterior saw nothing greater or more precious than these. On the interior, however, the whole tent of witness shone with gold and silver and precious stones. There were the pillars, the pedestals, the capitals, the censer, | the altar, the ark, the lamps, the mercy seat, the water basins, and the veils of the entrances, whose beauty was a blend of every sort of handsome dye: gold thread gorgeously woven together with blue and purple and flaxen and scarlet by delicate workmanship. A blend of all these, it made the brightness of the cloth shine like that of the rainbow.

My purpose in making this introduction will become completely clear to you from what I am about to say. Again it is the Song of Songs that lies

---

1. RSV: "tent of meeting." The expression "tent of witness" (ἡ τοῦ μαρτυρίου σκηνή; cf. Acts 7:44) recurs regularly in LXX Exodus after chapter 27. The description in the text draws on God's instructions (Exod 25–26) to Moses for the making of a "holy place" (ἁγίασμα). For other accounts of the tent of witness, compare Gregory's *Vit. Mos.* 1.49–50 (GNO 7.1:23), a parallel description, and, of course, Philo, *Mos.* 2.79ff.

εἰς πᾶσαν φιλοσοφίας τε καὶ θεογνωσίας ὑφήγησιν. αὕτη ἐστὶν ἡ ἀληθινὴ
τοῦ μαρτυρίου σκηνή, ἧς προκαλύμματα μὲν καὶ δέρρεις καὶ ἡ τῆς αὐλαίας
περιβολὴ ἐρωτικοί τινες γίνονται λόγοι καὶ ῥήματα τὴν πρὸς τὸ ποθούμενον
σχέσιν ἐμφαίνοντα καὶ κάλλους ὑπογραφὴ καὶ μνήμη σωματικῶν μελῶν, τῶν
5   τε προφαινομένων ἐν τῷ προσώπῳ καὶ τῶν ὑποκεκρυμμένων τῇ τῆς ἐσθῆτος
περιβολῇ. τὰ δὲ ἐντὸς πολύφωτός τίς ἐστιν ὡς ἀληθῶς λυχνία καὶ κιβωτὸς
μυστηρίων πλήρης. καὶ τὸ τῆς εὐωδίας θυμιατήριον καὶ τὸ καθάρσιον τῆς
ἁμαρτίας, τὸ πάγχρυσον ἐκεῖνο τῆς εὐσεβείας θυσιαστήριον, τό τε τῶν
καταπετασμάτων κάλλος, τὸ διὰ τῆς τῶν ἀρετῶν εὐχροίας εὐσχημόνως
10   ἐξυφαινόμενον, καὶ οἱ ἀκλινεῖς τῶν λογισμῶν στῦλοι καὶ αἱ ἀμετάθετοι τῶν
δογμάτων βάσεις | τό τε τῶν κεφαλίδων κάλλος, δι' ὧν ἡ περὶ τὸ ἡγεμονικὸν   45
τῆς ψυχῆς ἑρμηνεύεται χάρις καὶ οἱ τῶν ψυχῶν λουτῆρες καὶ πάντα ὅσα πρὸς
τὴν οὐρανίαν τε καὶ ἀσώματον πολιτείαν βλέπει, ἃ δι' αἰνιγμάτων ὁ νόμος
διακελεύεται, ἐν τοῖς ὑποκεκρυμμένοις τῇ λέξει νοήμασιν ἔστιν εὑρεῖν,
15   εἰ μόνον ἐπιτηδείους πρὸς τὴν εἰς τὰ ἅγια τῶν ἁγίων εἴσοδον ἑαυτοὺς δι'
ἐπιμελείας ποιήσαιμεν τῷ λουτῆρι τοῦ λόγου πάντα ῥύπον αἰσχρᾶς ἐννοίας
ἀποκλυσάμενοι, μήποτε θιγόντες παρὰ τὸ παράγγελμα τοῦ νόμου θνησιμαίου
νοήματος ἤ τινος τῶν ἀκαθάρτων ἐνθυμίων ἁψάμενοι ἀθέατοι τῶν ἐντὸς
τῆς σκηνῆς θαυμάτων ἀποκλεισθῶμεν. οὐ γὰρ παραδέχεται τῶν τοιούτων
20   τὴν εἴσοδον ὁ τοῦ πνεύματος νόμος, ἐὰν μή τις πλύνῃ τὸ τῆς συνειδήσεως
ἑαυτοῦ ἱμάτιον κατὰ τὸ Μωϋσέως παράγγελμα ὁ νεκρᾶς τινος καὶ βδελυκτῆς
ἐννοίας ἁψάμενος.

Ἄγει δὲ τὸν λόγον ἡ ἀκολουθία τῶν προεξητασμένων πρὸς τὴν θεωρίαν
τῶν παρὰ τῆς νύμφης πρὸς τὰς νεάνιδας εἰρημένων. ἔστι δὲ ταῦτα· Μέλαινά
25   εἰμι καὶ καλή, θυγατέρες Ἰερουσαλήμ, ὡς σκηνώματα κηδάρ, ὡς δέρρεις
Σολομών.

before us, for our guidance in all matters having to do with philosophy and the knowledge of God. This book is the true tent of witness. Its external veils and curtains and the drapes that cover it round are a set of erotic words and expressions that evince an orientation to an object of desire, offer a description of something beautiful, and make mention of bodily members, both those that are seen and those that are concealed by clothing. The things that belong to the interior, though, are a Person of many lights, full of mysteries as being the true Lampstand and the true Ark.[2] Then there is the censer of sweet fragrance; and the purifier from sin, that golden, reverend Mercy Seat; and the beauty of the veils, handsomely woven with the healthful coloring of the virtues; both the unswerving pillars that are reasoned thoughts and the immovable pedestals that are the dogmas; | both the beauty of the capitals (which evidence the loveliness of the soul's governing part) and the fonts for the washing of souls. Indeed, all the things, laid down in the law in figures, that look to the heavenly and incorporeal way of life can be found in the ideas hidden in the text. The condition for discerning them is that we take care to prepare ourselves for entrance upon the holy of holies by washing off in the bath of reason all the filth of shameful thinking, lest as persons blinded we be excluded from the wonders within the tent because we have violated the law's injunction by coming into contact with a corpse-like idea or by teaching some unclean notion. For the law of the Spirit does not allow entrance upon things of this order unless the person who has touched some dead and abominable thought washes the garment of conscience in accordance with Moses' injunction.

The thought sequence[3] of the matters into which we have already inquired brings our discourse to an investigation of what the Bride says to her maidens.[4] It goes as follows: *I am dark[5] and beautiful, O daughters of Jerusalem, as the tents of Kedar, as the curtains of Solomon.*

---

2. Compare Gregory's *Vit. Mos.* 2.174–175 (GNO 7.1:91), where the point—that the true Tabernacle or Tent of Witness is the Word of God who "tabernacled among us" (John 1:14)—is much the same as here.

3. Greek ἀκολουθία (= "sequence"). This is a key word in Gregory's exegetical vocabulary. It refers not so much to word order or an order of topics as to a *logical development* of ideas that underlies the text and informs it.

4. Origen (Baehrens 1925, 113.13–14) points out that the words to be considered here are addressed to the "daughters of Jerusalem," and contrary to Gregory he differentiates these from the "maidens" of v. 3.

5. Rufinus in his translation of Origen's commentary (Baehrens 1925, 113.10–12) renders the Greek μέλαινα as *fusca* and adds the explanation: "In other manuscripts we read: 'I am black and beautiful.'" He is probably referring, as R. P. Lawson indicates in his note (1956, 328), to the Latin versions.

καλῶς ἡ διδάσκαλος ἀφ' ὧν ἔδει ταῖς μαθητευομέναις ψυχαῖς | ἄρχεται   46
ποιεῖσθαι τῶν ἀγαθῶν τὴν ὑφήγησιν· αἱ μὲν γὰρ προθύμως ἔχουσι, δι' ὧν
ἐπαγγέλλονται, παντὸς ἀνθρωπίνου λόγου, ὃν οἶνον τροπικῶς ὀνομάζουσι,
προτιμοτέραν ποιεῖσθαι τὴν ἐκ τῶν λογικῶν αὐτῆς μαζῶν ἀπορρέουσαν χάριν
5   οὕτως εἰποῦσαι τῷ ῥήματι ὅτι Ἀγαπήσωμεν μαστούς σου ὑπὲρ οἶνον, ἐπειδὴ
σὲ ἡ εὐθύτης ἠγάπησεν, ἡ δὲ προσθήκην ποιεῖ ταῖς μαθητευομέναις τοῦ
περὶ αὐτὴν θαύματος, ὡς ἂν μᾶλλον μάθοιμεν τὴν ἀμέτρητον τοῦ νυμφίου
φιλανθρωπίαν τοῦ διὰ τῆς ἀγάπης ἐπιβάλλοντος τῇ ἀγαπηθείσῃ τὸ κάλλος·
μὴ θαυμάσητε γάρ φησι, ὅτι ἐμὲ ἡ εὐθύτης ἠγάπησεν, ἀλλ' ὅτι μέλαιναν
10   οὖσαν ἐξ ἁμαρτίας καὶ προσῳκειωμένην τῷ ζόφῳ διὰ τῶν ἔργων καλὴν διὰ
τῆς ἀγάπης ἐποίησε τὸ ἴδιον κάλλος πρὸς τὸ ἐμὸν αἶσχος ἀνταλλαξάμενος.
μεταθεὶς γὰρ πρὸς ἑαυτὸν τὸν τῶν ἐμῶν ἁμαρτιῶν ῥύπον μετέδωκέ μοι τῆς
ἑαυτοῦ καθαρότητος κοινωνόν με τοῦ ἑαυτοῦ κάλλους ἀπεργασάμενος, ὃς
πρῶτον ἐποίησεν ἐξ εἰδεχθοῦς ἐρασμίαν καὶ οὕτως ἠγάπησεν.
15   μετὰ ταῦτα προτρέπεται τὰς νεάνιδας καὶ αὐτὰς γενέσθαι καλὰς τὸ καθ'
ἑαυτὴν προδεικνύουσα κάλλος καθ' ὁμοιότητα τοῦ μεγάλου Παύλου τοῦ
λέγοντος Γίνεσθε ὡς ἐγώ, ὅτι καὶ ἐγὼ ὡς ὑμεῖς· καὶ Μιμηταί μου | γίνεσθε   47
καθὼς κἀγὼ Χριστοῦ. διὰ τοῦτο γὰρ οὐκ ἐᾷ τὰς μαθητευομένας αὐτῇ ψυχὰς
πρὸς τὸ παρῳχηκὸς τοῦ βίου βλεπούσας ἀπελπίζειν τοῦ γίνεσθαι καλάς,
20   ἀλλὰ πρὸς αὐτὴν ὁρώσας τοῦτο μανθάνειν διὰ τοῦ ὑποδείγματος, ὅτι τὸ
παρὸν γίνεται τοῦ παρῳχηκότος προκάλυμμα, ἐὰν ἄμωμον ᾖ. λέγει γὰρ
ὅτι κἂν νῦν μοι ἐπιλάμπῃ τὸ κάλλος, ὅ μοι διὰ τοῦ ἀγαπηθῆναι παρὰ τῆς
εὐθύτητος ἐπεμορφώθη, ἀλλ' οἶδα ἐμαυτὴν οὐ λαμπρὰν οὖσαν τὸ κατ' ἀρχὰς
ἀλλὰ μέλαιναν. τὸ δὲ τοιοῦτον εἶδος περὶ ἐμέ, τὸ σκοτεινὸν καὶ ζοφῶδες, ὁ
25   προλαβὼν βίος ἐποίησεν. ἀλλ' ὅμως ἐκεῖνο οὖσα τοῦτο εἰμι. μετεσκευάσθη
γὰρ τὸ ὁμοίωμα τοῦ σκότους εἰς κάλλους μορφήν. καὶ ὑμεῖς τοίνυν, ὦ
θυγατέρες Ἰερουσαλήμ, ἀναβλέψατε πρὸς τὴν μητέρα ὑμῶν Ἰερουσαλήμ. κἂν
σκηνώματα τοῦ κηδὰρ ἦτε διὰ τοῦ ἐνοικῆσαι ὑμῖν τὸν ἄρχοντα τῆς ἐξουσίας

Appropriately, the teacher[6] | starts off her account of the good by taking up matters that are requisite for souls in the status of learners. For these souls, because of the promises that have come to them, are eager to prefer the grace that pours out of their teacher's rational breasts to any human thought, which in a figure they call *wine*. Hence their word: *Let us love your breasts more than wine; for righteousness has loved you.*[7] The teacher, for her part, further sets forth for her disciples the marvel that has come about for her, in order that we may the better learn the Bridegroom's measureless love of humanity—the Bridegroom who in his love clothes his Beloved with beauty. For she says: "Do not marvel that Righteousness has loved me. Marvel rather that when I was dark with sin and at home in the dark because of my deeds, he by his love made me beautiful, exchanging his own beauty for my ugliness. For having transferred to himself the filth of my sins, he shared his own purity with me and constituted me a participant in his own beauty—he who first made something desirable[8] out of one who had been repulsive and in this way acted lovingly."[9]

After this, as she exhibits the beauty that is hers, she urges the young girls to become beautiful also—speaking after the example of the great Paul, who said "Become as I am, for I too was as you" (Gal 4:12), and "Become imitators | of me as I am of Christ" (1 Cor 11:1). Hence she does not permit the souls that are her disciples to dwell upon their past life and despair of becoming beautiful. Rather, they are to look upon her and from her example learn this: that the present, if it be without spot, covers over the past. For she says, "Even if beauty now illumines me, the beauty that was formed in me because I was loved by Righteousness, yet I know myself to have been, to start with, not gleaming but dark. This dark and gloomy aspect that I bear is the work of my earlier life. But at the same time as I am the latter, I am also the former. For the likeness of darkness was changed into the form of beauty. So now you, O daughters of Jerusalem, look up toward Jerusalem your mother. Although you were *tents of Kedar* because the ruler of the power of darkness

---

6. I.e., the Bride, who in Gregory's exegesis of the Song regularly appears in the role of a mistress to her apprentices.

7. Song 1:4, which Gregory comments on above, homily 1, p. 33 (Jaeger).

8. Greek ἐράσμιαν, an object of erotic desire.

9. Nyssen interprets the Bride's words in v. 4a as explaining how it is true of the Bride (i.e., the soul) that "Righteousness has loved" her. Origen (Baehrens 1925, 113.24–125.6), on the other hand, takes them as spoken "in the person" of the Gentile church, which defends itself against Jewish charges on the ground that, although it has never enjoyed the illumination of the Mosaic law, it has nevertheless now come to the Word of God. He briefly (125.6–9) notes that it can "be said, of any soul whatever which after abundant sins has turned to repentance," that it is "black on account of its sins and beautiful on account of its penitence" (cf. Theodoret [PG 81:69A], who repeats this in another context).

τοῦ σκότους (σκοτασμὸς γὰρ ἡ τοῦ κηδὰρ λέξις διερμηνεύεται), δέρρεις τοῦ
Σολομῶντος γενήσεσθε, τουτέστι ναὸς τοῦ βασιλέως ἔσεσθε ἐνοικήσαντος
ὑμῖν | τοῦ βασιλέως Σολομῶντος. Σολομὼν δὲ ὁ εἰρηνικός ἐστιν, ὁ τῇ εἰρήνῃ   48
ἐπώνυμος. δέρρεις γὰρ Σολομῶντος ἀπὸ μέρους πᾶσαν τὴν βασιλικὴν σκηνὴν
5   κατωνόμασεν.

τούτοις μοι δοκεῖ τοῖς νοήμασιν ὁ μέγας Παῦλος προσεχέστερον ἐν τῷ
πρὸς Ῥωμαίους φιλοχωρῆσαι λόγῳ, ἐν οἷς συνίστησι τοῦ θεοῦ τὴν περὶ ἡμᾶς
ἀγάπην, ὅτι ἁμαρτωλοὺς ὄντας ἡμᾶς καὶ μέλανας φωτοειδεῖς τε καὶ ἐρασμίους
διὰ τοῦ ἐπιλάμψαι τὴν χάριν ἐποίησεν. ὥσπερ γὰρ ἐν νυκτὶ πάντα τῷ
10   ἐπικρατοῦντι συμμελαίνεται ζόφῳ, κἂν λαμπρὰ κατὰ φύσιν ὄντα τύχῃ, φωτὸς
δὲ ἐπιλαβόντος οὐ παραμένει τοῖς ἐν τῷ ζόφῳ σκοτισθεῖσιν ἡ πρὸς τὸ σκότος
ὁμοίωσις, οὕτω μετατεθείσης τῆς ψυχῆς ἀπὸ τῆς πλάνης πρὸς τὴν ἀλήθειαν
καὶ ἡ σκοτεινὴ τοῦ βίου μορφὴ πρὸς τὴν φωτεινὴν χάριν συμμεταβάλλεται.

ταῦτα καὶ πρὸς τὸν Τιμόθεον, ὡς αὕτη πρὸς τὰς νεάνιδας, λέγει ἡ τοῦ
15   Χριστοῦ νύμφη, ὁ Παῦλος, ὁ λαμπρὸς ἐκ μέλανος μετὰ ταῦτα γενόμενος ὅτι
καλὸς ἠξιώθη καὶ αὐτὸς γενέσθαι τὸ πρότερον βλάσφημος ὢν καὶ διώκτης
καὶ ὑβριστὴς καὶ μέλας καὶ ὅτι Χριστὸς εἰς τὸν κόσμον ἦλθε | λαμπροὺς   49
ποιῆσαι τοὺς μέλανας, οὐ δικαίους πρὸς ἑαυτὸν καλῶν ἀλλὰ ἁμαρτωλοὺς εἰς
μετάνοιαν, οὓς τῷ λουτρῷ τῆς παλιγγενεσίας λάμπειν ὡς φωστῆρας ἐποίησε
20   τὸ ζοφῶδες αὐτῶν εἶδος ἀποκλύσας τῷ ὕδατι·

τὸ αὐτὸ τοῦτο καὶ ὁ τοῦ Δαβὶδ ὀφθαλμὸς ἐν τῇ ἄνω πόλει ὁρᾷ καὶ ἐν
θαύματι ποιεῖται τὸ θέαμα, πῶς ἐν τῇ πόλει τοῦ θεοῦ, περὶ ἧς τὰ δεδοξασμένα
λελάληται, Βαβυλὼν οἰκίζεται καὶ ἡ πόρνη Ῥαὰβ μνημονεύεται, ἀλλόφυλοί
τε καὶ Τύρος καὶ ὁ τῶν Αἰθιόπων λαὸς ἐν αὐτῇ γίνονται, ὡς μηκέτι τῶν
25   ἀνθρώπων τινὰ τῇ πόλει ταύτῃ τὴν τῶν οἰκητόρων ἐρημίαν ἐπονειδίζειν
λέγοντα Μή τις ἔτι τῇ Σιὼν ἐρεῖ· ἄνθρωπος ἐγεννήθη ἐν αὐτῇ; κἀκεῖ γὰρ

(cf. Eph 2:2; Col 1:13) dwelt in you (for the word "Kedar" means darkness),[10] you shall become *Solomon's curtains*—that is, you shall be the temple of the King[11] when King Solomon[12] | dwells within you." Now Solomon is the peaceable one, being named after peace. For the phrase *curtains of Solomon* names the entire royal tent after one of its parts.

It seems to me that the great Paul, in his letter to the Romans, makes much of a thought that is very close to this. There he establishes the love of God for us on the ground that, when we were sinners and *dark*, God made us full of light and lovely by shining upon us with his grace (cf. Rom 5:6–8). For just as at night everything, bright though it be by nature, shares the black look of the dominant darkness, but once the light comes, there remains no trace of darkness in things that had before been obscured by the night, just so when the soul has been transposed from error to truth, the dark form of her life is transformed into radiant beauty.

Paul, moreover, the bride of Christ who was dark and later became bright, says to Timothy the same thing that the Bride says to her maidens. He says that he, who earlier was a blasphemer and a persecutor and a man of pride and a dark one (cf. 1 Tim 1:13), was deemed worthy of beauty and further that Christ came into the world | to make dark ones bright (cf. 1 Tim 1:15), not calling the righteous to himself but calling sinners to repentance (cf. Matt 9:13 // Luke 5:32), whom he caused to shine like stars by the laver of rebirth (cf. Tit 3:5) when he had washed off their dark appearance with water.

Further, the eye of David sees this very same thing in the city on high and makes of his vision something to wonder at. He tells how, in the city of God, of which "glorious things are spoken" (Ps 86:3), Babylon is domiciled and Rahab the harlot is named, and there are foreigners within her, and Tyre, and the people of the Ethiopians—so that no one may ever reproach that city for being void of inhabitants by asking: "Shall any still say to Zion, 'A human being was born within her'?"[13] For there strangers become fellow tribesmen

---

10. Gregory the Great (*Exp. Cant.* 32, CCSL 144:33) notes that "Kedar" means *tenebrae* but also observes with Origen (Baehrens 1925, 114.13–14) that Kedar was the second son of Ishmael (Gen 25:13) and adds: "The dwellings of Esau were Kedar." On this analysis, to liken the Bride to "tents of Kedar," then, is to judge her a Gentile and a sinner.

11. See Origen's commentary (Baehrens 1925, 124.23ff.), which makes a distinction between two cases. The Bride compares either (1) her beauty or (2) her darkened aspect to Solomon's curtains. In the former case she refers to the heavenly tabernacle; in the latter, to its earthly image. Gregory the Great (*Exp. Cant.* 32, CCSL 144:33), however, understands "Solomon's curtains" as "all souls that adhere to God," sticking firmly by his identification of the Bride as church.

12. I.e., Christ.

13. This text of Ps 86:5a (LXX) probably reflects a variant found in Origen's Octapla; see the *apparatus criticus* in the Rahlfs edition of the LXX *ad loc.*

φυλέται τῆς πόλεως γίνονται οἱ ἀλλόφυλοι καὶ Ἱεροσολυμῖται οἱ Βαβυλώνιοι
καὶ παρθένος ἡ πόρνη καὶ λαμπροὶ οἱ Αἰθίοπες καὶ Τύρος ἡ ἄνω πόλις·
οὕτω καὶ ἐνταῦθα τὰς θυγατέρας Ἱερουσαλὴμ προθυμοποιεῖται ἡ νύμφη
συνιστῶσα τοῦ νυμφίου τὴν ἀγαθότητα, ὅτι κἂν μέλαινάν τινα λάβῃ ψυχήν,
5   τῇ πρὸς ἑαυτὸν κοινωνίᾳ καλὴν ἀπεργάζεται, κἂν τις σκήνωμα ἢ κηδάρ,
φωτὸς οἰκητήριον γίνεται τοῦ ἀληθινοῦ Σολομῶντος, τουτέστι τοῦ εἰρηνικοῦ
| βασιλέως ἐν αὐτῇ κατοικήσαντος. διὰ τοῦτό φησι Μέλαινά εἰμι καὶ καλή,   50
θυγατέρες Ἱερουσαλήμ, ἵνα πρὸς ἐμὲ βλέπουσαι καὶ ὑμεῖς γένησθε δέρρεις
Σολομῶντος, κἂν σκηνώματα ἦτε κηδάρ.
10   Εἶτα ἐπάγει τοῖς εἰρημένοις τὰ ἐφεξῆς, δι' ὧν ἀναγκαίως ἀσφαλίζεται
τὴν τῶν μαθητευομένων διάνοιαν μὴ τῷ δημιουργῷ τὴν αἰτίαν τοῦ
σκοτεινοῦ εἴδους ἀνατιθέναι ἀλλὰ τὴν ἑκάστου προαίρεσιν τοῦ τοιούτου
εἴδους τὰς ἀρχὰς καταβάλλεσθαι. Μὴ βλέψητε γὰρ πρός με, φησίν, ὅτι ἐγώ
εἰμι μεμελανωμένη. οὐ τοιαύτη γέγονα παρὰ τὴν πρώτην· οὐδὲ γὰρ εἰκὸς
15   ἦν ταῖς φωτειναῖς τοῦ θεοῦ χερσὶ πλασσομένην σκοτεινῷ τινι καὶ μέλανι
περιχρωσθῆναι τῷ εἴδει. οὐκ ἤμην τοίνυν τοιαύτη, φησίν, ἀλλὰ γέγονα. οὐ
γὰρ ἐκ φύσεώς εἰμι μεμελανωμένη, ἀλλ' ἐπείσακτόν μοι τὸ τοιοῦτον αἶσχος
ἐγένετο τοῦ ἡλίου πρὸς τὸ μέλαν ἐκ λαμπροῦ τὴν μορφὴν μεταχρώσαντος. Ὁ
ἥλιος γάρ, φησί, παρέβλεψέ με.

of the city, and the Babylonians become Jerusalemites, and the harlot a virgin, and the Ethiopians bright, and Tyre, the city on high.

And so it is that here the Bride, by manifesting the goodness of the Bridegroom, encourages the daughters of Jerusalem, saying that even if he were to take in a dark soul, he would render it beautiful by its communion with him, and even if some soul were a *tent of Kedar*, it would become the habitation of the light of the true Solomon—that is, of the peaceable | King who has come to dwell within it. That is why she says "*I am dark and beautiful, O daughters of Jerusalem,* in order that, looking to me, you too may become *curtains of Solomon,* though you are *tents of Kedar.*"

Then she adds the words that follow to her statements—and by their means, as is necessary, guards the minds of her disciples against making the Creator the source of the dark aspect. Instead, they are to assign the origin of that appearance to the individual's choice.[14] For she says "*Do not gaze at me, for I have been made dark.* I did not come to be so at the very first." It did not make sense, moreover, for one who was shaped by the radiant hands of God to have her appearance stained all over with some dark and gloomy color. "So therefore," she says, "that is not what I was, but what I became. For it is not because of my nature that I was blackened. Rather did such ugliness come to me from the outside, because the sun changed my appearance from radiant to black." For she says *The sun has looked askance at me.*[15]

---

14. So Origen (Baehrens 1925, 125.19): "is not such by nature, nor thus created by the Creator." Cf. the words of Lachesis, the daughter of Necessity, in Plato, *Resp.* 617E: "Virtue has no master, and each person will have more or less of her as he honors or despises her: the blame belongs to the one who does the choosing; God is without blame." This is a commonplace theme in the Platonist tradition, especially perhaps in its later anti-Stoic polemic, and the arguments thus developed served writers such as Origen well in their polemic against Valentinianism. See Amand 1945. See also below, homily 4, p. 102 (Jaeger), with the note there, for parallel passages in Gregory.

15. LXX: παρέβλεψέ με. Rufinus in his translation of Origen renders this verb by *despicere* (as against Jerome's *decolorare*), whose meaning coincides with that of παραβλέπω in the sense "despise" or "disdain." In fact, however, Origen had taken it to mean that the sun (i.e., the divine Wisdom) *does not directly illumine* the fallen soul (Baehrens 1925, 126.10; 128.8 [*oblique adspicere*]): it looks *aside* or *away* from such a soul. Hence Origen argues that, unlike dark bodily color (which is caused by the sun's looking at a person [*respicere*]), blackness of soul is acquired "not by birth but by neglect," i.e., by that idleness that occasions the soul's fall and the Sun's aversion. He and Nyssen thus agree that the soul's dark appearance is "accidental" (Baehrens 1925, 125.19) in the sense of stemming from choice, not nature. Their agreement, however, extends no further than this. Theodoret too (PG 81:69A) ascribes the Bride's darkening to sin but identifies the sin as idolatry, appealing to Rom 1:25: she worshiped "this perceptible sun" rather than "the Sun of Righteousness," and for that reason the sun that she worshiped "touched" her (reading καθήψατο for παρέβλεψε with Symmachus).

τί οὖν ἐστιν ὃ διὰ τούτων μανθάνομεν; λέγει διὰ παραβολῆς τοῖς ὄχλοις ὁ
κύριος ὅτι ὁ σπείρων τὸν λόγον οὐ τὴν ἀγαθὴν | μόνον κατασπείρει καρδίαν,   51
ἀλλὰ κἂν λιθώδης τις ἦ κἂν ταῖς ἀκάνθαις ὑλομανοῦσα κἂν παρόδιός τε καὶ
πεπατημένη, πᾶσιν ὑπὸ φιλανθρωπίας ἐπιβάλλει τοῦ λόγου τὰ σπέρματα.
5   καὶ ἑκάστου τὰ ἰδιώματα ἑρμηνεύων τῷ λόγῳ τοῦτό φησιν ἐπὶ τῆς λιθώδους
συμβαίνειν ψυχῆς, ὅτι οὐκ ἐν βάθει ῥιζοῦται τὸ ἐσπαρμένον, ἀλλὰ παραχρῆμα
μὲν δι' ἐπιπολαίου βλάστης τὸν στάχυν κατεπαγγέλλεται, θερμότερον δὲ
τοῦ ἡλίου τὸ ὑποκείμενον θάλψαντος τῷ μὴ ὑποκεῖσθαι ταῖς ῥίζαις ἰκμάδα
καταξηραίνεται. πειρασμὸν δὲ διὰ τῆς ἑρμηνείας ὀνομάζει τὸν ἥλιον.
10   οὐκοῦν τοῦτο παρὰ τῆς διδασκάλου τὸ δόγμα μανθάνομεν, ὅτι γέγονε
μὲν ἡ ἀνθρωπίνη φύσις τοῦ ἀληθινοῦ φωτὸς ἀπεικόνισμα πόρρω τῶν
σκοτεινῶν χαρακτήρων τῇ τοῦ ἀρχετύπου κάλλους ὁμοιότητι στίλβουσα,
ὁ δὲ πειρασμὸς τὸν φλογώδη καύσωνα δι' ἀπάτης ἐπιβαλὼν ἁπαλὴν ἔτι
καὶ ἄρριζον τὴν πρώτην βλάστην κατέλαβε καί, πρὶν ἕξιν τινὰ τοῦ ἀγαθοῦ
15   κτήσασθαι καὶ διὰ τῆς τῶν λογισμῶν γεωργίας δοῦναι ταῖς ῥίζαις τόπον ἐπὶ
τὸ βάθος, εὐθὺς διὰ τῆς παρακοῆς ἀποξηράνας τὸ χλοερόν τε καὶ εὐθαλὲς
εἶδος διὰ τῆς καύσεως μέλαν ἐποίησεν.
εἰ δὲ ἥλιος ἡ ἀντικειμένη τοῦ πειρασμοῦ προσβολὴ ὀνομάζεται, μηδεὶς
| ξενιζέσθω τῶν ἀκουόντων ἐν πολλοῖς τὸ τοιοῦτον παρὰ τῆς θεοπνεύστου   52
20   γραφῆς διδασκόμενος. καὶ γὰρ ἐν δευτέρᾳ τῶν ἀναβαθμῶν ᾠδῇ ταύτην
ποιεῖται τὴν εὐλογίαν τῷ τὴν βοήθειαν ἔχοντι παρὰ κυρίου, τοῦ ποιήσαντος
τὸν οὐρανὸν καὶ τὴν γῆν, τὸ μὴ συγκαίεσθαι αὐτὸν ὑπὸ τοῦ ἡλίου διὰ τῆς
ἡμέρας. καὶ ὁ προφήτης Ἡσαΐας τὴν τῆς ἐκκλησίας κατάστασιν προφητεύων
ὥσπερ τινὰ πομπὴν ὑπογράφει τὴν πολιτείαν φαιδρύνων τὸν λόγον τῷ
25   διηγήματι. λέγει γὰρ θυγατέρας ἐπ' ὤμων αἰρομένας καὶ παῖδας ἐν λαμπήναις
κομιζομένους καὶ σκιαδείοις τὸν φλογμὸν ἀποκρούοντας· δι' ὧν ἐν αἰνίγμασι

What, then, do we learn from these statements? In a parable (Matt 13:3–23; Luke 8:5–15), the Lord said to the crowds that the sower of the word does not plant solely | in the good heart. Even if a heart be stony, even if it be overgrown with thorns, even if it be alongside the path and trodden down, he casts the seed of the word into them all because of his love of humankind. Furthermore, explaining in his discourse the characteristics of each class, the Lord says that in the case of the stony heart what happens is this: the seed is not deeply rooted but gives promise of producing an early ear because of its surface shoot. It dries up, though, when the sun has heated up the soil, because there is no moisture beneath for the roots. In his interpretation of the parable, the Lord identifies the sun as "temptation."[16]

I take it, then, that the truth we gather from the lady who instructs us is this: human nature came into existence as a copy of the true light, far removed from the marks of darkness and resplendent in its likeness to the beauty of its archetype.[17] But temptation and trial, when they had deceitfully brought on their fiery heat, destroyed the shoot while it was still delicate and rootless. Before it had a firm hold on goodness and before it had provided depth for its roots to sink in by thoughtful reflection's husbandry, they straightway rendered it dark through disobedience, having dried up its verdant and thriving form with burning heat.

But if the hostile assault of temptation and trial is named "sun," let my hearers not | be puzzled, for they are taught this sort of thing by many texts in the inspired Scripture. In the second Song of Ascents, a blessing is conferred on the person who has the help of the Lord, "the Maker of heaven and earth," to the effect that he shall not be burned by the sun during the daytime (cf. Ps 120:6). Furthermore, the prophet Isaiah, prophesying the church's way of being, portrays its mode of life as a sort of procession and brightens his discourse with a narrative of it. He speaks of "daughters" lifted up "on shoulders" (Isa 49:22; 60:4) and of children being carried in "covered vehicles" and fending off the fiery blaze with "sunshades" (cf. Isa 66:20). By these expressions

---

16. Where Origen, by contrast, understands "sun" here of the "Sun of Righteousness" (Baehrens 1925, 126.9–10), the divine Wisdom, Theodoret takes it of the "perceptible" sun. Gregory the Great agrees with Origen in identifying the "sun" with Christ, but since he reads the Vulgate (*decoloravit* for παρέβλεψε), he understands the text to say: " the closer we come to grace, the more we know ourselves to be sinners," citing Gal 2:7 (*Exp. Cant.* 33, CCSL 144:34). Origen nevertheless in another place can speak of "the sun of temptation" (in connection with Song 1:16 and Ps 120:6; cf. *Comm. Cant.* 3.2 [Baehrens 1925, 176; trans. Lawson 1956, 173]).

17. Cf. Methodius, *Symp.* 6.1 (trans. Musurillo 1958, 91): "All of us ... come into this world with an extraordinary beauty which has a relationship and kinship with wisdom. And then it is that men's souls most clearly resemble Him who begot and formed them, when they continue to reflect the pure image of His likeness."

τὸν ἐν ἀρετῇ διαγράφει βίον διὰ μὲν τῆς νηπιώδους ἡλικίας ὑποδεικνύων
τὸ ἀρτιγενές τε καὶ ἄκακον, διὰ δὲ τῶν σκιαδείων τὴν ἐξ ἐγκρατείας τε καὶ
καθαρότητος προσγινομένην ταῖς ψυχαῖς παραμυθίαν τοῦ καύσωνος. δι᾽
ὧν μανθάνομεν ὅτι χρὴ ἐπ᾽ ὤμων αἴρεσθαι τὴν τῷ θεῷ νυμφοστολουμένην
5   ψυχήν, οὐ πατουμένην ὑπὸ τῆς σαρκὸς ἀλλ᾽ ἐπικαθημένην τῷ ὄγκῳ τοῦ
σώματος. λαμπήνην δὲ ἀκούοντες τὴν ἐκλαμπτικὴν τοῦ φωτίσματος χάριν
μανθάνομεν, δι᾽ ἧς παῖδες γινόμεθα οὐκέτι | τῇ γῇ τὸ ἴχνος ἐρείδοντες, ἀλλ᾽   53
ἀπ᾽ ἐκείνης πρὸς τὴν οὐρανίαν ζωὴν κομιζόμενοι. σκιερὸς δὲ γίνεται ἡμῖν
καὶ δροσώδης ὁ βίος διὰ τῶν τῆς ἀρετῆς σκιαδείων κατασβεννυμένου τοῦ
10   καύσωνος. οὗτος οὖν ἐστιν ὁ παραβλάπτων ἥλιος, ὅταν μὴ διατειχίζηται ὁ
παρ᾽ αὐτοῦ φλογμὸς τῇ νεφέλῃ τοῦ πνεύματος, ἣν διεπέτασε τοῖς τοιούτοις
ὁ κύριος εἰς σκέπην αὐτοῖς· οὗτος γάρ ἐστιν ὁ ἥλιος ὁ τὴν λαμπρὰν τοῦ
σώματος ἐπιφάνειαν τῇ προσβολῇ τῶν πειρασμῶν ἐπικαίων καὶ μελαίνων ἐν
δυσμορφίᾳ τὸ εἶδος.
15   Εἶτα διηγεῖται, ὅθεν τὴν ἀρχὴν ἔσχεν ἡ πρὸς τὸ μέλαν τῆς εὐχροίας
ἡμῶν μεταποίησις. Υἱοὶ μητρός μου, φησίν, ἐμαχέσαντο ἐν ἐμοί, ἔθεντό με
φυλάκισσαν ἐν ἀμπελῶσιν· ἀμπελῶνα ἐμὸν οὐκ ἐφύλαξα.
καί μοι τοῦτο παρασχέσθω ἡ ἀκοή, μὴ λίαν ἀκριβολογεῖσθαι πρὸς τὴν
τῆς λέξεως σύνταξιν ἀλλὰ πρὸς τὸν εἱρμὸν τοῦ νοήματος βλέπειν. εἰ δέ τι μὴ
20   ἀκριβῶς συνηρτημένον ἐστὶν ἐκ τῆς συμφράσεως, τῇ ἀσθενείᾳ λογισάσθω
τῶν τὴν Ἑβραίων γλῶτταν μεταβαλόντων εἰς τὴν Ἑλλάδα φωνήν· οἷς γὰρ
ἐν ἐπιμελείᾳ γέγονε παιδευθῆναι τὴν Ἑβραίων διάλεκτον, οὐδὲν εὑρίσκεται
τοιοῦτον, οἷον δοκεῖν ἀσυναρτήτως ἔχειν. ὁ δὲ σχηματισμὸς | τῆς ἡμετέρας   54
γλώττης μὴ συμβαίνων τῷ σχήματι τῆς Ἑβραϊκῆς εὐγλωττίας σύγχυσίν τινα
25   ποιεῖ τοῖς ἐπιπολαιότερον ἀκολουθοῦσι τῇ σημασίᾳ τῆς λέξεως.
ἡ μὲν οὖν διάνοια τῶν προκειμένων ῥημάτων αὕτη ἐστίν, ὅσον ἡμεῖς
κατειλήφαμεν, ὅτι· γέγονε τὸ κατ᾽ ἀρχὰς ὁ ἄνθρωπος οὐδενὸς τῶν θείων
ἀγαθῶν ἐνδεής, ᾧ ἔργον ἦν φυλάξαι μόνον τὰ ἀγαθά, οὐχὶ κτήσασθαι. ἡ δὲ

he pictures, in enigmas, the virtuous life. By the allusions to childhood he indicates that which is newborn and innocent, and by the "sunshades" the relief from summer heat that comes to souls through self-control and purity. From all this we learn that it is necessary to lift up "on the shoulders" the soul that is being led to God as a bride—the soul that is not trodden down under the flesh but elevated so as to be over the bulk of the body. And when we hear "covered vehicle," we understand the shining grace of the enlightenment[18] by means of which we become children who are no longer | earth-treaders but are carried up from earth toward the heavenly life. Our life, moreover, becomes shady and cool when the summer heat is quenched by the "sun-shade" of virtue. Here, then, is the sun that does damage—when the blaze that comes from it is not cut off by the cloud of the Spirit, which the Lord would spread out for such souls to serve them as a shelter. For this is the sun that scorches the shining appearance of the body by bringing temptation to it and darkens its appearance with ugliness.

Then she explains where the change of our good coloring into darkness took its origin. *The sons of my mother,* she says, *fought within me. They made me a guard in the vineyards. I did not guard my vineyard.*

May my audience allow me this, not to be too minute in following the syntax of a text but rather to attend to the way in which the thought hangs together. If there is some incoherence in the passage,[19] let it be reckoned to the account of those who translated the Hebrew tongue into Greek. People who have taken the trouble to learn the Hebrew language find nothing that is such as to appear incoherent, but the structure | of our tongue, since it does not agree with the form of good Hebrew speech, occasions an indistinctness for people who follow the sense of the text with too little attention.

Here, then, is the meaning of the words before us as far as we have grasped it. Humanity came into existence at the beginning lacking not a single one of the divine goods. Its task was simply to "guard" the good things, not to acquire them. But the treachery of the hostile powers stripped humanity

---

18. This is no doubt an allusion to baptism, for which φωτισμός ("illumination," "enlightenment") was a traditional designation. The connection of this with λαμπήνη (a covered vehicle of some sort, called "mule-drawn" at Isa 66:20 [LXX]) is obscure to me, unless Gregory is envisaging baptism (and the enlightenment it brings) as the "vehicle" that elevates the soul to new life, just as it provides protection against the power of temptation; see just below the reference to "the cloud of the Spirit" (who was understood to be given in baptism).

19. What Gregory is worried about is the suggestion that "the sons of my mother" may be taken to have been responsible not only for setting the Bride up as a "guard in the vineyards," as in the first clause of v. 5c, but also for giving her charge of the (singular) "vineyard" of the second clause. See his argument starting at the end of p. 57 (Jaeger) below.

τῶν ἐχθρῶν ἐπιβουλὴ γυμνὸν αὐτὸν τῶν προσόντων ἐποίησε μὴ φυλάξαντα τὴν δοθεῖσαν αὐτῷ φύσει παρὰ τῷ θεῷ εὐκληρίαν.

αὕτη μὲν οὖν ἐστιν ἡ τῶν ῥημάτων διάνοια, ἡ δὲ διὰ τῶν αἰνιγματικῶν λόγων τοῦ νοήματος τούτου παράδοσις τοῦτον ἔχει τὸν τρόπον· Υἱοὶ μητρός
5   μου, φησίν, ἐμαχέσαντο ἐν ἐμοί, ἔθεντό με φυλάκισσαν ἐν ἀμπελῶσιν· ἀμπελῶνα ἐμὸν οὐκ ἐφύλαξα.

πολλὰ δι' ὀλίγων δογματικῶς ἡμᾶς ἐκπαιδεύει ὁ λόγος. πρῶτον μὲν ὅπερ καὶ ὁ μέγας ἀποφαίνεται Παῦλος, ὅτι τὰ πάντα ἐκ τοῦ θεοῦ καὶ Εἷς θεὸς ὁ πατὴρ ἐξ οὗ τὰ πάντα, καὶ οὐδὲν τῶν ὄντων ἐστὶν ὃ μὴ δι' ἐκείνου τε καὶ ἐξ
10   ἐκείνου τὸ εἶναι ἔχει | (Πάντα γάρ, φησί, δι' αὐτοῦ ἐγένετο καὶ χωρὶς αὐτοῦ   55
ἐγένετο οὐδέν· ἀλλ' ἐπειδὴ πάντα ἐποίησεν ὁ θεός, καλὰ λίαν ἐστί. πάντα γὰρ ἐν σοφίᾳ ἐποίησεν), ἔδωκε δὲ τῇ λογικῇ φύσει τὴν αὐτεξούσιον χάριν καὶ προσέθηκε δύναμιν εὑρετικὴν τῶν καταθυμίων, ὡς ἂν τὸ ἐφ' ἡμῖν χώραν ἔχοι καὶ μὴ κατηναγκασμένον εἴη τὸ ἀγαθὸν καὶ ἀκούσιον, ἀλλὰ κατόρθωμα
15   προαιρέσεως γένοιτο.

τούτου δὲ τοῦ αὐτεξουσίου κινήματος αὐτοκρατορικῶς πρὸς τὸ δοκοῦν ἡμᾶς ἄγοντος ηὑρέθη τις ἐν τῇ φύσει τῶν ὄντων ὁ κακῶς τῇ ἐξουσίᾳ χρησάμενος καὶ κατὰ τὴν τοῦ ἀποστόλου φωνὴν κακῶν ἐφευρετὴς γενόμενος· ὃς τῷ μὲν ἐκ θεοῦ καὶ αὐτὸς εἶναι ἀδελφός ἐστιν ἡμέτερος, τῷ
20   δὲ τῆς τοῦ ἀγαθοῦ μετουσίας ἑκουσίως ἀπορρυῆναι τὴν τῶν κακῶν εἴσοδον καινοτομήσας καὶ πατὴρ ψεύδους γενόμενος εἰς πολεμίου τάξιν ἑαυτὸν κατέστησε πᾶσιν, οἷς ὁ σκοπὸς τῆς προαιρέσεως πρὸς τὸ κρεῖττον βλέπει.

διὰ τούτου τοίνυν καὶ τοῖς λοιποῖς τῆς τῶν ἀγαθῶν ἀποπτώσεως τῆς ἀφορμῆς ἐγγενομένης (ὃ δὴ καὶ τῇ φύσει τῶν ἀνθρώπων ἐγένετο) καλῶς ἡ
25   ποτὲ μὲν μέλαινα, | νῦν δὲ καλὴ τὴν αἰτίαν τῆς ζοφώδους ὄψεως εἰς τοὺς   56
τοιούτους τῆς μητρὸς υἱοὺς ἀνατίθησι παιδεύουσα διὰ τῶν λεγομένων ἡμᾶς, ὅτι μία μὲν πᾶσίν ἐστι τοῖς οὖσιν οἷόν τις μήτηρ ἡ τῶν ὄντων αἰτία. καὶ διὰ

of what belonged to it, when it did not guard the good fortune that had been given it by God as a natural endowment.

So here we have the meaning of these statements, but this sense is conveyed by means of enigmas, in the following manner. *The sons of my mother,* she says, *fought within me. They made me a guard in the vineyards. I did not guard my vineyard.*

The text teaches us many basic truths in few words. First of all, there is something that the great Paul declares, that all things are from God, that "There is one God the Father from whom are all things" (1 Cor 8:6), and also that there is none of the things that exist that does not have its being both through him and from him: | "For all things," it says, "came to be through him, and apart from him nothing came to be" (John 1:3). But since God made all things, they are "very good" (Gen 1:31), for he made all things by Wisdom. To the rational nature, however, he gave the grace of self-determination and added a capacity to detect what fits one's purposes. In this way space might be made for our responsibility, and the good should not be compelled and involuntary but come about as the product of choice.

Since the impulse of self-determination unavoidably leads us toward the apparent good, there was found in the order of Being one agent who used this power wrongly and, according to the word of the apostle, became the "inventor of mischief" (Rom 1:30). Because he too came from God, he is our brother, but since he brought about the entrance of evil by voluntarily shedding off his participation in the good and becoming "father of the lie" (John 8:44), he set himself up as an enemy to all whose choice aims at what is better.[20]

Since, therefore, through this agent opportunity was afforded the rest of falling away from the good things (which indeed came to pass for the human race), the Bride who once was dark | but now is beautiful is right to specify such *sons of* her *mother* as the cause of her dark aspect—teaching us in these words that there is, as it were, one Mother[21] of all things that belong to the

---

20. "Sons of my mother," then, refers to Satan (and his hosts). Origen, on the contrary, identifies them with the apostles, just as he identifies the "mother" as the heavenly Jerusalem (Baehrens 1925, 131.9–16). Cf. Theodoret (PG 81:69C) and Gregory the Great (*Exp. Cant.* 38, CCSL 144:37), who take the same line. Apollinarius (*apud* Procopius, *Cat. Cant.*; PG 87:1556CD), noting that Symmachus's version has "son" in the singular, suggests that the phrase refers to those who first persecuted the church but then taught it—and notably to the apostle Paul.

21. Here Nyssen takes a somewhat idiosyncratic view. See further his observations below in homily 7, pp. 212–13 (Jaeger). Origen identifies the "mother" of v. 5b as "the Jerusalem above," which is "free" (Gal 4:26); so too Theodoret (PG 81:69C). Gregory the Great follows Origen in one of his applications of this line (*Exp. Cant.* 38, CCSL 144:37) but in another identifies the mother as "benignitas et potentia Dei" (40, CCSL 144:39).

τοῦτο ἀδελφὰ πάντα ἐστὶν ἀλλήλων τὰ ἐν τοῖς οὖσι νοούμενα. ἡ δὲ τῆς
προαιρέσεως διαφορὰ πρὸς τὸ φίλιόν τε καὶ πολέμιον τὴν φύσιν διέσχισεν·
οἱ γὰρ ἀφεστῶτες τῆς πρὸς τὸ ἀγαθὸν σχέσεως καὶ διὰ τῆς τοῦ κρείττονος
ἀποστάσεως τὸ κακὸν ὑποστήσαντες (οὐδὲ γάρ ἐστιν ἄλλη τις κακοῦ
5   ὑπόστασις εἰ μὴ ὁ χωρισμὸς τοῦ βελτίονος) πᾶσαν ποιοῦνται σπουδὴν καὶ
ἐπίνοιαν τοῦ καὶ ἄλλους πρὸς τὴν τῶν κακῶν κοινωνίαν προσεταιρίσασθαι.
καὶ διὰ τοῦτό φησιν· οὗτοι οἱ υἱοὶ τῆς μητρός μου (τῇ γὰρ πληθυντικῇ σημασίᾳ
τὸ πολυσχιδὲς τῆς κακίας ἐνδείκνυται) πόλεμον ἐν ἐμοὶ συνεστήσαντο, οὐκ
ἔξωθεν ἐξ ἐπιδρομῆς πολεμοῦντες ἀλλ' αὐτὴν τὴν ψυχὴν ποιησάμενοι τοῦ ἐν
10   αὐτῇ | πολέμου μεταίχμιον· ἐν ἑκάστῳ γάρ ἐστιν ὁ πόλεμος, καθὼς ἑρμηνεύει   57
ὁ θεῖος ἀπόστολος λέγων ὅτι Βλέπω ἕτερον νόμον ἐν τοῖς μέλεσί μου
ἀντιστρατευόμενον τῷ νόμῳ τοῦ νοός μου καὶ αἰχμαλωτίζοντά με τῷ νόμῳ
τῆς ἁμαρτίας τῷ ὄντι ἐν τοῖς μέλεσί μου. ταύτης τοίνυν τῆς ἐμφυλίου μάχης
ἐν ἐμοὶ συστάσης παρὰ τῶν ἀδελφῶν μέν, ἐχθρῶν δὲ τῆς ἐμῆς σωτηρίας,
15   μέλαινα ἐγενόμην ἡττηθεῖσα τῶν πολεμίων καὶ τὸν ἀμπελῶνα τὸν ἐμὸν οὐκ
ἐφύλαξα.

ταὐτὸν δὲ χρὴ νοεῖν τῷ παραδείσῳ τὸν ἀμπελῶνα· καὶ γὰρ κἀκεῖ
φυλάσσειν ἐτάχθη ὁ ἄνθρωπος τὸν παράδεισον. ἡ δὲ τῆς φυλακῆς ἀμέλεια
ἐκβάλλει τοῦ παραδείσου τὸν ἄνθρωπον καὶ οἰκήτορα τῶν δυσμῶν ποιεῖ
20   τῆς ἀνατολῆς ἀποστήσασα. διὰ τοῦτο ἡ ἀνατολὴ ταῖς δυσμαῖς ἐπιφαίνεται·
Ψάλατε γάρ, φησί, τῷ κυρίῳ τῷ ἐπιβεβηκότι ἐπὶ δυσμῶν, ἵνα τοῦ φωτὸς ἐν τῇ

realm of Being, the cause of their existence. For this reason all things that are conceived as beings are brothers and sisters one of another, but difference of choice split the family up into a friendly and a hostile part. Those who departed from their disposition for the good and because of this departure from the better lent existence to evil (for evil has no other reality[22] than separation from what is better) turned every effort and thought to make others their companions in this fellowship with evil. That is why she says, "These *sons of my mother*" (for by use of the plural she indicates the many forms of evil) "set up a warfare within me,[23] not fighting by way of onslaught from without but making of the soul herself a territory in dispute with its interior | enemy. For the battle is within each of us, as the divine apostle explains when he says: 'I see in my members another law that fights against the law of my intellect and makes me a captive to the law of sin that is in my members' (Rom 7:23). Because this civil war has been generated within me by my brethren, enemies of my salvation, I became dark when defeated by my adversaries, and *I did not guard my vineyard.*"

It is necessary, however, to understand the vineyard to be the same as the garden,[24] for it is there that the human being was commanded to *guard* the paradise. Neglect of this duty cast the human being out of the garden and made him a dweller in the place of the setting sun, having removed him from the sunrise. That is why the rising sun shines upon the place of its setting. For the Scripture says, "Sing to the Lord, who has entered the place of the setting sun," so that when the light has shined in the darkness, the dark-

---

22. Or perhaps "subsistence." Cf. Aristotle, *Metaph.* 9.9 (1051a5ff., and esp. 17), where the principle is laid down that "the bad does not exist apart from bad things," i.e., does not exist on its own. This is a regular theme in Nyssen's writings; see, e.g., homily 12 below (pp. 349–50 [Jaeger]) and *Opif. hom.* 12 (164A): "This ... is the way in which evil comes to be. It has come to exist through a putting away of excellence."

23. Like Nyssen, Origen takes the LXX ἐν ἐμοί quite seriously, but he envisages the "fighting within" as a warfare conducted *within the church* by the apostles against the church's unbelief, vice, and false ideas (Baehrens 1925, 131.16–23) or else, when the text is applied to the individual soul, as the struggle between the angels ("the sons of my mother") and the demons (133.17–24) in the soul of the immature believer. Nyssen's interpretation seems to derive from this last line of thought, although he revises Origen's exegesis radically. The Vulgate has *contra me* for the LXX's ἐν ἐμοί, and Latin commentators therefore take a different line.

24. Origen, by contrast, identifies this vineyard as the "learning" or "culture" (*eruditio*) that the believer in Christ relinquishes and deserts after conversion (Baehrens 1925, 132.11–14). Theodoret (PG 81:72B–C) offers this as one of two possible explanations of the text; the other takes it to mean "the soul's profit." Gregory the Great (*Exp. Cant.* 35, CCSL 144) interprets the word variously of Judea, which believing Jews, under persecution, deserted in order to preach to the Gentiles; "the ancient tradition [*consuetudo*] of error," which the Gentile church deserts (38); and (the church's) soul or life or mind (40).

σκοτίᾳ λάμψαντος μεταποιηθῇ πρὸς τὴν ἀκτῖνα τὸ σκότος καὶ γένηται καλὴ πάλιν ἡ μέλαινα.

τὸ δὲ δοκοῦν ἀσυνάρτητον τῆς λέξεως ὡς πρὸς τὴν εὑρεθεῖσαν διάνοιαν τούτῳ τῷ τρόπῳ δυνατόν ἐστι παραμυθήσασθαι· Ἔθεντό με, φησί,
5 φυλάκισσαν ἐν ἀμπελῶσιν, ὅπερ ἴσον ἐστὶ τῷ Ἔθεντο τὴν Ἱερουσαλὴμ ὡς ὀπωροφυλάκιον. οὐ γὰρ ἐκεῖνοι κατέστησαν αὐτὴν φύλακα τοῦ θείου   58
ἀμπελῶνος, | ὡς ἄν τις ἐκ τοῦ προχείρου νοήσειεν, ἀλλ' ὁ καταστήσας μέν ἐστι θεός, ἐκεῖνοι δὲ ἐμαχέσαντο μόνον ἐν αὐτῇ καὶ ἔθεντο αὐτὴν Ὡς σκηνὴν ἐν ἀμπελῶνι καὶ ὡς ὀπωροφυλάκιον ἐν σικυηράτῳ. τῆς γὰρ φυλασσομένης
10 ὀπώρας διὰ τὴν παρακοὴν στερηθεῖσα ἄχρηστον θέαμα κατελείφθη τοῦ φυλασσομένου ἐν αὐτῇ μὴ ὄντος.

καὶ ἐπειδὴ ἔθετο ὁ θεὸς τὸν ἄνθρωπον ἐργάζεσθαι καὶ φυλάσσειν τὸν παράδεισον, τοῦτο εἶπεν ἡ νύμφη ὅτι τοῦ θεοῦ θεμένου τὴν ψυχήν μου εἰς ζωήν (ζωὴ γὰρ ἦν ἡ τοῦ παραδείσου τρυφή, ἐν ᾧ ἔθετο ὁ θεὸς τὸν ἄνθρωπον
15 ἐργάζεσθαι καὶ φυλάσσειν αὐτόν) οἱ ἐχθροὶ μετέστησαν αὐτὴν ἀπὸ τῆς τοῦ παραδείσου φυλακῆς εἰς τὸ σπουδάζειν περὶ τὸν αὐτῶν ἀμπελῶνα, οὗ ὁ βότρυς γεωργεῖ τὴν πικρίαν καὶ ἡ σταφυλὴ τὴν χολήν. τοιοῦτος ἀμπελὼν Σόδομα ἦν, τοιαύτη κληματὶς Γόμορρα ἡ συγκαταδικασθεῖσα Σοδόμοις, δι' ὧν ὁ τῶν δρακόντων θυμὸς ὁ ἀνίατος ἐν ταῖς πονηραῖς ληνοῖς τῶν Σοδομιτῶν
20 ὑπερεχέθη. ἔστι δὲ καὶ μέχρι τοῦ νῦν τῶν τοιούτων ἀμπελώνων ἐπιμελητάς τε καὶ φύλακας τοὺς πολλοὺς τῶν ἀνθρώπων ἰδεῖν, οἳ ἐν σπουδῇ τὰ πάθη παρ' ἑαυτοῖς τηροῦσιν ὥσπερ δεδοικότες μὴ τὸ κακὸν ἀπολέσωσιν. ὁρᾷς τοὺς πονηροὺς τῆς | εἰδωλολατρίας φύλακας τῆς τε κατὰ τὴν ἀσέβειαν καὶ τῆς   59
κατὰ τὴν πλεονεξίαν ἐνεργουμένης, πῶς ἐπαγρυπνοῦσι τῇ φυλακῇ τῶν κακῶν
25 ζημίαν τὸ στερηθῆναι τῆς ἀνομίας νομίζοντες. καὶ ἐπὶ τῶν ἄλλων ὡσαύτως ἔστιν ἰδεῖν τοὺς ἐν πάθει παραδεξαμένους τὴν ἡδονὴν ἢ ὑπερηφανίαν ἢ τῦφον ἢ ἄλλο τι τῶν τοιούτων, πῶς περιέχονται διὰ πάσης φυλακῆς τῶν τοιούτων κακῶν κέρδος ποιούμενοι τὸ μηδέποτε τῶν κακῶν τὴν ψυχὴν καθαρεῦσαι.

ταῦτα οὖν ἡ νύμφη ὀδύρεται λέγουσα ὅτι διὰ τοῦτο ἐγενόμην μέλαινα,
30 ἐπειδὴ τὰ ζιζάνια τοῦ ἐχθροῦ καὶ τὰς πονηρὰς αὐτῶν κληματίδας φυλάσσουσά τε καὶ περιέπουσα τὸν ἀμπελῶνα τὸν ἐμὸν οὐκ ἐφύλαξα. ὦ πόσον κινεῖ πένθος ἐν τοῖς αἰσθητικῶς ἐπαΐουσιν Ἀμπελῶνα ἐμὸν οὐκ ἐφύλαξα. θρῆνος ἀντικρύς ἐστιν ἡ φωνή, θρῆνος τοὺς τῶν προφητῶν στεναγμοὺς κινῶν εἰς συμπάθειαν· πῶς ἐγένετο πόρνη πόλις πιστὴ Σιὼν πλήρης κρίσεως; πῶς

ness may be transformed into brightness and the dark one may once again become beautiful.

As to the apparent incoherence in the text, so far as it affects the interpretation we have uncovered, it can be abated in the following way. *They made me*, she says, *a guard in the vineyards*. This is the same as saying, "They made Jerusalem a crop-watcher's hut" (Ps 78:1). For it was not these *sons* who established her as a guard of the divine vineyard, | as one might think from the surface meaning. The one who so established her was God, while these only fought against her and set her up "as a tent in a vineyard and as a crop-watcher's hut in a cucumber bed" (Isa 1:8).[25] For deprived by her disobedience of the crop she was guarding, she was left an empty spectacle, since the thing to be guarded was not within her.

And since it was God who had made the human being to work the garden and to watch over it, what the Bride said is: "Though God established my soul in life"—for "life" meant the delight of the garden in which God had placed the human being to work and to guard it—the enemies transferred it from care of the garden to a responsibility for their own vineyard, where the grape produces bitterness and the cluster, gall. Sodom was such a vineyard; Gomorrah, which was condemned together with Sodom, <was> such a vine. Through them the venom of the powers of evil overflowed in the wicked wine vats of the Sodomites. And to this day it is possible to see that the majority of human beings are keepers and guardians of just such vineyards. Enthusiastically they clutch to themselves the passions within them, like people who are afraid lest they suffer loss of evil. You see the wicked guardians | of idolatry, which works itself out in impiety and greed, how they keep their watch unsleeping, because they deem it a punishment to be deprived of their lawlessness. And in the case of others, one can in the same way see people who have passionately taken pleasure or arrogance or vanity or something else of that sort to themselves, how they hold on by every means possible to such evils, counting it all gain that their soul is never cleansed of evil.

These things, therefore, the Bride laments and says, "This is why I became dark—because I guarded the weeds and wicked vines of the Adversary and took care of them but did not guard the vineyard that is mine." O what sorrow moves in those who hear with understanding the words *I did not guard my vineyard*! The cry is an open lament, a lament that moves the sympathetic groans of the prophets. "How did the faithful city Zion, full of judgment,

---

25. Origen also distinguishes the "vineyards" of the first clause from the "vineyard" of the second, but for him the former are the books of the Hebrew and Christian Scriptures, which the apostles entrust to the Bride's keeping (Baehrens 1925, 132.4–11).

κατελείφθη ἡ θυγάτηρ Σιὼν ὡς σκηνὴ ἐν ἀμπελῶνι; πῶς ἐκάθισε μόνη ἡ πόλις ἡ πεπληθυμμένη λαῶν, ἄρχουσα ἐν χώραις ἐγενήθη εἰς φόρον; πῶς ἠμαυρώθη τὸ χρυσίον, | ἠλλοιώθη τὸ ἀργύριον τὸ ἀγαθόν; πῶς ἐγένετο μέλαινα ἡ τῷ   60
ἀληθινῷ φωτὶ τὰ πρῶτα συναναλάμπουσα; πάντα ταῦτα ἐγένετό μοι, φησί,
5   ὅτι τὸν ἀμπελῶνα τὸν ἐμὸν οὐκ ἐφύλαξα.
     ἀμπελών ἐστιν ἡ ἀθανασία, ἀμπελὼν ἡ ἀπάθεια καὶ ἡ πρὸς τὸ θεῖον ὁμοίωσις καὶ ἡ παντὸς κακοῦ ἀλλοτρίωσις. τούτου τοῦ ἀμπελῶνος καρπὸς ἡ καθαρότης, ὁ λαμπρὸς οὗτος καὶ ὥριμος βότρυς ὁ ἡλιάζων τῷ εἴδει καὶ καταγλυκαίνων ἐν ἁγνείᾳ τὰ τῆς ψυχῆς αἰσθητήρια, ἕλιξ δὲ τοῦ
10   ἀμπελῶνος ἡ πρὸς τὴν ἀΐδιον ζωὴν περιπλοκή τε καὶ συμφυῖα, κλήματα δὲ βλυζανόμενα τὰ τῶν ἀρετῶν ἐστιν ὑψώματα τὰ πρὸς τὸ ὕψος τῶν ἀγγέλων ἀναδενδρούμενα, φύλλα δὲ τεθηλότα καὶ τῷ ἠρεμαίῳ πνεύματι γλαφυρῶς τοῖς κλάδοις ἐπισειόμενα ὁ πολυειδὴς τῶν θείων ἀρετῶν ἐστι κόσμος τῶν συναναθαλλόντων τῷ πνεύματι. ταῦτα πάντα κεκτημένη, φησί, καὶ ἐν
15   τῇ ἀπολαύσει τούτων λαμπρυνομένη διὰ τὸ μὴ φυλάξαι τὸν ἀμπελῶνα κατεμελάνθην τῷ πένθει· τῆς γὰρ καθαρότητος ἐκπεσοῦσα τὸ ζοφῶδες εἶδος ἐνεδυσάμην (τοιοῦτος γὰρ τῷ εἴδει ὁ χιτὼν ὁ δερμάτινος), νῦν δὲ διὰ τὴν ἀγαπήσασάν με πάλιν εὐθύτητα καλή τε καὶ φωτοειδὴς γενομένη ὑποπτεύω τὴν εὐκληρίαν, μὴ πάλιν ἀπολέσω τὸ κάλλος ἀγνοίᾳ τοῦ κατὰ τὴν ἀσφάλειαν
20   τρόπου περὶ τὴν φυλακὴν ἀστοχήσασα.
     | Διὰ τοῦτο καταλιποῦσα τὸν πρὸς τὰς νεάνιδας λόγον πάλιν δι᾽ εὐχῆς   61
ἀνακαλεῖ τὸν νυμφίον ὄνομα ποιησαμένη τοῦ ποθουμένου τὴν πρὸς αὐτὸν ἐνδιάθετον σχέσιν. τί γάρ φησιν; Ἀπάγγειλόν μοι, ὃν ἠγάπησεν ἡ ψυχή μου, ποῦ ποιμαίνεις, ποῦ κοιτάζεις ἐν μεσημβρίᾳ, μήποτε γένωμαι ὡς
25   περιβαλλομένη ἐπ᾽ ἀγέλαις ἑταίρων σου.

become a whore" (Isa 1:21)? How was "the daughter of Zion" left "like a tent in a vineyard" (Isa 1:8)? "How does the city that was full of people sit in solitude, how has she who ruled among the territories become a tributary" (Lam 1:1)? "How did the gold lose its gleam | and the good silver get altered" (Lam 4:1)? How did she become dark who at the beginning shone with the true Light? "All these things happened to me," she says, "because *I did not guard my vineyard.*"

The vineyard is immortality, the vineyard is impassibility, and becoming like to the divine, and being removed from all evil. The fruit of this vineyard is purity, that ripe and gleaming cluster whose appearance is a shining like the sun's and that pleases the soul's senses by its chaste simplicity. The spiraling tendril that the vineyard produces is a weaving and growing together into eternal life. The branches that shoot out are the virtues in their exaltation, climbing up to the height that belongs to the angels. The abundant leaves, shaken delicately against the branches by a gentle wind, are the manifold adornment of the divine virtues, which belong to those who are sprouting up together in the Spirit.[26] "Possessed of all these things," she says, "and gleaming bright in the enjoyment of them, I was darkened with grief because *I did not guard my vineyard.* For fallen away from purity, I was clothed in my dark appearance (for such, in its look, is the coat of skin[27]), but now because of the Righteousness that loved me again, I have become lovely and full of light and look anxiously upon my good fortune, lest I lose my beauty again, because I have missed the mark out of ignorance of the sure way to keep guard."

| On this account she leaves off addressing the maidens and calls once more in prayer upon the Bridegroom, putting to the One she desires the name of the way she feels about him. For what does she say? *Speak to me, you whom my soul loves, where do you pasture your flock, where do you rest them at the noontide? Lest I become as one who is veiled*[28] *by the flocks of your companions.*

---

26. In order fully to understand this sentence, one must recognize that the word for "wind" is the same as that for "Spirit," i.e., πνεῦμα.

27. On the "coats of skin," which played a central role in Nyssen's picture of the fallen human condition, see Gen 3:21 (χιτῶνας δερματίνους).

28. It is interesting that Nyssen nowhere tries to explain this obscure phrase in the LXX. For Origen's speculations, see Baehrens 1925, 136.3–24; 141.12–15 (the Bride does not want to appear as "una ex philosophorum scholis," in which the truth is covered up). Cyril of Alexandria appeals to 2 Cor 3:15 and interprets the phrase of the "veil" that lies over the minds of the Jews; the Bride is, then, the "repentant synagogue" (PG 87:1557B–C). Theodoret (PG 81:73C), however, refers to Symmachus, who for "covered around" or "veiled" has "roaming" (ῥεμβομένη; cf. the Vulgate's "vagari … per greges").

ποῦ ποιμαίνεις ὁ ποιμὴν ὁ καλὸς ὁ αἴρων ἐπὶ τῶν ὤμων ὅλον τὸ ποίμνιον;
ἓν γάρ ἐστι πρόβατον πᾶσα ἡ ἀνθρωπίνη φύσις, ἣν ἐπὶ τῶν ὤμων ἀνέλαβες.
δεῖξόν μοι τὸν τόπον τῆς χλόης, γνώρισόν μοι τὸ ὕδωρ τῆς ἀναπαύσεως,
ἐξάγαγέ με πρὸς τὴν τρόφιμον πόαν, κάλεσόν με ἐκ τοῦ ὀνόματος, ἵνα
5   ἀκούσω τῆς σῆς φωνῆς, ἐγὼ τὸ σὸν πρόβατον, καὶ δός μοι διὰ τῆς φωνῆς σου
τὴν ζωὴν τὴν αἰώνιον. ἀπάγγειλόν μοι, ὃν ἠγάπησεν ἡ ψυχή μου. οὕτω γάρ
σε κατονομάζω, ἐπειδὴ τὸ ὄνομά σου ὑπὲρ πᾶν ἐστιν ὄνομα καὶ πάσῃ φύσει
λογικῇ ἄφραστόν τε καὶ ἀχώρητον. οὐκοῦν ὄνομά σοί ἐστι γνωριστικὸν τῆς
σῆς ἀγαθότητος ἡ τῆς ψυχῆς μου περὶ σὲ σχέσις. πῶς γάρ σε μὴ ἀγαπήσω
10   τὸν οὕτω με ἀγαπήσαντα καὶ ταῦτα μέλαιναν οὖσαν, ὥστε τὴν ψυχήν σου
ὑπὲρ τῶν προβάτων θεῖναι, ἃ σὺ ποιμαίνεις; μείζονα ταύτης ἀγάπην οὐκ ἔστιν
ἐπινοῆσαι ἢ τὸ τῆς σῆς ψυχῆς τὴν σωτηρίαν τὴν ἐμὴν ἀνταλλάξασθαι.
| δίδαξον οὖν με, φησί, ποῦ ποιμαίνεις, ἵνα εὑροῦσα τὴν σωτήριον   62
νομὴν ἐμφορηθῶ τῆς οὐρανίας τροφῆς, ἧς ὁ μὴ φαγὼν οὐ δύναται εἰς τὴν
15   ζωὴν εἰσελθεῖν, καὶ δραμοῦσα πρὸς σὲ τὴν πηγὴν σπάσω τοῦ θείου πόματος,
ὃ σὺ τοῖς διψῶσι πηγάζεις προχέων τὸ ὕδωρ ἐκ τῆς πλευρᾶς τοῦ σιδήρου
τὴν φλέβα ταύτην ἀναστομώσαντος, οὗ ὁ γευσάμενος πηγὴ γίνεται ὕδατος
ἁλλομένου εἰς ζωὴν αἰώνιον. ἐὰν γὰρ ἐν τούτοις με ποιμάνῃς, κοιτάσεις με
πάντως ἐν μεσημβρίᾳ, ὅταν ἐν εἰρήνῃ ἐπὶ τὸ αὐτὸ κοιμηθεῖσα ἐν τῷ ἀσκίῳ
20   φωτὶ ἀναπαύσωμαι· ἄσκιος γὰρ πανταχόθεν ἡ μεσημβρία τοῦ ἡλίου τῆς
κορυφῆς ὑπερλάμποντος, ἐν ᾗ σὺ κοιτάζεις τοὺς ὑπὸ σοῦ ποιμανθέντας, ὅταν
τὰ παιδία σου δέξῃ μετὰ σεαυτοῦ εἰς τὴν κοίτην.
οὐδεὶς δὲ τῆς ἀναπαύσεως τῆς μεσημβρινῆς ἀξιοῦται μὴ υἱὸς φωτὸς
καὶ υἱὸς ἡμέρας γενόμενος. ὁ δὲ κατὰ τὸ ἴσον ἑαυτὸν τοῦ τε ἑσπερινοῦ
25   καὶ τοῦ ὀρθρινοῦ σκότους χωρίσας (τουτέστιν ὅπου ἄρχεται τὸ κακὸν καὶ
εἰς ὃ καταλήγει) οὗτος ἐν τῇ μεσημβρίᾳ παρὰ τοῦ ἡλίου τῆς δικαιοσύνης
κοιτάζεται. γνώρισον οὖν μοι, φησί, ποῦ χρή με ποιμαίνεσθαι καὶ τίς ἡ
ὁδὸς τῆς μεσημβρινῆς ἀναπαύσεως, μήποτέ με τῆς ἀγαθῆς χειραγωγίας

"Where do you pasture your flock, O Good Shepherd, you who carry the whole flock on your shoulders? For the whole human race is one herd, which you have taken on your shoulders.[29] Show me the place where there is new-grown grass, make known to me the water of repose (cf. Ps 22:1), lead me out to the nourishing pasture, call me by name in order that I, I your sheep, may hear your voice, and by your voice give me eternal life. *Speak to me, you whom my soul loves*—for so shall I name you, since your name is above every name and cannot be spoken or grasped by any rational nature. Therefore your name, which declares your goodness, is my soul's attitude toward you.[30] For how shall I not love you, who so loved me—even when I was dark—as to lay down your life for the sheep that you shepherd? It is not possible to conceive a love greater than this: to give up the well-being of your life in exchange for mine.

| "Teach me, then," she says, "where you keep your flock, so that as I find the saving pasture I may be filled with heavenly nourishment (apart from the eating of which one cannot enter into life), and as I run to you, the Fountain, may I suck in the divine drink that you gush forth for those who are thirsty, pouring out water from your side after the iron spear gave that spring a mouth (cf. John 19:34)—the drink that, if one tastes of it, becomes a spring of water welling up to eternal life (cf. John 4:14). For if you pasture me in this way, you will assuredly give me rest at midday, when I shall take my sleep, having lain down in peace in the same place, in the unshadowed light. For the noonday, when the sun shines directly from overhead, is unshaded, and in it you give rest to those whom you shepherd, when you take your young ones with you into bed."

But no one is worthy of noonday rest who has not become a son of the light and a son of the day. One who has separated himself equally from both the evening darkness of the west and the morning darkness of the east (that is, from the place where evil begins and the place where it ceases)—this is the one who is given rest at noonday by the Sun of Righteousness. "So make known to me," she says, "where I must be pastured and which is the way that leads to noonday rest, lest if I have strayed from sound teaching, ignorance of

---

29. Contrast Origen, who identifies all the company of the Bridegroom (referring to Song 6:8–9), including the "sheep" of the present verse, as those who believe in Christ, i.e., the church in all the differentiations of its members (Baehrens 1925, 135.5–10). He seems, however, to distinguish these from the ἑταίρων ("companions") of v. 7c, who are the angels of the nations with their own herds (136.25–137.2).

30. That is, "love." Cf. Origen (Baehrens 1925, 137.21–24), who, however, lacks Nyssen's characteristic suggestion that "love" is not a name that declares the Bridegroom's *nature,* but only his effect on us.

ἀποσφαλεῖσαν ταῖς | ἀλλοτρίαις τῶν σῶν ποιμνίων ἀγέλαις ἢ τῆς ἀληθείας   63
ἄγνοια συναγελάσῃ. ταῦτα εἶπε περὶ τοῦ γενομένου κάλλους αὐτῇ θεόθεν
ἀγωνιῶσα καί, ὅπως ἂν εἰς τὸ διηνεκὲς αὐτῇ παραμένοι ἡ εὐμορφία, μαθεῖν
ἀξιοῦσα.

5   ἀλλ᾽ οὔπω καταξιοῦται τῆς τοῦ νυμφίου φωνῆς τοῦ θεοῦ περὶ αὐτῆς
κρεῖττόν τι προβλεψαμένου, ὡς ἂν εἰς μείζονα πόθον τὴν ἐπιθυμίαν αὐτῆς
ἀναφλέξειεν ἡ ἀναβολὴ τῆς ἀπολαύσεως, ὥστε συναυξηθῆναι τῷ πόθῳ τὴν
εὐφροσύνην.

Ἀλλ᾽ οἱ φίλοι τοῦ νυμφίου πρὸς αὐτὴν διαλέγονται τὸν τρόπον τῆς
10   τῶν προσόντων ἀγαθῶν ἀσφαλείας διὰ συμβουλῆς ὑφηγούμενοι. ἔστι
δὲ κεκαλυμμένος δι᾽ ἀσαφείας καὶ ὁ παρ᾽ ἐκείνων λόγος· ἔχει γὰρ οὕτως ἡ
λέξις Ἐὰν μὴ γνῷς σεαυτήν, ἡ καλὴ ἐν γυναιξίν, ἔξελθε σὺ ἐν πτέρναις τῶν
ποιμνίων καὶ ποίμαινε τὰς ἐρίφους ἐπὶ σκηνώμασι τῶν ποιμνίων. τούτων δὲ
τῶν ῥημάτων ἡ μὲν διάνοια πρόδηλος ἐκ τῆς τῶν ἐξετασθέντων ἀκολουθίας
15   ἐστίν, ἡ δὲ σύνταξις δοκεῖ πως τὴν ἀσάφειαν ἔχειν. τίς οὖν ἐστιν ἡ διάνοια;

ἀσφαλέστατόν ἐστι φυλακτήριον ἡμῶν τὸ ἑαυτὸν μὴ ἀγνοῆσαι μηδέ τι
ἄλλο τῶν περὶ αὐτὸν βλέποντα ἑαυτὸν οἴεσθαι βλέπειν. ὅπερ δὴ πάσχουσιν οἱ
ἑαυτῶν ἀνεπίσκεπτοι· ἰσχὺν ἢ κάλλος ἢ δόξαν ἢ δυναστείαν ἤ τινα πλούτου
περιουσίαν ἢ τῦφον ἢ ὄγκον ἢ σώματος μέγεθος ἢ μορφῆς εὐμοιρίαν ἢ | ἄλλο   64
20   τι ἐν ἑαυτοῖς τοιοῦτον ὁρῶντες τοῦτο ἑαυτοὺς εἶναι νομίζουσιν. διὰ τοῦτο
σφαλεροὶ φύλακές εἰσιν ἑαυτῶν τῇ περὶ τὸ ἀλλότριον σχέσει ἀφύλακτον
περιορῶντες τὸ ἴδιον. πῶς γὰρ ἄν τις φυλάξειέ τι, ὃ μὴ ἐπίσταται; οὐκοῦν
ἀσφαλεστάτη φρουρὰ τῶν ἐν ἡμῖν ἀγαθῶν τὸ ἑαυτοὺς μὴ ἀγνοῆσαι καὶ τὸ
γνῶναι ἕκαστον ἑαυτὸν ὅπερ ἐστὶ καὶ ἀκριβῶς ἑαυτὸν ἀπὸ τῶν περὶ αὐτὸν
25   διακρίνειν, ὡς ἂν μὴ λάθοι φυλάσσων ἀνθ᾽ ἑαυτοῦ τὸ ἀλλότριον·

the truth should gather me in | with the herds[31] that are alien to your flocks."
These things she said because she was anxious about the beauty that had
come to her from God and thought it vital to learn how her beauty might
abide with her permanently.

But she is not yet deemed worthy of the voice of the Bridegroom, since
God foresees something better for her: that delay of fruition will inflame her
desire to a higher point of yearning, and joy will be increased along with
yearning.

The friends of the Bridegroom, however, discuss with her the way of safe-
guarding the good things that she presently possesses; they instruct her by
giving her counsel. Their speech too, though, is veiled in obscurity, for this is
how the text runs: *If you do not know yourself, O beautiful one among women,
go forth in the footsteps of the flocks and tend the kids by the shepherds' tents.*
The point of these words is apparent from the thought sequence of the passages we have already studied, but the manner in which the words are ordered
seems to contain some unclarity. So what is the meaning?

Our greatest safeguard is not to be ignorant of oneself[32] and not to suppose that one is looking at oneself when in fact one is viewing something else,
something that hangs about the outer edges of oneself. This is the affliction
of those who do not seriously appraise themselves. They see in themselves
strength or beauty or glory or power or abundance of riches or pride or dig-
nity or bodily size or good looks or |some other such thing, and they take
it for themselves. For this reason they are unreliable keepers of themselves.
With their interest fixed on what is alien, they allow what is their own to go
unprotected. For how shall anyone guard what he has no knowledge of? So
the most secure watch over the good things within us is not to be ignorant of
ourselves and for each to know what he is and to distinguish clearly between
himself and the things around his edges, so that he may not end up keeping
guard over what is alien rather than over himself.

---

31. Nyssen seems to agree with Origen here, who sees the companions' flocks as the
nations, shepherded by their angels, who are neither so skillful nor so caring in their shepherd's
work as the Bridegroom. Theodoret (PG 81:73A) takes the same line but identifies these alien
herds as heresies, as does Gregory the Great (*Exp. Cant.* 42, CCSL 144:40), who observes that all
priests and teachers appear to be God's "companions" but that many are his adversaries as far as
their life goes.

32. No doubt Gregory here has the classical maxim "Know thyself" in mind. It had already
been appropriated by Clement of Alexandria (*Paed.* 3.1). Origen explicitly quotes it, taking
care to note that Solomon had anticipated the Greek sages in this matter. For him the requisite
knowledge is expressed in the proposition "You have been made after the image of God" (Baehrens 1925, 141.19–27). Nyssen comes to this theme toward the end of his exposition (see p. 68
[Jaeger] below).

ὁ γὰρ πρὸς τὴν ἐν τῷ κόσμῳ τούτῳ βλέπων ζωὴν καὶ τὰ ἐνταῦθα τίμια
φυλακῆς ἄξια κρίνων οὐκ οἶδε τὸ ἴδιον διακρῖναι τοῦ ἀλλοτρίου· οὐδὲν
γὰρ τῶν παρερχομένων ἐστὶν ἡμέτερον. πῶς γὰρ ἄν τις κρατήσειε τοῦ
παροδικοῦ τε καὶ ῥέοντος; ἐπεὶ οὖν ἓν μόνον ὡσαύτως ἔχει, ἡ νοητή τε καὶ
5   ἄϋλος φύσις, ἡ δὲ ὕλη παρέρχεται διὰ ῥοῆς τινος καὶ κινήσεως πάντοτε
ἀλλοιουμένη, ἀναγκαίως ὁ τοῦ ἑστῶτος χωριζόμενος τῷ ἀστατοῦντι πάντως
συμπαραφέρεται καὶ ὁ τὸ παρερχόμενον διώκων καὶ τὸ ἑστὼς καταλείπων
ἀμφοτέρων διαμαρτάνει τὸ μὲν | ἀφιείς, τὸ δὲ κατασχεῖν μὴ δυνάμενος. διὰ   65
τοῦτό φησιν ἡ τῶν φίλων τοῦ νυμφίου συμβουλὴ τὰ εἰρημένα ὅτι Ἐὰν μὴ
10   γνῷς σεαυτήν, ἡ καλὴ ἐν γυναιξίν, ἔξελθε σὺ ἐν πτέρναις τῶν ποιμνίων καὶ
ποίμαινε τὰς ἐρίφους ἐπὶ σκηνώμασι τῶν ποιμνίων.

τοῦτο δέ ἐστι τί; ὅτι ὁ ἑαυτὸν ἀγνοήσας ἐκπίπτει μὲν τῆς τῶν προβάτων
ἀγέλης, σύννομος δὲ γίνεται τοῖς ἐρίφοις, ὧν ἡ στάσις ἐπὶ τὸ σκαιὸν
ἀπεώσθη, οὕτω τοῦ καλοῦ ποιμένος ἐκ δεξιῶν μὲν τὰ πρόβατα στήσαντος,
15   ἀφορίσαντος δὲ τῆς κρείττονος λήξεως ἐπὶ τὸ ἀριστερὸν τὰ ἐρίφια. τοῦτο
τοίνυν ἐκ τῆς τῶν φίλων τοῦ νυμφίου συμβουλῆς παιδευόμεθα τὸ δεῖν εἰς
αὐτὴν βλέπειν τὴν τῶν πραγμάτων φύσιν καὶ μὴ πεπλανημένοις ἴχνεσι τῆς
ἀληθείας παραστοχάζεσθαι.

Σαφέστερον δὲ χρὴ τὸν περὶ τούτων ἐκθέσθαι λόγον. πολλοὶ τῶν
20   ἀνθρώπων οὐκ αὐτοὶ κρίνουσιν ὅπως ἔχει τὰ πράγματα φύσεως, ἀλλὰ πρὸς
τὴν συνήθειαν τῶν προβεβιωκότων ὁρῶντες τῆς ὑγιοῦς τῶν ὄντων κρίσεως
ἁμαρτάνουσιν οὐκ ἔμφρονά τινα λογισμὸν ἀλλὰ συνήθειαν ἄλογον τοῦ
καλοῦ κριτήριον προβαλλόμενοι· ὅθεν εἰς ἀρχάς τε καὶ δυναστείας ἑαυτοὺς
εἰσωθοῦσι καὶ τὰς ἐν τῷ κόσμῳ τούτῳ περιφανείας καὶ τοὺς ὑλικοὺς ὄγκους
25   περὶ πολλοῦ ποιοῦνται, ἄδηλον ὄν, εἰς ὅ τι τούτων ἕκαστον καταλήξει μετὰ
τὸν τῇδε | βίον· οὐ γὰρ ἀσφαλὴς τῶν μελλόντων ἐγγυητὴς ἡ συνήθεια, ἧς τὸ   66
πέρας ἐρίφων εὑρίσκεται πολλάκις οὐχὶ προβάτων ἀγέλη.

νοεῖς δὲ πάντως τὸν λόγον ἐκ τῆς τοῦ εὐαγγελίου φωνῆς. ὁ δὲ πρὸς τὸ
ἴδιον τῆς ἀνθρωπίνης φύσεως βλέπων (τοῦτο δέ ἐστιν ὁ λόγος) καταφρονήσει
30   μὲν τῆς ἀλόγου συνηθείας, οὐδὲν δὲ ὡς καλὸν αἱρήσεται, ὃ μὴ τῇ ψυχῇ φέρει
τι κέρδος. οὐκοῦν οὐ χρὴ πρὸς τὰ ἴχνη τῶν βοσκημάτων βλέπειν, ἃ τῷ γεώδει
βίῳ διὰ τῶν πτερνῶν ἐνσημαίνονται οἱ προωδευκότες τὸν βίον· ἀφανὴς γὰρ

Now the person who is concerned about the life of this world and who judges its honors worthy of being guarded does not know how to distinguish what is his own from what is alien, for none of the things that come and then go belongs to us. How can one master that which passes by and flows away? Since, then, only one thing—the intelligible and immaterial nature—exists self-identically, while matter, which is always in process of being altered by some flux and motion, passes away, the person who is separated from what is stable will necessarily be carried along with what is never at rest, and he who pursues that which passes away and deserts what is stable misses both. The one | he lets go of; the other he is unable to hold on to. That explains why the counsel of the friends of the Bridegroom is conveyed in these words: *If you do not know yourself, O beautiful one among women, go forth in the footsteps of the flocks and tend the kids by the shepherds' tents.*

What does this mean? That one who does not know herself is excluded from the flock of sheep and reckoned among the goats, whose place has been set off to the left. Thus the Good Shepherd locates the sheep on his right hand, while he keeps the goats on his left, separated from the better portion (cf. Matt 25:32–33).[33] So from the advice of the Bridegroom's friends we learn this: that it is necessary to look into the very nature of things and not to seek the truth with straying steps.

But we need to set out the implications of this principle more clearly. Most people do not judge for themselves how things stand by nature. Instead, they look to the customs of their forebears and fail to achieve a sound judgment about reality, because they set up an irrational habit as their criterion of the good rather than any intelligent consideration. Consequently, they thrust themselves into positions of authority and power and make much of prominence in this world and of material things, although it is unclear to what end any of these things will come after this | life. For habit is not a secure guarantor of things to come, since what it usually ends up with is a herd of goats, not of sheep.

The words of the Gospel make the point here plain. The person who takes account of what is proper to human nature (and that is reason) will despise irrational habit and will choose as good nothing that does not profit the soul. Therefore, it is wrong to look to the tracks of the cattle, which those who have gone through life before us stamp upon the earthly life with their

---

33. Origen (Baehrens 1925, 142.5–8) appeals to the same Gospel text but sees the Bride who does not know herself not as "among the goats" but as condemned to feed them.

34. See also Gregory the Great (*Exp. Cant.* 44, CCSL 144:43): "egredere et abi post vestigia gregum," which means "to follow, not my example, but the example of the nations." By contrast,

ἐκ τῶν φαινομένων ἡ τοῦ προτιμοτέρου κρίσις, ἕως ἂν ἔξω τοῦ βίου γενώμεθα
κἀκεῖ γνῶμεν, τίσιν ἠκολουθήσαμεν. ὁ τοίνυν μὴ ἐξ αὐτῶν τῶν πραγμάτων
διακρίνων τὸ καλὸν ἐκ τοῦ χείρονος ἀλλὰ τοῖς ἴχνεσι τῶν προωδευκότων
ἑπόμενος τὴν παρελθοῦσαν τοῦ βίου συνήθειαν διδάσκαλον τῆς ἰδίας ζωῆς
5   προβαλλόμενος λανθάνει πολλάκις κατὰ τὸν καιρὸν τῆς δικαίας κρίσεως
ἔριφος ἀντὶ προβάτου γενόμενος. οὐκοῦν ταῦτα λεγόντων ἔστιν ἀκούειν
τῶν φίλων ὅτι σύ, ὦ ψυχή, ἡ ἐκ μελαίνης γενομένη καλή, εἴ σοι μέλει τοῦ
διαιωνίζειν σοι τῆς εὐμορφίας | τὴν χάριν, μὴ τοῖς ἴχνεσιν ἐπιπλανῶ τῶν   67
προωδευκότων τὸν βίον· ἄδηλον γὰρ εἰ μὴ τρίβος ἐρίφων ἐστὶ τὸ φαινόμενον,
10   ἢ σὺ κατόπιν ἀκολουθοῦσα διὰ τὸ μὴ φαίνεσθαί σοι τοὺς διὰ τῶν ἰχνῶν τὴν
ἀτραπὸν τρίψαντας, ἐπειδὰν παρέλθῃς τὸν βίον καὶ κατακλεισθῇς ἐν τῇ τοῦ
θανάτου μάνδρᾳ, μήποτε προστεθῇς τῇ τῶν ἐρίφων ἀγέλῃ, οἷς ἀγνοοῦσα
διὰ τῶν ἰχνῶν τοῦ βίου κατόπιν ἐπηκολούθησας. Ἐὰν γὰρ μὴ γνῷς σεαυτήν,
φησίν, ἡ καλὴ ἐν γυναιξίν, ἔξελθε σὺ ἐν πτέρναις τῶν ποιμνίων καὶ ποίμαινε
15   τὰς ἐρίφους ἐπὶ σκηνώμασι τῶν ποιμνίων.

ὅπερ δι᾽ ἑτέρου τινὸς ἀντιγράφου σαφέστερόν ἐστι κατανοῆσαι, ὡς μηδὲ
τὴν σύνταξιν τῶν ῥημάτων δοκεῖν ἀσυναρτήτως ἔχειν. φησὶ γὰρ ὅτι Ἐὰν μὴ
γνῷς σεαυτήν, ἡ καλὴ ἐν γυναιξίν, ἐξῆλθες ἐκ τῶν πτερνῶν τοῦ ποιμνίου καὶ
ποιμαίνεις ἐρίφους ἀντὶ σκηνωμάτων ποιμνίων· ὥστε δι᾽ ἀκριβείας συμβαίνειν
20   τὴν ἐν τοῖς ῥήμασι τούτοις ἐμφαινομένην διάνοιαν τῇ προαποδοθείσῃ θεωρίᾳ
τοῦ λόγου.

οὐκοῦν ἵνα μὴ ταῦτα πάθῃς, πρόσεχε σεαυτῇ, φησὶν ὁ λόγος·τοῦτο γάρ
ἐστι τὸ ἀσφαλὲς τῶν | ἀγαθῶν φυλακτήριον· γνῶθι πόσον ὑπὲρ τὴν λοιπὴν   68
κτίσιν παρὰ τοῦ πεποιηκότος τετίμησαι. οὐκ οὐρανὸς γέγονεν εἰκὼν τοῦ
25   θεοῦ, οὐ σελήνη, οὐχ ἥλιος, οὐ τὸ ἀστρῷον κάλλος, οὐκ ἄλλο τι τῶν κατὰ
τὴν κτίσιν φαινομένων οὐδέν. μόνη σὺ γέγονας τῆς ὑπερεχούσης πάντα
νοῦν φύσεως ἀπεικόνισμα, τοῦ ἀφθάρτου κάλλους ὁμοίωμα, τῆς ἀληθινῆς
θεότητος ἀποτύπωμα, τῆς μακαρίας ζωῆς δοχεῖον, τοῦ ἀληθινοῦ φωτὸς
ἐκμαγεῖον, πρὸς ὃ βλέπουσα ἐκεῖνο γίνῃ, ὅπερ ἐκεῖνός ἐστι, μιμουμένη τὸν
30   ἐν σοὶ λάμποντα διὰ τῆς ἀντιλαμπούσης αὐγῆς ἐκ τῆς σῆς καθαρότητος.
οὐδὲν οὕτω τῶν ὄντων μέγα, ὡς τῷ σῷ μεγέθει παραμετρεῖσθαι. ὁ οὐρανὸς
ὅλος τῇ τοῦ θεοῦ σπιθαμῇ περιλαμβάνεται, γῆ δὲ καὶ θάλασσα τῇ δρακὶ
τῆς χειρὸς αὐτοῦ περιείργεται. ἀλλ᾽ ὅμως ὁ τοσοῦτος, ὁ τοιοῦτος, ὁ πᾶσαν
τῇ παλάμῃ περισφίγγων τὴν κτίσιν, ὅλος σοὶ χωρητὸς γίνεται καὶ ἐν σοὶ
35   κατοικεῖ καὶ οὐ στενοχωρεῖται τῇ σῇ φύσει ἐνδιοδεύων ὁ εἰπὼν Ἐνοικήσω

hooves.[34] For when based on appearances, judgment of what is most to be honored is uncertain, until we are outside of this life and there find out whom we have followed. So the person who does not discriminate good from evil on the basis of the things themselves but follows in the steps of those who have gone before, establishing transient habit as the guide of his own life, often turns out, all unawares, to be a goat and not a sheep in the day of righteous judgment. Hence you are in a position to hear what your friends are saying: "You, O soul, who from being dark have become beautiful, if you wish | the grace of your attractiveness to endure, do not err in the steps of those who have gone before you in life. For it is not plain that what appears before you is not a goat-track; and if you follow it from behind, since those whose footsteps made the path are not seen to you, when you have passed through life and are shut up in death's fold, you may be consigned to the herd of goats behind which you ignorantly followed on because of the tracks their life made." For *if you do not know yourself*, it says, *O beautiful one among women, go forth in the footsteps of the flocks and tend the kids by the shepherds' tents.*

It is possible to interpret this with greater clarity on the basis of a different way of rendering <the text>, and then the syntax of the words does not seem disjointed. It reads: *If you do not know yourself, O beautiful one among women,* you are *going forth from the footsteps of the flock, and you are tending kids* instead of *the shepherds' tents;* and the sense that is evident in these words agrees exactly with the previously given interpretation of the passage.

The passage says, then, "Have a care to yourself, for this is the sure safeguard |of <your> good things. Know how much you have been honored by the Maker above the rest of the creation. Heaven did not become the image of God, nor the moon, nor the sun, nor the beautiful stars—nor a single other one of the things that appear in the created order. Only you came into existence as a copy of the Nature that transcends every intellect, a likeness of the incorruptible Beauty, an impress of the true Deity—a model of that true Light in the contemplation of which you become what it is, imitating that which shines within you by the ray that shines forth in response from your purity. None of the things that exist is so great as to be compared to your greatness. The whole heaven is contained in the span of God's hand; earth and sea are encompassed by his hand. But at the same time this One, being such as he is and so great as he is, grasping the whole creation in the palm of his hand, becomes limited for your sake and dwells in you and is not confined as he penetrates your nature. For he is the One who says, 'I will dwell within them

---

Theodoret (PG 81:76A–B) thinks that following the tracks of the herds means looking to the way of life of the saints of the past.

ἐν αὐτοῖς καὶ ἐμπεριπατήσω. ἐὰν ταῦτα βλέπῃς, εἰς οὐδὲν τῶν περιγείων τὸν
ὀφθαλμὸν ἀσχολήσεις. τί τοῦτο λέγω; ἀλλ᾽ οὐδὲ ὁ οὐρανός σοι θαυμαστὸς
νομισθήσεται. πῶς γὰρ θαυμάσεις | τοὺς οὐρανούς, ὦ ἄνθρωπε, σεαυτὸν   69
βλέπων τῶν οὐρανῶν μονιμώτερον; οἱ μὲν γὰρ παρέρχονται, σὺ δὲ τῷ ἀεὶ
5   ὄντι συνδιαμένεις πρὸς τὸ ἀΐδιον. οὐ θαυμάσεις πλάτη γῆς οὐδὲ πελάγη πρὸς
ἄπειρον ἐκτεινόμενα, ὧν ἐπιστατεῖν ἐτάχθης ὥσπερ τινὸς ξυνωρίδος πώλων
ἡνίοχος εὐπειθῆ πρὸς τὸ δοκοῦν ἔχων τὰ στοιχεῖα ταῦτα καὶ ὑπεξούσια· ἥ
τε γὰρ γῆ σοι πρὸς τὰς τοῦ βίου χρείας ὑπηρετεῖται καὶ ἡ θάλασσα καθάπερ
τις πῶλος εὐήνιος ὑπέχει σοι τὰ νῶτα καὶ ἐπιβάτην ἑαυτῆς τὸν ἄνθρωπον
10 δέχεται.

Ἐὰν οὖν γνῷς σεαυτήν, ἡ καλὴ ἐν γυναιξίν, παντὸς τοῦ κόσμου
ὑπερφρονήσεις καὶ πρὸς τὸ ἄϋλον ἀγαθὸν διὰ παντὸς ὁρῶσα περιόψῃ τῶν
κατὰ τὸν βίον τοῦτον ἰχνῶν τὴν πλάνην. οὐκοῦν ἀεὶ πρόσεχε σεαυτῇ, καὶ οὐ
μὴ πλανηθήσῃ περὶ τὴν τῶν ἐρίφων ἀγέλην οὐδὲ ἔριφος ἀντὶ προβάτου ἐν τῷ
15 καιρῷ τῆς κρίσεως ἐπιδειχθήσῃ οὐδὲ τῆς ἐκ δεξιῶν στάσεως ἀφορισθήσῃ, ἀλλ᾽
ἀκούσῃ τῆς γλυκείας φωνῆς, ἥ φησι πρὸς τὰ ἐριοφόρα τε καὶ ἥμερα πρόβατα
ὅτι Δεῦτε οἱ εὐλογημένοι τοῦ πατρός μου, κληρονομήσατε τὴν ἡτοιμασμένην
ὑμῖν βασιλείαν πρὸ καταβολῆς κόσμου. ἧς καὶ ἡμεῖς ἀξιωθείημεν ἐν Χριστῷ
Ἰησοῦ τῷ κυρίῳ ἡμῶν,

20   ᾧ ἡ δόξα εἰς τοὺς αἰῶνας.
                      ἀμήν.

and will walk about among them' (2 Cor 6:16). If you see these things, you will not set your eye on anything earthly. Why do I say this? Because you will not reckon the heaven itself a thing that is wonderful for you. For how shall you marvel at | the heavens, O human, when you see that you yourself are more lasting than the heavens? For they pass away, but you remain forever in the company of that which always is. You will not marvel at the flat earth or at the seas as they stretch out beyond limit. You were commanded to have charge over them as a driver over a pair of foals, having these elements obedient to your purpose and subject to your power. For earth is your servant for the necessities of life, and the sea like a docile steed gives you its back and accepts the human being as its rider.

"If, then, you know yourself, *O beautiful one among women,* you will look down on the whole cosmos, and fixing your gaze in all circumstances on the immaterial good, you will be watchful concerning the error of the ways of this life. So always take heed to yourself, and you will not be led astray regarding the flock of goats or be shown up as a goat rather than a sheep at the time of judgment or be exiled from the station at the right hand. Rather, you will hear the sweet voice that says to the wool-bearing and tame sheep, 'Come, O blessed of my Father, and inherit the kingdom prepared for you from the foundation of the cosmos'"—of which may we be found worthy in Christ Jesus our Lord,

To whom be glory to the ages.
Amen.

Τῇ ἵππῳ μου ἐν ἅρμασι Φαραὼ   70
ὡμοίωσά σε, ἡ πλησίον μου.
Τί ὡραιώθησαν σιαγόνες σου ὡς τρυγόνος,
τράχηλός σου ὡς ὁρμίσκοι;

5   Ὁμοιώματα χρυσίου ποιήσομέν σοι μετὰ στιγμάτων τοῦ ἀργυρίου.
Ἕως οὗ ὁ βασιλεὺς ἐν ἀνακλίσει αὐτοῦ,

       νάρδος μου ἔδωκεν ὀσμὴν αὐτοῦ.
       Ἀπόδεσμος στακτῆς ἀδελφιδός μου ἐμοί,
       ἀνὰ μέσον τῶν μαστῶν μου αὐλισθήσεται·
10   Βότρυς τῆς κύπρου ἀδελφιδός μου ἐμοὶ
       ἐν ἀμπελῶσιν ἐν Γαδί.

Ὅσα πρὸ τῆς παρούσης ἀναγνώσεως ἐν τοῖς προοιμίοις τοῦ Ἄισματος
τῶν ᾀσμάτων ἡμῖν τεθεώρηται, ὁμοίως ἔχει τῇ γινομένῃ μετὰ τὴν νύκτα
περὶ τὸν ὄρθρον αὐγῇ. οὔτε γὰρ ἐκείνη καθαρὸν φῶς, ἀλλὰ φωτός ἐστι
15   προοίμιον· καὶ τὰ εἰρημένα τοιαῦτα, ὡς τὴν ἀνατολὴν μὲν ἡμῖν τοῦ ἀληθινοῦ
καταμηνύειν φωτός, οὐ μὴν ἐν ἑαυτοῖς ἔχειν αὐτὸν τοῦ ἡλίου τὸν κύκλον
τηλαυγῶς προφαινόμενον. ἐν ἐκείνοις μὲν γὰρ ἡ νύμφη φθέγγεται καὶ οἱ
φίλοι καὶ αἱ νεάνιδες, νῦν δὲ αὐτοῦ τοῦ νυμφίου φωνὴ καθάπερ τις κύκλος
ἡλιακὸς | ἀνατέλλει ἀποκρύπτων ταῖς τῶν ἀκτίνων αὐγαῖς πᾶσαν τῶν τε   71
20   προφανέντων ἀστέρων καὶ τοῦ ὑπαυγάσαντος ὄρθρου τὴν λαμπηδόνα.
       κάκεῖνα μὲν πάντα καθαρσίων τινῶν καὶ περιρραντηρίων δύναμιν ἔχει, δι᾽
ὧν ἀφαγνισθεῖσαι αἱ ψυχαὶ πρὸς τὴν ὑποδοχὴν τῶν θείων παρασκευάζονται,
ὁ δὲ νῦν λόγος αὐτῆς τῆς θεότητός ἐστι μετουσία αὐτοῦ τοῦ θεοῦ λόγου διὰ
τῆς ἰδίας φωνῆς μεταδιδόντος τῷ ἀκούοντι τῆς ἀκηράτου δυνάμεως τὴν
25   κοινωνίαν.
       καὶ ὥσπερ ἐπὶ τοῦ ὄρους Σινᾶ προπαρασκευασθεὶς τοῖς καθαρσίοις ὁ
Ἰσραὴλ ἐν ἡμέραις δύο τῇ τρίτῃ κατὰ τὸν ὄρθρον ἀξιοῦται τῆς θεοφανείας
οὐκέτι περὶ τὴν πλύσιν τῶν ἱματίων ἄσχολος ὤν, ἀλλ᾽ αὐτὸν δεχόμενος
ἐμφανῶς τὸν θεόν, οὗ χάριν τὸν τῆς ψυχῆς ῥύπον διὰ τῶν προλαβόντων
30   καθαρσίων ἀπεπλύνατο, οὕτω καὶ νῦν ἡ ἐν τοῖς φθάσασι λόγοις γεγενημένη
τῶν προοιμίων τοῦ Ἄισματος τῶν Ἀισμάτων θεωρία κατὰ τὰς προλαβούσας
δύο ἡμέρας τοσοῦτον ὠφέλησεν, ὅσον ἐκπλῦναι καὶ ἀποκλύσαι τοῦ ῥύπου

HOMILY 3
Song 1:9–14

| ⁹*I have likened you, my close one,*
to my horse among the chariots of Pharaoh.
¹⁰*Why are your cheeks made beauteous like a dove's,*
your neck like circlets?

¹¹*We will make you likenesses of gold with silver studs,*
¹²*until the king is in his bed.*

My spikenard gave off his scent.
¹³*My kinsman is for me a bundle of myrrh,*
he shall lie between my breasts.
¹⁴*My kinsman is for me a cluster of grape blossoms*
among the vineyards in Gad.

Everything in the introductory part of the Song of Songs, which we have treated of prior to the present reading, is like the glow that appears when night has ended but before the dawn. That is not a pure light but light's preface, and the things there stated were calculated to point us to the rising of the true light, but they did not contain in themselves the very disc of the sun bravely shining. In those passages the Bride spoke, and the friends, and the bridesmaids. Now, however, the voice of the Bridegroom himself, like a sun's orb, | rises up and eclipses with the light of its rays all the brightness both of the stars that shone earlier and of the glistening dawn.

To be sure, the previous passages all have the power that belongs to means of purification and lustration. By their agency souls that have been purified are prepared for the reception of the divine. But the words of the present passage are a participation in the Godhead itself, since the divine Word in his own voice confers on the hearer a fellowship with the undefiled Power.

And just as Israel, at Mount Sinai, was prepared beforehand for two days by rites of purification and then, at dawn on the third day, was judged worthy of the theophany (cf. Exod 19:10–11), being no longer busied with the cleansing of garments but openly receiving God himself, for whose sake the soul's filth had been washed away by the earlier purifications, so now, in our own case, the insight into the prefatory parts of the Song of Songs that we achieved on the preceding two days in our earlier homilies has been of profit to the extent that the sense contained in the words has been washed and scrubbed

τῆς σαρκὸς τὴν ἐν τοῖς λεγομένοις διάνοιαν. αὐτὸς δὲ ὁ θεὸς λόγος σήμερον, ἥτις ἐστὶ τρίτη μετὰ τὴν πρώτην τε καὶ δευτέραν, καθαρθεῖσιν ἐπιφανήσεται,   72 οὐ γνόφῳ καὶ θυέλλῃ καὶ σάλπιγγος ἤχῳ | καὶ πυρὶ φοβερῷ ἐκ πυθμένος εἰς ἀκρώρειαν τοῦ ὄρους τὴν περιοχὴν διασμύχοντι φανερὰν καὶ ἐπίδηλον 5 ἑαυτοῦ τὴν παρουσίαν ποιούμενος, ἀλλ᾽ ἡδὺς καὶ εὐπρόσιτος ἐκ τοῦ φοβεροῦ εἴδους ἐκείνου πρὸς τὴν νυμφικὴν εὐφροσύνην μεθαρμοσάμενος.

τῆς γὰρ νύμφης δεηθείσης μαθεῖν τοὺς τῆς ἀναπαύσεως τόπους, ἐν οἷς ὁ ἀγαθὸς ποιμὴν τὴν διατριβὴν ἔχει, ὥστε μή τι κατὰ ἄγνοιαν τῶν ἀβουλήτων παθεῖν, εἶτα τῶν φίλων τοῦ νυμφίου τὸ ἀσφαλὲς τῆς ἀληθείας κριτήριον 10 ὑφηγησαμένων τὸ πρὸς ἑαυτὴν βλέπειν τὴν ψυχὴν καὶ ἑαυτὴν γινώσκειν (τὸ γὰρ ἑαυτὴν ἀγνοεῖν ἀρχὴν ἀπεφήναντο καὶ ἀκολουθίαν εἶναι τοῦ μηδὲ ἄλλο τι τῶν δεόντων εἰδέναι. πῶς γὰρ ἄν τις ἄλλο τι μάθοι ἑαυτὸν ἀγνοῶν;) ἐπὶ τούτοις ὡς ἱκανῶς ἤδη τοῦ ἡγεμονικοῦ τῆς ψυχῆς κεκαθαρμένου ἐπανατέλλει τῇ ποθούσῃ ὁ λόγος προτροπὴν πρὸς τὸ τελειότερον ποιούμενος διὰ τῆς 15 ἀποδοχῆς τῶν παρόντων· ὁ γὰρ ἐπὶ τοῖς κατορθώμασιν ἔπαινος σφοδροτέραν   73 | τοῖς κατορθώσασι τὴν πρὸς τὸ κρεῖττον προθυμίαν ἐντίθησιν.

Τίς οὖν ὁ παρὰ τοῦ ἀληθινοῦ λόγου γεγονὼς πρὸς τὴν παρθένον λόγος; Τῇ ἵππῳ μου, φησίν, ἐν ἅρμασι Φαραὼ ὡμοίωσά σε, ἡ πλησίον μου. ἀλλ᾽ ἐπειδὴ οὐκ ἔστιν ἐκ τοῦ προχείρου τὴν τῶν εἰρημένων θεωρῆσαι διάνοιαν, 20 ἐξετάσαι προσήκει δι᾽ ἐπιμελείας καθὼς ἂν οἷόν τε ᾖ τὸ προκείμενον.

ἄλλην δύναμιν τὴν ἀντιταχθεῖσαν τῇ ἵππῳ τοῦ Φαραὼ παρὰ τῆς ἱστορίας ἐμάθομεν, νεφέλην καὶ ῥάβδον καὶ βίαιον ἄνεμον καὶ πέλαγος διχῇ διαιρούμενον καὶ βυθὸν ἐν κόνει καὶ τὴν ἐκ κυμάτων τειχοποιΐαν καὶ ξηρὰν ἄβυσσον τὴν διὰ τοῦ μέσου τῶν ἐξ ὕδατος τειχῶν χερσωθεῖσαν, δι᾽ ὧν 25 ἁπάντων ἐγίνετο τοῖς Ἰσραηλίταις ἡ σωτηρία πανστρατιᾷ τοῦ Φαραὼ μετὰ τῶν ἵππων τε καὶ ἁρμάτων συγκαλυφθέντος τοῖς κύμασιν. οὐδεμιᾶς τοίνυν ἱππικῆς δυνάμεως ἀντιταχθείσης τῷ Αἰγυπτίῳ στρατῷ ἄπορον ἂν εἴη μαθεῖν, ποία ἵππῳ τῇ διαφανείσῃ κατὰ τῶν Αἰγυπτίων ἁρμάτων ἡ νύμφη παρὰ τοῦ

to remove the filth of the flesh. But today—the third day[1] after the first and second—God the Word himself will be manifested to those who have been purified: not in cloud and wind and sound of trumpet, | not in the terrifying fire that smolders its way from the base of the mountain to its crown, but sweetly and agreeably, having given up that fearsome aspect so as to fit in with the joys of a wedding.

For the Bride had asked to discover the places of refreshment in which the Good Shepherd sojourns, so as not through ignorance to suffer anything contrary to her purpose. Then the friends of the Bridegroom taught her the sure standard of truth, which is for the soul to look upon itself and to know itself. (For they declared that ignorance of oneself is at once the source and the outcome of failure to know any of the other things that are needful. How can one learn anything else if one does not know oneself?) In addition, since the governing part of the soul has already been sufficiently purified, the Word dawns upon a soul full of love and desire. It begets incitement to what is more perfect by approval of her present state. For praise of achievements induces | in those who have accomplished them a more vehement desire for better things.

What, then, is the word that has come to the virgin from the true Word? *I have likened you, my close one*, he says, *to my horse[2] among the chariots of Pharaoh*. Since, however, it is not possible to discern the sense of these words by appeal to their surface meaning,[3] we are obliged, as far as we are able, to make diligent inquiry into the text before us.

From the scriptural narrative (cf. Exod 14:25–31) we learned of another force that was arrayed against Pharaoh's cavalry: a cloud, and a staff, and a strong wind, and a sea divided into two parts, and a dusty seabed, and walls made of waves, and a dry deep that had been turned into land between the watery walls. By the agency of all these, salvation came to the Israelites with their whole force, while Pharaoh with his horses and chariots was covered over by the waves. Since, then, there was no cavalry force arrayed against the Egyptian army, it seems hard to determine what kind of *horse* it was, showing itself in opposition to the Egyptian chariots, to which the Bride is now lik-

---

1. This passage suggests fairly clearly that Gregory's homilies—or at least the first three of them—were delivered on successive days, weekdays, no doubt, in the Lenten season.

2. The Greek word for "horse" (ἵππος) is here feminine by gender (ἡ ἵππος). In that form it can mean either "mare" or "horse" in the sense of "cavalry" (cf. the Old English expression "a body of horse"). Gregory takes advantage of this ambiguity: his "mare" (the soul or Bride) stands for a body of cavalry, which in turn, as becomes apparent, is to be identified as the angelic host.

3. The reason for this judgment appears from the next paragraph: the account in Exod 14 makes no mention of any cavalry that fought on the side of the Israelites.

λόγου νῦν προσεικάζεται· Τῇ ἵππῳ γάρ μου, φησί, τῇ ἐν τοῖς ἅρμασι τοῦ
Φαραὼ κατειργασμένῃ τὴν νίκην ὡμοίωσά σε, ἡ πλησίον μου.

ἡ δῆλόν ἐστιν ὅτι ὥσπερ οὐκ ἔστι διὰ ναυμαχίας ἡττηθῆναί τινας μὴ
ναυτικοῦ στρατοῦ τὴν ἐν ταῖς ναυσὶ τῶν ἐναντίων δύναμιν καταδύσαντος,
5   οὕτως οὐδὲ ἂν ἐν ἱππομαχίᾳ τις ἡττηθείη μή τινος | ἱππικῆς ἐκ τῶν ἐναντίων   74
ἀντιταχθείσης δυνάμεως; ἐπειδὴ τοίνυν τὸ κράτιστον τῆς τῶν Αἰγυπτίων
στρατιᾶς ἡ ἵππος ἦν, τὴν ἐπαχθεῖσαν αὐτῇ κατὰ τὸ ἀόρατον δύναμιν, δι᾽ ἧς ἡ
νίκη κατὰ τῶν Αἰγυπτίων ἐγένετο, ἵππον ὁ λόγος ὠνόμασεν· ᾐσθάνοντο γὰρ
κἀκεῖνοι τοῦ πολεμοῦντος καὶ πρὸς ἀλλήλους ἐβόων Κύριος πολεμεῖ τοὺς
10   Αἰγυπτίους καὶ Φύγωμεν ἀπὸ προσώπου κυρίου. δῆλον δὲ ὅτι καταλλήλως
τῇ παρασκευῇ τῶν ἐναντίων ὁ ἀληθινὸς ἀρχιστράτηγος τὴν ἰδίαν ἀνθώπλιζε
δύναμιν. οὐκοῦν ἦν τις ἀόρατος δύναμις ἡ διὰ τῶν περὶ τὴν θάλασσαν
θαυμάτων ἐνεργοῦσα τῶν Αἰγυπτίων τὸν ὄλεθρον, ἣν ἵππον ὁ λόγος
ὠνόμασεν.

15   ἀγγελικὴν δὲ στρατιὰν εἶναι ταύτην ὑπονοοῦμεν, περὶ ἧς φησιν ὁ
προφήτης ὅτι Ἐπιβήσῃ ἐπὶ τοὺς ἵππους σου, καὶ ἡ ἱππασία σου σωτηρία.
ἀλλὰ καὶ ἅρματος θεοῦ μνήμην ὁ Δαβὶδ ἐποιήσατο λέγων Τὸ ἅρμα τοῦ θεοῦ
μυριοπλάσιον, ᾧ ὑποζεύγνυνται τῶν εὐθηνούντων αἱ χιλιάδες. ἔτι δὲ καὶ ἡ τὸν
προφήτην Ἡλίαν μετάρσιον ἐκ γῆς ἐπὶ τὸν αἰθέριον χῶρον ἀναλαμβάνουσα
20   δύναμις τῷ τῶν ἵππων ὀνόματι παρὰ τῆς γραφῆς ὀνομάζεται καὶ αὐτὸν δὲ τὸν
προφήτην ἅρμα λέγει τοῦ Ἰσραὴλ καὶ ἱππέα ἡ ἱστορία καὶ τοὺς περιοδεύοντας
πᾶσαν τὴν οἰκουμένην, | δι᾽ ὧν ἡ γῆ κατοικίζεται καὶ ἡσυχάζει, Ζαχαρίας ὁ   75
προφήτης ἵππους ὠνόμασε διαλεγομένους πρὸς τὸν ἄνθρωπον τὸν μέσον
ἑστῶτα τῶν δύο ὁρῶν.

ened by the text. For it says: *I have likened you, my close one, to my horse* that achieved victory *among the chariots of Pharaoh.*

Surely, though, it is plain that, just as it is not possible for any fleet to be worsted in naval combat unless a fighting force has overcome the troops aboard the ships of its enemy, by the same token no one would be worsted in a cavalry battle unless an | opposing cavalry force had been arrayed against him. Since, then, the mightiest element in the Egyptian army was the horse, our text uses the term *horse* to refer to the invisible force by which victory was gained over the Egyptians. For those Egyptians also sensed the presence of this Fighter and cried out to one another, "The Lord fights against the Egyptians," and "Let us flee from the face of the Lord" (cf. Exod 14:25). Obviously, the true General of the armies outfitted forces of his own to meet the enemy array. It was, therefore, some invisible force that worked the destruction of the Egyptians through the marvels at the sea—and that the text calls *horse.*

My surmise is that this cavalry was the angelic host[4] of which the prophet says, "You will mount upon your horses, and your cavalry is salvation" (Hab 3:8).[5] David also mentioned God's chariot: "The chariot of God is ten-thousand-fold, to which thousands of thriving beasts are yoked" (Ps 67:18). Furthermore, the power that took the prophet Elijah up from the earth to the ethereal realm[6] is called "horses" by the Scripture, and the narrative calls the prophet himself "chariot of Israel" and "horseman" (4 Kgdms 2:12). And the prophet Zechariah called those who go about the inhabited world, | by whom the earth is settled and pacified, "horses" as they discoursed with the man who stood in the midst of the two mountains (Zech 1:8, 10).

---

4. Origen has the same exegetical problem as Gregory, that of identifying this "horse" of which no mention is made in Exodus. He and Gregory also make the same tacit assumption, that the exodus from Egypt is a historical symbol of Christian baptism. They differ, however, about the "horse." Origen concludes that "horse" is an allusion to "those souls who accept the bridle of his discipline, and bear the yoke of his sweetness, and are led by the Spirit of God"(Baehrens 1925, 151; trans. Lawson 1956, 141), and then, on the basis of the white horse of Rev 19:11–21, as the church, "since she, whom he has sanctified for himself by the laver of water, has neither spot nor wrinkle" (Baehrens 1925, 152; Lawson 1956, 142). Gregory disagrees in part with this line because he thinks that the Scriptures presuppose the existence of more than one sort of divine "horse," a point he makes in this and the next paragraphs.

5. Origen also quotes this text (Baehrens 1925, 151.20–22), as well as the passage below from 1 Kingdoms, but the others Nyssen has culled for himself, no doubt to show the different kinds of divine "horse" of which the Scriptures speak.

6. This refers to the region of the cosmos occupied by Aristotle's famous "fifth element," whose natural motion was circular and which therefore constituted the stuff of the heavens from the moon up: cf. *Cael.* 1.2 (269a20ff.). See also Philo, *Conf.* 156; Diogenes Laertius, *Lives of the Philosophers* 7.139.

οὐκοῦν ἔστι τις ἵππος τῷ τὸ πᾶν κεκτημένῳ· ἡ μὲν τὸν προφήτην ἀνάγουσα, ἡ δὲ τὴν οἰκουμένην οἰκίζουσα, ἡ δὲ ὑποζευγνυμένη τῷ ἅρματι, ἄλλη δὲ τὸν θεὸν ἔποχον ἐπὶ σωτηρίᾳ τῶν ἀνθρώπων λαμβάνουσα, ἄλλη δὲ τὴν Αἰγυπτίαν καταδύουσα δύναμιν.

5 πολλῆς τοίνυν οὔσης ἐν ταῖς θείαις ἵπποις τῆς διὰ τῶν ἐνεργειῶν φαινομένης διαφορᾶς τῇ καθαιρετικῇ τῆς Αἰγυπτίας δυνάμεως ἵππῳ παρεικάζεται ἡ διὰ τοῦ δρόμου τῆς ἀρετῆς τῷ θεῷ πλησιάσασα· οὕτω γάρ φησι πρὸς αὐτὴν ὁ λόγος ὅτι Τῇ ἵππῳ μου ἐν ἅρμασι Φαραὼ ὡμοίωσά σε, ἡ πλησίον μου.

πολλοὺς δὲ καὶ μεγάλους ἐπαίνους ὁ λόγος ἐν ἑαυτῷ περιείληφε καί τις
10 κατορθωμάτων κατάλογός ἐστιν ἡ πρὸς τὴν ἵππον ταύτην ὁμοίωσις· ὅσα γὰρ τοῦ Ἰσραὴλ ἐν τῇ παροικίᾳ τῶν Αἰγυπτίων μνημονεύεται, ἡ δουλεία, ἡ καλάμη, ὁ πηλός, ἡ πλινθεία, πᾶσα ἡ περὶ τὴν γῆν ἀσχολία, οἱ χαλεποὶ τῶν τοιούτων ἔργων ἐπιστάται, οἱ τὸν πήλινον αὐτοὺς καθ᾽ ἑκάστην ἡμέραν ἀπαιτοῦντες φόρον, δι᾽ οὓς τὸ ὕδωρ αἷμα γίνεται καὶ τὸ φῶς σκοτίζεται καὶ
15 βάτραχοι τοῖς οἴκοις | εἰσέρπουσι καὶ ἡ καμιναία κόνις τὰς φλυκτίδας ἐκ τῶν   76
σωμάτων ἀναζέειν ποιεῖ, καὶ τὰ καθ᾽ ἕκαστον πάντα, ἡ ἀκρίς, οἱ σκνῖπες, ὁ βροῦχος, ἡ χάλαζα, τῶν πρωτοτόκων τὰ πάθη, πάντα ταῦτα καὶ ὅσα πρὸς τὸ κρεῖττον ἡ ἱστορία διέξεισι, δι᾽ ὧν γίνεται τοῖς Ἰσραηλίταις ἡ σωτηρία, ἐπαίνων ἐστὶν ὑπόθεσις τῇ τῷ θεῷ συναπτομένῃ ψυχῇ· οὐ γὰρ ἂν ὡμοιώθη
20 τῇ δυνάμει ἐκείνῃ τῇ καθαιρετικῇ τῶν Αἰγυπτίων κακῶν, δι᾽ ἧς ἐλευθεροῦται ὁ Ἰσραὴλ τῆς πονηρᾶς τυραννίδος, εἰ μὴ πάντα ταῦτα καὶ ταύτῃ κατώρθωτο τά τε καθαιρετικὰ τῆς Αἰγύπτου καὶ τὰ παρασκευαστικὰ τῆς πρὸς τὸν θεὸν πορείας τῶν μετοικιζομένων πρὸς τὴν γῆν τῆς ἐπαγγελίας ἀπὸ τῆς Αἰγυπτίας ἰλύος. οὐκοῦν ἐπειδή, καθώς φησιν ὁ θεῖος ἀπόστολος, πάντα πρὸς νουθεσίαν
25 ἡμῶν ἀναγέγραπται, ὅσα ἡ θεόπνευστος περιέχει γραφή, οὐδὲν ἄλλο ἢ συμβουλεύει διὰ τῶν πρὸς τὴν νύμφην εἰρημένων ὁ λόγος ἡμῖν ὅτι χρὴ καὶ ἡμᾶς ἔποχον δεξαμένους ἐφ᾽ ἑαυτῶν τὸν λόγον καὶ καταγωνισαμένους τὴν Αἰγυπτίαν ἵππον αὐτοῖς ἅρμασι καὶ ἀναβάταις καὶ πᾶσαν αὐτῶν τὴν πονηρὰν

There is, then, a cavalry that belongs to the One who possesses the universe: on the one hand, it takes the prophet up on high; on the other, it colonizes the inhabited earth; then it is yoked to the chariot; and there is one troop that bears God mounted upon it for the salvation of humanity and another that drowns the forces of the Egyptians. Given, then, that there are significant differences of function among God's cavalries, differences that are marked by their varying activities, the Bride who has come close[7] to God by running the race of virtue is likened to that body of horse that destroyed the Egyptian force. That is why the Word says to her, *I have likened you, my close one, to my horse among the chariots of Pharaoh.*

Now this statement contains a plethora of high praises, and the likening of the Bride to this troop of horse amounts to a catalogue of great and righteous deeds. For whatever calls to mind Israel in its Egyptian sojourn—slavery, straw, clay, brickmaking, all the hard work of husbandry, the harsh overseers of such tasks, who demand a daily tribute of bricks from the Israelites and on whose account the water becomes blood and the light is darkened and frogs creep into the houses | and the dust of the furnace makes boils grow out on bodies, and there come all the individual plagues: the grasshopper, the gnats, the locust, the hail, the sufferings of the firstborn—all of these, and whatever the history recounts of happier events through which salvation comes to the Israelites, represent a ground on which praises can be accorded the soul that cleaves to God. For she would not have been likened to the force that destroyed the evil of the Egyptians and liberated Israel from the wicked tyrant unless all these things had been successfully accomplished in her case—both those by which Egypt was destroyed and those that enabled the people who were migrating from the slime of Egypt toward the land of promise to journey toward God. Since, therefore, as the divine apostle says, everything in the inspired Scriptures is written for "our admonition," this passage does nothing but counsel us, through the words spoken to the Bride, that we, who have accepted the Word as our own Rider[8] and have prevailed against the Egyptian cavalry by means of the same chariots and riders and have drowned all their

---

7. One must remember that, in the verse under consideration here (Song 1:9b), the Bridegroom refers to the Bride as "my close one" (ἡ πλησίον μου).

8. Cf. Origen (Baehrens 1925, 152.24; 153.4; trans. Lawson 1956, 143), for whom, however, it is above all the church, the body of the baptized, that is ridden by the Word of God. Nyssen thus ends up sounding the same themes as Origen but with the insistence that the successful traversing of the Red Sea—i.e., baptism—requires the assistance of the heavenly host, to which the Bride is compared.

δυναστείαν τῷ ὕδατι καταπνίξαντας οὕτως ὁμοιωθῆναι τῇ δυνάμει ἐκείνῃ
καθάπερ τινὰ ῥύπον τὴν ἀντικειμένην στρατιὰν ἐναφέντας τῷ | ὕδατι.   77
ὡς δ' ἂν σαφέστερον μάθοιμεν τὸ λεγόμενον, τοιοῦτόν ἐστιν· οὐκ
ἔστιν ὁμοιωθῆναι τῇ ἵππῳ, δι' ἧς τὰ ἅρματα τῶν Αἰγυπτίων τῷ βυθῷ
5   κατεποντίσθη, εἰ μή τις διὰ τοῦ μυστικοῦ ὕδατος τῆς τοῦ ἀντικειμένου
δουλείας ἐλευθερούμενος πᾶν Αἰγυπτιάζον νόημα καὶ πᾶσαν ἀλλόφυλον
κακίαν τε καὶ ἁμαρτίαν <ἐν> τῷ ὕδατι καταλιπὼν καθαρὸς ἀναδύῃ μηδὲν
τῆς Αἰγυπτίας συνειδήσεως τῷ μετὰ ταῦτα βίῳ συνεπαγόμενος· ὁ γὰρ
ἀκριβῶς πασῶν καθαρεύσας τῶν Αἰγυπτίων πληγῶν, αἵματος καὶ βατράχων
10   καὶ φλυκτίδων καὶ σκότους, ἀκρίδος τε καὶ σκνιπῶν καὶ χαλάζης καὶ τῆς τοῦ
πυρὸς ἐπομβρίας καὶ τῶν λοιπῶν, ὧν ὁ τῆς ἱστορίας μέμνηται λόγος, οὗτος
ἄξιός ἐστιν ὁμοιωθῆναι τῇ δυνάμει ἐκείνῃ, ἧς ἔποχος ὁ λόγος γίνεται.
πάντως δὲ οὐκ ἀγνοοῦμεν τὰ διὰ τῶν πληγῶν σημαινόμενα, πῶς γίνεται
τοῖς Αἰγυπτίοις τὸ αἷμα πληγὴ καὶ ἡ τῶν βατράχων ὀσμὴ καὶ ἡ τοῦ φωτὸς
15   εἰς τὸ σκότος μεταβολὴ καὶ τὰ καθ' ἕκαστον πάντα. τίς γὰρ οὐκ οἶδε, διὰ
ποταποῦ βίου αἷμά τις γίνεται ἐκ ποτίμου τοῦ πρότερον εἰς διαφθορὰν
ἀλλοιούμενος καὶ τί ποιῶν ζωογονεῖ τῷ ἰδίῳ οἴκῳ τὴν τῶν βατράχων
δυσωδίαν καὶ πῶς μεταποιεῖ τὸν φωτεινὸν βίον εἰς ἔργα νυκτὶ φίλα καὶ
ζοφώδη, δι' ὧν ἡ τῆς γεέννης κάμινος τὰς πονηρὰς τῆς κατακρίσεως
20   φλυκτίδας ἀναζέειν ποιεῖ; οὕτω δὲ καὶ τὰ καθ' ἕκαστον τῶν ἐν Αἰγύπτῳ
κακῶν ῥάδιον μεταλαβεῖν εἰς παίδευσίν τε καὶ σωφρονισμὸν τοῦ ἀκούοντος,
ἀλλὰ περιττὸν | ἂν εἴη μηκύνειν διὰ τῶν ὁμολογουμένων τὸν λόγον.   78
τούτων τοίνυν καὶ τῶν τοιούτων κρείττους γενόμενοι καὶ τῷ θεῷ
πλησιάσαντες καὶ αὐτοὶ πάντως ἀκουσόμεθα ὅτι Τῇ ἵππῳ μου ἐν ἅρμασι
25   Φαραὼ ὡμοίωσά σε, ἡ πλησίον μου.
Ἀλλὰ λυπεῖ τυχὸν τοὺς τὸν σώφρονα καὶ καθαρὸν ἐξησκηκότας βίον ἡ
πρὸς τὸν ἵππον ὁμοίωσις, διότι πολλοὶ τῶν προφητῶν ἀπαγορεύουσιν ἡμῖν
τὸ ὁμοιοῦσθαι τοῖς ἵπποις, τοῦ μὲν Ἱερεμίου τὴν μοιχικὴν λύσσαν τῷ ὀνόματι
τῶν ἵππων διασημάναντος, ἐν οἷς φησιν Ἵπποι θηλυμανεῖς ἐγενήθησαν,
30   ἕκαστος ἐπὶ τὴν γυναῖκα τοῦ πλησίον αὐτοῦ ἐχρεμέτιζεν, τοῦ δὲ μεγάλου
Δαβὶδ φοβερὸν ποιουμένου τὸ ὡς ἵππον τινὰ καὶ ἡμίονον γίνεσθαι, ὧν κελεύει
κατάγχειν ἐν κημῷ τε καὶ χαλινῷ τὰς σιαγόνας. διὰ τοῦτο παραμυθεῖται
τῷ ἐφεξῆς λόγῳ τὴν τοιαύτην διάνοιαν λέγων ὅτι οὐ τοιαῦταί σού εἰσιν αἱ
σιαγόνες, κἂν ἵππος ᾖς, ὡς κημοῦ χρῄζειν καὶ χαλινοῦ εἰς ἀγχόνην, ἀλλά σοι
35

evil power in the water,[9] should in this way be made like that Power, having left the opposing host, like some impurity, behind in | the water.

But so that we may the more clearly understand what is meant, it is something like this: one cannot become like the horse by which the chariots of the Egyptians were plunged into the deep unless, liberated by the mystical water from the enemy's enslavement, one leaves behind in the water every Egyptianizing thought and every alien sin and evil and rises up purified, bringing along in one's subsequent life nothing of the Egyptian self-awareness. For the person who has been completely cleansed of the Egyptian plagues— the blood and the frogs and the boils and the darkness; the locust and the gnats and the hail and the rain of fire and the rest of the things that the story mentions—this person is worthy to be likened to that power on which the Word is mounted.

Above all, we are not ignorant of what the plagues signify, of how it is that blood becomes a plague to the Egyptians, and the smell of frogs as well, and the changing of light into darkness, and all the other particular afflictions. For who does not know what sort of life it takes to turn someone into blood and turn what once was potable water into corruption? Or what deeds it is that one does to produce a stink of frogs in his own house? Or how one transforms the light-filled life into dark works that love the night and on whose account the furnace of Gehenna causes the evil boils of condemnation to burst out? Thus each of the evils that happened in Egypt is easily transposed into instruction and moral tutelage for the hearer, but it |would be excessive to stretch out our discourse with things that everyone acknowledges.

So when we have become better than these things and others like them and have come close to God we ourselves will certainly hear: *I have likened you, my close one, to my horse among the chariots of Pharaoh.*

This comparison to a body of horse, though, may trouble those who have exercised themselves in the pure and temperate life, since many of the prophets forbid us to become like horses. Jeremiah uses *horse* to refer to adulterous mania when he says: "You have become lustful horses; each of you neighed after his neighbor's wife" (Jer 5:8). And the great David thinks it a fearsome thing for someone to become like a horse or a mule, whose jaws he orders to be restrained by muzzle and bit (Ps 31:9). That is why the next statement qualifies this comparison when it says, "*Your jaws* are not such as they would be if you were a horse, so as to need restraint by muzzle and bit, but yours is

---

9. This is the point at which it becomes clear that Gregory, like Origen, has been interpreting this verse with the baptisms of the members of his audience in mind, for the water mentioned in this sentence is plainly the water of baptism, of which the Red Sea is a type.

διὰ τῆς καθαρότητος τῶν τρυγόνων ἡ σιαγὼν καλλωπίζεται. φησὶ γὰρ Τί ὡραιώθησαν σιαγόνες σου ὡς τρυγόνος;

μαρτυρεῖται δὲ παρὰ τῶν τὰ | τοιαῦτα τετηρηκότων τοῦτο τὸ ὄρνεον   79
μένειν, εἰ διαζευχθείη τῆς συζυγίας, εἰς τὸ ἐφεξῆς ἀσυνδύαστον, ὡς φυσικῶς
5   ἐν αὐτῷ κατορθοῦσθαι τὴν σωφροσύνην. διὰ τοῦτο τῷ αἰνίγματι τῶν ἐπαίνων
συμπαρελήφθη ὑπὸ τοῦ λόγου τοῦτο τὸ ὄρνεον, ὡς ἀντὶ χαλινοῦ γενέσθαι
τῇ σιαγόνι τῆς θείας ἵππου τὴν τῆς τρυγόνος ὁμοίωσιν, δι᾽ ἧς ἡ καθαρὰ ζωὴ
ἐπιπρέπειν τῇ τοιαύτῃ ἵππῳ διασημαίνεται.

διὸ θαυμαστικῶς φησι πρὸς αὐτὴν ὁ λόγος Τί ὡραιώθησαν σιαγόνες
10   σου ὡς τρυγόνος. Ἐπάγει δὲ τούτῳ καὶ ἕτερον δι᾽ ὁμοιώσεως ἔπαινον λέγων
Τράχηλός σου ὡς ὁρμίσκοι. ἅπαξ γὰρ ἐμπεσὼν τῇ τροπικῇ σημασίᾳ διὰ τῶν
περὶ τῶν ἵππων θεωρουμένων ἐπινοεῖ τῇ νύμφῃ τὸν ἔπαινον· ἐπαινεῖ γὰρ
τὸν τράχηλον τὸν ἐν σχήματι κύκλου γυρούμενον, ὃ δὴ περὶ τοὺς γαύρους
τῶν πώλων ὁρῶμεν γινόμενον· ἡ γὰρ τῶν ὁρμίσκων μνήμη τὸν κύκλον
15   ἐνδείκνυται, οὗ τὸ σχῆμα ἐπὶ τοῦ αὐχένος δεικνύμενον εὐπρεπέστερον
ἑαυτοῦ τὸν πῶλον ποιεῖ.

ὅρμος δὲ λέγεται κυρίως μὲν ἐπὶ τῶν παραλίων τόπων, ἐν οἷς ἡ ὄχθη
κατὰ τὸ ἐντὸς μηνοειδῶς κοιλανθεῖσα ὑποδέχεται τῷ κόλπῳ τὴν θάλασσαν
καὶ ἀναπαύει δι᾽ ἑαυτῆς τοὺς ἐκ τοῦ πελάγους προσπλέοντας, ἐκ μεταφορᾶς
20   δὲ διὰ τοῦ σχήματος | ὁ περιτραχήλιος κόσμος ὅρμος λέγεται. ὅταν δὲ   80
ὑποκοριστικῶς ὁρμίσκον ἀντὶ ὅρμου λέγωμεν, τὴν ἐν ὀλίγῳ τοῦ σχήματος
ὁμοιότητα διὰ τῆς τοιαύτης φωνῆς ἐνδεικνύμεθα.

πολλὰ τοίνυν εἰς ἐγκώμια συντελοῦντα τῇ νύμφῃ ἡ πρὸς τοὺς ὁρμίσκους
ὁμοιότης τοῦ τραχήλου ἐνδείκνυται·

25   πρῶτον μὲν ὅτι εἰς κύκλου σχῆμα κάμπτων ὁ πῶλος τὸν αὐχένα πρὸς τὰς
ἰδίας τῶν ποδῶν βάσεις ὁρᾷ, δι᾽ ὧν ἀπρόσκοπόν τε καὶ ἀσφαλῆ ποιεῖται τὸν
δρόμον μήτε τῷ λίθῳ προσπταίων μήτε κενεμβατῶν ἐν τῷ βόθρῳ (τοῦτο δὲ
οὐ μικρὸν εἰς εὐφημίαν ἐστὶ ψυχῆς τὸ πρὸς ἑαυτὴν βλέπειν καὶ δι᾽ ἀσφαλείας

the *cheek*[10] of turtledoves, made beautiful by purity."[11] For the text reads: *Why are your cheeks made beauteous like a dove's?*

It is testified by those who have observed | such things that if this bird has been separated from its mate, it remains without one, as though temperance just naturally had its way with it.[12] That is why this bird is introduced by the Word into the enigma of the praises, and it turns out that the jaw of the divine horse has, not a bit, but the likeness of the turtledove, which shows that the pure life is proper to a horse of this sort.

To this there is added still another word of praise in the form of a simile when it says, *Your neck is like circlets.* For having once fallen into figurative speech with the allegorical treatment of horses, he contrives a compliment for the Bride. He praises the neck that is bent in the shape of a curve, as we see happening in the play of young colts.[13] For the mention of *circlets* indicates something that is round, whose shape, exhibited in the neck, renders the colt more handsome than itself.[14]

The word "circle,"[15] though, is used mostly to refer to places along the seashore where the cliff, hollowed out in the shape of a crescent, receives the sea in its bosom and offers haven to those who approach it from the ocean. Yet | an adornment of the neck is called a "circle" metaphorically because of its shape, and when, using a diminutive, we say "circlet" instead of "circle," we indicate, by this way of talking, a small-scale likeness to this shape.

The comparison of her neck to "circlets," then, indicates many things that go to make up praise for the Bride.

First of all, there is the fact that the colt that bends its neck into the shape of a round curve is looking to the proper places for its feet. In this way, it makes its running safe and free of stumbling, since it neither hurts itself on a stone nor stumbles in a hole. And it is no small praise for the soul that she looks to herself and hastens her running toward the Divine by taking every

---

10. Gregory's thought here turns on the fact that the Greek σιαγών ("cheek") literally refers to a jaw or jawbone.

11. Cf. Origen, *Comm. Cant.* 2.6 (Baehrens 1925, 155; trans. Lawson 1956, 146), for whom also the Bride's cheek signifies "those members of the church who cultivate the integrity of chastity and virtue."

12. This idea is apparently taken over from Origen, *Comm. Cant.* 2.6 (Baehrens 1925, 155; trans. Lawson 1956, 146).

13. The appeal to the appearance of leaping colts is of course an extension of the earlier figure of the Bride as "horse."

14. That is to say, the praise of the Bride's neck intimated by the word "circlets" (ὁρμίσκοι) marks a further step in the soul's progress in perfection: she becomes better than her (previous) self.

15. I.e., ὅρμος, of which ὁρμίσκοι is, Gregory says, a diminutive.

πάσης πρὸς τὸν θεῖον δρόμον ἐπείγεσθαι πάντα τὰ ἐκ πειρασμῶν τινων
ἐγγινόμενα πρὸς τὸν δρόμον ἐμπόδια διαλλομένην καὶ ὑπερβαίνουσαν),
   ἔπειτα δὲ καὶ αὐτὸ τὸ πρωτότυπον τῶν ὅρμων ὄνομα, ὅθεν διὰ τὴν
τοῦ σχήματος ὁμοιότητα ὁ περιδέραιος κόσμος ὁρμίσκος ὠνόμασται,
5   μεγάλων τινῶν ἐγκωμίων ὑπερβολὴν περιέχει, ὅταν ὁμοιωθῇ τοῖς ὁρμίσκοις
ὁ τράχηλος. τίνα δέ ἐστι τὰ ἐγκώμια τὰ διὰ τούτων ἡμῖν ὑπὸ τοῦ λόγου
δηλούμενα;
   ἡδύ τι καὶ σωτήριόν ἐστι τοῖς καταπλέουσιν ὁ λιμὴν καὶ τὸ μετὰ τὴν
ἐν θαλάσσῃ κακοπάθειαν ὅρμον τινὰ καταλαβεῖν εὐδιάζοντα, ἐν ᾧ λήθην
10   ποιησάμενοι τῶν ἐν θαλάσσῃ κακῶν ὅλοι τῆς ἀναπαύσεως γίνονται τοὺς
μακροὺς πόνους δι᾽ ἡσυχίας | παραμυθούμενοι. οὐκ ἔστιν αὐτοῖς οὐκέτι   81
ναυαγίου φόβος οὔτε ἡ τῶν ὑφάλων ὑπόνοια οὔτε πειρατῶν κίνδυνος οὔτε
πνευμάτων ταραχὴ οὔτε ἐκ βυθῶν ἀνοιδαίνει διὰ τῶν ἀνέμων ἡ θάλασσα,
ἀλλὰ πάντων τῶν τοιούτων κινδύνων ἐκτὸς γίνονται οἱ χειμαζόμενοι τοῦ
15   πελάγους ἐν τῷ ὅρμῳ γαληνιάζοντες. εἰ τοίνυν οὕτω τις τὴν ἑαυτοῦ ψυχὴν
καταστήσειεν, ὡς αὐτήν τε γαλήνην ἔχειν ἐν ἀκύμονι τῇ ἡσυχίᾳ μηδὲν
παρακινουμένην ἐκ τῶν πνευμάτων τῆς πονηρίας μήτε δι᾽ ὑπερηφανίας
οἰδαίνουσαν μήτε τοῖς τοῦ θυμοῦ κύμασιν ἐξαφρίζουσαν μήτε κατ᾽ ἄλλο τι
πάθος κλυδωνιζομένην καὶ περιφερομένην παντὶ ἀνέμῳ τῷ τὰ ποικίλα κύματα
20   τῶν παθημάτων ἐγείροντι, εἰ τοίνυν αὐτή τε οὕτως ἔχοι καὶ τοὺς ἐν τῷ πελάγει
τοῦ βίου χειμαζομένους ἐν ταῖς παντοδαπαῖς τῶν κακῶν τρικυμίαις ἐν ἑαυτῇ
καταστέλλοι λείαν αὐτοῖς καὶ ἀκύμαντον τὴν δι᾽ ἀρετῆς ζωὴν ὑφαπλώσασα,
ὥστε τοὺς ἐν αὐτῇ γεγονότας ἐκτὸς γενέσθαι τῶν ἐκ ναυαγίου κακῶν,
καλῶς ὑπὸ τοῦ λόγου τοῖς ὁρμίσκοις ὁμοιοῦται τῆς πληθυντικῆς σημασίας
25   τὴν ἐν ἑκάστῳ εἴδει τῆς ἀρετῆς τελειότητα σημαινούσης· εἰ γὰρ ἦν ἑνὶ μόνῳ
προσεικασμένη ὁρμίσκῳ, ἀτελὴς ἂν πάντως ὁ ἔπαινος ἦν ὡς οὐ τὴν αὐτὴν | 82
καὶ ἐπὶ τῶν λοιπῶν ἀρετῶν μαρτυρίαν ἔχων· νῦν δὲ πασῶν συλλαμβάνει τῷ
λόγῳ τῶν ἀρετῶν τὴν μαρτυρίαν ἡ πρὸς τὸ πλῆθος τῶν ὁρμίσκων ὁμοίωσις.
   καὶ τοῦτο συμβουλή τίς ἐστι παρὰ τοῦ λόγου τῷ κοινῷ τῆς ἐκκλησίας
30   προσαγομένη τὸ μὴ δεῖν ἡμᾶς πρὸς ἕν τι τῶν ἀγαθῶν βλέποντας ἀμελῶς περὶ
τὰ λοιπὰ τῶν κατορθωμάτων ἔχειν, ἀλλ᾽ εἴ σοι γέγονεν ὅρμος ἡ σωφροσύνη
καθάπερ τισὶ μαργαρίταις τῷ καθαρῷ βίῳ λαμπρύνων τὸν τράχηλον, ἔστω
σοι καὶ ἕτερος ὅρμος ὁ τοὺς τιμίους λίθους τῶν ἐντολῶν ἐν ἑαυτῷ περιείργων
<ζῆλος> καὶ δι᾽ ἑαυτοῦ τῆς δέρης πλεονάζων τὸ κάλλος, ἔστω σοι καὶ ἄλλος
35   κόσμος περιαυχένιος ἡ εὐσεβής τε καὶ ὑγιαίνουσα πίστις κύκλῳ τὸν τῆς

care as she overleaps and transcends all the obstacles that beset her course because of the trials that come her way.

Then too the original word "circle" itself—by derivation from which, because of a similarity in shape, a necklace is called "circlet"—contains a superabundance of great compliments, given that the neck has been likened to a "circlet." But then what are the praises that our text thus opens up for us?

For those who are putting in to shore, the circle of the harbor is a thing of pleasure and safety—as also it is to reach a calm haven after troubles on the sea. There they contrive to forget the voyage's hardships and are wholly at rest and find relief from their great labors in quiet.[16] | No longer are they afraid of shipwreck, or suspicious of the deeps, or in danger from pirates, or tossed by winds; nor does the sea swell up from the depths because of gales. No, those who are storm-tossed on the sea find exemption from all such dangers as they repose in the harbor's circle. If, then, a person so establishes her soul that by reason of inner calm she has repose in stillness, being in no wise disturbed by the winds of evil, nor swelling with arrogance, nor foamed up by the waves of anger, nor, in obedience to some other affliction, tossed and carried about by every wind that raises the many waves of the passions—if, I say, she is in this state and within herself reduces to order whatever there is upon the sea of life that is distressed by the many billows of its evils because she has spread beneath them, smooth and undisturbed, the life of virtue, so that those who have entered her are removed from the troubles of shipwreck, then she is rightly likened by our text to *circlets*. The plural form of the word denotes perfection in each kind of virtue, for if she were likened only to a single circlet, the praise would be incomplete, since it would not contain the very same testimony | with regard to the rest of the virtues. As it is, however, the comparison to a multitude of circlets comprises in the statement a testimony to all the virtues.

Now this is a piece of advice addressed by our text to the general membership of the church. It instructs us that we must not focus attention on one good thing and be careless of other righteous actions; but if self-control is your "circle" and adorns your neck with purity of life as with a string of pearls, wear another necklace too: that zeal that bears the precious stones of the commandments and increases the beauty of the throat by its presence. And have yet another adornment for your neck: that religious and healthful

---

16. The Greek word here is ἡσυχία, and it recurs just below as (in English) "stillness." Such quiet or tranquility or (sometimes) interior silence, which is clearly the theme or subject of this paragraph, was understood to be a state in which the passions and the inward chatter of the mind are stilled and the individual can achieve a degree of contemplation.

ψυχῆς αὐχένα διαλαμβάνουσα. οὗτός ἐστιν ὁ κλοιὸς ὁ χρύσεος ὁ ἐκ τοῦ
ἀκηράτου τῆς θεογνωσίας χρυσίου τῷ τραχήλῳ περιλαμπόμενος, περὶ οὗ
φησιν ἡ Παροιμία ὅτι Στέφανον χαρίτων δέξῃ σῇ κορυφῇ καὶ κλοιὸν χρύσεον
περὶ σῷ τραχήλῳ.

5   Ἡ μὲν οὖν διὰ τῶν ὁρμίσκων συμβουλὴ τοιαύτη, καιρὸς δ᾽ ἂν εἴη καὶ
τὸν ἐφεξῆς λόγον προσθεῖναι τῇ θεωρίᾳ, ὃν οἱ φίλοι τοῦ νυμφίου πρὸς τὴν
παρθένον πεποίηνται. | ἔστι δὲ ἡ λέξις αὕτη· Ὁμοιώματα χρυσίου ποιήσομέν   83
σοι μετὰ στιγμάτων τοῦ ἀργυρίου, ἕως οὗ ὁ βασιλεὺς ἐν ἀνακλίσει αὐτοῦ.

       τούτων δὲ τῷ μὲν πρὸς τὸν εἱρμὸν βλέποντι τῆς προαποδοθείσης ἡμῖν
10   θεωρίας δοκεῖ πως ἡ διάνοια συνηρτῆσθαι καὶ τὸ ἀκόλουθον ἔχειν, ἡ δὲ λέξις
ἐμβαθύνουσα ταῖς τροπικαῖς σημασίαις δυσκατανόητον ποιεῖ τὸ διὰ τῶν
αἰνιγμάτων δηλούμενον.

       ἐπειδὴ γὰρ τὸ τῆς ψυχῆς κάλλος τῇ ἵππῳ τῇ καθαιρετικῇ τῶν Αἰγυπτίων
ἁρμάτων ἀφωμοιώθη (τουτέστι τῇ ἀγγελικῇ στρατιᾷ), τῇ δὲ ἵππῳ ἐκείνῃ
15   φησὶν ὁ καλὸς ἐπιβάτης χαλινὸν μὲν εἶναι τὴν καθαρότητα, ἣν διὰ τοῦ
ὁμοιῶσαι τὰς σιαγόνας ταῖς τῆς τρυγόνος ἐσήμανε, κόσμον δὲ περιαυχένιον
τοὺς ποικίλους ὅρμους τοὺς διὰ τῶν ἀρετῶν περιστίλβοντας, βούλονταί τινα
καὶ οἱ φίλοι προσθήκην τῷ κάλλει τῆς ἵππου ποιήσασθαι ἐξ ὁμοιωμάτων
χρυσίου κατακοσμοῦντες τὰ φάλαρα, οἷς ἐνστίζουσι καὶ τοῦ ἀργυρίου τὴν
20   καθαρότητα, ὡς ἂν μᾶλλον διαλάμποι τὸ κάλλος τοῦ προκοσμήματος τῆς
αὐγῆς τοῦ ἀργυρίου πρὸς τὴν λαμπηδόνα τοῦ χρυσίου συγκιρναμένης.

       ἀναγκαῖον δ᾽ ἂν εἴη τὰς τροπικὰς | ἐμφάσεις καταλιπόντας τῆς   84
ὠφελούσης ἡμᾶς διανοίας μὴ ἀποστῆσαι τὸν λόγον.

       προσεικάσθη μὲν ἐκείνη τῇ ἵππῳ ἡ διὰ τῶν ἀρετῶν κεκαθαρμένη ψυχή·
25   ἀλλ᾽ οὔπω τοῦ λόγου γέγονεν ὑποχείριος οὐδὲ ἐβάσταξεν ἐφ᾽ ἑαυτῆς τὸν ἐπὶ
σωτηρίᾳ τοῖς τοιούτοις ἐποχούμενον ἵπποις· χρὴ γὰρ πρῶτον διὰ πάντων
κατακοσμηθῆναι τὸν ἵππον, εἶθ᾽ οὕτω τὸν βασιλέα ἔποχον δέξασθαι. εἴτε
δὲ ἄνωθεν ἑαυτῷ ἐφαρμόζοι τὸν ἵππον ὁ κατὰ τὸν προφήτην ἐπιβαίνων ἐφ᾽
ἡμᾶς τοὺς ἵππους καὶ ἐπὶ σωτηρίᾳ ἡμῶν ἐφ᾽ ἡμῶν ἱππαζόμενος, εἴτε καὶ ἐν
30   ἡμῖν γένοιτο ὁ ἐνοικῶν τε καὶ ἐμπεριπατῶν καὶ ἐπὶ τὰ βάθη τῆς ψυχῆς ἡμῶν
διαδυόμενος, οὐδὲν διαφέρει κατὰ τὴν ἔννοιαν· ᾧ γὰρ ἂν τὸ ἓν ἐξ ἀμφοτέρων

faith that girdles the throat of the soul. This is the golden collar that shines about the neck with a glitter that comes from the gold of undefiled knowledge of God. Concerning it, the proverb says, "You shall receive a crown of beauty for your head and a golden collar about your neck" (Prov 1:9).

This, then, is the sort of counsel conveyed by the *circlets*. But it is time to subject the next statement, which the friends of the Bridegroom address to the virgin, to examination. | The text runs: *We will make you likenesses of gold with silver studs, until the king is in his bed.*

Now to someone who considers how our interpretation has unfolded hitherto, the meaning of this statement seems in some way to fit in and to follow along, but the text runs deep and by its figurative turns of speech makes the point of what its enigmas disclose difficult to grasp.

For since the beauty of the soul has earlier been likened to the mare—that is, the angelic host—that destroyed the chariots of the Egyptians, and since the good Rider says that for that horse purity serves as rein and bit (which is what he meant by comparing her cheeks to those of a dove) and that the adornment of her neck is the different necklaces that gleam with the virtues, the friends of the Bridegroom also want to contrive some enhancement of this mare's beauty in their own right, by adorning the bosses of her gear with likenesses of gold, into which they etch the purity of silver, so that the beauty that adorns her may the more intensely shine forth when the gleam of silver is mingled with the glitter of gold.

It would serve best, however, to set the figurative | expressions in the text to one side and not to divert our attention from the meaning that profits us.

Now the soul that has been purified by the virtues has been compared to that *horse,* but it has not yet come under the control of the Word, nor has she carried on herself the one who "rides" upon such horses "for salvation."[17] For the horse must first of all be adorned in every way and then, in this state, receive the King as its rider. Whether he—the one who, according to the prophet, mounts himself on us horses and rides us for our salvation (cf. Hab 3:8)—renders the horse docile from above, or whether he comes to be within us as one who at once indwells us and tarries within us and makes his way through to the depths of our soul, this makes no difference to the meaning. The person to whom one of these things happens has the other accomplished

---

17. See above, p. 75 (Jaeger), where Gregory has carefully distinguished the "horse" that overwhelmed the Egyptians from that on which God rides. Correcting Origen, who makes no such distinction, Gregory, as one might expect, sees these two steeds as representing different stages in the Bride's progress. She becomes the horse mentioned by Habakkuk (on which God rides "for salvation") only *after* she has conquered the Egyptians and been adorned with images of gold.

γένηται, συγκατωρθώθη καὶ τὸ λειπόμενον· ὅ τε γὰρ ἐφ᾽ ἑαυτοῦ τὸν θεὸν
ἔχων καὶ ἐν ἑαυτῷ πάντως ἔχει καὶ ὁ ἐν ἑαυτῷ δεξάμενος ὑπέβη τὸν ἐν αὐτῷ
γεγονότα. οὐκοῦν μέλλει ὁ βασιλεὺς τῷ ἵππῳ τούτῳ ἐπαναπαύεσθαι. ταὐτὸν
δέ ἐστιν ἐπὶ τῆς θείας δυνάμεως, καθὼς εἴρηται, καθέδρα τε καὶ ἀνάκλισις·
5   ὁπότερον γὰρ ἂν ἐξ ἀμφοτέρων ἐν ἡμῖν γένηται, τὸ ἴσον | ἡ χάρις ἔχει.   85
ἐπειδὴ τοίνυν οἱ ἑτοιμασταὶ τοῦ βασιλέως εὔθετον πρὸς ὑποδοχὴν αὐτῷ
διὰ τῶν προκοσμημάτων τὸν ἵππον ποιοῦσι, ταὐτὸν δέ ἐστιν ἐπὶ θεοῦ τὸ ἔν
τινι καὶ τὸ ἐπί τινος γενέσθαι, καταλιπόντες τὸ κατὰ τὴν τροπικὴν σημασίαν
ἀκόλουθον οἱ παρασκευασταὶ καὶ θεράποντες κλίνην τὸν ἵππον ἐποίησαν·
10 χρὴ γὰρ ἡμᾶς, φησίν, ὁμοιώματα χρυσίου ποιῆσαι μετὰ στιγμάτων τοῦ
ἀργυρίου τὰ τοῦ ἵππου τὴν μορφὴν ὡραΐζοντα, ἵνα γένηται ὁ βασιλεὺς οὐκ ἐν
καθέδρᾳ, φησίν, ἀλλ᾽ ἐν ἀνακλίσει αὐτοῦ.
Ἡ μὲν οὖν ἀκολουθία τῆς λέξεως, καθὼς ὁ λόγος ὑπέδειξεν, τοῦτον ἔχει
τὸν τρόπον, ἄξιον δὲ τοῦτο μὴ παραδραμεῖν ἀθεώρητον, τί δή ποτε οὐκ αὐτὸ
15 τὸ χρυσίον εἰς κόσμον παραλαμβάνεται ἀλλὰ τοῦ χρυσίου τὰ ὁμοιώματα καὶ
οὐκ αὐτὸς ὁ ἄργυρος ἀλλὰ τὰ ἐκ τῆς ὕλης ταύτης τῷ ὁμοιώματι τοῦ χρυσίου
ἐγκροτούμενα στίγματα.
ὃ τοίνυν περὶ τούτων ὑπενοήσαμεν τοιοῦτόν ἐστι· πᾶσα ἡ περὶ τῆς
ἀρρήτου φύσεως διδασκαλία, κἂν ὅτι μάλιστα δοκῇ θεοπρεπῆ τινα καὶ
20 ὑψηλὴν ἐμφαίνειν διάνοιαν, ὁμοιώματα χρυσίου ἐστίν, οὐκ αὐτὸ τὸ χρυσίον·
οὐ γὰρ ἔστι παραστῆσαι δι᾽ ἀκριβείας τὸ ὑπὲρ ἔννοιαν ἀγαθόν. κἂν Παῦλός
τις ᾖ ὁ ἐν παραδείσῳ μυηθεὶς τὰ ἀπόρρητα, κἂν τῶν ἀλαλήτων ῥημάτων
ἐπα|κροάσηται, ἀνέκφραστα μένει περὶ θεοῦ τὰ νοήματα· ἄρρητα γάρ φησιν   86
εἶναι τῶν νοημάτων τούτων τὰ ῥήματα. οἱ τοίνυν λογισμούς τινας ἡμῖν
25 ἀγαθοὺς ἐντιθέντες περὶ τῆς τῶν μυστηρίων κατανοήσεως αὐτὸ μὲν εἰπεῖν
ὅπως ἔχει φύσεως ἀδυνατοῦσι, λέγουσι δὲ ἀπαύγασμα δόξης, χαρακτῆρα
ὑποστάσεως, μορφὴν θεοῦ, λόγον ἐν ἀρχῇ, λόγον θεόν· ἅπερ πάντα ἡμῖν

for him as well. The individual who has God mounted upon him also has God within him in every sense, and he who receives God within him is beneath the One within. Hence the King will lie down to rest upon this horse, but where the divine power is concerned, sitting and reclining are one and the same, as has been said; for whichever of the two comes to pass within us, | the grace is the same.

Since, therefore, the King's grooms are readying a horse whose adornments suit it to receive him, and since it is the same thing for God to be within someone and to be mounted on someone, the grooms and attendants deserted the logic of their metaphor and turned the *horse* into a *bed*.[18] "For," it says, "we must *make likenesses of gold with silver studs,* which confer splendor on the horse's appearance, in order that the King may be, not on his seat, but *in his bed."*

So, then, the sequence of thought in the wording does indeed have this general drift, as the text indicates. But it is important not to pass over without examination the question why it is that not gold itself but likenesses of gold are taken as adornments and not silver itself but studs of that substance that are struck into the likenesses of gold.

The underlying meaning we detect here is this: even though it seems to exhibit an understanding that is noble and worthy of God, all teaching about the ineffable Nature amounts to *likenesses of gold,* not gold itself.[19] For it is not possible to set out with accuracy the Good that transcends our conception of it. Even though there was a certain Paul who, in paradise, was initiated into things unspeakable, and even though he heard unutterable words, | his intuitions concerning God remain inexpressible, for he asserts that the words for these intuitions cannot be spoken (cf. 2 Cor 12:3–6). Hence it is that teachers who provide us with fair thoughts relating to the mysteries are quite unable to articulate what they are with respect to their nature. Rather they say, "radiance of … glory," "stamp of the substance" (Heb 1:3), "form of God"

---

18. This is Gregory's way of conceding that to construe v. 12a with v. 11, as his reading does, produces a disconnection of thought in the form, as he takes it, of a mixed metaphor.

19. Origen explains that "gold symbolizes the perceptive [*intellegibilis*?] and incorporeal nature, whereas silver represents the power of speech and reason" (Baehrens 1925, 159; trans. Lawson 1956, 151). He then goes on to explain—and here Gregory follows him—that images or likenesses of gold are not gold itself, thus taking the phrase ὁμοιώματα χρυσίου to mean "things that image gold" rather than "images made of gold." Origen, however, then states that "images of gold" refers to "truth's shadow," i.e., the law as contrasted with the gospel (Baehrens 1925, 160; trans. Lawson 1956, 152). Gregory's line is more radical: for him the gold means the infinite and incomprehensible divine Nature, and the images or likenesses are "all teaching about the ineffable Nature."

μὲν τοῖς ἀθεάτοις ἐκείνου τοῦ θησαυροῦ χρυσίον δοκεῖ, τοῖς δὲ δυναμένοις ἀναβλέπειν πρὸς τὴν ἀλήθειαν ὁμοιώματά ἐστι χρυσίου καὶ οὐ χρυσὸς ἐν τοῖς λεπτοῖς τοῦ ἀργυρίου διαφαινόμενος στίγμασιν. ἀργύριον δὲ ἡ ῥηματικὴ σημασία ἐστί, καθώς φησιν ἡ γραφὴ Ἄργυρος πεπυρωμένος γλῶσσα δικαίου.

5   τὸ τοίνυν διὰ τούτων δηλούμενον τοιοῦτόν ἐστιν ὅτι ἡ θεία φύσις πάσης ὑπέρκειται καταληπτικῆς διανοίας. τὸ δὲ περὶ αὐτῆς ἡμῖν ἐγγινόμενον νόημα ὁμοίωμά ἐστι τοῦ ζητουμένου· οὐ γὰρ αὐτὸ δείκνυσιν ἐκείνου τὸ εἶδος, ὃ οὔτε τις εἶδεν οὔτε ἰδεῖν δύναται, ἀλλὰ δι' ἐσόπτρου καὶ δι' αἰνίγματος ἔμφασίν τινα σκιαγραφεῖ τοῦ ζητουμένου ἔκ τινος εἰκασμοῦ ταῖς ψυχαῖς ἐγγινομένην.

10   πᾶς δὲ λόγος τῶν τοιούτων νοημάτων σημαντικὸς στιγμῆς | τινος ἀμεροῦς   87
δύναμιν ἔχει μὴ δυνάμενος ἐμφῆναι ὅπερ ἡ διάνοια βούλεται· ὡς εἶναι πᾶσαν μὲν διάνοιαν κατωτέραν τῆς θείας κατανοήσεως, πάντα δὲ λόγον ἑρμηνευτικὸν στιγμὴν βραχεῖαν δοκεῖν μὴ δυνάμενον τῷ πλάτει τῆς διανοίας συνεπεκτείνεσθαι. τὴν οὖν διὰ τῶν τοιούτων νοημάτων χειραγωγουμένην

15   ψυχὴν πρὸς τὴν τῶν ἀλήπτων περίνοιαν διὰ μόνης πίστεως εἰσοικίζειν ἐν ἑαυτῇ λέγει δεῖν τὴν πάντα νοῦν ὑπερέχουσαν φύσιν. καὶ τοῦτό ἐστι τὸ παρὰ τῶν φίλων λεγόμενον, ὅτι σοὶ ποιήσομεν, ὦ ψυχή, τῇ καλῶς πρὸς τὴν ἵππον ἀπεικασθείσῃ ἰνδάλματά τινα τῆς ἀληθείας καὶ ὁμοιώματα (τοιαύτη γὰρ καὶ τοῦ τῶν λόγων ἀργυρίου ἡ δύναμις, ὡς ἐναύσματά τινα σπινθηροειδῆ δοκεῖν

20   εἶναι τὰ ῥήματα μὴ δυνάμενα δι' ἀκριβείας ἐμφῆναι τὸ ἐγκείμενον νόημα), σὺ δὲ ταῦτα δεξαμένη ὑποζύγιόν τε καὶ οἰκητήριον γενήσῃ διὰ πίστεως τοῦ σοι ἐνανακλίνεσθαι μέλλοντος διὰ τῆς ἐν σοὶ κατοικήσεως· τοῦ γὰρ αὐτοῦ καὶ θρόνος ἔσῃ καὶ οἶκος γενήσῃ.

τάχα δ' ἄν τις εἴποι τὴν τοῦ Παύλου ψυχὴν ἢ εἴ τις ἄλλη γέγονε κατ'

25   ἐκείνην τῶν τοιούτων ἀξιοῦσθαι | ῥημάτων· ἐκεῖνος γὰρ σκεῦος ἐκλογῆς   88
ἅπαξ γενόμενος καὶ ἐφ' ἑαυτοῦ καὶ ἐν ἑαυτῷ εἶχε τὸν κύριον ἐν μὲν τῷ βαστάζειν αὐτοῦ τὸ ὄνομα ἐναντίον ἐθνῶν καὶ βασιλέων ἵππος γενόμενος, ἐν δὲ τῷ μηκέτι αὐτὸν ζῆν, ἀλλ' ἐν ἑαυτῷ δεικνύειν ζῶντα ἐκεῖνον καὶ δοκιμὴν διδόναι τοῦ ἐν αὐτῷ λαλοῦντος Χριστοῦ οἶκος περιληπτικὸς τῆς ἀπεριλήπτου

30   γενόμενος φύσεως.

Ταῦτα τῶν φίλων τοῦ νυμφίου τῇ καθαρᾷ καὶ παρθένῳ χαρισαμένων ψυχῇ (εἶεν δ' ἂν οὗτοι τὰ Λειτουργικὰ πνεύματα τὰ εἰς διακονίαν ἀποστελλόμενα διὰ τοὺς μέλλοντας κληρονομεῖν σωτηρίαν) τελειοτέρα πως γίνεται τῇ προσθήκῃ τῶν χαρισμάτων ἡ νύμφη. καὶ μᾶλλον προσεγγίσασα

35   τῷ ποθουμένῳ, πρὶν τὸ κάλλος αὐτοῦ τοῖς ὀφθαλμοῖς ἐμφανῆναι, διὰ τῆς

(Phil 2:6), "Word in the beginning," "Word divine" (John 1:1). To us who are unseeing, all these expressions seem like the gold of that treasure, but to those who are able to look up toward the Truth, it is *likenesses of gold,* and not gold, that makes itself seen in between the delicate markings of silver. Silver means a verbal act of signifying, as when the Scripture says, "The tongue of a righteous person is silver tried in fire" (Prov 10:20).

What is conveyed, therefore, by these words is this: that the divine Nature transcends the mind's grasp. Our thought concerning it is a likeness or image of what we seek, for it does not manifest the form of that which no one has seen or can see. Rather, it sketches darkly, in a mirror and in an enigma, a reflection of what we seek that comes to birth in our souls on the basis of some conjecture. All speech, however, that refers to such intuitions has the function of | some indivisible mark, being unable to make clear what the mind intends. Thus all our thinking is inferior to the divine understanding, and every explanatory word of speech seems to be an abbreviated tracery mark that is unable to embrace the breadth of the act of understanding. Hence Paul says that the soul that is led by such intuitions to awareness of things that cannot be grasped must bring the Nature that transcends all intellect within herself by faith alone.[20] And this is what the friends of the Bridegroom say: "We shall make for you, O soul, rightly likened to the horse, certain manifestations and likenesses of truth (for this is the function of the *silver* of words: the things people say seem to be sparklike embers that cannot with accuracy express the intuition they carry), but you, when you have received these likenesses, shall become a dwelling place and a servant by faith of the One who is coming to recline within you by dwelling within you. You shall both be his throne and become his home."

Perhaps one might venture that the soul of Paul—or some other soul that is comparable to his—is worthy of being described in such | terms as these. For since he became a "vessel of election" (Acts 9:15) once for all, he had the Lord both upon him and within him and became the Lord's horse in that he bore his name before peoples and kings. He became the palpable dwelling of the impalpable Nature in that it was no longer he who lived, but he shows Christ living in him and gives proof of Christ speaking in him.

Once the friends of the Bridegroom have lavished these gifts upon the pure and virgin soul (for they must be the "ministering spirits" [cf. Heb 1:14] sent for the sake of those who are to inherit salvation), the Bride comes a step closer to perfection because of these further graces. And when she has approached the object of her desire more closely, but before his beauty is man-

---

20. See below, homily 6, p. 183 (Jaeger), for the same idea.

ὀσφραντικῆς αἰσθήσεως τοῦ ζητουμένου ἐφάπτεται οἷόν τινος χρωτὸς
ἰδιότητα τῇ ὀσφραντικῇ δυνάμει κατανοήσασα καί φησιν ἐπεγνωκέναι αὐτοῦ
τὴν ὀσμὴν τῇ εὐωδίᾳ τοῦ μύρου, ᾧ νάρδος ἐστὶ τὸ ὄνομα, ταύτῃ πρὸς τοὺς
φίλους τῇ φωνῇ χρησαμένη Νάρδος μου ἔδωκεν ὀσμὴν αὐτοῦ. ὡς γὰρ ὑμεῖς,
5   φησίν, οὐκ αὐτὸ τὸ ἀκήρατον τῆς θεότητος | χρυσίον ἀλλ᾽ ὁμοιώματα διὰ   89
τῶν χωρητῶν ἡμῖν νοημάτων τοῦ χρυσίου χαρίζεσθε, οὐ τηλαυγεῖ τῷ λόγῳ
τὰ κατ᾽ αὐτὸν ἐκκαλύπτοντες, ἀλλὰ διὰ τῆς βραχύτητος τῶν τοῦ λογικοῦ
ἀργυρίου στιγμάτων ἐμφάσεις τινὰς παρασχόμενοι τοῦ ζητουμένου, οὕτω
κἀγὼ διὰ τῆς εὐπνοίας τοῦ ἐμοῦ μύρου τὴν αὐτοῦ ἐκείνου εὐωδίαν τῇ
10   αἰσθήσει παρεδεξάμην.

τοιοῦτον δέ τινα νοῦν δοκεῖ μοι τὸ λεγόμενον ἔχειν· ἐπειδὴ πολλῶν καὶ
διαφόρων ἀρωμάτων ἄλλου κατ᾽ ἄλλην ἰδιότητα εὐπνοούντων τεχνική τις
καὶ ἔμμετρος μίξις τὸ τοιοῦτον ἀπεργάζεται μύρον μιᾶς τινος πόας εὐώδους
ἐκ τῶν συνεμβαλλομένων, ᾗ ὄνομα νάρδος ἐστίν, ὅλῳ τῷ σκευάσματι
15   παρεχομένης τὸ ὄνομα, τὸ δὲ ἐκ πάντων τῶν ἀρωματικῶν ἰδιωμάτων εἰς
μίαν συνερανιζόμενον εὔπνοιαν ὡς αὐτὴν τοῦ νυμφίου τὴν εὐωδίαν ἡ
κεκαθαρμένη αἴσθησις δέχεται,

ταῦτα διὰ τῶν εἰρημένων παιδεύειν ἡμᾶς τὸν λόγον οἰόμεθα ὅτι ἐκεῖνο
μέν, ὅ τί ποτε κατ᾽ οὐσίαν ἐστί, τὸ πάσης ὑπερκείμενον τῆς τῶν ὄντων
20   συστάσεώς τε καὶ διοικήσεως ἀπρόσιτόν τε καὶ ἀναφές ἐστι καὶ ἄληπτον, ἡ δὲ
ἐν ἡμῖν διὰ τῆς τῶν ἀρετῶν καθαρότητος μυρεψουμένη εὐωδία ἀντ᾽ ἐκείνου
ἡμῖν γίνεται μιμουμένη τῷ καθ᾽ ἑαυτὴν καθαρῷ τὸ τῇ φύσει ἀκήρατον καὶ
τῷ ἀγαθῷ τὸ ἀγαθὸν καὶ τῷ ἀφθάρτῳ τὸ ἄφθαρτον καὶ τῷ ἀναλλοιώτῳ τὸ | 90
ἀναλλοίωτον καὶ πᾶσι τοῖς κατ᾽ ἀρετὴν ἐν ἡμῖν κατορθουμένοις τὴν ἀληθινὴν

ifest to her eyes, she touches the one she seeks through her sense of smell, as if by her power of smell she recognized the distinctive quality of some color, and she says that she recognizes his fragrance by means of the sweetness of a perfume whose name is *spikenard*—saying to the friends of the Bridegroom, *My spikenard gave off his scent*.[21] "For," she says, "just as you confer not the pure gold of the Godhead | but, by way of concepts comprehensible to us, likenesses of gold and do not disclose what pertains to it in clear speech but furnish intimations of the Object of our search by means of the laconic tracings of the silver of rational speech, so too I, in the fragrance of my perfume, sense the sweetness of that very One himself."

The meaning that the statement seems to me to bear is as follows. It is an artful and balanced mixture of many different aromas—each with its proper sweetness—that produces this perfume, while of all those that are blended together it is one sweet-smelling herb called spikenard that lends its name to the entire preparation. Further, the purified sensibility receives what has been put together into one fragrance out of all the special aromas as the very sweetness of the Bridegroom.

Hence we judge that the words of the text are teaching us this, namely, that that Reality, whatever it is in its essence, which transcends the entire structure and order of Being, is unapproachable, impalpable, and incomprehensible but that, for us, the sweetness that is blended within us by the purity of the virtues takes its place because by its own purity it images that which is by nature the Undefiled[22]—and by its goodness, the Good; and by its incorruptibility, the Incorruptible; and by its unchangeability, | the Unchangeable; and by all the things within us that are rightly done in accordance with

---

21. Origen, careful as always for accuracy, notes that the words ὀσμήν αὐτοῦ in this line can mean either "his scent" or "its scent." It is not clear to what he would take "its" to refer (since, being neuter in gender, "its" cannot refer back to "spikenard," which in Greek is feminine). Gregory simply accepts the former alternative and thus is bound, as he says in the next sentence, to insist that it is the spikenard *of the Bride* that gives off the scent of the Bridegroom. (The problem arises from the fact that the LXX translation requires μου ["*my* spikenard"] to refer to the [feminine] Bride or soul but needs a masculine or neuter antecedent for αὐτοῦ ["*his/its* fragrance"]. In the Hebrew original the second possessive has "spikenard" as its antecedent and is feminine in gender, producing in English "My spikenard gave off its fragrance").

22. Gregory sees in this line, too, a statement that in its spiritual sense addresses the problem of how the infinite and incomprehensible God can be known to finite persons. He takes the Bride's spikenard to symbolize a balanced blend of the virtues that gives off "his"—i.e., the Bridegroom's—"scent" and that in that sense mirrors or reflects him in the medium of the human soul itself. This interpretation is no doubt in part derived from Origen's (cf. *Comm. Cant.* 2.9 [Baehrens 1925, 166; trans. Lawson 1956, 160–61]), but Nyssen puts Origen's idea—that the Bride receives back from Christ *her* nard bearing *his* scent—to a different use.

ἀρετήν, περὶ ἧς φησιν Ἀμβακοὺμ ὁ προφήτης ὡς τοὺς οὐρανοὺς πάντας διαλαβούσης. οὐκοῦν ἡ ταῦτα πρὸς τοὺς φίλους τοῦ νυμφίου διεξιοῦσα, ὅτι τὴν ὀσμὴν αὐτοῦ ἡ ἐμὴ νάρδος ἐμοὶ δίδωσι, ταῦτά μοι καὶ τὰ τοιαῦτα δοκεῖ φιλοσοφοῦσα λέγειν ὅτι,
5   εἴ τις πᾶν ἄνθος εὐωδίας ἢ ἄρωμα ἐκ τῶν ποικίλων τῆς ἀρετῆς λειμώνων ἀνθολογήσας καὶ πάντα ἑαυτοῦ τὸν βίον ἔμμυρον διὰ τῆς τῶν καθ᾽ ἕκαστον ἐπιτηδευμάτων εὐοσμίας ἀπεργασάμενος διὰ πάντων γένοιτο τέλειος, πρὸς αὐτὸν μὲν τὸν θεὸν λόγον ὡς πρὸς ἡλίου κύκλον ἀτενῶς ἰδεῖν φύσιν οὐκ ἔχει, ἐν ἑαυτῷ δὲ καθάπερ ἐν κατόπτρῳ βλέπει τὸν ἥλιον· αἱ γὰρ τῆς ἀληθινῆς
10   ἐκείνης καὶ θείας ἀρετῆς ἀκτῖνες τῷ κεκαθαρμένῳ βίῳ διὰ τῆς ἀπορρεούσης αὐτῶν ἀπαθείας ἐλλάμπουσαι ὁρατὸν ποιοῦσιν ἡμῖν τὸ ἀόρατον καὶ ληπτὸν τὸ ἀπρόσιτον τῷ ἡμετέρῳ κατόπτρῳ ἐνζωγραφοῦσαι τὸν ἥλιον.
      ταὐτὸν δέ ἐστιν ὡς πρὸς τὸ ἐγκείμενον νόημα ἢ ἀκτῖνας εἰπεῖν ἡλίου ἢ τῆς ἀρετῆς ἀπορροίας ἢ τὰς ἀρωματικὰς εὐωδίας· ὅ τι γὰρ ἂν ἐκ
15   τούτων πρὸς τὸν τοῦ λόγου σκοπὸν ὑποθώμεθα, ἓν ἐξ ἁπάντων | ἐστὶ τὸ   91
      ἐγγινόμενον νόημα τὸ διὰ τῶν ἀρετῶν ἡμῖν τοῦ πάντα νοῦν ὑπερέχοντος ἀγαθοῦ τὴν γνῶσιν ἐγγίνεσθαι, ὥσπερ ἔστι διά τινος εἰκόνος τὸ ἀρχέτυπον κάλλος ἀναλογίσασθαι. οὕτω καὶ Παῦλος, ἡ νύμφη, ὁ διὰ τῶν ἀρετῶν τὸν νυμφίον μιμούμενος καὶ ζωγραφῶν ἐν ἑαυτῷ διὰ τοῦ εὐώδους τὸ ἀπρόσιτον
20   κάλλος ἔκ τε τῶν καρπῶν τοῦ πνεύματος, ἀγάπης τε καὶ χαρᾶς καὶ εἰρήνης καὶ τῶν τοιούτων εἰδῶν, μυρεψῶν ταύτην τὴν νάρδον Χριστοῦ εὐωδίαν ἑαυτὸν ἔλεγεν εἶναι τὴν ἀπρόσιτον ἐκείνην καὶ ὑπερέχουσαν χάριν ἐν ἑαυτῷ ὀσφραινόμενος καὶ τοῖς ἄλλοις παρέχων ἑαυτὸν ὥσπερ τι θυμίαμα κατ᾽ ἐξουσίαν ἀντιλαμβάνεσθαι, οἷς κατὰ τὴν προσοῦσαν ἑκάστῳ διάθεσιν
25   ἢ ζωοποιὸς ἐγίνετο ἢ θανατηφόρος ἡ εὔπνοια· ὡς γὰρ τὸ αὐτὸ μύρον, εἰ κανθάρῳ καὶ περιστερᾷ προστεθείη, οὐ ταὐτὸν ἐφ᾽ ἑκατέρων ἐργάζεται, ἀλλ᾽ ἡ μὲν περιστερὰ ῥωμαλεωτέρα διὰ τῆς εὐπνοίας τοῦ μύρου γίνεται, ὁ δὲ κάνθαρος φθείρεται, οὕτω καὶ ὁ μέγας Παῦλος, τὸ θεῖον ἐκεῖνο θυμίαμα, εἰ μέν τις ἦν περιστερὰ κατὰ Τίτον ἢ Σιλουανὸν ἢ Τιμόθεον, συμμετεῖχεν
30   αὐτῷ | τῆς εὐωδίας τοῦ μύρου προκόπτων ἐν παντὶ καλῷ τοῖς κατ᾽ αὐτὸν   92

virtue, the true Virtue, concerning which the prophet Habakkuk says that it embraces all the heavens (cf. Hab 3:3). Therefore she who explains to the friends of the Bridegroom, "My *spikenard* gives off *his scent,*" seems to me to say, in her philosophic discourse, both these things and the following.

If a person, having gathered every sweet-smelling flower or scent from the various blooms of virtue and having rendered his whole life a perfume by the fragrance of his daily doings, should become perfect in all respects, he does not have it in him to look intently upon the divine Word itself any more than upon the disc of the sun. Nevertheless, he sees the sun within himself as in a mirror.[23] For the rays of that true and divine Virtue shine upon the purified life through the inward peace[24] that flows from them, and they make the Invisible visible for us and the Incomprehensible comprehensible, because they portray the Sun in the mirror that we are.

Where this idea is concerned, it is one and the same thing to speak of rays of the sun or of emanations of virtue or of sweet aromatic scents. For no matter which of these we adopt to express the point of our text, all of them give rise to | a single notion: that knowledge of the Good that transcends every intellect comes to us through the virtues, even as it is possible through some image to get a glimpse of the archetypal Beauty. So it was with the Bride Paul. He imitated the Bridegroom by his virtues and inscribed within himself the unapproachable Beauty by means of their sweetness, and out of the fruits of the Spirit—love and joy and peace and the like—he blended this *spikenard.* Hence he said that he was "the aroma of Christ" (2 Cor 2:15), capturing within himself the scent of that transcendent and unapproachable Grace and providing himself for others to have a part in according to their ability, as though he were an incense: others to whom, in accordance with the present disposition of each, the sweet smell became either life-giving or death-dealing. For the same unguent, if it be touched to a beetle and to a dove, does not have the same effect in each case, but the dove becomes stronger on account of the unguent's scent, while the beetle perishes. Similarly, if anyone were a dove on the model of Titus or Silvanus or Timothy, the great Paul, that divine incense, shared with him | the sweet scent of his perfume by the examples he provided

---

23. On the idea that one knows God by mirroring God, and indeed on this whole passage, see Gregory's discussion of the words "Blessed are the pure in heart, for they shall see God" (*Beat.* 6, esp. PG 44:1272B; trans. Graef 1954, 148; see also *De an.,* PG 46:89B). The principle that God is known as one comes to reflect God in oneself underlies this whole passage (see above, n. 19) and is basic for Gregory. See also below, pp. 98, 104, 150, 218–19 (Jaeger), where the idea recurs, as well as homily 4, p. 104 (Jaeger), where Gregory generalizes it.

24. Literally, "impassibility" (ἀπάθεια).

ὑποδείγμασιν, εἰ δὲ Δημᾶς τις ἦν ἢ Ἀλέξανδρος ἢ Ἑρμογένης, οὐ φέροντες τὸ
τῆς ἐγκρατείας θυμίαμα κανθάρων δίκην ὑπὸ τῆς εὐωδίας ἐφυγαδεύοντο. οὐ
χάριν ἔλεγεν ὁ τοῖς τοιούτοις εὔπνοῶν μύροις ὅτι Χριστοῦ εὐωδία ἐσμὲν ἐν
τοῖς σῳζομένοις καὶ ἐν τοῖς ἀπολλυμένοις, οἷς μὲν ὀσμὴ θανάτου εἰς θάνατον,
5   οἷς δὲ ὀσμὴ ζωῆς εἰς ζωήν.
    εἰ δέ τι συγγενὲς καὶ ἡ εὐαγγελικὴ νάρδος ἔχει πρὸς τὸ μύρον τῆς νύμφης,
ἔξεστι τῷ βουλομένῳ διὰ τῶν γεγραμμένων ἀναλογίσασθαι, τίς ἦν ἐκείνη ἡ
νάρδος ἡ πιστική, ἡ πολύτιμος, ἡ καταχεθεῖσα μὲν τῆς κεφαλῆς τοῦ κυρίου,
πάντα δὲ τὸν οἶκον τῆς εὐωδίας πληρώσασα· τάχα γὰρ οὐκ ἀπεξένωται τοῦ
10 μύρου τὸ μύρον, ὃ τῇ νύμφῃ μὲν τὴν ὀσμὴν τοῦ νυμφίου δίδωσιν, ἐν δὲ τῷ
εὐαγγελίῳ αὐτοῦ καταχεθὲν τοῦ κυρίου πληροῖ τῆς εὐωδίας τὸν οἶκον, ἐν ᾧ
τὸ συμπόσιον ἦν. δοκεῖ γάρ μοι κἀκεῖ προφητικῷ τινι πνεύματι προμηνῦσαι
διὰ τοῦ μύρου ἡ γυνὴ τὸ τοῦ θανάτου μυστήριον, καθὼς μαρτυρεῖ τοῖς
παρ' αὐτῆς γεγενημένοις ὁ κύριος λέγων ὅτι Προέλαβεν εἰς τὸ ἐνταφιάσαι
15 με. καὶ τὸν οἶκον τὸν πληρωθέντα τῆς εὐωδίας ἀντὶ παντὸς τοῦ κόσμου
καὶ ὅλης τῆς οἰκουμένης νοεῖν ὑποτίθεται εἰπὼν ὅτι | Ὅπου ἐὰν κηρυχθῇ   93
τὸ εὐαγγέλιον τοῦτο ἐν ὅλῳ τῷ κόσμῳ, ἡ ὀσμὴ τοῦ μύρου συνδιαδοθήσεται
τῷ τοῦ εὐαγγελίου κηρύγματι καὶ μνημόσυνον ἔσται, φησί, ταύτης τὸ
εὐαγγέλιον. οὐκοῦν ἐπειδὴ ἐν μὲν τῷ Ἄισματι τῶν ᾀσμάτων ἡ νάρδος τὴν
20 ὀσμὴν τοῦ νυμφίου τῇ νύμφῃ δίδωσιν, ἐν δὲ τῷ εὐαγγελίῳ ὅλου τοῦ σώματος
τῆς ἐκκλησίας ἐν πάσῃ τῇ οἰκουμένῃ καὶ ἐν παντὶ τῷ κόσμῳ χρῖσμα ἡ εὐωδία
γίνεται ἡ τότε τὸν οἶκον πληρώσασα, τάχα τις εὑρίσκεται κοινωνία διὰ
τούτων ἐν ἀμφοτέροις, ὡς ἓν τὰ δύο δοκεῖν.
    Καὶ ταῦτα μὲν εἰς τοσοῦτον. ἡ δὲ ἐφεξῆς ῥῆσις καταλλήλως μὲν τῇ τοῦ
25 ἐπιθαλαμίου δράματος ὑποθέσει ὡς παρὰ τῆς ἐν παστάδι παρεσκευασμένης
ἔχειν δοκεῖ, μείζονα δὲ καὶ τελειοτέραν ἐμφαίνει φιλοσοφίαν, ἣν κατορθῶσαι
μόνων τῶν ἤδη τετελειωμένων ἐστίν. τί οὖν ἐστι τὸ εἰρημένον; Ἀπόδεσμος
στακτῆς ἀδελφιδός μου ἐμοί· ἀνὰ μέσον τῶν μαστῶν μου αὐλισθήσεται·

as he advanced in every good thing, but if someone were a Demas or an Alexander or an Hermogenes, not enduring the incense of self-control, that one was put to flight by the sweet odor just like the beetle. That is why he who radiated such sweet scents said, "We are the aroma of Christ in those who are being saved and in those who are perishing, to one a fragrance from death to death, to the other a fragrance from life to life" (cf. 2 Cor 2:15–16).

Further, if the spikenard mentioned in the Gospel is akin to the perfume of the Bride, it is possible for one who so desires to discern what that faithful, valuable spikenard was that was poured down on the Lord's head and filled the whole house with its sweetness. For it may be that that perfume is not different from the perfume that provides the Bride with the scent of the Bridegroom, but in the Gospel, when poured out over the Lord, filled with its sweetness the house in which the supper was held. It seems to me that there, in a prophetic spirit, the woman foreshadowed with the perfume the mystery of the death—just as the Lord bore witness to those in her company when he said, "She has prepared me for burial" (Mark 14:8 // Matt 26:12). And he assumes that the house filled with sweetness stands for the entire cosmos and the whole inhabited world[25] when he says, | "Wherever this gospel is preached in the whole cosmos" (Matt 26:13), the perfume's sweetness will be absorbed with the preaching of the gospel and, he says, "the gospel will be a memorial of her" (Matt 26:13 // Mark 14:9). Since, then, in the Song of Songs, the spikenard conveys to the Bride the scent of the Bridegroom, while in the Gospel the sweetness that then filled the house becomes the ointment of the whole body of the church in the whole cosmos, this suggests that the two have something in common to the point of seeming to be the same.

So much, then, for that. The next statement seems to fit in well with the business of a wedding scene, as if stemming from a woman making preparations in the inner bridal chamber, yet it sets forth a higher and more perfect philosophy, and to get it right belongs only to those who are already being perfected. What, then, is said? *My kinsman*[26] *is for me a bundle of myrrh, he shall lie between my breasts.*

---

25. Compare Origen, *Comm. Cant.* 2.9 (Baehrens 1925, 166; trans. Lawson 1956, 160), from whom Gregory appears to get this way of understanding what the Gospel means when it relates (John 12:3) that Mary anointed the feet of Jesus with nard, so that "the house was filled with the fragrance of the ointment."

26. Origen takes time out here to note that the Bride calls the Bridegroom ἀδελφιδός here for the first time and to indicate that the term means a brother's son, i.e., a nephew. Origen explains the use of this word by suggesting that the brother of the Bride (who represents the Gentile church) is the Jewish people, whose son Jesus is "after the flesh." Gregory develops the same idea, but only a bit later, when he comes to Song 1:16; see below, homily 4, p. 107 (Jaeger).

φασὶν ἐπιμέλειαν εἶναι ταῖς φιλοκόσμοις τῶν γυναικῶν μὴ τοῖς ἔξωθεν
προκοσμήμασι μόνον ἐπινοεῖν ἑαυταῖς τὸ ἐπὶ τῶν συμβιούντων ἐράσμιον, | 94
ἀλλ᾽ ἐπιτηδεύειν διά τινος εὐπνοίας ἡδίω τὰ σώματα τοῖς ἑαυτῶν ἀνδράσι
φαίνεσθαι τὸ καταλλήλως ἐνεργοῦν πρὸς τὴν τοιαύτην χρείαν ἄρωμα ἐντὸς
5   τῆς κατὰ τὴν ἐσθῆτα περιβολῆς ἀποκρύπτουσαι· οὗ τὸν οἰκεῖον ἀτμὸν
ἐκδιδόντος καὶ τὸ σῶμα τῇ τοῦ ἀρώματος εὐπνοίᾳ συγκαταχρώννυται.
ταύτης δὲ οὔσης ἐν αὐταῖς τῆς συνηθείας οἷον τολμᾷ ἡ μεγαλόφρων αὕτη
παρθένος. ἐμοί, φησίν, ἀπόδεσμος, ὃν ἐξαρτῶ τοῦ αὐχένος ἐπὶ τὸ στῆθος, δι᾽
οὗ τὴν εὐοσμίαν παρέχω τῷ σώματι, οὐκ ἄλλο τι τῶν εὐπνοούντων ἀρωμάτων
10   ἐστίν, ἀλλ᾽ αὐτὸς ὁ κύριος στακτὴ γενόμενος ἔγκειται ἐν τῷ ἀποδέσμῳ τῆς
συνειδήσεως, αὐτῇ μου τῇ καρδίᾳ ἐναυλιζόμενος. ἡ γὰρ τοπικὴ τῆς καρδίας
θέσις ἐν τῷ μέσῳ τῶν μαζῶν παρὰ τῶν τὰ τοιαῦτα ἐπεσκεμμένων εἶναι
λέγεται. ἐκεῖ δέ φησιν ἡ νύμφη ἔχειν τὸν ἀπόδεσμον, ἐν ᾧ τόπῳ τὸ ἀγαθὸν
θησαυρίζεται. ἀλλὰ καὶ πηγήν τινα τοῦ ἐν ἡμῖν θερμοῦ τὴν καρδίαν φασίν,
15   ἀφ᾽ ἧς διὰ τῶν ἀρτηριῶν ἐφ᾽ ἅπαν ἡ θερμότης τὸ σῶμα καταμερίζεται, δι᾽
ἧς ἔνθερμά τε καὶ ζωτικὰ τὰ μέλη τοῦ σώματος γίνεται τῷ πυρὶ τῆς καρδίας
ὑποθαλπόμενα, ἡ τοίνυν ἐν τῷ ἡγεμονικῷ παραδεξαμένη τοῦ κυρίου τὴν
εὐωδίαν καὶ τὴν καρδίαν ἑαυτῆς ἔνδεσμον τοῦ τοιούτου ποιήσασα θυμιάματος
πάντα τὰ καθ᾽ ἕκαστον τοῦ βίου ἐπιτηδεύματα οἷόν τινος σώματος μέλη ζέειν
20 | παρασκευάζει τῷ ἐκ τῆς καρδίας διήκοντι πνεύματι μηδεμιᾶς ἀνομίας τὴν   95
πρὸς τὸν θεὸν ἀγάπην ἐν μηδενὶ μέλει τοῦ σώματος καταψυχούσης.
Ἀλλ᾽ ἐπὶ τὸν ἐφεξῆς λόγον μετέλθωμεν. ἀκούσωμεν, τί ἡ ἄμπελος ἡ
εὐθηνοῦσα περὶ τῶν καρπῶν ἑαυτῆς διαλέγεται ἡ ἐν πᾶσι τοῖς κλίτεσι τῆς
τοῦ θεοῦ οἰκίας, καθώς φησιν ὁ προφήτης, διηπλωμένη καὶ διὰ τῶν τῆς
25   ἀγάπης ἑλίκων περιελισσομένη τῇ θείᾳ τε καὶ ἀκηράτῳ ζωῇ. Βότρυς, φησί,
τῆς κύπρου ἀδελφιδός μου ἐμοὶ ἐν ἀμπελῶνι ἐν Γαδί.
τίς οὕτω μακάριος, μᾶλλον δὲ τίς οὕτω κρείττων πάσης μακαριότητος,
ὥστε τὸν ἴδιον καρπὸν βλέπων ἐν αὐτῷ τῷ βότρυϊ τῆς ἑαυτοῦ ψυχῆς ὁρᾶν
τὸν τοῦ ἀμπελῶνος δεσπότην; ἰδοὺ γὰρ ὅσον ηὐξήθη ἐν τῇ ἰδίᾳ νάρδῳ τοῦ
30   νυμφίου ἐπιγνοῦσα τὴν εὔπνοιαν· ἡ στακτὴν αὐτὸν εὐώδη ποιησαμένη καὶ
διαλαβοῦσα τῷ τῆς καρδίας ἐνδέσμῳ τὸ ἄρωμα, ὡς ἂν παραμένοι αὐτῇ τὸ
ἀγαθὸν διὰ παντὸς ἀδιάπνευστον, μήτηρ τοῦ θείου βότρυος γίνεται τοῦ πρὸ

People say that wives who love adornment are careful not to contrive what is attractive in the eyes of their spouses solely by means of ornaments worn on the outside | but by the use of some aromatic herb see to it that their bodies appear pleasing to their husbands—and conceal the herb that is suited to such use within the cover of their clothing. When this gives off its natural scent, the body too will be tinged by the sweet scent of the herb. Such being the custom among these women, see what the noble-minded virgin herself dares to say. "As to me," she says, "the bundle that I hang from my neck upon the breast and by which I give my body a sweet smell is not one of the other perfumed herbs, but the Lord himself, become myrrh, lies in the bundle of my conscience, dwelling in my very heart." For the experts in these matters say that the location of the heart is between the breasts. The Bride says that she keeps her receptacle there in the place where goodness is treasured up.[27] But they also say that the heart is a source of the heat within us. From it warmth is shared out through the arteries to the whole body, and by its means the body's limbs become warm and alive, secretly heated by the heart's fire. When, then, she has accepted the sweet scent of the Lord within her ruling part and has made of her heart a container for such incense, she accustoms all the several pursuits of her life, like the limbs of some body, | to simmer with the Spirit that spreads from her heart, and no lawlessness chills the love of God in any member of her body.

But let us go on to the next statement. Let us hear what "the fruitful vine" says about her fruits—she who is spread out, as the prophet says, within all the walls of God's house and by the tendrils of her love embraces the life that is divine and pure. *My kinsman is for me a cluster of grape blossoms*[28] *among the vineyards in Gad,*[29] she says.

Who is there so blessed—or rather so raised above blessedness—that, when he looks upon his own fruit, what he sees in the very cluster of his own heart is the Lord of the vineyard? For look how much the soul has increased now that she has known the sweet smell of the Bridegroom in her own nard: she makes him the scent of myrrh and receives his scent into the receptacle of her heart, so that the Good may abide with her forever unexhausted;

---

27. See Matt 6:21; Luke 12:34; and also Luke 6:45.

28. On the word κύπρος and the tendentious translation "grape blossoms," see below n. 30.

29. The LXX here has "in the vineyards of Engaddi" (and Origen takes the trouble to explain that Engaddi is a district better known for balsam trees than for grape vines; see *Comm. Cant.* 2.11 [Baehrens 1925, 170; trans. Lawson 1956, 26:166]), but Nyssen guesses that the proper text is ἐν Γαδί, which in English yields "among (*or* in) the vineyards in Gad." The Hebrew original is En-Gedi, the name of an oasis in the vicinity of the Dead Sea.

μὲν τοῦ πάθους κυπρίζοντος, ὅπερ ἐστὶν ἀνθοῦντος, ἐν δὲ τῷ πάθει τὸν οἶνον προχέοντος. ὁ γὰρ τὴν καρδίαν ἡμῶν εὐφραίνων οἶνος αἷμα σταφυλῆς | μετὰ   96
τὴν τοῦ πάθους οἰκονομίαν γίνεταί τε καὶ ὀνομάζεται.

    διπλῆς οὖν οὔσης ἐν τῷ βότρυϊ τῆς ἀπολαύσεως, τῆς μὲν ἐκ τοῦ ἄνθους,
5 ὅταν εὐφραίνῃ τῇ εὐοσμίᾳ τὰ αἰσθητήρια, τῆς δὲ διὰ τοῦ τελειωθέντος
ἤδη καρποῦ, ὅταν ὑπάρχῃ κατ᾽ ἐξουσίαν ἢ τῆς βρώσεως κατατρυφᾶν ἢ ἐν
συμποσίοις τῷ οἴνῳ φαιδρύνεσθαι ἐνταῦθα ἡ νύμφη ἔτι τὸν ἀνθοῦντα βότρυν
καρποφορεῖ κύπρον τὴν οἰνάνθην κατονομάζουσα·

    τὸ γὰρ γεννηθὲν <ἐν> ἡμῖν παιδίον, ὁ Ἰησοῦς ὁ ἐν τοῖς δεξαμένοις αὐτὸν
10 διαφόρως προκόπτων σοφίᾳ τε καὶ ἡλικίᾳ καὶ χάριτι οὐκ ἐν πᾶσιν ὁ αὐτός
ἐστιν, ἀλλὰ πρὸς τὸ μέτρον τοῦ ἐν ᾧ γίνεται, καθὼς ἂν ὁ χωρῶν αὐτὸν ἱκανῶς
ἔχῃ, τοιοῦτος φαίνεται ἢ νηπιάζων ἢ προκόπτων ἢ τελειούμενος κατὰ τὴν τοῦ
βότρυος φύσιν, ὃς οὐ πάντοτε μετὰ τοῦ αὐτοῦ εἴδους ἐπὶ τῆς ἀμπέλου ὁρᾶται,
ἀλλὰ συνεξαλλάσσει τῷ χρόνῳ τὸ εἶδος, ἀνθῶν, κυπρίζων, τελειούμενος,
15 πεπαινόμενος, οἶνος γενόμενος. ἐπαγγέλλεται τοίνυν ἡ ἄμπελος τῷ ἰδίῳ
καρπῷ, ὃς οὔπω μέν ἐστι πρὸς οἶνον ὥριμος, ἀλλ᾽ | ἀναμένει τὸ πλήρωμα τῶν   97
καιρῶν, οὐ μὴν ὡς εἰς τρυφὴν ἀναπόλαυστος· τὴν ὄσφρησιν γὰρ εὐφραίνει
ἀντὶ τῆς γεύσεως τῇ προσδοκίᾳ τῶν ἀγαθῶν τοῖς ἀτμοῖς τῆς ἐλπίδος ἡδύνων
τὰ τῆς ψυχῆς αἰσθητήρια· τὸ γὰρ πιστόν τε καὶ ἀναμφίβολον τῆς ἐλπιζομένης
20 χάριτος ἀπόλαυσις τοῖς δι᾽ ὑπομονῆς ἀπεκδεχομένοις τὸ προσδοκώμενον
γίνεται. οὗτος οὖν ὁ τῆς κύπρου βότρυς ἐστί, βότρυς οἶνον ἐπαγγελλόμενος,
οὔπω δὲ οἶνος γινόμενος, ἀλλὰ διὰ τοῦ ἄνθους (ἡ δὲ ἐλπὶς τὸ ἄνθος ἐστί) τὴν
ἐσομένην χάριν πιστούμενος.

    ἡ δὲ τοῦ <ἐν> Γαδὶ προσθήκη σημαίνει τὸν πίονα χῶρον, ᾧ ἐνριζωθεῖσα
25 ἡ ἄμπελος εὔτροφον καὶ ἡδὺν τὸν καρπὸν ἀπεργάζεται· οὕτω γὰρ οἱ τοπικῶς
ἱστορήσαντες λέγουσι τὸν κλῆρον τοῦ Γὰδ ἐπιτηδείως ἔχειν πρὸς εὐτροφίαν

she becomes mother of the cluster of divine fruit that blossoms[30]—that is, blooms—before the passion, but after the passion pours forth wine. For the wine that "makes our heart glad" (cf. Ps 103:15) becomes and is called, | after the economy of the passion, "blood of the grape."

So then there are two ways in which the grape gives pleasure: on the one hand, by its blossom, when it delights the senses with its smell; on the other, by its ripe fruit, when it serves, at one's will, either as food to give delight or by its wine to bring cheer at celebrations. In this case the Bride as yet bears the cluster in the form of a bloom, since she gives the name "blossom" to the vine's flower.

For the child who was born for us—Jesus, who within those who receive him grows in a variety of different ways in wisdom and stature and grace[31]— is not the same in all but indwells in a way that accords with the capacity of the one into whom he comes. He is manifested in a character that fits the ability of the one who takes him in, either as a babe or as making progress or as being perfected—and this accords with the nature of a grape cluster, which does not always have the same appearance on the vine but changes its character with time as it blossoms, takes on color, matures, ripens, and becomes wine. By its own fruit, then—which is not ripe enough to make wine but | awaits "the fullness of the times" (cf. Gal 4:4) and yet is not meant to be merely a useless luxury—the vine affords a promise. For in anticipating good things it delights smell rather than taste and gives pleasure to the soul's senses with the fragrances of hope; for to those who await it with eager patience there comes the trustworthy and unambiguous enjoyment of the grace that is hoped for. This, then, is the *cluster of grape blossoms*, a cluster that gives promise of wine because it has not yet become wine but by its blossom (and hope is the blossom) gives assurance of the grace to come.

The addition of (*in*) *Gad* signifies the land of abundance, in which the fertile vineyard has been planted and a sweet fruit is produced. Thus geographers have said that the portion assigned to Gad is well adapted to the

---

30. This translates the Greek verb κυπρίζω, from which, it seems, Gregory wants to derive the noun κύπρος (the noun in the text that I have rendered, in order to make Gregory's exegesis intelligible, as "grape blossoms"). Gregory takes it, on the ground of this derivation, that the "cluster" is composed of something that is blooming, and Theodoret (PG 81:81D) seems to follow him. Origen (at least in Rufinus's Latin translation) does not relate κύπρος to κυπρίζω but identifies κύπρος, whose reference he regards as ambiguous, as in this occurrence referring specifically to a grape cluster in bloom ("uva florens"; Baehrens 1925, 170).

31. See Methodius, *Symp.* 8.8 (trans. Musurillo 1958, 113): "Christ is spiritually begotten in each" individual who is "enlightened spiritually" (i.e., baptized; cf. Gregory's language above, homily 2, p. 52 [Jaeger], and n. 7).

βοτρύων. ἐπειδὴ τοίνυν ὁ τῷ νόμῳ τοῦ κυρίου σύμφωνον ἔχων τὸ θέλημα καὶ διὰ πάσης νυκτός τε καὶ ἡμέρας ταύτην τὴν μελέτην ποιούμενος ἀειθαλὲς γίνεται δένδρον ταῖς τῶν ὑδάτων ἐπιρροαῖς πιαινόμενος καὶ ἐν τῷ καθήκοντι καιρῷ τὸν καρπὸν παρεχόμενος, τούτου χάριν καὶ ἡ τοῦ νυμφίου ἄμπελος ἐν
5   τῷ | Γαδί, τῷ πίονι τούτῳ τόπῳ ἐρριζωμένη (τουτέστιν ἐν βαθείᾳ τῇ διανοίᾳ   98
τῇ διὰ τῶν θείων διδαγμάτων καταρδομένῃ) καὶ αὔξουσα τὸν εὐανθῆ τοῦτον καὶ κυπρίζοντα βότρυν ἐκαρποφόρησεν, ᾧ τὸν γεωργόν τε καὶ φυτηκόμον ἑαυτῆς ἐνορᾷ. ὡς μακάριον τὸ τοιοῦτον γεώργιον, οὗ ὁ καρπὸς πρὸς τὴν τοῦ νυμφίου ὁμοιοῦται μορφήν. ἐπειδὴ γὰρ φῶς ἀληθινόν ἐστιν ἐκεῖνος καὶ
10   ἀληθινὴ ζωὴ καὶ δικαιοσύνη ἀληθής, καθὼς ἡ Σοφία φησί, καὶ πάντα τὰ τοιαῦτα, ὅταν τις διὰ τῶν ἔργων ταῦτα γένηται, ἃ ἐκεῖνός ἐστιν, οὗτος τὸν τῆς ἰδίας συνειδήσεως βότρυν βλέπων αὐτὸν τὸν νυμφίον ἐν τούτῳ βλέπει τῇ φωτεινῇ τε καὶ ἀκηλιδώτῳ ζωῇ τὸ φῶς τῆς ἀληθείας ἐνοπτριζόμενος.

διὰ τοῦτό φησιν ἡ ἄμπελος ἡ εὐθηνοῦσα, ὅτι ἐμὸς βότρυς ὁ διὰ τοῦ
15   ἄνθους κυπρίζων αὐτὸς ἐκεῖνός ἐστιν ὁ ἀληθινὸς βότρυς, ὁ ἐπὶ τῶν ξυλίνων ἀναφορέων ἑαυτὸν δείξας, οὗ τὸ αἷμα τοῖς σῳζομένοις τε καὶ εὐφραινο|μένοις   99
πότιμόν τε καὶ σωτήριον γίνεται,

ᾧ ἡ δόξα εἰς τοὺς αἰῶνας τῶν αἰώνων.
ἀμήν.

cultivation of flourishing grapes. Since, then, the person whose will accords with the law of the Lord and who makes this his concern both night and day becomes an ever-blooming tree that is fed by the streams of waters and brings forth its fruit in due season—for this reason the Bridegroom's vineyard in | Gad, planted and growing in that place of abundance (that is, in the deep understanding that is watered by the divine teachings), bore this blossoming and blushing cluster in which she sees her own husbandman and vine-dresser. How happy such a garden is, whose fruit is made to be like the form of the Bridegroom! For since he is the true light and true life and true righteousness, as Wisdom says, and all such things, when a person becomes by his works these things that the Bridegroom is, he looks upon the cluster of his own conscience, and in it sees the Bridegroom himself, and he mirrors[32] the light of the Truth in his spotless and lightsome life.

This is why the flourishing vineyard says, "My grape cluster, blooming in its blossom, is that true Cluster who has manifested himself upon the poles of wood, whose blood becomes both drink and salvation to those who are being saved | and are of good cheer."

To him be glory to the ages of ages.

Amen.

---

32. See above, p. 90 (Jaeger), and n. 23 there.

Λόγος δ΄

Ἰδοὺ εἶ καλή, ἡ πλησίον μου,
ἰδοὺ εἶ καλή· ὀφθαλμοί σου περιστεραί.
Ἰδοὺ εἶ καλός, ἀδελφιδός μου, καί γε ὡραῖος.
πρὸς κλίνῃ ἡμῶν σύσκιος,
5   Δοκοὶ οἴκων ἡμῶν κέδροι,
φατνώματα ἡμῶν κυπάρισσοι.

Ἐγὼ ἄνθος τοῦ πεδίου,
κρίνον τῶν κοιλάδων.
Ὡς κρίνον ἐν μέσῳ ἀκανθῶν,
10   οὕτως ἀδελφή μου ἀνὰ μέσον τῶν θυγατέρων.
Ὡς μῆλον ἐν τοῖς ξύλοις τοῦ δρυμοῦ,
οὕτως ἀδελφιδός μου ἀνὰ μέσον τῶν υἱῶν·
ὑπὸ τὴν σκιὰν αὐτοῦ ἐπεθύμησα καὶ ἐκάθισα,
καὶ ὁ καρπὸς αὐτοῦ γλυκὺς ἐν τῷ λάρυγγί μου.
15   Εἰσαγάγετέ με εἰς οἶκον τοῦ οἴνου,
τάξατε ἐπ᾽ ἐμὲ ἀγάπην.
Στηρίσατέ με ἐν μύροις
στοιβάσατέ με ἐν μήλοις, ὅτι τετρωμένη ἀγάπης ἐγώ.
Εὐώνυμος αὐτοῦ ὑπὸ τὴν κεφαλήν μου
20 | καὶ ἡ δεξιὰ αὐτοῦ περιλήψεταί με.   100
Ὥρκισα ὑμᾶς, θυγατέρες Ἰερουσαλήμ,
ἐν δυνάμεσι καὶ ἐν ἰσχύσεσι τοῦ ἀγροῦ,
ἐὰν ἐγείρητε καὶ ἐξεγείρητε τὴν ἀγάπην, ἕως οὗ θελήσῃ.

Φασὶ τοὺς τὸ χρυσίον τεχνικῶς ἐκκαθαίροντας, εἰ διά τινος ῥυπαρωτέρας
25   ὕλης κατ᾽ ἐπιβουλὴν ἐμμιχθείσης ἀμαυρωθείη τῆς λαμπηδόνος τὸ κάλλος, τῇ
διὰ τοῦ πυρὸς χωνείᾳ θεραπεύειν τὴν δύσχροιαν καὶ πολλάκις τοῦτο ποιεῖν
καὶ καθ᾽ ἑκάστην χωνείαν ἐπισκοπεῖν, ὅσον παρὰ τὴν προτέραν ἐν τοῖς ἐφεξῆς
γέγονεν ὁ χρυσὸς εὐχρούστερος, καὶ μὴ πρότερον παύεσθαι τῷ πυρὶ τὴν ὕλην
ἀποκαθαίροντας, ἕως ἂν αὐτὸ τοῦ χρυσίου τὸ εἶδος ἑαυτῷ μαρτυρήσῃ τὸ
30   καθαρόν τε καὶ ἀκιβδήλευτον.

HOMILY 4
Song 1:15–2:7

[15]*Behold, you are beautiful, my close one,*
Behold, you are beautiful: your eyes are doves.
[16]*Behold, you are beautiful, my kinsman, and glorious,*
in the shadow by our bed.
[17]*The beams of our house are cedars,*
our coffered ceilings are of cypress.

[1]*I am a blossom of the plain,*
a lily of the valleys.
[2]*As a lily among thorns,*
so is my sister among the daughters.
[3]*As an apple tree among the trees of the wood,*
so is my kinsman among the sons.
Under his shadow I rejoiced and sat down,
and his fruit was sweet in my throat.
[4]*Bring me into the house of wine,*
Set love in order upon me.
[5]*Strengthen me with perfumes,*
Encompass me with apples, for I have been wounded by love.
[6]*His left hand is under my head,*
and his right hand shall embrace me.
[7]*I have charged you, O daughters of Jerusalem,*
by the powers and strengths of the field,
Do not rouse or wake love, until he please.

They say that people who know how to clean gold—if its glowing beauty has been obscured by the treacherous admixture of some base material—get rid of the bad coloring by smelting it down in fire. They do this repeatedly, moreover, and watch closely each time to observe the extent to which the gold has become fairer in the later smeltings as against the first, and they do not stop purifying the metal with fire until the very look of the gold bears witness for itself that it is pure and unadulterated.[1]

---

1. For this figure, see Gregory's treatise *De anima et resurrectione* (PG 46:100A), where it affords an analogy for the removal of a disposition to be absorbed in material concerns (εἰς τὴν πρὸς τὰ ὑλώδη σχέσιν [ibid., 97B]).

τίνος δὲ χάριν τῆς παρούσης τῶν ἀνεγνωσμένων θεωρίας ἁπτόμενοι τούτων τὴν μνήμην ἐποιησάμεθα, δῆλον ὑμῖν ἐξ αὐτῆς ἤδη τῆς διανοίας τῶν γεγραμμένων γενήσεται.

χρυσῖτις ἦν τὸ κατ' ἀρχὰς ἡ ἀνθρωπίνη φύσις καὶ λάμπουσα τῇ πρὸς
5   τὸ ἀκήρατον ἀγαθὸν ὁμοιότητι, ἀλλὰ δύσχρους καὶ μέλαινα μετὰ τοῦτο τῇ
ἐπιμιξίᾳ τῆς κακίας ἐγένετο, καθὼς ἐν τοῖς πρώτοις τοῦ Ἄισματος τῆς νύμφης
ἠκούσαμεν ὅτι μέλαιναν αὐτὴν ἐποίησεν ἡ τῆς φυλακῆς τοῦ ἀμπελῶνος
ὀλιγωρία· ἧς θεραπεύων τὴν δυσμορφίαν | ὁ πάντα ἐν σοφίᾳ τεχνιτεύων   101
θεὸς οὐ καινόν τι κάλλος ἐπ' αὐτῆς μηχανᾶται ὃ μὴ πρότερον ἦν, ἀλλ'
10 ἐπὶ τὴν πρώτην ἐπανάγει χάριν δι' ἀναλύσεως τὴν τῷ κακῷ μελανθεῖσαν
μεταχωνεύων πρὸς τὸ ἀκήρατον.

ὥσπερ τοίνυν οἱ ἀκριβεῖς χρυσογνώμονες μετὰ τὴν πρώτην χωνείαν
ἐπισκοποῦσιν, ὅσον ἐπέδωκεν εἰς κάλλος ἡ ὕλη τῷ πυρὶ τὸν ῥύπον
ἐνδαπανήσασα, καὶ πάλιν δευτέρας γενομένης χωνείας, εἰ μὴ ἱκανῶς παρὰ
15 τὴν πρώτην ἀπεκαθάρθη, τὸ προστεθὲν κάλλος ἐπιλογίζονται καὶ πολλάκις
τὸ ἴσον ποιοῦντες ἀεὶ τὰς τοῦ κάλλους προσθήκας διὰ τῆς ἐπιστημονικῆς
δοκιμασίας ἐπιγινώσκουσιν, οὕτω καὶ νῦν ὁ θεραπευτὴς τοῦ μελανθέντος
χρυσίου καθάπερ τινὶ χώνῃ τὴν ψυχὴν λαμπρύνας διὰ τῶν προσαχθέντων
αὐτῇ φαρμάκων ἐν μὲν τοῖς φθάσασιν ἵππου τινὸς εὐμορφίαν τῷ φαινομένῳ
20 προσεμαρτύρησε, νῦν δὲ ὡς παρθένου λοιπὸν ἀποδέχεται τὸ ἀναφανὲν αὐτῆς
κάλλος.

φησὶ γὰρ Ἰδοὺ εἶ καλή, ἡ πλησίον μου, ἰδοὺ εἶ καλή· ὀφθαλμοί σου
περιστεραί. παιδεύει δὲ διὰ τῶν εἰρημένων ὁ λόγος ταύτην εἶναι τοῦ κάλλους
τὴν ἐπανάληψιν τῷ προσεγγίσαι πάλιν τῷ ἀληθινῷ κάλλει, οὗ ἀπεφοίτησε·
25 φησὶ γὰρ Ἰδοὺ εἶ καλή, ἡ πλησίον μου· | ὅπερ ἐστὶν ὅτι διὰ τοῦτο πρότερον   102
οὐκ ἦσθα καλή, διότι τοῦ ἀρχετύπου κάλλους ἀποξενωθεῖσα τῇ πονηρᾷ
γειτνιάσει τῆς κακίας πρὸς τὸ εἰδεχθὲς ἠλλοιώθης.

τὸ δὲ λεγόμενον τοιοῦτόν ἐστι· δεκτικὴ τῶν κατὰ γνώμην ἡ ἀνθρωπίνη
γέγονε φύσις καὶ πρὸς ὅπερ ἂν ἡ ῥοπὴ τῆς προαιρέσεως αὐτὴν ἄγῃ, κατ'
30 ἐκεῖνο καὶ ἀλλοιοῦται· τοῦ τε γὰρ θυμοῦ παραδεξαμένη τὸ πάθος θυμώδης

Why we have made mention of these matters as we set out to construe today's portion of the materials we are reading will become apparent to you from the very sense of the written text.

At the beginning, human nature was golden and gleaming because of its likeness to the undefiled Good. But later, by reason of the admixture of evil,[2] it became discolored and dark—just as, at the opening of the Song, we heard the Bride say that negligence in keeping her vineyard made her *dark*. In curing her discoloration, | God, who contrives everything by Wisdom, does not devise for her some novel beauty that had never before existed. Rather, he restores her to her original loveliness by releasing it, recasting the one who had been darkened by vice so that she becomes undefiled.

Careful assessors of gold, once the first smelting is done, set about gauging the extent to which the metal, when it has surrendered its filth to the fire, has made progress toward beauty, and again, when a second smelting has taken place, if the gold has still not been sufficiently purified, they estimate the gain in beauty and, repeating the process over and over, closely observe the increments of beauty by making exact assessments. In exactly the same way here, the Restorer of the tarnished gold, having brightened the soul as in a smelting vessel by treating it with medicines, has, in an earlier part of the text, testified that her appearance has the handsome form of a *horse*. In this reading, however, he finally acknowledges that her beauty, once more manifest, is as that of a virgin.

For he says *Behold, you are beautiful, my close one, behold, you are beautiful: your eyes are doves.* By these expressions the Word teaches that restoration of the soul's beauty consists in her drawing near once again to the true Beauty from which she departed. For he says *Behold, you are beautiful, my close one,* | which is to say, "The reason why you were not beautiful before is that you had been estranged from the archetypal Beauty and had become ugly because of your wrongful association with evil."

And the point is this. Human nature came into being as something capable of becoming whatever it determines upon, and to whatever goal the thrust of its choice leads it, it undergoes alteration in accord with what it seeks.[3]

---

2. For this idea of an "admixture of evil," see *De anima et resurrectione* (PG 46:81B), where Macrina explains that Adam's fall consists in his choosing to eat of the tree of the knowledge of good and evil; i.e., "the life mixed out of opposites," having deserted his original "portion unmixed with the worse." Cf. also ibid. 116AB; below, homily 12, pp. 350–51 (Jaeger).

3. See Gregory's *Vit. Mos.* 2.3: "We are in some manner our own parents, giving birth to ourselves by our own free choice in accordance with whatever we wish to be, whether male or female, molding ourselves to the teaching of virtue or vice" (trans. Malherbe and Ferguson 1978, 55f–56; GNO 7.1:34, 11ff.). This point is a frequent one with Gregory; see above, homily 2, p. 50 (Jaeger), and n. 8 there.

γίνεται καὶ τῆς ἐπιθυμίας ἐπικρατησάσης εἰς ἡδονὴν διαλύεται, πρὸς
δειλίαν τε καὶ φόβον καὶ τὰ καθ' ἕκαστον πάθη τῆς ῥοπῆς γενομένης τὰς
ἑκάστου τῶν παθῶν μορφὰς ὑποδύεται, ὥσπερ δὴ καὶ ἐκ | τοῦ ἐναντίου τὸ   103
μακρόθυμον, τὸ καθαρόν, τὸ εἰρηνικόν, τὸ ἀόργητον, τὸ ἄλυπον, τὸ εὐθαρσές,
5   τὸ ἀπτόητον, πάντα ταῦτα ἐν ἑαυτῇ δεξαμένη ἑκάστου τούτων ἐπισημαίνει
τὸν χαρακτῆρα τῇ καταστάσει τῆς ψυχῆς ἐν ἀταραξίᾳ γαληνιάζουσα.
συμβαίνει τοίνυν ἀμέσως πρὸς τὴν κακίαν τῆς ἀρετῆς διεστώσης μὴ δύνασθαι
κατὰ ταὐτὸν ἀμφότερα τῷ ἑνὶ παραγίνεσθαι· ὁ γὰρ τοῦ σωφρονεῖν ἀποστὰς
ἐν τῷ ἀκολάστῳ πάντως γίνεται βίῳ καὶ ὁ τὸν ἀκάθαρτον βδελυξάμενος
10 βίον κατώρθωσεν ἐν τῇ ἀποστροφῇ τοῦ κακοῦ τὸ ἀμόλυντον. οὕτω καὶ τὰ
ἄλλα πάντα· ὁ ταπεινοφρονῶν τῆς ὑπερηφανίας κεχώρισται καὶ ὁ διὰ τοῦ
τύφου ἑαυτὸν ἐξογκώσας τὴν ταπεινοφροσύνην ἀπώσατο. καὶ τί χρὴ τὰ καθ'
ἕκαστον λέγοντα διατρίβειν, πῶς ἐπὶ τῶν ἀντικειμένων τῇ φύσει ἡ τοῦ ἑνὸς
ἀπουσία θέσις καὶ ὕπαρξις τοῦ ἑτέρου γίνεται;
15   οὕτω τοίνυν ἐχούσης ἡμῶν τῆς προαιρέσεως, ὡς κατ' ἐξουσίαν ἔχειν ὅπερ
ἂν ἐθέλῃ τούτῳ συσχηματίζεσθαι, καλῶς φησι πρὸς τὴν ὡραϊσθεῖσαν ὁ λόγος,
ὅτι ἀποστᾶσα μὲν τῆς τοῦ κακοῦ κοινωνίας ἐμοὶ προσήγγισας, πλησιάσασα
| δὲ τῷ ἀρχετύπῳ κάλλει καὶ αὐτὴ καλὴ γέγονας οἷόν τι κάτοπτρον τῷ ἐμῷ   104
χαρακτῆρι ἐμμορφωθεῖσα· κατόπτρῳ γὰρ ἔοικεν ὡς ἀληθῶς τὸ ἀνθρώπινον
20 κατὰ τὰς τῶν προαιρέσεων ἐμφάσεις μεταμορφούμενον· εἴ τε γὰρ πρὸς
χρυσὸν ἴδοι, χρυσὸς φαίνεται καὶ τὰς ταύτης αὐγὰς τῆς ὕλης διὰ τῆς
ἐμφάσεως δείκνυσιν, εἴ τέ τι τῶν εἰδεχθῶν ἐμφανείη, καὶ τούτου τὸ αἶσχος δι'
ὁμοιώσεως ἀπομάσσεται βάτραχόν τινα ἢ φρῦνον ἢ σκολόπενδραν ἢ ἄλλο
τι τῶν ἀηδῶν θεαμάτων τῷ οἰκείῳ εἴδει ὑποκρινόμενον, ὥπερ ἂν τούτων
25 εὑρεθῇ ἀντιπρόσωπον. ἐπειδὴ τοίνυν κατὰ νώτου τὴν κακίαν ποιησαμένη ἡ
κεκαθαρμένη ὑπὸ τοῦ λόγου ψυχὴ τὸν ἡλιακὸν ἐν ἑαυτῇ κύκλον ἐδέξατο καὶ
τῷ ὀφθέντι ἐν αὐτῇ φωτὶ συνεξέλαμψε, διὰ τοῦτό φησι πρὸς αὐτὴν ὁ λόγος,
ὅτι γέγονας ἤδη καλὴ πλησιάσασα τῷ ἐμῷ φωτὶ διὰ τοῦ προσεγγισμοῦ τὴν
κοινωνίαν ἐφελκυσαμένη τοῦ κάλλους. Ἰδοὺ εἶ καλή, φησίν, ἡ πλησίον μου.

When it takes into itself the passion of anger, it becomes angry. When desire reigns, it is dissolved into pleasure.[4] When impulse runs in the direction of cowardice and fear, it assumes the shape of the passions proper to each of these—just as, | contrariwise, when it receives into itself greatness of spirit, purity, peaceableness, calmness of temper, harmlessness, courage, high-spirit-edness—all of these—it shows the mark of each of them in that the soul is established in peace and inner tranquillity. Since virtue, then, is different from vice and there is no mean between them, virtue and vice cannot character-ize one subject in the same respect at the same time. One who departs from temperance comes to live a thoroughly unbridled life, while one who abomi-nates the impure life achieves, by turning from evil, a life that is undefiled. And so it is in all the other cases. The person who maintains a humble mind is segregated from arrogance, while someone who is puffed up with affectation has driven humility out. And why should we waste time by mentioning each individual case—how, where naturally contrary qualities are concerned, the absence of the one spells the establishment and presence of the other?

Since, then, our choice is so constituted that we are disposed to take on the shape of whatever we want, the Word rightly says to the Bride in her new glory, "You have drawn near to me as you have rejected the fellowship of evil, | and in drawing near to the archetypal Beauty, you too have become beautiful, informed like a mirror by my appearance." For in that it is trans-formed in accordance with the reflections of its choices, the human person is rightly likened to a mirror.[5] If it looks upon gold, gold it appears, and by way of reflection it gives off the beams of that substance; and if it has the look of some hateful thing, it is imitating that ugliness through a likeness, playing, in its own appearance, the part of a frog or a toad or a millipede or some other unpleasant sight—whichever of them it reflects. Having, then, put evil behind it, the soul purified by the Word has taken the sun's orb within itself and has been gleaming in company with the light that appears within it, and therefore the Word says to her: "You have already become beautiful by coming close to my light, making a participation in the beautiful your own by this drawing near." *Behold*, he says, *you are beautiful, my close one.*

---

4. The references to "anger" and "desire" indicate that Gregory is using Plato's division of the soul into three personified "parts"; see Plato, *Resp.* 439Cff.

5. This is a basic theme in Gregory's spirituality (though by no means either peculiar to it or unprecedented), closely related of course to the doctrine that humanity was created "after the image and likeness of God." Here, however, he generalizes the theme: it is not merely that humanity comes to mirror God by imitating God's qualities; it also appears that humanity becomes "like" whatever sort of thing upon which it focuses its choosing. This idea is reiterated just below (p. 105 [Jaeger]) with the support of an analogy from vision. See also above, homily 3, p. 90 (Jaeger), with n. 23 there; below, homily 5, p. 150 (Jaeger).

εἶτα ἐπισχὼν καὶ οἷον ἐν προσθήκῃ τινὶ | καὶ ἐπιτάσει γενομένην τοῦ   105
κάλλους αὐτὴν θεασάμενος πάλιν τὸν αὐτὸν ἐπαναλαμβάνει λόγον εἰπὼν
Ἰδοὺ εἶ καλή. ἀλλ' ἐν μὲν τῷ προτέρῳ τὴν πλησίον ὠνόμασεν, ἐνταῦθα δὲ
τὴν ἐκ τοῦ εἴδους τῶν ὀμμάτων γνωριζομένην· Ὀφθαλμοὶ γάρ σου, φησί,
5   περιστεραί· πρότερον μὲν γάρ, ὅτε τῇ ἵππῳ ἀφωμοιώθη, ἐν σιαγόνι τε καὶ
τραχήλῳ ὁ ἔπαινος ἦν, νῦν δὲ ὅτε τὸ ἴδιον αὐτῆς ἀνεφάνη κάλλος, ἡ τῶν
ὀφθαλμῶν χάρις ἐγκωμιάζεται.

ὁ δὲ τῶν ὀφθαλμῶν ἔπαινός ἐστι τὸ περιστερὰς εἶναι τὰ ὄμματα·
ὅπερ μοι δοκεῖ τοιαύτην ἐμφαίνειν διάνοιαν· ἐπειδὴ ταῖς καθαραῖς τῶν
10   ὀμμάτων κόραις ἐνορᾶται τῶν ἐνατενιζόντων τὰ πρόσωπα (φασὶ γὰρ οἱ τὰ
τοιαῦτα φυσιολογεῖν ἐπιστήμονες ὅτι τὰς τῶν εἰδώλων ἐμπτώσεις δεχόμενος,
αἳ τῶν ὁρατῶν ἀπορρέουσιν, οὕτως ἐνεργεῖ τὴν ὄψιν ὁ ὀφθαλμός), τούτου
χάριν ἔπαινος γίνεται τῆς τῶν ὀφθαλμῶν εὐμορφίας τὸ τῆς περιστερᾶς εἶδος
τὸ ταῖς κόραις αὐτῶν ἐμφαινόμενον. πρὸς ὃ γὰρ ἄν τις ἐνατενίσῃ, τούτου
15   δέχεται ἐν ἑαυτῷ τὸ ὁμοίωμα. ἐπεὶ οὖν ὁ μηκέτι πρὸς σάρκα καὶ αἷμα βλέπων
πρὸς τὸν πνευματικὸν βίον ὁρᾷ, καθώς φησιν ὁ ἀπόστολος, ζῶν πνεύματι
καὶ στοιχῶν πνεύματι καὶ τὰς πράξεις τοῦ σώματος θανατῶν τῷ πνεύματι καὶ
ὅλος δι' ὅλου πνευματικὸς γινόμενος, οὐ | ψυχικὸς οὐδὲ σαρκικός, τούτου   106
χάριν μαρτυρεῖται ἡ τῆς σωματικῆς προσπαθείας ἀπηλλαγμένη ψυχὴ τὸ
20   τῆς περιστερᾶς εἶδος ἐν τοῖς ὄμμασιν ἔχειν, τουτέστι τὸν χαρακτῆρα τῆς
πνευματικῆς ζωῆς τῷ διορατικῷ τῆς ψυχῆς ἐναυγάζεσθαι.

ἐπεὶ οὖν γέγονεν ὁ καθαρὸς αὐτῆς ὀφθαλμὸς δεκτικὸς τοῦ τῆς περιστερᾶς
χαρακτῆρος, διὰ τοῦτο χωρεῖ καὶ τὸ τοῦ νυμφίου κάλλος θεάσασθαι· νῦν
γὰρ πρώτως ἡ παρθένος ἀτενίζει τῇ τοῦ νυμφίου μορφῇ, ὅτε ἔσχε τὴν
25   περιστερὰν ἐν τοῖς ὄμμασιν (Οὐδεὶς γὰρ δύναται εἰπεῖν κύριον Ἰησοῦν εἰ μὴ
ἐν πνεύματι ἁγίῳ), καί φησιν Ἰδοὺ εἶ καλός, ἀδελφιδός μου, καί γε ὡραῖος·

Then pausing and, as it were, contemplating her in the increase | and
increment of her beauty, he repeats the same expression: *Behold, you are
beautiful.*[6] In the previous line, however, he named her *close one*, while here
she is identified by the appearance of her eyes. For he says *Your eyes are doves.*
Previously, the commendation was directed to her cheek and and her neck,[7]
but now that her characteristic and proper beauty has been manifested, it is
the loveliness of her eyes that is extolled.

The praise given to her eyes is to the effect that they are doves, and to
me the sense of this seems to be as follows. We see faces in the clear pupils
of eyes that are focused on someone (for people who can give the scientific
explanations of such things say that the eye activates its vision by receiving the impressions of the images given off by visible bodies), and for this
reason it becomes a commendation of the eyes' form that the shape of a dove
shows in their pupils. For people receive in themselves the likeness of whatever they gaze upon intently. Since, then, one who no longer gazes upon flesh
and blood looks toward the spiritual life, as the apostle says, and lives in the
Spirit, and walks by the Spirit (cf. Gal 5:25), and puts to death the deeds of the
body, and becomes wholly spiritual throughout (cf. Rom 8:13), not | psychic
or fleshly, it follows that the soul that has been delivered from bodily passion
is attested as having in its eyes the shape of the dove—that is, the imprint of
the spiritual life is beheld in the clear vision of the soul.[8]

Since, then, her purified eye has received the imprint of the dove, she
is also capable of beholding the beauty of the Bridegroom.[9] For now for the
first time, the virgin gazes upon the form of the Bridegroom,[10] now, that is,
that she has the dove in her eyes (for "No one can say, 'Jesus is Lord!' except
by the Holy Spirit" [1 Cor 12:3]), and she says *Behold, you are beautiful, my*

---

6. Origen finds the repetition of the words "Behold, you are beautiful," significant, as
Nyssen apparently does not. He suggests first that its repetition without "close one" assures the
Bride that she is beautiful "even if she happens to be away from him" (Baehrens 1925, 173.3),
but later he finds in it a still "deeper mystery": it indicates that the Bride will be beautiful even—
and also—in "the age to come," just as the first occurrence affirms her beauty in the present age
(174.7ff.).

7. See above, homily 3, pp. 78–79 (Jaeger).

8. Origen is much less vague. He too associates "dove" with the Holy Spirit but avers that
"to have the eyes of a dove" is "to understand the Law and the Prophets in a spiritual sense"
(trans. Lawson 1956, 170; cf. Baehrens 1925, 173.16–17). Nyssen for his part is no doubt pursuing his idea, introduced just above, that the soul is a mirror.

9. In *Comm. Cant.* 3.2 Origen says, "For of a truth nobody can perceive and know how
great is the splendour of the Word, until he receives the dove's eyes—that is, a spiritual understanding" (trans. Lawson 1956, 172; Baehrens 1925, 174–75).

10. At the opening of homily 3 (Jaeger, p. 70), Gregory called attention to the first hearing
of the Bridegroom's voice; here, then, the Bride passes from audition to vision.

ἀφ' οὗ γὰρ οὐδὲν ἄλλο μοι καλὸν εἶναι δοκεῖ, ἀλλ' ἀπεστράφην πάντα ὅσα
τὸ πρότερον ἐν καλοῖς ἐνομίζετο, οὐκέτι μοι πεπλάνηται ἡ τοῦ καλοῦ κρίσις,
ὥστε ἄλλο τι παρὰ σὲ καλὸν οἴεσθαι· οὐκ ἔπαινός τις ἀνθρώπινος, οὐ δόξα,
οὐ περιφάνεια, οὐ κοσμικὴ δυναστεία· ταῦτα γὰρ τοῖς πρὸς τὴν αἴσθησιν
5   βλέπουσιν ἐπικέχρωσται μὲν τῇ τοῦ καλοῦ φαντασίᾳ, οὐ μήν ἐστιν ὅπερ
νομίζεται. πῶς γὰρ ἄν τι εἴη καλόν, ὃ μηδὲ ὅλως ἔστι καθ' ὑπόστασιν; τὸ γὰρ
ἐν τῷ κόσμῳ τούτῳ τετιμημένον ἐν μόνῃ τῇ οἰήσει τῶν νομιζόντων εἶναι τὸ
εἶναι ἔχει. σὺ δὲ ἀληθῶς εἶ καλός, | οὐ καλὸς μόνον ἀλλ' αὐτὴ τοῦ καλοῦ ἡ   107
οὐσία, ἀεὶ τοιοῦτος ὑπάρχων, πάντοτε ὢν ὅπερ εἶ, οὔτε κατὰ καιρὸν ἀνθῶν
10   οὔτε ἐπὶ καιροῦ πάλιν ἀποβάλλων τὸ ἄνθος, ἀλλὰ τῇ ἀϊδιότητι τῆς ζωῆς
συμπαρατείνων τὴν ὥραν· ᾧ ὄνομα ἡ φιλανθρωπία ἐγένετο. ὅτι ἄρα ἐξ Ἰούδα
ἀνέτειλας ἡμῖν, ἀδελφὸς δὲ ὁ Ἰουδαίων λαὸς τοῦ ἐξ ἐθνῶν σοι προσιόντος,
καλῶς διὰ τὴν ἐν σαρκὶ γεγενημένην τῆς θεότητός σου φανέρωσιν ἀδελφιδὸς
τῆς ποθούσης κατωνομάσθης.
15   Εἶτα ἐπήγαγε Πρὸς κλίνῃ ἡμῶν σύσκιος. τουτέστιν ἔγνω σε ἤτοι
γνώσεται ἡ ἀνθρωπίνη φύσις σύσκιον τῇ οἰκονομίᾳ γενόμενον· ἦλθες
γάρ φησι σὺ ὁ καλὸς ἀδελφιδός, ὁ ὡραῖος, | πρὸς τῇ κλίνῃ ἡμῶν σύσκιος   108
γενόμενος. εἰ γὰρ μὴ συνεσκίασας αὐτὸς σεαυτὸν τὴν ἄκρατον τῆς θεότητος
ἀκτῖνα συγκαλύψας τῇ τοῦ δούλου μορφῇ, τίς ἂν ὑπέστη σου τὴν ἐμφάνειαν;
20   οὐδεὶς γὰρ ὄψεται πρόσωπον κυρίου καὶ ζήσεται. ἦλθες τοίνυν ὁ ὡραῖος,
ἀλλ' ὡς χωροῦμεν δέξασθαι τοιοῦτος γενόμενος· ἦλθες τὰς τῆς θεότητος
ἀκτῖνας τῇ περιβολῇ συσκιάσας τοῦ σώματος. πῶς γὰρ ἂν ἐχώρησε θνητὴ καὶ
ἐπίκηρος φύσις τῇ ἀκηράτῳ καὶ ἀπροσίτῳ συζυγίᾳ συναρμοσθῆναι, εἰ μὴ τοῖς
ἐν σκότῳ ζῶσιν ἡμῖν ἡ σκιὰ τοῦ σώματος πρὸς τὸ φῶς ἐμεσίτευσεν;

kinsman, and glorious. "From this point, nothing else seems lovely to me, but I have turned away from all things that were thought noble before. My judgment of what is noble no longer errs so as to deem anything lovely besides you: not human approval, not glory, not celebrity, not worldly power. For these things are tinged with a show of nobility for those whose attention is focused on sense perception, but they are not what they are reckoned to be. For how should something be noble when it lacks entire reality? That which is honored in this world, after all, has its being only in the heads of the people who make the judgment, but you are truly beautiful— | not only beautiful, but the very essence of the Beautiful, existing forever as such, being at every moment what you are, neither blooming when the appropriate time comes, nor putting off your bloom at the right time, but stretching your springtime splendor out to match the everlastingness of your life—you whose name is love of humankind. Since, then, you have risen upon us out of Judah, and the Jewish people is brother to the people that comes to you out of the Gentiles, you have rightly, on account of the manifestation of your Deity in the flesh, been named the kinsman[11] of the one who desires you."

Then she adds: *in the shadow by our bed.* That is, "Human nature knows you, or will know you, as the One who became shaded by the divine Economy.[12] For you came," she says, "as the beautiful *kinsman,* the glorious one, | who became present at our couch thickly shaded. For if you yourself had not shaded yourself, concealing the pure ray of your Deity by the 'form of a slave' (Phil 2:7), who could have borne your appearing? For no one shall see 'the face' of the Lord 'and live' (Exod 33:20). Therefore you, the glorious one, came, but you came in such wise as we are able to receive you. You came with the radiance of Divinity shaded by the garment of a body." For how could a mortal and perishable nature be adapted to live together with the imperishable and inaccessible, unless the shadow[13] of the body had mediated between the Light and us who live in darkness (cf. Isa 9:1)?

---

11. Or "beloved." The Greek word here translated as "kinsman" in the bride's address to the bridegroom is ἀδελφιδός (literally, "little brother" or "nephew"), and it renders the Hebrew for "beloved." Gregory, however, makes play, here and below, with both possible senses of the word. See above, homily 3 and n. 22 there.

12. Greek οἰκονομία, which connotes (roughly) "the plan that God has followed to effect human salvation" and in practice often denotes, as here, the central element in that plan, namely, the "enfleshing" (ἐνσάρκωσις) of the Word; cf. John 1:14; Eph 1:9.

13. On this idea see Origen, *Princ.* 2.6.7, where, however, the "shadow" of the Word is the created soul of Jesus. In his commentary on this verse of the Song, Origen only briefly refers to the incarnation, identifying the "bed" of Song 1:16 as Jesus's body, which is shared with the Bride (*Comm. Cant.* 3.2, Baehrens 1925, 176).

κλίνην δὲ ὀνομάζει ἡ νύμφη τῇ τροπικῇ σημασίᾳ τὴν πρὸς τὸ θεῖον
ἀνάκρασιν τῆς ἀνθρωπίνης φύσεως ἑρμηνεύουσα, ὡς καὶ ὁ μέγας ἀπόστολος
ἁρμόζεται τῷ Χριστῷ τὴν παρθένον, ἡμᾶς, καὶ νυμφοστολεῖ [τὴν ψυχὴν] καὶ
τὴν προσκόλλησιν τῶν δύο εἰς ἑνὸς σώματος κοινωνίαν τὸ μέγα μυστήριον
5   εἶναι λέγει τῆς τοῦ Χριστοῦ πρὸς τὴν ἐκκλησίαν ἑνώσεως· εἰπὼν γὰρ ὅτι
Ἔσονται οἱ δύο εἰς σάρκα μίαν ἐπήγαγεν ὅτι Τὸ μυστήριον τοῦτο μέγα ἐστίν,
ἐγὼ δὲ λέγω εἰς Χριστὸν καὶ εἰς τὴν ἐκκλησίαν. διὰ τοῦτο τοίνυν τὸ μυστήριον
κλίνην ἡ παρθένος ψυχὴ τὴν | πρὸς τὸ θεῖον κοινωνίαν ὠνόμασεν.   109
        ταύτην δὲ οὐκ ἄλλως ἦν δυνατὸν γενέσθαι εἰ μὴ διὰ τοῦ σύσκιον
10   ἡμῖν διὰ τοῦ σώματος ἐπιφανῆναι τὸν κύριον, ὃς οὐ νυμφίος μόνον ἀλλὰ
καὶ οἰκοδόμος ἐστίν, αὐτὸς ἐν ἡμῖν καὶ τεχνιτεύων τὸν οἶκον καὶ ὕλη τῆς
τέχνης γινόμενος· ὄροφον γὰρ ἐπιβάλλει τῷ οἴκῳ διὰ τῆς ἀσήπτου ὕλης
καλλωπίζων τὸ ἔργον. τοιαύτη δέ ἐστιν ἡ κέδρος καὶ ἡ κυπάρισσος, ὧν ὁ
ἐγκείμενος τοῖς ξύλοις τόνος πάσης σηπτικῆς αἰτίας κρείττων ἐστίν, οὐ
15   χρόνῳ εἴκων, οὐ σῆτας φύων, οὐκ εὐρῶτι φθειρόμενος. ἐκ τούτων κέδροι
μὲν διὰ τὸ ἐπιμήκεις εἶναι τὰ πλάτη τοῦ οἴκου τῷ ὀρόφῳ διαλαμβάνουσιν,
αἱ δὲ κυπάρισσοι διὰ τῆς λεγομένης φατνώσεως τὴν ἔνδοθεν κατασκευὴν
ὡραΐζουσιν. ἔχει δὲ ἡ λέξις οὕτως· Δοκοὶ οἴκων ἡμῶν κέδροι, φατνώματα
ἡμῶν κυπάρισσοι.
20   πάντως δὲ τὰ δηλούμενα διὰ τῶν ξύλων αἰνίγματα φανερὰ τοῖς
ἐπακολουθοῦσι τῷ εἱρμῷ τῆς διανοίας ἐστίν. βροχὴν ὀνομάζει τὰς ποικίλας
τῶν πειρασμῶν προσβολὰς ἐν τῷ εὐαγγελίῳ ὁ κύριος λέγων ἐπὶ τοῦ καλῶς
τὴν οἰκίαν ἐπὶ τῆς πέτρας οἰκοδομήσαντος ὅτι Κατέβη ἡ βροχὴ καὶ ἔπνευσαν
οἱ ἄνεμοι καὶ ἦλθον οἱ ποταμοὶ καὶ ἀπαθὲς ἔμεινεν ἐν τούτοις τὸ οἰκοδόμημα.
25   ταύτης οὖν ἕνεκεν τῆς κακῆς ἐπομβρίας χρεία τοιούτων ἡμῖν ἐστιν δοκῶν.

In a figurative turn of speech the Bride uses the word *bed* to mean the mingling of the human race[14] with the Divine,[15] just as the great apostle has the virgin—us—"betrothed" to Christ (2 Cor 11:2), and leads the soul in a bridal procession, and declares that the joining of the two in the communion of one body is the great mystery of the union of Christ with the church (cf. Eph 5:32). For when he said, "The two shall become one flesh," he added, "This is a great mystery, but I apply it to Christ and the church." So it is in view of this mystery that the virgin soul | gives the name *bed* to communion with the Divine.

But there was no way in which this communion could come to pass save by the Lord's manifestation to us by way of a shadow, by way of his body—the Lord who is not only Bridegroom but also Architect, who himself, dwelling within us, both constructs his dwelling and is the material that his art employs. For, you see, he adds a roof to the house and embellishes his work with wood that does not decay. Such are the cedar and the cypress. The strength in their timbers is stronger than anything that causes decay; it does not give in to time, nor engender worms, nor dissolve because of mold. Of these two, it is cedars that, because they are long, divide up the width of the house at the roof, while it is cypresses that adorn its interior structure with the carved ceiling that the text mentions: *The beams of our house are cedars, our coffered ceilings are of cypress.*

Now it is perfectly apparent, to those who are following the train of thought, what the enigma of the timbers signifies. In the Gospel, the Lord assigns the name "rain" to the varied assaults of temptations.[16] Of the person who happily builds his house upon a rock he says: "The rain came down and the winds blew and the floods came, and the foundation remained unharmed in the midst of these things" (Matt 7:25). It is, then, on account of this evil inundation that we have need of such "beams" as these. They will mean the

---

14. Literally, "human nature." But I think that here as in many other places Gregory uses this phrase to mean a collective and not a "form," just as in English "humankind" means not "the sort of thing a human is" but the totality of humanity.

15. Thus after all Gregory's interpretation of Song 1:16b follows Origen's. The latter, for whom the Bride here represents the church, takes "our bed" to mean the "body" that the Bride has in common with the Bridegroom, with allusion to 1 Cor 6:15 (Baehrens 1925, 175.19–20). Gregory too connects the enfleshing of Christ directly with the "marriage" in which Christ and church become one flesh, and hence with the κοινωνία of the soul with the Word. See the observations of Daniélou 1954, 24. Theodoret (PG 81:84D) takes an entirely different tack and identifies the "bed" as the holy Scripture, "in which the Bridegroom and the Bride ... are together in a spiritual fellowship."

16. Note that above in homily 2 (p. 51 [Jaeger]), where Gregory is referring to the parable of the sower, it is the sun that is to be identified as "the hostile assault of temptation and trial."

αὗται δ' ἂν εἶεν αἱ ἀρεταί, αἳ τὰς τῶν πειρασμῶν ἐπιρροὰς | ἐντὸς ἑαυτῶν οὐ   110
προσίενται στερραί τε οὖσαι καὶ ἀνένδοτοι καὶ τὸ πρὸς κακίαν ἀμάλακτον ἐν
τοῖς πειρασμοῖς διασῴζουσαι.

    μάθοιμεν δ' ἂν τὸ λεγόμενον τὴν ἐν τῷ Ἐκκλησιαστῇ ῥῆσιν τῷ
5 προκειμένῳ συνεξετάσαντες· ἐκεῖ γάρ φησιν Ἐν ὀκνηρίαις ταπεινωθήσεται
δόκωσις καὶ ἐν ἀργίᾳ χειρῶν στάξει οἰκία. ὥσπερ γὰρ εἰ ἀσθενῆ τε καὶ ἄτονα
ὑπὸ λεπτότητος εἴη τὰ ξύλα τὰ διειληφότα τὸν ὄροφον, ὀκνηρῶς δὲ ἔχοι
πρὸς τὴν τοῦ δώματος ἐπιμέλειαν ὁ τοῦ οἴκου δεσπότης, οὐδὲν ἀπώνατο τῆς
στέγης τοῦ ὄμβρου διὰ σταγόνων εἰσρέοντος (κοιλαίνεται γὰρ ἐξ ἀνάγκης
10 ὁ ὄροφος εἴκων τῷ βάρει τοῦ ὕδατος καὶ οὐκ ἀντέχει τῶν ξύλων ἡ ἀτονία
πρὸς τὴν τοῦ βάρους προσβολὴν ὑποκλάζουσα. διὰ τοῦτο ἐπὶ τὰ ἐντὸς
διαδίδοται τὸ ἐναπειλημμένον τῇ κοιλότητι ὕδωρ καὶ αἱ σταγόνες αὗται κατὰ
τὸν Παροιμιώδη λόγον ἐκβάλλουσι τοῦ οἴκου τὸν ἄνθρωπον ἐν τῇ ἡμέρᾳ
τοῦ ὑετοῦ), οὕτως ἡμῖν τῷ τῆς παραβολῆς αἰνίγματι διακελεύεται διὰ τῆς
15 τῶν ἀρετῶν εὐτονίας ἀνενδότους εἶναι πρὸς τὰς τῶν πειρασμῶν ἐπιρροάς,
μή ποτε μαλακισθέντες διὰ τῆς τῶν παθημάτων ἐμπτώσεως κοῖλοι γενώμεθα
καὶ τὴν ἐπιρροὴν τῶν τοιούτων ὑδάτων ἔξωθεν ἐπὶ τὴν καρδίαν εἰσρέουσαν
ἐντὸς τῶν ταμιείων παραδεξώμεθα, δι' ὧν | φθείρεται ἡμῖν τὰ ἀπόθετα.   111

    αἱ δὲ κέδροι αὗται τοῦ Λιβάνου, ἃς ἐφύτευσεν ὁ κύριος, αἷς ἐννοσσεύουσι
20 τὰ στρουθία, ὧν ἡ τοῦ ἐρωδιοῦ καλιὰ καθηγεῖται, αὗται τοίνυν αἱ κέδροι,
αἱ ἀρεταί, τὸν οἶκον τῆς νυμφικῆς παστάδος κατασφαλίζονται, αἷς
ἐννοσσεύουσιν αἱ ψυχαὶ στρουθία γινόμεναι καὶ τῶν παγίδων ὑπεριπτάμεναι,
ὧν καθηγεῖται ἡ τοῦ ἐρωδιοῦ καλιά, ἣν οἰκίαν ὀνομάζει ὁ λόγος. λέγουσι
δὲ ἀπεχθῶς περὶ τὰς μίξεις ἔχειν τοῦτο τὸ ὄρνεον καί τινι φύσεως ἀνάγκῃ
25 πρὸς ἄλληλα συνδυάζεσθαι, κράζοντά τε καὶ δυσανασχετοῦντα καὶ τὴν
ἀηδίαν ἐπισημαίνοντα. ὅθεν μοι δοκεῖ τὴν καθαρότητα ἐν αἰνίγματι διὰ τοῦ
ὀνόματος τούτου σημαίνειν ὁ λόγος.

    ταύτας οὖν τὰς δοκοὺς ἐπὶ τοῦ ὀρόφου τῆς καθαρᾶς παστάδος βλέπει
ἡ νύμφη, ὁρᾷ δὲ καὶ τὸν ἐκ τῆς κυπαρίσσου κόσμον διά τινος εὐξέστου τε
30 καὶ ἐναρμονίου συνθέσεως τὸ | ὁρώμενον κάλλος ἐπαγλαΐζοντα· κυπάρισσον   112

virtues,[17] which do not | give entrance to the downpour of the temptations because they are solid and do not give way and preserve, in the midst of trials, their intractability in the face of evil.

We may see the point of this if, together with the text before us, we have examined what is said in Ecclesiastes, for there it says, "Through sloth the roof has collapsed, and through the hands' idleness the house leaks" (Eccl 10:18). Just as, if the timbers that support the roof are thin and therefore slack, and the master of the house is slothful about the care of his dwelling, nothing is shed off the roof and the rain comes in drop by drop (for the roof inevitably gets hollowed out when it gives way to the weight of the water, and the slackness of the timbers, sinking under the assault of this weight, offers no resistance; hence the water caught in the depression is distributed on the inside, and the drops themselves, as Proverbs says, cast the man out of his house on the day of a rainstorm [Prov 27:15]), so in the enigma of this parable we are commanded to resist the assaults of temptation by the strength of the virtues, lest, when we are weakened by the passions that fall upon us, we become hollow and take the stream of those waters into our treasure chambers as it attacks the heart from without—waters through which our treasure | is spoiled and corrupted.

Now these same cedars of Lebanon—which the Lord "planted," in which "the birds build their nests," among which "the heron's dwelling" (Ps 103:16–17) is most prominent—these same cedars, I say, the virtues, safeguard the house of the bridal chamber, in which the souls that are becoming birds and are flying above the hunter's snare (cf. Ps 123:7) "build their nests," and among them the heron's nest, which our text calls "dwelling," is the highest. And they say that this bird has a distaste for sexual intercourse,[18] and it couples with others by a kind of compulsion of nature, screeching and showing frustration and giving signs of disgust. Hence it seems to me that by this name the text signifies purity by means of an enigma.

So the Bride looks upon these beams in the ceiling of the pure bridal chamber, but she also sees the decoration done in cypress-wood, which, by providing a nicely worked and harmonious pattern, contributes to the | beauty of the sight, for, she says, the *coffered ceilings* of the roof are *of cypress*.

---

17. Contrast Origen, who identifies the "cedars" as "those who protect the Church," and more specifically the bishops and elders (Baehrens 1925, 177.12–23; trans. Lawson 1956, 175–76). Gregory's exegesis, however, picks up on suggestions of Origen's and develops them lengthily, e.g., that the "beams" of the ceiling protect it from rain and heat. For another appropriation of Origen's hints, see the exegesis of Theodoret (PG 81:85AB).

18. See Aristotle, *Hist. an.* 609b23–24. The "ash-coloured" heron, says Aristotle, "submits with reluctance to the duties of incubation, or to union of the sexes; in fact, it screams during the union, and it is said drips blood from its eyes."

γὰρ εἶπεν εἶναι τὰ τοῦ ὀρόφου φατνώματα. φατνώματα δὲ λέγεται εὔρυθμός
τις καὶ διάγλυφος σανίδων πῆξις τὸ τῆς ὀροφῆς κάλλος διαποικίλλουσα.

τί οὖν διὰ τούτων μανθάνομεν; εὐπνοεῖ φυσικῶς ἡ κυπάρισσος· ἡ δὲ αὐτὴ
καὶ σηπεδόνος ἐστὶν ἀπαράδεκτος καὶ πρὸς πᾶσαν τεκτονικὴν φιλοτεχνίαν
5   ἐπιτηδείως ἔχει λεία τε γινομένη καὶ ἐναρμόνιος καὶ πρὸς τοὺς διὰ τῶν
γλυφίδων καλλωπισμοὺς ἐπιτήδειος. τοῦτο οὖν οἶμαι διὰ τῶν λεγομένων
ἡμᾶς παιδεύεσθαι μὴ μόνον ἐν τῇ ψυχῇ τὰς ἀρετὰς ἐν ἕξει κατορθοῦσθαι
κατὰ τὸ ἄδηλον, ἀλλὰ μηδὲ τῆς κατὰ τὸ φαινόμενον εὐσχημοσύνης ἀμελῶς
ἔχειν· χρὴ γὰρ προνοεῖν καλὰ ἐνώπιον θεοῦ καὶ ἀνθρώπων καὶ θεῷ μὲν
10   πεφανερῶσθαι, ἀνθρώπους δὲ πείθειν καὶ μαρτυρίαν καλὴν ἔχειν ἀπὸ τῶν
ἔξωθεν καὶ λάμπειν τοῖς φωτεινοῖς ἔργοις ἔμπροσθεν τῶν ἀνθρώπων καὶ
εὐσχημόνως περιπατεῖν πρὸς τοὺς ἔξωθεν. ταῦτά ἐστι τὰ φατνώματα τὰ διὰ
τῆς τοῦ Χριστοῦ εὐωδίας, ἧς αἴνιγμά ἐστιν ἡ κυπάρισσος, ἐν τῇ εὐσχημοσύνῃ
τοῦ βίου φιλοτεχνούμενα, καθὼς ᾔδει τὰ τοιαῦτα συντιθέναι καλῶς τε καὶ
15   ἐναρμονίως ὁ σοφὸς ἀρχιτέκτων Παῦλος ὁ λέγων Πάντα κατὰ τάξιν ἐν ὑμῖν
καὶ εὐσχημόνως γινέσθω.

| Τούτων δὲ οὕτω κατορθωθέντων ἐπαύξησις τοῦ ἐν ἡμῖν γίνεται κάλλους   113
τῆς πλατείας ἡμῶν φύσεως τὸ εὐῶδες καὶ καθαρὸν ἄνθος ἀναδιδούσης.
ὄνομα δὲ τῷ ἄνθει κρίνον ἐστίν, ᾧ ἡ φυσικῶς ἐνθεωρουμένη λαμπρότης
20   τὴν τῆς σωφροσύνης μαρμαρυγὴν ὑπαινίσσεται. ταῦτα γὰρ ἡ νύμφη περὶ
ἑαυτῆς διεξέρχεται λέγουσα· ἐγὼ μετὰ τὸ γενέσθαι πρὸς τῇ κλίνῃ ἡμῶν τὸν
νυμφίον συσκιασθέντα τῷ σώματι, ὃς ᾠκοδόμησεν ἑαυτῷ τὸν οἶκον, ἐμέ, ταῖς
τῶν ἀρετῶν κέδροις ὀροφώσας τὴν στέγην καὶ τῇ εὐπνοίᾳ τῶν κυπαρίσσων
καλλωπίσας τὸν ὄροφον, γέγονα ἐκ τοῦ πεδίου τῆς φύσεως ἄνθος εὐχροίᾳ τε
25   καὶ εὐωδίᾳ τῶν λοιπῶν ἀνθῶν διαφέρουσα· κρίνον γὰρ ἀνεφύην ἐκ τῶν
κοιλάδων.

ἔχει δὲ ἡ λέξις οὕτως· Ἐγὼ ἄνθος τοῦ πεδίου, κρίνον τῶν κοιλάδων.
ἀληθῶς γὰρ ἡ διὰ τῶν προθεωρηθέντων ἡμῖν <ἐν> τῷ πλάτει τῆς φύσεως
γεωργηθεῖσα ψυχή (πεδίον γὰρ ἀκούσαντες τὴν πλατύτητα τῆς ἀνθρωπίνης
30   φύσεως ἐνοήσαμεν διὰ τὸ πολλῶν τε καὶ ἀπείρων αὐτὴν δεκτικὴν εἶναι
νοημάτων τε καὶ πραγμάτων καὶ μαθημάτων) ἡ τοίνυν κατὰ τὸν εἰρημένον
τρόπον παρὰ τοῦ γεωργοῦντος τὴν φύσιν ἡμῶν ἐμπονηθεῖσα ψυχὴ ἄνθος
εὔοσμόν τε καὶ λαμπρὸν καὶ καθαρὸν ἀναφύεται ἐκ τοῦ τῆς φύσεως ἡμῶν
πεδίου.

Coffered ceilings, though, refers to well-proportioned, carved work done on wooden panels, which adds variety to the beauty of the roof.

What, then, do we learn from this? The cypress naturally gives off a fragrance. This same wood, moreover, is immune to decay and receptive of every sort of skilled craftsmanship, being at once smooth and handsome and suited to carving. So I think we are taught by these words that it is not only within the soul—invisibly—in the form of an abiding disposition that the virtues are established. We are also taught that the virtues are not averse to the visible manifestation of their loveliness. For it is necessary to take thought for things that are good in the sight of God and humanity (cf. Prov 3:4; 2 Cor 8:21), and also to make ourselves manifest to God while at the same time we persuade our fellow humans, and to have a good testimony from outsiders (1 Thess 4:12), and to shine in good works before humanity (cf. Matt 5:16), and to walk with the look of beauty before outsiders. These are the *coffered ceilings* that, through the sweet odor of Christ (of which the cypress is a figure), are artfully contrived by graciousness of life—just as Paul, the wise master builder, knew how to frame such things beautifully and harmoniously when he said, "Let all things be done among you decently and in order" (1 Cor 14:40).

| After these things have thus been successfully accomplished, there comes about an augmentation of the beauty within us. The broad meadow of our nature brings forth a pure and sweet-smelling blossom. The name of this flower is *lily*, and the brightness that is naturally seen in it gives a hint of the radiance that belongs to self-control. This is what the Bride relates about herself when she says: "After the Bridegroom came to our couch shaded by his body, the Bridegroom who built himself a house—me—and roofed it with the cedar trees of the virtues and adorned the ceiling with the sweet smell of cypress, after that, I say, I came up out of the fertile plain of my nature as a flower superior to all the others both in beauty of color and in sweetness of scent. I grew up out of the valleys as a lily."

The text goes on as follows: *I am a blossom of the plain, a lily of the valleys.* For truly the soul that has been cultivated, by the means we have already seen, in the breadth of its nature (for on hearing the word *plain,* what I thought of was the "broadness" of human nature, on account of its capacity to be the subject of many, indeed unlimited, thoughts, interests, and forms of knowledge)—this soul, then, worked on in the way we have said by the Tiller of our nature's soil, grows up out of the *plain* of our nature as a *blossom* that is fragrant and bright and pure.[19]

---

19. In Origen's view (*Comm. Cant.* 3.4; Baehrens 1925, 177.26), the words "I am a blossom of the plain, a lily of the valleys," are spoken by the Bridegroom, not the Bride, "about himself and about the Bride." Thus for him the Bridegroom is the lily, while the plain is "that … people

τὸ δὲ πεδίον τοῦτο, κἂν συγκρίσει τῆς | οὐρανίας διαγωγῆς κοιλὰς   114
ὀνομάζηται, οὐδὲν ἧττον πεδίον ἐστὶ καὶ οὐ κωλύεται ἡ ἐν αὐτῷ γεωργηθεῖσα
καλῶς ἄνθος γενέσθαι· ἐκ γὰρ τοῦ κοίλου ἐπὶ τὸ ὑψηλὸν ὁ βλαστὸς
ἀνατέλλει, καθὼς ἔστιν ἰδεῖν ἐπὶ τοῦ κρίνου γινόμενον· ἐπὶ πολὺ γὰρ ἐπὶ τὸ
5   ὄρθιον ἐκ τῆς ῥίζης καλαμοειδῶς ἀναδραμοῦσα ἡ βοτάνη τοῦ κρίνου τότε τὸ
ἄνθος ἐκ τῆς κορυφῆς ἀναδίδωσιν οὐκ ὀλίγῳ τῷ μεταξὺ διαστήματι τῆς γῆς
ἀποστήσασα, ὡς ἄν, οἶμαι, καθαρὸν ἐν μετεώρῳ διαμένοι τὸ κάλλος τῇ πρὸς
τὴν γῆν ἐπιμιξίᾳ μὴ μολυνόμενον.
   διὰ ταῦτα καὶ ὁ δίκαιος ὀφθαλμὸς τὴν τοῦτο γενομένην ἤτοι γενήσεσθαι
10   ποθήσασαν (ἀμφότερα γὰρ ἐκ τῶν εἰρημένων ὑπενοήσαμεν, ἢ ὅτι
μεγαλαυχεῖται ὡς ἤδη γεγενημένη ὅπερ ἐπόθησεν, ἢ ὅτι δεῖται τοῦ γεωργοῦ
ἄνθος γενέσθαι διὰ τῆς ἐκείνου σοφίας ἐκ τῶν κοιλάδων τῆς ἀνθρωπίνης
ζωῆς εἰς κρίνου κάλλος ἀναδραμοῦσα), εἴτε οὖν γενέσθαι βούλεται τοῦτο εἴτε
καὶ γέγονεν ὅπερ ἠθέλησε, καλῶς ὁ δίκαιος ὀφθαλμὸς τοῦ νυμφίου πρὸς τὴν
15   ἀγαθὴν ἐπιθυμίαν τῆς πρὸς αὐτὸν ὁρώσης ἰδὼν ἐπένευσε γενέσθαι κρίνον
αὐτὴν μὴ συμπνιγόμενον ταῖς τοῦ βίου ἀκάνθαις, ἃς θυγατέρας ὠνόμασεν
ἐνδειξάμενος, οἶμαι, κατὰ τὸ σιωπώμενον τὰς ἐχθρὰς τῆς ἀνθρωπίνης ζωῆς
δυνάμεις, ὧν πατὴρ ὁ τῆς | κακίας εὑρετὴς κατονομάζεται.   115

And even though this plain, should one compare it with the | heavenly way of life, might be called a hollow, it is nonetheless a plain for all that, and the soul that has been cultivated in it is not prevented from blossoming beautifully. For the shoot rises from the hollow to the height, as one can see in the case of the white lily. Straight up from the root for a great distance the lily plant ascends, not unlike a reed, and then puts out a flower from its top when it has been separated from the earth by no little distance—in order, I imagine, that its beauty, unsoiled by contact with the earth, may, in midair, remain pure.

On this account too, a soul that has arrived at this state or else has desired to arrive at it (for on the basis of the text I think both senses are possible: either she is boasting because she has already become what she desired; or else she is begging the husbandman that through his wisdom she may become a blossom and rise out of the hollows of the human way of life to attain the beauty of the lily)—whether, then, I say, she wants to become this or has become what she wanted, the righteous eye[20] of the Bridegroom, discerning the good desire of the soul that looks toward him, properly consents to her becoming a lily, and a lily that is not smothered by the *thorns* of life. These thorns he designated *daughters*, identifying them implicitly, as I see it, as the powers that threaten human life, whose father is styled | the inventor of evil.[21]

---

which was cultivated by the Prophets and the Law," and the valley is the "rocky and uncultivated place of the Gentiles" (Baehrens 1925, 177–78). It is only secondarily that he suggests that the individual soul may be the plain or the field or a lily blooming therein (178.15–19; 179.9–11, 13–14). Naturally enough, however, it is this idea that Gregory follows out and develops, along lines that Origen intimates.

20. This sentence, up to this point, cannot be put into comprehensible English as it stands in the Greek. Its subject ("the just eye") is named at its very start, but without any accompanying verb or any mention of the Bridegroom. The sentence is then cut off by the remarks set in parenthesis (which obviously occurred to Gregory suddenly, even as he was speaking), and it hangs incomplete and unintelligible until its opening is in effect repeated after the close of the parenthesis, this time together with its verb (ἐπένευσε: "consents") and a helpful indication of the person to whom the eye in question belongs. Some amanuensis no doubt took down Gregory's words exactly as he spoke them, and they have stood uncorrected.

21. I.e., Satan. Gregory notes the parallel between daughters and thorns and concludes (1) that the daughters, like the thorns, must be assigned a negative valence and (2) that they would not be called daughters in the text if their significance did not derive from the identity of their parent. He is not really much interested in this verse, but Origen takes more pains with it. For him the "thorns" are best understood as representing heretics, and they are also called "daughters" because heretics are souls that "begin by believing, and afterwards depart from the road of faith and the truth of the Church's teaching" (*Comm. Cant.* 3.4; trans. Lawson 1956, 178; cf. Baehrens 1925, 178–79).

Ὡς κρίνον οὖν φησιν ἐν μέσῳ τῶν ἀκανθῶν, οὕτως ἀδελφή μου ἀνὰ μέσον τῶν θυγατέρων. ὅσην ὁρῶμεν τῆς εἰς τὸ ὕψος ἀνόδου τὴν προκοπὴν ἐπὶ τῆς ψυχῆς γινομένην· πρώτη ἄνοδος τὸ πρὸς τὴν καθαιρετικὴν τῆς Αἰγυπτίας δυνάμεως ἵππον ὁμοιωθῆναι, δευτέρα ἄνοδος τὸ πλησίον αὐτὴν γενέσθαι
5   καὶ περιστερὰς ποιῆσαι τὰ ὄμματα, τρίτη νῦν ἄνοδος τὸ μηκέτι πλησίον, ἀλλ᾽ ἀδελφὴν τοῦ δεσπότου ὀνομασθῆναι· Ὃς γὰρ ἂν ποιήσῃ, φησί, τὸ θέλημα τοῦ πατρός μου τοῦ ἐν τοῖς οὐρανοῖς, οὗτος ἀδελφός μου καὶ ἀδελφὴ καὶ μήτηρ ἐστίν. ἐπεὶ οὖν γέγονεν ἄνθος μηδὲν ὑπὸ τῶν ἀκανθοφόρων πειρασμῶν πρὸς τὸ γενέσθαι κρίνον παραβλαβεῖσα, ἐπιλαθομένη δὲ τοῦ λαοῦ καὶ τοῦ
10   οἴκου τοῦ πατρὸς αὐτῆς πρὸς τὸν ἀληθινὸν εἶδε πατέρα (διὸ καὶ ἀδελφὴ τοῦ υἱοῦ ὀνομάζεται τῷ τῆς υἱοθεσίας πνεύματι πρὸς τὴν συγγένειαν ταύτην εἰσποιηθεῖσα καὶ τῆς πρὸς τὰς θυγατέρας τοῦ ψευδωνύμου πατρὸς κοινωνίας ἀπαλλαγεῖσα), | πάλιν ἑαυτῆς γίνεται ὑψηλοτέρα καὶ βλέπει τι μυστήριον διὰ   116
τῶν τῆς περιστερᾶς ὀφθαλμῶν (λέγω δὲ τῷ πνεύματι τῆς προφητείας).
15   ὃ δὲ βλέπει, τοῦτό ἐστιν· Ὡς μῆλον ἐν τοῖς ξύλοις τοῦ δρυμοῦ, οὕτως ἀδελφιδός μου ἀνὰ μέσον τῶν υἱῶν. τί οὖν ἐστιν, ὃ τεθέαται; δρυμὸν ὀνομάζει συνήθως ἡ θεία γραφὴ τὸν ὑλώδη τῶν ἀνθρώπων βίον τὸν τὰ ποικίλα εἴδη τῶν παθημάτων ὑλομανήσαντα, ἐν ᾧ τὰ φθαρτικὰ θηρία φωλεύει καὶ κατακρύπτεται, ὧν ἡ φύσις ἐν φωτὶ καὶ ἡλίῳ ἀνενέργητος
20   μένουσα διὰ σκότους τὴν ἰσχὺν ἔχει· μετὰ γὰρ τὸ δῦναι τὸν ἥλιόν φησιν ὁ προφήτης νυκτὸς ἐπιγενομένης ἐν αὐτῇ τὰ θηρία τοῦ δρυμοῦ τῶν φωλεῶν ἀναδύεσθαι. ἐπειδὴ τοίνυν ὁ μονιὸς ὁ ἐν τῷ δρυμῶνι τρεφόμενος τὴν καλὴν τῆς ἀνθρωπίνης φύσεως ἄμπελον ἐλυμήνατο, καθὼς φησιν ὁ προφήτης ὅτι Ἐλυμήνατο αὐτὴν ὗς ἐκ δρυμοῦ καὶ μονιὸς ἄγριος κατενεμήσατο αὐτήν, διὰ
25   τοῦτο ἐμφύεται τῷ δρυμῶνι τὸ μῆλον, ὃ τῷ μὲν ξύλον εἶναι τῆς ἀνθρωπίνης ὕλης ἐστὶν ὁμοούσιον (ἐπειράσθη γὰρ κατὰ πάντα | καθ᾽ ὁμοιότητα χωρὶς   117
ἁμαρτίας), τῷ δὲ τοιοῦτον φέρειν καρπόν, δι᾽ οὗ γλυκαίνεται τὰ τῆς ψυχῆς αἰσθητήρια, πλείονα ἔχει τὴν πρὸς τὸν δρυμὸν παραλλαγὴν ἢ ὅσην ἔχει πρὸς τὰς ἀκάνθας τὸ κρίνον· τὸ μὲν γὰρ κρίνον μέχρι τοῦ εἴδους καὶ τῆς
30   εὐπνοίας τὸ τερπνὸν ἔχει, ἡ δὲ τοῦ μήλου χάρις πρὸς τὰς τρεῖς αἰσθήσεις ἁρμοδίως καταμερίζεται καὶ ὀφθαλμὸν εὐφραίνουσα τῇ ὥρᾳ τοῦ εἴδους καὶ τὴν ὀσφραντικὴν ἡδύνουσα αἴσθησιν διὰ τῆς εὐπνοίας καὶ τροφὴ γινομένη καταγλυκαίνει τὰ γευστικὰ αἰσθητήρια.

Therefore just as he says *a lily among thorns*, so too he says *my sister*[22] *among the daughters*. We see how great the soul's progress is on its road upward. The first stage is to be made like the *horse* that destroyed the Egyptian power. The second stage is for the soul to become *close one* and to have its eyes made doves. Now, however, the third stage is no longer to be designated *close one* but rather "sister" of the Master. "For," he says, "whoever shall do the will of my Father in heaven, the same is my brother, and sister, and mother" (Matt 12:50). Since, then, in the course of becoming a lily, she became a blossom without being hindered by thorny trials and temptations, she has forgotten the household and people of her own father and looked to the true Father (which is why she is named the Son's sister when she has been adopted by "the Spirit of sonship" [Rom 8:15] into this kinship[23] and has been delivered from fellowship with the daughters of the "father" falsely so called), and | again she rises above herself and contemplates a mystery by means of the eyes of the dove (that is, by the Spirit of prophecy).

This is what she sees: *As an apple tree among the trees of the wood, so is my kinsman among the sons*. What is it, then, that she has seen? As its custom is, the Holy Scripture assigns the name "wood" to that material life of the human race that is bursting with the various sorts of passions, the wood in which destroyer beasts lurk and hide, whose kind accomplishes nothing in the light of the sun but takes its strength from darkness. For after the sun has set, the prophet says, when night has come, "the wild beasts of the wood" come out of their lairs (Ps 103:20). The wild boar that feeds in the thicket ravages the beautiful vineyard of human nature, as the prophet says: "The wild boar ravaged it, and the wild pig grazed over it" (Ps 79:14); and this explains why the *apple tree* is planted in the midst of the thicket. Because it is a tree, it is of the same substance as the stuff of humanity (he was tried "in every way | in accordance with his likeness to us, apart from sin" [Heb 4:15]), but because it bears a fruit by which the perceptive faculties of the soul are touched with sweetness, it differs to a greater degree from the *wood* than the *lily* does from the thorns. The *lily* is pleasing in its appearance and its scent, but the delight afforded by the apple is shared, in a way suited to each, among three senses: it gladdens the eye by the splendor of its appearance; by its scent, it gives pleasure to the sense of smell; and as food it provides sweetness to the organs of taste.

---

22. The word "sister" (ἀδελφή) is a reading peculiar to Gregory—and one to which he attaches great significance, as becomes manifest in what immediately follows. The manuscripts of the LXX known to us agree on "close one" (πλησίον).

23. Greek συγγένεια. This idea is based ultimately on Paul's argument in Gal 4.

καλῶς οὖν εἶδεν ἡ νύμφη τὸ ἑαυτῆς πρὸς τὸν δεσπότην διάφορον, ὅτι ἐκεῖνος μὲν ἡμῖν καὶ ὀφθαλμῶν γίνεται χάρις φῶς γινόμενος καὶ μύρον [ἐν] τῇ ὀσφρήσει καὶ ζωὴ τοῖς ἐσθίουσιν (ὁ γὰρ φαγὼν αὐτὸν ζήσεται, καθώς φησί που τὸ εὐαγγέλιον), ἡ δὲ ἀνθρωπίνη φύσις δι' ἀρετῆς τελειωθεῖσα ἄνθος
5   γίνεται μόνον, οὐ τὸν γεωργὸν τρέφουσα ἀλλ' ἑαυτὴν καλλωπίζουσα· οὐ γὰρ ἐκεῖνος ἐνδεὴς τῶν ἡμετέρων ἀγαθῶν, ἀλλ' ἡμεῖς τῶν ἐκείνου δεόμεθα, καθώς φησιν ὁ προφήτης Ὅτι τῶν ἀγαθῶν μου οὐ χρείαν ἔχεις.
       Διὰ τοῦτο βλέπει τὸν νυμφίον ἡ κεκαθαρμένη ψυχὴ μῆλον ἐν τοῖς τοῦ δρυμοῦ ξύλοις γενόμενον, ἵνα ἐγκεντρίσας | ἑαυτῷ πάντας τοὺς ἀγρίους τοῦ   118
10   δρυμῶνος κλάδους τῷ ὁμοίῳ καρπῷ βρύειν παρασκευάσῃ. ὥσπερ τοίνυν τὰς θυγατέρας διὰ τὸ ταῖς ἀκάνθαις ὁμοιωθῆναι τὰ τοῦ ψευδωνύμου πατρὸς ἐνοήσαμεν τέκνα, αἵτινες τῷ ἄνθει συμπαραφυεῖσαι τῷ χρόνῳ καὶ αὐταὶ πρὸς τὴν τοῦ κρίνου μεταβαίνουσι χάριν, οὕτω καὶ ἐνταῦθα τοὺς προσεικασθέντας τοῖς ξύλοις τοῦ δρυμοῦ ἀκούσαντες οὐ φίλους σημαίνεσθαι τοῦ νυμφίου ἀλλὰ
15   τοὺς ἐναντίους ὑπενοήσαμεν, οὓς υἱοὺς ὄντας τοῦ σκότους καὶ τέκνα ὀργῆς τῇ κοινωνίᾳ τοῦ καρποῦ εἰς υἱοὺς φωτὸς καὶ υἱοὺς εἰρήνης μετασκευάζει. διὰ τοῦτό φησιν ἡ γεγυμνασμένη τὰ αἰσθητήρια ὅτι Ὁ καρπὸς αὐτοῦ γλυκὺς ἐν τῷ λάρυγγί μου. καρπὸς δὲ ἡ διδασκαλία πάντως ἐστίν· Ὡς γλυκέα γάρ φησιν ὁ προφήτης τῷ λάρυγγί μου τὰ λόγιά σου, ὑπὲρ μέλι τῷ στόματί μου.
20   Ὡς μῆλον ἐν τοῖς ξύλοις τοῦ δρυμοῦ, οὕτως ἀδελφιδός μου ἀνὰ μέσον τῶν υἱῶν. ὑπὸ τὴν σκιὰν αὐτοῦ ἐπεθύμησα καὶ ἐκάθισα καὶ ὁ καρπὸς αὐτοῦ γλυκὺς ἐν τῷ λάρυγγί μου. τότε γὰρ ὡς ἀληθῶς γλυκαίνεται τῷ λόγῳ τὰ τῆς ψυχῆς αἰσθητήρια, ὅταν ἡμᾶς πρὸς τὸν ἐκ τῶν πειρασμῶν | φλογμὸν ἡ   119
       σκιὰ τοῦ μήλου διατειχίσῃ, ὡς μὴ συγκαίεσθαι ἡμᾶς ὑπὸ τοῦ τοιούτου ἡλίου
25   γυμνῆς τῆς κεφαλῆς ὑπερζέοντος.
       οὐκ ἔστι δὲ ἄλλως ὑπὸ τὴν σκιὰν τοῦ ξύλου τῆς ζωῆς ἀναψῦξαι μὴ τῆς ἐπιθυμίας πρὸς τοῦτο τὴν ψυχὴν ἀναγούσης. ὁρᾷς διὰ τί σοι ἡ ἐπιθυμητικὴ δύναμις ἔγκειται, ἵνα σοι πόθον ἐμποιήσῃ τοῦ μήλου, οὗ πολυειδὴς γίνεται τοῖς προσεγγίσασιν ἡ ἀπόλαυσις· ὅ τε γὰρ ὀφθαλμὸς τῇ ὥρᾳ τοῦ κάλλους
30   προσαναπαύεται καὶ ὁ μυκτὴρ ἀναπνεῖ τὴν εὐωδίαν καὶ τὸ σῶμα τρέφεται καὶ

The Bride was right, then, to discern the difference between herself and the Lord. He is joy to our eyes when he comes as light, perfume to our sense of smell, and life to those who eat him (for anyone who eats him will live, as the Gospel says somewhere [cf. John 6:51–52]). On the other hand, human nature, when through virtue it achieves its fulfilment, becomes no more than a flower, which does not feed its planter but adorns itself. For he stands in no need of our good things, but we stand in need of his, as the prophet says: "You have no need of my goods" (Ps 15:2).

Why is it that the soul that has been purified perceives the Bridegroom as *an apple tree* in the midst of the thicket's bushes? So that | when he has grafted all the wild branches into himself, he will equip them to abound with fruit like his own. Thus because they are likened to thorns, we understand *the daughters* to be children of the counterfeit father, but children who, when they have grown alongside the flower and together with it, are themselves changed as time goes on into the beauty of the lily. In the same way, when we hear of persons who resemble the trees of the wood, we presume that what is meant is not the friends but the enemies of the Bridegroom. Yet though they be sons of darkness and children of wrath, he transmutes them into sons of light and sons of peace by their sharing in the fruit he bears. This is the reason why the soul that has trained its organs of sense says, *His fruit was sweet in my throat.* The word *fruit,* certainly, means teaching, for the prophet says, "Thy words are sweet to my throat, better than honey to my mouth" (Ps 118:103).

As an apple tree among the trees of the wood, so is my kinsman among the sons. Under his shadow I rejoiced and sat down, and his fruit was sweet in my throat. For the sense organs of the soul are truly touched with sweetness by the Word when the apple tree's shadow[24] protects us from the fiery | blaze of temptations so that we are not burned up by such a sun as it seethes over our uncovered heads.[25]

There is no way in which it is possible to be cool under the shadow of the tree of life except as desire leads the soul up to it. You see why you have a faculty of desire, in order, namely, that you may conceive an appetite for the *apple,*[26] the delight of which takes many forms for those who have drawn near to it. For the eye rests upon the splendor of its beauty, and the nostril breathes its fragrance in, and the body is nourished, and the mouth is touched

---

24. Origen devotes much of his time to an explication of the apple tree's shadow, his exegesis turning on Lam 4:20. Gregory in this section follows out just one of Origen's developments of this theme.

25. For this symbolism, see above, homily 2, pp. 50–51 (Jaeger).

26. The Greek μῆλος means both an apple tree and its fruit, and in reading this passage it is well to keep this fact in mind.

τὸ στόμα γλυκαίνεται καὶ ὁ καύσων ἀποστρέφεται καὶ ἡ σκιὰ θρόνος γίνεται,
ᾗ ἐγκάθηται ἡ ψυχὴ ἡ τῶν λοιμῶν τὴν καθέδραν ἀρνησαμένη.

Εἶτά φησιν Εἰσαγάγετέ με εἰς οἶκον τοῦ οἴνου, τάξατε ἐπ' ἐμὲ ἀγάπην,
στηρίσατέ με ἐν μύροις, στοιβάσατέ με ἐν μήλοις, ὅτι τετρωμένη ἀγάπης ἐγώ.
5   ὢ πῶς τρέχει τὸν θεῖον δρόμον ἡ καλῶς τῇ ἵππῳ προσεικασθεῖσα ψυχή, ὡς
πυκνοῖς τε καὶ συντεταμένοις τοῖς ἅλμασι τοῖς ἔμπροσθεν ἐπεκτείνεται, πρὸς
δὲ τὸ κατόπιν οὐκ ἐπιστρέφεται· πόσων ἔτυχεν ἐν τοῖς φθάσασιν. καὶ ἔτι διψῇ.
καὶ τοσαύτη τοῦ δίψους ἐστὶν ἡ ἐπίτασις, ὅ τι οὐκ ἀρκεῖται τῷ τῆς σοφίας
κρατῆρι. | οὐδ' ἱκανὸν οἴεται πρὸς θεραπείαν τῆς δίψης ὅλον ἐγχέασθαι τὸν   120
10   κρατῆρα τῷ στόματι, ἀλλ' εἰς αὐτὸν τοῦ οἴνου τὸν οἶκον παραχθῆναι ζητεῖ καὶ
αὐταῖς ταῖς ληνοῖς ὑποσχεῖν τὸ στόμα, αἵ τὸν οἶνον τὸν ἡδὺν ὑπερβλύζουσι,
καὶ ἰδεῖν τὸν βότρυν τὸν ταῖς ληνοῖς ἐνθλιβόμενον καὶ τὴν ἄμπελον ἐκείνην
τὴν τὸν τοιοῦτον βότρυν ἐκτρέφουσαν καὶ τὸν γεωργὸν τῆς ἀληθινῆς
ἀμπέλου τὸν οὕτως εὔτροφον τὸν βότρυν καὶ ἡδὺν ἐργαζόμενον·
15   ὧν ἕκαστον περιττὸν ἂν εἴη διευκρινεῖσθαι φανερᾶς οὔσης τῆς ἑκάστῳ
τούτων ἐνθεωρουμένης τροπικῆς σημασίας. πάντως δὲ κἀκεῖνο βούλεται
κατιδεῖν τὸ μυστήριον, πῶς ἐρυθαίνεται τῷ πατητῷ τῆς ληνοῦ τὰ τοῦ
νυμφίου ἱμάτια, περὶ οὗ φησιν ὁ προφήτης Διὰ τί σου ἐρυθρὰ τὰ ἱμάτια καὶ
τὰ ἐνδύματά σου ὡς ἀπὸ πατητοῦ ληνοῦ; διὰ ταῦτα καὶ τὰ τοιαῦτα ἐντὸς
20   γενέσθαι τοῦ οἴκου ποθεῖ, ἐν ᾧ τὸ κατὰ τὸν οἶνόν ἐστι μυστήριον.

εἶτα ἐντὸς γενομένη πάλιν ἐπὶ τὸ μεῖζον ἐξάλλεται· ζητεῖ γὰρ ὑποταγῆναι
τῇ ἀγάπῃ. ἀγάπη δέ ἐστιν ὁ θεὸς κατὰ τὴν Ἰωάννου φωνήν, ᾧ τὸ ὑποταγῆναι
τὴν ψυχὴν σωτηρίαν εἶναι ὁ Δαβὶδ | ἀπεφήνατο. ἐπεὶ οὖν γέγονα, φησίν, ἐν   121
τῷ οἴκῳ τοῦ οἴνου, ὑποτάξατέ με τῇ ἀγάπῃ ἤτοι τάξατε ἐπ' ἐμὲ τὴν ἀγάπην.
25   ὅπως γὰρ ἂν χρήσῃ τῇ ἀναστροφῇ τοῦ λόγου, ταὐτόν ἐστι δι' ἑκατέρου τὸ
σημαινόμενον, ἔκ τε τοῦ ὑπὸ τὴν ἀγάπην ταχθῆναι καὶ ἐκ τοῦ τὴν ἀγάπην
αὐτῇ ἐπιταχθῆναι.

with sweetness, and burning heat is turned away, and the shadow becomes a throne on which there is set the soul that has repudiated the seat of pestilence (cf. Ps 1:1).

Next it says: *Bring me into the house of wine, set love in order upon me, strengthen me with perfumes, encompass me with apples, for I have been wounded by love.*" O how the soul—rightly likened to a mare—runs the divine race as with frequent, urgent leaps she stretches out toward that which lies ahead (cf. Phil 3:14) and is not turned back! How much she has already attained! May she thirst even more! And such is the vehemence of her thirst that the cup of Wisdom does not satisfy her (cf. Prov 2:9). | Nor, for the slaking of her thirst, does she think that it is enough to pour the entire cup into her mouth. No, she seeks to be brought into the very *house of wine,* and to hold her mouth under the winevats themselves as they overflow with sweet wine (cf. Prov 3:10), and to see the grape cluster being pressed in the vats and the vine that puts forth such a cluster and that Husbandman of the true vine whose work produces a cluster so sweet and thriving.

It would be superfluous to explicate the particular meaning of each of these items, for the symbolic sense discerned in each of them is evident.[27] But the Bride also wants, in every way, to see into this mystery, namely, how the Bridegroom's garments are made red with the trodden grapes in the winevat. It is with reference to this Bridegroom that the prophet says, "For what reason are your garments red, and your clothing, as from the trodden grapes of the winevat?" (Isa 63:2). For these and the like reasons, the soul wants to come inside *the house of wine,* in which the mystery of the wine is found.

And then, once inside, she leaps forward again in search of something better. She seeks to be subject to love. Now according to what John says, love means God (cf. 1 John 4:8, 16), and David declared that it is salvation for the soul to be subject to God (Ps 6:2). | "Since, then," she says, "I have entered the house of wine, subject me to love," or *set love in order upon me.*[28] For whichever turn of speech she employs—being subjected to love and having love "set in order" upon her—what is meant is the same.

---

27. It is evident in part at least because Origen had made it so. What is obvious to Gregory from the words of his text is that the "house of wine" is where the church or the soul can "enjoy the teachings of Wisdom and the mysteries of knowledge as the sweetness of a banquet and the gladness of wine" (*Comm. Cant.* 3.6; trans. Lawson 1956, 186–87; cf. Baehrens 1925, 185.24–27).

28. It should be noted that the verb translated here by "subject" or "be subjected" (ὑποτάσσω) is a compound form of τάσσω, "dispose" or "order." Again Gregory plays with alternative senses of the same word. Thus just below he discusses the proper "ordering" (τάξις) of love, taking a hint from 1 Cor 14:40 ("Let all things be done decently and in order [κατὰ τάξιν]). Cf. Origen, who explains that the Bride's words mean, "Teach me the different degrees of charity" (trans. Lawson 1956, 191; cf. Baehrens 1925, 188.20–21).

Ἢ τάχα τι καὶ δόγμα τῶν ἀστειοτέρων διὰ ταύτης τῆς φωνῆς
διδασκόμεθα, οἵαν ἀνατιθέναι προσήκει τῷ θεῷ τὴν ἀγάπην καὶ ὅπως πρὸς
τοὺς ἀνθρώπους ἔχειν· εἰ γὰρ χρὴ πάντα κατὰ τάξιν καὶ εὐσχημόνως γίνεσθαι,
πολὺ μᾶλλον ἐν τοῖς τοιούτοις ἡ τάξις ἁρμόδιος.

5   ού γὰρ ἂν οὐδὲ ὁ Κάϊν ἐπὶ
τῷ κακῶς διελεῖν κατεκρίθη, εἰ μετὰ τοῦ ὀρθῶς προσενεγκεῖν καὶ τὸ πρέπον
ἐν τῇ τάξει ἐφύλαξε τῶν αὐτῷ τε πρὸς τὴν χρείαν καταλειπομένων καὶ τῶν
τῷ θεῷ ἀφιερουμένων· δέον γὰρ ἐκ τῶν πρωτογενημάτων τῷ θεῷ τῆς θυσίας
ἀπάρξασθαι, αὐτὸς τῶν τιμιωτέρων ἐμφορηθεὶς τὸν θεὸν τοῖς λειψάνοις
ἐδεξιώσατο.

10   χρὴ τοίνυν | εἰδέναι τῆς ἀγάπης τὴν τάξιν, ἣν ὑφηγεῖται διὰ τοῦ νόμου,   122
πῶς μὲν ἀγαπᾶσθαι χρὴ τὸν θεόν, πῶς δὲ τὸν πλησίον καὶ τὴν γυναῖκα καὶ
τὸν ἐχθρόν, μήποτε ἄτακτός τις καὶ ἐνηλλαγμένη γένηται τῆς ἀγάπης ἡ
ἀποπλήρωσις· δεῖ γὰρ τὸν θεὸν μὲν ἀγαπᾶν ἐξ ὅλης καρδίας τε καὶ ψυχῆς καὶ
δυνάμεως καὶ αἰσθήσεως, τὸν δὲ πλησίον ὡς ἑαυτόν, τὴν γυναῖκα δέ, εἰ μέν

15   τις καθαρωτέρας ἐστὶ ψυχῆς, ὡς ὁ Χριστὸς τὴν ἐκκλησίαν, ὁ δὲ ἐμπαθέστερος,
ὡς τὸ ἴδιον σῶμα (οὕτω γὰρ κελεύει ὁ τῶν τοιούτων διατάκτης Παῦλος),
τὸν ἐχθρὸν δὲ ἐν τῷ μὴ κακὸν ἀντιδοῦναι κακοῦ, ἀλλὰ δι᾿ εὐεργεσίας τὴν
ἀδικίαν ἀμείψασθαι. νῦν δὲ συγκεχυμένην ἔστιν ἰδεῖν καὶ ἄτακτον ἐπὶ τῶν
πολλῶν τὴν ἀγάπην, διὰ τῆς ἀκαταλλήλου ἀναρμοστίας πεπλανημένως

20   ἐνεργουμένην, οἳ χρήματα μὲν καὶ τιμὰς καὶ γυναῖκας, ἂν τύχωσι θερμότερον
πρὸς αὐτὰς διακείμενοι, ἐξ ὅλης ἀγαπῶσι ψυχῆς καὶ δυνάμεως, ὡς καὶ τὴν
ζωὴν ἂν ὑπὲρ αὐτῶν ἐθελῆσαι προέσθαι, θεὸν δὲ τοσοῦτον ὅσον δοκεῖν· τῷ
δὲ πλησίον μόγις ἂν ἐπιδείξαιντο τὴν τοῖς ἐχθροῖς ἀφορισθεῖσαν ἀγάπην. ἡ
δὲ πρὸς τὸν μισοῦντα | σχέσις ἐστὶ τὸ μείζονι κακῷ τοὺς προλελυπηκότας   123

25   ἀμύνεσθαι. τάξατε οὖν, φησίν, ἐπ᾿ ἐμὲ τὴν ἀγάπην, ὥστε θεῷ μὲν ἀναθεῖναι
ὅσον ὀφείλεται, ἐπὶ δὲ τῶν ἄλλων ἑκάστου τοῦ προσήκοντος μέτρου μὴ
ἀστοχῆσαι.

ἢ καὶ τοῦτο τυχόν ἐστιν ὑπονοῆσαι διὰ τοῦ λόγου, ὅτι ἐπειδὴ ἀγαπηθεῖσα
παρὰ τὴν πρώτην διὰ τῆς παρακοῆς ἐν τοῖς ἐχθροῖς ἐλογίσθην, νυνὶ δὲ πάλιν

30   εἰς τὴν αὐτὴν ἐπανῆλθον χάριν δι᾿ ἀγάπης τῷ δεσπότῃ συναρμοσθεῖσα,
κυρώσατέ μοι τὸ τῆς χάριτος ταύτης τεταγμένον καὶ ἀμετάστατον, ὑμεῖς
οἱ φίλοι τοῦ νυμφίου, δι᾿ ἐπιμελείας καὶ προσοχῆς τῷ παγίῳ συντηροῦντές
μοι τὴν πρὸς τὸ κρεῖττον ῥοπήν;

Here, perhaps, by this turn of phrase, we are also taught a basic truth of unusual subtlety, namely, what sort of love we ought to extend to God and how we are to relate ourselves to other human persons. For if it is necessary that everything be done in order and decently (cf. 1 Cor 14:40), how much more is a fitting order required in such matters as these! For not even Cain would have been condemned for dividing his sacrifice wrongly, if, in addition to making his offering correctly, he had kept to what was proper where it was a question of what was consecrated to God and what was retained for his own use. He ought to have offered his sacrifice to God from the firstfruits, but he filled himself with the best things and honored God with what was left.

So one must | be aware of the order of love that the law lays down: how it is right for God to be loved on the one hand, and how it is right for neighbor, wife, and enemy to be loved on the other, lest one's fulfillment of love become something disordered and inverted. For one ought to love God with the whole heart and soul and power and perception; and one's neighbor as oneself; and one's wife, if one is truly pure in soul, as Christ loved the church (cf. Eph 5:25), or else, if one is more subject to passion, as one's own body (cf. Eph 5:28), for so Paul, the ordainer of such things, commands; and one's enemy by not returning evil for evil but by repaying injustice with kindness. As it is, though, anyone can see that love is in most instances confused and disordered—exercised in a way that goes wrong because it is inappropriate and contrary to the rule. People love things and honors and wives (if they happen to be warmly disposed toward them) with their entire soul and strength, so that they are willing to give up life on their account, but God they love as much as seems good to them. And where their neighbor is concerned, they scarcely even exhibit the love prescribed for enemies. Their disposition toward one who hates them | is to requite those who have injured them previously with a greater evil. So the Bride says: "*Set love in order upon me,* so that I may dedicate to God as much as is owed him and may not, in the case of each of the others, diverge from the proper measure of love."[29]

Further, it may be that in this saying there is a concealed meaning, to wit: "Even though I was loved at the beginning, because of my transgression I was reckoned among the enemies of God; but now, reconciled to the Master by love, I am restored to that very same grace. Do you, therefore, O friends of the Bridegroom, confirm for me that this love is something rightly ordered and unchangeable. By your care and your concern, preserve in steadfastness my impulse toward what is higher."

---

29. The above section is a brisk paraphrase of Origen's much longer and more detailed discussion of the proper "ordering" of love (Baehrens 1925, 186ff.; cf. trans. Lawson 1956, 187ff.).

Ταῦτα δὲ εἰποῦσα πάλιν πρὸς τὸ ὑψηλότερον μέτεισι· στηριχθῆναι γὰρ πρὸς τὴν τῶν ἀγαθῶν βεβαιότητα τοῖς μύροις ζητεῖ. Στηρίσατέ με, φησίν, ἐν μύροις.

ὦ παραδόξων στύλων καὶ καινῶν ἐρεισμάτων. πῶς τὰ μύρα στῦλοι τοῦ
5   οἴκου γίνονται; πῶς τῇ εὐπνοίᾳ τὸ πάγιον τῆς τοῦ ὀρόφου κατασκευῆς διερείδεται; ἢ δῆλον πάντως ἐστὶν ὅτι τὸ τῶν ἀρετῶν χρῆμα πολυειδῶς ἐν ἡμῖν κατορθούμενον κατὰ τὰς διαφορὰς τῶν ἐνεργημάτων καὶ ὀνομάζεται; ἀρετὴ γάρ ἐστιν οὐ | μόνον τὸ βλέπειν τὸ ἀγαθὸν καὶ τὸ ἐν μετουσίᾳ τοῦ   124 κρείττονος γίνεσθαι, ἀλλὰ καὶ τὸ ἀμετάπτωτον ἐν τῷ καλῷ διασῴζεσθαι. ὁ
10 τοίνυν στηριχθῆναι βουλόμενος ἐν τοῖς μύροις τὸ βέβαιον ἐν ταῖς ἀρεταῖς αὐτῷ προσγενέσθαι ζητεῖ· ἀρετὴ γὰρ τὸ μύρον, διότι πάσης δυσωδίας ἁμαρτημάτων κεχώρισται.

θαυμάσειε δ᾽ ἄν τις καὶ τὸ τῶν εἰρημένων ἀκόλουθον, διὰ τίνων στοιβασθῆναι τὸν ἑαυτῆς οἶκον ἐπιθυμεῖ· οὐ βάτοις τισὶ καὶ ἀκάνθαις καὶ
15 φορυτῷ καὶ καλάμῃ (μᾶλλον δὲ καθώς φησιν ὁ ἀπόστολος οὐ ξύλοις καὶ καλάμῃ καὶ χόρτῳ), οἷς οἱ ὑλώδεις οἶκοι κατασκευάζονται, ἀλλὰ στοιβῇ τῆς τοῦ οἴκου τούτου στέγης τὰ μῆλα γίνεται· λέγει γὰρ Στοιβάσατέ με ἐν μήλοις, ἵνα γένηται πάντα ἐν πᾶσιν αὐτῇ ὁ καρπὸς οὗτος· τὸ κάλλος, τὸ μύρον, ὁ γλυκασμός, ἡ τροφή, ἡ διὰ τῆς σκιᾶς ἀνάψυξις, ὁ ἀναπαύων θρόνος, ὁ
20 βεβαιῶν στῦλος, ὁ ἐπισκεπάζων ὄροφος. ὡς κάλλος γὰρ μετὰ ἐπιθυμίας ὁρᾶται, ὡς μύρον ἡδύνει τὴν ὄσφρησιν, ὡς τροφὴ πιαίνει τὸ σῶμα καὶ γλυκαίνει τὴν γεῦσιν, ὡς σκιὰ καταψύχει τὸν καύσωνα, ὡς θρόνος ἀναπαύει τὸν κόπον, ὡς στέγη τοῦ οἴκου σκέπη τῷ ἐνοικοῦντι γίνεται, ὡς στύλος παρέχει τὸ ἀμετάπτωτον, ὡς εὐφανὲς μῆλον ὡραΐζει τὸν ὄροφον. τί | γὰρ ἂν   125

And saying this, she moves again toward things more sublime. For she seeks to be strengthened and supported by means of *perfumes* for the sake of stability in the possession of these good things. *Strengthen me*, she says, *with perfumes*.

What unheard-of pillars and unprecedented props![30] How shall perfumes become the pillars of the house? How is the steadiness of the roof structure maintained by a fragrance? But then it is surely plain that our treasury of virtues—brought to maturity within us in a variety of forms—is also labeled in accordance with its varying effects. For virtue is not only | seeing the good and coming to have a share in what is nobler but also being kept unchangeably in the good. The person, then, who wants to be sustained by perfumes seeks to have steadfastness in the virtues he has acquired. For perfume means virtue, in that it is set apart from the foul smell of sins.

One might also wonder at what follows these words, at what she desires her house to be packed with. It is not with the brambles and thorns and rubbish and hay (or rather, as the apostle says, with the "wood and hay and stubble" [1 Cor 3:12]) with which material houses are built. No, the filling of the roof of this house turns out to be *apples*. For she says, *Encompass me with apples*, so that this fruit may become all in all to her: beauty, perfume, sweetness, nourishment, the respite of shade, the restful seat, the steadying pillar, the covering roof. For taken as beautiful the apple is contemplated with desire, taken as perfume it gives pleasure to the sense of smell, taken as food it fattens the body and pleases the taste, taken as shade it cools the midday heat, taken as a seat it gives rest from labor, taken as the house's roof it covers the one who dwells there, taken as a pillar it provides stability, taken as for its fair appearance the apple beautifies the ceiling. For | what lovelier sight can

---

30. Gregory is not alone in thinking it odd to speak of someone being supported by ointments or perfumes. His way of handling the difficulty by ingenious exegesis, however, does not suit more recent types, who prefer emendation. Although "perfumes" is the undoubted reading of the manuscripts of the lxx, Grabe proposed an emendation that the Rahlfs edition prints: ἀμόραις (sweet cakes) for μύροις (perfumes). The problem of the text here was apparently recognized by Origen as well. In this connection, see Rufinus's translation of Origen and Procopius's report of Origen's comment with its mention of texts that contained ἀμύροις (thistles? nonperfumed [plants]?) instead of μύροις (Baehrens 1925, 191.23–24). Grabe's emendation of the lxx text may, then, supply the solution to these confusions (on which see Lawson 1956, 348 n. 87). Origen, however, seems to go along with the idea suggested, or at least allowed, by the existence of texts containing ἀμύροις and by Symmachus's version of this stichos of the Song (ἐπανακλίνατε με οἰνάνθῃ: "lie me down upon a vine"). The Bride, he says, "seeks the consolation of trees and woods" ("arborum solacia silvarumque sectatur"), which of course makes sense in the light of the following stichos, with its mention of apple trees. The "perfumes" or "ointments" of the text then become "unfruitful trees" (ἀμύροις!).

τις ἐπινοήσειε περικαλλέστερον θέαμα μήλων συνθέσεως, ὅταν εὐδιάθετος
ἡ ὀπώρα κατὰ τὸ συνεχὲς ἐφ᾽ ὑπτίου τινὸς πρὸς ἑαυτὴν ἡνωμένη κατὰ τὴν
πέψιν ποικίλληται τοῦ ἐρυθήματος τῆς ὀπώρας καταμειγνυμένου πρὸς τὸ
ὑπόλευκον. εἰ τοίνυν δυνατὸν ἦν τὴν ἐξ ἐπιπέδου τῶν μήλων θέσιν ἄνωθεν
5   ἐπαιωρουμένην ὁρᾶσθαι, τί ἂν τῆς τοιαύτης ὄψεως ἦν γλαφυρώτερον;
        ὅπερ ἐπὶ τῆς τῶν νοητῶν ἀγαθῶν ἐπιθυμίας ἐστὶν οὐκ ἀδύνατον· οὐ γὰρ
βαρὺ τῆς ὀπώρας ἐκείνης τὸ εἶδος οὐδὲ εἰς γῆν βρῖθον καὶ καθελκόμενον,
ἀλλὰ πρὸς τὸ ὕψος τὴν ῥοπὴν ἐκ φύσεως ἔχει· ἀνωφυὴς γὰρ ἡ ἀρετὴ καὶ
πρὸς τὸ ἄνω βλέπει. διὸ τῷ κάλλει τῶν τοιούτων μήλων ἐπιθυμεῖ ἡ νύμφη
10   τὸν ὄροφον τοῦ ἰδίου οἴκου ἐνωραΐζεσθαι· οὐ γάρ μοι τοῦτο δοκεῖ κατὰ τὸ
προηγούμενον τῷ λόγῳ σπουδάζεσθαι, ὡς εὐφανές τι θέαμα διὰ τῆς τῶν
μήλων συνθέσεως ἐπὶ τῆς στέγης ὁρᾶσθαι. τίς γὰρ ἂν γένοιτο διὰ τούτων
πρὸς ἀρετὴν ὁδηγία, εἰ μή τι νόημα τῶν ὠφελούντων ἡμᾶς εἴη τοῖς εἰρημένοις
ἐνθεωρούμενον;
15   τί οὖν ἐστιν ὃ εἰκάζομεν; ὁ ἐν τῷ δρυμῶνι τῆς φύσεως ἡμῶν ὑπὸ
φιλανθρωπίας ἀναβλαστήσας διὰ τοῦ μετασχεῖν σαρκός τε καὶ αἵματος
μῆλον ἐγένετο· πρὸς ἑκάτερον γὰρ τούτων ἔστιν ἰδεῖν ἐν τῇ ὀπώρᾳ ταύτῃ
διὰ τῆς χρόας | τὴν ὁμοίωσιν· τῷ μὲν γὰρ ὑπολευκαίνοντι μιμεῖται τὴν τῆς   126
σαρκὸς ἰδιότητα, τὸ δὲ ἐπικεχρωσμένον ἐρύθημα συγγενῶς ἔχειν πρὸς τὴν
20   τοῦ αἵματος φύσιν διὰ τοῦ εἴδους μαρτυρεῖται. ὅταν τοίνυν ἡ ἐντρυφῶσα τοῖς
θείοις ψυχὴ κατὰ τὴν στέγην ταῦτα βλέπειν ἐπιθυμήσῃ, τοῦτο τῷ αἰνίγματι
παιδευόμεθα· ἐκ γὰρ τοῦ ἄνω βλέποντας ἡμᾶς προσέχειν τοῖς μήλοις πρὸς
τὴν οὐράνιον ἔστι πολιτείαν ὁδηγεῖσθαι διὰ τῶν εὐαγγελικῶν διδαγμάτων.
ἅπερ ὁ ἄνωθεν ἐρχόμενος καὶ ἐπάνω πάντων ὢν ὑπέδειξεν ἡμῖν διὰ τῆς ἐν
25   σαρκὶ φανερώσεως πάντων τῶν ἀγαθῶν πολιτευμάτων ἐν ἑαυτῷ δείξας τὰ
ὑποδείγματα, καθώς φησιν ὅτι Μάθετε ἀπ᾽ ἐμοῦ, ὅτι πρᾷός εἰμι καὶ ταπεινὸς
τῇ καρδίᾳ. τὸ δὲ αὐτὸ τοῦτο καὶ ὁ ἀπόστολος τὴν ταπεινοφροσύνην
ἡμῖν ὑφηγούμενος λέγει (δυνατὸν γὰρ δι᾽ ἑνὸς θεωρήματος πᾶσαν τὴν
ἀλήθειαν τοῦ λόγου πιστώσασθαι)· πρὸς γὰρ τοὺς τὰ ἄνω βλέποντας
30   Τοῦτο φρονείσθω, φησίν, ἐν ὑμῖν, ὃ καὶ ἐν Χριστῷ Ἰησοῦ, ὃς ἐν μορφῇ θεοῦ
ὑπάρχων οὐχ ἁρπαγμὸν ἡγήσατο τὸ εἶναι ἴσα θεῷ, ἀλλ᾽ ἑαυτὸν ἐκένωσε
μορφὴν δούλου λαβὼν ὁ διὰ σαρκὸς καὶ αἵματος ἐπιδημήσας τῷ βίῳ καὶ ἀντὶ
τῆς προκειμένης αὐτῷ χαρᾶς ἐν μετουσίᾳ τῆς ταπεινότητος ἡμῶν ἑκουσίως
γενόμενος καὶ μέχρι τῆς τοῦ θανάτου κατελθὼν πείρας. διὰ ταῦτά φησιν ἡ
35   νύμφη Στοιβάσατέ με ἐν μήλοις, ἵνα πάντοτε εἰς | ὕψος ὁρῶσα βλέπω στερρῶς   127
τὰ τῶν ἀγαθῶν ὑποδείγματα τὰ ἐν τῷ νυμφίῳ δεικνύμενα· ἐκεῖ ἡ πραότης,
ἐκεῖ τὸ ἀόργητον, ἐκεῖ τὸ πρὸς τοὺς ἐχθροὺς ἀμνησίκακον καὶ τὸ πρὸς τοὺς
λυποῦντας φιλάνθρωπον καὶ τὸ δι᾽ εὐεργεσίας τὴν κακίαν ἀμείβεσθαι, ἐκεῖ τὸ
ἐγκρατές, τὸ καθαρόν, τὸ μακρόθυμον, τὸ πάσης κενοδοξίας τε καὶ ἀπάτης
βιωτικῆς ἀνεπίμικτον.

one imagine than an arrangement of apples, when the fruit, nicely disposed and set closely together against a flat surface, varies in color as it ripens, the reddish flush of the fruit mingling with the white? So if it were possible to see the level arrangement of apples as it hovered from above, what would be more elegant than such a sight?

Now this is not impossible in the case of desire for intelligible goods. For that fruit is not heavy by quality, nor does it sink or descend to the earth. Its natural impulse is toward the heights, for virtue's natural growth is upwards, and it looks toward what is above. That is why the Bride desires to have the roof of her house made glorious by the beauty of this sort of apple. For it does not seem to me to take the text seriously along the lines of the foregoing interpretation, if it is said that what is seen is merely some fair sight created on the ceiling by an arrangement of apples. For what guidance in virtue would there be in this, unless there were some idea profitable for us contained in the words?

What is our conjecture, then? He who for love of humanity grew up in the woods of our nature became an apple by sharing flesh and blood. For in the coloring of this fruit one can see a likeness to | each of these. By its whiteness it copies a characteristic of flesh, while its reddish tinge by its appearance attests its kinship with the nature of blood. When, therefore, the soul that is nourished on things divine desires to see these things at its roof, what the symbol is teaching us is this: for us to be intent on the apples as we look to what is above is to be guided toward the celestial way of life by the teachings of the gospel. He who came from above and is above all things showed these teachings to us by his manifestation in the flesh, because in himself he furnished the patterns of all good forms of conduct—just as it says, "Learn from me, for I am meek and lowly of heart" (Matt 11:29). The apostle too says the very same thing when he is instructing us in humility (for the whole truth of the Word can be rendered believable by a single insight): to those who look upwards he says, "Let this mind be in you that was also in Christ Jesus, who, being in the form of God, did not think equality with God a thing to be snatched at but emptied himself and took the form of a slave" (Phil 2:5–7)—he who by means of flesh and blood sojourned in this world and instead of the "joy that was set before him" became the willing sharer of our lowliness and descended to the point of experiencing death (cf. Phil 2:8). That is why the Bride says, "*Encompass me with apples,* so that, looking on high, | I may gaze steadfastly upon the patterns of the good things that are made known in the Bridegroom. That is where gentleness is; that is where anger is absent; that is where we find forgiveness of enemies and love for those who do harm; there is self-control, purity, long-suffering; there is that which has no part in any vanity or deceit of this world."

Ταῦτα εἰποῦσα ἐπαινεῖ τὸν τοξότην τῆς εὐστοχίας ὡς καλῶς ἐπ' αὐτῆς τὸ
βέλος εὐθύνοντα· Τετρωμένη γάρ φησιν ἀγάπης ἐγώ. δείκνυσι δὲ τῷ λόγῳ τὸ
βέλος τὸ τῇ καρδίᾳ διὰ βάθους ἐγκείμενον. ὁ δὲ τοξότης τοῦ βέλους ἡ ἀγάπη
ἐστίν· τὴν δὲ ἀγάπην τὸν θεὸν εἶναι παρὰ τῆς ἁγίας γραφῆς μεμαθήκαμεν, ὃς
5   τὸ ἐκλεκτὸν ἑαυτοῦ βέλος, τὸν μονογενῆ θεόν, ἐπὶ τοὺς σῳζομένους ἐκπέμπει
τῷ πνεύματι τῆς ζωῆς τὴν τριπλῆν τῆς ἀκίδος ἀκμὴν περιχρώσας (ἀκὶς δὲ
ἡ πίστις ἐστίν), ἵνα, ἐν ᾧ ἂν γένηται, συνεισαγάγῃ μετὰ τοῦ βέλους καὶ τὸν
τοξότην, ὥς φησιν ὁ κύριος ὅτι ἐγὼ καὶ ὁ πατὴρ Ἐλευσόμεθα καὶ μονὴν παρ'
αὐτῷ ποιησόμεθα. ὁρᾷ τοίνυν ἡ διὰ τῶν θείων ἀναβάσεων ὑψωθεῖσα ψυχὴ
10   τὸ | γλυκὺ τῆς ἀγάπης βέλος ἐν ἑαυτῇ, ᾧ ἐτρώθη, καὶ καύχημα ποιεῖται τὴν   128
τοιαύτην πληγὴν λέγουσα ὅτι Τετρωμένη ἀγάπης ἐγώ.

ὢ καλοῦ τραύματος καὶ γλυκείας πληγῆς, δι' ἧς ἡ ζωὴ ἐπὶ τὰ ἐντὸς
διαδύεται ὥσπερ τινὰ θύραν καὶ εἴσοδον τὴν ἐκ τοῦ βέλους διαίρεσιν ἑαυτῇ
ὑπανοίξασα. ὁμοῦ τε γὰρ τὸ τῆς ἀγάπης βέλος ἐδέξατο καὶ παραχρῆμα εἰς
15   γαμικὴν θυμηδίαν ἡ τοξεία μετεσκευάσθη· φανερὸν γάρ ἐστιν ὅπως αἱ χεῖρες
τὸ τόξον μεταχειρίζονται μεριζόμεναι πρὸς τὴν χρείαν ταῖς ἐνεργείαις· ἡ
μὲν γὰρ εὐώνυμος τοῦ τόξου ἅπτεται, ἡ δεξιὰ δὲ τὴν νευρὰν πρὸς ἑαυτὴν
ἐπισπᾶται συνεφελκομένη διὰ τῶν γλυφίδων τὸ βέλος τῇ προσβολῇ τῆς
ἀριστερᾶς χειρὸς πρὸς τὸν σκοπὸν εὐθυνόμενον. ἡ τοίνυν πρὸ ὀλίγου σκοπὸς
20   γενομένη τοῦ βέλους νῦν ἑαυτὴν ἀντὶ βέλους ἐν ταῖς χερσὶ τοῦ τοξότου
βλέπει, ἄλλως τῆς δεξιᾶς καὶ ἑτέρως τῆς εὐωνύμου διαλαμβανούσης τὸ
βέλος. ἀλλ' ἐπειδὴ διὰ τῆς ἐπιθαλαμίου τροπῆς αἱ τῶν θεωρημάτων ἐμφάσεις
δι' ἀκολούθου προάγονται, οὐκ ἐποίησε τὴν ἀκίδα τοῦ βέλους ὑπὸ τῆς
ἀριστερᾶς ἀνεχομένην οὐδὲ τὴν δεξιὰν τὸ ἕτερον μέρος διαλαμβάνουσαν,
25   ὡς ἂν γένοιτο ἡ ψυχὴ βέλος ἐν τῇ χειρὶ τοῦ δυνατοῦ πρὸς τὸν ἄνω σκοπὸν
εὐθυνόμενον, ἀλλ' ἐποίησε τὴν μὲν εὐώνυμον ἀντὶ τῆς ἀκίδος τῇ κεφαλῇ
ὑποβάλλεσθαι,

| διαλαμβάνεσθαι δὲ τῇ δεξιᾷ τὸ λειπόμενον, ὡς ἄν, οἶμαι, κατὰ ταὐτὸν ἐν   129
τοῖς διπλοῖς αἰνίγμασι τὰ περὶ τῆς θείας ἀναβάσεως ὁ λόγος φιλοσοφήσειε,
30   δεικνὺς ὅτι ὁ αὐτὸς καὶ νυμφίος καὶ τοξότης ἐστὶν ἡμῶν, νύμφη τε καὶ βέλει
τῇ κεκαθαρμένῃ κεχρημένος ψυχῇ, ὡς βέλος πρὸς τὸν ἀγαθὸν εὐθύνων
σκοπόν, ὡς νύμφην εἰς μετουσίαν ἀναλαμβάνων τῆς ἀφθάρτου ἀϊδιότητος,
μῆκος βίου καὶ ἔτη ζωῆς διὰ τῆς δεξιᾶς χαριζόμενος, διὰ δὲ τῆς ἀριστερᾶς τὸν
τῶν αἰωνίων ἀγαθῶν πλοῦτον καὶ τὴν τοῦ θεοῦ δόξαν, ἧς οἱ τὴν τοῦ κόσμου

After she has said these things, she praises the accurate archer because he has directed his arrow straight at her, for she says, *I have been wounded by love.* By these words she signifies the arrow that lies deep in her heart. But the archer who discharges the arrow is love. From Holy Scripture, however, we have learned that God is love (cf. 1 John 4:8, 16), and he discharges his own chosen arrow (cf. Isa 49:2)—the Only Begotten God—at those who are being saved, having smeared over the triple point of the barb with the Spirit of life (the barb is faith), so that, in the person in whom it is planted, it may introduce the archer together with the arrow, as the Lord says: "I and my Father will come and make our dwelling with him" (John 14:23). See, then, the soul that has been exalted through the divine ascents sees in herself the | sweet arrow of love by which she is wounded and makes boast of such a blow by saying, *I have been wounded by love.*

O sweet and happy wound, by which life slips through to the inward parts, opening the arrow's cut to make itself a door and an entrance! As soon as she has taken love's arrow, archery is straightway changed into the joy of marriage. For obviously it is the two hands that hold the bow, and for the sake of this function their actions are distinct and different. The left hand holds the bow, while the right hand draws the string in its own direction and along with it, with the help of the notches, pulls the arrow, which is guided to its target by the pressure of the left hand. The soul, therefore, who a little before was the arrow's target, now sees herself, in the arrow's place, in the hands of the archer—with the right hand and the left hand grasping the arrow differently. But since it is the figure of a wedding that governs the way in which the description of the truths we discern moves along from one stage to another, the text does not have the point of the arrow supported by the left hand, nor the rest of it held by the right hand—which would mean that the soul becomes, in the hand of the strong archer, an arrow that is guided toward a heavenly target. Rather it is under the *head* (instead of the arrow point) that she makes the left hand to lie, while what remains is grasped by the right hand.

| The effect of this, I think, is to speak spiritually about the divine ascent by means of two enigmas at the same time: to show that one and the same is both our Bridegroom and our Archer, who handles the purified soul both as bride and as arrow. In that the soul is "arrow," he guides her toward the good target. In that the soul is "bride," he receives her into participation of his incorruptible eternity. With his right hand he gives "length of life and years of life,"[31] while with the left he gives the riches of eternal goods and the glory

---

31. The English "life" here translates two different Greek words: βίος and ζωή. The language is that of Prov 3:16.

ζητοῦντες δόξαν ἀμέτοχοι γίνονται. διὰ τοῦτό φησιν Εὐώνυμος αὐτοῦ ὑπὸ τὴν κεφαλήν μου, δι᾽ ἧς εὐθύνεται πρὸς τὸν σκοπὸν τὸ βέλος, ἡ δεξιὰ δὲ αὐτοῦ πρὸς ἑαυτήν με διαλαβοῦσα καὶ ἐφελκυσαμένη κούφην με πρὸς τὴν ἄνω φορὰν ἀπεργάζεται, κἀκεῖ πεμπομένην καὶ τοῦ τοξότου μὴ χωριζομένην, ὡς
5   ὁμοῦ τε φέρεσθαι διὰ τῆς βολῆς καὶ ταῖς χερσὶ τοῦ τοξότου ἐναναπαύεσθαι. τὰ δὲ τῶν χειρῶν τούτων ἰδιώματά φησιν ἡ Παροιμία ὅτι Μῆκος βίου καὶ ἔτη ζωῆς ἐν τῇ δεξιᾷ τῆς σοφίας, ἐν δὲ τῇ ἀριστερᾷ αὐτῆς πλοῦτος καὶ δόξα.
    Εἶτα πρὸς τὰς θυγατέρας τῆς ἄνω Ἰερουσαλὴμ τρέπει τὸν λόγον. ὁ δὲ λόγος παράκλησίς ἐστιν ἐνόρκως προσαγομένη | τοῦ πλεονάζειν καὶ   130
10 ἐπαύξειν ἀεὶ τὴν ἀγάπην, ἕως ἂν ἐνεργὸν ἑαυτοῦ ποιήσῃ τὸ θέλημα ὁ θέλων πάντας σωθῆναι καὶ εἰς ἐπίγνωσιν ἀληθείας ἐλθεῖν. ὁ δὲ λόγος οὗτός ἐστιν ὃν πεποίηται Ὥρκισα ὑμᾶς, θυγατέρες Ἰερουσαλήμ, ἐν δυνάμεσι καὶ ἐν ἰσχύσεσι τοῦ ἀγροῦ, ἐὰν ἐγείρητε καὶ ἐξεγείρητε τὴν ἀγάπην, ἕως οὗ θελήσῃ.
    ὅρκος ἐστὶ λόγος πιστούμενος δι᾽ ἑαυτοῦ τὴν ἀλήθειαν. διπλῆ δὲ ἡ κατὰ
15 τὸν ὅρκον ἐνέργεια· ἢ γὰρ αὐτός τις πιστοῦται τῷ ἀκούοντι τὴν ἀλήθειαν ἢ ἄλλοις διὰ τοῦ ὁρκισμοῦ τὴν ἀνάγκην ἐπάγει τοῦ μηδὲν παραψεύσασθαι, οἷον Ὥμοσε κύριος τῷ Δαβὶδ ἀλήθειαν καὶ οὐ μὴ ἀθετήσει αὐτήν. ἐνταῦθα τὸ πιστὸν τῆς ὑποσχέσεως ἐμπεδοῦται τῷ ὅρκῳ. ὅταν δὲ φροντίδα ποιούμενος ὁ Ἀβραὰμ τῆς εὐγενοῦς ἐπὶ τῷ μονογενεῖ συζυγίας προστάσσῃ τῷ ἰδίῳ
20 θεράποντι μή τινα τῶν τοῦ γένους Χαναὰν τῶν τῇ δουλείᾳ καταδεδικασμένων συνοικίσαι πρὸς γάμον τῷ Ἰσαάκ, ὡς ἂν μὴ λυμήναιτο τῇ εὐγενείᾳ τῆς διαδοχῆς ἡ τοῦ δουλικοῦ γένους ἐπιμιξία, ἀλλ᾽ ἐκ τῆς πατρῴας αὐτοῦ γῆς καὶ συγγενείας ἁρμόσασθαι τῷ παιδὶ τὴν συζυγίαν, ἀνάγκην ἐπάγει | τοῦ μὴ   131
    ῥᾳθυμῆσαι περὶ τὸ πρόσταγμα διὰ τοῦ ὁρκίσαι αὐτὸν ἦ μὴν ἐπιτελῆ ποιήσειν,
25 ὅσα περὶ τοῦ παιδὸς ἐδοκίμασεν. [ὁρκίζεται τοίνυν ὑπὸ τοῦ Ἀβραὰμ ὁ θεράπων, ἵνα τῷ Ἰσαὰκ τὴν πρέπουσαν συζυγίαν ἁρμόσηται.]
    διπλῆς τοίνυν οὔσης τῆς κατὰ τὸν ὅρκον ἐνεργείας ἐνταῦθα ἡ πρὸς τοσοῦτον ὕψος ἀναδραμοῦσα ψυχή, ὅσον ἐν τοῖς προεξητασμένοις ἐθεωρήσαμεν, ταῖς μαθητευομέναις ψυχαῖς τὴν πρὸς τὸ τέλειον πρόοδον
30 ὑφηγουμένη οὐχ ὧν αὐτὴ τετύχηκε παρέχει ταῖς ἀκουούσαις διὰ τοῦ ὅρκου τὸ ἀναμφίβολον, ἀλλ᾽ ἐκείνας διὰ τοῦ ὁρκισμοῦ πρὸς τὸν κατ᾽ ἀρετὴν χειραγωγεῖ βίον, μέχρι τότε ἀκοίμητόν τε καὶ ἐγρηγορυῖαν τὴν ἀγάπην ἔχειν, ἕως ἂν εἰς πέρας ἔλθῃ τὸ ἀγαθὸν αὐτοῦ θέλημα, τοῦτο δέ ἐστι τὸ πάντας σωθῆναι καὶ εἰς ἐπίγνωσιν ἀληθείας ἐλθεῖν. ὁ δὲ ὁρκισμὸς ὥσπερ ἐκεῖ ἐν τῷ μηρῷ τοῦ

of God—in which those who seek the world's glory have no share. That is why she says: "*His left hand is under my head*—the hand by which the arrow is directed toward its target, while his right hand, when it has grasped and drawn my light weight to itself, perfects me for the journey on high. And thither I am being dispatched, not separated from the archer, so as at once to be borne by the flight and to be at rest in the hands of the archer." Now the proverb speaks of the characteristics of these hands: "Length of life and years of life are in Wisdom's right hand, and in her left are riches and splendor" (Prov 3:16).

Then the Bride addresses the daughters of the Jerusalem on high. And what she utters is an exhortation, brought forward with an oath, | always to increase and multiply love until he who wills all to be saved and to come to knowledge of the truth (1 Tim 2:4) renders his will operative. This is what she says: *I have charged you, O daughters of Jerusalem, by the powers and virtues of the field, do not rouse or wake love, until he please.*

Now an oath is an utterance that of itself guarantees truth. The function of an oath, however, is twofold. Either a person, acting for himself, gives a hearer warrant of truth, or else he imposes upon others a compelling necessity to falsify nothing; for example, "The Lord swore truth to David and will not go back on it" (Ps 131:11). Here the trustworthiness of the promise is ratified by the oath. On the other hand, when Abraham, taking thought about a noble marriage for his only son, orders his own servant not to marry Isaac to one of that Canaanite race who were condemned to slavery (so that a mingling with slave stock would not injure the nobility of his line) but to arrange a marriage for the child from his ancestral homeland and his own kin, he imposes a absolute obligation | not to neglect the command by administering an oath to him that he would surely carry out whatever Abraham had sanctioned concerning the child (cf. Gen 24:2–9). [Therefore Abraham also had the servant swear to provide Isaac with an appropriate wife.][32]

Even though, then, the function of an oath is double, in this particular case the soul that has ascended to a height as great as that which we have seen in our previous investigations does not, as she teaches the way of perfection to the souls that are her disciples, use an oath to furnish her hearers with assurance regarding what she has attained. Rather does she, by her swearing, direct them to the life of virtue: to keep their loving sleepless and wakeful until the time when God's good will achieves its end, that is, until "all have been saved and have come to the knowledge of the truth" (1 Tim 2:4). And

---

32. These words occur only in the Syrian translation of the homilies and almost certainly represent a gloss; see the *apparatus criticus* in Langerbeck 1960.

πατριάρχου ἐγένετο, οὕτως ἐνταῦθα ἐν δυνάμεσι καὶ ἐν ἰσχύσεσι τοῦ | ἀγροῦ   132
γίνεται οὕτως εἰπόντος τοῦ λόγου Ὥρκισα ὑμᾶς, θυγατέρες Ἰερουσαλήμ, ἐν
δυνάμεσι καὶ ἐν ἰσχύσεσι τοῦ ἀγροῦ, ἐὰν ἐγείρητε καὶ ἐξεγείρητε τὴν ἀγάπην,
ἕως οὗ θελήσῃ.

5   Θεωρητέον τοίνυν ἐν τούτοις πρῶτον μὲν τίς ὁ ἀγρός, ἔπειτα δὲ τίς ἡ
ἰσχὺς τοῦ ἀγροῦ καὶ ἡ δύναμις καὶ εἰ διαφορὰν ἔχει ταῦτα πρὸς ἄλληλα ἢ
ἓν δι’ ἀμφοτέρων ἐστὶ τὸ σημαινόμενον· πρὸς τούτοις τί τὸ ἐγείρεσθαι καὶ
τί τὸ ἐξεγείρεσθαι τὴν ἀγάπην. τὸ γὰρ Ἕως οὗ θελήσῃ διὰ τῶν εἰρημένων
προαποδέδοται.

10   ὅτι μὲν οὖν διὰ τοῦ ἀγροῦ σημαίνει τὸν κόσμον ἡ τοῦ δεσπότου φωνή,
παντί που δῆλον ἐκ τῶν εὐαγγελίων ἐστίν, ὅτι δὲ παράγει τὸ σχῆμα τοῦ
κόσμου τούτου καὶ οὐδὲν πάγιον ἐν τῇ ἀστατούσῃ δείκνυται φύσει, δῆλον
ἐκ τῆς τοῦ Ἐκκλησιαστοῦ μεγαλοφωνίας ἐστίν, ὃς πᾶν τὸ φαινόμενόν τε
καὶ παρερχόμενον ἐν ματαίοις ἠρίθμησεν. τίς οὖν ἡ δύναμις τοῦ τοιούτου
15   ἀγροῦ, ὅς ἐστιν ὁ κόσμος, ἢ τίς ἡ ἰσχύς, ὧν ἡ μνήμη ἀπαράβατον ποιεῖ διὰ
τοῦ ὁρκισμοῦ ταῖς θυγατράσιν Ἰερουσαλὴμ τὸ παράγγελμα; εἰ μὲν γὰρ πρὸς
τὰ φαινόμενα βλέποιμεν ὡς οὔσης τινὸς ἐν τούτοις δυνάμεως, παραγράφεται
τὴν τοιαύτην ὑπόληψιν ὁ | Ἐκκλησιαστὴς μάταιον ὀνομάζων πᾶν τὸ ἐν   133
τούτοις δεικνύμενόν τε καὶ σπουδαζόμενον· τὸ γὰρ μάταιον οὐχ ὑφέστηκε,
20   τὸ δὲ μὴ ὑφεστὼς κατὰ τὴν οὐσίαν ἰσχὺν οὐκ ἔχει.

ἢ τάχα διὰ τῆς πληθυντικῆς σημασίας τῆς κατὰ τὴν δύναμιν ἔστι τινὰ
στοχασμὸν εὑρεῖν τοῦ νοήματος· τοιαύτην γὰρ εὕρομεν παρὰ τῇ ἁγίᾳ
γραφῇ διαφορὰν ἐπὶ τῶν τοιούτων ὀνομάτων· ὅταν μοναδικῶς ἡ δύναμις
λέγηται, πρὸς τὸ θεῖον ἀναπέμπεται διὰ ταύτης τῆς φωνῆς ἡ διάνοια, ὅταν
25   δὲ διὰ τοῦ πληθυντικοῦ σχήματος ἐκφωνῆται, τὴν ἀγγελικὴν φύσιν τῷ
λόγῳ παρίστησιν. οἷον Χριστὸς θεοῦ δύναμις καὶ θεοῦ σοφία. ἐνταῦθα
τῷ μοναδικῷ τὸ θεῖον ἐγνώρισεν. Εὐλογεῖτε τὸν κύριον, πᾶσαι αἱ δυνάμεις
αὐτοῦ. ὧδε τὸ πληθυντικὸν τῶν δυνάμεων τῆς νοητῆς τῶν ἀγγέλων φύσεως
τὴν σημασίαν ἐνδείκνυται. τὸ δὲ τῆς ἰσχύος ὄνομα συμπαραληφθὲν μετὰ τῆς
30   δυνάμεως ἐπίτασιν τῆς τοῦ νοήματος ἐμφάσεως ἔχει οὕτω τῆς γραφῆς διὰ
τῆς ἐπαναλήψεως τῶν ἰσοδυναμούντων ῥημάτων βεβαιότερον ἐμφαινούσης
ὃ βούλεται, ὡς τὸ Κύριε, ἡ ἰσχύς μου, κύριος στερέωμά μου· ταὐτὸν γὰρ
ἑκατέρου τῶν ῥημάτων τὸ σημαινόμενον, ἀλλ’ ἡ τῶν ἰσοδυναμούντων
συνθήκη ἔνδειξιν ποιεῖται τῆς κατὰ τὸ σημαινόμενον ἐπιτά|σεως.   134

just as back then the oath was taken by the patriarch's thigh (Gen 24:9), so now it is taken *by the powers and virtues of* | *the field.* Thus the text says: *I have charged you, O daughters of Jerusalem, by the powers and virtues of the field, do not rouse or wake love, until he please.*

So first of all, where these words are concerned, we must try to see what the *field* is, and then what the "strength" and the "power" of the field are, and whether the latter differ from each other or the same thing is signified by both. In addition to these tasks, we must ask what is meant by "wakening" and "stirring" love. For the expression *until he please* has already been treated in what was said above.

Well, then, it is entirely obvious from the Gospels that by *field* the Master's speech refers to the world;[33] on the other hand, from the lofty words of Ecclesiastes—who counted everything that appears and passes away as vanity (Eccl 1:2)—it is evident that "the form of this world is passing away" (1 Cor 7:32) and that in its unstable nature nothing abiding is discernible. Then what is the "power" or the "virtue" of this field that is the world, the "power" and "virtue" whose mention renders the order given to the daughters of Jerusalem inviolable by reason of the oath? For if we look to things that appear as though there were some power in them, | Ecclesiastes enters an objection against such an assumption when it labels everything that is brought to light or sought after among appearances as vanity. For what is vain has no reality, and what has no essential reality has no strength.

Maybe, though, it is possible to find a certain hint at the meaning by attending to the plural form of "power." For we find in Holy Scripture that there is a distinction made in the case of such terms, to wit: when power is spoken of as single, the understanding is referred by this language to the Divine, whereas it is the angelic nature that is present to the mind when the plural form is used. Take the case of Christ as "the power of God and the wisdom of God" (1 Cor 1:24). Here by the singular form Scripture makes the Divine known. "Praise the Lord, all you Powers of his" (Ps 102:21); in this case the plurality of the powers indicates a reference to the intelligible nature of the angels. Now the term "virtue," when taken together with "power," puts a strong emphasis on the meaning of the idea conveyed; in this way the Scripture, by repeating words of the same sense, shows more certainly what is intended—as when it says, "O Lord, my strength, the Lord is my stronghold" (Ps 17:2–3). For the meaning of each of the words is the same, but the combination of terms of the same sense renders what is signified | emphatic.

---

33. Contrast Origen, *Comm. Cant.* 2.10 (Baehrens 1925, 197–98, trans. Lawson 1956, 204), who appeals to Gen 27:27 for the meaning of "field" and takes it to mean either the soul's "life and … manner of living" or "the Church's faith and way of life."

ἡ τοίνυν τῶν δυνάμεων πληθυντικὴ σημασία καὶ ἡ ὁμοιότροπος τῶν
ἰσχύων μνήμη πρὸς τὴν ἀγγελικὴν ἔοικε φύσιν ἀπάγειν τῶν ἀκουόντων
τὴν ἔννοιαν, ὥστε τὸν ὁρκισμὸν τὸν ἐπὶ βεβαιώσει τῶν κεκριμένων παρὰ
τῆς διδασκάλου ταῖς μαθητευομέναις ψυχαῖς προσαγόμενον μὴ κατὰ τοῦ
5   παράγοντος γίνεσθαι κόσμου ἀλλὰ κατὰ τῆς ἐπιδιαμενούσης εἰς ἀεὶ φύσεως
τῶν ἀγγέλων, πρὸς οὓς βλέπειν διακελεύεται, ἵνα τὸ πάγιόν τε καὶ στάσιμον
τῆς κατ᾽ ἀρετὴν πολιτείας βεβαιώσῃ τῷ ὑποδείγματι. ἐπειδὴ γὰρ τὸν μετὰ τὴν
ἀνάστασιν βίον ὅμοιον ἐπήγγελται τῇ ἀγγελικῇ καταστάσει [τῶν ἀνθρώπων]
γενήσεσθαι (ἀψευδὴς δὲ ὁ ἐπαγγειλάμενος), ἀκόλουθον ἂν εἴη καὶ τὴν ἐν τῷ
10   κόσμῳ ζωὴν πρὸς τὴν ἐλπιζομένην μετὰ ταῦτα παρασκευάζεσθαι, ὥστε ἐν
σαρκὶ ζῶντας καὶ ἐν τῷ ἀγρῷ τοῦ κόσμου διάγοντας μὴ κατὰ σάρκα ζῆν μηδὲ
συσχηματίζεσθαι τῷ κόσμῳ τούτῳ, ἀλλὰ προμελετᾶν τὸν ἐλπιζόμενον βίον
διὰ τῆς ἐν τῷ κόσμῳ ζωῆς. διὰ τοῦτο τὴν διὰ τοῦ ὅρκου βεβαίωσιν ἐμποιεῖται
ταῖς ψυχαῖς τῶν μαθητευομένων ἡ νύμφη, ὥστε τὴν ζωὴν αὐτῶν τὴν ἐν τῷ
15   ἀγρῷ τούτῳ κατορθουμένην | πρὸς τὰς δυνάμεις βλέπειν, μιμουμένην διὰ   135
τῆς ἀπαθείας τὴν ἀγγελικὴν καθαρότητα· οὕτω γὰρ ἐγειρομένης τῆς ἀγάπης
καὶ ἐξεγειρομένης (ὅπερ ἐστὶν ὑψουμένης τε καὶ ἀεὶ διὰ προσθήκης πρὸς
τὸ μεῖζον ἐπαυξομένης) τὸ ἀγαθὸν εἶπε θέλημα τοῦ θεοῦ τελειοῦσθαι ὡς ἐν
οὐρανῷ καὶ ἐπὶ γῆς τῆς ἀγγελικῆς καὶ ἐν ἡμῖν ἀπαθείας κατορθουμένης.
20   ταῦτα κατενοήσαμεν εἰς τὸ Ὥρκισα ὑμᾶς, θυγατέρες Ἰερουσαλήμ, ἐν
δυνάμεσι καὶ ἐν ἰσχύσεσι τοῦ ἀγροῦ, ἐὰν ἐγείρητε καὶ ἐξεγείρητε τὴν ἀγάπην,
ἕως οὗ θελήσῃ. εἰ δέ τις εὑρεθείη λόγος ἕτερος μᾶλλον προσεγγίζων τῇ
ἀληθείᾳ τῶν ζητουμένων, δεξώμεθα τὴν χάριν καὶ εὐχαριστήσωμεν τῷ
ἀποκαλύπτοντι τὰ κεκρυμμένα μυστήρια διὰ τοῦ ἁγίου πνεύματος ἐν Χριστῷ
25   Ἰησοῦ τῷ κυρίῳ ἡμῶν,

ᾧ ἡ δόξα εἰς τοὺς αἰῶνας.
ἀμήν.

The plural significance of *powers,* therefore, and the mention of *strengths* in the same mode seems to point the understanding of the hearers to the angelic nature. Consequently the oath—brought before the disciple-souls to establish the judgments of their teacher—does not appeal to the world that is passing away but to the eternally abiding nature of the angels. It enjoins looking toward them in order that by their example it may establish the steadfastness and stability of the virtuous life. For since it has been proclaimed that our life after the resurrection will become like the angelic constitution (cf. Matt 22:30)—and he who made the announcement does not lie—it would be appropriate even for our life in the world to be made ready for the life we hope for, so that those who live in the flesh and lead an existence in the field of the world do not live according to the flesh and are not conformed to this world, but through their life in the world practice beforehand the life they are hoping for. This is why the Bride, by an oath, imparts strength to the souls of her disciples—so that, namely, their life, which is being set right in this "field," | may look to the powers, imitating the angelic purity by its impassibility. For when love is thus being wakened and stirred—which means being lifted up and always increasing through progress toward what is better—the good will of God is fulfilled, as in heaven, so on the angelic earth and within us, since impassibility is being achieved.

This is what we have understood by the words: *I have charged you, O daughters of Jerusalem, by the powers and strengths of the field, do not rouse or wake love, until he please.* But if some other interpretation has been found that comes closer to the truth of what we search for, we shall accept the gracious favor and give thanks to him who reveals the hidden mysteries through the Holy Spirit in Christ Jesus our Lord,

To whom be glory to the ages of ages.
Amen.

Λόγος ε'

Φωνὴ τοῦ ἀδελφιδοῦ μου·
ἰδοὺ οὗτος ἥκει πηδῶν ἐπὶ τὰ ὄρη,
διαλλόμενος ἐπὶ τοὺς βουνούς.
Ὅμοιός ἐστι ἀδελφιδός μου τῇ δορκάδι
5   ἢ νεβρῷ ἐλάφων ἐπὶ τὰ ὄρη Βαιθήλ.
| ἰδοὺ οὗτος ἔστηκεν ὀπίσω τοῦ τοίχου ἡμῶν   136
παρακύπτων διὰ τῶν θυρίδων,
ἐκκύπτων διὰ τῶν δικτύων.

Ἀποκρίνεται ὁ ἀδελφιδός μου καὶ λέγει μοι·
10   ἀνάστα ἐλθέ, ἡ πλησίον μου, καλή μου, περιστερά μου,
Ὅτι ἰδοὺ ὁ χειμὼν παρῆλθεν,
ὁ ὑετὸς ἀπῆλθεν, ἐπορεύθη ἑαυτῷ,
Τὰ ἄνθη ὤφθη ἐν τῇ γῇ,
καιρὸς τῆς τομῆς ἔφθακεν,
15   φωνὴ τοῦ τρυγόνος ἠκούσθη ἐν τῇ γῇ ἡμῶν,
Ἡ συκῆ ἐξήνεγκε τοὺς ὀλύνθους αὐτῆς,
αἱ ἄμπελοι κυπρίζουσιν, ἔδωκαν ὀσμήν.

ἀνάστα ἐλθέ, ἡ πλησίον μου, καλή μου, περιστερά μου,
Δεῦρο σεαυτῇ, περιστερά μου, ἐν σκέπῃ τῆς πέτρας
20   ἐχόμενα τοῦ προτειχίσματος.
δεῖξόν μοι τὴν ὄψιν σου
καὶ ἀκούτισόν με τὴν φωνήν σου,
ὅτι ἡ φωνή σου ἡδεῖα καὶ ἡ ὄψις σου ὡραία.
Πιάσατε ἡμῖν ἀλώπεκας μικροὺς ἀφανίζοντας ἀμπελῶνας,
25   καὶ αἱ ἄμπελοι ἡμῶν κυπρίζουσιν.

Ἀδελφιδός μου ἐμοὶ κἀγὼ αὐτῷ,
ὁ ποιμαίνων ἐν τοῖς κρίνοις,
Ἕως οὗ διαπνεύσῃ ἡ ἡμέρα καὶ κινηθῶσιν αἱ σκιαί.
| ἀπόστρεψον ὁμοιώθητι, ἀδελφιδέ μου,   137
30   τῇ δορκάδι ἢ νεβρῷ ἐλάφων
ἐπὶ τὰ ὄρη τῶν κοιλωμάτων.

HOMILY 5
Song 2:8–17

[8]*The voice of my kinsman:*
Behold, he comes leaping over the mountains,
bounding over the hills.
[9]*My kinsman is like a gazelle,*
or a young hart on the mountains of Bethel.
Behold, he stands behind our wall,
leaning through the windows,
peering through the lattices.

[10]*My kinsman answers and says to me,*
Rise up, come, my close one, my fair one, my dove.
[11]*For behold, the winter is past,*
the rain is gone, it has departed.
[12]*The flowers are seen on the earth,*
the time for cutting has come,
the voice of the dove is heard in our land.
[13]*The fig tree has put forth its early fruit,*
the vines blossom, they give off fragrance.

Rise up, come, my close one, my fair one, my dove.
[14]*Come for yourself, my dove, to the shelter of the rock,*
close by the wall.
Show me your face,
and let me hear your voice;
for your voice is sweet, and your countenance is glorious.
[15]*Catch us the little foxes that spoil the vines,*
and our vines blossom.

[16]*My kinsman is mine and I am his;*
he feeds his flock among the lilies,
[17]*until the day dawns and the shadows depart.*
Turn back, my kinsman,
be made like the gazelle or young hart
on the mountains of the plains.

Τὰ νῦν προτεθέντα διὰ τῆς ἀναγνώσεως ἡμῖν ἐκ τῆς τοῦ Ἄισματος τῶν
Ἀισμάτων φιλοσοφίας καὶ εἰς ἐπιθυμίαν ἄγει τῆς τῶν ὑπερκειμένων ἀγαθῶν
θεωρίας καὶ λύπην ἐντίθησιν ἡμῶν ταῖς ψυχαῖς ἀπόγνωσιν ἐμποιοῦντα
τρόπον τινὰ τῆς τῶν ἀλήπτων κατανοήσεως· πῶς γὰρ ἄν τις ἀλύπως
5   διατεθείη σκοπῶν ὅτι ἐν τοσαύταις ἀνόδοις ὑψωθεῖσα δι᾽ ἀγάπης πρὸς τὴν
τοῦ ἀγαθοῦ μετουσίαν ἡ κεκαθαρμένη ψυχὴ οὔπω, καθώς φησιν ὁ ἀπόστολος,
κατειληφέναι δοκεῖ τὸ ζητούμενον;
      καίτοι γε πρὸς τὰς ἀνόδους ἐκείνας βλέπων τὰς προδιηνυσμένας ἐν
τοῖς πρὸ τούτων λόγοις ἐμακάριζον αὐτὴν τῆς ἀναβάσεως, ὅτε τὸ γλυκὺ
10   μῆλον ἐπέγνω τῆς ἀκαρπίας τοῦ δρυμοῦ διακρίνασα καὶ ὡς ἐπιθυμητὴν
αὐτοῦ τὴν σκιὰν ἐποιήσατο καὶ τῷ καρπῷ καταγλυκανθεῖσα ἐν τοῖς ταμιείοις
τῆς εὐφροσύνης ἐγένετο (οἶνον δὲ ὀνομάζει τὴν | εὐφροσύνην, ᾧ ἡ καρδία   138
τῶν μετεχόντων εὐφραίνεται) καὶ ὡς ἐν τῇ ἀγάπῃ ταχθεῖσα τοῖς μύροις
στηρίζεται διαληφθεῖσα τῇ τῶν μήλων περιβολῇ καὶ ὡς ἐγκάρδιον δεξαμένη
15   τῆς ἀγάπης τὸ βέλος πάλιν ἐν ταῖς χερσὶ τοῦ τοξότου καὶ αὐτὴ βέλος γίνεται
πρὸς τὸν τῆς ἀληθείας σκοπὸν ἐν ταῖς χερσὶ τοῦ δυνατοῦ εὐθυνομένη· ταῦτα
καὶ τὰ τοιαῦτα βλέπων τοῦ ἀκροτάτου τῆς μακαριότητος ἐπειλῆφθαι τὴν διὰ
τοσούτων ὑψωθεῖσαν ἐλογιζόμην.
      ἀλλ᾽ ὡς ἔοικεν ἔτι προοίμια τῆς ἀνόδου τὰ προδιηνυσμένα ἐστί·
20   πάσας γὰρ τὰς ἀναβάσεις ἐκείνας οὐ θεωρίαν τε καὶ κατάληψιν ἐναργῆ
τῆς ἀληθείας ἀλλὰ φωνὴν τοῦ ποθουμένου κατονομάζει διὰ τῆς ἀκοῆς
χαρακτηριζομένην τοῖς ἰδιώμασιν, οὐ διὰ τῆς κατανοήσεως γινωσκομένην
τε καὶ εὐφραίνουσαν. εἰ οὖν ἐκείνη τοσοῦτον ὑψωθεῖσα, καθὼς περὶ τοῦ
μεγάλου Παύλου μανθάνομεν τοῦ τριῶν οὐρανῶν ὑπεραρθέντος, οὔπω
25   κατειληφέναι τὸ ζητούμενον δι᾽ ἀκριβείας ἐνδείκνυται, τί παθεῖν εἰκὸς ἡμᾶς ἢ
ἐν τίσιν εἶναι λογίσασθαι τοὺς μήπω τοῖς προθύροις τῶν ἀδύτων τῆς θεωρίας
ἐγγίσαντας;
      ἔξεστι δὲ δι᾽ αὐτῶν τῶν παρ᾽ αὐτῆς εἰρημένων κατιδεῖν τοῦ ζητουμένου
τὸ δυσθεώρη|τον· Φωνὴ τοῦ ἀδελφιδοῦ μου, φησίν, οὐκ εἶδος, οὐ πρόσωπον,   139
30   οὐ χαρακτὴρ ἐμφαίνων τοῦ ζητουμένου τὴν φύσιν, ἀλλὰ φωνὴ στοχασμὸν
μᾶλλον ἢ βεβαίωσιν ἐμποιοῦσα περὶ τοῦ φθεγγομένου,
      ὅστις ἐστίν, ὅτι γὰρ εἰκασμῷ μᾶλλον ἔοικε τὸ λεγόμενον καὶ οὐχὶ
ἀναμφιβόλῳ τινὶ πληροφορίᾳ τῆς καταλήψεως, δῆλόν ἐστιν ἐκ τοῦ μὴ μιᾷ
τινι προσφυῆναι διανοίᾳ τὸν λόγον μηδὲ πρὸς ἓν εἶδος ὁρᾶν, ἀλλ᾽ ἐπὶ πολλὰ
35   φέρεσθαι ταῖς ὀπτασίαις ἄλλοτε ἄλλως βλέπειν οἰομένην καὶ οὐ πάντοτε
τῷ αὐτῷ παραμένουσαν χαρακτῆρι τοῦ καταληφθέντος [δῆλον ἐκ τῶν

This reading from the philosophy of the Song of Songs sets out for us matters that evoke a desire for the contemplation of transcendent goods. At the very same time, it fills our soul with grief as, in a certain way, it creates despair of our grasping the Incomprehensible. For how is it possible to be without grief when one considers that the purified soul—even though through love she has been exalted toward participation in the Good by a whole series of ascents—does not yet seem, as the apostle says, to have laid hold on what she seeks?

It is true that when, in the addresses before this one, I was attending to the ascents already accomplished, I would pronounce the soul blessed on account of her progress toward the heights. She recognized the sweet apple tree, marking it out as different from the unfruitful thicket. She made herself a lover of its shade. Filled with sweetness by its fruit, she entered the treasure houses of gladness (for the name of | gladness is "wine," by which the hearts of those who share it are rejoiced [cf. Ps 103:15]). Disposed and ordered by love, she is sustained by perfumes, after being clothed about with apples. When in her heart she has taken the arrow of love, she herself, in the hands of the archer, becomes an arrow directed at the target of Truth by the hands of "the Strong One." Looking on these and the like things, I reckoned that the soul that had been exalted through so many stages had achieved the height of blessedness.

Yet it seems that what has already been accomplished is still the preliminary stage of her climb. For all these ascents are described, not in terms of contemplation or clear grasp of the Truth, but by reference to the "voice" of the One who is desired, and the characteristics of a voice are identified by hearing, not known and rejoiced in by understanding. If then the soul that has been exalted to this extent—as we learn concerning the great Paul when he was caught up above three heavens—is shown not truly to have seized her goal, what is likely to become of us, or in what category may those be reckoned who have not yet drawn near even to the entrances into the sanctuaries of contemplation?

From the things that the soul says, one can see that the object of her search is difficult to discern. | The voice of my beloved—that is what she says: not a form, not a countenance, not a property that manifests the nature of the One sought, but a voice that creates, not assurance, but plausible conviction about the identity of the One who speaks.

For something spoken is more like a probability than it is like unambiguous fullness of comprehension, and this is evident from the fact that what is said is not bound to any single meaning, nor does her eye see a single form. On the contrary, she is carried in many directions by her visions, believing that she sees something different at different moments and not always hold-

λεγομένων ἐστίν]· Ἰδοὺ γάρ φησιν οὗτος ἥκει, οὐχ ἑστὼς οὐδὲ παραμένων,
ὡς διὰ τῆς ἐπιμονῆς γνωρισθῆναι τῷ ἀτενίζοντι ἀλλ᾽ ἀφαρπάζων ἑαυτὸν
τῶν ὄψεων, πρὶν εἰς τελείαν γνῶσιν ἐλθεῖν· Πηδῶν γάρ φησιν ἐπὶ τὰ ὄρη καὶ
τοῖς βουνοῖς ἐφαλλόμενος. καὶ νῦν μὲν δορκὰς νομίζεται, πάλιν δὲ νεβρῷ
5   προσεικάζεται· Ὅμοιος γάρ φησιν ἀδελφιδός μού ἐστι τῇ δορκάδι ἢ νεβρῷ
ἐλάφων ἐπὶ τὰ ὄρη Βαιθήλ. οὕτως | τὸ ἀεὶ καταλαμβανόμενον ἄλλοτε ἄλλος   140
ἐστὶ χαρακτήρ.
     Ταῦτά ἐστιν, ἅ με κατὰ τὴν πρόχειρον ἔννοιαν εἰς λύπην ἄγει
ἀπόγνωσιν ἐμποιοῦντα τῆς ἀκριβοῦς τῶν ὑπερκειμένων κατανοήσεως.
10   πλὴν ἀλλὰ πειρατέον ἀναθέντας τῷ θεῷ τὴν ἐλπίδα, τῷ διδόντι ῥῆμα τοῖς
εὐαγγελιζομένοις δυνάμει πολλῇ, προσαρμόσαι τοῖς προκατανενοημένοις ἐν
εἱρμῷ τινι δι᾽ ἀκολούθου τὴν θεωρίαν.
     Φωνὴ τοῦ ἀδελφιδοῦ μού φησι καὶ εὐθὺς ἐπήγαγεν Ἰδοὺ οὗτος ἥκει.
τί οὖν ἐν τούτοις ὑπενοήσαμεν; προβλέπει τάχα τὴν διὰ τοῦ εὐαγγελίου
15   φανερωθεῖσαν ἡμῖν τοῦ θεοῦ λόγου οἰκονομίαν τὰ εἰρημένα, τὴν
προκαταγγελθεῖσαν μὲν διὰ τῶν προφητῶν, φανερωθεῖσαν δὲ διὰ τῆς κατὰ
σάρκα τοῦ θεοῦ ἐπιφανείας· μαρτυρεῖται γὰρ τοῖς ἔργοις ἡ θεία φωνὴ καὶ
συνάπτεται τῷ λόγῳ τῆς ἐπαγγελίας ἡ ἔκβασις, καθώς φησιν ὁ προφήτης
ὅτι Καθάπερ ἠκούσαμεν, οὕτω καὶ εἴδομεν. Φωνή, φησί, τοῦ ἀδελφιδοῦ μου·
20   τοῦτό ἐστιν ὃ ἠκούσαμεν. Ἰδοὺ οὗτος ἥκει· τοῦτο ὃ τοῖς ὀφθαλμοῖς
ἐδεξάμεθα. Πολυμερῶς καὶ πολυτρόπως πάλαι ὁ θεὸς λαλήσας τοῖς πατράσιν
ἐν τοῖς προφήταις· αὕτη ἡ τῆς φωνῆς ἀκοή. Ἐπ᾽ ἐσχάτων τῶν ἡμερῶν
ἐλάλησεν | ἡμῖν ἐν υἱῷ· τοῦτό ἐστι τὸ εἰρημένον Ἰδοὺ οὗτος ἥκει ἐπιπηδῶν   141
τοῖς ὄρεσι καὶ κατὰ τῶν βουνῶν διαλλόμενος, προσφυῶς καὶ καταλλήλως
25   τῇ τε δορκάδι κατά τινα ἴδιον λόγον καὶ πάλιν τῷ νεβρῷ τῶν ἐλάφων καθ᾽
ἑτέραν ἔννοιαν ὁμοιούμενος.
     ἡ δορκὰς σημαίνει τὴν ὀξυωπίαν τοῦ τὸ πᾶν ἐπιβλέποντος· φασὶ γὰρ
τοῦτο τὸ ζῷον ὑπερφυῶς δερκόμενον ἐκ τῆς ἐνεργείας ἔχειν τὸ ὄνομα. ἀλλὰ
μὴν ταὐτόν ἐστι τῷ θεᾶσθαι τὸ δέρκεσθαι. οὐκοῦν ὁ ἐφορῶν τὰ πάντα καὶ
ἐπιβλέπων ἐκ τοῦ θεᾶσθαι τὰ πάντα θεὸς τῶν πάντων ἐπονομάζεται. ἐπειδὴ
30   τοίνυν θεὸς ἐφανερώθη ἐν σαρκὶ ὁ ἐπὶ καθαιρέσει τῶν ἀντικειμένων δυνάμεων

ing to the same attribute of what she grasps.[1] That is why she says *Behold, he is coming*—not stopping or abiding, so as to be made known to an observer by standing still, but snatching himself out of sight before he is perfectly known. For she says *Leaping upon the mountains* and *bounding across the hills*. Moreover, he is a gazelle now but later is likened to a fawn. For she says *My beloved is like the gazelle, or like the fawn of a deer on the hills of Bethel*. Thus | what is ever and again being grasped is now one identifying feature and now another.

This is the language that, when taken in its obvious sense, occasions my grief because it induces despair about the possibility of a precise understanding of things transcendent. Yet we are bound to attempt—having dedicated our hope to God, who confers utterance on those who proclaim the gospel with great power—to conform our interpretation, within a connected sequence of thought, to what we have already understood.

The voice of my beloved, she says, and then straightway adds *Behold, he is coming*. What, then, are we to make of these words? Probably these expressions look forward to the economy of the divine Word, made known to us in the gospel, announced beforehand by the prophets but revealed through God's manifestation in the flesh. For the divine voice is attested by deeds, and to the word of promise its accomplishment is attached, just as the prophet says: "As we have heard, so also we have seen" (Ps 47:9). *The voice of my beloved:* this is what we have heard. *Behold, he is coming:* this is what the eyes see. "In many and various ways God spoke of old to our fathers by the prophets" (Heb 1:1): this is the hearing of the voice. "In the last days he spoke | to us by a Son" (Heb 1:2): this is what is meant by *Behold, he is coming, leaping upon the mountains, bounding across the hills*—likened suitably and appropriately to a gazelle for a special reason, and again, in accordance with another insight, to the fawn of a deer.

"Gazelle" signifies the sharp-sightedness of him who sees over the universe, for they say that this animal, surpassingly endowed with the ability to see, takes its name from this activity.[2] To see, however, is the same thing as to behold. Consequently, the one who looks and sees over all things is called "God" from the fact that he beholds everything.[3] Since, therefore, he who

---

1. Here the manuscripts add what appears to be a gloss: "It is clear from what is said."

2. The Greek word rendered here as "gazelle" is δορκάς, which is etymologically related to the verb δέρκομαι ("see" or "see clearly"), perhaps because the eyes of the animal in question are large in proportion to the rest of its face. See below, homily 7, p. 242 (Jaeger), and n. 12 there. Origen had made the same point; see *Comm. Cant.* 3.12 (Baehrens 1925, 214.30–31; cf. trans. Lawson 1956, 226).

3. Gregory thinks that the word θεός ("god") is cognate with the verb θεᾶσθαι (here rendered as "behold").

ἐπιφανεὶς τῷ βίῳ, διὰ τοῦτο δορκάδι μὲν ὁμοιοῦται ὁ ἐκ τῶν οὐρανῶν ἐπὶ
τὴν γῆν ἐπιβλέψας, νεβρῷ δὲ ὁ τὰ ὄρη καὶ τοὺς βουνοὺς διαλαμβάνων
τοῖς ἅλμασι, τουτέστιν ὁ καταπατῶν τε καὶ καταλύων τὰ πονηρὰ τῆς τῶν
δαιμόνων κακίας ὑψώματα· ὄρη μὲν γὰρ λέγει τὰ ἐν τῇ κραταιότητι αὐτοῦ
5   ταρασσόμενα, ὥς φησιν ὁ Δαβίδ, τὰ μετατιθέμενα ἐν καρδίᾳ θαλασσῶν καὶ
τῷ συγγενεῖ τόπῳ τῆς ἀβύσσου καταδυόμενα, περὶ ὧν πρὸς τοὺς μαθητὰς
εἶπεν ὁ κύριος ὅτι Ἐὰν ἔχητε | πίστιν ὡς κόκκον σινάπεως, ἐρεῖτε τῷ ὄρει   142
τούτῳ (δεικνὺς τῷ λόγῳ τὸ πονηρὸν ἐκεῖνο τὸ σεληναῖον δαιμόνιον), ὅτι
Ἄρθητι καὶ βλήθητι εἰς τὴν θάλασσαν.
10   ἐπειδὴ τοίνυν ἴδιον τῆς τῶν νεβρῶν ἐστι φύσεως τὸ ἀναλωτικὸν τῶν
θηρίων καὶ τὸ φυγαδεύειν τῷ ἄσθματι καὶ τῇ τοῦ χρωτὸς ἰδιότητι τὸ τῶν
ὄφεων γένος, διὰ τοῦτο δορκάδι μὲν ὁ ἐφορῶν τὰ πάντα ὡμοίωται, νεβρῷ
δὲ ἐλάφων ὡς πατῶν τε καὶ ἀναλίσκων τὴν ἐναντίαν ἐνέργειαν, ἣν ἡ τροπικὴ
σημασία ὄρη καὶ βουνοὺς κατωνόμασεν.
15   γέγονέ τε οὖν ἡ τοῦ νυμφίου φωνὴ διὰ τῶν προφητῶν, ἐν οἷς ἐλάλησεν ὁ
θεός, καὶ μετὰ τὴν φωνὴν ἦλθεν ὁ λόγος ἐπιπηδῶν τοῖς ἀντικειμένοις ὄρεσι
καὶ τῶν βουνῶν καθαλλόμενος, πᾶσαν ἐκ τοῦ ἴσου τὴν ἀποστατικὴν δύναμιν
ὑπόχιον ἑαυτῷ ποιῶν, τήν τε ὑποδεεστέραν καὶ τὴν προάγουσαν· τοῦτο γὰρ
ἡ τῶν βουνῶν πρὸς τὰ ὄρη διαστολὴ ὑπαινίσσεται ὅτι καὶ τὸ ἐξέχον ἐν τοῖς
20   ἀντικειμένοις ὁμοίως τῷ ὑποβεβηκότι καθαιρεῖται ἐν τῇ αὐτῇ δυνάμει τε καὶ
ἐξουσίᾳ πατούμενον· ὁμοίως γὰρ καταπατεῖται ὁ λέων τε καὶ ὁ δράκων, τὰ
ὑπερέχοντα, ὅ τε ὄφις καὶ ὁ σκορπίος, τὰ | δοκοῦντα καταδεέστερα.   143
οἷόν τι λέγω· ἣν ἐν τοῖς ἀκολουθοῦσιν αὐτῷ ὄχλοις ὄρη δαιμόνια, ἣν
ἐν ταῖς συναγωγαῖς, ἣν ἐν τῇ χώρᾳ τῶν Γερασηνῶν, ἣν ἐν ἑτέροις τόποις
25   πολλοῖς, κατὰ τῆς ἀνθρωπίνης φύσεως ὑψούμενά τε καὶ κορυφούμενα. ἐκ
τούτων ἦσαν καὶ βουνοὶ καὶ ὄρη, ὑπερέχοντές τε καὶ ὑποκείμενοι. ἀλλ' ὁ
νεβρὸς τῶν ἐλάφων, ὁ ἀναλωτικὸς τῶν ὄφεων, ὁ καὶ τοὺς μαθητὰς εἰς τὴν

appeared under the conditions of our life to destroy the opposing powers was manifested as God in flesh, for just this reason the one who from heaven looks over the earth is likened to a gazelle, while, on the other hand, he who marks out the mountains and hills with his leaps is likened to a fawn—that is, one who treads down and destroys the wicked heights of demonic evil.[4] For "mountains" means the things that are shaken "by his might," even as David says (Ps 45:4): the things "that are moved in the heart of the sea and sunk in the place of the abyss" (Ps 45:3). Concerning these, the Lord said to his disciples, "If you have | faith as a grain of mustard seed, you will say to this mountain,"—signifying by this word the evil demon that brings on lunacy— " 'Rise up and be cast into the sea' " (Matt 17:20).

Since, therefore, it is proper to the nature of the fawn to destroy wild things and, by its breath and the special character of its color, to put the serpent-kind to flight,[5] for this reason the one who oversees all things is on the one hand likened to a gazelle, but on the other hand, because he treads down and destroys the opposing Energy—which in figurative language is called "mountains and hills"—he is likened to a young hart.

The voice of the Bridegroom, moreover, was heard through the prophets, in whom God spoke, and after the voice there came the Word, leaping upon the opposing mountains and rushing down the hills, making the whole rebellious power equally subject to himself, both the inferior power and the power that takes the lead. For the distinction between hills and mountains hints at this: that even that which is preeminent among the opposing powers is destroyed in exactly the same way as that which is under it, being trodden down by the same might and the same authority. Both "lion and serpent" (Ps 90:13)—the exalted ones—are trampled, and so are the snake and the scorpion (cf. Luke 10:19, who | seem to be their inferiors.

What I mean is something like this: in the crowds that followed Jesus, in the synagogues, in the territory of the Gerasenes, in many other places, there were demonic Heights, exalted against humankind and towering. Among these there were both hills and mountains, the preeminent and the inferior. But the young hart—who destroys serpents and who likewise forms

---

4. Origen, on the contrary, identifies the mountains as the prophets and perhaps the apostles (Baehrens 1925, 201), a theme that Gregory exploits briefly just below without conceding his point about the meaning of the mountains and hills. There is of course just a hint of Gregory's line at one point in Origen's exegesis; see Baehrens 1925, 204.14ff., with its image of the Word of God overcoming kingdoms. For a different interpretation of this entire stichos, see Gregory, *Beat.*, homily 2 (trans. Graef 1954, 101).

5. See Origen, *Comm. Cant.* 3.11 (Baehrens 1925, 201, with the fragment from Procopius; cf. trans. Lawson 1956, 209), for the idea that young male deer attack snakes, which is reported in Pliny the Elder, *Nat.* 8.114; cf. Aelian, *Nat. an.* 2.9; 8.6.

τῶν ἐλάφων καταρτιζόμενος φύσιν, ἐν οἷς λέγει ὅτι Δέδωκα ὑμῖν ἐξουσίαν
τοῦ πατεῖν ἐπάνω ὄφεων καὶ σκορπίων, πᾶσιν ἐπίσης ἐπιβάλλει τὸ ἴχνος,
ταῦτά τε φυγαδεύων καὶ μεθαλλόμενος ἀπὸ τούτων πρὸς ἕτερα, ὡς διὰ
τούτων τὸ μέγεθος τῶν κατ' ἀρετὴν ὑψουμένων ἀναφανῆναι μηκέτι τοῖς
5   γεωλόφοις τῆς κακίας ἐπισκοτούμενον· τὰ γὰρ ὄρη Βαιθὴλ ἔοικεν ἐκ τῆς τοῦ
ὀνόματος ἑρμηνείας τὸν ὑψηλὸν καὶ οὐράνιον ἐνδείκνυσθαι βίον· οἶκον γὰρ
θεοῦ σημαίνειν τὴν λέξιν ταύτην φασὶν οἱ τῆς Ἑβραίων φωνῆς ἐπιστήμονες.
διὸ φησιν Ἐπὶ τὰ ὄρη Βαιθήλ.

Εἶδε ταῦτα ὁ κεκαθαρμένος τε καὶ διορατικὸς τῆς ψυχῆς | ὀφθαλμός,   144
10   ὁ τοῖς θείοις ἐκείνοις ἅλμασι τοῖς κατὰ τῶν ἀντικειμένων γεωλόφων
γινομένοις συμμεθαλλόμενος, καὶ περὶ τοῦ χρόνοις ὕστερον γενησομένου
ὡς ἤδη παρόντος ποιεῖται τὸν λόγον διὰ τὸ πιστόν τε καὶ ἀναμφίβολον τῆς
ἐλπιζομένης χάριτος ὡς ἔργον τὴν ἐλπίδα βλέπων· φησὶ γὰρ ὅτι ὁ κατὰ τῶν
ὀρέων πηδῶν ἐν εὐκινήτῳ τῷ τάχει καὶ εἰς βουνοὺς ἀπὸ βουνῶν διαλλόμενος
15   στάσιμον δείκνυσιν ἡμῖν ἑαυτὸν κατόπιν τοῦ τοίχου γενόμενος καὶ ἐκ τῶν
δικτύων τῶν θυρίδων διαλεγόμενος. ἔχει δὲ οὕτως ἡ λέξις· Ἰδοὺ οὗτος
ἕστηκεν ὀπίσω τοῦ τοίχου ἡμῶν παρακύπτων διὰ τῶν θυρίδων, ἐκκύπτων
διὰ τῶν δικτύων.

τὸ μὲν οὖν σωματικῶς ἐν τῷ λόγῳ ὑπογραφόμενον τοιοῦτόν ἐστι, ὅτι
20   ἔνδον οἰκουρούσῃ τῇ νύμφῃ διὰ τῶν θυρίδων ὁ ἐραστὴς διαλέγεται καὶ τοῦ
τοίχου κατὰ τὸ μέσον ἀμφοτέρους διείργοντος ἀνεμπόδιστος γίνεται τοῦ
λόγου ἡ κοινωνία διὰ μὲν τῶν θυρίδων τῆς κεφαλῆς παρακυπτούσης, διὰ δὲ
τῶν δικτύων τῶν ἐν ταῖς θυρίσι πρὸς τὰ ἐντὸς τοῦ ὀφθαλμοῦ διακύπτοντος,

ἡ δὲ κατὰ ἀναγωγὴν θεωρία τῆς προεξητασμένης ἔχεται διανοίας·
25   ὁδῷ γὰρ καὶ ἀκολουθίᾳ προσοικειοῖ τῷ θεῷ τὴν | ἀνθρωπίνην φύσιν ὁ   145
λόγος, πρῶτον μὲν αὐτὴν διὰ τῶν προφητῶν καταυγάζων καὶ τῶν νομικῶν
παραγγελμάτων (οὕτω γὰρ νοοῦμεν· θυρίδας μὲν τοὺς προφήτας τοὺς
τὸ φῶς εἰσάγοντας, δίκτυα δὲ τὴν τῶν νομικῶν παραγγελμάτων πλοκήν,
δι' ὧν ἀμφοτέρων ἡ αὐγὴ τοῦ ἀληθινοῦ φωτὸς ἐπὶ τὰ ἐντὸς παραδύεται)·

his disciples so that they may be deer when he says in their presence, "I have given you authority to tread on snakes and scorpions" (Luke 10:19)—sets his foot upon all of them equally, both putting them to flight and leaping from the one set to the other, so as through them to make it perfectly plain that the stature of those whom virtue lifts up is no longer overshadowed by the hillocks of evil. For the hills of Bethel seems, on the basis of the name's meaning, to denote the exalted and heavenly life, since those who know Hebrew say that the word means "house of God." That is why it says *on the hills of Bethel*.

The purified and discerning eye of the soul sees these things, | as it keeps company with those divine leaps over the opposing hills, and she discourses of the one who is coming in the future as if he were already present, contemplating her hope as something already accomplished, thanks to the trustiness and certainty of the hoped-for grace. For the text says, "He who treads upon the mountains with swift agility and leaps from hill to hill shows himself to us as stationary, standing behind the wall and conversing from behind the latticework of the windows." That is the point of its saying *Behold, he stands behind our wall, looking through the windows, peeping through the lattices.*"

Thus the situation that is literally described in the text is this: the Beloved converses through the windows with the Bride who keeps the house, and, though the wall between them separates the pair, their verbal communication is unimpeded, since his head looks in through the windows, while his eye peers through the latticework[6] of the windows upon the interior.

The anagogical sense of the words, however, adheres closely to the line of thought we have already uncovered, for the Word follows a certain path and a certain sequence in adapting | human nature to God. First of all he shines upon it by means of the prophets and the law's injunctions. (This is our interpretation: the windows are the prophets, who bring in the light, while the lattices are the network of the law's injunctions.[7] Through both of them

---

6. Origen (Baehrens 1925, 203; cf. trans. Lawson 1956, 212) takes the δίκτυα ("retia" in Rufinus's Latin) of Song 2:9 to be "nets," that is to say, Satan's snares, which the Word "tears and rends." In one place, to be sure, he envisages these "nets" as "latticework" (see n. 7 below), but further on he returns to his original idea and develops it (Baehrens 1925, 221.18–222.3).

7. Contrast Origen *Comm. Cant.* 3.13 (Baehrens 1925, 219.8ff.; cf. trans. Lawson 1956, 233), for whom vision "through the windows … [and] lattices" represents the sort of thing Paul meant by seeing "by means of a mirror in an enigma" (1 Cor 13:12). Thus further along he says: "But that he is said to 'look through the nets' of the windows doubtless points [to] the fact that so long as the soul is in the house of this body, she cannot receive the naked and plain wisdom of God, but beholds the invisible and the incorporeal by means of certain analogies and tokens and images of visible things" (trans. Lawson 1956, 234; cf. Baehrens 1925, 220.7ff.).

μετὰ ταῦτα δὲ ἡ τελεία τοῦ φωτὸς ἔλλαμψις γίνεται, ὅταν ἐπιφανῇ τὸ φῶς
τὸ ἀληθινὸν τοῖς ἐν σκότει καὶ σκιᾷ θανάτου καθημένοις διὰ τῆς πρὸς τὴν
φύσιν ἡμῶν συνανακράσεως. πρότερον οὖν αἱ αὐγαὶ τῶν προφητικῶν τε καὶ
νομικῶν νοημάτων ἐλλάμπουσαι τῇ ψυχῇ διὰ τῶν νοηθεισῶν ἡμῖν θυρίδων
5   τε καὶ δικτύων ἐπιθυμίαν ἐμποιοῦσι τοῦ ἰδεῖν ἐν ὑπαίθρῳ τὸν ἥλιον, εἶθ᾽ οὕτω
τὸ ποθούμενον εἰς ἔργον προέρχεται.

Ἀκούσωμεν δὲ οἷα πρὸς τὴν ἐκκλησίαν λαλεῖ ὁ μήπω ἐντὸς τοῦ
τοίχου γενόμενος ἀλλ᾽ ἔτι διὰ τῶν φωταγωγῶν αὐτῇ προσφθεγγόμενος·
Ἀποκρίνεται, φησίν, ὁ ἀδελφιδός μου καὶ λέγει μοι· Ἀνάστα, ἐλθέ, ἡ πλησίον
10   μου, καλή μου, περιστερά μου, ὅτι ἰδοὺ ὁ χειμὼν παρῆλθεν, ὁ ὑετὸς ἀπῆλθεν,
ἐπορεύθη ἑαυτῷ, τὰ ἄνθη ὤφθη ἐν τῇ γῇ, ὁ καιρὸς τῆς τομῆς ἔφθακεν, | φωνὴ   146
τοῦ τρυγόνος ἠκούσθη ἐν τῇ γῇ ἡμῶν, ἡ συκῆ ἐξήνεγκε τοὺς ὀλύνθους αὐτῆς,
αἱ ἄμπελοι κυπρίζουσιν, ἔδωκαν ὀσμήν.

Ὦ πῶς γλαφυρῶς ἡμῖν ὑπογράφει τὴν τοῦ ἔαρος χάριν ὁ πλάστης τοῦ
15   ἔαρος, πρὸς ὅν φησιν ὁ Δαβὶδ ὅτι Θέρος καὶ ἔαρ σὺ ἔπλασας αὐτά. λύει τὴν
τοῦ χειμῶνος κατήφειαν παρεληλυθέναι λέγων τὴν χειμερινὴν σκυθρωπότητα
καὶ τὴν τῶν ὑετῶν ἀηδίαν· λειμῶνας δείκνυσι βρύοντας καὶ ὡραϊζομένους
τοῖς ἄνθεσιν, τὰ δὲ ἄνθη ἐν ἀκμῇ εἶναι λέγει καὶ πρὸς τομὴν ἐπιτηδείως
ἔχειν, ὡς εἰς στεφάνου πλοκὴν ἢ μύρου κατασκευὴν ἀναιρεῖσθαι πάντως
20   τοὺς ἀνθολόγους. ἡδύνει δὲ τὸν καιρὸν ὁ λόγος καὶ ταῖς τῶν ὀρνίθων ᾠδαῖς
κατὰ τὰ ἄλση περιηχούμενον τῆς ἡδείας τῶν τρυγόνων φωνῆς ταῖς ἀκοαῖς
προσηχούσης, συκῆν δὲ λέγει καὶ ἄμπελον τὴν ἀπ᾽ αὐτῶν γενησομένην
τρυφὴν τοῖς φαινομένοις   προοιμιάζεσθαι, τὴν μὲν τοὺς ὀλύνθους
ἐκφέρουσαν, τὴν δὲ τῷ ἄνθει κυπρίζουσαν, ὡς κατατρυφᾶν τῆς εὐωδίας τὴν
25   ὄσφρησιν. οὕτω μὲν οὖν ἁβρύνεται τῇ ὑπογραφῇ τῆς ἐαρινῆς ὥρας ὁ λόγος τό
τε σκυθρωπὸν ἀποβάλλων καὶ τοῖς γλυκυτέ | ροις ἐμφιλοχωρῶν διηγήμασιν.

χρὴ δέ, οἶμαι, μὴ παραμεῖναι τὴν διάνοιαν τῇ τῶν γλαφυρῶν τούτων   147
ὑπογραφῇ, ἀλλὰ δι᾽ αὐτῶν ὁδηγηθῆναι πρὸς τὰ δηλούμενα διὰ τῶν λογίων
τούτων μυστήρια, ὥστε ἀνακαλυφθῆναι τὸν θησαυρὸν τῶν νοημάτων τὸν
30   ἐγκεκρυμμένον τοῖς ῥήμασιν.

τί οὖν ἐστιν ὃ φαμεν; πεπήγει ποτὲ τῷ τῆς εἰδωλολατρίας κρυμῷ τὸ
ἀνθρώπινον τῆς εὐκινήτου φύσεως τῶν ἀνθρώπων πρὸς τὴν τῶν ἀκινήτων
σεβασμάτων φύσιν μεταβληθείσης· Ὅμοιοι γάρ φησιν αὐτοῖς γένοιντο
οἱ ποιοῦντες αὐτὰ καὶ πάντες οἱ πεποιθότες ἐπ᾽ αὐτοῖς. καὶ τὸ εἰκὸς ἐν
35   τοῖς γινομένοις ἦν· ὥσπερ γὰρ οἱ πρὸς τὴν ἀληθινὴν θεότητα βλέποντες
ἐφ᾽ ἑαυτῶν δέχονται τὰ τῆς θείας φύσεως ἰδιώματα, οὕτως ὁ τῇ ματαιότητι

the beam of the true Light steals into the interior.) After that, however, comes the Light's perfect illumination, when, by its mingling with our nature, the true Light shows itself to those who are in darkness and the shadow of death. At an earlier stage, then, the beams of the prophetic and legal ideas, which illumine the soul by way of its windows and lattices, as we have understood, induce a desire to see the sun in the open air, and then, in the way indicated, the Desired steps forward to do his work.

But let us hear what sort of thing he speaks to the church[8] when he is not yet within the walls but is still addressing her through the channels of light. My beloved answers and says to me: *Rise up, come, my close one, my fair one, my dove. For behold, the winter is past, the rain has gone, it has departed. The flowers are seen on the earth, the time for cutting has come, the voice of the dove| is heard in our land. The fig tree has put forth its early fruit, the vines blossom, they give off fragrance.*

O how elegantly the Maker of the springtime describes its beauty for us! To him David said, "Summer and spring—you formed them" (Ps 73:17). He dissolves the winter's gloom and says that its melancholy has passed, together with the repellent rains. He shows us the meadows teeming and glorious with blossoms, while the blossoms, he says, are at their best and ready to be cut, so that the flower gatherers take them up to plait crowns or to make perfume. The text also embellishes the season with the songs of the birds in the groves, as the sweet call of the dove re-echoes in the ear. And he says that the fig and the vine presage by their appearance the delicacies they will bring forth, one bearing the early fig, while the other blossoms and delights the sense of smell with its fragrance. The Word thus speaks with elegance in its account of springtime's beauty, both casting out gloom and | dwelling fondly upon accounts of things that afford more pleasure.

It is best, though, I think, that our understanding not come to rest in the account of these sweet things but rather journey by their help toward the mysteries that these oracles reveal, so that the treasure of the ideas hidden in the words may be brought to light.

What are we saying? There was a time when humanity was frozen stiff by the chill of idolatry because the changeable nature of human beings had been altered to conform to that of unchangeable idols. For it is written: "Those who make them are like them; so are all who believe in them" (Ps 113:16). And what happened back there was equitable. For just as those who look upon the true Godhead take to themselves the characteristics of the divine

---

8. Two or three lines before this, the Bride was the soul; now, without warning, she is identified as "church."

τῶν εἰδώλων προσανέχων μετεστοιχειοῦτο πρὸς τὸ βλεπόμενον λίθος ἐξ
ἀνθρώπου γινόμενος. ἐπειδὴ τοίνυν ἀπολιθωθεῖσα διὰ τῆς τῶν εἰδώλων
λατρείας ἀκίνητος ἦν πρὸς τὸ κρεῖττον ἡ φύσις ἐμπεπηγυῖα τῷ τῆς
εἰδωλολατρίας κρυμῷ, τούτου χάριν ἐπανατέλλει τῷ χαλεπῷ τούτῳ χειμῶνι
5   ὁ τῆς δικαιοσύνης ἥλιος καὶ ἔαρ ποιεῖ τοῦ μεσημβρινοῦ πνεύματος, τοῦ τὴν
τοιαύτην διαλύοντος πῆξιν, ἅμα τῇ ἀνατολῇ τῶν ἀκτίνων συνεπιθάλποντος
ἅπαν τὸ ὑποκείμενον, ἵνα διαθερμανθεὶς τῷ πνεύματι ὁ διὰ τοῦ κρύους
λιθωθεὶς ἄνθρωπος καὶ ὑποθαλφθεὶς τῇ ἀκτῖνι | τοῦ λόγου πάλιν γένηται   148
ὕδωρ ἁλλόμενον εἰς ζωὴν αἰώνιον· Πνεύσεται γὰρ τὸ πνεῦμα αὐτοῦ
10   καὶ ῥυήσεται ὕδατα Στρεφομένης τῆς πέτρας εἰς λίμνας ὑδάτων καὶ τῆς
ἀκροτόμου εἰς πηγὰς ὑδάτων. ὅπερ γυμνότερον πρὸς τοὺς Ἰουδαίους ὁ
βαπτιστὴς ἀνεβόησε λέγων τοὺς λίθους τούτους ἐγείρεσθαι εἰς τὸ γενέσθαι
τέκνα τοῦ πατριάρχου δι᾽ ἀρετῆς ὁμοιούμενα.

ταῦτα τοίνυν ἀκούει τοῦ λόγου ἡ ἐκκλησία διὰ τῶν προφητικῶν θυρίδων
15   καὶ τῶν νομικῶν δικτύων δεχομένη τὴν τῆς ἀληθείας αὐγὴν ἔτι συνεστῶτος
τοῦ τυπικοῦ τῆς διδασκαλίας τοίχου, τοῦ νόμου λέγω, τοῦ τὴν σκιὰν
ποιοῦντος τῶν μελλόντων ἀγαθῶν, οὐκ αὐτὴν τὴν εἰκόνα τῶν πραγμάτων
δεικνύοντος, οὗ κατόπιν ἵσταται ἡ ἀλήθεια ἐχομένη τοῦ τύπου πρῶτον μὲν
διὰ τῶν προφητῶν ἐναυγάζουσα τῇ ἐκκλησίᾳ τὸν λόγον, μετὰ ταῦτα δὲ
20   τῇ φανερώσει τοῦ εὐαγγελίου πᾶσαν τοῦ τύπου τὴν σκιοειδῆ φαντασίαν
ἐξαναλίσκουσα, δι᾽ ἧς καθαιρεῖται μὲν τὸ μεσότοιχον, συνάπτεται δὲ ὁ ἐν
τῷ οἴκῳ ἀὴρ πρὸς τὸ αἴθριον φῶς, ὡς μηκέτι διὰ τῶν θυρίδων χρείαν ἔχειν
περιαυγάζεσθαι αὐτοῦ τοῦ ἀληθινοῦ φωτὸς διὰ τῶν εὐαγγελικῶν ἀκτίνων τὰ
ἔνδον πάντα καταφωτίζοντος.

25   διὰ τοῦτο ἐμβοᾷ διὰ τῶν φωταγωγῶν τῇ ἐκκλησίᾳ ὁ λόγος ὁ ἀνορθῶν
τοὺς κατερραγμένους | λέγων Ἀνάστηθι (δηλαδὴ ἐκ τοῦ πτώματος) ἡ τῷ   149
γλίσχρῳ τῆς ἁμαρτίας ἐνολισθήσασα, ἡ συμποδισθεῖσα διὰ τοῦ ὄφεως καὶ εἰς
γῆν πεσοῦσα καὶ ἐν τῷ πτώματι τῆς παρακοῆς γενομένη, ἀνάστα. οὐκ ἀρκεῖ
δέ σοι, φησί, τὸ ἀνορθωθῆναι μόνον ἐκ τοῦ πτώματος, ἀλλὰ καὶ πρόελθε διὰ
30   τῆς τῶν ἀγαθῶν προκοπῆς τὸν ἐν ἀρετῇ διανύουσα δρόμον.

ὅπερ δὴ καὶ ἐπὶ τοῦ παραλυτικοῦ μεμαθήκαμεν· οὐ γὰρ διανίστησι μόνον
ὁ λόγος τὸ ἐπικλίνιον ἄχθος ἐκεῖνο, ἀλλὰ καὶ περιπατεῖν ἐγκελεύεται. ὅπερ
μοι δοκεῖ τὴν πρὸς τὸ κρεῖττον πρόοδόν τε καὶ ἐπαύξησιν διὰ τῆς μεταβατικῆς

nature, so too the person who is devoted to the vanity of idols is transformed into the stone he looks upon and becomes other than human. Since, then, once it has been petrified by the worship of idols, human nature cannot be changed for the better because it is frozen stiff by the chill of idolatry, the Sun of Righteousness rises upon this harsh winter and brings the spring of the Spirit,[9] which melts such ice and, as its rays rise up, warms everything that lies beneath it. So it is that the person who has been petrified by the frost, once warmed by the Spirit and heated by the ray | of the Word, again becomes water that springs up to life eternal. For "His Spirit will blow, and the waters will flow" (Ps 147:7). This is what the Baptist cried out to the Jews plainly when he stated that "these stones" would arise to become children of the patriarch (Matt 3:9 // Luke 3:8), made like him by virtue.

These, therefore, are the things that the church hears from the Word when, through the prophetic windows and the lattices of the law, she receives the light of the Truth while the wall of the teaching, which has the character of a type, still stands. What I mean by this, of course, is the law.[10] It casts the shadow of the good things to come. It does not manifest the very image of the things; behind it, closely attached to the type, stands the Truth, which first radiates the Word upon the church in the prophets and then, by the revelation of the gospel, destroys the shadowy imagery of the type. This Truth takes away "the dividing wall" and unites the atmosphere within the house with the light of the open air, so that the Bride no longer needs to get light through the windows, since the beams of the gospel illumine the whole interior.

This explains why the Word, who raises up the fallen, calls out through the windows to the church | and says: "Rise up"—plainly it means from a fall—"you who have slipped and fallen on the slick surface of sin. You who have been bound by the serpent and have collapsed upon the earth and live in the fallen state of disobedience—arise! For you it is not sufficient," he says, "merely to be raised up from your fall. No, you are also to advance by making progress in the good as you finish your course in a state of virtue."

This we have also learned from the case of the paralytic (cf. Matt 9:5–6). For the Word does not only restore that prostrate burden but commands him to walk. And this seems to me to signify both progress toward the better and

---

9. What Gregory writes here, τοῦ μεσημβρινοῦ πνεύματος, can hardly be rendered in English; it means "the south wind," but πνεῦμα also means "spirit," and what Gregory intends is to associate the Spirit of God with the south wind that brings springtime in its wake.

10. This line of thought no doubt comes from Origen, who speaks of Christ's standing briefly "*behind the wall* of the Old Covenant's house" (*Comm. Cant.* 3.13; Baehrens 1925, 220.17).

κινήσεως σημαίνειν [ὁ λόγος]. Ἀνάστα οὖν φησι καὶ Ἐλθέ. ὦ προστάγματος
δύναμις. ὄντως φωνὴ δυνάμεώς ἐστιν ἡ φωνὴ τοῦ θεοῦ, καθὼς ἡ ψαλμῳδία
φησὶν ὅτι Ἰδοὺ δώσει τὴν φωνὴν αὐτοῦ, φωνὴν δυνάμεως· καὶ Αὐτὸς εἶπε
καὶ ἐγενήθησαν, αὐτὸς ἐνετείλατο καὶ ἐκτίσθησαν. ἰδοὺ καὶ νῦν εἶπε πρὸς
5   τὴν κειμένην ὅτι Ἀνάστηθι καὶ ὅτι Ἐλθὲ καὶ εὐθὺς ἔργον τὸ πρόσταγμα
γίνεται· ὁμοῦ γὰρ τῷ δέξασθαι τοῦ λόγου τὴν | δύναμιν καὶ ἵσταται καὶ   150
παρίσταται καὶ πλησίον γίνεται τοῦ φωτός, ὡς ὑπ᾽ αὐτοῦ τοῦ καλέσαντος
αὐτὴν μεμαρτύρηται οὕτως εἰπόντος τοῦ λόγου Ἀνάστα, ἐλθέ, ἡ πλησίον μου,
καλή μου, περιστερά μου.
10   τίς ἡ τάξις αὕτη τοῦ λόγου; πῶς ἔχεται τοῦ ἑτέρου τὸ ἕτερον; πῶς σῴζεται
καθ᾽ εἱρμὸν ὥσπερ ἐν ἁλύσει τινὶ τὸ τῶν νοημάτων ἀκόλουθον; ἀκούει τοῦ
προστάγματος, ἐνδυναμοῦται τῷ λόγῳ, ἐγείρεται, προέρχεται, πλησιάζει,
καλὴ γίνεται, περιστερὰ ὀνομάζεται.
πῶς γάρ ἐστι δυνατὸν καλὴν ὄψιν ἐν κατόπτρῳ γενέσθαι μὴ καλῆς
15   τινος μορφῆς δεξαμένῳ τὴν ἔμφασιν; οὐκοῦν καὶ τὸ τῆς ἀνθρωπίνης φύσεως
κάτοπτρον οὐ πρότερον ἐγένετο καλόν, ἀλλ᾽ ὅτε τῷ καλῷ ἐπλησίασε καὶ
τῇ εἰκόνι τοῦ θείου κάλλους ἐνεμορφώθη. ὥσπερ γὰρ τὸ τοῦ ὄφεως εἶχεν
εἶδος ἕως ἔκειτο ἐπὶ τῆς γῆς καὶ πρὸς αὐτὸν ἀφεώρα, κατὰ τὸν αὐτὸν τρόπον
ἐπειδὴ ἀνέστη καὶ τῷ ἀγαθῷ ἔδειξεν ἑαυτὴν ἀντιπρόσωπον κατὰ νώτου τὴν
20   κακίαν ποιησαμένη, πρὸς ὃ βλέπει κατ᾽ ἐκεῖνο καὶ σχηματίζεται· βλέπει δὲ
πρὸς τὸ ἀρχέτυπον κάλλος. διὰ τοῦτο τῷ φωτὶ προσεγγίσασα φῶς γίνεται,
τῷ δὲ φωτὶ τὸ καλὸν τῆς | περιστερᾶς εἶδος ἐνεικονίζεται, ἐκείνης λέγω τῆς   151
περιστερᾶς, ἧς τὸ εἶδος τὴν τοῦ ἁγίου πνεύματος παρουσίαν ἐγνώρισεν.
οὕτω τοίνυν αὐτῇ προσφωνήσας ὁ λόγος καὶ ὀνομάσας αὐτὴν καλὴν
25   μὲν διὰ τὸ πλησίον, περιστερὰν δὲ διὰ τὸ κάλλος, καὶ τὰ ἐφεξῆς διεξέρχεται
οὐκέτι λέγων κρατεῖν τοῦ χειμῶνος τῶν ψυχῶν τὴν κατήφειαν· οὐ γὰρ ἀντέχει
πρὸς τὴν ἀκτῖνα τὸ κρύος. Ἰδού, φησίν, ὁ χειμὼν παρῆλθεν, ὁ ὑετὸς ἀπῆλθεν,
ἐπορεύθη ἑαυτῷ.

growth by way of a process of transformation.[11] That is why he says, *Arise!* and *Come!* O the power of this command! Truly the voice of God is a voice of power, just as the psalm says: "He will put forth his voice, a voice of power" (Ps 67:34); and again, "He spoke, and they came to be; he commanded, and they were created" (Ps 32:9). Behold, at this very point he addresses the prostrate one and says *Arise!* and then *Come!* and straightway the command becomes reality. For at the moment in which she receives the | power of the Word, she stands up, and hands herself over, and comes close to the light—as is testified by the very One who calls her: for the Word says: *Arise! Come! my close one, my beauty, my dove.*

What is the point of this order of words in our text? How is one element in it tied in with another? How is the logical sequence of the ideas kept connected as in a chain? She hears the command. She is empowered by the Word. She rises up. She moves forward. She is brought close. She becomes a beauty. She is named dove.

How after all is it possible for a beautiful image to appear in a mirror unless the mirror has received the impression of a lovely form? Hence the mirror that is human nature does not become beautiful until it has drawn close to the Beautiful and been formed by the image of the divine Beauty. For just as human nature took the form of the serpent as long as it lay prostrate upon the earth and directed its gaze on him, in the same way, when it has risen up and shown itself to be face to face with the Good by turning its back upon evil, it is shaped in accordance with that which it looks upon—and what it looks upon is the archetypal Beauty.[12] When, therefore, it has drawn close to the Light, it becomes light, and in this light the beautiful | form of the dove is imaged—and the dove I am talking about is the one whose form makes known the presence of the Holy Spirit.[13]

So, then, the Word has spoken to her and called her *fair one* because she is close to him and *dove* because of her beauty. And he continues in the words that follow by saying that the misery of the soul's winter does not triumph, because the frost fails to withstand the radiance. *For behold*, he says, *the winter is past, the rain is gone, it has departed.*

---

11. Contrast Origen, *Comm. Cant.* 3.13 (Baehrens 1925, 220.24–25, with the fragment cited there from Procopius), who sees in the Bridegroom's words a summons to move "from the letter to the Spirit": "Vocat ergo eam et invitat a carnalibus ad spiritalia, a visibilibus ad invisibilia, a lege 'venire' ad evangelium."

12. On this whole sequence of ideas, see above, homily 3, p. 90 (Jaeger), and n. 22 there; homily 4, p. 104 (Jaeger), with n. 5.

13. See above, homily 4, pp. 106–7 (Jaeger), with nn. 8 and 9; Origen, *Comm. Cant.* 3(4).14 (Baehrens 1925, 223–24; cf. trans. Lawson 1956, 240)—a passage that nicely shows the basic affinity of thought between Gregory and Origen.

πολυώνυμον ποιεῖ τὸ κακὸν κατὰ τὰς διαφορὰς τῶν ἐνεργημάτων
ὀνομαζόμενον· ὁ αὐτὸς γὰρ καὶ χειμὼν καὶ ὑετὸς καὶ σταγόνες, καθ᾽
ἕκαστον τῶν ὀνομάτων πειρασμοῦ τινος κατὰ τὸ ἰδιάζον σημαινομένου·
χειμὼν λέγεται διὰ τὴν πολυειδῆ τῶν κακῶν σημασίαν· ἐν γὰρ τῷ χειμῶνι
5   τὰ τεθηλότα μαραίνεται, τὸ ἐπὶ τῶν δένδρων κάλλος, ὃ διὰ τῶν φύλλων
φυσικῶς ὡραΐζεται, ἀπορρεῖ τῶν κλάδων καὶ τῇ γῇ καταμίγνυται, σιγᾷ
τῶν μουσικῶν ὀρνίθων ἡ μελῳδία, φεύγει ἡ ἀηδών, ναρκᾷ ἡ χελιδών,
ἀποξενοῦται τῆς καλιᾶς ἡ τρυγών, μιμεῖται τὰ πάντα τὴν τοῦ θανάτου
κατήφειαν, νεκροῦται ὁ βλαστός, ἀποθνήσκει ἡ πόα· ὥσπερ ὀστέα σαρκῶν
10 κεχωρισμένα οὕτως οἱ κλάδοι τῶν φύλλων γυμνωθέντες εἰδεχθὲς θέαμα
γίνονται ἀντὶ τῆς | προσούσης αὐτοῖς ἐκ τῶν βλαστῶν ἀγλαΐας. τί δ᾽ ἄν τις   152
λέγοι τὰ κατὰ θάλασσαν πάθη, τὰ διὰ τοῦ χειμῶνος γινόμενα, πῶς ἐκ βυθῶν
ἀναστρεφομένη καὶ διοιδαίνουσα σκοπέλους καὶ ὄρη μιμεῖται πρὸς τὸ ὄρθιον
σχῆμα κορυφουμένη τῷ ὕδατι, πῶς ἐφορμᾷ καθάπερ πολεμία τῇ γῇ ὑπὲρ τὰς
15 ἠϊόνας ἑαυτὴν ἐπεκβάλλουσα καὶ ταῖς ἐπαλλήλοις τῶν κυμάτων πληγαῖς
οἷόν τισι μηχανημάτων προσβολαῖς αὐτὴν κατασείουσα;
       ἀλλά μοι νόει τὰ τοῦ χειμῶνος πάθη ταῦτα καὶ τὰ τοιαῦτα πάντα
μεταλαμβάνων εἰς τροπικὴν σημασίαν, τί ἐστιν ἐν χειμῶνι τὸ ἀπανθοῦν τε καὶ
μαραινόμενον, τί τὸ εἰς γῆν ἐκ τῶν ἀκρεμόνων ἀναλυόμενον, τίς ἡ σιωπῶσα
20 τῶν ᾠδικῶν ὀρνίθων φωνή, τίς ἡ θάλασσα ἡ ἐπωρυομένη τοῖς κύμασι, τίς ἐπὶ
τούτοις ὁ ὑετός, τίνες τοῦ ὑετοῦ αἱ σταγόνες, πῶς ἑαυτῷ πορεύεται ὁ ὑετός·
διὰ τούτου γὰρ τὸ ἔμψυχόν τε καὶ προαιρετικὸν τοῦ τοιούτου χειμῶνος
ὑποσημαίνει τὸ αἴνιγμα. τάχα γὰρ κἂν μὴ τὰ καθ᾽ ἕκαστον διασαφήσῃ ὁ
λόγος, πρόδηλός ἐστι τῷ ἀκούοντι ἡ ἑκάστῳ τούτων ἐμφαινομένη διάνοια,
25 πῶς τεθήλει τὸ κατ᾽ ἀρχὰς ἡ ἀνθρωπίνη φύσις, ἕως ἐν τῷ παραδείσῳ ἦν τῷ
τῆς πηγῆς ἐκείνης ὕδατι πιαινο|μένη καὶ θάλλουσα, ὅτε ἦν ἀντὶ φύλλων ὁ τῆς   153
ἀθανασίας βλαστὸς ὡραΐζων τὴν φύσιν· ἀλλὰ τοῦ χειμῶνος τῆς παρακοῆς
τὴν ῥίζαν ἀποξηράναντος ἀπετινάχθη τὸ ἄνθος καὶ εἰς γῆν ἀνελύθη, καὶ
ἐγυμνώθη τοῦ κάλλους τῆς ἀθανασίας ὁ ἄνθρωπος καὶ ἡ τῶν ἀρετῶν πόα
30 κατεξηράνθη τῆς πρὸς τὸν θεὸν ἀγάπης διὰ τὸ πληθυνθῆναι τὴν ἀνομίαν
καταψυγείσης, ὅθεν τὰ ποικίλα παθήματα τοῖς ἀντικειμένοις πνεύμασιν ἐν
ἡμῖν ἐκορυφώθη, δι᾽ ὧν τὰ πονηρὰ τῆς ψυχῆς ναυάγια γίνεται.
       ἀλλὰ ἐλθόντος τοῦ τὸ ἔαρ ἡμῖν τῶν ψυχῶν ἐμποιήσαντος, ὃς τοῦ
πονηροῦ ἀνέμου τὴν θάλασσάν ποτε διεγείραντος καὶ τοῖς πνεύμασιν ἐπιτιμᾷ
35 καὶ τῇ θαλάσσῃ λέγει Σιώπα πεφίμωσο, πάντα εἰς γαλήνην καὶ νηνεμίαν
μετεσκευάσθη, καὶ πάλιν ἀναθάλλειν ἄρχεται καὶ τοῖς ἰδίοις ἄνθεσιν ἡ φύσις
ἡμῶν ὡραΐζεσθαι. ἄνθη δὲ τῆς ζωῆς ἡμῶν αἱ ἀρεταὶ νῦν μὲν ἀνθοῦσαι, τὸν

He gives many names to evil in accordance with its different workings. Winter and rain and "drops" are the same; each of the names labels some particular trial in a way that corresponds to its special character. It is called winter because that term connotes a multitude of bad things. In the winter, things that have grown up wither away: the splendor that hangs upon the trees, which naturally adorns itself with leaves, drops from its branches and is mingled with the earth. The melody of the songbirds is silenced: the nightingale flees away; the swallow is benumbed; the turtledove is exiled from its nest. All things mimic the misery of death: the blossom is killed; the grass of the field dies. Like bones denuded of flesh, so the branches stripped of their leaves become an ugly sight that contrasts with | the splendor that their blossoms lend them. And then what shall one say of the turbulence that winter brings to the sea? Swelling and churning up from the depths, it imitates peaks and mountains, brought by its waters to a standing head. It rushes like a foe upon the earth, throwing itself up and over the sands and shaking the earth with blow upon blow of its waves, like so many volleys of siege engines.

But understand these afflictions of the winter season, and everything that is like them, by taking them in a transferred, figural sense. What is it that fades and wastes away in the winter? What is it that falls from the boughs to the earth? What is the now-silent voice of the songbirds? What is the sea that rises up and attacks with its waters? And further, what is the rain, and what the drops of rain, and how does the rain carry itself off? By all this, the enigma of a winter like this points, at a deeper level, to the situation of beings that are ensouled and endowed with the power of choice. Even if my discourse does not clarify every individual detail, the sense that shines through in each of these images is clear to anyone who pays close attention: how the human race flourished at the beginning, while it was lodged in the paradise, nurtured by the water of that spring | and flourishing. At that time, its nature was adorned not with leaves but with the blossom of immortality. But the winter of disobedience dried up the root. The blossom was shaken off and fell to the earth; the human being was stripped of the beauty of immortality, and the green grass of the virtues was dried up as love for God became cold in the face of burgeoning lawlessness. Consequently the varied turbulences, as a result of which the soul's shipwrecks come about, were brought to their peaks within us by the opposing spirits.

But then there came the One who works in us the springtime of souls, the One who, when an evil wind was agitating the sea, both rebuked the spirits and to the sea said, "Peace! Be still!" (Mark 4:39)—and all became calm and still. Once again our nature began to flourish and to be adorned with its own blossoms. But the blossoms that are proper to our life are the virtues, which

δὲ καρπὸν αὐτῶν τῷ ἰδίῳ καιρῷ παρεχόμεναι. διὰ τοῦτό φησιν ὁ λόγος Ὁ χειμὼν παρῆλθεν, ὁ ὑετὸς ἀπῆλθεν, ἐπορεύθη ἑαυτῷ, τὰ ἄνθη ὤφθη ἐν τῇ γῇ, καιρὸς τῆς τομῆς ἔφθακεν. ὁρᾷς, φησί, τὸν | λειμῶνα τὸν διὰ τῶν ἀρετῶν   154
ἀνθοῦντα, ὁρᾷς τὴν σωφροσύνην, τουτέστι τὸ λαμπρόν τε καὶ εὐῶδες κρίνον,
5   ὁρᾷς τὴν αἰδῶ, τὸ ῥόδον, ὁρᾷς τὸ ἴον, τοῦ Χριστοῦ τὴν εὐωδίαν. τί οὖν οὐ στεφανηπλοκεῖς διὰ τούτων; οὗτός ἐστιν ὁ καιρός, ἐν ᾧ χρὴ δρεψάμενον τῇ πλοκῇ τῶν τοιούτων στεφάνων ἐγκαλλωπίσασθαι. ὁ καιρὸς τῆς τομῆς αὐτῶν ἔφθακεν.

τοῦτό σοι διαμαρτύρεται ἡ φωνὴ τοῦ τρυγόνος, τουτέστιν ἡ φωνὴ τοῦ
10 βοῶντος ἐν τῇ ἐρήμῳ· Ἰωάννης γάρ ἐστιν ὁ τρυγὼν οὗτος, ὁ τοῦ φαιδροῦ τούτου ἔαρος πρόδρομος ὁ τὰ καλὰ τῆς ἀρετῆς ἄνθη τοῖς ἀνθρώποις δεικνύων καὶ τοῖς βουλομένοις ἀνθολογεῖν προτείνων, δι᾽ ὧν ὑπεδείκνυε τὸ ἐκ τῆς ῥίζης τοῦ Ἰεσσαὶ ἄνθος, τὸν ἀμνὸν τοῦ θεοῦ τὸν αἴροντα τὴν ἁμαρτίαν τοῦ κόσμου, καὶ ὑπετίθετο τὴν ἐκ τῶν κακῶν μετάνοιαν καὶ τὴν κατ᾽ ἀρετὴν
15 πολιτείαν· Ἠκούσθη γάρ φησιν ἡ φωνὴ τοῦ τρυγόνος ἐν τῇ γῇ ἡμῶν.

τάχα γῆν τοὺς κατεγνωσμένους ἐν κακίᾳ κατονομάζει, οὓς τελώνας τε καὶ πόρνας λέγει τὸ εὐαγγέλιον, ἐν οἷς ἠκούσθη τοῦ Ἰωάννου ὁ λόγος τῶν λοιπῶν οὐ παραδεξαμένων τὸ κήρυγμα.

τὸ δὲ περὶ τῆς συκῆς εἰρημένον ὅτι Ἐξήνεγκε τοὺς ὀλύνθους αὐτῆς οὑτωσὶ
20 τῷ λόγῳ κατανοήσωμεν· ἑλκτικὴ τῆς ἐν τῷ βάθει νοτίδος | διαφερόντως   155
ὑπὸ θερμότητός ἐστιν ἡ συκῆ, πολλῆς δὲ κατὰ τὰς ἐντεριώνας τῆς ἰκμάδος συνισταμένης ἀναγκαίως ἡ φύσις διὰ τῆς τῶν ὑγρῶν πέψεως τῆς ἐν τῷ φυτῷ γινομένης τὸ ἀχρεῖόν τε καὶ γεῶδες τῆς ἰκμάδος ἐκ τῶν ἀκρεμόνων ἀποσκευάζεται, καὶ πολλάκις τοῦτο ποιεῖ, ἕως ἂν τὸ εἰλικρινές τε καὶ τρόφιμον
25 ἐν τῷ καθήκοντι καιρῷ προβάλῃ κεκαθαρμένον τῆς ἀχρήστου ποιότητος. τὸ τοίνυν πρὸ τοῦ γλυκέος τε καὶ τελείου καρποῦ ὑπὸ τῆς συκῆς ἐν καρπῶν εἴδει προβαλλόμενον ὄλυνθος λέγεται, ὅπερ καὶ αὐτὸ μὲν ἐδώδιμον ἔσθ᾽ ὅτε τοῖς βουλομένοις ἐστίν. οὐ μὴν ἐκεῖνό ἐστιν ὁ καρπός, ἀλλὰ τοῦ καρποῦ προοίμιον γίνεται· ὁ ταῦτα τοίνυν θεασάμενος καὶ τὸν καρπὸν ὅσον οὐδέπω
30 πάντως ἐκδέχεται· σημεῖον γὰρ τῶν ἐδωδίμων σύκων οἱ ὄλυνθοι γίνονται, οὓς ἐξενηνοχέναι φησὶ τὴν συκῆν.

ἐπειδὴ γὰρ τὸ πνευματικὸν ἔαρ ὑπογράφει τῇ νύμφῃ ὁ λόγος, ὁ δὲ καιρὸς οὗτος μεθόριός ἐστι τῶν δύο καιρῶν, τῆς τε χειμερινῆς κατηφείας καὶ τῆς ἐν τῷ θέρει τῶν καρπῶν μετουσίας, διὰ τοῦτο τὸ μὲν παρῳχηκέναι τὰ
35 κακὰ διαρρήδην εὐαγγελίζεται, τοὺς δὲ καρποὺς τῆς ἀρετῆς οὔπω τελείως

put forth flowers now but bear their fruit in their own time. That is why the Word says: *The winter is past, the rain is gone, it has departed. The flowers are seen on the earth, the time for cutting*[14] *has come.* "You see," he says, "the | meadow blooming because of the virtues; you see self-control, that is, the bright and fragrant lily; you see reverence, the red rose; you see the violet, the sweet smell of Christ. Why, then, do you not employ these to make wreaths? This is the time at which it is right, the time when the cutting is done, to take pleasure in the plaiting of such wreaths. The time for their cutting has come."

This is what the voice of the dove attests for you, that is, the voice of him who cries out in the wilderness. For this dove is John. He is the forerunner of our bright springtime, who shows people the beautiful blossoms of virtue and proffers them to those who want to gather flowers, by which he signifies, at a deeper level, the sprout from the root of Jesse (cf. Isa 11:1), "the Lamb of God who takes away the sin of the world," and by which he enjoins repentance from evil and a way of life in accordance with virtue. For it says: *The voice of the dove is heard in our land.*

By "land" here it probably means people who are accused of evil, whom the Gospel refers to as tax collectors and harlots, who heard John's word while the rest ignored his message.

Now as to what it says about the fig tree: it *has put forth its early fruit.* This we understand, with the guidance of reason, in the following fashion. The fig tree draws into itself | an unusual amount of the moisture stored in the ground because of its internal warmth, but when a great deal of moisture is collected in its pith, its nature necessarily—by means of the working of the juices in the shoot—rids itself of the useless and solid elements in this moisture and discharges them from its branches. Moreover, it does this frequently, until, at the proper time, it puts forth a fruit that is pure and nourishing, cleansed of any improper quality. Therefore that which the fig tree puts forth in the form of a fruit prior to its sweet and perfect fruit is called "early fruit," and this itself is edible from time to time for those who like it. But it is not the fruit; it comes as the fruit's precursor. Someone who sees these summer figs, therefore, is still waiting for the real fruit, for the summer figs, which the fig tree is said to bring forth, are a sign of the edible figs to come.

For since the Word is describing the spiritual springtime to the Bride, and since this season is a halfway house between two others—between wintry desolation and the summer's sharing in the harvest—for just that reason, while he openly proclaims the passing of evil things, he does not yet point

---

14. Greek: καιρὸς τῆς τομῆς. The LXX translators no doubt had pruning in mind, but Gregory thinks of plucking flowers and weaving them into wreaths.

προδείκνυσιν. ἀλλὰ τούτους μὲν ἐν τῷ καθήκοντι καιρῷ ταμιεύσεται, ὅταν ἐνστῇ τὸ θέρος (οἶδας δὲ πάντως τὸ διὰ τοῦ θέρους δηλούμενον ἐκ τῆς τοῦ κυρίου φωνῆς, ἢ τοῦτό φησιν ὅτι Ὁ θερισμὸς συντέλεια τοῦ αἰῶνός | ἐστιν),   156
νῦν δὲ τὰς ἐλπίδας δείκνυσι διὰ τῶν ἀρετῶν ἀνθούσας, ὧν ὁ καρπός, καθώς
5   φησιν ὁ προφήτης, ἐν τῷ καιρῷ τῷ ἰδίῳ προφαίνεται.

τῆς τοίνυν ἀνθρωπίνης φύσεως κατὰ τὴν μνημονευθεῖσαν ἐνταῦθα συκῆν πολλὴν διὰ τοῦ νοηθέντος ἡμῖν χειμῶνος τὴν κακὴν ἰκμάδα συλλεξαμένης καλῶς ὁ τὸ ψυχικὸν ἔαρ ἡμῖν ἐργαζόμενος καὶ τῇ καθηκούσῃ γεωπονίᾳ φυτηκομῶν τὸ ἀνθρώπινον πρῶτον μὲν ἐκβάλλει τῆς φύσεως πᾶν ὅσον
10   γεῶδες καὶ ἄχρηστον ἀντὶ ἀκρεμόνων δι’ ἐξομολογήσεως ἀποσκευάζων τὰ περιττώματα, εἶθ’ οὕτως χαρακτῆρά τινα τῆς ἐλπιζομένης μακαριότητος διὰ τῆς ἀστειοτέρας ζωῆς ἐπιβάλλων τῷ βίῳ οἷόν τισιν ὀλύνθοις τὴν μέλλουσαν γλυκύτητα τῶν σύκων εὐαγγελίζεται. καὶ τοῦτό ἐστι τὸ λεγόμενον ὅτι Ἡ συκῆ ἐξήνεγκε τοὺς ὀλύνθους αὐτῆς.

15   Οὕτω μοι νόησον καὶ τὴν κυπρίζουσαν ἄμπελον, ἧς ὁ μὲν οἶνος ὁ τὴν καρδίαν εὐφραίνων πληρώσει ποτὲ τὸν τῆς σοφίας κρατῆρα καὶ προκείσεται τοῖς συμπόταις ἐκ τοῦ ὑψηλοῦ κηρύγματος κατ’ ἐξουσίαν ἀρύεσθαι εἰς ἀγαθήν τε καὶ νηφάλιον μέθην. ἐκείνην λέγω τὴν μέθην, δι’ ἧς τοῖς ἀνθρώποις ἐκ τῶν ὑλικῶν πρὸς τὸ θειότερον ἡ ἔκστασις γίνεται. νῦν μέντοι κυπρίζει διὰ
20   τοῦ ἄνθους ἡ ἄμπελος καί | τις ἐκδίδοται παρ’ αὐτῆς ἀτμὸς εὐωδιάζων, ἡδὺς   157
καὶ προσηνής, πρὸς τὸ περιέχον πνεῦμα κατακιρνάμενος. οἶδας δὲ τὸ πνεῦμα πάντως, ὃ τὴν εὐωδίαν ταύτην τοῖς σῳζομένοις ἐργάζεται, παρὰ τοῦ Παύλου μαθών.

Ταῦτα προδείκνυσι τῇ νύμφῃ ὁ λόγος τοῦ καλοῦ τῶν ψυχῶν ἔαρος τὰ
25   γνωρίσματα καὶ ἐπισπεύδει πρὸς τὴν τῶν προκειμένων ἀπόλαυσιν διεγείρων αὐτὴν τῷ λόγῳ Ἀνάστα, λέγων, ἐλθέ, ἡ πλησίον μου, καλή μου, περιστερά μου. ὅσα δόγματα δι’ ὀλίγων ἐν τοῖς ῥήμασι τούτοις ὁ λόγος ἡμῖν ὑποδείκνυσιν. οὐ γὰρ κατά τινα περιττὴν καὶ παρέλκουσαν ματαιολογίαν τοῖς αὐτοῖς ῥήμασιν ἐμφιλοχωρεῖν τὴν θεόπνευστον διδασκαλίαν ἐστὶν εἰκός, ἀλλά τι μέγα καὶ
30   θεοπρεπὲς νόημα διὰ τῆς παλιλλογίας ἡμῖν ὑποδείκνυται.

to the full fruits of virtue. These, however, he will dispense at the proper season, when the summer is come (and what "summer" means, you know well enough from the words of the Lord, which say: "The harvest is the consummation of the age"). | But now what he manifests is the hopes that come to blossom through the virtues, whose fruit (as the prophet says) is brought forth in due season (Ps 1:3).

Since, then, our human nature, like the fig tree that is mentioned here, has gathered to itself, during the winter that is grasped as an intelligible reality, a great deal of harmful moisture, it is right that he who works in us the springtime of the soul and who cultivates the soil of our humanity by his husbandry should first of all cast out of our nature everything that is earthy and inappropriate, getting rid not of boughs but of transgressions through the act of confession, and then should proclaim the coming sweetness of the figs as he stamps in our being an impress of the hoped-for happiness by means of a more honorable life—an impress not unlike the early figs. This is what it means to say: *the fig tree has put forth its early fruit.*

Interpret the blossoming vine[15] in this way too. Its wine, rejoicing the heart, will one day fill up wisdom's chalice (cf. Prov 9:2–5) and, as warranted by "the exalted summons," be set before the fellowship of its drinkers, to be drawn at their pleasure for the sake of a good and sober drunkenness. What I am referring to is the drunkenness that occasions that self-transcendence[16] by which people move out of the material sphere toward what is more divine. So now the vine blossoms with its flower and from it | gives out a fragrant scent, sweet and gentle, that is mingled with the Spirit that contains it. And you surely know the Spirit that works that fragrance in those who are being saved; you have learned of it from Paul.

The Word shows the Bride these marks of the fruitful spring of souls, and he urges her on to enjoyment of the things that lie ahead, wakening her with the cry: *Come, rise up, my close one, my beauty, my dove.* What a quantity of teaching in how small a compass does the Word indicate for us with these words! For it is unlikely that, in the manner of vain, superfluous and spun-out talk, the inspired teaching should choose to dwell once more upon the very same words.[17] No, some great thought, worthy of God, is indicated to us by the repetition of this line.

---

15. This is Gregory's comment on Song 1:13b ("the vines blossom").

16. Literally "ecstasy" (ἔκστασις), a standing outside oneself. Gregory, however, applies this word not to "being beside oneself" in a mystical experience of some sort but to the process of moral transformation by which the self comes to mirror God.

17. I.e., the "same words" as in Song 2:10b. The Spirit does not repeat itself.

τὸ δὲ λεγόμενον τοιοῦτόν ἐστιν· ἡ μακαρία καὶ ἀΐδιος καὶ πάντα νοῦν
ὑπερέχουσα φύσις πάντα τὰ ὄντα ἐν ἑαυτῇ περιείργουσα ὑπ' οὐδενὸς
περιέχεται ὅρου· οὐδὲν γάρ ἐστι περὶ αὐτὴν θεωρούμενον, οὐ χρόνος,
οὐ τόπος, οὐ χρῶμα, οὐ σχῆμα, οὐκ εἶδος, οὐκ ὄγκος, οὐ πηλικότης, οὐ
5   διάστημα, οὐδὲ ἄλλο τι περιγραπτικὸν ὄνομα ἢ πρᾶγμα ἢ νόημα, ἀλλὰ πᾶν
τὸ περὶ αὐτὴν νοούμενον ἀγαθὸν εἰς ἄπειρόν τε καὶ ἀόριστον πρόεισιν.
ὅπου γὰρ κακία χώραν οὐκ ἔχει, ἀγαθοῦ | πέρας ἐστὶν οὐδέν. ἐπὶ γὰρ τῆς   158
τρεπτῆς φύσεως διὰ τὸ ἴσην ἐγκεῖσθαι τὴν δύναμιν τῇ προαιρέσει πρὸς τὴν
ἐφ' ἑκάτερα τῶν ἐναντίων ῥοπὴν τό τε ἀγαθὸν τὸ ἐν ἡμῖν καὶ τὸ κακὸν ταῖς
10 διαδοχαῖς ἀλλήλων ἐναπολήγει καὶ γίνεται τοῦ ἀγαθοῦ ὅρος ἡ ἐπιγινομένη
κακία καὶ πάντα τὰ τῶν ψυχῶν ἡμῶν ἐπιτηδεύματα, ὅσα κατὰ τὸ ἐναντίον
ἀλλήλοις ἀντικαθέστηκεν, εἰς ἄλληλα λήγει καὶ ὑπ' ἀλλήλων ὁρίζεται· ἡ δὲ
ἁπλῆ καὶ καθαρὰ καὶ μονοειδὴς καὶ ἄτρεπτος καὶ ἀναλλοίωτος φύσις ἀεὶ
ὡσαύτως ἔχουσα καὶ οὐδέποτε ἑαυτῆς ἐξισταμένη διὰ τὸ ἀπαράδεκτος εἶναι
15 τῆς πρὸς τὸ κακὸν κοινωνίας ἀόριστος ἐν τῷ ἀγαθῷ μένει, οὐδὲν ἑαυτῆς
βλέπουσα πέρας διὰ τὸ μηδὲν περὶ ἑαυτὴν τῶν ἐναντίων βλέπειν.

ὅταν τοίνυν ἐφέλκηται πρὸς μετουσίαν ἑαυτῆς τὴν ἀνθρωπίνην ψυχήν,
ἀεὶ τῷ ἴσῳ μέτρῳ κατὰ τὴν πρὸς τὸ κρεῖττον ὑπεροχὴν τῆς μετεχούσης
ὑπερανέστηκεν· ἡ μὲν γὰρ ψυχὴ μείζων ἑαυτῆς πάντοτε διὰ τῆς τοῦ
20 ὑπερέχοντος μετουσίας γίνεται καὶ αὐξομένη οὐχ ἵσταται, τὸ δὲ μετεχόμενον
ἀγαθὸν ἐν ἴσῳ μένει ὡσαύτως ὑπὸ τῆς ἐπὶ πλεῖον ἀεὶ μετεχούσης ἐν ἴσῃ
πάντοτε τῇ ὑπεροχῇ εὑρισκόμενον.

ὁρῶμεν τοίνυν ὥσπερ ἐν βαθμῶν ἀναβάσει χειραγωγουμένην διὰ τῶν τῆς
ἀρετῆς ἀνόδων ἐπὶ τὰ ὕψη παρὰ τοῦ λόγου τὴν νύμφην, ἣ ἐνίησι | πρῶτον   159
25 διὰ τῶν προφητικῶν θυρίδων καὶ τῶν δικτυωτῶν τοῦ νόμου παραγγελμάτων
τὴν ἀκτῖνα ὁ λόγος καὶ προσκαλεῖται αὐτὴν ἐγγίσαι τῷ φωτὶ καὶ καλὴν
γενέσθαι πρὸς τὸ εἶδος τῆς περιστερᾶς ἐν τῷ φωτὶ μορφωθεῖσαν. εἶτα
μετασχοῦσαν τῶν καλῶν ὅσον ἐχώρησε πάλιν ἐξ ὑπαρχῆς ὡς ἔτι τῶν καλῶν
οὖσαν ἀμέτοχον πρὸς τὴν τοῦ ὑπερκειμένου κάλλους μετουσίαν ἐφέλκεται,
30 ὥστε αὐτῇ κατὰ τὴν ἀναλογίαν τῆς προκοπῆς πρὸς τὸ ἀεὶ προφαινόμενον
καὶ τὴν ἐπιθυμίαν συναύξεσθαι καὶ διὰ τὴν ὑπερβολὴν τῶν πάντοτε κατὰ τὸ
ὑπερκείμενον εὑρισκομένων ἀγαθῶν πρώτως ἅπτεσθαι τῆς ἀνόδου δοκεῖν.
διὰ τοῦτό φησι πάλιν πρὸς τὴν ἐγηγερμένην ὅτι Ἀνάστηθι καὶ πρὸς τὴν
ἐλθοῦσαν ὅτι Ἐλθέ·
35   οὔτε γὰρ τῷ οὕτως ἀνισταμένῳ λείψει ποτὲ τὸ ἀεὶ ἀνίστασθαι οὔτε τῷ
τρέχοντι πρὸς τὸν κύριον ἢ πρὸς τὸν θεῖον δρόμον εὐρυχωρία δαπανηθήσεται.
ἀεί τε γὰρ ἐγείρεσθαι χρὴ καὶ μηδέποτε διὰ τοῦ δρόμου προσεγγίζοντας

What is meant is this: the blessed and eternal nature that transcends every intellect, since it encompasses all things in itself, is contained by no limit. For there is nothing that mind can discern that contains it: not time or place or color or shape or form or bulk or magnitude or interval or any other confining thing, be it name or thing or idea. No, but every good thing that the mind attributes to it runs out to infinity and beyond all limit. For where there is no place for evil, there is no limit | set to the good. In the case of the mutable sort of being, both the good that is in us, and the evil as well, are limited by each other's effects, because our capacity to choose has an equal power for motion in the direct of each of the opposites. So the evil that supervenes sets a limit to the good, and all the habits of our souls, to the extent that they oppose one another, bring one another to a halt and are limited by one another. But the simple and pure and uniform and unalterable Nature, being always so, stands unlimited in its goodness and is never alienated from itself because it is not open to participation in evil. It sees no limit of itself, because it sees none of its contraries in itself.

As, therefore, it draws human nature to participation in itself, it always surpasses that which participates in it to the same degree, in conformity with its superabundance of goodness. For the soul is always becoming better than itself on account of its participation in the transcendent. It does not stop growing, but the Good that is participated remains in unaltered degree as it is, since the being that ever more and more participates in it discovers that it is always surpassed to the same extent.

We see, then, that the Bride is being led by the Word through the ascents of virtue up to the heights, just as if she were climbing stairs. To this Bride the Word first of all sends in, | through the prophetic windows and the law's lattices, the ray of the commandments and summons her to draw near to the light and to become beautiful once, in the light, she has been given the shape of the dove. Then, when she has shared, as far as is possible for her, in the good things, he draws her toward participation in the transcendent Beauty just as though she had hitherto had no part in them at all. The result is that it seems to her that desire increases in proportion to her progress toward that Light which eternally shines out and at the same time that her ascent is just beginning, on account of the transcendence of the good things, which are always beyond her. That is why he says once again to the awakened soul, *Rise up,* and to the soul that is coming, *Come!*

For to one who has risen up in this manner there will never be wanting an up-rising without end; nor for one who runs to the Lord will opportunity for the divine race be used up. For it is always necessary to rise up, and it is never right for those who are drawing near by their running to halt. For that

παύεσθαι. ὥστε ὁσάκις ἂν λέγῃ τὸ Ἀνάστηθι καὶ τὸ Ἐλθέ, τοσαυτάκις τῆς πρὸς τὸ κρεῖττον ἀναβάσεως τὴν δύναμιν δίδωσιν.

οὕτω νόει καὶ τὰ | ἐφεξῆς τῷ λόγῳ προσκείμενα· ὁ γὰρ καλὴν ἐκ καλῆς   160
γενέσθαι κελεύων τὸ ἀποστολικὸν ἄντικρυς ὑποτίθεται τὴν αὐτὴν εἰκόνα
5   προστάσσων ἀπὸ δόξης εἰς δόξαν μεταμορφοῦσθαι, ὡς πάντοτε δόξαν
εἶναι τὸ λαμβανόμενον καὶ τὸ ἀεὶ εὑρισκόμενον, κἂν ὅτι μάλιστα μέγα τε
καὶ ὑψηλὸν ᾖ, μικρότερον εἶναι τοῦ ἐλπιζομένου πιστεύεσθαι. οὕτω τοίνυν
περιστερὰν οὖσαν ἐν τοῖς προκατωρθωμένοις οὐδὲν ἧττον περιστερὰν αὐτὴν
πάλιν διὰ τῆς πρὸς τὸ κρεῖττον μεταμορφώσεως γενέσθαι διακελεύεται καί,
10   εἰ τοῦτο γένοιτο, τὸ ὑπὲρ τοῦτο πάλιν ὁ λόγος καθεξῆς διὰ τοῦ ὀνόματος
ὑποδείξει· λέγει γὰρ Δεῦρο σεαυτῇ, περιστερά μου, ἐν σκέπῃ τῆς πέτρας
ἐχόμενα τοῦ προτειχίσματος.

τίς οὖν ἡ πρὸς τὸ τέλειον ἄνοδος, ἥτις τοῖς νῦν εἰρημένοις ἐμφαίνεται;
τὸ μηκέτι πρὸς τὴν τῶν ἐφελκομένων βλέπειν σπουδήν, ἀλλ᾽ ὁδηγὸν πρὸς
15   τὸ κρεῖττον τὴν ἰδίαν ἐπιθυμίαν ἔχειν. Δεῦρο, γάρ φησι, σεαυτῇ, μὴ ἐκ λύπης
μηδὲ ἐξ ἀνάγκης, ἀλλὰ σεαυτῇ, τοῖς ἰδίοις λογισμοῖς τὴν ἐπιθυμίαν πρὸς τὸ
καλὸν ἐπιρρώσασα, οὐκ ἀνάγκης καθηγουμένης· ἀδέσποτον | γὰρ ἡ ἀρετὴ   161
καὶ ἑκούσιον καὶ ἀνάγκης πάσης ἐλεύθερον. τοιοῦτος ἦν ὁ Δαβὶδ ὁ τὰ ἑκούσια
μόνα τῶν παρ᾽ αὐτοῦ γινομένων εὐδοκηθῆναι τῷ θεῷ προσευχόμενος καὶ
20   ἑκουσίως θύειν ἐπαγγελλόμενος· τοιοῦτος ἕκαστος τῶν ἁγίων ἑαυτὸν τῷ
θεῷ προσάγων, οὐκ ἐξ ἀνάγκης ἀγόμενος, καὶ σὺ τοίνυν δεῖξον τὴν τελείαν
κατάστασιν ἐν τῷ σεαυτῇ τῆς πρὸς τὸ κρεῖττον ἀνόδου τὴν ἐπιθυμίαν λαβεῖν.
τοιαύτη δὲ γενομένη, φησίν, ἥξεις ἐπὶ τὴν σκέπην τῆς πέτρας ἐχόμενα τοῦ
προτειχίσματος.

25   τὸ δὲ λεγόμενον τοιοῦτόν ἐστιν (χρὴ γὰρ μεταβαλεῖν τὸν λόγον ἀπὸ τῶν
αἰνιγμάτων πρὸς τὸ σαφέστερον)· μία σκέπη τῆς ἀνθρωπίνης ἐστὶ ψυχῆς
τὸ ὑψηλὸν εὐαγγέλιον, ἐν ᾧ ὁ γενόμενος τῆς σκιοειδοῦς διδασκαλίας διὰ
τῶν τυπικῶν τε καὶ συμβολικῶν νοημάτων οὐκέτι προσδέεται φανερούσης
τῆς ἀληθείας τὰ κεκαλυμμένα τῶν προσταγμάτων αἰνίγματα· πέτραν δὲ
30   τὴν εὐαγγελικὴν ὀνομάζεσθαι χάριν οὐδεὶς ἂν ἀντείποι τῶν ὁπωσοῦν
μετεχόντων τῆς πίστεως· πολλαχόθεν γὰρ ἔστιν ἐκ τῆς γραφῆς τοῦτο
μαθεῖν τὸ πέτραν εἶναι τὸ εὐαγγέλιον. τὸ τοίνυν λεγόμενον τοιοῦτόν ἐστι·
εἰ ἐνεγυμνάσθης, ὦ ψυχή, τῷ νόμῳ, εἰ τὰς διὰ τῶν προφητικῶν θυρίδων
αὐγὰς τῇ διανοίᾳ τεθέασαι, μηκέτι ὑπὸ τὴν τοῦ νομικοῦ | τοίχου σκιὰν μένε   162
35   (σκιὰν γὰρ ὁ τοῖχος ποιεῖ τῶν μελλόντων ἀγαθῶν, οὐκ αὐτὴν τὴν εἰκόνα τῶν

reason, as often as he says *Rise up!* and *Come!* he confers the capacity for an ascent toward what is better.

This is also the meaning | of what comes next in the passage, for he who commands virtue to be born of virtue straightway appends the apostolic counsel by prescribing that the same image "be transformed from glory to glory" (2 Cor 3:16), meaning that glory is always being received and that what is forever being discovered, no matter how great and exalted it is, is believed to be less than what is hoped for. So it is, then, that the bride is commanded, dove though she was in her former achievements, to become nothing less than a dove again by being transformed for the better; and if this comes to pass, the Word, when next he uses the word *dove,* will again refer to what lies beyond this. For he says, *Come for yourself, my dove, to the shelter of the rock, close by the wall.*

What step upward toward perfection is shown us in these words? No longer to focus attention on making an effort to attain the things that attract but to take one's own desire as a guide toward what is better. For he says, "*Come for yourself*—not out of grief or compulsion but for yourself, not shown the way by compulsion but with your own thoughts lending strength to your desire for the good." For virtue has no master. | It is voluntary and free of all compulsion. Such a one was David, who prayed that only his voluntary deeds might find approval with God (cf. Ps 118:108) and promised to sacrifice of his own will (cf. Ps 53:8). Such was each of the saints who brought himself to God without being compelled. So, then, do you demonstrate your mature state by taking up for yourself this desire for an ascent toward what is higher. And having become this sort of person," he says, "you will have come *to the shelter of the rock, close by the wall.*"

The meaning is something on this order (for we have to transpose what is said from its enigmatic form to one of greater clarity): one shelter of the human soul is the exalted gospel. Whoever is within it no longer has need of the shadowy teaching that comes through types and symbols, for the truth has brought the hidden enigmas of the law's regulations to light, while none of those who have any part whatever in faith can deny that the gospel's grace is named "rock." For from many places in the Scripture it is possible to discover this, that the gospel is a rock.[18] The point of the text, then, is this: "If, O soul, you have been exercised in the law, if in your understanding you have beheld the rays of light that come through the prophetic windows, remain no longer under the shadow of | the law's wall (for the wall creates a shadow of

---

18. Perhaps Gregory has Matt 7:24 and Luke 6:48 in mind and doubtless Rom 9:33 and 1 Cor 10:4. The rock that is the gospel is also, as Gregory observes two paragraphs below, to be identified as Christ.

πραγμάτων), ἀλλ' ἐπὶ τὴν πέτραν ἐκ τοῦ σύνεγγυς ἀπὸ τοῦ τοίχου μετάβηθι· ἔχεται γὰρ ἡ πέτρα τοῦ προτειχίσματος, ἐπειδὴ τῆς εὐαγγελικῆς πίστεως ὁ νόμος προτείχισμα γέγονε, καὶ ἔχεται ἀλλήλων τὰ δόγματα γειτνιῶντα κατὰ τὴν δύναμιν. τί γὰρ ἐγγύτερον τοῦ Μὴ μοιχεῦσαι τῷ Μὴ ἐπιθυμῆσαι καὶ τοῦ
5 καθαρεύειν ἀπὸ φόνου τῷ μηδὲ ὀργῇ τὴν καρδίαν μολύνεσθαι; ἐπεὶ οὖν ἔχεται τοῦ προτειχίσματος ἡ σκέπη τῆς πέτρας, ἀδιάστατός ἐστί σοι ἡ ἀπὸ τοῦ τοίχου ἐπὶ τὴν πέτραν μετάστασις·

περιτομὴ ἐν τῷ τοίχῳ καὶ περιτομὴ ἐν τῇ πέτρᾳ, πρόβατον καὶ πρόβατον, αἷμα καὶ αἷμα, πάσχα καὶ πάσχα, καὶ πάντα σχεδὸν τὰ αὐτὰ καὶ διὰ τῶν αὐτῶν
10 ἀλλήλων ἐχόμενα, πλὴν ὅσον πνευματικὴ μὲν ἡ πέτρα, χοϊκὸς δὲ ὁ τοῖχος, ᾧ συναναπέπλασται τὸ σωματικὸν καὶ γεῶδες. ἡ δὲ εὐαγγελικὴ πέτρα τὸν σαρκώδη τῶν νοημάτων πηλὸν οὐκ ἔχει (ἀλλὰ καὶ περιτομὴν λαμβάνει ὁ ἄνθρωπος καὶ ὅλος ὑγιὴς μένει μηδεμιᾶς λώβης ἀκρωτηριαζούσης τὸ πλάσμα τῆς φύσεως καὶ φυλάσσει ἐν τῇ τῶν κακῶν ἀπραξίᾳ τὸ σάββατον καὶ τὴν
15 πρὸς τὸ καλὸν ἀργίαν οὐ καταδέχεται | μαθὼν ὅτι Ἔξεστι τῷ σαββάτῳ καλὸν 163 ποιεῖν, καὶ ἀδιάκριτον ποιεῖται τῆς τροφῆς τὴν μετουσίαν καὶ ἀκαθάρτου οὐχ ἅπτεται· οὐδὲν γὰρ τῶν εἰσερχομένων διὰ τοῦ στόματος κοινὸν εἶναι παρὰ τῆς πέτρας παιδεύεται), ἀλλὰ διὰ πάντων τὰς σωματικὰς τοῦ νόμου παρατηρήσεις ἀπωσαμένη πρὸς τὸ πνευματικόν τε καὶ νοητὸν μεταλαμβάνει
20 τῶν ῥημάτων τὴν διάνοιαν, οὕτως εἰπόντος τοῦ Παύλου ὅτι Ὁ νόμος πνευματικός ἐστιν. ὁ γὰρ οὕτως ἐκλαβὼν τὸν νόμον ὑπὸ τὴν σκέπην τῆς εὐαγγελικῆς γίνεται πέτρας τὴν ἐχομένην τοῦ σωματικοῦ προτειχίσματος.

Ταῦτα τοῦ λόγου διὰ τῶν θυρίδων αὐτῇ ἐμβοήσαντος καλῶς ἀποκρίνεται ἡ περιστερὰ ἡ περιλαμφθεῖσα διὰ τῆς τῶν νοημάτων αὐγῆς καὶ τὴν πέτραν
25 νοήσασα, ἥτις ἐστὶν ὁ Χριστός· λέγει γὰρ Δεῖξόν μοι τὴν ὄψιν σου καὶ ἀκούτισόν με τὴν φωνήν σου, ὅτι ἡ φωνή σου ἡδεῖα καὶ ἡ ὄψις σου ὡραία. τὸ δὲ λεγόμενον τοιοῦτόν ἐστι· μηκέτι μοι διαλέγου διὰ τῶν προφητικῶν τε καὶ νομικῶν αἰνιγμάτων, ἀλλ' ὡς ἰδεῖν δύναμαι, οὕτω μοι δεῖξον σαυτὸν ἐμφανῶς, ἵνα ἐντὸς γένωμαι τῆς εὐαγγελικῆς πέτρας καταλιποῦσα τὸ τοῦ νόμου
30 προτείχισμα, καὶ ὡς χωρεῖ ἡ ἀκοή μου, οὕτω δὸς τὴν φωνήν σου ἐν τοῖς ὠσί μου γενέσθαι· εἰ γὰρ ἡ διὰ | τῶν θυρίδων φωνὴ τοσοῦτόν ἐστιν ἡδεῖα, πολὺ 164 μᾶλλον ἡ κατὰ πρόσωπόν σου ἐμφάνεια τὸ ἐράσμιον ἕξει.

ταῦτα λέγει ἡ νύμφη νοήσασα τὸ κατὰ τὴν εὐαγγελικὴν πέτραν μυστήριον, εἰς ὅπερ αὐτὴν ὁ πολυμερῶς καὶ πολυτρόπως ἐν ταῖς θυρίσι γενόμενος λόγος

the good things to come, and not the very image of the realities), but rather make the short move from the wall to the rock. For the rock lies close by the wall, since the law stands as the wall of the evangelical faith: the essential teachings [i.e., of law and gospel] are closely involved with one another, resembling one another in their force. For what is closer to 'Thou shalt not lust' than 'Thou shalt not commit adultery' and to not defiling one's heart with anger than being clean of murder? Since, then, the shelter of the rock is close by the wall, your move from the wall to the rock is uninterrupted."

There is circumcision in the wall, and circumcision in the rock; sheep and sheep, blood and blood, Pasch and Pasch. All these things are more or less the same and close to one another because of their common elements—save to the extent that the rock is spiritual, while the wall, in which the corporeal and the earthy are mingled, is of earth. The rock of the gospel does not contain the fleshly clay of these ideas. On the contrary, the human person receives circumcision and remains wholly in a state of health without any mutilation to maim its natural form; and keeps the Sabbath by refraining from evil deeds; and is not open to idleness in pursuit of the good, | having learned that "It is lawful to do good on the Sabbath" (Matt 12:12); and partakes of food without distinction and yet without touching the unclean: for by the Rock it is taught that nothing that enters by the mouth is common, but rejecting in every case the corporeal observance of the law, it transposes the sense of the words to the spiritual and intelligible plane. Thus Paul says, "The law is spiritual" (Rom 7:14). The person who receives the law in this fashion comes under the shelter of the gospel rock, which is close by the corporeal wall.

When the Word has called out to her in this way through the windows, the dove answers appropriately—the dove who had been illumined by the beam of these thoughts and had understood the meaning of the rock, which is Christ. For she[19] says: *Show me your face, and let me hear your voice, for your voice is sweet, and your countenance is glorious.* The meaning is this: "Speak to me no longer by way of the enigmas of the prophets and the law, but show me yourself clearly so that I may see. In that way I can leave the outworks of the law behind and come to be within the rock of the gospel. And let your voice sound in my ears to the extent that my hearing can take it in. For if the | voice through the windows is so pleasing, your manifestation face to face will all the more evoke love."

This is what the Bride says when she has grasped the mystery of the gospel rock, into which the Word, coming within the windows "in many and

---

19. It is almost inevitable that Gregory should put these words in the mouth of the Bride, but in fact, as Origen, for one, recognizes, they apppear to be a continuation of the Bridegroom's speech.

ἐχειραγώγησε, καὶ ἐν ἐπιθυμίᾳ γίνεται τῆς διὰ σαρκὸς θεοφανείας, ὥστε τὸν
λόγον γενέσθαι σάρκα καὶ τὸν θεὸν ἐν σαρκὶ φανερωθῆναι καὶ παραθέσθαι
ταῖς ἀκοαῖς ἡμῶν τὰς θείας φωνὰς τὰς ἐπαγγελλομένας τοῖς ἀξίοις τὴν
αἰωνίαν μακαριότητα. πῶς συμβαίνουσι τῇ εὐχῇ τῆς νύμφης αἱ τοῦ Συμεῶνος
5   φωναί, ὅς φησι Νῦν ἀπολύεις τὸν δοῦλόν σου, δέσποτα, κατὰ τὸ ῥῆμά σου
ἐν εἰρήνῃ, ὅτι εἶδον οἱ ὀφθαλμοί μου τὸ σωτήριόν σου; εἶδε γὰρ ἐκεῖνος, ὡς
ἰδεῖν ἐπεπόθησεν αὕτη. τὴν δὲ φωνὴν αὐτοῦ τὴν ἡδεῖαν οἱ δεξάμενοι τοῦ
εὐαγγελίου τὴν χάριν ἐπιγινώσκουσιν οἱ εἰπόντες ὅτι Ῥήματα ζωῆς αἰωνίου
ἔχεις.
10   Διὰ ταῦτα δέχεται τὴν εὐχὴν τῆς νύμφης δικαίαν οὖσαν ὁ καθαρὸς
νυμφίος καὶ μέλλων δεικνύειν ἑαυτὸν ἐμφανῶς πρῶτον τοὺς θηρευτὰς
παρορμᾷ πρὸς τὴν ἄγραν τῶν ἀλωπέκων, ὡς μηκέτι τὸν ἀμπελῶνα δι᾽
αὐτῶν πρὸς τὸν κυπρισμὸν ἐμποδίζεσθαι, λέγων Πιάσατε ἡμῖν ἀλώπεκας,
μικροὺς μὲν ὄντας, ἀφανιστικοὺς δὲ τῶν ἀμπελώνων· ἀνθήσουσι | γὰρ αἱ   165
15   ἄμπελοι, εἰ μηκέτι εἴη τὰ λυμαινόμενα. Πιάσατε ἡμῖν ἀλώπεκας μικροὺς
ἀφανίζοντας ἀμπελῶνας, καὶ αἱ ἄμπελοι ἡμῶν κυπρίζουσιν.
ἆρ᾽ ἔστι δυνατὸν κατ᾽ ἀξίαν ἐφικέσθαι τῆς μεγαλοφυΐας τῶν νοημάτων;
ὅσον θαῦμα τῆς θείας μεγαλειότητος περιέχει ὁ λόγος, ὅσην ἐμφαίνει
τῆς δυνάμεως τοῦ θεοῦ τὴν ὑπερβολὴν ἡ τῶν εἰρημένων διάνοια.
20   πῶς ἐκεῖνος, περὶ οὗ τὰ τηλικαῦτα λέγεται, ὁ ἀνθρωποκτόνος, ὁ ἐν κακίᾳ
δυνατός, οὗ ἡ γλῶσσα ὡσεὶ ξυρὸν ἠκονημένον, περὶ οὗ φησιν ὁ προφήτης
ὅτι Τὰ βέλη τοῦ δυνατοῦ ἠκονημένα σὺν τοῖς ἄνθραξι τοῖς ἐρημικοῖς, καὶ
Ἐνεδρεύει ὡς λέων ἐν τῇ μάνδρᾳ αὐτοῦ, ὁ δράκων ὁ μέγας, ὁ ἀποστάτης, ὁ
ᾅδης ὁ πλατύνων τὸ στόμα αὐτοῦ, ὁ κοσμοκράτωρ τῆς ἐξουσίας τοῦ σκότους,
25   ὁ ἔχων τοῦ θανάτου τὸ κράτος, καὶ ὅσα ἐκ προσώπου αὐτοῦ διηγεῖται ἡ
προφητεία, ὁ ἀφαιρούμενος ὅρια ἐθνῶν ἃ ἔστησε (δηλονότι ὁ ὕψιστος) κατ᾽
ἀριθμὸν ἀγγέλων αὐτοῦ, ὁ καταλαμβάνων τὴν οἰκουμένην ὡς νοσσιὰν καὶ
ὡς καταλελειμμένα ᾠὰ αἴρων αὐτήν, ὁ λέγων τιθέναι ἐπάνω τῶν νεφελῶν
τὸν θρόνον αὐτοῦ καὶ ὅμοιος γίνεσθαι τῷ ὑψίστῳ, καὶ ὅσα ἐν τῷ Ἰὼβ ὁ λόγος
30   περὶ | αὐτοῦ διεξέρχεται τὰ φοβερὰ καὶ φρικώδη, οὗ χαλκαῖ μὲν αἱ πλευραί,   166
σίδηρος δὲ χυτὸς ἡ ῥάχις, ἔγκατα δὲ αὐτοῦ σμιρίτης λίθος, καὶ πάντα τὰ
τοιαῦτα, δι᾽ ὧν τὴν φοβερὰν φύσιν ἐκείνην ὑπογράφει ὁ λόγος, οὗτος οὖν ὁ
τοσοῦτος καὶ τοιοῦτος, ὁ στρατηγὸς τῶν ἐν τοῖς δαίμοσι λεγεώνων,

various ways" (cf. Heb 1:1), brought her, and she becomes desirous of the fleshly theophany—that the Word become flesh, and that God be manifested in flesh, and that the divine utterances that promise eternal blessedness to the worthy be offered to our hearing. How well does the voice of Simeon agree with the Bride's prayer. He says: "Now, O Lord, you let your servant depart in peace in accordance with your word. For my eyes have seen your salvation" (Luke 2:29–30). For he saw, even as she desired to see. And those who hear his sweet voice know the grace of the gospel—the ones who say, "You have the words of eternal life" (John 6:68).

Thus the pure Bridegroom accepts the prayer of the Bride because she is righteous, and meaning to show himself openly, he first of all urges the hunters to chase down the foxes so that they will no longer prevent the vineyard from blooming. "Catch us ... foxes, he says, which, small though they be, destroy vineyards. For the | vines will blossom, when there is nothing left that harms them. *Catch us the little foxes that destroy vineyards, and our vines blossom.*"

Can we then fittingly attain the loftiness of these ideas? How great a display of the majesty of God does this text contain! How great a preeminence of the divine power does the sense of its words evince!

How is he described[20]—he, I mean, of whom such things as these are said, that he is humanity's slayer (cf. John 8:44) powerful in doing evil, with a tongue like a whetted razor (Ps 51:3–4)? Of him the prophet says, "The arrows of the Mighty One, sharpened with the coals of the desert" (Ps 119:4); and, "Like a lion he lies in wait in his lair" (Ps 9:30). He is the great dragon (cf. Ezek 29:3), the Apostate, Hades that opens its mouth (cf. Isa 5:14), the World Ruler of the power of darkness (cf. Eph 6:12), he who has the power of death (cf. Heb 2:14). Then prophecy describes him speaking for himself. He is the one who removes the borders of the nations (cf. Isa 10:13), which he—obviously this refers to the Most High—established according to the number of his angels (Deut 32:8). He is the one who seizes the inhabited earth as if it were a nest and takes it up like forsaken eggs (cf. Isa 10:14). He is the one who says that his throne sits above the clouds and that he is like the Most High God (Isa 14:13–14). Then there are all the fearful and awful things that the Word narrates about | him in the book of Job: his ribs are of bronze and his limbs of cast iron (cf. Job 40:18), and his entrails are powdered stone (cf. Job 41:7)—and all the statements of this sort by whose means the scriptural text sketches that fearsome nature. Such he is, then, and so great, the commanding general of the legions of demons.

---

20. Satan is meant here.

πῶς ὀνομάζεται παρὰ τῆς ἀληθινῆς τε καὶ μόνης δυνάμεως; μικρὸν
ἀλωπέκιον. καὶ οἱ περὶ αὐτὸν πάντες, ἡ ὑποχείριος αὐτῷ στρατιά, πάντες
κατὰ τὸ ἴσον ἐξευτελισθέντες κατονομάζονται παρὰ τοῦ παρορμῶντος πρὸς
τὴν κατ᾽ αὐτῶν ἄγραν τοὺς θηρευτάς.

5   εἶεν δ᾽ ἂν οὗτοι τάχα μὲν αἱ ἀγγελικαὶ δυνάμεις αἱ τῆς δεσποτικῆς
παρουσίας ἐπὶ τὴν γῆν προπομπεύουσαι καὶ τὸν βασιλέα τῆς δόξης ἐντὸς
τοῦ βίου παράγουσαι, αἱ τοῖς ἀγνοοῦσιν ὑποδεικνύουσαι, Τίς ἐστιν οὗτος
ὁ βασιλεὺς τῆς δόξης, ὁ κραταιὸς καὶ δυνατὸς ἐν πολέμῳ, ἴσως δ᾽ ἄν τις
εἴποι καὶ τὰ Λειτουργικὰ πνεύματα τὰ εἰς διακονίαν ἀποστελλόμενα διὰ
10   τοὺς μέλλοντας κληρονομεῖν σωτηρίαν, τάχα δὲ θηρευτὰς εἴποι τις ἂν
καὶ τοὺς ἁγίους ἀποστόλους εἶναι τοὺς εἰς τὴν ἄγραν τῶν θηρίων τούτων
ἐκπεμπομένους, | πρὸς οὓς εἶπεν ὅτι Ποιήσω ὑμᾶς ἁλιεῖς ἀνθρώπων· οὐ   167
γὰρ ἂν ἐνήργησαν τὴν ἀνθρωπίνην ἁλείαν τῇ τῶν λόγων περιβολῇ τὰς τῶν
σῳζομένων ψυχὰς σαγηνεύοντας, εἰ μὴ πρότερον ἐκ τῶν φωλεῶν τὰ θηρία
15   ταῦτα ἐξέβαλον, τοὺς μικροὺς ἐκείνους ἀλώπεκας ἐκ τῶν καρδιῶν λέγω, αἷς
ἐνεφώλευον, ὥστε ποιῆσαι τόπον τῷ υἱῷ τοῦ θεοῦ, ὅπου ἑαυτοῦ τὴν κεφαλὴν
ἀναπαύσει, μηκέτι τοῦ γένους τῶν ἀλωπέκων ἐν ταῖς καρδίαις φωλεύοντος.
πλὴν οὕσπερ ἂν ὑποθῆται τοὺς ἀγρευτὰς εἶναι ὁ λόγος, τὸ μεγαλεῖον καὶ
ἄφραστον τῆς θείας δυνάμεως διὰ τῶν προστεταγμένων αὐτοῖς διδασκόμεθα·
20   οὐ γὰρ εἶπεν ὅτι θηράσατε τὸν ὗν τὸν ἐκ τοῦ δρυμοῦ τὴν ἄμπελον τοῦ θεοῦ
λυμαινόμενον ἢ τὸν μονιὸν τὸν ἄγριον ἢ τὸν ὠρυόμενον λέοντα ἢ τὸ μέγα
κῆτος ἢ τὸν ὑποβρύχιον δράκοντα (ἢ γὰρ ἄν τινα δύναμιν τῶν ἀντιμαχούντων
διὰ τῶν τοιούτων ὁ λόγος τοῖς θηρευταῖς ἐνεδείκνυτο), ἀλλὰ πᾶσαι, φησίν,
ἐκεῖναι αἱ περίγειοι δυναστεῖαι, πρὸς ἃς ἡ πάλη τοῖς ἀνθρώποις ἐστίν, ἀρχαί τε
25   καὶ ἐξουσίαι καὶ κοσμοκράτορες σκότους καὶ πνεύματα πονηρίας, ἀλωπεκιά
ἐστι μικρά, δολερά τε καὶ δύστηνα, πρὸς τὴν ὑμετέραν κρινόμενα δύναμιν.
| ἐὰν ἐκείνων κατακρατήσητε, τότε ἀπολήψεται τὴν ἰδίαν χάριν ὁ ἀμπελὼν   168
ὁ ἡμέτερος, ἡ ἀνθρωπίνη φύσις, καὶ τὴν τῶν βοτρύων φορὰν διὰ τοῦ ἄνθους
τῆς ἐναρέτου πολιτείας προοιμιάσεται. Πιάσατε οὖν ἡμῖν ἀλώπεκας μικροὺς
30   ἀφανίζοντας ἀμπελῶνας καὶ αἱ ἄμπελοι ἡμῶν κυπρίζουσιν.

Ἤκουσε τοῦ θείου προστάγματος ἡ ἄμπελος, ἡ γυνή, περὶ ἧς φησιν ὁ
Δαβὶδ ὅτι Ἡ γυνή σου ὡς ἄμπελος εὐθηνοῦσα, καὶ εἶδεν ἑαυτὴν ἐν τῇ δυνάμει
τοῦ κελεύσαντος τῆς ἐκ τῶν θηρίων τούτων λύμης κεκαθαρμένην καὶ εὐθὺς
δίδωσιν ἑαυτὴν τῷ γεωργῷ τῷ τὸ μεσότοιχον τοῦ φραγμοῦ λύσαντι· οὐκέτι
35   γὰρ τῷ τοίχῳ τοῦ νόμου πρὸς τὴν συνάφειαν τοῦ ποθουμένου διατειχίζεται,
ἀλλά φησιν Ἐγὼ τῷ ἀδελφιδῷ μου καὶ ὁ ἀδελφιδός μου ἐμοί, ὁ ποιμαίνων

But how is this one named by the true and only Power? He is a little fox![21] And all those who are about him, the army that is under his orders, all are disparagingly named in the same way by the one who urges the hunters to chase them down.

No doubt these hunters would be the angelic powers, those who precede the Lord's advent on the earth, who lead the King of Glory's way into this life and who make it plain to the ignorant "Who this King of Glory is, the one who is strong and mighty in battle" (Ps 23:8). By the same token, one might also say "the ministering spirits" (Heb 1:4), dispatched in the service of those who shall inherit salvation; and no doubt one might say that the hunters are the holy apostles sent forth to chase these wild animals, the apostles | to whom the Lord said, "I will make you fishers of men" (Matt 4:19), for they would not have carried out this fishing for men with the net of their words, catching the souls of the saved, unless they had first of all cast these wild beasts out of their lairs—the little foxes, I mean—out of the hearts in which they lay hid, so as to make a place where the Son of God may lay his head because the fox-breed is no longer lurking there. Besides, the very ones whom the Word commands to be hunters are taught the greatness and the wonder of the divine power by the things enjoined upon them. For he did not say, "Hunt the wild pig that 'ravages' God's vineyard from its thicket, or 'the wild boar' (cf. Ps 79:14), or the roaring lion, or the great Leviathan, or the monster of the deep" (though indeed the Word showed the hunters, in such beasts, something of the power of the opposing forces). No, "All these earthly powers," he says, "with whom humans struggle—princes and authorities and world rulers of darkness and spirits of wickedness—are little foxes, wretched and treacherous, consigned under your power. | If you overcome them, then our vineyard, our human nature, will receive the grace proper to it and will begin the harvest of grapes with the blossom of virtuous conduct." Therefore catch us little foxes that destroy the vineyards, and our vines blossom.

The command of God was heard by the vineyard, by the wife, of whom David said, "Your wife is as a flourishing vineyard" (Ps 127:3), and she saw herself cleansed, through the power of him who commanded, from the ravages of these wild beasts, and straightway she gives herself to the husbandman who "has broken down the dividing wall of hostility" (cf. Eph 2:14). For no longer is she cut off from union with the one she desires by the wall of the law. On the contrary, she says: *My beloved is mine and I am his; he feeds his flock among*

---

21. Contrast Origen, *Comm. Cant.* 3(4).15 (Baehrens 1925, 238.18–19; cf. trans. Lawson 1956, 256), who take the advice to capture "little foxes" to mean that bad thoughts must be squelched when they are still immature. Otherwise he and Gregory broadly agree in their interpretations of this verse.

ἐν τοῖς κρίνοις, ἕως οὗ διαπνεύσῃ ἡ ἡμέρα καὶ κινηθῶσιν αἱ σκιαί. τοῦτο δέ
ἐστιν· εἶδον, φησί, πρόσωπον πρὸς πρόσωπον τὸν ἀεὶ μὲν ὄντα ὅπερ ἐστί,
δι᾽ ἐμὲ δὲ ἐκ τῆς ἀδελφῆς μου τῆς συναγωγῆς ἀνθρωπικῶς ἀνατείλαντα
καὶ ἐν αὐτῷ ἀναπαύομαι καὶ γίνομαι αὐτῷ οἰκητήριον. οὗτος γάρ ἐστιν
5   ὁ ποιμὴν ὁ καλός, ὃς οὐχὶ χόρτον ποιεῖται τὴν τῶν ποιμνίων νομήν, ἀλλὰ
       | καθαροῖς κρίνοις τρέφει τὰ πρόβατα· ἀληθῶς γὰρ ὁ μηκέτι τῷ χόρτῳ   169
       τρέφων τὸν χόρτον· ἰδίᾳ γὰρ τροφὴ τῆς ἀλόγου φύσεως ὁ χόρτος ἐστίν, ὁ δὲ
       ἄνθρωπος λογικὸς ὢν τῷ ἀληθινῷ τρέφεται λόγῳ, εἰ δὲ τοῦ τοιούτου χόρτου
       ἐμφορηθείη, καὶ αὐτὸς γίνεται χόρτος· Πᾶσα γάρ φησι σὰρξ χόρτος ἐστίν, ἕως
10   ἂν ᾖ σάρξ. εἰ δέ τις πνεῦμα γένοιτο γεννηθεὶς ἐκ τοῦ πνεύματος, οὐκέτι τὸν
       χορτώδη ἐπιβοσκηθήσεται βίον, ἀλλὰ τὸ πνεῦμα ἔσται αὐτοῦ τροφή, ὅπερ ἡ
       καθαρότης καὶ ἡ εὔπνοια τοῦ κρίνου αἰνίσσεται. ἔσται οὖν καὶ αὐτὸς κρίνον
       καθαρὸν καὶ εὔπνουν πρὸς τὴν φύσιν τῆς τροφῆς ἀλλοιούμενος.
            τοῦτό ἐστιν ἡ διαχεομένη ταῖς ἀκτῖσιν ἡμέρα ἤτοι διαπνέουσα, καθὼς
15   ὠνόμασεν ἡ θεία φωνὴ τὴν διὰ τοῦ πνεύματος τῶν ἀκτίνων γινομένην
       διάχυσιν διαπνοὴν ὀνομάσασα, ὅθεν αἱ τοῦ βίου μετακινοῦνται σκιαί,
       περὶ ἃς κατὰ σπουδὴν ὁρῶσιν | οἱ μήπω τῷ φωτὶ τῆς ἀληθείας τὸν τῆς   170
       ψυχῆς ὀφθαλμὸν καταυγάσαντες, οἱ τὴν σκιὰν καὶ τὸ μάταιον ὡς ὑφεστὼς
       ὁρῶντες καὶ τὸ ἀληθῶς ὂν ὡς μὴ ὂν παραβλέποντες. ἀλλ᾽ οἱ διὰ τῶν κρίνων
20   τρεφόμενοι (τουτέστιν οἱ τῇ καθαρᾷ τε καὶ εὐπνοούσῃ τροφῇ τὴν ψυχὴν
       πιαινόμενοι) πᾶσαν ἀπατηλήν τε καὶ σκιοειδῆ φαντασίαν τῶν κατὰ τὸν
       βίον τοῦτον σπουδαζομένων ἑαυτῶν ἀποστήσαντες πρὸς τὴν ἀληθινὴν τῶν
       πραγμάτων ὑπόστασιν ὄψονται υἱοὶ φωτὸς καὶ υἱοὶ ἡμέρας γινόμενοι.
            Ταῦτα βλέπει ἡ νύμφη καὶ κατεπείγει τὸν λόγον διὰ τάχους εἰς ἔργον
25   προαγαγεῖν τῶν ἀγαθῶν τὴν ἐλπίδα Ἀπόστρεψον λέγουσα τῶν κακῶν
       τὴν φοράν, ὦ ἀδελφιδέ, ὁμοιώθητι τῇ δορκάδι ἢ νεβρῷ ἐλάφων ἐπὶ τὰ ὄρη
       τῶν κοιλωμάτων, ἴδε ὡς δορκὰς ὁ τὰς ἐνθυμήσεις τῶν ἀνθρώπων βλέπων,
       ὁ τοὺς διαλογισμοὺς τῶν καρδιῶν ἀναγινώσκων, ἀφάνισον τὴν γονὴν τῆς
       κακίας ὡς νεβρὸς ἐλάφων ἐξαναλίσκων τὸ γένος τοῦ ὄφεως· ὁρᾷς τὰ κοῖλα
30   ὄρη τοῦ ἀνθρωπίνου βίου, ὧν τὰ ἐπαναστήματα οὐχὶ ἀκρώρειαί εἰσιν ἀλλὰ
       φάραγγες. τρέχει τοίνυν ἕως τάχους ὁ λόγος ἐπὶ τὰ κοῖλα ὄρη· πᾶν γὰρ τὸ
       κατὰ τῆς ἀληθείας ὑψούμενον βάραθρόν ἐστι καὶ οὐχὶ | ὄρος, κοίλωμα   171
       καὶ οὐκ ἀνάστημα. ἐὰν οὖν ἐπιδράμῃς ἐπὶ ταῦτα, φησί, πᾶσα ἡ τοιαύτη
       φάραγξ πληρωθήσεται καὶ πᾶν τὸ τοιοῦτον ὄρος ταπεινωθήσεται. ταῦτα
35   φθέγγεται ἡ ψυχή, ἣν ποιμαίνει ὁ λόγος οὐκ ἐν ἀκάνθαις τισὶν ἢ χόρτοις
       ἀλλ᾽ ἐν τῇ εὐοδμίᾳ τῶν κρίνων τῆς καθαρᾶς πολιτείας. ὧν γένοιτο καὶ ἡμᾶς
       ἐμφορηθῆναι ποιμαινομένους ὑπὸ τοῦ λόγου,

            ᾧ ἡ δόξα καὶ τὸ κράτος εἰς τοὺς αἰῶνας τῶν αἰώνων.
            ἀμήν.

the lilies, until the day dawns and the shadows depart. That is, "I have seen," she says, "the One who is eternally what he is face to face. I have seen him rising up in human form on my account out of the synagogue my sister, and I am resting in him and am becoming a member of his household. For he is the Good Shepherd, who no longer gives his flock grass to feed upon but nourishes his sheep | with pure lilies." For truly the good shepherd is the one who no longer nourishes grass with grass. Grass is the food proper to the nonrational nature, while the human person, being rational, is nourished by the true Word; but if a person fills up on this sort of grass, he himself becomes grass. "For," it says, "all flesh is grass," as long as it is flesh. But if a person becomes spirit by being born of the Spirit, that person will no more graze upon the life of grass. His nourishment will be the Spirit, which is signified by the purity and sweet scent of the lily. Therefore that person too will be a lily, pure and sweet-scented, once he has been changed into the nature of that which nourishes him.

This Spirit is that day that is poured—or rather breathed—out by the radiance, for the divine voice gave a name to the outpouring of the radiance by the Spirit by calling it "breathing out," and by it the shadows of this life are removed—the shadows upon which those persons gaze | who have not yet illumined the eye of the soul with the light of truth, who perceive shadow and vanity as substantive things and mistake what truly is for what is not. But those who are nourished by the lilies (that is, those who fatten their souls with the pure and sweet-scented nourishment) have put away from themselves any deceptive and shadowy imagining, which belongs to people who are busied about this life. They will look toward the true ground of the being of things, having become sons of light and sons of the day.

The Bride sees these things, and she urges the Word to be swift in bringing the hope of good things to realization, saying: "*Turn back* the stream of evil things, my beloved: *be made like the gazelle or the fawn of a deer upon the hills of the plains.* O you who have your eye on people's desires and read the thoughts of our hearts, see like the gazelle! Like the fawn of a deer that destroys the tribe of serpents, eradicate the offspring of evil! You perceive the hollow hills of human life, whose crests are not ridges but chasms." Swiftly, therefore, the Word runs to the hollow hills. For everything that is exalted against the truth is a hollow pit and not | a hill, a cavity and not a crest. "So if you run to these hills," she says, "every such chasm will be filled and every such hill will be made low." This is what the soul utters, whom the Word tends, not with thorns or grasses, but with the fragrance of the lilies that are the life of purity. And let us, shepherded by the Word, be filled with these lilies.

To him be glory and power to the ages of ages.
Amen.

Λόγος ζ'

Ἐπὶ κοίτην μου ἐν νυξὶν
ἐζήτησα ὃν ἠγάπησεν ἡ ψυχή μου,
ἐζήτησα αὐτὸν καὶ οὐχ εὗρον αὐτόν,
ἐκάλεσα αὐτὸν καὶ οὐχ ὑπήκουσέ μου.
5 Ἀναστήσομαι δὴ καὶ κυκλώσω ἐν τῇ πόλει
ἐν ταῖς ἀγοραῖς καὶ ἐν ταῖς πλατείαις
καὶ ζητήσω ὃν ἠγάπησεν ἡ ψυχή μου·
ἐζήτησα αὐτὸν καὶ οὐχ εὗρον αὐτόν.
εὕροσάν με οἱ τηροῦντες οἱ κυκλοῦντες ἐν τῇ πόλει.
10 | Μὴ ὃν ἠγάπησεν ἡ ψυχή μου εἴδετε;   172
ὡς μικρὸν ὅτε παρῆλθον ἀπ' αὐτῶν,
Ἕως οὗ εὗρον ὃν ἠγάπησεν ἡ ψυχή μου.
ἐκράτησα αὐτὸν καὶ οὐκ ἀφῆκα αὐτόν,
ἕως οὗ εἰσήγαγον αὐτὸν εἰς οἶκον μητρός μου
15 καὶ εἰς ταμιεῖον τῆς συλλαβούσης με.

Ὥρκισα ὑμᾶς, θυγατέρες Ἰερουσαλήμ,
ἐν ταῖς δυνάμεσι καὶ ἐν ταῖς ἰσχύσεσι τοῦ ἀγροῦ,
ἐὰν ἐγείρητε καὶ ἐξεγείρητε τὴν ἀγάπην, ἕως οὗ θελήσει.

Τίς αὕτη ἡ ἀναβαίνουσα ἀπὸ τῆς ἐρήμου
20 ὡς στελέχη καπνοῦ, τεθυμιαμένη σμύρνα καὶ λίβανος,
ἀπὸ πάντων κονιορτῶν μυρεψοῦ;
Ἰδοὺ ἡ κλίνη τοῦ Σαλωμών,
ἑξήκοντα δυνατοὶ κύκλῳ αὐτῆς
ἀπὸ δυνατῶν Ἰσραήλ,
25 Πάντες κατέχοντες ρομφαίαν,
δεδιδαγμένοι πόλεμον,
ἀνὴρ ρομφαία αὐτοῦ ἐπὶ τὸν μηρὸν αὐτοῦ
ἀπὸ θάμβους ἐν νυξίν.

Πάλιν τὰ μεγάλα τε καὶ ὑψηλὰ δόγματα παρὰ τοῦ Ἄισματος τῶν
30 ἀσμάτων διὰ τῆς παρούσης ἀναγνώσεως παιδευόμεθα. φιλοσοφία γάρ ἐστι
τὸ τῆς νύμφης διήγημα, δι' ὧν τὰ περὶ ἑαυτῆς διεξέρχεται, ὅπως χρὴ περὶ
τὸ θεῖον ἔχειν τοὺς | ἐραστὰς τοῦ ὑπερκειμένου κάλλους δογματιζούσης. 173
ὃ δὲ μανθάνομεν διὰ τῶν προκειμένων λογίων τοιοῦτόν ἐστιν (χρὴ γὰρ
οἶμαι προεκθέσθαι πρότερον τὴν τοῖς ρητοῖς ἐγκειμένην διάνοιαν, εἶθ'

HOMILY 6
Song 3:1–8

¹*Upon my bed by night*
I sought him whom my soul loves,
I sought him and did not find him,
I called him, and he did not hearken to me.
²*I will arise, then, and go around in the city,*
in the markets and in the streets,
and I will seek him whom my soul loves.
I sought him and did not find him.
³*The watchmen making their rounds in the city found me.*
"Have you not seen him whom my soul loves?"
⁴*It was but a moment after I parted from them*
that I found him whom my soul loves.
I seized him and did not let him go,
until I brought him into my mother's house,
and into the chamber of her who conceived me.

⁵*I have charged you, O daughters of Jerusalem,*
by the powers and by the virtues of the field,
[not] to rouse love or waken it until it desires.

⁶*Who is this coming up from the wilderness,*
like tree trunks of smoke, myrrh being burnt and frankincense,
from all the powders of the perfumer?
⁷*Behold Solomon's bed:*
sixty mighty men surround it
out of the mighty men of Israel.
⁸*They all bear a sword,*
being instructed in war;
each man has his sword on his thigh,
because of fear by night.

Once again, in the present lection, we are given weighty and exalted teachings by the Song of Songs. For the Bride's narrative, in which she tells about things that have happened to her, is philosophy, in that she teaches how | lovers of the transcendent Beauty are to relate themselves to the Divine. What we learn from these oracles is something of the following sort (for in my judgment one must first of all set forth the meaning contained in what is

-183-

οὕτως ἐφαρμόσαι τοῖς προθεωρηθεῖσι τὰ θεόπνευστα ῥήματα), ἔστι τοίνυν, ὡς ἐν ὀλίγῳ συνελόντα φράσαι, τοιοῦτόν τι δόγμα διὰ τῶν εἰρημένων ἀναφαινόμενον·

διχῇ τέτμηται κατὰ τὴν ἀνωτάτω διαίρεσιν ἡ τῶν ὄντων φύσις· τὸ μὲν
5   γάρ ἐστιν αἰσθητὸν καὶ ὑλῶδες, τὸ δὲ νοητόν τε καὶ ἄϋλον. αἰσθητὸν μὲν οὖν λέγομεν ὅσον τῇ αἰσθήσει καταλαμβάνεται, νοητὸν δὲ τὸ ὑπερπῖπτον τὴν αἰσθητικὴν κατανόησιν.

ἐκ τούτων τὸ μὲν νοητὸν ἄπειρόν ἐστι καὶ ἀόριστον, τὸ δὲ ἕτερον πάντως τισὶ διαλαμβάνεται πέρασιν. πάσης γὰρ ὕλης τῷ ποσῷ τε καὶ τῷ ποιῷ
10   διειλημμένης ἐν ὄγκῳ καὶ εἴδει καὶ ἐπιφανείᾳ καὶ σχήματι, πέρας γίνεται τῆς περὶ αὐτὴν κατανοήσεως τὰ περὶ αὐτὴν θεωρούμενα, ὡς μηδὲν ἔχειν τὸν τὴν ὕλην διερευνώμενον ἔξω τι τούτων ἐν φαντασίᾳ λαβεῖν· τὸ δὲ νοητόν τε καὶ ἄϋλον τῆς τοιαύτης περιοχῆς καθαρεῦον ἐκφεύγει τὸν ὅρον ἐν οὐδενὶ | 174 περατούμενον.

15   πάλιν δὲ καὶ τῆς νοητῆς φύσεως διχῇ διῃρημένης ἡ μὲν ἄκτιστός ἐστι καὶ ποιητικὴ τῶν ὄντων, ἀεὶ οὖσα ὅπερ ἐστὶ καὶ πάντοτε ὡσαύτως ἔχουσα, κρείττων τε προσθήκης ἁπάσης καὶ τῆς ἐλαττώσεως τῶν ἀγαθῶν ἀνεπίδεκτος, ἡ δὲ διὰ κτίσεως παραχθεῖσα εἰς γένεσιν πρὸς τὸ πρῶτον αἴτιον ἀεὶ βλέπει τῶν ὄντων καὶ τῇ μετουσίᾳ τοῦ ὑπερέχοντος διὰ παντὸς ἐν τῷ ἀγαθῷ συντηρεῖται

said and then fit the inspired words to what has already been discerned)—it is, I say, to speak summarily, some such teaching as the following that is conveyed by what is said.

The nature of things that exist is divided, at the highest level of generality, into two kinds. On the one hand, there is that which is perceptible and material; on the other, that which is intelligible and nonmaterial.[1] Hence we reckon something to fall into the category of the perceptible to the extent that it is grasped by sense perception, but we reckon as intelligible that which falls beyond the observation of the senses.

Of these two, the intelligible has neither limit nor bound,[2] while the other is entirely contained by particular limits. For since matter in its totality is grasped in terms of quantity and quality, which determine its bulk and form and surface and shape, what one sees of it constitutes, in its case, a limit to what is known about it, so that the person who is investigating materiality has nothing apart from some one of these characteristics to lay hold of in the imagination. Contrariwise, that which is intelligible and immaterial, being released from such confines, escapes limit and is | bounded by nothing

But again, the intelligible nature is also divided into two kinds.[3] The first is uncreated and is that which brings intelligible realities into being. It is what it is eternally and is in every respect self-identical. Further, it is beyond any addition to, and incapable of any diminution of, the goods it possesses. The second, however, has been brought into existence by an act of creation. It looks eternally upon the First Cause of the things that are and is preserved in

---

1. For such a division of reality, see Plato, *Tim.* 27D–28A. For Plato, however, the fundamental division is between that-which-is and that-which-comes-to-be, a division that in his account coincides with that between the intelligible and the perceptible. Christian tradition, however, worked with a different fundamental distinction, that between the creative (God) and the creaturely (everything else), and the question how, or whether, the distinction between Creator and creature coincides with Plato's division between Being and Becoming was a confusing if not, in the end, a difficult one.

2. This idea, that the intelligible realm of Forms (which by Gregory's day had come to mean the order of mind-with-its-intellectual-objects) is as such infinite (ἄπειρος) and boundless (ἀόριστος), would have made little sense to Plato, since for him intelligibility is *stability in a definable identity that the mind can grasp clearly* (hence the identification of Being with the intelligible; see n. 1 above). It is true that Plotinus when interpreting Plato applies the adjective ἄπειρος to the intelligible order—but only to indicate that it is all-inclusive and "never expends any of itself, since it has no past or future" (*Enn.* 3.7.5 ad fin.). Gregory, however, intends to say that the realm of the "intelligible" itself, and therefore the "beings" or "realities" (τὰ ὄντα) that constitute it, are always beyond complete or adequate knowledge.

3. Here Gregory introduces what is for him the basic distinction; see above, n. 1. For a particularly eloquent statement of the difference between Creator and creature, see Gregory, *Eun.* 2(12B).69–70 (in GNO 1:246–47; cf. NPNF[2] 5:257).

καὶ τρόπον τινὰ πάντοτε κτίζεται διὰ τῆς ἐν τοῖς ἀγαθοῖς ἐπαυξήσεως πρὸς
τὸ μεῖζον ἀλλοιουμένη, ὡς μηδὲ ταύτῃ τι πέρας ἐνθεωρεῖσθαι μηδὲ ὅρῳ
τινὶ τὴν πρὸς τὸ κρεῖττον αὔξησιν αὐτῆς περιγράφεσθαι ἀλλ᾽ εἶναι πάντοτε
τὸ ἀεὶ παρὸν ἀγαθόν, κἂν ὅτι μάλιστα μέγα τε καὶ τέλειον εἶναι δοκῇ,
5   ἀρχὴν τοῦ ὑπερκειμένου καὶ μείζονος, ὡς καὶ ἐν τούτῳ τὸν ἀποστολικὸν
ἀληθεύεσθαι λόγον διὰ τῆς τῶν ἔμπροσθεν ἐπεκτάσεως ἐν λήθῃ γινομένων
τῶν προδιηνυσμένων· τὸ γὰρ ἀεί τι μεῖζον καὶ καθ᾽ ὑπερβολὴν ἀγαθὸν
εὑρισκόμενον, περὶ ἑαυτὸ κατέχον τὴν τῶν μετεχόντων διάθεσιν, οὐκ ἐᾷ πρὸς
τὰ παρῳχηκότα βλέπειν τῇ τῶν προτιμοτέρων ἀπολαύσει τῶν καταδεεστέρων
10   τὴν μνήμην παρακρουόμενον.
| Τὸ μὲν οὖν νόημα τὸ τῇ φιλοσοφίᾳ τοῦ νυμφικοῦ διηγήματος ἡμῖν   175
δογματιζόμενον τοιοῦτον εἶναι νομίζομεν, καιρὸς δ᾽ ἂν εἴη πρῶτον μὲν αὐτῆς
ἐπιμνησθῆναι τῆς λέξεως τῶν θεοπνεύστων λογίων, εἶθ᾽ οὕτως ἐφαρμόσαι
τοῖς προθεωρηθεῖσι τὴν τοῖς ῥητοῖς ἐγκειμένην διάνοιαν. Ἐπὶ κοίτην μου ἐν
15   νυξὶν ἐζήτησα, φησίν, ὃν ἠγάπησεν ἡ ψυχή μου, ἐζήτησα αὐτὸν καὶ οὐχ εὗρον
αὐτόν, ἐκάλεσα αὐτὸν καὶ οὐχ ὑπήκουσέ μου. ἀναστήσομαι δὴ καὶ κυκλώσω
ἐν τῇ πόλει, ἐν ταῖς ἀγοραῖς καὶ ἐν ταῖς πλατείαις καὶ ζητήσω ὃν ἠγάπησεν
ἡ ψυχή μου. ἐζήτησα αὐτὸν καὶ οὐχ εὗρον αὐτόν. εὕροσάν με οἱ τηροῦντες,
οἱ κυκλοῦντες ἐν τῇ πόλει. μὴ ὃν ἠγάπησεν ἡ ψυχή μου εἴδετε; ὡς μικρὸν
20   ὅτε παρῆλθον ἀπ᾽ αὐτῶν, ἕως οὗ εὗρον ὃν ἠγάπησεν ἡ ψυχή μου· ἐκράτησα
αὐτὸν καὶ οὐκ ἀφῆκα αὐτόν, ἕως οὗ εἰσήγαγον αὐτὸν εἰς οἶκον μητρός μου
καὶ εἰς ταμιεῖον τῆς συλλαβούσης με.
Πῶς τοίνυν ἐν τοῖς εἰρημένοις εὑρίσκομεν τὰ δογματικῶς ἡμῖν
προθεωρηθέντα νοήματα; γέγονεν ἐν ταῖς προλαβούσαις ἀνόδοις πρὸς
25   λόγον τῆς ἑκάστοτε γινομένης αὐξήσεως ἀεὶ πρὸς τὸ κρεῖττον ἀλλοιουμένη
καὶ οὐδέποτε ἐπὶ τοῦ καταληφθέντος ἀγαθοῦ ἱσταμένη, νῦν μὲν ἵππῳ

every respect in the good by its participation in what transcends it. It is also, in a certain fashion, always being created as it is changed for the better by being enhanced in goodness.[4] For this reason, no end point can be conceived for it either, and its growth toward the better is not confined by any limit, but the good that is given at any particular time is always a starting point for something more and better, even though it already appears to be as great and as complete as possible. In its case, too, then, the apostle's word is confirmed, because it stretches forward in forgetfulness of things that have already been accomplished (cf. Phil 3:13). For that good which is now and again discovered to be a better thing, not to say something surpassing, focuses the attention of those who have a share in it upon itself and does not permit [them] to look toward what is past, since it voids the recollection of inferior things by the enjoyment of those that are to be honored more highly.

| So we think that the truth that is conveyed to us by the philosophy of the Bride's tale is of this order, but it is no doubt appropriate first of all to quote the very text of the inspired words, and then by this means to fit their meaning to what we have already looked into. *Upon my bed by night, she says, I sought him whom my soul loves, I sought him and did not find him, I called him, and he did not hearken to me. I will arise, then, and go around in the city, in the markets and in the streets, and I will seek him whom my soul loves. I sought him and did not find him. The watchmen making their rounds in the city found me. "Have you not seen him whom my soul loves?" It was but a moment after I parted from them that I found him whom my soul loves. I seized him and did not let him go, until I brought him into my mother's house, and into the chamber of her who conceived me.*

How, then, do we find in these words the ideas we treated of earlier as basic principles? In the ascents previously accomplished, the soul was always being changed for the better by comparison with each current stage of growth, and so never stopping at the good she had already grasped.[5] Thus at one

---

4. This statement and those that immediately follow seem to define Gregory's distinctive point of view regarding the nature of Intellect (i.e., of mind-and-its-objects). Intellect or intellects exist as part of the created order (see n. 1 above). Thus for him the late Platonist version of the Platonic realm of Forms falls unmistakably—and paradoxically—within Plato's category of that-which-comes-to-be, i.e., that whose very nature it is to change. What is peculiar to Nyssen is that he takes this circumstance, somewhat optimistically, to imply that intellectual creatures are inherently self-transcending in their approximation to the (infinite) Good. The notion that creation *continues* is not, however, unique to Gregory; it is found earlier in Irenaeus, who speaks of the originating act of creation as "initium creationis."

5. This sentence states the theme of the next section, which finishes only on p. 180 (Jaeger) and which reviews in summary fashion the steps in the Bride's progress as Gregory's exegesis has discovered them in homilies 1–5.

παραβαλλομένη τῇ καταστρεψαμένῃ τὸν Αἰγύπτιον τύραννον, πάλιν δὲ
ὁρμίσκοις τε καὶ τρυγόσιν εἰκαζομένη κατὰ τὸν περιαυχένιον κόσμον. | εἶτα   176
ὡς οὐκ ἀρκεσθεῖσα τούτοις ἔτι πρὸς τὸ ἀνώτερον πρόεισι· διὰ γὰρ τῆς ἰδίας
νάρδου τὴν θείαν ἐπιγινώσκει εὐωδίαν καὶ οὐδὲ ἐν τούτῳ μένει, ἀλλὰ πάλιν
5   αὐτὸν τὸν ποθούμενον οἷόν τι ἄρωμα εὔπνουν ἑαυτῇ περιάπτει μεταξὺ τῶν
λογικῶν μαζῶν, ὅθεν βρύει τὰ θεῖα διδάγματα, τῷ χωρήματι τῆς καρδίας
ἐνδησαμένη, μετὰ τοῦτο καρπὸν ἑαυτῆς ποιεῖται τὸν γεωργὸν βότρυν αὐτὸν
ὀνομάζουσα ἡδύ τι καὶ προσηνὲς διὰ τοῦ ἄνθους εὐωδιάζοντα, καὶ οὕτως
αὐξηθεῖσα διὰ τῶν τοιούτων ὁδῶν καλὴ λέγεται καὶ πλησίον γίνεται καὶ
10   περιστεραῖς τὸ ἐν τοῖς ὄμμασιν αὐτῆς παρεικάζεται κάλλος.

εἶτα πάλιν πρὸς τὸ μεῖζον χωρεῖ· διορατικωτέρα γὰρ γινομένη κἀκείνη
τοῦ λόγου καταμανθάνει τὴν ὥραν καὶ θαυμάζει, πῶς σύσκιος ἐπὶ τὴν
κλίνην τῆς κάτω ζωῆς καταβαίνει τῇ ὑλικῇ τοῦ ἀνθρωπίνου σώματος φύσει
συσκιαζόμενος. πρὸς τούτοις τὸν τῆς ἀρετῆς οἶκον διαγράφει τῷ λόγῳ,
15   οὗ γίνεται ἡ ἐρέψιμος ὕλη κέδρος τε καὶ κυπάρισσος σηπεδόνος | τε καὶ   177
διαφθορᾶς ἀνεπίδεκτος, δι᾽ ὧν τὸ μόνιμόν τε καὶ ἀμετάβλητον τῆς πρὸς τὸ
ἀγαθὸν σχέσεως διερμηνεύει τῷ λόγῳ. ἐπὶ τούτοις διὰ συγκρίσεως ἡ πρὸς τὸ
κρεῖττον αὐτῆς παραλλαγὴ διαδείκνυται καὶ κρίνον ἐν ἀκάνθαις δοκεῖ. καὶ
πάλιν παρ᾽ ἐκείνης καθορᾶται τοῦ νυμφίου τὸ πρὸς τοὺς ἄλλους διάφορον·
20   μῆλον γὰρ ὀνομάζεται μεταξὺ δρυμῶνος ἀκάρπου τῇ εὐχροίᾳ τῆς ὀπώρας
ὡραϊζόμενον, οὗ τὴν σκιὰν ὑπελθοῦσα ἐν τῷ οἴκῳ τοῦ οἴνου γίνεται. καὶ
μύροις στηρίζεται καὶ τοῖς καρποῖς τοῦ μήλου στοιβάζεται καὶ τὸ ἐκλεκτὸν
βέλος ἐν τῇ καρδίᾳ δεξαμένη διὰ τῆς γλυκείας πληγῆς πάλιν καὶ αὐτὴ γίνεται
βέλος ἐν ταῖς χερσὶ τοῦ τοξότου τῆς μὲν εὐωνύμου τὴν κεφαλὴν πρὸς τὸν
25   ἄνω σκοπὸν εὐθυνούσης, τῆς δεξιᾶς δὲ πρὸς ἑαυτὴν διαλαμβανούσης τὸ
βέλος. μετὰ ταῦτα ὡς ἤδη πρὸς τὸ τέλειον φθάσασα καὶ ταῖς λοιπαῖς τὴν
ἐπὶ τὰ αὐτὰ προθυμίαν ὑφηγεῖται τῷ λόγῳ δι᾽ ὁρκισμοῦ τινος τὴν περὶ τὴν
ἀγάπην αὐτῶν σπουδὴν ἐπεγείρουσα.

τίς οὖν οὐκ ἂν εἴποι τὴν ἐπὶ τοσοῦτον ὑψωθεῖσαν ψυχὴν ἐν τῷ ἀκροτάτῳ
30   γεγενῆσθαι ὅρῳ τῆς τελειότητος; ἀλλ᾽ ὅμως τὸ πέρας τῶν προδιηνυσμένων
ἀρχὴ γίνεται τῆς ἐπὶ | τὰ ὑπερκείμενα χειραγωγίας· πάντα γὰρ ἐκεῖνα φωνῆς   178
ἦχος ἐνομίσθη πρὸς τὴν τῶν μυστικῶν θεωρίαν τὴν ψυχὴν διὰ τῆς ἀκοῆς
ἐπιστρεφούσης.

καὶ βλέπειν ἄρχεται τὸν ποθούμενον ἄλλῳ εἴδει τοῖς ὀφθαλμοῖς
35   ἐμφαινόμενον· δορκάδι γὰρ ὁμοιοῦται καὶ νεβρῷ παρεικάζεται, καὶ
οὐχ ἕστηκεν οὔτε ἐπὶ τῆς μιᾶς ὄψεως οὔτε ἐπὶ τοῦ τόπου τοῦ αὐτοῦ τὸ
φαινόμενον, ἀλλ᾽ ἐπιπηδᾷ τοῖς ὄρεσιν ἀπὸ τῶν ἀκρωρειῶν ἐπὶ τὰς τῶν

moment she is compared to the horse that overthrew the Egyptian tyrant, but then further she is likened to circlets and to doves because of the adornment about her neck. | Then, as though not satisfied with these achievements, she continues to progress to a higher stage. By means of her own spikenard she becomes aware of the divine fragrance, and she does not stop even with this, but now she applies the beloved One himself like a sweet perfume between her rational breasts, from which she gushes divine teachings, having held him in the chamber of her heart. Next she makes the husbandman her own fruit, calling him a bunch of grapes because through his blossom he gives off a sweet and gentle fragrance. And when she has undergone growth by following these paths, she is called "beautiful" and becomes the beloved, and the beauty in her eyes is likened to doves.

Then once more she journeys toward better things. Our Bride becomes more clear-sighted and discerns the glory of the Word and marvels at how he descends as a comrade upon the couch of this life below, shadowed about by the material nature of the human body. In addition, she describes the house of virtue in her discourse, the house whose roof is made of cedar and cypress, which is not subject to decay | or corruption; here her words convey the stability and unchangeability of her disposition for the good. Furthermore, her change for the better is indicated by use of a comparison, and she appears as a lily among thorns. Again, she discerns the way in which the Bridegroom differs from the others, for he is called an apple tree in the midst of a barren thicket—an apple beautified by summer's bloom—and when she comes under its shadow, she finds herself in the house of wine. Moreover, she is supported with perfumes and is filled with the fruit of the apple tree. And when she has received in her heart the elect arrow, she herself in turn, by this sweet wound, becomes an arrow in the hands of the archer, as the hand on the left directs her head toward the goal on high, while the right hand pulls the arrow to itself. After this, as one who has already come to perfection, she instructs the rest in her discourse about eagerness for the same goal, arousing their zeal for love by using an oath.

Who, then, would not say that a soul exalted to such a degree had come to the highest peak of perfection? Nevertheless the limit that defines the things that have already been accomplished becomes the starting point of | her being led to realities that transcend them. For all the former things are reckoned to be the sound of a voice that uses the soul's hearing to turn it toward discernment of things hidden.

She starts, in an additional step, to see the One whom she desires when he appears to her eyes in a form other than his own. For he is likened to a gazelle and compared to a fawn—and he is not stationary. He appears neither under a single aspect nor in one and the same place but leaps upon the

βουνῶν ἐξοχὰς μεθαλλόμενος. καὶ πάλιν ἐν μείζονι καταστάσει ἡ νύμφη
γίνεται φωνῆς δευτέρας πρὸς αὐτὴν ἐλθούσης, δι᾿ ἧς παρορμᾶται καταλιπεῖν
τὴν ἐκ τοῦ τοίχου σκιὰν καὶ ἐν ὑπαίθρῳ γενέσθαι καὶ τῇ σκέπῃ τῆς πέτρας
ἐναναπαύσασθαι τῆς ἐχομένης τοῦ προτειχίσματος καὶ τῆς ἐαρινῆς ὥρας
5   κατατρυφῆσαι δρεπομένην τοῦ καιροῦ τὰ ἄνθη ἀκμαῖα ὄντα καὶ ὥρια καὶ
πρὸς τομὴν ἐπιτήδεια καὶ ὅσα ἄλλα πρὸς ἀπόλαυσιν ὁ καιρὸς τοῖς τρυφῶσι
χαρίζεται ἐν ταῖς τῶν μουσικῶν ὀρνίθων φωναῖς. δι᾿ ὧν πάλιν τελειοτέρα
γινομένη ἡ νύμφη αὐτὴν ἀξιοῖ τοῦ φθεγγομένου τὴν ὄψιν ἰδεῖν ἐμφανῶς καὶ
τὸν λόγον παρ᾿ αὐτοῦ δέξασθαι μηκέτι δι᾿ ἑτέρων φθεγγόμενον.
10   πάλιν εἰκός ἐστιν ἐπὶ τούτοις μακαρισθῆναι τὴν ψυχὴν τῆς ὑψηλῆς
ἀναβάσεως, τοῦ ἀκροτάτου τῶν ποθουμένων ἐφικομένην· τί γὰρ ἄν τις
μεῖζον εἰς μακαρισμὸν ἐννοήσειε τοῦ ἰδεῖν τὸν θεόν; ἀλλὰ καὶ τοῦτο | τῶν   179
μὲν προδιηνυσμένων πέρας ἐστί, τῆς δὲ τῶν ὑπερκειμένων ἐλπίδος ἀρχὴ
γίνεται· πάλιν γὰρ τῆς φωνῆς ἀκούει τῆς διακελευομένης τοῖς θηρευταῖς
15   ἐπὶ σωτηρίᾳ τῶν λογικῶν ἀμπελώνων ἀγρεῦσαι τὰ βλαπτικὰ τῶν καρπῶν
θηρία, τοὺς μικροὺς ἐκείνους ἀλώπεκας. καὶ τούτου γενομένου μεταχωρεῖ
τὰ δύο εἰς ἄλληλα· ὅ τε γὰρ θεὸς ἐν τῇ ψυχῇ γίνεται καὶ πάλιν εἰς τὸν θεὸν
ἡ ψυχὴ μετοικίζεται. λέγει γὰρ ὅτι Ἀδελφιδός μου ἐμοὶ κἀγὼ αὐτῷ, τῷ ἐν
κρίνοις ποιμαίνοντι καὶ μετατιθέντι τὴν ἀνθρωπίνην ζωὴν ἀπὸ τῶν σκιοειδῶν
20   φαντασμάτων ἐπὶ τὴν τῶν ὄντων ἀλήθειαν.
       ὁρᾷς εἰς ὅσον ἀναβέβηκεν ὕψος ἡ ἐκ δυνάμεως εἰς δύναμιν κατὰ τὸν
προφητικὸν λόγον πορευομένη, ὡς τοῦ ἀκροτάτου τῆς τῶν ἀγαθῶν ἐλπίδος
τετυχηκέναι δοκεῖν· τί γὰρ ἀνώτερον τοῦ ἐν αὐτῷ γενέσθαι τῷ ποθουμένῳ
καὶ ἐν ἑαυτῷ τὸν ποθούμενον δέξασθαι; ἀλλ᾿ ὅμως ἐν τούτῳ γενομένη πάλιν
25   ὡς ἐνδεὴς οὖσα τοῦ ἀγαθοῦ ὀδύρεται καὶ ὡς μήπω ἔχουσα τὸ τῇ ἐπιθυμίᾳ
προκείμενον ἀμηχανεῖ τε καὶ δυσχεραίνει καὶ τὴν τοιαύτην τῆς ψυχῆς
ἀμηχανίαν δημοσιεύει τῷ διηγήματι καὶ ὅπως εὗρε τὸ ζητούμενον ὑπογράφει
τῷ λόγῳ.
       Ταῦτα δὲ πάντα διὰ τῆς τῶν προκειμένων ἡμῖν ῥητῶν θεωρίας
30   μανθάνομεν, δι᾿ ὧν σαφῶς διδασκόμεθα τὸ μήτε | τινὶ πέρατι τὸ μεγαλεῖον   180
τῆς θείας ὁρίζεσθαι φύσεως μήτε τι γνώσεως μέτρον ὅρον γίνεσθαι τῆς τῶν
ζητουμένων κατανοήσεως, μεθ᾿ ὃν στῆναι χρὴ τῆς ἐπὶ τὸ πρόσω φορᾶς τὸν
τῶν ὑψηλῶν ὀρεγόμενον, ἀλλ᾿ οὕτως ἔχειν τὸν διὰ τῆς τῶν ὑπερκειμένων

mountains, bounding from the ridges to the heights of the hills. And now again the Bride attains a higher state as a second voice comes to her. It incites her to depart from the shadow that is made by the wall, to enter the open air, to find rest in the shelter of the rock that the outwork surrounds, and to take delight in the splendor of the springtime as she plucks the seasonal blossoms when they are at their gorgeous best and ready for cutting—and in whatever else the season lavishes by way of pleasure upon those who revel in the music of its songbirds. By this means the Bride approaches yet closer to perfection. She prays to see the very countenance of the One who addresses her, and she receives from him a word that no longer comes by way of intermediaries.

Once again, after all this, it seems that the soul has been blessed with ascent to the heights and has attained the highest of her desires. For what greater blessing can be conceived than that of seeing God? Yet this too | marks a limit set to what has already been accomplished: it comes as the dawning of a hope for what lies beyond it. For now once more she hears the voice. It summons the hunters, for the salvation of the rational vines, to capture the wild animals that harm the fruit—those *little foxes*. When this has come to pass, the two actors move into one another. God comes into the soul, and correspondingly the soul is brought into God. For she says, "*My beloved is mine, and I am his*. He does his pasturing among the lilies and transfers human life from the realm of shadowy images to the truth of that which is."

You see to what a height she has climbed, this soul that, in accordance with the prophetic word, is going "from strength to strength" (Ps 83:8): she seems to attain the hope of the very highest good. For what is higher than to be in the One who is the object of desire and to receive the object of desire within oneself? But in this situation too she bewails the fact that she is needy for the Good. As one who does not yet have what is present to her desire, she is perplexed and dissatisfied, and she broadcasts this perplexity of her soul in her story, describing in her account how she found the one she sought.

All this we learn by a discerning consideration of the words before us. By their means we are taught plainly that | the greatness of the divine Nature knows no limit, and that no measure of knowledge sets bounds to a seeker's looking—bounds beyond which one who is reaching for the heights must cease to move ahead.[6] On the contrary, the intelligence that makes its course

---

6. This is Gregory's point. See above, n. 3. This whole theme is introduced in the very first of the homilies, in Nyssen's exegesis of the words "Your name is perfume poured out"; see above, pp. 36–37 (Jaeger). It is interesting to contrast the way in which the exegesis attributed to Gregory the Great takes this passage. The words "I sought him and did not find him" reflect, the author thinks, the fact "that she never completely finds the one she seeks *in this world*" (PL 79:502B, emphasis added).

κατανοήσεως ἐπὶ τὸ ἄνω τρέχοντα νοῦν, ὡς πᾶσαν τελειότητα γνώσεως τὴν
ἐφικτὴν τῇ ἀνθρωπίνῃ φύσει ἀρχὴν γίνεσθαι τῆς τῶν ὑψηλοτέρων ἐπιθυμίας.

καί μοι σκόπει δι᾽ ἀκριβείας τὸν προκείμενον τῇ θεωρίᾳ λόγον τοῦτο
προκατανοήσας ὅτι θάλαμός ἐστιν ἡ σωματικὴ τοῦ λόγου ὑπογραφὴ καὶ
5   γαμική τις διασκευή, ἢ δίδωσι τῇ θεωρίᾳ τὰς ὕλας, ὧν ἡ φιλοσοφία πρὸς τὸ
καθαρόν τε καὶ ἄϋλον μετενεγκοῦσα τὰς τῶν νοημάτων ἐμφάσεις διὰ τῶν
ἐν αὐτοῖς ἐπιτελουμένων προάγει τὰ δόγματα τοῖς τῶν γινομένων αἰνίγμασι
συγχρησαμένη πρὸς τὴν τῶν δηλουμένων σαφήνειαν.

ἐπεὶ τοίνυν νύμφην μὲν ὑπέθετο τὴν ψυχὴν ὁ λόγος, ὁ δὲ ἐξ ὅλης καρδίας
10   τε καὶ ψυχῆς καὶ δυνάμεως παρ᾽ αὐτῆς ἀγαπώμενος νυμφίος κατονομάζεται,
ἀκολούθως ἡ | ἐπὶ τὸ ἀκρότατον ὡς ᾤετο τῶν ἐλπιζομένων ἐλθοῦσα καὶ   181
ἤδη πρὸς τὸν ποθούμενον ἀνακεκρᾶσθαι νομίσασα κοίτην ὀνομάζει τὴν
τελειοτέραν τοῦ ἀγαθοῦ μετουσίαν καὶ νύκτα λέγει τὸν τῆς κοίτης καιρόν.
διὰ δὲ τοῦ ὀνόματος τῆς νυκτὸς ἐνδείκνυται τῶν ἀοράτων τὴν θεωρίαν
15   καθ᾽ ὁμοιότητα Μωϋσέως τοῦ ἐν τῷ γνόφῳ γεγονότος ἐν ᾧ ἦν ὁ θεός, ὃς
Ἔθετο, καθώς φησιν ὁ προφήτης, σκότος ἀποκρυφὴν αὐτοῦ κύκλῳ αὐτοῦ.
ἐν ᾧ καταστᾶσα τότε διδάσκεται ὅτι τοσοῦτον ἀπέσχε τοῦ ἐπιβῆναι τῆς
τελειότητος ὅσον οἱ μηδὲ τὴν ἀρχὴν ἐγχειρήσαντες· ἤδη γάρ φησιν ὡς
τῶν τελείων ἀξιωθεῖσα καθάπερ ἐπὶ κοίτης τινὸς τῆς τῶν ἐγνωσμένων
20   καταλήψεως ἐμαυτὴν ἀναπαύουσα ὅτε τῶν ἀοράτων ἐντὸς ἐγενόμην
καταλιποῦσα τὰ αἰσθητήρια, ὅτε περιεσχέθην τῇ θείᾳ νυκτὶ τὸν ἐν τῷ γνόφῳ
κεκρυμμένον ἀναζητοῦσα, τότε τὴν μὲν ἀγάπην πρὸς τὸν ποθούμενον εἶχον,
αὐτὸ δὲ τὸ ἀγαπώμενον διέπτη τῶν λογισμῶν τὴν λαβήν· ἐζήτουν γὰρ αὐτὸν
ἐπὶ τὴν κοίτην μου ἐν ταῖς νυξίν, ὥστε γνῶναι τίς ἡ οὐσία, πόθεν ἄρχεται, εἰς
25   τί καταλήγει, ἐν τίνι τὸ εἶναι ἔχει· ἀλλ᾽ οὐχ εὗρον αὐτόν. ἐκάλουν αὐτὸν ἐξ
ὀνόματος ὡς ἦν μοι δυνατὸν ἐξευρεῖν ἐπὶ τοῦ ἀκατονομάστου ὀνόματα, ἀλλ᾽
οὐκ ἦν ὀνόματος ἔμφασις ἡ καθικνουμένη τοῦ ζητουμένου.

upward by searching into what lies beyond it is so constituted that every fulfillment of knowledge that human nature can attain becomes the starting point of desire for things yet more exalted.

Now consider in detail, if you will, the speech that offers itself for our study and discernment—but only after you have first understood this, that what the text describes at the bodily level is a bridal chamber and the business of a marriage, and these provide the matter for our inquiry. Philosophical treatment of these matters transposes the surface meaning of the thoughts into the key of the pure and the immaterial and sets forth the teachings of the faith, using the enigmas provided by the events narrated in order to arrive at a clear grasp of what is revealed.

Since, then, the text represents the soul as a Bride and designates him whom she loves with her entire "heart and soul ... and strength" (Mark 12:30) as a Bridegroom, it is logical that she | —who in her own mind has attained the highest of her hopes and has already, in her own judgment, been united with the One she desires—should call her more perfect participation in the Good a *bed* and should term the time of her going to bed *night*. Now the word *night* points to contemplation of things unseen, just like Moses, who entered into the darkness in which God was[7] (cf. Exod 20:21)—God who, as the prophet says, "Made darkness his hiding place round about him" (Ps 17:2). And once the soul was there, she learned that she was as far from arriving at perfection as those who had not yet made a beginning. For she says: "Even when, as one judged worthy of perfection, I am taking my rest as upon some *bed* of the comprehension of what I have known;[8] when I have entered into the Invisible, with the world of sense left behind me; when, surrounded by the divine night, I am seeking what is hidden in the darkness—that is when I have indeed laid hold on love for the one I desire, but the object of my love has flown from the net of my thoughts. For I was seeking him *upon my bed by night,* so as to know what his essence is, whence he has his beginning, where he reaches his end, by what means he has existence. But I did not find him. I was calling him by name, as far as I was able to discover names for the Nameless, but there was no name whose sense could attain the one I was seeking."

---

7. This is a favorite theme of Gregory's. For a similar passage, see below, homily 12, pp. 354–55 (Jaeger); cf. *Vit. Mos.* 2.162ff.

8. This understanding of the Bride's "bed" is peculiar to Nyssen. Nilus of Ancyra, for example, wants it to represent something like "taking one's ease" (and so naturally concludes that the Bride must leave her bed before she can find the One she desires; see Procopius of Gaza, *Cat. Cant.*; PG 87:1617C–D), while Theodoret ignores the bed and focuses attention on the absence of the Bridegroom as an illustration of God's "training ... souls with trials" (PG 81:113A).

| πῶς γὰρ ἂν ὁ ὑπὲρ πᾶν ὄνομα ὢν διὰ τῆς ὀνομαστικῆς κλήσεως   182
ἐξευρεθείη; οὗ χάριν φησὶν ὅτι Ἐκάλεσα αὐτὸν καὶ οὐχ ὑπήκουσέ μου.
τότε ἔγνων ὅτι τῆς μεγαλοπρεπείας, τῆς δόξης, τῆς ἁγιωσύνης αὐτοῦ οὐκ ἔστι
πέρας. διὸ πάλιν ἀνίστησιν ἑαυτὴν καὶ περιπολεῖ τῇ διανοίᾳ τὴν νοητήν τε
5 καὶ ὑπερκόσμιον φύσιν, ἣν πόλιν κατονομάζει, ἐν ᾗ αἱ ἀρχαί τε καὶ κυριότητες
καὶ οἱ ταῖς ἐξουσίαις ἀποτεταγμένοι θρόνοι ἥ τε τῶν ἐπουρανίων πανήγυρις,
ἣν ἀγορὰν ὀνομάζει, καὶ τὸ ἀπερίληπτον ἀριθμῷ πλῆθος, ὃ τῷ τῆς πλατείας
διασημαίνει ὀνόματι, εἰ ἄρα ἐν τούτοις εὑρεθείη τὸ ἀγαπώμενον. ἡ μὲν οὖν
περιῄει διερευνωμένη πᾶσαν ἀγγελικὴν διακόσμησιν καὶ ὡς οὐκ εἶδεν ἐν τοῖς
10 εὑρεθεῖσιν ἀγαθοῖς τὸ ζητούμενον τοῦτο καθ᾽ ἑαυτὴν ἐλογίσατο· ἆρα κἂν
ἐκείνοις ληπτόν ἐστι τὸ παρ᾽ ἐμοῦ ἀγαπώμενον; καί φησι πρὸς αὐτούς· μὴ κἂν
ὑμεῖς ὃν ἠγάπησεν ἡ ψυχή μου εἴδετε; σιωπησάντων δὲ πρὸς τὴν τοιαύτην
ἐρώτησιν καὶ διὰ τῆς σιωπῆς ἐνδειξαμένων τὸ κἀκείνοις ἄληπτον εἶναι τὸ
παρ᾽ αὐτῆς ζητούμενον, ὡς διεξῆλθε τῇ πολυπραγμοσύνῃ τῆς διανοίας πᾶσαν
15 ἐκείνην τὴν ὑπερκόσμιον πόλιν καὶ οὐδὲ ἐν τοῖς νοητοῖς τε καὶ | ἀσωμάτοις   183
εἶδεν οἷον ἐπόθησεν, τότε καταλιποῦσα πᾶν τὸ εὑρισκόμενον οὕτως
ἐγνώρισε τὸ ζητούμενον, τὸ ἐν μόνῳ τῷ μὴ καταλαμβάνεσθαι τί ἐστιν ὅτι ἔστι
γινωσκόμενον, οὗ πᾶν γνώρισμα καταληπτικὸν ἐμπόδιον τοῖς ἀναζητοῦσι
πρὸς τὴν εὕρεσιν γίνεται.
20   διὰ τοῦτό φησι Μικρὸν ὅτε παρῆλθον ἀπ᾽ αὐτῶν ἀφεῖσα πᾶσαν τὴν κτίσιν
καὶ παρελθοῦσα πᾶν τὸ ἐν τῇ κτίσει νοούμενον καὶ πᾶσαν καταληπτικὴν
ἔφοδον καταλιποῦσα, τῇ πίστει εὗρον τὸν ἀγαπώμενον καὶ οὐκέτι μεθήσω
τῇ τῆς πίστεως λαβῇ τοῦ εὑρεθέντος ἀντεχομένη, ἕως ἂν ἐντὸς γένηται τοῦ
ἐμοῦ ταμείου. καρδία δὲ πάντως τὸ ταμεῖόν ἐστιν, ἣ τότε γίνεται δεκτικὴ τῆς
25 θείας αὐτοῦ ἐνοικήσεως, ὅταν ἐπανέλθῃ πρὸς τὴν κατάστασιν ἐκείνην, ἐν ᾗ

| How, after all, could the One who is above every name be discovered by calling out a name for him? That is why she says *I called him, but he gave no answer.* At that point she knew that there is no limit of his splendor, his glory, and his holiness. Hence she bestirs herself again and in her understanding moves about the intelligible and supracosmic nature[9] (which she calls *the city*), in which are the Rulers and Lordships and the Thrones set over the Powers and the assembly of the heavenly beings (which she calls *the square*) as well as the unnumbered multitude (which she denotes by the word *street*)—to see if she can find the Beloved among these. So she went about, searching every angelic order; and since she did not see the one she sought among the good beings she found, she mused thus within herself: "May it be that the one I love is known to them?" And she said to them, *Have you not seen the one whom my soul loves?* But they fell silent in the face of this inquiry and by their silence showed that the One she sought was imperceptible even to them. As, then, she went, in the persistent curiosity of her understanding, through the whole of that supracosmic city and even among intelligible and | incorporeal beings did not see the object of her desire—at that point she left behind everything she had already found and in this way recognized the object of her search, whose existence is known only in incomprehension of what it is, in whose case every conceptual trait is an obstacle to its discovery for those who seek it.[10]

So she says, "*No sooner had I passed them by,* having departed from the whole created order and passed by everything in the creation that is intelligible and left behind every conceptual approach, than I found the Beloved by faith,[11] and holding on by faith's grasp to the one I have found, I will not let go until he is within my *chamber*." Now the *chamber* is surely the heart, which at that moment became receptive of his divine indwelling—at the moment, that

---

9. Gregory here identifies the realm of the intelligible (the "Forms" of Platonist tradition) with the angelic orders. This equation makes perfect sense in the light of the tendency in later Platonism to fuse intelligence(s) and intelligible(s). Gregory's "city" is a rough equivalent of Plotinus's realm of Intellect—with this crucial difference, that it is fitted into the Creator/creature dichotomy, and the Platonist order of Being is—partially (?)—located in the category of the creaturely. See above, nn. 1–3.

10. God, then, like Plotinus's One, can scarcely be included in the class of "intelligible and incorporeal beings," and strictly speaking Gregory must, like Plotinus, deny that God, whose being (τὶ ἐστίν) cannot be conceptually grasped, can in the usual Platonist sense be said to *be*.

11. For the same idea, see Gregory, *Vit. Mos.* 2.163 (GNO 7.1:87); *Eun.* 2(12B).88–93 (GNO 1:252ff.). It is interesting that Cyril of Alexandria (see Procopius of Gaza, *Cat. Cant.*; PG 87:1620C) likens the Bride in this passage to "the women who … went to the tomb of Jesus … but did not find him" and the "guards" who went about the city to the angels that appeared at the tomb. Thus it is not until the angels are left behind that the risen Christ is found.

τὸ κατ᾽ ἀρχὰς ἦν ὅτε ἐπλάσθη ὑπὸ τῆς συλλαβούσης. μητέρα δὲ πάντως τὴν
πρώτην τῆς συστάσεως ἡμῶν αἰτίαν νοῶν τις οὐχ ἁμαρτήσεται.

Καιρὸς δ᾽ ἂν εἴη πάλιν ἐπ᾽ αὐτῆς τῆς λέξεως παραθέσθαι τὰς θείας
φωνάς, ὥστε τοῖς θεωρηθεῖσιν ἐφαρμοσθῆναι τὰ ῥήματα· Ἐπὶ κοίτην μου
5   ἐν νυξὶν ἐζήτησα ὃν ἠγάπησεν | ἡ ψυχή μου, ἐζήτησα αὐτὸν καὶ οὐχ εὗρον   184
αὐτόν, ἐκάλεσα αὐτὸν καὶ οὐχ ὑπήκουσέ μου. ἀναστήσομαι δὴ καὶ κυκλώσω
ἐν τῇ πόλει ἐν ταῖς ἀγοραῖς καὶ ἐν ταῖς πλατείαις καὶ ζητήσω ὃν ἠγάπησεν
ἡ ψυχή μου. ἐζήτησα αὐτὸν καὶ οὐχ εὗρον αὐτόν. εὕροσάν με οἱ τηροῦντες
οἱ κυκλοῦντες ἐν τῇ πόλει. μὴ ὃν ἠγάπησεν ἡ ψυχή μου εἴδετε; ὡς μικρὸν
10 ὅτε παρῆλθον ἀπ᾽ αὐτῶν, ἕως οὗ εὗρον ὃν ἠγάπησεν ἡ ψυχή μου. ἐκράτησα
αὐτὸν καὶ οὐκ ἀφῆκα αὐτόν, ἕως οὗ εἰσήγαγον αὐτὸν εἰς οἶκον μητρός μου
καὶ εἰς ταμιεῖον τῆς συλλαβούσης με.

Ἐπὶ τούτοις πάλιν ὑπὸ φιλανθρωπίας καὶ ταῖς θυγατράσιν Ἰερουσαλὴμ
διαλέγεται, ἃς ἐν τοῖς ἔμπροσθεν συγκρίσει τοῦ τῆς νύμφης κάλλους τοῦ
15 παρεικασθέντος τῷ κρίνῳ ἀκάνθας ὁ λόγος ὠνόμασε, καὶ διὰ τοῦ ὅρκου τῶν
ἐν τῷ κόσμῳ δυνάμεων πρὸς τὸ ἴσον τῆς ἀγάπης διανίστησι μέτρον, ὥστε
τὸ θέλημα τοῦ νυμφίου καὶ ἐπ᾽ αὐτῶν ἐνεργὸν γενέσθαι. εἴρηται δὲ ἐν τοῖς
φθάσασι τίς τε ὁ κόσμος, ἐν ᾧ αἱ ἰσχύες καὶ αἱ δυνάμεις, καὶ τί τὸ θέλημα
τοῦ ἐξ ὅλης καρδίας τε καὶ ψυχῆς ἀγαπωμένου, ὡς μὴ χρείαν εἶναι πάλιν διὰ
20 τῶν | αὐτῶν τὸν λόγον μηκύνεσθαι τῆς προθεωρηθείσης ἡμῖν ἐν τοῖς ῥήμασι   185
διανοίας καὶ τὸ ἐν τῷ τόπῳ τούτῳ νοούμενον ἱκανῶς φανερούσης.

ἀλλὰ πρὸς τὸ ἐφεξῆς τῷ λόγῳ προΐωμεν, εἴ πως γένοιτο δυνατὸν καὶ ἡμῖν
συναναβῆναι τῇ τελείᾳ περιστερᾷ πρὸς τὸ ὕψος ἀνιπταμένῃ καὶ ἀκοῦσαι τῆς
τῶν φίλων τοῦ νυμφίου φωνῆς ἐν θαύματι ποιουμένων τὴν ἀνάβασιν αὐτῆς
25 τὴν ἐκ τῆς ἐρήμου, ὃ δὴ καὶ μᾶλλον πλεονάζει τοῖς θεαταῖς τὴν ἔκπληξιν, εἰ
τοιαύτην ἡ ἔρημος ἀναδίδωσι, ὡς μιμεῖσθαι δένδρων κάλλος τῶν ἐν τῇ ἐρήμῳ
διὰ τὸν ἀτμὸν τοῦ θυμιάματος γεωργουμένων.

τὰ δὲ θυμιάματα σμύρνα καὶ λίβανος ἦν. τῷ δὲ ἀπὸ τούτων ἀτμῷ καὶ
κονιορτός τις διὰ τῶν λεπτοποιηθέντων ἀρωμάτων συνηγείρετό τε καὶ
30 συνανέβαινεν, ὡς ἀντὶ κόνεως εἶναι τῆς ἀνακεκραμένης πρὸς τὸν ἀέρα

is, when it returned to that condition in which it was at the beginning when it was formed by the *mother* who gave it birth. We shall not go wrong to conceive the *mother* as the First Cause of our constitution.[12]

But maybe now it is time once more to set the divine utterances alongside the text itself, so as to conform the words to what the mind has discerned. *Upon my bed by night I sought him whom | my soul loves, I sought him and did not find him, I called him, and he did not hearken to me. I will arise and go about in the city, in the markets and in the streets, and I will seek him whom my soul loves. I sought him but did not find him. The watchmen making their rounds in the city found me. "Have you not seen the one whom my soul loves?" It was but a moment after I parted from them that I found him whom my soul loves. I seized him and would not let him go until I had brought him into my mother's house, and into the chamber of her who bore me.*

Then once again, out of goodwill, she addresses the *daughters of Jerusalem*—those whom, in the preceding passage, the Word called *thorns* by comparison with the beauty of the Bride, which was likened to that of a lily, and by an oath that invokes the powers within the cosmos she arouses them to an equal measure of love, so that the will of the Bridegroom may become operative in their case too. It has already been said both what that cosmos is in which the Virtues and Powers are, and what is the will of the One who is loved with the whole heart and soul,[13] and therefore there is no need to prolong our speech on the | same subject, since the meaning that we have already discovered in the words sufficiently illuminates the sense of this passage too.

But let us move on to the next verse. Maybe it will be possible for us too to *come up* in the company of the perfect dove as she wings her way toward the heights and to hear the voice of the Bridegroom's friends as they marvel at her ascent out of *the wilderness*; and it increases the astonishment of the witnesses still more, when the wilderness yields up one who imitates the beauty of trees—trees raised and tended in the wilderness by the vapor of incense.

Now the incense consists of *myrrh and frankincense*. Together with the vapor stemming from these, a powder of aromatic herbs ground fine was also stirred up, and it mounted up, so that instead of dust that had been mixed

---

12. For an expansion and defense of this idea, see below, homily 7, pp. 212–13 (Jaeger). The commentary attributed to Cassiodorus, whose interpretation of these words may reflect earlier tradition, takes "mother" to refer to "the synagogue," which "the church gathered out of the nations" calls "my spiritual mother" (PL 70:1068C).

13. See above, homily 4, pp. 132–36 (Jaeger).

τὴν λεπτομερῆ τῶν ἀρωμάτων διάχυσιν, δι' ἧς ὄρθιος ὁ κονιορτὸς ἦν καὶ μετέωρος.

ἔχει δὲ οὕτως ἡ λέξις· Τίς αὕτη ἡ ἀναβαίνουσα ἐκ τῆς ἐρήμου ὡς στελέχη καπνοῦ τεθυμιαμένη σμύρνα καὶ λίβανος ἀπὸ πάντων κονιορτῶν μυρεψοῦ;
5　εἴ τις ἀκριβῶς ἐπιστήσειε τοῖς εἰρημένοις τὸν νοῦν, εὑρήσει τοῦ προκατανοηθέντος ἡμῖν δόγματος τὴν ἀλήθειαν· ὥσπερ γὰρ ἐν ταῖς πομπαῖς τῶν θεάτρων, κἂν οἱ αὐτοὶ ὦσιν οἱ τὴν προτεθεῖσαν αὐτοῖς ἱστορίαν ὑποκρινό|μενοι, ὅμως ἕτεροι ἐξ ἑτέρων νομίζονται φαίνεσθαι οἱ τῇ διαφορᾷ　186
τῶν προσωπείων τὸ εἶδος τὸ περὶ αὐτοὺς ἐναμείβοντες καὶ ὁ νῦν δοῦλος
10　ἢ ἰδιώτης φαινόμενος μετ' ὀλίγον ἀριστεύς τε καὶ στρατιώτης ὁρᾶται καὶ πάλιν καταλιπὼν τὸ ὑποχείριον σχῆμα στρατηγικὸν εἶδος ἀναλαμβάνει ἢ καὶ βασιλέως μορφὴν ὑποδύεται, οὕτω καὶ ἐν ταῖς κατὰ τὴν ἀρετὴν προκοπαῖς οὐ πάντοτε τῷ αὐτῷ παραμένουσι χαρακτῆρι οἱ ἀπὸ δόξης εἰς δόξαν διὰ τῆς τῶν ὑψηλοτέρων ἐπιθυμίας μεταμορφούμενοι, ἀλλὰ πρὸς λόγον τῆς
15　ἀεὶ κατορθωθείσης ἑκάστῳ διὰ τῶν ἀγαθῶν τελειότητος ἴδιός τις τῷ βίῳ χαρακτὴρ ἐπιλάμπει ἄλλος ἐξ ἄλλου γινόμενός τε καὶ φαινόμενος διὰ τῆς τῶν ἀγαθῶν ἐπαυξήσεως.

διό μοι δοκοῦσι ξενίζεσθαι πρὸς τὸ φαινόμενον οἱ φίλοι τοῦ νυμφίου οἱ πρότερον μὲν αὐτὴν ἐγνωκότες καλὴν ἀλλ' ὡς ἐν γυναιξὶ καλήν, μετὰ
20　ταῦτα δὲ δι' ὁμοιότητος χρυσίου μετὰ στιγμάτων ἀργυρίου τὸ κάλλος αὐτῆς ὡραΐζοντες. νυνὶ δὲ μηδὲν τῶν προλαβόντων σημείων περὶ αὐτὴν καθορῶντες ἀλλ' ἀπὸ τῶν ὑψηλοτέρων χαρακτηρίζοντες θαυμάζουσιν οὐ μόνον τὴν ἄνοδον ἀλλὰ καὶ ὅθεν ἀνέδραμεν· τοῦτο γάρ ἐστιν ὃ τὴν ἐπίτασιν ποιεῖ τῆς ἐκπλήξεως· μία ὁρᾶται ἡ ἀναβαίνουσα, καὶ ἄλσει δένδρων τὸ φαινόμενον
25　παραβάλλεται· στελέχη γὰρ | ὁρᾶσθαι νομίζεται εἰς ὕψος ἀνατρέχοντα καὶ　187
αὐξανόμενα, τὸ δὲ ὑποτρέφον τὰ στελέχη ταῦτα οὐ πίων τίς ἐστι γῆ καὶ κατάρρυτος, ἀλλ' αὐχμηρὰ καὶ διψώδης καὶ ἔρημος. τίνι τοίνυν ἐνριζοῦται τὰ στελέχη ταῦτα καὶ πόθεν αὔξεται; ῥίζα μὲν αὐτοῖς ἡ τῶν ἀρωμάτων κόνις ἐστίν, ἀρδεία δὲ ὁ ἐκ τῶν θυμιαμάτων ἀτμὸς ἐπιδροσίζων διὰ τῆς εὐωδίας
30　τοῦτο τὸ ἄλσος.

ὅσον ἔπαινον περιέχει τῆς ἐπὶ τοῖς τοιούτοις μαρτυρηθείσης ὁ λόγος. τό τε γὰρ ἀλλήλους διερωτᾶν περὶ τῆς ὀφθείσης ὡς ἐν ἄλλῳ δεικνυμένης τῷ εἴδει καὶ οὐ κατὰ τὴν προτέραν μορφὴν ἐγκώμιόν ἐστι τῆς κατ' ἀρετὴν προκοπῆς τελεώτατον πολλὴν αὐτῇ μαρτυροῦν τὴν πρὸς τὸ κρεῖττον παραλλαγὴν καὶ
35　μετάστασιν· ξενιζομένων γάρ ἐστιν ἡ φωνὴ παρὰ τὸ σύνηθες εἶδος ἐν θαύματι ποιουμένων τὴν ἐπανθοῦσαν μορφὴν ὅτι· αὕτη ἡ ἀναβαίνουσα ἐκ τῆς ἐρήμου

into the air, there was an array of tiny bits of these herbs, and so the powder stood high and straight up in the air.

This is how the text goes: *Who is this coming up from the wilderness like tree trunks of smoke, myrrh being burnt and frankincense, from all the powders of the perfumer?*

Anyone who looks closely into the meaning of these words will discover the truth of the fundamental teaching that we thought through earlier. For consider an example: in theatrical performances, even though it is the same actors who take the parts assigned them in the drama, | nevertheless different persons seem to appear in different instances as the actors alter their look by changing their masks, and one who appears now as a slave or an ordinary citizen is shortly seen as a valorous man and a soldier, and again, putting off the look of a subject, takes on the appearance of one fitted for command or even assumes the aspect of a king. In the same way, where progress in virtue is concerned, those who are being transformed from glory to glory (cf. 2 Cor 3:18) because of their desire for higher things do not always persist in the very same character. Rather, in proportion to the perfection that each has attained for the moment through good things, some special quality illumines his manner of life, one such appearing and succeeding to another by reason of his increase in good things.

That, it seems to me, is why the friends of the Bridegroom are astonished at what appears to their eyes. First they knew her as beautiful—but as beautiful *among women*. Then they glorified her beauty on account of its similarity to gold stippled with silver. Now, however, they discern none of the signs that they had previously seen in her but mark her out by reference to more exalted things. They marvel not only at her ascent but also at the place from which she has climbed. For this is what brings about their intense amazement. One person is seen coming upwards, and yet what shows itself is likened to a grove of trees. For they conclude that they are | seeing *tree trunks* that shoot up on high and grow in size, but what nourishes these trunks is not some rich, well-watered soil but a soil that is dry and thirsty and desolate. In what, then, are these trunks rooted, and what do they grow out of? Their root is the powder of the spices, and what waters them is the vapor of fragrances that bedews this grove with its sweet smell.

How splendid, then, is the praise that this passage contains for the one to whom such witness is borne! For they ask one another about the one who is manifested to them as if she is being shown to them in another form and not according to her former appearance; and this is praise of her progress in virtue—praise that perfectly attests the extent of her change and alteration for the better. For their words are the words of people who are astonished, amazed at the Bride's blooming appearance as compared with her usual look.

μέλαινα τὸ πρότερον ἡμῖν ἑωρᾶτο. πῶς τὴν σκοτεινὴν μορφὴν ἀπεκλύσατο;
πῶς αὐτῇ χιονῶδες ἐπαστράπτει τὸ κάλλος;
      ἡ ἔρημός ἐστιν ὡς ἔοικεν αἰτία τούτων, ἡ καθάπερ τι ἔρνος ἀναδραμεῖν
αὐτὴν εἰς ὕψος ποιήσασα καὶ πρὸς τὸ τοιοῦτον | μεταβάλλουσα κάλλος·   188
5   οὐ γὰρ ἐξ αὐτομάτου τινὸς συντυχίας οὐδὲ κατ᾽ ἄκριτόν τινα ἀποκλήρωσιν
γέγονεν αὐτῇ ἡ πρὸς τὸ ὕψος ἀναδρομή, ἀλλ᾽ ἐξ οἰκείων πόνων δι᾽ ἐγκρατείας
τε καὶ ἐπιμελείας τὸ κάλλος ἐκτήσατο. οὕτω ποτὲ καὶ ἡ τοῦ προφήτου ψυχὴ
διψώδης ἐγένετο τῆς θείας πηγῆς, ἐπειδὴ αὐτῷ ἡ σὰρξ ἔρημός τε καὶ ἄβατος
καὶ ἄνυδρος γενομένη τὸ θεῖον δίψος ἐν ἑαυτῇ παρεδέξατο.
10   τὸ τοίνυν ἐκ τῆς ἐρήμου ἀναβαίνειν αὐτὴν μαρτυρίαν περιέχει τοῦ διὰ
προσοχῆς τε καὶ ἐγκρατείας εἰς τοσοῦτον ὕψος ἀναδραμεῖν, ὡς καὶ τοῖς
φίλοις τοῦ νυμφίου θαῦμα γενέσθαι, οἳ διὰ πολλῶν ὑποδειγμάτων τὸ κάλλος
αὐτῆς ἑρμηνεύουσιν, ἐπειδὴ δι᾽ ἑνὸς ἅπαν περιληφθῆναι οὐχ οἷόν τε ἦν·
      πρῶτον μὲν γὰρ στελέχει τὴν ὥραν εἰκάζουσι καὶ οὐδὲ τοῦτο ἑνί, ἀλλ᾽ εἰς
15 πλῆθος δένδρων ἄγεται τῶν ἐν αὐτῇ θαυμάτων ἡ εἰκασία, ὡς ἂν τὸ πολυειδὲς
καὶ ποικίλον τῶν ἀρετῶν τῇ ὑπογραφῇ τοῦ ἄλσους διαδεικνύοιτο· εἶτα
καπνὸς ἐκ θυμιαμάτων εἰς τὴν εἰκόνα τοῦ κάλλους παραλαμβάνεται καὶ οὐδὲ
οὗτος ἁπλοῦς ἀλλὰ σμύρνης καὶ λιβάνου συγκεκραμένων, ὡς μίαν ἐξ ἀμφοῖν
γενέσθαι τῶν ἀτμῶν τὴν χάριν, δι᾽ ὧν τὸ τῆς νύμφης | ὑπογράφεται κάλλος·   189
20 ἄλλος ἔπαινος αὐτῆς ἡ τῶν ἀρωμάτων τούτων γίνεται μίξις· ἡ σμύρνα πρὸς
τὸν ἐνταφιασμὸν τῶν σωμάτων ἐπιτηδείως ἔχει, ὁ δὲ λίβανος κατά τινα λόγον
ἀφιέρωται τῇ τοῦ θείου τιμῇ. ὁ τοίνυν ἑαυτὸν μέλλων ἀνατιθέναι τῇ τοῦ

"This one who is coming up out of the wilderness is she whom we saw earlier as *dark*. How was her darkness cleansed? How does a snow-white beauty lighten upon her?"

It seems that *the wilderness* is the cause of this![14] It makes her shoot up on high like a young tree[15] and | makes her over into a beauty of this sort. It is not by some spontaneous coincidence nor by blind chance that this upward ascent becomes hers. No, the beauty becomes hers through her own labors in the way of self-control and diligence. Thus did the soul of the prophet once become thirsty for the divine spring, because his flesh, being dry and desolate and unwatered, took the divine thirst into itself (cf. Ps 62:2).

Thus the Bride's ascent out of the wilderness shows that she mounts up to such a height by care and self-control[16] and so becomes a source of wonder to the friends of the Bridegroom. They in turn convey her beauty by the use of many examples and illustrations, for it was not possible for the whole scope of it to be grasped in a single image.

First of all they liken her splendor to a *tree trunk*—and not just to one, but the wonders within her are likened to a multitude of trees, so that by the description of the grove the many types and varieties of her virtues may be indicated. Then a smoke cloud of fragrances is employed to provide an image of her beauty, nor is this portrayed as uniform but as mingled together out of myrrh and frankincense, so that a single aroma is produced from a pair of scents, and by them the beauty of the Bride | is portrayed. The mixture of these fragrances becomes yet another way of praising her: myrrh is appropriate for the preparation of bodies for burial, while frankincense is naturally set apart for the honoring of the Divine.[17] Hence the person who intends to

---

14. The wilderness, then, signifies the rigors of the ascetic life. The commentary attributed to Cassiodorus has a less complicated way of explaining "wilderness" here. The author takes his cue from the story of the exodus and sees the wilderness of the Song as representing the "desert" of the nations, through which the church must make its way in order to be nourished by heavenly manna and to enter its land of promise.

15. In the *apparatus criticus* here Langerbeck 1960 adduces Homer, *Il.* 18.56–57: "He shot up like a young tree, / and I nurtured him, like a tree grown in the pride of the orchard" (trans. Lattimore 1962).

16. Nilus of Ancyra (in Procopius, *Cat. Cant.*; PG 87:1624Af.) asserts that the ascent of the Bride from the desert as a pillar of smoke generated by the burning of myrrh and frankincense "signifies withdrawal [ἀναχώρησις] from earthly things." He compares the soul that thus withdraws with a column of smoke that rises from the ground, and of course the mention of myrrh evokes the thought of mortification of the body. This line of interpretation is closely related to Nyssen's (who in fact merely decorates it somewhat fancifully) and may reflect the themes of Origen's exegesis of the passage.

17. See below, homily 7, p. 243 (Jaeger); homily 12, pp. 343ff. (Jaeger). See n. 16 above for the same interpretation as presented by Nilus of Ancyra.

θεοῦ θεραπείᾳ οὐκ ἄλλως ἔσται λίβανος τῷ θεῷ θυμιώμενος, εἰ μὴ πρότερον
σμύρνα γένοιτο, τουτέστιν εἰ μὴ τὰ ἐπὶ τῆς γῆς ἑαυτοῦ μέλη νεκρώσειε
συνταφεὶς τῷ ὑπὲρ ἡμῶν ἀναδεξαμένῳ τὸν θάνατον καὶ τὴν σμύρναν ἐκείνην
τὴν εἰς τὸν ἐνταφιασμὸν τοῦ κυρίου παραληφθεῖσαν τῇ σαρκὶ τῇ ἰδίᾳ διὰ τοῦ
5   νεκρῶσαι τὰ μέλη καταδεξάμενος. ὧν γενομένων πᾶν εἶδος τῶν κατ' ἀρετὴν
ἀρωμάτων ἐν τῷ κύκλῳ τοῦ βίου καθάπερ ἐν θυΐᾳ τινὶ λεπτοποιηθέντων τὸν
ἡδὺν ἐκεῖνον κονιορτὸν ἀπεργάζεται, ὃν ὁ ἀναλαβὼν ἐν τῷ ἄσθματι εὔπνους
γίνεται τοῦ μεμυρισμένου πνεύματος πλήρης γενόμενος.

Μετὰ δὲ τὴν ἐπὶ τῷ κάλλει μαρτυρίαν οἱ φίλοι τοῦ νυμφίου καὶ
10   παρασκευασταὶ τοῦ ἁγνοῦ θαλάμου καὶ τῆς καθαρᾶς | νύμφης προμνήστορες   190
ὑποδεικνύουσιν αὐτῇ τῆς βασιλικῆς κλίνης τὸ κάλλος, ὡς ἂν μᾶλλον εἰς
ἐπιθυμίαν τὴν νύμφην ἀγάγοιεν τῆς θείας τε καὶ ἀχράντου μετ' αὐτοῦ
συμβιώσεως. ἡ δὲ ὑπογραφὴ τῆς τοῦ βασιλέως κλίνης αὕτη ἐστίν, ἣν τῷ
δεικτικῷ λόγῳ ὑπ' ὄψιν ἄγουσιν αὐτῇ δι' ὧν διεξέρχονται· λέγουσι γάρ· Ἰδοὺ
15   ἡ κλίνη τοῦ Σαλωμών, ἑξήκοντα δυνατοὶ κύκλῳ αὐτῆς ἀπὸ δυνατῶν Ἰσραήλ,
πάντες κατέχοντες ῥομφαίαν, δεδιδαγμένοι πόλεμον· ἀνὴρ ῥομφαία αὐτοῦ
ἐπὶ τὸν μηρὸν αὐτοῦ ἀπὸ θάμβους ἐν νυξίν.

ὅτι μὲν οὖν οὐκ ἐκ τῆς ἱστορίας ὁ περὶ τῆς κλίνης λόγος ἐστί, παντὶ
δῆλον ἂν γένοιτο διὰ τῶν σωματικῶς περὶ τοῦ Σολομῶνος ἱστορηθέντων, οὗ
20   καὶ τὰ βασίλεια καὶ τὴν τράπεζαν καὶ τὴν λοιπὴν ἐν τῇ βασιλείᾳ διαγωγὴν
μετὰ πάσης ἀκριβείας ὁ λόγος ὑπέγραψεν. καινὸν δέ τι καὶ παρηλλαγμένον
εἶπε περὶ τῆς κλίνης οὐδέν, ὡς πᾶσαν ἀνάγκην εἶναι μὴ παραμεῖναι τῷ
γράμματι τὴν ἐξήγησιν, ἀλλὰ διά τινος ἐπιμελεστέρας κατανοήσεως
μεταλαβεῖν τὸν λόγον εἰς πνευματικὴν θεωρίαν τῆς ὑλικῆς ἐμφάσεως τὸν
25   νοῦν ἀποστήσαντας.

τίς γὰρ ἂν ἐξ ὁπλιτῶν ἑξήκοντα καλλωπισμὸς γένοιτο κλίνης νυμφικῆς,
οἷς μάθημα μὲν τὰ φοβερὰ τοῦ πολέμου, κόσμος δὲ ἡ ῥομφαία | προβεβλημένη   191
τοῦ σώματος, θάμβος δὲ περὶ αὐτοὺς νυκτερινόν; (τὴν γὰρ φοβερὰν ἔκπληξιν
τὴν ἐκ δειμάτων τινῶν νυκτερινῶν γινομένην διὰ τῆς τοῦ θάμβους λέξεως
30   ὁ λόγος ἐνδείκνυται, ἣν τοῖς ὁπλίταις τούτοις προσεῖναι λέγει.) οὐκοῦν
παντὶ τρόπῳ ζητητέον ἂν εἴη διάνοιάν τινα διὰ τῶν ῥητῶν τούτων τοῖς
προτεθεωρημένοις ἀκόλουθον.

τίς οὖν ἐστιν ἡ διάνοια; ἔοικε τὸ θεῖον κάλλος ἐν τῷ φοβερῷ τὸ ἐράσμιον
ἔχειν ἀπὸ τῶν ἐναντίων τῷ σωματικῷ κάλλει δεικνύμενον· ἐνταῦθα μὲν γὰρ
35   ἑλκτικὸν εἰς ἐπιθυμίαν ἐστὶ τὸ προσηνὲς τῇ ὄψει καὶ μειλίχιον καὶ πάσης
φοβερᾶς τε καὶ θυμώδους διαθέσεως κεχωρισμένον, τὸ δὲ ἀκήρατον κάλλος

dedicate himself to the worship of God will not be frankincense burned for God unless he has first become myrrh—that is, unless he mortifies his earthly members, having been buried together with the one who submitted to death on our behalf and having received in his own flesh, through mortification of its members, that myrrh which was used to prepare the Lord for burial. When these things have come to pass, every species of the fragrances that belong to virtue[18]—once they have been ground fine in the bowl of life as in some mortar—produces that sweet cloud of dust, and he who inhales it becomes sweet-smelling because he has become full of the fragrant Spirit.

After they have attested the Bride's beauty, the friends of the Bridegroom and furnishers of the chaste bridal chamber and intermediaries with the pure | Bride point out to her the beauty of the royal bed, so as to induce the Bride to desire a divine and unspotted cohabitation with Bridegroom. The description given of the King's bed is this—and they bring it before her eyes in ostensive language by means of the things they enumerate: *Behold Solomon's bed: sixty mighty men surround it, out of the mighty men of Israel. All of them bear a sword, being instructed in war; each man has his sword on his thigh because of fear by night.*

Now what is said about the "litter" does not derive from any history, and this ought to be evident to everyone from the data[19] that have been recorded about Solomon. With perfect accuracy the scriptural text described his palace and his table and the rest of his way of life in the palace. But concerning his bed it said nothing novel or special, and hence there is compelling reason why in this case interpretation should not stick with the letter but, by a more deliberate and laborious way of understanding, transpose what is said to the level of spiritual comprehension, after distancing the mind from the literal sense.

For what ornamentation can be supplied for a bridal bed by sixty hoplites, whose study is the terror of battle, whose finery is a sword | held before the body, whose terror is that which comes by night? (By the term *fear,* after all, the text indicates the fearful consternation aroused by certain nocturnal terrors, and this is what it attributes to these hoplites.) So we ought by all means to look for a sense in these expressions that is consonant with our earlier interpretations.

What sense is that, then? It seems that the divine beauty evokes love because it is fearsome; it reveals itself as coming from elsewhere than any corporeal beauty. For here it is what is pleasant to the eye and gentle and set apart from any fierce or fearsome disposition that induces passionate desire

---

18. Cf. Cassiodorus (PL 70:1069D): "congerie virtutum."
19. Literally, "what has been recorded corporeally [σωματικῶς]."

ἐκεῖνο ἡ φοβερά τε καὶ κατάπληκτος ἀνδρεία ἐστίν. ἐπειδὴ γὰρ ἡ ἐμπαθὴς
καὶ ῥυπῶσα τῶν σωμάτων ἐπιθυμία τοῖς τῆς σαρκὸς μέλεσιν ἐγκαθημένη
καθάπερ τι σύνταγμα ληστρικὸν ἐνεδρεύει τὸν νοῦν καὶ αἰχμάλωτον ἄγει
πολλάκις πρὸς τὸ ἑαυτῆς βούλημα συναρπάσασα, ἐχθρὸν δὲ τῷ θεῷ τὸ
5   γινόμενον, καθώς φησιν ὁ ἀπόστολος ὅτι Τὸ φρόνημα τῆς σαρκὸς ἔχθρα εἰς
θεόν, διὰ τοῦτο ἀκόλουθόν ἐστιν ἐκ τῶν | ἐναντίων τῇ σωματικῇ ἐπιθυμίᾳ   192
τὸν θεῖον ἔρωτα γίνεσθαι, ὥστε εἰ ταύτης καθηγεῖται ἔκλυσις καὶ ἄνεσις καὶ
βλακώδης διάχυσις, ἐκεῖ τὴν ἐπίφοβόν τε καὶ κατάπληκτον ἀνδρείαν ὕλην
τοῦ θείου ἔρωτος γίνεσθαι· τοῦ γὰρ ἀνδρώδους θυμοῦ τὸν τῆς ἡδονῆς
10   λόχον καταπτοήσαντός τε καὶ φυγαδεύσαντος οὕτω τὸ καθαρὸν τῆς ψυχῆς
ἀναφαίνεται κάλλος μηδενὶ πάθει σωματικῆς ἐπιθυμίας καταρρυπούμενον.
      οὐκοῦν ἀναγκαίως ἡ νυμφικὴ τοῦ βασιλέως κλίνη τοῖς ὁπλίταις ἐν κύκλῳ
διαλαμβάνεται, ὧν ἡ τοῦ πολεμεῖν ἐμπειρία καὶ τὸ πρόχειρον ἔχειν ἐπὶ τοῦ
μηροῦ τὴν ῥομφαίαν θάμβος καὶ ἔκπληξιν ἐμποιεῖ τοῖς σκοτεινοῖς λογισμοῖς
15   τοῖς ἐν νυξί τε καὶ σκοτομήνῃ τοὺς εὐθεῖς τῇ καρδίᾳ λοχῶσί τε καὶ τοξεύουσιν.
ὅτι γὰρ ἀναιρετικὴ τῶν ῥυπαρῶν ἡδονῶν ἐστιν ἡ τῶν περιεστοιχισμένων τὴν
κλίνην ἐξόπλισις, δῆλον ἂν γένοιτο διὰ τῆς ὑπογραφῆς τοῦ λόγου ὅς φησιν
ὅτι Πάντες δεδιδαγμένοι πόλεμον, ἀνὴρ ῥομφαία αὐτοῦ ἐπὶ τὸν μηρὸν αὐτοῦ·
ἀληθῶς γὰρ εἰδότων ἐστίν, ὅπως ἀντιστρατεύεσθαι χρὴ τῇ σαρκί τε καὶ
20   τῷ αἵματι, τὸ τὴν ῥομφαίαν τῷ μηρῷ ἔχειν ἐφηρμοσμένην. νοεῖ δὲ πάντως
ὁ τῶν γραφικῶν αἰνιγμάτων | οὐκ ἄπειρος ἔκ τε τῆς τοῦ μηροῦ μνήμης τὸ   193
σημαινόμενον καὶ ὅτι ῥομφαία ὁ λόγος ἐστίν. ὁ τοίνυν τὸ φοβερὸν ὅπλον,
λέγω δὲ τὴν τῆς σωφροσύνης ῥομφαίαν, διεζωσμένος οὗτός ἐστι τῇ ἀφθάρτῳ
κλίνῃ ἐράσμιος, εἷς τῶν δυνατῶν Ἰσραὴλ καὶ τοῦ καταλόγου τῶν ἑξήκοντα
25   ἄξιος.
      τὸν δὲ ἀριθμὸν τοῦτον ἔχειν μέν τινα μυστικὸν λόγον οὐκ ἀμφιβάλλομεν,
ἀλλὰ μόνοις ἐκείνοις δῆλον, οἷς ἀποκαλύπτει τὰ κεκρυμμένα μυστήρια
ἡ τοῦ πνεύματος χάρις, ἡμεῖς δὲ καλῶς ἔχειν φαμὲν τῶν προχείρων τοῦ
λόγου νοημάτων ἐμφορηθέντας, καθὼς ἐπὶ τοῦ πάσχα νομοθετεῖ Μωϋσῆς
30   τῶν προφαινομένων σαρκῶν ἐμφαγόντας ἀπολυπραγμόνητον ἐᾶσαι τὸ
τοῖς ὀστέοις τῆς ἀσαφείας ἐγκεκρυμμένον. εἰ δέ τίς ἐστιν ἐπιθυμητὴς
τῶν κρυφίων μυελῶν τοῦ λόγου, ζητείτω παρὰ τοῦ τὰ κεκρυμμένα τοῖς
ἀξίοις ἀποκαλύπτοντος. ὡς δ᾽ ἂν μὴ δοκοίημεν ἀγύμναστον παρατρέχειν
τὸν λόγον μηδὲ καταρραθυμεῖν τοῦ θείου προστάγματος τοῦ ἐρευνᾶν

in us, but that unsullied Beauty is a fearsome and terrible strength. For since the passionate and filthy lust for things bodily, which resides in the fleshly members like a band of robbers,[20] lays snares for the intellect and frequently seizes it and carries it off captive to its own will, which has become hostile to God, as the apostle says: "the mind of the flesh is hostile toward God" (Rom 8:7), on this account it is appropriate for a divine love and longing[21] to originate out of | what stands in opposition to corporeal desire, so that wherever feebleness and indulgence and lazy relaxation give rise to such desire, in that place a terrible and astonishing strength may become the stuff of divine love. For it is when manly strength has given fright to that which mothers pleasure, and has put it to flight, that the soul's pure beauty is revealed, it being unsullied by any affliction [πάθος] of corporeal desire.

That is why the King's marriage bed must be surrounded by a circle of hoplites.[22] Their skill in fighting and their possession of a sword ready on the thigh breeds astonishment and terror in the dark thoughts that waylay and assault, at night and by moonlight, those who are upright of heart. That the arming of the men who surround the bed signifies riddance of base pleasures should be evident from the description in the text that says: *All … being instructed in war; each man with a sword on his thigh.* For to have the sword fitted to the thigh is truly for those who are aware that one must fight against flesh and blood. Anyone who has | some experience of interpreting the Scripture's enigmas is well aware both of what is to be gathered from the mention of "thigh" and that "sword" means "the Word." So the one who is girt with a weapon that inspires fear (I mean the sword of temperance), this one is the beloved of the incorruptible bed, one of *Israel's strong ones,* worthy to be included in the list of the sixty.

Now we may be sure that this number has a mystical meaning, but it is only apparent to those to whom the grace of the Spirit reveals hidden mysteries, and we say that all is well with those who are satisfied by the surface meanings of the text—in the same way that, referring to the Passover, Moses decrees that those who eat of the flesh that appears are to leave untouched that which is concealed in the hidden bones (cf. Num 9:11–12). So should anyone be desirous of the secret marrow of the text, let it be sought from the One who reveals hidden things to those who are worthy of them. Lest, however, we appear to be content with the naked text or to neglect the divine

---

20. For a parallel, see Methodius, *Res.* 2.4.8.

21. "Love" here is, of course, ἔρως.

22. Note that the "hoplites" represent, in the commentary attributed to Cassiodorus, public teachers in the church: "sanctos doctores, fortes et animo constantes" (PL 70:1070B).

τὰς θείας διακελευομένου γραφάς, οὑτωσὶ τὸν περὶ τῶν ἑξήκοντα λόγον διασκοπήσωμεν·

δώδεκα ῥάβδοι κατ' ἀριθμὸν τῶν φυλῶν τοῦ Ἰσραὴλ | κατὰ πρόσταγμα   194
θεῖον παρὰ τοῦ Μωϋσέως λαμβάνονται, ἀλλὰ μία τῶν πασῶν προετιμήθη
5   μόνη παρὰ τὰς ἄλλας βλαστήσασα. πάλιν παρὰ τοῦ τοῦ Ναυὴ Ἰησοῦ
ἰσάριθμοι ταῖς φυλαῖς τοῦ Ἰσραὴλ λίθοι ἐκ τοῦ Ἰορδάνου λαμβάνονται, ὧν
οὐδὲ εἷς ἀπόβλητος γίνεται πάντων ὁμοτίμως εἰς μαρτυρίαν τοῦ κατὰ τὸν
Ἰορδάνην μυστηρίου παραληφθέντων.

καὶ πολὺ τὸ ἀκόλουθον ἐν τοῖς ἱστορουμένοις ἐστίν· προκοπὴν γάρ τινα
10   τοῦ λαοῦ πρὸς τὸ τελειότερον ὁ λόγος ἐνδείκνυται, ὡς ἐν ἀρχαῖς μὲν τῆς
νομοθεσίας μίαν εὑρεθῆναι ῥάβδον ζῶσάν τε καὶ βλαστάνουσαν, τὰς δὲ λοιπὰς
ὡς ξηράς τε οὔσας καὶ ἀκάρπους ἀποβληθῆναι. πλείονος δὲ διαγεγονότος
χρόνου καὶ τῶν νομικῶν αὐτοῖς παραγγελμάτων ἐν ἀκριβεστέρᾳ κατανοήσει
γεγενημένων, ὡς καὶ τὴν ἐκ δευτέρου περιτομὴν τὴν παρὰ τοῦ Ἰησοῦ αὐτοῖς
15   ἐπαγομένην καὶ νοῆσαι καὶ δέξασθαι τῆς πετρίνης μαχαίρας περιελούσης
αὐτῶν πᾶν τὸ ἀκάθαρτον (νοεῖ δὲ πάντως ὁ συνετὸς ἀκροατὴς τῆς τε
πέτρας καὶ τῆς μαχαίρας τὸ σημαινόμενον), εἰκὸς ἦν βεβαιωθείσης ἐν αὐτοῖς
τῆς νομίμου τε καὶ ἐναρέτου ζωῆς μηδένα τῶν λίθων τῶν ἐπ' ὀνόματι τῶν
Ἰσραηλιτικῶν φυλῶν παραληφθέντων εὑρεθῆναι ἀπόβλητον.

20   ἐπεὶ δὲ χρὴ πάντοτε τῶν ἀγαθῶν τὰς ἐπαυξήσεις ἐπιζητεῖν, ὅτε προῆλθεν
ὁ | χρόνος, καὶ ἡ δύναμις τοῦ Ἰσραὴλ μείζων ἐγένετο· οὕτω γάρ φησιν ἐν   195
τοῖς προκειμένοις ἡμῖν ῥητοῖς ὁ λόγος ὅτι ἀπὸ δυνατῶν Ἰσραὴλ τότε οὐκέτι
εἷς ἀπὸ φυλῆς λίθος ἢ μία ῥάβδος λαμβάνεται, ἀλλὰ πέντε ἀντὶ ῥάβδων
ἢ λίθων ἀφ' ἑκάστης φυλῆς ἄνδρες πολεμισταί, δεδιδαγμένοι πόλεμον,
25   αἴροντες ῥομφαίαν, ἀπὸ δυνατῶν Ἰσραὴλ τὴν θείαν κλίνην περιστοιχίζονται,
ὧν διὰ τοῦτο οὐδεὶς ἀπόβλητος γίνεται, διότι πάσης φυλῆς ἀπαρχὴ οἱ πέντε
γίνονται, ὧν ὁ ἀριθμὸς δωδεκάκις κεφαλαιούμενος τὸ πλήρωμα ποιεῖ τῶν
ἑξήκοντα. χρὴ τοίνυν πέντε ἀφ' ἑκάστης φυλῆς φοβεροὺς ὁπλομάχους
φύλακας τῆς τοῦ βασιλέως κλίνης γενέσθαι, ὡς, εἴ γε λείποι τῷ ἀριθμῷ τῶν
30   πέντε, ἀπαράδεκτον εἶναι καὶ τὸ λειπόμενον.

command to search the divine Scriptures, we shall consider what is said about the "sixty."[23]

Now twelve rods, in accord with the number of the tribes of Israel, | were received by Moses at God's command, but of the whole number, one alone was preferred before the others because it blossomed (cf. Num 17:1–11).[24] Further, stones from the Jordan, equal in number to the tribes of Israel, were received by Jesus[25] the son of Nun. Of these not one was cast aside, since all were accepted with equal honor as a testimony to the mystery that occurred by the Jordan (cf. Josh 4).

Between these stories there is a significant connection, for the text indicates progress toward perfection on the part of the people. At the beginning of the giving of the law, one rod is found that is alive and blossoms, while the others are set aside as being dried out and sterile. But after much time had passed and they had understood the injunctions of the law more exactly, so as both to understand and accept the second circumcision that Jesus introduced for them (cf. Josh 5:2–9),[26] the stone knife having removed all uncleanness from them (the wise hearer will perfectly understand what is meant by the stone and the knife[27]), it was right and reasonable that after the lawful and virtuous life had been fixed in them, none of the stones that had been endowed with the names of the Israelite tribes should turn out to be rejected.

Since however it is of necessity that we seek the increase of things that are good, the strength of Israel grew greater as | time went on, for so the Word says in the text that lies before us: *out of the mighty men of Israel* it is no longer, at that time, a single stone or a single rod that is taken from a tribe, but from each tribe five fighting men—instead of rods or stones—*out of the mighty men of Israel, instructed in war* and bearing the sword, surround the divine bed. Hence not one of these is rejected, and the reason is that the five become the firstfruits of every tribe, since their number, if multiplied by twelve, makes up the full total of sixty. It is therefore strictly necessary that five fearsome warriors from each tribe become the guards of the royal bed, since if any of the five is lacking, the remainder too will be unacceptable.

---

23. For a different numerological interpretation, less ingenious and therefore perhaps more likely to be traditional, see Cassiodorus (PL 70:1070A), where the analogy of the six days of creation is adduced.

24. Gregory also refers to this incident in *Vit. Mos.* 1.70 (GNO 7.1:30).

25. It is not unimportant to note that in the Greek of the LXX version of the Former Prophets, as in Gregory's writings, the Hebrew name "Joshua" becomes "Jesus."

26. Gregory is referring to a form of the LXX text of Josh 5:2 that we know only from the Codex Alexandrinus, which adds at the end of the verse "for a second time," thus conforming the Greek version to the Masoretic Text of the Hebrew.

27. Presumably Gregory means to intimate that circumcision is a type of baptism.

Ἆρ' ἐστι λοιπὸν κατατολμῆσαι τοῦ ἐνθυμήματος, πῶς ἀφ' ἑκάστης
φυλῆς οἱ πέντε ὁπλίζονται, ἵνα τῆς βασιλικῆς κλίνης φύλακες γένωνται,
πῶς ἕκαστος τῶν πέντε τούτων φοβερὸς τοῖς ἀντιτεταγμένοις διὰ τῆς
ὁπλίσεως γίνεται τὴν ῥομφαίαν τοῦ μηροῦ προβαλλόμενος; ἢ δῆλόν ἐστιν
5   ὅτι ὁ εἷς ἄνθρωπος οἱ πέντε οὗτοι ὁπλῖταί εἰσιν ἑκάστης αἰσθήσεως | τὴν   196
πρόσφορον ἑαυτῇ ῥομφαίαν εἰς κατάπληξιν τῶν ἐναντίων προβαλλομένης;
ὀφθαλμοῦ ῥομφαία τὸ διὰ παντὸς ὁρᾶν πρὸς τὸν κύριον καὶ ὀρθὰ βλέπειν
καὶ μηδενὶ τῶν ῥυπαρῶν θεαμάτων καταμολύνεσθαι, ἀκοῆς ὅπλον ὡσαύτως
ἡ τῶν θείων διδαγμάτων ἀκρόασις καὶ τὸ μηδέποτε μάταιον λόγον ἐν ἑαυτῇ
10   παραδέξασθαι. οὕτως ἔστιν ὁπλίσαι καὶ τὴν γεῦσιν καὶ τὴν ἁφὴν καὶ τὴν
ὄσφρησιν τῇ τῆς ἐγκρατείας ῥομφαίᾳ καταλλήλως ἑκάστην τῶν αἰσθήσεων
θωρακίζοντα, δι' ὧν γίνεται θάμβος καὶ ἔκπληξις τοῖς σκοτεινοῖς ἐχθροῖς,
ὧν καιρὸς εἰς τὴν κατὰ τῶν ψυχῶν ἐπιβουλὴν ἡ νὺξ γίνεται καὶ τὸ σκότος.
ἐν ταύτῃ γὰρ εἶπεν ὁ προφήτης τὰ θηρία τοῦ ἀγροῦ τὴν πονηρὰν βρῶσιν
15   ἑαυτοῖς ἐκ τῶν τοῦ θεοῦ ποιμνίων περιεργάζεσθαι· Ἔθου γάρ, φησί, σκότος
καὶ ἐγένετο νύξ· ἐν αὐτῇ διελεύσονται πάντα τὰ θηρία τοῦ δρυμοῦ, σκύμνοι
ὠρυόμενοι ἁρπάσαι.

ἐπειδὴ τοίνυν Ἰσραὴλ γίνεται πᾶς ὁ σωζόμενος (Οὐ γὰρ πάντες οἱ ἐξ
Ἰσραὴλ οὗτοι Ἰσραήλ, ἀλλ' ὅσοι βλέπουσι τὸν θεὸν ἐκ τῆς ἐνεργείας | κυρίως   197
20   τῇ προσηγορίᾳ ταύτῃ κατονομάζονται), ἴδιον δὲ τοῦ ὁρῶντός ἐστι τὸν θεὸν
τὸ μηδενὶ τῶν αἰσθητηρίων πρὸς ἁμαρτίαν βλέπειν (οὐδεὶς γὰρ δύναται πρὸς
δύο κυρίους ὁρᾶν, ἀλλὰ χρὴ τὸν ἕνα μισηθῆναι πάντως, εἰ μέλλοι ἀγαπᾶσθαι
ὁ ἕτερος), τούτου χάριν μία κλίνη τοῦ βασιλέως γίνεται πᾶν τὸ σωζόμενον· εἰ
γὰρ πάντες ὄψονται τὸν θεὸν οἱ καθαροὶ τῇ καρδίᾳ γενόμενοι, οἱ δὲ τὸν θεὸν
25   ἰδόντες Ἰσραὴλ κυρίως γίνονταί τε καὶ ὀνομάζονται, δώδεκα δὲ διαιρεῖται
φυλαῖς κατά τινα λόγον ἀπόρρητον τοῦτο τὸ ὄνομα, καλῶς τὸ πλήρωμα τῶν
σωζομένων τῷ ἀριθμῷ τῶν ἑξήκοντα κεφαλαιοῦται ἑνὸς μὲν ἀφ' ἑκάστου
μέρους λαμβανομένου, εἰς πέντε δὲ ὁπλίτας κατὰ τὸν ἀριθμὸν τῶν αἰσθήσεων
τοῦ ἑνὸς τούτου μεριζομένου.
30   οὐκοῦν πάντες οἱ τὴν θείαν ἐνδυσάμενοι πανοπλίαν μίαν κυκλοῦσι τοῦ
βασιλέως κλίνην εἷς Ἰσραὴλ οἱ πάντες γενόμενοι καὶ διὰ τῶν δώδεκα φυλῶν
τῆς πενταχῇ νοουμένης ἀριστείας εἰς τὸν ἀριθμὸν τῶν ἑξήκοντα πάντως
ἀνακεφαλαιουμένου τοῦ τῶν ἀριστέων πληρώματος μία παράταξις καὶ
στρατὸς εἷς καὶ μία κλίνη, τουτέστιν ἐκκλησία μία καὶ λαὸς εἷς καὶ νύμφη μία
35   οἱ πάντες γενήσονται ὑφ' ἑνὶ | ταξιάρχῃ καὶ ἐκκλησιαστῇ καὶ νυμφίῳ πρὸς   198
ἑνὸς σώματος κοινωνίαν συναρμοζόμενοι.

Is it possible further to venture upon the question how the five men from each tribe equip themselves to become guards of the royal bed, how, by reason of his equipment, each of these five becomes fearsome to his opponents as he holds his sword before his thigh? Now is it not plain that these five warriors are the one human being, with each of its senses deploying | the weapon proper to it for the consternation of its enemies? The eye's sword is to look across and through everything toward the Lord, and to contemplate what is right, and not to be defiled by any unseemly sight. Hearing's weapon, similarly, is hearkening to the divine teachings and refusal to take in vain talk. In this way it is also possible to arm taste and touch and smell with the sword of self-control, protecting each of the senses in the appropriate manner. So come terror and amazement upon the dark enemies, whose plot against souls finds its opportunity in darkness and at night. For the prophet says that it is at night that the beasts of the field are busy getting themselves evil food from the flocks of the Lord: "You bring darkness, and night comes. In it all the beasts of the forest go about, lions roaring for prey" (Ps 103:20–21).

Since, therefore, *Israel* means each and every person who is saved (for not every offspring of Israel is Israel; those who are called by this name | in its proper sense are those who actively see God[28]), and what marks out the person who looks upon God is never to contemplate sin with any of the sense organs (for no one can look to two lords, but one of them must be entirely hated if the other is to be loved [cf. Matt 6:24 // Luke 16:13])—for this reason the *one* royal bed means every single individual who is saved. For if all who have become "pure in heart … shall see God" (cf. Matt 5:8), and those who see God properly are, and are called, Israel, and this name is, in accordance with some ineffable principle, divided into twelve tribes, then it is entirely appropriate for the full body of those who are saved to be summed up by the number sixty: there is one person taken from each part, while each such person is divided into five warriors in accordance with the number of the senses.

So it is that all who have put on the divine armor surround the royal bed. They have become, as a whole group, the one Israel; and since, because there are twelve tribes that constitute this body of the brave in its fivefold form, the full total of the brave is completely summed up in the number sixty; they make up one formation and one army and one bed—that is, all shall become one church, one people, and one bride, fitted together into the communion of one body by one | Commander, one Head of the church, one Bridegroom.

---

28. See Origen, *Princ.* 4.3.9: "we understand that it is a race of souls that is called Israel…, for Israel means 'the mind seeing God' or 'man seeing God'" (trans. Butterworth 1966, 300). See also Philo, *Ebr.* 82–83.

τὸ δὲ κλίνην τὴν ἀνάπαυσιν εἶναι τῶν σῳζομένων καὶ ἐκ τῆς τοῦ κυρίου φωνῆς διδασκόμεθα, ὅς φησι πρὸς τὸν ἀναιδῶς ἐν νυκτὶ θυροκρουστοῦντα ὅτι Ἤδη ἡ θύρα κέκλεισται καὶ τὰ παιδία μετ' ἐμοῦ ἐπὶ τῆς κοίτης ἐστίν. καλῶς δὲ τοὺς διὰ τῶν ὅπλων τῆς δικαιοσύνης τὸ ἀπαθὲς ἑαυτοῖς κατορθώσαντας

5   παιδία κατονομάζει ὁ λόγος δόγμα διὰ τούτων ἡμῖν ὑφηγούμενος, ὅτι τὸ ἐξ ἐπιμελείας προσγινόμενον ἡμῖν ἀγαθὸν οὐκ ἄλλο τί ἐστι παρὰ τὸ ἐξ ἀρχῆς ἐναποτεθὲν τῇ φύσει· ὅ τε γὰρ τῷ μηρῷ τὴν ῥομφαίαν διαζωσάμενος διὰ προσοχῆς τοῦ κατ' ἀρετὴν βίου τὸ πάθος ἀπεσκευάσατο τό τε νήπιον τῇ ἡλικίᾳ ἀναισθήτως ἔχει τοῦ τοιούτου πάθους· οὐ γὰρ χωρεῖ τὸ πάθος ἡ

10   νηπιότης. οὐκοῦν ταὐτόν ἐστιν ὁπλίτας τε περὶ τὴν κλίνην εἶναι μαθεῖν καὶ νήπια ἐπὶ τῆς κοίτης ἀναπαυόμενα· μία γὰρ ἐπ' ἀμφοτέρων ἡ ἀπάθεια τῶν τε μὴ παραδεξαμένων καὶ τῶν ἀπωσαμένων τὸ πάθος· οἱ μὲν γὰρ οὔπω ἔγνωσαν, οἱ δὲ πρὸς τὴν τοιαύτην κατάστασιν ἑαυτοὺς ἐπανήγαγον στραφέντες καὶ παιδία τῇ ἀπαθείᾳ γενόμενοι, ὡς μακάριον τὸ ἐν τούτοις | εὑρεθῆναι ἢ   199

15   παιδίον ἢ ὁπλίτην ἢ ἀληθινὸν Ἰσραηλίτην γενόμενον, ὡς μὲν Ἰσραηλίτην ἐν καθαρᾷ καρδίᾳ τὸν θεὸν ὁρῶντα, ὡς δὲ ὁπλίτην ἐν ἀπαθείᾳ καὶ καθαρότητι τὴν τοῦ βασιλέως κλίνην, τουτέστιν τὴν ἑαυτοῦ καρδίαν φυλάσσοντα, ὡς δὲ παιδίον ἐπὶ τῆς μακαρίας κοίτης ἀναπαυόμενον ἐν Χριστῷ Ἰησοῦ τῷ κυρίῳ ἡμῶν,

20   ᾧ ἡ δόξα εἰς τοὺς αἰῶνας τῶν αἰώνων.
ἀμήν.

Now it is from the very voice of the Lord that we learn that the bed means the repose of those who are saved. To the one who shamelessly knocks on the door at night he says: "The door is already shut, and the children are with me in the bed" (Luke 11:7). Rightly does the Word give the name "children" to those who by the weapons of righteousness attain invulnerability [τὸ ἀπαθές], and in this way he instructs us that the good thing that accrues to us through diligent labor is nothing other than what was deposited in our nature from the beginning. For the person who has girded *his sword on his thigh* has been stripped of passion [τὸ πάθος] by devotion to the virtuous life and possesses youth in his freedom from such passion, since youth makes no room for passion. Hence it is one and the same thing to know that there are armed men around the bed and that there are children at rest in the bed. For in both cases the invulnerability is the same: it is that of people who have not taken passion into their lives but have cast it out. For there are some who have not yet come to their senses, but there are others who have brought themselves to just such a condition of life, because they have turned and become children through invulnerability to passion, so that in them | there is found the child, or warrior, or true Israelite who has come to blessedness: the Israelite who with a pure heart sees God; the warrior who stands guard in invulnerability and purity over the royal bed—that is, his own heart; the child taking rest upon the blessed bed, in Christ Jesus our Lord,

To whom be glory to the ages of ages.
Amen.

Λόγος ζ'

Φορεῖον ἐποίησεν ἑαυτῷ ὁ βασιλεὺς Σαλωμὼν
ἀπὸ ξύλων τοῦ Λιβάνου,
Στύλους αὐτοῦ ἐποίησεν ἀργύριον
καὶ τὸ ἀνάκλιτον αὐτοῦ χρυσίον,
5   ἐπιβάσεις αὐτοῦ πορφύραν,
ἐντὸς αὐτοῦ λιθόστρωτον
ἀγάπην ἀπὸ θυγατέρων Ἰερουσαλήμ.
Ἐξέλθετε καὶ ἴδετε, θυγατέρες Σιών,
ἐν τῷ βασιλεῖ Σαλωμών,
10   ἐν τῷ στεφάνῳ, ᾧ ἐστεφάνωσεν αὐτὸν ἡ μήτηρ αὐτοῦ
ἐν ἡμέρᾳ νυμφεύσεως αὐτοῦ
| καὶ ἐν ἡμέρᾳ εὐφροσύνης καρδίας αὐτοῦ.   200

Ἰδοὺ εἶ καλή, ἡ πλησίον μου, ἰδοὺ εἶ καλή.
ὀφθαλμοί σου περιστεραὶ ἐκτὸς τῆς σιωπήσεώς σου.
15   τρίχωμά σου ὡς ἀγέλαι τῶν αἰγῶν,
αἵ ἀπεκαλύφθησαν ἀπὸ τοῦ Γαλαάδ.
Ὀδόντες σου ὡς ἀγέλαι τῶν κεκαρμένων,
αἵ ἀνέβησαν ἀπὸ τοῦ λουτροῦ,
αἱ πᾶσαι διδυμεύουσαι,
20   καὶ ἀτεκνοῦσα οὐκ ἔστιν ἐν αὐταῖς.
Ὡς σπαρτίον κόκκινον χείλη σου,
καὶ ἡ λαλιά σου ὡραία.
ὡς λέπυρον ῥόας μῆλόν σου ἐκτὸς τῆς σιωπήσεώς σου.
Ὡς πύργος Δαβὶδ τράχηλός σου
25   ὁ ᾠκοδομημένος ἐν θαλπιώθ·
χίλιοι θυρεοὶ κρέμανται ἐπ᾽ αὐτόν,
πᾶσαι βολίδες τῶν δυνατῶν.
Δύο μαστοί σου ὡς δύο νεβροὶ δίδυμοι δορκάδος
οἱ νεμόμενοι ἐν τοῖς κρίνοις,
30   Ἕως οὗ διαπνεύσῃ ἡ ἡμέρα καὶ κινηθῶσιν αἱ σκιαί.
πορεύσομαι ἐμαυτῷ πρὸς τὸ ὄρος τῆς σμύρνης
| καὶ πρὸς τὸν βουνὸν τοῦ λιβάνου.   201
Ὅλη καλὴ εἶ, ἡ πλησίον μου, καὶ
μῶμος οὔκ ἐστιν ἐν σοί.

HOMILY 7
Song 3:9–4:7a

[9]*King Solomon made himself a palanquin*
of the woods of Lebanon.
[10]*He made the pillars of it silver,*
and the backrest of it gold;
the seat of it was purple,
its interior a mosaic of stones,
love from the daughters of Jerusalem.
[11]*Come forth, you daughters of Jerusalem, and behold*
King Solomon,
in the crown with which his mother crowned him,
on the day of his wedding,
and on the day of his heart's gladness.

[1]*Behold you are beautiful, my close one, behold you are beautiful.*
Your eyes are doves outside your veil.
Your hair is like flocks of goats
that have been revealed from Gilead.
[2]*Your teeth are like flocks of shorn ewes*
that have come up from their washing,
all bearing twins,
and not one of them barren.
[3]*Your lips are like a scarlet thread,*
and your speech is radiant.
Like the rind of a pomegranate is your cheek outside your silence.
[4]*Your neck is like a tower of David,*
which was built in Thalpioth.
A thousand shields hang upon it,
all the darts of the mighty men.
[5]*Your breasts are like two twin fawns*
that feed among the lilies,
[6]*Until the day breathes and the shadows are moved.*
I will betake myself to the mountain of myrrh,
and to the hill of frankincense.
[7]*You are beautiful through and through, my close one,*
and there is no flaw in you.

Ἐν πολλοῖς ὁ βασιλεὺς Σολομὼν εἰς τύπον τοῦ ἀληθινοῦ βασιλέως παραλαμβάνεται, πολλοῖς δέ φημι τοῖς πρὸς τὸ κρεῖττον περὶ αὐτοῦ παρὰ τῆς ἁγίας γραφῆς ἱστορουμένοις· εἰρηνικός τε γὰρ λέγεται, καὶ ναὸν οἰκοδομεῖ καὶ σοφίαν ἀμέτρητον ἔχει, βασιλεύει τε τοῦ Ἰσραὴλ καὶ κρίνει τὸν λαὸν ἐν
5   δικαιοσύνῃ καὶ ἐκ τοῦ σπέρματός ἐστι τοῦ Δαβίδ, ἀλλὰ καὶ ἡ τῶν Αἰθιόπων βασίλισσα πρὸς αὐτὸν φοιτᾷ. ταῦτα γὰρ πάντα καὶ τὰ τοιαῦτα περὶ αὐτοῦ μὲν λέγεται τυπικῶς, προδιαγράφει δὲ τοῦ εὐαγγελίου τὴν δύναμιν.

τίς γὰρ οὕτως εἰρηνικὸς ὡς ὁ ἀποκτείνας τὴν ἔχθραν καὶ τῷ σταυρῷ προσηλώσας, ὁ τοὺς ἐχθροὺς ἑαυτοῦ ἡμᾶς, μᾶλλον δὲ τὸν κόσμον ὅλον
10   ἑαυτῷ καταλλάξας καὶ τὸ μεσότοιχον τοῦ φραγμοῦ λύσας, Ἵνα τοὺς δύο κτίσῃ ἐν ἑαυτῷ εἰς ἕνα καινὸν ἄνθρωπον ποιῶν εἰρήνην, ὁ κηρύξας τοῖς μακράν τε καὶ τοῖς ἐγγὺς τὴν εἰρήνην διὰ τῶν εὐαγγελιζομένων τὰ ἀγαθά;

τίς δὲ | τοιοῦτος οἰκοδόμος ναοῦ ὁ τοὺς θεμελίους μὲν αὐτοῦ τιθεὶς ἐν   202 τοῖς ὄρεσι τοῖς ἁγίοις, τουτέστιν ἐν τοῖς προφήταις τε καὶ τοῖς ἀποστόλοις,
15   ἐποικοδομῶν δέ, καθώς φησιν ὁ ἀπόστολος, Ἐπὶ τῷ θεμελίῳ τῶν ἀποστόλων καὶ προφητῶν τοὺς ζῶντάς τε καὶ ἐμψύχους λίθους τοὺς δι' ἑαυτῶν πρὸς τὴν τῶν τοίχων ἁρμονίαν κατὰ τὸν προφητικὸν λόγον κυλιομένους, ὥστε συναρμοσθέντας ἐν τῇ ἑνότητι τῆς πίστεως καὶ τῷ συνδέσμῳ τῆς εἰρήνης αὐξῆσαι δι' ἑαυτῶν τὸν ναὸν τὸν ἅγιον εἰς τὸ γενέσθαι κατοικητήριον θεοῦ
20   ἐν πνεύματι;

ὅτι δὲ καὶ τῇ σοφίᾳ τῇ ἑαυτοῦ ὁ Σολομὼν τὴν ἀληθινὴν μηνύει σοφίαν, οὐδεὶς ἂν ἀντείποι πρός τε τὴν ἱστορίαν καὶ πρὸς τὴν ἀλήθειαν βλέπων· μαρτυρεῖται μὲν γὰρ ὑπὸ τῆς ἱστορίας ἐκεῖνος, ὅτι παρῆλθε τοὺς τῆς ἀνθρωπίνης σοφίας ὅρους πάντων τὴν γνῶσιν ἐν τῷ πλάτει τῆς καρδίας
25   χωρήσας, ὡς καὶ τοὺς προλαβόντας παραδραμεῖν καὶ τοῖς ἐφεξῆς γενέσθαι ἀνέφικτος, ὁ δὲ κύριος κατὰ τὴν ἑαυτοῦ φύσιν αὐτό, ὅπερ ἐστὶν ἀλήθειά τε καὶ σοφία καὶ δύναμις, οὐσίᾳ | ἐστίν. διὰ τοῦτο τοῦ Δαβὶδ εἰπόντος ὅτι   203 Πάντα ἐν σοφίᾳ ἐγένετο, ἑρμηνεύων τὸν προφήτην ὁ θεῖος ἀπόστολος Ἐν αὐτῷ ἐκτίσθαι τὰ πάντα λέγει, ὡς τοῦτον τοῦ προφήτου διὰ τῆς σοφίας
30   σημαίνοντος.

τὸ δὲ βασιλέα τοῦ Ἰσραὴλ εἶναι τὸν κύριον καὶ παρὰ τῶν ἐχθρῶν μεμαρτύρηται τῶν ὑπογεγραφηκότων τῷ σταυρῷ τὴν ὁμολογίαν τῆς βασιλείας αὐτοῦ ὅτι Οὗτός ἐστιν ὁ βασιλεὺς τῶν Ἰουδαίων· δεχόμεθα γὰρ τὴν μαρτυρίαν, εἰ καὶ κατασμικρύνειν νομίζεται τὸ μεγαλεῖον τοῦ κράτους τῇ
35   τῶν Ἰσραηλιτῶν βασιλείᾳ τὴν δεσποτείαν ὁρίζουσα. οὐ γὰρ οὕτως ἔχει, ἀλλ' ἀπὸ μέρους τὴν κατὰ πάντων ἀρχὴν ἡ ἐπιγραφὴ αὕτη τῷ σταυρῷ ἀνατίθησι τῷ μὴ προσθεῖναι ὅτι μόνων τῶν Ἰουδαίων οὗτός ἐστι βασιλεύς· ἀπολύτως

King Solomon qualifies in many ways as a type of the true King—I mean, in the many nobler things that the Scriptures record about him. For he is called peaceable, and builds a temple, and is possessed of immeasurable wisdom. He also rules Israel and judges the people in righteousness, and he is of the seed of David. What is more, the queen of the Ethiopians visits him. Now all these things—and whatever others may be like them—are said about him *typically*: they sketch out, in an anticipatory way, the power of the gospel.

Who, after all, is as peaceable as he who "brought the hostility to an end" (cf. Eph 2:16) and "nailed it to the cross" (cf. Col 2:14); he who reconciled to himself us, his enemies—or better, the whole cosmos—and "has broken down the dividing wall ... in order that he might create in himself one new humanity, so making peace" (Eph 2:14–15); he who "preached peace," through those who brought the message of good things, to people who were "far off" and to people who were "near at hand" (Eph 2:17)?

And who | is such a temple builder as the one who has set his "foundations ... upon the holy mountains" (Ps 86:1), that is, upon the prophets and the apostles, but laying, as the apostle says, "upon the foundation of the apostles and prophets" (Eph 2:20) stones that are living (cf. 1 Pet 2:5) and ensouled, which by their own agency are rolled up to contribute to the structure of the walls, as the prophet says, so that, being "joined together" in the unity of the faith and in the "bond of peace" (Eph 4:3) they have of themselves so increased the holy temple that it has become "the dwelling place of God in the Spirit" (Eph 2:22)?

Furthermore, no one who considers the biblical narrative and the truth can deny that Solomon by his own wisdom points to the true Wisdom. The biblical narrative indeed attests that this man transcended the heights of human wisdom, by accommodating in the wideness of his heart the knowledge of all things, so that he outstripped those who were before him and could not be touched by those who came after him. But the Lord is this thing—Truth and Wisdom and Power— | by his very own nature, in essence. Hence when David says, "Everything came to be in Wisdom" (Ps 103:24), the divine apostle interprets him by saying, "In him all things were created" (cf. Col 1:16), believing that the Lord is the one whom the prophet denotes by "Wisdom."

And that the Lord is King of Israel was attested even by his enemies, who on the cross endorsed in writing the confession of his kingship: "This is the king of the Jews" (cf. Matt 27:37 // Luke 23:38). We accept this witness, even though it is thought to diminish the greatness of his rule by confining his sway to the kingdom of the Israelites. In fact this is not the case. On the contrary, this same inscription, in that it does not go on to say that the person referred to is king *only* of the Jews, attributes to the cross a universal rule on

γὰρ αὐτῷ προσμαρτυρήσας ὁ λόγος τὴν τῶν Ἰουδαίων ἀρχὴν καὶ τὸ κατὰ
πάντων κράτος κατὰ τὸ σιωπώμενον τῇ ὁμολογίᾳ ταύτῃ συμπεριέλαβεν· ὁ
γὰρ βασιλεὺς πάσης τῆς γῆς καὶ τοῦ μέρους πάντως | τὴν δεσποτείαν ἔχει.   204
    ἡ δὲ περὶ τὴν δικαίαν κρίσιν τοῦ Σολομῶνος σπουδὴ τὸν ἀληθινὸν
5   κριτὴν τοῦ παντὸς κόσμου διασημαίνει, ὅς φησιν ὅτι Ὁ πατὴρ κρίνει οὐδένα,
ἀλλὰ τὴν κρίσιν πᾶσαν δέδωκε τῷ υἱῷ· καὶ ὅτι Οὐ δύναμαι ἀπ᾽ ἐμαυτοῦ
ποιεῖν οὐδέν, ἀλλὰ καθὼς ἀκούω κρίνω καὶ ἡ κρίσις ἡ ἐμὴ δικαία ἐστίν. οὗτος
γὰρ ὁ ἀκρότατος τῆς δικαίας κρίσεως ὅρος τὸ μὴ ἀφ᾽ ἑαυτοῦ τι κατά τινα
προσπάθειαν ἢ ἀποκλήρωσιν τοῖς κρινομένοις νέμειν, ἀλλὰ πρῶτον ἀκούειν
10 τῶν ὑποδίκων τῇ κρίσει, εἶθ᾽ οὕτω τὴν ἐπ᾽ αὐτοῖς ψῆφον ἐκτίθεσθαι. οὗ χάριν
ἡ τοῦ θεοῦ δύναμίς τινα ὁμολογεῖ καὶ μὴ δύνασθαι· τὸ γὰρ ἔξω τοῦ δικαίου
παρατρέψαι τὴν κρίσιν ἀδυνατεῖ ἡ ἀλήθεια.
    τὸ δὲ ἐκ τοῦ σπέρματος Δαβὶδ εἶναι τὸ κατὰ σάρκα τὸν κύριον παρὰ
τοῦ γεγονότος ἐκ τοῦ Δαβὶδ προμηνύεσθαι ὡς ὁμολογούμενον τῷ λόγῳ
15 παρήσομεν.
    τὸ δὲ κατὰ τὴν Αἰθιοπίδα μυστήριον, πῶς καταλιποῦσα τῶν | Αἰθιόπων   205
τὴν βασιλείαν καὶ τοσοῦτον διαβᾶσα τὸν ἐν τῷ μέσῳ τόπον πρὸς τὸν
Σολομῶνα διὰ τὸ κλέος τῆς σοφίας ἐπείγεται λίθοις τε τιμίοις καὶ χρυσῷ καὶ
τοῖς τῶν ἀρωμάτων ἡδύσμασι δεξιουμένη τὸν βασιλέα, δῆλον ἂν γένοιτο
20 τῷ ἐπιστήσαντι, πρὸς ὅ τι τῶν εὐαγγελικῶν βλέπει θαυμάτων· τίς γὰρ οὐκ
οἶδεν ὅτι μέλαινα ἦν ἐξ εἰδωλολατρίας τὸ κατ᾽ ἀρχὰς ἡ ἐξ ἐθνῶν ἐκκλησία
πρὶν ἐκκλησία γενέσθαι πολλῷ μεταξὺ τῷ τῆς ἀγνοίας διαστήματι τῆς πρὸς
τὸν ἀληθινὸν θεὸν γνώσεως ἀπῳκισμένη; ἀλλ᾽ ὅτε ἐπεφάνη ἡ χάρις τοῦ θεοῦ
καὶ ἡ σοφία διέλαμψε καὶ τὸ φῶς τὸ ἀληθινὸν πρὸς τοὺς ἐν σκότει καὶ σκιᾷ
25 θανάτου καθημένους τὴν ἀκτῖνα διέπεμψε, τότε τοῦ Ἰσραὴλ πρὸς τὸ φῶς
ἐπιμύσαντος καὶ τῆς τῶν ἀγαθῶν μετουσίας ἑαυτὸν ἀποστήσαντος ἔρχονται
οἱ Αἰθίοπες, οἱ ἐξ ἐθνῶν τῇ πίστει προστρέχοντες καὶ οἵ ποτε ὄντες μακρὰν
ἐγγὺς γίνονται τῷ μυστικῷ ὕδατι τὴν μελανίαν ἀποκλυσάμενοι, ὥστε τὴν
Αἰθιοπίαν προφθάσαι χεῖρα αὐτῆς τῷ θεῷ καὶ προσαγαγεῖν δῶρα τῷ βασιλεῖ
30 τά τε τῆς εὐσεβείας ἀρώματα καὶ τὸ τῆς θεογνωσίας χρυσίον καὶ τοὺς τιμίους
λίθους τῆς τῶν ἐντολῶν τε καὶ τῶν ἀρετῶν ἐργασίας.
    | Ἀλλὰ πρὸς ὅ τι βλέπων ἐντεῦθεν ἄρχομαι τῆς προκειμένης ἡμῖν τῶν   206
ῥητῶν θεωρίας, ἤδη διασαφήσω τῷ λόγῳ αὐτὴν προεκθέμενος τὴν λέξιν τῶν
θείων λογίων ἔχουσαν οὕτω· Φορεῖον ἐποίησεν ἑαυτῷ ὁ βασιλεὺς Σαλωμὼν

the basis of its partial rule. For by attesting in unqualified terms his rule over the Jews, the statement implicitly included in this confession a universal sway, for the king of the whole earth certainly has | dominion also over a part of it.

The zeal of Solomon for just judgment, however, signifies the Judge of the whole cosmos, who says, "The Father judges no one, but he has given all judgment to the Son" (John 5:22); and "I cannot do anything of myself, but I judge according as I hear, and my judgment is just" (John 5:30).[1] For this is the highest norm of just judgment: not "of oneself" to make assignment to the parties, on the basis of some arbitrary decision or feeling of sympathy, but first of all to "hear" those who are on trial in the judgment and then in this way to set out the verdict upon them. That is why the Power of God acknowledges that he cannot do certain things, for Truth cannot turn judgment away from what is just.

Since it is acknowledged by the scriptural word, I pass over the fact that David's offspring [i.e., Solomon] points ahead to the Lord's being of the seed of David after the flesh.

As to the mystery of the Ethiopian queen, how she left | the kingdom of the Ethiopians, and journeyed over a huge spread of intervening territory to Solomon's side on account of the fame of his wisdom, and greeted the king with costly gems and gold and the piquancy of spices (cf. 3 Kgdms 10:1–13)— it should be plain to anyone who has paid attention to the matter which of the wonders of the gospel this story contemplates. For who does not know that because of idolatry the Gentile church was dark to begin with and before it became church was far removed, by a great intervening space of ignorance, from the knowledge that leads to the true God? But when the grace of God was revealed and Wisdom shone forth and the true light transmitted its radiance to "those who sat in darkness and the shadow of death" (cf. Luke 1:79), then, while Israel closed its eyes to the light and banished itself from sharing in the good things, the Ethiopians come. Those of the Gentiles who approach by way of faith and who once were far off draw near, having washed off their darkness in the mystical water. Thus Ethiopia extends her hand to God and offers gifts to the King: the spices of piety and the gold of the knowledge of God and the precious gems of the commandments and of the work of the virtues.

| My aim in beginning today's interpretation of the words of the Song with these matters I shall immediately make plain by setting out the very text of the divine oracles, which goes like this: *King Solomon made himself a palan-*

---

1. In his citation of this verse, Gregory appears to follow a text identical with that of Tatian's *Diatessaron.*

ἀπὸ ξύλων τοῦ Λιβάνου, στύλους αὐτοῦ ἐποίησεν ἀργύριον καὶ τὸ ἀνάκλιτον αὐτοῦ χρυσίον, ἐπιβάσεις αὐτοῦ πορφύραν, ἐντὸς αὐτοῦ λιθόστρωτον ἀγάπην ἀπὸ θυγατέρων Ἱερουσαλήμ.

ὥσπερ τοίνυν ἐν τοῖς προεξητασμένοις περὶ τοῦ Σολομῶνος εὗρεν
5   ὁ λόγος δι' ὧν τὸ περὶ τοῦ κυρίου μυστήριον ἐν ἐκείνῳ τῷ προσώπῳ προδιαγράφεται, οὕτω καὶ διὰ τῆς τοῦ φορείου κατασκευῆς ἡ περὶ ἡμῶν οἰκονομία τοῦ κυρίου διασημαίνεται· πολυτρόπως γὰρ ὁ θεὸς ἐν τοῖς ἀξίοις ἑαυτοῦ γίνεται, καθὼς ἂν ἕκαστος ἔχῃ δυνάμεώς τε καὶ ἀξίας οὕτως ἐν ἑκάστῳ γινόμενος. ὁ μὲν γάρ τις γίνεται θεοῦ τόπος, ὁ δὲ οἶκος, ἄλλος
10 δὲ θρόνος καὶ ἕτερος ὑποπόδιον. ἔστι δέ τις ὁ καὶ ἅρμα γινόμενος ἢ ἵππος εὐήνιος δεχόμενος ἐφ' ἑαυτοῦ τὸν ἀγαθὸν ἀναβάτην καὶ πρὸς τὸ δοκοῦν τῷ εὐθύνοντι διανύων τὸν δρόμον. ὡς δὲ νῦν διδασκόμεθα καὶ φορεῖον | 207
αὐτοῦ τις γίνεται ὁ κατὰ τὴν ἐκείνου σοφίαν οὐ μόνον τοῖς ἐκ τοῦ Λιβάνου κατασκευαζόμενος ξύλοις ἀλλὰ καὶ χρυσῷ καὶ ἀργύρῳ καὶ πορφύρᾳ καὶ
15 λίθοις καταλλήλως ἐν ἑκάστῳ μέρει καλλωπιζόμενος· δι' ὧν ἡ ἀγάπη αὐτοῦ ἐνεργὸς γίνεται οὐ πάντων χωρούντων τὴν τῆς ἀγάπης ἐνέργειαν, ἀλλ' εἴ τις θυγάτηρ τῆς ἄνω Ἱερουσαλὴμ τῆς ἐλευθέρας διὰ τοῦ βίου γνωρίζοιτο.

ὅτι μὲν οὖν ὁ τὸν θεὸν ἐν ἑαυτῷ φέρων φορεῖόν ἐστι τοῦ ἐν αὐτῷ καθιδρυμένου, δῆλον καὶ πρὸ τῶν ἡμετέρων λόγων ἂν εἴη· ὁ γὰρ κατὰ τὸν
20 ἅγιον Παῦλον μηκέτι αὐτὸς ζῶν ἀλλὰ ζῶντα ἔχων ἐν ἑαυτῷ τὸν Χριστὸν καὶ δοκιμὴν διδοὺς τοῦ ἐν αὐτῷ λαλοῦντος Χριστοῦ οὗτος κυρίως φορεῖον λέγεταί τε καὶ γίνεται τοῦ ἐν αὐτῷ φερομένου καὶ ὑπ' αὐτοῦ βασταζομένου.

Ἀλλ' οὐ τοῦτό ἐστι τὸ ζητούμενον. ἐκεῖνο δὲ μᾶλλον προσήκει δι' ἐπιμελείας κατανοῆσαι, τί βούλεται τὸ τῆς ὕλης ποικίλον τε καὶ πολυειδὲς καὶ
25 πῶς συμπαραλαμβάνεται χρυσῷ καὶ ἀργύρῳ καὶ πορφύρᾳ καὶ λίθοις καὶ ἡ τοῦ ξύλου φύσις εἰς τὴν κατασκευὴν τοῦ φορείου. καίτοι γε τὸ ξύλον | 208
ἀρχιτέκτων Παῦλος μετὰ τοῦ χόρτου καὶ τῆς καλάμης εἰς τὴν οἰκοδομὴν τοῦ οἴκου κρίνει ἀπόβλητον ὡς τῇ ἀναλωτικῇ τοῦ πυρὸς δυνάμει τῇ δοκιμαζούσῃ τὸ ἔργον ἐνδαπανώμενον. ἀλλ' οἴδαμέν τινα ξύλου φύσιν μὴ διαμένουσαν

quin of the woods of Lebanon. He made the pillars of it silver, and the backrest of it gold; the seat of it was purple, its interior a mosaic of stones, love from the daughters of Jerusalem.

So just as reason discerned, in the preceding scrutiny of the figure of Solomon, how the mystery concerning the Lord was sketched out ahead of time in Solomon's person, so also by the appointments of the litter the Lord's plan for our salvation [οἰκονομία] is signified. For there are many ways in which God comes within those who are worthy of him. He comes to be in each individual in a way that corresponds with that person's power and worthiness. One becomes God's "place," another his "house," another his "throne," another his "footstool." There is one who even becomes his chariot or the docile steed that receives the good rider on its back and finishes its course in obedience to what seems good to the one who guides it. Accordingly, we now learn | that there is also one who becomes his *palanquin,* one who in accord with Solomon's wisdom is not only fitted out with pieces of wood from Lebanon but is also adorned appropriately in every part with gold and silver and scarlet and stones. By means of these this individual's *love* becomes active, though not all have room for the working of love, but only those who become known through their lives as daughters of "the Jerusalem above," which is "free" (cf. Gal 4:26).

Hence the fact that one who bears God within is the *palanquin* of him who is throned within should be evident even before these words of ours; for he who, according to the holy Paul, is no longer living himself but has Christ living within him (cf. Gal 2:20) and gives proof of the Christ who speaks within him (cf. 2 Cor 13:3), this person is preeminently said to be, and becomes in truth, the *palanquin* of the One borne within him and carried by him.

But this is not the thing we are looking for. Rather, the thing we want diligently to apprehend is the meaning of the variety and multiformity of the litter's material and how it is that wood[2] is included with gold and silver and scarlet and gemstones in the appointments of the litter. After all, | that "wise architect" Paul judges that wood, together with hay and stubble, can be dispensed with in the building of the house: it is destroyed by the consuming power of the fire that tests the work (cf. 1 Cor 3:10–15). On the other

---

2. Gregory writes ἡ τοῦ ξύλου φύσις (literally, "the nature of wood"). It needs to be noted here and in the following discussion of this stichos (Song 3:9b) that the Greek ξύλον basically means "timber," "wood," or "log," but it can also mean "tree." Thus Paul at 1 Cor 3:12 uses it to mean wood considered as a material, but at Gen 2:16–17 the translators of the LXX employed it to mean "tree." Gregory, who writes with both of these passages in mind, thus uses the word ambiguously.

ἐν ᾧ ἐστιν ἀλλὰ πρὸς χρυσὸν ἢ ἄργυρον ἢ ἄλλο τι τῶν τιμίων ἑαυτὴν
μεταβάλλουσαν· ἐν γὰρ τῇ μεγάλῃ τοῦ θεοῦ οἰκίᾳ φησὶν ὁ ἀπόστολος τὰ μὲν
εἶναι σκεύη χρυσᾶ τῇ φύσει καὶ ἀργυρᾶ, τὴν ἀσώματον ὡς οἶμαι καὶ νοερὰν
κτίσιν διὰ τούτων ὑπαινισσόμενος, τὰ δὲ ξύλινά τε καὶ ὀστράκινα, ἡμᾶς τάχα
5   διὰ τούτων ἀποσημαίνων, οὓς ἀπεγέωσε μὲν ἡ παρακοὴ καὶ ὀστρακίνους
ἐποίησεν, ἡ δὲ διὰ τοῦ ξύλου ἁμαρτία ξύλινα ἡμᾶς σκεύη ἀντὶ χρυσῶν
ἀπειργάσατο. μεμέρισται δὲ πρὸς τὴν ἀξίαν τῆς ὕλης καὶ ἡ τῶν σκευῶν
χρῆσις· τὰ μὲν γὰρ τῆς τιμιωτέρας ὕλης εἰς τιμὴν ἀποτέτακται, τὰ δὲ εἰς τὴν
ἄτιμον ὑπηρεσίαν ἀπέρριπται. ἀλλὰ τί φησι περὶ τῶν τοιούτων ὁ Παῦλος; ὅτι
10   ἐξουσίαν ἔχει τὸ σκεῦος ἐκ τῆς ἰδίας προαιρέσεως ἢ χρύσεον ἀπὸ ξυλίνου
ἢ ἀργύρεον ἐξ ὀστρακίνου γενέσθαι· Ἐὰν γάρ τις, φησίν, ἐκκαθάρῃ ἑαυτόν,
ἔσται σκεῦος εἰς | τιμὴν τῷ δεσπότῃ πρὸς πᾶν ἔργον ἀγαθὸν ἡτοιμασμένον.   209
τάχα τοίνυν διὰ τῶν εἰρημένων προσαγόμεθά πως τῇ προκειμένῃ θεωρίᾳ τοῦ
λόγου·
15   τὸ ὄρος ὁ Λίβανος ἐν πολλοῖς τῆς ἁγίας γραφῆς εἰς ἔνδειξιν τῆς
ἀντικειμένης δυνάμεως μνημονεύεται, ὡς ὅταν λέγῃ διὰ τοῦ προφήτου ὅτι
Συντρίψει κύριος τὰς κέδρους τοῦ Λιβάνου καὶ λεπτυνεῖ αὐτάς τε καὶ τὸν
Λίβανον ὡς τὸν μόσχον, ἐκεῖνον δηλαδὴ τὸν ἐν τῇ ἐρήμῳ καταλεανθέντα
ὑπὸ τοῦ Μωϋσέως καὶ πότιμον διὰ λεπτότητα τοῖς Ἰσραηλίταις γενόμενον.
20   δηλοῦται γὰρ ὧδε διὰ τῆς προφητείας ὅτι οὐ μόνον τὰ ἐκφυέντα παρὰ τῆς
ἀντικειμένης δυνάμεως κακὰ ἀλλὰ καὶ αὐτὸ τὸ ὄρος, ἡ πρώτη τοῦ κακοῦ
ῥίζα, ὁ Λίβανος ὁ ὑποτρέφων τῶν τοιούτων κέδρων τὴν ὕλην εἰς τὸ μὴ ὂν
περιστήσεται. οὐκοῦν ἡμεῖς ἦμέν ποτε τοῦ Λιβάνου τὰ ξύλα, ἕως ἐν ἐκείνῳ
ἦμεν ἐρριζωμένοι διά τε τοῦ πονηροῦ βίου καὶ τῆς τῶν εἰδώλων ἀπάτης. ἀλλ'
25   ἐπειδὴ ἐκεῖθεν ὑπὸ τῆς λογικῆς ἀξίνης ἐτμήθημεν καὶ ἐν ταῖς τοῦ τεχνίτου
χερσὶν ἐγενόμεθα, φορεῖον ἑαυτοῦ ἡμᾶς ἐποίησε μεταστοιχειώσας τοῦ ξύλου
τὴν φύσιν διὰ τῆς παλιγγενεσίας εἰς ἀργύριόν τε καὶ χρυσίον καὶ εἰς εὐανθῆ
πορφύραν καὶ εἰς τὰς τῶν λίθων αὐγάς.
και ὥσπερ φησὶν ὁ ἀπόστολος ὅτι καταλλήλως ἐμέρισεν ὁ θεὸς ἑκάστῳ
30 | τὰς τοῦ ἁγίου πνεύματος δωρεὰς καὶ ᾧ μὲν δίδωσι προφητείαν κατὰ τὴν   210

hand, we know of a kind of wood that does not remain as it is but changes itself into gold or silver or some other precious thing; for the apostle says that in the great household of God there are vessels that are gold and silver by nature—alluding by these, in my judgment, to the incorporeal and intelligent creation—and others of wood and clay, most likely denoting by these us whom disobedience has turned into earth and rendered things of clay, while the sin occasioned by the tree[3] has made us wooden rather than golden vessels. But the use of the vessels also differs, in accordance with the worth of their material, for those of more precious material are set apart for honor, while those destined for dishonorable service are cast aside. What is it, though, that Paul says about the latter sort? That the vessel has the power, on the basis of its own capacity for choice, to become gold from wood or silver from clay. "For," he says, "if a person purify himself, he will be a vessel | for honor, made ready by the master of the house for every good work" (2 Tim 2:21). Perhaps, then, by what has been said we are somehow being brought close to the requisite discernment of the sense of our text.

Mount Lebanon is mentioned in many scriptural texts to indicate the opposing Power, as when it says through the prophet, "The Lord will shatter the cedars of Lebanon, and he makes both them and Lebanon thin like a calf" (Ps 28:5–6), which obviously means the calf that was pulverized by Moses in the wilderness and became drinkable by the Israelites because of its lack of solidity (cf. Exod 32:20). Now the prophecy in this case shows that not only the evils that issue from the opposing Power but the very Mountain itself, the primary root of evil, the Lebanon that nourishes the substance of such cedars as these, comes to nonbeing. We, then, were once *trees of Lebanon,* as long as we were rooted in it by an evil life and by the vanity of idols. But because, after that, we were felled by the axe of the Logos[4] and came into the hands of the Artisan, he has made us his own *palanquin* and by the regeneration[5] changed the nature of wood into that of silver and gold, and into bright purple and the radiance of stones.

Now the apostle says that God measured | the gifts of the Holy Spirit appropriately to each individual and gives to one the gift of prophecy accord-

---

3. Ξύλον: see n. 2 above. Gregory means "the tree of the knowledge of good and evil," from which Adam and Eve ate at the serpent's behest.

4. Gregory writes ὑπὸ τῆς λογικῆς ἀξίνης, which might strictly speaking be rendered as "by the rational axe." This, however, would miss Gregory's point: it is the Logos or Word of God who is intimated by λογικῆς here. Perhaps Gregory has Heb 4:12 lurking in the back of his mind.

5. Παλιγγενεσία; cf. Tit 3:5. The reference is, of course, to baptism.

ἀναλογίαν τῆς πίστεως, ἄλλῳ δὲ ἄλλο τι τῶν ἐνεργημάτων, πρὸς ὃ πέφυκέ
τε καὶ δύναται ἕκαστος τὴν χάριν δέξασθαι ἢ ὀφθαλμὸς τοῦ σώματος τῆς
ἐκκλησίας γινόμενος ἢ εἰς χεῖρα τασσόμενος ἢ ἀντὶ ποδὸς ὑποστηρίζων,
οὕτω καὶ ἐν τῇ τοῦ φορείου κατασκευῇ ὁ μέν τις στῦλος, ὁ δὲ ἐπίβασις
5   γίνεται, ἕτερος δὲ τὸ πρὸς τῇ κεφαλῇ μέρος, ὃ ἀνάκλιτον προσηγόρευσεν,
εἰσὶ δέ τινες οἱ εἰς τὸ ἐντὸς τεταγμένοι. ὧν ἁπάντων κατά τινα λόγον ὁ
τεχνίτης οὐ μονοειδῆ πρὸς τὸν καλλωπισμὸν ἐπινοεῖ τὴν ὕλην, ἀλλὰ πάντα
μὲν κατακοσμεῖταί τῳ κάλλει, διάφορος δὲ καὶ κατάλληλος ἑκάστῳ τούτων
ἐπινοεῖται ἡ ὥρα. εἰσὶ τοίνυν ἀργύριον μὲν οἱ στῦλοι τοῦ φορείου, αἱ δὲ
10   τούτων ἐπιβάσεις πορφύρα, ἐκ χρυσίου δὲ τὸ ἀνάκλιτον τὸ τὴν κεφαλὴν
ὑποβαῖνον, ἐν ᾧ κλίνει τὴν ἑαυτοῦ κεφαλὴν ὁ νυμφίος, τοῖς δὲ τιμίοις λίθοις
τὸ ἔνδον ἅπαν καταποικίλλεται.

οὐκοῦν στύλους μὲν νοητέον τοὺς στύλους τῆς ἐκκλησίας, οἷς ἀκριβῶς
ἀργύριον καθαρόν τε καὶ πεπυρωμένον ὁ λόγος ἐστίν, οἳ τῆς βασιλείας ἐν τῷ
15   ὑψηλῷ τῆς πολιτείας ἐπιβεβήκασιν (ἐξαίρετον γὰρ γνώρισμα τῆς βασιλείας
ἡ πορφύρα | νομίζεται), τὸ δὲ ἡγεμονικὸν αὐτῶν, ἐν ᾧ τὴν κεφαλὴν ἑαυτοῦ   211
κλίνει ὁ τὸ φορεῖον κατασκευάσας, τὸ τῶν καθαρῶν δογμάτων χρυσίον
ἐστίν, ὅσα δὲ ἀφανῆ τε καὶ κρύφια, τῇ καθαρᾷ συνειδήσει τῶν τιμίων λίθων
ἐνωραΐζεται, δι' ὧν ἁπάντων ἀπὸ τῶν θυγατέρων Ἰερουσαλὴμ ἡ ἀγάπη
20   συνίσταται.

εἰ δὲ βούλοιτό τις φορεῖον μὲν πᾶσαν λέγειν τὴν ἐκκλησίαν, καταμερίζοι
δὲ κατὰ τὰς τῶν ἐνεργειῶν διαφορὰς εἰς πρόσωπά τινα τοῦ φορείου τὰ μέρη
ὡς ἤδη περὶ τούτου προείρηται, πολλὴν καὶ οὕτως εὐκολίαν ὁ λόγος ἔχει
ἑκάστῳ τάγματι τῶν κατὰ τὴν ἐκκλησίαν τεταγμένων ἐφαρμόσαι τοῦ φορείου
25   τὰ μέρη (καθώς φησιν ὁ ἀπόστολος ὅτι Ἔθετο ὁ θεὸς ἐν τῇ ἐκκλησίᾳ πρῶτον
ἀποστόλους δεύτερον προφήτας τρίτον διδασκάλους ἔπειτα τὰ καθ' ἕκαστον
πάντα πρὸς τὸν καταρτισμὸν τῶν ἁγίων), ὡς διὰ τῶν ὀνομάτων τούτων
τῶν πρὸς τὴν τοῦ φορείου κατασκευὴν συντελούντων ἱερέας νοεῖσθαι καὶ
διδασκάλους καὶ τὴν σεμνὴν παρθενίαν τὴν ἐντὸς τοῦ φορείου τῇ καθαρότητι
30   τῶν ἀρετῶν οἷόν τισι λίθων αὐγαῖς ἐναστράπτουσαν.

Ἀλλὰ περὶ μὲν τούτων τοσαῦτα. ὁ δὲ ἐφεξῆς λόγος προτροπὴν περιέχει
πρὸς τὰς θυγατέρας Ἰερουσαλὴμ παρὰ τῆς νύμφης γινόμενος. ὡς γὰρ ὁ
μέγας Παῦλος ζημίαν | ἡγεῖτο, εἰ μὴ πᾶσι τῶν ἰδίων ἀγαθῶν ἐκοινώνησεν (διὸ   212
τὰ τοιαῦτα πρὸς τοὺς ἀκούοντας ἔλεγεν ὅτι Γίνεσθε ὡς ἐγώ, καὶ γὰρ αὐτὸς
35   ἤμην ποτὲ καθ' ὑμᾶς· καὶ ὅτι Μιμηταί μου γίνεσθε καθὼς κἀγὼ Χριστοῦ),
οὕτω καὶ ἡ φιλάνθρωπος αὕτη νύμφη τῶν θείων τοῦ νυμφίου μυστηρίων
ἀξιωθεῖσα, ὅτε τὴν κλίνην εἶδε καὶ φορεῖον τοῦ βασιλέως ἐγένετο, βοᾷ πρὸς
τὰς νεάνιδας (αὗται δ' ἂν εἶεν αἱ τῶν σῳζομένων ψυχαί) ἕως πότε λέγουσα

ing to the proportion of faith, while to another he gives some other function, according as each has the natural disposition and the ability to receive grace— either becoming an eye of the body of the church, or being assigned the role of a hand, or supplying support in the place of a foot (cf. Rom 12:3–8; 1 Cor 12:7–11, 14–28). In the same way, one person becomes, in the structure of the *palanquin,* a *post,* another becomes the seat, while another becomes the part where the head is (called *backrest*), and some, further, are meant for the interior. The Artisan conceives the material that is to be used for all of these according to a design for the litter's ornamentation, but it is not all of a single sort. On the contrary, though everything is handsomely adorned, the beauty contrived for each part is different and appropriate. Hence the posts of the palanquin are silver, while its base is scarlet, and the backrest, on which the Bridegroom rests his head, is gold, and the interior is variegated in color with precious stones.

So then one must conceive the posts as the "pillars of the church" (cf. Gal 2:9; Rev 3:12), whose speech, in its precision, is fired and purified silver. They have entered upon the way of life of the kingdom on high (for purple is thought | to be the special mark of regal status). But in their case the governing part of the soul, on which the one who built the litter rests his head, is the gold of the pure dogmas, while whatever is hidden and invisible from without is adorned by that pure conscience represented by the precious stones, out of which *love* is fashioned at the hands of *the daughters of Jerusalem.*

If, though, someone should wish to assert that the palanquin stands for the whole church, while the parts of the palanquin (as has already been said in this regard) are assigned to particular roles that correspond to differences of function—even taken in this sense, our text has no difficulty at all in matching the parts of the litter to each rank of those who are ordered in the church (as the apostle says: "God has appointed in the church first apostles, second prophets, third teachers, then" [1 Cor 12:28] all functions individually "for the equipment of the saints" [Eph 4:12]). Thus by these names that accomplish the fitting-out of the litter, we understand priests and teachers and that holy virginity that flashes within the litter with the purity of the virtues like the gleaming of so many precious stones.

But enough for that. The next verse contains an exhortation addressed by the Bride to the daughters of Jerusalem. For as the great Paul judges it | a loss if he does not share his own good things with all (which is why he said to his hearers: "Become as I am, for I was once as you are" [Gal 4:12]; and then, "Become imitators of me as I am of Christ" [1 Cor 11:1]), so too the Bride herself, a lover of humanity who has been made worthy of the divine mysteries of the Bridegroom, when she has seen the couch and has become the litter of the King, calls to the young women (who no doubt represent the

τῷ σπηλαίῳ τοῦ βίου ἐναποκλείεσθε; ἐξέλθετε τῶν προκαλυμμάτων τῆς
φύσεως καὶ ἴδετε τὸ θαυμαστὸν θέαμα Σιὼν θυγατέρες γενόμεναι, θεάσασθε
περιπρέποντα τῇ κεφαλῇ τοῦ βασιλέως τὸν στέφανον, ὃν ἡ μήτηρ αὐτῷ
περιέθηκε κατὰ τὴν τοῦ προφήτου φωνήν, ὅς φησιν Ἔθηκας ἐπὶ τὴν κεφαλὴν
5   αὐτοῦ στέφανον ἐκ λίθου τιμίου.

πάντως δὲ οὐδεὶς τῶν κρίνειν τοὺς περὶ θεοῦ λόγους ἐπεσκεμμένων
ἀκριβολογεῖται περὶ τὴν τοῦ ὀνόματος ἔμφασιν, ὅτι μήτηρ ἀντὶ τοῦ πατρὸς
μνημονεύεται, μίαν | ἀφ᾽ ἑκατέρας φωνῆς ἀναλαμβάνων διάνοιαν. ἐπειδὴ γὰρ   213
οὔτε ἄρρεν οὔτε θῆλυ τὸ θεῖόν ἐστιν (πῶς γὰρ ἂν ἐπὶ τῆς θεότητός τι νοηθείη
10   τοιοῦτον, ὁπότε οὐδὲ ἡμῖν τοῖς ἀνθρώποις τοῦτο εἰς τὸ διηνεκὲς παραμένει,
ἀλλ᾽ ὅταν ἐν Χριστῷ πάντες εἷς γενώμεθα, τὰ σημεῖα τῆς διαφορᾶς ταύτης
μετὰ ὅλου τοῦ παλαιοῦ ἀνθρώπου συνεκδυόμεθα;), τούτου χάριν ἰσοδυναμεῖ
πρὸς τὴν ἔνδειξιν τῆς ἀφράστου φύσεως πᾶν τὸ εὑρισκόμενον ὄνομα οὔτε
θήλεος οὔτε ἄρρενος τὴν σημασίαν τῆς ἀκηράτου καταμολύνοντος φύσεως.
15   διὰ τοῦτο ἐν μὲν τῷ εὐαγγελίῳ ὁ πατὴρ λέγεται ποιεῖν τῷ υἱῷ τοὺς γάμους,
ὁ δὲ προφήτης πρὸς τὸν θεὸν λέγει ὅτι Ἔθηκας ἐπὶ τὴν κεφαλὴν αὐτοῦ
στέφανον ἐκ λίθου τιμίου, ἐνταῦθα δὲ παρὰ τῆς μητρός φησιν ἐπιτεθεῖσθαι
τῷ νυμφίῳ τὸν στέφανον. ἐπεὶ οὖν εἷς ἐστιν ὁ γάμος καὶ μία ἡ νύμφη καὶ παρὰ
ἑνὸς ἐπιβάλλεται τῷ νυμφίῳ ὁ στέφανος, διαφέρει πάντως οὐδὲν ἢ υἱὸν τοῦ
20   θεοῦ τὸν μονογενῆ λέγειν θεὸν ἢ υἱὸν τῆς ἀγάπης αὐτοῦ κατὰ τὴν Παύλου
φωνὴν μιᾶς οὔσης καθ᾽ | ἑκάτερον ὄνομα τῆς νυμφοστολούσης αὐτὸν ἐπὶ τῇ   214
ἡμετέρᾳ συνοικήσει δυνάμεως.

ἐξέλθετε οὖν φησὶν ἡ νύμφη πρὸς τὰς νεάνιδας, καὶ θυγατέρες Σιὼν
γένεσθε, ὥστε ἀπὸ σκοπιᾶς ὑψηλῆς (οὕτω γὰρ ἡ Σιὼν ἑρμηνεύεται) δυνηθῆναι
25   τὸ θαυμαστὸν ἰδεῖν θέαμα στεφανηφοροῦντα τὸν νυμφίον. στέφανος δὲ
αὐτῷ ἡ ἐκκλησία γίνεται διὰ τῶν ἐμψύχων λίθων τὴν κεφαλὴν ἐν κύκλῳ
διαλαμβάνουσα, στεφανηπλόκος δὲ τοῦ τοιούτου στεφάνου ἡ ἀγάπη ἐστίν,
ἣν εἴτε μητέρα εἴτε ἀγάπην τις λέγοι, οὐχ ἁμαρτήσεται· θεὸς γάρ ἐστιν ἡ
ἀγάπη κατὰ τὴν Ἰωάννου φωνήν. τούτῳ δὲ τῷ στεφάνῳ ἐνευφραίνεσθαι λέγει
30   αὐτὸν ἡ νύμφη τῷ νυμφικῷ κόσμῳ ἐναγαλλόμενον· χαίρει γὰρ ὡς ἀληθῶς ὁ
σύνοικον τὴν ἐκκλησίαν ἑαυτῷ ποιησάμενος ταῖς ἀρεταῖς τῶν διαπρεπόντων
ἐν αὐτῇ στεφανούμενος. κρεῖττον δ᾽ ἂν εἴη αὐτὰς παραθέσθαι τὰς θείας
φωνὰς ἐπὶ λέξεως ἐχούσας οὕτως· Ἐξέλθετε καὶ ἴδετε, θυγατέρες Σιών, ἐν τῷ
βασιλεῖ Σαλωμὼν ἐν τῷ στεφάνῳ, ᾧ ἐστεφάνωσεν αὐτὸν ἡ μήτηρ αὐτοῦ ἐν
35   ἡμέρᾳ νυμφεύσεως αὐτοῦ καὶ ἐν ἡμέρᾳ εὐφροσύνης καρδίας αὐτοῦ.

souls of those who are being saved), saying, "How long will you be shut up in the cavern[6] of this life? Come out, when you have become daughters of Zion, from among the shadows of nature, and behold the wondrous sight. You will see the crown that adorns the head of the King, which his mother placed on his brow in accordance with the word of the prophet, 'You have placed on his brow a crown of precious stone' " (Ps 20:4).

Now no one who has given thought to the way we talk about God is going to be overprecise about the sense of the name—that "mother" is mentioned instead of "father," | for he will gather the same meaning from either term. For the Divine is neither male nor female.[7] (How, after all, could any such thing be conceived in the case of Deity, when this condition is not permanent even for us human beings, but when we all become one in Christ, we put off the signs of this difference along with the whole of the old humanity?) For this reason, every name we turn up is of the same adequacy for purposes of pointing to the unutterable Nature, since neither "male" nor "female" defiles the meaning of the inviolate Nature. Hence in the Gospel a father is said to give a marriage feast for a son, while the prophet addresses God, saying, "You have put a crown of precious stone on his head" and then asserts that the crown was put on the Bridegroom's head by his mother. So there is one wedding feast, and the Bride is one, and the crown is placed on the head of the Bridegroom by one agent. Hence it makes no difference whether God calls the Only Begotten "Son of God" or "Son of his love" (Col 1:13), as Paul has it, since whichever | name is used it is one Power who escorts the Bridegroom to our marriage.

So the Bride says to the young women: "Come out, and become daughters of Zion, so that you will be able to see, from an exalted height (for so 'Zion' is translated), the marvelous sight of the Bridegroom wearing his crown." Now the church becomes his crown because of the "living stones" with which she encircles his head, and the One who plaits a crown of this sort is Love, whom one may call either "mother" or "love" without risk of error, for according to John's word God is love. Now the Bride says that he rejoices in this crown as he delights in the bridal splendor. For the one who has taken the church for himself as a partner is joyful when he is crowned with the virtues of those who stand out within her. But it would be more effective to set out the divine words themselves, which go exactly like this: *Go forth, you daughters of Jerusalem, and see King Solomon in his crown with which his mother crowned him, on the day of his wedding, and on the day of his heart's rejoicing.*

---

6. This is no doubt Plato's famous cave; see *Resp.* 514Aff.

7. For similar denials that the differences of sex apply to God (or to humanity "after the image" of God), see, e.g., Gregory, *Opif. hom.* 16 (PG 44:185A); *Virg.* 5 (PG 46:348A).

Τὴν οὖν τοιαύτην φιλανθρωπίαν τῆς νύμφης ὁ λόγος ἀποδεξάμενος, ὅτι
κατὰ μίμησιν τοῦ δεσπότου καὶ | αὐτὴ Πάντας θέλει σωθῆναι καὶ εἰς ἐπίγνωσιν   215
ἀληθείας ἐλθεῖν, σεμνοτέραν αὐτὴν ἀπεργάζεται κῆρυξ τοῦ κάλλους αὐτῆς
καὶ ζωγράφος γινόμενος· οὐ γὰρ ἁπλῶς ὁ τῆς ὥρας ἔπαινος γίνεται καθολικήν
5   τινα τὴν εὐφημίαν περιέχων τοῦ κάλλους, ἀλλ᾽ ἐμφιλοχωρεῖ τῷ λόγῳ τοῖς
καθ᾽ ἕκαστον μέλεσιν ἴδιον ἑκάστῳ μέλει διὰ συγκρίσεώς τε καὶ ὁμοιώσεως
χαριζόμενος τὸ ἐγκώμιον.
    λέγει δὲ οὕτως· Ἰδοὺ εἶ καλή, ἡ πλησίον μου, ἰδοὺ εἶ καλή· ἡ γὰρ
μιμησαμένη τοῦ δεσπότου τὸ φιλάνθρωπον βούλημα καὶ ἐξελθεῖν
10   ἐγκελευσαμένη καθ᾽ ὁμοιότητα τοῦ Ἀβραὰμ τὰς νεάνιδας, ἑκάστην ἀπὸ τῆς
γῆς ἑαυτῆς καὶ ἀπὸ τῆς περὶ τὰ αἰσθητήρια συγγενείας αὐτῆς, ὥστε ἰδεῖν
τὸν καθαρὸν νυμφίον στεφανηφοροῦντα τὴν ἐκκλησίαν, ἀληθῶς πλησίον
γίνεται τῆς δεσποτικῆς ἀγαθότητος διὰ τῆς πρὸς τὸν πλησίον ἀγάπης τῷ θεῷ
προσεγγίσασα. καλὴ οὖν εἶ, φησὶ πρὸς αὐτὴν ὁ λόγος, τῇ ἀγαθῇ προαιρέσει
15   τῷ καλῷ πλησιάσασα. ἡ δὲ ἐπανάληψις τοῦ ἐπαίνου τὸ ἄψευστον τῆς
μαρτυρίας ἐνδείκνυται· ἐν γὰρ τῇ διπλῇ μαρτυρίᾳ βεβαιοῦσθαι τὴν ἀλήθειαν
ὁ θεῖος ἀποφαίνεται | νόμος. διὰ τοῦτό φησιν Ἰδοὺ εἶ καλή, ἡ πλησίον μου,   216
ἰδοὺ εἶ καλή.
    Ἀλλ᾽ ἐπειδὴ ἓν σῶμα τοῦ Χριστοῦ ἡ ἐκκλησία πᾶσα, ἐν δὲ τῷ ἑνὶ σώματι,
20   καθώς φησιν ὁ ἀπόστολος, μέλη ἐστὶ πολλά, πάντα δὲ τὰ μέλη οὐ τὴν
αὐτὴν ἔχει πρᾶξιν, ἀλλὰ τὸν μὲν ὀφθαλμὸν ἔπλασεν ὁ θεὸς ἐν τῷ σώματι,
ἕτερος δέ τις οὓς ἐφυτεύθη, εἰσὶ δέ τινες διὰ τῆς ἐνεργείας τῶν δυνάμεων
χεῖρες γινόμενοι καὶ πόδες λέγονταί τινες οἱ τὰ βάρη βαστάζοντες, εἴη δ᾽
ἄν τι καὶ γεύσεως ἔργον καὶ ὀσφρήσεως καὶ τὰ καθ᾽ ἕκαστον πάντα, δι᾽ ὧν
25   τὸ ἀνθρώπινον σύγκειται σῶμα, δυνατόν ἐστιν εὑρεῖν ἐν τῷ κοινῷ σώματι
τῆς ἐκκλησίας χείλη τε καὶ ὀδόντας καὶ γλῶσσαν, μαζούς τε καὶ κοιλίαν καὶ
τράχηλον, ὡς δὲ ὁ Παῦλός φησι καὶ αὐτὰ τὰ δοκοῦντα ἀσχήμονα εἶναι τοῦ
σώματος. τούτου χάριν ὁ ἀκριβὴς τοῦ κάλλους δοκιμαστὴς τῶν ἀρεσάντων
αὐτῷ μελῶν ἐξ ὅλου τοῦ σώματος ἴδιόν τε καὶ πρόσφορον ἑκάστῳ ποιεῖται
30   τὸν ἔπαινον.
    ἄρχεται δὲ τῶν ἐγκωμίων ἀπὸ τῶν κυριωτέρων μελῶν. τί γὰρ ὀφθαλμῶν
ἐν τοῖς μέλεσιν ἡμῶν ἐστι τιμιώτερον, δι᾽ ὧν ἡ τοῦ φωτὸς ἀντίληψις γίνεται,
παρ᾽ ὧν ἐστιν ἡ τῶν φιλίων τε καὶ πολεμίων ἐπίγνωσις, οἷς τὸ ἴδιόν τε καὶ τὸ | 217
ἀλλότριον διακρίνομεν, οἳ πάσης ἐργασίας ὑφηγηταὶ καὶ διδάσκαλοι γίνονται
35   καὶ τῆς ἀπλανοῦς ὁδοιπορίας ὁδηγοὶ συμφυεῖς καὶ ἀχώριστοι, ὧν ἡ θέσις τῶν

When the Word, then, has taken account of the Bride's love of human-ity—a love of such a kind that after the pattern of the Lord | she too "wants everyone to be saved and to come to the knowledge of truth" (cf. 1 Tim 2:4)—he assigns her the more prestige by assuming the role of a herald and portraitist of her beauty. For his praise of her glory is not a simple one that honors her beauty in general terms. Rather, he dwells lovingly on her individ-ual members, lavishing on each the honor proper to it by way of comparisons and analogies.

This is what he says: *Behold you are beautiful, my close one; behold you are beautiful.* For she who imitates the loving will of the Master and commands the young women to *go forth* after the fashion of Abraham, each from her own land and from her kinship with the faculties of sense, so as to see the pure bridegroom wearing the church as a crown—she truly becomes *close* to the goodness of her Lord because she has drawn near to God by love of neigh-bor. Therefore the Word says to her, "*You are beautiful* now that by your good choice you have drawn close to Beauty." The repetition of the praise demon-strates the sincerity of the testimony, for the divine law declares that the truth is established by a double testimony (cf. Deut 19:15).[8] | That is why he says, *Behold you are beautiful, my close one, behold you are beautiful.*

Since, however, the whole church is one body of Christ, but in the one body, as the apostle says, there are many members, and all the members do not have the same function (cf. 1 Cor 12:12–26), but God forms one as an eye for the body and another was implanted as an ear, and some become hands on account of what they are able to do, and some that carry our weight are called feet, but there will also have to be a job of tasting and smelling, not to mention all the individual parts of which the human body is composed— since this is so, I say, it is possible to find in the common body of the church lips as well as teeth and tongue, breasts and womb and neck and, as Paul says, also those members of the body that appear unseemly. Hence the one who praises beauty with precision gives to each of the members of the body that please him the honor that is proper and fitting.

He begins his encomium with the noblest members. For which among our members is worthy of greater honor than the eyes? Through them we receive light, with their help we recognize friend and foe, by their means we distinguish what is native from what is | alien. They are the tutors and instruc-tors of every work we undertake and the natural and inseparable guides of

---

8. The text of Deuteronomy that Gregory alludes to here speaks of "two witnesses," not of one testimony repeated a second time.

ἄλλων αἰσθητηρίων ὑπερκειμένη τὸ προτιμότερον τῆς ἀπ' αὐτῶν γινομένης ἡμῖν πρὸς τὸν βίον ὠφελείας ἐνδείκνυται.

πάντως δὲ πρόδηλόν ἐστι τοῖς ἀκούουσιν εἰς ποῖα μέλη τῆς ἐκκλησίας ὁ τῶν ὀφθαλμῶν ἔπαινος βλέπει· ὀφθαλμὸς ἦν Σαμουὴλ ὁ βλέπων (οὕτω 5 γὰρ ὠνομάζετο), ὀφθαλμὸς Ἰεζεκιὴλ ὁ σκοπεῖν ὑπὸ τοῦ θεοῦ τεταγμένος ἐπὶ τῇ τῶν φυλασσομένων παρ' αὐτοῦ σωτηρίᾳ, ὀφθαλμὸς Μιχαίας ὁ ὁρῶν καὶ Μωϋσῆς ὁ θεώμενος ὁ διὰ τοῦτο καὶ θεὸς ὠνομασμένος, ὀφθαλμοὶ πάντες ἐκεῖνοι οἱ εἰς ὁδηγίαν τοῦ λαοῦ τεταγμένοι. οὓς καὶ ὁρῶντας ὠνόμαζον οἱ τότε ἄνθρωποι· καὶ νῦν οἱ τὸν ἐκείνων τόπον ἀναπληροῦντες <ἐν> τῷ 10 σώματι τῆς ἐκκλησίας ὀφθαλμοὶ κυρίως κατονομάζονται, ἐὰν ἀκριβῶς πρὸς τὸν τῆς δικαιοσύνης βλέπωσιν ἥλιον μηδαμοῦ τοῖς ἔργοις τοῦ σκότους ἐναμβλυώττοντες, καὶ εἰ διακρίνοιεν τοῦ ἀλλοτρίου τὸ ἴδιον ἐν τῷ γινώσκειν ὅτι πᾶν ἀλλότριόν ἐστι τῆς φύσεως ἡμῶν τὸ φαινόμενόν τε καὶ πρόσκαιρον, ἴδιον δὲ τὸ δι' ἐλπίδος | προκείμενον, οὗ ἡ κτῆσις μένει πρὸς τὸ διηνεκὲς 218 15 ἀναφαίρετος.

ὀφθαλμῶν ἔργον καὶ τὸ διαγινώσκειν τὸ φίλιόν τε καὶ τὸ πολέμιον, ὥστε ἀγαπᾶν μὲν τὸν ἀληθινὸν φίλον ἐξ ὅλης καρδίας τε καὶ ψυχῆς καὶ δυνάμεως, τέλειον δὲ μῖσος κατὰ τοῦ ἐχθροῦ τῆς ζωῆς ἡμῶν ἐπιδείκνυσθαι. ἀλλὰ καὶ ὁ τῶν πρακτέων ὑφηγητὴς καὶ τῶν συμφερόντων διδάσκαλος καὶ τῆς ἐπὶ 20 τὸν θεὸν πορείας χειραγωγὸς τοῦ καθαροῦ τε καὶ ὑγιαίνοντος ὀφθαλμοῦ τὸ ἔργον δι' ἀκριβείας ποιεῖ καθ' ὁμοιότητα τῶν σωματικῶν ὀμμάτων διὰ τῆς ὑψηλῆς πολιτείας τῶν λοιπῶν προφαινόμενος.

διὰ τοῦτο ἐντεῦθεν ἐπαινεῖν ὁ λόγος τὸ τῆς νύμφης ἄρχεται κάλλος καί φησιν Ὀφθαλμοί σου περιστεραί· ἀκεραίους γὰρ εἰς τὸ κακὸν τοὺς ἐν 25 ὀφθαλμῶν τάξει προβεβλημένους ὁρῶν τὴν ἁπλότητά τε καὶ τὸ ἀκέραιον τοῦ ἤθους αὐτῶν ἀποδεξάμενος περιστερὰς αὐτοὺς κατωνόμασεν· ἴδιον γάρ ἐστι περιστερῶν τὸ ἀκέραιον. ἢ τάχα καὶ τοιοῦτόν τινα ὁ λόγος μαρτυρεῖ τοῖς ὄμμασιν ἔπαινον· ἐπειδὴ γὰρ πάντων τῶν ὁρατῶν αἱ εἰκόνες τῷ καθαρῷ τῆς κόρης ἐμπίπτουσαι τὴν ὁρατικὴν ἐνέργειαν ἀποτελοῦσιν, ἀνάγκη πᾶσα πρὸς 30 ὅ τις ὁρᾷ, τούτου τὴν μορφὴν ἀναλαμβάνειν διὰ τοῦ ὀφθαλμοῦ κατόπτρου

inerrant walking. Their location above the other sense organs manifests the fact that their usefulness to us for the conduct of life is of the greatest worth.

To those who have ears, though, it is perfectly apparent which members of the church are contemplated by this praise of the eyes. Samuel "the seer" (1 Kgdms 9:11),[9] for so was he named, was an eye; Ezekiel, who was set by God to watch over the salvation of those in his charge (cf. Ezek 3:17), was an eye; Micah "the seer"[10] was an eye; and Moses the overseer, who for just this reason was called "god" (Exod 7:1)[11]—all of those who were assigned to lead the people were eyes. The folk of their time called them "seers," and even now those who fill their places in the body of the church are properly termed eyes, on condition that they look undeviatingly upon the Sun of Righteousness and never dim their sight with the works of darkness and that they make a distinction between what is native and what is alien, in the knowledge that everything that appears and is ephemeral is alien to our nature, while what is available | through hope is native to us, because its possession is inalienable for all eternity.

Another work of the eyes is to recognize friend and foe, so that we may love our true Friend with all our heart and soul and strength while manifesting a ripe hatred for the enemy of life. Furthermore, the one who provides instruction in what to do and teaches what is fitting and gives guidance for the journey God-ward—such a one does with exactitude the work of a pure and healthful eye, being, after the likeness of our bodily eyes, conspicuous beyond others because of the exalted character of his mode of life.

That is why the Word begins his praise of the Bride's beauty from that point and says, *Your eyes are doves.* For seeing that those who are set to the front in the place of eyes are unstained by evil, and noting the purity and simplicity of their ways, he calls them doves, for purity is a native characteristic of doves. Or perhaps the Word attests such praise as the following with regard to eyes: for since the images of all visible things, when they make contact with a pure pupil <of the eye>, bring about vision, it is necessary that one assume the form of that toward which one looks, receiving through the

---

9. In the Greek of 1 Kgdms (1 Sam) 9:11, it is explained that a prophet had been called "one who sees," ὁ βλέπων. English would render both this expression—as well as ὁ ὁρῶν, which Gregory uses just below to describe "Micah"—by the word "seer." See below, n. 10.

10. It is Amos, not Micah, who is called ὁ ὁρῶν ("the see-er") at Amos 7:12. Perhaps Gregory's memory failed him here. He repeats this idea in homily 13 (p. 394 [Jaeger]) but without supplying names.

11. Moses was to be a "god" to Pharaoh, says Exod 7:1, and Gregory explains this by reference to his theory that θεός ("god") is etymologically derived from θεᾶσθαι ("see"). See above, p. 141 (Jaeger) on Song 2:9, with the note there.

δίκην τοῦ ὁρατοῦ τὸ εἶδος | ἀναμασσόμενον. ὅταν τοίνυν ὁ τὴν ὀπτικὴν   219
ταύτην ἐξουσίαν ἐπὶ τῆς ἐκκλησίας λαβὼν πρὸς μηδὲν ὑλῶδες καὶ σωματικὸν
βλέπῃ, ὁ πνευματικός τε καὶ ἄϋλος ἐν αὐτῷ κατορθοῦται βίος. ἡ δὲ τοιαύτη
ζωὴ τῇ τοῦ ἁγίου πνεύματος χάριτι καταμορφοῦται. οὐκοῦν ὁ τελεώτατος
5   τῶν ὀφθαλμῶν ἐστιν ἔπαινος τὸ πρὸς τὴν τοῦ πνεύματος τοῦ ἁγίου χάριν
μεμορφῶσθαι αὐτῶν τῆς ζωῆς τὸ εἶδος· περιστερὰ γὰρ τὸ πνεῦμα τὸ ἅγιον.
    ἡ δὲ δυὰς τῶν ὀφθαλμῶν ἐπαινεῖται, ὡς ἂν ὅλος γένοιτο ἐν ἐπαίνῳ ὁ
ἄνθρωπος, ὁ φαινόμενός τε καὶ νοούμενος. διὰ τοῦτο γὰρ προσέθηκε τῷ
ἐπαίνῳ καὶ ἄλλην ὑπερβολὴν εἰπὼν ὅτι Ἐκτὸς τῆς σιωπήσεώς σου· τοῦ
10   γὰρ ἀγαθοῦ βίου τὸ μέν τι πρόδηλόν ἐστιν, ὡς καὶ ἀνθρώποις γνώριμον
εἶναι, τὸ δὲ κρύφιόν τε καὶ ἀπόρρητον μόνῳ θεῷ καθορώμενον. ὁ τοίνυν
τὸ ἀκατέργαστον βλέπων καὶ εἰς τὰ κρύφια καθορῶν μαρτυρεῖ ἐπὶ τοῦ
ἐπαινουμένου προσώπου πλέον εἶναι τοῦ ὁρωμένου τὸ σιωπώμενον. δι' ὧν
φησιν ὅτι Ὀφθαλμοί σου περιστεραὶ ἐκτὸς τῆς σιωπήσεώς σου· ἔξωθεν γάρ
15   ἐστι τοῦ ἐπαινεθέντος ἤδη τὸ διὰ τῆς σιωπῆς θαυμαζόμενον.
    Ὁδῷ δὲ προάγει καθεξῆς τὸ τοῦ κάλλους ἐγκώμιον ἐπὶ τὰς τρίχας
μεταγαγὼν τὸν λόγον καί φησι Τρίχωμά | σου ὡς ἀγέλαι τῶν αἰγῶν, αἳ   220
ἀνεκαλύφθησαν ἀπὸ τοῦ Γαλαάδ. νοῆσαι δὲ προσήκει πρῶτον τῆς τριχὸς
τὴν φύσιν, εἶθ' οὕτως ἐπιγνῶναι τὸν ἔπαινον, ὃν διὰ τῶν τριχῶν ὁ λόγος
20   τῇ νύμφῃ χαρίζεται. οὐκοῦν δόξα μὲν γυναικὸς ἡ θρὶξ παρὰ τοῦ Παύλου
ὠνόμασται καὶ ἀντὶ περιβολαίου δεδόσθαι τῇ γυναικὶ τὴν κόμην λέγει. αἰδῶ
δὲ καὶ σωφροσύνην τὸ πρέπον εἶναί φησι ταῖς γυναιξὶ περιβόλαιον οὕτω
γράψας τῷ ῥήματι ὅτι Ὡς πρέπει γυναιξὶν ἐπαγγελλομέναις θεοσέβειαν Μετὰ
αἰδοῦς καὶ σωφροσύνης κοσμεῖν ἑαυτάς, ὡς διὰ τούτων τὰς ἐπὶ τῆς κεφαλῆς
25   τρίχας, αἷς κομᾷ ἡ γυνή, αἰδῶ καὶ σωφροσύνην διὰ τῆς τοῦ Παύλου σοφίας
καταλαμβάνεσθαι· οὐδὲ γὰρ ἄλλην τινὰ πρέπει δόξαν ὀνομάζεσθαι ἐπὶ τῆς
ἐπαγγελλομένης θεοσέβειαν ψυχῆς εἰ μὴ τὴν αἰδῶ τε καὶ σωφροσύνην, ἣν
κόμην ὠνόμασεν, ἣν ὅταν μὴ ἔχῃ Καταισχύνει τὴν κεφαλὴν ἑαυτῆς, καθώς
φησιν ὁ ἀπόστολος. εἰ δὲ ταῦτα περὶ τῶν τριχῶν ὁ Παῦλος ἐφιλοσόφησε,
30 | προσακτέον ἂν εἴη τὰ τοῦ ἀποστόλου νοήματα τῷ ἐπαίνῳ τῆς ἐκκλησίας   221

eye, in the fashion of a mirror,[12] the form of the visible thing. | When therefore one who has received this eyelike authority over the church gazes upon nothing material and corporeal, the spiritual and immaterial life is established within him. Hence the most perfect praise of eyes is that the form of their life is shaped in conformity with the grace of the Holy Spirit, for the Holy Spirit is a dove.[13]

Now the eyes are praised as a pair so that the entire human being may be included in the praise—the phenomenal as well as the noumenal.[14] That explains why the Word adds yet a further lavish note to his praise and says *outside your veil*. For where the good life is concerned, there is a portion of it that is manifest, so as to be known to human beings, and there is a portion that is hidden and ineffable, seen only by God. He, therefore, who looks upon what is unfinished and discerns the things that are hidden testifies, regarding the subject of these praises, that what is kept in silence[15] is greater than what is seen. Hence he says: *Your eyes are doves outside your veil*. For that which is marveled at in silence is set apart from that which has been praised.

But the Word moves his praise of the Bride's beauty ahead to another stage and turns the discourse to her hair. It says: *Your hair | is like flocks of goats that have been revealed from Gilead*. Now it is best first of all to understand the nature of hair and then, in this way, to learn what praise it is that the Word lavishes upon the Bride. Hair is called a woman's "glory" by Paul, and he says that the hair of the head was given woman "in place of a covering" (1 Cor 11:15). And he said that modesty and temperance are the proper covering for women, thus writing (to quote exactly), "As befits women who profess piety," they are to "adorn themselves with modesty and temperance" (1 Tim 2:9–10). Thus, according to Paul's wisdom, the hair of the head that crowns a woman is to be understood as modesty and temperance. For in the case of the soul that professes true religion, it is not fitting for any glory to be mentioned save modesty and temperance, which he calls "hair of the head," and should she not possess it, she "dishonors her head," as the apostle says. But if Paul philosophizes in this way about hair, | doubtless the apostle's ideas

---

12. See above homily 3 (p. 90 [Jaeger]), with n. 23; homily 4 (p. 104 [Jaeger]), with n. 5.

13. Here Gregory in effect repeats what he has already said in homily 5 above (pp. 150–51 [Jaeger]). The identification of "dove" as meaning the Holy Spirit is also to be found in homily 13, p. 395 (Jaeger).

14. Gregory means the human person as perceptible (corporeal), on the one hand, and as intelligible (immaterial), on the other.

15. The word for a veil (σιώπησις) literally means "a keeping silence" and is related to the verb σιωπάω ("keep silence," "be silent about," hence "conceal"). For Gregory, then, what is "behind the veil" is both hidden from sight and *unspoken*. See below, pp. 230–31 (Jaeger), with n. 24; homily 15, p. 456 (Jaeger), with n. 23.

ἐν τῷ περὶ τοῦ τριχώματος λόγῳ κατὰ τὴν προκειμένην φωνὴν ἥ φησιν ὅτι
Τρίχωμά σου ὡς ἀγέλαι τῶν αἰγῶν, αἳ ἀνεκαλύφθησαν ἀπὸ τοῦ Γαλαάδ· διὰ
τούτων γὰρ τὴν ἐνάρετον πολιτείαν ἐν ἐπαίνῳ ποιεῖται ὁ λόγος.

ἀλλὰ κἀκεῖνο προστεθῆναι τῷ περὶ τῶν τριχῶν λόγῳ προσήκει ὅτι
5   πάσης αἰσθήσεως ζωτικῆς ἀμοιροῦσιν αἱ κόμαι· οὐ μικρὸν γὰρ εἰς ἐπαύξησιν
ἐγκωμίων καὶ τοῦτο τὸ μήτε πόνου μήτε ἡδονῆς αἴσθησιν ἐν ταῖς θριξὶν
εἶναι· τὸ μὲν γὰρ σῶμα, ὅθεν ἐκφύονται, ὀδυνᾶται παρατιλλόμενον, αὐτὴ
δὲ ἡ θρὶξ οὔτε εἰ τέμνοιτο οὔτε εἰ φλέγοιτο οὔτε εἰ διά τινος κομμωτικῆς
ἐπιμελείας καταλεαίνοιτο τῶν γινομένων αἴσθησιν δέχεται. τὸ δὲ ἀμοιρεῖν
10   τῆς αἰσθήσεως τῶν νεκρῶν ἐστιν ἴδιον. οὐκοῦν ὁ μηδεμίαν τῶν ἐν τῷ κόσμῳ
τούτῳ σπουδαζομένων παραδεχόμενος αἴσθησιν μήτε ὑπὸ δόξης τε καὶ
τιμῆς ἐξογκούμενος μήτε δι' ὕβρεώς τε καὶ ἀτιμίας ἀλγεινῶς διατιθέμενος,
ἀλλ' ἐν ὁμοίῳ καθ' ἑκάτερον τῶν ἐναντίων ἑαυτὸν φυλάσσων, οὗτός ἐστιν
ἡ ἐπαινουμένη τῆς νύμφης κόμη, νεκρὸς ἄντικρυς καὶ ἀκίνητος πρὸς τὰ τοῦ
15   κόσμου φαινόμενος πράγματα, εἴτε οὕτως εἴτε ὡς ἑτέρως ἔχοι.

Εἰ δὲ τὸ πλεονέκτημα τῶν τριχῶν ἀγέλαις αἰγῶν παρα|βάλλεται ταῖς   222
ἀπὸ τοῦ Γαλαάδ ἀνακαλυφθείσαις, ἃ μὲν χρὴ δι' ἀκριβείας περὶ τούτων
γινώσκειν, οὔπω καταλαβεῖν ἠδυνήθημεν, στοχαζόμεθα δὲ ὅτι ὥσπερ τὰ ξύλα
τοῦ Λιβάνου εἰς χρυσόν τε καὶ ἄργυρον καὶ πορφύραν καὶ λίθους τιμίους
20   μεταποιήσας φορεῖον ὁ βασιλεὺς κατεσκεύασεν ἑαυτῷ, οὕτως οἶδεν ὁ ποιμὴν
ὁ καλὸς αἰγῶν ἀγέλας παραλαβὼν εἰς ποίμνια μεταβαλεῖν τὰ αἰπόλια τοῦ
Γαλαάδ ὄρους. ἀλλοφύλου δὲ ὄρους ὄνομα τοῦτο τοῦ τὴν τοιαύτην χάριν
ἀνακαλύπτοντος, ὥστε τοὺς ἐξ ἐθνῶν τῷ καλῷ ποιμένι ἀκολουθήσαντας εἰς
τὸ τρίχωμα συντελέσαι τοῦ τῆς νύμφης κάλλους, δι' ὧν σωφροσύνη τε καὶ
25   αἰδὼς καὶ ἐγκράτεια καὶ ἡ τοῦ σώματος νέκρωσις κατὰ τὸν προθεωρηθέντα
λόγον διασημαίνεται.

ἢ τάχα συμβάλλεταί τι πρὸς τὴν τῶν αἰγῶν θεωρίαν καὶ ὁ Ἠλίας τῷ ὄρει
τῷ Γαλαάδ ἐμφιλοσοφήσας χρόνον πολύν, ὃς μάλιστα τοῦ κατ' ἐγκράτειαν
καθηγήσατο βίου αὐχμηρὸς τὸ εἶδος, λάσιος τὴν τρίχα, ἀντὶ μαλακῆς τινος

should be applied to the commendation of the church as that is contained in the remarks about hair in the statement before us, that is, *Your hair is like herds of goats that have been revealed from Gilead*. For by their means the text accords praise to the virtuous way of life.

But one ought to add this too to what is said about hair: that it has no share in the sense experience that belongs to living things.[16] For there is no small enhancement of these praises in the fact that in hair there is sensation neither of pain nor of pleasure. The body out of which hairs grow suffers pain when they are plucked out; the hair itself, however, has no sensation if it is cut or if it is burned or if it is combed and arranged out of some concern for good looks. Now to have no part in sensation is proper to beings that are dead. So one who has no sensation of the things that are much valued in this world, and is not elated by glory and honor, and is not pained by outrage and dishonor, but maintains herself in the same state with regard to both of the contraries, this one is the hair of the Bride that is praised—undisguisedly dead and unmoved with regard to the affairs of the world, whether they go this way or that.

If, however, the abundance of hair is compared | to *herds of goats* that have been *revealed* from Gilead, I have not yet been able to grasp what we are meant, by our careful efforts, to see about them. My guess is, however, that just as the King constructed his palanquin after he had changed the wood of Lebanon into gold and silver and purple and precious stones, so the Good Shepherd knows how to take herds of goats to himself and turn the herds on Mount Gilead into sheep. This, however, is the name of a foreign mountain, and it *reveals* a work of grace such as this: that those of the Gentiles[17] who have followed the Good Shepherd make up the hair that beautifies the Bride and by which temperance and modesty and self-control and bodily mortification are indicated, in accordance with our earlier interpretation.

On the other hand, might it be helpful for understanding this business of the goats that Elijah practiced the philosophical life[18] for a long time on Mount Gilead,[19] Elijah who, dried up in appearance, with shaggy hair, clothed

---

16. For the same idea, which seems to be a favorite with Gregory, see below, homily 15, p. 451 (Jaeger); *Vit. Mos.* 2.183 (GNO 7.1:95; trans. Malherbe and Ferguson 1978, 101).

17. Namely, persons "foreign" to Israel.

18. "Philosophy" or "the philosophical life" meant, for Gregory and his contemporaries, the ascetical life.

19. At 3 Kgdms (1 Kgs) 17:1, Elijah is described as "the Tishbite, of Tishbe in Gilead," and the text of the LXX says that when the messenger of King Ahaziah came to see him, Elijah "was seated at the top of the mountain" (2 Kgdms [2 Sam] 1:9). Gregory may have taken this mountain to be Mount Gilead on the ground that the latter was Elijah's home, and he may have thought that the prophet practiced the ascetical life there, but there is no explicit biblical reference to Elijah doing anything on Mount Gilead.

234   GREGORY OF NYSSA: *HOMILIES ON THE SONG OF SONGS*

ἐσθῆτος δέρματι αἰγὸς σκεπαζόμενος; πάντες οὖν οἱ κατὰ τὸν προφήτην
ἐκεῖνον τὸν ἑαυτῶν κατορθοῦντες βίον κόσμος γίνονται τῆς ἐκκλησίας,
ἀγεληδὸν | κατὰ τὸν νῦν ἐπικρατοῦντα τῆς φιλοσοφίας τρόπον μετ' ἀλλήλων   223
τὴν ἀρετὴν ἐκπονοῦντες. τὸ δὲ ἐκ τοῦ Γαλαὰδ τὰς τοιαύτας ἀποκαλυφθῆναι
5   ἀγέλας μείζονα τοῦ θαύματος τὴν ὑπερβολὴν ἔχει, ὅτι ἐκ τοῦ ἐθνικοῦ βίου
γέγονεν ἡμῖν ἡ πρὸς τὴν κατὰ θεὸν φιλοσοφίαν μετάστασις· οὐ γὰρ Σιὼν
ὄρος τὸ ἅγιον αὐτοῦ τῆς τοιαύτης καθήγησατο πολιτείας, ἀλλὰ τὸ τοῖς
εἰδώλοις ἀνακείμενον ἔθνος εἰς τοσαύτην ἦλθε τοῦ βίου μεταβολήν, ὥστε
τὴν κεφαλὴν κοσμῆσαι τῆς νύμφης τοῖς κατ' ἀρετὴν προτερήμασιν.
10   Εἶτα τοὺς ὀδόντας τῇ ἀκολουθίᾳ τῶν ἐπαίνων ὁ λόγος προτίθησι
παραδραμὼν τοῦ στόματός τε καὶ τῶν χειλῶν τὰ ἐγκώμια, ὅπερ ἄξιον μὴ
παριδεῖν ἀνεξέταστον. τί δή ποτε τῶν χειλῶν οἱ ὀδόντες ἐν τοῖς ἐπαίνοις
προτίθενται; τάχα μὲν οὖν εἴποι τις ἂν γλαφυρώτερον τὸ κάλλος δεῖξαι
βουλόμενος μειδίαμα στόματος διὰ τῆς τῶν ὀδόντων ὑπογραφῆς κατὰ τὸ
15   λεληθὸς συνενδείκνυσθαι, ἐγὼ δὲ πρὸς ἕτερον βλέπων προτερεύειν ἐν τοῖς
ἐπαίνοις τὸ τῶν ὀδόντων κάλλος πρὸ τῶν τοῦ στόματος ἐγκωμίων λογίζομαι·
μετὰ τοῦτο γὰρ οὐδὲ τὸ χεῖλος ἀφῆκεν ἀνεγκωμίαστον, σπαρτίον εἰπὼν
κόκκινον εἶναι τὰ χείλη αὐτῆς καὶ τὴν λαλιὰν ὡραίαν. τί οὖν ἐστιν ὃ περὶ
τούτου στοχάζομαι;
20   ἀρίστη τάξις ἐστὶν | ἐν τοῖς μαθήμασι πρῶτον διδάσκεσθαι καὶ τότε   224
φθέγγεσθαι. τὰ δὲ μαθήματα ψυχῆς βρώματά τις εἰπὼν εἶναι τοῦ εἰκότος οὐχ
ἁμαρτήσεται. ὥσπερ δὲ τὴν σωματικὴν τροφὴν τοῖς ὀδοῦσι καταλεάναντες
κατάλληλον αὐτὴν τοῖς σπλάγχνοις γενέσθαι παρασκευάζομεν, κατὰ τὸν
αὐτὸν τρόπον ἔστι τις λεπτοποιητικὴ τῶν διδαγμάτων δύναμις ἐν τῇ ψυχῇ,
25   δι' ἧς ὠφέλιμον γίνεται τῷ δεχομένῳ τὸ μάθημα. τοὺς τοίνυν κριτικούς τε καὶ
διαιρετικοὺς τῶν διδαγμάτων καθηγητάς, δι' ὧν εὔληπτος γίνεται ἡμῖν καὶ
ἐπωφελὴς ἡ διδασκαλία, ὀδόντας ὑπὸ τοῦ λόγου φημὶ τροπικῶς ὀνομάζεσθαι.
οὗ χάριν προλαμβάνει τῶν ὀδόντων ὁ ἔπαινος, εἶθ' οὕτως ἐπάγεται τῶν
χειλῶν τὸ ἐγκώμιον· οὐ γὰρ ἂν ἐπήνθιστο τῷ λογικῷ κάλλει τὸ χεῖλος μὴ τῶν
30   ὀδόντων ἐκείνων διὰ τῆς φιλοπονωτέρας τῶν μαθημάτων κατανοήσεως τὴν
ἐν τοῖς λόγοις χάριν ἐπιβαλλόντων τοῖς χείλεσιν, αἰτίαν μὲν οὖν τῆς ἐν τοῖς
ἐπαίνοις ἀκολουθίας ταύτην ἐπὶ τῶν ὀδόντων κατενοήσαμεν.
κασρὸς δ' ἂν εἴη καὶ αὐτὸν ἐξετάσαι τὸν ἔπαινον, πῶς παραβάλλει τὸ ἐν
τοῖς ὀδοῦσι κάλλος ταῖς κεκαρμέναις ἀγέλαις, αἳ νῦν τοῦ λουτροῦ ἀναδυεῖσαι
35   διδύμοις ἐπαγάλλονται τόκοις κατὰ τὸ ἴσον αἱ πᾶσαι. ἔχει δὲ κατὰ | τὴν λέξιν   225

in goatskin rather than in soft raiment, demonstrated the continent life? Thus all those who rightly order their lives after the manner of that prophet become the ornament of the church, practicing virtue with one another in herds,[20] | in accordance with the manner of the philosophical life that now prevails. That *herds* of this sort have been revealed *from Gilead* contains an extravagance greater than any wonder—that it is a life foreign to Israel that was the starting point of our migration toward the life of godly philosophy. For it was not God's holy Mount Zion that showed the way to such a manner of life; on the contrary, it was the nation dedicated to idols that came to a change of life so great as to adorn the head of the Bride with the distinctions that virtue brings.

Then, in the sequence of praises, the text takes up the Bride's *teeth*, passing over any commendation of her mouth and her lips—a circumstance it were well not to leave unexamined. Why, then, are the teeth preferred to the lips in this list of praises? Someone might say—wanting to manifest her beauty more subtly—that by the portrayal of the teeth the mouth's smile is implicitly signified. I, however, taking account of another factor, reckon that in the list of praises the beauty of the teeth precedes the commendations of the mouth. For after this <verse> it does not leave the lip without its need of commendation but says that her lips are a scarlet cord and her speech beautiful. What, then, am I hinting at here?

Where knowledge is concerned, | the best order is first to be taught and then to speak, and if someone says that the subjects of knowledge are the food of the soul,[21] he will not be far from the truth. When we chew corporeal food with our teeth, however, we get it ready to adapt to the intestines. In the same way, there is a certain power in the soul that breaks up the things we learn into small bits, and through this power knowledge becomes useful to the one who takes it in. Hence I say that it is teachers whom the text calls—figuratively—*teeth*, since they have the capacity for making distinctions and divisions and through them instruction becomes easy to grasp and profitable. This is why the list of praises puts the teeth first and then adds its commendation of the lips. For the lip would not glow with a rational beauty unless the teeth, by their laborious mastering of the subjects of knowledge, supplied the lips with grace of speech; and therefore we conceive this to be the reason for the order and sequence of the praises where the teeth are concerned.

But it is surely time to inquire into the terms of the praise here given the Bride, how the loveliness of her teeth is likened to shorn herds, which now—all equally—rejoice in twin offspring as they come up from the wash-

---

20. Gregory understands the herds of goats as a symbol for ascetics living in community.
21. See Plato, *Prot.* 313C.

οὕτως ὁ ἔπαινος· Ὀδόντες σου ὡς ἀγέλαι τῶν κεκαρμένων, αἳ ἀνέβησαν ἀπὸ
τοῦ λουτροῦ, αἱ πᾶσαι διδυμεύουσαι καὶ ἀτεκνοῦσα οὐκ ἔστιν ἐν αὐταῖς.

τοῦτο τοίνυν εἰ πρὸς τὸ σωματικὸν τοῦ ὑποδείγματος βλέποιμεν, οὐκ οἶδα
πῶς ἄν τις ἐπαινεῖσθαι τοὺς ὀδόντας εἴποι διὰ τῆς πρὸς τὰς πολυγονούσας
5   ἀγέλας συγκρίσεως· ὀδόντων μὲν γὰρ ἔπαινος ἡ στερρότης ἐστὶ καὶ ἡ
ἐναρμόνιος θέσις καὶ τὸ παγίως δι᾽ ὁμαλῆς καὶ ἀκολούθου τῆς ἁρμονίας
ἐμπεφυκέναι τοῖς οὔλοις, αἱ δὲ ἀναβαίνουσαι τοῦ λουτροῦ ἀγέλαι μετὰ τῆς
διδύμου γονῆς ἐπισκεδασθεῖσαι ταῖς νάπαις ποίαν ὀδόντων ὑπογράφουσιν
ὥραν τῷ καθ᾽ ἑαυτὰς ὑποδείγματι, οὐκ ἔστιν ἐκ τοῦ προχείρου κατανοῆσαι·
10   οὗτοι στοιχηδὸν συνεστήκασιν ἐναρμονίως ἀλλήλων ἐχόμενοι, ἐκεῖναι δὲ
ἀπ᾽ ἀλλήλων διασκεδάννυνται πρὸς τὴν χρείαν τῆς νομῆς ἀραιούμεναι.
ἀλλὰ καὶ γυμνῷ τῷ ὀδόντι κατὰ φύσιν ὄντι εἰς σύγκρισιν τὸ ἐριοφοροῦν οὐκ
εὐάρμοστον. οὐκοῦν ἐρευνητέον ἂν εἴη, πῶς ὁ κοσμῶν δι᾽ ἐγκωμίων τὴν τῶν
ὀδόντων εὐαρμοστίαν ταῖς διδυμοτόκοις ἀγέλαις παραβάλλει τὸ κάλλος,
15   ταῖς ἀποκειραμέναις τὸ ἔριον καὶ λουτρῷ τὸν ῥύπον ἀποκλυσαμέναις τοῦ
σώματος. τί οὖν περὶ τούτων ὑπενοήσαμεν;

οἱ τὰ θεῖα μυστήρια διὰ σαφεστέρας ἐξηγήσεως λεπτοποιοῦντες,
ὡς εὐπαράδεκτον τὴν πνευματικὴν ταύτην τροφὴν γενέσθαι τῷ σώματι
τῆς ἐκκλησίας, οὗτοι τὸ τῶν ὀδόντων ἔργον ἀποτελοῦσι παχύν τε καὶ
20   συνεστῶτα τοῦ λόγου τὸν ἄρτον τῷ ἑαυτῶν λαμβάνοντες στόματι καὶ διὰ
| τῆς λεπτομερεστέρας θεωρίας εὔβρωτον ταῖς ψυχαῖς τῶν δεχομένων   226
παρασκευάζοντες, οἷον (κρεῖττον γὰρ ἐπὶ ὑποδειγμάτων παραστῆσαι τὸ
νόημα) ὁ μακάριος Παῦλος νῦν μὲν ἁπλῶς τε καὶ ἀκατασκεύως ὥσπερ τινὰ
ψωμὸν ἀκατέργαστον προτίθησιν ἡμῖν τὸ τοῦ νόμου παράγγελμα λέγων
25   Οὐ φιμώσεις βοῦν ἀλοῶντα, πάλιν δὲ διὰ τῆς ἐπεξηγήσεως ἀπαλύνας
εὐπαράδεκτον ποιεῖ τοῦ νόμου τὸ βούλημα λέγων Μὴ τῶν βοῶν μέλει τῷ θεῷ;
ἢ δι᾽ ἡμᾶς πάντως ἐγράφη καὶ ἄλλα τοιαῦτα πολλά, οἷον Ἀβραὰμ δύο υἱοὺς
ἔσχεν, ἕνα ἐκ τῆς παιδίσκης καὶ ἕνα ἐκ τῆς ἐλευθέρας. τοῦτο ὁ ἀκατέργαστος
ἄρτος. ἀλλὰ πῶς αὐτὸν διαλεπτύνων ἐδώδιμον ποιεῖ τοῖς τρεφομένοις; εἰς
30   δύο διαθήκας μεταλαμβάνει τὴν ἱστορίαν, τὴν μὲν εἰς δουλείαν γεννῶσαν,
τὴν δὲ τῆς δουλείας ἐλευθεροῦσαν. οὕτω καὶ πάντα τὸν νόμον (ἵνα μὴ τὰ
καθ᾽ ἕκαστον λέγοντες διατρίβωμεν) παχυμερὲς σῶμα λαβὼν λεπτύνει διὰ

ing. The terms | of the praise are as follows: *Your teeth are like herds of shorn ewes that have come up from their washing, all bearing twins, and not one of them barren.*

Now if we were to attend to the literal sense of this image, I do not understand how anyone could say that praise is being given her teeth by comparing them with prolific flocks. What is commended in teeth is their hardness, and their appropriate placement, and their being firmly fixed in the gums in an even and consistent arrangement. But as to *flocks* that are coming up from the *washing*, having been scattered over the glens with pairs of offspring, it is not possible easily to understand what sort of attractiveness they indicate to belong to teeth by the image they provide. Teeth stand together in a row, joined to one another harmoniously, while flocks are scattered about, separated because of their need of pasture. Furthermore, it makes no sense to compare something that bears wool to a tooth, which is naturally naked. So one is bound to inquire how it is that one who lavishes praise on the nice arrangement of teeth can compare their beauty to flocks of ewes that bear twins, flocks whose wool is close shorn and whose bodily filth has been washed off. What, then, are we to make of this?

Those who grind the divine mysteries up small by interpreting them more lucidly, so that this spiritual nourishment can the more easily be taken in by the church's body,[22] these people carry out the work of *teeth*. They take the thick and compact bread of the Word into their own mouth and by | an interpretation that divides it into small bits they supply it to the souls of its recipients in a more edible form. Thus—for it is easier to get an idea across by using an illustration—the blessed Paul simply and without preparation sets before us the law's commandment in the form of an indigestible morsel when he says, "You shall not muzzle the ox that is treading out grain," but then he goes back and, after tenderizing it by his exegesis, he makes the intent of the law easy to grasp when he says: "Is it for oxen that God is concerned? … It was written" entirely "for our sake" (1 Cor 9:9–10). And he says many other things of the same sort, as for example, "Abraham had two sons, one of a slave girl and the other of a free woman" (Gal 4:22). This is the untouched loaf. But then how does he grind it up to make it edible for learners? He interprets the story as referring to two covenants, one that "bears children for slavery" (Gal 4:24), while the other liberates from slavery.[23] In the same fashion—lest we waste time on details—he takes the coarsely structured body of the law as a whole and cuts it up into fine pieces by his insightful and discerning treat-

---

22. For this figure, see Origen, *Hom. Exod.* 10.4 (on Exod 21:23).

23. For this whole passage, see Origen, *Princ.* 4.2.6, where the two texts adduced by Gregory are cited as justifying figural exegesis.

τῆς θεωρίας πνευματικὸν αὐτὸν ἐκ σωματικοῦ ἐργαζόμενος, Οἴδαμεν, λέγων,
ὅτι ὁ νόμος πνευματικός ἐστιν.

ὅπερ τοίνυν ἐπὶ τοῦ Παύλου κατενοήσαμεν | ὡς ὀδόντων χρείαν τῇ   227
ἐκκλησίᾳ πληροῦντος ἐν τῷ διαλεπτύνειν τὴν τῶν δογμάτων σαφήνειαν,
5   τοῦτο καὶ ἐπὶ παντὸς τοῦ κατὰ μίμησιν ἐκείνου διασαφοῦντος ἡμῖν τὰ
μυστήρια λέγομεν. οὐκοῦν ὀδόντες εἰσὶ τῆς ἐκκλησίας οἱ τὴν ἀκατέργαστον
τῶν θείων λογίων πόαν λεπτοποιοῦντες ἡμῖν καὶ μηρυκίζοντες.

ὥσπερ τοίνυν ὑπογράφει τῶν τοῦ καλοῦ ἔργου τῆς ἐπισκοπῆς
ὀρεγομένων τὸν βίον ὁ θεῖος ἀπόστολος λέγων τὰ καθ᾽ ἕκαστον, οἷον
10   εἶναι προσήκει τὸν τῆς ἱερωσύνης ἐπειλημμένον, ὡς μετὰ πάντων καὶ
τὴν διδακτικὴν χάριν ἔχειν, οὕτως ἐνταῦθα τοὺς εἰς ὀδόντων ὑπηρεσίαν
τεταγμένους ἐν τῇ ἐκκλησίᾳ βούλεται ὁ λόγος πρῶτον κεκαρμένους εἶναι,
τουτέστι πάσης ὑλικῆς ἀχθηδόνος γεγυμνωμένους, εἶτα τῷ λουτρῷ τῆς
συνειδήσεως παντὸς μολυσμοῦ σαρκὸς καὶ πνεύματος καθαρεύοντας, πρὸς
15   τούτοις ἀεὶ διὰ προκοπῆς ἀναβαίνοντας καὶ μηδέποτε πρὸς τὸ ἔμπαλιν
κατασυρομένους ἐπὶ τὸ βάραθρον, ἐπὶ πᾶσι δὲ διπλαῖς ταῖς τῶν ἀγαθῶν
κυημάτων γοναῖς κατὰ πᾶν εἶδος ἀρετῆς ἐπαγάλλεσθαι καὶ ἐν μηδενὶ τῶν
καλῶν ἐπιτηδευμάτων ἀγονεῖν. τὸ δὲ διπλοῦν κύημα αἴνιγμα γίνεται τῆς καθ᾽
ἑκάτερον τῶν ἐν ἡμῖν | νοουμένων εὐδοκιμήσεως, ὥστε διδυμοτόκους εἶναι   228
20   τοὺς τοιούτους ὀδόντας, τῇ μὲν ψυχῇ τὴν ἀπάθειαν, τῷ δὲ σωματικῷ βίῳ τὴν
εὐσχημοσύνην γεννῶντας.

Ἐπάγει τούτοις δι᾽ ἀκολούθου τὸν ἐπιπρέποντα τοῖς χείλεσιν ἔπαινον
σπαρτίῳ κοκκοβαφεῖ παρεικάζων τὸ κάλλος, οὗ τὴν ἑρμηνείαν αὐτὸς ἐπήγαγε
λαλιὰν ὡραίαν τὸ σπαρτίον κατονομάσας. τοῦτο δὲ ἐν τοῖς φθάσασιν ἤδη
25   προτεθεώρηται, ὅπως τῇ τῶν ὀδόντων ὑπηρεσίᾳ τὸ ἐν τοῖς χείλεσιν ὡραΐζεται
κάλλος· τῇ γὰρ τῶν ὀδόντων (τουτέστι τῇ τῶν διδασκάλων) ὑφηγήσει τὸ
στόμα τῆς ἐκκλησίας συμφθέγγεται. διὰ τοῦτο πρῶτον οἱ ὀδόντες κείρονται
καὶ λούονται καὶ οὐκ ἀτεκνοῦσι καὶ διδυμεύουσι, καὶ τότε τῷ κοκκίνῳ εἴδει
τὰ χείλη περιανθίζεται, ὅταν γένηται πᾶσα ἡ ἐκκλησία κατὰ τὴν τοῦ ἀγαθοῦ
30   συμφωνίαν χεῖλος ἓν καὶ φωνὴ μία.

διπλοῦν δὲ τοῦ κάλλους ἐστὶ τὸ ὑπόδειγμα· οὐ γὰρ μόνον ἁπλῶς
σπαρτίον φησὶν εἶναι τὰ χείλη, ἀλλὰ προσέθηκε καὶ τῆς εὐχροίας τὸ ἄνθος,
ὥστε δι᾽ ἀμφοτέρων καλλωπισθῆναι τῆς ἐκκλησίας τὸ στόμα διά τε τοῦ
σπαρτίου καὶ τοῦ κοκκίνου ἰδιαζόντως καθ᾽ ἑκάτερον μέρος· τῷ μὲν γὰρ
35   σπαρτίῳ τὴν ὁμογνωμοσύνην παιδεύεται, ὥστε πᾶσαν αὐτὴν ἓν σπαρτίον καὶ
μίαν γενέσθαι σειρὰν ἐκ διαφόρων νημάτων συγκεκλωσμένην, | διὰ δὲ τοῦ   229
κοκκίνου πρὸς τὸ αἷμα δι᾽ οὗ ἐλυτρώθημεν βλέπειν διδάσκεται καὶ ἀεὶ τὴν
ὁμολογίαν διὰ στόματος φέρειν τοῦ ἐξαγοράσαντος ἡμᾶς διὰ τοῦ αἵματος·
δι᾽ ἀμφοτέρων γὰρ τούτων ἐστὶ πληρουμένη τοῖς τῆς ἐκκλησίας χείλεσιν ἡ

ment of it, rendering it spiritual where it had been corporeal, for he says, "We know that the law is spiritual" (Rom 7:14).

What we observe, then, in the case of Paul, | that he fulfills the church's need of *teeth* by grinding the open truth of the teachings up small, we say also in the case of everyone who, after his example, clarifies the mysteries for us. So indeed the church's *teeth* are those who chop up the indigestible fodder of the divine oracles for us and chew it as their cud.

Just as the divine apostle, then, describes the way of life of those who desire "the noble task" (1 Tim 3:1) of the episcopate, specifying point by point what sort of person the recipient of the priesthood ought to be, so as also, along with everything else, to possess the gift of teaching, even so in this text the Word wishes those who are assigned to perform the service of *teeth* in the church first of all to be *shorn* (that is, stripped of every material burden) and second, in virtue of the *washing* of conscience, to be free of any fleshly or spiritual spot. In addition to this, they are always to be making their way upwards in virtue of their progress and never to be dragged backwards, down to perdition—but above all to take pleasure in all the *twin* descendants of their high-born offspring in every form of virtue and to be *barren* in no good habits. As to the twin birth, that is an enigma for what is estimable in each of the two elements that are | discernible in us; it means that *teeth* of this sort are twin-bearers, giving birth to impassibility for the soul, and for the bodily life, to "decorum."

Next in order, the Word adds to these statements the praise that is proper to the Bride's lips. He likens their beauty to that of a scarlet *thread,* and he himself provides the interpretation of this when he identifies the *thread* as *graceful speech.* This point, however, has already been explained in what we have just said, namely, that by the service that the *teeth* perform the beauty proper to the lips blooms. For the mouth of the church gives voice to the guidance furnished by the *teeth* (that is to say, by teachers). Hence first of all the *teeth* are shorn and washed and are not barren and give birth to twins, and after this the lips produce a *scarlet* bloom, when the whole church becomes one lip and one voice speaking in accordance with the harmony of goodness.

Now the portrayal of this beauty is twofold, for he does not simply say that the lips are *a thread,* but to this description there is added the bloom of their color, so that the mouth of the church is beautified by both—at once by the *thread* and by the *scarlet*—and by each in its special way. For by the epithet *thread* agreement in mind is taught, so that the church as a whole is one *thread* and one cord, woven together out of different strands; | but by the epithet *scarlet* we are taught to consider the blood by which we have been redeemed and ever to confess with the mouth the one who ransomed us by his blood. For the comeliness that belongs to the church's lips is ful-

εὐπρέπεια, ὅταν καὶ ἡ πίστις τῆς ὁμολογίας προλάμπῃ καὶ ἡ ἀγάπη τῇ πίστει συμπλέκηται.

καὶ εἰ χρὴ ὥσπερ ὁρισμῷ τινι περιλαβεῖν τὸ ὑπόδειγμα, οὕτω τὸ ῥηθὲν ὁριούμεθα· κόκκινον σπαρτίον ἐστὶ Πίστις δι᾽ ἀγάπης ἐνεργουμένη, ὡς τῇ
5   πίστει μὲν δηλοῦσθαι τὸ κόκκινον, τῇ δὲ ἀγάπῃ τὸ σπαρτίον διερμηνεύεσθαι. τούτοις κεκοσμῆσθαι τὰ χείλη τῆς νύμφης μαρτυρεῖ ἡ ἀλήθεια.

ἡ δὲ ὡραία λαλιὰ θεωρίας τινὸς λεπτοτέρας ἢ ἑρμηνείας ἄλλης οὐκ ἐπιδέεται· φθάσας γὰρ διεσάφησεν ὁ ἀπόστολος ὅτι ἡ λαλιὰ αὕτη τὸ ῥῆμα τῆς πίστεώς ἐστιν ὃ κηρύσσομεν, λέγων Ἐὰν ὁμολογήσῃς τῷ στόματί σου κύριον
10   Ἰησοῦν καὶ πιστεύσῃς ἐν τῇ καρδίᾳ σου ὅτι ὁ θεὸς αὐτὸν ἤγειρεν ἐκ νεκρῶν, σωθήσῃ· καρδίᾳ γὰρ πιστεύεται εἰς δικαιοσύνην, στόματι δὲ ὁμολογεῖται εἰς σωτηρίαν. αὕτη ἐστὶν ἡ ὡραία λαλιά, δι᾽ ἧς τὰ χείλη τῆς ἐκκλησίας κατὰ τὸ κόκκινον ἐκεῖνο σπαρτίον εὐπρεπῶς ἐπανθίζεται.

Ἀρέσκεται δὲ μετὰ τὴν τοῦ στόματος ὥραν ὁ νυμφίος καὶ τῷ τῆς παρειᾶς
15   ἐρυθήματι. μῆλον δὲ τοῦτο τοῦ προσώπου τὸ μέρος ἐκ καταχρήσεως καλεῖ ἡ συνήθεια. προσεικάζει | τοίνυν τὸ τῆς παρειᾶς μῆλον τῷ λεπύρῳ τῆς ῥόας   230 γράψας οὕτω τὸν ἔπαινον αὐτὸν ἐπὶ λέξεως· Ὡς λέπυρον ῥόας μῆλόν σου ἐκτὸς τῆς σιωπήσεώς σου.

ὅτι μὲν οὖν αἰδώς ἐστι τὸ ἐπαινούμενον παντὶ ῥάδιον ἐκ τῆς ἀκολουθίας
20   τῶν τεθεωρημένων λογίσασθαι· σωματοποιήσας γὰρ τὴν ἐκκλησίαν ὁ λόγος εἰς τὸ τῆς νύμφης εἶδος καὶ τὰς καθ᾽ ἕκαστον ἀρετὰς καταλλήλως τῇ ὑπογραφῇ τῆς κατὰ τὸ πρόσωπον ὥρας ἐπιμερίσας νῦν διὰ τοῦ ἐρυθήματος τοῦ ταῖς παρειαῖς ἐπιζέοντος προσφόρως ἐπαινεῖ τὴν σωφροσύνην αἰδοῖ κατακοσμήσας ἐν τῷ τῆς ῥόας αἰνίγματι· ὁ γὰρ καρπὸς οὗτος στυφῇ τε
25   καὶ ἀβρώτῳ τῇ ἐπιφανείᾳ ἐντρέφεται. διὸ καλῶς τε καὶ οἰκείως εἰς τὸ τῆς σωφροσύνης κατόρθωμα διὰ τῆς θεωρίας μεταλαμβάνεται· ὡς γὰρ ἡ στύψις τοῦ τῆς ῥόας λεπύρου τρέφει τε καὶ φυλάσσει τοῦ ἐμπεριεχομένου καρποῦ τὴν γλυκύτητα, οὕτως ὁ στυφός τε καὶ ἐγκρατὴς καὶ κατεσκληκὼς βίος φύλαξ γίνεται τῶν τῆς σωφροσύνης καλῶν. διπλοῦς δὲ καὶ ἐνταῦθα
30   τῆς ἀρετῆς ταύτης ὁ ἔπαινος γίνεται διά τε τῶν προφαινομένων κατὰ τὸν εὐσχήμονα βίον καὶ διὰ τῶν ἐν τῇ τῆς ψυχῆς ἀπαθείᾳ κατορθουμένων, ὧν Ὁ ἔπαινος, καθὼς φησιν ὁ ἀπόστολος, οὐκ ἐξ ἀνθρώπων ἀλλ᾽ ἐκ | θεοῦ· ἡ   231 γὰρ ἐπιλάμπουσα τοῖς γινομένοις αἰδὼς ἴδιον μὲν ἐκ τῶν προδήλων ἔχει τὸν

filled when both the faith of the confession shines forth and love is woven together with faith.

And if we need to capture the point of all this in some definitive phrase, we will mark out the meaning of the text in this way: *scarlet thread* means "Faith working by love." By "faith," *scarlet* is explained, while "love" interprets *thread.* The truth bears witness that this is the way in which the lips of the Bride are adorned.

As to *graceful speech,* it stands in no need of any narrower interpretation or of any alternative reading; the apostle has already made it plain that this very speech is the word of faith that we preach. He says: "If you confess with your lips that Jesus is Lord and believe in your heart that God raised him from the dead, you will be saved; for with the heart one believes, and so is justified, and with the mouth one confesses, and so is saved" (Rom 10:9). This is itself the *graceful speech* by which the church's lips are adorned with that *scarlet thread.*

After the beauty of the Bride's mouth, the Bridegroom also takes delight in the blush of her cheek. Custom refers to this part of the face, by catachresis, as *apple.*[24] Thus he likens | the *apple* of the cheek to *the skin of a pomegranate,* phrasing his commendation in these words: *Your apple is like the skin of a pomegranate outside your veil.*

Now it is easy for anyone to figure out, in light of the course and logic of our interpretations up to this point, that what is being praised is modesty. For once the Word has personified the church in the shape of a bride and has enumerated her individual virtues one after another by describing the beauty of her countenance, he now fitly praises her temperance by mentioning the blush that comes up on her cheeks, after adorning her with modesty by employing the enigma of the pomegranate. For this fruit grows up looking hard and inedible. Hence it is right and appropriate to interpret it, by way of spiritual interpretation, as the product of temperance; for just as the harshness of the pomegranate's skin fosters and protects the sweetness of the fruit it encloses, so a life that is harsh and self-controlled and austere is the protector of the good things that flow from temperance. In this case too, moreover, the praise of this virtue comes about in a twofold manner: both by what is manifested in a decorous manner of life and by what is achieved through the soul's interior impassibility. And the "praise" of these things, as the apostle says, "is not from human beings but from | God" (Rom 2:29). For the modesty that shines forth in outward events has its own, proper commendation of a mani-

---

24. The text of the LXX here has "apple" (μῆλον), and Gregory explains that, by a customary "misuse" or substitution of one word for another, this Greek word is employed to refer to the human cheek.

ἔπαινον, ἐκτὸς δὲ τῶν σιωπωμένων ἐστὶ καὶ ὑποκεκρυμμένων θαυμάτων, ἃ
μόνῳ καθορᾶται τῷ ὀφθαλμῷ ἐκείνῳ τῷ εἰς τὰ κρύφια βλέποντι.

Διὰ δὲ τῶν μετὰ ταῦτα μανθάνομεν ὅτι πᾶν τὸ παρὰ τῶν θεοφορουμένων
ἁγίων γινόμενον τύπος τις καὶ διδασκαλία τῶν εἰς ἀρετὴν κατορθουμένων
5   ἐγίνετο· οἱ γάμοι, αἱ ἀποικίαι, οἱ πόλεμοι, αἱ τῶν οἰκοδομημάτων κατασκευαί,
πάντα κατά τινα λόγον εἰς νουθεσίαν τῷ μετὰ ταῦτα προδιετυποῦτο βίῳ·
Ἐγράφη γὰρ ταῦτα, φησί, πρὸς νουθεσίαν ἡμῶν, εἰς οὓς τὰ τέλη τῶν αἰώνων
κατήντησεν· ὁ μὲν γὰρ κατὰ τῶν ἀλλοφύλων πόλεμος συμβουλεύει κατὰ τῆς
κακίας ἡμᾶς ἀνδρίζεσθαι, ἡ δὲ κατὰ τοὺς γάμους σπουδὴ τὴν τῶν ἀρετῶν
10   συνοίκησιν δι᾽ αἰνιγμάτων ἡμῖν ὑποτίθεται. ὡσαύτως δὲ καὶ ἡ ἀποικία τοῦ
ἐναρέτου βίου τὸν οἰκισμὸν ὑποβάλλει, τὰ δὲ ὅσα περὶ τὰς κατασκευὰς
τῶν οἰκοδομημάτων παρ᾽ αὐτῶν ἐσπουδάζετο, τῶν ἡμετέρων οἴκων τῶν δι᾽
ἀρετῆς οἰκοδομουμένων ἐπιμέλειαν ποιεῖσθαι διακελεύεται. διό μοι δοκεῖ
κἀκεῖ τὸν περιφανῆ πύργον ἐκεῖνον, <ἐν> ᾧ τὰ ἀκροθίνια τῶν λαφύρων
15   ἀνέθηκεν ὁ Δαβίδ, | πρὸς τὴν προκοπὴν τῆς ἐκκλησίας βλέπων [τῶν τι κατ᾽   232
ἀρετὴν σπουδαζομένων] προδιατυπῶσαι τούτῳ τῷ ἔργῳ, ὃς ὑπερφαίνεται
μὲν ἀκρωρείας τινὸς εἰς ὕψος ἀνατεινόμενος, ἐπιτήδειος δὲ κατὰ τὸν χρόνον
ἐκεῖνον πρὸς τὴν τῶν λαφύρων φυλακὴν ἐνομίσθη, ὅσα δουλωσάμενος
τοὺς ἀλλοφύλους μετὰ τῶν λοιπῶν χρημάτων ἴδιον κέρδος ὁ βασιλεὺς
20   ἐποιήσατο.

Ἔδειξεν οὖν διὰ τῆς ἑαυτοῦ σοφίας ὁ βασιλεὺς πρὸς ὅ τι βλέπων ὁ Δαβὶδ
ἀγαθὸν τῇ τῶν ἀνθρώπων ζωῇ ὥσπερ τινὰ συμβουλὴν τῷ μετὰ ταῦτα βίῳ
διὰ τῆς τοῦ πύργου κατασκευῆς προαπέθετο· παντὸς γὰρ τοῦ σώματος
τῆς ἐκκλησίας τῶν καθ᾽ ἕκαστον μελῶν διὰ τῆς πρός τι παραθέσεώς τε καὶ
25   ὁμοιώσεως ἐγκωμιάζειν τὸ κάλλος μέλλων δι᾽ ἀκολούθου τοὺς ἐν τῷ λαῷ
τὸν τοῦ τραχήλου τόπον ἐπέχοντας οἵους τινὰς εἶναι προσήκει διαγράφων τῷ
λόγῳ τοῦ πύργου μέμνηται τούτου, ᾧ ἐπονομάζεται μὲν ὁ Δαβίδ, ἔχει δὲ καὶ
ἀπὸ τῶν ἐπάλξεων τὸ γνώριμον· θαλπιὼθ γὰρ αἱ ἐπάλξεις κατονομάζονται.

fest and public sort. It stands *outside* the hidden and unspoken[25] marvels that are seen only by the Eye that gazes on hidden things.

From the words that follow these, we learn that whatever came to pass at the instance of the holy persons whom God inspired came to pass as a type and a teaching concerned with things accomplished for the sake of virtue. The marriages, the emigrations, the battles, the constructions of buildings—all prefigure, by way of analogy, the mode of life that comes after them, with intent to provide instruction. For "these things were written down," it says, "for our instruction, upon whom the end of the ages has come" (1 Cor 10:11). Battle against alien peoples counsels us to be courageous in the struggle against evil, while attention given to marriage enjoins upon us, in a riddling manner, cohabitation with the virtues. In the same way, emigration points to the settling and establishment of the virtuous life, while whatever these holy people seriously undertook by way of the construction of buildings enjoins upon us earnestness regarding our own dwellings as they are being built through virtue. That explains why I judge that in this text also that conspicuous *tower,* in which David stored the firstfruits of his spoils, | looking toward the increase of the church,[26] is prefigured by this work of construction.[27] This tower, reaching on high, overtops the ridge of a mountain and in that day was reckoned suitable and safe as a depository for the spoils of war—whatever spoils the king, when he had subjected alien peoples, kept for his own benefit over and above the rest.

Hence by this wisdom of his the king[28] indicates the good for human life that David had in mind when he provided, by the construction of his tower, what amounts to counsel for the mode of life that was coming. His intent is to heap praise on the beauty of each of the members of the church's body by setting each of them alongside something else and comparing the two. Accordingly, he describes what is proper for those who occupy the neck's place among the people, and in doing so he makes mention of this tower, to which the name of David is given and which is made notable by its battlements, for *thalpiôth* means "battlements." Here then is the text: *Your neck is*

---

25. Σιωπωμένων; see above, p. 219 (Jaeger), and n. 15.

26. At this point in the Greek text the majority of manuscripts (see the apparatus of Langerbeck 1960, 232, *ad loc.*) add the words τῶν τι κατ' ἀρετὴν σπουδαζομένων ("of those who are seriously concerned about virtue"). Langerbeck regards them as a later insertion in the text intended to explain "this work."

27. I.e., the work of constructing our own buildings by means of virtue. I have added the words "of construction."

28. I.e., King Solomon, who is (1) the preeminent possessor of wisdom, (2) the author of the Song, and (3) a type of the Word of God. See above, homily 1, on Song 1:1.

οὕτω δὲ ἡ λέξις ἔχει· Ὡς πύργος Δαβὶδ τράχηλός σου ὁ ᾠκοδομημένος ἐν
θαλπιώθ· χίλιοι θυρεοὶ κρέμανται ἐπ' αὐτόν, πᾶσαι βολίδες τῶν δυνατῶν.

| ἡ μὲν οὖν σωματικὴ τοῦ πύργου κατασκευὴ τὸ περίβλεπτον ἔχει ἔκ τε   233
τοῦ ἔργον εἶναι τοῦ βασιλέως Δαβὶδ καὶ ἐκ τῆς περιφανείας τοῦ τόπου καὶ
5   ἐκ τῶν ἀνατεθέντων ὅπλων ἐν αὐτῷ, τῶν θυρεῶν τε καὶ τῶν βολίδων, ὧν τὸ
πλῆθος ἐνδείκνυται ὁ λόγος τῷ τῆς χιλιάδος ὀνόματι, ἡμῖν δὲ σκοπός ἐστι
κατανοῆσαι τοῦ θείου λογίου τὴν δύναμιν. πῶς παραβάλλεται τῷ πύργῳ
τούτῳ τὸ μέρος ἐκεῖνο τῆς ἐκκλησίας, ᾧ τράχηλός ἐστι τὸ ὄνομα; πρῶτον
τοίνυν ἐξετάσαι προσήκει, ποῖον ἐν τῷ καθ' ἡμᾶς σώματι μέρος τῷ ὀνόματι
10   τοῦ τραχήλου προσαγορεύεται, εἶθ' οὕτως ἐφαρμόσαι τῷ τῆς ἐκκλησίας μέλει
τὸ ὄνομα.

οὐκοῦν τὸ ἐρριζωμένον μὲν ἐν τῷ μέσῳ τῶν ὤμων, ἀνέχον δὲ τὴν
κεφαλὴν ἐφ' ἑαυτοῦ καὶ ἀντὶ βάσεως τοῦ ὑπερκειμένου γινόμενον τράχηλος
ὀνομάζεται, οὗ τὸ κατόπιν μὲν ὀστέοις ἐρείδεται, τὸ δὲ προβεβλημένον
15   ἐλεύθερόν ἐστι τῆς τῶν ὀστέων περιβολῆς. ἡ δὲ τοῦ ὀστέου φύσις οὐ
καθ' ὁμοιότητα τοῦ πήχεος ἢ τῆς κνήμης συνεχὴς πρὸς ἑαυτήν ἐστι καὶ
ἀδιαίρετος, ἀλλὰ πολλαχῇ τῶν ὀστέων ἐν σπονδύλων σχήματι διῃρημένων
διὰ τῶν περιπεφυκότων αὐτοῖς νεύρων τε καὶ μυῶν καὶ συνδέσμων ἡ ἕνωσις
αὐτῶν πρὸς ἄλληλα γίνεται καὶ διὰ τοῦ μυελοῦ τοῦ αὐλοειδῶς κατὰ τὸ μέσον
20   διήκοντος. οὗ ἡ περιοχὴ μὲν πρὸς τὰς μήνιγγας αὐτὸ δὲ τὸ ἐγκείμενον πρὸς
τὸν ἐγκέφαλον ἥνωται. ἐν δὲ τοῖς ἔμπροσθεν περιέχει μὲν τὴν ἀρτηρίαν ὁ
τράχηλος, ἣ | δοχεῖόν ἐστι τοῦ πνεύματος τοῦ ἔξωθεν ἡμῖν εἰσοικιζομένου   234
τε καὶ εἰσρέοντος, δι' οὗ τὸ ἐγκάρδιον πῦρ πρὸς τὴν ἐνέργειαν αὐτοῦ τὴν
κατὰ φύσιν ἀναρριπίζεται, περιέχει δὲ καὶ τῆς τροφῆς τὰς εἰσόδους διὰ τοῦ
25   λαιμοῦ τε καὶ τοῦ λάρυγγος πᾶν τὸ διὰ τοῦ στόματος εἰσαγόμενον πρὸς τὴν
κοιλότητα τὴν δεκτικὴν τούτων διαπορθμεύων. ἔχει δὲ καὶ ἄλλο παρὰ τὰ
λοιπὰ τῶν μελῶν ἐξαίρετόν τι ὁ τράχηλος· κατὰ γὰρ τὴν ἄνω τῆς ἀρτηρίας
θέσιν ἐστὶν ἐν αὐτῷ τὸ τῆς φωνῆς ἐργαστήριον, ἐν ᾧ τὰ φωνητικὰ πάντα
παρεσκεύασται ὄργανα, δι' ὧν ἀπογεννᾶται ὁ ἦχος τῷ ἀναδιδομένῳ πνεύματι
30   περιδονουμένης ἐν κύκλῳ τῆς ἀρτηρίας.

οὕτω δὲ τοῦ σωματικοῦ μέλους ἡμῖν διαγραφέντος εὔκολον ἂν εἴη διὰ
τῶν ἐνταῦθα θεωρηθέντων καὶ τὸν τοῦ ἐκκλησιαστικοῦ σώματος τράχηλον
κατανοῆσαι, ὅστις ἐστὶν ὁ διὰ τῶν καταλλήλων ἐνεργειῶν τὸ ὄνομα τοῦτο
κυρίως ἀναλαμβάνων τράχηλός τε ὀνομαζόμενος καὶ τῷ πύργῳ τοῦ Δαβὶδ
35   ὁμοιούμενος. πρῶτον μὲν οὖν ὃ δὴ καὶ πρῶτόν ἐστιν, εἴ τις τὴν ἀληθινὴν τοῦ
παντὸς κεφαλὴν ἐφ' ἑαυτοῦ βαστάζοι (ἐκείνην λέγω τὴν κεφαλὴν ἥτις ἐστὶν
ὁ Χριστός, ἐξ οὗ πᾶν τὸ σῶμα συναρμολογεῖται καὶ συμβιβάζεται), οὗτος
κυρίως ἐφ' ἑαυτοῦ φέρει τοῦτο τὸ ὄνομα. πρὸς τούτοις εἰ τοῦ πνεύματός ἐστι
δεκτικὸς τοῦ τὴν καρδίαν ἡμῶν πυροειδῆ ποιοῦντος καὶ | ἐκθερμαίνοντος   235
40   καὶ εἰ διὰ τῆς εὐήχου φωνῆς ὑπηρετεῖ τῷ λόγῳ· οὐδὲ γὰρ ἄλλου τινὸς ἕνεκεν
τὴν ἀνθρωπίνην φωνὴν ὁ θεὸς τῇ φύσει τῶν ἀνθρώπων ἐνετεκτήνατο ἢ ἵνα

like a tower of David, which was built in thalpiôth. *A thousand shields hang*
upon it, all the darts of the mighty men.

| The corporeal structure of the tower, therefore, evokes admiration, at
once because it is the work of David the king, because of the conspicuousness
of its location, and because of the weapons that are attached to it, the shields
and the javelins, whose multitude the text indicates by the term "thousand."
Our aim, though, is to understand the force of the divine oracle. In what way
is that part of the church that we call "neck" compared to this *tower*? Hence
we have first of all to inquire, with regard to that part of the human body to
which the word "neck" is applied, what sort of thing it is and then in this way
to apply the word to the member of the church that it suits.

Now we apply the word "neck" to that which is rooted between the shoulders, while it holds the head up and acts as a base for what lies above it. At
its rear it is supported by bones, but on the front it is free of the garment of
bones. The bone in question, however, is not, like that of the forearm or the
shank, integral and all of one piece. Rather, since the bones are divided from
one another in the form of numerous vertebrae, their unity with one another
is effected by the nerves and muscles and ligaments that grow around them
and by the marrow that runs through them as through a channel. Its outer
side is united to the membranes of the brain, and its inner side, to the brain
itself. Now in front, the neck contains the windpipe that is | the receptacle of
the breath [πνεῦμα] that comes from outside and rushes in to make its home
in us and by which the fire within the heart is rekindled to fulfill its natural
operation. The neck also contains the entrances for food; through the throat
and the larynx it transmits everything that comes in through the mouth to
the cavity that receives it. And there is also another characteristic that sets
the neck apart from the other members of the body: within it, beneath the
site of the wind-pipe, is the plant in which voice production takes place, and
in it there stand ready all the instruments of speech that give rise to sound by
means of the exhaled breath [πνεῦμα] as the windpipe is agitated all around it.

When the bodily member is portrayed for us in this fashion, it should
be easy, by reference to the matters we have treated of here, to identify the
"neck" of the church's body as well: what it is that on account of its analogous
operations most properly receives this name and in fact is named "neck" and
likened to the *tower of David*. Taking first things first, if there is a member
that bears up the true head of the whole body (I mean "the Head," which is
"Christ, from whom the ... body" is "joined and knit together" [cf. Eph 4:15–
16]), then it will be this member that most properly carries the name. Further,
if it is receptive of the Spirit [πνεῦμα] that sets our heart afire and | warms it,
and if it serves the ends of intelligible speech by its euphonious voice, for God
provided human nature with a voice for no other reason than that it should

ὄργανον ἢ τοῦ λόγου διαρθροῦσα δι᾽ ἑαυτῆς τὰ τῆς καρδίας κινήματα. ἐχέτω
δὲ οὗτος ὁ τράχηλος καὶ τὴν θρεπτικὴν ἐνέργειαν, τὴν διδασκαλίαν λέγω,
δι᾽ ἧς παντὶ τῷ σώματι τῆς ἐκκλησίας συντηρεῖται ἡ δύναμις· ἐπιρρεούσης
γὰρ ἀεὶ τῆς τροφῆς ἐν τῷ εἶναι διαμένει τὸ σῶμα, ἐπιλειπούσης δὲ φθίνει καὶ
5   διαφθείρεται. μιμείσθω δὲ καὶ τὴν ἐναρμόνιον τῶν σπονδύλων θέσιν ἐν τῷ
τοὺς καθ᾽ ἕκαστον τῷ λαῷ συντελοῦντας διὰ τοῦ συνδέσμου τῆς εἰρήνης ἓν
ἀπεργάζεσθαι μέλος κλινόμενόν τε καὶ ἀνορθούμενον καὶ καθ᾽ ἑκάτερον τῶν
πλαγίων εὐκινήτως μεταστρεφόμενον.
    τοιοῦτος τράχηλος ὁ Παῦλος ἦν καὶ εἰ δή τις ἄλλος κατὰ μίμησιν ἐκείνου
10   τὸν βίον κατώρθωσεν, ὃς ἐβάστασε μὲν τὸ ὄνομα τοῦ κυρίου σκεῦος ἐκλογῆς
τῷ δεσπότῃ γενόμενος, καὶ οὕτως αὐτῷ δι᾽ ἀκριβείας ἡ κεφαλὴ τῶν ὅλων
ἐφήρμοστο, ὥστε καὶ ὅσα ἐλάλει μηκέτι αὐτὸν εἶναι τὸν λαλοῦντα, ἀλλὰ τὴν
κεφαλὴν αὐτοῦ φθέγγεσθαι, καθὼς ἐπέδειξε τοῖς Κορινθίοις τὸν Χριστὸν ἐν
αὐτῷ λαλοῦντά τε καὶ φθεγγόμενον. οὕτως αὐτοῦ εὔφωνός τε καὶ εὔηχος ἦν
15   ἡ ἀρτηρία διὰ τοῦ ἁγίου | πνεύματος διαρθροῦσα τῆς ἀληθείας τὸν λόγον,   236
οὕτως αὐτῷ πάντοτε τοῖς θείοις λογίοις ὁ λάρυγξ κατεγλυκαίνετο τρέφων
ὅλον δι᾽ ἑαυτοῦ τὸ σῶμα τοῖς ζωοποιοῖς ἐκείνοις διδάγμασιν. εἰ δὲ καὶ τὸ τῶν
σπονδύλων ζητεῖς, τίς οὕτω τοὺς πάντας εἰς ἓν σῶμα συνήρμοσε τῷ συνδέσμῳ
τῆς εἰρήνης καὶ τῆς ἀγάπης; τίς οὕτως ἐδίδαξε κλίνεσθαι τὸν τράχηλον ἐν
20   τῷ τοῖς ταπεινοῖς συμπεριφέρεσθαι καὶ ἀνορθοῦσθαι πάλιν ἐν τῷ τὰ ἄνω
φρονεῖν καὶ πρὸς τὰ πλάγια περισκοπεῖν εὐστρόφως τε καὶ εὐκινήτως ἐν τῷ
τὰς ποικίλας τοῦ διαβόλου μεθοδείας ἐκκλίνειν καὶ ἀσφαλίζεσθαι;
    ὁ τοιοῦτος οὖν τράχηλος ὄντως παρὰ τοῦ Δαβὶδ ᾠκοδόμηται. νόει
δὲ διὰ τοῦ Δαβὶδ τὸν βασιλέα, τὸν τοῦ βασιλέως πατέρα, ὃς ἐξ ἀρχῆς τὸν
25   ἄνθρωπον κατεσκεύασε πύργον εἶναι καὶ οὐχὶ σύμπτωμα καὶ διὰ τῆς χάριτος
αὐτὸν πάλιν ἀνῳκοδόμησεν ἀσφαλισάμενος τοῖς πολλοῖς θυρεοῖς, ὥστε
μηκέτι αὐτὸν ταῖς τῶν πολεμίων ἐφόδοις εὐεπίβατον εἶναι· οἱ γὰρ κρεμάμενοι
θυρεοί, οὐκ ἐπὶ γῆς κείμενοι ἀλλὰ διαέριοι περὶ αὐτὸν θεωρούμενοι, καὶ μετὰ
τῶν θυρεῶν αἱ τῶν δυνατῶν βολίδες φόβον ἐμποιοῦσι τοῖς πολεμίοις, ὥστε
30   μηδὲ τὴν ἀρχὴν ἐγχειρῆσαι καταδραμεῖν τοῦ πύργου. οἶμαι δὲ τὴν ἀγγελικὴν
φρουρὰν ἐν κύκλῳ περιεστοιχισμένην τὸν τοιοῦτον | πύργον τῷ πλήθει τῶν   237
θυρεῶν ἡμῖν διασημαίνεσθαι.
    δείκνυσι δὲ καὶ ἡ τῶν βολίδων μνήμη τὴν τοιαύτην διάνοιαν· οὐ γὰρ
ἁπλῶς εἶπε βολίδας, ἀλλὰ τῇ τῶν δυνατῶν προσθήκῃ τοὺς ὑπερμαχοῦντας
35   ἡμῶν ἐνεδείξατο, ὥστε συμβαίνειν τὸ λεγόμενον τῷ τῆς ψαλμῳδίας ῥητῷ
ὅτι Παρεμβαλεῖ ἄγγελος κυρίου κύκλῳ τῶν φοβουμένων αὐτὸν καὶ ῥύσεται

be an instrument to articulate the motions of the heart.[29] Also let this "neck" be the subject of an activity of providing nourishment, by which I mean teaching, through which strength is sustained for the whole body of the church; for when there is a constant flow of food, the body remains in being, but if food be lacking, it wastes away and is destroyed. Further let it imitate the harmonious disposition of the vertebrae by individually taking those who make up the people and by "the bond of peace" making them a single member in bowing and standing erect and turning gracefully to either side.

Such a neck was Paul, and anyone else who conducts his life rightly in imitation of Paul. He bore up the name of the Lord as the Master's "vessel of election" (Acts 9:15), and in this manner the Head of all was closely fitted upon him, with the result that it was no longer he who spoke whatever he said, but his Head gave utterance—just as he shows the Corinthians that the Christ "speaks" and gives utterance "in him" (2 Cor 13:3). Thus his windpipe sounded nobly and beautifully on account of the Holy | Spirit and articulated the word of truth; thus his larynx was ever sweetened for him by the divine oracles, and he gave nourishment to the whole body through those life-giving teachings. And if you ask about the vertebrae—well, who so fitted everyone together in one body by the "bond of peace" and love? And who so taught the neck to bow in accommodation to humble things, and to stand erect in taking account of things on high, and to look to the sides easily and gracefully in turning away and warding off the craft of the devil?

A neck of this sort, therefore, really was built by David. By David we understand the King who is Father of the King that from the beginning constructed the human being[30] to be a *tower* and not a collapsed pile and who by grace rebuilt him again and secured him with a multitude of *shields,* so that he might no longer be easy for his enemies to attack. For those hanging *shields*—not lying on the ground but surrounding it in the air—and with the *shields, the javelins of the mighty,* work fear in enemies, so that they do not attempt to attack the tower in the first place. So I suspect | that the multitude of the *shields* signifies to us the angelic garrison that walls such a *tower.*

The mention of *javelins* also points to such an interpretation, for the text did not simply say *javelins,* but by adding *of the mighty* it indicates those who fight on our behalf. Thus the words agree with the statement of the psalm: "The angel of the Lord encamps around those who fear him and protects

---

29. For Gregory's understanding of the relation between the human body and the activity of rational speech, see his earlier treatise *Opif. hom.* 8.1–2, 8; 9 (PG 44:144A–C, 148C–152A).

30. Solomon, as we have seen, is for Gregory a type of Christ (see above p. 232 [Jaeger] and homily 1, pp. 16–17 [Jaeger]); David, therefore, as Solomon's father, can be allegorized as God, the Father of the divine Son.

αὐτούς. ὁ δὲ τῶν χιλίων ἀριθμὸς οὔ μοι δοκεῖ δι' ἀκριβείας σημαίνειν τὴν τῶν
ἑκατοντάδων δεκάδα, ἀλλ' εἰς πλήθους ἔνδειξιν παρελήφθη ὑπὸ τοῦ λόγου·
σύνηθες γάρ ἐστιν ἐκ τῆς καταχρήσεως τῆς γραφικῆς τῷ ἀριθμῷ τούτῳ
τὸ πλῆθος ἐνδείκνυσθαι, ὥς φησιν ὁ Δαβὶδ ἀντὶ τοῦ πλήθους ὅτι Χιλιάδες
5   εὐθηνούντων, καὶ Ὑπὲρ χιλιάδας χρυσίου καὶ ἀργυρίου.
        Οὕτω μὲν οὖν τὸν τράχηλον τὸν ἐπὶ τῶν ὤμων ἐρριζωμένον
κατενοήσαμεν. ὤμους δὲ νοοῦμεν, οἷς ἐπιπέφυκε, τὰς πρακτικάς τε καὶ
ἐνεργητικὰς σπουδάς, δι' ὧν οἱ βραχίονες ἡμῶν τὴν σωτηρίαν ἑαυτῶν
κατεργάζονται.
10   τὴν δὲ πρὸς τὸ μεῖζον ἐπαύξησιν τῆς κατὰ θεὸν ὑψουμένης ψυχῆς
σύνοιδε πάντως ὁ ἐπιστατικῶς τοῖς λεγομένοις ἀκολουθῶν, ὅτι πρότερον μὲν
ἀγαπητὸν ἦν τῇ νύμφῃ ἵππῳ ὁμοιωθῆναι τῇ καταγωνισαμένῃ τὸν Αἰγύπτιον
τύραννον καὶ πρὸς τοὺς ὁρμίσκους ἐμφερῶς ἔχειν τὴν ἐπὶ τοῦ τραχήλου | 238
εὐπρέπειαν· νυνὶ δὲ πόσην αὐτῇ μαρτυρεῖ τὴν πρὸς τὸ ἀγαθὸν τελειότητα, ὅτι
15   οὐχ ὁρμίσκοις τισὶ περιδεραίοις προσεικάζει τοῦ τραχήλου τὴν ὥραν, ἀλλὰ
πύργος εἶναι διὰ τὸ μέγεθος λέγεται, ὃν περίβλεπτον ποιεῖ καὶ τοῖς πόρρωθεν
ἀφεστηκόσιν ἀποσκοπούμενον οὐ μόνον ἡ περὶ τὴν οἰκοδομὴν φιλοτιμία
ἐφ' ὅ τι μήκιστον τὸ ὕψος ἐγείρουσα, ἀλλὰ καὶ ἡ τοῦ τόπου θέσις φυσικῶς
ὑπερανεστῶσα τῶν γειτνιώντων; ὅταν τοίνυν βασιλέως μὲν ἔργον ὁ πύργος
20   ᾖ, ἐπὶ δὲ τῆς ὑψηλῆς πολιτείας βεβηκὼς τύχῃ, τότε ἀληθὲς ἐπιδείκνυται τὸ
παρὰ τοῦ κυρίου λεγόμενον ὅτι Οὐ δύναται πόλις κρυβῆναι ἐπάνω ὄρους
κειμένη. νόει δέ μοι τὸν πύργον ἀντὶ τῆς πόλεως.
        Καιρὸς δ' ἂν εἴη καὶ τοὺς δύο νεβροὺς τῆς δορκάδος κατανοῆσαι, οἳ
περὶ τὴν καρδίαν τῆς νύμφης αὐλίζονται μαστοὶ κληθέντες παρὰ τοῦ λόγου
25   [καθώς φησι Δύο μαστοί | σου ὡς δύο νεβροὶ δίδυμοι δορκάδος οἱ νεμόμενοι   239
ἐν τοῖς κρίνοις] διὰ τὸ μεταξὺ τούτων εἶναι τῆς καρδίας τὴν θέσιν, ὧν ἡ
νομὴ οὐ χόρτος ἐστὶν ἢ ἄκανθα ἀλλὰ κρίνα παντὶ τῷ τῆς νομῆς χρόνῳ τὸ
ἄνθος ἑαυτῶν παρατείνοντα καὶ οὐ κατὰ καιρὸν ἀνθοῦντα οὐδὲ ἐπὶ καιροῦ
μαραινόμενα, ἀλλὰ διαρκῆ παρεχόμενα τοῖς νεβροῖς τούτοις δι' ἑαυτῶν τὴν
30   τροφήν, ἕως ἂν μηκέτι αἱ σκιαὶ κρατῶσι τῆς σπουδαζομένης περὶ τὸν βίον
ἀπάτης, ἀλλ' ἤδη τοῦ φωτὸς πανταχῇ διαλάμψαντος καταυγασθῇ τὰ πάντα
διὰ τῆς ἡμέρας τῆς ὅπου θέλει διαπνεούσης τὸ φῶς. [οὕτω γάρ φησιν ὁ

them" (Ps 33:8). And the number *thousands* does not seem to me mean exactly "tens of hundreds" but to be employed by the Word to indicate a multitude; for it is customary, given the Scriptures' metaphorical use of words, for multitude to be denoted by this number. Thus David, instead of saying "a multitude," says, "Thousands of those that flourish" (Ps 67:18) and "more than thousands of gold and silver pieces" (Ps 118:72).

This, then, is the way in which we understand the *neck* that is implanted upon the shoulders. As to the shoulders out of which it grows, them we understand to be the active and operative exertions through which our arms work their own salvation.

Now the reader who is following the text attentively understands at any rate the growth for the better that belongs to the soul that is being exalted toward God. Earlier on, the Bride was content to be likened to *the horse* that fought the Egyptian tyrant and to have the comeliness of her neck compared to *circlets*. | Now, though, the text attests for her an amazing degree of perfection in relation to the good. The beauty of her neck is not likened to any circlets but is called a *tower* because of its height. This tower is rendered prominent and visible even to those at a distance—not only by the builder's ambition for the edifice, which elevates it as high as possible, but also by its location in a place that naturally looms above the adjacent land. Since, then, the tower is the work of a king, and it has attained the manner of life proper to citizens[31] of the realm on high, what the Lord said is shown to be true: "A city set on a hill cannot be hid" (Matt 5:14). Think of the tower, then, as standing for the city.

It must be time, though, to give thought to the *two … fawns* that lodge about the heart of the Bride and that the text calls *breasts*[32]—just as it says, *Your breasts | are like two twin fawns that feed among the lilies*—because the heart is located between them. Their pasture is not grass or thorns but *lilies* that put out their blossom throughout the entire time of grazing. They do not bloom or wither away seasonally but in and of themselves provide sufficient food for these *fawns*—until *the shadows* of that deceit which is much valued in the business of human life no longer bear sway, but, the light having already dawned, all things are illumined by the day, which *breathes* out light where it

---

31. The Greek term that this expression ("manner … citizens") translates is πολιτεία, which for Gregory intimates the idea of a "city" (πόλις).

32. At this point, as Langerbeck has argued (see the *apparatus criticus* at Langerbeck 1960, 238), someone has inserted the text of Song 4:5, preceded by "As it says." Langerbeck—rightly, I judge—brackets the words on the ground that the insertion interrupts the sequence of thought, and I have omitted it in this translation.

λόγος Ἕως οὗ διαπνεύσῃ ἡ ἡμέρα καὶ κινηθῶσιν αἱ σκιαί.] οἶδας δὲ πάντως
παρὰ τοῦ εὐαγγελίου μαθὼν ὅτι τὸ πνεῦμά ἐστι τὸ ἅγιον τὸ διὰ τοῦ πνεῖν
ὅπου βούλεται φῶς ἐμποιοῦν τοῖς ἐπισταμένοις ὅθεν ἔρχεται καὶ ποῦ ὑπάγει·
περὶ οὗ νῦν ὁ λόγος οὑτωσὶ διεξέρχεται Δύο μαστοί σου ὡς δύο νεβροὶ
5   δίδυμοι δορκάδος οἱ νεμόμενοι ἐν τοῖς κρίνοις, ἕως οὗ διαπνεύσῃ ἡ ἡμέρα καὶ
κινηθῶσιν αἱ σκιαί.

ἀλλὰ τὸ μὲν ἡμέραν λέγεσθαι τὸ πνεῦμα τὸ ἅγιον, φῶς πνέον οἷς ἂν | 240
ἐγγένηται, οὐκ οἶμαί τινα τῶν νοῦν ἐχόντων ἐπιδιστάσαι τῷ λόγῳ· εἰ γὰρ υἱοὶ
φωτὸς καὶ υἱοὶ ἡμέρας γίνονται οἱ γεννηθέντες παρὰ τοῦ πνεύματος, τί ἄλλο
10   χρὴ νοεῖν τὸ πνεῦμα τὸ ἅγιον ἢ φῶς καὶ ἡμέραν, ἧς ἡ πνοὴ φυγαδευτικὴ τῶν
σκιῶν τῆς ματαιότητος γίνεται; ἀνάγκη γὰρ πᾶσα τοῦ ἡλίου φανέντος τὰς
σκιὰς μὴ μένειν ἀλλὰ μεταχωρεῖν τε καὶ μετανίστασθαι.

τὸ δὲ περὶ τῶν δύο νεβρῶν τῆς δορκάδος μυστήριον εὔκαιρον ἂν εἴη
προσθεῖναι τῇ ἐξετάσει τοῦ λόγου, ὧν δίδυμος μέν ἐστιν ἡ γένεσις, τροφὴ
15   δὲ τὸ κρίνον, τόπος δὲ νομῆς ἡ ἀγαθή τε καὶ πίειρα γῆ. αὕτη δ' ἐστὶν ἡ
καρδία κατὰ τὸν τῆς παραβολῆς τοῦ κυρίου λόγον· ἐν αὐτῇ δὲ νεμόμενοι
καὶ τοὺς καθαροὺς ἐξ αὐτῆς λογισμοὺς ἀνθολογοῦντες πιαίνονται. τὸ
δὲ ἄνθος τῶν κρίνων διπλῆν ἔχει τὴν χάριν παρὰ τῆς φύσεως εὐπνοίας τῇ
εὐχροίᾳ συμμεμιγμένης, ὡς καθ' ἑκάτερον εἶναι τοῖς δρεπομένοις ἐράσμιον,
20   εἴτε τῇ ὀσφρήσει προσάγοιεν εἴτε τοῖς ὀφθαλμοῖς τοῦ κάλλους τῆς ὥρας
κατατρυφῶεν· ἡ μὲν γὰρ ὄσφρησις τῆς τοῦ Χριστοῦ εὐωδίας πλήρης γίνεται,
διὰ δὲ τοῦ εἴδους ἐνδείκνυται τὸ καθαρόν τε καὶ ἀκηλίδωτον.

Τάχα τοίνυν ἤδη διὰ τῶν εἰρημένων σεσαφήνισται ἡμῖν τὸ ὑπὸ τοῦ λόγου
δηλούμενον ὅτι δύο ἀνθρώπων ἐν τοῖς | καθ' ἕκαστον θεωρουμένων, τοῦ   241
25   μὲν σωματικοῦ τε καὶ φαινομένου, τοῦ δὲ νοητοῦ τε καὶ ἀοράτου, δίδυμος
μὲν ἀμφοτέρων ἐστὶν ἡ γένεσις κατὰ ταὐτὸν ἀλλήλοις συνεπιδημούντων
τῷ βίῳ· οὔτε γὰρ προϋπάρχει τοῦ σώματος ἡ ψυχὴ οὔτε προκατασκευάζεται
τῆς ψυχῆς τὸ σῶμα, ἀλλ' ὁμοχρόνως ἐν τῇ ζωῇ γίνονται. τροφὴ δὲ τούτοις
κατὰ φύσιν μέν ἐστιν ἡ καθαρότης καὶ ἡ εὐωδία καὶ πάντα τὰ τοιαῦτα, ὧν
30   εὐφοροῦσιν αἱ ἀρεταί, ἔστι δὲ ὅτε τὸ δηλητήριόν τισιν ἀντὶ τοῦ τροφίμου
σπουδάζεται, οἳ οὐχὶ τὰ ἄνθη τῶν ἀρετῶν ἐπιβόσκονται, ἀλλ' ἀκάνθαις
ἐπιτέρπονται καὶ τριβόλοις· οὕτω γὰρ τῆς παραβολῆς τοῦ εὐαγγελίου
ὀνομαζούσης τὰς ἁμαρτίας ἠκούσαμεν, ὧν ἡ κατάρα τοῦ ὄφεως τὴν κακὴν

will.[33] Now having been to school with the Gospel, you well know that it is the Holy Spirit that, because it breathes "where it wills," enlightens those who know "whence it comes" and "whither it goes" (cf. John 3:8), and our text has the Spirit in mind even now as it specifies: *Your breasts are like two twin fawns that feed among the lilies, until the day breathes and the shadows are moved.*

But that the Holy Spirit is called *day,* breathing light | within those in whom he has come to dwell, on this score I suppose that no rational person entertains any doubt in his mind. For if those who have been born of the Spirit become "sons of light" and "sons of the day" (cf. 1 Thess 5:5), what else can one understand the Spirit to be save "light" and "day"—whose breath banishes the shadows of illusion? For it is utterly inevitable that when the sun has appeared, the shades of darkness should no longer abide, but that they should move away and be dispersed.

This will surely be the right time to introduce the mystery of the two fawns into our scrutiny of the passage, the fawns whose birth is that of twins, whose food is the lily, whose pasture is the good and plenteous earth. According to the word of the Lord's parable, this earth is the heart (cf. Luke 8:15), and they are fattened as they graze on it and from it gather the flowers of pure thoughts. Now the blossom of the lily naturally has a double beauty: it mingles an appealing scent with lovely coloration, so that in both respects it is an object of desire for those who pluck it; either it will draw people by its scent, or it will delight the eyes with the splendor of its beauty. For the smell is full of the sweet scent of Christ, while its appearance signifies what is pure and spotless.

Perhaps, then, these words have already made it plain to us—what the passage makes manifest—that there are two human beings | to be discerned in each individual. The one is corporeal and visible, while the other is intelligible and invisible; yet the birth of the two is *twin,* since they come jointly into life at the same time. For the soul does not exist before the body, nor is the body constituted before the soul, but they come into life simultaneously. Now the food that naturally suits these is purity and fragrance and the like, which are born of the virtues, but there comes a time when certain folk set a higher value on what harms them than on what nourishes them. These do not feed on the flowers of the virtues but take delight in "thorns and thistles" (Matt 7:16)—for this is the name that the parable in the Gospel assigns to sins—whose evil shoot was introduced by the curse laid on the serpent. Since,

---

33. Here someone has seen fit to insert the text of Song 4:6a—perhaps the same someone who was responsible for the insertion of 4:5 above (see n. 32). Obviously some scribe thought that Gregory's allusive, not to say labored, introduction of these verses would confuse a reader unless the text he was referring to were supplied.

βλάστην ἐδημιούργησεν. ἐπειδὴ τοίνυν διακριτικῶν ὀφθαλμῶν ἐστι χρεία
τῶν δυναμένων ἐν ἀκριβείᾳ διαγνῶναι τὸ κρίνον τε καὶ τὴν ἄκανθαν καὶ
τὸ μὲν σωτήριον προελέσθαι, τὸ δὲ φθοροποιὸν ἀποπέμψασθαι, διὰ τοῦτο
τὸν καθ᾽ ὁμοιότη|τα τοῦ μεγάλου Παύλου μαζὸν τοῖς νηπίοις γινόμενον καὶ   242
5   γαλακτοτροφοῦντα τοὺς ἀρτιγενεῖς τῆς ἐκκλησίας δυάδα μαζῶν ἀλλήλοις
συγγεννηθέντων τῶν τοῖς νεβροῖς τῆς δορκάδος ἀπεικαζομένων ὠνόμασεν
διὰ πάντων μαρτυρῶν τῷ τοιούτῳ μέλει τῆς ἐκκλησίας τὸ δόκιμον, ὅτι τε
καθ᾽ ἑκάτερον εὐοδοῦται πρὸς τὴν τῶν καθαρῶν κρίνων νομὴν ὀξὺ δεδορκὼς
καὶ διακρίνων τοῦ τροφίμου τὴν ἄκανθαν καὶ ὅτι περὶ τὸ ἡγεμονικὸν
10   ἀναστρέφεται, οὗ σύμβολον ἡ καρδία ἐστιν ἡ δι᾽ ἑαυτῆς τοὺς μαζοὺς
ὑποτρέφουσα καὶ ἔτι πρὸς τούτοις ὅτι οὐκ ἐν ἑαυτῷ κατακλείει τὴν χάριν,
ἀλλ᾽ ἐπέχει τοῖς δεομένοις τοῦ λόγου τὴν θηλήν, Ὡς ἐὰν τροφὸς θάλπῃ τὰ
ἑαυτῆς τέκνα, καθὼς ἐποίει τε καὶ ἔλεγεν ὁ ἀπόστολος.
    Μέχρι τούτων δὲ τῶν μελῶν τῆς ἐκκλησίας προαγαγὼν ὁ λόγος τὸν
15   ἔπαινον ἐν τοῖς ἐφεξῆς ὁλοσώματον ποιεῖται αὐτῆς τὸ ἐγκώμιον, ὅταν Διὰ τοῦ
θανάτου καταργήσῃ τὸν τὸ κράτος ἔχοντα τοῦ θανάτου καὶ πάλιν ἐπαναγάγῃ
ἑαυτὸν πρὸς τὴν ἰδίαν δόξαν τῆς θεότητος, ἣν εἶχεν ἀπ᾽ ἀρχῆς πρὸ τοῦ τὸν
κόσμον εἶναι· εἰπὼν γὰρ ὅτι Πορεύσομαι | ἐμαυτῷ εἰς τὸ ὄρος τῆς σμύρνης   243
καὶ εἰς τὸν βουνὸν τοῦ λιβάνου, διὰ μὲν τῆς σμύρνης τὸ πάθος, διὰ δὲ τοῦ
λιβάνου τὴν δόξαν τῆς θεότητος ἐνδειξάμενος προσέθηκεν Ὅλη καλὴ εἶ,
20   ἡ πλησίον μου, καὶ μῶμος οὐκ ἔστιν ἐν σοί, διδάσκων διὰ τῶν εἰρημένων
πρῶτον μὲν ὅτι οὐδεὶς αἴρει τὴν ψυχὴν αὐτοῦ ἀπ᾽ αὐτοῦ, ἀλλ᾽ ἐξουσίαν ἔχει
θεῖναι αὐτὴν καὶ ἐξουσίαν ἔχει πάλιν λαβεῖν αὐτὴν πορευόμενος ἑαυτῷ ἐπὶ
τὸ ὄρος τῆς σμύρνης, οὐκ ἐκ τῶν ἡμετέρων ἔργων ἵνα μή τις καυχήσηται,
ἀλλ᾽ ἐξ ἰδίας χάριτος τὸν ὑπὲρ τῶν ἁμαρτωλῶν ἀναδεχόμενος θάνατον·
25   ἔπειτα δὲ ὅτι οὐκ ἔστιν ἄλλως καθαρθῆναι τοῦ μώμου τὴν ἀνθρωπίνην φύσιν
μὴ τοῦ ἀμνοῦ τοῦ αἴροντος τὴν ἁμαρτίαν τοῦ κόσμου πᾶσαν δι᾽ ἑαυτοῦ τὴν
κακίαν ἐξαφανίσαντος. ὁ τοίνυν εἰπὼν ὅτι Ὅλη καλὴ εἶ, ἡ πλησίον μου, καὶ
μῶμος οὐκ ἔστιν ἐν σοί· καὶ ἐπαγαγὼν τὸ κατὰ τὸ πάθος μυστήριον διὰ τοῦ

then, the business of discerning eyes that can distinguish exactly between lily and thorn is to choose what is saving but dismiss what is destructive, for this reason our text refers to the person who, after the fashion | of the great Paul, becomes a breast for the little ones and feeds the church's newborn with milk as a pair of breasts that are born together and likened to the fawns of a deer. In this way it bears witness to the esteem that belongs to such a member of the church: both because in each case, seeing[34] sharply and distinguishing the thorn from nourishing food, he shows the way toward the pasture of pure lilies; and also because he refers himself back to the ruling power, whose symbol is the heart that itself gives nourishment to the breasts—and further still because he does not imprison grace within himself but offers the teat of the Word to those in need of it "as a wet nurse takes care of her own children" (1 Thess 2:7), just as the apostle said and did.[35]

Up to this point the Word has been pronouncing the praise of the church's individual members. In what follows he contrives an encomium on her whole body, since "through death he destroyed him who has the power of death" (Heb 2:14) and was restored again to the glory proper to the Godhead, which he possessed from the beginning, before the cosmos existed. For when he had said: *I will betake myself* | *to the mountain of myrrh, and to the hill of frankincense,* indicating by *myrrh* his suffering and by *frankincense* the glory of the Godhead, he added: *You are beautiful through and through, my close one, and there is no flaw within you.* By these words he teaches first that no one takes his life from him but that he has the power to lay it down and the power to take it up again as he makes his journey *to the mountain of myrrh,* accepting death on behalf of sinners not as a result of any deeds of ours, "lest anyone boast" (Eph 2:8), but out of his own graciousness; and then that it is not possible for human nature to be purified of its *flaw* unless "the lamb … that takes away the sin of the cosmos" (John 1:29) destroys the evil himself. Therefore the one who says *You are beautiful through and through, my close one, and there is no flaw within you,* and who introduces the mystery

---

34. Here there is an evident pun, which incidentally reveals some of the logic of Gregory's rather obscure argument here. The word rendered as "seeing" (δεδορκώς) is reminiscent of the word for "deer" (δορκάς), and no doubt for that reason Gregory regularly associates deer with clear vision.

35. This elaborate allegory is intended to show why "breasts" and "fawns" are likened to each other in the text of the Song. The "fawn" of the gazelle is symbolic, here as above, of vision and the attendant ability to discern good from evil, while the breast is symbolic of feeding with the grace of the Word. Both of these functions are carried out in the church by one who like Paul is a "twin"—i.e., a human person in whom corporeal and incorporeal components are joined—who knows thorns and weeds from lilies and at the same time dispenses the nourishment of truth.

κατὰ τὴν σμύρναν αἰνίγματος εἶτα τοῦ λιβάνου μνησθείς, δι' οὗ τὸ θεῖον ἐνδείκνυται, τοῦτο παιδεύει ἡμᾶς ὅτι ὁ συμμετασχὼν αὐτῷ τῆς σμύρνης συμμεθέξει πάντως καὶ τοῦ λιβάνου· ὁ γὰρ συμπαθὼν καὶ συνδοξάζεται πάντως, ὁ δὲ ἅπαξ ἐν τῇ θείᾳ δόξῃ γενόμενος ὅλος γίνεται καλὸς ἔξω τοῦ
5   ἀντικειμένου μώμου γενόμενος, οὗ καὶ ἡμεῖς χωρισθείημεν | διὰ τοῦ ὑπὲρ   244
ἡμῶν ἀποθανόντος καὶ ἐγερθέντος,

ᾧ ἡ δόξα εἰς τοὺς αἰῶνας τῶν αἰώνων.
ἀμήν.

of his suffering under the figure of *myrrh,* and then makes mention of *frank-incense*—this one is instructing us that the one who shares *myrrh* with him will also fully share in his *frankincense;* for the one who suffers with him will be fully glorified with him, and the one who has once for all entered into the divine glory becomes *all beautiful,* having been separated from the inimical *flaw.* May we too be segregated from it | through the one who died for us and was raised,

To whom be glory to the ages of ages.
Amen.

Λόγος η′

Δεῦρο ἀπὸ Λιβάνου, νύμφη, δεῦρο ἀπὸ Λιβάνου·
ἐλεύσῃ καὶ διελεύσῃ ἀπὸ ἀρχῆς πίστεως,
ἀπὸ κεφαλῆς Σανὶρ καὶ Ἑρμών,
ἀπὸ μανδρῶν λεόντων, ἀπὸ ὀρέων παρδάλεων.
5   Ἐκαρδίωσας ἡμᾶς, ἀδελφὴ ἡμῶν νύμφη,
ἐκαρδίωσας ἡμᾶς ἑνὶ ἀπὸ ὀφθαλμῶν σου,
ἐν μιᾷ, ἐνθέματι τραχήλου σου.

Τί ἐκαλλιώθησαν μαστοί σου, ἀδελφή μου νύμφη,
τί ἐκαλλιώθησαν μαστοί σου ἀπὸ οἴνου;
10   καὶ ὀσμὴ ἱματίων σου ὑπὲρ πάντα τὰ ἀρώματα.
Κηρίον ἀποστάζουσι χείλη σου, νύμφη,
μέλι καὶ γάλα ὑπὸ τὴν γλῶσσάν σου,
καὶ ὀσμὴ ἱματίων σου ὡς ὀσμὴ λιβάνου.
| Κῆπος κεκλεισμένος ἀδελφή μου νύμφη,   245
15   κῆπος κεκλεισμένος, πηγὴ ἐσφραγισμένη.
Ἀποστολαί σου παράδεισος ῥοῶν
μετὰ καρποῦ
κύπροι μετὰ νάρδων, ἀκροδρύων,
Νάρδος καὶ κρόκος,
20   κάλαμος καὶ κιννάμωμον
μετὰ πάντων ξύλων τοῦ Λιβάνου,
σμύρνα, ἀλόη μετὰ πάντων πρωτομύρων,
Πηγὴ κήπων, φρέαρ ὕδατος ζῶντος
καὶ ῥοιζοῦντος ἀπὸ τοῦ Λιβάνου.

25   Ὁ τὰς μεγάλας ὀπτασίας διεξελθὼν πρὸς τοὺς Κορινθίους, ὁ μέγας
ἀπόστολος, ὅτε καὶ ἀμφίβολος περὶ τῆς ἑαυτοῦ φύσεως ἔφησεν εἶναι εἴτε
σῶμα ἦν εἴτε νόημα ἐν τῷ καιρῷ τῆς ἐν τῷ παραδείσῳ μυσταγωγίας, ταῦτα
διαμαρτυράμενος λέγει ὅτι Ἐμαυτὸν οὔπω λογίζομαι κατειληφέναι, ἀλλ' ἔτι

HOMILY 8
Song 4:8–9

⁸*Come away from frankincense,*¹ *my bride, come away from frankincense.*
You shall come and pass through from the beginning of faith,
from the peak of Sanir and Hermon,
from the lions' dens, from the mountains of the leopards.
⁹*You have heartened us, O my sister bride,*
you have heartened us with one of your eyes,
in one, by the ornament of your neck.

[¹⁰*How your breasts have been made beautiful, my sister bride!*
How your breasts have been made beautiful from wine!
And the fragrance of your perfumed ointments is above all spices.
¹¹*Your lips drop honey, my bride,*
honey and milk are under your tongue,
and the fragrance of your garments is as the fragrance of frankincense.
¹²*My sister bride is an enclosed garden,*
a garden enclosed, a fountain sealed.
¹³*Your outsendings are a paradise of pomegranate trees*
with the produce of fruit trees,
henna with spikenard,
¹⁴*spikenard and saffron,*
calamus and cinnamon,
with all the frankincense trees,
myrrh, aloe with all the finest perfumes,
¹⁵*a fountain of gardens, a spring of living water*
that pours forth from frankincense.]²

After his account to the Corinthians of his sublime visions (cf. 2 Cor 12:1–4)—in the course of which he also observed that he was uncertain of his own state at the time of his mystic initiation into paradise, whether he was body or thought—the grand apostle makes a solemn acknowledgment:

---

1. See below, n. 5.

2. The majority of manuscripts, including the old Syriac version of Gregory's homilies, here write out the text of Song 4:10–15, which, however, Gregory does not treat in this sermon. Apparently he had intended to treat these verses but stopped short of his original goal (homily 8 is the shortest of the fifteen). They are taken up in homily 9. See below, p. 260 [Jaeger] *ad fin.*, and n. 22 there.

τοῖς ἔμπροσθεν ἐπεκτείνομαι τῶν προδιηνυσμένων λήθην ποιούμενος, δηλῶν
ὅτι καὶ μετὰ τὸν τρίτον οὐρανὸν ἐκεῖνον ὃν αὐτὸς ἔγνω μόνος (οὐ γάρ τι
Μωϋσῆς ἐν τῇ κοσμογενείᾳ περὶ αὐτοῦ διηγήσατο) καὶ μετὰ τὴν ἄρρητον τῶν
τοῦ παραδείσου μυστηρίων ἀκρόασιν ἔτι ἐπὶ τὸ ἀνώτερον ἵεται καὶ οὐ λήγει
5   τῆς ἀναβάσεως οὐδέποτε τὸ καταλαμβανόμενον ἀγαθὸν ὅρον τῆς ἐπιθυμίας
ποιούμενος,
      διδάσκων οἶμαι διὰ τούτων ἡμᾶς ὅτι τῆς μακαρίας ἐκείνης τῶν ἀγαθῶν
| φύσεως πολὺ μέν ἐστι τὸ ἀεὶ εὑρισκόμενον, ἀπειροπλάσιον δὲ τοῦ πάντοτε   246
καταλαμβανομένου τὸ ὑπερκείμενον καὶ τοῦτο εἰς τὸ διηνεκὲς γίνεται
10   τῷ μετέχοντι ἐν πάσῃ τῇ τῶν αἰώνων ἀϊδιότητι διὰ τῶν ἀεὶ μειζόνων τῆς
ἐπαυξήσεως τοῖς μετέχουσι γινομένης· ὁ μὲν γὰρ καθαρὸς τὴν καρδίαν κατὰ
τὴν ἀψευδῆ τοῦ δεσπότου φωνὴν ὁρᾷ τὸν θεόν, ἀεὶ κατὰ τὴν ἀναλογίαν
τῆς δυνάμεως ὅσον χωρῆσαι δύναται τοσοῦτον τῇ κατανοήσει δεχόμενος.
τὸ μέντοι ἀόριστόν τε καὶ ἀπερίληπτον τῆς θεότητος ἐπέκεινα πάσης
15   καταλήψεως διαμένει· οὐ γὰρ τῆς μεγαλοπρεπείας τῆς δόξης οὐκ ἔστι πέρας,
καθὼς ὁ προφήτης μαρτύρεται, τοῦτο πάντοτε ὡσαύτως ἔχει ἐν τῷ αὐτῷ ὕψει
διὰ παντὸς θεωρούμενον.
      ὥσπερ δὴ καὶ ὁ μέγας Δαβὶδ ὁ τὰς καλὰς ἀναβάσεις ἐν τῇ καρδίᾳ
διατιθέμενος καὶ ἐκ δυνάμεως εἰς δύναμιν ἀεὶ πορευόμενος τοῦτο πρὸς τὸν
20   θεὸν ἀνεβόησεν ὅτι Σὺ δὲ ὕψιστος εἰς τὸν αἰῶνα, κύριε· τοῦτο οἶμαι διὰ τῆς
φωνῆς ταύτης σημαίνων ὅτι ἐν πάσῃ τῇ τοῦ ἀτελευτήτου αἰῶνος ἀϊδιότητι
ὁ μὲν πρὸς σὲ τρέχων ἑαυτοῦ μείζων πάντοτε καὶ ἀνώτερος γίνεται ἀεὶ
διὰ τῆς τῶν ἀγαθῶν ἀναβάσεως ἀναλόγως αὐξόμενος, σὺ δὲ ὁ αὐτὸς εἶ
ὕψιστος εἰς τὸν αἰῶνα μένων, οὐδέποτε χθαμαλώτερος τοῖς ἀνιοῦσι φανῆναι
25   δυνάμενος τῷ κατὰ τὸ ἴσον ἀνώτερος πάντοτε καὶ ὑψηλότερος | εἶναι τῆς   247
τῶν ὑψουμένων δυνάμεως.
      ταῦτα τοίνυν περὶ τῆς φύσεως τῶν ἀφράστων ἀγαθῶν δογματίζειν τὸν
ἀπόστολον ὑπειλήφαμεν λέγοντα ὅτι τὸ ἀγαθὸν ἐκεῖνο Ὀφθαλμὸς οὐκ εἶδεν,
κἂν ἀεὶ βλέπῃ (οὐ γὰρ ὅσον ἐστὶ βλέπει, ἀλλ’ ὅσον τῷ ὀφθαλμῷ δυνατόν
30   ἐστι δέξασθαι), Καὶ οὓς οὐκ ἤκουσεν, καθ’ ὅσον ἐστὶ τὸ δηλούμενον, κἂν
πάντοτε δέχηται τῇ ἀκοῇ τὸν λόγον, Καὶ ἐπὶ καρδίαν ἀνθρώπου οὐκ ἀνέβη,

"I do not consider that I have made it my own, but straining forward to what lies ahead, I forget what has already been accomplished" (Phil 3:13).[3] By this he shows that after that "third heaven" that he alone knew (for Moses told nothing about it in his cosmogony) and after the ineffable audition of the mysteries of paradise, he is still hastening toward something higher and never leaves off his ascent by setting the good he has already grasped as a limit to his desires.

In this way, as I see it, [Paul] teaches us, on the one hand, that what is ever and again discovered of that blessed | Nature that is the Good is something great but, on the other hand, that what lies beyond what is grasped at any particular point is infinitely greater; and during the entire eternity of the ages this becomes the case for the person who participates in the Good, since those who participate in it receive increase and growth in that they encounter ever greater and better things. For according to the Master's true statement, the person who is pure in heart sees God (cf. Matt 5:8), ever grasping in the mind as much as he is able to take in, in proportion to his capacity. Nevertheless, the infinity and incomprehensibility of the Godhead remains beyond all direct apprehension. For that reality, "the splendor" of whose "glory" knows no "limit," as the prophet testifies (Ps 145:3, 5 LXX) exists forever unchanging, forever discerned in the same exalted height.

So the great David—though "in the heart" he has traced out the glad "ascents" and always goes "from strength to strength" (Ps 83:6, 8)—cries out to God: "You, O Lord, are the Most Exalted for eternity" (Ps 91:9); and in my opinion what he means by his cry is this: "In the entire eternity of the unending age, the person who bends his course toward you is always becoming greater and higher than he is, making relative growth because of his 'ascent' through good things, but you are the same and remain eternally the Most Exalted. You can never, to those making their ascent, be revealed as on a lower level than they, for you are always, by comparison, higher and | more exalted than the reach of those who are being raised up."

Hence we find that the apostle taught this truth[4] concerning the nature of the inexpressible goods when he said: "eye has not seen" that Good even if it be ever gazing upon it (for it does not see as much as there is, but only as much as the eye is capable of taking in); and "ear has not heard" the full extent of what is revealed, even though its hearing be ever receiving the Word; and "it has not entered into the human heart" (1 Cor 2:9), even though persons

---

3. It should be noted that Gregory here is partially quoting and partially paraphrasing, which is natural enough in light of the centrality of this passage from Philippians for his spirituality and anthropology.

4. Greek δογματίζειν, meaning essentially "state a basic truth."

κἂν διὰ παντὸς ὁ καθαρὸς τῇ καρδίᾳ ὅσον δύναται βλέπῃ· τὸ γὰρ ἀεὶ
καταλαμβανόμενον τῶν μὲν προκαταληφθέντων πάντως μεῖζόν ἐστιν, οὐ μὴν
ὁρίζει ἐν ἑαυτῷ τὸ ζητούμενον, ἀλλὰ τὸ πέρας τοῦ εὑρεθέντος ἀρχὴ πρὸς
τὴν τῶν ὑψηλοτέρων εὕρεσιν τοῖς ἀναβαίνουσι γίνεται καὶ οὔτε ὁ ἀνιὼν ποτε
5   ἵσταται ἀρχὴν ἐξ ἀρχῆς μεταλαμβάνων οὔτε τελεῖται περὶ ἑαυτὴν ἡ τῶν ἀεὶ
μειζόνων ἀρχή· οὐδέποτε γὰρ ἐπὶ τῶν ἐγνωσμένων ἡ τοῦ ἀνιόντος ἐπιθυμία
μένει, ἀλλὰ διὰ μείζονος πάλιν ἑτέρας ἐπιθυμίας πρὸς ἑτέραν ὑπερκειμένην
κατὰ τὸ ἐφεξῆς ἡ ψυχὴ ἀνιοῦσα πάντοτε διὰ τῶν ἀνωτέρων ὁδεύει πρὸς τὸ
ἀόριστον.
10   Τούτων δὲ ἡμῖν οὕτω διῃρημένων καιρὸς ἂν εἴη | προθεῖναι τῶν θείων   248
λογίων τὴν θεωρίαν· Δεῦρο ἀπὸ λιβάνου, νύμφη, δεῦρο ἀπὸ λιβάνου·
ἐλεύσῃ καὶ διελεύσῃ ἀπὸ ἀρχῆς πίστεως, ἀπὸ κεφαλῆς Σανὶρ καὶ Ἑρμών, ἀπὸ
μανδρῶν λεόντων, ἀπὸ ὀρέων παρδάλεων.
τί τοίνυν ἐν τούτοις ὑπενοήσαμεν; ἀεὶ τῶν ἀγαθῶν ἡ πηγὴ πρὸς ἑαυτὴν
15   τοὺς διψῶντας ἐφέλκεται, καθὼς ἐν τῷ εὐαγγελίῳ φησὶν ἡ πηγὴ ὅτι Εἴ τις
διψᾷ, ἐρχέσθω πρός με καὶ πινέτω· ἐν τούτοις γὰρ οὔτε τῆς δίψης οὔτε
τῆς πρὸς αὐτὸν ὁρμῆς οὔτε τῆς ἐν τῷ πίνειν ἀπολαύσεως ἔδωκεν ὅρον,
ἀλλὰ τῷ παρατατικῷ τοῦ προστάγματος πρὸς τὸ διηνεκὲς ποιεῖται τὴν
προτροπὴν καὶ τοῦ διψῆν καὶ τοῦ πίνειν καὶ τοῦ πρὸς αὐτὸν τὴν ὁρμὴν
20   ἔχειν. τοῖς δὲ γευσαμένοις ἤδη καὶ τῇ πείρᾳ μαθοῦσιν ὅτι χρηστὸς ὁ κύριος
οἷόν τις προτροπὴ πρὸς τὴν τοῦ πλείονος μετουσίαν ἡ γεῦσις γίνεται. διὰ
τοῦτο οὐδέποτε λείπει τῷ ἀναβαίνοντι ἡ γινομένη πρὸς αὐτὸν προτροπὴ ἡ
πάντοτε πρὸς τὸ μεῖζον ἐφελκομένη· ὑπομνησθῶμεν γὰρ τῆς πολλάκις ἐν
τοῖς φθάσασιν ἤδη γεγενημένης παρορμήσεως παρὰ τοῦ λόγου τῇ νύμφῃ.
25 | Ἐλθέ, ἡ πλησίον μου, λέγει καὶ πάλιν Δεῦρο περιστερά μου, καὶ Δεῦρο   249
σεαυτῇ ἐν σκέπῃ τῆς πέτρας. καὶ ἄλλας τοιαύτας φωνὰς προτρεπτικάς τε καὶ
ἑλκτικὰς τῆς τῶν μειζόνων ἐπιθυμίας ὁ λόγος πρὸς τὴν ψυχὴν ποιησάμενος
καὶ μαρτυρήσας ἤδη τῇ πρὸς αὐτὸν ἀνιούσῃ τὸ διὰ πάντων ἀμώμητον εἰπὼν
ὅτι Ὅλη καλὴ εἶ καὶ μῶμος οὐκ ἔστιν ἐν σοί, ὡς ἂν μὴ τῇ μαρτυρίᾳ ταύτῃ
30   ἐγχαυνωθεῖσα πρὸς τὴν τῶν μειζόνων ἄνοδον ἐμποδισθείη, πάλιν διὰ τῆς

who are pure in heart may regularly see as much as they are capable of. For that which is apprehended at any given time is in all respects greater than anything that has been apprehended previously, but it does not in and of itself set limits to the object of the search. On the contrary, for those who are in process of ascent, the outer limit of what has been discovered becomes the starting point of a search after more exalted things. Neither, moreover, does the one who is mounting up ever cease to promote one starting point into another, nor does the starting point of ever-greater things find fulfillment simply in itself. For the desire of the soul that is ascending never rests content with what has been known. In turn mounting upwards by way of one greater desire toward another that surpasses it, that soul is always journeying toward the infinite by way of higher things.

With these matters clarified, no doubt it is time | to set out our understanding of the divine oracles: *Come away from frankincense,*[5] *my bride, come away from frankincense. Come and pass through from the beginning of faith, from the peak of Sanir and Hermon, from the lions' dens, from the mountains of the leopards.*

What meaning, then, did we detect in these words? The wellspring of good things always draws the thirsty to itself—just as in the Gospel the wellspring says: "If anyone thirst, let him come to me and drink" (John 7:37). For in using these words, he sets no limit, whether to thirst, or to the urge to come to him, or to the enjoyment of the drinking. Rather, by the open-endedness of his injunction, he issues a continuing invitation to thirst and to drink and to be impelled toward him. To those who have already "tasted" and have learned from experience "that the Lord is good" (cf. Ps 33:9; 1 Pet 2:3), the tasting becomes, as it were, an invitation to partake of yet more. On this account the invitation to come to him that has been offered, and that ever and again draws us to better things, is never lacking to the person who is journeying upwards. Let us not be forgetful of the urging that the Word addressed to the Bride in earlier passages: | *Come, my close one,* he says, and again, *Come, my dove,* and *Come for yourself … to the shelter of the rock.* Indeed the Word has also addressed other such sayings to the soul, sayings calculated to exhort her and to bring her to the desire for greater things, and he has already attested her perfect flawlessness for her as she mounts toward him, saying: *You are beautiful through and through, my close one, and there is no flaw in you.* But lest she be filled with conceit by this testimony and be hindered in her ascent, he enjoins her once again, in these words of exhorta-

---

5. The Greek word is λίβανος, which can be taken either as a place name ("Lebanon") or as a common noun meaning "frankincense." Since Gregory takes it in the latter sense, I have so translated it here and at the beginning of the homily.

προτρεπτικῆς ταύτης φωνῆς ἐπὶ τὴν τῶν ὑπερκειμένων ἐπιθυμίαν ἀναβῆναι
παρακελεύεται λέγων Δεῦρο ἀπὸ λιβάνου, νύμφη.

τὸ δὲ λεγόμενον τοιοῦτόν ἐστι· καλῶς, φησίν, ἐν τοῖς φθάσασιν
ἠκολούθησας, ἦλθες μετ᾽ ἐμοῦ πρὸς τὸ ὄρος τῆς σμύρνης (συνετάφης γάρ μοι
5   διὰ τοῦ βαπτίσματος εἰς τὸν θάνατον), συνανῆλθές μοι καὶ ἐπὶ τὸν βουνὸν
τοῦ λιβάνου (συνανέστης γάρ μοι καὶ ὑψώθης ἐν τῇ τῆς θεότητος κοινωνίᾳ,
ἣν ἐνδείκνυται τοῦ λιβάνου τὸ ὄνομα), ἀνάβηθί μοι καὶ ἀπὸ τούτων ἐπὶ ἕτερα
ὄρη προκόπτουσά τε καὶ ὑψουμένη διὰ τῆς ἐνεργοῦς γνώσεως, δεῦρο τοίνυν
ἀπὸ τοῦ λιβάνου, φησίν, οὐκέτι μνηστὴ ἀλλὰ νύμφη. οὐ γάρ ἐστι δυνατὸν ἐμοὶ
10   συζῆσαι μὴ ἀλλοιωθέντα διὰ τῆς τοῦ θανάτου σμύρνης πρὸς τὴν τοῦ λιβάνου
θεότητα. ἐπεὶ οὖν ἐν τούτῳ γέγονας | ἤδη τῷ ὕψει, μὴ στῇς ἀνιοῦσα ὡς ἤδη   250
διὰ τούτων ἐπιβᾶσα τῆς τελειότητος· ἀρχὴ γάρ σοι πίστεως ὁ λίβανος οὗτος
γίνεται, οὗ μετέσχες διὰ τῆς ἀναστάσεως, ἀρχὴ δὲ τῆς ἐπὶ τὰ ὑψηλότερα τῶν
ἀγαθῶν πορείας. ἀπὸ τοίνυν τῆς ἀρχῆς ταύτης, ἥτις ἐστὶν ἡ πίστις, ἐλεύσῃ
15   καὶ διελεύσῃ· τουτέστι καὶ νῦν ἥξεις καὶ εἰς ἀεὶ διερχομένη διὰ τῶν τοιούτων
ἀνόδων οὐκ ἀπολήξεις.

Ἔχει δὲ ἡ λέξις οὕτως· Ἐλεύσῃ καὶ διελεύσῃ ἀπὸ ἀρχῆς πίστεως, ἀπὸ
κεφαλῆς Σανὶρ καὶ Ἑρμών. διὰ τούτων δὲ τὸ τῆς ἄνωθεν γεννήσεως ὑποφαίνει
μυστήριον· ἐντεῦθεν γὰρ προχεῖσθαί φασι τὰς τοῦ Ἰορδάνου πηγάς, ὧν
20   ὑπέρκειται τοῦτο τὸ ὄρος δύο λοφιαῖς μεριζόμενον, αἷς ταῦτα ἐπίκειται τὰ
ὀνόματα Σανὶρ καὶ Ἑρμών. ἐπεὶ οὖν τὸ ἐκ τῶν πηγῶν τούτων ῥεῖθρον ἀρχὴ
γέγονεν ἡμῖν τῆς πρὸς τὸ θεῖον μεταποιήσεως, τούτου χάριν ἀκούει τοῦ πρὸς
ἑαυτὸν καλοῦντος αὐτὴν ὅς φησι Δεῦρο ἀπὸ λιβάνου καὶ ἀπὸ ἀρχῆς πίστεως
καὶ ἀπὸ κεφαλῆς τῶν ὀρέων τούτων, ὅθεν σοι γεγόνασιν αἱ τοῦ μυστηρίου
25   πηγαί.

καλῶς δὲ προστίθησι τὴν τῶν λεόντων τε καὶ παρδάλεων μνήμην, ἵνα διὰ
τῆς τῶν λυπηρῶν παραθέσεως γλυκυτέραν ποιήσῃ | τὴν τῶν εὐφραινόντων   251
ἀπόλαυσιν· ἐπειδὴ γὰρ ἀποθέμενός ποτε τὸ θεῖον εἶδος ὁ ἄνθρωπος πρὸς

tion, to mount up to a desire for that which lies beyond: *Come away from frankincense, my bride.*

The point of his words is something on this order: "Rightly," he says, "have you followed me in what has gone before. You accompanied me to the mountain of myrrh (for you were 'buried' with me 'by baptism into death' [cf. Rom 6:4]), and you came with me too to the hill of frankincense (for you rose with me and were exalted to communion with the Godhead, which is what the word *frankincense* indicates). Now come up with me, come away from these to yet further heights, as you progress and are uplifted by the knowledge that works in you. Come away, then, from frankincense," he says, "no longer as one betrothed, but as a bride. For it is not possible to live together with me until you have been changed by the myrrh of death into the deity of frankincense. Since, then, you have | already attained this height, do not stop in your ascent as though you have already achieved perfection by these accomplishments. For this frankincense, which you have come to share through the resurrection, is for you the beginning of faith,[6] the beginning of a journey toward higher levels of goodness. So come and pass through from this beginning which is faith; that is, even now you shall come, and you shall not cease[7] passing forever through such ascents."

The text runs as follows: *Come and pass through from the beginning of faith, from the peak of Sanir and Hermon.* With these words, however, he intimates the mystery of the birth from above,[8] for it is from there, they say, that the springs of the Jordan flow, over which there looms this mountain that divides into two peaks with the names Sanir and Hermon. Since, then, the stream that flows out of these springs is for us the beginning of our being remodeled for existence at the level of the divine, the soul hears the one who is calling her to himself, and he says: "Come away from frankincense and from the beginning of faith and from the peak of these mountains, whence there come for you the springs of the mystery."

Moreover, it is aptly that he adds the mention of lions and leopards, so as to make | the pleasure of those who rejoice even sweeter by contrasting it with things that give pain. For humanity, once it had put off its divine aspect,

---

6. This phrase—"the beginning of faith" (with which the LXX renders—or replaces—the Hebrew "peak of Amana")—seems to explain why Gregory takes this passage in the way he does. It suggests *baptism* to him, as indeed, does the juxtaposition of "myrrh" and "frankincense" when interpreted in the light of Paul's remarks in Rom 6, where baptism is said to involve death to sin and resurrection with Christ. The burden of the exegesis is to argue that baptism is the beginning of the person's ascent to God, not its completion.

7. There is ringing rhyme-effect here: ἥξεις ("you shall come") and ἀπολήξεις ("you shall not cease").

8. This is another allusion to baptism.

τὴν ὁμοιότητα τῆς ἀλόγου φύσεως ἐθηριώθη πάρδαλις καὶ λέων διὰ τῶν
πονηρῶν ἐπιτηδευμάτων γενόμενος (ὁ γὰρ ὑπὸ τοῦ λέοντος ἑλκυσθεὶς τοῦ
ἐνεδρεύοντος ἐν τῇ μάνδρᾳ, καθώς φησιν ὁ προφήτης, καὶ ἐν τῇ παγίδι
αὐτοῦ ταπεινωθεὶς πρὸς τὴν ἐκείνου φύσιν μεταμορφοῦται κατακρατήσαντος
5   τοῦ θηρίου τῆς φύσεως· Ὅμοιοι γὰρ αὐτοῖς, φησί, γένοιντο οἱ ποιοῦντες
αὐτὰ καὶ πάντες οἱ πεποιθότες ἐπ᾽ αὐτοῖς. ὁμοίως δὲ καὶ πάρδαλις γίνεται
ὁ διὰ τῶν τοῦ βίου κηλίδων τὴν ψυχὴν στιγματίσας), ἐπεὶ οὖν ἦν ποτε ὅτε
ἐν τούτοις ἦν τὸ ἀνθρώπινον διὰ τῆς εἰδωλολατρίας καὶ τῆς Ἰουδαϊκῆς
ἀπάτης καὶ τῆς ποικίλης τῶν ἁμαρτιῶν κακίας πλανώμενον, μετὰ ταῦτα δὲ
10 διὰ τοῦ Ἰορδάνου καὶ τῆς σμύρνης καὶ τοῦ λιβάνου πρὸς τοσοῦτον ὑψώθη,
ὥστε αὐτῷ ἤδη συμμετεωροπορεῖν τῷ θεῷ, τούτου χάριν πλεονάζει τῶν
παρόντων ἀγαθῶν τὴν εὐφροσύνην ὁ λόγος διὰ τῆς τῶν ποτε γεγενημένων
ἀνιαρῶν παραθέσεως προφέρων, ἐν τίσιν ἦν ἡ ψυχὴ πρὸ τοῦ λιβάνου καὶ
τῆς ἀρχῆς τῆς πίστεως καὶ πρὸ τῶν ἐπὶ τοῦ Ἰορδάνου γνωρισθέντων ἡμῖν
15 μυστηρίων· ὡς γὰρ ἡ κατ᾽ εἰρήνην ζωὴ γλυκυτέρα μετὰ τὸν πόλεμον γίνεται
τοῖς σκυθρωποῖς διηγήμασιν ἡδυνομένη καὶ τὸ τῆς ὑγείας ἀγαθὸν μᾶλλον
καταγλυκαίνει τὰ τοῦ σώματος ἡμῶν αἰσθητήρια, εἰ ἔκ τινος ἀρρωστημάτων
| ἀηδίας πρὸς ἑαυτὴν ἐπανέλθοι πάλιν ἡ φύσις, τὸν αὐτὸν τρόπον ἐπίτασίν   252
τινα καὶ πλεονασμὸν τῆς ἐν τοῖς ἀγαθοῖς εὐφροσύνης οἰκονομῶν ὁ ἀγαθὸς
20 νυμφίος τῇ πρὸς αὐτὸν ἀνιούσῃ ψυχῇ οὐ μόνον τὸ ἑαυτοῦ κάλλος τῇ νύμφῃ
προδείκνυσιν, ἀλλὰ καὶ τοῦ φρικωδεστάτου τῶν θηρίων εἴδους ὑπομιμνήσκει
τῷ λόγῳ, ἵνα μᾶλλον ἐντρυφήσῃ τοῖς παροῦσι καλοῖς μανθάνουσα διὰ τῆς
παραθέσεως, οἷα ἀνθ᾽ οἵων ἠλλάξατο.

τάχα δέ τι καὶ ἕτερον διὰ τούτων ἐκ προνοίας ἀγαθὸν τῇ νύμφῃ
25 κατασκευάζεται· ἐπειδὴ γὰρ βούλεται ἡμᾶς ὁ λόγος τρεπτοὺς ὄντας κατὰ
τὴν φύσιν μὴ πρὸς τὸ κακὸν διὰ τῆς τροπῆς ἀπορρέειν, ἀλλὰ διὰ τῆς ἀεὶ
πρὸς τὸ κρεῖττον γινομένης αὐξήσεως συνεργὸν τὴν τροπὴν πρὸς τὴν
τῶν ὑψηλοτέρων ἄνοδον ἔχειν, ὥστε κατορθωθῆναι διὰ τοῦ τρεπτοῦ τῆς
φύσεως ἡμῶν τὸ πρὸς τὸ κακὸν ἀναλλοίωτον, τούτου χάριν ὥσπερ τινὰ
30 παιδαγωγὸν καὶ φύλακα πρὸς τὴν τῶν κακῶν ἀλλοτρίωσιν τὴν μνήμην τῶν
ποτε κατακρατησάντων θηρίων ὁ λόγος προήνεγκεν, ἵνα τῇ | ἀποστροφῇ τῶν   253

was brutalized and approached likeness to the irrational nature and through its evil habits became a leopard and a lion.[9] (For the person who is dragged off by the "lion" that lurks "in his den," as the prophet says, and is brought down "in his snare" [Ps 9:30–31] is transformed into that nature because the beast-nature has prevailed over him, for it says, "All who make them and all who put trust in them become like them" [Ps 113:16]. In the same way, someone who has spotted his soul with life's blemishes becomes a leopard.) There was a time, then, when humanity found itself in just such a state: going astray on account of its idolatry, and the Jewish error, and the manifold evil of its sins. Afterwards, though, it was brought, by the Jordan and the myrrh and the frankincense, to so great a height as already to be walking on high with God. That, moreover, is why our passage magnifies the joy of present goods by setting them alongside the grievous circumstances of time past, displaying the soul's situation prior to the frankincense and the beginning of faith and before the mysteries made known to us at the Jordan.[10] For a life of peace is the more delectable, once warfare is done with, for being sweetened with tales of troubles past, and good health delights the body's sense organs the more if the organism | has been restored to its natural state after some distasteful illness; and in the same way the good Bridegroom effects intensity and superabundance of joy over good things in the soul that is climbing toward him, not only by showing the Bride her own beauty but also by recalling to her mind the awful image of wild beasts, so that she may the more exult in her present blessedness as she learns from the contrast what good things have taken the place of those evils.

Maybe too by these words he is, in his providence, preparing the Bride for a further gift. For the Word wishes us, mutable as we are by nature, not to decline into evil by our changing, but through unending growth for the better to make change cooperate in our ascent toward higher things.[11] In this way, by means of the very mutability of our nature, we will be confirmed in an incapacity for evil. This is the reason why the Word evokes our memory of the wild beasts that once controlled us, namely, to be a kind of guide and guard to assure our aversion from evil things, so that | by turning away from

---

9. See Origen, *Princ.* 1.8.4.

10. I.e., in the baptism of Jesus.

11. Gregory is perhaps the first Christian teacher to state a positive view of the mutability that was taken to be proper to human beings in virtue of their createdness. Origen seems to have pictured changeability simply as a perpetual liability to departure from the good. Gregory, by contrast, envisages it as empowering an unending process of approximation to the Divine, the limitless Good, with the result that changeability becomes, perhaps somewhat paradoxically, the mirror in human nature of God's infinity.

χειρόνων τὸ ἀκλινές τε καὶ ἀπαράτρεπτον ἐν τοῖς ἀγαθοῖς κατορθώσωμεν
οὔτε ἱστάμενοι τῆς ἐπὶ τὸ κρεῖττον τροπῆς οὔτε πρὸς τὸ κακὸν ἀλλοιούμενοι.
διὰ ταῦτα καὶ ἐλθεῖν ἐγκελεύεται ἀπὸ τοῦ λιβάνου τὴν νύμφην καὶ τῆς
μάνδρας τῶν λεόντων ὑπομιμνήσκει, ἧ ἐνηυλίζετο, καὶ τὰ τῶν παρδάλεων
5   ὄρη προφέρει τῷ λόγῳ, οἷς ἐνδιέτριβεν ὅτε τοῖς θηρίοις ὁμοδίαιτος ἦν.
Ἀλλ' ἐπειδὴ πάντοτε ἡ τοῦ λόγου φωνὴ δυνάμεώς ἐστι φωνή, καθάπερ
ἐπὶ τῆς πρώτης κτίσεως συνεξέλαμψε τὸ φῶς τῷ προστάγματι καὶ συνυπέστη
πάλιν τῷ προστακτικῷ ῥήματι τὸ στερέωμα καὶ ἡ λοιπὴ πᾶσα κτίσις ὡσαύτως
τῷ ποιητικῷ συνανεφαίνετο λόγῳ, τὸν αὐτὸν τρόπον καὶ νῦν τοῦ λόγου
10   τὴν ψυχὴν κρείττονα γενομένην πρὸς ἑαυτὸν ἐλθεῖν ἐγκελευσαμένου
ἀδιαστάτως δυναμωθεῖσα τῷ προστάγματι τοιαύτη γίνεται, οἵαν ὁ νυμφίος
ἐβούλετο, μεταποιηθεῖσα πρὸς τὸ θειότερον καὶ ἀπὸ τῆς δόξης ἐν ᾗ ἦν πρὸς
τὴν ἀνωτέραν δόξαν μεταμορφωθεῖσα διὰ τῆς ἀγαθῆς ἀλλοιώσεως, ὡς θαῦμα
γενέσθαι τῷ περὶ τὸν νυμφίον τῶν ἀγγέλων χορῷ καὶ πάντας εὐφήμως πρὸς
15   αὐτὴν τὴν θαυμαστικὴν ταύτην προέσθαι φωνὴν ὅτι Ἐκαρδίωσας ἡμᾶς,
ἀδελφὴ | ἡμῶν νύμφη· ὁ γὰρ τῆς ἀπαθείας χαρακτὴρ ὁμοίως ἐπιλάμπων   254
αὐτῇ τε καὶ τοῖς ἀγγέλοις εἰς τὴν τῶν ἀσωμάτων αὐτὴν ἄγει συγγένειάν τε
καὶ ἀδελφότητα τὴν ἐν σαρκὶ τὸ ἀπαθὲς κατορθώσασαν. διὰ τοῦτό φασι
πρὸς αὐτὴν ὅτι Ἐκαρδίωσας ἡμᾶς, ἀδελφὴ ἡμῶν νύμφη, κυρίως ἑκατέρῳ
20   τῶν ὀνομάτων σεμνυνομένη· ἀδελφὴ μὲν ἡμετέρα διὰ τὴν τῆς ἀπαθείας
συγγένειαν, νύμφη δὲ διὰ τὴν πρὸς τὸν λόγον συνάφειαν. τοῦ δὲ ἐκαρδίωσας
τὸ σημαινόμενον τοιοῦτον εἶναι νομίζομεν οἷόν ἐστι καὶ τὸ ἐψύχωσας, ὡς εἰ
ἔλεγον πρὸς αὐτὴν ὅτι καρδίαν ἡμῖν ἐνέθηκας.
σαφηνείας δὲ χάριν, ὡς ἂν γένοιτο μᾶλλον καταφανὲς ἡμῖν τὸ
25   λεγόμενον, τὸν θεῖον ἀπόστολον πρὸς τὴν τῶν μυστηρίων τούτων
ἑρμηνείαν παραληψόμεθα· φησὶ γάρ που τῶν ἑαυτοῦ λόγων ἐκεῖνος πρὸς
Ἐφεσίους γράφων, ὅτε τὴν μεγάλην οἰκονομίαν τῆς διὰ σαρκὸς γεγενημένης
θεοφανείας ἡμῖν διηγήσατο, ὅτι οὐ μόνον ἡ ἀνθρωπίνη φύσις ἐπαιδεύθη τὰ
θεῖα διὰ τῆς χάριτος ταύτης μυστήρια, ἀλλὰ καὶ ταῖς ἀρχαῖς καὶ ταῖς ἐξουσίαις
30   ἐν τοῖς ἐπουρανίοις ἐγνωρίσθη ἡ πολυποίκιλος σοφία τοῦ θεοῦ διὰ τῆς κατὰ
Χριστὸν ἐν τοῖς ἀνθρώποις οἰκονομίας φανερωθεῖσα. ἔχει δὲ ἡ λέξις οὕτως·
Ἵνα γνωρισθῇ νῦν ταῖς ἀρχαῖς καὶ ταῖς ἐξουσίαις ἐν τοῖς ἐπουρανίοις διὰ | 255
τῆς ἐκκλησίας ἡ πολυποίκιλος σοφία τοῦ θεοῦ κατὰ πρόθεσιν τῶν αἰώνων ἣν

evil we may be wholly unswerving and unchangeable in the good—neither coming to a stop in our change for the better nor being altered for the worse. That is why he orders the Bride to come away from Lebanon and reminds her of the lions' den, in which she made her home, and mentions the hills of the leopards, where she spent her days when she was the companion of wild beasts.

The voice of the Word is always a voice of power. Hence just as in the first creation the light shone forth even as the command was given, and the firmament in its turn came into being simultaneously with the word of command, and all the rest of the creation was in the same way manifested together with the creative Word—so too now, when the Word commands the soul in its newfound goodness to come to him, she is instantly empowered by the command and comes to be what the Bridegroom willed. She is changed into something more divine and on account of her glad alteration she is transformed from the glory that she had already reached to a higher glory (cf. 1 Cor 3:18), with the result that she becomes a source of wonder to the chorus of angels about the Bridegroom, and propitiously all of them address her with this expression of wonder: *You have given us heart, O bride | our*[12] *sister.* For the mark of impassibility, which illuminates her just as it does the angels, brings the soul that has achieved impassibility in the flesh into a relation of kinship and sisterhood with incorporeal beings. That is why they say to her: "*You have heartened us,* O bride our sister, and you are honored with each of these titles in its most proper sense. Our sister you are in virtue of our kinship in impassibility, and bride you are in virtue of your being joined to the Word." As to the meaning of *heartened,* we judge it to signify much the same as "enlivened," as if they were saying to her, "You have put heart in us."

For the sake of clarity, however, and so that the meaning may become more transparent for us, we will attend to the divine apostle in order to understand these mysteries. For at one point in the Letter to the Ephesians, after he had set out for us the great economy of the theophany that came about in the flesh, Paul stated that it was not to the human race alone that the divine mysteries were taught by this act of grace but that the manifold wisdom of God was also made known to the heavenly rulers and powers, having been revealed through the economy that was carried out in Christ among us human beings. These are his words: "That through | the church the multiform wisdom of God might now be made known to the principalities and powers in the heavenly places. This was according to the eternal purpose that he has

---

12. Gregory adjusts the text to suit his idea of who the speakers are here; the LXX actually reads "*my* sister."

ἐποίησεν ἐν Χριστῷ Ἰησοῦ τῷ κυρίῳ ἡμῶν, ἐν ᾧ ἔχομεν τὴν παρρησίαν καὶ
προσαγωγὴν ἐν πεποιθήσει διὰ τῆς πίστεως αὐτοῦ·
    τῷ ὄντι γὰρ διὰ τῆς ἐκκλησίας γνωρίζεται ταῖς ὑπερκοσμίοις δυνάμεσιν
ἡ ποικίλη τοῦ θεοῦ σοφία ἡ διὰ τῶν ἐναντίων θαυματουργήσασα τὰ μεγάλα
5   θαυμάσια, πῶς γέγονε διὰ θανάτου ζωὴ καὶ δικαιοσύνη διὰ τῆς ἁμαρτίας καὶ
διὰ κατάρας εὐλογία καὶ δόξα διὰ τῆς ἀτιμίας καὶ διὰ τῆς ἀσθενείας ἡ δύναμις·
μόνην γὰρ ἐν τοῖς πρὸ τούτου χρόνοις τὴν ἁπλῆν τε καὶ μονοειδῆ τοῦ θεοῦ
σοφίαν αἱ ὑπερκόσμιοι δυνάμεις ἐγίνωσκον καταλλήλως ἐνεργοῦσαν τῇ
φύσει τὰ θαύματα (καὶ ποικίλον ἦν ἐν τοῖς ὁρωμένοις οὐδὲν ἐν τῷ δύναμιν
10 οὖσαν τὴν θείαν φύσιν πᾶσαν τὴν κτίσιν κατ’ ἐξουσίαν ἐργάζεσθαι ἐν μόνῃ τῇ
ὁρμῇ τοῦ θελήματος τὴν τῶν ὄντων φύσιν εἰς γένεσιν ἄγουσαν καὶ ποιεῖν τὰ
πάντα καλὰ λίαν τὰ ἀπὸ τῆς τοῦ καλοῦ πηγῆς ἀναβρύοντα), τὸ δὲ ποικίλον
τοῦτο τῆς σοφίας εἶδος τὸ ἐκ τῆς πρὸς τὰ ἐναντία διαπλοκῆς συνιστάμενον
νῦν διὰ τῆς ἐκκλησίας σαφῶς ἐδιδάχθησαν, πῶς ὁ λόγος σὰρξ γίνεται, πῶς ἡ
15 ζωὴ θανάτῳ μίγνυται, πῶς τῷ ἰδίῳ μώλωπι τὴν ἡμετέραν ἐξιᾶται πληγήν, πῶς
τῇ ἀσθενείᾳ τοῦ σταυροῦ καταπαλαίει τοῦ ἀντικειμένου τὴν δύναμιν, πῶς τὸ
ἀόρατον | ἐν σαρκὶ φανεροῦται, πῶς ἐξωνεῖται τοὺς αἰχμαλώτους αὐτός τε   256
ὢν ὁ ὠνούμενος καὶ αὐτὸς χρῆμα γινόμενος (ἑαυτὸν γὰρ ἔδωκε λύτρον ὑπὲρ
ἡμῶν τῷ θανάτῳ), πῶς καὶ ἐν τῷ θανάτῳ γίνεται καὶ τῆς ζωῆς οὐκ ἐξίσταται,
20 πῶς καὶ τῇ δουλείᾳ καταμίγνυται καὶ ἐν τῇ βασιλείᾳ μένει· ταῦτα γὰρ πάντα
καὶ τὰ τοιαῦτα ποικίλα ὄντα καὶ οὐχ ἁπλᾶ τῆς σοφίας ἔργα διὰ τῆς ἐκκλησίας
οἱ φίλοι τοῦ νυμφίου μαθόντες ἐκαρδιώθησαν, ἄλλον χαρακτῆρα τῆς θείας
σοφίας ἐν τῷ μυστηρίῳ κατανοήσαντες.
    εἰ δὲ μὴ τολμηρόν ἐστιν εἰπεῖν, τάχα κἀκεῖνοι διὰ τῆς νύμφης τὸ τοῦ
25 νυμφίου κάλλος ἰδόντες ἐθαύμασαν τὸ πᾶσι τοῖς οὖσιν ἀόρατόν τε καὶ
ἀκατάληπτον· ὃν γὰρ Οὐδεὶς ἑώρακε πώποτε, καθώς φησιν Ἰωάννης, Οὐδὲ
ἰδεῖν τις δύναται, καθὼς ὁ Παῦλος μαρτύρεται, οὗτος σῶμα ἑαυτοῦ τὴν
ἐκκλησίαν ἐποίησε καὶ διὰ τῆς προσθήκης τῶν σῳζομένων οἰκοδομεῖ ἑαυτὸν
ἐν ἀγάπῃ, Μέχρις ἂν καταντήσωμεν οἱ πάντες εἰς ἄνδρα τέλειον, εἰς μέτρον
30 ἡλικίας τοῦ πληρώματος τοῦ Χριστοῦ. εἰ οὖν σῶμα τοῦ Χριστοῦ ἡ ἐκκλησία,
κεφαλὴ δὲ τοῦ σώματος ὁ Χριστὸς τῷ ἰδίῳ χαρακτῆρι μορφῶν τῆς ἐκκλησίας
τὸ πρόσωπον, τάχα διὰ τοῦτο πρὸς ταύτην βλέποντες οἱ φίλοι τοῦ νυμφίου
ἐκαρδιώθησαν, ὅτι τρανότερον ἐν αὐτῇ τὸν | ἀόρατον βλέπουσιν· καθάπερ οἱ   257
αὐτὸν τοῦ ἡλίου τὸν κύκλον ἰδεῖν ἀδυνατοῦντες, διὰ δὲ τῆς τοῦ ὕδατος αὐγῆς

realized in Christ Jesus our Lord, in whom we have boldness and confidence of access through our faith in him" (Eph 3:10–11).

For in truth it is through the church that "the multiform wisdom of God," which has worked its great marvels by the instrumentality of contraries, is made known to the powers above the cosmos: how life came through death, and righteousness through sin, and blessing through curse, and glory through shame, and strength through weakness. In previous times, the powers above the cosmos knew only the simple and uniform wisdom of God, which works wonders in agreement with the nature of each; and there was nothing "multiform" among the things that were to be seen—when the divine Nature, powerful as it is, fashioned the entire created order by fiat, bringing the system of things into being by a mere act of will and made all the things that gushed from the fount of goodness "very good" (Gen 1:31). But they were brought to clear knowledge of this manifoldness of wisdom, which consists in the knitting together of contraries, through the church: how the Word becomes flesh; how life is mingled with death; how by his own stripe our calamity is healed; how by the weakness of the cross the power of the Adversary was overthrown; how the invisible | was revealed in flesh; how he redeemed the captives, being himself both the purchaser and the price (for he gave himself as a ransom to death on our account); how he died and did not depart from life; how he shared in the condition of a slave and remained in his kingly state. For all of these things, and whatever is like them, are "multiform," not simple, works of Wisdom, and learning of them through the church, the friends of the Bridegroom were *heartened*, grasping in the mystery another mark of the divine wisdom.

And if it is not too venturesome a thing to say, perhaps those powers marveled at what is invisible and incomprehensible to all beings because they discerned the beauty of the Bridegroom by the agency of the Bride. For the One whom "no one has seen at any time," as John says (John 1:18), whom "no one can see," as Paul bears witness (1 Tim 6:16)—this One established the church as his body and by the addition of those who are being saved builds it up "in love," "until we all attain ... to mature humanity, to the measure of the stature of the fullness of Christ" (Eph 4:13). If, then, the church is Christ's body, while Christ is Head of the body, forming the countenance of the church with the stamp of his own identity,[13] maybe the reason why the friends of the Bridegroom were *heartened* as they looked upon her was that in her they | saw the Invisible more clearly. Just as those who cannot look upon the disc

---

13. For this idea, see Methodius, *Symp.* 8.8 (trans. Musurillo 1958, 113), where, however, it is applied not to the church as such but to those who are baptized, i.e., the members of the church severally.

εἰς αὐτὸν ὁρῶντες, οὕτω κἀκεῖνοι ὡς ἐν κατόπτρῳ καθαρῷ τῇ ἐκκλησίᾳ τὸν τῆς δικαιοσύνης ἥλιον βλέπουσι τὸν διὰ τοῦ φαινομένου κατανοούμενον.

τούτου χάριν οὐχ ἅπαξ εἴρηται τῇ νύμφῃ παρὰ τῶν φίλων τὸ ἐκαρδίωσας ἡμᾶς (ὅπερ ἐστὶν ὅτι ψυχήν τινα καὶ διάνοιαν πρὸς τὴν τοῦ φωτὸς κατανόησιν

5   δι' ἑαυτῆς ἡμῖν ἐνεποίησας), ἀλλὰ καὶ πάλιν τὸν αὐτὸν ἐπαναλαμβάνουσι λόγον ἀξιοπιστίαν προστιθέντες τῷ λεγομένῳ διὰ τῆς δευτερώσεως· λέγουσι γὰρ ἐπαναλαμβάνοντες ὅτι Ἐκαρδίωσας ἡμᾶς ἑνὶ ἀπὸ ὀφθαλμῶν σου.

τοῦτό ἐστι μάλιστα ὃ τὴν θαυμαστικὴν ἐνεποίησε τοῖς φίλοις περὶ τῆς νύμφης διάθεσιν· διπλῆς γὰρ οὔσης τῇ ψυχῇ τῆς ὀπτικῆς ἐνεργείας καὶ τῆς

10   μὲν τὴν ἀλήθειαν ὁρώσης, τῆς δὲ ἑτέρας περὶ τὰ μάταια πλανωμένης, ἐπειδὴ περὶ μόνην τοῦ ἀγαθοῦ τὴν φύσιν ἀνέῳκται τῆς νύμφης ὁ καθαρὸς ὀφθαλμός, ἀργεῖ δὲ ὁ ἕτερος, τούτου χάριν τῷ ἑνὶ τῶν ὀφθαλμῶν | προσάγουσιν οἱ   258 φίλοι τὸν ἔπαινον, δι' οὗ μόνου θεωρεῖ τὸν μόνον, ἐκεῖνον λέγω τὸν μόνον τὸν ἐν τῇ ἀτρέπτῳ τε καὶ ἀϊδίῳ καταλαμβανόμενον φύσει, τόν τε ἀληθινὸν

15   πατέρα καὶ τὸν μονογενῆ υἱὸν καὶ τὸ ἅγιον πνεῦμα· μόνον γάρ ἐστιν ὡς ἀληθῶς τὸ ἐν μιᾷ θεωρούμενον φύσει, μηδένα χωρισμὸν ἢ ἀλλοτρίωσιν τῆς κατὰ τὰς ὑποστάσεις διαφορᾶς ἐμποιούσης. εἰσὶ γάρ τινες οἳ διαφόροις ὀφθαλμοῖς κακῶς περὶ τὸ ἀνύπαρκτον ὀξυωποῦσιν εἰς πολλὰς φύσεις τὸ ἓν ταῖς τῶν ἐνδιαστρόφων ὀφθαλμῶν φαντασίαις καταμερίζοντες. οὗτοί εἰσιν οἱ

20   λεγόμενοι πολυβλέποντες, οἱ διὰ τοῦ πολλὰ βλέπειν ὁρῶντες οὐδέν. καὶ ὅσοι νῦν μὲν πρὸς τὸν θεὸν ὁρῶσι, πάλιν δὲ ταῖς ὑλικαῖς φαντασίαις ἐπιπλανῶνται,

of the sun see it by means of the water's gleaming,[14] so too these powers look upon the Sun of Righteousness as in the clear mirror of the church,[15] grasping it through its manifestation.

That is why it is not just once that the friends tell the Bride *You have heartened us* (which means: "By your own agency you have worked within us a soul and a mentality that enable comprehension of the light"); no, they use the same expression again, adding by this repetition to the force of what they say. For they repeat the phrase when they say: *You have given us heart with one of your eyes.*

It is this above all that fills the friends with wonder concerning the Bride's state. For the soul's work of seeing is twofold:[16] there is one operation by which it sees the truth, and another that is led astray by attending to things that amount to nothing. And since the Bride's pure eye is open only to the nature of the good, while the other is inactive, the friends for this reason give praise | to *one* of her eyes, by whose sole means she contemplates the only One[17]—that One, I mean, which is known in its immutable and eternal nature: the true Father, the Only Begotten Son, and the Holy Spirit. For that is truly "only" which is contemplated in a single nature, without the introduction of any division or estrangement on the ground that the hypostases are distinct.[18] For there are people[19] who, by making wrong use of different eyes, have a clear vision of what is not real and divide the One into many natures because of the fantasies conjured by their perverse eyes. These are the so-called "many-seeing"; they see nothing because they perceive many things.[20] And all who look toward God but are then once more led astray

---

14. See Plato, *Resp.* 7 (516AB), where the image of the sun and of "reflections in water" occurs in the development of the story of the cave.

15. For the image of the mirror, see Wisd 7:26.

16. For this idea, see also Methodius, *Symp.* 7.2 (trans. Musurillo 1958, 98), with its distinction between bodily and psychic faculties of sight.

17. Cf. the famous words of Plotinus (*Enn.* 6.9.11 *ad fin.*): "the flight of the alone to the Alone." Gregory may well be making an allusion to this phrase here (see Daniélou 1954, 38).

18. Gregory here refers to the doctrine of the Trinity in the Nicene and orthodox form, which, not least because of the work of Basil the Great (Gregory's brother), Gregory of Nazianzus, and Gregory of Nyssa himself, triumphed at the Council of Constantinople (381). According to this formula, the Deity is *one* in respect of nature and *three* in respect of hypostasis (ὑπόστασις), the Latin counterpart of which was *persona*.

19. I.e., the neo-Arians represented by Eunomius of Cyzicus, who understood the terms "Father," "Son," and "Spirit" to refer to three different natures (so that if the Father was said to be God by nature, the same could not be true of the other two members of the Trinity).

20. The word translated "blind" literally meant, as Langerbeck points out in his critical apparatus *ad loc.* (1960, 258), "seeing a multitude of things" and was employed as a euphemism for "blind." Gregory here plays on this ambiguity to characterize his neo-Arian opponents.

ἀνάξιοι τῆς τῶν ἀγγέλων εὐφημίας εἰσὶ ταῖς τῶν ἀνυπάρκτων φαντασίαις
ἐμματαιάζοντες, ὁ δὲ πρὸς μόνον τὸ θεῖον ὀξυωπῶν τυφλὸς ἐν τοῖς ἄλλοις
πᾶσίν ἐστιν, πρὸς ἅπερ αἱ τῶν πολλῶν βλέπουσιν ὄψεις. διὰ τοῦτο τῷ ἑνὶ τῶν
ὀφθαλμῶν ποιεῖ τοῖς φίλοις ἡ νύμφη τὸ θαῦμα. οὐκοῦν τυφλὸς μέν ἐστιν ὁ
5   πολυόμματος ὁ πρὸς τὰ μάταια πολλοῖς ὀφθαλμοῖς βλέπων, ὀξυδερκὴς δὲ
καὶ διορατικὸς ἐκεῖνος ὁ δι' ἑνὸς τοῦ τῆς ψυχῆς ὀφθαλμοῦ πρὸς μόνον τὸ
ἀγαθὸν βλέπων.

Τίς δὲ ἐκείνη ἐστὶν ἡ μία ἢ τί τὸ ἔνθεμα τοῦ τραχήλου τῆς νύμφης, οὐ
χαλεπὸν ἂν εἴη διὰ τῶν ἐξητασμένων | ἐπιλογίσασθαι, κἂν δοκῇ πως ἀσαφὴς   259
10   ἡ λέξις εἶναι, κατὰ τὴν σύμφρασιν· οὕτω γὰρ ὁ λόγος φησὶν ὅτι Ἐκαρδίωσας
ἡμᾶς ἑνὶ ἀπὸ ὀφθαλμῶν σου, ἐν μιᾷ, ἐνθέματι τραχήλου σου, ὡς τὸ μὲν Ἐν μιᾷ
σύμφωνον εἶναι τῷ Ἑνὶ ἀπὸ ὀφθαλμῶν σου, νοούντων ἡμῶν κατὰ παράλειψιν
τὸ Ἐν μιᾷ ψυχῇ.

πολλαὶ γὰρ ἐν ἑκάστῳ γίνονται τῶν ἀπαιδεύτων ψυχαί, ἐν οἷς τὰ πάθη
15   διὰ τῆς ἐπικρατήσεως εἰς τὸν τῆς ψυχῆς τόπον ἀντιμεθίσταται πρὸς λύπην
καὶ ἡδονὴν ἢ θυμὸν καὶ φόβον καὶ δειλίαν καὶ θράσος μεταβαλλομένου τοῦ
τῆς ψυχῆς χαρακτῆρος. ἡ δὲ πρὸς τὸν λόγον ὁρῶσα τῷ μονοειδεῖ τῆς κατ'
ἀρετὴν ζωῆς μιᾷ ψυχῇ συζῆν μεμαρτύρηται. οὐκοῦν οὕτω διασταλτέον τὸν
λόγον, ὡς τὸ μὲν Ἐν μιᾷ τῷ προλαβόντι συνημμένον εἶναι κατὰ τὴν ἔννοιαν
20   νοούντων ἡμῶν ἢ ἐν μιᾷ ψυχῇ ἢ ἐν μιᾷ καταστάσει, τὸ δὲ ἐφεξῆς ἑτέραν ἔχειν
διάνοιαν τὸ Ἐνθέματι τραχήλου σου.

ὡς ἄν τις ὅλον πρὸς τὸ σαφέστερον μεταλαβὼν εἴποι ὅτι σου καὶ
ὀφθαλμὸς εἷς ἐστιν ἐν τῷ πρὸς τὸ ἓν βλέπειν | καὶ ψυχὴ μία διὰ τὸ μὴ πρὸς   260
διαφόρους διαθέσεις μερίζεσθαι καὶ ἡ θέσις τοῦ τραχήλου σου τὸ τέλειον ἔχει
25   τὸν θεῖον ζυγὸν ἐφ' ἑαυτῆς ἀραμένη. ἐπεὶ οὖν ἐπὶ ὄψει ἐν μὲν τῷ ἐνθέματι τοῦ
τραχήλου σου τὸν τοῦ Χριστοῦ ὁρῶμεν ζυγόν, ἐν δὲ τῇ περὶ τὸ ὄντως ἀγαθὸν
διαθέσει ἕνα ὀφθαλμὸν καὶ μίαν ψυχήν, διὰ τοῦτο ὁμολογοῦμεν ὅτι τοῖς σοῖς

by material imaginings are unworthy of the angels' praise because they waste their time with images of things that have no reality. On the other hand, the person whose vision is keen solely where the Divine is concerned is blind in respect of all of those other things on which the vision of the multitude is focused. Hence the Bride inspires wonder in the friends of the Bridegroom by reason of the "one" of her eyes. And so too the many-eyed person, who looks on empty things with a multitude of eyes, is blind, while the one who through one eye—that of the soul—looks upon the Good is sharp and clear of sight.

But who does that second *one* refer to, and what is the *ornament* of the Bride's neck? It should not be difficult, on the basis of our investigations up to this point, | to come to a conclusion about these questions, even though there is some uncertainty about the words in relation to their context.[21] Here is the passage: *You have given us heart by one of your eyes, by one, with the ornament of your neck*—so that the phrase *by one* fits in with the expression *with one of your eyes,* and we are going to understand it as an elliptical expression standing for "by one soul."

For in everyone who has been without discipline there are many souls; in such a person the passions, because they have taken control, occupy the soul's territory, and so the character of the soul is altered to become pain and pleasure or anger and fear and cowardice and rashness. But the person who looks toward the Word by undeviating practice of the virtuous life is acknowledged to live with only one soul. Hence the text ought to be divided so that the phrase *in one* is construed with what precedes it, since we take it, in accordance with the sense of the passage, to mean either "in one soul" or "in one condition"; while the expression *by the ornament of your neck,* which follows, has a different sense.

Thus one might restate the whole thing in clearer fashion by saying: "Your eye is one because it looks toward the One; | and your soul is one because it is not divided among differing dispositions; and your neck sits perfectly because it bears the divine yoke. Since, therefore, on looking we see in the ornament of your neck the yoke of Christ, and in your disposition toward the true Good one eye and one soul, we confess that by these marvels you have

---

21. The question for Gregory is whether the phrase ἐν μίᾳ ("in one" or "by one") should—or could—be taken with ἐνθέματι ("ornament") or, as Gregory proposes, be read as an elliptical phrase echoing the "one" of "one of your eyes." He speculates that the elided word is ψυχή ("soul"), and the justification of this speculation—a justification he does not state—is twofold: that it is consistent with his understanding of the general sense of the passage; and that μίᾳ does not agree in gender with ἐνθέματι. The real problem, of course, lies in the Septuagint's unhappy translation of the original Hebrew.

ἡμᾶς θαύμασιν ἐκαρδίωσας ἕνα δεικνύουσα ὀφθαλμὸν καὶ μίαν ψυχὴν ἐν τῷ ἐνθέματι τοῦ τραχήλου σου. [ἔνθεμα δὲ τοῦ τραχήλου τῆς νύμφης ὁ ζυγός ἐστι καθὼς εἴρηται.]

5   αὕτη μὲν οὖν ἡ τῶν ἀγγέλων ἐστὶν εὐφημία ἣν ἐπὶ τῷ κάλλει τῆς νύμφης πεποίηνται (τούτους γὰρ εἶναι τοὺς φίλους τοῦ νυμφίου κατελαβόμεθα), ὡς δ' ἂν μὴ δοκοίη ἄκριτός τις αὐτῶν εἶναι καὶ διημαρτημένος ὁ ἔπαινος, κυροῖ τῶν φίλων τὴν ἐπὶ τῷ κάλλει τῆς νύμφης κρίσιν ἐπιψηφίσας ὁ λόγος καὶ προστίθησι καὶ αὐτὸς τὰ μείζω θαύματα τῇ μαρτυρίᾳ τοῦ κάλλους τὴν αὐτοῖς τοῖς μέλεσιν ἐπιφαινομένην ὥραν διαγράφων τῷ λόγῳ, ἃ ἐν τοῖς ἐφεξῆς

10   θεοῦ διδόντος προσθήσομεν, εἴ γέ τις γένοιτο ἡμῖν ἐκ τῆς ἄνωθεν συμμαχίας δύναμις πρὸς τὴν κατανόησιν | τοῦ μυστηρίου εἰς ἐπίγνωσιν τοῦ κάλλους τῆς   261 ἐκκλησίας καὶ εἰς ἔπαινον τῆς δόξης τῆς χάριτος αὐτοῦ ἐν Χριστῷ Ἰησοῦ τῷ κυρίῳ ἡμῶν,

ᾧ πρέπει ἡ δόξα εἰς τοὺς αἰῶνας τῶν αἰώνων.
15   ἀμήν.

given us heart, demonstrating your one eye and your one soul by the ornament of your neck."

These, then, are the laudatory words of the angels, directed to the beauty of the Bride (we understand these angels to be the friends of the Bridegroom); but in order that their praise may not seem confused and faulty, the Word, who put the question, confirms the judgment of his friends on the Bride's beauty. He himself adds yet greater marvels to the attestation of her beauty by speaking of the splendor that appears in her limbs. These matters, if God be willing, we shall set out in our next sermon[22]—if power is given us from our friends on high for the interpretation | of the mystery, so that we may have knowledge of the church's beauty and praise the glory of his grace in Christ Jesus our Lord,

Whom glory befits to the ages of ages.
Amen.

---

22. It seems that Gregory breaks off at this point, perhaps because of considerations of time, without covering as much of the text as he had originally intended. See above, n. 1, on the citation of the text of the Song that precedes this homily.

Λόγος θ'

Τί ἐκαλλιώθησαν μαστοί σου, ἀδελφή μου νύμφη,
τί ἐκαλλιώθησαν μαστοί σου ἀπὸ οἴνου;
καὶ ὀσμὴ μύρων σου ὑπὲρ πάντα τὰ ἀρώματα.
Κηρίον ἀποστάζουσι χείλη σου, νύμφη,
5   μέλι καὶ γάλα ὑπὸ τὴν γλῶσσάν σου,
καὶ ὀσμὴ ἱματίων σου ὡς ὀσμὴ λιβάνου.

Κῆπος κεκλεισμένος ἀδελφή μου νύμφη,
κῆπος κεκλεισμένος, πηγὴ ἐσφραγισμένη.
Ἀποστολαί σου παράδεισος ῥοῶν μετὰ καρποῦ
10   κύπρος μετὰ νάρδου, ἀκροδρύων,
Νάρδος καὶ κρόκος,
κάλαμος καὶ κιννάμωμον
μετὰ πάντων ξύλων τοῦ λιβάνου,
σμύρνα, ἀλόη μετὰ πάντων πρωτομύρων,
15   Πηγὴ κήπων, φρέαρ ὕδατος ζῶντος
καὶ ῥοιζοῦντος ἀπὸ τοῦ λιβάνου.

| Εἰ συνηγέρθητε τῷ Χριστῷ, τὰ ἄνω φρονεῖτε, μὴ τὰ ἐπὶ τῆς γῆς. λέγει 262
ταῦτα πρὸς ἡμᾶς ὁ ἐν Παύλῳ λαλῶν· Ἀπεθάνετε γάρ, φησί, καὶ ἡ ζωὴ ὑμῶν
κέκρυπται σὺν τῷ Χριστῷ ἐν τῷ θεῷ. ὅταν ὁ Χριστὸς φανερωθῇ ἡ ζωὴ ὑμῶν,
20   τότε καὶ ὑμεῖς σὺν αὐτῷ φανερωθήσεσθε ἐν δόξῃ.
εἰ τοίνυν νεκροὶ τῇ κάτω φύσει γεγόναμεν εἰς οὐρανὸν ἀπὸ γῆς τὴν
ἐλπίδα τῆς ζωῆς μετοικίσαντες καὶ ἡ διὰ σαρκὸς ζωὴ κέκρυπται ἀφ' ἡμῶν
κατὰ τὸν παροιμιώδη λόγον ὅς φησιν ὅτι Σοφοὶ κρύψουσιν αἴσθησιν,
ἀναμένομεν δὲ τὴν ἀληθινὴν ἐν ἡμῖν φανερωθῆναι ζωήν, ἥτις ἐστὶν ὁ Χριστός,
25   ὥστε καὶ ἡμᾶς ἐν δόξῃ φανερωθῆναι μεταποιηθέντας πρὸς τὸ θειότερον,
οὕτω τῶν παρόντων ἀκούσωμεν ὡς ἀποθανόντες τῷ σώματι πρὸς μηδεμίαν
σαρκώδη διάνοιαν ἐκ τῶν λεγομένων κατασυρόμενοι· ὁ γὰρ νεκρὸς τοῖς
παθήμασι καὶ ταῖς ἐπιθυμίαις ἐπὶ τὸ καθαρὸν καὶ ἀκήρατον μετοίσει τὰς τῶν
ῥημάτων ἐμφάσεις τὰ ἄνω φρονῶν, Οὗ ὁ Χριστός ἐστιν ἐν δεξιᾷ τοῦ πατρὸς
30   καθήμενος, ἐν ᾧ πάθος οὐκ ἔστι τῶν ταπεινῶν τε καὶ χαμαιζήλων νοημάτων
λήθην ποιούμενος.

HOMILY 9
Song 4:10–15

¹⁰How your breasts have been made beautiful, my sister bride!
How your breasts have been made beautiful from wine!
And the fragrance of your perfumed ointments is above all spices.
¹¹Your lips drop honey, my bride,
honey and milk are under your tongue,
and the fragrance of your garments is as the fragrance of frankincense.

¹²My sister bride is an enclosed garden,
a garden enclosed, a fountain sealed.
¹³Your outsendings are a paradise of pomegranate trees
with the produce of fruit trees,
henna with spikenard,
¹⁴spikenard and saffron,
calamus and cinnamon,
with all the frankincense trees,
myrrh, aloe with all the finest perfumes,
¹⁵a fountain of gardens, a spring of living water
that pours forth from frankincense.

"If you have been raised with Christ…, set your minds on things above, not on things that are on earth." The one who speaks in Paul addresses these words to us. "For you have died," says he, "and your life is hid with Christ in God. When Christ who is our life appears, then you also will appear with him in glory" (Col 3:1–4).

Well, then, if we have died to the nature below, having transferred our hope of life from earth to heaven, and if the fleshly life is concealed from us (as the proverb says: "The wise shall conceal sense knowledge" [Prov 10:14]), and we are waiting for the true life, which is Christ, to be manifested in us, so that we too may appear in glory when we have been transformed into a more divine state of being—in that case, let us attend to today's passage as persons who are dead to the body and draw out no fleshly meaning from its words. For a person who is dead to passions and desires will transpose the outward meaning of the words into the key of what is pure and undefiled, setting his mind on "things that are above, where Christ is seated at the right hand" of the Father. In him there is no passion, because he has been made forgetful of low and earthly thoughts.

ἀκούσωμεν τοίνυν τῶν θείων ῥημάτων, δι' ὧν ὑπογράφει ὁ λόγος τῆς ἀμιάντου νύμφης τὸ κάλλος, ἀκούσωμεν δὲ ὡς ἔξω γεγονότες ἤδη σαρκός τε καὶ αἵματος, εἰς δὲ τὴν πνευματικὴν μεταστοιχειωθέντες φύσιν.

| Τί ἐκαλλιώθησαν μαστοί σου, ἀδελφή μου νύμφη; τί ἐκαλλιώθησαν   263
5   μαστοί σου ἀπὸ οἴνου καὶ ὀσμὴ μύρων σου ὑπὲρ πάντα τὰ ἀρώματα; ὅτι μὲν
οὖν πᾶς ὁ ποιῶν τὸ θέλημα τοῦ κυρίου ἀδελφὸς αὐτοῦ καὶ ἀδελφὴ καὶ μήτηρ
ἐστὶ καὶ ὅτι ἡ ἁρμοσθεῖσα τῷ κυρίῳ παρθένος ἁγνὴ πρὸς μετουσίαν τῆς
ἀχράντου παστάδος νύμφη κυρίως κατονομάζεται, παντὶ δῆλον ἂν εἴη τοῦτο
τῷ μὴ ἀγνοοῦντι τὰς θεοπνεύστους φωνάς· ἐγὼ δὲ τῶν θείων ῥητῶν τούτων
10 διερευνώμενος τὴν διάνοιαν οὐ ψιλὸν ἔπαινον ἐκ τῆς τοιαύτης κλήσεως ὁρῶ
προσαγόμενον παρὰ τοῦ λόγου τῇ νύμφῃ, ἀλλὰ τὰς αἰτίας τῆς εἰς τὸ κάλλος
αὐτῆς ἐπιδόσεως διεξιέναι τὸν νυμφίον φημί, ὡς οὐκ ἂν αὐτῆς καλλιωθείσης
ἐν ταῖς τῶν ἀγαθῶν διδαγμάτων πηγαῖς, ἃς μαζοὺς διὰ τῆς τροπικῆς σημασίας
κατονομάζει, εἰ μὴ πρῶτον ἀδελφὴν ἑαυτὴν τοῦ κυρίου διὰ τῶν ἀγαθῶν
15 ἔργων ἐποίησε καὶ εἰς παρθενίαν διὰ τῆς ἄνωθεν γεννήσεως ἀνακαινισθεῖσα
μνηστὴ καὶ νύμφη τοῦ ἁρμοσαμένου ἐγένετο. ὁ τοίνυν ἀδελφὴν ἑαυτοῦ καὶ
νύμφην αὐτὴν κατονομάσας τὴν αἰτίαν λέγει τῆς πρὸς τὸ κρεῖττόν τε καὶ
τελειότερον τῶν μαζῶν αὐτῆς ἀλλοιώσεως, οἳ οὐκέτι γάλα βρύουσι τὴν τῶν
νηπίων τροφήν, ἀλλὰ | τὸν ἀκήρατον οἶνον ἐπὶ εὐφροσύνῃ τῶν τελειοτέρων   264
20 πηγάζουσιν, οὗ τὴν χάριν τὸ τῶν καπήλων ὕδωρ οὐκ ἐλυμήνατο.

σῴζεται δέ πως ἐν τοῖς λεγομένοις ὡς ἐν γαμικῇ θυμηδίᾳ ἡ ἀγαπητικὴ
φιλοφροσύνη δι' ἀμοιβῆς παρ' ἀμφοτέρων ἀλλήλοις τὴν ἐρωτικὴν
ἀντιχαριζομένων διάθεσιν· ταῖς γὰρ ὁμοίαις φωναῖς ἀντιδεξιοῦται ὁ
νυμφίος τὴν ἐκκλησίαν, οἵαις ἐκείνη προλαβοῦσα τὸ ἐκείνου κάλλος ἐν
25 τοῖς προοιμίοις ἀνύμνησεν· εὐθὺς γὰρ ἐν ταῖς πρώταις φωναῖς, ὅτε τὸν ἀπὸ
τοῦ θείου στόματος λόγον τῷ στόματι ἑαυτῆς ἐγγενέσθαι ἐπόθησε τῷ τοῦ
φιλήματος αἰνίγματι τοῦτο διασημάνασα, τὴν αἰτίαν τῆς τοιαύτης ἐπιθυμίας
εἶπε τὸ ἀγαθοὺς εἶναι αὐτοῦ τοὺς μαστοὺς νικῶντας τῇ παρ' ἑαυτῶν χορηγίᾳ
τὴν τοῦ οἴνου φύσιν καὶ παριόντας πᾶσαν μύρων τε καὶ ἀρωμάτων εὐωδίαν
30 οὕτως εἰποῦσα τῷ λόγῳ Ὅτι ἀγαθοὶ μαστοί σου ὑπὲρ οἶνον καὶ ὀσμὴ μύρων
σου ὑπὲρ πάντα τὰ ἀρώματα.

Let us then attend to the divine sayings by which the Word traces out the beauty of the undefiled Bride, and let us attend to them as people who have already come apart from flesh and blood and been transformed into a spiritual nature.

How your breasts have been made beautiful, my sister bride! How your breasts have been made beautiful from wine! And the fragrance of your perfumed ointments is above all spices. Now everyone who does the will of the Lord is his "brother and sister and mother" (cf. Mark 3:35), and the hallowed virgin who is betrothed to the Lord (cf. 2 Cor 11:2) in order to have a place in the undefiled marriage chamber is properly called "bride"—so much is obvious to everyone who does not fail to understand the inspired words. I, however, as I explore the sense of these divine sayings, do not perceive that the Word is bringing the Bride mere praise when he applies these titles to her. On the contrary, I say that the Bridegroom is here specifying what it is that occasions the increase of her beauty: the wellsprings of good teaching—which in a figurative turn of speech he calls "breasts"—do not beautify her unless she has first of all by her good works made herself the Lord's *sister* and, renewed for virginity by the birth from above,[1] has become her Lord's intended spouse and Bride. Hence the One who is calling her *sister* and *bride* is explaining why her breasts have been changed for the better and become more perfect, breasts that no longer put forth milk, the food of babes (cf. 1 Cor 3:1–2), but | gush forth pure wine, whose delights the tavern keeper's water has not diluted—for the delight of those who have made progress toward perfection.

In the speeches made, just as at a wedding celebration, both parties sustain a mood of loving[2] gaiety by a mutual exchange in which they express one to the other the love with which they desire each other. For the Bridegroom returns the church's greeting in words that are much the same as she had used to proclaim his beauty in the prelude of the Song. In the very opening lines [cf. Song 1:2–3], when she sought to have the word from the divine mouth come to birth in her own—signifying this with the enigma of a kiss—she specifies as the reason for her desire the fact that his *breasts* are good, superior to wine in the abundance that flows from them, and surpassing any sweetness of perfumes and spices. This is what she said: *Your breasts are better than wine, and the fragrance of your perfumed ointments is better than all spices.*

---

1. I.e., baptism.

2. "Loving" here translates the Greek ἀγαπητική. On the other hand, the phrase "love with which they desire each other" just below renders τὴν ἐρωτικὴν … διάθεσιν. This is about as close as one can come in English to noting the difference of connotation between ἀγάπη and ἔρως—and their virtual equivalence here.

ἐπειδὴ τοίνυν καὶ ἐν τοῖς ἄλλοις πᾶσι τοῦτο παρὰ τῆς θείας φιλοσοφίας
τὸ δόγμα μανθάνομεν ὅτι τοιοῦτον ἀεὶ γίνεται τὸ θεῖον ἡμῖν, οἵους ἂν ἑαυτοὺς
| τῷ θεῷ διὰ τῆς προαιρέσεως δείξωμεν (ἀγαθὸν μὲν γὰρ αὐτὸν εἶναι τοῖς   265
ἀγαθοῖς ὁ Δαβὶδ ἐν τῇ προφητείᾳ μαρτύρεται, τοῖς δὲ θηριωθεῖσι διὰ τοῦ βίου
5   ἕτερός τις τῶν προφητῶν ἄρκον αὐτὸν λέγει καὶ πάρδαλιν δι᾽ αἰνιγμάτων τὰ
εὐαγγελικὰ προεκτιθέμενος δόγματα, ἐν οἷς ἄλλος τοῖς δεξιοῖς καὶ ἕτερος τοῖς
εὐωνύμοις ὁ τῶν λόγων τοῦ βασιλέως χαρακτὴρ καθορᾶται, τοῖς μὲν ἀγαθός
τε καὶ μείλιχος, τοῖς δὲ φοβερὸς καὶ ἀμείλικτος καταλλήλως τῇ προαιρέσει
τῶν κρινομένων ἑαυτὸν μεθαρμόζων), τούτου χάριν καὶ νῦν πρόσφορος τῇ
10   νύμφῃ παρὰ τοῦ λόγου ἡ ἀντίδοσις γίνεται· ἐν οἷς ὕμνησε τοῦ δεσπότου
τὸ κάλλος, ἐν τοῖς ὁμοίοις αὐτῇ τοῦ κυρίου ἀντιχαρισαμένου τὸν ἔπαινον·
ἀποδέχεται γὰρ καὶ αὐτὸς τῶν μαζῶν αὐτῆς τὴν διὰ τῆς ἐνεργείας πρὸς τὸ
κρεῖττον γεγενημένην ἀλλοίωσιν, ὅτι τοῦ γαλακτοφορεῖν παυσάμενοι οἶνον
καὶ οὐχὶ γάλα προχέουσι, δι᾽ οὗ ταῖς τελειοτέραις | καρδίαις ἡ εὐφροσύνη   266
15   γίνεται τῶν μηκέτι ὑπὸ νηπιότητος κλυδωνιζομένων, ἀλλ᾽ ἐκ τοῦ κρατῆρος
τῆς σοφίας ἐμφορεῖσθαι δυναμένων τῷ στόματι τὰ ἀγαθὰ καὶ ἐφέλκεσθαι.
Ἐπαινέσας τοίνυν τοὺς μαζοὺς διὰ τὴν τοῦ οἴνου φορὰν προστίθησι
καὶ τῆς εὐοδμίας τὸν ἔπαινον εἰπὼν ὅτι Καὶ ὀσμὴ μύρων σου ὑπὲρ πάντα τὰ
ἀρώματα.
20   νοῆσαι δὲ χρὴ τὸν τοιοῦτον ἔπαινον ἐκ τῆς ἁγίας γραφῆς τῶν
ὀνομασθέντων ἀρωμάτων διδαχθέντας τὴν φύσιν. πᾶν τὸ εὔπνουν ἄρωμα τῆς
ὀσφραντικῆς αἰσθήσεως ἡδονὴ γίνεται. οὐκοῦν ἐκεῖνα λέγειν ἀρώματα τὸν
λόγον νοήσομεν, ὅσα παρὰ τῆς γραφῆς εὐπνοεῖν ἐδιδάχθημεν· οἷον προσάγει
Νῶε τῷ θεῷ τὴν θυσίαν Καὶ ὠσφράνθη κύριος ὀσμὴν εὐωδίας. οὐκοῦν
25   ἀρώματα γίνεται τῷ θεῷ ἡ θυσία. πολλαὶ καὶ μετὰ ταῦτα προσάγονται τῷ θεῷ
διὰ τοῦ νόμου ἱλεωτικαὶ θυσίαι, χαριστήριοί τε καὶ σωτήριοι καὶ καθάρσιοι
καὶ περὶ ἁμαρτίας· πάντα ταῦτα τίθει ἐν τοῖς ἀρώμασι, καὶ τὰς ὁλοκαρπώσεις
καὶ τὰς ὁλοκαυτώσεις καὶ τὰς μερικὰς τῶν ἀφαιρεμάτων ἀφιερώσεις, τὸ
στηθύνιον τοῦ ἱερείου, τὸν λοβὸν τοῦ ἥπατος, τὸ ἐπινεφρίδιον στέαρ καὶ   267
30   ἔτι πρὸς τούτοις τὸν λίβανον, τὴν τῷ ἐλαίῳ διαβεβρεγμένην σεμίδαλιν, τὸ
θυμίαμα τῆς συνθέσεως, καὶ τὰ ἄλλα πάντα ὅσα διὰ πυρὸς εἶχε τὴν ἁγιστείαν
ἐν τῷ καταλόγῳ τῶν ἀρωμάτων ἔστω.
ὅταν οὖν ἀκούσωμεν τὸ τῆς νύμφης μύρον πλείονος ὑπὲρ πάντα τὰ
ἀρώματα τῆς ἀποδοχῆς ἀξιούμενον, τοῦτο τῷ λόγῳ μανθάνομεν, ὅτι τὸ τῆς

Now since we everywhere learn from the divine philosophy this essential truth, that God is always for us what by our own choice we show ourselves to be | for God (David, after all, attests in his prophecy that God is good to the good [cf. Ps 72:1], but another prophet says that he is "a bear" and "a leopard" [Hos 13:7–8] to those whose way of life has made wild animals of them—and thus sets forth in an enigma the Gospel teachings in which the King's words have one meaning for those on his right hand, and another for those on his left, being good and kind for one set but fearsome and harsh for the other [cf. Matt 25:34–46], adapting his words to fit the choice made by those being judged), hence in this case too, the response that comes from the Word is suited to the Bride. In his turn, the Lord lavishes praise upon her in words like those in which she sang of the Master's beauty, for he approves of the change that has come to her breasts through her efforts to be better, in that they have ceased to give milk and pour out wine in its stead; and in the more mature |hearts of those who are no longer subject to the disturbances of youth but are capable of filling themselves from Wisdom's chalice and of drinking in her good things with their mouth, this wine occasions gladness.

So, then, when he has praised her breasts for their flow of wine, he also adds a tribute to her fragrance and says: *and the fragrance of your perfumed ointments is above all spices.*

Those who have learned the nature of the spices named here must still interpret a commendation like this on the basis of the Holy Scriptures. Every sweet-smelling spice produces pleasure for the sense of smell. We shall therefore understand that the text uses *spices* to designate whatever things Scripture teaches us to be sweet-smelling, as, for example, when Noah brings a sacrifice to God, "and the Lord smelled the sweet smell" (Gen 8:20). *Spices,* then, means sacrifice brought to God. Furthermore, the law subsequently brings many expiatory sacrifices to God, as well as offerings of thanksgiving and offerings for deliverance, purifying sacrifices, and sacrifices for sin. All of these are included among the *spices,* and also whole offerings and burnt offerings and hallowings of particular portions—the breast of the victim, the lobe of the liver, | the fat on the kidney; and in addition to these, frankincense, wheaten bread soaked in oil, the incense that is compounded,[3] and all the other things that through fire are offered to God belong to the list of *spices.*

When, therefore, we hear that the Bride's perfume is valued more highly than *all spices,* what we learn from the text is that the mystery of truth—which

---

3. Τὸ θυμίαμα τῆς συνθέσεως; cf. Lev 4:18 (which, however, has the plural θυμιαμάτων) and Exod 30:37 (θυμίαμα κατὰ τὴν σύνθεσιν ταύτην: "incense in accordance with this combination [of ingredients]"). Gregory's phrase is probably a shorthand expression that conforms to the language of Leviticus and stands for whatever the phrase in Exod 30:37 refers to.

ἀληθείας μυστήριον τὸ διὰ τῆς εὐαγγελικῆς διδασκαλίας ἐπιτελούμενον
μόνον εὐῶδές ἐστι τῷ θεῷ, πάντων τῶν νομικῶν ἀρωμάτων προκεκριμένον,
ἅτε μηκέτι τύπῳ τινὶ καὶ σκιᾷ καλυπτόμενον ἀλλὰ τῇ φανερώσει τῆς
ἀληθείας εὔπνουν γινόμενον· εἰ γάρ τι καὶ τῶν προλαβόντων ἀρωμάτων
5   ὠσφράνθη κύριος εἰς ὀσμὴν εὐωδίας, κατὰ τὸν ἐμφαινόμενον λόγον τοῖς
γινομένοις ἕκαστον αὐτῶν τῆς ἀποδοχῆς ἠξιώθη οὐ κατὰ τὸ πρόχειρόν τε καὶ
σωματικὸν εἶδος τῶν γινομένων. καὶ τοῦτο δῆλόν ἐστι ἐκ τῆς μεγάλης τοῦ
προφήτου φωνῆς ἥ φησιν ὅτι Οὐ δέξομαι ἐκ τοῦ οἴκου σου μόσχους οὐδὲ ἐκ
τῶν ποιμνίων σου χιμάρους· οὐ γὰρ φάγομαι κρέα ταύρων οὐδὲ αἷμα τράγων
10   πίομαι.
κ</br>αίτοι πάλαι πολλάκις αἱ ζωοθυσίαι γεγόνασιν. ἀλλὰ κἂν γένηται ταῦτα,
ἕτερόν ἐστι τὸ διὰ τούτων ἐν αἰνίγματί σοι νομοθετούμενον τὸ | δεῖν τὰ πάθη   268
τὰ ἐν σοὶ σφαγιάζεσθαι· Θυσία γάρ, φησί, τῷ θεῷ πνεῦμα συντετριμμένον,
καρδίαν συντετριμμένην καὶ τεταπεινωμένην ὁ θεὸς οὐκ ἐξουδενώσει. ὅθεν
15   γίνεται ἡ θυσία τῆς αἰνέσεως ἡμῶν ἡ δοξάζουσα τὸν τὴν τοιαύτην ὀσμὴν
ὀσφραινόμενον.
ἐπειδὴ τοίνυν τὰ τυπικὰ πάντα τοῦ νόμου ἀρώματα ὑπερβᾶσα ἡ
πνευματικῶς εὐπνοοῦσα κατὰ τὸν Παῦλον ψυχή, ὃς Χριστοῦ εὐωδία ἦν,
αὕτη διὰ τοῦ βίου ἐγένετο καὶ τὸ μύρον τῆς ἱερωσύνης καὶ τὸ θυμίαμα τῆς
20   συνθέσεως διὰ τῆς ποικίλης τῶν ἀρετῶν συνεισφορᾶς τε καὶ μίξεως καλῶς
εὐπνοήσασα, ἧς ὁ βίος ἐφάνη τῇ ὀσφρήσει τοῦ νυμφίου εἰς ὀσμὴν εὐωδίας,
διὰ τοῦτο ἡ θεία αἴσθησις, καθὼς ὁ Σολομὼν ὀνομάζει, τῶν σωματικῶν
ἀρωμάτων τοῦ νόμου προτίθησι τὴν ἄυλον ἐκείνην καὶ καθαρὰν τὴν διὰ τῶν
ἀρετῶν μυρεψουμένην εὐωδίαν λέγων Καὶ ὀσμὴ μύρων σου ὑπὲρ πάντα τὰ
25   ἀρώματα.
Ὁ δὲ ἐφεξῆς λόγος πρὸς τὸ ὑψηλότερον προάγει τὸν ἔπαινον τὴν ἐκ
μελέτης τε καὶ προσοχῆς γενομένην αὐτῇ τῶν πνευματικῶν χαρισμάτων
περιουσίαν μαρτυρῶν τῷ | λόγῳ·   269
ἐπειδὴ γὰρ παρὰ τὴν μέλισσαν φοιτᾶν τὸν τῆς σοφίας μαθητὴν ὁ
30   παροιμιακὸς βούλεται λόγος (νοεῖς δὲ πάντως ἐκ τῶν μαθημάτων τὴν
διδάσκαλον ἥτις ἐστίν) λέγων τοῖς ἐρασταῖς τῆς σοφίας Πορεύθητι πρὸς τὴν
μέλισσαν καὶ μάθε ὡς ἐργάτις ἐστὶ τήν τε ἐργασίαν ὡς σεμνὴν ἐμπορεύεται,
ἧς τοὺς πόνους βασιλεῖς τε καὶ ἰδιῶται πρὸς ὑγείαν προσφέρονται (ποθεινὴν
δὲ λέγει πᾶσιν εἶναι αὐτὴν καὶ ἐπίδοξον, ἀσθενοῦσαν μὲν κατὰ τὴν ῥώμην,

comes to its fulfillment in the teaching of the gospel—is for God the only thing that is "sweet-smelling." It is preferred above all the *spices* of the law in that it is no longer veiled by type and shadow;[4] for even if the Lord "smelled" this or that one of the aforementioned *spices* as a "sweet smell," he judged each of them to be acceptable because of the principle [λόγος] manifested in what was done, and not because of the superficial and perceptible appearance of what was done. This is shown, moreover, by the great cry of the prophet: "I will accept no bull calves from your house, not he goats from your flocks … for I do not eat the flesh of bulls or drink the blood of goats" (Ps 49:9, 13).

Yet sacrifices of living victims were frequently performed in those days. Nevertheless, even if they did take place, the admonition that comes to you "in an enigma" through them is another thing altogether, namely, | that your business is to slaughter the passions that are within you. "The sacrifice for God is a broken spirit; God will not despise a broken and humbled heart" (Ps 50:19).

Since, then, the soul that breathes out spiritual fragrance like Paul (who was "the aroma of Christ" [2 Cor 2:15]) transcends all the *spices* of the law, foreshadowings as they are, and since this same soul, by its way of life, becomes the perfumed ointment of priesthood and the "incense that is compounded"[5] and gives off a fine fragrance on account of the tying in together and blending of the different virtues, and since, too, it is manifested to the Bridegroom's senses as a sweet-smelling fragrance—for this reason, I say, the divine sense perception, as Solomon names it, prefers that pure and immaterial scent that is blended of the virtues to the corporeal *spices* of the law and says: *and the scent of your perfumed ointment is above all spices.*

Now the next statement elevates the praise of the Bride to a still higher level in that the abundance of spiritual graces that become hers through diligence and carefulness is attested | by the language of the text.

Proverbs, after all, desires the disciple of Wisdom to resort for instruction to the bee—and you are perfectly well aware, on the basis of what you have learned, of the identity of this teacher. It says to the lovers of Wisdom (Prov 6:8): "Make your way to the bee, and learn that she is a worker and makes a serious business of her labors;[6] and both kings and simple folk consume what she produces for their health's sake." It also says that she is "sought after" and "of high repute," weak in body to be sure but one who honors Wisdom and is

---

4. See 1 Cor 10:6, 11 ("type"); Heb 10:1 ("shadow"); and 2 Cor 3:15–16.

5. On this expression, see n. 3 above.

6. See the same association of ideas in Aristotle, *Hist. an.* 625b24.

τὴν δὲ σοφίαν τιμήσασαν καὶ διὰ τοῦτο προαχθεῖσαν εἰς ὑπόδειγμα βίου τοῖς ἐναρέτοις· Τὴν γὰρ σοφίαν, φησί, τιμήσασα προήχθη),

συμβουλεύει δὴ διὰ τῶν εἰρημένων μηδενὸς ἀπέχεσθαι τῶν ἀγαθῶν μαθημάτων, ἀλλὰ τῷ λειμῶνι τῶν θεοπνεύστων ἐφιπτάμενον λόγων, ἀφ᾽
5   ἑκάστου τι πρὸς τὴν κτῆσιν τῆς σοφίας ἀπανθιζόμενον κηροπλαστεῖν ἑαυτῷ τὸ κηρίον, οἷον ἐν σίμβλῳ τινὶ τῇ ἑαυτοῦ καρδίᾳ τὴν φιλεργίαν ταύτην ἀποτιθέμενον, ὥσπερ τινὰς ἐν κηρίῳ σύριγγας τῶν πολυειδῶν μαθημάτων ἀσυγχύτους ἐν τῇ μνήμῃ τὰς θήκας δημιουργήσαντα, καὶ οὕτω κατὰ μίμησιν τῆς σοφῆς ἐκείνης μελίσσης, ἧς ἡδὺ μὲν τὸ κηρίον ἄπληκτον δὲ τὸ
10 κέντρον, τὴν σεμνὴν ταύτην τῶν ἀρετῶν ἐργασίαν διὰ παντὸς ἐμπορεύεσθαι. ἐμπορεύεται γὰρ ὡς ἀληθῶς ὁ τὰ ἀγαθὰ τὰ αἰώνια τῶν τῇδε πόνων διαμειβόμενος καὶ τοὺς ἰδίους πόνους εἰς ψυχικὴν ὑγείαν βασιλεῦσί τε καὶ ἰδιώταις νέμων, ὥστε ποθεινὴν | τῷ νυμφίῳ τὴν τοιαύτην γενέσθαι ψυχὴν   270 καὶ τοῖς ἀγγέλοις ἐπίδοξον ἐν ἀσθενείᾳ τελειοῦσαν τὴν δύναμιν διὰ τὴν τῆς
15 σοφίας τιμήν.

ἐπειδὴ τοίνυν παιδεύσεώς ἐστι καὶ φιλοπονίας ὑποδείγματα τὰ περὶ τὴν σοφὴν ἐκείνην μέλισσαν διηγήματα καὶ αἱ ποικίλαι τῶν πνευματικῶν χαρισμάτων διαιρέσεις κατὰ τὴν τῆς σπουδῆς ἀναλογίαν τοῖς πεπονηκόσι προγίνονται, διὰ τοῦτό φησι πρὸς τὴν νύμφην ὅτι πλήρης σοι γέγονεν ἡ
20 καρδία τῶν ἐκ τῆς παντοδαπῆς παιδεύσεως κηρίων, ὅθεν προφέρεις ἐκ τοῦ ἀγαθοῦ θησαυροῦ τῆς καρδίας τὰς μελιχρὰς τῶν λόγων σταγόνας, ὡς εἶναί σοι μέλι τὸν λόγον συναναμεμιγμένον τῷ γάλακτι· Κηρίον γάρ, φησίν, ἀποστάζει χείλη σου, νύμφη, μέλι καὶ γάλα ὑπὸ τὴν γλῶσσάν σου. παρεσκεύασται γάρ σοι ὁ λόγος οὐ μονοειδῶς τοῖς ἀκούουσι τὴν ὠφέλειαν ἐπιδεικνύμενος ἀλλὰ
25 καταλλήλως πρὸς τὴν τῶν δεχομένων δύναμιν ἁρμοζόμενος, ὡς καὶ τοῖς τελειοτέροις καὶ τοῖς νηπιάζουσιν οἰκείως ἔχειν, τοῖς μὲν τελείοις μέλι, τοῖς δὲ νηπίοις γάλα γινόμενος.

οἷος ὁ Παῦλος ἦν, τοῖς μὲν ἁπαλωτέροις τῶν λόγων τοὺς ἀρτιγενεῖς τιθηνούμενος, σοφίαν δὲ λαλῶν ἐν τοῖς τελείοις ἐν μυστηρίῳ τὴν
30 ἀποκεκρυμμένην ἀπὸ τῶν αἰώνων, ἣν οὐ χωρεῖ ὁ αἰὼν οὗτος οὐδὲ οἱ ἄρχοντες τοῦ αἰῶνος τούτου. τὴν οὖν τοιαύτην παρα|σκευὴν τοῦ μέλιτός τε καὶ τοῦ   271 γάλακτος ὑποκεῖσθαι λέγει τῇ γλώσσῃ τὴν τεταμιευμένην τε καὶ εὔκαιρον τῶν λόγων χρῆσιν διὰ τῆς τοιαύτης φωνῆς ἐνδεικνύμενος· ὁ γὰρ εἰδώς, πῶς δεῖ ἑνὶ ἑκάστῳ ἀποκρίνεσθαι, ἔχων ὑπὸ τὴν γλῶσσαν τὴν ποικίλην ταύτην
35 τοῦ λόγου δύναμιν ἁρμοδίως ἑκάστῳ τῶν ἀκουόντων τὸ πρὸς τὴν χρείαν ἐπὶ καιροῦ προχειρίζεται.

therefore brought forward as an example to the virtuous, for it says, "Having honored Wisdom, she has been brought to honor" (Prov 6:8).[7]

In these words Proverbs counsels that one should not depart from any of the good teachings but, flying to the grassy meadow of the inspired words, should suck from each of them something that assists the acquisition of Wisdom and make oneself into a honeycomb, storing the fruit of this labor in one's heart as in some beehive, fashioning for the manifold teachings separate storage places in the memory, like the hollow cells in a honeycomb. In this way one will make a business of this noble work of the virtues, in imitation of that wise bee, whose honeycomb is sweet and whose sting does not wound. For the person who exchanges hard work here for eternal goods, and who dispenses the fruit of his own labors to kings and to common folk alike for the sake of their souls' health, truly obtains a reward, so that a soul of this sort becomes |an object of the Bridegroom's desire and glorious in the sight of the angels, because she has made "strength perfect in weakness" (2 Cor 12:9) by giving honor to Wisdom.

Since, then, what is related about that wise bee affords us models for formation through learning and for devotion to work, and since it is in proportion to their zeal that the varying shares of spiritual gifts make their appearance in those who labor, for this very reason the Bridegroom says to the Bride, "Your heart has been filled with honeycombs built of a many-sided learning, and from the good treasure of your heart you bring forth, drop by drop, words as sweet as honey, so that your speech is honey mingled with milk." He says, then, *Your lips drop honey, my Bride, honey and milk are under your tongue*—for your discourse is not adapted to benefit its hearers in one way only, but it conforms itself to the several capacities of those who receive it, so that it suits both those who are more advanced and those who are beginners, serving as honey for the mature but as milk for beginners."

Paul was an example of this. He nourished the newborn with gentler words, while "among the mature" he spoke "in a mystery" a wisdom that was hidden from the age—a wisdom that neither this age nor "the rulers of this age" take in (cf. 1 Cor 2:6–8). Hence the Bridegroom says that such a | provision both of honey and of milk lies under the Bride's tongue, and by this expression he indicates the apt and measured use of words, for he who knows how each individual must be answered and has this power of varied speech under his tongue, supplies in an appropriate manner, to each of his hearers, what is necessary for the occasion.

---

7. The verb here—προάγειν—can mean both "bring forward" and "promote."

Τοιοῦτον δὲ προσαγαγὼν τῷ στόματί τε καὶ τῇ γλώσσῃ τῆς νύμφης
τὸν ἔπαινον πάλιν πρὸς τὰ μείζω τῶν ἐγκωμίων μετέρχεται λέγων ὅτι Ὀσμὴ
ἱματίων σου ὡς ὀσμὴ λιβάνου.

ὁ δὲ λόγος οὗτος φιλοσοφία τίς ἐστιν εἰς ὅτι βλέπει τοῖς ἀνθρώποις ὁ
5   κατ᾽ ἀρετὴν βίος ὑποδεικνύων· πέρας γὰρ τῆς ἐναρέτου ζωῆς ἡ πρὸς τὸ θεῖόν
ἐστιν ὁμοίωσις· καὶ τούτου χάριν ἥ τε τῆς ψυχῆς καθαρότης καὶ τὸ πάσης
ἐμπαθοῦς διαθέσεως ἀνεπίμικτον δι᾽ ἐπιμελείας κατορθοῦται τοῖς ἐναρέτοις,
ὥστε τινὰ χαρακτῆρα τῆς ὑπερκειμένης φύσεως διὰ τῆς ἀστειοτέρας ζωῆς καὶ
ἐν αὐτοῖς γενέσθαι.

10   ἐπειδὴ τοίνυν οὐ μονοειδής τίς ἐστιν οὐδὲ μονότροπος ἡ κατ᾽ ἀρετὴν
πολιτεία, ἀλλ᾽ ὥσπερ ἐπὶ τῆς τῶν ὑφασμάτων κατασκευῆς διὰ πολλῶν
νημάτων, τῶν μὲν ἐπ᾽ εὐθείας ἀνατεταμένων τῶν δὲ κατὰ τὸ πλάγιον
διῃρμένων, ἡ ὑφαντικὴ τέχνη τὴν ἐσθῆτα ποιεῖ, οὕτω καὶ ἐπὶ τῆς ἐναρέτου
ζωῆς πολλὰ χρὴ συνδραμεῖν, δι᾽ ὧν ὁ ἀστεῖος ἐξυφαίνεται βίος, καθὼς
15   ἀπαριθμεῖται τὰ τοιαῦτα νήματα ὁ θεῖος ἀπόστολος, δι᾽ ὧν | ἡ τῶν καθαρῶν   272
ἔργων ἱστουργία συνίσταται, ἀγάπην λέγων καὶ χαρὰν καὶ εἰρήνην,
μακροθυμίαν τε καὶ χρηστότητα καὶ πάντα τὰ τοιαῦτα, οἷς κατακοσμεῖται ὁ
ἐκ τοῦ φθαρτοῦ τε καὶ γηΐνου βίου τὴν οὐράνιον ἀφθαρσίαν μετενδυόμενος,
τούτου χάριν ἀποδέχεται τὸν ἐν τῇ ἐσθῆτι κόσμον τῆς νύμφης ὡς τῷ λιβάνῳ
20   κατὰ τὴν ὀσμὴν ὁμοιούμενον.

καίτοι γε πρὸ τούτου πάντων εἶπε τῶν ἀρωμάτων προέχειν τὴν τοῦ
μύρου τῆς νύμφης εὐωδίαν, ὡς δοκεῖν ἐν τούτῳ καθαίρεσιν εἶναι τῶν
ἐγκωμίων, εἴπερ ἡ παντὸς ἀρώματος ὑπερτεθεῖσα νῦν πρὸς ἓν τῶν ἀρωμάτων
ὁμοιοῦται διὰ συγκρίσεως, οὕτως εἰπόντος τοῦ λόγου ὅτι κατὰ τὴν ὀσμὴν
25   τοῦ λιβάνου ἡ τῶν ἱματίων σού ἐστιν εὐωδία. ἀλλ᾽ ἐπειδὴ ἰδιαζόντως κατά
τινα λόγον εἰς τὴν τοῦ θείου τιμὴν ἀποτεταγμένον ἦν τὸ τοῦ λιβάνου
θυμίαμα, τούτου χάριν ἡ ὑπὲρ πάντα τὰ ἀρώματα εἶναι κριθεῖσα ἀξιοῦται
τῆς πρὸς τὸ ἓν ἄρωμα ὁμοιώσεως τὸ τῷ θεῷ ἀνακείμενον, ὡς τὸ νόημα τοῦ
αἰνίγματος τοιοῦτον εἶναι ὅτι· σοί, ὦ νύμφη, τῶν ἀρετῶν ἡ περιβολὴ τὴν
30   θείαν μιμεῖται μακαριότητα διὰ καθαρότητός τε καὶ ἀπαθείας τῇ ἀπροσίτῳ
φύσει ὁμοιουμένη· τοιαύτη γάρ, φησίν, ἡ τῶν σῶν ἱματίων ὀσμή, ὡς πρὸς τὸν
λίβανον ἐμφερῶς ἔχειν τὸν ἀνακείμενον εἰς τὴν τοῦ θείου τιμήν.

Πάλιν μανθάνομεν διὰ τῶν ἐφεξῆς ἐπαίνων, πῶς ἄν | τις γένοιτο τοῦ   273
κυρίου ἀδελφὴ καὶ ὁμόζυγος, δι᾽ ὧν φησιν ὅτι Κῆπος κεκλεισμένος ἀδελφή
35   μου νύμφη. οὐκοῦν εἴ τις μεταποιεῖται νύμφη μὲν διὰ τοῦ προσκολληθῆναι
τῷ κυρίῳ γενέσθαι, ἀδελφὴ δὲ διὰ τοῦ τὸ θέλημα αὐτοῦ κατεργάζεσθαι,

Having praised the Bride's mouth and tongue in this way, he once again moves on to a higher order of commendation as he says: *The fragrance of your garments is as the fragrance of frankincense.*

This statement is an observation of the philosophical order. It indicates what the goal of the life of virtue is for human beings. For the limit that the virtuous life approaches is likeness to the Divine,[8] and for the sake of this goal both the soul's purity and its separation from any passionate disposition are in virtuous persons carefully realized, so that a certain impress of the transcendent Nature comes to them also, on account of the nobler quality of their life.

Now the virtuous manner of life is not uniform or marked by a single style, but just as in the making of a fabric the weaver's art creates the garment by using many threads, some of which are stretched vertically and others are carried horizontally, so too, in the case of the virtuous life, many things must twine together if a noble life is to be woven. Just so the divine apostle enumerates threads of this sort, threads by means of which | pure works are woven together; he mentions love and joy and peace, patience and kindness (cf. Gal 5:22) and all the sorts of thing that adorn the person who is putting on the garment of heavenly incorruptibility in place of a corruptible and earthly life (1 Cor 15:53). This is why the Bridegroom acknowledges that the adornment of the Bride's garment is, as far as its fragrance goes, like frankincense.

No doubt the Bridegroom said, earlier on, that the sweet smell of the Bride's perfume excelled *all* the *spices*, and therefore, if indeed she who surpassed all spices is now likened, in a comparison, to one particular spice—for what the Word says is, "The sweet smell of your clothing conforms to the fragrance of frankincense"—this seems to nullify his previous tributes. Since, however, frankincense was for some reason set apart especially for the honor of the Deity, she who was deemed to be *above all spices* is reckoned worthy of being likened to the particular spice that is dedicated to God. Thus the meaning of the enigma is this: "In your case, O Bride, the garment of virtues imitates the divine blessedness because it has been made like the unapproachable Nature by its purity and impassibility. For," he says, "the scent of your garments is such as to bear a resemblance to that frankincense that is dedicated to the honoring of God."

Once more, from the next set of praises, where the Bridegroom says *My bride is an enclosed garden,* we learn how | one can become the Lord's sister and yokefollow. If, then, someone is so changed as to become *bride* because he has been joined to the Lord (cf. Eph 5:31) and *sister* because she has done

---

8. Cf. Plato, *Theaet.* 176A–B, not to mention Gen 1:26–27. For the association of frankincense with likeness to God, see below, p. 280 (Jaeger).

καθὼς λέγει τὸ εὐαγγέλιον, κῆπος εὐθαλὴς γενέσθω πάντων ἔχων ἐν ἑαυτῷ
τῶν φυτῶν τὴν ὥραν, τήν τε γλυκεῖαν συκῆν καὶ τὴν κατάκαρπον ἐλαίαν καὶ
τὸν ὑψίκομον φοίνικα καὶ τὴν εὐθηνοῦσαν ἄμπελον, μὴ θάμνον ἀκανθώδη
τινὰ μηδὲ κόνυζαν, ἀλλὰ κυπάρισσον ἀντ' αὐτῶν καὶ μυρσίνην. οὕτω γὰρ τὸν
5   τοιοῦτον κῆπον οἶδεν ὡραΐζειν ὁ μέγας τε Δαβὶδ καὶ ὁ ὑψηλὸς Ἡσαΐας, ὁ
μὲν λέγων Δίκαιος ὡς φοῖνιξ ἀνθήσει· καὶ Ἐγὼ δὲ ὡσεὶ ἐλαία κατάκαρπος·
καὶ Ἡ γυνή σου ὡς ἄμπελος εὐθηνοῦσα· ὁ δὲ Ἡσαΐας ἀντὶ θάμνου μὲν τὴν
κυπάρισσον, ἀντὶ δὲ κονύζης τὴν μυρσίνην φησὶν ἀναβήσεσθαι· καὶ παρ' ἑτέρῳ
τινὶ προφήτῃ μακαρίζεται ὁ ὑποκάτω τῆς συκῆς τῆς ἰδίας ἀναπαυόμενος.
10   τὰ δὲ καθ' ἕκαστον περὶ τῶν δένδρων τούτων αἰνίγματα τῶν | ὑπὸ τῆς   274
προφητείας ἡμῖν ὑποδειχθέντων παρέλκον ἂν εἴη δι' ἀκριβείας ἐκτίθεσθαι,
προδήλου πᾶσιν ὄντος, τίς μὲν ὁ γλυκὺς τῆς συκῆς ἐστι καρπὸς ὁ ἐκ τοῦ
δριμυτάτου ὀποῦ πεπαινόμενος, ὁ κατ' ἀρχὰς μὲν πικρός τε καὶ ἄβρωτος,
ὕστερον δὲ καρπὸς εἰρηνικὸς γινόμενος καὶ καταγλυκαίνων τὰ τῆς ψυχῆς
15   αἰσθητήρια, τί δὲ ἡμῖν ἡ τῆς ἐλαίας καρπογονία χαρίζεται διὰ τοῦ δριμυτάτου
τε καὶ πικροτάτου χυμοῦ τοῦ κατ' ἀρχὰς ἐντρεφομένου τῇ ὀπώρᾳ μετὰ ταῦτα
διὰ τῆς καταλλήλου πεπάνσεώς τε καὶ γεωργίας εἰς ἐλαίου μεταβάλλουσα
φύσιν ὃ τοῦ φωτὸς γίνεται ὕλη καὶ καμάτων λυτήριον καὶ πόνων ἄνεσις καὶ
κεφαλῆς φαιδρότης καὶ πρὸς τοὺς ἀγῶνας τοῖς νομίμως ἀθλοῦσι συνέργεια,
20   πῶς δὲ δυσεπιχείρητον ποιεῖ τὸν ἑαυτοῦ καρπὸν τοῖς κλέπταις ὁ φοῖνιξ ἄνω
θησαυρίζων καὶ οὐχὶ πρόσγειον αὐτὸν ἐκφέρων· ἥ τε τῆς ἀμπέλου χάρις καὶ
ἡ εὐώδης κυπάρισσος καὶ τὸ ἡδὺ τῆς μυρσίνης· ταῦτα πάντα διὰ τροπικῆς
θεωρίας πρὸς τὸν κατ' ἀρετὴν μεταληφθέντα λόγον πρόδηλα πᾶσίν ἐστι τοῖς
νουνεχῶς ἐπαΐουσι πρὸς ὅ τι βλέπει.
25   οὐκοῦν ὁ τῶν τοιούτων δένδρων κῆπος γεγονὼς εὐθαλὴς καὶ κατάφυτος
καὶ τῷ τῶν ἐντολῶν ἑρκίῳ πανταχόθεν ἠσφαλισμένος, ὡς | μηδεμίαν καθ'   275
ἑαυτοῦ παρασχεῖν τῷ κλέπτῃ καὶ τοῖς θηρίοις τὴν πάροδον (ὁ γὰρ ἐν κύκλῳ
τῷ φραγμῷ τῶν ἐντολῶν διειλημμένος ἀνεπίβατός ἐστι τῷ μονιῷ τῷ ἀγρίῳ
καὶ ὁ ἐκ τοῦ δρυμοῦ αὐτὸν ὗς οὐ λυμαίνεται), εἴ τις τοίνυν καὶ κῆπός ἐστι
30   καὶ ἠσφαλισμένος, οὗτος ἀδελφὴ καὶ νύμφη γίνεται τοῦ πρὸς τὴν τοιαύτην
εἰπόντος ψυχὴν ὅτι Κῆπος κεκλεισμένος ἀδελφή μου νύμφη.
Ἀλλὰ τῷ κήπῳ τούτῳ καὶ πηγῆς ἐστι χρεία, ὡς ἂν εὐθαλὲς διαμένοι
τὸ ἄλσος τῷ ὕδατι πρὸς τὸ διηνεκὲς πιαινόμενον. διὰ τοῦτο συνέζευξεν

his will as the Gospel says (cf. Mark 3:35), let her become a thriving garden that contains the splendor of all the plants: the sweet fig tree with the fruitful olive, the lofty-headed date palm, and the flourishing vine—and no thorn or briar, but instead cypress and myrtle. For both the great David and the noble Isaiah knew how to give honor to such a garden; the one says, "The righteous shall flourish like the palm tree" (Ps 31:19) and "I am like a fruitful olive tree" (Ps 51:8) and "Your wife is like a flourishing vine" (Ps 127:3); and then Isaiah says: "The cypress will rise up in place of" the thorn, and "in place of the briar, the myrtle" (Isa 55:13). In another prophet, moreover, the person who rests beneath his own fig tree is pronounced blessed (Mic 4:4).

Now it would be superfluous to explain one by one, in detail, the enigmas | that prophecy sets out for us as touching these trees. Surely it is evident to all what the sweet fruit of the fig tree stands for. It matures as it is fed by the most bitter of saps, and at the beginning it is sour and inedible; but in the end it becomes a mellow fruit, affording sweetness to the soul's senses. It is equally clear what a gift the olive's fruitfulness bestows upon us by means of a juice that is thoroughly sharp and acid, a juice that begins by being formed in the fruit and afterwards, by proper maturing and cultivation, changes into olive oil—at which point it becomes the stuff of illumination;[9] the deliverer from weariness and cure of toils; the gleam that radiates from the head; and the helper of those who compete in athletic contests according to the rules. It is clear too how the date palm, hoarding its fruit up on high and never bringing it forth near the earth, makes it all but inaccessible to thieves, not to mention the beauty of the vine, the happy scent of the cypress, and the sweetness of the myrtle. All these things, when they have been changed by a figural interpretation into discourse that deals with virtue, are open books to all who bring good sense to the task of seeing what they intend.

So, then, the person who has become a garden with trees like these, flourishing and fully planted and protected on every side by the fence of the commandments, so that | there is no entry afforded to the thief or to wild beasts (for the person who is encircled by the bar of the commandments is inaccessible to the "savage pig," and the "boar from the forest" does not "ravage" him [Ps 79:14])—if, then, I say, someone is both a garden and a garden that is protected, that person becomes *sister* and *bride* of the One who says to such a soul: *My sister bride is an enclosed garden.*

A garden like this, though, has need of a spring so that the grove may continue to flourish by being fed with a continuous supply of water. That is

---

9. Literally, "light." Gregory is thinking, of course, of the oil lamp, in which burning olive oil provides light.

ἐν τοῖς ἐπαίνοις τὴν πηγὴν τῷ κήπῳ εἰπὼν ὅτι Κῆπος κεκλεισμένος, πηγὴ
ἐσφραγισμένη. τὸν δὲ περὶ τῆς πηγῆς λόγον ἡ Παροιμία διδάσκει ἡμᾶς
δι' αἰνίγματος ἐν οἷς φησιν ὅτι Ἡ πηγὴ τοῦ ὕδατός σου ἔστω σοι ἰδία· καὶ
Ἔστω σοι μόνῳ καὶ μηδεὶς ἀλλότριος μετασχέτω σοι. ὡς γὰρ ἐκεῖ κωλύει
5   τοῖς ἀλλοτρίοις ἐνδαπανᾶσθαι τῆς πηγῆς τὸ ὕδωρ, οὕτως ἐνταῦθα τὸ
μηδαμοῦ διαχεῖσθαι πρὸς ἀλλοτρίους τὴν πηγὴν μαρτυρεῖ διὰ τοῦ εἰπεῖν ὅτι
Ἐσφραγισμένη, ὅπερ ἴσον ἐστὶ τῷ εἰπεῖν ὅτι πεφυλαγμένη.

τὸ δὲ λεγόμενον τοιοῦτόν ἐστι· πηγὴ κυρίως κατονομάζεται κατά γε τὸν
ἐμὸν λόγον ἡ διανοητικὴ τῆς ψυχῆς ἡμῶν δύναμις ἡ παντοίους λογισμοὺς ἐν
10 ἡμῖν βρύουσά τε καὶ πηγάζουσα. ἀλλὰ τότε ἡμέτερον γίνεται τῆς διανοίας
τὸ κίνημα, ὅταν πρὸς τὰ συμφέροντα ἡμῖν | κινῆται πᾶσαν ἡμῖν συνεργίαν   276
πρὸς τὴν κτῆσιν τῶν ἀγαθῶν παρεχόμενον. ὅταν δέ τις τρέψῃ τῶν λογισμῶν
τὴν ἐνέργειαν πρὸς κακίας ἐπίνοιαν, τότε τοῖς ἀλλοτρίοις ἐνδαπανᾶται τὸ
ῥεῖθρον, ὡς εὐτροφεῖν μὲν τὸν ἀκανθώδη βίον τῇ συμμαχίᾳ τῶν λογισμῶν
15 καταρδόμενον, ἀποξηραίνεσθαι δὲ καὶ μαραίνεσθαι τὴν κρείττω φύσιν
μηδεμιᾶς τῆς ἐκ λογισμῶν ἰκμάδος ὑποτρεφούσης τὴν ῥίζαν. ἐπειδὴ τοίνυν
ἡ σφραγὶς τὸ ἄσυλον τῷ δι' αὐτῆς φυλασσομένῳ χαρίζεται φοβοῦσα τῷ
σημάντρῳ τὸν κλέπτην, πᾶν δὲ τὸ μὴ κλεπτόμενον τῷ δεσπότῃ μένει
ἀκέραιον, τὴν ἀκροτάτην ἔοικεν ἀρετὴν μαρτυρεῖν τῇ νύμφῃ ἐνταῦθα ὁ
20 ἔπαινος, ὅτι ἀνέπαφος αὐτῆς μένει τοῖς ἐχθροῖς ἡ διάνοια ἐν καθαρότητι καὶ
ἀπαθείᾳ φυλασσομένη τῷ ἰδίῳ δεσπότῃ· σφραγίζεται γὰρ τὴν πηγὴν ταύτην
ἡ καθαρότης μηδεμιᾷ νοημάτων ἰλύϊ τὸ διαυγές τε καὶ ἀερῶδες τῆς καρδίας
ἐπιθολώσασα.

ὡς δ' ἄν τις ἐπὶ τὸ σαφέστερον προαγάγοι τὸ νόημα, τοιοῦτόν ἐστιν·
25 ἐπειδὴ τῶν ἐν ἡμῖν τὰ μὲν ὡς ἀληθῶς ἐστιν ἡμέτερα, ὅσα τῆς ψυχῆς ἐστιν ἴδια,
τὰ δὲ οἰκειούμεθα ὡς ἡμέτερα, τὰ περὶ τὸ σῶμά τε καὶ τὰ | ἔξωθεν λέγω, διὰ   277
τινος ἡμαρτημένης ὑπολήψεως ἴδια νομίζοντες τὰ ἀλλότρια (τί γὰρ κοινὸν
τῇ ἀΰλῳ τῆς ψυχῆς φύσει πρὸς τὴν ὑλικὴν παχυμέρειαν;), τούτου χάριν ὅ γε
παροιμιώδης συμβουλεύει λόγος μὴ τοῖς ἀλλοτρίοις ἡμῶν, τοῖς περὶ τὸ σῶμά
30 φημι καὶ τὰ ἔξωθεν, τὴν πηγὴν τῆς διανοίας ἐναναλίσκεσθαι, ἀλλὰ περὶ τὸν
ἴδιον ἀναστρέφεσθαι κῆπον τὴν τοῦ θεοῦ φυτείαν πιαίνουσαν. ἀρετὰς δὲ εἶναι

why the Bridegroom conjoins a *fountain* with the *garden* in his praises and
says *a garden enclosed, a fountain sealed*. Regarding the significance of the
fountain, Proverbs instructs us in an enigma where it says, "Let your fountain
of water be your own," and "Let it be yours only and let no stranger share
it with you" (Prov 5:17–18). For just as in Proverbs the Bridegroom[10] for-
bids the fountain's waters to be spent on strangers, so here, by the expression
sealed, which amounts to the same thing as "has been kept safe," it testifies
that the stream from the fountain is not dispersed just anywhere for the sake
of strangers.

What it means is something like this. As I see the matter, what is most
properly termed "fountain" is the soul's faculty of reasoning,[11] which teems
within us with all sorts of thoughts and, fountain-like, gushes them forth.
But the motion of the reasoning faculty becomes properly *ours* only when it
is going in the direction of what is beneficial for us | and when it assists us
in every way to possess what is good. But should a person divert the working of his thoughts toward the contrivance of evil, that is the point at which
the stream spends itself on things alien; and so it is the life of thorns that
flourishes, watered as it is by the alliance of his thoughts, while the higher
nature withers and dries up because its root is not nourished by the water of
his thoughts. Since, then, the seal, which inspires the thief with terror by its
mark, confers inviolability upon whatever is guarded by it, and since whatever is not stolen remains the unspoiled property of its owner, the praise
accorded here seems to ascribe the highest possible virtue to the Bride,
namely, that her mind remains untouched by her enemies because it is preserved for its proper owner in purity and impassibility.[12] For this fountain is
sealed by purity, and no turbid thoughts muddy the transparency and clarity
of its heart.

But in order to make our thought as clear as possible, it comes to this:
of the things that are within us, there are some, whatever is proper to the
soul, that are truly *ours;* and there are some, things associated with the body,
I mean, and | things outside of us, that we appropriate as though they were
ours because, by reason of some erroneous notion, we deem what is alien to
be our own. (What, after all, does the immaterial nature of the soul have in
common with the coarse crudity of matter?) This is why Proverbs counsels
us that our mind's fountain is not to be spent upon what is alien to us—I
mean things that concern the body and things outside of us—but to mind our
own garden and give increase to God's planting. We have learned, however,

---

10. The Logos, that is, in the character of Wisdom; see above, homily 1, p. 23 (Jaeger).

11. Δύναμις διανοητική, i.e., the capacity for linear "thinking through" of things.

12. Compare the exegesis of Methodius, *Symp.* 7.1 (trans. Musurillo 1958, 98).

τὴν φυτείαν τοῦ θεοῦ μεμαθήκαμεν, περὶ ἃς ἡ διανοητικὴ τῆς ψυχῆς ἡμῶν δύναμις ἀσχολουμένη καὶ πρὸς οὐδὲν τῶν ἔξωθεν ἀπορρέουσα τῷ χαρακτῆρι τῆς ἀληθείας σφραγίζεται, τῇ πρὸς τὸ ἀγαθὸν σχέσει ἐμμορφουμένη.

Ἴδωμεν δὲ καὶ τῶν ἐφεξῆς ἐπαίνων τὴν δύναμιν· Ἀποστολαί σου, φησί,
5   παράδεισος ῥοῶν μετὰ καρποῦ ἀκροδρύων, κύπρος μετὰ νάρδου, νάρδος καὶ κρόκος, κάλαμος καὶ κιννάμωμον μετὰ πάντων ξύλων τοῦ λιβάνου, σμύρνα, ἀλόη μετὰ πάντων πρωτομύρων, πηγὴ κήπων, φρέαρ ὕδατος ζῶντος καὶ ῥοιζοῦντος ἀπὸ τοῦ λιβάνου.

ὅτι μὲν οὖν παμμέγεθές τι καὶ ἐξαίσιον τοῖς εἰρημένοις ἔγκειται | νόημα, δι'   278
10   οὗ τῆς κατὰ θεὸν ὑψωθείσης τὸ κάλλος ἐν θαύματι γίνεται ταῖς πολυτρόποις τῶν ἐπαίνων ὑπερβολαῖς εὐφημουμένης, δῆλον καὶ ἐκ τῆς προχείρου λέξεως τῶν εἰρημένων ἐστίν. τίς δὲ ἡ ἀληθής ἐστι διάνοια, ἣν διασημαίνει ταῦτα τὰ ῥήματα μόνου ἂν εἴη σαφῶς εἰδέναι τοῦ κατὰ τὸν ἅγιον Παῦλον ἐπισταμένου πνεύματι λαλεῖν τὰ θεῖα μυστήρια· πῶς γὰρ τὸ ἀποστελλόμενον παρὰ τῆς
15   νύμφης ῥοῶν ἐστι παράδεισος; πῶς δὲ ἐκ τῶν ῥοῶν ὁ καρπὸς τῶν ἀκροδρύων προφέρεται; πῶς δὲ τὰ ἀκρόδρυα μύρων γίνεται καὶ ἀρωμάτων κατάλογος; ἐν γὰρ τοῖς τῶν ἀκροδρύων καρποῖς κύπρος καὶ νάρδος καὶ κρόκος ἐστί, κάλαμός τε καὶ κιννάμωμον καὶ πᾶν τοῦ λιβάνου ξύλον ὡς οὐδεμιᾶς τῆς κατὰ τὸ ἄρωμα τοῦ λιβάνου διαφορᾶς ἐν τοῖς ἀπηριθμημένοις λειπούσης. οἷς
20   προστίθεται σμύρνα τε καὶ ἀλόη καὶ τὰ πρωτόμυρα πάντα· καὶ ἡ πρότερον κῆπος [ἐν τοῖς ἄνω] παρὰ τοῦ ἐπαινοῦντος ὀνομασθεῖσα νῦν πηγὴ λέγεται κήπων καὶ φρέαρ ὕδατος ζῶντος καὶ ῥοιζοῦντος ἀπὸ τοῦ λιβάνου.

ἀλλὰ τὸν μὲν ἀληθῆ περὶ τούτων λόγον εἰδεῖεν ἄν, καθὼς προεῖπον, οἱ τὸ βάθος τοῦ πλούτου καὶ τῆς σοφίας καὶ τῆς γνώσεως τοῦ θεοῦ διερευνᾶσθαι
25   δυνάμενοι, ἡμεῖς δέ, ὡς ἂν μὴ παντελῶς | ἄγευστοι τῶν ἐν τῷ τόπῳ τούτῳ   279
προκειμένων ἀγαθῶν καὶ ἀναπόλαυστοι καταλειφθείημεν, δι' ὀλίγων τῷ λόγῳ προσάξομεν αὐτὸν τὸν θεὸν λόγον καθηγεμόνα τῆς σπουδῆς ποιησάμενοι.

that God's planting is the virtues, and when the thinking faculty of the soul is occupied with these and not flowing off toward something external, it is sealed with the mark of truth and shaped by a disposition for the good.

But let us move ahead and discern the force of the next set of praises. *Your outsendings*[13] *are a paradise*[14] *of pomegranate trees with the produce of fruit trees, henna with spikenard, spikenard and saffron, calamus and cinnamon, with all the frankincense trees, myrrh, aloe with all the finest perfumes, a fountain of gardens, a well of living waters that pours forth from frankincense.*

That there is contained in these words some great and extraordinary | idea, an idea whereby the beauty of the soul that has been exalted as though she were a god becomes an object of astonishment as she is honored with a variety of hyperbolic praises, so much is obvious even from the plain sense of the words. But what the true meaning of these words is, to know that clearly belongs only to one who, like Saint Paul, knows how to speak divine mysteries by the Spirit (cf. 1 Cor 14:2). For how is that which is sent forth by the Bride *a paradise of pomegranate trees*? And how is *the produce of fruit trees* brought forth out of the pomegranate trees? And how do the fruit trees become a series of perfumes and spices? For among the fruits of the trees are henna and spikenard, calamus and cinnamon, and every frankincense tree (which means that among the trees included under "every," no distinctive form of the of the scent of frankincense has been omitted). And to these myrrh and aloe and all the finest perfumes are added. What is more, the "garden," as it was previously named by the praise singer, is now called *a fountain of gardens* and *a well of living waters* and is said to pour forth from frankincense.

But as I said before, it is those who are able to search the depth of the riches and of the wisdom and knowledge of God (cf. Rom 11:33; 1 Cor 2:10) who would know the true account of these matters. As for us, lest we be left with absolutely | no taste or enjoyment of the good things that are set before us in this text, we shall address it briefly, having taken the divine Word himself as the guide for our earnest effort.

---

13. This awkward term has been used in the translation of Song 4:13 in order to suggest why Gregory interprets the verse as he does. The Greek word so translated is ἀποστολαί, which literally connotes "things [fem.] sent forth" and represents the LXX's attempt to render a Hebrew word that means "shoots" or "buds." Just below (p. 278 [Jaeger]), however, Gregory paraphrases it with the expression τὸ ἀποστελλόμενον, "that which is sent forth," and of course he inevitably associates it with its cognate ἀπόστολος ("apostle"!). See below, pp. 281–82 (Jaeger), and n. 15.

14. The Greek word παράδεισος (whence the English "paradise") means a garden in the sense of an enclosed park or pleasure ground, like Central Park in New York City (see Gregory's definition of the word below, p. 282 [Jaeger]); the word translated as "garden" toward the end of this quotation is κῆπος, which refers to any rich and cultivated area.

ἔοικεν ἅπας ὁ τῶν ἐπαίνων κατάλογος, ὅ τε πρὸ τούτων εἰρημένος καὶ
ὅσα νῦν περὶ αὐτῆς ἡμῖν ὁ λόγος παρέθετο, μὴ πρὸς εὐφημίαν τινὰ ψιλὴν
κατὰ τὸ προηγούμενον βλέπειν, ἀλλὰ δύναμιν ἐντιθέναι διὰ τῶν λεγομένων
πρὸς τὴν ἐπὶ τὰ μείζω τε καὶ ὑψηλότερα τῆς καρδίας ἀνάβασιν· οἷον ἀδελφὴ
5   καὶ νύμφη τοῦ λόγου κατονομάζεται, ἀλλὰ συνάπτει τῶν ὀνομάτων τούτων
ἑκάτερον τὴν ψυχὴν τῷ νυμφίῳ τῆς μὲν κατὰ τὴν νύμφην σημασίας σύσσωμον
αὐτήν, καθὼς ὀνομάζει ὁ Παῦλος, ποιούσης τῷ ἀφθάρτῳ νυμφίῳ, τῆς δὲ
περὶ τὰ θελήματα σπουδῆς εἰς ἀδελφικὴν ἀγχιστείαν προσαγούσης κατὰ τὴν
τοῦ εὐαγγελίου φωνήν· εἶτα ἐπαινεῖται φύσις μαζῶν ἡ ἀντὶ γάλακτος οἶνον
10   προχέουσα καὶ δῆλον ὅτι ἔργον ὁ ἔπαινος γίνεται (οὐ γὰρ ἐγκωμιάζεται τὸ
ἀνύπαρκτον)· πρὸς τούτοις τὸ μύρον αὐτῆς πάντων τῶν ἀρωμάτων ὑπέρτερον
κρίνεται, ὅπερ οὐκ ἂν οὕτως ἔχειν ἐκρίθη μὴ κατ᾽ ἀλήθειαν πρὸς ἐκεῖνο τὸ
ὕψος αὐτῆς διὰ τῆς ἐν τῷ κρείττονι προκοπῆς ἀναδραμούσης· θαυμάζεται
μετὰ τοῦτο τὰ κηρία τοῦ λόγου τὰ τοῦ στόματος αὐτῆς | ἀποστάζοντα καὶ ἡ   280
15   σύγκρατος τῆς σοφίας παρασκευὴ ἡ ὑποκειμένη τῇ γλώσσῃ γάλακτος πρὸς
μέλι συγκεκραμένου· καὶ ταῦτα δύναμίς ἐστιν οὐ ῥήματα· πρὸς γὰρ τὴν τῶν
ὑψηλοτέρων ἄνοδον χειραγωγουμένη ὑπὸ τοῦ λόγου τοσοῦτον ηὐξήθη,
ὥστε μέλιτος ποιῆσαι πηγὴν τὸ στόμα καὶ ταμιεῖον τῆς συμμίκτου σοφίας τὴν
γλῶσσαν, ᾗ ἐνθεωρεῖται ἡ γῆ τῆς ἐπαγγελίας ἡ ῥέουσα γάλα καὶ μέλι·
20   τοσοῦτον δὲ αὐτὴν διὰ τῶν ἀναβάσεων ὑψώσας ὁ λόγος ἔτι πρὸς τὸ
ὑψηλότερον ἄγει τὴν ἐσθῆτα αὐτῆς εὐπνοεῖν λέγων κατὰ τὴν τοῦ λιβάνου
ὀσμήν, δι᾽ οὗ τὸ ἐνδεδῦσθαι αὐτὴν τὸν Χριστὸν μαρτυρεῖ ὁ λόγος· παντὸς
γὰρ ἐναρέτου βίου τέλος ἡ τοῦ θεοῦ μετουσία γίνεται (διὰ γὰρ τοῦ λιβάνου
τὸ θεῖον ἐνδείκνυται)· καὶ οὐδὲ ἐν τούτοις ἔστη ἡ πρὸς τὸ ὑψηλότερον ἀεὶ
25   χειραγωγουμένη ὑπὸ τοῦ λόγου ψυχή, ἀλλὰ μετὰ τὸ ὁμοιωθῆναι τῷ λιβάνῳ
τὴν εὐωδίαν κῆπος γίνεται καθ᾽ ὁμοιότητα τοῦ παραδείσου, κῆπος οὐχ ὡς
ἐν τοῖς πρώτοις ἀνθρώποις ἦν ἄνετός τε καὶ ἀφύλακτος, ἀλλὰ τῇ μνήμῃ τῆς
ἐντολῆς πανταχόθεν τετειχισμένος.
Ὁρᾷς ὅσην προσέλαβεν εἰς τὸ ἄνω τὴν δύναμιν. πάλιν ὅρα μοι τὴν
30   ὑπὲρ τοῦτο ἀνάβασιν· οὐ γὰρ μόνον κῆπος κεκλεισμένος ἐγένετο τὴν ἰδίαν
καρποφοροῦσα τροφήν, ἀλλὰ καὶ πότιμος γίνεται τοῖς διψῶσιν εἰς πηγῆς
φύσιν μετατεθεῖσα καὶ ταύτης ἐσφραγισμένης.
καὶ οὐδὲ ἐν τούτοις | ἔστη, ἀλλ᾽ εἰς τοσοῦτον ἔφθασε τῆς ἐπὶ τὸ   281
μεῖζον αὐξήσεως, ὡς ἐκ τοῦ στόματος αὐτῆς βλαστάνειν παράδεισον (ὁ
35   γὰρ ἀκριβέστερον προσσχὼν τῇ τῆς Ἑβραϊκῆς λέξεως ἐμφάσει ἀντὶ τοῦ
εἰπεῖν· Ἀποστολαί σου ἐκ στόματός σου, φησί· Παράδεισος ῥοῶν, ὅπερ

The whole catalogue of praises—both those spoken earlier on and everything the Word is now telling us about the Bride—does not appear to intend, in the first instance, mere commendation but to implant, by the words it uses, a power that enables the heart to ascend to better and nobler realities. For example, she is named a *sister* and *bride* of the Word, but each of these designations attaches the soul to the Bridegroom: the sense of the term "bride" makes her, as Paul puts it, "one body with" (Eph 3:6; cf. 5:30–31) the incorruptible Bridegroom; while according to the word of the Gospel, zeal for his will promotes her to a sister's kinship with him (cf. Mark 3:35). Later on there comes praise for breasts that naturally pour forth wine instead of milk, and it is plain enough that the content of the praise becomes reality; for one does not commend what is nonexistent. In addition, her perfume is judged to be superior to all the spices—which would not be thought to be the case unless she were truly running an upward course toward that height by her progress in the good. After this, wonder is expressed at the honeycombs of thoughtful speech that drip from her mouth, | and at the blend of wisdom that lies under her tongue, where milk is mixed with honey. Nor are these things a matter of mere talk, but of power; for as she was being conducted by the Word in her ascent to higher things, she underwent growth to such an extent that her mouth was made a fountain of honey, and her tongue, a store of wisdom that has been mixed together, in which the mind can discern the land of promise that flows with milk and honey.

And when through these ascents the Word has exalted her thus far, he brings her along still further in the direction of the heights when he says that her garments give off a scent like that of frankincense—a statement that testifies that she has put on Christ (Gal 3:27). For the goal of the whole life of virtue is participation in God, and it is Deity that frankincense signifies. Yet the soul that is ever being led by the Word toward something more sublime does not come to a halt even here, but after her fragrance has become similar to that of frankincense, she becomes a garden after the likeness of the paradise—not a garden untended and unguarded, as among the first human beings, but a garden walled on every side by recollection of the commandment.

You see how much power she has received for her journey on high. But notice, please, that she ascends even beyond this. She does not only become a *locked garden* that produces its own food, but she is also transformed into a *fountain*—and that *sealed*—and becomes water that the thirsty can drink.

Nor does she | stop even there. She has reached such a point in her growth and betterment that a paradise sprouts from her mouth (for the reader who attends painstakingly to the sense of the Hebrew text reads *from your mouth* [*comes*] *a paradise of pomegranate trees* instead of *Your outsendings are* [*a*

τοιοῦτόν ἐστιν ὅτι ὁ λόγος σου, ὁ διὰ τοῦ στόματός σου ἀποστελλόμενος, παράδεισός ἐστι ῥοῶν. αἱ δὲ ῥόαι παγκαρπίαν τινὰ τῶν ἀκροδρύων ἐκφύουσι, τὰ δὲ ἀκρόδρυα κύπρος μετὰ νάρδου, νάρδος καὶ κρόκος, κάλαμός τε καὶ κιννάμωμον καὶ πᾶν εἶδος τοῦ λιβάνου καὶ σμύρνα καὶ ἀλόη καὶ τὰ
5 πρωτόμυρα). ἐπειδὴ τοίνυν κατὰ τὸν ἐν τῇ ψαλμῳδίᾳ μακαρισμὸν τῆς ἀντιλήψεως αὐτῇ παρὰ τοῦ θεοῦ γινομένης τὰς καλὰς ταύτας ἀναβάσεις ἐν τῇ καρδίᾳ διέθετο πάντοτε ἐκ δυνάμεως πορευομένη εἰς δύναμιν, καλῶς ἐπὶ τῆς τελειοτέρας καταστάσεως ῥοῶν παράδεισος αἱ τοῦ στόματος αὐτῆς ἀποστολαὶ ὀνομάζονται. προσφυῶς δὲ τῷ ὑποκειμένῳ νοήματι ἡ λέξις τῆς
10 ἀποστολῆς ἐφηρμόσθη· τὸ γὰρ ἀποστελλόμενον ἀπὸ τοῦ πέμποντος εἰς τὸν ὑποδεχόμενον μεταβαίνει. καὶ τοῦτο ἐκ τῆς συνήθους τοῦ ῥήματος | 282 καταχρήσεως ἔστι μαθεῖν, ὡς καὶ τὸ εὐαγγέλιον λέγει, ὅτι τοὺς μαθητὰς τοὺς πρὸς τὸ κήρυγμα τῆς ἀληθείας ἐκπεμπομένους ἀποστόλους ὁ λόγος ὠνόμασεν. τί οὖν ἐστιν ὃ ἀποστέλλει τὸ στόμα τῆς νύμφης; δῆλον ὅτι τὸν
15 λόγον τῆς πίστεως, ὃς ἐν τοῖς ὑποδεχομένοις γενόμενος παράδεισος γίνεται διὰ τῆς ἀκοῆς ταῖς καρδίαις ἐμφυτευόμενος. τὸ δὲ κατάφυτον καὶ συνηρεφὲς τοῖς δένδροις ἄλσος παράδεισον εἴωθε καλεῖν ἡ συνήθεια.

ὡς ἂν οὖν καὶ τὸ γένος μάθοιμεν τῶν φυτῶν, ὅπερ διὰ τοῦ λόγου ταῖς ψυχαῖς τῶν πεπιστευκότων κηπεύεται, ῥόας ὀνομάζει τὰ δένδρα, ἃς
20 φυτηκομεῖ ὁ λόγος ὁ παρὰ τοῦ στόματος τῆς νύμφης ἀποστελλόμενος. ἡ δὲ ῥόα δυσεπιχείρητός ἐστι τῷ κλέπτῃ ἀκανθώδεις προβαλλομένη τοὺς ὄρπηκας καὶ τὸν καρπὸν αὐστηρῷ τινι καὶ πικραίνοντι κατὰ τὴν γεῦσιν τῷ προκαλύμματι περιέχουσά τε καὶ ὑποτρέφουσα, ὃς κατὰ τὸν ἴδιον καιρὸν μετὰ τὸ πεπανθῆναι τοῦ ἐλύτρου περιρραγέντος ἔνδοθεν διαφαίνεται,
25 ἡδὺς μὲν τὴν ὄψιν καὶ εὐδιάθετος, μελιηδὴς δὲ τὴν γεῦσιν καὶ ἄλυπος, ὁ καταγλυκαίνων τῷ οἰνώδει χυμῷ τὰ γευστικὰ αἰσθητήρια.

διὰ τοῦτό μοι δοκεῖ ῥοῶν παραδείσους ἐν ταῖς τῶν ἀκουόντων ψυχαῖς ὁ ἀποστελλόμενος ἐκ τοῦ στόματος τῆς νύμφης λόγος ἐργάζεσθαι, ἵνα διδαχθῶμεν διὰ τῶν λεγομένων μὴ διά τινος ἐκλύσεως | καὶ τρυφῆς κατὰ τὴν   283
30 παροῦσαν ζωὴν μαλακίζεσθαι, ἀλλὰ τὸν κατεσκληκότα διὰ τῆς ἐγκρατείας αἱρεῖσθαι βίον· οὕτω γὰρ ἂν ἀπρόσιτος γένοιτο τοῖς κλέπταις ὁ τῆς ἀρετῆς

paradise of pomegranates],[15] which is to say, "Your speech, which is sent forth through your mouth, is a garden of pomegranate trees." Pomegranate trees, however, produce an assortment of the *produce of fruit trees,* and this fruit is *henna with spikenard, spikenard and saffron,* both *calamus and cinnamon,* and every sort of *frankincense* and *myrrh* and *aloe* and the finest perfumes). Since, therefore, in accordance with the Psalter's praise of "the succor" that comes to her "from God," she establishes "in her heart" those lovely "ascents," going ever "from strength to strength" (Ps 83:6–8), it is appropriate, given her more perfect state, that *the outsendings* from her mouth are called *a garden of pomegranates.* Indeed the term "outsending" fits the underlying idea most aptly, for what is sent out makes its way from sender to recipient. From, moreover, the customary | improper use of the word, one can also learn this, that, as the Gospel also says, it was to those disciples who were "sent out" to proclaim the truth that the Word gave the name "apostles."[16] But what is it that the mouth of the Bride sends forth? Plainly it is the word of faith, which, when it has reached its recipients, becomes a paradise planted in their hearts by the sense of hearing. By the dictate of custom, however, "paradise" normally refers to a grove full of plants and shaded by trees.

In order, then, that we may also learn the sort of plants that the Word cultivates in the hearts of those who have come to faith, the text names them—that is, the trees that the word issuing from the Bride's mouth plants and tends—*pomegranates.* Now the pomegranate is hard for a thief to take. It puts forth shoots that are full of thorns and both encases and nourishes its fruit within a husk that is harsh and bitter to the taste. The fruit appears—in its proper season, after it has ripened and its sheath has been torn open from within—fair and pleasing to the eye, honey-like and inoffensive to the taste, conveying sweetness to the taste buds with juices that are like wine.[17]

It seems to me, then, that the word that is sent forth from the Bride's mouth creates gardens of pomegranates in the souls of her hearers to this end: that we may learn from our text not, in this present life, to make ourselves weak | through laxity or softness but to prefer a form of life that has been rendered firm and severe by self-control. In this way, the fruit that is virtue

---

15. On the LXX text, see above, n. 13. Gregory has not actually consulted the Hebrew text or even, necessarily, consulted and repeated Origen (which is nevertheless entirely possible). His emendation, which takes ἀποστολαί ("outsendings," "sent forths") to mean "what is sent forth *from the mouth,*" might well spring from a marriage of (1) the natural association in his mind of ἀποστολαί with ἀποστόλοι, and (2) the further association in his mind between ἀποστόλοι and speaking or proclaiming.

16. On this sentence, see n. 15 above.

17. For this account of the pomegranate and its symbolic meaning, see also above, homily 7, p. 230 (Jaeger).

καρπὸς τῇ στυφῇ τῆς ἐγκρατείας περιβολῇ πεφραγμένος καὶ διὰ τῆς σεμνῆς
τε καὶ ἀμειδοῦς καταστάσεως οἷόν τισιν ἀκανθῶν ἀκμαῖς ἀμύσσων τοὺς
ἐπὶ κακῷ προσεγγίζοντας. ἀλλ᾽ ὅταν ὁ καιρὸς παράσχῃ τῆς ἀπολαύσεως
τῶν καρπῶν τὸ ἐνδόσιμον, παγκαρπία τῆς τρυφῆς ἐκ παντὸς γένους τῶν
5   ἀκροδρύων ἡ ῥόα γίνεται οὐκ ἐν βραβύλοις ἢ βαλάνοις ἤ τισι τοιούτοις
τῆς τῶν καρπῶν ἀπολαύσεως γινομένης, ἀλλὰ ποικίλη τις καὶ πολυειδὴς
ἀρωμάτων φύσις ἐν τοῖς ἀκροδρύοις εὑρίσκεται·

κύπρος γάρ ἐστι μετὰ νάρδου ἡ καλὴ συζυγία, τὸ μὲν θερμὸν τὸ δὲ
εὐῶδες· οὐ γὰρ ἐπαινετὸν ἐφ᾽ ἑαυτοῦ τὸ θερμόν, ὅταν δυσώδης πύρωσις
10   ἡ θερμότης ᾖ, ἀλλὰ συμμαρτυρεῖσθαι χρὴ τῷ θερμῷ διὰ τῆς εὐπνοίας τὴν
καθαρότητα, ἵνα γένηται τῷ ἁγίῳ πνεύματι ζέων ὁ τῆς ἀηδοῦς θερμότητος
κεκαθαρμένος.

ἐν τούτοις ἔστιν εὑρεῖν τοῖς ἀκροδρύοις καὶ ἄλλα ἀρώματα· νάρδον φησὶ
καὶ κρόκον. ἀλλὰ τῆς μὲν νάρδου τὴν εὔπνοιαν ἐν τοῖς ἄνω μεμαθήκαμεν
15   λόγοις, ὑπόλοιπον δ᾽ ἂν εἴη τοῦ κρόκου τὸ αἴνιγμα παραστῆσαι τῷ λόγῳ.
φασὶ μὲν οὖν οἱ | τὴν δύναμιν τοῦ ἄνθους τούτου κατανοήσαντες μέσως   284
ἔχειν ψύξεώς τε καὶ θερμότητος καὶ τῷ φεύγειν τὴν ἐφ᾽ ἑκάτερον ἀμετρίαν
παρηγορικὴν τῶν ὀδυνῶν ἔχειν τὴν δύναμιν, ὡς διὰ τούτου τάχα τὸν περὶ τῆς
ἀρετῆς ἡμῖν λόγον φιλοσοφεῖν τῷ αἰνίγματι, διότι πᾶσα ἀρετὴ δύο κακιῶν
20   ἐστι μέση, τῆς τε ἐλλείψεως τοῦ καλοῦ καὶ τῆς ὑπερπτώσεως. οἷον τὴν
ἀνδρείαν ἢ τὴν ἐλευθερίαν φασί, τὴν μὲν δειλίας τε καὶ θρασύτητος, τὴν δὲ
μικρολογίας τε καὶ ἀσωτίας ἐν μέσῳ θεωρεῖσθαι· καὶ τὴν μὲν δειλίαν τε καὶ
μικρολογίαν κατ᾽ ἔλλειψιν τοῦ καθήκοντος ἐν κακίᾳ λέγουσι γίνεσθαι, τὴν δὲ
ἀσωτίαν καὶ τὴν θρασύτητα κατὰ πλεονασμὸν καὶ ὑπέρπτωσιν, τῆς δὲ καθ᾽
25   ἑκάτερον ἀμετρίας τὸ μέσον ἀρετὴν ὀνομάζουσιν. οὐκοῦν ἔχοι ἄν τι πρὸς τὴν
ἀρετὴν ὁ περὶ τοῦ κρόκου λόγος ἀκόλουθον τῇ τῆς δυνάμεως μεσότητι τὸ
ἀνελλιπές τε καὶ τὸ ἀπέριττον τῆς ἐναρέτου καταστάσεως ἑρμηνεύων,

ἐγὼ δέ φημι, κἂν ἰδιωτικώτερον ᾖ τὸ λεγόμενον, τάχα μᾶλλον πρὸς τὸν
τῆς πίστεως λόγον οἰκειότερον τὸ αἴνιγμα τοῦ κρόκου παραλαμβάνεσθαι·
30   τριπλῷ μὲν | γὰρ ὑποτρέφεται τὸ ἄνθος τῷ κάλυκι καὶ αὐτὸς δὲ ὁ κάλυξ ἐν   285
ἀεροειδεῖ τῇ χρόᾳ ἄνθος ἐστίν, ἐκδυθείσης δὲ τῆς τῶν καλύκων περιβολῆς

can be inaccessible to thieves because it is secured from without by the harsh sheathing of self-control, and because by its stern and noble demeanor it lacerates, as though with sharp thorns, those who draw near with evil intent. But when the season signals the time for enjoyment of the fruit, the pomegranate becomes a vast assortment of delights derived from fruit trees of every kind; for the enjoyment of the fruits is not occasioned by the wild plum or acorns or things of that sort; no, but one encounters, among these fruit trees, a variegated and multiform species of spices.

For *henna with spikenard* makes a happy marriage, the one being hot and the other fragrant; for what is hot is not praiseworthy in itself, when the heat is a burning that gives off a bad smell, but purity with its fragrance must speak up in harmony with what is hot, in order that the person who has been cleansed of the repellent heat may glow with the warmth of the Holy Spirit.[18]

And there are more spices to seek among these fruits: *spikenard,* it says, *and saffron.* But we have already learned the meaning of the fragrance of nard in what was said just now; what remains is to convey in words the enigma represented by saffron. Those | who have become acquainted with the potency of this blossom say that it strikes a mean between cold and heat and that it has the power of assuaging pain by reason of its avoidance of the extremes to which each of the latter can go. Perhaps, then, on the basis of this, one can use the enigma of saffron to philosophize on the subject of virtue, to assert, namely, that every virtue is a mean between two evils, that which falls short of the good and that which exceeds it.[19] Courage, for example, and liberality, they say, are to be defined as the means respectively between terror and rashness and between meanness and prodigality; and they say that terror and meanness are evils because they fall short of what is right, while prodigality and rashness are evils because they exceed and exaggerate it. Virtue, though, they call the mean between each of the extremes. Hence what is said of saffron may well contain some analogy with virtue and, on the basis of saffron's tendency to produce a median state, interpret for us the absence of defect and excess in the condition of virtue.

My own view, however, inexpert though the statement may be, is that it might perhaps be more apposite to take the enigma of saffron to bear on our understanding of the faith. For this flower | is nourished within a threefold corolla, and the corolla itself is a flower of the color of the sky; and when the

---

18. See Rom 12:11 and also Paul's reference to the "burning" (πυροῦσθαι) of desire at 1 Cor 7:9.

19. See Aristotle, *Eth. nic.* 2.6 (1107a2), which is the classical statement of this view. Gregory states this same principle in earlier writings; see, e.g., *Vit. Mos.* 2.288 (GNO 7.1:284: trans. Malherbe and Ferguson 1978, 128).

τρία εὑρίσκεται πάντως τὰ εὐπνοοῦντα καὶ χρησιμεύοντα πρὸς τὰς ἰάσεις
ἄνθη τὰ ὑποκεκρυμμένα τοῖς κάλυξι, μεγέθει καὶ κάλλει καὶ εὐπνοίᾳ καὶ
τῇ τῆς δυνάμεως ἰδιότητι ὡσαύτως πρὸς ἄλληλα ἔχοντα καὶ ἓν τὰ τρία διὰ
πάντων δεικνύμενα εὐχροίᾳ τε, καθὼς εἴρηται, καὶ εὐπνοίᾳ καὶ τῷ ποιῷ
5   τῆς δυνάμεως. οἷς συμπαραπέφυκεν ἕτερα τρία, ξανθὰ μὲν ἰδεῖν ἄποια δὲ
πρὸς πᾶσαν ὑγιεινὴν εὐχρηστίαν. περὶ ἃ γίνεται τοῖς ἀπείροις ἡ πλάνη τοῖς
διὰ τὴν εὔχροιαν τὸ νόθον δρεπομένοις ἀντὶ τοῦ κρείττονος. ὅπερ καὶ νῦν
ποιοῦσιν οἱ περὶ τὴν πίστιν ἐξαμαρτάνοντες τὰς σεσοφισμένας ἀπάτας πρὸ
τῶν ὑγιεινῶν δογμάτων αἱρούμενοι.
10   ἐλέσθω δὲ ἐξ ἑκατέρων ἡ τοῦ ἀκροατοῦ κρίσις ὃ βούλεται, εἴτε τὸ ἕτερον
ἐξ αὐτῶν εἴτε ἀμφότερα· ἓν γὰρ τρόπον τινά ἐστιν ἀμφότερα ἥ τε τῆς τελείας
ἀρετῆς καὶ ἡ τῆς θεότητος κτῆσις· οὐ γὰρ ἔξω ἡ ἀρετὴ τῆς θεότητος.
Ἡμεῖς δὲ ἐπὶ τὴν τῶν λοιπῶν ἀρωμάτων θεωρίαν μετέλθωμεν τῶν
δι' ἀκολούθου μνημονευθέντων ὑπὸ τοῦ λόγου. κάλαμος, φησί, καὶ
15   κιννάμωμόν ἐστι τὰ ἀκρόδρυα τὰ ἐκ τῶν ῥοῶν τοῦ παραδείσου τῆς νύμφης
καρποφορούμενα. ἀλλὰ τὸν μὲν κάλαμον εὐπνοίᾳ προέχειν ὑπὲρ τὰ ἄλλα | 286
φασίν, ὡς καὶ πρὸς τὸ ἱερατικὸν θυμίαμα ὑπὸ τοῦ νόμου παραλαμβάνεσθαι,
τὸ δὲ κιννάμωμον πολυειδῆ τινα καὶ ποικίλην ἐνέργειαν διά τινος φυσικῆς
δυνάμεως ἐπαγγέλλεσθαι, ὧν τὰ πολλὰ καὶ ὑπὲρ πίστιν εἶναι δοκεῖ· καὶ γὰρ
20   ζέοντός φασι τοῦ ἐν τῷ λέβητι ὕδατος εἴπερ θίγοι μόνον τοῦτο τὸ ἄρωμα,
εὐθὺς καταψύχειν τὸ ὕδωρ καὶ λουτρῷ ἐπεισενεχθὲν διαπύρῳ μεταποιεῖν
τὸν ἐν τῷ ἀέρι φλογμὸν εἰς ψυχρότητα καὶ ἀφανιστικὴν τῶν ἐκ φθορᾶς τινος
ζωογονουμένων τὴν φύσιν ἔχειν. καὶ ἄλλα τοιαῦτα περὶ αὐτοῦ διεξέρχονται,
ἃ ὑπὲρ τὴν πίστιν τῶν ἀκουόντων εἶναι δοκεῖ· λέγουσι γάρ, εἰ ἐντεθείη τῷ
25   στόματι τοῦ καθεύδοντος, μηδὲν ἐμποδίζεσθαι πρὸς τὴν τῶν πυνθανομένων
ἀπόκρισιν τὸν καθεύδοντα, ἀλλὰ καὶ ἐν τῷ ὕπνῳ μένειν αὐτὸν καὶ νηφαλίους
καὶ διηρθρωμένας ποιεῖσθαι πρὸς ἔπος τὰς ἀποκρίσεις.
περὶ ὧν διαβεβαιώσασθαι μὲν οὕτως ἔχειν τὸν μὴ διὰ τῆς πείρας
μαθόντα τῶν ἱστορουμένων περὶ αὐτοῦ τὴν ἀλήθειαν προπετὲς ἂν εἴη καὶ
30   ἀνεπίσκεπτον· πλὴν ἀλλ' ἐπειδὴ κατά τινα μυστικὸν λόγον ἐνηριθμήθη
τῷ καταλόγῳ τῶν ἀκροδρύων καὶ τοῦτο τὸ ἄρωμα οὐκ ἀληθῶς ῥοῶν
ἐκφυόμενον (οὐδὲ γὰρ ὄντως αἰσθητοὺς παραδείσους τὸ στόμα τῆς νύμφης

covering of these outer petals is removed, three flowers, previously hidden by the petals, are revealed, full of fragrance and useful in healing. They are like one another in size, beauty, fragrance, and the special quality of their potency, and the three are manifested as one in every respect: in the freshness of their appearance and, as has been said, in fragrance and in the special quality of their potency. Another threesome grows alongside these, golden to look upon but without any quality that makes them useful for purposes of healing. Where the last-mentioned threesome is concerned, error seizes the inexperienced, who, because of its appealing color, pluck the inferior instead of the nobler set. Even now, those who err concerning the faith do the very same thing by choosing clever deceits over the health-giving truths of faith.[20]

Let the judgment of the hearer choose from the two interpretations as it will, either one of them or both, for in a certain way, both are one—possession of perfect virtue and possession of the Godhead—since there is no virtue outside the Godhead.

Let us move on, however, to discern the significance of the remainder of the spices that the text goes on to mention in a sequence. *Calamus*, it says, *and cinnamon* are the fruit trees that bud and flower from the pomegranates of the Bride's paradise. But in virtue of its sweet scent, calamus stands out above the others, | people say, and so is employed by the law for priestly incense (cf. Exod 30:23), while cinnamon, by reason of a natural potency, gives promise of performing various and multiform functions. The greater part of the latter appear incredible. Indeed they say that if this spice should no more than touch water as it boils in the kettle, the water instantly cools down, and that if introduced into a blazing hot bathhouse, it will cool the heat of the air, and that it has the natural capacity to destroy the creatures generated out of something in a state of decay. Other things of this sort are also related concerning it, things that seem beyond the belief of their hearers. Thus it is said that if it is placed in the mouth of someone who is asleep, the sleeper is in no wise hindered from answering people who put questions but even in slumber remains present and returns sober and articulate answers to all queries.

Now where these reports are concerned, it would be rash and thoughtless to maintain that the claims are correct, unless one has learned so from the experience of people who look into the truth of the matter. On the other hand, this spice like the others was included in the list of fruit trees on the basis of some mystical logic, since after all it does not grow out of pomegranate trees (for neither does the Bride's mouth really put forth perceptible paradises, but

---

20. This is, of course, a reference to Gregory's *bêtes noires*, the neo-Arians as represented in particular by Eunomius of Cyzicus, who emphatically denied the identity of the "nature" of the persons of the Trinity.

προΐεται, ἀλλ᾽ ὥστε σύμβολον γενέσθαι | νοήματός τινος τῶν εἰς ἔπαινον   287
συντελούντων τῇ νύμφῃ), οὐκ οἶμαι καλῶς ἔχειν ἀποβαλεῖν τὰ περὶ τοῦ
κινναμώμου μυθολογούμενα, ταῦτά τε ἃ νῦν περὶ αὐτοῦ διεξῆλθεν ὁ λόγος
καὶ εἴ τι μετὰ τούτων ἄλλο τοῖς τὰ περὶ αὐτοῦ διηγουμένους διεξιέναι
5   δοκεῖ· γένοιτο γὰρ ἄν τις πρὸς τὸν κατ᾽ ἀρετὴν ἔπαινον ἐκ τῶν λεγομένων
συνεισφορὰ ἑκάστου τῶν ἱστορηθέντων εὐσήμως μεταλαμβανομένου πρὸς
ἔνδειξιν τῆς τοῦ βίου τοῦ κατ᾽ ἀρετὴν τελειότητος·
    ἔστι γὰρ ἐν τοῖς πεπαιδευμένοις τε καὶ λελογισμένοις τοῦτο εὑρεῖν
ἐν τῇ ψυχῇ τὸ κιννάμωμον· ὅταν τις ἤτοι δι᾽ ἐπιθυμίας ζέων ἢ τῷ θυμῷ
10   πυρακτούμενος τῷ λογισμῷ κατασβέσῃ τὰ πάθη ἢ ἐν τῷ ὕπνῳ τοῦ βίου διὰ
στόματος ἔχων τὸ νηφάλιον τοῦτο τοῦ λογισμοῦ κιννάμωμον παραπλησίως
τοῖς ἀΰπνοις τε καὶ ἐγρηγορόσιν ἀγγέλοις ἀπλανῆ καὶ ἀσύγχυτον ἐπιδεικνύῃ
τὴν τῶν λεγομένων διάνοιαν μιμούμενος διὰ τῆς ἀληθείας τοῦ λόγου τὴν
ἄϋπνον τῶν ἀγγέλων φύσιν, οὓς οὐδεμία φαντασίας ἀνάγκη τῆς ἀληθείας
15   ἐξίστησιν, οὗτος λέγοιτο ἂν βρύειν διὰ τοῦ στόματος τὸ κιννάμωμον, δι᾽ οὗ
καὶ τῆς ἐπιθυμίας ἡ πύρωσις καὶ ἡ περικάρδιος | τοῦ θυμοῦ κατασβέννυται   288
ζέσις, καὶ πάσης τῆς κατὰ τὸν βίον τούτου ὀνειρώδους φαντασίας τε καὶ
συγχύσεως καθαρεύειν τῷ λόγῳ.
    καὶ μηδεὶς πρὸς τὸ ἀπίθανον βλέπων τῶν περὶ τοῦ κινναμώμου λεγομένων
20   διαβαλλέτω τὸν λόγον ὡς οὐκ ἐκ τῶν ἀληθῶν προσάγοντα τῇ νύμφῃ τὸν
ἔπαινον· οἶδε γὰρ πολλάκις ἡ ἁγία γραφὴ καὶ μύθους τινὰς ἐκ τῶν ἔξωθεν
συμπαραλαμβάνειν εἰς τὴν τοῦ ἰδίου σκοποῦ συνεργίαν καὶ ἀνεπαισχύντως ἐκ
τῆς μυθικῆς ἱστορίας ὀνομάτων μνημονεύειν τινῶν εἰς ἐναργεστέραν ἔνδειξιν
τοῦ προκειμένου νοήματος, ὡς ἐπὶ τῶν τοῦ Ἰὼβ θυγατέρων, ὧν τὸ κάλλος
25   ὑπερθαυμάσας ὁ λόγος καὶ διὰ τῶν ὀνομάτων τὴν ὑπερβολὴν τοῦ περὶ αὐτῶν
θαύματος ἐνεδείξατο λέγων τὴν μὲν Ἡμέραν λέγεσθαι τὴν δὲ Κασίαν τὴν δὲ
τρίτην Ἀμαλθείας Κέρας. τοῦτο δὲ παντὶ δῆλόν ἐστιν ὅτι μῦθος Ἑλληνικὸς
ἔπλασε τὸ κατὰ τὴν Ἀμάλθειαν διήγημα, ἣν αἶγα οὖσαν τροφὸν γενέσθαι

this is stated in order to serve as a symbol of | one of the ideas that contribute to the praise of the Bride).[21] Hence I doubt whether it is a good thing to reject out of hand the fables that are told regarding cinnamon—be it the ones my address has just related or any other of their sort that seems, to those who relate such stories, to be worth the telling. After all, there might emerge from what is said a contribution to the praise of virtue, if everything narrated is transposed in a distinct manner so as to point to the perfection of the virtuous life.

For there is a kind of "cinnamon" to be found in the souls of those who have been trained and gifted with reflection. Suppose that a person who is either seething with desire or burning up with anger quenches the passions by articulate thinking. Or suppose that someone who exists in the sleep of this life but possesses in his mouth the sober "cinnamon" of articulate thought[22] evinces, in a manner similar to that of the sleepless and wakeful angels, unerring and sure understanding of the sense of what is said and so imitates, by the truth of what he says, the sleepless nature of the angels, whom no force of the imagination alienates from truth—such a person might well be said to produce cinnamon through the mouth, by which the burning of desire and the seething | of anger around the heart are quenched, and to be purified by articulate thought from all the deceptive imaginings and confusions of this life.

Let no one, moreover, with mind fixed on the implausibility of the tales told about cinnamon, attack what I am saying on the ground that it constructs the praises of the Bride out of things that have no substance. The Holy Scripture, after all, can enlist even alien myths in the service of its aim and, in order to make its thought the more clear, make blameless and explicit mention of names drawn from a mythical narrative. Consider the example of Job's daughters. Having expressed great wonder at their beauty, the text indicates the surpassing degree of its admiration for them by saying that one of them was called "Day," another "Cinnamon," and the third "Amaltheia's Horn."[23] Now everyone knows that a Greek myth shaped the tale of Amaltheia, of whom they tell the story that she was a goat and became the wet-nurse of that

---

21. In other words, Gregory denies that what he has earlier on explained as the literal sense of this passage is empirically "true." He then goes on to insist that even empirical falsehood can, if allegorically rendered, point to truth on a higher level of understanding.

22. "Articulate thought" here is my translation of λόγος. It is intended to call attention to the way in which Gregory automatically associates *rational thinking* with *speaking*. The association is of course built into the Greek term λόγος but not into the English "reason." See further Gregory's characterization of λόγος in his treatise *Opif. hom.* 8.2, 8 (PG 44:144B, 148C–149A).

23. Gregory is, of course, referring to the LXX text of Job 42:14 (*q.v.*). In the Hebrew, the names are Jemimah ("little dove"), Keziah ("cassia" = "cinnamon"), and Kerenhappuch ("horn of eye-shadow").

τοῦ Κρητὸς ἐκείνου μυθολογοῦσιν, ἧς τοῦ ἑνὸς ἐκπεσόντος κέρως βρύειν ἐκ
τοῦ κοίλου τὴν παγκαρπίαν ὁ μῦθος ἐποίησεν. ἆρ' οὖν ἐπίστευσε τοῖς περὶ
τῆς Ἀμαλθείας μυθολογουμένοις ἡ ἁγία γραφή; οὐκ ἔστι ταῦτα. ἀλλὰ τὸ | 289
πάμφορον τῶν κατ' ἀρετὴν ἀγαθῶν μαρτυροῦσα τῇ θυγατρὶ τοῦ Ἰὼβ διὰ τοῦ
5   ὀνόματος τούτου παρίστησιν, ὥστε τὸν λελογισμένως τῆς γραφῆς ἐπαΐοντα
τὸν σκοπὸν τοῦ ἐπαίνου νοῆσαι μόνον ἐκ τοῦ ὀνόματος, τὰς δὲ μυθικὰς
τερατείας χαίρειν ἐᾶσαι·

ὡς καὶ τὴν Κασίαν καὶ τὴν Ἡμέραν ἀκούσαντες οὔτε τὴν ἀρωματικὴν
ὕλην οὔτε τὸν ὑπὲρ γῆς τοῦ ἡλίου δρόμον διὰ τῶν ὀνομάτων ἐμάθομεν, ἀλλὰ
10   τῆς κατ' ἀρετὴν αὐτῶν πολιτείας ἔνδειξιν περιέχειν φαμὲν τὰ ὀνόματα· ὧν ἡ
μὲν Κασία τὸ καθαρόν τε καὶ εὐῶδες τῶν ἐπιτηδευμάτων ἐνδείκνυται, ἡ δὲ
Ἡμέρα τὸ εὔσχημον, καθώς φησιν ὁ ἀπόστολος τοὺς καθαρῶς βιοτεύοντας
τέκνα φωτὸς καὶ υἱοὺς ἡμέρας κατονομάζεσθαι. οὕτως οὖν καὶ ἐνταῦθα
οὐκ ἀσυντελῆ πρὸς τοὺς ἐπαίνους τῆς νύμφης ἐστὶ τὰ περὶ τοῦ κινναμώμου
15   λεγόμενα διὰ τῆς τροπικῆς ἐξηγήσεως μεταλαμβανόμενα εἰς ἐγκωμίων
ὑπόθεσιν.

Ὁ δὲ τοσοῦτος ἤδη γενόμενος καὶ πρὸς τοῦτο φθάσας τῶν ἐγκωμίων τὸ
ὕψος διὰ τοῦ βίου διὰ πάντων τῆς θείας εἰκόνος ἐφ' ἑαυτοῦ δείκνυσι τοὺς
χαρακτῆρας· τοῦτο γὰρ ἐνδείκνυται ὁ εἰπὼν ὅτι Ἀπὸ πάντων ξύλων τοῦ
20   λιβάνου· οὐ γὰρ μονοειδὲς τοῦ λιβάνου τὸ ξύλον εἶναί φασιν οἱ τὰ τοιαῦτα
παρατηρήσαντες, ὅθεν ὁ λιβανωτὸς ἀπορρέει, ἀλλ' ἔστι | τις ἐν τοῖς ξύλοις   290
διαφορὰ τὸ τοῦ ἀρώματος σχῆμα τῷ εἴδει τοῦ ξύλου συνεξαλλάσσουσα. ὁ
τοίνυν ἐν πᾶσι τοῖς ἐπιτηδεύμασι τοῦ βίου ἐπισημαίνων ἐν ἑαυτῷ τὸ θεοειδὲς
πάντων δείκνυσιν ἐν ἑαυτῷ τῶν τοῦ λιβάνου ξύλων τὸ κάλλος, δι' ὧν τὸ
25   θεῖον εἶδος χαρακτηρίζεται.

Οὐδεὶς δὲ κοινωνὸς τῆς τοῦ θεοῦ γίνεται δόξης μὴ σύμμορφος πρῶτον
τῷ ὁμοιώματι τοῦ θανάτου γενόμενος. διὸ φησι καὶ τοῦτο ἐν τῷ καταλόγῳ
τῶν ἀρωμάτων ὁ ἔπαινος ὅτι ῥοῶν ἀκρόδρυα τά τε λοιπὰ τῶν ἀρωμάτων
ἐστὶν ἃ διεξῆλθεν ὁ λόγος καὶ μετ' αὐτῶν ἡ σμύρνα τε καὶ ἡ ἀλόη καὶ τὰ
30   πρωτόμυρα· δι' ἐκείνων μὲν γάρ, τῆς σμύρνης λέγω καὶ τῆς ἀλόης, τὴν τῆς
ταφῆς κοινωνίαν ἐνδείκνυται (καθώς φησι τὸ ὑψηλὸν εὐαγγέλιον ὅτι διὰ

Cretan.[24] When her single horn fell out, the story has her give abundant birth from the cavity to all kinds of fruits. Well then, did the Holy Scripture believe the tales told about Amaltheia? Not at all. But by this name it attests and represents | the fruitfulness of Job's daughter in the good things that belong to virtue, in order that someone who pays intelligent attention to Scripture will from that name grasp only the intent of the praise, while dismissing from his mind the mythic talk of wonders.

In the same way, when we hear "Cinnamon" and "Day," we do not think of an aromatic substance or of the sun's course above the earth but say that the names contain an indication of the virtuous mode of life. "Cinnamon" points to the purity and fragrance of their way of life, while "Day" indicates its nobility. Does not the apostle say that those who live in purity are called "children of light" and "children of day" (1 Thess 5:5)? Similarly in this case, then, the things that are said about cinnamon are not without usefulness for singing the Bride's praises if they are changed by figural interpretation into an opportunity for her commendation.

The person who has already become as great as this and has attained such exalted praises by her manner of life exhibits everywhere the marks of the divine image. This is what is indicated by the one who says *from*[25] *all the frankincense trees*. For those who have observed such trees closely to see whence the frankincense gum flows down say that the frankincense tree is not of one single variety but that between the trees | there is a difference in the character of the scent, which changes from tree to tree. Hence the person who in all the pursuits of human life manifests in his own self likeness to God exhibits in himself the beauty of *all the frankincense trees,* by which the divine form is marked.

But no one becomes a participant in the divine glory without first being conformed to the likeness of death (cf. Rom 6:5; Phil 3:10, 21). Hence the encomium of the Bride conveyed in the list of spices also says this: it is not only the other spices enumerated in the text that qualify as fruit trees springing from pomegranates but also, together with them, *myrrh and aloe and the finest perfumes*. For by these—I mean myrrh and aloe—is meant a sharing in

---

24. The name of the Cretan in question was Zeus, but Gregory is not disposed to mention it.

25. This reading ("from" instead of "with," for which see the standard LXX text as translated at the beginning of this homily and on p. 277 [Jaeger]) probably derives, as Langerbeck has suggested in his apparatus *ad loc.*, from a note of the scribe who, in taking Gregory's dictation, was hurried and abbreviated the text of Song 4:14b–15, merely indicating with the word "from" the beginning of the quotation. A later copyist, missing the point, then removed the preposition "with," which belongs in the text of the Song, leaving "from" in its place.

τούτων ἐγένετο ὁ ἐνταφιασμὸς τῷ ὑπὲρ ἡμῶν γευσαμένῳ θανάτου), διὰ δὲ
τῶν πρωτομύρων τὸ καθαρόν τε καὶ ἀμιγὲς πάσης καπηλικῆς ῥᾳδιουργίας
ὁ λόγος ἐνδείκνυται, ὥσπερ καὶ Ἀμὼς τοῖς διὰ τούτων τρυφῶσι τὰ τοιαῦτα
προφέρει λέγων Οἱ τὸν διυλισμένον πίνοντες οἶνον καὶ τὰ πρωτόμυρα   291
5   χριόμενοι καὶ πρὸ τούτων Οἱ ἐσθίοντες, φησίν, | ἐρίφους ἐκ ποιμνίου καὶ
μοσχάρια ἐκ μέσου βουκολίων γαλαθηνὰ καὶ οἱ ἐπικροτοῦντες πρὸς τὴν
φωνὴν τῶν ὀργάνων, ὡς οὔτε τὸν οἶνον τρυγίας ἀναθολούσης οὔτε ἐπὶ τοῦ
μύρου μίξεώς τινος τὸ ἀκραιφνὲς τῆς εὐοδμίας διαφθειρούσης. ἀλλ᾽ ἐκεῖ
μὲν πάντως ὀνειδίζειν οἴεσθαι χρὴ τοῖς Ἰσραηλίταις τὴν προφητείαν, ὅτι
10 ἄκρατον τὸν τῆς γραφῆς ἐμφορούμενοι λόγον πάσης τρυγίας διυλισμένον καὶ
ἀδόλωτον ἔχοντες τῶν μύρων τὴν εὐοδμίαν καὶ διὰ πάντων κατατρυφῶντες
τῆς πνευματικῆς πανδαισίας οὐδὲν ἀπώναντο τῆς τοιαύτης τρυφῆς τῆς
κακῆς αὐτῶν προαιρέσεως καὶ τὸ διαυγὲς τοῦ οἴνου εἰς ἀνατροπὴν θολερὰν
μεταποιούσης καὶ τὸ καθαρὸν τῶν πρωτομύρων διὰ τῆς τῶν πονηρῶν
15 νοημάτων ἐπιμιξίας λυμαινομένης, ἐνταῦθα μέντοι τὸ ἀκιβδήλευτόν τε καὶ
καθαρὸν τῶν δογμάτων μαρτυρεῖ τῇ νύμφῃ ὁ λόγος διὰ τῆς τῶν πρωτομύρων
καρποφορίας.

Καὶ οὐδὲ ἐν τούτοις ἔστη οὔτε ἡ νύμφη τοῖς ὑψηλοτέροις ἑαυτὴν
ἐπεκτείνουσα οὔτε ὁ λόγος συνεργῶν αὐτῇ πρὸς τὴν ἄνοδον· ἧς γὰρ αἱ ἐκ
20 τοῦ στόματος ἀποστολαὶ ῥοῶν εἰσι καὶ ἀρωμάτων παράδεισοι, αὕτη νῦν πηγὴ
γίνεται τοὺς ἐξ αὐτῆς ἀναφυέντας παραδείσους κατάρδουσα· οὐχ ὡς ἐπὶ τοῦ
Παύλου τε καὶ Ἀπολλὼ μεμαθήκαμεν ὡς τοῦ μὲν φυτεύοντος τοῦ δὲ ἑτέρου
ποτίζοντος, ἀλλ᾽ αὐτὴ τὰ δύο ἐργάζεται φύουσά τε τοὺς παραδείσους ὁμοῦ
καὶ ποτίζουσα.   292
25 | ἢ τάχα καὶ ὑψηλότερόν τινα λόγον περιέχει ὁ ἔπαινος· πηγὴν γὰρ αὐτὴν
οὐ νάματος προχεομένου τινὸς ἀλλὰ κήπων εἶναί φησιν, οὐχ ὑδάτων τινὰς
ἀπορροὰς ἀλλ᾽ αὐτοὺς κήπους πηγάζουσάν τε καὶ ἀναβρύουσαν. οὕτως
ἀνέβρυε τοὺς ἐμψύχους κήπους ὁ θεῖος ἀπόστολος, παρ᾽ οἷς ἂν ἐγένετο τὸν
τῆς ἐκκλησίας παράδεισον διὰ τῆς διδασκαλίας ἐκφύων.
30 εἶτα πρὸς τὸ ἀκρότατον ἄγει τὴν νύμφην διὰ τῶν ἐπαίνων ὁ λόγος
φρέαρ αὐτὴν ὀνομάσας ὕδατος ζῶντος καὶ ῥοιζοῦντος ἀπὸ τοῦ λιβάνου· ἃ
γὰρ περὶ τῆς ζωοποιοῦ μεμαθήκαμεν φύσεως παρὰ τῆς ἁγίας γραφῆς, νῦν
μὲν τῆς προφητείας λεγούσης ἐκ προσώπου τοῦ θεοῦ ὅτι Ἐμὲ ἐγκατέλιπον
πηγὴν ὕδατος ζῶντος, πάλιν δὲ τοῦ κυρίου πρὸς τὴν Σαμαρεῖτιν εἰπόντος Εἰ
35 ᾔδεις τὴν δωρεὰν τοῦ θεοῦ καὶ τίς ἐστιν ὁ λέγων σοι· δός μοι πιεῖν, σὺ ἂν

burial (even as the sublime Gospel records that the One who tasted death on our behalf [Heb 2:9] was prepared for his burial by these very spices [John 19:39]). By *finest perfumes,* on the other hand, the text signifies purity and liberation from unprincipled villainy. Amos brings a corresponding reproach against those who make use of such perfumes in order to live luxuriously. He says, "Those who drink filtered wine and are anointed with the finest perfumes...;" and before this, "Those who eat," says he, | "goats from the flock and young lambs from the herds, and those who beat time with musical instruments" (Amos 6:4–7). The assumption is that no dregs render the wine cloudy and that no adulteration spoils the purity of the perfume's fragrance. In the case of this text, however, one must suppose that the prophecy is upbraiding the Israelites on the ground that, even though they filled themselves with the unmixed word of the Scriptures, from which any sediment had been filtered out, and possessed the unadulterated fragrance of the perfumes, and took their pleasure in the spiritual feast, they had no profit from these luxuries because their choice of wrong transformed the clarity of the wine into its turgid contrary and spoiled the purity of the *finest perfumes* by adulterating them with evil thoughts. In the case of our text, however, the Word attests the integrity and purity of the Bride's teachings by allusion to the fruitfulness of the chief perfumes.

But not even here does the Bride come to a halt in her "stretching forward" (cf. Phil 3:13) to higher things, nor does the Word cease to work together with her in her ascent. For she who puts forth from her mouth gardens of pomegranates and spices now becomes a *fountain* that waters the gardens that stem from her. It is not, as we learn in the case of Paul and Apollos (cf. 1 Cor 3:6), that one person plants and another waters. On the contrary, it is the Bride who does both jobs, at once planting the gardens and watering them.

| Or perhaps this word of praise contains a message that is more sublime still. For it does not say that she is the source of a running stream but *of gardens:* she gushes and shoots forth, not streams of water, but actual gardens. It is in this way that the divine apostle gushed forth ensouled "gardens," among whom he came, giving birth by his teaching to the paradise that is the church.

The Word with his praises brings the Bride to her greatest height by calling her *a spring of water that is living and that flows from frankincense.* As to these things, we know from the Scriptures that they pertain to the life-giving Nature, since on the one hand the prophecy says, in the very person of God, "They have deserted me, the fountain of living waters" (Jer 2:13); and then, on the other hand, the Lord says to the Samaritan woman, "If you knew the gift of God and who it is that is saying to you, 'Give me a drink,' you would

ἤτησας αὐτὸν καὶ ἔδωκεν ἄν σοι ὕδωρ ζῶν· καὶ Εἴ τις διψᾷ, ἐρχέσθω πρός με καὶ πινέτω· ὁ γὰρ πιστεύων εἰς ἐμέ, καθὼς εἶπεν ἡ γραφή, ποταμοὶ ἐκ τῆς κοιλίας αὐτοῦ ῥεύσουσιν ὕδατος ζῶντος. τοῦτο δὲ ἔλεγε περὶ τοῦ πνεύματος   293 οὗ ἤμελλον λαμβάνειν οἱ πιστεύοντες εἰς αὐτόν—πανταχοῦ τοίνυν τῆς θείας 5   φύσεως διὰ τοῦ ζῶντος ὕδατος νοουμένης | ἐνταῦθα ἡ ἀψευδὴς μαρτυρία τοῦ λόγου φρέαρ ὕδατος ζῶντος τὴν νύμφην εἶναι συνίστησιν, ᾧ ἐκ τοῦ λιβάνου ἐστὶν ἡ φορά. τοῦτο δὲ τὸ πάντων παραδοξότατον· πάντων γὰρ τῶν φρεάτων ἐν συστήματι τὸ ὕδωρ ἐχόντων μόνη ἡ νύμφη διεξοδικὸν ἐν ἑαυτῇ ἔχει τὸ ὕδωρ, ὥστε τὸ μὲν βάθος ἔχειν τοῦ φρέατος, τοῦ ποταμοῦ δὲ τὸ ἀεικίνητον. 10   τίς ἂν κατ᾽ ἀξίαν ἐφίκοιτο τῶν ὑποδεικνυμένων θαυμάτων ὡς διὰ τῆς νῦν γενομένης αὐτῇ ὁμοιώσεως; τάχα οὐκέτι ἔχει ὅπου ἑαυτὴν ὑπεράρῃ διὰ πάντων ὁμοιωθεῖσα πρὸς τὸ ἀρχέτυπον κάλλος· μεμίμηται γὰρ δι᾽ ἀκριβείας τῇ μὲν πηγῇ τὴν πηγήν, τῇ δὲ ζωῇ τὴν ζωήν, τὸ δὲ ὕδωρ τῷ ὕδατι· ζῶν γὰρ ὁ λόγος ἐστὶ τοῦ θεοῦ, ζῇ καὶ ἡ τὸν λόγον δεξαμένη ψυχή· ἐκεῖνο τὸ ὕδωρ ἐκ 15   τοῦ θεοῦ ῥεῖ, καθώς φησιν ἡ πηγὴ ὅτι Ἐκ τοῦ θεοῦ ἐξῆλθον καὶ ἥκω, αὕτη δὲ περιέχει τὸ εἰσρέον τῷ τῆς ψυχῆς φρέατι καὶ διὰ τοῦτο γίνεται ταμιεῖον τοῦ ζῶντος ἐκείνου ὕδατος τοῦ ἐκ τοῦ λιβάνου ῥέοντος, μᾶλλον δὲ ῥοιζοῦντος, καθὼς ὁ λόγος ὠνόμασεν· οὗ καὶ ἡμεῖς γενοίμεθα μέτοχοι κτησάμενοι τὸ φρέαρ ἐκεῖνο, ἵνα κατὰ τὸ τῆς σοφίας παράγγελμα ἡμέτερον πίνωμεν ὕδωρ 20   καὶ μὴ ἀλλότριον ἐν Χριστῷ Ἰησοῦ   294

| τῷ κυρίῳ ἡμῶν, ᾧ ἡ δόξα εἰς τοὺς αἰῶνας τῶν αἰώνων. ἀμήν.

ask him, and he would give you living water" (John 4:10)—not to mention, "If anyone is thirsty, let him come to me and drink; for those who believe in me, as the Scripture says, 'Rivers of water shall flow from their hearts.' Now this he said concerning the Spirit, whom those who believe in him were going to receive" (John 7:37–38). Everywhere, then, it is the divine Nature that is understood when living water is mentioned, | and here in our text the truthful witness of the Word constitutes the Bride *a well of living water,* the direction of whose flow is *from frankincense.* And the most unbelievable thing of all is this: that of all the wells that contain a mass of water, only the Bride contains within herself water that is in transit, so as to possess a well's depth, but at the same time a river's unceasing motion.

Who could worthily attain to the wonderful things that are signified by the likeness[26] that now attaches to the Bride? Perhaps she no longer has anywhere further to be lifted up to, now that she has been made like to the archetypal Beauty—for by the fountain, the Fount is exactly imitated; by her life, the life; by her water, the Water. The Word of God is living, and the soul that has received the Word is alive. That water flows out from God, even as the Fount says: "I have come from God, and to God I go" (John 8:42); and she contains the inflow within the well of her soul and so becomes the storehouse of that living water that flows *from frankincense*—or rather *gushes,* as the Word has phrased it. And may we too, having taken possession of that well, become participants in that water, so that in accordance with Wisdom's injunction, we may drink not of strange water but of the water that is ours (cf. Prov 5:15) in Christ Jesus |our Lord,

To whom glory belongs to the ages of ages.
Amen.

---

26. I.e., the divine likeness.

Λόγος ι'

Ἐξεγέρθητι, βορρᾶ, καὶ ἔρχου, νότε,
διάπνευσον κῆπόν μου καὶ ῥευσάτωσαν ἀρώματά μου.
καταβήτω ὁ ἀδελφιδός μου εἰς κῆπον αὐτοῦ

καὶ φαγέτω καρπὸν ἀκροδρύων αὐτοῦ.
5   Κατέβην εἰς κῆπόν μου, ἀδελφή μου νύμφη,

ἐτρύγησα σμύρναν μου μετὰ ἀρωμάτων μου
ἔφαγον ἄρτον μου μετὰ μέλιτός μου,
ἔπιον οἶνόν μου μετὰ γάλακτός μου.
φάγετε, οἱ πλησίον μου,
10   καὶ πίετε καὶ μεθύσθητε, ἀδελφοί μου.

Ἐγὼ καθεύδω καὶ ἡ καρδία μου ἀγρυπνεῖ.

    Τῆς νῦν προτεθείσης ἡμῖν τῶν θείων ῥητῶν θεωρίας ἐκ τῆς τοῦ Ἄισματος
τῶν Ἀισμάτων ἀκολουθίας δυσεφικτά τινα καὶ κεκαλυμμένα δι' ἀσαφείας ἐν
ἀπορρήτοις περιεχούσης νοήματα μείζονος ἡμῖν προσοχῆς ἐστι χρεία, μᾶλλον
15   δὲ πλείονος τῆς διὰ τῶν εὐχῶν συνεργίας καὶ τῆς παρὰ τοῦ ἁγίου πνεύματος
ὁδηγίας, ὡς ἂν μὴ ταὐτὸν πάθοιμεν | ἐπὶ τῆς τῶν ὑψηλῶν τούτων θαυμάτων   295
ἐκπλήξεως, ὅπερ καὶ ἐπὶ τῶν ἀστέρων πάσχειν εἰώθαμεν· καὶ γὰρ ἐκείνων
πόρρωθεν τὸ κάλλος θαυμάζοντες οὐδεμίαν μηχανὴν πρὸς τὴν κτῆσιν αὐτῶν
ἐπινοῆσαι δυνάμεθα, ἀλλὰ μία τοῦ κάλλους αὐτῶν ἐστιν ἡμῖν ἡ ἀπόλαυσις
20   τὸ θαυμαστικῶς περὶ τὸ φαινόμενον ἔχειν. ἀστέρες γάρ τινές εἰσιν ἀτεχνῶς
αἱ τῶν θείων τούτων λογίων μαρμαρυγαί τε καὶ λαμπηδόνες τῶν τῆς ψυχῆς
ὀμμάτων ὑπερλάμπουσαί τε καὶ ὑπερκείμεναι Κατὰ τὸ ὕψος τοῦ οὐρανοῦ ἀπὸ
τῆς γῆς, ὥς φησιν ὁ προφήτης.
    εἰ δὲ γένοιτο καὶ περὶ τὴν ἡμετέραν ψυχήν, ὃ περὶ τὸν Ἠλίαν ἀκούομεν,
25   καὶ ἀναληφθεῖσα τῷ πυρίνῳ ἅρματι ἡμῶν ἡ διάνοια μετάρσιος πρὸς τὰ
οὐράνια κάλλη μετατεθείη (πνεῦμα δὲ ἅγιον εἶναι τὸ πῦρ ἐννοήσομεν,
ὅπερ βαλεῖν ἐπὶ τὴν γῆν ἦλθεν ὁ κύριος, τὸ ἐν γλωσσῶν εἴδει τοῖς μαθηταῖς
μεριζόμενον), οὐκ ἀπ' ἐλπίδος ἡμῖν γενήσεται τὸ πλησιάσαι τούτοις τοῖς
ἄστροις, τοῖς θείοις λέγω νοήμασι, τοῖς διὰ τῶν οὐρανίων τε καὶ πνευματικῶν
30   λογίων τὰς ψυχὰς ἡμῶν | περιαστράπτουσιν.   296

HOMILY 10
Song 4:16–5:2a

¹⁶*Away, north wind, and come, south wind!*
And blow through my garden,
and let my fragrances flow out.

¹*Let my kinsman come down into his garden,*
and eat the fruit of his fruit trees.

I am come into my garden, my sister, my bride:
I have gathered my myrrh with my spices;
I have eaten my bread with my honey;
I have drunk my wine with my milk.
You who are close to me, eat!
And you, my brethren, drink and be drunken!

²*I sleep, but my heart is awake.*

The task now set before us of probing these divine words taken from the Song of Songs involves thoughts that are difficult to understand and, because of their obscurity, hidden and ineffable. We have need, therefore, of greater diligence—or better, of greater assistance through prayer and of guidance on the part of the Holy Spirit—lest we suffer the same paralysis of mind | in the case of these sublime wonders that we regularly undergo in the face of the stars. For when we marvel from afar at the beauty of the stars, we are unable to conceive any method for laying hold on them, but our one way of delighting in their beauty is to be seized with wonder at their appearance. Yet the sparklings and shinings of these divine oracles truly are, after all, stars of a sort, which shine out in a way that, in the words of the prophet, transcends the eyes of the soul "as the height of the heaven is high above the earth" (Ps 102:11).

Should it, though, come to pass for our soul, as we learn that it did for Elijah (4 Kgdms 2:11), to have our understanding seized up in a fiery chariot and carried on high toward the beauty of the heavens (and we know that the fire is the Holy Spirit that the Lord came to cast upon the earth [Luke 12:49] and that was shared among the disciples in the form of tongues [Acts 2:3]), it will not be beyond hope that we should draw near to these stars—and I mean the divine thoughts that in the heavenly and spiritual oracles | flash about our souls.

ἀνάβλεψον γὰρ τῷ τῆς ψυχῆς ὀφθαλμῷ, πρὸς σὲ λέγω τὸν ἀκροατὴν
τὴν πρὸς τὸν πατριάρχην γενομένην παρὰ τοῦ κυρίου φωνήν, Ἀνάβλεψον
εἰς τὸν οὐρανὸν τοῦτον καὶ ἴδε τοὺς ἀστέρας τούτους, εἰ δύνασαι αὐτῶν
ἐκμετρῆσαι τῶν νοημάτων τὸ ὕψος, βλέπε τὴν ἐξουσίαν τῆς βασιλίδος ἐκ τῶν
5   προσταγμάτων αὐτῆς τὴν δυναστείαν κατανοήσας, ὡς αὐτοκρατορική τις
αὐθεντία τοῖς λεγομένοις ἐμφαίνεται· οὐ δι᾽ εὐχῆς κατορθοῖ ὅπερ βούλεται
ἀλλὰ κατὰ τὴν ἀψευδῆ τοῦ ἐπαγγειλαμένου φωνήν, ὅς φησι τὸν πιστὸν καὶ
φρόνιμον οἰκονόμον πάντων τῶν ὑπαρχόντων τῷ δεσπότῃ κύριον γίνεσθαι.
ταύτης ἐπιλαβομένη τῆς ἐξουσίας βασιλικῶς ἑαυτῇ διοικεῖται τὰ καταθύμια
10   τῶν δύο ἀνέμων, τὸν μὲν βορρᾶν διὰ προστάγματος ἑαυτῆς ἀφορίζουσα, τὸν
δὲ νότον φιλοφρόνως καλοῦσα καὶ πρὸς ἑαυτὴν ἐλθεῖν κατεπείγουσα.
Ἔχει δὲ ἡ λέξις οὕτως· Ἐξεγέρθητι, βορρᾶ, καὶ ἔρχου, νότε. τάχα τι
συγγενὲς ἔστι τοῖς λεγομένοις εὑρεῖν ἐν τοῖς τοῦ ἑκατοντάρχου λόγοις, οὓς
αὐτὸς ὁ θεὸς λόγος ἐθαύμασε, καθὼς ὁ εὐαγγελιστὴς διηγήσατο λέγων ὅτι
15   Ἀκούσας δὲ ὁ Ἰησοῦς ἐθαύμασε καὶ ὑπερέθηκε τῆς τοῦ | Ἰσραὴλ πίστεως τὴν   297
τοῦ ἑκατοντάρχου φωνήν· οὐ γὰρ πρὸς τὸν λαόν μοι δοκεῖ τὸν Ἰσραηλιτικὸν
ποιεῖσθαι τοῦ ἑκατοντάρχου τὴν σύγκρισιν ἐν τῷ τῆς πίστεως λόγῳ ἀλλὰ
πρὸς αὐτὸν ἐκεῖνον τὸν Ἰσραήλ, ὃς ἐν τῇ πρὸς τὸν ἀντικείμενον πάλῃ
μετὰ τῆς τοῦ θεοῦ συμμαχίας μόγις τὸ πτῶμα διέφυγεν οὐκ ἀκριβῶς τῆς
20   τοῦ ἀντιπάλου βλάβης ἔξω γενόμενος· ἐν γὰρ τῷ μηρῷ τὸ πάθος ἐδέξατο.
οὗτος δὲ ὁ ἑκατοντάρχης, περὶ οὗ νῦν ὁ λόγος ἐστί, βασιλικῇ τινι δυνάμει
τὸ ἀλλότριον κατ᾽ ἐξουσίαν ἀποπεμπόμενος οἰκειοῦται τὸ καταθύμιον· ἐπὶ
τούτῳ γάρ μοι δοκεῖ μάλιστα τετυχηκέναι τοῦ θαύματος ὁ ἀνήρ, ὅτι φησὶν ἐν
τοῖς ὑποχειρίοις αὐτοῦ στρατιώταις ἐν αὐθεντικῇ ἐξουσίᾳ ἀποπέμπεσθαί τε ὃν
25   βούλεται καὶ προσκαλεῖσθαι τὸν καταθύμιον καὶ τῷ δούλῳ τὴν καθήκουσαν
ἐπιτάττειν ὑπηρεσίαν.
κἀκεῖ γὰρ φιλοσοφία τίς ἐστιν ἡ τοῦ ἑκατοντάρχου φωνή, ὅτι τὸν ἅπαξ
ἀποπεμφθέντα οὐκέτι πρὸς ἑαυτὸν ἐπανάγει, ἀλλὰ τούτου ἀποφοιτήσαντος
ἕτερον ἀντ᾽ αὐτοῦ εἰσοικίζεται (Τούτῳ γὰρ εἰπὼν ὅτι πορεύθητι, καὶ
30   πορεύεται, ἄλλον προσκαλεῖσθαί φησιν, οὐχ ὃν ἀπεπέμψατο) παιδεύοντος

Gaze upward with the eye of the soul! To you who have heard the word
that came to the patriarch from the Lord I say: "Gaze upward into this heaven
and see if you can measure out the sublimity of the thoughts that these stars
signify" (cf. Gen 15:5). Contemplate the mighty authority of the Queen[1]
when, from the commands she gives, you have grasped the extent of her
power and seen how her sovereign authority is manifested in her words. For
she does not bring about what she wills by praying, but in a way that accords
with the truthful saying of the One who has made a promise—and his word
is that the wise and faithful steward became the lord of all his master's possessions (cf. Luke 12:42–48 // Matt 24:45–51). Once she has received this power,
she royally rules the minds of the two winds for her own purposes. By her
very own command she dismisses the north wind while in a friendly manner
she calls to the south wind and urges it to come to her.

So the text runs: *Away,*[2] *north wind, and come, south wind!* Perhaps there
is a parallel to these words in those of the centurion, at which the Word of
God himself was astonished, even as the Evangelist relates when he says,
"When Jesus heard this, he was astonished" (Matt 8:10), and ranked the
words of the centurion above | the faith of Israel.[3] For it does not seem to me
that the Lord's observation about faith compares the centurion to the Israelite
people but to Israel himself,[4] who with the aid of God only just escaped being
defeated in his wrestling match with the Adversary and did not actually avoid
harm at his rival's hand but was hurt in his thigh. As to this centurion whom
we are now discussing, he obtains his wish by dispatching, with a power royal
in character, another agent under his authority. For it also seems to me that
the man got his miracle precisely because of his assertion that with genuine
authority he dispatched whomever he wished and summoned whomever he
wanted, and also set his slave the appropriate task of service.

And here the centurion's statement (cf. Matt 8:9; Luke 7:8) contains a
word of philosophy, for he does not recall the soldier who has once been
sent away, but when the one has departed, he takes another to himself in the
former's stead (for when he has said "to this one, 'Go,' and he goes," he states

---

1. I.e., here, the Bride of the Song, who is given the title "queen" because she gives commands to the winds.

2. The Greek ἐξεγέρθητι would to almost anyone but Gregory mean "Rise up!" or "Awake!"
Gregory, however, for reasons that appear in his discussion of the connotations of "north" in the
Scriptures (see below, pp. 300–301 [Jaeger]), stresses the preposition ἐξ- with which the verb is
compounded and takes it to mean something like "Up and out with you!"

3. Matt. 8:10. Gregory evidently reads the text known to us from the Codex Sinaiticus, the
Codex Ephraemi, and others: "nor have I found such faith in Israel." Nestle preferred the reading of the Codex Vaticanus: "Nor have I found such faith with anyone in Israel."

4. I.e., the patriarch Jacob (cf. Gen 32:28).

οἶμαι τοῦ λόγου τὸ τοιοῦτον δόγμα ὅτι τὰ ἀλλήλοις ἀντικείμενα τῷ αὐτῷ μετ'
ἀλλήλων | συνεπιχωριάζειν φύσιν οὐκ ἔχει· οὐδεμία γὰρ κοινωνία φωτὶ πρὸς   298
σκότος, φησὶν ὁ ἀπόστολος, ἀλλ' ἀνάγκη πᾶσα τοῦ σκότους ἐκχωρήσαντος
φῶς εἶναι τὸ ἀντ' ἐκείνου ὁρώμενον καὶ τῆς κακίας ἐκποδὼν γενομένης
5   τὴν ἀρετὴν ἀντεισάγεσθαι, τούτου δὲ κατορθωθέντος μηκέτι τὸ φρόνημα
τῆς σαρκὸς ἀνταίρειν τῷ πνεύματι (μηδὲ γὰρ δύνασθαι νεκρωθείσης αὐτοῦ
τῆς εἰς τὸ ἀντιτείνειν δυνάμεως), ἀλλὰ πρὸς πᾶσαν καθήκουσαν ὑπηρεσίαν
εὔθετον γίνεσθαι τῇ δυναστείᾳ τοῦ πνεύματος ἐπιπειθὲς ὑπάρχον καὶ
ὑποχείριον. ὅταν γὰρ ἀποδιωχθῇ μὲν ὁ τῆς κακίας σύμμαχος στρατιώτης,
10   ἀντεισέλθῃ δὲ ὁ τῆς ἀρετῆς ὁπλίτης ἐνδεδυκὼς τὸν θώρακα τῆς δικαιοσύνης
καὶ τὴν μάχαιραν τοῦ πνεύματος διὰ χειρὸς φέρων, προβαλλόμενος δὲ τὰ
σκεπαστήρια τῶν ὅπλων· τήν τε περικεφαλαίαν τοῦ σωτηρίου καὶ τὸν θυρεὸν
τῆς πίστεως, καὶ πᾶσαν φέρων ἐν ἑαυτῷ τὴν πνευματικὴν πανοπλίαν, τότε
φοβεῖται τὸν ἑαυτοῦ κύριον τὸν νοῦν ὁ δοῦλος τὸ σῶμα καὶ προθύμως τὰ τοῦ
15   κρατοῦντος παραγγέλματα δέχεται, δι' ὧν ἡ ἀρετὴ κατορθοῦται τῇ ὑπουργίᾳ
τοῦ σώματος. τοῦτο γὰρ ἐνδείκνυται τοῦ ἑκατοντάρχου ὁ λόγος εἰπὼν ὅτι
Καὶ τῷ δούλῳ μου λέγω· ποίησον τοῦτο, καὶ ποιεῖ.
    Ἀλλ' ἀκούσωμεν τῆς βασιλίδος, ὅπως ἀπανίστησιν ἀφ' ἑαυτῆς τὸν
βορρᾶν εἰς τὸ ἔμπαλιν αὐτοῦ τὴν πνοὴν ἀναστρέψασα· οὐ γὰρ ἠρεμεῖν
20   ἐπιτάσσει, καθάπερ ἐπὶ | τοῦ κλυδωνίου τῆς θαλάσσης ὁ κύριος εἰς ἡσυχίαν   299
ἄγει τὴν λαίλαπα σιωπᾶν παραγγείλας τοῖς κύμασιν, ἀλλ' ἀποχωρεῖν καὶ
φεύγειν παρακελεύεται, ὡς ἂν ἀκωλύτως ὁ νότος ῥέοι μηδεμιᾶς ἀντιπνοίας
ἐμποδιζούσης αὐτοῦ τὴν φοράν, Ἐξεγέρθητι λέγουσα τῷ βορρᾷ.
    τίς δὲ ἡ αἰτία τῆς τοῦ ἀνέμου τούτου μεταναστάσεως; Σκληρὸς ἄνεμος
25   ὁ βορρᾶς ἐστι, φησὶ [ποῦ τοῦτο;] τῆς Παροιμίας ὁ λόγος, ὀνόματι δὲ
ἐπιδέξιος καλεῖται. ἀλλ' οὐδενὶ δεξιὸς ὁ βορρᾶς πλὴν εἴ τις κατὰ νώτου τὴν
ἀνατολὴν ἔχοι πρὸς τὰς δυσμὰς τὸν δρόμον ποιούμενος. νοεῖς δὲ πάντως
τῶν λεγομένων τὸ αἴνιγμα, ὅτι ὁ τῆς ἀνατολῆς ἀποστάς (οὕτω γὰρ παρὰ τῆς
προφητείας ὁ Χριστὸς ὀνομάζεται) καὶ πρὸς τὰς δυσμὰς τοῦ φωτὸς ἑαυτὸν
30   συνελαύνων, ὅπου ἐστὶν ἡ ἐξουσία τοῦ σκότους, δεξιὸν ἔχει ἐφ' ἑαυτοῦ τὸν

that he summons another, and not the one he sent away). By this, I think, the Word teaches us the basic truth that things that are contrary to one another cannot naturally | be together in the same place. For "darkness and light," says the apostle, have nothing "in common" (2 Cor 6:14), but when darkness departs it is strictly necessary that light be visible in its place, and when evil has gone away, that good be introduced in its stead—and once this has been accomplished, that "the mind of the flesh" (Rom 8:7; cf. 7:23) no longer rebel against the spirit (for it cannot do so when its power of resistance has been killed), but that instead it become available for every appropriate service, rendered obedient and submissive by the spirit's power. For when the mercenary in alliance with evil has been put to flight, virtue's soldier enters in his place, having put on "the breastplate of righteousness" and bearing in his hand "the sword of the spirit," with his defenses—"the helmet of salvation" and "the shield of faith" (Eph 6:14–15)—ready and bearing within himself the whole spiritual panoply. And then the slave that is the body trembles before its lord, the intellect,[5] and eagerly accepts the commands of its ruler, by which, with the body's assistance, virtue is achieved. This is what is indicated by the centurion's saying: "I say to my slave, 'Do this,' and he does it" (Matt 8:9 // Luke 7:8).

But let us attend to the Queen and hear how she sends the north wind away from her, turning its blast backwards. For she does not order it to be silent as, | in the storm at sea, the Lord quieted the great storm by commanding the waves to be silent (cf. Luke 8:23–24). Rather, by saying *Away!* to the north wind she enjoins it to retire and flee,[6] so that the south wind may blow uninhibited, with no contrary blast to impede its course.

But what is the reason for this wind's dismissal? "The north is a harsh wind," says the book of Proverbs <where?[7]>, "and its name is called 'On the Right Hand'" (Prov 27:16). But the north wind is not to the right of anyone unless it is someone whose back is to the east and who is heading to the west. So now you grasp the concealed meaning of the saying: that he who has departed from the east (for so the Christ is named in the prophecy [cf. Zech 6:12]) and impels himself toward the setting sun, where the power of

---

5. Here Gregory seems to identify the human "intellect" (νοῦς) with the "spirit" of which he has been speaking. The equivalence of *human* spirit with intellect was in Gregory's day a commonplace, whose origin apparently lay in the writings of Philo of Alexandria and whose acceptance was not discouraged by the language of Rom 7.

6. See above, n. 2.

7. As Langerbeck notes in his *apparatus* (1960, 299), this expression—in the Greek, ποῦ τοῦτο;—is probably the insertion of a scribe who did not know where in Proverbs the quotation was to be found.

βορρᾶν τοῖς πονηροῖς ἐφοδίοις αὐτὸν δεξιούμενον, δι' ὧν ὁ πρὸς τὸ σκότος γίνεται δρόμος. οὕτως εὑρίσκει τὸν βορρᾶν ἑαυτοῦ δεξιὸν ὁ ἀκόλαστος τῷ πάθει τῆς ἀτιμίας συμπνέοντα, οὕτω γίνεται τῷ πλεονέκτῃ δεξιὸν τὸ πνεῦμα τοῦτο τῆς πονηρίας, ὅταν αὐτῷ τὰς ὕλας | τῆς πλεονεξίας οἷόν τινα ψάμμον ἢ   300
5   κόνιν περισωρεύῃ, οὕτω πρὸς ἕκαστον τῶν πλημμελημάτων τὴν παρ' ἑαυτοῦ συνεργίαν χαριζόμενος ἐπιδέξιος γίνεται, οἷς ἂν γένηται, σκληρὸς μὲν κατὰ τὴν φύσιν ὤν, ἐπικρύπτων δὲ ταῖς ἡδοναῖς τὸ ἀντίτυπον.
      διὰ τοῦτο φυγαδεύει τῆς ἰδίας ἀρχῆς τὸν βορρᾶν ἡ κατὰ τῶν παθῶν ἀναδησαμένη τὸ κράτος Ἐξεγέρθητι λέγουσα ὦ βορρᾶ. διὰ τί δὲ τῷ
10 ὀνόματι τούτῳ ἡ ἀντικειμένη διασημαίνεται δύναμις, παντὶ δῆλον ἂν εἴη τῷ κατανενοηκότι τὴν τῶν ὄντων φύσιν. τίς γὰρ οὐκ οἶδε τοῦ ἡλίου τὴν κίνησιν, ὅτι ἐκ τῶν ἀνατολῶν διὰ τοῦ νοτίου τὸν δρόμον ποιούμενος πρὸς τὰς δυσμὰς ἐπικλίνεται; τὸ δὲ σχῆμα τῆς γῆς σφαιροειδὲς ὄν, καθώς φασιν οἱ τὰ τοιαῦτα κατανοήσαντες, ἐν ᾧπερ ἂν τῷ ἡλίῳ περιλαμφθῇ, κατὰ πᾶσαν ἀνάγκην ἐν
15 τῷ ἀντικειμένῳ σκοτίζεται τῇ ἀντιφράξει τοῦ ναστοῦ σκιαζόμενον. ἐπεὶ οὖν ἀφεγγὴς ὁ τόπος ἐκεῖνος καὶ κατεψυγμένος εἰς ἀεὶ διαμένει μήτε λαμπόμενος ὑπὸ τῶν ἡλιακῶν ἀκτίνων μήτε θαλπόμενος, διὰ τοῦτο τὸν ἄρχοντα τῆς ἐξουσίας τοῦ σκότους, τὸν τὴν ἁπαλὴν τῶν ψυχῶν φύσιν | ὕδατος δίκην   301 ἀπολιθοῦντα διὰ τῆς πήξεως καὶ σκληρὰν ἐργαζόμενον, βορρᾶν τε καὶ
20 σκληρὸν ὀνομάζει ὁ λόγος, τὸν τῆς κατηφείας τοῦ χειμῶνος ἐργάτην, ἐκείνου λέγω τοῦ χειμῶνος, ἐν ᾧ τὴν φυγὴν τῶν κινδύνων ἀμήχανον λέγει τὸ εὐαγγέλιον· ἐν αὐτῷ γὰρ τῶν κατ' ἀρετὴν ἀνθούντων ἡ ὥρα μαραίνεται.
      Καλῶς οὖν ἀπελαύνει τοῦτον κατ' ἐξουσίαν ἡ τῆς βασιλίδος φωνή, προσκαλεῖται δὲ τὸ μεσημβρινὸν πνεῦμα τὸ θερμόν τε καὶ ἀείφεγγες, ὅπερ
25 ὀνομάζει νότον, δι' οὗ ὁ χειμάρρους τῆς τρυφῆς ῥέει, λέγουσα Καὶ ἔρχου, νότε, διάπνευσον κῆπόν μου καὶ ῥευσάτωσαν ἀρώματά μου, ὥστε τῇ βιαίᾳ πνοῇ, καθὼς ἐν τῷ ὑπερῴῳ γεγενῆσθαι τοῖς μαθηταῖς ἀκούομεν, τοῖς ἐμψύχοις

darkness resides, has the north wind at his right hand to welcome him by providing the evil things he needs for his journey toward darkness. Thus the intemperate person finds the north wind at his right hand gusting in unison with his ignoble passion. In the same way this wicked wind comes to the right hand of the greedy individual and heaps up about him the matter | for his greed, like so much sand or dust. In the same way the north wind is at hand to bestow its cooperation freely in each and every sin or fault, and for those to whom it comes, since it is "harsh" by nature, it cloaks its repellent character with pleasures.

For this reason she who is restraining the power of the passions banishes the north wind from her realm, saying *Away, north wind!* And as to the reason why the opposing Power is referred to by this title,[8] that must be obvious to everyone who has an understanding of the nature of things. Who does not know how the sun moves, how, starting from the east, it inclines toward the west, making its way through the south? Now since the earth is shaped like a sphere,[9] as the experts in such matters tell us, it is strictly necessary that the side of the earth opposite to that illumined by the sun should be in darkness, cast into shadow by the interposed mass. Since, then, that place is without light and remains forever cold, neither lit nor warmed by the sun's rays, the scriptural text sets the names *north wind* and "harsh" to the Prince of the power of darkness. He hardens the malleable nature of souls by freezing them | like water and so renders them "harsh." He is the one who contrives the gloom of winter, that winter, I mean, in which, as the Gospel says, flight from danger is impossible (Matt 24:20 // Mark 13:18). In that winter, the splendor of virtue's flowers withers away.

So it is a good thing that the voice of the Queen, in tones of authority, should send him packing, while summoning to her presence the warm and ever bright noontide wind.[10] This wind, which makes the pleasant streams of the springtime thaw flow forth, she calls "south," and she says, "*Come, O south wind, blow through my garden, and let my fragrances be made to flow,* so that with that 'mighty blast' (Acts 1:15)[11]—just as we hear it happened for the

---

8. See Origen, *Princ.* 2.8.3, which seems to be a source, directly or indirectly, of Gregory's explanation here.

9. This was the common view of Greek science since before the time of Plato, whose dialogue *Timaeus* presupposes such an idea.

10. The Greek word translated by "wind" here is πνεῦμα, which of course can be rendered by "spirit" as well as by "wind" or "breath." Having thus slipped the term into his discourse, Gregory proceeds to play on its ambiguity by taking the south wind as the allegorical equivalent of the divine Spirit.

11. See Acts 2:2, where the "mighty wind [πνοή]" from heaven betokens the descent of "the Holy Spirit" (2:4) upon the disciples.

φυτοῖς ἐπιπεσόντα κινῆσαι τὴν τοῦ θεοῦ φυτείαν πρὸς τὴν τῶν ἀρωμάτων
φορὰν καὶ ῥέειν παρασκευάσαι διὰ τοῦ στόματος τὴν εὐώδη προφητείαν καὶ
τὰ σωτήρια τῆς πίστεως δόγματα κατὰ πᾶν εἶδος γλώσσης ἀκωλύτως τὴν
εὐωδίαν τῶν διδαγμάτων προχέοντα. οὕτως οἱ ἑκατὸν καὶ εἴκοσι μαθηταὶ οἱ
5   ἐν τῷ οἴκῳ τοῦ θεοῦ πεφυτευμένοι τῇ πνοῇ τοῦ τοιούτου νότου τὴν διὰ τῶν
γλωσσῶν διδασκαλίαν ἐξήνθησαν.

διὰ τοῦτο τοίνυν | φησὶ τῷ τοιούτῳ νότῳ ἡ νύμφη ὅτι Διάπνευσον   302
κῆπόν μου, ἐπειδὴ μήτηρ κήπων ἐγένετο παρὰ τῆς τοῦ νυμφίου φωνῆς τοῦ
ποιήσαντος αὐτήν, καθὼς περιέχει ὁ λόγος, Κήπων πηγήν. οὗ χάριν τὸν κῆπον
10   αὐτῆς τὴν ἐκκλησίαν τὴν τοῖς ἐμψύχοις βρύουσαν δένδροις διαπνευσθῆναι
βούλεται, ὥστε ῥεῦσαι ἀπ᾽ αὐτῶν τὰ ἀρώματα· ὁ μὲν γὰρ προφήτης φησὶν ὅτι
Πνεύσεται τὸ πνεῦμα αὐτοῦ καὶ ῥυήσεται ὕδατα, ἡ δὲ τῷ βασιλικῷ πλούτῳ
κομῶσα νύμφη πρὸς τὸ μεγαλοφυέστερον ἐξαλλάσσει τὰ ῥεύματα ἀρωμάτων
ποταμοὺς ποιοῦσα τῶν τοῦ κήπου δένδρων ἐκρέοντας διὰ τῆς βίας τοῦ
15   πνεύματος,

ὥστε διὰ τούτου μαθεῖν τῆς παλαιᾶς διαθήκης πρὸς τὴν καινὴν τὸ
διάφορον, ὅτι ὁ μὲν προφητικὸς ποταμὸς ἐπληρώθη ὑδάτων, ὁ δὲ εὐαγγελικὸς
ἀρωμάτων. τοιοῦτος ποταμὸς ἀρωμάτων ἦν ἐκ τοῦ κήπου τῆς ἐκκλησίας
ῥέων διὰ τοῦ πνεύματος ὁ μέγας Παῦλος, οὗ τὸ ῥεῖθρον Χριστοῦ εὐωδία ἦν,
20   τοιοῦτος ἄλλος ὁ Ἰωάννης, ὁ Λουκᾶς, ὁ Ματθαῖος, ὁ Μᾶρκος καὶ οἱ ἄλλοι
πάντες, τὰ εὐγενῆ φυτὰ τοῦ κήπου τῆς νύμφης, οἳ τῷ φωτεινῷ ἐκείνῳ τῷ
μεσημβρινῷ νότῳ | διαπνευσθέντες πηγαὶ ἀρωμάτων ἐγένοντο βρύοντες τὴν   303
τῶν εὐαγγελίων εὐωδίαν.

Καταβήτω, φησίν, ὁ ἀδελφιδός μου εἰς κῆπον αὐτοῦ καὶ φαγέτω
25   καρπὸν ἀκροδρύων αὐτοῦ. ὢ πεπαρρησιασμένης φωνῆς. ὢ φιλοτίμου τε
καὶ μεγαλοδώρου ψυχῆς πᾶσαν ὑπερβολὴν μεγαλοφροσύνης νικώσης.
τίνα δεξιοῦται πρὸς εὐωχίαν τοῖς ἰδίοις καρποῖς; τίνι παρασκευάζει διὰ τῶν
ἰδίων ἀγαθῶν τὴν πανδαισίαν; τίνα καλεῖ πρὸς τὴν τῶν παρεσκευασμένων
ἑστίασιν; τὸν ἐξ οὗ τὰ πάντα καὶ δι᾽ οὗ τὰ πάντα καὶ ἐν ᾧ τὰ πάντα, τὸν
30   διδόντα τοῖς πᾶσι τροφὴν ἐν εὐκαιρίᾳ, τὸν ἀνοίγοντα τὴν χεῖρα αὐτοῦ καὶ
πληροῦντα πᾶν ζῷον εὐδοκίας, τὸν ἄρτον τὸν ἐκ τοῦ οὐρανοῦ καταβαίνοντα
καὶ ζωὴν διδόντα τῷ κόσμῳ, τὸν πᾶσι τοῖς οὖσι τὴν ζωὴν ἐκ τῆς ἰδίας πηγῆς

disciples—you may fall upon the ensouled plants and move God's plantation to bring forth fragrances, and prepare them, as you pour out the sweet savor of the doctrines, to let sweet-smelling prophecy and the saving teachings[12] of the faith flow from their mouths freely in every type of language. In this way the hundred and twenty disciples who have been planted in the house of God will put forth, by the help of the 'blast' of such a south wind, the blossom of articulate instruction."

Here then is the reason why | the Bride says to such a south wind: *Blow through my garden.* It is because the voice of the Bridegroom, her Creator, constituted her mother of the gardens,[13] as is conveyed by the expression *fountain of gardens* (Song 4:15).[14] Hence she wants her garden, which is the church burgeoning with living trees, to have the wind blow through it so that its fragrances may flow out. The prophet says, after all, "He makes his wind blow, and the waters flow" (Ps 147:7), while the Bride for her part, resplendent with a royal opulence, makes the streams of fragrances ever greater, creating by the power of the wind veritable rivers flowing out from the trees of her garden.

In this way she teaches the difference between the old and the new covenants, that is, that the prophetic river was filled with waters, but the river of the gospel, with fragrances. The great Paul was himself such a river of fragrances (cf. 2 Cor 2:15) issuing from the garden of the church by the agency of the Spirit [πνεῦμα], and his stream was the sweet savor of Christ; and the same can be said of John, of Luke, of Matthew, of Mark, and of all the others, the noble plants of the Bride's garden. Breathed through by that bright noonday wind, | they became fountains of fragrance, bursting with the scent of the Gospels.

Let my kinsman, so it runs, *come down into his garden, and let him eat the fruit of his fruit trees.* What free and outspoken speech! What a generous and munificent soul that has overreached all arrogant extravagance! Whom does she welcome to a feast of her own fruits? For whom does she lay out an ideal banquet with her own good things? Whom does she call to a repast of things ready and prepared? It is the One from whom and through whom and in whom are all things (Rom 11:36), the One who opens his hand and fills every living thing with satisfaction (Ps 144:16), the One who comes down as the bread from heaven and gives life to the cosmos (John 6:33), the One who

---

12. The Greek word here is δόγματα, by which Gregory appears to mean the basic and characteristic teachings of the Christian "school."

13. See Methodius's description of "our Mother the Church" in *Symp.* 8.11 (trans. Musurillo 1958, 116).

14. See above, homily 9, p. 291–92 (Jaeger).

ἐπιρρέοντα· τούτῳ ἡ νύμφη προτίθησι τράπεζαν. κῆπος δέ ἐστιν ἡ τράπεζα ὁ
διὰ τῶν ἐμψύχων δένδρων πεφυτευμένος, ἡμεῖς δὲ τὰ δένδρα, εἴπερ δὴ καὶ
ἡμεῖς, οἱ τροφὴν αὐτῷ προτιθέντες τὴν τῶν ψυχῶν ἡμῶν σωτηρίαν οὕτως
εἰπόντος τοῦ τὴν ἡμετέραν εὐωχουμένου ζωὴν ὅτι Ἐμὸν βρῶμά ἐστιν, ἵνα
5   ποιῶ τὸ θέλημα τοῦ πατρός μου. δῆλος δὲ ὁ σκοπὸς τοῦ θείου θελήματος,
|Ὃς πάντας ἀνθρώπους θέλει σωθῆναι καὶ εἰς ἐπίγνωσιν ἀληθείας ἐλθεῖν.   304
αὕτη οὖν ἐστιν ἡ ἑτοιμασθεῖσα βρῶσις αὐτῷ τὸ σωθῆναι ἡμᾶς. καρπὸς δὲ
ἡμῶν ἡ προαίρεσις γίνεται ἡ τῷ δρεπομένῳ ἡμᾶς θεῷ δι᾽ ἑαυτῆς ὡς διά τινος
ἀκρεμόνος τὴν ψυχὴν ἐγχειρίζουσα. χρὴ δὲ διὰ τούτων ἰδεῖν ὅτι πρότερον ἡ
10 νύμφη τῷ καρπῷ τοῦ μήλου καταγλυκαίνεται εἰποῦσα· Καὶ ὁ καρπὸς αὐτοῦ
γλυκὺς ἐν τῷ λάρυγγί μου· καὶ τότε καρπὸς καὶ αὐτὴ γίνεται ὡραῖός τε καὶ
γλυκάζων καὶ τῷ γεωργῷ πρὸς εὐφροσύνην προκείμενος.

ἡ δὲ τοῦ Καταβήτω λέξις εὐκτικὴν ἔχει τὴν σημασίαν ὁμοιοτρόπως
ἐκφωνηθεῖσα τῷ Ἁγιασθήτω τὸ ὄνομά σου καὶ Γενηθήτω τὸ θέλημά σου· ὡς
15 γὰρ ἐκεῖ τὴν εὐκτικὴν ἔμφασιν ὁ τῶν ῥητῶν ἐκείνων σχηματισμὸς περιέχει,
οὕτω καὶ ἐνταῦθα τὸ Καταβήτω εὐχὴ τῆς νύμφης ἐστὶν ἐπιδεικνυμένης τῷ
θεῷ τῶν τῆς ἀρετῆς ἀκροδρύων τὴν εὐφορίαν.

ἡ δὲ κατάβασις τὸ τῆς φιλανθρωπίας ἔργον διασημαίνει· ἐπειδὴ γὰρ οὐκ
ἔστιν ἄλλως ἀναληφθῆναι ἡμᾶς πρὸς τὸν ὕψιστον, εἰ μὴ πρὸς τὸ χθαμαλὸν
20 ἐπικλιθείη ὁ Ἀναλαμβάνων τοὺς πραεῖς κύριος, διὰ τοῦτο ἡ ἀνιοῦσα πρὸς
τὸ ἄνω ψυχὴ τὴν παρὰ τοῦ ὑπερκειμένου χειραγωγίαν | προσκαλουμένη   305
ὑποκαταβῆναι αὐτὸν τοῦ ἰδίου μεγέθους εὔχεται, ἵνα τοῖς κάτω ἐφικτὸς
γένηται.

ὁ δὲ εἰπὼν διὰ τοῦ προφήτου ὅτι Ἔτι λαλοῦντός σου ἐρεῖ· ἰδοὺ πάρειμι,
25 πρὶν ἐπεξελθεῖν τῇ εὐχῇ τὴν νύμφην, καὶ ἤκουσεν ὧν ἐδεήθη καὶ τῇ ἑτοιμασίᾳ
τῆς καρδίας αὐτῆς προσέσχε καὶ ἐν τῷ κήπῳ ἐγένετο τῷ διαπνευσθέντι ὑπὸ
τοῦ νότου καὶ τοὺς καρποὺς τῶν ἀρωμάτων ἐδρέψατο καὶ τῶν τῆς ἀρετῆς
ἀκροδρύων ἐνεφορήθη καὶ διήγημα τὴν εὐωχίαν πεποίηται λέγων οὑτωσὶ
πρὸς τὴν νύμφην· Κατέβην εἰς κῆπόν μου, ἀδελφή μου νύμφη, ἐτρύγησα
30 σμύρναν μου μετὰ ἀρωμάτων μου, ἔφαγον ἄρτον μου μετὰ μέλιτός μου,
ἔπιον οἶνόν μου μετὰ γάλακτός μου. φάγετε, οἱ πλησίον μου, καὶ πίετε καὶ
μεθύσθητε, ἀδελφοί μου.

from his own wellspring pours life into all beings. For him the Bride sets her table. And the table is a *garden* planted with trees that have souls, and we are the trees—if indeed we are the ones—who have set before him as food the salvation of our souls because the one who feasts on our life has said, "My food is to do the will of my Father" (John 4:34). Now the aim of God's will is clear: | he "wants all people to be saved and to come to a knowledge of truth" (1 Tim 2:4). This, then, is the food that has been readied for him: our salvation. And our *fruit* is the faculty of choice that of its own accord entrusts its soul, as with a branch, to the God who plucks us.[15] In this connection, it is essential to see that prior to this the Bride is filled with sweetness by the apple tree's fruit, when she says: *And his fruit is sweet in my throat* (2:3). And that is the moment when she herself becomes a fruit at once beautiful and sweet-tasting and available for the delight of the husbandman.

The expression *Let ... come down*, though, has an optative sense and says the same sort of thing as "Let your name be hallowed" and "Let your will be done" (Matt 6:9–10); for just as in those cases the grammatical form of the words directly implies a wish or hope, so too in this case the expression *Let ... come down* is a prayer of the Bride as she manifests to God the abundant produce of virtue's trees.

As to the coming down, however, it signifies that which the divine love of humanity brings about. For since there is no way in which we can be seized up on high unless the Lord who "lifts up the meek" (Ps 146:6) bends down to the lowly, the soul that is mounting on high offers a prayer for guidance to the transcendent One, |summoning him to descend from the grandeur that is proper to him in order that he may be accessible to those below.

Now the One who said by the prophet, "While you are still speaking, he will say: 'Behold, I am here'" (Isa 58:9), will at once, before the Bride has completed her petition, have heard what she needs, and taken note of her heart's readiness, and taken his place in her garden through which the south wind has blown, and plucked the aromatic fruits, and filled himself with the produce of virtue, and made his feasting a recital as he says to the Bride: *I have come down*[16] *into my garden, my sister, my bride: I have gathered my myrrh with my spices; I have eaten my bread with my honey; I have drunk my wine with my milk. You who are close to me, eat! And you, my brethren, drink and be drunken!*

---

15. For Methodius (*Symp.* 7.1 [trans. Musurillo 1958, 98]) it is "Christ alone" who plucks "the spices of heaven's fragrance" that grow in the sealed garden of the Bride.

16. Here Gregory substitutes κατέβην for the lxx's εἰσῆλθον, perhaps unconsciously. It fits his exegesis to assimilate "entered" here to the "come down" of the previous verse.

Ὁρᾷς πῶς ὑπερβάλλει τῇ μεγαλοδωρεᾷ τὴν αἴτησιν· ἀρωμάτων ηὔξατο γενέσθαι πηγὰς ἡ νύμφη τὰ ἑαυτῆς ἐν τῷ κήπῳ φυτὰ διαπνευσθέντα τῷ ἐκ μεσημβρίας ἐπιπνέοντι νότῳ καὶ τῷ καρπῷ τῶν ἀκροδρύων τὸν γεωργὸν δεξιώσασθαι (τοῦτο δὲ παντὶ δῆλον ὅτι πᾶσα εὔπνοια τῆς ὀσφραντικῆς
5   αἰσθήσεως ἡδονὴ γίνεται, τὰ δὲ ἀκρόδρυα τῆς τοῦ ἄρτου δυνάμεως κατὰ τὴν βρῶσιν ὡς πρὸς τὴν τῶν τρεφομένων εὐεξίαν ἐστὶν ἀτονώτερα), ὁ δὲ καταβὰς ἐπὶ τὸν ἑαυτοῦ κῆπον καὶ πρὸς τὸ μεῖζόν τε καὶ τιμιώτερον τὴν τῶν καρπῶν μεταβαλὼν φύσιν δρέπεται μὲν ἐκ τοῦ κήπου σμύρναν | 306
εὑρὼν μετὰ ἀρωμάτων αὐτοῦ (παρ' αὐτοῦ γὰρ εἶναι εἴ τι καλόν, ἐν ᾧπερ ἂν
10 εὑρεθῇ, ὁ προφητικὸς ὕμνησε λόγος), ἀντὶ δὲ τῶν ἀκροδρύων ἄρτῳ βρίθειν παρασκευάζει τὰ δένδρα συναναμεμιγμένῳ μετὰ τοῦ μέλιτος αὐτοῦ (καὶ τούτῳ τὸ προφητικὸν συνεκφωνείσθω ὅτι αὐτοῦ τὸ μέλι ὡς καὶ τὰ λοιπὰ τῶν καλῶν) καὶ τὸν οἶνον ἀπ' αὐτοῦ ἀρύεται συνανακεκραμένον τῷ γάλακτι αὐτοῦ· Ἐξ αὐτοῦ γὰρ καὶ δι' αὐτοῦ καὶ εἰς αὐτὸν τὰ πάντα.
15   ὦ μακαρίων κήπων ἐκείνων, ὧν τὰ φυτὰ τοιούτοις βρύειν καρποῖς μεμαρτύρηται, ὡς πρὸς ἅπαν εἶδος τρυφῆς κατὰ τὴν ἐπιθυμίαν τῆς ἀπολαύσεως ἁρμοδίως μεταποιεῖσθαι. τῷ μὲν γὰρ διὰ τῆς εὐωδίας τρυφῶντι σμύρνα γίνεται μετὰ ἀρωμάτων διὰ τῆς τῶν ἐπιγείων μελῶν νεκρότητος τὸν καθαρὸν καὶ εὐώδη μυρεψοῦντα βίον τὸν ἐκ ποικίλων τε καὶ διαφόρων τῶν
20 τῆς ἀρετῆς ἀρωμάτων συγκεραννύμενον, τῷ δὲ τὴν τελειοτέραν ἐπιζητοῦντι τροφὴν ἄρτος γίνεται οὐκέτι ἐπὶ πικρίδων ἐσθιόμενος, ὡς ὁ νόμος διακελεύεται | (πρὸς γὰρ τὸ παρόν ἐστιν ἡ πικρία), ἀλλ' ὄψον ἑαυτοῦ τὸ μέλι   307
ποιούμενος, ὅταν ἐν τῷ ἰδίῳ καιρῷ ὁ καρπὸς τῆς ἀρετῆς καταγλυκαίνῃ τὰ τῆς ψυχῆς αἰσθητήρια (οὗ ἀπόδειξις ὁ μετὰ τὴν ἀνάστασιν τοῦ κυρίου προφανεὶς
25 τοῖς μαθηταῖς ἄρτος ἐστί) τῷ κηρίῳ τοῦ μέλιτος ἡδυνόμενος, τῷ διψῶντι δὲ κρατὴρ γίνεται πλήρης οἴνου καὶ γάλακτος, οὐ σπογγιὰ χολῇ τε καὶ ὄξει διάβροχος, οἵαν οἱ Ἰουδαῖοι τῷ εὐεργέτῃ τὴν φιλοτησίαν διὰ τοῦ καλάμου προτείνουσιν.
         πάντως δὲ οὐκ ἀγνοοῦμεν τὰ τῶν εἰρημένων αἰνίγματα· πῶς δένδρον
30 ἦν σμυρνοφόρον ὁ Παῦλος ὁ καθ' ἡμέραν ἀποθνήσκων καὶ αὐτὸς ἑαυτῷ διδοὺς τὸ τοῦ θανάτου ἀπόκριμα καὶ διὰ καθαρότητός τε καὶ ἀπαθείας ἀρωματίζων ὀσμὴ ζωῆς τοῖς σῳζομένοις γινόμενος, πῶς δὲ σιτοποιεῖ [τῷ κυρίῳ] τὰ ἔμψυχα τοῦ κήπου φυτὰ τῷ δεσπότῃ τοῦ κήπου, οἷς μαρτυρεῖ ὁ

You see how in his generosity he does more than the Bride requested. The Bride prayed that the plants in her garden, breathed through by the wind that blows from the south, might become wellsprings of fragrance and that the husbandman might be welcomed by the fruit of her fruit trees (plain as it is to everyone that though any sweet scent gives pleasure to the sense of smell, fruits are, from the point of view of the health of those who feed on them, less nutritious as nourishment than bread). But the husbandman came down to his garden and changed the nature of the fruit so that they became better and of more worth. | Finding myrrh, he plucked it from the garden with fragrant spices *of his own*[17] (for he is the source of anything lovely, in whatever subject it be found, as the prophetic word once sang [cf. Zech 9:17 LXX]); and instead of fruit, he made the trees hang heavy with bread tinctured with *his* honey (and let the prophetic word be uttered in unison with this as well: the honey is *his* as are the other lovely things); and their wine he draws off mixed with *his* milk. For "from him and through him and for him are all things" (Rom 11:36).

Happy indeed are those gardens whose plants are attested to burgeon so with fruit that they are fit to be turned into every kind of delicacy to accommodate the desire for pleasure! For to one who delights in the sweet scent there comes *myrrh with … fragrances* by way of the mortification of earthly members, fashioning the pure and sweet-scented life that is blended out of the many differing spices of virtue. Then for the one who is seeking more perfect nourishment, bread appears, and it is no longer eaten with "bitter herbs" (Exod 12:8) as the law commands | (for the bitterness is a matter of the here and now) but with honey as its relish, whenever, in its own season, the fruit of virtue, touched with honey, conveys sweetness to the soul's senses (which is demonstrated by the bread that was manifested to the disciples after the Lord's resurrection [John 21:9–14]). And for the one who drinks, the bowl is full of wine and milk. It is not a sponge soaked with vinegar and gall (cf. Matt 27:48), which is the sort of loving-cup that the Jews offered on a reed to the Benefactor.

Nor are we in any way unaware of the enigmatic statements that hint at the sense of these words. Thus Paul, the one who died daily (cf. 1 Cor 15:31), was a myrrh-bearing tree who passed sentence on himself (cf. 2 Cor 1:9) and so, giving off a sweet scent in virtue of his purity and impassibility, became a "fragrance" of life "for those who are being saved" (2 Cor 2:14–15). The

---

17. Gregory notes that throughout Song 5:1 it is the Bridegroom's myrrh, fragrances, bread, and so forth, that are spoken of, not the Bride's; this leads him to the idea that the descent of the Bridegroom into the "garden" of the Bride effects an enhancement or elevation of her "produce."

ἐπὶ τοῦ θρόνου καθήμενος ὅτι Ἐπείνασα καὶ ἐδώκατέ μοι φαγεῖν (ἄρτος γὰρ
εὐφροσύνης ἐστὶν ἡ εὐποιΐα τῷ μέλιτι τῆς ἐντολῆς γλυκαινόμενος), πῶς δὲ
πάλιν οἰνοχοεῖ τῷ νυμφίῳ τὰ εὐερνῆ τοῦ κήπου φυτά, πρὸς οὓς τοῦτό φησιν
ὅτι Ἐδίψησα καὶ ἐποτίσατέ με, γάλακτι τὸν οἶνον | κεράσαντες, οὐχ ὕδατι   308
5   κατὰ τὴν τῶν καπήλων συνήθειαν. τὸ δὲ γάλα ἡ πρώτη τῆς ἀνθρωπίνης
φύσεώς ἐστι τροφή, ἡ καθαρά τε καὶ ἁπλῆ καὶ ὄντως νηπιώδης καὶ ἄδολος
καὶ πάσης πονηρᾶς αἰτίας κεκαθαρμένη.

Ταῦτα εἰπὼν πρὸς τὴν νύμφην ὁ λόγος παρατίθεται τοῖς πλησίον τὰ
τοῦ εὐαγγελίου μυστήρια λέγων Φάγετε, οἱ πλησίον μου, καὶ πίετε καὶ
10   μεθύσθητε, ἀδελφοί μου· τῷ γὰρ ἐπισταμένῳ τὰς μυστικὰς τοῦ εὐαγγελίου
φωνὰς οὐδεμία φανήσεται διαφορὰ τῶν ἐνταῦθα ῥητῶν πρὸς τὴν ἐκεῖ
τοῖς μαθηταῖς γινομένην μυσταγωγίαν· ὡσαύτως γὰρ ἐκεῖ τε καὶ ἐνταῦθά
φησιν ὁ λόγος τὸ Φάγετε καὶ τὸ Πίετε. ἡ δὲ πρὸς τὴν μέθην προτροπή,
ἣν ἐνταῦθα τοῖς ἀδελφοῖς ὁ λόγος πεποίηται, δόξειεν ἂν τοῖς πολλοῖς
15   πλεῖόν τι παρὰ τὸ εὐαγγέλιον ἔχειν. εἰ δέ τις ἀκριβῶς ἐξετάσειεν, καὶ τοῦτο
σύμφωνον τοῖς εὐαγγελικοῖς εὑρεθήσεται· ὅπερ γὰρ ἐνταῦθα τῷ λόγῳ
τοῖς φίλοις παρεκελεύσατο, τοῦτο ἐκεῖ διὰ τῶν ἔργων ἐποίησεν, διότι πᾶσα
μέθη ἔκστασιν εἴωθε ποιεῖν τῆς διανοίας τοῖς κεκρατημένοις ὑπὸ τοῦ οἴνου.
οὐκοῦν ὅπερ ἐνταῦθα προτρέπεται, τοῦτο διὰ τῆς θείας ἐκείνης βρώσεώς τε
20   καὶ πόσεως καὶ τότε ἐγένετο καὶ πάντοτε γίνεται | συνεισιούσης τῇ βρώσει τε   309
καὶ τῇ πόσει τῆς ἀπὸ τῶν χειρόνων πρὸς τὰ βελτίω μεταβολῆς καὶ ἐκστάσεως.
οὕτω μεθύουσι, καθὼς ἡ προφητεία φησίν, οἱ τὴν πιότητα τοῦ οἴκου τοῦ θεοῦ
πίνοντες καὶ τῷ χειμάρρῳ τῆς τρυφῆς ποτιζόμενοι.

ὥσπερ ἐμεθύσθη ποτὲ καὶ ὁ μέγας Δαβίδ, ὅτε ἐκβὰς αὐτὸς ἑαυτοῦ καὶ ἐν
25   ἐκστάσει γενόμενος εἶδε τὸ ἀθέατον κάλλος καὶ τὴν ἀοίδιμον ἐκείνην φωνὴν
ἐξεβόησεν ὅτι Πᾶς ἄνθρωπος ψεύστης, ὁ λόγῳ τῶν ἀφράστων ἀγαθῶν
ἐπιτρέπων τὴν ἑρμηνείαν. οὕτως ἐμεθύσθη καὶ ὁ νεώτερος Βενιαμὶν Παῦλος,
ὅτε ἐν ἐκστάσει ἐγένετο λέγων Εἴτε γὰρ ἐξέστημεν, θεῷ (πρὸς ἐκεῖνον γὰρ
αὐτῷ ἡ ἔκστασις ἦν), Εἴτε σωφρονοῦμεν, ὑμῖν, οἷς ἐδείκνυεν ἐν τοῖς πρὸς τὸν
30   Φῆστον λόγοις ἑαυτὸν μὴ μαινόμενον, ἀλλὰ σωφροσύνης τε καὶ δικαιοσύνης
ἀποφθεγγόμενος ῥήματα. οἶδα καὶ τὸν μακάριον Πέτρον ἐν τῷ τοιούτῳ τῆς

ensouled plants of the garden make bread for its Lord—to whom the One who sits on the throne bears witness when he says, "I was hungry and you gave me food" (Matt 25:35); for the performance of good deeds is the bread of gladness when it is rendered sweet by the honey of the commandment. Again, how the flourishing plants of the garden pour out wine for the Bridegroom— to whom he says, " 'I was thirsty and you gave me drink' (Matt 25:35), mixing | your wine with milk and not with water as the hucksters invariably do." Now milk is the first nourishment of the human race—pure and simple and truly childlike and guileless and purified of every cause of evil.

With these words said to the Bride, the Word sets forth to those nearby the mysteries of the Gospel: *You who are close to me, eat! And you, my brethren, drink and be drunken!* For to one who has known the mystical utterances of the Gospel, no difference will be discerned between the words of this text and the mystagogical instruction given to the disciples there. Just as is the case there (cf. Matt 26:26),[18] so also here the Word says "Eat!" and "Drink!" As to the exhortation to drunkenness that the Word addresses to his brethren in our text, it may well seem to most people to contain something beyond what the Gospel says. But if one looks closely into the matter, this too will be found consonant with the content of the Gospels. For what the Word prescribes for his friends here, he there brought about by his deeds, since all drunkenness tends, in those who have been mastered by wine, to bring about a displacement [*ekstasis*] of discursive thought. Hence what he prescribes here came to pass then because of that divine food and drink, and indeed always comes to pass | when a change and displacement from worse to better accompany the food and the drink. To be drunken in this manner is, as the prophecy says, for those who drink the fatness of God's house and water themselves at the stream of delight (cf. Ps 35:9).

The great David too was drunken in this way on one occasion, when, having gone out of himself and entered into ecstasy [*ekstasis*], he saw the invisible Beauty and cried out that famous word, "Every human being is a liar" (Ps 115:2), and so committed to speech an account of inexpressible things. In the same way Paul as well, the younger Benjamin,[19] was drunken when he entered into ecstasy and said, "For if I am beside myself, it is for God" (since his ecstasy was directed upon God), "and if I am in control of myself, it is for you" (2 Cor 5:13)—the people to whom, in his speech before Festus (cf. Acts 26:24–25), he showed that he was not out of his mind but was speaking words of self-control and righteousness. Think too of the blessed

---

18. The "mystagogical instruction" in question is, of course, the one treating the Eucharist.
19. Paul, like David, was of the tribe of Benjamin; see Rom 11:1 and Phil 3:5.

μέθης εἴδει πρόσπεινόν τε ὄντα ὁμοῦ καὶ | μεθύοντα· πρὶν γὰρ τὴν σωματικὴν   310
τροφὴν προσενέγκασθαι, ὅτε Ἐγένετο πρόσπεινος καὶ ἤθελε γεύσασθαι,
παρασκευαζόντων αὐτῷ τῶν ἰδίων τὴν τράπεζαν γίνεται αὐτῷ ἡ θεία τε καὶ
νηφάλιος μέθη, δι᾽ ἧς ἐξίσταται αὐτὸς ἑαυτοῦ καὶ θεωρεῖ τὴν εὐαγγελικὴν
5   ὀθόνην τέσσαρσιν ἀρχαῖς ἄνωθεν καθιεμένην πᾶν γένος ἀνθρώπων ἐν ἑαυτῇ
περιέχουσαν ἐν μυρίοις εἴδεσι πετεινῶν τε καὶ τετραπόδων καὶ ἑρπετῶν καὶ
θηρίων κατὰ τὰς τῶν σεβασμάτων διαφορὰς μεμορφωμένων, ὧν τὸ θηριῶδές
τε καὶ ἄλογον εἶδος θῦσαι τῷ Πέτρῳ ὁ λόγος διακελεύεται, ἵνα καθαρθέντων
αὐτῶν τὸ λειπόμενον ἐδώδιμον γένηται, ὅτε καὶ γυμνὸς ὁ τῆς εὐσεβείας
10 παραδίδοται λόγος οὐχ ἅπαξ εἰπούσης τῆς θείας φωνῆς ὅτι οὐκ ἔστι κοινόν,
ὅπερ ὁ θεὸς ἐκαθάρισεν, ἀλλ᾽ εἰς τρὶς γενομένου τοῦ τοιούτου κηρύγματος,
ἵνα μάθωμεν τῇ μιᾷ φωνῇ θεὸν καθαρίζοντα τὸν πατέρα καὶ ἐν τῇ ἑτέρᾳ
ὡσαύτως τὸν καθαρίζοντα θεὸν τὸν μονογενῆ θεὸν εἶναι καὶ ἐν τῇ ἄλλῃ
παραπλησίως ὅτι ὁ πᾶν ἀκάθαρτον καθαρίζων θεὸς τὸ πνεῦμά ἐστι τὸ ἅγιον.
15   τοιαύτης τοίνυν γινομένης τῆς ἐκ τοῦ οἴνου μέθης, ὃν προτίθησι τοῖς
συμπόταις ὁ κύριος, δι᾽ ἧς πρὸς τὰ θειότερα τῇ ψυχῇ ἡ ἔκστασις γίνεται, | 311
καλῶς παρακελεύεται τοῖς πλησίον διὰ τῶν ἀρετῶν γεγονόσιν, οὐ τοῖς
πόρρωθεν ἀφεστηκόσιν [ὁ κύριος] ὅτι Φάγετε, οἱ πλησίον μου, καὶ πίετε
καὶ μεθύσθητε· Ὁ γὰρ ἀναξίως ἐσθίων καὶ πίνων κρίμα ἑαυτῷ ἐσθίει καὶ
20 πίνει, καλῶς δὲ τοὺς ἀξίους τῆς βρώσεως ἀδελφοὺς προσηγόρευσεν· ὁ γὰρ
ποιῶν τὰ θελήματα αὐτοῦ καὶ ἀδελφὸς καὶ ἀδελφὴ καὶ μήτηρ ὑπὸ τοῦ λόγου
κατονομάζεται.
Ἀκολούθως δὲ διαδέχεται τὴν μέθην ὁ ὕπνος, ὡς ἂν διὰ τῆς πέψεως
ἀναδοθείη τοῖς δαιτυμόσιν εἰς εὐεξίαν ἡ δύναμις. διὰ τοῦτο μετὰ τὴν
25 πανδαισίαν ἐκείνην ἐν τῷ ὕπνῳ ἡ νύμφη γίνεται. ξένος δέ τις οὗτος ὁ ὕπνος
ἐστὶ καὶ τῆς φυσικῆς συνηθείας ἀλλότριος· ἐπὶ μὲν γὰρ τοῦ συνήθους ὕπνου
οὔτε ὁ καθεύδων ἐγρήγορεν καὶ ὁ ἐγρηγορὼς οὐ καθεύδει, ἀλλ᾽ ἐν ἀλλήλοις
λήγει ἀμφότερα ὅ τε ὕπνος καὶ ἡ ἐγρήγορσις ταῖς διαδοχαῖς ἀλλήλων
ὑπεξιστάμενα καὶ ἀνὰ μέρος ἑκάστῳ παραγινόμενα, ἐνταῦθα δέ τις καινὴ καὶ
30 παράδοξος μίξις τῶν ἐναντίων καὶ σύνοδος περὶ αὐτὴν θεωρεῖται· Ἐγὼ γάρ,
φησί, καθεύδω καὶ ἡ καρδία μου ἀγρυπνεῖ.
τίνα οὖν χρὴ διάνοιαν περὶ τούτων λαβεῖν; ὕπνος θανάτου ἐστὶν ὁμοίωμα·
λύεται γὰρ ἐν αὐτῷ πᾶσα αἰσθητικὴ τῶν σωμάτων ἐνέργεια, οὐκ ὄψεως, οὐκ
ἀκοῆς, οὐκ ὀσφρή|σεως, οὐ γεύσεως, οὐχ ἁφῆς παρὰ τὸν τοῦ ὕπνου καιρὸν   312
35 ἐνεργούσης τὸ ἴδιον· ἀλλὰ καὶ λύει τὸν τόνον τοῦ σώματος, ποιεῖ δὲ καὶ
λήθην τῶν ἐν τῷ ἀνθρώπῳ φροντίδων καὶ κατευνάζει τὸν φόβον καὶ ἡμεροῖ
τὸν θυμὸν καὶ ὑποχαλᾷ τῶν πικραινομένων τὸ σύντονον καὶ πάντων τῶν
κακῶν ἀναισθησίαν ποιεῖ, ἕως ἂν κατακρατῶν τύχῃ τοῦ σώματος. οὐκοῦν

Peter in a drunken state of this sort, at once hungry and | drunken. For before the corporeal food was set before him, when "he became hungry and wanted something to eat," the divine and sober drunkenness came upon him while his people "were preparing" a table, and it caused him to go out of himself and to see the evangelical "cloth ... being let down upon the earth" from above "by its four corners" (Acts 10:10–16). Within itself it contained every race of human beings appearing under thousands of forms of birds and four-footed creatures and reptiles and wild animals, given shapes to accord with the different objects of their worship, and the Word enjoined Peter to kill the wild and nonrational species, so that when they had been cleansed, the remainder might become edible once the Word of piety was openly transmitted. So it was not just once that the divine voice said, "What God has cleansed is not common," but the proclamation came three times. The intent of this was that we should learn from the one utterance God the Father cleansing, and from the second that the God who cleanses is the Only Begotten God, and from the final utterance, in much the same way, that the one who cleanses everything unclean is the Holy Spirit.

Since then it is a drunkenness of this sort that is occasioned by the wine that the Lord sets before his companions—a drunkenness that causes the soul to move out of itself in the direction of things more divine— | it is entirely right that his command is for those who have drawn near to him in virtue, and not those who have stood apart at a distance: *You who are close to me, eat!* and *Drink and be drunken!* For he who eats and drinks unworthily eats and drinks judgment for himself (cf. 1 Cor 11:29), but he rightly addresses those worthy of the food as brethren and sisters; for the Word calls the person who does his will at once brother and sister and mother (Mark 3:35).

Sleep naturally succeeds drunkenness, so that by the processes of digestion guests may have their capacity for well-being restored. Hence the Bride falls asleep after this feast. This sleep, though, is a stranger and alien to the ordinary course of nature. For in the usual sort of sleep, the sleeper is not awake, nor does one who is waking sleep; rather, sleep and wakefulness both come to an end in each other—they alternate in withdrawal from each other and come to each person by turns. In this text, however, one discerns in the Bride a novel and surprising mixture and coalescence of these opposites. For *I sleep*, it says, *but my heart lies awake.*

Now what sense are we to make of this? Sleep is an image of death, for in death every perceptive activity of bodies is dissolved. There is no activity of seeing, or of hearing, or of | smelling or tasting, or of touching in the season of sleep. What is more, it relaxes the body's tension and brings about forgetfulness of the person's thoughts. It puts fear to sleep and tames aggression and relaxes the intensity of bitterness and effects an insensibility to all evils, as

τοῦτο διὰ τῶν εἰρημένων μανθάνομεν ὅτι ὑψηλοτέρα γέγονεν ἑαυτῆς ἡ ταῦτα μεγαλαυχουμένη καὶ λέγουσα ὅτι Ἐγὼ καθεύδω καὶ ἡ καρδία μου ἀγρυπνεῖ.

τῷ ὄντι γὰρ ἐφ᾽ ὧν μόνος ὁ νοῦς ἐφ᾽ ἑαυτοῦ βιοτεύει οὐδενὶ τῶν αἰσθητηρίων παρενοχλούμενος, ὡς ὕπνῳ τινὶ καὶ κώματι πάρετος ἡ τοῦ

5   σώματος γίνεται φύσις καὶ ἀληθῶς ἔστιν εἰπεῖν ὅτι κοιμᾶται δι᾽ ἀπραξίας ἡ ὅρασις ἀτιμαζομένων τῶν θεαμάτων ἐκείνων, ὅσα τὰς παιδικὰς ὄψεις ἐκπλήττειν εἴωθεν. οὐ ταῦτα λέγω μόνα ἃ τῆς γεώδους ὕλης ἐστίν, οἷον χρυσίον τε καὶ ἀργύριον καὶ τῶν λίθων ἐκεῖνα ὅσα διά τινος εὐχροίας κινεῖ τοῖς ὀφθαλμοῖς τὴν λιχνείαν, ἀλλὰ καὶ τὰ περὶ τὸν οὐρανὸν φαινόμενα

10   θαύματα, αἵ τε τῶν ἀστέρων αὐγαὶ καὶ τοῦ ἡλίου ὁ κύκλος καὶ τὸ πολύμορφον τῆς σελήνης εἶδος καὶ εἴ τι ἄλλο τοῖς ὀφθαλμοῖς ἡδονὴν φέρει διὰ τὸ μηδὲν εἰς ἀεὶ μένειν ἀλλὰ συμμετακινεῖσθαι τῇ παρόδῳ | τοῦ χρόνου καὶ   313 συμπαράγεσθαι. πάντων τῶν τοιούτων ὑπεροφθέντων διὰ τὴν τῶν ἀληθινῶν ἀγαθῶν θεωρίαν πάρετός ἐστιν ὁ τοῦ σώματος ὀφθαλμὸς πρὸς οὐδὲν τῶν

15   παρ᾽ αὐτοῦ ὑποδεικνυμένων τῆς τελειοτέρας ψυχῆς καθελκομένης διὰ τὸ μόνα βλέπειν τῇ διανοίᾳ τὰ τῶν ὁρατῶν ὑπερκείμενα. οὕτω καὶ ἡ ἀκοὴ νεκρά τις καὶ ἀνενέργητος γίνεται πρὸς τὰ ὑπὲρ λόγον τῆς ψυχῆς ἀσχολουμένης.

τὰς δὲ κτηνωδεστέρας τῶν αἰσθήσεων οὐδὲ λέγειν ἄξιον ὅτι πόρρωθεν καθάπερ τις νεκρώδης δυσωδία τῆς ψυχῆς ἀπορρίπτεται ἥ τε ῥινηλατοῦσα

20   τὰς ὀδμὰς ὄσφρησις καὶ ἡ τῇ λατρείᾳ τῆς κοιλίας προσκαθημένη γεῦσις καὶ ἡ ἁφὴ πρὸς τούτοις, τὸ ἀνδραποδῶδες καὶ τυφλὸν αἰσθητήριον ὃ τάχα διὰ τοὺς τυφλοὺς μόνον ἡ φύσις ἐποίησεν, ὧν πάντων ὥσπερ ἐν ὕπνῳ τινὶ δι᾽ ἀπραξίας κεκρατημένων καθαρὰ τῆς καρδίας ἐστὶν ἡ ἐνέργεια καὶ πρὸς τὸ ἄνω βλέπει ὁ λογισμὸς ἀπερίηχητος μένων ἐκ τῆς αἰσθητικῆς κινήσεως καὶ ἀθόλωτος.

25   διπλῆς γὰρ οὔσης ἐν τῇ ἀνθρωπίνῃ φύσει τῆς ἡδονῆς, τῆς μὲν ἐν ψυχῇ δι᾽ ἀπαθείας ἐνεργουμένης, τῆς δὲ διὰ πάθους ἐν σώματι, ἥνπερ ἂν ἐξ ἀμφοτέρων ἡ προαίρεσις ἕληται, αὕτη κατὰ τῆς ἑτέρας τὸ κράτος ἔχει. ὡς εἴ τις πρὸς τὴν αἴσθησιν βλέποι τὴν δι᾽ αὐτῆς ἐμφυομένην τῷ σώματι ἡδονὴν ἐφελκόμενος, ἄγευστος τῆς θείας εὐφροσύνης διαβιώσεται, διότι πέφυκέ πως

30   ἐπισκοτεῖσθαι τὸ κρεῖττον ὑπὸ τοῦ χείρονος. οἷς δ᾽ ἂν ἡ ἐπιθυμία τὴν πρὸς τὸ | θεῖον ἔχῃ ῥοπήν, τούτοις ἀνεπισκότητον μένει τὸ ἀγαθὸν καὶ φευκτὸν ἅπαν   314 εἶναι νομίζεται τὸ καταγοητεῦον τὴν αἴσθησιν. διὰ τοῦτο ἡ ψυχή, ὅταν μόνῃ τῇ θεωρίᾳ τοῦ ὄντος εὐφραίνηται, πρὸς οὐδὲν ἐγρήγορε τῶν ἐνεργουμένων

long as it prevails over the body. Hence from our text we learn this: that she who makes the boast that *I sleep, but my heart lies awake* has risen higher than herself.

For the truth is that insofar as only the intellect in itself is alive, without any distraction from the organs of sense perception, the bodily nature becomes inactive, as in slumber or profound sleep,[20] and it is truly possible to say that through disuse the capacity to see all those shameful objects that regularly trouble childish eyes is put to sleep. I do not mean merely those objects that fall in the class of the material and earthly, like silver and gold and stones that fill the eye with greed because of their fine colors, but also the objects of vision that appear in the heaven: the stars' shining and the sun's disc and the manifold show of the moon and anything else that pleasures the eyes because it nowise abides forever but alters and passes on with | the lapse of time. When vision of the truly good leads us to look beyond all such things, the bodily eye is inactive, for then the more perfect soul, which uses its understanding to look only on matters that are beyond seeing, is not drawn to any of the things to which that eye directs its attention. In the same way too the faculty of hearing becomes a dead thing and goes out of operation when the soul occupies itself with things beyond speech.

As to the more bestial of the senses, they are hardly worth mentioning. Long since, like some graveyard stench attached to the soul, they have been put away: the sense of smell, scenting out odors; and the sense of taste, bound to the belly's service; and the sense of touch as well, the blind and servile organ that nature, we may think, created only for the sake of the blind. When all these are as it were bound in sleep by disuse, then the working of the heart is pure, and its discourse is focused on what is above it, untroubled and unaccompanied by the noise that stems from the stirrings of sense perception.

For in the human constitution there is a double pleasure, one that is in the soul and is activated by impassibility and another that is occasioned in the body by passion, and whichever of the two our choosing shall elect is the one that prevails over the other. Thus if one focuses attention on sense perception and seeks for oneself the pleasure it grafts into the body, one's life is spent without tasting the divine gladness, since the better is automatically overshadowed by the worse. But for those whose desire flows in the direction of | the divine, the good stands unshadowed, and judgment flees everything that bewitches the senses. Hence it is that the soul, when its only delight lies

---

20. This whole passage, beginning with the above comparison of sleep to death and continuing to the very end of the homily, should be compared with Plato, *Phaed.* 64C–67B, and especially perhaps 66D–E: "if we are ever going to know anything purely, it [the body] must be got rid of, and things must be contemplated for themselves by the soul for itself."

καθ᾽ ἡδονὴν δι᾽ αἰσθήσεως, ἀλλὰ πᾶσαν σωματικὴν κατακοιμήσασα κίνησιν γυμνῇ τε καὶ καθαρᾷ τῇ διανοίᾳ διὰ τῆς θείας ἐγρηγόρσεως δέχεται τοῦ θεοῦ τὴν ἐμφάνειαν·

ἧς καὶ ἡμεῖς ἀξιωθείημεν διὰ τοῦ εἰρημένου ὕπνου κατορθοῦντες τῆς
5   ψυχῆς τὴν ἐγρήγορσιν ἐν Χριστῷ Ἰησοῦ τῷ κυρίῳ ἡμῶν

ᾧ πρέπει ἡ δόξα εἰς τοὺς αἰῶνας τῶν αἰώνων.
ἀμήν.

in contemplation of what is real, wakens to none of the pleasurable stirrings of the senses. It has put to sleep every corporeal notion, and wakened by the divine, it embraces the revelation of God by pure and naked thought.

And may we too be judged worthy of this revelation, having accomplished by means of the aforesaid sleep the wakening of our soul in Jesus Christ our Lord,

to whom be glory to the ages of ages.
Amen.

Φωνὴ τοῦ ἀδελφιδοῦ μου κρούει ἐπὶ τὴν θύραν·
ἄνοιξόν μοι, ἀδελφή μου, ἡ πλησίον μου,
περιστερά μου, τελεία μου,
ὅτι ἡ κεφαλή μου ἐπλήσθη δρόσου
5   καὶ οἱ βόστρυχοί μου ψεκάδων νυκτός.
Ἐξεδυσάμην τὸν χιτῶνά μου, πῶς ἐνδύσομαι αὐτόν;
ἐνιψάμην τοὺς πόδας μου, πῶς μολυνῶ αὐτούς;
| Ἀδελφιδός μου ἀπέστειλε χεῖρα αὐτοῦ διὰ τῆς ὀπῆς   315
καὶ ἡ κοιλία μου ἐθροήθη ἐπ' αὐτόν.
10   Ἀνέστην ἐγὼ ἀνοῖξαι τῷ ἀδελφιδῷ μου,
<αἱ> χεῖρές μου ἔσταξαν σμύρναν,
οἱ δάκτυλοί μου σμύρναν πλήρη.
ἐπὶ χεῖρας τοῦ κλείθρου
Ἤνοιξα ἐγὼ τῷ ἀδελφιδῷ μου,
15   ἀδελφιδός μου παρῆλθεν·
ἡ ψυχή μου ἐξῆλθεν ἐν λόγῳ αὐτοῦ.
ἐζήτησα αὐτὸν καὶ οὐχ εὗρον αὐτόν,
ἐκάλεσα αὐτὸν καὶ οὐχ ὑπήκουσέ μου.
Εὕροσάν με οἱ φύλακες οἱ κυκλοῦντες ἐν τῇ πόλει,
20   ἐπάταξάν με, ἐτραυμάτισάν με,
ἦραν τὸ θέριστρον ἀπ' ἐμοῦ οἱ φύλακες τῶν τειχέων.

Ἓν καὶ τοῦτο τῶν μεγάλων παραγγελμάτων ἐστὶ τοῦ κυρίου, δι' ὧν ἡ
διάνοια τῶν μαθητευομένων τῷ λόγῳ καθάπερ τινὰ χοῦν ἅπαν τὸ ὑλῶδες
τῆς φύσεως ἀφ' ἑαυτῆς ἐκτινάξασα πρὸς τὴν ἐπιθυμίαν τῶν ὑπερκειμένων
25   ἐπαίρεται, [τοῦτο δέ ἐστι] τὸ δεῖν κρείττους εἶναι τοῦ ὕπνου τοὺς πρὸς
τὴν ἄνω ζωὴν ἀναβλέποντας καὶ διὰ παντὸς ἐγρηγορέναι τῇ διανοίᾳ οἷον
ἀπατεῶνά τινα τῶν ψυχῶν καὶ τῆς ἀληθείας ἐπίβουλον τὸν νυσταγμὸν τῶν
ὀφθαλμῶν ἀπελαύνοντας.

| ἐκεῖνον λέγω τὸν νυσταγμὸν καὶ τὸν ὕπνον, δι' ὧν πλάσσεται τοῖς 316
30   ἐμβαθύνουσι τῇ τοῦ βίου ἀπάτῃ τὰ ὀνειρώδη ταῦτα φαντάσματα· αἱ ἀρχαί,

²*The voice of my kinsman knocks at the door:*
"Open to me, my sister, my close one,
my dove, my perfect one,
for my head is covered with dew
and my locks with the drops of the night."
³*"I have removed my tunic. How shall I put it on?*
I have washed my feet. How shall I soil them?"
⁴*My kinsman has put his hand through the opening,*
and my belly has cried out for him.
[⁵*I rose up to open to my kinsman;*
my hands dropped myrrh,
my fingers choice myrrh.
Hands on the bar,
⁶*I opened to my kinsman,*
my kinsman passed me by,
my soul went out at his word.
I sought him, and I did not find him,
I called him, but he did not answer me.
⁷*The watchmen that go their rounds in the city found me,*
they struck me, they wounded me,
the watchmen of the walls took my veil away from me.]¹

One, and one of the weightiest, of the Lord's admonitions, by which the mind of the Word's disciples shakes off the materiality of their nature like so much dust and is elevated to a desire for things transcendent, is this: that those who look toward the life above must be stronger than sleep and ever wakeful in mind,² fighting off the eyes' drowsiness as if it were some cheater of souls or plotter against the truth.

| I refer to that drowsiness and that sleep that manufacture, for those who are sunk deep in life's deceits, dream images of high offices, treasures,

---

1. The original text of this homily includes Song 5:5–7 as part of the preliminary lection. Clearly the preacher ran out of time before treating these verses, as is indicated by the hurried manner of the ending of homily 11 and by the fact that these verses are handled in homily 12.

2. See above, homily 10, pp. 311ff. (Jaeger), with Gregory's explanation of Song 5:2a (*I sleep, but my heart lies awake*). The opening of the present homily recalls and continues the theme of mental wakefulness.

οἱ πλοῦτοι, αἱ δυναστεῖαι, ὁ τῦφος, ἡ διὰ τῶν ἡδονῶν γοητεία, τὸ φιλόδοξόν
τε καὶ ἀπολαυστικὸν καὶ φιλότιμον καὶ πάντα ὅσα κατὰ τὸν βίον τοῦτον
τοῖς ἀνεπισκέπτοις διά τινος φαντασίας μάτην σπουδάζεται, ἃ τῇ παροδικῇ
τοῦ χρόνου συμπαραρρέοντα φύσει ἐν τῷ δοκεῖν ἔχει τὸ εἶναι οὔτε ὄντα
5   ὅπερ νομίζεται οὔτε ἐν αὐτῷ τῷ νομίζεσθαι πρὸς τὸ διηνεκὲς παραμένοντα
ἀλλ' ὁμοῦ γίνεσθαί τε δοκοῦντα καὶ ἀπολλύμενα κυμάτων δίκην τῶν
ἐγκορυφουμένων τοῖς ὕδασιν, ἃ πρὸς καιρὸν τῇ κινήσει τῶν ἀνέμων
συνδιογκούμενα ἀβέβαιον εἰς διαμονὴν ἔχει τὸν ὄγκον· ἐν βραχεῖ γὰρ τῇ
ῥοπῇ συναναστάντα τοῦ πνεύματος πάλιν ἐν ὁμαλῷ τὴν τῆς θαλάσσης
10   ἐπιφάνειαν δείκνυσι συγκατασταλέντα τῷ πνεύματι.

ὡς ἂν οὖν ἔξω τῶν τοιούτων γένοιτο | φαντασμάτων ἡμῖν ἡ διάνοια, τὸν   317
βαρὺν τοῦτον ὕπνον ἀποσείεσθαι τῶν τῆς ψυχῆς ὀμμάτων διακελεύεται, ἵνα
μὴ τῇ περὶ τὸ ἀνύπαρκτον σπουδῇ τῶν ὑφεστώτων τε καὶ ὡς ἀληθῶς ὄντων
ἀπολισθήσωμεν. διὰ τοῦτο καὶ ὑποτίθεται ἡμῖν ἐπίνοιαν τῆς ἐγρηγόρσεως
15   λέγων Ἔστωσαν ὑμῶν αἱ ὀσφύες περιεζωσμέναι καὶ οἱ λύχνοι καιόμενοι· τοῖς
τε γὰρ ὀφθαλμοῖς τὸ φῶς ἐμφαινόμενον ἀποσοβεῖ τῶν ὀμμάτων τὸν ὕπνον
καὶ ἡ ὀσφῦς διεσφιγμένη διὰ τῆς ζώνης ἀπαράδεκτον τοῦ ὕπνου παρασκευάζει
τὸ σῶμα οὐ προσιεμένης τὴν ἐκ τοῦ ὕπνου ἄνεσιν τῆς τῶν πόνων αἰσθήσεως.
σαφῆ δὲ πάντως ἐστὶ τὰ διὰ τῶν αἰνιγμάτων δηλούμενα, ὅτι ὁ τῇ σωφροσύνῃ
20   διεζωσμένος ἐν φωτὶ ζῇ τοῦ καθαροῦ συνειδότος τῷ λύχνῳ τῆς παρρησίας
τὸν βίον περιαυγάζοντος, δι' ὧν τῆς ἀληθείας προφαινομένης ἄϋπνός τε
καὶ ἀνεξαπάτητος ἡ ψυχὴ διαμένει οὐδενὶ τῶν ἀπατηλῶν τούτων ὀνείρων
ἐμματαιάζουσα.

εἰ δὲ τοῦτο κατορθωθείη κατὰ τὴν τοῦ λόγου ὑφήγησιν, ἀγγελικός τις
25   ἡμᾶς διαδέξεται βίος· τούτοις γὰρ ἡμᾶς ὁμοιοῖ τὸ θεῖον παράγγελμα, δι' ὧν
φησιν ὅτι Καὶ ὑμεῖς ὅμοιοι ἀνθρώποις προσδεχομένοις τὸν κύριον ἑαυτῶν,
| πότε ἀναλύσει ἐκ τῶν γάμων, ἵνα ἐλθόντος καὶ κρούσαντος εὐθέως   318
ἀνοίξωσιν αὐτῷ· ἐκεῖνοι γάρ εἰσιν οἱ προσδεχόμενοι τοῦ κυρίου τὴν ἐκ τῶν
γάμων ἐπάνοδον καὶ ταῖς ἐπουρανίαις πύλαις ἐγρηγορότι τῷ ὀφθαλμῷ
30   προσκαθήμενοι, ἵνα πάλιν εἰσέλθῃ δι' αὐτῶν ἀναλύσας ἐκ τῶν γάμων ὁ
βασιλεὺς τῆς δόξης εἰς τὴν ὑπερουράνιον ἐκείνην μακαριότητα. ὅθεν κατὰ
τὴν ψαλμῳδίαν ὡς ἐκ παστάδος ὁ νυμφίος ἐκπορευθεὶς ἡρμόσατο ἑαυτῷ
τὴν παρθένον, ἡμᾶς, διὰ τῆς μυστικῆς ἀναγεννήσεως, τὴν τοῖς εἰδώλοις
ἐκπορνευθεῖσαν, εἰς ἀφθαρσίαν παρθενικὴν ἀναστοιχειώσας τὴν φύσιν.
35   τῶν οὖν γάμων ἤδη τετελεσμένων καὶ νυμφευθείσης ὑπὸ τοῦ λόγου τῆς
ἐκκλησίας, καθώς φησιν ὁ Ἰωάννης ὅτι Ὁ ἔχων τὴν νύμφην νυμφίος ἐστί, καὶ
εἰς τὸν τῶν μυστηρίων θάλαμον αὐτῆς παραδεχθείσης ἀνέμενον οἱ ἄγγελοι

lordships, self-conceit, bewitching pleasures, of lust for fame and luxury and vanity—and all things whatsoever that people without awareness chase after vainly in this life at the behest of some fantasy. These things, which flow away with time as it passes, have their being in seeming. They are not what they are esteemed to be, nor do they continue permanently to be thus esteemed. On the contrary, no sooner do they seem to come into being than they perish, like billows that raise their heads on the waters: they are massed together for a moment by the wind's motion, but their mass is too unstable to endure. Raised up momentarily by the gusting wind, they are calmed down along with the wind and allow the even surface of the sea to be seen again.

In order, then, that our mind may be free of such | fantasies, he orders that this heavy sleep be banished from the eyes of the soul, lest devotion to what is unreal cause us to bid farewell to true and substantive realities. That is why he enjoins upon us the notion of wakefulness when he says, "Let your loins be girded and your lamps burning" (Luke 12:35), for light shining in the eyes drives sleep from them, and loins tightly belted make the body unreceptive to sleep, since the experience of laborious exertion inhibits the relaxation that sleep brings. It is apparent in any case what is conveyed by these enigmatic statements, namely, that the person who is girt about with self-control lives by the light of a purified conscience, with her life illumined by the lamp of candor; and when by these means truth becomes apparent, the soul of such a person abides untouched by sleep or by any deception and does not dally with any of these misleading dreams.

And if this is accomplished under the guidance of the Word, a life of angelic quality accrues to us, for the divine command likens us to angels when he says: "And be like people who are waiting for their Lord | to come home from the marriage feast, so that they may open to him at once when he comes and knocks" (Luke 12:36). For it is the angels who wait for the return of their Lord from the marriage feast and sit at the heavenly portals with sleepless eye, in order that the King of Glory, when he comes back from the marriage feast, may enter with their help into that supercelestial blessedness. Hence, as the hymn in the Psalms (Ps 18:6) would have it, the Bridegroom, having emerged as from the bridal chamber, espoused the virgin—that is to say, us— in the mystic rebirth,[3] even though she had been prostituted to idols, and restored her nature to virginal incorruptibility. Since, then, the marriage rites have already been carried out and the church has been taken by the Word as his Bride (just as John says: "He who has the bride is the bridegroom" [John 3:29]), and the Bride has been taken into the inner chamber of the mysteries,

---

3. The reference is clearly to baptism.

τὴν ἐπάνοδον τοῦ βασιλέως τῆς δόξης ἐπὶ τὴν κατὰ φύσιν μακαριότητα.

τούτοις οὖν εἶπε δεῖν ὁμοιοῦσθαι κατὰ τὸν ἡμέτερον βίον, ἵνα καθάπερ ἐκεῖνοι πόρρω κακίας καὶ ἀπάτης πολιτευόμενοι πρὸς ὑποδοχὴν εἰσιν εὐτρεπεῖς τῆς δεσποτικῆς παρουσίας, | οὕτω καὶ ἡμεῖς τοῖς προθύροις τῶν καταγωγίων   319
5   ἡμῶν προσαγρυπνοῦντες ἑτοίμους πρὸς ὑπακοὴν ἑαυτοὺς ποιήσωμεν, ὅταν ἐπιστὰς κρούῃ τὴν θύραν· Μακάριοι γάρ, φησίν, οἱ δοῦλοι ἐκεῖνοι, οὓς ἐλθὼν ὁ κύριος εὑρήσει ποιοῦντας οὕτως.

ἐπεὶ οὖν μακάριόν ἐστι τὸ ὑπακούειν τῷ κρούοντι, τούτου χάριν ἡ διὰ παντὸς πρὸς τὴν μακαριότητα βλέπουσα αἰσθάνεται τοῦ παρεστῶτος τῇ
10   θύρᾳ, ἡ καλῶς τοῖς ἰδίοις θησαυροῖς ἐπαγρυπνοῦσα ψυχή, καί φησιν Φωνή τοῦ ἀδελφιδοῦ μου κρούει ἐπὶ τὴν θύραν.

πῶς ἄν τις τὴν πρὸς τὰ θειότερα τῆς νύμφης ἄνοδον διὰ τῶν λεγομένων ἀξίως κατανοήσειεν; ἡ μετὰ τοσαύτης ἐξουσίας τε καὶ πεποιθήσεως τὸν σκληρὸν ἐκεῖνον βορρᾶν ἀφ᾽ ἑαυτῆς ἐξοικίσασα καὶ τὸ φωτεινὸν πνεῦμα πρὸς
15   ἑαυτὴν ἐφελκυσαμένη, ἡ παραδείσους ῥοῶν διὰ τοῦ στόματος ἐργαζομένη ὧν ἀρώματα ἦν τὰ ἀκρόδρυα, ἡ τὸν κῆπον ἑαυτῆς τράπεζαν προθεῖσα τῷ δεσπότῃ τῆς κτίσεως, ἧς ἀπόβλητον ἐφάνη τῶν προτεθέντων οὐδέν, ἀλλὰ πάντα καλὰ εἶναι ἐμαρτυρήθη· ἡ σμύρνα, τὸ ἄρωμα, ὁ μετὰ τοῦ μέλιτος ἄρτος, ὁ μετὰ τοῦ γάλακτος οἶνος, ᾗ ἐμαρτύρησεν ὁ λόγος τὸ τέλειον ὁ εἰπὼν
20   ὅτι Ὅλη | καλὴ εἶ καὶ μῶμος οὐκ ἔστιν ἐν σοί, αὕτη νῦν οὕτω διάκειται· ὡς   320
πρώτως μέλλουσα δέχεσθαι τοῦ θεοῦ τὴν ἐμφάνειαν καὶ ὡς οὐδέπω τὸν νῦν ἐστῶτα πρὸ τῶν θυρῶν λόγον εἰσδεξαμένη καὶ εἰσοικίσασα ἐν θαύματι τῆς φωνῆς ποιεῖται τὴν δύναμιν. διὰ τοῦτό φησιν οὔπω ἑαυτῆς ἀλλὰ τῆς θύρας αὐτῆς ἅπτεσθαι τὴν τοῦ νυμφίου φωνήν· Φωνὴ γάρ, φησί, τοῦ ἀδελφιδοῦ μου
25   κρούει ἐπὶ τὴν θύραν.

Ὁρᾷς, πῶς ἀόριστός ἐστι τοῖς πρὸς τὸν θεὸν ἀνιοῦσιν ὁ δρόμος, πῶς τὸ ἀεὶ καταλαμβανόμενον ἀρχὴ πρὸς τὸ ὑπερκείμενον γίνεται· ὅτε γὰρ στάσιν τινὰ τοῦ δρόμου τῆς ἐπὶ τὰ ὑψηλὰ πορείας διὰ τῶν πρὸς αὐτὴν εἰρημένων ἠλπίσαμεν (τί γὰρ ἄν τις μετὰ τὴν τῆς τελειότητος μαρτυρίαν
30   πλέον ζητήσειεν;) τότε βλέπομεν ἔτι ἔνδον οὖσαν αὐτὴν καὶ οὔπω τῶν θυρῶν ἐκτὸς γεγενημένην οὐδὲ τῆς κατὰ πρόσωπον ἐμφανείας κατατρυφήσασαν ἀλλ᾽ ἔτι διὰ τῆς ἀκοῆς πρὸς τὴν τῶν ἀγαθῶν μετουσίαν ὁδηγουμένην. τοῦτο οὖν διὰ τῶν εἰρημένων τὸ δόγμα μανθάνομεν, ὅτι πάντοτε τοῖς ἐπὶ τὸ μεῖζον

the angels are awaiting the return of the King of Glory to the blessedness that belongs to him by nature. And the point is that in our living we are to become like them, in order that just as they, dwelling far from evil and error, are ready to greet their Lord at his coming, | so we also, sitting wakeful by the gates of our dwellings, may render ourselves ready to hear when he arrives and knocks at the door, "for," he says, "blessed are those servants whom their Lord finds doing this when he comes" (cf. Luke 12:37, 43).

Since, then, it is a blessed thing to hear and answer the one who knocks, the soul that ever seeks blessedness and that rightly watches over her treasures detects the one who stands at her door, and she says *The voice of my kinsman knocks at the door.*

Now how can we, in the light of these words, rightly understand the Bride's ascent to things nobler and more divine? With great authority and boldness she has banished the harsh north wind and drawn to herself the luminous Spirit.[4] With her mouth she has made herself gardens *of pomegranate trees* whose fruits are fragrances. She has set her garden as a table before the Lord of creation, and not one of the things presented there appeared worthy of rejection, but all were attested as good—the myrrh, the fragrance, the bread with honey, the wine with milk; and the Word bore witness of her perfection, saying *You are all | beautiful, my close one, there is no flaw within you.*[5] Yet now she herself is found in the state of one who is about to receive the manifestation of God for the first time and, having never before welcomed and taken in the Word who now stands at her door, is astounded at the strength of his voice. That is why the text says that the voice of the Bridegroom comes in contact not with her, but with her door: *The voice of my kinsman,* says she, *knocks at the door.*

You perceive how, for those who are making their way upwards toward God, the course they run has no end, how everything that is laid hold on becomes a starting point for something yet higher. Just when we have anticipated, on account of the words addressed to the Bride, that there will come a halting place in the course of her journey on high (for what more can one seek in the face of the witness borne to her perfection?), at that point we see that she is still inside and has not yet come outside the doors or enjoyed a face-to-face revelation but is still making her way by hearing[6] toward participation in the good things. The words of the text, then, teach us this: that to those who are making progress toward what is better the word of the apostle

---

4. For this and the following allusions, see above homily 10.

5. Song 4:7. See above, homily 7, p. 243 (Jaeger).

6. For Gregory's reflections in passing on the business of hearing and seeing, see above, homily 3, pp. 70–71 (Jaeger); homily 5, p. 138 (Jaeger).

προκόπτουσιν ἁρμόδιός ἐστιν ἡ τοῦ ἀποστόλου φωνὴ ἡ λέγουσα ὅτι Εἴ τις
δοκεῖ ἐγνωκέναι τι, οὔπω ἔγνω καθὼς δεῖ γνῶναι·

ἔγνω μὲν γὰρ αὐτὸν ἐν | τοῖς φθάσασιν ἡ ψυχὴ τοσοῦτον ὅσον κατέλαβεν,   321
ἀλλ᾽ ἐπειδὴ τὸ μήπω κατειλημμένον ἀπειροπλάσιον τοῦ καταληφθέντος ἐστί,
5   διὰ τοῦτο καὶ ὤφθη πολλάκις τῇ ψυχῇ ὁ νυμφίος καὶ ὡς μηδέπω ἐν ὀφθαλμοῖς
γενόμενος ὀφθήσεσθαι τῇ νύμφῃ διὰ τῆς φωνῆς ἐπαγγέλλεται.

ὡς δ᾽ ἂν σαφέστερον ἡμῖν τὸ νόημα γένοιτο, εἰκόνα τινὰ δι᾽ ὑποδείγματος
προσθήσω τῷ λόγῳ· ὥσπερ γὰρ εἴ τις πλησίον ἐκείνης γένοιτο τῆς πηγῆς,
ἣν ἀναβαίνειν εἶπεν ἐκ τῆς γῆς κατ᾽ ἀρχὰς ἡ γραφὴ τοσαύτην οὖσαν τὸ
10   πλῆθος ὡς ἅπαν τῆς γῆς ἐπικλύζειν τὸ πρόσωπον, θαυμάσει μὲν ὁ τῇ πηγῇ
πλησιάσας τὸ ἄπειρον ὕδωρ ἐκεῖνο τὸ πάντοτε αὐτῆς ἀνομβροῦν τε καὶ
προχεόμενον, οὐ μὴν εἴποι ἂν ὅλον ἑωρακέναι τὸ ὕδωρ (πῶς γὰρ ἂν ἴδοι τὸ
ἔτι τοῖς κόλποις τῆς γῆς ἐγκρυπτόμενον; ὥστε κἂν ἐπὶ πολὺ παραμείνῃ τῷ
βρύοντι, ἀεὶ ἐν ἀρχαῖς ἐστι τῆς θεωρίας τοῦ ὕδατος· οὐ γὰρ παύεται τὸ ὕδωρ
15   ἀεί τε ῥέον καὶ ἀεὶ τοῦ βρύειν ἀρχόμενον), οὕτως ὁ πρὸς τὸ θεῖον ἐκεῖνο καὶ
ἀόριστον κάλλος βλέπων, ἐπειδὴ τὸ πάντοτε εὑρισκόμενον καινότερόν τε
καὶ παραδοξότερον πάντως παρὰ τὸ ἤδη κατειλημμένον ὁρᾶται, θαυμάζει
μὲν τὸ ἀεὶ προφαινόμενον, οὐδέποτε δὲ ἵσταται τῆς τοῦ ἰδεῖν ἐπιθυμίας διὰ
τὸ πάντως τοῦ ἑωραμένου μεγαλοπρεπέστερόν τε καὶ θειότερον εἶναι τὸ
20   προσδοκώμενον. διὰ τοῦτο οὖν καὶ ἐνταῦθα ἡ νύμφη ἀεὶ θαυμάζουσά τε
καὶ ἐκπληττομένη τὸ γινωσκόμενον οὐδέποτε ἐν τοῖς ἐγνωσμένοις ἵστησι
τοῦ θεωρουμένου τὸν πόθον. οὗ χάριν καὶ νῦν ὡς ἔτι | θυροκρουστοῦντος   322
τοῦ λόγου αἰσθάνεται καὶ πρὸς τὴν ὑπακοὴν διανίσταται καί φησι Φωνὴ τοῦ
ἀδελφιδοῦ μου κρούει ἐπὶ τὴν θύραν.

25   Εἶτα ἡσυχίαν ταῖς ἀκοαῖς ἐνδοῦσα ἀκούει τοῦ διὰ τῆς φωνῆς
προσηχήσαντος λόγου. ὁ δὲ λόγος τοιοῦτός ἐστιν· Ἄνοιξόν μοι, ἀδελφή μου,
ἡ πλησίον μου, περιστερά μου, τελεία μου, ὅτι ἡ κεφαλή μου ἐπλήσθη δρόσου
καὶ οἱ βόστρυχοί μου ψεκάδων νυκτός.

τούτου δὲ τὴν διάνοιαν οὕτως ἄν τις καταλάβοι τῇ θεωρίᾳ. τῷ μεγάλῳ
30   Μωϋσῇ διὰ φωτὸς ἤρξατο ἡ τοῦ θεοῦ ἐπιφάνεια, μετὰ ταῦτα διὰ νεφέλης
αὐτῷ ὁ θεὸς διαλέγεται, εἶτα ὑψηλότερος καὶ τελειότερος ἤδη γενόμενος
ἐν γνόφῳ τὸν θεὸν βλέπει. ὃ δὲ διὰ τούτου μανθάνομεν τοιοῦτόν ἐστιν·

always applies, the word that says, "If anyone seems to know something, he does not yet know as he ought to know" (1 Cor 8:2).

For the soul has known him—to the extent that she has comprehended him—in | what has already come to pass, but since that which is not yet comprehended is infinitely greater than that which has been comprehended, the Bridegroom is manifested to the soul frequently and promises the Bride by his voice that he will be revealed as one who has not yet been seen.

In order that this idea may be the clearer to us, I shall set forth an image by way of illustration. Suppose that someone draws near to that fountain that the Scripture says welled up out of the earth at the beginning, and so abundantly that it flooded the whole face of the earth (cf. Gen 2:6). The person who has drawn near to the fountain will marvel at that limitless supply of water that ever gushes out and flows from it, yet he would not say that he has seen all of the water. (For how can he see the water that is still concealed in earth's bosom? The fact is that even if he remains for a long time at the gushing spring, he is always just beginning to contemplate the water, for the water never stops in its everlasting flow nor does it ever cease beginning to gush forth.) In the same way, the person who looks toward that divine and infinite Beauty glimpses something that is always being discovered as more novel and more surprising than what has already been grasped, and for that reason she marvels at that which is always being manifested, but she never comes to a halt in her desire to see, since what she looks forward to is in every possible way more splendid and more divine than what she has seen. This, then, is the reason why, in our present case, the Bride, ever amazed and marveling at what is known, never brings her desire for the object of her vision to a halt at what has already been apprehended. So it is that now too she senses the Word | knocking, as it were, at her door and rises to answer him, saying, *The voice of my kinsman knocks at the door.*

Next, bringing her sense of hearing to a state of calm, she makes out the words that the sound conveys, and this is what is said. *Open to me, my sister, my close one, my dove, my perfect one, for my head is covered with dew and my locks with the drops of the night.*

By dint of careful discernment, one might take the meaning of these words to be this: the revelation of God to the great Moses began with light as its medium, but afterwards God spoke to him through the medium of a cloud, and when he had become more lifted up and more perfect, he saw God in darkness.[7] What we learn from this is something like the following: the

---

7. See Daniélou 1954, 18–19, and Gregory of Nyssa, *Vit. Mos.* 1.58 (GNO 7.1:26), where Gregory informs us that Moses spent forty days in the darkness, during which he "shared in that eternal life" and was "outside of [his human] nature." Cf. *Vit. Mos.* 2.162–163 (7.1:86.16ff.; trans. Malherbe and Ferguson, 95): "Scripture teaches ... that religious knowledge comes at first

ἡ πρώτη ἀπὸ τῶν ψευδῶν καὶ πεπλανημένων περὶ θεοῦ ὑπολήψεων
ἀναχώρησις ἡ ἀπὸ τοῦ σκότους εἰς φῶς ἐστι μετάστασις, ἡ δὲ προσεχεστέρα
τῶν κρυπτῶν κατανόησις ἡ διὰ τῶν φαινομένων χειραγωγοῦσα τὴν ψυχὴν
πρὸς τὴν ἀόρατον φύσιν οἷόν τις νεφέλη γίνεται τὸ φαινόμενον μὲν ἅπαν
5   ἐπισκιάζουσα πρὸς δὲ τὸ κρύφιον | βλέπειν τὴν ψυχὴν χειραγωγοῦσα καὶ   323
συνεθίζουσα, ἡ δὲ διὰ τούτων ὁδεύουσα πρὸς τὰ ἄνω ψυχή, ὅσον ἐφικτόν
ἐστι τῇ ἀνθρωπίνῃ φύσει καταλιποῦσα, ἐντὸς τῶν ἀδύτων τῆς θεογνωσίας
γίνεται τῷ θείῳ γνόφῳ πανταχόθεν διαληφθεῖσα, ἐν ᾧ τοῦ φαινομένου τε
καὶ καταλαμβανομένου παντὸς ἔξω καταλειφθέντος μόνον ὑπολείπεται τῇ
10 θεωρίᾳ τῆς ψυχῆς τὸ ἀόρατόν τε καὶ ἀκατάληπτον, ἐν ᾧ ἐστιν ὁ θεός, καθώς
φησι περὶ τοῦ νομοθέτου ὁ λόγος ὅτι Εἰσῆλθε δὲ Μωϋσῆς εἰς τὸν γνόφον οὗ
ἦν ὁ θεός.

Τούτων δὲ ἡμῖν οὕτω θεωρηθέντων σκεπτέον ἂν εἴη καὶ τῶν
προκειμένων ἡμῖν ῥητῶν τὴν πρὸς τὰ εἰρημένα συγγένειαν. ἦν ὅτε μέλαινα
15 ἦν ἡ νύμφη τοῖς ἀφωτίστοις δόγμασιν ἐσκοτισμένη παραβλέψαντος αὐτὴν
τοῦ ἡλίου τοῦ διὰ τῶν πειρασμῶν τὴν ἄρριζον ἐπὶ τῶν πετρῶν σπορὰν
ἐπικαίοντος, ὅτε τῶν ἐν αὐτῇ μαχεσαμένων ἡττηθεῖσα τὸν ἀμπελῶνα τὸν
ἑαυτῆς οὐκ ἐφύλαξεν, ὅτε ἑαυτὴν ἀγνοήσασα τὰς τῶν ἐρίφων ἀγέλας ἀντὶ
τῶν προβάτων ἐποίμαινεν. ἀλλ᾽ ἐπειδὴ τῆς πρὸς τὸ κακὸν συμφυΐας ἑαυτὴν
20 ἀποσπάσασα διὰ τοῦ μυστικοῦ ἐκείνου φιλήματος τῇ πηγῇ τοῦ φωτὸς
προσαγαγεῖν τὸ στόμα ἐπόθησε, τότε καλὴ γίνεται τῷ | φωτὶ τῆς ἀληθείας   324
περιλαμφθεῖσα καὶ τὸ μέλαν τῆς ἀγνοίας ἀποκλυσαμένη τῷ ὕδατι. εἶτα ἵππῳ

first withdrawal[8] from false and erroneous notions about God takes the form of a transition from darkness to light. More attentive apprehension of hidden realities, which leads the soul to the invisible realm by way of what appears, is like a cloud that casts a shadow on everything that appears but yet induces and accustoms the soul | to look upon what is hidden. But the soul that has made its way through these stages to higher things, having left behind whatever is accessible to human nature, enters within the innermost shrine of the knowledge of God and is entirely seized about by the divine darkness; and in this darkness, since everything that appears and is comprehended has been left outside, only the invisible and the incomprehensible remain for the soul's contemplation[9]—and in them God is, just as the Word says concerning the Lawgiver: "Moses entered into the darkness where God was" (Exod 20:21).

Now that we have thus interpreted these statements, we are bound to ask whether the words before us are compatible with what I have been saying. There was a time when the Bride was *dark,* cast into darkness by unenlightened beliefs, by reason of the fact that the sun looked askance at her and by temptations scorched the seed that lay rootless on the rocks;[10] when she did not *guard* her *vineyard,* being weakened by the forces waging their war within her; when, ignorant of herself, she shepherded the herds of goats instead of sheep. But when she separated herself from any kinship with evil and sought, in that mystical kiss, to bring her mouth to the fount of light, then she became beautiful and good, illumined by the | light of truth and cleansed by water

---

to those who receive it as light.... But as the mind progresses and, through an ever greater and more perfect diligence, comes to apprehend reality, as it approaches more nearly to contemplation, it sees more clearly what of the divine nature is uncontemplated. For leaving behind everything that is observed, not only what sense comprehends but also what intelligence thinks it sees, it keeps on penetrating deeper until by the intelligence's yearning for understanding it gains access to the invisible and the incomprehensible, and there it sees God. This is the true knowledge of what is sought; this is the seeing that consists in not seeing, because that which is sought transcends all knowledge, being separated on all sides by incomprehensibility as by a kind of darkness."

8. Greek ἀναχώρησις: a technical term of Christian asceticism, usually employed to mean withdrawal from the world (see Gregory, *Vit. Mos.* 1.19 [GNO 7.1:8]), but here applied to withdrawal from falsehood and evil.

9. Origen's interpretation of the *four* stages of the soul's progress as he sees it in the Song of Songs is indicated by Ambrose of Milan, *Isaac* 6.50, and it is worth contrasting with the three-stage picture that Gregory outlines here. Gregory's interpretation here turns on themes suggested by the word "night," whereas Origen, though he notes the "swiftness" of the Word, which causes the soul to lose track of the Word for a moment (Song 5:5b), acknowledges her final success in grasping the Word.

10. For this and what immediately follows, see Song 1:5–8 and above, homily 2, pp. 48–65 (Jaeger).

ὁμοιοῦται διὰ τὸ εὔδρομον καὶ τῇ περιστερᾷ διὰ τὸ τάχος τῆς πτήσεως. δι᾽
ὧν πᾶν τὸ καταλαμβανόμενόν τε καὶ φαινόμενον ὡς ἵππος διαδραμοῦσα
καὶ ὡς περιστερὰ διαπτᾶσα πρότερον μὲν τῇ σκιᾷ τοῦ μήλου μετὰ ἐπιθυμίας
ἐπαναπαύεται μῆλον ἀντὶ νεφέλης τὸ ἐπισκιάζον κατονομάσασα, νῦν δὲ
5   ἤδη ὑπὸ τῆς θείας νυκτὸς περιέχεται, καθ᾽ ἣν ὁ νυμφίος παραγίνεται μὲν οὐ
φαίνεται δέ.

πῶς γὰρ ἂν ἐν νυκτὶ φανείη τὸ μὴ ὁρώμενον; ἀλλ᾽ αἴσθησιν μέν τινα
δίδωσι τῇ ψυχῇ τῆς παρουσίας, ἐκφεύγει δὲ τὴν ἐναργῆ κατανόησιν τῷ
ἀοράτῳ τῆς φύσεως ἐγκρυπτόμενος.

10   τίς τοίνυν ἐστὶν ἡ γινομένη τῇ ψυχῇ διὰ τῆς νυκτὸς ταύτης μυσταγωγία;
ἅπτεται τῆς θύρας ὁ λόγος. θύραν δὲ νοοῦμεν τὴν στοχαστικὴν τῶν ἀρρήτων
διάνοιαν, δι᾽ ἧς εἰσοικίζεται τὸ ζητούμενον. ἔξω τοίνυν ἑστῶσα τῆς φύσεως
ἡμῶν ἡ ἀλήθεια διὰ τῆς ἐκ μέρους γνώσεως, καθώς φησιν ὁ ἀπόστολος, ἐν
ὑπονοίαις τισὶ καὶ αἰνίγμασι θυροκρουστεῖ τὴν διάνοιαν Ἄνοιξον λέγουσα
15   καὶ μετὰ τῆς προτροπῆς ὑποτιθεμένη τὸν τρόπον, ὅπως ἀνοιγῆναι προσήκει
τὴν θύραν, οἷόν τινας κλεῖς ὀρέγουσα τὰ καλὰ ταῦτα ὀνόματα, δι᾽ ὧν τὸ
κεκλεισμένον ἀνοίγεται· κλεῖδες γάρ εἰσιν ἄντικρυς αἱ τῶν ὀνομάτων | τούτων   325
ἐμφάσεις αἱ τὰ κρυπτὰ διανοίγουσαι· ἀδελφὴ καὶ πλησίον καὶ περιστερὰ καὶ
τελεία. εἰ γὰρ βούλει σοι, φησίν, ἀνοιγῆναι τὴν θύραν καὶ ἐπαρθῆναι τῆς
20   ψυχῆς σου τὰς πύλας, ἵνα εἰσέλθῃ ὁ βασιλεὺς τῆς δόξης, χρή σε ἀδελφήν
μου γενέσθαι ἐν τῷ τὰ θελήματά μου τῇ ψυχῇ παραδέξασθαι, καθὼς ἐν τῷ
εὐαγγελίῳ φησὶν ἀδελφὸν αὐτοῦ καὶ ἀδελφὴν γίνεσθαι τὸν ἐν τοῖς θελήμασιν

from the darkness of ignorance.[11] Then she is likened to a horse for swiftness and to a dove for the speed of her flight.[12] On this account, galloping like a horse and flying like a dove through everything that appears and is comprehended, she first rests, full of desire, in the shadow of the apple tree,[13] calling that which shades her "apple tree" rather than "cloud." Now, however, she is already surrounded by the divine night, in which the Bridegroom draws near but is not manifest.[14]

But how may that which is not seen appear in the night? It confers on the soul some perception of its presence, but it escapes clear and distinct intellectual grasp in being concealed by the invisibility of its nature.

What is the initiatory process, then, that this night causes the soul to undergo? The Word touches her *door*.[15] Now by *door* we signify that intuitive[16] understanding of things inexpressible[17] through which the object of our search is brought into our home. So it is that Truth, which stands outside of our nature because our knowledge is "partial," as the apostle says (cf. 1 Cor 13:9), knocks at the door of our understanding by way of certain hints and enigmas,[18] saying *Open,* and she supplies, together with encouragement, the way in which the door is to be opened, for she provides the following beautiful names to serve as keys to open what is closed; for | the meanings of these words are plainly keys by which hidden matters are opened up—*sister,* I mean, and *close one,* and *dove,* and *perfect one.* "If it is your desire," we are told, "that the door be opened and that 'the gates' of your soul be lifted up, in order that 'the King of Glory' may come in (cf. Ps 23:7, 9), you must become my sister by accepting my will in your soul," just as in the Gospel it says that the person who lives by his will becomes his brother and sister (cf. Mark 3:35).[19] "Further, you must draw near to Truth and become in the fullest

---

11. This is a reference to baptism as "illumination," a commonplace theme since the second century and before.

12. See Song 1:10–11 (2:10?) and above, homily 3, pp. 73–79 (Jaeger), where, however, there is no allusion to the dove's swiftness.

13. See Song 2:3–5 and above, homily 4, pp. 115–19 (Jaeger).

14. For the significance of the above sentences for an understanding of Gregory's three stages of the soul's growth, see Daniélou 1954, 20ff.

15. See Aristotle, *Metaph.* 12.7 (1072b20–21): νοητὸς γὰρ γίγνεται θιγγάνων καὶ νοῶν, ὥστε ταὐτὸν νοῦς καὶ νοητόν.

16. Greek: στοχαστικήν. Gregory does not mean "operating by guesswork" but something more like "divinatory."

17. Theodoret (PG 81:149C) disagrees; the "soul's doors" are "the body's senses."

18. Greek: ἐν ... αἰνίγμασι. Cf. 1 Cor 13:12 (βλέπομεν ... δι' ἐσόπτρου ἐν αἰνίγματι).

19. Origen, if Ambrose's *Isaac* 6.51 is good evidence for his line of thought here, explained that "sister" indicates that "the marriage of the Word and the soul is spiritual," since "souls do not know covenants of wedlock or the ways of bodily union, but they are like the angels in

αὐτοῦ ζῶντα, χρὴ δέ σε καὶ προσεγγίσαι τῇ ἀληθείᾳ καὶ πλησίον ἀκριβῶς
γενέσθαι, ὥστε μηδενὶ μέσῳ διατειχίζεσθαι καὶ ἐν τῇ φύσει τῆς περιστερᾶς
ἔχειν τὸ τέλειον, τοῦτο δέ ἐστι τὸ ἀνελλιπῆ τε καὶ πεπληρωμένην εἶναι
πάσης ἀκακίας καὶ καθαρότητος. ταῦτα λαβοῦσα, ὦ ψυχή, οἷόν τινας κλεῖς

5   τὰ ὀνόματα ἄνοιξον δι' αὐτῶν τῇ ἀληθείᾳ τὴν εἴσοδον ἀδελφὴ γενομένη καὶ
πλησίον καὶ περιστερὰ καὶ τελεία. ἔσται δέ σοι τὸ κέρδος ἐκ τοῦ εἰσδέξασθαί
με καὶ εἰσοικίσασθαι ἡ ἐκ τῆς κεφαλῆς μου δρόσος, ἧς πλήρης εἰμί, καὶ αἱ τῆς
νυκτὸς ψεκάδες αἱ τῶν βοστρύχων τῶν ἐμῶν ἀπορρέουσαι.

ἐκ τούτων δὲ τὸ μὲν ἴασιν εἶναι τὴν δρόσον παρὰ τοῦ προφήτου σαφῶς
10   μεμαθήκαμεν ὅς φησιν ὅτι Ἡ δρόσος ἡ παρὰ σοῦ ἴαμα αὐτοῖς ἐστιν, αἱ δὲ
τῆς νυκτὸς ψεκάδες τῆς προθεωρηθείσης ἔχονται διανοίας· οὐ γάρ ἐστι
δυνατὸν τὸν ἐντὸς τῶν ἀδύτων τε | καὶ ἀθεωρήτων γενόμενον ὄμβρῳ τινὶ τῆς   326
γνώσεως ἐντυχεῖν ἢ χειμάρρῳ, ἀλλ' ἀγαπητὸν εἰ λεπταῖς τισι καὶ ἀμυδραῖς
διανοίαις ἐπιψεκάζοι τὴν γνῶσιν αὐτῶν ἡ ἀλήθεια διὰ τῶν ἁγίων τε καὶ
15   θεοφορουμένων τῆς λογικῆς σταγόνος ἀπορρεούσης. βοστρύχους γὰρ οἶμαι
τῆς τοῦ παντὸς κεφαλῆς ἐξηρτημένους τροπικῶς ὀνομάζεσθαι προφήτας καὶ
εὐαγγελιστὰς καὶ ἀποστόλους, ὧν ἕκαστος ὅσον ἐχώρουν ἐκ τῶν σκοτεινῶν
τε καὶ ἀποκρύφων καὶ ἀοράτων θησαυρῶν ἀρυόμενοι ἡμῖν μὲν ποταμοὶ
γίνονται πλήρεις ὑδάτων. ὡς δὲ πρὸς τὴν ὄντως ἀλήθειαν δροσώδεις εἰσὶ
20   ψεκάδες, κἂν τῷ πλήθει τε καὶ μεγέθει τῆς διδασκαλίας πλημμύρωσιν.

οἷος ὁ Παῦλος ἦν ποταμὸς ὑπὲρ τὸν οὐρανὸν τοῖς τῶν νοημάτων κύμασι
κορυφούμενος ἕως τρίτου οὐρανοῦ, ἕως τοῦ παραδείσου, ἕως τῶν ἀρρήτων
τε καὶ ἀνεκφωνήτων ῥημάτων καὶ διὰ πάσης τῆς τοιαύτης μεγαληγορίας
πελαγίζων τῷ λόγῳ δείκνυσι πάλιν ὅτι ψεκάς τίς ἐστι δροσώδης ὁ λόγος
25   οὗτος συγκρίσει τοῦ ὄντως λόγου, δι' ὧν φησιν ὅτι Ἐκ μέρους γινώσκομεν
καὶ ἐκ μέρους προφητεύομεν· καὶ Εἴ τις δοκεῖ ἐγνωκέναι τι, οὔπω ἔγνω καθὼς
δεῖ γνῶναι· καὶ Ἐγὼ ἐμαυτὸν οὔπω λογίζομαι κατειληφέναι. εἰ τοίνυν ἡ ἰκμὰς
τῆς δρόσου καὶ ἡ τῶν βοστρύχων ψεκὰς ποταμοὶ δοκοῦσι | καὶ πελάγη καὶ   327
κύματα πρὸς τὴν ἡμετέραν κρινόμενα δύναμιν, τί χρὴ περὶ τῆς πηγῆς ἐκείνης

sense 'close' to it, so that there is nothing between you and it and you possess the dove's perfection in your own nature—that is, you are full, lacking nothing, of innocence and purity. When, O soul, you have accepted these words as keys, use them to give entrance to the Truth, having become *sister* and *close one* and *dove* and *perfect*. And when you have received me, and taken me into your home, your reward will be the *dew* from my head, of which I am full, and *the drops of the night* that flow from my locks."

Now we have learned from the prophet that of this pair the dew symbolizes healing, for he says, "The dew that comes from you is healing for them." As to *the drops of the night,* they are connected with the line of thought we discerned above. It is not possible, after all, for one who has entered the place of things beyond our grasp and | vision to take in some great torrent or deluge of knowledge, but it is enough if Truth drizzle down knowledge of them[20] by way of thoughts that are subtle and only just discernible, pouring out reason's drop through persons who are holy and inspired. For it is my belief that the *locks* that hang from the head of the All should be taken to figure prophets and evangelists and apostles; for each of them draws in as much as he can absorb of the dark, hidden, and invisible treasures, and for us they become rivers full of waters. To be sure they are drops of dew as measured by the authentic Truth, yet they overflow with a teaching that is at once multifarious and profound.

Paul was such a river. He soared above the sky until he reached the third heaven, the paradise,[21] even the "things that cannot be told" or uttered (cf. 2 Cor 12:2–4). And flooded with all this deep talk as he was, he still indicates by what he says that by comparison with the true Word, this speech is on the order of a dewdrop. Hence he says: "We know in part, and we prophesy in part" (1 Cor 13:9); and "If someone thinks he knows something, he does not yet know as he ought to know" (1 Cor 8:2); and "I do not yet reckon myself to have understood" (Phil 3:13). If therefore the moisture of the dew, and the drop that rests on the hair, seem to be rivers | and seas and billows when measured by the standard of our abilities, what is one to think about that Wellspring who says: "If anyone thirst, let him come to me and drink"?

---

heaven." Theodoret's line of interpretation is closer to Gregory's: "And I also call you my sister, not only because of our affinity of nature ... but also because of our shared devotion" (τὴν τῆς εὐσέβειας οἰκειότητα; PG 81:152B).

20. Cf. Philo, *Her.* 42.204. Philo is referring to the cloud of Exod 14:20, which, because it protected the Israelites from the Egyptians, he envisages as raining wisdom on virtuous souls but "blizzards of vengeance" (Colson and Whitaker 1932) on the wicked.

21. See 2 Cor 12:2–4, where Paul appears to equate the third heaven (v. 2) with paradise (v. 3); cf. Clement of Alexandria, *Exc.* 51.1, where, however, it is the fourth heaven that is identified as the Garden.

λογίσασθαι τῆς εἰπούσης ὅτι Εἴ τις διψᾷ, ἐρχέσθω πρός με καὶ πινέτω; αὐτὸς
ἕκαστος τῶν ἀκουόντων δι᾽ ἀναλογίας τῶν εἰρημένων στοχασμὸν λαμβανέτω
τοῦ θαύματος. εἰ γὰρ ἡ ψεκὰς εἰς ποταμῶν ἐξήρκεσε γένεσιν, τί αὐτὸν τὸν τοῦ
θεοῦ ποταμὸν διὰ τῆς ψεκάδος ταύτης ἔστιν ἀναλογίσασθαι;

5   Ἴδωμεν δὲ καὶ πῶς ὑπακούει τῷ λόγῳ ἡ νύμφη, πῶς ἀνοίγει τῷ
νυμφίῳ τὴν εἴσοδον. Ἐξεδυσάμην, φησί, τὸν χιτῶνά μου· πῶς ἐνδύσομαι
αὐτόν; ἐνιψάμην τοὺς πόδας μου· πῶς μολυνῶ αὐτούς; καλῶς ἤκουσε τοῦ
κελεύσαντος ἀδελφὴν αὐτὴν καὶ πλησίον γενέσθαι καὶ περιστερὰν καὶ
τελείαν, ἵνα διὰ τούτων εἰσοικισθῇ τῇ ψυχῇ ἡ ἀλήθεια· ἐποίησε γὰρ ἅπερ
10   ἤκουσεν ἐκδυσαμένη τὸν δερμάτινον ἐκεῖνον χιτῶνα, ὃν μετὰ τὴν ἁμαρτίαν
περιεβάλετο, καὶ ἀπονιψαμένη τῶν ποδῶν τὸ γεῶδες, ᾧ ἐνειλήθη ἀπὸ τῆς ἐν
παραδείσῳ διαγωγῆς εἰς τὴν γῆν ἀναλύσασα, ὅτε ἤκουσεν ὅτι Γῆ εἶ καὶ εἰς
γῆν ἀπελεύσῃ.

διὰ τούτων ἤνοιξεν ἐπὶ τὴν ψυχὴν τῷ λόγῳ τὴν εἴσοδον διασταλέντος
15   τοῦ τῆς | καρδίας παραπετάσματος, τουτέστι τῆς σαρκός. σάρκα δὲ εἰπὼν τὸν   328
παλαιὸν λέγω ἄνθρωπον, ὃν ἐκδύσασθαί τε καὶ ἀποθέσθαι κελεύει ὁ θεῖος
ἀπόστολος τοὺς μέλλοντας τῷ λουτρῷ τοῦ λόγου τὸν ῥύπον τῶν βάσεων
τῆς ψυχῆς ἀποκλύζεσθαι. οὐκοῦν ὁ τὸν παλαιὸν ἀπεκδυσάμενος ἄνθρωπον
καὶ περιελὼν τῆς καρδίας τὸ κάλυμμα, ἤνοιξε τῷ λόγῳ τὴν εἴσοδον, ὃν ἐντὸς
20   γενόμενον ἔνδυμα ποιεῖται ἑαυτῆς ἡ ψυχὴ κατὰ τὴν τοῦ ἀποστόλου ὑφήγησιν,
ὃς κελεύει τὸν ἐκδυσάμενον τὴν ῥακώδη τοῦ παλαιοῦ ἀνθρώπου περιβολὴν
Ἐνδύσασθαι τὸν καινὸν χιτῶνα τὸν κατὰ θεὸν κτισθέντα ἐν ὁσιότητι καὶ
δικαιοσύνῃ· Ἰησοῦν δὲ λέγει εἶναι τὸ ἔνδυμα.

ἡ δὲ ὁμολογία τῆς νύμφης τοῦ μηκέτι τὸν ἀποβληθέντα χιτῶνα πάλιν
25   ἀναλαμβάνειν, ἀλλ᾽ ἀρκεῖσθαι τῷ ἑνὶ χιτῶνι κατὰ τὸν δοθέντα τοῖς μαθηταῖς
νόμον, ὃν διὰ τῆς ἄνωθεν γεννήσεως ἀνακαινισθεῖσα μετημφιάσατο, βεβαιοῖ
τοῦ κυρίου τὸν λόγον τὸν κελεύοντα τοὺς ἅπαξ τῷ θείῳ κοσμηθέντας

Let every hearer make for himself an estimate of the wonder that bears some proportion to what has been said. For if a <single> drop is enough to give rise to rivers, what, on the basis of this drop, can one reckon the river of God itself to be?

But let us further see how the Bride is obedient to the Word, how she opens a door for the Bridegroom. *I have removed my tunic,* she says, *How shall I put it on? I have washed my feet. How shall I soil them?* Rightly did she hear the One who had commanded her to become *sister* and *close one* and *dove* and *perfect,* in order that in this way Truth might take up residence in her soul, for she did what she heard. She put off that "tunic of skin" that she had put on after the sin (cf. Gen 3:21),[22] and from her feet she washed the earthy stuff that covered them after she returned to the earth from her sojourn in the Garden, when she heard the words: "Earth thou art and to earth thou shalt return" (Gen 3:19).

These are the ways in which she opened a way into her soul for the Word, having rent the veil of | her heart, that is, the flesh. When I say "flesh," what I mean is "the old humanity" (Col 3:9),[23] which the divine apostle commands to be stripped off and put aside by those who are going to wash off the filth of the soul's feet in the bath of the Word.[24] So whoever has taken off the old humanity and rent the veil of the heart has opened an entrance for the Word. And when the Word has entered her, the soul makes him her garment in accordance with the instruction of the apostle; for he commands the person who has taken off the rags of the old humanity "to put on the new" tunic that "has been created after the likeness of God in holiness and righteousness" (Eph 4:24); and he says that this garment is Jesus (cf. Rom 13:14).

As to the Bride's affirmation that she will never again take up the tunic she has put off but will be content, in accordance with the command given to the disciples (cf. Matt 10:10), with the one tunic[25] that she put on when she was renewed through the rebirth from above—this confession, I say, confirms the Lord's word, which commands that those who have once for all been dressed

---

22. Cf. Ambrose of Milan, *Isaac* 6.52: "she took off that robe of skins that Adam and Eve had received after their sin, the robe of corruption, the robe of the passions." And see below, homily 12, p. 351 ("dead form of existence"), as well as *De anima et resurrectione* (PG 46:148C): δέρμα δὲ ἀκούων τὸ σχῆμα τῆς ἀλόγου φύσεως νοεῖν μοι δοκῶ, ᾧ πρὸς τὸ πάθος οἰκειώθεντες περιεβλήθημεν.

23. Cf. Theodoret (PG 81:152C), who alludes to the same Pauline text.

24. Clearly in this whole passage Gregory has baptism, the beginning of the Christian way, in his mind, not only as a washing but as a "putting off" of one identity and the assumption of a new identity. For a parallel, see the opening words of homily 1, and note, just below, the reference to renewal "through the rebirth from above."

25. See Mark 6:9, with Matt 10:10 and Luke 9:3.

ἐνδύματι μηκέτι ἐπενδύσασθαι τὸν τῆς ἁμαρτίας χιτῶνα, μηδὲ δύο χιτῶνας
ἔχειν, ἀλλὰ τὸν ἕνα μόνον, ἵνα μὴ δύο περὶ τὸν αὐτὸν ὦσιν οἱ ἀσύμβατοι πρὸς
ἀλλήλους χιτῶνες. τίς γὰρ κοινωνία τῷ σκοτεινῷ ἐνδύματι πρὸς τὸ φωτοειδές
| τε καὶ ἄϋλον;   329
5   οὐ μόνον δὲ τοῦτό φησιν ὁ νόμος τὸ μὴ δεῖν δύο χιτῶνας ἔχειν, ἀλλὰ
μηδὲ ἐπιρράπτειν τὸ καινὸν ὕφασμα τῷ παλαιῷ ἱματίῳ, ἵνα μὴ χείρων γένηται
ἡ ἀσχημοσύνη τοῦ τὸ τοιοῦτον περιβαλλομένου μήτε τοῦ ἐνραφέντος
μείναντος καὶ τοῦ παλαιοῦ χεῖρον τὸ σχίσμα παθόντος καὶ δυσθεράπευτον·
Αἴρει γάρ, φησί, τὸ πλήρωμα τὸ καινὸν τοῦ παλαιοῦ καὶ χεῖρον σχίσμα
10   γίνεται, ὡς δημοσιεύεσθαι δι᾽ αὐτοῦ τὰ ἀσχήμονα. διὰ τοῦτό φησιν
Ἐξεδυσάμην τὸν χιτῶνά μου· πῶς ἐνδύσομαι αὐτόν; τίς γὰρ ἂν βλέπων περὶ
ἑαυτὸν τὸν ἡλιοειδῆ τοῦ κυρίου χιτῶνα τὸν διὰ καθαρότητος καὶ ἀφθαρσίας
ἱστουργηθέντα, οἷον ἐπὶ τῆς <ἐπὶ> τοῦ ὄρους μεταμορφώσεως ἔδειξεν, εἶτα
καταδέχεται τὸ πτωχόν τε καὶ ῥακῶδες ἱμάτιον ἑαυτῷ περιθεῖναι, ὅπερ ὁ
15   μέθυσος καὶ πορνοκόπος, καθὼς ἡ Παροιμία φησί, περιβάλλεται;
        Ἀλλ᾽ οὐδὲ τοὺς πόδας νιψαμένη πάλιν τῇ βάσει τὸν ἐκ τῆς γῆς μολυσμὸν
παραδέχεται· Ἐνιψάμην γάρ, φησί, τοὺς πόδας μου· πῶς μολυνῶ αὐτούς;
οὐδὲ γὰρ Μωϋσῆς τῷ θείῳ προστάγματι τῆς νεκρᾶς τῶν δερμάτων περιβολῆς
ἐλευθερώ|σας τοὺς πόδας, ὅτε τῆς ἁγίας τε καὶ πεφωτισμένης ἐπέβαινε   330
20   γῆς, πάλιν ἱστορεῖται διαλαβὼν τοὺς πόδας τοῖς ὑποδήμασιν, ὅς γε καὶ τὴν
ἱερατικὴν ἐσθῆτα κατὰ τὸν τύπον τὸν ἐν τῷ ὄρει δειχθέντα φιλοτεχνήσας,
χρυσοῦ καὶ πορφύρας καὶ βύσσου καὶ ὑακίνθου καὶ κόκκου τὰς αὐγὰς
συγκεράσας ἐν τῷ ὑφάσματι, ὥστε σύμμικτον ἐκ πάντων ἀπαστράπτειν τὸ
κάλλος, οὐδένα τοῖς ποσὶ κόσμον ἐπετεχνήσατο, ἀλλ᾽ ἦν καλλωπισμὸς τοῦ
25   ἱερατικοῦ ποδὸς τὸ γυμνὸν εἶναι πάσης περιβολῆς καὶ ἐλεύθερον· χρὴ γὰρ
τὸν ἱερέα πάντως ἐπὶ τῆς ἁγίας βεβηκέναι γῆς, ἧς μετὰ νεκρῶν δερμάτων
ἐπιβατεύειν οὐ θέμις. διὰ τοῦτο καὶ τοῖς μαθηταῖς ὁ κύριος ἀπαγορεύει τὰ
ὑποδήματα, ἐπειδὴ κελεύει αὐτοὺς εἰς ὁδὸν ἐθνῶν μὴ πορεύεσθαι ἀλλὰ διὰ
τῆς ἁγίας ὁδοῦ προϊέναι.

up in the divine garment shall never again put on sin's tunic, nor possess two tunics, but only the one, lest there be two conflicting garments on one person. For what does the garment of mourning have in common with the one that is full of light | and immaterial?

The law, though, does not say merely that one must not have two tunics but also that one must not sew new cloth on an old cloak; otherwise the shabby look of the person who wears it becomes even worse when the patch fails to hold, and the old garment suffers a tear that is worse and all but impossible to mend. For he says, "The new patch will tear away from the old cloth, and the result will be a worse tear" (Mark 2:21), which will put the disgrace on public display. Hence she says, *I have removed my tunic. How shall I put it on?* Who is there, after all, who sees himself garbed in the Lord's glistening tunic—woven out of purity and incorruptibility as he manifested it in his transfiguration on the mount—and then allows himself to assume the poor, ragged garment in which "the drunkard and whoremonger," as Proverbs (23:21) says, attires himself?

Nor does she whose feet have been washed ever again contract, in her walking, the defilement of things earthy. For, says she, *I have washed my feet. How shall I soil them?"* Furthermore, it is related that Moses, after, at God's command, he had liberated | his feet from their dead clothing of skins upon entering the holy and luminous ground (cf. Exod 3:5), did not put those shoes back on.[26] And when he had made the priestly garment after the pattern shown him on the mountain—mixing the gleaming colors of "gold and purple and scarlet and linen" (cf. Exod 28:5, 8, 15) in the robe, so that it was refulgent with a beauty mingled out of all of these—he made nothing to adorn the feet. No, the adornment of the priest's foot was its nakedness and its freedom from any covering, for the priest must ever walk on holy ground, and it is not right to enter holy ground wearing dead skins. Hence too the Lord forbade his disciples to wear sandals when he ordered them not to travel "the way of the Gentiles" (Matt 10:9, 5) but to take the holy way.

And you are in no wise unacquainted with this holy way by which he orders his disciples to go, for you have learned about it from him who said, "I

---

26. Cf. *Vit. Mos.* 2.22 (GNO 7.1:39.22ff.), where the shoes that Moses removed from his feet (Exod 3:5) are described as "the dead and earthy wrapping of skins that was put around our species [φύσις] at the beginning." Gregory, as Daniélou observed, employs the image of the shoes as an equivalent for that of the "tunics of skin" (Daniélou 1954, 27), and thus the theophany at the burning bush becomes for Gregory another symbol of baptism, i.e., of the transition from death (putting off of the "dead" self represented by Moses' shoes) to resurrection (here portrayed as enlightenment). See below, p. 331 (Jaeger): "she who has once and for all, through baptism, taken off her sandals."

οὐκ ἀγνοεῖς δὲ πάντως τὴν ἁγίαν ὁδόν, δι' ἧς οἱ μαθηταὶ τρέχειν κελεύονται, μαθὼν παρὰ τοῦ εἰπόντος ὅτι Ἐγώ εἰμι ἡ ὁδός, ἧς οὐκ ἔστιν ἅψασθαι τὸν μὴ ὑπολυσάμενον τὴν τοῦ νεκροῦ ἀνθρώπου περιβολήν. ἐπεὶ οὖν ἐν ταύτῃ ἐγένετο τῇ ὁδῷ ἡ νύμφη, ἐν ᾗ τῶν δι' αὐτῆς περιπατούντων ὁ κύριος

5   νίπτει τοὺς πόδας τῷ ὕδατι καὶ ἐκμάσσει τῷ λεντίῳ ᾧ διεζώσατο (δύναμις δέ ἐστι καθαρτικὴ τῶν ἁμαρτιῶν τὸ τοῦ κυρίου διάζωσμα· Ἐνεδύσατο γάρ, φησί, κύριος δύναμιν καὶ περιεζώσατο), διὰ τοῦτο καθαρθεῖα τοὺς πόδας ἐπὶ τῆς ὁδοῦ τῆς βασιλικῆς ἑαυτὴν φυλάσσει οὐκ | ἐκκλίνουσα εἰς δεξιὰ ἢ εἰς   331 ἀριστερά, ἵνα μὴ καθ' ἑκάτερον ἔξω τῆς ὁδοῦ παρενεγκοῦσα τὸ ἴχνος μολύνῃ

10   τῷ πηλῷ τὸν πόδα.

νοεῖς δὲ πάντως τὸ διὰ τῶν εἰρημένων δηλούμενον ὅτι ἡ ἅπαξ διὰ τοῦ βαπτίσματος ὑπολυσαμένη τὰ ὑποδήματα (ἴδιον γὰρ τοῦ βαπτίζοντος ἔργον τὸ λύειν τοὺς ἱμάντας τῶν ὑποδεδεμένων, καθὼς Ἰωάννης διεμαρτύρατο μὴ δύνασθαι τοῦτο ἐπὶ μόνου τοῦ κυρίου ποιῆσαι· πῶς γὰρ ἂν ἔλυσε τὸν μηδὲ

15   τὴν ἀρχὴν τῷ ἱμάντι τῆς ἁμαρτίας ἐνδεδεμένον;) αὕτη τοὺς πόδας ἐνίψατο πάντα γήϊνον ῥύπον συναποβαλοῦσα τοῖς ὑποδήμασιν. φυλάσσει τοίνυν ἐπὶ τῆς πεπλακωμένης ὁδοῦ τὴν βάσιν ἀμόλυντον, ὡς καὶ ὁ Δαβὶδ ἐποίει, ὅτε τοῦ πηλοῦ τὴν ἰλὺν ἀποκλυσάμενος ἐπὶ τῆς πέτρας ἔστησε τοὺς ἑαυτοῦ πόδας οὕτως εἰπὼν τῷ λόγῳ ὅτι Ἀνήγαγέ με ἐκ λάκκου ταλαιπωρίας καὶ ἀπὸ πηλοῦ

20   ἰλύος καὶ ἔστησεν ἐπὶ πέτραν τοὺς πόδας μου καὶ κατεύθυνε τὰ διαβήματά μου. πέτραν δὲ νοοῦμεν τὸν κύριον ὅς ἐστι φῶς καὶ ἀλήθεια καὶ ἀφθαρσία καὶ δικαιοσύνη, δι' ὧν ἡ πνευματικὴ | ὁδὸς διαπλακοῦται. ὧν ὁ μὴ παρατραπεὶς   332 καθ' ἑκάτερον καθαρὸν διασῴζει τὸ ἴχνος οὐδαμόθεν τῷ πηλῷ τῆς ἡδονῆς μολυνόμενον.

25   ταῦτά ἐστι κατά γε τὸν ἐμὸν λόγον, δι' ὧν ἡ θύρα τῷ λόγῳ παρὰ τῆς νύμφης ἀνοίγεται· ἡ γὰρ ὁμολογία τοῦ μηκέτι ἀναλαβεῖν τὸν ἀποβληθέντα πηλὸν μηδὲ τῇ πορείᾳ τοῦ βίου τὸν γεώδη μολυσμὸν παραδέξασθαι εἴσοδος γίνεται τοῦ ἁγιασμοῦ ἐπὶ τὴν οὕτω παρεσκευασμένην ψυχήν. ἁγιασμὸς δὲ ὁ κύριος. καὶ τοῦτο μὲν τοῖς εἰρημένοις ἐπεραιώθη τὸ νόημα.

30   Πάλιν δὲ μετὰ τοῦτο τῆς ὑπερκειμένης ἀναβάσεως ἅπτεται ἡ ψυχὴ οὐκέτι φωνῆς τὴν καρδίαν θυροκρουστούσης ἀλλ' αὐτῆς τῆς θείας χειρὸς διὰ τῆς ὀπῆς ἐπὶ τὰ ἐντὸς παραδύσης· Ἀδελφιδός μου γάρ, φησίν, ἀπέστειλε τὴν χεῖρα αὐτοῦ διὰ τῆς ὀπῆς, καὶ ἡ κοιλία μου ἐθροήθη ἐπ' αὐτόν.

δῆλον δὲ πάντως ἐστὶ τῷ συνετῶς ἐπαΐοντι, ὅσον πλεονάζει τῷ ὕψει τὰ

35   νῦν εἰρημένα παρὰ τὰ πρότερον· Ἄνοιξον λέγει πρὸς τὴν νύμφην ὁ λόγος· δίδωσιν αὐτῇ διὰ τῶν θείων ὀνομάτων τοῦ ἀνοῖξαι τὴν δύναμιν· ὑπακούει τῷ λόγῳ ἡ νύμφη (γίνεται γὰρ ὅπερ ἤκουσεν· ἀδελφὴ καὶ πλησίον καὶ περιστερὰ καὶ τελεία)· ἀποδύεται τὸν δερμάτινον ἐκεῖνον χιτῶνα καὶ τὸν ῥύπον τῶν ποδῶν ἀπονίπτεται καὶ οὔτε τὸ εἰδεχθὲς καὶ ῥωγαλέον ἐκεῖνο ἱμάτιον

am the way," the way upon which no one can set a foot who has not removed the garment of our dead humanity. Since, then, the Bride finds herself on this very road, on which the Lord washes with water the feet of those who walk it and dries them with the towel that girds his waist (and the belt that girds the Lord's waist has the power to cleanse away sin, for it says, "The Lord is robed, he is girded with power" [Ps 92:1])—for this reason, I say, once her feet are cleansed, she keeps herself on the royal road. She does not | stray to the right or to the left, lest she step off the road on either hand and defile her foot with mud.

You perceive clearly, then, what these words convey: that she who has once and for all, through baptism, taken off her sandals (for it is the proper business of a baptizer to loose the thongs of those who are wearing sandals, just as John testified that he was unable to do this in the sole case of the Lord, for how could he loose one who had never been bound by the thong of sin?), she has had her feet washed and has shed, with her sandals, all earthy filth. Therefore she keeps her undefiled feet to the paved road, just as David did when he washed off the slimy clay and fixed his feet on the rock, as he says: "He drew me up from the pit of distress, out of the miry bog, and set my feet upon a rock and made my steps straight" (Ps 39:3). The rock we understand to be the Lord, who is light and truth and incorruption and righteousness; and with these qualities the spiritual | road is paved. The soul that does not turn aside in either direction keeps her feet clean and pure, entirely unsullied by the mire of pleasure.

These, as I see it, are the means by which the Bride opens her door to the Word. Testimony to the effect that one has not once more taken on the muck that had been removed nor, by the conduct of one's life, made room for earthy pollution—this allows holiness to enter the soul that is thus prepared. But holiness means the Lord. And it is this idea that the words of the text convey.

Thereupon the soul once again takes in hand the ascent on high—no longer in response to a voice knocking at the door of her heart but to the divine hand itself as it slips in through the opening to the interior. For she says: *My kinsman has put his hand through the opening, and my heart has cried out for him.*

Now to anyone whose ear is attuned to understanding, it is perfectly plain how much more exalted in tone these words are than those that were spoken earlier. The Word says to the Bride, *Open.* By according her names of divine import, he gives her the power to open. The Bride obeys the Word (for she becomes what she has heard: *sister* and *beloved* and *dove* and *perfect*). She puts off that "tunic of skin" and washes the dirt from her feet, and she neither puts that ragged and ugly garment back on | nor sets her foot further upon the earth. She has heard his voice, then, and has obeyed his command:

πάλιν ἑαυτῇ περιτίθησιν | οὔτε τῇ γῇ πρὸς τὸ λοιπὸν ἐναπερείδει τὸ ἴχνος· 333
ἤκουσεν οὖν αὐτοῦ τῆς φωνῆς καὶ τῷ προστάγματι πείθεται· ἀνοίγει τὴν
θύραν περιελομένη τῆς καρδίας τὸ κάλυμμα· διέσχε τῆς θύρας τὸ τῆς σαρκὸς
παραπέτασμα· πᾶσα ἠνοίγη τῆς ψυχῆς ἡ πύλη, ἵνα εἰσέλθῃ ὁ βασιλεὺς τῆς
5   δόξης. ἀλλ᾽ ἡ τῆς πύλης εὐρυχωρία μικρά τις ἀπεδείχθη τρυμαλιὰ στενὴ
καὶ βραχεῖα, δι᾽ ἧς οὐκ αὐτὸς ὁ νυμφίος ἀλλ᾽ ἡ χεὶρ αὐτοῦ μόγις ἐχώρησεν,
ὥστε δι᾽ αὐτῆς ἐπὶ τὸ ἐντὸς γενέσθαι καὶ ἅψασθαι τῆς ἐπιθυμούσης τὸν
νυμφίον ἰδεῖν, ἢ τοσοῦτον ἐκέρδανε μόνον ὅσον γνῶναι ὅτι ἡ χεὶρ ἐκείνη τοῦ
ποθουμένου ἐστίν.
10   οἷα δὲ ἡμῖν ὑποδείκνυται δόγματα διὰ τῆς ἐν τοῖς εἰρημένοις φιλοσοφίας
μάθοιμεν ἄν, εἰ μικρὸν τῷ λόγῳ προσδιατρίψαιμεν· ἡ ἀνθρωπίνη ψυχὴ δύο
φύσεων οὖσα μεθόριος, ὧν ἡ μὲν ἀσώματός ἐστι καὶ νοερὰ καὶ ἀκήρατος ἡ δὲ
ἑτέρα σωματικὴ καὶ ὑλώδης καὶ ἄλογος, ἐπειδὰν τάχιστα τῆς πρὸς τὸν παχύν
τε καὶ γεώδη βίον σχέσεως | ἐκκαθαρθεῖσα δι᾽ ἀρετῆς ἀναβλέψῃ πρὸς τὸ 334
15   συγγενὲς καὶ θειότερον, οὐ παύεται διερευνωμένη καὶ ἀναζητοῦσα τὴν τῶν
ὄντων ἀρχήν, τίς ἡ τοῦ κάλλους τῶν ὄντων πηγή, πόθεν βρύει ἡ δύναμις, τί τὸ
πηγάζον τὴν ἐμφαινομένην τοῖς οὖσι σοφίαν. πάντας δὲ λογισμοὺς καὶ πᾶσαν
ἐρευνητικὴν νοημάτων δύναμιν ἀνακινοῦσα καὶ περιεργαζομένη καταλαβεῖν
τὸ ζητούμενον ὅρον ποιεῖται τῆς καταλήψεως τοῦ θεοῦ τὴν ἐνέργειαν μόνην
20   τὴν μέχρις ἡμῶν κατιοῦσαν, ἧς διὰ τῆς ζωῆς ἡμῶν αἰσθανόμεθα.
      καὶ ὥσπερ τὸ τῷ ὕδατι συναναδιδόμενον ἐκ τῆς γῆς πνεῦμα οὐχ ἵσταται
περὶ τὸν πυθμένα τῆς λίμνης, ἀλλὰ πομφόλυξ γενόμενον ἐπὶ τὸ ἄνω πρὸς τὸ
συγγενὲς ἀνατρέχει καί, ὅταν διέλθῃ τὴν ἄκραν τοῦ ὕδατος ἐπιφάνειαν καὶ
καταμιχθῇ πρὸς τὸν ἀέρα, τότε τῆς ἐπὶ τὸ ἄνω κινήσεως ἵσταται, τοιοῦτόν
25   τι πάσχει καὶ ἡ τὰ θεῖα διερευνωμένη ψυχή· ἐπειδὰν ἐκ τῶν κάτωθεν πρὸς
τὴν τῶν ὑπερκειμένων γνῶσιν ἑαυτὴν ἀνατείνῃ, τὰ τῆς ἐνεργείας αὐτοῦ
θαύματα καταλαβοῦσα περαιτέρω προελθεῖν διὰ τῆς πολυπραγμοσύνης τέως
οὐ δύναται, ἀλλὰ θαυμάζει καὶ | σέβεται τὸν ὅτι ἔστι μόνον δι᾽ ὧν ἐνεργεῖ 335
γινωσκόμενον.
30   ὁρᾷ τὸ οὐράνιον κάλλος, τὰς τῶν φωστήρων αὐγάς, τὴν ὀξεῖαν τοῦ πόλου
κυκλοφορίαν, τὴν εὔτακτόν τε καὶ ἐναρμόνιον τῶν ἐντὸς ἄστρων περιφοράν,
τὸν ἐνιαύσιον κύκλον τέσσαρσι καιροῖς εἰς ἑαυτὸν ἀναστρέφοντα, τὴν

she opens the door when she has drawn back the veil of her heart. She has pulled away from the door the curtain of the flesh. The gateway of the soul is thrown fully open, in order that the King of Glory may come in. But the generous space that the gateway affords turns out to be a tiny hole, narrow and confined. Through it the hand of the Bridegroom will scarcely pass, and least of all the Bridegroom himself, so as to come inside and touch the soul who wants to see the Bridegroom. Her gain consists in no more than this: to know that that hand belongs to the One she longs for.

We shall grasp the truths[27] conveyed by the philosophy contained in these statements if we dwell a bit longer on the message. The human soul stands on the borderline between two kinds of reality. One of them is incorporeal and intelligent and pure, while the other is corporeal and material and nonrational. When, therefore, cleansed as soon as possible of her inclination toward a gross and earthly life, | the soul looks up with the help of virtue toward what is akin to her and closer to the divine, she never stops searching and seeking after the Principle of the things that are, after the Wellspring of their beauty, after the Source of the power that fills them, after whatever it is that pours forth the wisdom displayed in them. Stirring all her thought processes and all the exploratory power of her concepts, and striving earnestly to comprehend what she is seeking, she attains, as the limit of her apprehension of God, nothing more than that divine activity [energeia] that comes down and reaches to us,[28] and which we sense through the medium of our life.

Consider how the breath that comes along with water out of the earth does not stay at the bottom of the pool but becomes a bubble and makes its way up to what is akin to it; and only when it has got to the surface of the water and is mingled with the air does its upward course come to a halt. Something like this happens also to the soul in search of things divine. When she stretches herself out from things below toward the knowledge of things on high, once she has grasped the marvels produced by God's working, she cannot for a while progress further by her busy search for knowledge, but is filled with wonder and | worships the One who is known to exist only through the things that his activity brings about.

She sees the beauty of the heavens, the radiance of the lights, the precise revolution of the celestial sphere, the orderly and harmonious circular movement of the stars within it, the annual cycle of the four seasons returning upon itself, the earth adapting itself to what encompasses it and changing its own doings in accord with the variance in the motion of the heavens. She

---

27. The Greek is δόγματα, fundamental or essential teachings.

28. Cf. the language of Theodoret (PG 81:153A): εἰσαγαγὼν τὴν χεῖρα τουτέστι τὴν ἐνέργειαν. See above, homily 1, p. 33 (Jaeger), and n. 19 there.

γῆν συνδιατιθεμένην τῷ περιέχοντι καὶ τῇ διαφορᾷ τῆς τῶν ὑπερκειμένων
κινήσεως τὰς ἰδίας ἐνεργείας συνεξαλλάσσουσαν, τάς τε πολυειδεῖς ἐν
τοῖς ζῴοις φύσεις τῶν τε καθ' ὕδατος διαιτωμένων καὶ τῶν τὴν διαέριον
ἀπολαχόντων φορὰν καὶ οἷς χερσαῖος ὁ βίος, τάς τε παντοδαπὰς τῶν φυτῶν
5   ἰδέας καὶ τὰς ποικίλας πόας ποιότητι καὶ δυνάμει καὶ σχήματι ἀλλήλων
διαφερούσας καὶ τὰς τῶν καρπῶν τε καὶ χυμῶν ἰδιότητας· <ταῦτα τοίνυν>
καὶ τὰ ἄλλα, δι' ὧν ἡ ἐνέργεια τοῦ θεοῦ διαδείκνυται, βλέπουσα ἡ ψυχὴ διὰ
τοῦ θαύματος τῶν φαινομένων ἀναλογίζεται τῇ διανοίᾳ τὸν διὰ τῶν ἔργων
νοούμενον ὅτι | ἔστιν.   336
10   ἴσως δὲ κατὰ τὸν αἰῶνα τὸν μέλλοντα, ὅταν παρέλθῃ πᾶν τὸ ὁρώμενον
κατὰ τὴν τοῦ κυρίου φωνήν, ὅς φησιν ὅτι Ὁ οὐρανὸς καὶ ἡ γῆ παρελεύσεται,
καὶ εἰς ἐκείνην μετέλθωμεν τὴν ζωήν, ἣ ὑπὲρ ὀφθαλμόν τέ ἐστι καὶ ἀκοὴν
καὶ διάνοιαν, τότε οὐκέτι ἐκ μέρους διὰ τῶν ἔργων ἐπιγνωσόμεθα τὴν τοῦ
ἀγαθοῦ φύσιν ὥσπερ καὶ νῦν οὐδὲ διὰ τῆς τῶν φαινομένων ἐνεργείας τὸ
15   ὑπερκείμενον νοηθήσεται, ἀλλ' ἑτέρως καταληφθήσεται πάντως τὸ εἶδος
τῆς ἀφράστου μακαριότητος καὶ ἄλλος τρόπος τῆς ἀπολαύσεως, ὃς νῦν Ἐπὶ
καρδίαν ἀνθρώπου ἀναβῆναι φύσιν οὐκ ἔχει.

τέως δὲ νῦν ὅρος τῇ ψυχῇ τῆς τοῦ ἀφράστου γνώσεώς ἐστιν ἡ
ἐμφαινομένη τοῖς οὖσιν ἐνέργεια, ἣν χεῖρα λέγεσθαι τροπικῶς ἐνοήσαμεν.
20   τοῦτο τοίνυν ἡμῖν τὸ δόγμα διὰ τῶν θείων τούτων λογίων πεφιλοσόφηται,
δι' ὧν ἡ καθαρὰ ψυχή, οὐκέτι τοῦ γηΐνου τε καὶ ὑλικοῦ βίου ἐπιβατεύουσα,
ἵνα μὴ μολύνῃ ἑαυτῆς τὸ ἴχνος τοῖς κάτω ἐνερειδόμενον, προσδοκήσασα
αὐτὸν ὑποδέξασθαι τὸν νυμφίον ὅλον ἐν τῷ οἴκῳ γενόμενον, ἠγάπησε μόνην
τέως τὴν χεῖρα θεασαμένη, δι' ἧς ἑρμηνεύεται ἡ ἐνεργητικὴ αὐτοῦ δύναμις·
25   Ἀδελφιδός μου γάρ, φησίν, ἀπέστειλε τὴν χεῖρα | αὐτοῦ διὰ τῆς ὀπῆς. οὐ γὰρ   337
χωρεῖ ἡ ἀνθρωπίνη πενία τὴν ἀόριστόν τε καὶ ἀπερίληπτον φύσιν ἐν ἑαυτῇ
δέξασθαι.

Ἡ δὲ κοιλία μου, φησίν, ἐθροήθη ἐπ' αὐτόν. ἔκπληξίν τινα σημαίνει καὶ
ξενισμὸν ἐπὶ τῷ φανέντι θαύματι τὸ τῆς θροήσεως ὄνομα· πᾶσα γὰρ αὐτῆς
30   ἡ διανοητικὴ δύναμις συνεκινήθη πρὸς τὸ θαῦμα τῶν διὰ τῆς θείας χειρὸς
ἐνεργουμένων, ὧν ἡ κατανόησις ὑπερκειμένη τῆς ἀνθρωπίνης δυνάμεως
τὸ ἀκατάληπτόν τε καὶ ἀχώρητον τῆς τοῦ ἐνεργοῦντος φύσεως δι' ἑαυτῆς
ἑρμηνεύει. πᾶσα γὰρ ἡ τῶν ὄντων κτίσις τῆς χειρὸς ἐκείνης τῆς διὰ τῆς ὀπῆς
ἡμῖν φανερωθείσης ἔργον ἐστίν, ὡς ὁ Ἰωάννης τε βοᾷ λέγων καὶ ὁ προφήτης
35   τῷ εὐαγγελίῳ συμφθέγγεται· ὁ μὲν γάρ φησιν ὅτι Πάντα δι' αὐτοῦ ἐγένετο, ὁ
δὲ προφήτης χεῖρα ὀνομάζει τὴν ποιητικὴν τῶν ὄντων δύναμιν εἰπὼν ὅτι Ἡ
χείρ μου ἐποίησε ταῦτα πάντα. εἰ οὖν τῆς ἐνεργείας ἐκείνης ἔργα τά τε ἄλλα
πάντα καὶ τὰ οὐράνια κάλλη, οὔπω δὲ κατείληφεν ἡ ζητητικὴ τοῦ ἀνθρώπου

also sees, among living things, the multiform natures at once of those that live in water, of those whose way is in the air, and those that live their life on dry land—the plants in their unnumbered forms, the various herbs, differing from one another in character and function and appearance, and the special qualities of the fruit and their juices. The soul, then, seeing these and other phenomena through which the working of God is signified, reckons, on account of their marvelous character, that the One who is apprehended through his work in fact | exists.

In the same way, in the age to come, when everything that is seen passes away in accordance with the Lord's word to the effect that "the heaven and the earth shall pass away" (Matt 24:35), and we are transported into that life that transcends sight and hearing and thinking, then no longer shall we know the Good's nature "in part" (cf. 1 Cor 13:9) as we do now, nor shall the transcendent be conceived by way of the workings of things that appear. On the contrary, the form of the ineffable Blessedness shall be apprehended in another fashion, and the mode of its fruition will be different, a mode that cannot now "enter into the human heart" (cf. 1 Cor 2:9).

Up until now, though, the limit of the soul's knowledge of the Ineffable is God's activity manifested in existent things, what we figuratively understand as God's Hand. It is this truth, then, that constitutes the wisdom conveyed by the divine oracles. With their help the pure soul—no longer walking the way of an earthy and material life, lest her steps be defiled by being planted down below—has indeed looked forward to welcoming her Bridegroom entire when he enters her house; yet so far all she has loved is the mere sight of his hand, by which we understand the power of his working. For she says: *My kinsman has put his hand | through the opening.* Human poverty lacks the capacity to receive within itself the infinite and uncircumscribed Nature.

But she adds: *My belly has cried out for him.* The expression "cries out" signifies a profound disturbance and wonder in the face of the manifest marvel, for all her mental powers are stirred up at once by the marvelous things that the divine Hand works—the understanding of which, in the very fact that it lies beyond human intellectual capacity, conveys the incomprehensibility and the unlimited character of the Nature that works them. For the whole realm of created beings is the work of that Hand that has been made manifest to us *through the opening.* This is what John proclaims and what the prophet speaks in agreement with the Gospel, for the one says, "All things were made by him" (John 1:3), while the prophet sets a name to the power that creates the beings when he says, "My hand made all of these" (Isa 66:2). If, then, the human mind in its searching has so far failed to comprehend the things accomplished by that divine working—what is the nature of the heaven or of the sun or of any other of the marvels manifest in the

διάνοια, τί κατ᾿ οὐσίαν ὁ οὐρανός ἐστιν ἢ ὁ ἥλιος ἢ ἄλλο τι τῶν φαινομένων
ἐν τῇ κτίσει θαυμάτων, τούτου χάριν θροεῖται πρὸς τὴν θείαν ἐνέργειαν ἡ
καρδία, ὅτι εἰ ταῦτα καταλαβεῖν οὐ χωρεῖ, πῶς τὴν ὑπερκειμένην τούτων
καταλήψεται φύσιν;

5 | Τάχα δέ τις καὶ ἄλλως μεταλαβὼν τὰ τῶν εἰρημένων αἰνίγματα οὐκ ἔξω   338
τοῦ εἰκότος προάξει τὴν θεωρίαν· οἶμαι γὰρ οἶκον νοεῖσθαι τῆς νύμφης πᾶσαν
τὴν ἀνθρωπίνην ζωήν, ταύτῃ δὲ τὴν χεῖρα τὴν πάντων τῶν ὄντων ποιητικὴν
ἐνδημήσασαν πρὸς τὸ βραχύ τε καὶ οὐτιδανὸν τοῦ ἀνθρωπίνου βίου ἑαυτὴν
συστεῖλαι διὰ τοῦ μετασχεῖν τῆς φύσεως ἡμῶν Κατὰ πάντα καθ᾿ ὁμοιότητα
10   χωρὶς ἁμαρτίας, ἐν ἡμῖν δὲ γενομένην θρόησιν ἐμποιῆσαι καὶ ξενισμὸν ταῖς
ψυχαῖς· πῶς ὁ θεὸς ἐν σαρκὶ φανεροῦται; πῶς ὁ λόγος γίνεται σάρξ; πῶς ἐν
παρθενίᾳ τόκος καὶ ἐν μητρὶ παρθενία; πῶς τῷ σκότει τὸ φῶς καταμίγνυται
καὶ τῷ θανάτῳ ἡ ζωὴ κατακίρναται; πῶς χωρεῖ ἡ βραχεῖα τοῦ βίου τρυμαλιὰ
τὴν περιεκτικὴν πάντων τῶν ὄντων χεῖρα ἐν ἑαυτῇ δέξασθαι, ᾗ πᾶς ὁ οὐρανὸς
15   ἐκμετρεῖται καὶ ἡ γῆ πᾶσα καὶ τὸ ὕδωρ ἅπαν ἐμπεριέχεται;

εἰκὸς τοίνυν τὴν τοῦ εὐαγγελίου χάριν διὰ τοῦ τῆς χειρὸς αἰνίγματος
προφητικῶς ἡμῖν ὑπὸ τῆς νύμφης διασημαίνεσθαι· ὅτε γὰρ ἐπὶ τῆς γῆς ὤφθη
καὶ τοῖς ἀνθρώποις συνανεστράφη ὁ κύριος, τὸ καθαρόν τε καὶ ἄϋλον τοῦ
νυμφίου κάλλος καὶ τὴν τοῦ λόγου θεότητα καὶ τὴν τοῦ ἀληθινοῦ φωτὸς
20   λαμπηδόνα διὰ τῆς τῶν ἐνεργειῶν χειρὸς ἐγνωρίσαμεν· χεῖρα γὰρ νοοῦμεν
τὴν τῶν θαυμάτων ἀπεργαστικὴν αὐτοῦ δύναμιν, | δι᾿ ἧς ἐζωοποιοῦντο μὲν   339
οἱ νεκροὶ καὶ τῶν τυφλῶν αἱ ὄψεις ἀποκαθίσταντο καὶ τὸ τῆς λέπρας πάθος
ἐφυγαδεύετο καὶ πᾶν εἶδος ἀνιάτου καὶ χαλεπῆς ἀρρωστίας ἀπεχώρει τῶν
σωμάτων διὰ προστάγματος.

25   Προτεθείσης δὲ ἡμῖν τῆς διπλῆς ταύτης ἐπὶ τῇ χειρὶ θεωρίας, ὧν ἡ μὲν
ὑποτίθεται τὴν θείαν φύσιν ἀκατάληπτον οὖσαν παντελῶς καὶ ἀνείκαστον
διὰ μόνης τῆς ἐνεργείας γινώσκεσθαι, ἡ δὲ τὴν εὐαγγελικὴν χάριν
προαναφωνεῖσθαι λέγει διὰ τῶν λόγων τούτων ὑπὸ τῆς νύμφης, ἐπὶ τῷ
ἀκροατῇ ποιησόμεθα τὴν προσφυεστέραν τε καὶ μᾶλλον τοῖς ὑποκειμένοις
30   ἁρμόζουσαν πρὸ τῆς ἑτέρας ἐκλέξασθαι. πλὴν ὅτιπερ ἂν νομισθῇ
ψυχωφελέστερον εἶναι, γένοιτο ἂν ἡμῖν δι᾿ ἑκατέρου τῶν εἰρημένων αὐτάρκης
ἡ πρὸς τὸ ἀγαθὸν ὁδηγία· ἐκ μὲν γὰρ τοῦ γνῶναι, ὅτι τοῦ θεοῦ τὸ γνωστὸν
κατὰ τὴν τοῦ Παύλου φωνὴν διὰ τῆς τοῦ κόσμου κτίσεως νοούμενον
καθορᾶται, τῆς περὶ τῶν ἀκαταλήπτων πολυπραγμοσύνης φεισόμεθα, ὡς
35   ἂν μὴ διὰ τοῦ φυσιολογεῖσθαι τὴν ἀνέφικτόν τε καὶ ἀνεκφώνητον φύσιν
ὕλην λάβοι κατὰ τῆς ἀληθείας ἡ αἵρεσις· εἰ δὲ πρὸς τὸ εὐαγγέλιον βλέπειν
τὸ αἴνιγμα τῆς χειρὸς ὑποθώμεθα, καὶ οὕτω βεβαιοτέρα ἡμῖν τῶν μυστικῶν

created order—this explains why the heart, confronted with the working of God, cries out, "If these things cannot be understood, how shall the nature that transcends them be understood?"

| Perhaps, though, someone who takes the verbal enigmas of the Bride's statement in a different way will propound—and plausibly enough—the following interpretation. For I think that the Bride's house can be taken to mean the whole of human life, and thus the hand that makes all things, taking up residence in the confined and barren conditions of human existence, has contracted itself by sharing our nature, "Like us in every way apart from sin," and by being among us has generated dismay and astonishment in our souls. How is God manifested in flesh? How does the Word become flesh? How does birth come about in virginity, and virginity in a mother? How is light mixed in with darkness, and life mingled with death? How can the limited aperture of our life accommodate the hand that contains all things, by which the whole of heaven and earth is measured, and all the water is contained?

It makes sense, then, for the Bride, speaking as a prophet, to refer to the grace of the gospel under the figure of the hand. For when the Lord was revealed on earth and had converse with human beings, we, through the hand that is God in action, became aware of the pure and immaterial beauty of the Bridegroom, of the deity of the Word, and of the incandescence of the true light. In that hand we see the power that brings about his marvels— | the power through which the dead are brought to life, the eyes of the blind are restored, the disease of the leper is put to flight, and every sort of serious and incurable sickness is dismissed from people's bodies by a word of command.

Here, then, is a twofold interpretation of the hand. One of them lays it down that the divine nature is altogether incomprehensible and incomparable and so is known solely by its activity [energeia]. The second asserts that in these words the grace of the gospel was announced ahead of time by the Bride. We leave it to the hearer to choose the interpretation that is the more appropriate and better suited to the subject matter of the Song. Nevertheless, whichever is adjudged the more profitable to souls, each of them supplies us with sufficient guidance toward the good. For if we understand that "what is known of God," as Paul has said, "has been clearly perceived" through the world's creation, we will be spared idle curiosity about things that are incomprehensible, and heresy shall not find occasion against the truth on account of our theorizing on the subject of the Nature that is unattainable and unutterable. And if we take it that the figure of the hand concerns the gospel, in this way too our belief in | the mystical teachings will be made the stronger

δογμάτων ἡ πίστις γενήσεται διὰ | τῆς προαναφωνήσεως τῶν δογμάτων   340
προσλαβοῦσα τὸ ἀναμφίβολον, ἐν Χριστῷ Ἰησοῦ,

ᾧ ἡ δόξα εἰς τοὺς αἰῶνας.
ἀμήν.

and our doubtfulness reduced by the fact of their being announced beforehand, in Christ Jesus,

to whom be glory to the ages of ages.
Amen.

Λόγος ιβ'

Ἀνέστην ἐγὼ ἀνοῖξαι τῷ ἀδελφιδῷ μου,
<αἱ> χεῖρές μου ἔσταξαν σμύρναν,
οἱ δάκτυλοί μου σμύρναν πλήρη.
ἐπὶ χεῖρας τοῦ κλείθρου
5   Ἤνοιξα ἐγὼ τῷ ἀδελφιδῷ μου,
ἀδελφιδός μου παρῆλθεν,
ἡ ψυχή μου ἐξῆλθεν ἐν λόγῳ αὐτοῦ.
ἐζήτησα αὐτὸν καὶ οὐχ εὗρον αὐτόν,
ἐκάλεσα αὐτὸν καὶ οὐχ ὑπήκουσέ μου.
10   Εὕροσάν με οἱ φύλακες οἱ κυκλοῦντες ἐν τῇ πόλει,
ἐπάταξάν με, ἐτραυμάτισάν με,
ἦραν τὸ θέριστρον ἀπ᾽ ἐμοῦ οἱ φύλακες τῶν τειχέων.

Οἱ τὴν διαπόντιον ἀποδημίαν κατ᾽ ἐλπίδα πλούτου στελλόμενοι, ὅταν
ἤδη τὴν ὁλκάδα τοῦ λιμένος ἀποσαλεύσωσι | καὶ πρὸς τὸ πέλαγος στρέψῃ διὰ   341
15   τῶν πηδαλίων τὴν πρῶραν ὁ τῶν οἰάκων ὑπερκαθήμενος, εὐχὴν ποιοῦνται
τῆς ναυτιλίας προοίμιον θεὸν γενέσθαι καθηγεμόνα σφίσι τῆς εὐπλοίας
αἰτούμενοι. τὸ δὲ κεφάλαιόν ἐστιν αὐτοῖς τῆς εὐχῆς πνεῦμα προσηνές τε καὶ
πλόϊμον ἐμπεσεῖν τῷ ἱστίῳ πρὸς τὸν σκοπὸν τοῦ κυβερνήτου, κατὰ πρύμναν
ἱστάμενον· οὗ καταθυμίως αὐτοῖς ἐπιπνέοντος ἡδεῖα μὲν ἡ θάλασσα γίνεται
20   τοῖς ἠρεμαίοις κύμασι γλαφυρῶς ὑποφρίσσουσα, ἄλυπα δὲ τοῦ πελάγους τὰ
πλάτη δι᾽ εὐκολίας τῆς νεὼς ἐφιπταμένης καὶ ἐπολισθαινούσης τοῖς ὕδασι,
πρὸ ὀφθαλμῶν δὲ ὁ πλοῦτος ὁ διὰ τῆς ἐμπορίας αὐτοῖς ἐλπιζόμενος ἤδη τῆς
εὐπλοίας ἐγγυωμένης καὶ πρὸ τῆς πείρας τὴν εὐπορίαν.
ἀλλὰ πρὸς ὅ τι βλέπων ἐντεῦθεν προοιμιάζομαι, δῆλον πάντως ἐστὶ τοῖς
25   εὐμαθεστέροις τῶν ἀκροατῶν τὸ τῷ σκοπῷ τοῦ προοιμίου προκείμενον· μέγα
πρόκειται τῷ λόγῳ τὸ πέλαγος τῆς τῶν θείων ῥητῶν θεωρίας, πολὺς δὲ διὰ
τῆς ναυτιλίας ταύτης ὁ τῆς γνώσεως πλοῦτος ἐλπίζεται, ἡ δὲ ἔμψυχος αὕτη
ναῦς, ἡ ἐκκλησία, ἐν παντὶ τῷ ἰδίῳ πληρώματι πρὸς τὸν πλοῦν τῆς ἐξηγήσεως
βλέπει μετέωρος. | ἀλλ᾽ οὐ πρότερον ἅπτεται τῶν οἰάκων ὁ κυβερνήτης   342
30   λόγος, πρὶν ἂν ἐκ κοινοῦ γένηται τοῦ πληρώματος τῆς νεὼς πρὸς τὸν θεὸν ἡ
εὐχή, ὡς ἐπιπνεῦσαί τε ἡμῖν τὴν τοῦ ἁγίου πνεύματος δύναμιν καὶ ἀνακινῆσαι

HOMILY 12
Song 5:5–7

> [5]*I rose up to open to my kinsman;*
> *my hands dropped myrrh,*
> *my fingers choice myrrh.*
> *Hands on the bar,*
> [6]*I opened to my kinsman,*
> *my kinsman passed me by,*
> *my soul went out at his word.*
> *I sought him, and I did not find him,*
> *I called him, but he did not answer me.*
> [7]*The watchmen who go their rounds in the city found me,*
> *they struck me, they wounded me,*
> *the watchmen of the walls took my veil away from me.*

Think of people who are getting themselves ready for a journey across the sea in the hope of finding riches. As soon as they work their ship out of the harbor and the helmsman with his rudder has turned the prow | toward the open sea, they offer a prayer to open their venture and ask a god to be their guide for a fair voyage. The heart of their prayer is that a gentle and favorable wind may strike the sail for the sake of the course the steersman, in his station at the stern, has set. And should the wind blow in accordance with their wishes, the sea becomes pleasant and bristles nicely with gentle waves; its great distances afford no trouble because the ship moves easily as it flies and glides over the waters; and their eyes already see the riches they hope for from their trading, since the fair voyage gives assurance of abundance even before they experience it.

What we intend in making this our starting point is entirely plain to those of our hearers who are quicker to grasp what is intimated by the message of this prologue. Before our discourse there stretches the vast ocean of insight and inquiry into the divine words. From this venture we hope for great riches in the way of knowledge, and this animate ship of ours, the church, with its own full crew, looks expectantly forward to its voyage of explication. | But no sooner does the helmsman, who is our reason, lay a hand on the tiller than a common prayer is raised to God by the whole company aboard the ship: that the power of the Holy Spirit may blow upon us[1] and stir up the

---

1. For this figure of a voyage, with its likening of a favorable wind (πνεῦμα) to the Holy Spirit, see Methodius, *Symp.* 7.1 (trans. Musurillo 1958, 96).

τῶν νοημάτων τὰ κύματα καὶ δι᾽ αὐτῶν εὐπλοοῦντα προαγαγεῖν δι᾽ εὐθείας
τὸν λόγον, ἵνα οὕτω πελάγιοι διὰ τῆς θεωρίας γενόμενοι τὸν τῆς γνώσεως
πλοῦτον ἐμπορευσώμεθα, εἴπερ ἔλθοι διὰ τῶν εὐχῶν ὑμῶν τὸ πνεῦμα τὸ
ἅγιον ἐπὶ τὸν λόγον πλησίστιον.

5   Ἀρχὴ δὲ γενέσθω τοῦ λόγου τῶν θεοπνεύστων ῥημάτων ἡ μνήμη ἐπὶ
λέξεως ἔχουσα οὕτως· Ἀνέστην ἐγὼ ἀνοῖξαι τῷ ἀδελφιδῷ μου· <αἱ> χεῖρές
μου ἔσταξαν σμύρναν, οἱ δάκτυλοί μου σμύρναν πλήρη.

       ὅτι μὲν οὖν οὐκ ἔστιν ἄλλως ἐν ἡμῖν γενέσθαι τὸν ζῶντα λόγον (τὸν
καθαρὸν λέγω καὶ ἀσώματον νυμφίον τὸν δι᾽ ἀφθαρσίας καὶ ἁγιότητος
10   ἑαυτῷ τὴν ψυχὴν συνοικίζοντα), εἰ μή τις διὰ τοῦ νεκρῶσαι τὰ μέλη τὰ ἐπὶ
τῆς γῆς περιέλοιτο τὸ τῆς σαρκὸς παραπέτασμα καὶ οὕτως | ἀνοίξοι τῷ λόγῳ   343
τὴν θύραν, δι᾽ ἧς εἰς τὴν ψυχὴν εἰσοικίζεται, δῆλόν ἐστιν οὐ μόνον ἐκ τῶν
θείων τοῦ ἀποστόλου δογμάτων ἀλλὰ καὶ ἐκ τῶν νῦν εἰρημένων παρὰ τῆς
νύμφης· Ἀνέστην γάρ, φησίν, ἀνοῖξαι τῷ ἀδελφιδῷ μου διὰ τοῦ ποιῆσαι τὰς
15   χεῖράς μου τῆς σμύρνης πηγὰς ἀφ᾽ ἑαυτῶν ῥεούσας τὸ ἄρωμα καὶ πλήρωμα
τῶν δακτύλων δεῖξαι τὴν σμύρναν. τὸν γὰρ τρόπον, δι᾽ οὗ ἀνοίγεται τῷ
νυμφίῳ ἡ θύρα, φησὶ διὰ τῶν εἰρημένων ὅτι διὰ τοῦ Συνταφῆναι αὐτῷ διὰ τοῦ
βαπτίσματος εἰς τὸν θάνατον ἀνέστην· οὐ γὰρ ἂν ἐνήργησεν ἡ ἀνάστασις μὴ
προκαθηγησαμένης τῆς ἑκουσίου νεκρότητος. ἐνδείκνυται δὲ τὸ ἑκούσιον ἡ
20   ἐκ τῶν χειρῶν αὐτῆς ἀπορρέουσα τῆς σμύρνης σταγὼν καὶ τὸ πεπληρῶσθαι
τοὺς δακτύλους αὐτῆς τοῦ ἀρώματος τούτου· οὐ γὰρ ἑτέρωθεν ἐγγενέσθαι
τῇ χειρὶ λέγει τὴν σμύρναν (ἢ γὰρ ἂν ἐνομίσθη διὰ τούτου περιστατικὸν
αὐτῇ καὶ ἀκούσιον συμβῆναι τὸ διὰ τῆς σμύρνης δηλούμενον), ἀλλ᾽ αὐτάς
φησι τὰς χεῖρας (σημαίνει δὲ διὰ τῶν | χειρῶν τὰς ἐνεργητικὰς τῆς ψυχῆς   344
25   κινήσεις) ἀφ᾽ ἑαυτῶν στάξαι τὴν σμύρναν, τὴν οἴκοθεν ἐκ προαιρέσεως τῶν
σωματικῶν παθημάτων γινομένην νέκρωσιν διὰ τούτου σημαίνων, ἣν ἐν πᾶσι
τοῖς δακτύλοις πεπληρῶσθαι λέγει, τὰ καθ᾽ ἕκαστον εἴδη τὰ διῃρημένως δι᾽
ἀρετῆς σπουδαζόμενα τῷ τῶν δακτύλων διερμηνεύων ὀνόματι·

       ὡς εἶναι πάντα τὸν νοῦν τῶν λεγομένων τοιοῦτον, ὅτι ἔλαβον δύναμιν
30   ἀναστάσεως διὰ τοῦ νεκρῶσαι τὰ μέλη μου τὰ ἐπὶ τῆς γῆς ἑκουσίως μοι τῆς

waves of our thoughts, and that by their means it may prosper the voyage of our discourse and lead it on a direct course. In this way, finding ourselves on the high seas in our search for insight, we will traffic in the riches of knowledge, always supposing that in response to your prayer the Holy Spirit comes to fill the sails of our discourse.

Let the beginning of our address be a quotation of the divinely inspired words, the text of which goes like this: *I rose up to open to my kinsman; my hands dropped myrrh, my fingers choice myrrh.*

Now there is only one way in which the living Word comes within us: I refer to the pure and incorporeal Bridegroom who makes the soul dwell with him by means of incorruptibility and holiness, namely, if one removes the veil of the flesh (cf. 2 Cor 3:16) by mortifying one's earthly members (cf. Col 3:5) and in this way |opens to the Word the door through which he makes the soul his home. This is apparent not only from the divine teachings of the apostle but also from what the Bride says in this text. For, says she, "*I rose up to open to my kinsman* by making my hands founts of myrrh from which its spicy scent pours forth and by showing my fingers to be full of myrrh." For by these words she states the way in which the door is opened to the Bridegroom: "I have risen up by being 'buried with him through baptism into his death' (cf. Rom 6:4),[2] for the resurrection does not become actual if it is not preceded by voluntary death." The voluntary character of this death is indicated by the drop of myrrh that pours from her hands and by the fact that her fingers are full of its spicy scent, for she does not state that the myrrh comes onto her hand from an outside source (for that surely would make one suppose that what the myrrh signifies happened to her accidentally and involuntarily). No, she says that her hands themselves (and | by "hands" she means those motions of the soul that bring actions about) drip myrrh by their very own agency—and by "myrrh" she refers to the mortification of bodily passions that comes about through choice that originates in oneself. She further states that this mortification attains its full measure in all her fingers; and by the term "fingers" she signifies the particular types of mortification that are variously sought in the practice of virtue.

Thus, in sum, the sense of what she says is this: "I have received the power of the resurrection by mortifying my earthly members, and the mortification

---

2. The citation of this passage from Rom 6 is no doubt explained by the close association in Gregory's mind between myrrh and death. See above, homily 7, p. 243 (Jaeger), where myrrh is interpreted as signifying the suffering and death of Christ. It also indicates clearly the way in which the soul's progress through "mortification" (purification from passions) to resurrection is rooted in an understanding of baptism; see Daniélou 1954, 26. In this passage resurrection is understood as the dwelling of the soul with the Word.

τῶν τοιούτων μελῶν ἐνεργηθείσης νεκρώσεως, οὐ παρ' ἄλλου ταῖς χερσὶν
ἐντεθείσης τῆς σμύρνης ἀλλ' ἐκ τῆς ἐμῆς προαιρέσεως ἀπορρεούσης, ὡς καὶ
πᾶσι τοῖς κατ' ἀρετὴν ἐπιτηδεύμασιν, ἅπερ δακτύλους ὠνόμασεν, ἀνελλιπῆ
τὴν τοιαύτην ἐνορᾶσθαι διάθεσιν·
5   ἔστι γὰρ ἐπὶ τῶν ἀτελῶς τὴν ἀρετὴν μετιόντων ἰδεῖν ἑνὶ μὲν αὐτούς τινι
τεθνεῶτας πάθει ἐν ἑτέροις δὲ ζῶντας, καθάπερ ὁρῶμέν τινας νεκροῦντας
μὲν ἐν ἑαυτοῖς τὸ ἀκόλαστον, ἂν οὕτω τύχῃ, τρέφοντας δὲ δι' ἐπιμελείας τὸν
τῦφον ἢ ἕτερόν τι πάθος τὸ τῇ ψυχῇ λυμαινόμενον, οἷον τὸ φιλοχρήματον ἢ
τὸ ὀργίλον ἢ τὸ φιλόδοξον ἢ ἄλλο τι τοιοῦτον, οὗ κακῶς ἐν τῇ ψυχῇ ζῶντος
10   οὐκ ἔστι | πλήρεις τοὺς δακτύλους ἐπιδεῖξαι τῆς σμύρνης· οὐ γὰρ διὰ πάντων   345
φαίνεται τῶν ἐπιτηδευμάτων ἡ τοῦ κακοῦ νέκρωσίς τε καὶ ἀλλοτρίωσις,
πάντων δὲ πληρωθέντων τῶν τοιούτων δακτύλων τῆς νοηθείσης σμύρνης
καὶ ἀνίσταται ἡ ψυχὴ καὶ ἀνοίγει τῷ νυμφίῳ τὴν εἴσοδον.
     διὰ τοῦτο τάχα καὶ ὁ μέγας Παῦλος καλῶς νοήσας τὴν τοῦ δεσπότου
15   φωνὴν ἥ φησιν ὅτι οὐκ ἔστι φυῆναι στάχυν, ἐὰν μὴ προδιαλυθῇ τῷ θανάτῳ
ὁ κόκκος, τοῦτο κηρύσσει τῇ ἐκκλησίᾳ τὸ δόγμα ὅτι χρὴ θάνατον τῆς ζωῆς
καθηγήσασθαι, ὡς οὐκ ἐνδεχόμενον ἄλλως ἐν ἀνθρώπῳ τὴν ζωὴν γενέσθαι,
εἰ μὴ διὰ θανάτου λάβοι τὴν πάροδον·
     διπλῆς γὰρ ἐν ἡμῖν οὔσης τῆς φύσεως, τῆς μὲν λεπτῆς τε καὶ νοερᾶς καὶ
20   κούφης, τῆς δὲ παχείας καὶ ὑλικῆς καὶ βαρείας, ἀνάγκη πᾶσα ἀσύμβατον
πρὸς τὴν ἑτέραν ἐν ἑκατέρᾳ τούτων τὴν ὁρμὴν εἶναι καὶ ἰδιάζουσαν· τὸ
μὲν γὰρ νοερόν τε καὶ κοῦφον οἰκείαν ἔχει τὴν ἐπὶ τὸ ἄνω φοράν, τὸ δὲ
βαρὺ καὶ ὑλῶδες ἀεὶ πρὸς τὸ κάτω ῥέπει καὶ φέρεται. ἐξ ἐναντίου τοίνυν
γινομένης αὐτοῖς φυσικῶς τῆς κινήσεως οὐκ ἔστιν εὐοδωθῆναι τὸ ἕτερον μὴ
25   ἀτονήσαντος τοῦ ἄλλου πρὸς τὴν κατὰ φύσιν φοράν. μέση δὲ ἀμφοῖν ἐστῶσα
ἡ αὐτεξούσιος ἡμῶν δύναμίς τε καὶ προαίρεσις δι' ἑαυτῆς ἐμποιεῖ καὶ τόνον
τῷ κάμνοντι καὶ | ἀτονίαν τῷ κατισχύοντι· ἐν ᾧ γὰρ ἂν γένηται μέρει, τούτῳ   346
δίδωσι κατὰ τοῦ ἄλλου τὰ νικητήρια. οὕτως ἐν τῷ εὐαγγελίῳ ἐπαινεῖται μὲν
ὁ πιστὸς καὶ φρόνιμος οἰκονόμος (οὗτος γάρ ἐστι κατά γε τὸν ἐμὸν λόγον ἡ
30   καλῶς τῶν ἐν ἡμῖν ἐπιστατοῦσα προαίρεσις· ἐπαινεῖται γὰρ ὅτι τρέφει τὴν
οἰκετείαν τοῦ δεσπότου διὰ τῆς τῶν ἐναντίων νεκρώσεως· ἡ γὰρ ἐκείνων
φθορὰ τροφή τε καὶ εὐεξία τῶν κρειττόνων ἐστίν), κατηγορεῖται δὲ ὁ κακὸς
δοῦλος ἐκεῖνος ὁ διὰ τοῦ τοῖς μεθύουσι συνεῖναι πληγαῖς αἰκιζόμενος τὴν τοῦ

of such members was effected voluntarily. The myrrh was not placed on my hands by another agent, but it flowed from my own choice, so that in all virtuous pursuits," which she calls fingers, "a disposition of this kind is unfailingly discerned."

For one can see, in the case of people who share only imperfectly in virtue, that they have died indeed to one passion but are living in others. We see, for example, people who are putting intemperance to death in themselves but are earnestly nourishing arrogance or some other passion that wounds the soul: love of wealth, perhaps, or bad temper, or ambition, or some other such thing; and if that carries on its unwholesome life within the soul, | it is not possible to exhibit fingers full of myrrh, for the mortification of vice and estrangement from it are not manifest throughout one's pursuits. If, however, all one's fingers—understanding the word in this sense—have been filled with myrrh of the intelligible order, the soul both rises up and opens an entrance for the Bridegroom.

Perhaps that is why the great Paul, who correctly understood the Lord's words to the effect that the plant cannot grow unless the seed has first been dissolved in death (cf. John 12:24), declared to the church the doctrine that death must precede life, so that life cannot find a place within the human person unless it make its entrance by way of death.

For in us there is a dual nature. The one is fine and intelligent and light, while the other is coarse and material and heavy.[3] Hence it is inevitable that in each of these there be a dynamic that is proper to itself and irreconcilable with the other. For that in us which is intelligent and light has its native course upwards, but the heavy and material is ever borne, and ever flows, downwards. Since, then, their motions are naturally opposed, it is not possible for the one to follow its natural course successfully unless the other has been weakened. But our power of choice and self-governance, which is stationed in the middle between these, works both strength in the one that is sickly and | weakness in the one that is strong, for it assigns the reward of victory to whichever side it takes. Even so in the Gospel there is praise for the faithful and prudent steward, for he, as I see it, represents our faculty of choice as it presides rightly over what goes on within us, since he is praised on the ground that he feeds his master's "household" (Matt 24:45 // Luke 12:42) by doing its adversaries to death; for their destruction spells the sustenance and good health of their betters. But there is condemnation for that "wicked slave" who afflicts God's household with blows because he keeps company

---

3. See also, on this point, Gregory's discussion in *Beat.*, homily 3 *ad fin.* (trans. Graef 1954, 15–16), with its allusion to two forms of life.

θεοῦ οἰκετείαν· πληγὴ γάρ ἐστιν ὡς ἀληθῶς κατὰ τῶν ἀρετῶν ἡ τῆς κακίας
εὐημερία.

ουκοῦν καλῶς ἔχει τὸν προφητικὸν ζηλώσαντας λόγον πρῶαν ἑαυτοῖς
ποιεῖν διὰ τοῦ ἀποκτεῖναι Πάντας τοὺς ἁμαρτωλοὺς τῆς γῆς τοῦ ἐξολεθρεῦσαι
5   ἐκ πόλεως κυρίου (ψυχὴ δὲ ἡ πόλις) πάντας τοὺς λογισμοὺς τοὺς
ἐργαζομένους τὴν ἀνομίαν, ὧν ὁ ὄλεθρος ζωὴ γίνεται τῶν ἀμεινόνων. οὕτως
οὖν διὰ τοῦ θανάτου ζῶμεν, ὅταν τῶν ἐν ἡμῖν, καθώς φησιν ὁ προφήτης, τὸ
μὲν ἀποκτείνῃ τὸ δὲ ζωοποιήσῃ ὁ λόγος ὁ εἰπὼν ὅτι Ἐγὼ ἀποκτενῶ καὶ ζῆν
| ποιήσω, ὡς καὶ ὁ Παῦλος ἀποθανὼν ἔζη καὶ ἀσθενῶν ἴσχυε καὶ δεδεμένος   347
10   ἐνήργει τὸν δρόμον καὶ πτωχεύων ἐπλούτιζε καὶ πάντα κατεῖχεν ἔχων οὐδέν,
Πάντοτε τὴν νέκρωσιν τοῦ Ἰησοῦ ἐν τῷ ἰδίῳ σώματι περιφέρων καὶ πάντοτε
τὴν ζωὴν αὐτοῦ ἐν ἑαυτῷ φανερῶν.

Ἀλλ' ἐπὶ τὸ προτεθὲν ἐπανέλθωμεν· ὅτι διὰ θανάτου ἡ ψυχὴ ἐκ τοῦ
θανάτου ἀνίσταται (ἐὰν γὰρ μὴ ἀποθάνῃ, νεκρὰ διὰ παντὸς μένει καὶ τῆς
15   ζωῆς ἀπαράδεκτος· ἐκ δὲ τοῦ ἀποθανεῖν ἐν ζωῇ γίνεται πᾶσαν ἀποθεμένη
νεκρότητα), καὶ τοῦτο ἡμῖν ἐκ τοῦ προκειμένου ῥητοῦ βεβαιοῦται τὸ δόγμα
οὕτως εἰπούσης τῆς νύμφης ὅτι Ἀνέστην ἐγὼ ἀνοῖξαι τῷ ἀδελφιδῷ μου· αἱ
χεῖρές μου ἔσταξαν σμύρναν, οἱ δάκτυλοί μου σμύρναν πλήρη. θανάτου δὲ
σύμβολον εἶναι τὴν σμύρναν οὐκ ἄν τις ἀμφιβάλοι τῶν ταῖς θείαις ὡμιληκότων
20   γραφαῖς. πῶς οὖν ὁ θάνατος ἡμᾶς ἐκ τοῦ θανάτου ἀνίστησιν, ἐπιζητεῖν οἶμαί
τινας τὸν περὶ τούτου λόγον εὐκρινηθῆναι σαφέστερον. ἐροῦμεν τοίνυν ὅπως
ἂν οἷόν τε ᾖ τάξιν τινὰ δι' ἀκολουθίας ἐπιθέντες τῷ λόγῳ.

πάντα ὅσα ἐποίησεν ὁ θεὸς καλὰ λίαν εἶναι ὁ τῆς κοσμογενείας λόγος
μαρτύρεται. ἐν δὲ τῶν λίαν καλῶν ἦν καὶ ὁ ἄνθρωπος, μᾶλλον δὲ πλεῖον | 348
25   τῶν ἄλλων κεκοσμημένος τῷ κάλλει· τί γὰρ ἂν ἕτερον οὕτως εἴη καλὸν ὡς
τὸ τοῦ ἀκηράτου κάλλους ὁμοίωμα· εἰ δὲ πάντα καλὰ λίαν, ἐν δὲ τοῖς πᾶσιν
ἢ καὶ πρὸ πάντων ὁ ἄνθρωπος ἦν, οὐκ ἦν πάντως ἐν τῷ ἀνθρώπῳ ὁ θάνατος·
οὐ γὰρ ἂν καλόν τι ὁ ἄνθρωπος ἦν, εἴπερ εἶχεν ἐν ἑαυτῷ τῆς τοῦ θανάτου
κατηφείας τὸν σκυθρωπὸν χαρακτῆρα. ἀλλὰ τῆς ἀϊδίου ζωῆς ἀπεικόνισμα
30   ὢν καὶ ὁμοίωμα καλὸς ἦν ὡς ἀληθῶς καὶ λίαν καλὸς τῷ φαιδρῷ τῆς ζωῆς
χαρακτῆρι καλλωπιζόμενος. ἦν δὲ αὐτῷ καὶ ὁ θεῖος παράδεισος διὰ τῆς

with drunkards (Matt 24:48–49 // Luke 12:45), for in truth a blow marks the flourishing of vice as over against the virtues.

Therefore it is well for those who emulate the prophetic word (Ps 100:8) to make for themselves an "early morning" by killing "all the earth's sinners, to root out from the city of the Lord"—"city" meaning the soul—"all" thoughts "that work lawlessness," whose destruction makes for the life of better things. Here, then, is the way in which we live by the agency of death: when (in the words of the prophet), of the two tendencies within us, the Word who says "I will kill, and I will | work life" (Deut 32:9) does the one to death and brings the other to life—just as Paul too lived in dying (cf. 2 Cor 6:9), and was strong in weakness (cf. 2 Cor 12:10), and though bound ran the course (cf. Acts 20:22, 24), and though poor made people rich, and possessed all things though he had nothing (cf. 2 Cor 6:10), always bearing the dying of Jesus in his own body (cf. 2 Cor 4:10), and always manifesting his light within himself.

But let us get back to our theme: that it is through death that the soul is raised up (for if it does not die, it remains for all time dead and incapable of life, but by dying it emerges into life once it has put off all its deadness), and this basic belief is confirmed for us by what is said here, when the Bride states: *I rose up to open to my kinsman; my hands dropped myrrh, my fingers choice myrrh.* No one who is in touch with the divine Scriptures will have any doubt that myrrh is a symbol of death. As to how death raises us up from death, I am sure there are some who seek to have our reasoning on this subject clarified further. So we shall say as much as we are able by imposing on our reasoning a strict logical order.

The creation narrative attests that everything God made is "very good" (Gen 1:31). Now one of these very good things was humanity; or rather, humanity was more greatly adorned with goodness | than the other creatures. For which of the others was so beautiful in its goodness[4] as to be the likeness of the undefiled Beauty? But if all were "very good" and humanity was included among them or even set above them, there was assuredly no death in the human person.[5] For humanity would not have been something good, if it had had within it the melancholy mark of death's downcasting. But being the copy and likeness of unending Life, it was truly good and very good, because embellished with the joyous mark of life. Humanity's too was the divine paradise, which teemed with life on account of the fruitfulness of its

---

4. Note that the Greek adjective καλός, here translated as "beautiful in goodness" and elsewhere in this passage simply as "good," has the original sense of "beautiful"; this sense lurks in the background here and elsewhere in Gregory's use of it, as no doubt also in the Septuagint's use of it at Gen 3:21.

5. On this point, see Wisd 2:23–24.

εὐκαρπίας τῶν δένδρων βρύων ζωήν, καὶ ἡ ἐντολὴ τοῦ θεοῦ ζωῆς ἦν νόμος τὸ μὴ ἀποθανεῖν παραγγέλλουσα.

ὄντος δὲ κατὰ τὸ μέσον τῆς τοῦ παραδείσου φυτείας τοῦ τὴν ζωὴν βρύοντος ξύλου, τί ποτε χρὴ τὸ ξύλον νοεῖν ἐκεῖνο οὗ ὁ καρπὸς ἡ ζωή, καὶ
5   τοῦ θανατηφόρου δὲ ξύλου, οὗ καλὸν ἅμα καὶ κακὸν εἶναι τὸν καρπὸν ἀποφαίνεται ὁ λόγος, καὶ | αὐτοῦ κατὰ τὸ μέσον ὄντος τοῦ παραδείσου,   349
ἀδυνάτου δὲ ὄντος ἐν τῷ μεσαιτάτῳ τοῖς δύο ξύλοις χώραν γενέσθαι; ὁπότερον γὰρ ἂν δῶμεν ἐξ ἀμφωτέρων ἐπέχειν τὸ μέσον, κατὰ πᾶσαν ἀνάγκην τὸ ἕτερον τῆς τοῦ μέσου χώρας πάντως ἐξείργεται· πρὸς γὰρ τὸ
10   περιέχον ἡ ἀκριβὴς τοῦ μέσου θέσις καταλαμβάνεται, ὅταν ἴσοις ἀπαντοχόθεν τοῖς διαστήμασιν ἀπέχῃ τοῦ πέρατος. ἐπειδὰν τοίνυν ἓν δι᾽ ἀκριβείας ᾖ τοῦ κύκλου τὸ μέσον, οὐκ ἂν γένοιτο μηχανὴ τοῦ αὐτοῦ μένοντος κύκλου δύο κέντρα κατὰ τὸ μέσον χώραν εὑρεῖν· εἰ γὰρ ἕτερον παρατεθείη κέντρον τῷ προλαβόντι, πρὸς τοῦτο κατ᾽ ἀνάγκην συμμετατεθέντος τοῦ κύκλου ἔξω τοῦ
15   μέσου τὸ πρότερον γίνεται τῆς τοῦ κύκλου περιοχῆς τῷ δευτέρῳ κέντρῳ περιγραφείσης. ἀλλὰ μὴν ἐν τῷ μέσῳ φησὶν εἶναι τοῦ παραδείσου καὶ τοῦτο καὶ τοῦτο, καίτοι ἐναντίως πρὸς ἄλληλα κατὰ τὴν δύναμιν ἔχοντα, τό τε ζωοποιὸν λέγω ξύλον καὶ οὗ θάνατος ἦν ὁ καρπός, ὅπερ ἁμαρτίαν ὁ Παῦλος ὠνόμασεν εἰπὼν ὅτι Καρπὸς ἁμαρτίας ὁ θάνατος.

20   νοῆσαι ἄρα προσήκει διὰ τῆς τῶν εἰρημένων φιλοσοφίας τοῦτο τὸ δόγμα ὅτι τῆς μὲν τοῦ θεοῦ φυτείας τὸ μεσαίτατόν ἐστιν ἡ ζωή, ὁ δὲ θάνατος ἀφύτευτος καθ᾽ ἑαυτόν ἐστι καὶ ἄρριζος ἰδίαν οὐδαμοῦ χώραν ἔχων, τῇ δὲ στερήσει τῆς ζωῆς | ἐμφυτεύεται, ὅταν ἀργήσῃ τοῖς ζῶσιν ἡ μετουσία τοῦ   350
κρείττονος.

25   ἐπεὶ οὖν ἐν τῷ μέσῳ τῶν θείων φυτῶν ἐστιν ἡ ζωή, τῇ δὲ ἀποπτώσει ταύτης ἐνυφίσταται ἡ τοῦ θανάτου φύσις, διὰ τοῦτο καὶ τὸ θανατηφόρον ξύλον ὁ τὸ δόγμα τοῦτο δι᾽ αἰνιγμάτων φιλοσοφήσας ἐν τῷ μέσῳ εἶναι τοῦ παραδείσου λέγει, οὗ τὸν καρπὸν εἶπε σύμμικτον ἔχειν ἐκ τῶν ἐναντίων τὴν δύναμιν· τὸ γὰρ αὐτὸ καλόν τε εἶναι ἅμα καὶ κακὸν διωρίσατο, τῆς ἁμαρτίας
30   οἶμαι διὰ τούτου τὴν φύσιν ὑπαινιττόμενος. ἐπειδὴ γὰρ πάντων τῶν διὰ κακίας ἐνεργουμένων ἡδονή τις καθηγεῖται πάντως καὶ οὐκ ἔστιν εὑρεῖν ἁμαρτίαν ἡδονῆς διεζευγμένην, ὅσα τε διὰ θυμοῦ καὶ ὅσα δι᾽ ἐπιθυμίας γίνεται πάθη, τούτου χάριν καὶ καλὸς ὁ καρπὸς ὀνομάζεται κατὰ τὴν ἡμαρτημένην τοῦ καλοῦ κρίσιν τοῖς τὸ καλὸν ἐν ἡδονῇ τιθεμένοις τοιοῦτος δοκῶν.

plants, and the commandment of God was a law of life, promising that there would be no death.

Now in the middle of the Garden there was a tree that teemed with life. What then is a reader to make of this tree whose fruit is life, given that the death-dealing tree—whose fruit, the text tells us, is at once good and evil— also stood | in the middle of the paradise,[6] even though there could not have been room for both trees at the very middle? For no matter which one of the two is accorded the position in the middle, the other is necessarily excluded altogether from that spot. The precise location of the middle, after all, is ascertained relatively to a circumference, when it is equidistant on every side from the outer limit of the circle. Since, then, the middle of a circle is exactly one in number, there will be no way of finding two centers at the midpoint if the circle remains as it is. For if another center is set alongside the one that was there before, then, since the circle is also shifted, the previous center falls outside the midpoint of the circumference of the circle that embraces the second center. Yet the text asserts that in the midst of the Garden there are found this tree as well as that one, even though their powers are opposite to each other—I mean the tree that makes for life and the one whose fruit is death, which Paul called "sin" when he said, "The fruit of sin is death."

On the basis of the philosophy contained in these words, then, we are meant to grasp the following principle: that life is the very center of God's plantation. Death on the contrary is, in and of itself, rootless and unplanted, since it has no place of its own. It is in consequence of the absence of life that death | gets planted, when living beings lack participation in the nobler condition.

Life, then, stands at the midpoint of the divine plantings, while death exists as the result of a falling away from life. Hence we can see why the One who has conveyed this principle to us in enigmas says that the death-dealing tree too—whose fruit, he says, possesses a power mixed together out of opposites—stands at the center. He has laid it down, in effect, that good and evil are one and the same thing, and in doing so hinted darkly at the nature of sin. For some pleasure or other is the instigator of all vicious actions that get carried out, and there is no such thing as sin that is disjoined from pleasure (whether the affects [πάθη] stem from spiritedness or from desire[7]). Hence the fruit is called "good" because of an erroneous judgment regarding what is good, for

---

6. Gregory reads Gen 2:9 (which asserts that both "the tree of life" and "the tree of the knowledge of good and evil" were "in the midst of the garden") as though "in the midst of" meant "at the exact geometrical center." See above, preface, pp. 10–11 (Jaeger); Norris 2002.

7. "Spiritedness" and "desire" are terms Plato had associated with the two lower "parts" of the soul; see, e.g., *Resp.* 439D–440E.

πονηρὸς δὲ μετὰ ταῦτα τῇ πικρᾷ τῆς βρώσεως ἀναδόσει εὑρίσκεται κατὰ τὴν παροιμιώδη φωνὴν ἥ φησι Μέλι τῶν χειλέων τῆς κακίας ἀποστάζειν, ἢ πρὸς καιρὸν μὲν λιπαίνει τὸν φάρυγγα, μετὰ ταῦτα δὲ πικρότερον χολῆς τοῖς κακῶς γλυκανθεῖσιν εὑρίσκεται.

5   ἐπειδὴ τοίνυν ἀποστὰς τῆς τῶν ἀγαθῶν παγκαρπίας ὁ ἄνθρωπος τοῦ φθοροποιοῦ καρποῦ διὰ τῆς παρακοῆς ἐνεπλήσθη (ὄνομα δὲ τοῦ καρποῦ τούτου ἡ θανατοποιὸς ἁμαρτία), εὐθὺς ἐνεκρώθη τῷ κρείττονι | βίῳ τὴν   351 ἄλογον καὶ κτηνώδη ζωὴν τῆς θειοτέρας ἀνταλλαξάμενος. καὶ καταμιχθέντος ἅπαξ τοῦ θανάτου τῇ φύσει συνδιεξῆλθε ταῖς τῶν τικτυμένων διαδοχαῖς 10   ἡ νεκρότης. ὅθεν νεκρὸς ἡμᾶς διεδέξατο βίος αὐτῆς τρόπον τινὰ τῆς ζωῆς ἡμῶν ἀποθανούσης· νεκρὰ γὰρ ἄντικρύς ἐστιν ἡμῶν ἡ ζωὴ τῆς ἀθανασίας ἐστερημένη. διὰ τοῦτο ταῖς δύο ταύταις ζωαῖς μεσιτεύει ὁ Ἐν μέσῳ τῶν δύο ζωῶν γινωσκόμενος, ἵνα τῇ ἀναιρέσει τῆς χείρονος δῷ τῇ ἀκηράτῳ τὰ νικητήρια. ὥσπερ τοίνυν τῷ ἀποθανεῖν τῇ ἀληθινῇ ζωῇ ὁ ἄνθρωπος εἰς 15   τὸν νεκρὸν τοῦτον μετέπεσε βίον, οὕτως ὅταν ἀποθάνῃ τῇ νεκρᾷ ταύτῃ καὶ κτηνώδει ζωῇ, πρὸς τὴν ἀεὶ ζῶσαν ἀντιμεθίσταται, ὡς ἀναμφίβολον εἶναι ὅτι οὐκ ἔστιν ἐν τῇ μακαρίᾳ γενέσθαι ζωῇ μὴ νεκρὸν τῇ ἁμαρτίᾳ γενόμενον.

οὗ χάριν ἐν τῷ αὐτῷ κατὰ τὸ μέσον ἑκάτερον τῶν ξύλων εἶναι ὑπὸ τοῦ λόγου πεφιλοσόφηται ὡς τοῦ μὲν φύσει ὄντος, τοῦ δὲ ἐπιγινομένου 20   τῷ ὄντι διὰ στερήσεως· ἐκ γὰρ τοῦ αὐτοῦ ἐπὶ τοῦ αὐτοῦ διὰ μετουσίας τε καὶ στερήσεως ἡ ἀντιμετάστασις γίνεται καὶ ζωῆς καὶ θανάτου ἐπειδὴ ὁ νεκρωθεὶς τῷ ἀγαθῷ ζῇ τῷ κακῷ καὶ ὁ νεκρὸς ἐν κακίᾳ | γενόμενος πρὸς   352 τὴν ἀρετὴν ἀνεβίω. οὐκοῦν καλῶς πλήρεις δείκνυσι τῆς σμύρνης τὰς ἑαυτῆς χεῖρας ἡ νύμφη διὰ τῆς ἐν πάσῃ τῇ κακίᾳ νεκρότητος ἀνισταμένη πρὸς τὸ 25   ἀνοῖξαι τῷ λόγῳ τὴν εἰς ἑαυτὴν εἴσοδον· ζωὴ δὲ ὁ λόγος ὃν εἰσοικίζεται.

such it seems to people who identify the good with pleasure. Later on, however, it occasions sour digestion and is found to be bad, just as Proverbs says:
"For the lips" of vice "drip honey, which" at the time "is as smooth as oil in
the throat" but later is found to be "more bitter than gall" for those who are
wrongly delighted by it (cf. Prov 5:3–4).[8]

Now the human being who had turned away from the rich assortment of
fruits that are good was filled, because of this disobedience, with the fruit that
works corruption (whose name is "sin the death-dealer"); and for this reason
humanity was straightway done to death as far as the higher | existence is con-
cerned, having taken on the nonrational and brutish life in place of the more
divine. And once death had been mingled with human nature, deadness, in
step with the successions of offspring to parents, made its way everywhere.
Hence a dead form of existence enfolded us, since life itself was, in a certain
sense, dying; for as soon as our life is deprived of immortality, it is a dead
thing. For this reason, the One who is made known "in the midst between
the two forms of life" (Hab 3:2)[9] stands in between these two kinds of life, in
order that by removal of the worse he may award the spoils of victory to the
one that is undefiled. So just as by dying to the true life humanity fell instead
into this dead form of existence, so too when it dies to this dead and animal
life,[10] it is redirected toward life eternal—and this stands as a certainty, that
one cannot live the blessed life without having become dead to sin.

This is the reason why our text, speaking philosophically, says that each
of the two trees is located in the same place at the midpoint: one of them
is there because of what it is by nature, while the other, coming along secondarily, is there by privation. For the interchange of life and death begins
from and ends with the same subject[11] by way at once of participation and of
privation, since the person who has been deadened to the good lives to vice,
and the one who has become dead in vice | is alive again to virtue. The Bride,
then, is right to indicate that her hands are full of myrrh, for by her deadness
to vice of all sorts she has been raised so as to open up an entrance into herself for the Word, and the Word whom she makes at home is life.

---

8. Gregory in effect paraphrases this passage in order to generalize its point. The original
refers not to vice but to a "loose woman" (RSV).

9. Hab 3:2c in the LXX reads "In the midst between two living creatures you shall be
known" (ἐν μέσῳ δύο ζῴων γνωσθήσῃ). Gregory reads ζωῶν (from ζωή) instead of ζῴων (from
ζῷον).

10. Elsewhere equated with the "old humanity" or "the flesh" and with the "tunics of skin"
of Gen 3:21 (homily 11, pp. 327ff. [Jaeger], q.v.); see further *Beat.*, homily 3 (trans. Graef 1954,
115), with its contrast between βίος and ζωή.

11. Reading, with the Greek manuscript tradition, ἐπὶ τὸ αὐτό for ἐπὶ τοῦ αὐτοῦ; see Dünzl's
remark at 1994b, 3:633 n. 28. The next clause ("since … virtue") seems to require this.

Πρὸς τοσοῦτον δὲ μέγεθος ἐπαρθεῖσα διὰ τῶν θεωρηθέντων ἡμῖν ἡ πρὸς τὸν θεὸν ὁρῶσα ψυχὴ Οὔπω, καθώς φησιν ὁ Παῦλος, οὕτως ἔγνω καθὼς δεῖ γνῶναι, οὐδὲ λογίζεται ἑαυτὴν κατειληφέναι, ἀλλ᾽ ἔτι πρὸς τὸ ὑπερκείμενον τρέχει Τοῖς ἔμπροσθεν ἑαυτὴν ἐπεκτείνουσα. ἡ γὰρ ἀκολουθία τῶν ἐφεξῆς
5   λόγων ταῦτα νοεῖν περὶ αὐτῆς ὑποτίθεται· Ἐπὶ χεῖρας τοῦ κλείθρου ἤνοιξα ἐγὼ τῷ ἀδελφιδῷ μου, καὶ ἐπήγαγεν ὅτι Ἀδελφιδός μου παρῆλθεν, ἡ ψυχή μου ἐξῆλθεν ἐν λόγῳ αὐτοῦ.

διδάσκει γὰρ διὰ τούτων ἡμᾶς ὅτι ἐπὶ τῆς πάντα νοῦν ὑπερεχούσης δυνάμεως εἷς καταλήψεώς ἐστι τρόπος οὐ τὸ στῆναι περὶ τὸ κατειλημμένον
10   ἀλλὰ τὸ ἀεὶ ζητοῦντα τὸ πλεῖον τοῦ καταληφθέντος μὴ ἵστασθαι. ἡ γὰρ πλήρης γενομένη τῆς σμύρνης πᾶσι τοῖς τοῦ βίου ἐπιτηδεύμασιν, ἅπερ δακτύλους τροπικῶς ὀνομάζει, τὴν | πρὸς τὸ κακὸν ἐπισημαίνουσα νέκρωσιν   353
καὶ τὸ ἑκούσιον τῆς ἀρετῆς διὰ τοῦ οἴκοθεν ἀποστάξαι τῶν χειρῶν τὴν σμύρναν ἐνδειξαμένη ἅψασθαί φησι τὰς χεῖρας ἑαυτῆς τοῦ κλείθρου,
15   τουτέστι τὰ ἔργα ἑαυτῆς ἐγγίσαι λέγει τῇ στενῇ καὶ τεθλιμμένῃ εἰσόδῳ ἧς τὸ κλεῖθρον ἐγχειρίζει τοῖς κατὰ Πέτρον ὁ λόγος. ἀνοίγει τοίνυν δι᾽ ἑκατέρων ἑαυτῇ τῆς βασιλείας τὴν θύραν, διά τε τῶν χειρῶν δι᾽ ὧν τὰ ἔργα δηλοῦται καὶ διὰ τοῦ κλείθρου τῆς πίστεως· δι᾽ ἀμφοτέρων γὰρ τούτων, ἔργων τε λέγω καὶ πίστεως, ἡ κλεὶς τῆς βασιλείας ἡμῖν ὑπὸ τοῦ λόγου κατασκευάζεται.

20   ὅτε τοίνυν ἤλπισε κατὰ τὸν Μωϋσέα γνωστῶς ἐμφανήσεσθαι αὐτῇ τοῦ ποθουμένου τὸ πρόσωπον, τότε παρῆλθε τὴν κατάληψιν αὐτῆς ὁ ζητούμενος. φησὶ γὰρ ὅτι Ἀδελφιδός μου παρῆλθεν, οὐ καταλιπὼν τὴν ἑπομένην αὐτῷ ψυχὴν ἀλλὰ πρὸς ἑαυτὸν ἐφελκόμενος· Ἡ ψυχὴ γάρ μού φησιν ἐξῆλθεν ἐν λόγῳ αὐτοῦ.

25   ὢ μακαρίας ἐξόδου ἐκείνης ἣν ἐξέρχεται ἡ τῷ λόγῳ ἑπομένη ψυχή. Κύριος φυλάξει τὴν ἔξοδόν σου καὶ τὴν εἴσοδόν σου, φησὶν ὁ προφήτης. αὕτη ἐστὶν

Exalted to such a height in the ways we have discerned, the soul that looks toward God "has not yet known," in Paul's words, "as she ought to know" (1 Cor 8:2), nor does she reckon herself "to have apprehended," but she continues to run after that which lies beyond her, "straining forward to what lies ahead" (Phil 3:13). For the thought sequence of the next words requires us to make this judgment about her: *Hands on the bar,*[12] *I opened to my kinsman,* and she adds, *My kinsman passed me by, my soul went forth at his word.*

By these words she teaches us that, where the Power that transcends every intellect is concerned, there is only one mode of apprehension and that is not to stand pat with what has been apprehended but never to cease searching after something greater than what has been apprehended. For she who has become full of myrrh, who by all the habits of her life (which she figuratively calls "fingers") indicates her death | to vice, who shows that her virtue is a free and voluntary thing by the fact that the myrrh dripping from her fingers stems from within her—she, I say, says that her very own *hands* touch *the bar,* which is to say that her own works have drawn near to the "narrow and hard" entrance (cf. Matt 7:14) whose bar the Word has entrusted to people of Peter's sort.[13] It follows that she opens the door of the kingdom for herself by a double means: by the hands that signify her works, and by the *bar* that is faith. For it is by both of these—by works, I mean, and by faith—that the Word equips us with the key of the kingdom.

When, therefore, she came to hope, just as Moses had, that the countenance of the One she desired would be manifested to her so that she might know him, at that very instant the One she sought escaped her apprehension.[14] For she says, *My kinsman passed me by,* not deserting the soul that followed after him but drawing her to himself,[15] for she goes on, *My soul went forth at his word.*

What a happy exodus is this, which the soul makes that is following the Word! "The Lord will preserve your exodus and your entrance" (Ps 120:8),

---

12. More properly, "On the handles of the lock," the LXX here reproducing the Hebrew literally. Gregory, however, seems to have been able to make little sense of this and understands the line as it has been translated in the text. See the words of the Bride below, p. 353 (Jaeger), and the remarks of Dünzl 1994b, 3:614 and n. 5.

13. To understand this statement, one must note the allusion to Matt 16:18–20 and "the keys [κλεῖδας] of the kingdom of heaven," which Gregory associates with the "bar" (κλεῖθρον) that locks the Bride's door. Gregory takes it that it is in virtue of his faith that the "keys" are entrusted to Peter. Thus entrance to the kingdom is dependent on faith as well as works, and "Peter's sort" (τοῖς κατὰ Πέτρον) are those who have faith.

14. Cf. Exod 33:13–22. Moses experienced God's presence but could not see his face.

15. Just so, in the LXX text of Exod 33:22, the "glory" of God "passes by" Moses; see below, p. 354 (Jaeger).

ὡς ἀληθῶς ἡ ὑπὸ τοῦ θεοῦ φυλασσομένη τοῖς ἀξίοις ἔξοδος ἅμα καὶ | εἴσοδος   354
γινομένη· ἡ γὰρ ἀπὸ τοῦ ἐν ᾧ ἐσμεν ἔξοδος τῶν ὑπερκειμένων ἀγαθῶν
εἴσοδος γίνεται. ταύτην οὖν ἐξῆλθεν ἡ ψυχὴ τὴν ἔξοδον ὁδηγῷ κεχρημένη
τῷ λόγῳ τῷ εἰπόντι ὅτι Ἐγώ εἰμι ἡ ὁδὸς καὶ ἡ θύρα, καὶ ὅτι Δι' ἐμοῦ ἐάν τις
5   εἰσέλθῃ, καὶ εἰσελεύσεται καὶ ἐξελεύσεται, οὐδέποτε οὔτε τοῦ εἰσιέναι λήγων
οὔτε τοῦ ἐξιέναι παυόμενος, ἀλλὰ πάντοτε διὰ προκοπῆς εἰς τὰ ὑπερκείμενα
εἰσιὼν καὶ ἀεὶ τῶν κατειλημμένων ἔξω γινόμενος.

οὕτω παρῆλθέ ποτε καὶ τὸν Μωϋσέα τὸ ποθούμενον ἐκεῖνο πρόσωπον
τοῦ κυρίου καὶ οὕτως ἡ ψυχὴ τοῦ νομοθέτου ἀεὶ ἔξω ἐγίνετο τοῦ ἐν ᾧ ἦν
10   ἑπομένη προϊόντι τῷ λόγῳ. τίς γὰρ οὐκ οἶδε τὰς ἀναβάσεις ἐκείνας ἃς ἀνέβη
ὁ Μωϋσῆς, ὁ ἀεὶ μέγας γινόμενος καὶ μηδέποτε ἱστάμενος τῆς ἐπὶ τὸ μεῖζον
αὐξήσεως; ηὐξήθη κατ' ἀρχὰς ὅτε τῆς τῶν Αἰγυπτίων βασιλείας ὑψηλότερον
τὸν ὀνειδισμὸν τοῦ Χριστοῦ ἐποιήσατο Μᾶλλον ἑλόμενος συγκακουχεῖσθαι
τῷ λαῷ τοῦ θεοῦ ἢ πρόσκαιρον ἔχειν ἁμαρτίας ἀπόλαυσιν· ηὐξήθη πάλιν ὅτε
15   καταπονοῦντος τὸν Ἑβραῖον τοῦ Αἰγυπτίου θανατοῖ τὸν ἀλλόφυλον ὑπὲρ
τοῦ Ἰσραηλίτου ἀγωνιζόμενος. νοεῖς δὲ πάντως ἐν τούτοις τὸν τῆς αὐξήσεως
τρόπον μεταβαλὼν τὴν ἱστορίαν εἰς τροπικὴν θεωρίαν. πάλιν | ἑαυτοῦ μείζων   355
ἐγένετο ἀπεριήχητον τὴν ζωὴν φυλάσσων διὰ τῆς ἐν τῇ ἐρήμῳ φιλοσοφίας
ἐν χρόνῳ πολλῷ. εἶτα τῷ πυρὶ τῷ ἐπὶ τῆς βάτου φωτίζεται. μετὰ τοῦτο καὶ
20   τὴν ἀκοὴν ταῖς τοῦ φωτὸς ἀκτῖσι διὰ τοῦ λόγου περιαυγάζεται. γυμνοῖ πρὸς
τούτοις τῆς νεκρᾶς περιβολῆς τὰς ἑαυτοῦ βάσεις, ἀναλίσκει τῇ ῥάβδῳ τοὺς
Αἰγυπτίους δράκοντας, ἐξαιρεῖται τῆς τυραννίδος τοῦ Φαραὼ τὸ ὁμόφυλον,
ὁδηγεῖται διὰ νεφέλης, διαιρεῖ τὸ πέλαγος, ὑποβρύχιον ποιεῖ τὴν τυραννίδα,
γλυκαίνει τὴν Μερράν, παίει τὴν πέτραν, ἐμφορεῖται τῆς τῶν ἀγγέλων τροφῆς,
25   τῶν σαλπίγγων ἀκούει, τοῦ καιομένου ὄρους κατατολμᾷ, τῆς ἀκρωρείας
ἅπτεται, τὴν νεφέλην ὑπέρχεται, ἐντὸς τοῦ γνόφου γίνεται ἐν ᾧ ἦν ὁ θεός,
τὴν διαθήκην δέχεται, ἥλιος γίνεται ἀπροσπέλαστον τοῖς προσεγγίζουσιν ἐκ
τοῦ προσώπου τὸ φῶς ἀπαστράπτων.

says the prophet. This is truly at one and the same time the exodus and | the entrance that God keeps for those that are worthy, since the exodus from our present state becomes an entrance upon the good things that lie beyond. This then is the exodus that the soul makes when it takes the Word as its guide, the Word who says "I am the way" (John 14:6) and "the door," and "Whoever enters by way of me ... will both come in and go out" (John 10:9). That soul neither leaves off coming in nor ceases going out but is ever entering into what lies beyond by the progress she makes and always taking leave of what she has already apprehended.

In just this way did that longed-for face of the Lord once pass by Moses, and just so did the soul of the Lawgiver ever and again take leave of the situation she was in as she followed the Word that went on ahead of her. Who does not observe the upward steps that Moses climbed, Moses who was ever in process of growing up[16] and never ceased from growth toward the better? He increased at the beginning, when he preferred the reproach of Christ over the kingdom of the Egyptians, "Choosing rather to share ill treatment with the people of God than to enjoy the fleeting pleasures of sin" (Heb 11:25). He increased again when, because an Egyptian was maltreating a Hebrew, he fought for the Israelite and killed the foreigner (cf. Exod 2:11–12). The manner of his growth in these events you understand fully by shifting the narrative to the level of figurative interpretation. Yet again he became | greater than himself when he kept his life undisturbed for a long space by living the philosophical life in the wilderness (cf. Exod 3:1).[17] Then he was enlightened by the fire that played over the bush (cf. Exod 3:2). After that his hearing too was illumined by the beams of light through the agency of the Word (cf. Exod 3:4–6). Further, he strips his feet of their dead covering (Exod 3:5); he destroys the Egyptian snakes with his staff (Exod 7:12); he frees his people from the tyrant Pharaoh; he is guided by a cloud (Exod 13:21); he divides the sea (cf. Exod 14:21); he drowns the tyrant (Exod 14:28); he makes Marah sweet (Exod 15:25); he smites the rock (Exod 17:6); he is filled with the food of angels (Ps 77:25; Exod 16:14–15); he hears the trumpets (Exod 19:16, 19); he dares the burning mountain (cf. Exod 19:18); he attains its pinnacle (Exod 19:20); the cloud comes down; he enters the darkness in which God dwells (Exod 24:16–18); he receives the covenant (cf. Exod 24:7); he becomes a sun, flashing unapproachable light from his countenance upon those who draw near him (Exod 34:29–35).

---

16. This is an allusion to Heb 11:24 (Μωϋσῆς μέγας γενόμενος: "when Moses had grown up"), but Gregory recasts the participle into the present form (γινόμενος).

17. Literally, "with the help of an extended [period of] philosophy in the wilderness." "Philosophy" here, as often in the Cappadocians, refers to an ascetic mode of life.

καὶ πῶς ἄν τις πάσας αὐτοῦ τὰς ἀναβάσεις καὶ τὰς ποικίλας θεοφανείας διεξέλθοι τῷ λόγῳ; ἀλλ' ὅμως ὁ τοσοῦτος, ὁ τοιοῦτος, ὁ ἐν τοσούτοις γενόμενος καὶ διὰ τοσούτων πρὸς τὸν θεὸν | ὑψωθεὶς ἔτι ἀπλήστως τῆς 356 ἐπιθυμίας ἔχει τοῦ πλείονος καὶ τοῦ κατὰ πρόσωπον ἰδεῖν τὸν θεὸν ἱκέτης
5 γίνεται καίτοι μαρτυρήσαντος ἤδη τοῦ λόγου τῆς κατὰ πρόσωπον αὐτὸν ὁμιλίας ἠξιῶσθαι. ἀλλ' ὅμως οὔτε τὸ ὡς φίλον φίλῳ προσδιαλέγεσθαι οὔτε ἡ στόμα κατὰ στόμα γινομένη αὐτῷ πρὸς τὸν θεὸν ὁμιλία τῆς τῶν ἀνωτέρων αὐτὸν ἐπιθυμίας ἵστησιν, ἀλλ' Εἰ εὕρηκα χάριν, φησίν, ἐνώπιόν σου, ἐμφάνισόν μοι σεαυτὸν γνωστῶς. καὶ ὁ τὴν αἰτηθεῖσαν χάριν δώσειν ἐπαγγειλάμενος,
10 ὁ εἰπὼν Ἔγνων σε παρὰ πάντας, παρέρχεται αὐτὸν ἐπὶ τοῦ θείου τόπου ἐν τῇ πέτρᾳ ὑπὸ τῆς θείας χειρὸς σκεπαζόμενον, ὥστε μόγις ἰδεῖν μετὰ τὴν πάροδον αὐτοῦ τὰ ὀπίσθια, διδάσκων, οἶμαι, διὰ τούτων ὁ λόγος ὅτι ὁ ἰδεῖν τὸν θεὸν ἐπιθυμῶν ἐν τῷ ἀεὶ αὐτῷ ἀκολουθεῖν ὁρᾷ τὸν ποθούμενον καὶ ἡ τοῦ προσώπου αὐτοῦ θεωρία ἐστὶν ἡ ἄπαυστος πρὸς αὐτὸν πορεία διὰ τοῦ
15 κατόπιν ἔπεσθαι τῷ λόγῳ κατορθουμένη.

οὕτω τοίνυν καὶ νῦν ἡ ψυχή, ὅτε ἀνέστη διὰ τοῦ θανάτου, ὅτε ἐπληρώθη τῆς σμύρνης, ὅτε προσήγαγε τῷ κλείθρῳ διὰ τῶν ἔργων τὰς χεῖρας καὶ εἰσοικίσασθαι τὸν ποθούμενον ἤλπισε, τότε ὁ μὲν παρέρχεται, | ἡ δὲ ἐξέρχεται 357 οὐκέτι μένουσα ἐν οἷς ἦν, ἀλλὰ τῷ λόγῳ ἐπὶ τὰ πρόσω προηγουμένῳ
20 ἐφεπομένη.

Ὁ δὲ ἐφεξῆς λόγος μᾶλλον ἡμῖν βεβαιοῖ τὴν προθεωρηθεῖσαν διάνοιαν ὅτι οὐκ ἐν τῷ καταλαμβάνεσθαι τὸ μέγεθος τῆς θείας γνωρίζεται φύσεως ἀλλ' ἐν τῷ παριέναι πᾶσαν καταληπτικὴν φαντασίαν καὶ δύναμιν· ἡ γὰρ ἐκβᾶσα ἤδη τὴν φύσιν ψυχή, ὡς ἂν μηδενὶ τῶν συνήθων πρὸς τὴν γνῶσιν τῶν ἀοράτων
25 κωλύοιτο, οὔτε ζητοῦσα τὸ μὴ εὑρισκόμενον ἵσταται οὔτε καλοῦσα τὸ ἀνεκφώνητον παύεται, φησὶ γὰρ ὅτι Ἐζήτησα αὐτὸν καὶ οὐχ εὗρον αὐτόν. πῶς γὰρ ἂν εὑρεθείη ὃν μηνύει τῶν γινωσκομένων οὐδέν, οὐκ εἶδος, οὐ χρῶμα, οὐ περιγραφή, οὐ ποσότης, οὐ τόπος, οὐ σχῆμα, οὐ στοχασμός, οὐκ εἰκασμός, οὐκ ἀναλογία; ἀλλὰ πάσης καταληπτικῆς ἐφόδου ἐξώτερος ἀεὶ εὑρισκόμενος
30 ἐκφεύγει πάντως τὴν τῶν ζητούντων λαβήν, διὰ τοῦτό φησιν Ἐζήτησα αὐτόν, διὰ τῶν ἐρευνητικῶν τῆς ψυχῆς δυνάμεων ἐν λογισμοῖς καὶ νοήμασι, καὶ πάντων ἐξώτερος ἦν τὸν προσεγγισμὸν τῆς διανοίας διαδιδράσκων. ὁ δὲ παντὸς γνωριστικοῦ χαρακτῆρος ἐξώτερος ἀεὶ εὑρισκόμενος πῶς ἂν διὰ

All these his upward steps and all the varied theophanies he experienced—how can words tell them? Yet for all that, it is such and so great a person as this—one whose life was so full of sublime events and who through them | was raised up toward God—who nevertheless still possesses an insatiable desire for something greater and comes to supplicate that he may see God face to face, even though the Scripture had already attested that he was judged worthy of speaking with God face to face (cf. Deut 34:10). But neither the fact that he addressed God as friend to friend nor his intimate conversation with God put a stop to his desire for higher things. On the contrary, his word is: "If I have found grace in your sight, manifest yourself to me in such wise that I may know you" (Exod 33:13). And the One who had promised to confer the asked-for gift, the One who said, "You have I known above all others" (Exod 33:12), passes Moses by as he is stationed upon the rock at the divine place and shielded by the divine hand, so that he can scarcely see God's back after God has passed by (Exod 33:21–23). By this, as I judge the matter, the Scripture teaches that a person who desires to see God catches sight of the One he seeks by always following after him and that the contemplation of God's face is an unceasing journey toward him that is brought to fulfillment by following behind the Word.

So it is in our present case. The soul, at the moment when through death she has been raised, when she has been filled with myrrh, when by her deeds she has touched her hands to the bar and hoped to bring the One she longs for into her house—at just that moment he passes her by, | while she, no longer remaining where she was, moves out, but following the Word who leads her forward.

The next statement further confirms the meaning we have already discerned in this passage, namely, that the greatness of the divine nature is not known in being apprehended but in its eluding every image or faculty that might apprehend it.[18] For the soul, who has already departed from her nature so as not to be prevented from knowing things unseen, neither ceases from seeking after what is not found nor stops calling for the unutterable. Thus she says: *I sought him, and I did not find him.* For how shall he be found whom none of the things we know declares—not look, nor color, nor outline, nor size, nor location, nor shape, nor conjecture, nor likelihood, nor analogy? No, the place where he is found is outside of every move to apprehend him, and hence he wholly escapes the grasp of those who seek him. That is why she says, "*I sought him*—by means of the soul's tracking powers, by reasonings and concepts, and he was outside them all, fleeing the mind's approach." For

---

18. Here Gregory employs the classical Stoic expression, καταληπτικὴ φαντασία.

τινος ὀνοματικῆς σημασίας περιληφθείη; τούτου χάριν ἐπινοεῖ | μὲν παντοίαν   358
ὀνομάτων δύναμιν εἰς τὴν τοῦ ἀφράστου ἀγαθοῦ σημασίαν, ἡττᾶται δὲ πᾶσα
φραστικὴ λόγου δύναμις καὶ τῆς ἀληθείας ἐλάττων ἐλέγχεται. διό φησιν ὅτι
ἐγὼ μὲν ἐκάλουν ὡς ἐδυνάμην ἐπινοοῦσα φωνὰς ἐνδεικτικὰς τῆς ἀφράστου
5   μακαριότητος, ὁ δὲ κρείττων ἦν τῆς τῶν σημαινομένων ἐνδείξεως.

οἷον δὴ ἐποίει πολλάκις καὶ ὁ μέγας Δαβὶδ μυρίοις ὀνόμασι τὸ θεῖον
καλῶν καὶ ἡττᾶσθαι τῆς ἀληθείας ὁμολογῶν· Σὺ γάρ, φησίν, ὁ θεὸς οἰκτίρμων
καὶ ἐλεήμων, μακρόθυμος καὶ πολυέλεος καὶ ἀληθινός, καὶ ἰσχὺς καὶ
στερέωμα καὶ καταφυγὴ καὶ δύναμις καὶ βοηθὸς καὶ ἀντιλήπτωρ καὶ κέρας
10   σωτηρίας καὶ τὰ τοιαῦτα. καὶ πάλιν ὁμολογεῖ ὅτι τὸ ὄνομα αὐτοῦ ἐν πάσῃ
τῇ γῇ οὐχὶ γινώσκεται ἀλλὰ θαυμάζεται· Ὡς θαυμαστὸν γάρ, φησί, τὸ ὄνομά
σου ἐν πάσῃ τῇ γῇ. οὕτω φησὶ καὶ πρὸς τὸν Μανωὲ ὁ περὶ τοῦ παιδὸς αὐτῷ
χρηματίσας, ὅτε ἠρωτήθη περὶ τοῦ ὀνόματος, ὅτι θαυμαστόν ἐστι τοῦτο καὶ
κρεῖττον ἢ ὥστε ὑπ᾽ ἀνθρωπίνης ἀκοῆς χωρηθῆναι. διὰ τοῦτο καὶ ἡ ψυχὴ
15   τὸν λόγον καλεῖ μὲν ὡς δύναται, δύναται δὲ οὐχ ὡς βούλεται· βούλεται γὰρ
πλεῖον ἢ δύναται. οὐ μὴν οὐδὲ θελῆσαι τοσοῦτον δύναται, | ὅσον ἐκεῖνος   359
ἐστιν, ἀλλ᾽ ὅσον βουληθῆναι ἡ προαίρεσις δύναται. ἐπεὶ οὖν ἀνέφικτός ἐστιν
ὁ καλούμενος τῇ τοῦ καλοῦντος ὁρμῇ, διὰ τοῦτό φησιν· Ἐκάλεσα αὐτὸν καὶ
οὐχ ὑπήκουσέ μου.

20   Ὅσα δὲ τοῖς εἰρημένοις ἡ νύμφη προστίθησι, κἂν σκυθρωποτέραν κατὰ
τὸ πρόχειρον ἔχῃ τὴν ἔνδειξιν, ἀλλ᾽ ἐμοὶ δοκεῖ πρὸς τὸν αὐτὸν σκοπὸν
βλέπειν καὶ τῆς τῶν ὑψηλοτέρων ἀναβάσεως ἔχεσθαι· φησὶ γὰρ ὅτι Εὕροσάν
με οἱ φύλακες οἱ κυκλοῦντες ἐν τῇ πόλει, ἐπάταξάν με, ἐτραυμάτισάν με, ἦραν
τὸ θέριστρον ἀπ᾽ ἐμοῦ οἱ φύλακες τῶν τειχέων.

25   ταῦτα γὰρ ἴσως δόξει τισὶν ὀδυρομένης μᾶλλον ἤπερ εὐφραινομένης
εἶναι τὰ ῥήματα, τὸ Ἐπάταξαν καὶ Ἐτραυμάτισαν καὶ Ἦραν τὸ θέριστρον·
τῷ δὲ ἀκριβῶς ἐπεσκεμμένῳ τὴν τῶν λεγομένων διάνοιαν μεγαλαυχουμένης
ἐπὶ τοῖς καλλίστοις εἰσὶν αἱ φωναί. οὑτωσὶ δὲ γένοιτ᾽ ἂν ἡμῖν καταφανὲς τὸ
λεγόμενον·

30   μικρὸν πρὸ τούτων ἐν τοῖς κατόπιν καθαρεύειν αὐτὴν παντὸς
προκαλύμματος ὁ λόγος μαρτύρεται, ἐν οἷς φησιν ἐκ προσώπου τῆς νύμφης
ὅτι Ἐξεδυσάμην τὸν χιτῶνά μου, πῶς ἐνδύσομαι αὐτόν; ἐνταῦθα δὲ πάλιν
ἀφῃρῆσθαι αὐτῆς λέγει τὸ θέριστρον. περιβόλαιον δὲ νυμφικόν ἐστι τὸ

how shall he be grasped by the sense of some label when he stands apart from any characteristic that can identify him? For this reason, she contrives | all sorts of word meanings to signify the unutterable Good, but every expressive power that belongs to rational speech falls short and is exposed as being less than the truth. Hence she says, "I indeed called out, as far as I was able, inventing utterances to designate the unutterable Blessedness, but he was greater than the power of the ideas to designate him."

The great David himself often does the same sort of thing: calling the Divine by a thousand names and then confessing that he has fallen short of the truth. "You," he says, "are a merciful and gracious God, generous and full of compassion and true" (Ps 85:15)—and "strength" and "rock" and "refuge" (Ps 17:2–3) and "power" and "helper" (Ps 45:2) and "protector" and "horn of salvation" (Ps 17:3c), and the like. Again he confesses that God's name is not known in all the earth but rather wondered at: "How wonderful," he says, "is your name in all the earth" (Ps 8:2, 10). In this manner too spoke the One who responded to Manoah's question about his child when [Manoah] asked his name: " 'It is to be wondered at' (Judg 13:18) and is greater than anything that human hearing can take in." That is why the soul too names the Word in whatever way she can, but her ability does not match her aim. She seeks more than she is capable of. Nor indeed is she able to want | all that he is, but only as much as her faculty of choice can intend. Since, then, the One called upon is beyond the reach of the caller's desire, she says: *I called upon him, but he did not answer me.*

Now the things that the Bride adds at this point refer in their plain sense to very unhappy circumstances, yet for all that they seem to me to serve the very same purpose and to be concerned with ascent to higher and nobler things. For she says: *The watchmen who go their rounds in the city found me, they struck me, they wounded me, the guards of the walls took my veil away from me.*

Now to some these expressions will seem to be suited more to one who is bewailing her lot than to one who is rejoicing—*struck*, I mean, and *wounded* and *took my veil away.* But for one who looks closely into the meaning of the statements, they are the utterances of a person who is glorying in things of the greatest beauty. This will become clear to us in the following manner.

Shortly before this, in the previous lection, the text attests that she is free of any covering, when it says, speaking in the person of the Bride: *I have removed my tunic. How shall I put it on?*[19] In the present passage it says again that her *veil* has been taken off her. Now the veil is a bridal garment

---

19. See above, homily 11, p. 327 (Jaeger).

θέριστρον συγκαλύπτον μετὰ τῆς | κεφαλῆς καὶ τὸ πρόσωπον, καθὼς περὶ τῆς   360
Ῥεβέκκας λέγει ἡ ἱστορία. πῶς οὖν ἡ γυμνωθεῖσα παντὸς περιβλήματος ἔτι
τὸ θέριστρον ἔχει ὅπερ νῦν αὐτῆς ἀφαιροῦνται οἱ φύλακες; ἢ δῆλον διὰ τῶν
εἰρημένων ἐστίν, ὅσον ἀπ' ἐκείνου πάλιν ἐπὶ τὸ ὑψηλότερον διὰ προκοπῆς
5   ἀνελήλυθεν; ἡ γὰρ ἀπεκδυσαμένη τὸν παλαιὸν χιτῶνα καὶ πάσης περιβολῆς
καθαρεύσασα τοσοῦτον ἑαυτῆς γίνεται καθαρωτέρα, ὡς συγκρίσει τῆς ἄρτι
γενομένης αὐτῇ καθαρότητος μὴ δοκεῖν ἀποδεδῦσθαι τὸ περιβόλαιον, ἀλλ'
εὑρεῖν τι πάλιν μετὰ τὴν γύμνωσιν ἐκείνην περὶ ἑαυτὴν ὃ ἀποθῆται. οὕτως
ἡ πρὸς τὸ θεῖον ἄνοδος τοῦ ἀεὶ εὑρισκομένου τὸ περὶ αὐτὴν παχύτερον
10   δείκνυσιν. διὰ τοῦτο συγκρίσει τῆς νῦν καθαρότητος ἡ προγενομένη
τοῦ χιτῶνος ἐκείνου γύμνωσις ὡς κάλυμμα πάλιν περιαιρεῖται παρὰ τῶν
εὑρισκόντων αὐτήν.

οὗτοι δέ εἰσιν οἱ φύλακες οἱ κυκλοῦντες τὴν πόλιν (ψυχὴ δὲ ἡ πόλις)
οἱ διὰ τοῦ πατάξαι καὶ τραυματίσαι περιελόντες τὸ θέριστρον, ὧν ἔργον
15   ἐστὶ τὸ φυλάσσειν τὰ τείχη τῆς πόλεως. ὅτι μὲν οὖν ἀγαθόν τί ἐστιν ἡ τοῦ
θερίστρου περιαίρεσις, ὥστε ἐλεύθερον τοῦ προκαλύμματος τὸν ὀφθαλμὸν
ἀπαραποδίστως ἐνατενίζειν τῷ ποθουμένῳ κάλλει, οὐκ ἄν τις ἀμφιβάλοι
| πρὸς τὸν ἀπόστολον βλέπων, ὃς τῇ δυνάμει τοῦ πνεύματος τὴν τοῦ   361
καλύμματος περιαίρεσιν ἀνατίθησι λέγων· Ὅταν δὲ ἐπιστρέψῃ πρὸς κύριον
20   περιαιρεῖται τὸ κάλυμμα· ὁ δὲ κύριος τὸ πνεῦμά ἐστιν. ὅτι δὲ τὸ τοῦ ἀγαθοῦ
παρασκευαστικὸν καὶ αὐτὸ πάντως ἐστὶν ἀγαθόν, οὐκ ἄν τις ἀμφιβάλοι
τῶν ἐπισταμένων πρὸς τὸ ἀκόλουθον βλέπειν. εἰ τοίνυν ἀγαθὸν ἡ τοῦ
καλύμματος περιαίρεσις, ἀγαθὸν ἂν εἴη πάντως καὶ ἡ πληγὴ καὶ τὸ τραῦμα
δι' ὧν κατορθοῦται ἡ περιαίρεσις. ἀλλ' ἐπειδὴ κατὰ τὴν πρόχειρον ἔννοιαν
25   ἀηδία τις ἐμφαίνεται τοῖς ῥήμασι τούτοις (ἄλγημα γὰρ ἐνδείκνυται ἡ φωνὴ
τοῦ Ἐπάταξάν με καὶ Ἐτραυμάτισάν με), καλῶς ἂν ἔχοι κατανοῆσαι πρῶτον
τῆς ἁγίας γραφῆς τὴν τῶν τοιούτων ῥημάτων χρῆσιν, εἴ που πρὸς τὸ κρεῖττον
αὐτῶν τὴν μνήμην πεποίηται, εἶθ' οὕτω θεωρῆσαι τῶν ἐνταῦθα λεγομένων
τὴν δύναμιν.

30   Πῶς ῥύεται ἡ σοφία τὴν τοῦ νέου ψυχὴν ἀπὸ θανάτου; τί συμβουλεύει
ποιεῖν, ἵνα μὴ ἀποθάνῃ ὁ νέος; αὐτῆς ἀκούσωμεν τῆς σοφίας· Ἐὰν πατάξῃς
αὐτόν, φησί, ῥάβδῳ, οὐ μὴ ἀποθάνῃ· σὺ μὲν γὰρ ῥάβδῳ πατάξεις αὐτόν, τὴν
δὲ ψυχὴν αὐτοῦ ῥύσῃ ἐκ θανάτου. ἔοικε τοίνυν ἀθανασίαν ἑρμηνεύειν ἡ
τοῦ Ἐπάταξάν με λέξις, καθὼς ὁ λόγος φησὶν ὅτι Ἐὰν πατάξῃς τῇ ῥάβδῳ,
35   οὐ μὴ ἀποθάνῃ, καὶ ὅτι οὐκ ἔστιν ἄλλως ῥυσθῆναι τὴν ψυχὴν ἐκ θανάτου
ἐὰν μὴ παταχθῇ | τῇ ῥάβδῳ. καλὸν ἄρα τὸ παταχθῆναι διὰ τῶν εἰρημένων   362

that covers | the face as well as the head, as the story of Rebecca says (cf. Gen 24:65).[20] How, then, does one who has been stripped of all covering still wear the *veil* that the *guards* now remove from her? But is it not the case that these words show how much progress upward she has made from that previous state? She who had removed that old tunic and been freed of all covering becomes so much purer than herself that by comparison with the purity that now becomes hers she does not seem to have taken off that clothing but again, even after that former stripping, finds something on her to be taken off. Thus the ascent to the Divine shows that what she wears about her is coarser and heavier than what is forever being discovered. Hence by comparison with her present purity the previous removal of that tunic is itself like a veil, which in its turn is stripped away by those who find her.

Now the latter are *the watchmen who go their rounds in the city*, "city" standing for the soul. They have removed her veil by striking and wounding her, and their job is to keep the walls of the city. And the removal of the veil, so that the eye, freed of what obscures it, gazes without interference on the Beauty it desires, is a good thing, as none can doubt | who pays attention to the apostle. He attributes the removal of the veil to the power of the Spirit when he says: "But when one turns to the Lord, the veil is removed; and the Lord is the Spirit" (2 Cor 3:16–17). Furthermore, no one who has the sense to attend to the way things hang together logically can doubt that what prepares the way for the good is itself in every sense a good. If then the removal of the veil is a good thing, so too, in every way, will be the blow and the wound by which its removal is accomplished. But since it is something repellent that is indicated by these terms in their ordinary sense (for to say *they struck me* and *they wounded me* suggests suffering), it will be proper first of all to examine the Holy Scriptures' use of such terms, to see whether they are employed to refer to something nobler and then to interpret the sense of this text accordingly.

How does Wisdom free the soul of a youth from death? What does she plan to do to prevent the youth from dying? Let us hear Wisdom herself. "If you strike him with a rod," says she, "he will not die. For you will strike him with a rod, and you will free his soul from death" (Prov 23:13–14). The expression *They struck me*, then, appears to signify immortality, in accordance with the Word's statement: "If you strike him with a rod, he will not die," and "It is not possible for the soul to be freed from death except it be struck | with the

---

20. With this passage compare Ambrose, *Isaac* 6.55 (CSEL 32.1.2:679), where the Bride of the Song is also compared with Rebecca in that "she came as a bride wearing a veil that covered her head." The idea no doubt reflects Origen's exegesis, but Gregory again puts his own twist on it.

ἡμῖν ἀποδέδεικται, διότι καλόν ἐστιν ὡς ἀληθῶς τὸ ἐκ θανάτου τὴν ψυχὴν
ῥυσθῆναι. οὕτω ποιεῖν καὶ τὸν θεὸν ὁ προφήτης φησὶ διὰ τοῦ ἀποκτέννειν
ζωοποιοῦντα καὶ διὰ τοῦ πατάσσειν ἰώμενον· Ἐγὼ γάρ φησιν ἀποκτενῶ καὶ
ζῆν ποιήσω, πατάξω κἀγὼ ἰάσομαι. διὰ τοῦτο καὶ ὁ μέγας Δαβὶδ οὐχὶ πληγὴν
5   εἶπεν ἀλλὰ παράκλησιν ἐκ τῆς τοιαύτης γίνεσθαι ῥάβδου, λέγων Ἡ ῥάβδος
σου καὶ ἡ βακτηρία σου, αὗταί με παρεκάλεσαν· δι' ὧν γίνεται ἡ τῆς θείας
αὐτῷ τραπέζης ἑτοιμασία καὶ ὅσα κατὰ τὸ ἀκόλουθον περιέχει ἡ ψαλμῳδία·
καὶ τὸ ἐπὶ τῆς κεφαλῆς ἔλαιον καὶ ὁ τοῦ ποτηρίου ἄκρατος, ὁ τὴν νηφάλιον
μέθην ἀπεργαζόμενος, καὶ ὁ καλῶς αὐτὸν καταδιώκων ἔλεος καὶ ἡ ἐν τῷ οἴκῳ
10   τοῦ θεοῦ μακροβίωσις. εἰ οὖν ταῦτα παρέχει ἡ γλυκεῖα ἐκείνη πληγὴ κατά τε
τὴν παροιμιώδη διδασκαλίαν καὶ κατὰ τὴν τοῦ προφήτου φωνήν, ἀγαθὸν ἄρα
ἐστὶ τὸ παταχθῆναι τῇ ῥάβδῳ, ἀφ' ἧς ἐστιν ἡ τῶν τοσούτων ἀγαθῶν εὐθηνία.

Μᾶλλον δὲ τὸ παρεθὲν πρὸ τῶν εἰρημένων διεξετάσωμεν· παρῆλθε τὴν
νύμφην ὁ λόγος ἀνέφικτος τῇ λαβῇ τῆς ποθούσης | γενόμενος· παρῆλθε δὲ   363
15   οὐχ ὥστε καταλιπεῖν ἣν παρέδραμεν, ἀλλ' ὥστε μᾶλλον αὐτὴν πρὸς ἑαυτὸν
ἐπισπάσασθαι· φησὶ γὰρ ὅτι Ἡ ψυχή μου ἐξῆλθεν ἐν λόγῳ αὐτοῦ. ἐξέρχεται
τοίνυν πρῶτον ἀπὸ τοῦ ἐν ᾧ ἦν ἡ ψυχὴ καὶ οὕτως ὑπὸ τῶν φυλασσόντων
τὴν πόλιν εὑρίσκεται· Εὕροσαν γάρ με, φησίν, οἱ φύλακες οἱ κυκλοῦντες ἐν
τῇ πόλει. εἰ μὲν οὖν ἢ Κίνδυνοι ᾅδου εὗρον αὐτὴν ἢ λῃσταῖς αὐτὴν εὑρῆσθαι
20   ἔλεγε, χαλεπὸν ἦν τὸ τῶν τοιούτων αὐτὴν εὕρημα γενέσθαι (Ὁ γὰρ κλέπτης
οὐκ ἔρχεται, εἰ μὴ ἵνα κλέψῃ καὶ θύσῃ καὶ ἀπολέσῃ), εἰ δὲ οἱ φύλακες αὐτὴν
εὑρίσκουσιν οἱ κυκλοῦντες ἐν τῇ πόλει, μακαριστὴ πάντως ἐστὶ τῆς τοιαύτης
εὑρέσεως· ὁ γὰρ ὑπὸ τοῦ φύλακος εὑρεθεὶς ὑπὸ λῃστῶν κλαπῆναι οὐ δύναται.
τίνες οὖν εἰσιν οἱ φύλακες;

25   τίνες ἄλλοι ἢ πάντως οἱ ὑπηρέται τοῦ φυλάσσοντος τὸν Ἰσραήλ, τοῦ
διὰ τῆς | φυλακῆς τὴν δεξιὰν χεῖρα σκεπάζοντος, τοῦ ἀπὸ παντὸς κακοῦ τὴν   364
ψυχὴν φυλάσσειν πεπιστευμένου, ὃς καὶ εἰσόδου καὶ ἐξόδου γίνεται φύλαξ;
ἐκεῖνός ἐστιν ὁ φύλαξ τῆς πόλεως περὶ οὗ φησιν ὅτι Ἐὰν μὴ κύριος φυλάξῃ
πόλιν, εἰς μάτην ἠγρύπνησεν ὁ φυλάσσων. τὰ τοίνυν Λειτουργικὰ πνεύματα,
30   τὰ εἰς διακονίαν ἀποστελλόμενα διὰ τοὺς μέλλοντας κληρονομεῖν σωτηρίαν,
ἐνδείκνυται διὰ τῶν φυλάκων ὁ λόγος τῶν κυκλούντων τὴν πόλιν. ψυχὴ δέ,
καθὼς εἴρηται, ἡ πόλις ἐστί, τὸ τοῦ θεοῦ οἰκητήριον. παρὰ τούτων οὖν εὑρέθη,
φησίν, ἡ ψυχή, ὡς εὑρέθη ποτὲ παρὰ τοῦ καλοῦ ποιμένος τὸ πρόβατον, ἐφ' οὗ
πᾶσαι τῶν ἀγγέλων αἱ χορεῖαι πρὸς εὐφροσύνην συνεκινήθησαν κατὰ τὴν
35   τοῦ κυρίου φωνήν. οὕτως εὑρέθη ποτὲ καὶ ἡ δραχμὴ ὑπὸ τοῦ λύχνου, ἐφ' ᾗ
χαίρουσι πάντες οἱ φίλοι τε καὶ οἱ γείτονες. τοιοῦτον εὕρημα καὶ Δαβίδ, ὁ
δοῦλος τοῦ κυρίου, γίνεται, καθὼς ἡ ψαλμῳδία φησὶν ἐκ προσώπου τοῦ θεοῦ

rod." We are shown, then, by these words that it is a fine thing to be struck, precisely because it is truly a fine thing for the soul to be freed from death. The prophet says that God too acts in this way: by killing he gives life, and by striking, heals. For it says: "I will kill and I will make alive; I will strike and I will heal" (Deut 32:39). That is why David said that the effect of a rod of this sort is not affliction but comfort: "Your rod and your staff, they comfort me" (Ps 22:5–6). Through them the divine table is prepared for him, and all the other things that this psalm mentions in the lines that follow this one: both the oil that anoints his head and the unmixed wine in the cup, which works a sober drunkenness; and the mercy that happily pursues him; and length of life in God's house. If, then, that sweet blow supplies these good things according to both the teaching of Proverbs and the word of the prophet, it is assuredly a good thing to be struck by the rod that is the source of the abundance of so many good things.

But let us rather take careful account of what is set forth just before these lines. The Word *passed by* the Bride in the sense that he became unattainable for the one who desired him. | He did not however *pass her by* so as to leave the one he outpaced behind, but rather so as to draw her to himself. For she says: *My soul went forth in his word.* First of all, then, the soul departs from her given state, and it is in this way that she is found by those who guard the city. *The watchmen who make their rounds in the city found me,* she says. To be sure, if either "the dangers of Hades" (Ps 114:3) found her or it said that she had been come upon by thieves, it would have been a hard thing indeed for her to be found by such as these (for "The thief comes only to steal and kill and destroy" [John 10:10]); but if *the watchmen who make their rounds in the city* find her, to be apprehended in that way is the happiest thing possible. For the person that has been found by the watcher cannot be robbed by thieves.

Who, then, are the watchmen? Who indeed, but the servants of the one who guards Israel, whose | guarding protects your right hand, who is trusted to keep the soul "from all evil," who is also the keeper of both "entrance … and exodus" (Ps 120:4–8). He is the keeper of that city of which it is said: "Unless the Lord keep the city, the watchman wakes but in vain" (Ps 126:1). So then by *the watchmen who go about the city* the Word indicates the "ministering spirits" who "are sent out to serve on behalf of those who are to inherit salvation" (Heb 1:14). But "city," as I have said, means the soul, the dwelling place of God. These then are the ones by whom, it says, the soul is found, even as once the Good Shepherd found the sheep over which, as the Lord said, all the songs of the angels were moved to rejoicing (cf. Luke 15:4–7). In the same way too was the drachma once found with the help of a lamp, and all the friends and neighbors rejoiced at it (cf. Luke 15:8–10). David too, the Lord's servant, was such a find, as the psalm says, speaking in God's person:

ὅτι Εὗρον Δαβὶδ τὸν δοῦλόν μου, ἐν ἐλαίῳ ἁγίῳ μου ἔχρισα αὐτόν. ὃς ἐπειδὴ κτῆμα τοῦ εὑρόντος ἐγένετο, ἀκούσωμεν οἵων ἀξιοῦται· Ἡ χείρ μου, φησίν, συναντιλήψεται αὐτῷ καὶ ὁ βραχίων μου | κατισχύσει αὐτόν· οὐκ ὠφελήσει   365 ἐχθρὸς ἐν αὐτῷ καὶ υἱὸς ἀνομίας οὐ κακώσει αὐτόν, καὶ συγκόψω ἀπὸ

5   προσώπου αὐτοῦ τοὺς ἐχθροὺς αὐτοῦ καὶ τοὺς μισοῦντας αὐτὸν τροπώσομαι· καὶ ὅσα ἄλλα ὁ τῆς εὐλογίας περιέχει κατάλογος.

οὐκοῦν καλόν ἐστι τὸ εὑρεθῆναι ὑπὸ τῶν κυκλούντων τὴν πόλιν, τὴν ψυχήν, ἀγγέλων. οὕτω γὰρ νοεῖν ὁ μέγας Δαβὶδ ὑποτίθεται λέγων Παρεμβαλεῖ ἄγγελος κυρίου κύκλῳ τῶν φοβουμένων αὐτὸν καὶ ῥύσεται αὐτούς.

10   οὐκοῦν ἡ εἰποῦσα ὅτι οἱ φύλακές με ἐπάταξαν, προσθήκην τινὰ γεγενῆσθαι αὐτῇ τῆς ἐπὶ τὸ ἄνω προκοπῆς ἐκαυχήσατο. εἰ δὲ καὶ ἐν τραύματι γεγενῆσθαι λέγει, τὸν ἐν βάθει γενόμενον αὐτῇ διὰ τῆς θείας ῥάβδου τύπον τῷ λόγῳ παρίστησιν· οὐ γὰρ ἐπιπολαίως τῆς πνευματικῆς ῥάβδου τὴν ἐνέργειαν ἐφ᾽ ἑαυτῆς δέχεται, ὡς μὴ ἐπιγνωσθῆναι τὸν τόπον ἐν ᾧ τὴν ῥάβδον

15   ἐδέξατο, ἀλλ᾽ ἐπίσημος διὰ τοῦ τραύματος γίνεται ἡ πληγὴ ᾗ ἐγκαυχᾶται ἡ νύμφη.

τὸ δὲ λεγόμενον τοιοῦτόν ἐστιν· ἡ θεία ῥάβδος ἐκείνη καὶ ἡ παρακλητικὴ βακτηρία, ἡ διὰ τοῦ πατάσσειν ἐνεργοῦσα τὴν ἴασιν, τὸ πνεῦμά ἐστιν, οὗ καρπὸς τά τε ἄλλα τῶν ἀγαθῶν ὅσα ὁ Παῦλος | ἠρίθμησε, καὶ μετὰ τῶν ἄλλων   366

20   ἡ παιδαγωγὸς τῆς ἐναρέτου πολιτείας ἐγκράτεια. οὕτω γὰρ καὶ Παῦλος, ὁ τῶν τοιούτων πληγῶν στιγματίας, τοῖς τραύμασι τούτοις ἐπαγαλλόμενος ἔλεγεν ὅτι Τὰ στίγματα τοῦ Χριστοῦ ἐν τῷ σώματί μου περιφέρω, δεικνὺς τὴν ἐν παντὶ κακῷ ἀσθένειαν, δι᾽ ἧς ἡ κατὰ Χριστὸν δύναμις ἐν ἀρετῇ τελειοῦται. καλὸν οὖν καὶ τὸ τραῦμα διὰ τῶν εἰρημένων ἡμῖν ἀναπέφηνε, δι᾽ οὗ γέγονεν

25   αὐτῇ τοῦ θερίστρου ἡ περιαίρεσις, ὥστε ἀνακαλυφθῆναι τὸ τῆς ψυχῆς κάλλος μηκέτι ἐπισκοτοῦντος τοῦ ἐπιβλήματος.

Ἀλλ᾽ ἐπαναλάβωμεν πάλιν ἀνακεφαλαιωσάμενοι τὴν τῶν εἰρημένων διάνοιαν· ἡ πρὸς τὸν θεὸν ὁρῶσα ψυχὴ καὶ τὸν ἀγαθὸν ἐκεῖνον πόθον τοῦ ἀφθάρτου κάλλους ἀναλαμβάνουσα ἀεὶ νέαν τὴν πρὸς τὸ ὑπερκείμενον

30   ἐπιθυμίαν ἔχει οὐδέποτε κόρῳ τὸν πόθον ἀμβλύνουσα. διὰ τοῦτο πάντοτε τοῖς ἔμπροσθεν ἐπεκτεινομένη οὐ παύεται καὶ ἀπὸ τοῦ ἐν ᾧ ἐστιν ἐξιοῦσα καὶ πρὸς τὸ ἐνδότερον εἰσδυομένη ἐν ᾧ οὔπω ἐγένετο καὶ τὸ πάντοτε θαυμαστὸν αὐτῇ καὶ μέγα φαινόμενον κατώτερον ποιουμένη τοῦ ἐφεξῆς

"I found David my servant; I anointed him with my holy oil" (Ps 88:21). And since David became the possession of the one who had found him, let us hear what he was counted worthy of: "My hand," it says, "will help him, and my right hand | will strengthen him. His enemy will gain nothing from him, and the son of lawlessness will not harm him, and I will cut his enemies to pieces before his face and put those who hate him to flight" (Ps 88:22–24)—not to mention the rest of blessings that the list contains.

Well, then, it is a fine thing for the soul to be found by the angels that go about the city. The great David commends this thought when he says: "The angel of the Lord deploys himself round about[21] those who fear him and delivers them" (Ps 33:8).

So the Bride who said *the watchmen ... struck me* was boasting that something further had been added to her in the way of progress upwards. And if she says that this came to her by way of a wound, what her words refer to is the mark left in the depth of her being by the divine rod; for it was not superficially that she felt the operation of the spiritual rod, so as to be ignorant of the place where it struck her. No, the blow of which the Bride boasts marked her because of the wound it caused.

And the meaning is this: that divine rod and comforting staff, which by a blow works healing, is the Spirit, whose fruit is those good things that Paul | enumerates, and among their number continence, the teacher of the virtuous life. For Paul too, who bore the mark of such blows, similarly exulted in wounds of this sort when he said, "I bear on my body the marks of Christ" (Gal 6:17), displaying that weakness in every vice by which the power that belongs to Christ is brought to perfection in virtue. By these words, then, he shows us that the wound too is an admirable thing. It occasions the stripping off of the Bride's *veil*,[22] so that the soul's beauty is revealed once her covering no longer obscures it.

But let us go back and summarize the sense of what has been said. The soul that looks toward God and regains the noble yearning for incorruptible Beauty possesses an ever-renewed desire for what lies beyond her, and she never dulls that desire because of satiety. For this reason she always "strains forward toward what lies ahead" (Phil 3:13). She does not stop departing from where she is, or working her way inwards where she has not yet been, or judging that what at every point appears great and marvelous to her is

---

21. Παρεμβαλεῖ ἄγγελος κυρίου κύκλῳ. Gregory was doubtless reminded of this verse not only by its mention of "the angel of the Lord" but also because it contains the word κύκλος ("circle, cycle"), which is reminiscent of the κυκλοῦντες ("going about, circling") of Song 5:7.

22. See above, p. 359 (Jaeger). There Gregory makes it clear that he associates this "veil" with the "tunics of skin" of Gen 3:21. Cf. homily 11, p. 327 (Jaeger).

διὰ τὸ περικαλλέστερον πάντως εἶναι τοῦ προκατειλημμένου τὸ ἀεὶ
εὑρισκόμενον, καθὼς καὶ ὁ Παῦλος καθ᾽ ἡμέραν ἀπέθνῃσκεν, ἐπειδὴ πάντοτε
πρὸς καινήν τινα μετῄει ζωὴν νεκρὸς ἀεὶ τῷ παρῳχηκότι γινόμενος καὶ λήθην
τῶν προδιηνυσμένων ποιούμενος.

5   διὰ τοῦτο καὶ ἡ πρὸς τὸν νυμφίον τρέχουσα νύμφη | στάσιν τινὰ τῆς   367
ἐπὶ τὸ μεῖζον προκοπῆς οὐχ εὑρίσκει· παραδείσους ποιεῖ ῥοῶν διὰ στόματος
ἀρώματα ῥέοντας, τροφὴν ἑτοιμάζει τῷ δεσπότῃ τῆς κτίσεως τοῖς ἰδίοις
αὐτὸν δεξιουμένη καρποῖς, πηγάζει κήπους, φρέαρ γίνεται ὕδατος ζῶντος,
ὅλη καλὴ καὶ ἄμωμος δείκνυται κατὰ τὴν μαρτυρίαν τοῦ λόγου. πάλιν ὑπὲρ
10   ταῦτα γενομένη αἰσθάνεται μεγαλοπρεπέστερον προσιόντος τοῦ λόγου,
πληρουμένου κατὰ τὴν κεφαλὴν τῆς δρόσου καὶ τῶν τῆς νυκτὸς ψεκάδων
τῶν ἐν τοῖς βοστρύχοις γινομένων, νίπτεται τοὺς πόδας, τὸν χιτῶνα ἐκδύεται,
σμύρναν διὰ τῶν χειρῶν ἀποστάζει, προσάγει τῷ κλείθρῳ τὰς χεῖρας,
ἀνοίγει τὴν εἴσοδον, ζητεῖ τὸν μὴ καταλαμβανόμενον, φωνεῖ τὸν ἀνέφικτον,
15   εὑρίσκεται ὑπὸ τῶν φυλάκων, δέχεται ἐφ᾽ ἑαυτῆς τὴν πατάσσουσαν ῥάβδον,
μιμεῖται τὴν πέτραν περὶ ἧς φησιν ὁ προφήτης ὅτι Ἐπάταξε πέτραν καὶ
ἐρρύησαν ὕδατα. ὁρᾷς εἰς ὅσον ἀνέδραμεν ὕψος ἡ νύμφη·

διὰ τοῦτο πατασσομένη ὥσπερ ἡ ἀκρότομος ὑπὸ τοῦ Μωϋσέως, ἵνα καθ᾽
ὁμοιότητα ἐκείνης καὶ αὕτη πηγάσῃ τοῖς διψῶσι τὸν | λόγον ἐκ τῆς πληγῆς   368
20   ἀνομβρήσαντα. εἶτα ἐπὶ τούτοις γυμνοῖ τὸ κάλλος τῆς ὄψεως τῶν φυλάκων
αὐτῆς περιελόντων τὸ θέριστρον. ταῦτά ἐστιν ἃ κατὰ τὸν τόπον τοῦτον
ἡμεῖς καταλαβεῖν ἠδυνήθημεν. φθόνος δὲ οὐδεὶς γενέσθαι τινὶ παρὰ τοῦ
ἀποκαλύπτοντος τὰ κεκρυμμένα μυστήρια ψυχωφελεστέραν τινὰ θεωρίαν ἐν
τοῖς προκειμένοις.

25   Ἴσως δὲ φήσει τις καὶ τοῦ Ἡσαΐου τὴν ὀπτασίαν ἔχειν τινὰ πρὸς τὰ
προκείμενα ῥητὰ κοινωνίαν· ἐκείνην λέγω τὴν ὀπτασίαν, ὅτε ἀποθανόντος
τοῦ λεπροῦ βασιλέως ἑωρακέναι φησὶ τὸν ἐπὶ τοῦ ὑψηλοῦ τε καὶ ἐπηρμένου
θρόνου μεγαλοπρεπῶς προκαθήμενον, οὗ σχῆμα μὲν καὶ εἶδος καὶ μέγεθος
ἰδεῖν οὐκ ἐχώρησεν (ἢ γὰρ ἂν εἶπε πάντως, εἴπερ ἐχώρησε, καθάπερ καὶ ἐπὶ
30   τῶν ἄλλων ὧν εἶδεν ἐποίησε πτέρυγας ἀριθμήσας καὶ στάσιν καὶ πτῆσιν
διηγησάμενος), φωνῆς δὲ μόνης ἀκηκοέναι φησίν, ὅτε ἐπήρθη τὸ ὑπέρθυρον
ὑπὸ τῆς τῶν Σεραφὶμ ὑμνῳδίας καὶ ὁ οἶκος ἐπλήσθη καπνοῦ καὶ δι᾽ ἑνὸς
τῶν Σεραφὶμ ἐπεβλήθη τῷ στόματι τοῦ προφήτου διάπυρος ἄνθραξ, οὗ

nonetheless inferior to what comes after it; for that which is ever in process of being discovered is at every point more lovely than what has already been apprehended. Just so Paul also died every day, since at every point he was going over into a new life, dying to the past and forgetting things that were already over and done.

That is why the Bride who runs toward the Bridegroom | does not find any stopping place in her progress toward the better. She creates gardens of pomegranate trees that pour out aromatic spices. She prepares food for the Master of the created order, making him welcome with the fruit she has produced. Like a spring she gushes forth plantings. She becomes a wellspring of living water. By the testimony of the Word she is shown to be wholly beautiful and spotless. Elevated in turn beyond these things, she becomes aware of the Word drawing near in his grandeur, his head soaked with dew and with the raindrops of the night on his curls. She cleanses her feet. She takes off her tunic. She drips myrrh from her hands. She touches her hands to the lock. She opens the entrance. She seeks the one who is not apprehended. She calls upon the unattainable. She is found by the watchmen. She receives the blow of the rod. She imitates the rock of which the prophet says: "He smote the rock, and waters gushed out" (Ps 77:20).

You see to what heights the Bride has ascended: she was struck just as the precipice was struck by Moses, in order that she too, like it, might gush forth, for those who are thirsty, | the Word who poured water forth from his wound. Then in addition to this, she bares the beauty of her appearance when the watchmen have stripped off her veil. These are the things that we have been able to comprehend in this text. But there is no ill will should anyone derive some more profitable interpretation at the hand of the One who reveals hidden mysteries.

Then no doubt someone will say that Isaiah's vision[23] has something in common with the text at hand, the vision, namely, when, after the death of the king who had leprosy,[24] he says that he saw One of great majesty seated "upon a throne high and lifted up," whose appearance and form and size he was unable to discern (for surely if he had been able he would have said so, as he did in the case of the other beings he saw, whose wings he enumerates and whose rest and flight he tells of), but says that he only heard a voice, when "the lintel of the door was shaken" by the song of the seraphim, and "the house was filled with smoke," and one of the seraphim touched the mouth of

---

23. For what follows, see Isa 6:1–7.

24. That King Uzziah was stricken with leprosy as a result of his usurpation of priestly functions is the testimony of 2 Chr 26:19, 21, 23. No such circumstance is alleged in the text of Isaiah.

γενομένου οὐ τὰ χείλη μόνον ἀλλὰ καὶ ἡ ἀκοὴ πρὸς τὴν τοῦ λόγου ὑποδοχὴν
καθαρίζεται. ὡς γὰρ | ἐνταῦθα παταχθῆναι λέγει καὶ τραυματισθῆναι παρὰ   369
τῶν φυλάκων ἡ νύμφη καὶ οὕτω γυμνωθῆναι τῆς τοῦ θερίστρου περιβολῆς,
οὕτω κἀκεῖ ἀντὶ μὲν τοῦ θερίστρου τὸ ὑπέρθυρον αἴρεται, ὥστε ἀνεμπόδιστον
5   αὐτῷ γενέσθαι τῶν ἐν τοῖς ἀδύτοις τὴν θεωρίαν, ἀντὶ δὲ τῶν φυλάκων τὰ
Σεραφὶμ ὀνομάζεται, ἀντὶ δὲ τῆς ῥάβδου ὁ ἄνθραξ. ἀντὶ δὲ τῆς πληγῆς ἡ
καῦσις. κοινὸν δὲ τὸ πέρας ἐπί τε τῆς νύμφης καὶ ἐπὶ τῆς τοῦ προφήτου ψυχῆς
ἡ καθαρότης ἐστίν. ὡς οὖν ὁ προφήτης διὰ τοῦ ἄνθρακος οὐχὶ ἀλγύνεται
καιόμενος, ἀλλὰ δοξάζεται λαμπρυνόμενος, οὕτω καὶ ἐνταῦθα ἡ νύμφη, οὐκ
10   ὀδύνην ἐκ τῆς πληγῆς αἰτιᾶται, ἀλλ' ἐπικαυχᾶται τῇ τῆς παρρησίας προσθήκῃ
ἐν τῇ ἀφαιρέσει τοῦ προκαλύμματος, ὃ θέριστρον ὁ λόγος ὠνόμασεν.
    Ἔστι δέ τινα καὶ ἄλλην διάνοιαν ἐν τοῖς προκειμένοις εὑρεῖν οὐδὲν
τῶν τεθεωρημένων ἀπάδουσαν· ἡ γὰρ ἐξελθοῦσα ψυχὴ ἐν τῷ λόγῳ αὐτοῦ
καὶ ζητοῦσα μὲν τὸν οὐχ εὑρισκόμενον, ἀνακαλοῦσα δὲ τὸν τῇ σημασίᾳ τῶν
15   ὀνομάτων ἀνέφικτον διδάσκεται παρὰ τῶν φυλάκων ὅτι τοῦ ἀνεφίκτου ἐρᾷ
καὶ τοῦ ἀκαταλήπτου ἐφίεται. δι' ὧν τρόπον τινὰ πλήσσεται καὶ τραυματίζεται
τῇ ἀνελπιστίᾳ τοῦ ποθουμένου ἀτελῆ τε καὶ ἀναπόλαυστον τοῦ καλοῦ τὴν
ἐπιθυμίαν νομίσασα. ἀλλὰ περιαιρεῖται τὸ τῆς λύπης θέριστρον διὰ τοῦ μαθεῖν
ὅτι τὸ ἀεὶ προκόπτειν ἐν τῷ ζητεῖν καὶ τὸ μηδέποτε τῆς | ἀνόδου παύεσθαι   370
20   τοῦτό ἐστιν ἡ ἀληθὴς τοῦ ποθουμένου ἀπόλαυσις τῆς πάντοτε πληρουμένης
ἐπιθυμίας ἑτέραν ἐπιθυμίαν τοῦ ὑπερκειμένου γεννώσης. ὡς οὖν περιείλετο
τῆς ἀνελπιστίας τὸ θέριστρον καὶ εἶδε τὸ ἀόριστόν τε καὶ ἀπερίγραπτον
τοῦ ἀγαπωμένου κάλλος ἐν πάσῃ τῇ ἀϊδιότητι τῶν αἰώνων κρεῖττον ἀεὶ
εὑρισκόμενον, ἐν σφοδροτέρῳ τείνεται πόθῳ καὶ μηνύει τῷ ἀγαπωμένῳ διὰ
25   τῶν τῆς Ἰερουσαλὴμ θυγατέρων τὴν τῆς καρδίας διάθεσιν, ὅτι τὸ ἐκλεκτὸν
τοῦ θεοῦ βέλος ἐν ἑαυτῇ δεξαμένη διὰ τῆς κατὰ τὴν πίστιν ἀκίδος βέβληται
τὴν καρδίαν ἐν τῷ καιρίῳ δεξαμένη τὴν τῆς ἀγάπης τοξείαν. θεὸς δέ ἐστιν ἡ
ἀγάπη, κατὰ τὴν Ἰωάννου φωνήν,

        ᾧ πρέπει ἡ δόξα καὶ τὸ κράτος εἰς τοὺς αἰῶνας τῶν αἰώνων.
30   ἀμήν.

the prophet with a fiery coal; and when this happened, not only were his lips purified but his hearing as well, for the reception of the Word. For just as in our text | the Bride says that she was struck and wounded by the watchmen and that in this way she was stripped of the covering of her veil, so in the case of Isaiah's vision, instead of the veil the "lintel of the door" was lifted[25] so that he might have an unhindered vision of the shrine, while instead of watchmen the seraphim are mentioned, instead of the rod, a coal, and instead of the blow, a burning. What is more, the purpose is the same, both in the case of the Bride and in that of the prophet's soul, namely, purity. Hence just as the prophet was not hurt when burned by the coal but was made splendid and bright, so too in this case the Bride is not occasioned any suffering by the blow she receives but glories in the freedom of access accorded her by the removal of the curtain, which is here called a veil.

One can find yet another meaning in this text, one that is not inconsistent with the things we have already discerned in it. For the soul that goes out at his word, seeking the One who is not found and calling upon the One whom words cannot attain, is taught by the watchmen that she is in love with the Unattainable and is directing herself toward the Incomprehensible. At their hands she is, in a certain sense, struck and wounded by the hopelessness of what she seeks, judging that her desire for the good is imperfect and falls short of its fruition. But the veil of her grief is removed when she learns that the true fruition of what she seeks is ever to make progress in seeking and never | to halt on the upward path, since her fulfilled desire ever generates a further desire for what is beyond her. As, then, the veil of hopelessness is lifted and she sees the infinite and unlimited beauty of her Beloved, a beauty that for all the eternity of the ages is ever and again discovered to be greater, she is pulled by a yet more intense yearning, and through the daughters of Jerusalem she discloses the state of her heart to her Beloved: how in the sting of faith she has received in herself God's chosen arrow (cf. Isa 49:2) and has been struck in the heart by receiving love's shot in her vital part. But John teaches us that God is love,

To whom be glory and dominion to the ages of ages.
Amen.

25. Gregory's point here depends on an ambiguity occasioned by the fact that the Septuagint uses a form of ἐπαίρω to describe the disturbing or shaking of the "lintel" in Isa 6:4. This verb is a compound form of αἴρω ("raise, lift"), but it also bears the additional sense of "excite" or "disturb." Gregory, however, takes it to mean roughly the same as αἴρω.

Λόγος ιγ΄

Ὤρκισα ὑμᾶς, θυγατέρες Ἰερουσαλήμ,
ἐν ταῖς δυνάμεσι καὶ ἐν ταῖς ἰσχύσεσι τοῦ ἀγροῦ,
ἐὰν εὕρητε τὸν ἀδελφιδόν μου, ἀπαγγείλατε αὐτῷ,
| ὅτι τετρωμένη ἀγάπης εἰμὶ ἐγώ.   371
5   Τί ἀδελφιδός σου, ἡ καλὴ ἐν γυναιξίν;
τί ἀδελφιδός σου ἀπὸ ἀδελφιδοῦ, ὅτι οὕτως ὤρκισας ἡμᾶς;
Ἀδελφιδός μου λευκὸς καὶ πυρρός,
ἐκλελοχισμένος ἀπὸ μυριάδων·
Κεφαλὴ αὐτοῦ χρυσίον κεφάζ,
10   βόστρυχοι αὐτοῦ ἐλάται, μέλανες ὡς κόραξ,
Ὀφθαλμοὶ αὐτοῦ ὡς περιστεραὶ ἐπὶ πληρώματα ὑδάτων
λελουμέναι ἐν γάλακτι
καθήμεναι ἐπὶ πληρώματα ὑδάτων.

Ὁ διὰ Μωϋσέως μὲν νομοθετήσας τὰ τοῦ νόμου μυστήρια, πληρώσας δὲ
15 δι᾽ ἑαυτοῦ ὅλον τὸν νόμον καὶ τοὺς προφήτας, καθὼς ἐν τῷ εὐαγγελίῳ φησὶν
ὅτι Οὐκ ἦλθον καταλῦσαι τὸν νόμον, ἀλλὰ πληρῶσαι, ὁ τῇ μὲν ἀναιρέσει τῆς
ὀργῆς συνεξαλείψας τὸν φόνον, τῷ δὲ ἀφανισμῷ τῆς ἐπιθυμίας συνεξελὼν
τῆς μοιχείας τὸ ἄγος, οὗτος ἐκβάλλει τοῦ βίου καὶ τὴν ἐκ τῆς ἐπιορκίας
κατάραν τῇ ἀπαγορεύσει τοῦ ὅρκου πεδήσας ἐν ἀπραξίᾳ τὸ δρέπανον· οὐ
20 γάρ ἐστι δυνατὸν ὅρκου γενέσθαι παράβασιν μὴ ὄντος ὅρκου. διό φησιν | 372
Ἠκούσατε ὅτι ἐρρέθη τοῖς ἀρχαίοις· οὐκ ἐπιορκήσεις, ἀποδώσεις δὲ κυρίῳ

HOMILY 13
Song 5:8–12

⁸I have adjured you, O daughters of Jerusalem,
By the powers and virtues of the field:
If you should find my kinsman, say to him
That I am wounded by love.
⁹What is your kinsman more than another,¹ O fair among women?
What is your kinsman more than another, that you have charged us so?
¹⁰My kinsman is white and ruddy,
set apart [in his birth²] from myriads.
¹¹His head is as very fine gold,³
His locks are firs, black as a raven.
His eyes are as doves by full pools of waters,
¹²Washed in milk,
sitting by pools of waters.

He who on the one hand laid down the mysteries of the law through Moses, who on the other hand did himself fulfill the entire law and the prophets (as he says in the Gospel: "I did not come to destroy the law but to fulfill it" [Matt 5:17]), who by removing wrath abolished murder (cf. Matt 5:21–26), who by destroying lust removed the stain of adultery with it (cf. Matt 5:27–32)—this one, I say, also cast out the curse attached to false swearing by his prohibition of the oath and bound the sickle⁴ up in idleness, for it is not possible for an oath to be violated when there is no oath. Hence he says, | "You have heard that it was said to the folk of old, 'You shall not swear falsely

---

1. Langerbeck (1960, 371) removes the words ἀπὸ ἀδελφιδοῦ ("more than another [*sc.* kinsman]") from Gregory's text of Song 5:9a because they are not cited at the appropriate points in the text of homily 13 (i.e., pp. 379.3, 380.9 [Jaeger]). They stand in the manuscripts of the LXX text, however.

2. On this translation, required not by the LXX text but by Gregory's exegesis, see below, n. 25.

3. The LXX here has "golden and *phaz*" (χρυσίον καὶ φαζ), φαζ being a transcribed Hebrew term signifying "pure" or "refined" gold. Gregory's text seems to have had κεφάζ ("like fine gold") instead of καὶ φαζ, which would suggest that his LXX text had been "corrected" by some puzzled scribe. The English translation here renders the text so as to make it accord with Gregory's understanding of it.

4. The LXX text of Zech 5:1–2 speaks of a "flying sickle" rather than a "flying scroll" (RSV), and it is to this sickle, which represented a curse and was to bring death to thieves and people who swore false oaths, that Gregory alludes here.

τοὺς ὅρκους σου. ἐγὼ δὲ λέγω σοι, φησί, μὴ ὀμόσαι ὅλως· μήτε ἐν τῷ
οὐρανῷ, ὅτι θρόνος ἐστὶ τοῦ θεοῦ, μήτε ἐν Ἱεροσολύμοις, ὅτι πόλις ἐστὶ τοῦ
μεγάλου βασιλέως, μήτε ἐν τῇ κεφαλῇ σου ὀμόσῃς, ὅτι οὐ δύνασαι ποιῆσαι
τρίχα λευκὴν ἢ μέλαιναν. ἔστω δὲ ὑμῶν ὁ λόγος τὸ ναὶ ναὶ καὶ τὸ οὒ οὔ· τὸ δὲ
5   περισσὸν τούτων ἐκ τοῦ διαβόλου ἐστίν.

ἡ δὲ διὰ τοῦ Ἄισματος τῶν Ἀισμάτων ἐπὶ τελειότητι μεμαρτυρημένη
ψυχὴ καὶ περιελομένη μὲν τῆς καρδίας τὸ κάλυμμα ἐν τῇ ἀπεκδύσει τοῦ
παλαιοῦ χιτῶνος, τοῦ δὲ προσώπου τὸ θέριστρον ἀποβαλοῦσα, ὅπερ νοοῦμεν
πᾶσαν διστάζουσάν τε καὶ κραδαινομένην διάνοιαν, ὥστε καθαρῶς τε καὶ
10 ἀναμφιβόλως πρὸς τὴν ἀλήθειαν βλέπειν, ὀρκίζει τὰς θυγατέρας Ἱερουσαλὴμ
οὔτε κατὰ τοῦ θείου θρόνου, ὃν οὐρανὸν ὀνομάζει ὁ λόγος, οὔτε κατὰ τῶν τοῦ
θεοῦ βασιλείων, οἷς ὄνομά ἐστιν Ἱεροσόλυμα, οὐ μὴν οὐδὲ κατὰ | τῆς κεφαλῆς   373
τῆς τιμίας, ἧς αἱ τρίχες οὔτε λευκαὶ οὔτε μέλαιναι γενέσθαι δύνανται, ἀλλ᾽ ἐπὶ
τὸν ἀγρὸν μεταφέρει τὸν ὅρκον κατὰ τῶν ἐν αὐτῷ δυνάμεων τὸν ὁρκισμὸν
15 ἐπάγουσα ταῖς νεάνισι λέγουσα· Ὥρκισα ὑμᾶς, θυγατέρες Ἱερουσαλήμ, ἐν
ταῖς δυνάμεσι καὶ ἐν ταῖς ἰσχύσεσι τοῦ ἀγροῦ.

ὅτι μὲν οὖν ἡ δι᾽ ὅλου μαρτυρηθεῖσα εἶναι καλὴ καὶ παντὸς καθαρεύουσα
μώμου οὐδὲν φθέγγεται τῶν περιττῶν, ὃ τῆς τοῦ διαβόλου μερίδος ἐστίν, ἀλλ᾽
ἐκ τοῦ θεοῦ ποιεῖται τὸν λόγον, παρ᾽ οὗ κατὰ τὸν Μιχαίαν εἴ τι ἀγαθόν ἐστι
20 καὶ εἴ τι καλὸν καὶ παρὰ ταῦτα οὐδέν, παντὶ δῆλόν ἐστι τῷ διὰ τῆς δεσποτικῆς
μαρτυρίας διδαχθέντι τὰ προσόντα τῇ νύμφῃ πλεονεκτήματα.

ἢ γάρ; ἀφεῖσα πάντα τὰ ἀπηγορευμένα εἴδη τοῦ ὅρκου καὶ μήτε τὴν
βασιλεύουσαν πόλιν μήτε τὸν θρόνον τοῦ μεγάλου βασιλέως ὅρκιον ταῖς
νεάνισι ποιησαμένη (διὰ τούτου γὰρ παιδευόμεθα πόσον ἀπέχειν ἡμᾶς χρὴ
25 τοῦ κατατολμᾶν τοῦ θεοῦ ἐν τοῖς ὅρκοις, ὅτι οὔτε τὸν θρόνον οὔτε τὴν πόλιν
ἐν τῷ ὅρκῳ παραλαμβάνειν ἐπιτρεπόμεθα) φεισαμένη τε πρὸς τούτοις τῆς
κεφαλῆς τῆς τιμίας, ἣν ἐν τοῖς ἐφεξῆς χρυσῆν εἶναι διαγράφει τῷ λόγῳ, ἧς
αἱ τρίχες οὔτε λευκαί εἰσιν οὔτε μέλαιναι (πῶς γὰρ ἂν ἢ μελανθείη χρυσὸς ἢ
πρὸς τὸ λευκὸν εἶδος μεταχρωσθείη;); πάντως, ὅτι τοιοῦτόν τινα προτείνει
30 τὸν | ὁρκισμὸν ταῖς παρθένοις, ὃς οὔτε τῷ εὐαγγελικῷ μάχεται νόμῳ καὶ   374
ἐπαίνου γίνεται τοῖς ὀμωμοκόσιν ὑπόθεσις κατὰ τὴν τοῦ προφήτου φωνὴν

but shall perform to the Lord what you have sworn.' But I say to you, 'Do not swear at all, either by heaven, for it is the throne of God, or by the earth, for it is his footstool, or by Jerusalem, for it is the city of the great King. And do not swear by your head, for you cannot make one hair white or black. Let what you say be simply "yes" or "no"; anything more than this comes from evil' " (cf. Matt 5:33–37).

But the soul that the Song of Songs attests as perfect, the soul that removed the curtain of her heart by putting off her old garment and threw off the veil from before her face—by which we understand every hesitant and timorous thought—so as to gaze purely and without uncertainty toward the truth, this soul does not adjure the daughters of Jerusalem by the divine throne, which the Gospel text calls "heaven," nor by God's kingdom, whose name is "Jerusalem," nor yet by the worshipful | head whose hairs are incapable of being either white or black.[5] No, she transfers the oath to *the field* and administers her oath to the young women by the *powers* that are in it. She says: *I have adjured you, O daughters of Jerusalem, by the powers and virtues of the field.*

Now she who is everywhere attested as beautiful and cleansed of every blemish does not utter anything of the "more"[6] that is the devil's portion. Rather does she speak from God, from whom there comes whatever is good and beautiful, and nothing more, as Micah says.[7] This is plain enough to anyone who has, from the Lord's testimony, learned of the excellences that belong to the Bride.

Is it indeed so? Has she put away all the forbidden kinds of oath, and made the young women swear neither by the royal city nor by the throne of the great King (for we learn how true it is that we must not presume upon God in swearing from the very fact that we are not suffered to name either the throne or the city in an oath), and has she refrained in addition from naming the treasured head, which she describes in the next bit of her discourse as being golden, whose hair is neither white nor black (for how could gold be darkened or be changed to the color of white?)? Yes indeed! For the | oath she proposes to the virgins is such as does not contradict the law of the Gospel and at the same time becomes a reason to praise those who have sworn it,

---

5. Gregory (ignoring the presence of the possessive pronoun "your," which seems to refer to the disciples) takes the "head" of Matt 5:36 to refer to Christ's head, no doubt in anticipation of his exegesis of Song 5:11, where the Bridegroom's head is said to be golden (and hence can scarcely be thought to have white or black hair).

6. I.e., more than "yes" and "no"; see Matt 5:37, cited just above.

7. Gregory has mixed up his prophets. It is from Zech 9:17, not from Micah, that he remembers the words εἴ τι ἀγαθόν ... εἴ τι καλόν as referring to works or gifts of God.

ἤ φησιν ὅτι Ἐπαινεθήσεται πᾶς ὁ ὀμνύων ἐν αὐτῷ, ὥστε τὴν τῶν λεγομένων διάνοιαν μὴ ἔξω εἶναι τοῦ ναὶ οὔ, ᾧ πιστοῦσθαι βούλεται τὴν ἀλήθειαν ὁ εὐαγγελικὸς νόμος λέγων Ἔστω δὲ ὑμῶν ὁ λόγος τὸ ναὶ [ναὶ καὶ τὸ οὔ] οὔ.

εἰ τοίνυν ἐν τοῖς ὁρκίοις ὀνόμασι κωλύεται μὲν ὁ θρόνος τοῦ βασιλέως
5 παραλαμβάνεσθαι, κωλύεται δὲ καὶ ἡ πόλις ἐν ᾗ τὰ βασίλεια, κωλύεται δὲ ὡσαύτως καὶ ἡ ἀληθινὴ κεφαλὴ πρὸς τὴν τοῦ ὅρκου παράληψιν, μόνον δὲ τὸ ναὶ καὶ τὸ οὔ συγκεχώρηται δι' ἀμφοτέρων κατὰ τὸ ἴσον τῆς ἀληθείας ἐν τῷ ναὶ θεωρουμένης, δῆλον ἂν εἴη ὅτι καὶ νῦν ὁ ταῖς νεάνισιν ἐπαγόμενος ὁρκισμὸς παρὰ τῆς νύμφης περὶ τὴν τοῦ ναὶ διάνοιαν ἀναστρέφεται, ὅπου
10 χρὴ ἐρηρεισμένην ἡμῶν εἶναι τὴν τῆς ψυχῆς συγκατάθεσιν. ἔχει δὲ ἡ λέξις οὕτως· Ὥρκισα ὑμᾶς, θυγατέρες Ἱερουσαλήμ, ἐν ταῖς δυνάμεσι καὶ ἐν ταῖς ἰσχύσεσι τοῦ ἀγροῦ, ἐὰν εὕρητε τὸν ἀδελφιδόν μου, ἀπαγγείλατε αὐτῷ ὅτι τετρωμένη ἀγάπης εἰμὶ ἐγώ.

| Ταῦτα δὲ τεθεώρηται μὲν ἤδη καὶ ἐν τοῖς φθάσασιν ὡς ἡ ἀκολουθία   375
15 τῶν νοημάτων ὑπέβαλεν, εἰρήσεται δὲ καὶ νῦν διὰ βραχέων τὰ εὑρισκόμενα. ἀμετάθετόν τι πρᾶγμα τὸν ὅρκον εἶναί φησιν ὁ ἀπόστολος βεβαιοῦντα δι' ἑαυτοῦ τὴν ἀλήθειαν καὶ πάσης αὐτὸν ἀντιλογίας εἶναι πέρας ὁρίζεται εἰς τὴν τῶν ἐγνωσμένων βεβαίωσιν. ἐπάγει τοίνυν τὸν ὁρκισμὸν ταῖς παρθένοις ἡ νύμφη ὥστε ἀπαράβατον φυλαχθῆναι αὐταῖς τὸ λεγόμενον. ἀλλ' ἐπειδὴ
20 πᾶς ὅρκος κατὰ τοῦ μείζονος γίνεται καθὼς φησιν ὁ ἀπόστολος (οὐ γὰρ ἄν τις ὅρκιον ποιήσαιτο τὸ ἑαυτοῦ ἀτιμότερον), σκοπῆσαι προσήκει, τί ταῖς νεάνισιν ἐν τῷ ὅρκῳ παρὰ τῆς νύμφης μεῖζον προτείνεται. Ὥρκισα, φησίν, ὑμᾶς, θυγατέρες Ἱερουσαλήμ, ἐν ταῖς δυνάμεσι καὶ ἐν ταῖς ἰσχύσεσι τοῦ ἀγροῦ. τί οὖν τὸ ὑπὲρ ἡμᾶς ἐν τούτοις ἐστίν; ἀγρὸν γὰρ τὸν κόσμον διὰ
25 τῆς τροπικῆς σημασίας νοεῖσθαι οὐκ ἀμφιβάλλομεν οὕτω τοῦ κυρίου καὶ ὀνομάσαντος τὸν κόσμον καὶ ἑρμηνεύσαντος. αἱ τοίνυν πολλαὶ δυνάμεις τε καὶ ἰσχύες τοῦ κόσμου τίνες εἰσίν, αἱ τῷ ὅρκῳ προκείμεναι, ἃς χρὴ μείζονας ἡμῶν νομισθῆναι, ἵνα ἰσχὺν λάβῃ πρὸς βεβαίωσιν τῆς ἀληθείας ὁ ὅρκος κατὰ τῶν μειζόνων γινόμενος;

30 οὐκοῦν | ἀναγκαῖον ἂν εἴη παραθέσθαι πρὸς τὴν σαφήνειαν τῶν   376
προκειμένων ἑτέραν ἔκδοσιν ἑρμηνευτικὴν τῶν ῥητῶν ἔχουσαν οὕτως·

even as the prophet says: "Everyone who swears by it shall be praised" (Ps 62:12). Consequently, the sense of the [Bride's] words does not transgress the limits of the "yes" or "no," by which the Gospel law wants the truth to be guaranteed when it says: "Let your word be 'yes yes' and 'no no.'"

If, then, it is forbidden in swearing to invoke the King's throne, and the city that contains the royal dwellings is also forbidden for invocation in an oath, as likewise is the true head, and only "yes" and "no" are allowed, seeing as the truth in the "yes" is equally discerned through both,[8] it should be obvious that here too the oath administered to the young women by the Bride turns on the meaning of the "yes," and upon that the assent of our soul must be based. The text is as follows: *I have adjured you, O daughters of Jerusalem, by the powers and virtues of the field: If you should find my kinsman, tell him that I am wounded by love.*

| In previous homilies we have already treated these matters as the sequence of ideas prompted us, but now we will summarize our findings briefly. The apostle says that an oath is something "unalterable" (Heb 6:17) that in and of itself guarantees the truth, and he lays it down that it "sets a limit to all ... dispute so as to guarantee" (Heb 6:16) what is known. The Bride, therefore, administers her oath to the virgins so that what she says may be kept by them as inviolable. But since every oath, as the apostle says (Heb 6:16), is "by a greater thing" (for none would swear by something less noble than himself), we ought to inquire what "greater thing" it is that the Bride proposes to the young women in the oath. Now her words are: *I have adjured you, O daughters of Jerusalem, by the powers and virtues of the field.*[9] So, then, what is there here that is superior to us? There is no doubt that the figurative reference of "field" is the cosmos, since the Lord named and rendered the cosmos in just this fashion (cf. Matt 13:24, 38). What, then, are the many powers and virtues of the cosmos, set out in the oath, which are to be reckoned greater than we in order that the oath, sworn by greater things, may be strong enough to guarantee the truth?

| One must, therefore, for the clarification of this text, set alongside it another version[10] that makes sense of the words. It runs as follows: "I have

---

8. What Gregory means by this deliberate obscurity is revealed below (p. 376 [Jaeger]) when he indicates what he understands by the "virtues" and the "powers" of the field respectively, associating the one with the "yes" and the other with the "no" and insisting that the latter serves the former.

9. See Song 2:7 (homily 4, pp. 130–35 [Jaeger]) and 3:5 (homily 6, pp. 184–85 [Jaeger]), where the words "by the powers and virtues of the field" follow "I have adjured you." At this point they are an addition to the text.

10. Whatever the source of this other version was (Origen's *Hexapla*?), it gives the correct translation of the Hebrew text of Song 2:7 and 3:5, though Gregory does not, at least explicitly,

Ὥρκισα ὑμᾶς, θυγατέρες Ἰερουσαλήμ, κατὰ τῶν δορκάδων καὶ κατὰ τῶν ἐλάφων τοῦ ἀγροῦ. διδασκόμεθα τοίνυν διὰ τῶν ὀνομάτων τούτων, ἐν τίνι ἐστὶν ἡ τοῦ κόσμου τούτου ἰσχὺς καὶ ἐν τίνι ἡ δύναμις, ἃ πρὸς βεβαίωσιν τῆς ἀληθείας διὰ τοῦ ὅρκου παραλαμβάνεται.

5   δύο ἐστὶ τὰ τῷ θεῷ προσοικειοῦντα τὸν ἄνθρωπον· ἓν μὲν τὸ ἀπλανὲς τῆς περὶ τὸ ὄντως ὂν ὑπολήψεως, ὡς μὴ ταῖς ἠπατημέναις ὑπονοίαις εἰς ἐθνικάς τε καὶ αἱρετικὰς περὶ τοῦ θείου δόξας ἐκφέρεσθαι, ὅπερ ἐστὶν ὡς ἀληθῶς τὸ ναί, ἕτερον δὲ ὁ καθαρὸς λογισμὸς πᾶσαν ἐμπαθῆ διάθεσιν τῆς ψυχῆς ἐξορίζων, ὅπερ οὐδὲ αὐτὸ τοῦ ναὶ ἠλλοτρίωται. τῆς τοίνυν διπλῆς

10   ταύτης τῶν ἀγαθῶν ἕξεως, ὧν ἡ μὲν πρὸς τὸ ὄντως ὂν ἀναβλέπειν ποιεῖ, ἡ δὲ φυγαδεύει τὰ πάθη τὰ τὴν ψυχὴν λυμαινόμενα, ἡ τῶν δορκάδων τε καὶ τῶν ἐλάφων μνήμη διὰ συμβόλων γνωρίζει τὴν δύναμιν· τούτων γὰρ ἡ μὲν ἀπλανῶς ὁρᾷ, ἡ δὲ βρωτικήν τινα καὶ ἀναλωτικὴν τῶν θηρίων δύναμιν ἔχει.

       τοῦτο τοίνυν προτείνει ταῖς παρθένοις ἡ νύμφη τὸ ναί· τό τε εὐσεβῶς
15   δεῖν πρὸς τὸ θεῖον βλέπειν | καὶ τὸ καθαρῶς ἐν ἀπαθείᾳ παρατρέχειν τὸν   377
       βίον. ὧν κατορθουμένων τὸ ἀμετάθετον πρᾶγμα ἐν ἡμῖν βεβαιοῦται τὸ ναί. οὗτος γάρ ἐστιν ὁ τὴν ἀλήθειαν πιστούμενος ὅρκος, ὃν Πᾶς ὁ ὀμνύων ἐν αὐτῷ ἐπαινεῖται, καθὼς φησιν ὁ προφήτης· ἀληθῶς γὰρ ὁ ἐν τοῖς δύο τούτοις τὸ ἀσφαλὲς ἐν ἑαυτῷ κατορθώσας ἔν τε τῷ λόγῳ τῆς πίστεως, ὅταν ἀπλανῶς

20   πρὸς τὴν ἀλήθειαν βλέπῃ, καὶ ἐν τῷ τρόπῳ τῆς ζωῆς, ὅταν παντὸς καθαρεύῃ τοῦ ἐκ πονηρίας μολύσματος, οὗτος ὀμνύει τῷ κυρίῳ μὴ ἀναβῆναι ἐπὶ κλίνης στρωμνῆς, μὴ δοῦναι ὕπνον τοῖς ὀφθαλμοῖς αὐτοῦ μηδὲ νυσταγμὸν τοῖς βλεφάροις, ἕως οὗ εὕρῃ ἐν ἑαυτῷ τόπον τῷ κυρίῳ σκήνωμα τοῦ ἐν αὐτῷ οἰκοῦντος γενόμενος.

25   Εἰ τοίνυν ἐσμὲν καὶ ἡμεῖς τῆς ἄνω Ἰερουσαλὴμ τέκνα, ἀκούσωμεν τῆς διδασκάλου, πῶς ἔστιν ἰδεῖν τὸν ποθούμενον. τί οὖν φησιν; ἐὰν ὅρκιον ἑαυτοῖς τοῦτο ποιήσωμεν τὸ ἐν ταῖς δυνάμεσιν εἶναι τῶν διορατικῶν δορκάδων καὶ ἐν ταῖς ἰσχύσεσι τῶν ἀφανιστικῶν τῆς κακίας ἐλάφων, ἔστι διὰ τούτων ἰδεῖν

adjured you, O daughters of Jerusalem, by the gazelles and the deer of the field." By these names we are taught in what lies the "virtue" of this cosmos and in what its "power," which are invoked by the oath to guarantee the truth.

There are two things that bring humanity into close affinity with God. One of these is the truthfulness of one's idea of that which authentically *is*, so that one is not carried off by erroneous notions into heretical and Gentile opinions about the Divine; and this is in truth the "yes." The other is pure thinking that banishes every chronic disorder of the soul; and this is consistent with the "yes."[11] The power of these two modes of possessing what is good—one of which makes us look toward what genuinely *is*, while the other sets to flight the passions that damage the soul—is symbolically made known to us by the mention of "gazelles" and "deer." For of these two, the one sees with perfect clarity, while the other possesses a capacity to eat and finish off wild beasts.[12]

This then is the "yes" that the Bride proposes to the virgins: the necessity both of looking toward the Divine with religious affection | and of making one's way through life in purity and in freedom from the disturbance of passion. If these be carried through, the "something 'unalterable,'" the "yes," is confirmed, for this is the oath that gives substance to the truth, such that "everyone who swears" it "by it shall be praised" (Ps 62:12), as the prophet says. For truly the person who in these two ways cultivates stability within—by the word of faith, in looking toward the truth without erring, and by manner of life, in being cleansed of any taint of wickedness—this person swears to the Lord not to climb into bed nor to give sleep to his eyes or slumber to his eyelids until he has found within himself "a place for the Lord" and become a dwelling place of the One who resides within him (cf. Ps 131:3–5).

If, then, we too are children of "the Jerusalem above" (cf. Gal 4:26), let us attend to our teacher to learn how it is possible to see the one we desire. What does she say? If we bind ourselves by this oath, taken by the powers of the clear-sighted gazelles and by the virtues of the vice-destroying deer, it is pos-

---

refer to it in his exposition of either of those verses (see above n. 9). It is not impossible that Gregory discovered this version only after delivering homilies 4 and 6 and took the opportunity afforded him here of supplementing his earlier exegesis of what he doubtless took to be a customary form of oath in the Song.

11. The banishing of every "chronic disorder" (ἐμπαθῆ διάθεσιν), i.e., of the passions that have settled into the soul, is the equivalent of a "no"—a negative action—that supports the affirmation of Truth.

12. See above, homily 5 on Song 2:8, for another reference to the "gazelle" (δορκάς, from δέρκομαι, "see" or "see clearly") and the "deer" (ἔλαφος); see esp. pp. 141–42 (Jaeger), where the "deer" is credited not with the power to consume but to "destroy wild things and ... to put the serpent kind to flight."

τὸν καθαρὸν νυμφίον, τὸν τῆς ἀγάπης τοξότην, καὶ εἰπεῖν πρὸς αὐτὸν τὴν
ἑκάστου ψυχὴν ὅτι Τετρωμένη ἀγάπης εἰμί.

καλὰ δὲ εἶναι τῆς ἀγάπης τὰ τραύματα καὶ παρὰ τῆς Παροιμίας
ἐμάθομεν ἥ φησιν Αἱρετὰ μὲν τοῦ φίλου τὰ τραύματα, κακὰ δὲ τῆς ἔχθρας
5   καὶ τὰ φιλήματα. | τίς δὲ ὁ φίλος οὗ τὰ τραύματα τῶν φιλημάτων τοῦ ἐχθροῦ   378
προτιμότερα, παντὶ δῆλόν ἐστι τῷ μὴ ἀγνοοῦντι τὰ τῆς σωτηρίας μυστήρια.
φίλος μὲν γάρ ἐστιν ἀληθινός τε καὶ βέβαιος ὁ καὶ ἐχθροὺς γενομένους ἡμᾶς
τοῦ ἀγαπᾶν μὴ παυσάμενος, ἐχθρὸς δὲ ἄπιστός τε καὶ ἀνήμερος ὁ μηδὲν
ἠδικηκότας ὑπαγαγὼν τῷ θανάτῳ. τραῦμα τοῖς πρωτοπλάστοις ἐδόκει ἡ διὰ
10   τῆς ἐντολῆς γενομένη τοῦ κακοῦ ἀπαγόρευσις (τραῦμα γὰρ ἐνομίσθη τοῦ
ἡδέος ἡ ἀλλοτρίωσις), φίλημα δὲ ἡ πρὸς τὸ ἡδὺ καὶ εὐφανὲς προτροπή. ἀλλ᾽
ἔδειξεν ἡ πεῖρα ὅτι τὰ νομιζόμενα τοῦ φίλου τραύματα τῶν φιλημάτων ἦν τοῦ
ἐχθροῦ λυσιτελέστερά τε καὶ αἱρετώτερα.

ἐπεὶ οὖν συνέστησεν ἑαυτοῦ τὴν ἀγάπην ὁ καλὸς ἐραστὴς τῶν ἡμετέρων
15   ψυχῶν, δι᾽ ἣν καὶ Ἁμαρτωλῶν ὄντων ἡμῶν Χριστὸς ὑπὲρ ἡμῶν ἀπέθανε,
διὰ τοῦτο ἀντερασθεῖσα ἡ νύμφη τοῦ ἀγαπήσαντος δείκνυσιν ἐν ἑαυτῇ
ἐγκείμενον διὰ βάθους τῆς ἀγάπης τὸ βέλος, τουτέστι τὴν τῆς θεότητος
αὐτοῦ κοινωνίαν· ἡ γὰρ ἀγάπη ἐστὶν ὁ θεός, καθὼς εἴρηται, ἡ διὰ τῆς κατὰ
τὴν πίστιν ἀκίδος τῇ καρδίᾳ ἐγγενομένη. εἰ δὲ χρὴ καὶ ὄνομα τοῦ βέλους
20   εἰπεῖν τούτου, ἐροῦμεν ὃ παρὰ τοῦ Παύλου ἐμάθομεν ὅτι τὸ βέλος τοῦτό ἐστι
Πίστις δι᾽ ἀγάπης ἐνεργουμένη.

| Ἀλλὰ ταῦτα μὲν ἐχέτω ὡς ἄν τῳ δοκῇ, ἴδωμεν δὲ καὶ τὴν παρὰ τῶν   379
παρθένων προσαχθεῖσαν ἐρώτησιν τῇ διδασκάλῳ· Τί ἀδελφιδός σου, ἡ καλὴ
ἐν γυναιξίν; τί ἀδελφιδός σου ἀπὸ ἀδελφιδοῦ, ὅτι οὕτως ὥρκισας ἡμᾶς;
25   τοιαύτην δέ μοί τινα δοκεῖ περιέχειν ἡ ῥῆσις διάνοιαν, καθὼς ἡ ἀκολουθία
τῶν προεξητασμένων εἰκάζειν δίδωσιν· ἐπειδὴ γὰρ εἶδον αἱ παρθένοι τὴν
καλὴν ἔξοδον τῆς ψυχῆς, τῆς νύμφης, ὅτε προσεφύη τῷ λόγῳ ἡ εἰποῦσα
ὅτι Ἐξῆλθεν ἡ ψυχή μου ἐν λόγῳ αὐτοῦ, καὶ ἔγνωσαν ὅτι ἐζήτει ἐξελθοῦσα
τὸν διὰ σημείων οὐχ εὑρισκόμενον καὶ ἐκάλει βοῶσα τὸν οὐχ ὑπακούοντα

sible by their means to see the pure Bridegroom, love's archer,[13] and for each person's soul to say to him *I am wounded by love*.

That the wounds of love are things to be cherished we learn already from Proverbs, which says: "The wounds of a friend are desirable, but even the kisses of a foe are evils" (cf. Prov 27:6).[14] | As to who the friend is whose wounds are more generous than the kisses of a foe, the answer is plain to anyone who is not ignorant of the mysteries of salvation. "Friend" signifies that true and unshakable One who has never stopped loving us even when we have been his foes. "Foe" indicates that savage and unreliable one who brings down to death those who have done him no ill. To the first humans, the prohibition of evil expressed in the commandment was a "wound" (for separation from what gives pleasure is reckoned to be a wound), while "kiss" meant incitement to what gives pleasure and appears good. Experience, however, has shown that from a friend things reckoned as wounds are more profitable and more to be desired than kisses from an enemy.

Since, then, the beautiful Lover[15] of our souls has commended his love, on account of which "Christ died for us" even "when we were sinners" (Rom 5:8), the Bride, having returned her Lover's love, discloses the arrow of love deeply lodged within her, that is to say, her fellowship with Deity itself. For love is God, as we have said,[16] come to inhabit the heart by the agency of the arrow of faith. And if it is right to set a name to this arrow, we repeat what we have learned from Paul, that this arrow is "faith working through love" (Gal 5:6).

| But let these words be held to say what one takes them to mean, and let us consider the question that the virgins put to their teacher: *What is your kinsman, O fair among women? What is your kinsman more than another, that you have charged us so?* As I see it, these words contain a meaning that the sequence of thought in earlier parts of the Song allows us to gather. For the virgins have observed the happy exodus[17] of the soul that is the Bride, when she attached herself to the Word in saying *My soul went forth in his word*; and they recognized that in going forth she was seeking One who is not found

---

13. For this theme, see homily 4 above, pp. 127–28 (Jaeger).

14. The Greek text cited (or remembered?) by Gregory differs widely from that of the LXX, which reads: "The wounds of a friend are more trustworthy than the voluntary kisses of an enemy."

15. The Greek word is ἐραστής. Gregory in this passage as elsewhere appears to make no distinction between ἔρως, ἀγάπη, and φιλία. He employs all three terms to indicate God's love of humanity, on the one hand, and humanity's love for God, on the other. In this connection, see the preface to Origen's commentary on the Song of Songs (trans. Lawson 1956, 24–34).

16. See homily 7, p. 214 (Jaeger), and esp. homily 4, p. 127 (Jaeger).

17. For this theme, see above, homily 12, pp. 353–54 (Jaeger).

τοῖς ὀνόμασι, διὰ τοῦτό φασι· πῶς ἐπιγνῶμεν αὐτὸν ἡμεῖς τὸν μηδενὶ σημείῳ
γνωριστικῷ εὑρισκόμενον, ὃς οὔτε ὑπακούει καλούμενος οὔτε κρατεῖται
ζητούμενος; περίελε τοίνυν καὶ σὺ τῶν ὀφθαλμῶν τῶν ἡμετέρων τὰ θέριστρα,
ὅπερ ἐποίησαν ἐπὶ σοὶ οἱ τῆς πόλεως φύλακες, ἵνα τις γένηται ἡμῖν ὁδηγία
5   πρὸς τὸ ζητούμενον. εἰπὲ τί ἐστιν ὁ ἀδελφιδός σου, καθ' ὃ ἔστιν ἐν τῷ λόγῳ
τῆς φύσεως· δὸς ἡμῖν ἔφοδον τῆς ἐπιγνώσεως αὐτοῦ διὰ γνωριστικῶν | 380
τινων τεκμηρίων, σὺ ἡ τοῦ καλοῦ πληρωθεῖσα καὶ διὰ τοῦτο γενομένη καλὴ
ἐν γυναιξί· γνώρισον ἡμῖν τὸ ζητούμενον· δίδαξον ἡμᾶς δι' ὧν εὑρίσκεται
σημείων ὁ μὴ ὁρώμενος, ὡς μηνῦσαι αὐτῷ περὶ τοῦ βέλους τῆς ἀγάπης, ᾧ
10   μέσην τέτρωσαι τὴν καρδίαν διὰ τῆς γλυκείας ὀδύνης τὸν πόθον ἐπαύξουσα.
Κρεῖττον δ' ἂν εἴη πάλιν τὴν αὐτὴν ῥῆσιν ἐπαναλαβεῖν ἐπὶ λέξεως, ὡς ἂν
ἐφαρμοσθείη τοῖς ῥητοῖς ἡ ἐκτεθεῖσα διάνοια· Τί ἀδελφιδός σου, ἡ καλὴ ἐν
γυναιξί; τί ἀδελφιδός σου ἀπὸ ἀδελφιδοῦ, ὅτι οὕτως ὥρκισας ἡμᾶς;
ἀκούσωμεν τοίνυν τῆς ἀκριβῶς περιελομένης τὸ θέριστρον καὶ
15   ἀνακεκαλυμμένῳ τῷ τῆς ψυχῆς ὀφθαλμῷ βλεπούσης πρὸς τὴν ἀλήθειαν. πῶς
ὑπογράφει αὐταῖς τὸ ζητούμενον; πῶς ζωγραφεῖ τῷ λόγῳ τοῦ ποθουμένου
τὸν χαρακτῆρα; πῶς ὑπ' ὄψιν ἄγει ταῖς παρθένοις τὸν ἀγνοούμενον; ἐπειδὴ
γὰρ τοῦ Χριστοῦ τὸ μὲν κτιστόν ἐστι τὸ δὲ ἄκτιστον (λέγομεν δὲ ἄκτιστον
μὲν εἶναι αὐτοῦ τὸ ἀΐδιόν τε καὶ προαιώνιον καὶ ποιητικὸν πάντων τῶν ὄντων,
20   κτιστὸν δὲ τὸ κατὰ τὴν ὑπὲρ ἡμῶν οἰκονομίαν συσχηματισθὲν τῷ σώματι
τῆς ταπεινώσεως ἡμῶν. μᾶλλον δὲ δι' αὐτῶν τῶν θείων ῥημάτων τὴν περὶ
τούτου διάνοιαν βέλτιον ἂν εἴη παραθέσθαι τῷ λόγῳ· | ἄκτιστον λέγομεν τὸν   381
ἐν ἀρχῇ ὄντα λόγον καὶ ἀεὶ πρὸς τὸν θεὸν ὄντα καὶ θεὸν ὄντα λόγον, τὸν
δι' οὗ τὰ πάντα ἐγένετο καὶ οὗ χωρὶς τῶν γεγονότων ἔστιν οὐδέν, κτιστὸν
25   δὲ τὸν σάρκα γενόμενον καὶ ἐν ἡμῖν σκηνώσαντα, οὗ καὶ σαρκωθέντος ἡ
ἐμφαινομένη δόξα δηλοῖ, ὅτι Θεὸς ἐφανερώθη ἐν σαρκί, θεὸς δὲ πάντως ὁ
μονογενής, ὁ ἐν τοῖς κόλποις ὢν τοῦ πατρός, οὕτως εἰπόντος τοῦ Ἰωάννου
ὅτι Ἐθεασάμεθα τὴν δόξαν αὐτοῦ, καίτοι τὸ φαινόμενον ἄνθρωπος ἦν, ἀλλὰ
τὸ δι' αὐτοῦ γνωριζόμενον Δόξαν φησὶν ὡς μονογενοῦς παρὰ πατρός, πλήρης
30   χάριτος καὶ ἀληθείας) ἐπειδὴ τοίνυν τὸ μὲν ἄκτιστον αὐτοῦ καὶ προαιώνιον
καὶ ἀΐδιον ἄληπτον μένει καθ' ὅλου πάσῃ φύσει καὶ ἀνεκφώνητον, τὸ δὲ διὰ

by signs and in crying out was calling upon One who does not answer to names. That is why they ask: "How shall we find him who is not detected by any sign of recognition, who neither answers when called upon nor is secured when sought? Take away, then, you yourself, the veils from our eyes as the city watchmen did from yours, so that we may have some guidance on our way to the One we seek. Tell us what your kinsman is, how he is to be classed by nature. Give us a way of finding him by means of | some signs that will identify him, you who overflow with beauty and so are *fair among women*! Make known to us the One we seek. Teach us by what tokens the invisible One is detected, so that we may acquaint him with the arrow of love with which your heart is wounded in its heart, increasing your desire by its sweet pain."

It will doubtless be better, though, to go back over this passage word for word, so that the meaning we have set forth may be reconciled with the words. *What is your kinsman, O fair among women? What is your kinsman more than others, that you should charge us so?*

Let us attend, then, to the one who has had her veil quite removed and looks toward the Truth with the uncovered eye of the soul. How does she describe for them the One she seeks? How does she portray in speech that which marks out the One she desires? How does she bring the Unknown One within the sight of her virgins? For since Christ is in one respect creature and in another respect uncreated. (We say that he is uncreated in that he is eternal and prior to the ages and the Maker of everything that is, but created in that he was conformed to our lowly body in the economy he carried out for our sakes. But it would be better to set out our understanding of this matter by means of the divine words themselves: | "uncreated" we call the Word who was in the beginning and is always with God and is God the Logos, the One through whom everything came to be and apart from whom none of the things that have come to be exists; but "created" we call the One who became flesh and tabernacled[18] among us, whose glory shining forth in his incarnate state reveals that God has been "manifested in flesh," the Only Begotten God who is in the bosom of the Father. For John says, "We have seen his glory," and even though what was observable was a human being, nevertheless what was made known through him, says John, was "glory as of the Only Begotten of the Father, full of grace and truth" [John 1:14]) Now that of him which is uncreated and before the ages and eternal is by nature completely incapable of being grasped and unutterable, while what is manifested for us through

---

18. It is the image suggested by this word "tabernacled" (ἐσκήνωσεν) in John 1:14 that occasions Gregory's christological interpretation of the "tent [σκηνή] of witness" in Exodus. See Gregory's *Vit. Mos.* 2.174 (GNO 7.1:91; trans. Malherbe and Ferguson 1978, 98), and above, homily 2, p. 44 (Jaeger). The flesh is the "tent" in which the Deity "tabernacles."

σαρκὸς ἡμῖν φανερωθὲν δύναται ποσῶς καὶ εἰς γνῶσιν ἐλθεῖν, τούτου χάριν
πρὸς ταῦτα ἡ διδάσκαλος βλέπει καὶ περὶ τούτων ποιεῖται τὸν λόγον ὅσα
δύναται γενέσθαι χωρητὰ τοῖς ἀκούουσιν.

    λέγω δὲ Τὸ μέγα τῆς εὐσεβείας μυστήριον, δι᾽ οὗ ὁ θεὸς ἐφανερώθη ἐν
5   σαρκί, ὁ ἐν μορφῇ θεοῦ ὑπάρχων καὶ τῷ δουλικῷ προσωπείῳ διὰ σαρκὸς
συναναστραφεὶς τοῖς ἀνθρώποις, ὃς ἐπειδὴ ἅπαξ πρὸς ἑαυτὸν διὰ τῆς ἀπαρχῆς
ἐπεσπάσατο τὴν ἐπίκηρον τῆς σαρκὸς φύσιν, ἣν διὰ τῆς ἀφθόρου παρθενίας
ἀνέλαβεν, ἀεὶ τῇ ἀπαρχῇ συναγιάζει τὸ κοινὸν τῆς φύσεως φύραμα διὰ | τῶν 382
ἑνουμένων αὐτῷ κατὰ τὴν κοινωνίαν τοῦ μυστηρίου τρέφων τὸ ἑαυτοῦ σῶμα,
10 τὴν ἐκκλησίαν, καὶ καταλλήλως τὰ ἐμφυόμενα διὰ τῆς πίστεως αὐτῷ μέλη
τῷ κοινῷ σώματι ἐναρμόζων εὐπρεπὲς τὸ πᾶν ἀπεργάζεται εἰς ὀφθαλμοὺς
καὶ στόμα καὶ χεῖρας καὶ τὰ λοιπὰ μέλη πρεπόντως τε καὶ ἁρμοδίως διατιθεὶς
τοὺς πιστεύοντας.

    οὕτω γάρ φησιν ὁ Παῦλος ὅτι Ἕν μέν ἐστι σῶμα, πολλὰ δὲ μέλη. Τὰ
15 δὲ μέλη πάντα οὐ τὴν αὐτὴν ἔχει πρᾶξιν, ἀλλ᾽ ἔστι τις καὶ ὀφθαλμὸς ἐν τῷ
σώματι μὴ καταφρονῶν τῆς χειρὸς καὶ κεφαλή τις ὢν οὐκ ἀπωθεῖται τοὺς
πόδας, ἀλλὰ συγκέκραται πρὸς ἑαυτὸ τῇ ποικιλίᾳ τῶν ἐνεργειῶν ἅπαν διὰ
τῶν μελῶν τὸ σῶμα, ἵνα μὴ στασιάζῃ πρὸς τὸ ὅλον τὰ μέρη. ταῦτα δὲ δι᾽
αἰνιγμάτων προθεὶς τὰ νοήματα ἐπὶ τὸ σαφέστερον προάγει τὸν λόγον εἰπὼν
20 ὅτι Ἔθετο ὁ θεὸς ἐν τῇ ἐκκλησίᾳ ἀποστόλους καὶ προφήτας καὶ διδασκάλους
καὶ ποιμένας Πρὸς τὸν καταρτισμὸν τῶν ἁγίων, εἰς ἔργον διακονίας, εἰς
οἰκοδομὴν τοῦ σώματος τοῦ Χριστοῦ, μέχρι καταντήσωμεν οἱ πάντες εἰς τὴν
ἑνότητα τῆς πίστεως καὶ τῆς ἐπιγνώσεως τοῦ υἱοῦ τοῦ θεοῦ εἰς ἄνδρα τέλειον
εἰς μέτρον ἡλικίας τοῦ πληρώματος τοῦ Χριστοῦ. καὶ πάλιν Αὐξήσωμεν,
25 φησίν, εἰς αὐτὸν τὰ πάντα, ὅς ἐστιν ἡ κεφαλή, ὁ Χριστός, ἐξ οὗ πᾶν τὸ σῶμα
συναρμολογούμενον καὶ συμβιβαζόμενον | διὰ πάσης ἁφῆς τῆς ἐπιχορηγίας 383
κατ᾽ ἐνέργειαν ἐν μέτρῳ ἑνὸς ἑκάστου μέρους τὴν αὔξησιν τοῦ σώματος
ποιεῖται εἰς οἰκοδομὴν ἑαυτοῦ ἐν ἀγάπῃ.

    οὐκοῦν ὁ πρὸς τὴν ἐκκλησίαν βλέπων πρὸς τὸν Χριστὸν ἄντικρυς
30 βλέπει τὸν ἑαυτὸν διὰ τῆς προσθήκης τῶν σῳζομένων οἰκοδομοῦντα καὶ
μεγαλύνοντα. ἡ τοίνυν ἀποθεμένη τῶν ὀμμάτων τὸ θέριστρον καθαρῷ τῷ
ὀφθαλμῷ τὸ ἄφραστον ὁρᾷ τοῦ νυμφίου κάλλος καὶ διὰ τοῦτο τρωθεῖσα
τῷ ἀσωμάτῳ καὶ διαπύρῳ βέλει τοῦ ἔρωτος· ἐπιτεταμένη γὰρ ἀγάπη ὁ ἔρως
λέγεται, ᾧ οὐδεὶς ἐπαισχύνεται ὅταν μὴ κατὰ σαρκὸς γένηται παρ᾽ αὐτοῦ
35 ἡ τοξεία, ἀλλ᾽ ἐπικαυχᾶται μᾶλλον τῷ τραύματι ὅταν διὰ τοῦ βάθους τῆς

the flesh can to a degree come into our knowledge; and for this reason our teacher focuses on the latter and in that regard speaks as much as her hearers are capable of taking in.

What I mean is "the great … mystery of our religion," in which God "was manifested in flesh" (1 Tim 3:16), in which he who "was in the form of God" also, in the role of a slave, held converse with human beings through his flesh (Phil 2:6–7). And since he once for all, through its firstfruits, drew to himself the mortal nature of flesh, which he took on by means of an uncorrupted virginity, he ever sanctifies the common dough of that nature through its firstfruits, nourishing his body, the church, in the persons | of those who are united to him in the fellowship of the mystery; and those members that are grafted into him through faith he fits into the common body, and he fashions a comely whole by fitly and appropriately assigning believers to roles as eyes and mouth and hands and the other members.

For Paul says that the body is one but the members many. Yet all the members do not have the same function. Instead, there is one member that is an eye in the body, though it does not look down on the hand, and another, though it is the head, does not spurn the feet; but through its members the whole body is bound together with itself by their various functions, lest the parts be at odds with the whole (cf. 1 Cor 12:12–27). Once he has set forth these thoughts in enigmatic symbols, Paul becomes more explicit when he says that God established in the church apostles and prophets and teachers and shepherds "for the equipment of the saints, for the work of ministry, for the building up of the body of Christ, until we all attain to the unity of the faith and of the knowledge of the Son of God, to mature manhood, to the measure of the stature of the fullness of Christ" (Eph 4:11–13). And again, "We are to grow up in every way into him who is the head, into Christ, from whom the whole body, joined and knit together | by every joint with which it is supplied, when each part is working properly, makes bodily growth and upbuilds itself in love" (Eph 4:15–16).

Anyone, therefore, who focuses attention on the church is in fact looking at Christ—Christ building himself up and augmenting himself by the addition of people who are being saved. She, then, who has put the veil off from her eyes sees the unspeakable beauty of the Bridegroom with a pure eye and in this way is wounded by the incorporeal and fiery arrow of love, for *agapē* when intensified is called love.[19] This occasions people no shame if love's archery is not fleshly; on the contrary, they boast the more in their wound

---

19. I.e., ἔρως. Gregory here takes ἀγάπη to be, as it were, a *general* term for love or affection and ἔρως to denote the same thing in a more acute form. See above, n. 15, with its reference to Origen's commentary.

καρδίας δέξηται τὴν τοῦ ἀΰλου πόθου ἀκίδα. ὅπερ δὴ καὶ αὕτη πεποίηκε ταῖς νεάνισι λέγουσα ὅτι Τετρωμένη ἀγάπης εἰμὶ ἐγώ.

Ἡ τοίνυν εἰς τοσοῦτον τελειότητος προελθοῦσα, ἐπειδὴ ἔδει καὶ ταῖς παρθένοις ὑποδεῖξαι τοῦ νυμφίου τὸ κάλλος, οὐκ ἐκεῖνο λέγει ὃ ἦν ἐν ἀρχῇ
5   (οὐδὲ γὰρ οἷόν τε ἦν δυνάμει λόγων φανερωθῆναι τὸ ἄρρητον), ἀλλὰ πρὸς τὴν διὰ σαρκὸς γενομένην ἡμῖν θεοφάνειαν χειραγωγεῖ τὰς παρθένους (ὅπερ δὴ καὶ ὁ μέγας Ἰωάννης πεποίηκεν, Ὃ μὲν ἦν ἀπ᾽ ἀρχῆς σιωπήσας, Ὃ δὲ ἑωράκαμεν καὶ ἀκηκόαμεν καὶ αἱ χεῖρες ἡμῶν ἐψηλάφησαν περὶ τοῦ λόγου τῆς ἀληθείας τοῦτο | μετ᾽ ἐπιμελείας διηγησάμενος).   384
10 φησὶν οὖν πρὸς αὐτὰς ἡ νύμφη· Ἀδελφιδός μου λευκὸς καὶ πυρρός, ἐκλελοχισμένος ἀπὸ μυριάδων. κεφαλὴ αὐτοῦ χρυσίον κεφάζ, βόστρυχοι αὐτοῦ ἐλάται, μέλανες ὡς κόραξ, οἱ ὀφθαλμοὶ αὐτοῦ ὡς περιστεραὶ ἐπὶ πληρώματα ὑδάτων λελουμέναι ἐν γάλακτι, καθήμεναι ἐπὶ πληρώματα ὑδάτων. σιαγόνες αὐτοῦ ὡς φιάλαι τοῦ ἀρώματος φύουσαι μυρεψικά, χείλη
15 αὐτοῦ κρίνα στάζοντα σμύρναν πλήρη, χεῖρες αὐτοῦ τορευταί, χρυσαῖ, πεπληρωμέναι θαρσεῖς, κοιλία αὐτοῦ πυξίον ἐλεφάντινον ἐπὶ λίθου σαπφείρου, κνῆμαι αὐτοῦ στῦλοι μαρμάρινοι, τεθεμελιωμένοι ἐπὶ βάσεις χρυσᾶς. εἶδος αὐτοῦ ὡς Λίβανος ἐκλεκτός, ὡς κέδροι, φάρυγξ αὐτοῦ γλυκασμὸς καὶ ὅλος ἐπιθυμία. οὗτος ἀδελφιδός μου καὶ οὗτος πλησίον μου,
20 θυγατέρες Ἰερουσαλήμ.

ταῦτα γὰρ πάντα, δι᾽ ὧν ἡ τοῦ κάλλους γέγονεν ὑπογραφή, οὐ τῶν ἀοράτων τε καὶ ἀκαταλήπτων τῆς θεότητός ἐστιν ἐνδεικτικὰ ἀλλὰ τῶν κατ᾽ οἰκονομίαν φανερωθέντων, ὅτε ἐπὶ τῆς γῆς ὤφθη καὶ τοῖς ἀνθρώποις συνανεστράφη τὴν ἀνθρωπίνην ἐνδυσάμενος φύσιν, δι᾽ ὧν κατὰ τὸν
25 ἀποστολικὸν λόγον καὶ τὰ ἀόρατα αὐτοῦ τοῖς ποιήμασι νοούμενα καθορᾶται διὰ τῆς τοῦ ἐκκλησιαστικοῦ κόσμου κατασκευῆς φανερούμενα. κόσμου γὰρ κτίσις ἐστὶν ἡ τῆς ἐκκλησίας κατασκευή, ἐν ᾗ | κατὰ τὴν τοῦ προφήτου   385
φωνὴν καὶ οὐρανὸς κτίζεται καινός (ὅπερ ἐστὶ τὸ στερέωμα τῆς εἰς Χριστὸν πίστεως καθὼς ὁ Παῦλός φησι) καὶ γῆ καινὴ κατασκευάζεται, Ἡ πίνουσα
30 τὸν ἐπ᾽ αὐτὴν ἐρχόμενον ὑετόν, καὶ ἄνθρωπος πλάσσεται ἄλλος, ὁ διὰ τῆς

when they receive the dart of immaterial desire in the very depth of the heart. And this is exactly what the Bride did when she said to the young women: *I am wounded by love.*

So, then, she who had advanced to such a degree of perfection, obliged as she is to show her virgins the beauty of the Bridegroom, does not speak of that which was "in the beginning" (John 1:1)—for it is not possible for the unutterable to be made manifest by the power of words—but she leads her virgins to the theophany that came to us through the medium of the flesh (and this is precisely what the great John did: he was silent about "that which was from the beginning," but he expounds "what we saw and heard and our hands touched concerning the Word of truth" [1 John 1:1] | with great care).

So the Bride says to them: *My kinsman is white and ruddy, set apart [in his birth] from myriads. His head is as very fine gold, his locks are firs, black as a raven. His eyes are as doves by pools of waters, washed in milk, sitting by pools of waters. [His cheeks are as bowls of spice pouring forth perfumes. His lips are lilies, dropping choice myrrh. His hands are skilled workers, golden, full of courage. His belly is an ivory tablet on a sapphire stone. His legs are marble pillars set upon bases of gold. His form is like Lebanon, choice like cedars. His throat is sweetness and entire desire. This is my kinsman, and this my close one, ye daughters of Jerusalem.]*[20]

Now all these statements, with their description of the Bridegroom's beauty, point not to the invisible and incomprehensible realities of the Godhead but to the things that were revealed in the economy,[21] when Deity, having put on human nature, was revealed on the earth and held converse with human beings. By their means, as the apostle says, "the invisible things of him ... have been clearly apprehended in his works" (Rom 1:20) as revealed through the foundation of the cosmos that is the church. For the creation of the cosmos signifies the foundation of the church, in which, | according to the word of the prophet, both a new heaven is created (which is "the firmament of faith in Christ" [cf. Col 2:5],[22] as Paul says) and a new earth is established (cf. Isa 65:17), which drinks "the rain that ... falls upon it" (cf. Heb 6:7), and another humanity, renewed by the birth from above "after the

---

20. The verses here enclosed in brackets (Song 5:13–16) are not treated in homily 13, nor indeed are they present in the portion of the Song (i.e., 5:8–12) read out at the beginning of the sermon. The citation of them here suggests that Gregory regards verses 8–16 as a single literary unit even though he cannot comment on the whole of it in one sermon.

21. I.e., God's plan and work of salvation, at the heart of which lies the incarnation of the Word.

22. Colossians speaks of the "firmness" (rsv) of believers' faith in Christ, but the Greek word (στερέωμα) is the very one employed at Gen 1:6 (lxx): "And God said, 'Let there be a *firmament* in the midst of the water.'"

ἄνωθεν γεννήσεως ἀνακαινιζόμενος κατ᾽ εἰκόνα τοῦ κτίσαντος αὐτόν, καὶ
φωστήρων φύσις ἑτέρα γίνεται, περὶ ὧν φησιν ὅτι Ὑμεῖς ἐστε τὸ φῶς τοῦ
κόσμου, καὶ Ἐν οἷς φαίνεσθε ὡς φωστῆρες ἐν κόσμῳ, καὶ ἀστέρες πολλοί, οἱ
ἐν τῷ στερεώματι τῆς πίστεως ἀνατέλλοντες.

5   καὶ οὔπω τοῦτο θαυμαστόν, εἰ
πλήθη ἄστρων ἐστὶν ἐν τῷ καινῷ τούτῳ κόσμῳ ὑπὸ τοῦ θεοῦ ἀριθμούμενα
καὶ ὀνομαζόμενα, ὧν τὰ ὀνόματα ὁ ποιητὴς τῶν τοιούτων ἄστρων ἐν τοῖς
οὐρανοῖς ἀπογεγράφθαι λέγει (οὕτω γὰρ ἤκουσα τοῦ δημιουργοῦ τῆς καινῆς
κτίσεως πρὸς τοὺς ἰδίους αὐτοῦ φωστῆρας λέγοντος ὅτι Τὰ ὀνόματα ὑμῶν
ἐγγέγραπται ἐν τοῖς οὐρανοῖς), οὐ τοῦτο τοίνυν μόνον τῆς καινῆς κτίσεώς

10   ἐστι τὸ παράδοξον ὅτι ἄστρων πλῆθος ἐν αὐτῇ δημιουργεῖται παρὰ τοῦ
λόγου, ἀλλ᾽ ὅτι καὶ ἥλιοι πολλοὶ κτίζονται ταῖς τῶν ἀγαθῶν ἔργων ἀκτῖσι
τὴν οἰκουμένην φωτίζοντες οὕτως εἰπόντος τοῦ ποιητοῦ τῶν τοιούτων
ἡλίων· Λαμψάτω τὸ φῶς ὑμῶν ἔμπροσθεν τῶν ἀνθρώπων, καὶ Τότε οἱ δίκαιοι
λάμψουσιν ὡς ὁ ἥλιος.

15   ὥσπερ τοίνυν ὁ πρὸς τὸν | αἰσθητὸν ἀπιδὼν κόσμον καὶ τὴν ἐμφαινομένην   386
τῷ κάλλει τῶν ὄντων σοφίαν κατανοήσας ἀναλογίζεται διὰ τῶν ὁρωμένων
τό τε ἀόρατον κάλλος καὶ τὴν πηγὴν τῆς σοφίας, ἧς ἡ ἀπόρροια τὴν τῶν
ὄντων συνεστήσατο φύσιν, οὕτω καὶ ὁ πρὸς τὸν καινὸν τοῦτον κόσμον
τῆς κατὰ τὴν ἐκκλησίαν κτίσεως βλέπων ὁρᾷ ἐν αὐτῷ τὸν πάντα ἐν πᾶσιν

20   ὄντα τε καὶ γινόμενον διὰ τῶν χωρητῶν τε καὶ καταλαμβανομένων ὑπὸ τῆς
φύσεως ἡμῶν χειραγωγῶν τὴν γνῶσιν πρὸς τὸ ἀχώρητον. οὗ χάριν ἐπειδὴ
ταύτην προσάγουσι τῇ πρὸς τὸ τέλειον ἀναδραμούσῃ ψυχῇ τὴν αἴτησιν
αἱ παρθένοι ψυχαὶ τοῦ γνωρισθῆναι αὐταῖς τὸν ποθούμενον, διὰ τῶν ἐπὶ
σωτηρίᾳ φανερωθέντων ἡμῖν ὑπογράφει ταῖς παρθένοις τὰ τοῦ ζητουμένου

25   γνωρίσματα καὶ πᾶσαν τὴν ἐκκλησίαν ἓν σῶμα τοῦ νυμφίου ποιήσασα ἴδιόν
τι νόημα δι᾽ ἑκάστου τῶν μελῶν ἐν τῇ ὑπογραφῇ τοῦ κάλλους ἐνδείκνυται,
δι᾽ ὧν ὅλον ἐκ τῶν κατὰ μέρος θεωρουμένων τὸ τοῦ σώματος κάλλος
συναπαρτίζεται.

Ἀρχὴν οὖν ποιεῖται τῆς διδασκαλίας τὴν προσεχῆ καὶ οἰκείαν ἡμῖν· ἐκ γὰρ

30   τοῦ σώματος τῆς κατηχήσεως ἄρχεται. ὥσπερ δὴ καὶ ὁ Ματθαῖος πεποίηκεν·
ἐκ τοῦ Ἀβραάμ τε καὶ Δαβὶδ γενεαλογήσας τὸ κατὰ σάρκα μυστήριον
τῷ μεγάλῳ Ἰωάννῃ ἐταμιεύσατο τοῖς ἤδη διὰ τούτων στοιχειωθεῖσι τὴν
ἐξ ἀϊδίου νοουμένην ἀρχὴν καὶ τὸν τῇ ἀρχῇ | συγκατανοούμενον λόγον   387
εὐαγγελίσασθαι.

35   διὰ τούτων τοίνυν τῶν νοημάτων ἡ νύμφη μυσταγωγεῖ τὰς νεάνιδας ὅτι·
οὐ πρότερον ἐπὶ τὸ ἄληπτόν τε καὶ ἀόριστον ἀναχθήσεται ὑμῶν ἡ διάνοια
πρὶν τοῦ ὀφθέντος διὰ τῆς πίστεως περιδράξασθαι. τὸ δὲ ὀφθὲν ἡ τῆς σαρκὸς
ἐστι φύσις· εἰποῦσα γὰρ ὅτι Ἀδελφιδός μου λευκὸς καὶ πυρρός, διὰ τῆς τῶν
δύο τούτων χρωμάτων μίξεως τὸ τῆς σαρκὸς ἰδίωμα ὑπογράφει τῷ λόγῳ.

image of its Creator" (cf. Col 3:10) is fashioned, and a different race of heavenly lights comes to be, about which it says, "You are the light of the cosmos" (Matt 5:14), and "Among whom you shine as lights in the cosmos" (Phil 2:15), and many stars, which rise in the firmament of faith. Nor is it a matter for wonder if in this new cosmos there is "a multitude of stars" that are numbered and named by God (Ps 146:4), whose names, says the Creator of such stars, have been written in heaven (for so have I heard the Artisan of the new creation saying to his own "lights": "Your names have been written in heaven" [Luke 10:20]). So, then, the marvel of the new creation lies not only in the fact that a multitude of stars are fashioned within it by the Word but also in the fact that many suns are created that light the inhabited world with the beams of good works—as the Maker of these suns said: "Let your light shine before humanity" (Matt 5:16), and "Then shall the righteous shine like the sun" (Matt 13:43).

Well, then, just as | the person who looks upon the perceptible cosmos and has grasped the Wisdom that is displayed in the beauty of these beings infers, on the basis of what the eye sees, the invisible Beauty and the wellspring of Wisdom, whose outflow contrived the natural order of what is, so too the person who attends to this new cosmos that appears in the creation of the church sees in it the One who is and is becoming "all in all" (cf. 1 Cor 15:28) as, by way of the things our nature can take in and comprehend, he directs our knowledge toward that which cannot be contained. Hence when the virgin souls request the soul that is ascending to perfection to make the One they desire known to them, she describes for the virgins the marks of the One they seek by appealing to the things that have been revealed to us for the sake of our salvation. She treats of the church as the one body of the Bridegroom, and by referring to each individual member, she indicates, in her account of his beauty, some one of his attributes and in this way, starting from the particular characteristics she has examined, sums up the beauty of the body as a whole.

As the starting point of her teaching, then, she takes what is close and native to us, for she begins her instruction with the body. And this is just what Matthew did. In a genealogy, he traced the beginnings of the mystery of the incarnation from Abraham and David (cf. Matt 1:2–17), and he left it to the great John to proclaim to those already instructed in these basics the eternal Beginning and | the Word that is thought together with the Beginning (cf. John 1:1).

By these ideas, then, the Bride initiates the young women into the truth: "Our understanding will not reach up to the incomprehensible and the infinite until it has first, by faith, laid hands on what has been made visible." But what is visible is the nature of the flesh, for she says *My kinsman is white and ruddy,* and by the mingling of these two colors she describes in words the

τοῦτο δὲ καὶ ἐν τοῖς ἄνω ἐποίησε μῆλον αὐτὸν ὀνομάσασα, οὗ πρὸς ἑκάτερον τῶν χρωμάτων σύγκρατον καθορᾶται τὸ εἶδος· λευκόν τε γάρ ἐστι τὸ μῆλον καὶ ἐρυθραίνεται, τὴν τοῦ αἵματος οἶμαι φύσιν συμβολικῶς ἐνδεικνυμένου τοῦ ἐρυθήματος.

5   Ἀλλ' ἐπειδὴ πᾶσα σὰρξ ἐν τόκῳ συνίσταται γάμου πάντως ὁδοποιοῦντος τὸν τόκον τοῖς εἰς τὴν ζωὴν ταύτην παριοῦσι διὰ γεννήσεως, ὡς ἂν μή τις σαρκὸς γένεσιν περὶ τὸ μυστήριον τῆς εὐσεβείας παραδεξάμενος πρὸς τὰ τῆς φύσεως ἔργα καὶ πάθη τῇ διανοίᾳ κατολισθήσειεν ὁμοιογενῆ τοῖς πᾶσι κἀκείνης τῆς σαρκὸς ἐννοήσας τὴν γένεσιν, τούτου χάριν τὸν κοινωνήσαντα
10   σαρκὸς καὶ αἵματος λευκὸν μὲν εἶναι καὶ πυρρὸν ὡμολόγησε διὰ τῶν δύο χρωμάτων τὴν τοῦ σώματος φύσιν αἰνισσομένη, οὐ μὴν ὁμοιότροπον αὐτοῦ τὴν λοχείαν τῷ κοινῷ τόκῳ γεγενῆσθαι λέγει. ἀλλ' ἐκ | πασῶν τῶν μυριάδων,   388 τῶν ἀφ' οὗ γεγόνασιν ἄνθρωποι καὶ εἰς ὅσον προελεύσεται ῥέουσα διὰ τοῦ τόκου τῶν ἐπιγινομένων ἡ φύσις, μόνος οὗτός ἐστι τῷ καινῷ τῆς λοχείας εἴδει
15   τῆς ζωῆς ταύτης ἁψάμενος, ᾧ οὐχὶ συνήργησε πρὸς τὸ γενέσθαι ἡ φύσις ἀλλ' ὑπηρέτησεν. διὰ τοῦτό φησιν ὅτι ὁ λευκὸς οὗτος καὶ πυρρός, ὁ διὰ σαρκὸς καὶ αἵματος ἐπιδημήσας τῷ βίῳ, μόνος ἐστὶν ἐκ πασῶν τῶν μυριάδων ἐκ τῆς παρθενικῆς καθαρότητος ἐκλελοχισμένος· οὗ ἀσυνδύαστος μὲν ἡ κυοφορία, ἀμόλυντος δὲ ἡ λοχεία, ἀνώδυνος δὲ ἡ ὠδίς· οὗ θάλαμος ἡ τοῦ ὑψίστου
20   δύναμις οἷόν τις νεφέλη τὴν παρθενίαν ἐπισκιάζουσα, πυρσὸς δὲ γαμήλιος ἡ τοῦ ἁγίου πνεύματος ἔλλαμψις, κλίνη δὲ ἡ ἀπάθεια καὶ γάμος ἡ ἀφθαρσία. ὁ τοίνυν ἐκ τῶν τοιούτων γενόμενος καλῶς ἐκλελοχισμένος ἐκ πασῶν τῶν μυριάδων κατωνομάσθη, ὅπερ τὸ μὴ ἐκ λοχοῦς αὐτὸν εἶναι σημαίνει· τούτου γὰρ μόνου χωρὶς λοχείας ἡ γέννησις ὥσπερ καὶ χωρὶς γάμου ἡ σύστασις. οὗ

characteristic trait of flesh. Furthermore, she made the same point above when she called him an "apple,"[23] whose distinctive appearance is made out as a blending of both of these colors; for the apple is white and it blushes—and the blush, I venture, points symbolically to the nature of blood.

But all flesh is constituted by childbirth,[24] and marriage paves the way to birth for everyone that enters this life through generation. For this reason—lest anyone who has accepted the fleshly generation that belongs to the mystery of godliness should descend mentally to the works and passions of nature by conceiving that this fleshly generation is of the same sort as all others—the Bride indeed confesses that the One who shared our flesh and blood is white and ruddy and by these two colors hints at the nature of the body, but she does not say that his birth came about in the same manner as ordinary childbirth. | Rather, out of all the *myriads* whence human beings have sprung and however far nature proceeds as it flows on through the birth of new generations, this individual alone it is that takes hold on this life by a new species of birth. In his case, nature did not contribute to his generation but acted in the role of a helper. That is why she says that this *white and ruddy* One who made our life his own through flesh and blood is the only one out of the *myriads* who was *set apart* in being born[25] of virginal purity. His mother's pregnancy was unique, his birth was unstained, and its pangs, painless. The bridal chamber was "the power of the Most High" overshadowing virginity like some cloud, the torch for the wedding feast was the radiance of the Holy Spirit, the bed was impassibility, and the marriage, incorruptibility. Hence he who was born in such circumstances was rightly named *set apart* [*in his birth*] *from* all *myriads*—which signifies that he is not from the process of childbirth,[26] for to him alone belongs a birth apart from parturition, just as

---

23. See above, homily 4, pp. 116–19 (Jaeger).

24. The Greek here uses the word τόκος, but the reason why the subject of Christ's birth is raised for Gregory at this point is the appearance of the participle ἐκλελοχισμένος in Song 5:10b (on which see the following note).

25. Or "was chosen," ἐκλελοχισμένος. This form is the perfect passive participle of ἐκλοχίζω, a verb that normally means "pick out" (of a group), and the natural way of rendering the LXX text of Song 5:10b might therefore be something like "chosen out of myriads." Gregory, however, sees in it an additional allusion to childbirth (λοχεία or even λόχος), perhaps because he takes [ἐκ]λοχίζειν to be related to λοχεύειν. In any case, he assigns the verb an unaccustomed meaning, best rendered perhaps by some phrase like "set apart by [manner of] birth."

26. Λοχοῦς or perhaps λέχους (see the *apparatus criticus* in Langerbeck 1960, *ad loc.*). In either case, Gregory is again playing on (or with) the participle ἐκλελοχισμένος, which he here interprets as meaning that "of the myriads" (*sc.*, of people born) only Christ is ἐκ λοχοῦς ("outside of childbirth" and its processes). See above, n. 14.

γὰρ ἔστιν ἐπὶ τῆς ἀφθόρου τε καὶ ἀπειρογάμου κυρίως τὸ ὄνομα τῆς λοχείας
εἰπεῖν, διότι παρθενίας τε καὶ λοχείας ἀσύμβατά ἐστι περὶ τὴν αὐτὴν τὰ
ὀνόματα. ἀλλ' ὥσπερ υἱὸς ἐδόθη ἡμῖν ἄνευ πατρός, οὕτω καὶ τὸ παιδίον ἄνευ
λοχείας γεγέννηται. ὡς γὰρ οὐκ ἔγνω ἡ παρθένος ὅπως ἐν τῷ σώματι αὐτῆς
5   τὸ θεοδόχον συνέστη σῶμα, οὕτως οὐδὲ τοῦ τόκου ᾔσθετο μαρτυρούσης
τῆς προφητείας αὐτῇ τὸ ἀνώδυνον | τῆς ὠδῖνος· φησὶ γὰρ Ἡσαΐας ὅτι   389
Πρὶν ἐλθεῖν τοὺς πόνους τῶν ὠδίνων ἐξέφυγε καὶ ἔτεκεν ἄρσεν. διὰ τοῦτο
ἐκλελοχισμένος καὶ ξενίζων καθ' ἑκάτερον τὴν ἀκολουθίαν τῆς φύσεως, οὔτε
ἀρξάμενος ἐξ ἡδονῆς οὔτε προελθὼν διὰ πόνων.
10   καὶ τοῦτο κατὰ τὸ ἀκόλουθόν τε γίνεται καὶ οὐκ ἔξω τοῦ εἰκότος ἐστίν·
ἐπειδὴ γὰρ ἡ τὸν θάνατον διὰ τῆς ἁμαρτίας ἐπεισαγαγοῦσα τῇ φύσει ἐν
λύπαις καὶ πόνοις τίκτειν κατεδικάσθη, ἔδει πάντως τὴν τῆς ζωῆς μητέρα ἀπὸ
χαρᾶς τε τῆς κυοφορίας ἄρξασθαι καὶ διὰ χαρᾶς τελειῶσαι τὸν τόκον. Χαῖρε
γάρ, φησί, κεχαριτωμένη, πρὸς αὐτὴν ὁ ἀρχάγγελος ἐκβαλὼν τῇ φωνῇ τὴν
15   λύπην τὴν ἐξ ἀρχῆς ὑπὸ τῆς ἁμαρτίας ἀποκληρωθεῖσαν τῷ τόκῳ.
οὗτος μὲν οὖν ὁ τῷ καινῷ τε καὶ ἰδιάζοντι τῆς γεννήσεως ἐκ πασῶν τῶν
μυριάδων μόνος τοιοῦτος γενόμενος, ὁ λευκός τε καὶ πυρρὸς διὰ τὴν σάρκα
καὶ τὸ αἷμα καλῶς ὠνομασμένος, καὶ ἐκλελοχισμένος ἀπὸ μυριάδων διὰ τὴν
ἄφθαρτόν τε καὶ ἀπαθῆ τοῦ τόκου παρὰ τοὺς λοιποὺς ἰδιότητα. ἢ τάχα καὶ διὰ
20   τὰ λοιπὰ τῆς γεννήσεως εἴδη, τὰ δίχα λοχείας γενόμενα, ταύτην ἐφήρμοσεν
αὐτῷ τὴν φωνὴν ἡ νύμφη. οὐκ ἀγνοεῖς δὲ πάντως, ὁσάκις ἐγεννήθη ὁ τῆς
καινῆς κτίσεως πάσης πρωτότοκος ὁ ἐν πολλοῖς ἀδελφοῖς πρωτότοκος, ὁ ἐκ
νεκρῶν πρωτότοκος, ὁ πρῶτος λύσας | τὰς ὠδῖνας τοῦ θανάτου καὶ πᾶσι τὸν   390
ἐκ νεκρῶν τόκον ὁδοποιήσας διὰ τῆς ἀναστάσεως. ἐν πᾶσι μὲν γὰρ τούτοις
25   ἐγεννήθη, οὐ μὴν διὰ λοχείας παρῆλθεν εἰς γέννησιν· ἥ τε γὰρ ἐκ τοῦ ὕδατος
γέννησις τὸ τῆς λοχείας πάθος οὐ παρεδέξατο καὶ ἡ ἐκ νεκρῶν παλιγγενεσία
καὶ ἡ τῆς θείας ταύτης κτίσεως πρωτοτοκία, ἀλλ' ἐν πᾶσι τούτοις καθαρεύει
τῆς λοχείας ὁ τόκος. διὰ τοῦτό φησιν Ἐκλελοχισμένος ἀπὸ μυριάδων.
Οἷον δὲ αὐτοῦ τὸ κάλλος ἐν τοῖς καθ' ἕκαστον μέλεσι διηγεῖται, καιρὸς
30   ἂν εἴη κατανοῆσαι διὰ τῶν εἰρημένων.

he was brought into being apart from marriage. For since the terms "virginity" and "childbirth" are inconsistent when used of the same person, it is not right to speak of parturition in the case of a woman who is pure and without experience of marriage. But just as a son was given to us without a father, so too the child was born apart from parturition. For as the virgin did not know how the God-receiving body came to be in her body, by the same token she did not experience childbirth, the prophecy attesting | that her birth pangs were painless. For Isaiah says: "Before she was in painful labor she gave birth and bore a male" (Isa 66:7). Hence he was *set apart* and altered the natural sequence of things at both ends, neither originating in pleasure nor coming forth at the cost of pain.

Furthermore, this is logical and not beyond likelihood. For since she who by sinning brought death down on human nature[27] was condemned to bear children in pain and distress, it was surely necessary and right that the mother of life should originate her childbearing in joy and with joy bring the birth to its completion. "Rejoice, O favored one," said the archangel to her (Luke 1:28)—by his word casting out the pain assigned from the beginning to childbearing because of sin.

This, then, is the One who by reason of the new and special mode of his birth became the only One of his sort out of all the *myriads*, the One who is rightly called both *white and ruddy* because of his flesh and blood and *set apart* [*in birth*] *from myriads* because of the incorruptible and impassible character of his birth as compared with that of others. Or perhaps the Bride applies this expression to him because of the remaining forms of birth, those that occur apart from parturition. You cannot be ignorant of how often he was born: the firstborn of the whole new creation (cf. Col 1:15), the "firstborn among many brothers" (Rom 8:29), the "firstborn from the dead" (Col 1:18), | the first to have "loosed the pangs of death" (Acts 2:24) and to have pioneered for all, through his resurrection, the birth from death. For he was born in all these ways but did not come to birth through parturition. The birth out of water (John 3:5) did not involve the suffering of childbirth, nor did the rebirth from the dead, nor did his being firstborn of this new creation. In all these instances the birth was free of parturition, and that is why it says *set apart* [*in birth*] *from myriads*.

But now it is time for us to gather from the text we have read out how the Bridegroom's beauty is characterized by way of each several member.

---

27. "Nature" (φύσις) here functions more as a collective than as an abstract noun and might well be translated as "race."

Κεφαλὴ αὐτοῦ, φησί, χρυσίον κεφάζ. ἡ δὲ Ἑβραϊκὴ λέξις, εἰ πρὸς τὴν
ἡμετέραν μεταληφθείη φωνήν, τὸ καθαρόν τε καὶ ἄπεφθον καὶ πάσης ἐπιμιξίας
ἀλλότριον χρυσίον διὰ τῆς φωνῆς ταύτης ἐνδείκνυται. ἀνερμήνευτον δέ μοι
δοκοῦσι καταλελοιπέναι τὴν τοῦ κεφὰζ λέξιν οἱ τὰς φωνὰς τῶν Ἑβραίων
5   ἐξελληνίσαντες διὰ τὸ μὴ εὑρεῖν ἐν τοῖς Ἑλληνικοῖς ῥήμασι μηδεμίαν φωνὴν
ἐξαγγελτικὴν τῆς ἐμφάσεως τῆς ἐνθεωρουμένης τῇ Ἑβραΐδι φωνῇ. ἡμεῖς
δὲ τοῦτο μαθόντες ὅτι τὸ εἰλικρινῶς καθαρὸν καὶ πάσης ὕλης ῥυπαρᾶς
ἀμιγές τε καὶ ἀπαράδεκτον ἡ τοιαύτη λέξις ἐνδείκνυται, ταῦτα περὶ τοῦ
προκειμένου ῥητοῦ νοεῖν ἐναγόμεθα ὅτι κεφαλὴ τοῦ σώματος τῆς ἐκκλησίας
10   ἐστὶν ὁ Χριστός. Χριστὸν δὲ | νῦν λέγομεν οὐ πρὸς τὸ ἀΐδιον τῆς θεότητος   391
ἀναπέμποντες τοῦτο τὸ ὄνομα ἀλλὰ πρὸς τὸν θεοδόχον ἄνθρωπον, τὸν
ἐπὶ γῆς ὀφθέντα καὶ τοῖς ἀνθρώποις συναναστραφέντα, τὸν τῆς παρθενίας
βλαστόν, ἐν ᾧ Κατῴκησε πᾶν τὸ πλήρωμα τῆς θεότητος σωματικῶς, τὴν
ἀπαρχὴν τοῦ κοινοῦ φυράματος, δι' οὗ ὁ λόγος τὴν φύσιν ἡμῶν περιεβάλετο
15   ποιήσας αὐτὴν ἀκήρατον, πάντων τῶν συμπεφυκότων αὐτῇ παθημάτων
ἐκκαθαρθεῖσαν. οὕτω γάρ φησι περὶ αὐτοῦ ὁ προφήτης ὅτι Ἁμαρτίαν οὐκ
ἐποίησεν, οὐδὲ εὑρέθη δόλος ἐν τῷ στόματι αὐτοῦ, τοῦ πεπειραμένου κατὰ
πάντα καθ' ὁμοιότητα τῆς φύσεως ἡμῶν χωρὶς ἁμαρτίας.
       ἡ μὲν οὖν κεφαλὴ τοῦ σώματος τῆς ἐκκλησίας, ἡ πάσης τῆς φύσεως
20   ἡμῶν ἀπαρχή, τὸ καθαρόν τε καὶ πάσης κακίας ἀμιγές τε καὶ ἀπαράδεκτον
χρυσίον ἐστίν, οἱ βόστρυχοι δέ, οἵ ποτε ζοφώδεις καὶ μέλανες καὶ τοῖς κόραξιν
ὡμοιωμένοι τῷ εἴδει (ἐκείνοις λέγω τοῖς κόραξιν, οἷς ἔργον ἐστὶ τὸ τοὺς
ὀφθαλμοὺς ἐκκόπτειν κατὰ τὸν παροιμιώδη λόγον καὶ τοῖς νεοσσοῖς τῶν
ἀετῶν βρῶμα τοὺς πηρωθέντας τῶν ὁρατικῶν αἰσθητηρίων παρασκευάζειν),
25   οὗτοι ἐλάται, τὰ ὑψηλά τε καὶ οὐρανομήκη δένδρα, γενόμενοι διὰ τοῦ
ἀναδραμεῖν ἐκ γῆς ἐπὶ τὸ οὐράνιον ὕψος προσθήκη τοῦ κάλλους γίνονται τοῦ
νυμφίου τῆς θείας κεφαλῆς ἑαυτοὺς | ἐξαρτήσαντες. οὐκ ἀγνοεῖς δὲ πάντως,   392
τί τῶν βοστρύχων τούτων ἔργον ἐστίν, ἐν τοῖς ἄνω μαθὼν παρ' αὐτῆς τῆς
τοῦ νυμφίου φωνῆς ὅτι Οἱ βόστρυχοί μου ἐπλήσθησαν ψεκάδων νυκτός.
30   ἐκεῖνοι οὖν εἰσιν οἱ ψεκάζοντες βόστρυχοι, οἱ παρὰ τῶν προφητῶν νεφέλαι
ὠνομασμένοι, ἀφ' ὧν γίνεται τῆς διδασκαλίας ὁ ὄμβρος, ὁ τὰς ἐμψύχους
ἀρούρας ποτίζων πρὸς τὴν εὐκαρπίαν τῶν τοῦ θεοῦ γεωργίων.

His head, it says, *is as very fine gold.* The Hebrew word, when translated into our language, signifies by this expression[28] gold that is pure and refined and free of all alloys. Now it seems to me that the people who rendered the Hebrew into Greek left the word *kephaz* untranslated because they did not find in the vocabulary of Greek any word that expressed the plain sense of the Hebrew word. We, however, have learned that this word signifies that which is completely pure and unmixed with any base material whatever; and with regard to the statement before us we are further led to see that the *head* of the body that is the church is Christ. At this point, however, | when we speak of Christ we are not using that name to refer to the Deity in its eternity but to the human being that receives the Deity—him who was seen on earth and lived among us humans, the offspring of virginity, in whom "all the fullness of the Deity dwelt bodily" (Col 2:9), the firstfruits of the common lump of dough (cf. Rom 11:16), through whom the Word put on our nature and rendered it undefiled, having cleansed it of all the passions that have grown to be part of it. For so the prophet says regarding him, "He did no sin, neither was guile found in his mouth" (1 Pet 2:22; cf. Isa 53:9), he who was tempted in all respects after the likeness of our nature but without sin (cf. Heb 4:15).

Therefore the head of the body that is the church, the firstfruits of our entire nature, is this pure *gold,* unreceptive of any form of evil and unmixed with it, while *his locks,* which are dark-hued and black and like ravens in appearance (those ravens, I mean, whose work it is, as Proverbs has it, to pick out eyes and to furnish those deprived of the organs of sight as food to "the nestlings of eagles"[29]), his locks, I say, are become *firs,* lofty and upward-reaching trees, which because they mount from earth to the height of heaven become an enhancement of the Bridegroom's beauty | as they attach themselves to his divine head. And you cannot be unaware what the function of these locks is, for you have learned earlier on from the voice of the Bridegroom himself that *My locks* are filled *with the drops of the night.*[30] These dripping locks, then, are what the prophets call "clouds," from which there comes the shower of teaching that waters the living earth to assure the fruitfulness of God's fields.

---

28. Gregory, of course, was speaking Greek, but his text of Song 5:11a contains the Hebrew expression *kephaz,* which would have been incomprehensible to his hearers. See above n. 3.

29. This thought is a product of Gregory's imagination. Prov 30:17 in the Septuagint version, which is concerned with persons who fail properly to respect their parents, envisages their *eyes,* not themselves, being fed to "nestlings of eagles."

30. See above, homily 11, p. 325 (Jaeger).

ἀποστόλους δὲ οἶμαι τροπικῶς τοὺς βοστρύχους ὑπὸ τοῦ λόγου
σημαίνεσθαι, ὧν τινες ἦσαν πρότερον ζοφώδεις τοῖς τοῦ βίου ἐπιτηδεύμασιν·
ὁ τελώνης, ὁ λῃστής, ὁ διώκτης, καὶ εἴ τις ἄλλος τοιοῦτος κατὰ τὸν μέλανά
τε καὶ σαρκοβόρον, τὸν τῶν ὀφθαλμῶν ἀφανιστικὸν κόρακα, λέγω δὲ τὸν
5   ἄρχοντα τῆς ἐξουσίας τοῦ σκότους, καθώς φησιν ὁ ἀπὸ κόρακος ἐλάτη
γενόμενος καὶ διὰ τοῦτο βόστρυχος τῆς θείας κεφαλῆς χρηματίσας ὅτι Τὸ
πρότερον ὢν βλάσφημος καὶ διώκτης καὶ ὑβριστής, ἕως ἦν κόραξ, πρὸς
τὴν χάριν ταύτην μετεσκευάσθη βόστρυχος γενόμενος τῇ οὐρανίᾳ δρόσῳ
διάβροχος, ὁ παντὶ τῷ σώματι | τῆς ἐκκλησίας τὸν τῶν ἀποκρύφων τε καὶ   393
10   σκοτεινῶν μυστηρίων λόγον ἐπιψεκάζων.

τούτους μὲν οὖν λέγεσθαι παρὰ τῆς νύμφης βοστρύχους ὑπενοήσαμεν, οἳ
τῆς χρυσῆς κεφαλῆς ἀπηρτημένοι οὐ μικρὰν δι' ἑαυτῶν ποιοῦσι προσθήκην
τῆς ὥρας τῇ τοῦ πνεύματος αὔρᾳ περισοβούμενοι. οὗτοι στέφανος γίνονται
κάλλους τῇ ἀκηράτῳ κεφαλῇ κοσμοῦντες αὐτὴν τῷ ἰδίῳ κυκλώματι· περὶ
15   τούτων γάρ μοι δοκεῖ λέγειν ἡ προφητεία ὅτι Ἔθηκας ἐπὶ τὴν κεφαλὴν αὐτοῦ
στέφανον ἐκ λίθου τιμίου. ὥστε αὐτοὺς δι' ἑκατέρων νοεῖσθαι τῶν ὀνομάτων·
εὐπρεπεῖς τε βοστρύχους καὶ λίθους τιμίους δι' ἑαυτῶν τὴν κεφαλὴν
καλλωπίζοντας.

Ἀκόλουθον δ' ἂν εἴη καὶ τὰ περὶ τῶν ὀφθαλμῶν εἰρημένα θεωρῆσαι τῷ
20   λόγῳ. ἔστι δὲ ἡ λέξις αὕτη· Ὀφθαλμοὶ αὐτοῦ ὡς περιστεραὶ ἐπὶ πληρώματα
ὑδάτων, λελουμέναι ἐν γάλακτι, καθήμεναι ἐπὶ πληρώματα ὑδάτων. ἡ δὲ τῶν
εἰρημένων διάνοια τῆς μὲν καταλήψεως ἡμῶν ἐστιν ὑψηλοτέρα (ὃ γὰρ ἂν
ἐννοήσωμεν περὶ τούτων, ἔλαττον εἶναι τῆς ἀληθείας οἰόμεθα), σκοπουμένοις
δὲ δι' ἐπιμελείας ἡμῖν τοιαύτη τις ἔδοξεν εἶναι·

25   φησί που τῶν ἑαυτοῦ λόγων ὁ θεῖος ἀπόστολος μὴ δύνασθαι λέγειν
τὸν ὀφθαλμὸν τῇ χειρὶ Χρείαν σου οὐκ ἔχω, δόγμα διὰ τούτων ποιούμενος
ὅτι δι' ἀμφοτέρων προσήκει τὸ σῶμα τῆς ἐκκλησίας πράττειν | καλῶς τοῦ   394
διορατικοῦ τῆς ἀληθείας συγκεκραμένου πρὸς τὸ δραστήριον, οὔτε τῆς
θεωρίας καθ' ἑαυτὴν τὴν ψυχὴν τελειούσης, εἰ μὴ καὶ τὰ ἔργα παρείη, τὰ
30   τὸν ἠθικὸν κατορθοῦντα βίον, οὔτε τῆς πρακτικῆς φιλοσοφίας αὐτάρκη
παρεχομένης τὴν ὠφέλειαν μὴ τῆς ἀληθινῆς εὐσεβείας τῶν γινομένων
καθηγουμένης. εἰ τοίνυν ἀναγκαία τῶν ὀφθαλμῶν πρὸς τὰς χεῖρας ἐστιν ἡ
συζυγία, τάχα προσαγόμεθα διὰ τῶν εἰρημένων πρῶτον μὲν τοὺς ὀφθαλμούς,
οἵτινές εἰσι, κατανοῆσαι, ἔπειτα δὲ καὶ τὸν περὶ αὐτῶν ἔπαινον ἐν θεωρίᾳ
35   λαβεῖν. τὸν δὲ περὶ τῶν χειρῶν λόγον τῷ ἰδίῳ ταμιευσόμεθα τόπῳ.

My own opinion is that by *locks* here the Word refers figuratively to the apostles, some of whom in their earlier lives and habits were dark-hued: the tax-collector (cf. Matt 10:3), the robber, the persecutor (cf. 1 Tim 1:13), and any other with a likeness to the black, carnivorous, eye-destroying raven, that is, to the Ruler of the power of darkness, as he says who was indeed a raven but who became a fir tree and hence is styled a "drop" on the divine head. He who "formerly"—for as long as he was a raven—was "a blasphemer and persecutor and mocker" (1 Tim 1:13) was transformed into a recipient of the grace of being a lock of hair soaked with the heavenly dew, who rains upon the whole body | of the church the word of dark and hidden mysteries.

We conjecture, then, that by *locks* the Bride means these individuals[31] who hang down from the golden Head and in their own right contribute no little enhancement of his beauty as they are tossed about by the breeze of the Spirit. These become a crown upon the unspotted head and adorn it with their nimbus, for it is, I think, about them that the prophecy says, "You have set a crown of precious stone upon his head." Thus they are named in both ways: they are at once comely locks and precious stones that contribute to the beauty of the head.

But let us move on in order and give consideration to what is said about the Bridegroom's eyes. Here is the text: *His eyes are as doves by full pools of waters, washed in milk, sitting by full pools of waters.* The meaning of these sayings is loftier than our understanding (for we judge that what we will comprehend of them is something less than the truth), but to us as we examined the text the sense seemed to be something like the following.

The divine apostle observes somewhere in his letters that the eye cannot say to the hand, "I have no need of you" (1 Cor 12:21). In these words he formulates a basic teaching, that it is the business of the body which is the church to do well at two sorts of activity, | to combine discernment of the truth with action, for contemplation does not of itself bring the soul to perfection unless it makes room for works that further the practice of the moral life, any more than practical wisdom is profitable in its own right unless, in the face of events, true and reverent belief guide what comes to pass. If, then, this cooperation of eyes and hand is necessary, it may be that this text[32] is leading us, first of all, to a grasp of what *eyes* refers to and then to a discerning comprehension of the praise that is accorded them. As to what is said about hands, that we postpone to its proper occasion.

---

31. He means, presumably, the apostles.
32. Gregory means the words of the Song, not the words of Paul in 1 Corinthians.

ὀφθαλμῶν γὰρ ἴδιον ἐκ φύσεως ἔργον ἐστὶ τὸ ὁρᾶν. διὸ κατὰ τὴν
τοπικὴν θέσιν πάντων ὑπέρκεινται τῶν αἰσθητηρίων εἰς ὁδηγίαν τοῦ παντὸς
σώματος προτεταγμένοι παρὰ τῆς φύσεως. ὅταν οὖν τοὺς τῆς ἀληθείας
καθηγουμένους παρὰ τῆς θείας γραφῆς οὕτως ὀνομαζομένους ἀκούσωμεν,
5 ὧν ὁ μέν τις ἐλέγετο ὁ βλέπων, ἕτερος δὲ ὁ ὁρῶν, ἄλλος δὲ σκοπός, οὕτω
παρὰ τοῦ θεοῦ διὰ τῆς προφητείας ὠνομασμένος, ἐναγόμεθα διὰ τούτων
τοὺς ἐφορᾶν καὶ ἐπιβλέπειν καὶ ἐπισκοπεῖν τεταγμένους ὀφθαλμοὺς ἐνταῦθα
νομίζειν κατονομάζεσθαι. τὸ δὲ περὶ αὐτοὺς θαῦμα καθ' ὁμοιότητά τινα
συγκριτικὴν γίνεσθαι διδασκόμεθα τῆς πρὸς | τὸ κρεῖττον παραθέσεως τὸ 395
10 κάλλος αὐτῶν ὑπογραφούσης· φησὶ γὰρ ὅτι Ὀφθαλμοὶ αὐτοῦ ὡς περιστεραί.

καλὸς γὰρ ὡς ἀληθῶς τῶν τοιούτων ὀμμάτων ἔπαινος ἡ ἀκακία, ἣν
κατορθοῦσιν οἱ μηκέτι τῷ σαρκώδει βίῳ ἐμμολυνόμενοι ἀλλὰ ζῶντές τε
καὶ στοιχοῦντες τῷ πνεύματι· ὁ γὰρ πνευματικός τε καὶ ἄϋλος βίος τῷ τῆς
περιστερᾶς εἴδει χαρακτηρίζεται, ἐπειδὴ καὶ αὐτὸ τὸ πνεῦμα τὸ ἅγιον οὕτως
15 ὤφθη παρὰ τοῦ Ἰωάννου ἐκ τῶν οὐρανῶν ἐπὶ τὸ ὕδωρ ἱπτάμενον. οὐκοῦν
τὸν ἀντὶ ὀφθαλμοῦ τῷ σώματι τῆς ἐκκλησίας ὑπὸ τοῦ θεοῦ τεταγμένον,
εἰ μέλλοι καθαρῶς ἐπισκοπεῖν τε καὶ ἐφορᾶν καὶ ἐπιβλέπειν, πᾶσαν τὴν
ἐκ κακίας λήμην ἀποκλύζεσθαι προσήκει τῷ ὕδατι. ἔστι δὲ οὐχ ἓν ὕδωρ
ῥυπτικὸν τῶν ὀμμάτων, ἀλλὰ πολλὰ τῶν τοιούτων ὑδάτων εἶναί φησι τὰ
20 πληρώματα. ὅσαι γάρ εἰσιν ἀρεταί, τοσαύτας χρὴ τὰς τῶν καθαρσίων ὑδάτων
ἐννοῆσαι πηγάς, δι' ὧν οἱ ὀφθαλμοὶ γίνονται ἀεὶ ἑαυτῶν καθαρώτεροι·
οἷον πηγὴ τοῦ καθαρσίου ὕδατός ἐστιν ἡ σωφροσύνη, ἄλλη τοιαύτη πηγὴ
ἡ ταπεινοφροσύνη ἡ ἀλήθειά τε καὶ ἡ δικαιοσύνη καὶ ἡ ἀνδρεία καὶ ἡ τοῦ
ἀγαθοῦ ἐπιθυμία καὶ ἡ τοῦ κακοῦ ἀλλοτρίωσις. | ταῦτα καὶ τὰ τοιαῦτα ὕδατά 396
25 ἐστιν ἐκ μιᾶς μὲν πηγῆς, διαφόρων δὲ ῥείθρων εἰς ἓν ἀθροιζόμενα πλήρωμα,
δι' ὧν πάσης ἐμπαθοῦς λήμης γίνεται τοῖς ὀφθαλμοῖς τὰ καθάρσια.

ἀλλ' εἰσὶ μὲν ἐπὶ τὰ πληρώματα τῶν ὑδάτων οἱ ὀφθαλμοί, οἱ διὰ τῆς
ἀκεραιότητός τε καὶ ἀκακίας ταῖς περιστεραῖς ὡμοιωμένοι, λουτρὸν δὲ αὐτῶν
εἶναι τὸ γάλα φησὶν οὕτως εἰπόντος τοῦ λόγου ὅτι Λελουμέναι ἐν γάλακτι.
30 πρέπων δὲ τοῖς τοιούτοις ὄμμασιν ἔπαινος τὸ τῷ γάλακτι τὴν τοιαύτην
περιστερὰν λουομένην ἐνωραΐζεσθαι· ἀληθὴς γὰρ ἡ τοῦ γάλακτός ἐστι
παρατήρησις ὅτι μόνον τῶν ὑγρῶν τοῦτο τοιαύτην ἔχει τὴν ἰδιότητα τὸ μὴ
ἐμφαίνεσθαι αὐτῷ εἴδωλόν τινος καὶ ὁμοίωμα. πάντα γὰρ ὅσα τῆς ὑγρᾶς ἐστι
φύσεως καθ' ὁμοιότητα τῶν κατόπτρων διὰ τοῦ λείου τῆς ἐπιφανείας τῶν εἰς
35 αὐτὰ βλεπόντων ἀντιφαίνεσθαι παρασκευάζει τὰ ὁμοιώματα, ἐν μόνῳ δὲ τῷ
γάλακτι ἡ τοιαύτη εἰδωλοποιΐα χώραν οὐκ ἔχει. οὗ χάριν τοιοῦτος τῶν τῆς
ἐκκλησίας ὀφθαλμῶν ἐστιν ὁ τελεώτατος ἔπαινος τὸ μηδὲν ἀνυπόστατόν τε
καὶ πεπλανημένον καὶ μάταιον παρὰ τὴν τῶν ὄντων ἀλήθειαν σκιαγραφεῖν

Now the distinctive natural function of eyes is seeing.[33] Hence they are located above all the other organs of perception, positioned by nature to provide guidance for the whole body. Therefore when we hear the teachers of truth named in this way by the divine Scripture—one of whom is called "the looker" (1 Sam 9:9), another "the seer" (Amos 7:12), and yet another "watchman" (Ezek 3:17; 33:7) because God called him this in the prophetic writings—we are led to think that in the text before us it is those who are ordained to oversee, to inspect, and to supervise who are called "eyes." We are taught, however, that amazement at the eyes derives from a similarity and the comparison it suggests. Their beauty is portrayed | by a comparison with something nobler, for it says *His eyes are like doves.*

Truly the fairest commendation of such eyes as these is innocence, which those persons attain who are no longer polluted by the life of the flesh but live by, and walk in, the Spirit. What sets the spiritual and nonmaterial life apart, after all, is the form of the dove, since the Holy Spirit itself was seen by John in this form, flying down from heaven upon the water. Hence the person to whom God assigns the place of the eye in the church's body must wash away all the teary haze of vice with water, if he is to supervise, oversee, and inspect in purity. There is not, however, one single water that flushes the eyes clean. No, our text says that there are many *pools of* such *waters,* for we must conceive that there are as many wellsprings of purifying waters—by whose means the eyes are ever becoming clearer than themselves—as there are virtues. One such wellspring of purifying waters is temperance; others are humility, truth and justice, and courage, and desire for the good, and alienation from evil. | These and similar waters come from a single wellspring, and they are gathered together into one pool in different streams, and through them the eyes are cleansed of every haze of passion.

Well, then, the *eyes*—likened as they are to doves because of their integrity and innocence—are located *by full pools of waters,* but it says that what washes them is milk; for so the text says: *washed in milk.* Fitting is the praise accorded such eyes as these, praise proclaiming that such a dove is made beautiful by being washed in milk. For it is truly observed of milk that of all fluids it alone has the property that in it no image or likeness appears. Things that are naturally liquid, as we know, behave like mirrors in that, because of their smooth surfaces, they cause the likenesses of those who look into them to be reflected back; only milk has no such capacity for imaging. Hence the highest praise of the church's eyes is this: that they do not mistakenly image anything unreal and counterfeit and empty that is contrary to what truly is

---

33. With this whole passage, compare what Gregory says in homily 7, pp. 216–17 (Jaeger).

ἐν ἑαυτοῖς δι' ἀπάτης ἀλλὰ τὸ ὄντως ὂν βλέπειν, τὰς δὲ ἠπατημένας τοῦ
τῇδε βίου ὄψεις τε καὶ | φαντασίας μὴ παραδέχεσθαι. διὰ τοῦτο πρὸς τὴν   397
καθαρότητα τῶν ὀμμάτων ὑπὸ τῆς τελείας ψυχῆς τὸ τοῦ γάλακτος λουτρὸν
ἀσφαλὲς ἐκρίθη.

5   Ὁ δὲ ἐφεξῆς λόγος νόμος ἐστὶ τοῖς ἐπαΐουσι περὶ ἃ χρὴ τοὺς ὀφθαλμοὺς
τὴν σπουδὴν ἔχειν· Καθήμεναι γάρ, φησίν, ἐπὶ πληρώματα ὑδάτων.
τὴν γὰρ διηνεκῆ προσεδρείαν τῆς περὶ τὰ θεῖα μαθήματα προσοχῆς ὁ
τοιοῦτος ὑποτίθεται λόγος, δι' ὧν ἐπαινεῖ τοὺς καθαροὺς ὀφθαλμοὺς καὶ
ἡμᾶς διδάσκων, ὅπως ἂν τὸ ἴδιον κάλλος τῶν ὀφθαλμῶν ἀναλάβοιμεν
10   ἀεὶ προσκαθήμενοι τοῖς τῶν ὑδάτων πληρώμασιν, ὡς οἵ γε πολλοὶ τῶν
εἰς ὀφθαλμοὺς τεταγμένων καταλιπόντες τὸ τοῖς τοιούτοις πληρώμασι
προσεδρεύειν τοῖς Βαβυλωνίοις ποταμοῖς παρακάθηνται πληροῦντες
τὴν ἐκ προσώπου τοῦ θεοῦ γενομένην ἐπὶ τῶν τοιούτων κατηγορίαν
Ἐμὲ ἐγκατέλιπον, πηγὴν ὕδατος ζῶντος, καὶ ὤρυξαν ἑαυτοῖς λάκκους
15   συντετριμμένους, οἳ οὐ μὴ δύνωνται ὕδωρ συνέχειν.

μάθημα τοίνυν ἐστίν, ὅπως ἂν γένοιτο καλὸς ὀφθαλμός, ἐμπρέπων τε
καὶ ἐναρμόζων τῇ χρυσῇ κεφαλῇ, τὸ εἶναι αὐτὸν ἀκέραιον μὲν κατὰ τὴν
περιστερὰν, ἀπλανῆ τε καὶ ἀνεξαπάτητον κατὰ τὴν τοῦ γάλακτος φύσιν,
μηδεμιᾷ | πλάνῃ τῶν ἀνυποστάτων φαντασιούμενον, προσκαθῆσθαι δὲ   398
20   διὰ παραμονῆς καὶ προσεδρείας τοῖς πληρώμασι τῶν θείων ὑδάτων καθ'
ὁμοιότητα τοῦ ξύλου τοῦ παρὰ τὰς διεξόδους τῶν ὑδάτων πεφυτευμένου
καὶ μὴ μεθισταμένου· οὕτω γὰρ ὅ τε καρπὸς ἐπὶ τοῦ ἰδίου καιροῦ
προβληθήσεται καὶ ὁ κλάδος ἀειθαλὴς φυλαχθήσεται τῇ εὐχροίᾳ τῶν φύλλων
περισοβούμενος.

25   νυνὶ δὲ πολλοὶ τῶν ὀφθαλμῶν τῶν πνευματικῶν τούτων ὑδάτων
καταμελοῦντες καὶ τῆς τοῦ λόγου προσεδρείας μικρὰ φροντίζοντες ἤτοι τὸν
τῆς φιλοχρηματίας ἑαυτοῖς λάκκον ὀρύσσουσιν ἢ τὴν κενοδοξίαν λατομοῦσιν
ἢ τὴν ὑπερηφανίαν φρεωρυχοῦσιν ἢ ἄλλους τινὰς λάκκους ἀπάτης μετ'
ἐπιμελείας ὀρύσσουσιν, οἳ συνέχειν εἰς τὸ διηνεκὲς τὸ σπουδαζόμενον αὐτοῖς
30   ὕδωρ φύσιν οὐκ ἔχουσιν ἀεὶ τῆς ὧδε τιμῆς τε καὶ δυναστείας καὶ δόξης, περὶ
ἥν ἐστιν ἡ σπουδὴ τοῖς πολλοῖς, ὁμοῦ τῷ συστῆναι διαρρεούσης καὶ οὐδὲν
ἴχνος τῆς ματαίας σπουδῆς ἐν τοῖς ἠπατημένοις καταλειπούσης. τοιούτους
εἶναι βούλεται τοὺς ὁρῶντάς τε καὶ ἐπισκοποῦντας ὁ λόγος ὧν χρὴ
προβεβλῆσθαι μὲν οἷόν τινα ὀφρύων περιβολὴν τὴν τῶν θείων διδαγμάτων
35   ἀσφάλειαν, ἐπικαλύπτεσθαι δὲ τῇ ταπεινοφροσύνῃ καθάπερ τινὶ βλεφάρων
περιβολῇ τὸ καθαρόν τε καὶ στίλβον τῆς πολιτείας, μή ποτε ἡ τῆς οἰήσεως
δοκὸς ἐμπεσοῦσα τῷ καθαρῷ τῆς κόρης ἐμποδὼν γένηται πρὸς τὴν ὅρασιν.

but look upon what *is* in the full and proper sense of that word. They do not take in the deceitful sights and | fantasies of the present life. For this reason, the perfect soul judges that it is the bath in milk that most surely purifies the eyes.

The next phrase is, for those who hear and understand, a law that specifies what the eyes must diligently attend to, for it says: *sitting by full pools of waters*. This expression, as it praises the pure eyes, enjoins unremitting assiduity[34] in attending to the divine teachings. It teaches us how, in sitting by the pools of waters, we can restore the proper beauty of the eyes, seeing that the majority of those who are assigned the place of eyes[35] have given up watching beside such waters as these and have seated themselves by the rivers of Babylon, justifying the indictment God has brought against such persons: "They have deserted me, the wellspring of living waters, and they have dug themselves broken cisterns that cannot hold water" (Jer 2:13).

The lesson is, then, how the eye may become beautiful when suited and adapted to the golden Head: it will, on the one hand, be pure after the manner of the dove, inerrant and undeceived like milk, not | confusedly forming images of the unreal for itself; and, on the other, it will by persistence and assiduity, take its seat by the pools of divine waters—just like the tree that has been planted by the streams of waters and has not been moved (cf. Ps 1:3). For in this way it will bring forth its fruit in due season, and its shoot, decked out in the fine color of its leaves, will be kept ever blooming.

As it is, however, many eyes, neglecting these spiritual waters and despising engagement with the Word, either dig themselves the cistern of love for money, or quarry vain conceits, or sink the well of arrogance, or devote themselves to digging other unreliable cisterns, which cannot permanently contain the water so eagerly sought for them; for honor and power and reputation in this life, in which the majority invest themselves, run off as soon as they are achieved, and there is not a single trace left of their vain investment in goods that deceive. The Word wants the seers and watchers to be people who set the surety of the divine teachings before them like the brow of an encompassing wall but conceal by a humility like an enclosing eyelid the purity and radiance of their way of life, lest the beam of self-conceit, falling upon the pure pupil of the eye, become an obstacle to sight.

---

34. Προσεδρεία, the Greek word used here, means literally "the state of being seated close up to (something)," which echoes, as Gregory plainly recognizes, the language of the Song ("sitting by pools of water"). The English "assiduity," which has roughly the same etymological sense, renders it with near exactness.

35. I.e., persons who have been appointed to the principal teaching offices in the church, specifically bishops.

τίς δὲ μετὰ τοὺς ὀφθαλμοὺς | τῶν μελῶν τοῦ νυμφίου ἐστὶν ὁ ἔπαινος,   399
ἐν τοῖς ἐφεξῆς θεοῦ διδόντος ἐπελευσόμεθα χάριτι τοῦ κυρίου ἡμῶν Ἰησοῦ
Χριστοῦ,

ᾧ ἡ δόξα εἰς τοὺς αἰῶνας.
5   ἀμήν.

As to the praise ascribed | to those of the Bridegroom's members that come after the eyes, if God permits we will come to them in the next homily by the grace of our Lord Jesus Christ,

To whom be glory throughout all ages.
Amen.

Λόγος ιδ΄

Σιαγόνες αὐτοῦ ὡς φιάλαι τοῦ ἀρώματος φύουσαι μυρεψικά,
χείλη αὐτοῦ κρίνα στάζοντα σμύρναν πλήρη,
Χεῖρες αὐτοῦ τορευταὶ χρυσαῖ πεπληρωμέναι θαρσεῖς,
κοιλία αὐτοῦ πυξίον ἐλεφάντινον ἐπὶ λίθου σαπφείρου,
5   Κνῆμαι αὐτοῦ στῦλοι μαρμάρινοι
τεθεμελιωμένοι ἐπὶ βάσεις χρυσᾶς,
εἶδος αὐτοῦ ὡς Λίβανος ἐκλεκτός, ὡς κέδροι,
Φάρυγξ αὐτοῦ γλυκασμὸς καὶ ὅλος ἐπιθυμία.
 οὗτος ἀδελφιδός μου
10   καὶ οὗτος πλησίον μου, θυγατέρες Ἰερουσαλήμ.

Ὁ τῷ ἀδόλῳ γάλακτι τρέφων τὸ νηπιάζον ἔτι τῆς πνευματικῆς ἡλικίας,
τροφός, καθώς φησιν αὐτὸς ὁ ἀπόστολος, τῶν ἀρτιγενῶν ἐν τῇ ἐκκλησίᾳ
γινόμενος, ταμιεύεται τὸν τῆς σοφίας ἄρτον τοῖς τελειωθεῖσι κατὰ τὸν ἔσω
ἄνθρωπον εἰπών· Σοφίαν δὲ λαλοῦμεν ἐν τοῖς τελείοις, οἳ διὰ τὴν | τῶν   400
15   ἀγαθῶν διδαγμάτων ἕξιν γεγυμνασμένα ἔχοντες τὰ τῆς ψυχῆς αἰσθητήρια
τοῦ ἄρτου τῆς σοφίας εὐπαράδεκτοι γίνονται τῆς λεπτοποιούσης ἐν τοῖς
ὀδοῦσι τῶν λογισμῶν σιαγόνος εἰς τροφὴν προσδεόμενοι.
χρὴ τοίνυν εἶναι καὶ σιαγόνας ἐν τῷ σώματι τοῦ Χριστοῦ τοῖς μηκέτι
προσανέχουσι τῇ θηλῇ τοῦ λόγου ἀλλ᾽ ἤδη τῆς στερροτέρας ἐφιεμένοις
20   τροφῆς, περὶ ὧν νῦν ποιεῖται τὸν λόγον ἡ νύμφη λέγουσα οὕτως· Σιαγόνες
αὐτοῦ ὡς φιάλαι τοῦ ἀρώματος φύουσαι μυρεψικά.
τὸ μὲν οὖν ἀκολούθως ἔχειν τὸν περὶ τῶν σιαγόνων λόγον τοῖς περὶ
τῶν ὀφθαλμῶν θεωρηθεῖσι παντὶ δῆλον ἂν εἴη τῷ συνετῶς ἐπαΐοντι· διὰ
τοῦτο γὰρ χρὴ τὸν ὀφθαλμὸν τῷ πληρώματι τῶν πνευματικῶν ὑδάτων
25   προσεδρεύοντα τῷ ἀπλανεῖ τε καὶ ἀδόλῳ λούεσθαι γάλακτι τῇ ἀκάκῳ

HOMILY 14
Song 5:13–16

¹³*His jaws are like bowls of spice pouring forth perfumes.*
His lips are lilies, dropping abundant myrrh.
¹⁴*His hands are skillfully sculpted, golden, filled, tharseis.*
His belly is an ivory tablet on a sapphire stone.
¹⁵*His legs are marble pillars*
resting upon golden pedestals.
His look is like Lebanon the chosen, like cedars.
¹⁶*His throat is sweetness, and [he is] totally desire.*
This is my kinsman,
and this is my close one, O daughters of Jerusalem.

He who nourishes those who are still children in spiritual age with pure milk (cf. 1 Pet 2:2)—the wet nurse (cf. 1 Thess 2:7), as the apostle himself says, of newborns in the church—reserves the bread of wisdom for those who have been made mature in their inner selves,[1] saying, "But among those who are mature we speak wisdom" (1 Cor 2:6), those who | have become able to ingest the bread of wisdom because the perceptive faculties of their souls have been kept in training by possession of good teachings (cf. Heb 5:14) but who, for the sake of their nourishment, stand in further need of that jaw which, with the teeth of its thoughts, grinds such food small.[2]

So there must be jaws too in the body of Christ, for the benefit of those who are no longer attached to the breasts of the Word but are already longing for more solid food, and it is about these that the Bride is now speaking as she says: *His jaws are like bowls of spice pouring forth perfumes.*

Now anyone who lends it an understanding ear can see that this statement about the jaws fits in with what we have already seen regarding the eyes.[3] Why, after all, must the eye that sits by the pool of spiritual waters be washed in pure and inerrant milk and be likened to an innocent dove? It is in order

---

1. Greek: κατὰ τὸν ἔσω ἄνθρωπον. For this expression of Paul's, see Rom 7:22, where it seems to be roughly equivalent to "the mind" (cf. Rom 7:23); and Eph. 3:16.

2. The Greek word σιαγών can be rendered in English both as "jaw" (as Gregory seems to take it here) and as "cheek" (the sense it bears in Song 5:13). English has no word that conveys both of these senses indiscriminately. See above, homily 3, pp. 78–79 (Jaeger), and n. 10 there.

3. See above, pp. 395–98 (Jaeger). Gregory has opened this homily not with his normal rather elaborate introductory remarks but with an immediate turn to the text of Song 5:13. It looks as though he considers it a simple continuation of the previous homily, separate from it only because of considerations of time in delivery. See the closing words of homily 13.

περιστερᾷ ὁμοιούμενον, ἵνα κοινωνοὺς ποιήσῃ τῶν ἰδίων ἀγαθῶν πάντας τοὺς εἰς τὸ σῶμα συντελοῦντας τῆς ἐκκλησίας. οὗ χάριν καὶ ὁ μέγας Ἡσαΐας τὸν ἐπὶ τὸ ὄρος τὸ ὑψηλὸν ἀναβάντα διὰ τῆς πολιτείας βοᾶν διακελεύεται λαμπρᾷ τῇ φωνῇ, ὥστε γνῶναι δι' αὐτοῦ τοὺς ἀκούοντας τὸν μετὰ
5   ἰσχύος ἐρχόμενον κύριον καὶ τὸν ἐξουσιάζοντα τῶν ὄντων βραχίονα, τὸν ποιμαίνοντα τὸ ποίμνιον καὶ τοὺς ἄρνας συνάγοντα καὶ τὰς καλῶς διὰ τῶν ἀγαθῶν ἐλπίδων κυοφορού|σας παρακαλοῦντα, τὸν διειληφότα τὸν οὐρανὸν   401
σπιθαμῇ καὶ πᾶσαν τὴν γῆν δρακὶ περισφίγγοντα, καὶ ὅσα ἄλλα πρὸς τούτοις ἡ προφητεία φησὶ δεῖν παρὰ τοῦ τῆς ἀκρωρείας ἐπιβεβηκότος κηρύσσεσθαι.
10   εἰ τοίνυν ἐπὶ τούτῳ γίνεται τοῖς ὀφθαλμοῖς ἡ ἐκ τῶν ὑδάτων τε καὶ τοῦ γάλακτος δύναμις πρὸς τὴν τῆς ἀληθείας ἐπίγνωσιν, ἀκολούθως ἐπαινοῦνται μετ' ἐκείνους αἱ σιαγόνες, ὧν ἔργον ἐστὶ τὸ λεπτοποιεῖν τὴν τροφὴν δι' ἧς ἡ τοῦ σώματος συντηρεῖται φύσις καὶ δύναμις.
     Ἴδωμεν τοίνυν ἐν τίνι τῶν σιαγόνων ἔστιν ὁ ἔπαινος. αὐτῆς ἀκούσωμεν
15   τῆς νύμφης οἷα περὶ αὐτῶν διεξέρχεται· Σιαγόνες αὐτοῦ, φησίν, ὡς φίάλαι τοῦ ἀρώματος φύουσαι μυρεψικά.
     εἰ τὸ διηπλωμένον τῶν ἐκπωμάτων εἶδος ὁ λόγος σημαίνει τῷ τῆς φιάλης ὀνόματι, ἐν ᾧ κλέπτεται διὰ τῆς κατασκευῆς ἡ κοιλότης οὔτε ἄγαν βαθυνομένου τοῦ σχήματος οὔτε δι' εὐθείας ἐξυπτιάζοντος, ὡς μήτε κοῖλον
20   ἀκριβῶς εἶναι δοκεῖν μήτε ἐπίπεδον, εἰ τοίνυν τὸ τοιοῦτον εἶδος ὑποδείκνυσι διὰ τῆς φιάλης ἡ νύμφη, ἴδιον ἂν ἔχοι λόγον ἐκ τοῦ σχήματος τούτου τῶν σιαγόνων ὁ ἔπαινος. εἴποι γὰρ ἄν τις τὸ ἁπλοῦν τε καὶ διηπλωμένον καὶ ἄδολον τῆς διδασκαλίας ἐπαινέσαι τὸν λόγον βουλόμενον μνήμην τῆς φιάλης ποιήσασθαι, ἐν ᾗ τὸ ἀπηγορευμένον ὑπὸ τοῦ προφήτου | βάθος συστῆναι οὐ   402
25   δύναται τοῦ εἰπόντος· Ῥυσθείην ἐκ τῶν μισούντων με καὶ ἐκ τῶν βαθέων τῶν ὑδάτων. τὴν οὖν ἐν ἁπλότητι φανερουμένην ἀλήθειαν δίχα τινὸς δολερᾶς κοιλότητός φαμεν διὰ τοῦ ὀνόματος τῆς φιάλης σημαίνεσθαι, ἧς ὕλη μέν ἐστι τὸ ἄρωμα, ἔργον δὲ τὸ φύειν μυρεψικά· Σιαγόνες γὰρ αὐτοῦ ὡς φίάλαι τοῦ ἀρώματος, οὐκ ἐξ ἀργύρου γενόμεναι ἢ χρυσοῦ ἢ ὑέλου ἤ τινος ἑτέρας
30   ὕλης τοιαύτης, ἀλλ' αὐτοῦ τοῦ ἀρώματος, ταῦτα ἐξ ἑαυτῶν φύουσαι, δι' ὧν τὰ μύρα κατασκευάζεται.
     σαφὴς δὲ πάντως διὰ τῶν εἰρημένων ἐστὶν ἡ τοῖς ῥητοῖς τούτοις ἐνθεωρουμένη διάνοια ὅτι τῶν καθαρῶν τῆς ἐκκλησίας ὀμμάτων ἔστι τοιαύτην παρασκευάζειν τῷ σώματι τὴν τροφὴν τῇ λεαντικῇ τῶν σιαγόνων
35   δυνάμει ὡς μηδὲν βαθύ τε καὶ ὕπουλον ἐν τοῖς λεγομένοις ὁρᾶσθαι, ἀλλ' εἶναι πάντα τηλαυγῆ τε καὶ ἐλεύθερα καὶ πάσης δολερᾶς ἐπικρύψεως καὶ

that it may make all those who constitute the body of the church participants in its own good things. For this same reason the great Isaiah commands the person who because of his way of life has gone up to the "high mountain" to cry out in a clear voice, and the aim of this is that those who hear because of him may know the Lord who is coming "with might" and the right arm that exercises authority over what is—the Lord who shepherds the flock, who gathers the lambs, who comforts those that are | with young because of their high hopes, who holds "the heaven in a span" (cf. Isa 40:9–12), and all the other things that the prophecy says are to be proclaimed by one who has gained the height of the mountain. If, then, a power that stems from both the waters and the milk is given to the eyes for the sake of the knowledge of truth, it is appropriate for the jaws to be praised along with them, for their job is to grind small the food by which the body's nature and power are preserved.

Let us see, then, in what the praise of the jaws consists. Let us listen to the Bride and hear what sorts of things she tells about them. *His jaws,* says she, *are like bowls of spices pouring forth perfumes.*

Now assume that by the word "bowl" the scriptural word denotes the opened-out shape of drinking cups. The hollow form of such cups is obscured because of the way they are made, for they are neither markedly deep nor do they stand straight up; and the consequence is that they seem to be neither quite hollow nor quite flat. So if this is the sort of thing the Bride means by "bowl," the praise given the jaws will doubtless assume a particular character from the shape attributed to them. For one might say that the text makes mention of "bowl" with the intent of praising the simplicity and openness[4] and guilelessness of the teaching, in which there cannot exist the sort of | "depth" that the prophet forbids when he says, "Save me from those who hate me, and from the abyss of the waters" (Ps 68:15). We say, then, that the term "bowl" signifies the truth manifesting itself in simplicity, apart from any fraudulent hollowness, and that the material it is made of is spice, while its function is to pour forth perfumes. For *his jaws are like bowls of spice*—not made of gold or silver or glass or some other such material but of spice itself—*pouring forth* from themselves that by which *perfumes* are made.

Now the sense we see in these words is plain from what we have said, namely, that it belongs to the church's pure eyes, by the agency of the jaws with their ability to soften what they chew, to provide the body with food of such a sort that in what is said there is nothing deep-buried or deceptive to be discerned but everything is lucid and open and free from any buried

---

4. The words "simplicity" (τὸ ἁπλοῦν) and "openness" (τὸ διηπλωμένον) share the same root in Greek, and this helps Gregory to slither from the "opened-out" (διηπλωμένον) shape of a drinking cup to the "simplicity" of the teaching.

βαθύτητος κεχωρισμένα, ὡς καὶ νηπίοις εἶναι κατάδηλα, καθώς φησιν ὁ
προφήτης ὅτι Ἡ μαρτυρία κυρίου πιστή, σοφίζουσα νήπια· καὶ Ἡ ἐντολὴ
κυρίου τηλαυγής, φωτίζουσα ὀφθαλμούς. εἰ γὰρ τοιαῦται εἶεν αἱ φιάλαι τοῦ
λόγου, οὐκ ἐκ τῆς γηΐνης ὕλης δηλονότι συστήσονται, ἀλλ᾽ ἐκ τοῦ ἀρώματος
5   αὐτοῖς ἔσται ἡ φύσις, ἐκείνου λέγω τοῦ ἀρώματος ὃ ὑπὲρ πάντα τὰ ἀρώματά
φησιν εἶναι ἡ νύμφη ἐν τοῖς προοιμίοις τοῦ Ἄισματος.
    τοιαύτη φιάλη ὁ Παῦλος ἦν, ὁ μὴ ἐν πανουργίᾳ τὸν λόγον | δολῶν ἀλλὰ   403
τῇ φανερώσει τῆς ἀληθείας ἑαυτὸν συνιστάνων. οὐ ἡ ὕλη τὸ ἐκ γῆς εἶναι
ἀπέθετο, ἀφ᾽ οὗ διὰ τοῦ βαπτισμοῦ τὰς λεπίδας τῶν ὀφθαλμῶν τῇ σαρκὶ
10   συναπέβαλεν, ἀλλ᾽ ἐκ τοῦ εὐπνοοῦντος ἀρώματος ἀνεσκευάσθη τοῦ ἁγίου
πνεύματος τέκνον γενόμενος· ὃς ἐπειδὴ διὰ τῆς τοιαύτης χαλκείας ἐκλογῆς
σκεῦος κατεσκευάσθη, πρὸς τὴν οἰνοχοΐαν τοῦ λόγου φιάλη γενόμενος
οὐκέτι χρείαν ἔσχεν ἀνθρώπου τὴν γνῶσιν αὐτῷ τῶν μυστηρίων ἐγχέοντος
(Οὐ γὰρ προσανέθετο σαρκὶ καὶ αἵματι), ἀλλ᾽ αὐτὸς ἔφυεν ἐν ἑαυτῷ καὶ
15   ἀνέβρυε τὸ θεῖον ποτὸν διὰ τῆς τοῦ Χριστοῦ εὐωδίας τὰ ποικίλα τῶν ἀρετῶν
ἄνθη μυρεψῶν τοῖς ἀκούουσιν, ὥστε κατὰ τὰς διαφοράς τε καὶ ἰδιότητας
τῶν δεχομένων τὸν λόγον κατάλληλον εὑρίσκεσθαι πρὸς τὴν τοῦ ζητοῦντος
χρείαν τὸ ἄρωμα τοῖς Ἰουδαίοις, τοῖς Ἕλλησι, ταῖς γυναιξί, τοῖς ἀνδράσι,
τοῖς δεσπόταις, τοῖς δούλοις, τοῖς γονεῦσι, τοῖς τέκνοις, τοῖς ἀνόμοις, τοῖς
20   ὑπὸ νόμον. οὕτως αὐτῷ πολυειδὴς ἦν διὰ πάσης ἀρετῆς κεκραμένη τῆς
διδασκαλίας ἡ χάρις, διὰ τῶν ποικίλων διδαγμάτων καταλλήλως τῇ ἑκάστου
χρείᾳ μυρεψούσης τῆς φιάλης τοῖς δεχομένοις τὸν λόγον. τὰς οὖν τοιαύτας
ἐπαινεῖ σιαγόνας ἡ τὸ τοῦ σώματος τοῦ νυμφίου κάλλος διαζωγραφοῦσα τῷ
λόγῳ.
25   Καὶ ὅτι πρὸς τοῦτο βλέπει τῶν σιαγόνων ὁ ἔπαινος, ὁ ἐφεξῆς λόγος διὰ
τῆς ἀκολουθίας μαρτύρεται· ἐπαινεῖται γὰρ μετὰ τὰς σιαγόνας τὰ χείλη δι᾽ ὧν
ὁ ἀρωματίζων | λόγος προέρχεται. οὕτω δὲ ὁ ἔπαινος ἔχει· Χείλη αὐτοῦ κρίνα   404
στάζοντα σμύρναν πλήρη.
        δύο κατὰ ταὐτὸν ἀρετὰς μαρτυρεῖ τῷ λόγῳ διὰ τοῦ διπλοῦ ὑποδείγματος,
30   ὧν ἓν μέν ἐστιν ἡ ἀλήθεια λαμπρά τε καὶ φωτοειδὴς ἐν τοῖς λεγομένοις
θεωρουμένη (τοιοῦτον γὰρ τοῦ κρίνου τὸ εἶδος, οὗ ἡ λαμπρότης αἴνιγμα
τῆς τῶν λεγομένων καθαρότητός τε καὶ ἀληθείας ἐστίν), ἕτερον δὲ τὸ μόνην

and deceitful depths, and thus plain even to babes, as the prophet says: "The testimony of the Lord is trustworthy, giving wisdom to babes"; and "The commandment of the Lord is bright, giving light to the eyes." For if the bowls of the word[5] are like this, then they do not consist of earthly materials, but their nature is made of spice—that spice, I mean, which the Bride in the proem of the Song of Songs says is *better than all spices.*[6]

Paul was such a bowl as this. He did not tamper with the word | by cunning but commended himself by "the open statement of the truth" (2 Cor 4:2). The material of which he was made put off its earthly character from the time when, in baptism, he cast off the scales on his eyes together with the flesh. He was reconstituted of fragrant[7] spice by becoming a child of the Holy Spirit. After he had been constituted a "vessel of election" (cf. Acts 9:15) through this fashioning and had become a bowl for pouring out the wine of the word, he no longer had need of a human being to infuse into him a knowledge of the mysteries (for he did not "confer with flesh and blood" [Gal 1:16]). Instead, he himself brought the divine drink forth within himself and through the "sweet savor of Christ" (2 Cor 2:15) poured it out, like a perfumer blending for his hearers the varied blossoms of the virtues. Thus the message was found to be a spice suited to the need of the one who sought it, in accord with the different characters and peculiarities of its recipients: for Jews, Greeks, women, men, masters, slaves, parents, children, those without the law, those under the law. He had, then, a gift of teaching that was multiform, mixed with every virtue; for this bowl blended the word for its recipients out of a variety of teachings in a way calculated to profit each individual. So it is jaws of this sort that are praised by her who pictures in words the beauty of the Bridegroom's body.

And the next statement, by the way it fits in logically, confirms that this is the intent of the praise accorded the jaws. For what is praised after the jaws have been mentioned are the lips, through which the sweet-scented | message is brought forth. The praise goes like this: *His lips are lilies, dropping choice myrrh.*

By this two-membered description, two excellences at once are acknowledged to characterize the message. The first of these is the radiant and luminous truth that is discerned in what the lips say (for such is the appearance of the lily, whose radiance is an enigma standing for the purity and truth of what is

---

5. Or, as Dünzl 1994b, 3:718 n. 14, rightly argues, "the bowl of the [word of] teaching" (i.e., as given by the church's "eyes"). In the following paragraphs of this passage I have sometimes rendered *logos* by "word" and sometimes by "message."

6. Song 1:3; cf. homily 1, pp. 35–36 (Jaeger).

7. Greek εὐπνοοῦντος, literally, "free-breathing." "Holy Spirit" in the next phrase picks up the sense and echoes the sound of this participle.

τὴν νοητήν τε καὶ ἄϋλον ζωὴν ὑπὸ τῆς διδασκαλίας προδείκνυσθαι, διὰ
τῆς τῶν νοητῶν θεωρίας ἀπονεκρουμένης τῆς κάτω ζωῆς τῆς διὰ σαρκός
τε καὶ αἵματος ἐνεργουμένης. ἡ γὰρ ἀπορρέουσα τοῦ στόματος σμύρνα
καὶ πλήρη ποιοῦσα ἑαυτῆς τὴν τοῦ δεχομένου ψυχὴν τῆς τοῦ σώματος

5   νεκρώσεως ἔμφασις γίνεται· πολλαχῇ γὰρ τὸ τοιοῦτον ἐν τῇ καταχρήσει τῶν
θεοπνεύστων λόγων παρατετήρηται τὸ τοῦ θανάτου σημαντικὸν εἶναι τῆς
σμύρνης τὸ ὄνομα. ὁ τοίνυν τέλειος καὶ καθαρὸς ὀφθαλμός, ὁ τὴν σιαγόνα
φιάλην ποιῶν τὴν τὰ μύρα ἐξ ἑαυτῆς φύουσάν τε καὶ πηγάζουσαν οὗτος
ἀνθεῖ τὰ κρίνα τῶν λόγων διὰ τοῦ στόματος τῶν τῇ θείᾳ κεκαλλωπισμένων

10   λαμπρότητι· οὕτω γὰρ τοὺς καθαρούς τε καὶ δι' ἀρετῆς εὐπνοοῦντας ὀνομάζει
ὁ λόγος, ἀφ' ὧν γίνεται ἡ τῆς σμύρνης σταγὼν ἀνελλιπῶς πληροῦσα τὴν τῶν
δεχομένων διάνοιαν, ὅπερ ἐστὶν ἡ τῆς ὑλικῆς ζωῆς ὑπεροψία πάντων τῶν τῇδε
σπουδαζομένων διὰ τὴν τῶν ὑπερκειμένων ἀγαθῶν ἐπιθυμίαν ἀνενεργήτων
τε καὶ νεκρῶν γινομένων.

15 | τοιαύτην ὁ Παῦλός ποτε σμύρναν προέχει τοῦ στόματος μεμιγμένην τῷ   405
καθαρῷ κρίνῳ τῆς σωφροσύνης ἐν ἀκοαῖς τῆς ἁγίας παρθένου (Θέκλα δὲ
ἦν ἡ παρθένος), ἢ καλῶς τῇ ψυχῇ τὰς ἀπορρεούσας τοῦ κρίνου σταγόνας
ἐν ἑαυτῇ δεξαμένη θανάτῳ διαλαμβάνει τὸν ἔξωθεν ἄνθρωπον πᾶσαν
σαρκώδη διάνοιάν τε καὶ ἐπιθυμίαν ἑαυτῆς ἀποσβέσασα. ἧς μετὰ τὴν ἀγαθὴν

20   διδασκαλίαν νεκρὰ μὲν ἦν ἡ νεότης, νεκρὸν δὲ τὸ ἐπιφαινόμενον κάλλος,
νεκρὰ δὲ πάντα τὰ σωματικὰ αἰσθητήρια μόνου ζῶντος ἐν αὐτῇ τοῦ λόγου, δι'
οὗ τεθνήκει μὲν αὐτῇ ἅπας ὁ κόσμος, τεθνήκει δὲ καὶ ἡ παρθένος τῷ κόσμῳ.

said). The other is the fact that the intelligible and nonmaterial life alone is the subject of the teaching, since the life below, which is carried on by flesh and blood, is done to death by the contemplation of intelligible reality.[8] For the myrrh that flows from the mouth and fills the receptive soul is an image for the mortification of the body, since it is often observed that in the improper usage of the inspired text the term "myrrh" signifies death.[9] Therefore the pure and perfect eye, which makes of the jaw a bowl that pours and gushes perfumes out of itself, this eye blossoms with lilies in the form of words that proceed from the mouth of those who have been beautified by the divine radiance; for so does the text identify those who are pure and who breathe out the perfume of virtue, from whom there is unendingly distilled the drop of myrrh that fills the mind of its recipients—that is to say, disdain for the material life, which appears when everything that people work for in this life becomes inoperative and dead on account of their desire for transcendent goods.

| Now Paul pours just such myrrh as this, mingled with the pure lily of temperance, into the ears of the holy virgin named Thecla.[10] With her soul she received within herself the drops that poured out from the lily, and she treated her outward self[11] to death by quenching her every fleshly thought and desire. Once she had received the good teaching, her youthful folly was dead, as was her outward show of beauty, and dead were all her corporeal senses. All that was alive in her was the word,[12] through which the whole cosmos died to her even as she, the virgin, died to the cosmos (cf. Gal 6:14).

---

8. For the sense of this expression in Gregory, see Daniélou 1970, 15.

9. The use of "myrrh" to signify death (a commonplace with Gregory; see above, homily 6, p. 189 [Jaeger]) is here described, in the technical language of Greek rhetoric, as a case of catachresis (κατάχρησις), a linguistic "impropriety" created by the substitution of one word for another word that has a different reference.

10. Thecla, to whom a famous martyrium near Seleucia was dedicated in Gregory's day, is known to us only from the *Acts of Paul and Thecla*, a second-century Christian romance that relates Paul's conversion of a young woman named Thecla and her subsequent martyrdom. The account is almost certainly legendary, but the *Acts* circulated widely in the ancient church, and Thecla was celebrated as an archetypical virgin and martyr (and was remembered as such in the eucharistic canon of the Roman Church). For the narrative, see Hennecke and Schneemelcher 1963–65, 2:353–64. See further Gregory's *Vit. Macr.* (GNO 8.1:372), with its account of the vision afforded Gregory's mother before the birth of her eldest daughter, a vision in which Macrina is addressed with the name "Thecla."

11. See above, n. 1, on Paul's "inner self." Gregory deduces from the apostle's language the existence of a corresponding ἔξωθεν ἄνθρωπος, a phrase that, strictly interpreted, means not "outward self" but "self that derives from without." For a possible clue to his meaning, see *Opif. hom.* 16 (PG 44:181B–C).

12. "Word" here might refer to the divine Logos (the Bridegroom). In this context, however, it seems more likely that it is an allusion to the "myrrh" that Paul speaks into the virginal

οὕτω ποτὲ παρὰ Κορνηλίῳ καὶ ὁ μέγας Πέτρος τὰ λαμπρὰ τοῦ λόγου κρίνα φθεγγόμενος πλήρεις τῆς σμύρνης τὰς τῶν ἀκουόντων ψυχὰς παρεσκεύασεν, οἳ παραχρῆμα τὸν λόγον δεξάμενοι τῷ Χριστῷ διὰ τοῦ βαπτίσματος συνετάφησαν νεκροὶ τῷ βίῳ γενόμενοι. καὶ μυρία πρὸς τούτοις
5   ἔστιν τῶν ἁγίων εὑρεῖν ὑποδείγματα, πῶς τοῦ κοινοῦ σώματος τῆς ἐκκλησίας στόμα γενόμενοι τῆς νεκρωτικῆς τῶν παθημάτων σμύρνης πλήρεις τοὺς ἀκροωμένους ἐποίουν ἀνθοφοροῦντες διὰ τῶν κρίνων τοῦ λόγου, δι' ὧν οἱ μεγάλοι τῆς πίστεως πρόμαχοι διὰ τῆς ἀγαθῆς ὁμολογίας κατὰ τὸν τῆς μαρτυρίας καιρὸν ἐν τοῖς ὑπὲρ | εὐσεβείας ἀγῶσι κατεσμυρνώθησαν. καὶ   406
10 τί χρὴ διὰ πλειόνων μηκύνειν τὸν περὶ τούτων λόγον φανερᾶς διὰ τῶν εἰρημένων γενομένης ἡμῖν τῆς διανοίας, πῶς τὸ στόμα τῆς ἐκκλησίας κρίνον γίνεται καὶ πῶς ἀποστάζει τοῦ κρίνου ἡ σμύρνα καὶ πῶς πληροῦται τῆς τοιαύτης σταγόνος ἡ τῶν δεχομένων ψυχή.
    Ἀλλὰ πρὸς τὸν ἐφεξῆς ἤδη λόγον μετέλθωμεν. φησὶ γάρ· Χεῖρες αὐτοῦ
15 τορευταί, χρυσαῖ, πεπληρωμέναι θαρσεῖς. ὅτι μὲν οὖν ἀτελής ἐστιν ἐπὶ τοῦ σώματος τῆς ἐκκλησίας ἡ τοῦ ὀφθαλμοῦ χάρις τῆς τῶν χειρῶν ὑπουργίας διεζευγμένη, σαφῶς παρὰ τοῦ μεγάλου μεμαθήκαμεν Παύλου ὅς φησιν ὅτι Οὐ δύναται ὁ ὀφθαλμὸς εἰπεῖν τῇ χειρί· χρείαν σου οὐκ ἔχω. τότε γὰρ μάλιστα ἡ τῶν ὀφθαλμῶν ἐνέργεια δείκνυται, ὅταν τὰ ἔργα μαρτυρῇ τὴν ὀξυωπίαν τῷ
20 ὄμματι διὰ τῆς περὶ τὰ καλὰ σπουδῆς τὴν ἀγαθὴν ὁδηγίαν ἐπισημαίνοντα. ἐπεὶ δὲ χρὴ προθέντας τὸν περὶ τῶν χειρῶν τοῦ θείου σώματος ἔπαινον ὁδηγηθῆναι διὰ τῶν εἰρημένων, ὅπως προσήκει κατηρτίσθαι τοὺς ἀντὶ χειρῶν ὄντας ἐπὶ τῆς ἐκκλησίας, αὐτὸ προθέντες τὸ θεῖον λόγιον, ὅπως ἂν οἷόν τε ᾖ, τὴν ἐγκειμένην αὐτῷ θεωρῆσαι διάνοιαν διδόντος θεοῦ πειρασόμεθα.
25   Χεῖρες αὐτοῦ, φησί, τορευταί, χρυσαῖ. τέως μὲν οὖν τοσοῦτον πρόδηλόν ἐστιν ἐκ τῶν εἰρημένων τὸ νόημα, ὅτι οἷς τὸ τῆς κεφαλῆς εἶδος ἐγκωμιάζεται διὰ τῶν αὐτῶν | καὶ ταῖς χερσὶ πληροῦται ὁ ἔπαινος. κεφαλὴν δὲ τὸν κατὰ   407
    σάρκα Χριστὸν ἐνοήσαμεν, ἐν ᾧ ὁ θεὸς ἦν τὸν κόσμον ἑαυτῷ καταλλάσσων κατὰ τὴν τοῦ Παύλου φωνήν, ὁ ἐν τῇ σαρκὶ διὰ τῶν δυνάμεών τε καὶ τῶν
30 θαυμάτων ἑαυτὸν φανερώσας. εἰ οὖν ἡ νοηθεῖσα ἡμῖν αὕτη κεφαλὴ χρυσίον ἀκήρατον παρὰ τοῦ λόγου κατωνομάσθη διὰ τὸ πάσης ἁμαρτίας ἐκτὸς εἶναι (Ὃς ἁμαρτίαν γάρ, φησίν, οὐκ ἐποίησεν οὐδὲ εὑρέθη δόλος ἐν τῷ στόματι αὐτοῦ), χρυσᾶς δὲ εἶναί φησι καὶ τὰς χεῖρας ὁ λόγος, πρόδηλόν ἐστι τὸ διὰ

In the same way did the great Peter give utterance once before Cornelius to the radiant lilies of the message and filled the souls of his auditors with myrrh; and they, as soon as they had received the word, were buried together with Christ by baptism, becoming dead to ordinary life. And one can find thousands of additional examples of saints who, blossoming out with the lilies of the word, became a mouth for the common body of the church and filled their hearers with the myrrh that does the passions to death. By their agency the great champions of the faith were imbued with myrrh through the good confession at the time of their martyrdom in the | contest for true religion. But there is no need to spin out our discourse about these matters. The meaning has become plain through what has already been said: how the church's mouth becomes a lily, and myrrh drips from the lily, and the soul of its recipients is filled with these drops.

But let us go on to the next line. It says: *His hands are skillfully sculpted, golden, filled, tharseis.* From the great Paul we have learned that in the body which is the church the gift of the eye falls short of its purpose when it is not associated with the service of the hands, for he states, "The eye cannot say to the hand, 'I have no need of you'" (1 Cor 12:21). The function of the eyes is shown to the greatest advantage when deeds bear witness to the acuteness of their vision, deeds that, by the zeal they exhibit for what is excellent, give evidence of being soundly guided. But since any who set forth the praise of the divine body's hands must be guided by what has been said about how those who have the role of hands in the church ought to be equipped, let us set out the divine oracle itself and attempt with God's help to discern, as far as we are able, the meaning that lies hidden within it.

His hands, it says, *are skillfully sculpted, golden.* From this language one truth is perfectly evident to start with: that the praise accorded | the hands is conveyed in the same terms in which the appearance of the head is celebrated.[13] But we have seen that the head is Christ incarnate, in whom "God was ... reconciling the cosmos to himself," as Paul says (2 Cor 5:19), manifesting himself in the flesh by acts of power and wonders. If, then, this very head, understood by us at the level of intelligible reality, has been called untarnished gold by the text of the Song on account of its exclusion of all sin (for it is said, "who did no sin, neither was guile found in his mouth" [1 Pet 2:22]), and the text further says that his hands are golden, the conclusion is obvious that the

---

ear of Thecla, the word that commends the death (mortification) of the "outer self" and corresponds to the "cross" by which Paul himself had died "to the cosmos." The words of Gal 6:14 seem to lie in the background of this statement and to govern its sense.

13. See Song 5:11 and above, homily 13, pp. 390–91 (Jaeger).

τούτων νοούμενον ὅτι τὸ καθόλου καθαρόν τε καὶ ἀναμάρτητον καὶ πάσης κακίας ἀμιγές τε καὶ ἀπαράδεκτον νομοθετεῖ τῇ χειρὶ ὁ λόγος.

χεῖρα δὲ νοοῦμεν πάντως τὴν τὰ κοινὰ τῆς ἐκκλησίας εἰς τὰς τῶν ἐντολῶν χρείας διαχειρίζουσαν, ἧς ἔπαινός ἐστι τὸ ὁμοιωθῆναι τῇ τῆς
5   κεφαλῆς φύσει κατὰ τὸ καθαρόν τε καὶ ἀναμάρτητον. καθαρὰ δὲ γίνεται τότε ἡ χείρ, ὅταν διὰ τῆς τορείας ἅπαν ἀποξύσηται τὸ ἐμποδίζον τῷ κάλλει· καθάπερ γὰρ οἱ πρός τινα ζῴου μορφὴν ἀποτυποῦντες τὸ μάρμαρον ἐκεῖνα διὰ τῆς τορείας ἐγλύφουσι τοῦ λίθου | καὶ ἐκκολάπτουσιν ὧν   408 περιαιρεθέντων πρὸς τὸ ἀρχέτυπον εἶδος ἀποτυποῦται τὸ μίμημα, οὕτω καὶ
10   ἐπὶ τοῦ κάλλους τῶν τοῦ σώματος τῆς ἐκκλησίας χειρῶν πολλὰ χρὴ διὰ τῆς τῶν λογισμῶν τορείας ἀποξυσθῆναι, ἵνα γένηται ἡ χεὶρ χρυσῆ ὡς ἀληθῶς καὶ ἀκήρατος. πάντως δὲ πρόδηλα πᾶσίν ἐστιν, ὅσα μὴ περιαιρεθέντα τῆς χειρὸς τῷ κάλλει λυμαίνεται, οἷον τὸ ἀνθρωπάρεσκον, τὸ φιλοκερδές, τὸ φιλόδοξον, τὸ μόνον πρὸς τὸ φαινόμενον βλέπειν, τὸ περιφανείας τινὰς ἑαυτῷ διὰ τῶν
15   ἐν χερσὶ πραγματεύεσθαι, τὸ εἰς τρυφὴν καὶ ἀπόλαυσιν ἰδίαν τῇ τῶν ἐντολῶν ἀποκεχρῆσθαι παρασκευῇ· ἃ χρὴ πάντα ταῦτα καὶ τὰ τοιαῦτα τοῖς τῶν λογισμῶν ὀργάνοις περιξυσάμενον ἐκεῖνο καταλιπεῖν μόνον τὸ καθαρόν τε καὶ ἀκιβδήλευτον χρυσίον τῆς προαιρέσεως τὸ τῇ ἀκηράτῳ κεφαλῇ ὁμοιούμενον.

20   σαφέστερον δ' ἂν γένοιτο ἡμῖν τὸ λεγόμενον διὰ τῆς τοῦ ἀποστόλου φωνῆς, ὃς πιστὸν τὸν θεὸν ὀνομάσας οὐδὲν ἄλλο καὶ ἐν τοῖς οἰκονόμοις ζητεῖν ἀξιοῖ ἢ τὸ πιστὸν εὑρεθῆναι, οὑτωσὶ γράψας τῷ ῥήματι· Ὧδε λοιπὸν ζητεῖται ἐν τοῖς οἰκονόμοις, ἵνα πιστός τις εὑρεθῇ. οὐκοῦν ὁ πιστὸς καὶ φρόνιμος οἰκονόμος ἀντὶ χειρὸς ὢν τῇ ἐκκλησίᾳ χρυσῆν καθ' ὁμοιότητα τῆς
25   κεφαλῆς δείκνυσι τὴν χεῖρα τοῦ σώματος τὸν σοφὸν ἑαυτοῦ δεσπότην διὰ τοῦ βίου μιμούμενος. οὐκ ἦν τοιαύτη χεὶρ ἐν τῷ τῶν ἀποστόλων σώματι ὁ Ἰούδας ἐκεῖνος ὁ ἐλεεινός τε καὶ δείλαιος, μᾶλλον δὲ ὁ στυγητός τε καὶ ἀποτρόπαιος, ὃς οἰκονομίαν | πτωχῶν πεπιστευμένος τὸν τῆς φιλοχρηματίας λίθον οὐκ   409 ἀπεξύσατο, ἀλλὰ φύλαξ ὢν τοῦ γλωσσοκόμου διὰ τοὺς κλέπτοντας αὐτὸς
30   ἑαυτοῦ κλέπτης ἐγένετο, ὃ ἐν ταῖς ἑαυτοῦ χερσὶν εἶχε διὰ τῶν ἰδίων χειρῶν ὑφαιρούμενος καὶ οὐ πρὸς τὴν ἐντολὴν ἀλλὰ πρὸς τὰ χρήματα βλέπων. ὧν ἡ ἀπόλαυσις ἐγένετο τίς; ἀγχόνη ἑκούσιος, ζωῆς ἀλλοτρίωσις, πανωλεθρία

text lays it down as a law for the hand that it be entirely pure and without sin, untouched by evil and unreceptive of it.

By "hand" here we understand the one who administers the common goods of the church in the service of the commandments and whose commendation it is to be likened to the character of the head in respect of purity and sinlessness. The hand becomes pure when everything that obscures its beauty is scraped off by its being *sculpted*. For just as those who inscribe the form of some living being into marble dig out | and remove from the stone, by a process of sculpting, those bits by whose removal the image is conformed to the appearance of its original, so too, where it is a question of the beauty of the hands that belong to the body of the church, there is a great deal that must be scraped off by the sculpting work of thoughts, so that the hand may become truly golden and untarnished. For anyone can see how many things there are that ruin the beauty of the hand if they are not removed: trying to please people, for example, or greed, or ambition, or caring only for what appears, or contriving status and reputation for oneself by means of the goods entrusted to one's hands, or misusing what has been provided to serve the commandments for one's own pleasure and enjoyment. All these dispositions, and any others that may be like them, are to be scraped away by the tools of one's thoughts until the only thing left is that pure and genuine gold, the gold that is proper to free choice, the gold that is conformed to the likeness of the untarnished Head.

This might be further clarified by the saying of the apostle, who after he has called God "trustworthy" sees fit to look for nothing else "in stewards" than that they be found trustworthy—and so he writes, in as many words, "Moreover it is required in stewards that a person be found trustworthy" (1 Cor 1:9). Therefore the trustworthy and wise steward, who in the church plays the role of a hand, shows the body's hand to be golden after the likeness of its head by imitating his wise master in the mode of his life. No such hand as this was Judas in the body of the apostles: Judas the pitiable and wretched, or better, the hateful and ill-omened. Entrusted with the care[14] | of the poor, he did not scrape down the stone of money-loving. He was the guardian of the chest against thieves but himself stole from himself and with his very own hands pirated that which he held in his hands, looking not to the commandment but to the money that was in it for him. And what enjoyment did he derive from this? Suicide by strangulation, alienation from life, total destruc-

---

14. The Greek word here is οἰκονομία. Judas was entrusted with the *management of affairs* as concerned the poor. This allusion merely confirms that what Gregory has in mind throughout this passage concerning the church's "hands" is those entrusted with money and other goods for the care of the poor, i.e., the deacons primarily.

ψυχῆς, μνημόσυνον πονηρὸν παντὶ τῷ μετ᾽ αὐτὸν χρόνῳ συνεκτεινόμενον.
οὐκοῦν χρὴ τορευτὰς εἶναι καὶ διαγλύφους τὰς χεῖρας, ἵνα περιαιρεθέντων
τῶν κακῶς συμπεφυκότων τὸ λειπόμενον χρυσὸς ᾖ τῷ τῆς κεφαλῆς κάλλει
κατὰ τὸ εἶδος συμβαῖνον.

5   Ἡ δὲ τοῦ θαρσεῖς λέξις πολύσημός ἐστιν ἐν τῇ γραφικῇ συνηθείᾳ οὐ
κατὰ τῆς αὐτῆς πάντοτε διανοίας εὑρισκομένη· ἀλλὰ πολλάκις μὲν πρὸς
τὸ κατεγνωσμένον, πολλάκις δὲ πρὸς τὸ θεῖόν τε καὶ μακάριον ἡ σημασία
μεταλαμβάνεται. οἷον ὅτε φεύγει ἀπὸ προσώπου τοῦ θεοῦ Ἰωνᾶς ὁ προφήτης,
ζητεῖ πλοῖον ἐπὶ θαρσεῖς πορευόμενον· καὶ ὁ μέγας Δαβὶδ πλοῖα θαρσεῖς
10   βιαίῳ πνεύματι λέγει συντρίβεσθαι, βίαιον πνεῦμα ὡς οἶμαι λέγων τὸ τοῖς
μαθηταῖς ἐπιφανέν, τοῖς | ἐν τῷ ὑπερῴῳ συνειλεγμένοις, ὃ πρότερον μὲν δι᾽   410
ἀκοῆς προεγνώσθη ὥσπερ φερομένης πνοῆς βιαίας, μετὰ ταῦτα δὲ καὶ τοῖς
ὀφθαλμοῖς ἐφανερώθη εἰς γλωσσῶν σχῆμα τυπούμενον καὶ τῇ ἐκλαμπτικῇ
φύσει τοῦ πυρὸς ὁμοιούμενον, δι᾽ οὗ συντρίβεται ἡ πολυσχιδῶς ἐπιπολάζουσα
15   τῇ ἀνθρωπίνῃ φύσει κακία, ἣν πλοῖα θαρσεῖς ὁ προφήτης ὠνόμασεν.

ταῦτα μὲν οὖν ἐστι δι᾽ ὧν τῷ ὀνόματι τούτῳ τὰ χείρω σημαίνεται, ὁ δὲ
μέγας Ἰεζεκιὴλ εἰς ὑπογραφὴν ἄγων τῆς γενομένης αὐτῷ ποτε θεοφανείας
τὴν ὀπτασίαν ἑνὸς τῶν θείων θεαμάτων τὸ εἶδος τῇ λέξει ταύτῃ διασημαίνει
λέγων· Καὶ τὸ εἶδος αὐτῶν ὡς εἶδος θαρσεῖς. φασὶ δὲ οἱ δι᾽ ἀκριβείας τῶν
20   Ἑβραϊκῶν λέξεων τὰς ἐμφάσεις ἐπεσκεμμένοι τὸ ἀχρωμάτιστόν τε καὶ νοητὸν
καὶ ἀσώματον διὰ τῆς λέξεως ταύτης ἐν τῇ προφητείᾳ σημαίνεσθαι. διπλῆς
τοίνυν οὔσης ἐν τῇ λέξει ταύτῃ τῆς σημασίας, ἐπειδὴ πρόδηλόν ἐστιν ὅτι
πρὸς τὸ κρεῖττον νῦν παρελήφθη τὸ ταύτης τῆς φωνῆς σημαινόμενον (οὐ γὰρ
ἂν εἰς ἔπαινον ἐλαμβάνετο τὸ ὑπαίτιον), ἀκόλουθον ἂν εἴη τοῦτο περὶ τῶν
25   ἐγκωμιαζομένων ἐννοῆσαι χειρῶν ὅτι ἀκριβῶς ἀφ᾽ ἑαυτῶν πᾶν τὸ περιττόν

tion of his soul, an evil memorial reaching down to every generation that should succeed him. The hands, then must be *graven* and carved out, so that by the removal of evil growths what remains will be gold, whose appearance fits in with the beauty of the head.

Now the term *tharseis*,[15] in scriptural usage, has more than one sense. It is not always found with the same meaning. Frequently it is used to signify something that is condemned, but often its reference is altered to denote that which is divine and blessed. For example, when Jonah the prophet flees from the face of God, he seeks a vessel that is traveling to *tharseis* (Jonah 1:3), and the great David says that the ships [of] *tharseis* will be destroyed by a powerful wind[16] (Ps 47:8)—calling "powerful," I suggest, the wind that was manifested to the disciples | when they were together in the upper room. This was first made known by its sound, "as of a rushing mighty wind," but afterwards it became manifest to the eyes, shaped after the form of tongues and made like to the glowing nature of fire (cf. Acts 2:2–4). By it the vice that sits in many-fingered form atop the human race is destroyed, the vice that the prophet called "ships [of] *tharseis*."

These are cases in which the term signifies something bad, but the great Ezekiel, when describing the vision of the theophany that once came to him, uses this expression to indicate the appearance of one of the divine manifestations: "And their[17] appearance was as the appearance [of] *tharseis*" (Ezek 1:16). Now close students of the meanings of Hebrew expressions say that in the prophecy this term refers both to that which is without color and to that which is intelligible and incorporeal.[18] So given the fact that in the text before us the meaning of the word is twofold, since it is apparent that what the word signifies is now something positive and good (for what is blameworthy would not be taken up into an expression of praise), it would seem to follow that what one understands about the hands that are being commended is this: they have scraped off from themselves everything that is superfluous

---

15. Θαρσεῖς (as Gregory reads the text) or θαρσίς (according to the standard text of the LXX) is part of the final phrase of Song 5:14. Neither word has any meaning in Greek, and Gregory has no notion what it signifies (although in many places in the LXX θαρσίς transliterates the Hebrew for "Tarshish"), but he enjoys exercising his ingenuity upon it.

16. Here again Gregory plays on the double meaning of πνεῦμα as denoting both wind and Spirit.

17. The LXX text of Ezek 1:16 has: "the appearance *of the wheels* is like the appearance of θαρσίς." But Gregory is not interested here in wheels and so drops the word in his quotation of the text.

18. Gregory, it appears, thinks that in its second and positive sense *tharseis* refers to a precious stone of some sort, which in turn symbolizes "that which is intelligible and incorporeal"; cf. the example of emeralds that Gregory gives below.

τε καὶ σωματῶδες ἀποτορεύσασαι πρὸς τὸ θεῖόν τε καὶ νοητὸν μεταβαίνουσι
τὴν ὑλώδη πᾶσαν καὶ βαρεῖαν περὶ τὰ πράγματα σχέσιν ἐκτιναξάμεναι.

οἷον δή φασι καὶ ἐπὶ τῆς | σμαραγδίνης βώλου τοὺς λιθογλύφους   411
ἐργάζεσθαι· τὸ γὰρ ἀφεγγὲς καὶ γεῶδες διὰ τῆς ἀκόνης ἐκδαπανήσαντές τε
5   καὶ ἀποψήξαντες ἐκεῖνο μόνον καταλείπουσιν ἀδαπάνητον, ᾧ καθορᾶταί τις
αὐγὴ χλοερά τε ἅμα καὶ ἐλαιάζουσα. ὅπερ μοι δοκεῖ σαφέστερον ἑρμηνεύων
ὁ θεῖος ἀπόστολος τοῦτο συμβουλεύειν ἔν τινι τῶν ἑαυτοῦ λόγων ὅτι χρὴ
ἀποσκευάζεσθαι τὴν περὶ τὰ βλεπόμενα σχέσιν, πρὸς δὲ τὸ ἀόρατον ταῖς
ἐπιθυμίαις ὁρμᾶν· Μὴ σκοπούντων γὰρ ἡμῶν, φησί, τὰ βλεπόμενα, ἀλλὰ τὰ
10   μὴ βλεπόμενα· τὰ γὰρ βλεπόμενα πρόσκαιρα, τὰ δὲ μὴ βλεπόμενα αἰώνια.

ταῦτα μὲν οὖν ἐν τῷ ἐπαίνῳ τῶν χειρῶν ἐνοήσαμεν, πῶς τῆς ὑλώδους
προσπαθείας ἐκπορευθεῖσαι ἀκήρατοι γίνονται πρὸς τὸ ἄϋλόν τε καὶ νοητὸν
ἀλλοιούμεναι διὰ τῆς προαιρέσεως· Χεῖρες γὰρ αὐτοῦ, φησί, τορευταί,
χρυσαῖ, πεπληρωμέναι θαρσεῖς.

15   Ἀκόλουθον δ᾽ ἂν εἴη καὶ τὸν ἐφεξῆς λόγον διασκοπῆσαι, ὃν περὶ τῆς
κοιλίας πεποίηται. ἔχει δὲ οὕτως ὁ λόγος· Κοιλία αὐτοῦ πυξίον ἐλεφάντινον
ἐπὶ λίθου σαπφείρου.

ὅτε τῷ Μωϋσῇ τὸν ταῖς λιθίναις δέλτοις ἐγχαραχθέντα νόμον ὁ τῆς
φύσεως δίδωσι νομοθέτης, πυξία λίθινα τὰς πλάκας ὠνόμασεν, αἷς ἐνετυπώθη
20   τὰ θεῖα χαράγματα, | οὕτως εἰπόντος τοῦ πρὸς τὸν Μωϋσέα περὶ αὐτῶν   412
χρηματίσαντος ὅτι Ἀνάβηθι πρός με εἰς τὸ ὄρος καὶ ἴσθι ἐκεῖ, καὶ δώσω σοι
τὰ πυξία τὰ λίθινα, τὸν νόμον καὶ τὰς ἐντολάς. μετὰ ταῦτα δέ, ἐπειδὴ πᾶν τὸ
σωματικὸν καὶ γεῶδες ἀπεξύσατο διὰ τῆς εὐαγγελικῆς σαφηνείας ὁ νόμος,
οὐκέτι λίθινον τὸ δεχόμενον τὰ γράμματα πυξίον ἐστὶν ἀλλ᾽ ἐκ τοῦ λαμπροῦ
25   τε καὶ νεοξύστου ἐλέφαντος· τὸ γὰρ δεκτικὸν τῶν ἐντολῶν καὶ τῶν νόμων,
ὅπερ κοιλίαν ὠνόμασε, πυξίον εἶναί φησιν ἐλεφάντινον ἐπὶ λίθου σαπφείρου.

πρῶτον δὲ οἶμαι χρῆναι τὸ σωματικὸν ὑπόδειγμα φανερὸν τῷ λόγῳ
ποιῆσαι, εἶθ᾽ οὕτως ἐπὶ τὴν θεωρίαν τῶν εἰρημένων ἐλθεῖν. πυκνόν τι ξύλον
ἡ πύξος ἐστὶ καὶ ὑπόλευκον, ἀφ᾽ ἧς φιλοτεχνοῦσιν ἑαυτοῖς πίνακας οἷς τῶν
30   γραμμάτων μέλει. τὸ τοίνυν τοιοῦτον πινάκιον τὸ πρὸς τὴν τῶν γραμμάτων
χρείαν κατεσκευασμένον, κἂν ἀφ᾽ ἑτέρας ὕλης τύχῃ γενόμενον, πυξίον

and corporeal, and they have moved in the direction of the divine and intelligible, having shaken off every heavy, material disposition.

It is, people say, something like this that jewel-cutters do | with a lump of ore containing emeralds. What is dark and earthy they remove and buff away with their tool, and all that they leave behind untouched is that in which one can see the stone's oily-smooth, green gleam. To me it seems that the divine apostle renders this idea more clearly when in one of his own discourses he advises his readers to rid themselves of their inclination to things that are seen and to focus their desires on the invisible. "We look," he says, "not to the things that are seen but to the things that are unseen, for the things that are seen are transient, but the things that are unseen are eternal" (2 Cor 4:18).

So, then, what we see in the praise of the hands is this: how by the power of choice they have had the encrustation of materiality dug away and are changed into the immaterial and intelligible. For *his hands*, it says, *are graven, golden, filled,*[19] *tharseis*.

But after this, it is surely logical to look into the next statement, which [the Bride] devised to describe the belly. This is how it goes: *His belly is an ivory tablet on a sapphire stone.*

When nature's Lawgiver presented to Moses the law engraved on stone tablets, he called these flat surfaces "writing tablets of stone"[20] on which the divine characters were stamped, | for the One who gave Moses orders regarding them said, "Come up the mountain to me and stay there, and I will give you the writing tablets of stone, the law and the commandments" (Exod 24:12). But later, when the law had been scraped clean of everything corporeal and earthy by the clarity of the gospel, the writing tablet that took the letters was no longer made of stone but of gleaming and newly polished ivory, for it says that the recipient of the commandments and laws—which is called *belly*—is an *ivory tablet on a sapphire stone.*

Now first of all, I think, we ought to clarify in explicit terms the sense of the corporeal sign and then by this route arrive at a discerning understanding of the words. Boxwood is a hardwood of off-white color, out of which scribes fashion themselves flat boards for writing. Such a small board, which has been constructed for purposes of writing, is by analogy called a writing tablet[21] even if it happens to have been made of some other material. So when

---

19. It is worth noticing that Gregory evades any discussion of "filled" (πεπληρωμέναι) in his exegesis of this line. Perhaps he saw no way of fitting it into the logic of his interpretation of the other words.

20. Πυξία λίθινα, but see below, n. 21.

21. Greek πυξίον. Exod 24:12, cited above in the text, calls the tablets of the law πυξία (which means literally tablets made of boxwood [πύξος]) and then describes them as made of

καταχρηστικῶς ὀνομάζεται. οὐκοῦν πυξίον ἀκούσαντες λεῖόν τι σκεῦος ἐπιτήδειον πρὸς γραμμάτων ὑποδοχὴν ἐνοήσαμεν. ἐπεὶ τοίνυν γενικόν τι τῶν τοιούτων πινάκων ὄνομα τὸ πυξίον ἐστίν, ἐνταῦθα καὶ τὸ εἶδος τῆς ὕλης τῷ | ὑποδείγματι ὁ λόγος προστίθησι, οὐκ ἀπὸ ξύλου λέγων ἀλλ᾽ ἐξ   413
ἐλέφαντος εἶναι τὴν κατασκευὴν τοῦ πυξίου. φασὶ δὲ διὰ πολλὴν πυκνότητα καὶ στερρότητα τὸ τοιοῦτον ὀστέον ἀδιάφθορον διαμένειν ἐφ᾽ ὅτι μήκιστον μηδεμίαν ἐκ χρόνου βλάβην παραδεχόμενον. ὁ δὲ σάπφειρος τῷ κυανοειδεῖ τῆς χρόας εἰς παραμυθίαν τοῦ καμάτου τῶν ὀφθαλμῶν ἐπινοεῖται, τοῖς φιλοπόνως προσανέχουσι τῷ καταγεγραμμένῳ πυξίῳ φυσικῶς τῆς τοιαύτης
10 αὐγῆς τὰς ὄψεις δι᾽ ἑαυτῆς ἀναπαυούσης.

τὸ μὲν οὖν ὑπόδειγμα, ᾧ διὰ συγκρίσεως ὁμοιοῦται ἡ ἐγκωμιαζομένη τῆς ἐκκλησίας κοιλία, τοιοῦτόν ἐστιν, ἐγὼ δὲ παρὰ τῆς προφητείας ἀκούσας τοῦτο διακελευομένης ἐκ προσώπου τοῦ θεοῦ ὅτι Γράψον ὅρασιν καὶ σαφῶς εἰς πυξίον, ἔννοιαν λαμβάνω, τί διὰ τοῦ ὀνόματος τῆς κοιλίας ἐν τῷ ἐπαινουμένῳ
15 σώματι τοῦ κυρίου προσήκει νοεῖν· εἰ γὰρ τὴν θείαν ὅρασιν σαφῶς ἐγγράφειν τῷ πυξίῳ ὁ λόγος διακελεύεται, τάχα τὸ καθαρὸν τῆς καρδίας, ᾧ διὰ τῆς μνήμης τὰς θείας ὁράσεις ἀπογραφόμεθα, τῷ τῆς κοιλίας ὀνόματι διασημαίνει. καθάπερ καὶ ὁ διαστείλας τὸ στόμα τοῦ μεγάλου Ἰεζεκιὴλ καὶ ἐνθεὶς αὐτῷ τὴν κεφαλίδα τοῦ βιβλίου πλήρη γραμμάτων καθ᾽ ἑκάτερον οὖσαν, κατά τε
20 τὸ ἔξωθεν αὐτοῦ καὶ τὸ ἔσωθεν, φησὶ πρὸς αὐτὸν ὅτι Τὸ στόμα σου φάγεται καὶ ἡ κοιλία σου πλησθήσεται, τὸ | διανοητικὸν καὶ τὸ λογιστικὸν τῆς ψυχῆς,   414
ᾧ ἐναπέθετο τὰ θεῖα μαθήματα, κοιλίαν προσαγορεύσας. παραπλησίως δὲ καὶ τὸν μέγαν Ἰερεμίαν τὴν ὑπὸ τῶν σκυθρωπῶν ἐκείνων νοημάτων ὀδυνωμένην καρδίαν κοιλίαν ἔγνωμεν ὀνομάζοντα, δι᾽ ὧν φησιν ὅτι Τὴν κοιλίαν μου ἀλγῶ
25 καὶ τὰ αἰσθητήρια τῆς καρδίας μου μαιμάσσει. εἰ δὲ χρὴ τὸ κυριώτερον τῶν εἰς τὴν διάνοιαν ταύτην ὁδηγούντων ἡμᾶς ἀπὸ τῆς θείας παραθέσθαι φωνῆς, τοῦτό φαμεν ὅπερ πρὸς τοὺς πεπιστευκότας εἶπεν ὁ κύριος ποταμοὺς λέγων ἐκ τῆς κοιλίας ἀπορρέειν ὕδατος ζῶντος τῶν εἰς αὐτὸν πιστευόντων. ἔχει δὲ οὕτως ἡ λέξις· Ὁ πιστεύων εἰς ἐμέ, καθὼς εἶπεν ἡ γραφή, ποταμοὶ ἐκ τῆς
30 κοιλίας αὐτοῦ ῥεύσουσιν ὕδατος ζῶντος.

we hear "writing tablets," we think of a smooth-surfaced device for writing. Since, then, "writing tablet" is a generic name for such flat boards, the Word in our text adds a mention of the specific kind of material that characterizes | this instance and says that the writing tablet is made not of wood but of ivory. Now they say that because this kind of bone is very hard and solid, it endures without decay for the longest possible period and is unharmed by time. For its part, the sapphire, in virtue of its deep blue color, is contrived so as to afford relief to the tired eyes of those who labor devotedly at reading the written-over tablet, since its glow naturally and of itself gives rest to the eyes.

Such, then, is the model to which the church's belly is likened for purposes of praise. But hearing from the prophecy this command spoken as from God, "Write down the vision, and plainly on a writing tablet" (Hab 2:2), I am led to wonder what one should understand by the word "belly" as it pertains to the body of the Lord that is being praised. For if the Word instructs us to write the divine vision down clearly on a tablet, it may be the case that by "belly" it means the purity of heart by which our memory registers the divine visions in writing. Further, the One who as it were opened the mouth of the great Ezekiel and put into it the scroll of the book that was full of letters on either side, both inside and outside, said to him, "Your mouth shall eat and your belly shall be filled" (Ezek 3:3), thus giving the name "belly" to | that in the soul which thinks and reasons, in which the divine teachings are deposited. Similarly we note that the great Jeremiah sets the name "belly" to the heart that is afflicted by those melancholy thoughts of his, on whose account he says, "My belly is pained, and the sense organs of my heart quiver" (Jer 4:19)![22] And if it is necessary for us to set out the principal scriptural testimony that leads us to this idea, we say what the Lord said to those who believed when he asserted that rivers of living water flow from the belly of those who believe in him. Here are his words: "He who believes in me, as the scripture has said, 'Out of his belly'[23] shall flow rivers of living water'" (John 7:38).

---

stone. Gregory explains that scribes tend to make a "flat board" for writing (πινάκιον) out of boxwood but that small writing tablets are called πυξία even if they are made of some other material. English cannot capture the relation between the Greek words for "boxwood" and for "tablet."

22. Gregory makes "sense organs" (αἰσθητήρια) the subject of the verb "quiver" (μαιμάσσει), which is more usually taken to belong to the next statement. He may be quoting by heart.

23. It is interesting that the RSV translates κοιλία ("belly") in John 7:38 as though it were καρδία ("heart"), thus perhaps lending verisimilitude to Gregory's exegesis. Compare the AV, which is stricter in rendering the Greek.

διὰ πάντων τοίνυν τῶν εἰρημένων τὴν καθαρὰν καρδίαν διὰ τοῦ τῆς κοιλίας ὀνόματος νοεῖν ἐναγόμεθα, ἥτις πυξίον τοῦ θείου γίνεται νόμου, τῶν, καθώς φησιν ὁ ἀπόστολος, Ἐνδεικνυμένων τὸ ἔργον τοῦ νόμου γραπτὸν ἐν ταῖς καρδίαις αὐτῶν, Οὐ μέλανι ἀλλὰ πνεύματι θεοῦ ζῶντος ἐγχαρασσομένων
5   τῇ ψυχῇ τῶν τοιούτων γραμμάτων, Οὐκ ἐν πλαξὶ λιθίναις, καθώς φησιν ὁ ἀπόστολος, ἀλλ' ἐν τῷ τῆς καρδίας πυξίῳ | καθαρῷ τε ὄντι καὶ λείῳ καὶ   415 στίλβοντι· τοιοῦτον γὰρ εἶναι χρὴ τὸ ἡγεμονικὸν τῆς ψυχῆς, ὥστε τρανὴν ἐν αὐτῷ καὶ ἀσύγχυτον τῶν θείων λογίων ἐντυποῦσθαι τὴν μνήμην οἷόν τισι γράμμασιν εὐσήμοις διηρθρωμένην.
10   καλῶς δὲ συμπαρείληπται τῷ τοιούτῳ πυξίῳ πρὸς τὸν τῆς κοιλίας ἔπαινον καὶ ὁ σάπφειρος· οὐρανοειδὴς γὰρ ἡ τοῦ σαπφείρου αὐγή. τὸ δὲ τοιοῦτον αἴνιγμα σύμβολον γίνεται τοῦ τὴν καρδίαν ἡμῶν τὰ ἄνω φρονεῖν τε καὶ βλέπειν, ὅπου τὸν θησαυρὸν ἀποτίθεται, κἀκεῖ τὰς ὄψεις προσαναπαύειν, ὥστε μὴ κάμνειν ἐν τῇ προσοχῇ τῶν θείων παραγγελμάτων τῆς οὐρανίας
15   ἐλπίδος τὸ ὀπτικὸν τῶν τῆς ψυχῆς ὀμμάτων ἀναπαυούσης.
Εἶτα διαδέχεται τὸν τῆς κοιλίας ἔπαινον τὰ τῆς κνήμης ἐγκώμια· φησὶ γὰρ ὅτι Κνῆμαι αὐτοῦ στῦλοι μαρμάρινοι τεθεμελιωμένοι ἐπὶ βάσεις χρυσᾶς.
πολύστυλος μέν ἐστι τῆς σοφίας ὁ οἶκος ὃν ἑαυτῇ ᾠκοδόμησε, πολλοὶ δὲ καὶ οἱ τὴν τοῦ μαρτυρίου σκηνὴν διερείδοντες στῦλοι διαφόροις ὕλαις
20   κεκοσμημένοι, ὧν κεφαλίδες μὲν ἦσαν καὶ βάσεις χρυσαῖ, τὸ δὲ μέσον τῇ τοῦ ἀργυρίου περιβολῇ κεκαλλώπιστο. τοὺς δὲ τῆς ἐκκλησίας στύλους (οἶκος δέ ἐστιν ἡ ἐκκλησία, καθώς φησιν ὁ ἀπόστολος ὅτι Πῶς δεῖ ἐν οἴκῳ θεοῦ ἀναστρέφεσθαι) μαρμαρίνους εἶναί φησιν ἡ νύμφη ἐπὶ | χρυσῶν βεβηκότας   416 τῶν βάσεων, ὅτι μὲν οὖν συμφωνεῖ τῇ τοῦ Βεσελεὴλ σοφίᾳ ἡ νύμφη κατὰ
25   τὴν τοῦ κάλλους ὑπογραφὴν παραπλησίως ἐκείνῳ τὴν κεφαλὴν καὶ τὰς βάσεις τῷ χρυσίῳ κοσμήσασα, παντὶ δῆλόν ἐστι τῷ τοῖς περὶ τῆς σκηνῆς εἰρημένοις καθομιλήσαντι· ὡς γὰρ ἐκεῖνος χρυσῆν ἑκάστῳ τῶν στύλων τὴν κεφαλὴν ἐφαρμόσας ἐπὶ χρυσῆς ἵστησι βάσεως, οὕτω καὶ ἐνταῦθά φησιν ἡ καθαρῶς πρὸς τὸ τοῦ νυμφίου βλέπουσα κάλλος κεφαλὴν μὲν αὐτοῦ εἶναι

So by all of these testimonies we are led to understand the pure heart when the word "belly" is used, and this becomes the tablet of the divine law in those who, as the apostle says, show "that they have the requirement of the law written in their hearts" (Rom 2:15), who have such letters graven in their soul not by ink but by the Spirit of the living God, "not on tablets of stone" (2 Cor 3:3), as the apostle says, but on the pure, white, and polished | writing tablet of the heart. For such must the governing part of the soul be if it is to be stamped with a clear and distinct memory of the divine oracles, spelled out in clear letters.[24]

And rightly too is the sapphire associated with such a tablet for praise of the belly, for the sapphire's gleam is the color of the sky. This enigma of the sapphire signifies that our heart thinks and looks upon things above, where our treasure is stored, and there rests its eyes, so that as the heavenly hope refreshes the power of the soul's eyes, we do not falter in attentiveness to the divine injunctions.

Then after praise of the belly there comes the commendation of the legs, for it says, *His legs are marble pillars resting upon golden pedestals.*

The house that Wisdom "built for herself" (Prov 9:1) has many pillars, and many too are the pillars, decorated with a variety of materials, that uphold the tent of witness, whose capitals and pedestals are of gold, while their central portions are embellished with a covering of silver. But the Bride says that the pillars of the church (and the church too is a house, even as the apostle says: "How one ought to behave in the house of God" [1 Tim 3:15]) are made of marble and seated | upon pedestals of gold. Hence it is plain to anyone who is familiar with what is said about the tent that the Bride in her description of its beauty is in agreement with the wisdom of Bezalel in that, similarly to him, she decorates the capital[25] and the pedestals with gold.[26] For just as Bezalel, having fitted each of the pillars with a golden capital, set it upon a golden pedestal, so too in our text she who contemplates the Bridegroom's beauty

---

24. See the similar image in Plato, *Theaet.* 194C-D (which is interesting here especially for its analogy for memory: imprints on a waxen tablet), and of course in Jer 31:33.

25. The word "capital"—which would ordinarily render the Greek κεφαλίς, as indeed it does at the beginning of this paragraph—here translates the Greek κεφαλή, which more normally means "head." Thus Gregory's move from the "capital" of a pillar to the "head" of the Bridegroom seems less implausible in Greek, in which it qualifies as an admirable pun, than it does in English.

26. The account of the work of Bezalel the son of Uri on the tent and the ark are found in Exod 37–38 (lxx, the order and detail of whose account are not the same as those of the Masoretic Text). According to 37:4, the "capitals" of the poles (στύλους) were of gold, but the pedestals were of silver. Perhaps Gregory is remembering wishfully.

χρυσίον καθαρὸν καὶ ἀκήρατον (τοῦτο γὰρ ἡ τοῦ κεφὰζ λέξις ἐνδείκνυται), τεθεμελιῶσθαι δὲ τὰς κνήμας ἐπὶ χρυσῶν λέγει τῶν βάσεων.

πρὸς ὅ τι δὲ χρὴ μεταληφθῆναι τὰ περὶ τῶν στύλων αἰνίγματα, τῷ ἁγίῳ Παύλῳ μαθητευόμενοι τῆς ἀληθοῦς ἐννοίας οὐκ ἐκπεσούμεθα, ὃς τοὺς
5 προέχοντας ἐν τοῖς ἀποστόλοις Πέτρον καὶ Ἰάκωβον καὶ Ἰωάννην στύλους τῆς ἐκκλησίας ὠνόμασεν. ἐπεὶ δὲ καὶ τοῦτο προσήκει μαθεῖν, πῶς ἔστι γενέσθαι στῦλον, ὡς ἂν καὶ ἡμεῖς ἄξιοι τῆς τοιαύτης γενοίμεθα κλήσεως, πάλιν καὶ τοῦτο παρὰ τῆς τοῦ Παύλου σοφίας ἀκούομεν, ὅς φησι στῦλον εἶναι τὸ ἑδραίωμα τῆς ἀληθείας. οὐκοῦν χρυσίον μέν ἐστιν ἡ ἀλήθεια, ἡ καὶ βάσις τῶν
10 κνημῶν γινομένη καὶ τὰς χεῖρας καὶ τὴν κεφαλὴν δι᾽ ἑαυτῆς καλλωπίζουσα, τὸ δὲ ἑδραίωμα εἰς τὴν τοῦ μαρμάρου | φύσιν μεταλαβών τις οὐχ ἁμαρτήσεται.   417 ὡς εἶναι τοιαύτην τὴν τῶν λεγομένων διάνοιαν ὅτι αἱ κνῆμαι τοῦ σώματος, οἱ μαρμάρινοι στῦλοι (τουτέστιν οἱ τῷ λαμπρῷ βίῳ καὶ τῷ ὑγιαίνοντι λόγῳ τὸ κοινὸν σῶμα τῆς ἐκκλησίας βαστάζοντές τε καὶ διερείδοντες, δι᾽ ὧν ἥ
15 τε βάσις τῆς πίστεως ἔχει τὸ πάγιον καὶ ὁ κατ᾽ ἀρετὴν δρόμος ἀνύεται καὶ ἐν τοῖς ἅλμασι τῶν θείων ἐλπίδων ὅλον τὸ σῶμα μετέωρον γίνεται) διὰ τῶν δύο κατορθοῦνται τούτων, ἀληθείας καὶ βεβαιότητος, τοῦ μὲν χρυσοῦ μεταλαμβανομένου πρὸς τὴν ἀλήθειαν, ἥτις κατὰ τὴν τοῦ Παύλου φωνὴν θεμέλιος τῆς θείας οἰκοδομῆς γίνεταί τε καὶ ὀνομάζεται (οὕτω γάρ φησιν ὅτι
20 Θεμέλιον ἄλλον οὐδεὶς δύναται θεῖναι παρὰ τὸν κείμενον, ὅς ἐστιν Ἰησοῦς Χριστός. Ἰησοῦς Χριστὸς δέ ἐστιν ἡ ἀλήθεια, ᾗ ἐνθεμελιοῦνται αἱ κνῆμαι, οἱ στῦλοι τῆς ἐκκλησίας), διὰ δὲ τοῦ μαρμάρου νοούντων ἡμῶν τό τε λαμπρὸν τοῦ βίου καὶ τὸ πρὸς τὴν τῶν ἀγαθῶν διάθεσιν ἐμβριθές τε καὶ ἀμετάθετον.

ἀλλ᾽ ἐπειδὴ πολλοὶ μὲν οἱ στῦλοι τῆς τοῦ μαρτυρίου σκηνῆς, πολλοὶ δὲ
25 καὶ οἱ τὸν τῆς σοφίας οἶκον διαβαστάζοντες, δύο δὲ νῦν ἐξαρκοῦσιν ὅλον ἀνέχειν ἐφ᾽ ἑαυτῶν τὸ σῶμα, τάχα πρὸς ἄλλην τινὰ διάνοιαν χρὴ μεταγαγεῖν τὸν σκοπὸν τοῦ αἰνίγματος· οἶμαι γὰρ διὰ | τούτων ἐκεῖνο κατασκευάζεσθαι   418 τὸ πολυειδεῖς μὲν γίνεσθαι τὰς ἐκ τοῦ νόμου πρὸς ἀρετὴν ὁδηγίας, πολλὰ δὲ καὶ τῆς σοφίας εἶναι τὰ παραγγέλματα πρὸς τὸν αὐτὸν ὁρῶντα σκοπόν,
30 τὸν δὲ συντετμημένον τοῦ εὐαγγελίου λόγον εἰς εὐαρίθμητόν τε καὶ συνεσταλμένον ἀγαγεῖν πᾶσαν τοῦ κατ᾽ ἀρετὴν βίου τὴν τελειότητα οὕτως εἰπόντος τοῦ κυρίου ὅτι Ἐν ταύταις ταῖς δυσὶν ἐντολαῖς ὅλος ὁ νόμος καὶ οἱ προφῆται κρέμανται.

in purity asserts that his head is pure, untarnished gold (for this is what the word *kephaz* shows[27]), while his legs rest upon golden pedestals.

As to the question into what terms this enigma of the pillars is to be transposed, we shall not miss the true meaning if we are taught by Saint Paul, who called Peter and James and John, preeminent ones among the apostles, "pillars" of the church. But since it is also important to find out how someone can become a pillar, so that we too may be made worthy of such a title, once again we hear our answer in Paul's wisdom, for he says that a "pillar" is the "support of the truth" (1 Tim 3:15). Hence the truth is *golden*.[28] It also becomes that on which the legs stand and itself lends its beauty to the arms and the head. Moreover, it will not be a mistake to interpret "support" as signifying the | natural quality of marble. Thus the sense of the words is this: that the body's legs, the marble pillars (that is to say, those who by their shining life and healthful speech bear up the common body of the church and support it and by whose work the pedestal of faith retains its steadfast character, and virtue's race is completed, and the whole body, in its leaps of a divine hope, touches the heavens), these legs, I say, are made straight by this pair: truth and firmness. The gold, on the one hand, is a figure for truth, which according to Paul's word becomes and is called the foundation of the divine edifice (for that is what he says: "Other foundation can no one lay than that which has been laid, which is Jesus Christ" [1 Cor 3:11]; but Jesus Christ is the truth [cf. John 14:6] on which the legs, the church's pillars, are grounded). On the other hand, the marble leads us to think of a shining life and of firmness and constancy in devotion to good things.

But the pillars of the tent of witness are many in number, and many too are those that uphold Wisdom's house. In the case of our text, however, two are sufficient by themselves to hold up the entire body. It may be, then, that one ought to understand the enigma's point in a different way. For my view is that by | these many pillars what is established is, on the one hand, the multiform character of the teaching by which the law brings us to virtue and, on the other, the multitude of Wisdom's injunctions to the same purpose. Yet the brisk and concise word of the Gospel renders the entire perfection of the virtuous life something brief and easily itemized, for the Lord says, "On these two commandments hang all the Law and the Prophets" (Matt 22:40).

---

27. See above, homily 13, pp. 390–91 (Jaeger), where Gregory explains that the Hebrew word *kephaz*, transliterated in the LXX text of the Song, means "gold that is pure and refined and free of all alloys."

28. Evidently Gregory reads the phrase in 1 Tim 3:15—ἑδραίωμα τῆς ἀληθείας—to mean not "that which supports the truth" but "the support [*or* 'bulwark'] that the truth is."

ἴσον δὲ πάντως ἐστὶν εἰς δύναμιν ἢ ὑποκρεμάμενον ἀνέχειν τὸ βάρος ἢ
ἐπικείμενον· εἷς γὰρ δι᾽ ἀμφοτέρων ὁ τῆς δυνάμεως θεωρεῖται τόνος τοῦ καθ᾽
ἑκάτερον τρόπον τὸ ἄχθος βαστάζοντος· φέρει γὰρ ὁμοίως δι᾽ ἑαυτοῦ, εἴτε
ἀπηρτημένον ἔχει τὸ βάρος εἴτε ὑπολαμβάνει τῇ παλάμῃ τὸ βασταζόμενον.
5   ἐπεὶ οὖν ὁ μὲν κύριος ἐν ταύταις φησὶ ταῖς δυσὶν ἐντολαῖς ὅλον τὸν νόμον
κρέμασθαι καὶ τοὺς προφήτας, νῦν δὲ ἡ νύμφη δύο στύλοις ἐπὶ χρυσῶν
θεμελίων βεβηκόσι βαστάζεσθαι λέγει τὸ σῶμα, καλῶς ἂν ἔχοι πρὸς τὴν
θεωρίαν τοῦ κατὰ τὰς κνήμας αἰνίγματος συμπαραλαβεῖν τὰς δύο ἐντολὰς
ἐκείνας, ὧν τὴν μὲν πρώτην ὀνομάζει ὁ κύριος, τὴν δὲ ὁμοίαν τῇ πρώτῃ,
10 λέγων τὸ μὲν ἀγαπᾶν τὸν θεὸν ἐξ ὅλης καρδίας τε καὶ ψυχῆς καὶ δυνάμεως
τὴν πρώτην ἐντολὴν εἶναι, τὸ δὲ τὸν πλησίον ὡς ἑαυτὸν | ἰσοδυναμεῖν τῇ   419
πρώτῃ. ἀλλὰ καὶ ὁ Παῦλος οἷόν τινα οἶκον δεκτικὸν τοῦ θεοῦ κατασκευάζων
τὸν μέγαν Τιμόθεον τοὺς δύο τούτους ἐν αὐτῷ ἵστησι στύλους, τῷ μὲν ὄνομα
θέμενος πίστιν τῷ δὲ ἑτέρῳ συνείδησιν, διὰ μὲν τῆς πίστεως τὴν εἰς θεὸν
15 ἀγάπην τὴν ἐξ ὅλης καρδίας τε καὶ ψυχῆς καὶ δυνάμεως σημαίνων, διὰ δὲ τῆς
ἀγαθῆς συνειδήσεως τὴν ἀγαπητικὴν εἰς τὸν πλησίον διάθεσιν.

τάχα δὲ οὐκ ἐναντιοῦται τῷ προτέρῳ νοήματι ἡ νῦν ἐφευρεθεῖσα διάνοια·
δι᾽ ἀμφοτέρων γὰρ τούτων ἐστὶ τὸ γενέσθαι στύλους τοὺς κατὰ Πέτρον
καὶ Ἰάκωβον καὶ Ἰωάννην καὶ εἰ δή τις ἄλλος κατ᾽ ἐκείνους τοῦ τοιούτου
20 ὀνόματος ἄξιος ἢ γέγονεν ἢ γενήσεται· ὁ γὰρ ἐν ταύταις ταῖς δυσὶν ἐντολαῖς
τελειωθεὶς στῦλος καὶ ἑδραίωμα τῆς ἀληθείας κατασκευάζεται κατὰ τὴν τοῦ
ἀποστόλου φωνήν, ὥστε τοῖς δύο τούτοις κατορθώμασιν ὅλον τὸ σῶμα τῆς
ἀληθείας καθάπερ κνήμαις τισὶν ἐπερείδεσθαι, τοῦ χρυσοῦ θεμελίου τῆς
κατὰ τὴν πίστιν βάσεως τὸ ἀκλινές τε καὶ ἀμετάθετον καὶ τὸ ἐν παντὶ ἀγαθῷ
25 πάγιον τοῖς λογισμοῖς ἐμποιοῦντος.

Μετὰ δὲ τοὺς ἐπαίνους τούτους καθάπερ ἀνακεφαλαιουμένη ὅλον τοῦ
νυμφίου τὸ κάλλος φησίν· Εἶδος αὐτοῦ ὡς Λίβανος ἐκλεκτός, ὡς κέδροι·
φάρυγξ αὐτοῦ γλυκασμὸς καὶ ὅλος ἐπιθυμία, οὗτος ἀδελφιδός μου καὶ οὗτος
πλησίον | μου, θυγατέρες Ἱερουσαλήμ. ἐν τούτῳ γὰρ οἶμαι σαφέστερον   420
30 αὐτὴν διασημαίνειν ὅτι περὶ τὸ βλεπόμενον τοῦ νυμφίου κάλλος ἐστὶν ὁ
ἔπαινος (ἐκεῖνό φημι τὸ βλεπόμενον, ὃ διὰ τῶν καθ᾽ ἕκαστον μελῶν τῶν
συμπληρούντων τὴν ἐκκλησίαν σωματοποιεῖ ὁ ἀπόστολος)· ἓν γὰρ εἶδος
αὐτοῦ φησιν εἶναι τὰς μυριάδας τῶν κέδρων, αἷς διείληπται πανταχόθεν ὁ

But there is hardly any difference, as far as the strength exerted is concerned, between carrying a weight that hangs down and bearing a weight that presses down. No matter which method is used, one observes the same exertion of strength on the part of the person who bears the load, for he does the same job of carrying whether he has his burden hanging down or supports the weight by placing a hand under it. Since then the Lord says that the whole of the Law and the Prophets *hangs* upon "these two commandments," and in our text the Bride states that the body *is supported* by two pillars set on golden pedestals, it will surely be correct to adduce those two commandments in order to construe the enigma of the legs. The Lord calls one of them "first" and the other "like" the first. He states that to love God with one's whole heart and soul and strength is the first commandment and that to love one's neighbor as oneself | is as important as the first. But Paul too, in the process, as it were, of making the great Timothy a house to receive God, erects in him these two pillars, assigning to one of them the name "faith" and to the other that of "conscience" (cf. 1 Tim 1:19). When he says "faith," he means loving God with one's whole heart and soul and strength, and when he says "good conscience," he means a disposition to love one's neighbor.

But is this newly discerned interpretation really contrary to our earlier idea?[29] After all, it is through both of these that people are able to become pillars like Peter and James and John—and anyone else who has or will become worthy, like them, of this title. For by these two commandments the perfected "pillar and support of the truth" is set up (as the apostle says). Thus the whole body of the truth is stayed upon these two uprights as though they were a pair of legs, and the golden foundation, the pedestal of faith, by its thoughts makes the body steady, immovable, constant in every good thing.

After these praises, as though summing up the whole beauty of the Bridegroom, she says: *His appearance is like Lebanon the chosen, like cedars. His throat is sweetness, and [he is] through and through desire. This is my kinsman, and this is my close one,| O daughters of Jerusalem.* For by these words, I take it, the Bride indicates more explicitly that her praise concerns the visible aspect of the Bridegroom's beauty (and by "visible" I refer to that which the apostle shapes into a single body out of the individual members that make up the church).[30] For she says that his appearance—that of a single individual—

---

29. The "earlier idea" is the interpretation of the whole of Song 1:14 given above on pp. 417–18 (Jaeger).

30. Gregory is responding here to the presence of the Greek word εἶδος (whose root sense is "that which is seen" of something, its "appearance," and hence its shape, form, or figure) in the text of Song 5:15c. For the point of this observation, see above, homily 13, pp. 383–84 (Jaeger). It is the *human* Christ fulfilled in his members, not the Deity, that the Bride's praises describe.

Λίβανος, δηλοῦσα διὰ τῶν λεγομένων ὅτι οὐδὲν ταπεινὸν καὶ χαμαίζηλον
συντελεῖ πρὸς τὴν εὐμορφίαν τοῦ σώματος, ἐὰν μή τι κατὰ τὴν κέδρον
ὑψηλὸν ᾖ καὶ πρὸς τὸ ἄνω τῇ κορυφῇ ἐπειγόμενον.
      Μᾶλλον δὲ τὸ παρατεθὲν ἐν τοῖς εἰρημένοις πρῶτον κατανοήσωμεν·
5   Εἶδος αὐτοῦ, φησίν, ὡς Λίβανος ἐκλεκτός. ἐκλογὴ δὲ παντὸς πράγματος διὰ
τῆς τοῦ ἐναντίου παραθέσεως γίνεται. ἐπεὶ οὖν ὁμώνυμόν ἐστι τὸ ἀγαθὸν
ἐπί τε τοῦ ὄντως ὄντος τοιούτου καὶ ἐπὶ τοῦ μὴ ὄντος μέν, ὑποκρινομένου δὲ
δι’ ἀπάτης καὶ δοκοῦντος εἶναι ὃ οὐκ ἔστιν, ὁ μὴ διαμαρτὼν τῆς τοῦ καλοῦ
κρίσεως τὸ ἐξειλεγμένον ἀγαθὸν ἀντὶ τοῦ ἠπατημένου προείλετο. ἐπεὶ οὖν
10 ἐνταῦθα τῷ ἐκλεκτῷ Λιβάνῳ τὸ εἶδος τοῦ νυμφίου προσείκασε, δύο κατὰ τὸ
ἀκόλουθον Λιβάνους ὁ λόγος νοεῖν ὑποτίθεται· ἕνα μὲν τὸν | πονηρὸν καὶ   421
ἀπόβλητον, τὸν ἴσα τῷ μόσχῳ κατὰ τὴν προφητείαν μετὰ τῶν κέδρων τῶν ἐφ’
ἑαυτοῦ συντριβόμενον, ἕτερον δὲ τὸν ἐκλεκτόν τε καὶ τίμιον, οὗ τὸ κάλλος
θεοπρεπές ἐστι καὶ θεοείκελον.
15   ὃ δὲ νοοῦμεν διὰ τῶν εἰρημένων τοιοῦτόν ἐστιν· εἷς βασιλεὺς κυρίως τε
καὶ ἀληθινῶς καὶ πρώτως ἐστὶν ὁ βασιλεὺς πάσης τῆς κτίσεως. ἀλλ’ ὅμως
καὶ ὁ κοσμοκράτωρ τοῦ σκότους σεμνύνει ἑαυτὸν τῷ τῆς βασιλείας ὀνόματι.
λεγεῶνες ἀγγέλων παρὰ τῷ ἀληθινῷ βασιλεῖ καὶ λεγεῶνες δαιμόνων παρὰ
τῷ ἄρχοντι τῆς ἐξουσίας τοῦ σκότους. ἀρχαὶ καὶ ἐξουσίαι καὶ δυνάμεις ὑπὸ
20 τὸν βασιλέα τῶν βασιλευόντων καὶ κύριον τῶν κυριευόντων. ἔχει κἀκεῖνος
κατὰ τὴν τοῦ ἀποστόλου φωνὴν ἀρχάς τε καὶ ἐξουσίας καὶ δυνάμεις τὰς
καταργουμένας, ὅταν μέλλῃ τὸ κακὸν εἰς τὸ μὴ ὂν ἀφανίζεσθαι (Ὅταν γὰρ
καταργήσῃ, φησί, πᾶσαν ἀρχὴν καὶ ἐξουσίαν καὶ δύναμιν). ἐπὶ θρόνου βλέπει
ὁ προφήτης τὸν βασιλέα τῆς δόξης καθήμενον ὑψηλοῦ τε καὶ ἐπηρμένου.
25 κἀκεῖνος ἐπαγγέλλεται θήσειν ἐπάνω τῶν ἄστρων τὸν ἴδιον θρόνον,
ὥστε εἶναι ὅμοιον τῷ ὑψίστῳ. σκεύη ἐκλογῆς ἐν τῇ μεγάλῃ ἑαυτοῦ οἰκίᾳ
ὁ τοῦ παντὸς ἔχει δεσπότης. ἔχει κἀκεῖνος σκεύη ὀργῆς κατηρτισμένα εἰς
ἀπώλειαν. πάλιν ζωὴν καὶ εἰρήνην δι’ ἀγγέλων|χορηγεῖ τοῖς ἀξίοις ὁ τῶν   422
ἀγγέλων κύριος. κἀκεῖνος θυμὸν καὶ ὀργὴν καὶ θλῖψιν ἀποστέλλει διὰ τῶν
30 ἀγγέλων τῶν πονηρῶν. καὶ τί χρὴ τὰ καθ’ ἕκαστον λέγειν, δι’ ὧν κατὰ τὸ
ἐναντίον ἀντεπαίρεται πρὸς τὴν τοῦ ἀγαθοῦ φύσιν ὁ ἀντικείμενος;

is like the myriads of cedars by which Lebanon is girt on every side, and she shows by her words that nothing low or dwarfed contributes to the beauty of the body's form, but only what is tall like the cedar and presses upward with its crown.

But first let us turn our minds to what is stated in the words. *His appearance*, it says, *is like Lebanon the chosen*. Now the choice of anything whatsoever occurs as a result of comparison with its contrary. Since, then, "good" is ambiguous, being applied on the one hand to what really *is* good and on the other to what is not but which because of a mistake presents the appearance of being what it is not,[31] the person who is unerring in judgment of what is good prefers the good that has been chosen to one that deceives. So since in our text the Bride likens the *look* of the Bridegroom to Lebanon *the chosen*, it follows that the Word requires us to think of two Lebanons. One of them is | bad and worthless and according to the prophecy is destroyed, just like the bull calf, together with the cedars that are upon it, but the other is chosen and precious, and its beauty is worthy of God and godlike.

What we gather from these words is something along the following lines. Properly and truly and primarily there is one King, and this is the King of the whole creation. Yet at the same time "the world ruler of darkness" (cf. Eph 6:12) exalts himself by claiming the title of kingship. There are legions of angels in the company of the true King (cf. Matt 26:53) and legions of demons in the company of the ruler of the dominion of darkness (cf. Mark 5:9; Luke 8:30). There are rules and authorities and powers (cf. Eph 1:21) under "the King of kings and the Lord of lords" (1 Tim 6:15). That other one too, as the apostle tells us, has rules and authorities and powers that are destroyed when evil shall be reduced to nothing (for it says, "When he destroys every rule, authority, and power" [1 Cor 15:24]). The prophet sees the King of glory seated upon a throne high and lifted up (cf. Isa 6:1). That other one too promises to set his own throne above the stars, so that he will be like the Most High (Isa 14:13–14). The Master of the universe has "vessels of election" (cf. Acts 9:15) in his great household, and that other one too has vessels of wrath destined for destruction (Rom 9:22). Again, the Lord of the angels provides the worthy with life and peace | by the ministry of angels (cf. Luke 2:14). And that other one too dispatches, by the hand of the wicked angels, "wrath, indignation, and distress" (Ps 77:49). What need more is there to attend to the detail of the deeds by which the Adversary rises up in his opposition to the realm of the good?

---

31. On the doctrine of the "apparent good," see above, homily 3, p. 55 (Jaeger); homily 12, p. 350 (Jaeger).

ἐπεὶ οὖν κατὰ τὸ αἰσθητὸν περιφανές ἐστι θέαμα τὸ ὄρος ὁ Λίβανος πανταχόθεν ταῖς ὑψηλαῖς κέδροις συνηρεφής τε καὶ δάσκιος, τούτου χάριν πρὸς τὰς ἐναντίας ἐννοίας διὰ τῶν κατὰ τὸ φαινόμενον ὑποδειγμάτων ὑπὸ τῆς γραφῆς τὸ ὄρος μερίζεται προσφόρως λαμβανόμενον καθ' ἑκάτερον.

5   καὶ οὕτως ἔστι παρὰ τοῖς αὐτοῖς προφήταις ἰδεῖν τὸ αὐτὸ ὄνομα κατὰ τὴν τῶν δηλουμένων διαφορὰν ἐπαινούμενόν τε καὶ κακιζόμενον· νῦν μὲν γὰρ συντρίβει κύριος τὰς κέδρους τοῦ Λιβάνου καὶ ὅλον τὸν Λίβανον μετὰ τῶν ἐν αὐτῷ κέδρων λεπτύνει καθ' ὁμοιότητα τοῦ εἰδωλοποιηθέντος μόσχου ἐν τῇ ἐρήμῳ (δι' οὗ τοῦτο ἡ προφητεία παρίστησιν ὅτι αὐτή τε ἡ κακία καὶ

10   πᾶν ἐξ αὐτῆς ὕψωμα τὸ κατὰ τῆς γνώσεως τοῦ θεοῦ ἐπαιρόμενον εἰς τὸ μὴ ὂν περιστήσεται), νῦν δὲ πρὸς τὸ κρεῖττον αὐτοῦ μεταλαμβάνει | τὴν   423 σημασίαν λέγων· Δίκαιος ὡς φοῖνιξ ἀνθήσει, ὡσεὶ κέδρος ἡ ἐν τῷ Λιβάνῳ πληθυνθήσεται· ὁ γὰρ ἀληθῶς δίκαιος (κύριος δέ ἐστιν ὁ δίκαιος ὁ δι' ἡμᾶς ἐκ γῆς ἀνασχών), ἐκεῖνος ὁ ὑψίκομος φοῖνιξ ὁ ἐν τῇ ὕλῃ τῆς φύσεως ἡμῶν

15   ἀνατείλας ὄρος γίνεται ταῖς κέδροις τῶν ῥιζουμένων διὰ πίστεως ἐν αὐτῷ πληθυνόμενος, αἵτινες ὅταν ἐν τῷ οἴκῳ τοῦ θεοῦ φυτευθῶσιν, Ἐν ταῖς αὐλαῖς τοῦ θεοῦ ἐξανθήσουσιν. οἶκον δὲ τὴν ἐκκλησίαν κατὰ τὴν τοῦ ἀποστόλου ὑφήγησιν ἐνοήσαμεν, ἐν ᾧ γίνεται ἡ τῶν κέδρων τοῦ θεοῦ φυτεία, αὐλὰς δὲ τὰς αἰωνίους σκηνάς, ἐν αἷς ἡ τῶν ἀγαθῶν ἐλπίδων ἐξάνθησίς τε καὶ

20   φανέρωσις τοῖς καθήκουσι χρόνοις γενήσεται.

ἐπειδὴ τοίνυν τὸ σῶμα τοῦ Χριστοῦ διὰ τῶν καθ' ἕκαστον ἐκπληροῦται μελῶν (τὰ γὰρ πολλὰ μέλη ἓν σῶμα γίνεται, καθώς φησιν ὁ ἀπόστολος), τούτου χάριν ὅλον τὸ τοῦ νυμφίου κάλλος τὸν ἐκλεκτὸν ὠνόμασε Λίβανον τὴν πρὸς τὸν ἀπόβλητον Λίβανον διαφορὰν τῷ ἐκλεκτὸν διαστείλασα· ἐκεῖνος

25   γάρ ἐστιν ὁ Λίβανος ὁ κατὰ τὸν Ἡσαΐαν σὺν τοῖς ὑψηλοῖς πεσούμενος, ὅταν ἐκ τῆς τοῦ Ἰεσσαὶ ῥίζης ἀνατείλῃ τὸ ἄνθος καὶ ἡ τῆς ἐξουσίας ῥάβδος ἀναφύῃ, δι' ἧς μεταβάλλε|ται τοῦ τε λέοντος καὶ τῆς παρδάλεως καὶ τῶν   424 ἀσπίδων ἡ φύσις πρὸς τὸ τιθασόν τε καὶ ἥμερον, ὥστε συνδιαιτᾶσθαι μὲν τῷ

Now in the perceptible order Mount Lebanon is a conspicuous sight, densely covered on every side with tall cedars. For this reason, because of the illustrative examples its appearance affords, the mountain is presented by the Scripture in differing lights to correspond with the contrary meanings it can bear and is usefully understood in either way. Thus it is possible to turn to the very same prophets and observe that this very same name is both praised and reproached because of the difference in the way it is perceived. For on one occasion (cf. Ps 28:5–6) the Lord destroys the cedars of Lebanon and grinds up the whole of Lebanon, together with the cedars upon it, like the idolatrous calf in the wilderness (by which the prophecy teaches that evildoing itself, and every Height[32] that is born of it and sets itself up against the knowledge of God, will be reduced to nothing). On another occasion, however, it changes the reference of the name for the better | and says: "The righteous shall bloom like the palm tree, like a cedar in Lebanon shall he abound" (Ps 91:13). For the truly righteous one (and the Lord is the righteous one who rose from the earth for our sake), the towering palm tree that rose up in the stuff[33] of our nature, became a mountain abounding in the cedars that are people rooted in him by faith; and when these have been planted "in the house" of God, "they shall bloom in the courts of … God" (Ps 91:14). Now we have seen that it is the church that, according to the teaching of the apostle, is "the house" in which God's cedar garden is planted, but "the courts" are the "eternal habitations" (see, e.g., Ps 83:2–3) in which there will occur, at the proper time, at once the blooming and the revelation of good hopes.

But the body of Christ is filled out by its individual members (for the many members become one body [cf. 1 Cor 12:12], as the apostle says), and this is why the Bride calls the beauty of the Bridegroom in its totality *Lebanon the chosen*, distinguishing the worthless Lebanon from the one that is *chosen*, for the former Lebanon is the one that according to Isaiah will collapse together with its lofty ones (cf. Isa 10:34) when from the root of Jesse a bloom will spring up, and the rod of power will grow up (cf. Isa 11:1); and by it the nature of the lion, the leopard, and the asps will | be changed and become tame and gentle, so that the lion will live in company with the calf,

---

32. ὕψωμα: Gregory often takes mountains or hills as symbols of the evil powers. See his comments on Song 2:8 in homily 5, p. 143 (Jaeger).

33. See above, homily 4, p. 116 (Jaeger), where Gregory comments on Song 2:3. There as here Gregory plays on the ambiguity of the word ὕλη, whose basic sense is that of "woods" or "[a] wood," whence its derivative senses of "wood" (i.e., what trees are made of) and "stuff" or "matter" (i.e., what anything whatever is made of). The phrase ὁ ἐν τῇ ὕλῃ τῆς φύσεως ἡμῶν ("the 'stuff' of our nature") might therefore just as well be rendered as something like "the forest of our nature," and Gregory appears to intend this play of thought.

μόσχῳ τὸν λέοντα, συναναπαύεσθαι δὲ τῷ ἐρίφῳ τὴν πάρδαλιν, ἐπιστατεῖν δὲ
τούτων τὸ παιδίον ἐκεῖνο τὸ νήπιον ὃ ἐγεννήθη ἡμῖν, οὗ ἡ χεὶρ ἐν τῇ τρώγλῃ
τῶν ἀσπίδων γίνεται καὶ τῶν ἐγγόνων τῆς ἀσπίδος ἐφαπτομένη καὶ τὸν ἰὸν
αὐτῶν ἀπαμβλύνουσα, ὧν γινομένων φησὶν ὁ προφήτης ὅτι καὶ Ὁ Λίβανος
5   σὺν τοῖς ὑψηλοῖς πεσεῖται.
        ὅσα δὲ μηνύει διὰ τῶν αἰνιγμάτων τούτων ἡ προφητεία, ὡς πρόδηλα
πᾶσιν ὄντα περιττὸν ἂν εἴη δι' ἀκριβείας ἐκτίθεσθαι. τίς γὰρ οὐκ οἶδε τὸ
γεννηθὲν ἡμῖν παιδίον τὸ τῶν ἀσπίδων τῇ χειρὶ ἐφαπτόμενον, οὗ ἡ ἐπιστασία
τὰ δηλητήρια τῶν θηρίων ποιεῖ τοῖς ἡμέροις ὁμόσκηνα τῆς φυσικῆς πικρίας
10   λήθην ποιούμενα; ἐπεὶ οὖν πίπτει διὰ τούτων ὁ Λίβανος, ἡ κακία, καὶ
συγκαταπίπτει τῇ πρώτῃ τῶν κακῶν ἀρχῇ τὰ κατὰ τῆς ἀληθείας ὑψώματα,
διὰ τοῦτο τῷ ἐκλεκτῷ Λιβάνῳ παρεικάζει ἡ νύμφη τοῦ κυρίου τὸ κάλλος
οὕτως εἰποῦσα τοῖς ῥήμασιν· Εἶδος αὐτοῦ ὡς Λίβανος ἐκλεκτός, ὡς κέδροι.
        Προστίθησι δὲ καὶ τῷ φάρυγγι τὸν κατάλληλον ἔπαινον γλυκασμόν
15   τε αὐτὸν καὶ ἐπιθυμίαν ὀνομάσασα. ἔχει δὲ ἡ λέξις οὕτως· Φάρυγξ αὐτοῦ
γλυκασμὸς καὶ ὅλος ἐπιθυμία.
        ὃ δὲ περὶ τούτου νοοῦμεν, τοιοῦτόν ἐστι· τὸ ὑπὸ τὸν ἀνθερεῶνα μέρος
φάρυγγα καλεῖ ἡ συνήθεια, ᾧ φασι | τὸν ἦχον τῇ προσπτώσει τοῦ ἐκ τῆς   425
ἀρτηρίας πνεύματος ἀπογεννᾶσθαι περιδονούμενον. ἐπεὶ οὖν κηρία μέλιτος
20   οἱ καλοί εἰσι λόγοι, λόγου δὲ ὄργανόν ἐστιν ἡ φωνή, ἧς ἡ γένεσίς ἐστιν ἐκ
φάρυγγος, τάχα τοὺς ὑπηρέτας τε καὶ ὑποφήτας τοῦ λόγου ἐν οἷς λαλεῖ ὁ
Χριστὸς τῷ ὀνόματι τούτῳ σημαίνεσθαι νοῶν τις οὐχ ἁμαρτήσεται· καὶ γὰρ ὁ
μέγας Ἰωάννης ἐρωτηθεὶς ὅστις εἴη φωνὴν ἑαυτὸν κατωνόμασεν, ἐπειδὴ τοῦ
λόγου πρόδρομος ἦν, καὶ ὁ μακάριος Παῦλος δοκιμὴν ἐδίδου τοῦ ἐν αὐτῷ
25   λαλοῦντος Χριστοῦ, ᾧ τὴν φωνὴν ἑαυτοῦ χρήσας γλυκασμὸς ἦν δι' ἐκείνου
φθεγγόμενος, καὶ πάντες οἱ προφῆται τὰ φωνητικὰ ἑαυτῶν ὄργανα τῷ
ἐνηχοῦντι αὐτοῖς πνεύματι παραχωρήσαντες γλυκασμὸς ἐγίνοντο τὸ θεῖον
μέλι διὰ τοῦ λάρυγγος τοῦ ἰδίου πηγάζοντες, ὃ Βασιλεῖς τε καὶ ἰδιῶται πρὸς
ὑγείαν προσφέρονται, οὗ ἡ ἀπόλαυσις οὐκ ἐπικόπτει τὴν ἐπιθυμίαν τῷ κόρῳ,
30   ἀλλὰ τρέφει μᾶλλον διὰ τῆς τῶν ἐπιθυμουμένων μετουσίας τὸν πόθον.
        διὰ τοῦτο καὶ ὅλον αὐτὸν ἐπιθυμίαν κατονομάζει οἷόν τινι ὁρισμῷ τὸ
τοῦ ζητουμένου κάλλος διὰ ταύτης τῆς | φωνῆς ὑπογράφουσα· Ὅλος γάρ,   426
φησίν, ἐπιθυμία. ὡς μακάρια τὰ μέλη ἐκεῖνα, δι' ὧν τὸ ὅλον ἐπιθυμία γίνεται,
διὰ τῆς ἐν παντὶ ἀγαθῷ τελειότητος σύγκρατον ἐκ πάντων τὸ ἐράσμιον

and the leopard will sleep with the kid, and in charge of them is that young "child" who "was born for us," whose hand enters the asps' nest and grasps the snake's offspring and makes their venom harmless (cf. Isa 11:6–8). And when these things have come to pass, says the prophet, "Lebanon with its lofty ones will collapse" (Isa 10:34).

Now it would be pointless to explain in detail all the things that the prophecy is setting forth by way of these enigmas, for they are apparent to everyone. Who does not know the child, "born to us," who handled the asps, and under whose oversight the harmful beasts shared the same home as the tame, because their natural rancor had been forgotten? In this way, then, the Lebanon of wickedness is brought to collapse, and together with the Origina-tor of evils the Heights raised up against truth also collapse. Hence the Bride likens the Lord's beauty to the chosen Lebanon in these words: *His appear-ance is like Lebanon the chosen, like cedars.*

She goes on to assign an appropriate praise to the throat, naming it "sweetness" and "desire." Here is how the text goes: *His throat is sweetness and entire desire.*

We understand this as follows. Convention calls the part of the body under the chin "throat," and they say that | by it sound is produced as it is whirled by the pressure of the breath that comes from the windpipe. Now "fine words" are "honeycombs" (Prov 16:24), and the instrument of such rational speech is the voice, which originates from the throat. Perhaps, then, one will not be mistaken if one understands this term "throat" to signify the servants and interpreters of the Word, in whom Christ speaks. The great John the Baptist, after all, when asked who he was, called himself a "voice" (John 1:23) because he was the forerunner of the Word, and the blessed Paul gave proof of the Christ speaking in him (cf. 2 Cor 13:3), and, having lent Christ his own voice, he gave voice to *sweetness.* Further, all the prophets, in handing over their organs of speech to the Spirit[34] that sounded within them, became *sweetness* as they poured the divine honey forth through their throat. Kings and common folk alike consumed it to their benefit. The pleasure of it did not check desire through surfeit; rather did it nourish longing by affording a taste of what desire seeks.

That is why she names the whole of him *desire,* as if she were capturing the beauty of the One she sought in a kind of definition | by this word, for it says *totally desire.* How blessed are the members through whose contributions the whole body becomes *desire*! By their perfection in every good thing they

---

34. πνεῦμα, which is the same word translated just above as "breath" in Gregory's account of the physiology of voice production.

ἀπεργαζόμενα κάλλος, ὥστε ὅλον, μὴ ἐν ὀφθαλμῷ μόνον καὶ κέρασιν
[ἢ βοστρύχοις] ἀλλὰ καὶ ἐν ποσὶ καὶ ἐν χερσὶ καὶ ἐν κνήμαις καὶ κατὰ τὸν
φάρυγγα παραπλησίως ἐπιθυμητὸν εἶναι μηδενὸς ἐν τοῖς μέλεσι κατὰ τὴν
ὑπερβολὴν τοῦ κάλλους ἐλαττουμένου.

5   Οὗτος, φησίν, ἀδελφιδός μου καὶ οὗτος πλησίον μου, θυγατέρες
Ἰερουσαλήμ· πάντα γὰρ ὑπ' ὄψιν αὐταῖς ἀγαγοῦσα διὰ τῆς τοῦ λόγου γραφῆς·
τὰ γνωρίσματα, δι' ὧν ἦν δυνατὸν γενέσθαι τὴν τοῦ ζητουμένου φανέρωσιν,
τότε τῷ δεικτικῷ | κέχρηται λόγῳ, οὗτός ἐστι, λέγουσα, ὁ ζητούμενος, ὃς   427
διὰ τοῦ ἀδελφὸς γενέσθαι ἐξ Ἰούδα ἡμῖν ἀνατείλας πλησίον ἐγένετο τοῦ
10   ἐμπεπτωκότος εἰς τοὺς λῃστὰς ἐλαίῳ καὶ οἴνῳ καὶ ἐπιδέσμοις τὰς πληγὰς
ἰασάμενος καὶ ἐπὶ τοῦ ἰδίου ἄρας ὑποζυγίου καὶ τῷ πανδοχείῳ ἐναναπαύσας
καὶ τὰ δύο δηνάρια πρὸς τὴν ζωὴν παρασχόμενος καὶ ἐν τῇ ἐπανόδῳ αὐτοῦ
τὸ προστεθὲν εἰς τὸ τῆς ἐντολῆς ἔργον ἀποδώσειν ἐπαγγειλάμενος.

       πάντως δὲ φανερόν ἐστι τούτων ἕκαστον εἰς ὅ τι βλέπει· τῷ γὰρ
15   ἐκπειράζοντι τὸν κύριον νομικῷ βουλομένῳ ὑπὲρ τοὺς ἄλλους ἑαυτὸν
δεῖξαι καὶ ἐν ὑπερηφανίᾳ τὸ πρὸς τοὺς λοιποὺς ὁμότιμον διαπτύοντι ἐν
τῷ λέγειν· Καὶ τίς ἐστί μου πλησίον; τότε ἐν διηγήματος εἴδει πᾶσαν τὴν
φιλάνθρωπον οἰκονομίαν ὁ λόγος ἐκτίθεται, τὴν ἄνωθεν κάθοδον τοῦ
ἀνθρώπου διηγησάμενος καὶ τὴν τῶν λῃστῶν ἐνέδραν καὶ τὴν τοῦ ἀφθάρτου
20   ἐνδύματος περιαίρεσιν καὶ τὰ τῆς ἁμαρτίας τραύματα καὶ τὸ εἰς ἥμισυ τῆς
φύσεως προχωρῆσαι τὸν θάνατον τῆς ψυχῆς ἀθανάτου διαμεινάσης καὶ τοῦ
νόμου τὴν ἀνωφελῆ πάροδον οὔτε ἱερέως οὔτε Λευΐτου τὰς πληγὰς τοῦ
παραπεπτωκότος τοῖς λῃσταῖς θεραπεύσαντος· ἀδύνατον γὰρ αἷμα ταύρων
καὶ τράγων ἀφελεῖν ἁμαρτίας,

25   ἀλλὰ τὸν πᾶσαν τὴν ἀνθρωπίνην φύσιν διὰ τῆς ἀπαρχῆς τοῦ φυράματος
περιθέμενον, ἐν ᾗ παντὸς | ἦν ἔθνους τὸ μέρος, Ἰουδαίου τε καὶ Σαμαρείτου   428
καὶ Ἕλληνος καὶ πάντων ἅπαξ ἀνθρώπων, τοῦτον μετὰ τοῦ σώματος, ὅπερ
ἐστὶν ὑποζύγιον, τῷ τόπῳ τῆς τοῦ ἀνθρώπου κακώσεως ἐπιστάντα καὶ
θεραπεῦσαι τὰ τραύματα καὶ ἐπὶ τοῦ ἰδίου αὐτὸν κτήνους ἐπαναπαῦσαι καὶ
30   καταγώγιον ποιῆσαι αὐτῷ τὴν ἰδίαν φιλανθρωπίαν, ᾗ πάντες οἱ κοπιῶντες
καὶ πεφορτισμένοι ἐναναπαύονται. ὁ δὲ ἐν αὐτῷ γενόμενος δέχεται πάντως
ἐν ἑαυτῷ τὸν ἐν ᾧ ἐγένετο οὕτως εἰπόντος τοῦ λόγου ὅτι Ὁ μένων ἐν ἐμοὶ
κἀγὼ ἐν αὐτῷ. δεξάμενος οὖν τῷ ἰδίῳ χωρήματι πανδοχεύει ἐν ἑαυτῷ τὸν
ἀχώρητον, παρ' οὗ δέχεται τὰ δύο νομίσματα, ὧν τὸ μέν ἐστιν ἡ ἐξ ὅλης ψυχῆς
35   εἰς τὸν θεὸν ἀγάπη, τὸ δὲ ἕτερον ἡ εἰς τὸν πλησίον ὡς ἑαυτόν, καθὼς καὶ ὁ
νομικὸς ἀπεκρίνατο. ἀλλ' ἐπειδὴ Οὐχ οἱ ἀκροαταὶ τοῦ νόμου δίκαιοι παρὰ
τῷ θεῷ, ἀλλ' οἱ ποιηταὶ τοῦ νόμου δικαιωθήσονται, χρὴ μὴ μόνον δέξασθαι

produce a fascinating beauty blended out of all of them, and the result is that the whole body—not only the eye and the hair but also the feet and hands and legs and around the throat—is desirable, and, because of the transcendence of its beauty, none of the members is counted inferior.

This, says she, *is my kinsman, and this is my close one, O daughters of Jerusalem,* for when by the language of her description she has brought to their attention all of the distinctive qualities by which it is possible for the One they seek to be manifest, she then makes use of | ostensive language: "This," she says, "is the one you are looking for. This is he who to become our brother rose up for us out of Judah, who became a neighbor to the man who fell among thieves, treated his blows with oil and wine and bandages, set him upon his own beast, furnished two denarii for his support, and promised that on his return he would repay whatever more was spent for the work of the commandment."

Now the point of every detail of this is plain to see. For here is a scribe testing the Lord because he wants to show himself superior to the others and loftily refusing his equality with the rest by asking, "And who is my neighbor?" (Luke 10:29). For him the Word then sets forth, in the form of a story, the entire economy of God's love for humanity. He relates the downward journey of the human being, the thieves' ambush, the stripping off of the incorruptible garment, the wounds of sin, death's occupation of the half of human nature[35] (the soul remains immortal), and the law's feckless passing-by (neither priest nor Levite treated the blows of the man who fell among thieves), for it was not possible for "the blood of bulls and of goats" to take away sins (Heb 10:4).

But he who wrapped the whole of humanity[36] about him through the firstfruits of the loaf, in which there was a portion | of every nation, of Jew and Samaritan and Greek and all human beings at once, he, I say, together with his body, represented by the beast, stopped at the place where humanity had been hurt and treated its wounds, and rested it upon his own mule, and made his own love of humanity a hostelry, in which "all who labor and are heavy laden" (cf. Matt 11:28) find repose. But anyone who comes to be in him receives within himself the One in whom he is; for the Word says, "Whoever abides in me, I also abide in him" (John 15:5). Hence anyone who has received him within is host to the Uncontained, from whose hand that pair of coins is received, one of which is to love God with one's whole soul, and the other, to love one's neighbor as oneself, even as the law required. But since "it is not the hearers of the law who are righteous before God, but the doers of

---

35. Cf. Luke 10:30, where it is said that the thieves left their victim "half-dead."

36. πᾶσαν τὴν ἀνθρωπίνην φύσιν means "the entire human race," since φύσις here appears once again to bear a collective as well as a general sense.

τὰ δύο ταῦτα νομίσματα (τὴν πίστιν λέγω τὴν εἰς τὸ θεῖον καὶ τὴν ἀγαθὴν
πρὸς τοὺς ὁμοφύλους συνείδησιν), | ἀλλά τι καὶ αὐτὸν συνεισενεγκεῖν διὰ   429
τῶν ἔργων πρὸς τὴν τῶν ἐντολῶν τούτων ἐκπλήρωσιν. διὰ τοῦτό φησιν πρὸς
τὸν πανδοχέα ὁ κύριος ὅτι πᾶν τὸ περὶ τὴν θεραπείαν τοῦ κεκακωμένου παρ'
5   αὐτοῦ γενόμενον ἐν τῇ δευτέρᾳ αὐτοῦ παρουσίᾳ κατὰ τὴν ἀξίαν τῆς σπουδῆς
ἀπολήψεται.

ὁ τοίνυν πλησίον ἡμῶν γεγονὼς διὰ τῆς τοιαύτης φιλανθρωπίας, ὁ διὰ
τοῦ ἐξ Ἰούδα ἡμῖν ἀνατεῖλαι ἀδελφιδὸς γενόμενος οὗτός ἐστιν, ὃν μηνύει ταῖς
νεάνισιν ὁ τῆς νύμφης λόγος, οὗτός ἐστιν ὁ ταῖς θυγατράσιν Ἰερουσαλὴμ
10   παρὰ τῆς ἀχράντου νύμφης δηλούμενος, δι' ὧν φησιν ὅτι Οὗτος ἀδελφιδός
μου καὶ οὗτος πλησίον μου, θυγατέρες Ἰερουσαλήμ· ὃν καὶ ἡμεῖς διὰ τῶν
δηλωθέντων γνωρισμάτων εὕροιμέν τε καὶ καταλάβοιμεν ἐπὶ σωτηρίᾳ τῶν
ψυχῶν ἡμῶν διὰ τῆς τοῦ ἁγίου πνεύματος χειραγωγίας,

ᾧ ἡ δόξα εἰς τοὺς αἰῶνας τῶν αἰώνων.
15   ἀμήν.

the law who will be justified" (Rom 2:15), it is necessary not only to receive that pair of coins (I mean faith in the Divine and a good conscience toward one's fellows) | but also by works to make one's own contribution toward the fulfillment of these commandments. That is why the Lord says to the inn-keeper that everything the latter does for the healing of the wounded man will be rewarded appropriately at his second coming.

So he who out of such love for humanity has become our neighbor, who has become our kinsman because he rises up for us out of Judah, this is the One whom the Bride's words declare to the young maidens. This is the One who is revealed to the daughters of Jerusalem by the immaculate Bride, who for their sake says: *This is my kinsman, and this is my close one, O daughters of Jerusalem*. And may we too both discover him by the marks shown us and receive him to the salvation of our souls, through the guidance of the Holy Spirit,

to whom be glory to the ages of ages.
Amen.

Λόγος ιε′

Ποῦ ἀπῆλθεν ὁ ἀδελφιδός σου, ἡ καλὴ ἐν γυναιξίν;
ποῦ ἀπέβλεψεν ὁ ἀδελφιδός σου;
καὶ ζητήσομεν αὐτὸν μετὰ σοῦ.
| Ἀδελφιδός μου κατέβη εἰς κῆπον αὐτοῦ   430
εἰς φιάλας τοῦ ἀρώματος
ποιμαίνειν ἐν κήποις καὶ συλλέγειν κρίνα.
Ἐγὼ τῷ ἀδελφιδῷ μου καὶ ὁ ἀδελφιδός μου ἐμοί,
ὁ ποιμαίνων ἐν τοῖς κρίνοις.
Καλὴ εἶ, ἡ πλησίον μου, ὡς εὐδοκία,
ὡραία ὡς Ἰερουσαλήμ,
θάμβος ὡς τεταγμέναι.
Ἀπόστρεψον ὀφθαλμούς σου ἀπεναντίον ἐμοῦ
ὅτι αὐτοὶ ἀνεπτέρωσάν με.
τρίχωμά σου ὡς ἀγέλαι τῶν αἰγῶν
αἳ ἀνεφάνησαν ἀπὸ τοῦ Γαλαάδ,
Ὀδόντες σου ὡς ἀγέλαι τῶν κεκαρμένων
αἳ ἀνέβησαν ἀπὸ τοῦ λουτροῦ,
αἱ πᾶσαι διδυμεύουσαι
καὶ ἀτεκνοῦσα οὐκ ἔστιν ἐν αὐταῖς,
Ὡς σπαρτίον κόκκινον χείλη σου
καὶ ἡ λαλιά σου ὡραία,
ὡς λέπυρον ῥόας μῆλόν σου
ἐκτὸς τῆς σιωπήσεώς σου.
Ἐξήκοντά εἰσι βασίλισσαι καὶ ὀγδοήκοντα παλλακαὶ
καὶ νεάνιδες ὧν οὐκ ἔστιν ἀριθμός.
Μία ἐστὶ περιστερά μου, τελεία μου,
μία ἐστὶ τῇ μητρὶ αὐτῆς,
ἐκλεκτή ἐστι τῇ τεκούσῃ αὐτήν.

HOMILY 15
Song 6:1–9

¹*Where has your kinsman gone, O beautiful among women?*
Where has your kinsman turned his regard?
And we shall seek him with you.
²*My kinsman has descended into his garden,*
into bowls of spice,
to graze among the gardens and to gather lilies.
³*I am for my kinsman, and my kinsman is for me;*
he grazes his flock among the lilies.
⁴*You are beautiful, my close one, like goodwill,*
lovely, like Jerusalem,
an object of terror, like serried ranks drawn up.
⁵*Turn your eyes away from that which is opposed to me,*
for they give me wings.
Your hair is like flocks of goats
that have appeared from the direction of Gilead.
⁶*Your teeth are like flocks of shorn sheep*
that have come up from the bath,
all of them bearing twins
and without a barren one among them.
⁷*Your lips are like a scarlet cord,*
and your speech is seasonable.[1]
Your cheek is like the skin of a pomegranate
outside your veil.
⁸*There are sixty queens and eighty concubines*
and young maidens without number.
⁹*One is my dove, my perfect one,*
one is she for her mother,
she is a chosen one for the woman who bore her.

---

1. These two lines (Song 6:7a–b) are not in the Hebrew text that we know. They seem to have been introduced by analogy with Song 4:3a–b, where they occur in a longer passage (Song 4:1c–3) whose other lines are also repeated here. Song 6:7b ("your speech is seasonable") is translated differently here than the same words in Song 4:3b (see above, homily 7, pp. 228–29 [Jaeger]) for reasons having to do with Gregory's way of interpreting it in this homily; see below, n. 26.

| Ὁ ἐκ τῆς πόλεως Ἀνδρέου καὶ Πέτρου μαρτυρηθεὶς εἶναι Φίλιππος ὁ   431
ἀπόστολος (ἐγκώμιον γάρ μοι δοκεῖ τοῦ Φιλίππου τὸ πολίτην αὐτὸν τῶν
ἀδελφῶν ἐκείνων εἶναι τῶν προθαυμασθέντων ἐν τῷ εὐαγγελίῳ διὰ τῆς περὶ
αὐτῶν ἱστορίας· ὁ μὲν γὰρ Ἀνδρέας ὑποδείξαντος τοῦ βαπτιστοῦ, τίς ἐστιν ὁ
5   ἀμνὸς ὁ αἴρων τὴν ἁμαρτίαν τοῦ κόσμου, αὐτός τε τὸ μυστήριον κατενόησε
κατόπιν τοῦ δειχθέντος ἀκολουθήσας καὶ ὅπου μένει μαθὼν καὶ τῷ ἰδίῳ
ἀδελφῷ παρεῖναι τὸν προμηνυθέντα παρὰ τῆς προφητείας εὐαγγελίζεται,
ὁ δὲ φθάσας μικροῦ δεῖν τῇ πίστει τὴν ἀκοὴν ὅλῃ τῇ ψυχῇ προστίθεται τῷ
ἀμνῷ καὶ διὰ τῆς τοῦ ὀνόματος ὑπαλλαγῆς μεταποιεῖται παρὰ τοῦ κυρίου
10 πρὸς τὸ θειότερον ἀντὶ Σίμωνος Πέτρος καὶ ὀνομασθεὶς καὶ γενόμενος.

καίτοι τῷ Ἀβραὰμ καὶ τῇ Σάρρᾳ πολλοῖς ὕστερον χρόνοις μετὰ πολλὰς
θεοφανείας τῆς ἐκ τῶν ὀνομάτων μεταδίδωσιν εὐλογίας ὁ κύριος τὸν μὲν
πατέρα τὴν δὲ ἄρχουσαν διὰ τῆς τῶν ὀνομάτων μεταποιήσεως χειροτονήσας.
ὡσαύτως δὲ καὶ ὁ Ἰακὼβ μετὰ τὴν παννύχιον πάλην ἀξιοῦται τῆς τοῦ | 432
15 Ἰσραὴλ ἐπωνυμίας τε καὶ δυνάμεως. ὁ δὲ μέγας Πέτρος οὐ κατὰ μικρὸν δι᾽
αὐξήσεως προῆλθεν ἐπὶ τὴν χάριν ταύτην, ἀλλ᾽ ὁμοῦ τε ἤκουσε τοῦ ἀδελφοῦ
καὶ ἐπίστευσε τῷ ἀμνῷ καὶ ἐτελειώθη διὰ τῆς πίστεως καὶ προσφυεὶς τῇ
πέτρᾳ Πέτρος ἐγένετο)

οὗτος τοίνυν ὁ Φίλιππος ὁ ἄξιος τῶν τοσούτων τε καὶ τηλικούτων
20 πολίτης, ἐπειδὴ εὕρεμα τοῦ κυρίου γενόμενος, καθώς φησι τὸ εὐαγγέλιον ὅτι
Εὑρίσκει τὸν Φίλιππον ὁ Ἰησοῦς, ἀκόλουθος ἐχειροτονήθη τοῦ λόγου τοῦ
εἰπόντος ὅτι Ἀκολούθει μοι καὶ τῷ φωτὶ τῷ ἀληθινῷ προσεγγίσας καθάπερ
τις λύχνος ἐκεῖθεν ἔσπασε πρὸς ἑαυτὸν τὴν τοῦ φωτὸς κοινωνίαν, καὶ

The daughters saw her, and they bless her.
The queens and concubines praise her.[2]

| Philip the apostle is declared to be from the city of Andrew and Peter. I mention this because to me at any rate it seems to be a way of honoring Philip to report that he is a fellow-citizen of that pair of brothers who have been made subjects of wonder and admiration by the Gospel account of them. For when the Baptist pointed out the identity of "the Lamb of God that takes away the sin of the world" (John 1:29), Andrew both grasped the mystery and, after following the One to whom John had pointed and learning where he lived, brought his own brother the good news that the One foretold by prophecy had arrived. His brother, in turn, all but anticipated the hearing of this message by his faith and attached himself to the Lamb with his entire soul. By changing his name—for he was both called and in fact became Peter instead of Simon—the Lord transmuted him into something more divine.

It is indeed true that, at a much more mature age[3] and after many theophanies, the Lord gave Abraham and Sarah a share in the blessing that stems from names: through a change of names he constituted the one of them a father and the other a ruler.[4] In the same way, Jacob too, but after a night-long wrestling match, was judged worthy|of the name and aptitude[5] of Israel. That great one, Peter, however, did not progress toward this grace bit by bit but at one and the same moment heard his brother and believed in the Lamb and was perfected by faith and, having attached himself to the Rock, became a rock.

As to this Philip, then, a worthy fellow-citizen of persons of such distinction and eminence, once he had become the Lord's "find" (as the Gospel says, Jesus *"found* Philip" [John 1:43]), he was made a follower of the Word who said to him, "Follow me" [John 1:43]. And when he had drawn near to the

---

2. The last two lines of Song 6:9, which are found in both the MT and LXX, are not given in the GNO text. They are included here in the translation because Gregory comments on them at the end of this homily.

3. Literally "later time," but Gregory means later relative to the length of their lives. He takes it that Peter was the more honored because he was a youngish man at the time of his calling.

4. See Philo, *Abr.* 99: "but the name of [Abraham's] wife was 'virtue,' her name being 'Sarra' in Chaldaean but in Greek 'ruler' (ἄρχουσα), because there is nothing that rules and governs more than virtue." Philo repeats this interpretation of Sarah's name in *Cher.* 7 and in *Mut.* 77, in both of which passages he explains (somewhat obscurely) the meanings of Sarah's successive names. Gregory no doubt gets the idea that Sarra means ἄρχουσα not directly from Philo but from the sixth of Origen's *Homilae in Genesim.*

5. See above, homily 6 (p. 197 [Jaeger]), where "Israel" is explained as meaning "one who sees God." Presumably, then, the δύναμις intended here is an "aptitude" for the vision of God.

περιλάμπει τὸν Ναθαναὴλ δᾳδουχήσας αὐτῷ τὸ τῆς εὐσεβείας μυστήριον δι᾽ ὧν φησιν·Ὃν ἔγραψε Μωϋσῆς καὶ οἱ προφῆται εὑρήκαμεν, Ἰησοῦν τὸν ἀπὸ Ναζαρὲτ τῆς Γαλιλαίας.

τοῦ δὲ Ναθαναὴλ | ἐπιστατικῶς δεξαμένου τὸ εὐαγγέλιον διὰ τὸ μετὰ   433
5   πάσης ἀκριβείας κατηχῆσθαι παρὰ τῆς προφητείας αὐτὸν τὸ περὶ τοῦ κυρίου μυστήριον καὶ εἰδέναι μὲν ὅτι ἐκ Βηθλεὲμ ἡ πρώτη διὰ σαρκὸς γενήσεται θεοφάνεια, διὰ δὲ τὴν ἐν Ναζαροῖς διαγωγὴν Ναζωραῖος κληθήσεται, πρὸς ἀμφότερα τοίνυν ἀποσκοποῦντος καὶ λογιζομένου, ὅτι ἐν μὲν τῇ τοῦ Δαβὶδ Βηθλεὲμ διὰ τὴν οἰκονομίαν τῆς κατὰ σάρκα γεννήσεως ἀναγκαῖον ἦν
10 γενέσθαι τὸ κατὰ τὸ σπήλαιον καὶ τὰ σπάργανα καὶ τὴν φάτνην μυστήριον, ἡ δὲ Γαλιλαία (ἐθνῶν δὲ τόπος ἡ Γαλιλαία) ἐπονομασθήσεταί ποτε τῷ τοῖς ἔθνεσιν ἐμφιλοχωρήσαντι λόγῳ, καὶ διὰ τοῦτο συνθεμένου τῷ τὸ φῶς αὐτῷ τῆς γνώσεως φήναντι καὶ εἰπόντος ὅτι Ἐκ Ναζαρὲτ δύναταί τι ἀγαθὸν εἶναι, τότε ὁδηγὸς πρὸς τὴν χάριν ὁ Φίλιππος γίνεται λέγων· Ἔρχου καὶ ἴδε. διὸ
15 καταλιπὼν ὁ Ναθαναὴλ τὴν τοῦ νόμου συκῆν, ἧς ἡ σκιὰ πρὸς τὴν μετουσίαν τοῦ φωτὸς διεκώλυε, καταλαμβάνει τὸν τὰ φύλλα τῆς συκῆς διὰ τὴν τῶν ἀγαθῶν ἀκαρπίαν | ἀποξηραίνοντα. διὸ καὶ μαρτυρεῖται παρὰ τοῦ λόγου   434 γνήσιος εἶναι καὶ οὐχὶ νόθος Ἰσραηλίτης ἐν τῷ ἀδόλῳ τῆς προαιρέσεως καθαρὸν ἐφ᾽ ἑαυτοῦ δεικνὺς τοῦ πατριάρχου τὸν χαρακτῆρα·Ἴδε γάρ, φησίν,
20 ἀληθινὸς Ἰσραηλίτης ἐν ᾧ δόλος οὐκ ἔστιν.

Πρὸς ὅ τι δὲ βλέπει τὸ ἐν τῷ προοιμίῳ διήγημα, φανερόν ἐστι πάντως τοῖς εὐμαθεστέροις ἀκροαταῖς ἐκ τῆς προτεθείσης κατὰ τὸ ἀκόλουθον ἡμῖν ἀναγνώσεως τῶν ἐκ τοῦ Ἄισματος τῶν Ἀισμάτων· ὡς γὰρ ὁ μὲν Ἀνδρέας τῇ φωνῇ τοῦ Ἰωάννου πρὸς τὸν ἀμνὸν ὡδηγήθη, ὁ δὲ Ναθαναὴλ φωταγωγηθεὶς
25 παρὰ τοῦ Φιλίππου καὶ τῆς περιεχούσης αὐτὸν τοῦ νόμου σκιᾶς ἔξω γενόμενος ἐν τῷ φωτὶ τῷ ἀληθινῷ γίνεται, οὕτω καὶ αἱ νεάνιδες πρὸς τὴν εὕρεσιν τοῦ μηνυθέντος αὐταῖς ἀγαθοῦ καθηγεμόνι χρῶνται τῇ τελειωθείσῃ διὰ τοῦ κάλλους ψυχῇ λέγουσαι πρὸς αὐτήν· Ποῦ ἀπῆλθεν ὁ ἀδελφιδός σου,

true light, like some lamp he drew from it a share of its light; then he enlightened Nathanael by illuminating for him the mystery of true religion in these words: "We have found the one of whom Moses wrote…, and the prophets, Jesus from Nazareth" (John 1:45) of Galilee.

Nathanael for his part | received the glad news with discernment because prophecy had taught him the mystery of the Lord with great accuracy, and he knew that the first revelation of God in the flesh would come from Bethlehem but that [the Lord] would be called a Nazarene because of his stay in Nazareth. Therefore he paid close attention to both of these truths and reasoned that for the sake of the economy of the fleshly birth it was necessary for the mystery of the cave and the swaddling clothes and the manger to occur in David's Bethlehem, but on the other hand that Galilee—which means "the place of the Gentiles"—would be given its name because of the Word who had delighted to dwell among the Gentiles. For this reason he agreed with the man who had revealed the light of knowledge to him and said, "From Nazareth something good can come" (John 1:46).[6] At this point, Philip becomes his guide toward grace and says, "Come and see." Therefore Nathanael leaves behind the fig tree of the law, whose shade was preventing his participation in the light, and lays hold on the One who withers the leaves of the fig tree because they fail to produce good fruit. | Therefore the Word also declares that he is a genuine, and not a counterfeit, Israelite, who demonstrates by the guilelessness of his choice that in his case the distinctive trait of the patriarch[7] is unsullied, "for behold," he says, "a true Israelite in whom there is no guile."

To instructed listeners, the point of this introductory narrative is entirely clear from the reading in the Song of Songs that has just been set before us following the order of the text. For just as Andrew was led to the Lamb by the voice of John, and just as Nathanael came within the true light when he had been introduced into the light by Philip and freed from the shadow of the law that enveloped him, so too the young maidens make use of their guide, the soul who has been brought to perfection by her comeliness, to help them find the Good that had been announced to them, and they say to her: *Where*

---

6. Gregory takes Nathanael's words not as a question ("Can anything good come out of Nazareth?") but as an assertion that agrees with (συνθεμένου) Philip's description of Jesus as "from Nazareth of Galilee" (cf. John 1:45). Cf. Dünzl 1994b, 3:770 n. 13 and the useful citation of Origen by Langerbeck 1960, 433, *ad loc.*

7. The patriarch in question is presumably Jacob (renamed "Israel," as Gregory has just noted), though whether it is his character as ἄπλαστος ("unaffected," perhaps "forthright"; see Gen 25:27, with the suggestion of Dünzl 1994b 3:773.7) that Gregory has in mind must remain a matter for speculation. Nevertheless, one must concede that it is difficult to portray Jacob as, in the strict sense, guileless.

ἡ καλὴ ἐν γυναιξίν; ποῦ ἀπέβλεψεν ὁ ἀδελφιδός σου; καὶ ζητήσομεν αὐτὸν μετὰ σοῦ.

ἀκολούθως δὲ προσάγουσι τῇ διδασκάλῳ τὴν πεῦσιν αἱ παρθένοι ψυχαί·
πρῶτον γὰρ τὸν περὶ τοῦ τί ἐστιν ἐποιήσαντο λόγον ἐν τῷ πρὸ ταύτης τῆς
5 ῥήσεως ἐρωτήματι λέγουσαι· Τί ἀδελφιδός σου, ἡ καλὴ ἐν γυναιξίν; ὅπερ
διδαχθεῖσαι διὰ τῶν εἰρημένων σημείων ὅτι λευκὸς καὶ πυρρὸς καὶ τὰ λοιπά,
δι᾽ ὧν ὑπεγράφη τὸ εἶδος | τοῦ ζητουμένου, περὶ τοῦ ποῦ πυνθάνονται. διὸ   435
λέγουσι· Ποῦ ἀπῆλθεν ὁ ἀδελφιδός σου; ἢ Ποῦ ἀπέβλεψεν; ἵνα πάντως ὅπου
μέν ἐστι μαθοῦσαι προσκυνήσωσιν εἰς τὸν τόπον οὗ ἔστησαν οἱ πόδες αὐτοῦ,
10 ὅπου δὲ ἀποβλέπει διδαχθεῖσαι οὕτω στήσωσιν ἑαυτάς, ὥστε καὶ αὐταῖς
ἐποφθῆναι τὴν δόξαν αὐτοῦ, οὗ ἡ ἐπιφάνεια σωτηρία τῶν ἐποπτευόντων
γίνεται, καθώς φησιν ὁ προφήτης ὅτι Ἐπίφανον τὸ πρόσωπόν σου καὶ
σωθησόμεθα.

καὶ ἡ διδάσκαλος καθ᾽ ὁμοιότητα Φιλίππου τοῦ εἰπόντος· Ἔρχου καὶ
15 ἴδε καθηγεῖται τῶν παρθένων πρὸς τὴν τοῦ ζητουμένου κατάληψιν ἀντὶ τοῦ
εἰπεῖν τὸ Ἴδε τὸν τόπον ὑποδεικνύουσα ἐν ᾧ ἐστιν ὁ ζητούμενος καὶ ὅπου
βλέπει· φησὶ γὰρ ὅτι Ἀδελφιδός μου κατέβη εἰς κῆπον αὐτοῦ εἰς φιάλας τοῦ
ἀρώματος. ἕως τούτου τὸ ἐν ᾧ ἐστιν ὑπὸ τοῦ λόγου σημαίνεται, τὸ δὲ ἀπὸ
τούτου, τί ὁρᾷ καὶ ὅπου βλέπει, τῷ λόγῳ δείκνυσιν ἡ διδάσκαλος εἰποῦσα ὅτι
20 Ποιμαίνει ἐν κήποις καὶ συλλέγει κρίνα. αὕτη μὲν οὖν ἡ σωματικὴ τοῦ λόγου
πρὸς τὰς νεάνιδάς ἐστιν ὁδηγία, δι᾽ ὧν μανθάνουσι καὶ ὅπου ἐστὶ καὶ ὅπου
βλέπει.

| Χρὴ δὲ πάντως καὶ τὸ ὠφέλιμον τῆς θεοπνεύστου ταύτης ἐπιγνῶναι   436
γραφῆς διὰ τῆς πνευματικῆς θεωρίας. οὐκοῦν ὅταν ἀκούσωμεν ὅτι Ἀδελφιδός
25 μου κατέβη εἰς κῆπον αὐτοῦ, τὸ εὐαγγελικὸν μυστήριον διὰ τῶν εἰρημένων
μανθάνομεν ἑκάστου τῶν ὀνομάτων τούτων τὸν μυστικὸν λόγον ἡμῖν
σαφηνίζοντος·

ὁ ἐν σαρκὶ φανερωθεὶς θεὸς διὰ τὸ ἐξ Ἰούδα μὲν ἀνατεῖλαι, λάμψαι δὲ
τοῖς ἔθνεσι τοῖς ἐν σκότει καὶ σκιᾷ θανάτου καθημένοις καλῶς καὶ προσφυῶς
30 τῷ ὀνόματι τοῦ ἀδελφιδοῦ παρὰ τῆς μνηστευθείσης αὐτῷ πρὸς ἀΐδιον
συζυγίαν κατονομάζεται ἀδελφῆς οὔσης τοῦ ἐξ Ἰούδα λαοῦ, τὸ δὲ Κατέβη

has your kinsman gone, O beautiful among women? Where has your kinsman turned his regard? And we shall seek him with you.

In bringing this question before their teacher, the virgin souls follow a logical order. In the first instance, in the question they posed before this one, they took up the issue of his "what" and asked, *What is your kinsman, O beautiful among women?*[8] Taught their answer by the clues stated above—that he is white and red and so on—in which the appearance of the | One they sought was described, they now ask about his "where." The reason why they say *Where has your kinsman gone?* or *Where has your kinsman turned his regard?* is so that they may, once they have learned where he is, make obeisance toward the place where his feet have stood (cf. Ps 131:7) and, once they have been taught where he turns his regard, may so station themselves that his glory may be revealed to them as well—that glory whose epiphany is the salvation of those who behold it, even as the prophet says: "Show[9] us your face, and we shall be saved" (Ps 79:4).

Then, like Philip, who said, "Come and see" (John 1:46), the teacher[10] leads the virgins toward a comprehension of the One they seek. She does not say "See," but she points out the place where the One sought for is and where he is looking, for she says: *My kinsman has descended into his garden, into bowls of spice.* Up to this point the text is indicating where he is located, but from this point on the teacher's language shows what he sees and where he is looking, since she says: "He pastures his flock *among the gardens and gathers lilies.*" This, then, is the outward and literal[11] guidance with which the text provides the maidens; from it they learn both where he is and where he is looking.

| It is also strictly neccessary, however, to descry, by spiritual inquiry and discernment, what is profitable for us in this inspired Scripture-passage. Hence when we hear *My kinsman has descended into his garden,* we learn the mystery of the gospel, since each of these terms illuminates the mystical meaning of the passage.

Because he arose out of Judah (cf. Heb 7:14) and brought light to the nations that dwelt in darkness and the shadow of death (cf. Luke 1:79), it is right and appropriate that God-manifest-in-flesh be assigned the title "kinsman"[12] by the one who has been betrothed to him for an everlasting

---

8. See Song 5:9, which with the following seven verses makes up the passage that Gregory interprets in homilies 13 and 14.

9. Greek ἐπίφανον. Cf. 2 Cor 4:6, which may have been in Gregory's mind.

10. I.e., the Bride, the soul that is approaching perfection.

11. Literally, "literal" is "corporeal" (Greek σωματική).

12. On this translation of ἀδελφιδός, see above, homily 4, p. 107 (Jaeger), with n. 11 there; homily 3, p. 93 (Jaeger), with n. 26 there.

δηλοῖ ὅτι διὰ τὸν ἀπὸ Ἱεροσολύμων εἰς Ἱεριχὼ καταβάντα καὶ ἐν τοῖς λῃσταῖς
γενόμενον ἄνθρωπον καὶ αὐτὸς τῇ καθόδῳ τοῦ ἐμπεσόντος τοῖς πολεμίοις
συγκατέρχεται, δι' ὧν σημαίνει τὴν ἐκ τῆς ἀφράστου μεγαλειότητος
γενομένην ἐπὶ τὸ ταπεινὸν τῆς φύσεως ἡμῶν συγκατάβασιν·

5   διὰ δὲ τοῦ κατὰ τὸν κῆπον αἰνίγματος τοῦτο μανθάνομεν ὅτι ἀναφυτεύει
τὸ ἑαυτοῦ γεώργιον ὁ ἀληθινὸς γεωργός, ἡμᾶς τοὺς ἀνθρώπους (ἡμεῖς γάρ
ἐσμεν αὐτοῦ τὸ γεώργιον κατὰ τὴν τοῦ Παύλου φωνήν. | ἐπεὶ οὖν ἐκεῖνός   437
ἐστιν ὁ κατ' ἀρχὰς ἐν τῷ παραδείσῳ γεωργήσας τὴν ἀνθρωπίνην φυτείαν
ἣν ἐφύτευσεν ὁ πατὴρ ὁ οὐράνιος, διὰ τοῦτο τοῦ μονιοῦ τοῦ ἀγρίου
10   κατανεμηθέντος ἡμᾶς, τὸν κῆπον, καὶ λυμηναμένου τὸ θεῖον γεώργιον κατέβη
τοῦ πάλιν ποιῆσαι κῆπον τὴν ἔρημον τῇ τῶν ἀρετῶν φυτείᾳ καλλωπιζόμενον
τὴν καθαρὰν καὶ θείαν τῆς διδασκαλίας πηγὴν ἐπὶ τὴν τῶν τοιούτων φυτῶν
ἐπιμέλειαν ὀχετηγήσας τῷ λόγῳ)·

αἱ δὲ τοῦ ἀρώματος φιάλαι ἐν μὲν τῇ τοῦ κάλλους ὑπογραφῇ πρὸς τὸ
15   τῶν σιαγόνων ἐγκώμιον παρελήφθησαν, δι' ὧν καταλεαίνεται τὰ πνευματικὰ
σιτία τοῖς τρεφομένοις, ἐνταῦθα δὲ τόπος εἶναι τοῦ νυμφίου καὶ ἐνδιαίτημα
παρὰ τοῦ λόγου μηνύεται τοῦτο μανθανόντων ἡμῶν ὅτι οὔτε ἐν ἐρήμῳ τῶν
ἀρετῶν ψυχῇ ὁ νυμφίος αὐλίζεται καί, εἴ τις κατὰ τὸν προαποδοθέντα λόγον
φιάλη ἀρώματος γένοιτο φύουσα τὰ μυρεψικά, ὁ τοιοῦτος κρατὴρ τῆς σοφίας
20   γενόμενος δέχεται ἐν ἑαυτῷ τὸν θεῖόν τε καὶ ἀκήρατον οἶνον δι' οὗ γίνεται
τῷ δεξαμένῳ ἡ εὐφροσύνη. ὁ δὲ ἐφεξῆς λόγος διδάσκει ἡμᾶς ποίαις νομαῖς τὰ
ποίμνια τοῦ καλοῦ ποιμένος πιαίνεται·

οὐ γὰρ εἰς ἐρήμους τινὰς καὶ ἀκανθοφόρους τόπους ἐξελαύνει | τὰ   438
πρόβατα, ὥστε τὴν χορτώδη δρέψασθαι πόαν, ἀλλὰ τροφὴ πρόκειται
25   αὐτοῖς τὰ ἐκ τῶν κήπων ἀρώματα, ἀντὶ δὲ χόρτου τὸ κρίνον γίνεται ὅπερ
φησὶ παρὰ τοῦ ποιμένος εἰς διατροφὴν τῶν προβάτων συλλέγεσθαι, ταῦτα
φιλοσοφοῦντος ἡμῖν διὰ τούτων τοῦ λόγου ὅτι ἡ περιεκτικὴ τῶν ὄντων
φύσις καὶ δύναμις πάντα ἐν ἑαυτῇ περιείρουσα τόπον ἑαυτῆς καὶ χώρημα
ποιεῖται τῶν δεχομένων τὴν καθαρότητα, ἐν οἷς ὁ πολυειδῶς διὰ τῶν ἀρετῶν
30   γεωργούμενος κῆπος κομᾷ μὲν τοῖς τῶν κρίνων ἄνθεσι, βρύει δὲ τῇ τῶν
ἀρωμάτων καρπογονίᾳ· τὰ μὲν γὰρ κρίνα τοῦ λαμπροῦ καὶ καθαροῦ τῆς

union, since she is herself a "kinswoman" who stems from Judah. As to the expression *has descended,* it reveals that he himself, for the sake of the man who "descended from Jerusalem to Jericho" (Luke 10:30) and found himself among thieves, did indeed accompany the descent of the one who fell among foes, and these things signify his coming down from unutterable majesty to the lowliness of our nature.

From the enigma of the garden, on the other hand, we learn that what the true Husbandman plants is we human beings (for according to Paul's statement, we are his field). | Now he is the one who in the paradise at the beginning tended the human planting that the heavenly Father had planted. That is why, once the wild boar had ravaged the garden—which is to say, us—and ruined the divine field, he *descended* in order once again to make the desert, beautified by the planting of the virtues, a garden and by the Word channeled the pure and divine spring waters of the teaching with the aim of fostering such plants.[13]

As to the *bowls of spice,* they were used in the description of the Bridegroom's beauty to praise his jaws,[14] by which spiritual foodstuffs are ground fine for those who are fed on them. In the present passage, however, our text declares that they represent the place, the dwelling place, of the Bridegroom, and what we learn is this: that the Bridegroom does not lodge in a soul that lacks[15] the virtues and, further still, that if a person should become, in the sense required by the earlier text, a bowl of spice that produces fragrant ointments, such a person has become a mixing bowl of Wisdom's (cf. Prov 9:2) and receives within himself the divine and unadulterated wine that brings gladness to its recipient (cf. Ps 103:15).

The text that follows this, however, teaches us on what pasturage the Good Shepherd's flocks are fattened. For he does not drive | his sheep into desert places to feed on grass where thorn bushes grow. Rather are spices from the gardens set before them to feed on, and in place of grass comes the lily, which, it says, is gathered by the shepherd as sustenance for his sheep. In these words the text philosophizes for us to the effect that the Nature that contains whatever is and the Power that encompasses all things takes as its place and its proper lodging the purity of those who receive it—those in whom the garden that is richly and variously cultivated by the virtues undulates with the blossoms of lilies and burgeons with the fruitfulness of spices. For the lilies

---

13. On this whole passage, see Ps 79:4, 14–20.

14. See above, homily 14, p. 401 (Jaeger); Song 5:13.

15. The Greek is ἔρημος, the word commonly translated as "empty territory," i.e., "desert." The Word is not attached to deserts, then, but prefers to dwell in paradises and gardens, i.e., souls in which the virtues have been planted and cultivated.

διανοίας αἴνιγμα γίνεται, ἡ δὲ τῶν ἀρωμάτων εὔπνοια τοῦ πάσης ἁμαρτιῶν δυσωδίας ἀλλοτρίως ἔχειν. τούτοις οὖν φησι τὸν τῶν λογικῶν ἐπιστάτην ποιμνίων ἐναναστρέφεσθαι, ἐν μὲν τοῖς κήποις νομεύοντα, τὰ δὲ κρίνα πρὸς τὴν τῶν προβάτων διατροφὴν κείροντά τε καὶ συλλέγοντα, ἅπερ διὰ
5   τοῦ μεγάλου Παύλου τοῖς προβάτοις προτίθησι τοῦ ἐκ τῆς θείας ἀποθήκης προβάλλοντος ἡμῖν τὴν ἐκ τῶν κρίνων διατροφήν. ἔστι δὲ ταῦτα Ὅσα ἀληθῆ, ὅσα σεμνά, ὅσα δίκαια, ὅσα ἁγνά, ὅσα προσφιλῆ, ὅσα εὔφημα, εἴ τις ἀρετὴ καὶ εἴ τις ἔπαινος. ταῦτά ἐστι κατά γε τὸν ἐμὸν | λόγον τὰ κρίνα οἷς διατρέφεται   439
παρὰ τοῦ καλοῦ ποιμένος τε καὶ διδασκάλου τὰ ποίμνια.
10   Ὁ δὲ ἐφεξῆς λόγος, ὃν ἡ καθαρὰ καὶ ἀκηλίδωτος νύμφη πεποίηται λέγουσα· Ἐγὼ τῷ ἀδελφιδῷ μου καὶ ὁ ἀδελφιδός μου ἐμοί, κανὼν καὶ ὅρος τῆς κατ' ἀρετὴν ἐστι τελειότητος· μανθάνομεν γὰρ διὰ τούτων τὸ μὴ δεῖν πλὴν τοῦ θεοῦ μηδὲν ἐν ἑαυτῷ ἔχειν μηδὲ πρὸς ἄλλο τι βλέπειν τὴν κεκαθαρμένην ψυχήν, ἀλλ' οὕτως ἑαυτὴν ἐκκαθᾶραι παντὸς ὑλικοῦ πράγματός τε καὶ
15   νοήματος, ὡς ὅλην διόλου μετατεθεῖσαν πρὸς τὸ νοητόν τε καὶ ἄϋλον ἐναργεστάτην εἰκόνα τοῦ ἀρχετύπου κάλλους ἑαυτὴν ἀπεργάσασθαι.
καὶ ὥσπερ ὁ ἐπὶ τοῦ πίνακος ἰδὼν τὴν γραφὴν δι' ἀκριβείας πρός τι τῶν ἀρχετύπων μεμορφωμένην, μίαν ἀμφοτέρων εἶναι τὴν μορφὴν ἀποφαίνεται καὶ τὸ ἐπὶ τῆς εἰκόνος κάλλος τοῦ πρωτοτύπου λέγων εἶναι καὶ τὸ ἀρχέτυπον
20   ἐναργῶς ἐν τῷ μιμήματι καθορᾶσθαι, τὸν αὐτὸν τρόπον ἡ εἰποῦσα ὅτι Ἐγὼ τῷ ἀδελφιδῷ μου καὶ ὁ ἀδελφιδός μου ἐμοί, συμμεμορφῶσθαι λέγει τῷ Χριστῷ τὸ ἴδιον κάλλος ἀπολαβοῦσα, τὴν πρώτην τῆς φύσεως ἡμῶν μακαριότητα, κατ' εἰκόνα καὶ ὁμοίωσιν τοῦ πρώτου καὶ μόνου καὶ ἀληθινοῦ κάλλους ὡραϊσθεῖσα.
25 | καὶ οἷον ἐπὶ τοῦ κατόπτρου γίνεται, ὅταν τεχνικῶς τε καὶ καταλλήλως   440
τῇ χρείᾳ κατεσκευασμένον ἐν καθαρᾷ τῇ ἐπιφανείᾳ δι' ἀκριβείας ἐν ἑαυτῷ δείξῃ τοῦ ἐμφανέντος προσώπου τὸν χαρακτῆρα, οὕτως ἑαυτὴν ἡ ψυχὴ προσφόρως τῇ χρείᾳ κατασκευάσασα καὶ πᾶσαν ὑλικὴν ἀπορριψαμένη κηλῖδα καθαρὸν τοῦ ἀκηράτου κάλλους ἑαυτῇ τὸ εἶδος ἐνετυπώσατο. λέγει
30   οὖν τὴν φωνὴν ταύτην τὸ προαιρετικόν τε καὶ ἔμψυχον κάτοπτρον ὅτι· ἐπειδὴ ἐγὼ ὅλῳ τῷ κύκλῳ τὸ τοῦ ἀδελφιδοῦ πρόσωπον βλέπω, διὰ τοῦτο ὅλον τῆς ἐκείνου μορφῆς τὸ κάλλος ἐν ἐμοὶ καθορᾶται. ταύτας ἄντικρυς μιμεῖται τὰς φωνὰς ὁ Παῦλος λέγων τῷ θεῷ ζῆν ὁ νεκρὸς τῷ κόσμῳ γενόμενος καὶ ὅτι ζῇ ἐν αὐτῷ ὁ Χριστὸς μόνος· ὁ γὰρ εἰπὼν ὅτι Ἐμοὶ τὸ ζῆν Χριστός, τοῦτο διὰ
35   τοῦ λόγου βοᾷ ὅτι οὐδὲν τῶν ἀνθρωπίνων τε καὶ ὑλικῶν παθημάτων ἐν αὐτῷ ζῇ, οὔτε ἡδονὴ οὔτε λύπη οὔτε θυμὸς οὔτε φόβος οὔτε δειλία οὔτε πτόησις οὔτε τῦφος οὔτε θράσος, οὐ μνησικακία οὐ φθόνος οὐκ ἀμυντική τις διάθεσις οὐ φιλοχρηματία οὐ φιλοδοξία οὐ φιλοτιμία, οὐκ ἄλλο τι τῶν τὴν ψυχὴν διά τινος σχέσεως κηλιδούντων, ἀλλ' ἐκεῖνός μοι μόνος ἐστὶν ὃς οὐδὲν τούτων

represent, in the manner of an enigma, the mind's radiance and purity, and the sweet scent of the spices stands for estrangement from all the rank stench of sin. It is in such souls, then, that the Overseer of the flocks is said to dwell, grazing in the gardens while cutting and gathering lilies for the sustenance of the sheep—lilies that he puts before the sheep by the hand of the great Paul, who sets out for us the sustenance of lilies taken from the storehouse of God. These are "whatever is true, whatever is honorable, whatever is just, whatever is pure, whatever is lovely, whatever is gracious, if there is any virtue, if there is any praise" (Phil 4:8). According to my | reckoning, these are the lilies with which the Good Shepherd and teacher feeds his flocks.

The next line, though, which the pure and spotless Bride speaks when she says *I am for my kinsman, and my kinsman is for me,* is the norm and definition of perfection in virtue. For through these words we learn that the purified soul is to have nothing within her save God and is to look upon nothing else. Rather must she so cleanse herself of every material concern and thought that she is entirely, in her whole being, transposed into the intelligible and immaterial realm and makes of herself a supremely vivid image of the prototypical Beauty.

Thus the person who sees on the flat surface of a board a sketch that closely approximates the form of a particular prototype declares that the form of both is the same: he will say both that the beauty of the image is that of the prototype and that the original is palpably discerned in its copy. In the same way, she who says *I am for my kinsman, and my kinsman is for me* asserts that she is conformed to Christ, that she has recovered her very own beauty, the primordial blessedness of the human race, that is, to be arrayed in a beauty that conforms to the image and likeness of the first, the sole, and the true beauty.

| The same thing comes about with a mirror when—granted that it is put together with skill and in conformity with its function—it displays in itself on its clear surface the exact imprint of the face it reflects. In just this way, the soul, when she has put herself together in a way suited to her function and cast off every material defilement, has graven into herself the pure look of the inviolate beauty. Hence the life-endued and choice-endowed mirror has this word to say: "Since I focus upon the face of my kinsman with my entire being, the entire beauty of his form is seen in me." Paul openly echoes these words when he says that he, who has died to the world, lives to God and that Christ alone lives in him. For one who says, "To me, to live is Christ" (Phil 1:21), by this statement affirms for all the world to hear that in him not a single one of the human and material passions is alive, not pleasure or grief, not anger or fear or cowardice or agitation or vanity or rashness, not vengefulness or envy, nor yet a vindictive disposition or love of money, of glory, or of honors, or

ἐστίν· πᾶν γὰρ τὸ ἔξω τῆς ἐκείνου φύσεως θεωρούμενον ἀποξυσάμενος
οὐδὲν ἔχω ἐν ἐμαυτῷ τοιοῦτον | οἷον ἐν ἐκείνῳ οὐκ ἔστιν. οὗ χάριν Ἐμοὶ τὸ   441
ζῆν Χριστός, ἤ, καθὼς ἡ νύμφη, Ἐγὼ τῷ ἀδελφιδῷ μου καὶ ὁ ἀδελφιδός μου
ἐμοί, ὅς ἐστιν ἁγιασμὸς καὶ καθαρότης καὶ ἀφθαρσία καὶ φῶς καὶ ἀλήθεια καὶ
5   τὰ τοιαῦτα ὅσα.
    ποιμαίνει τὴν ἐμὴν ψυχὴν οὐκ ἐν χόρτοις τισὶν ἢ φρυγάνοις ἀλλ' ἐν
ταῖς λαμπρότησι τῶν ἁγίων· ἡ γὰρ τῶν κρίνων φύσις ἐν τῷ λαμπρῷ τῆς
εὐχροίας ταύτην ὑπαινίσσεται ἡμῖν τὴν διάνοιαν. οὐκοῦν διὰ τοῦτο ἐπὶ τοὺς
λειμῶνας τῶν κρίνων ἄγει τὸ ἑαυτοῦ ποίμνιον ὁ ἐν τοῖς κρίνοις ποιμαίνων,
10 ἵνα γένηται Ἡ λαμπρότης κυρίου τοῦ θεοῦ ἡμῶν ἐφ' ἡμᾶς· τῷ γὰρ εἴδει τῆς
τροφῆς συνδιατίθεται πάντως καὶ τὸ τρεφόμενον. οἷον τί λέγω; ἔστω καθ'
ὑπόθεσιν κοῖλόν τι σκεῦος ἐξ ὑέλου πεποιημένον, ἐν ᾧ πᾶν τὸ βαλλόμενον
διαφαίνεται οἱονδὴ ἂν ᾖ, εἴτε ἀσβόλη τὸ ἐγκείμενον εἴη εἴτε τι τῶν
καθαρωτέρων τε καὶ λαμπροτέρων. οὐκοῦν τὴν λαμπρότητα τῶν κρίνων ταῖς
15 ψυχαῖς ἐντιθεὶς λαμπρὰς δι' αὐτῶν τὰς ψυχὰς ἀπεργάζεται διαφαινομένου
τοῦ ἐγκειμένου εἴδους ἐπὶ τὸ ἔξωθεν. ὡς δ' ἂν πρὸς τὸ σαφέστερον ἡμῖν
προαχθείη τὸ νοητόν, τοῦτό φαμεν ὅτι τρέφεται μὲν διὰ τῶν ἀρετῶν ἡ ψυχή,
κρίνα δὲ κατονομάζει τὰς ἀρετὰς δι' αἰνίγματος, | ὧν ὁ διὰ τῆς ἀγαθῆς   442
πολιτείας ἐμφορηθεὶς ἐπίδηλον ποιεῖ διὰ τοῦ βίου ἑκάστης ἀρετῆς τὸ εἶδος
20 διὰ τοῦ ἤθους ἐπιδεικνύμενος. ἔστω κρίνον καθαρὸν ἡ σωφροσύνη τε καὶ
δικαιοσύνη καὶ ἀνδρεία καὶ φρόνησις καὶ Ὅσα φησὶν ὁ ἀπόστολος ἀληθῆ
καὶ ὅσα σεμνὰ καὶ ὅσα προσφιλῆ, ὅσα δίκαια, ὅσα ἁγνά, ὅσα εὔφημα, εἴ τις
ἀρετὴ καὶ εἴ τις ἔπαινος· πάντα γὰρ ταῦτα ἐντὸς τῆς ψυχῆς γενόμενα τῷ
καθαρῷ διαδείκνυται βίῳ, καλλωπίζοντά τε τὸν περιέχοντα καὶ αὐτὰ διὰ τοῦ
25 εἰσδεξαμένου καλλωπιζόμενα.
    Ἡ τοίνυν ἀναθεῖσα ἑαυτὴν τῷ ἀδελφιδῷ καὶ δεξαμένη τοῦ ἀγαπηθέντος
τὸ κάλλος ἐν τῇ ἰδίᾳ μορφῇ οἵων ἀξιοῦται παρὰ τοῦ τοὺς δοξάζοντας αὐτὸν
δοξάζοντος, ἀκούσωμεν διὰ τῆς προσκειμένης τοῖς εἰρημένοις ἀκολουθίας·
φησὶ γὰρ πρὸς τὴν νύμφην ὁ λόγος· Καλὴ εἶ, ἡ πλησίον μου, ὡς εὐδοκία,
30 ὡραία ὡς Ἰερουσαλήμ, θάμβος ὡς τεταγμέναι.
    ὅτι μὲν οὖν ἡ δόξα παρὰ τῆς οὐρανίου στρατιᾶς ἀναπέμπεται τῷ ἐν
ὑψίστοις θεῷ ὑπὲρ τῆς ἐν ἀνθρώποις εὐδοκίας ἐν ταῖς ἀκοαῖς τῶν ποιμένων,
ὅτε εἶδον γεννηθεῖσαν ἐπὶ γῆς τὴν | εἰρήνην, καὶ ὅτι πόλις τοῦ μεγάλου   443
βασιλέως ἡ Ἰερουσαλὴμ παρὰ τοῦ δεσπότου πάσης κτίσεως ὀνομάζεται,
35 παντὶ δῆλον ἂν εἴη τῷ τοῖς εὐαγγελικοῖς καθομιλήσαντι λόγοις, ὡς διὰ
τούτων μὴ ἀγνοῆσαι, ποῖον μαρτυρεῖ τῇ νύμφῃ κάλλος ὁ λόγος διὰ τῆς πρὸς

anything else that stains the soul by means of some attachment. "But he alone is mine who is none of these things. I have scraped off everything that is discerned as alien to that nature of his, and I have in me nothing |such as is not found in him. For that reason 'To me, to live is Christ'"—or, in the words of the Bride, *I am for my kinsman, and my kinsman is for me,* he who is sanctification, and purity, and incorruptibility, and light, and truth, and all the like.

He pastures my soul not on shrubs and grasses but on the splendors of the saints, for by the brightness of its handsome coloring the lily species points to this meaning. Therefore he—the one who grazes *among the lilies*—leads his flock to meadows full of lilies to this end, that "the brightness of the Lord our God may be upon us" (Ps 89:17). For the one who is fed is surely brought, by the sort of food consumed, to share its state of being. What is an apt illustration of this? Imagine a hollow vessel made of glass. Everything that is placed in it shows through for whatever it is, whether the contents be soot or something purer and more shining. Well then, when Christ has filled souls with the splendor of lilies, by their means he renders the souls shining in splendor as the nature of their contents shows through to the outside. And in order to make this idea clearer, I say this, that the soul's nourishment is the virtues and that the name "lilies" is assigned to the virtues to serve as an enigma of them; and when| people are filled up with them on account of their leading a good life, they manifest in life the quality of every virtue by displaying it in their habitual conduct. Let self-control be a pure lily—and courage and practical wisdom and, as the apostle says, "Whatever is true, whatever is honorable, whatever is lovely, whatever is just, whatever is pure, whatever is gracious, if there is any virtue, if there is any praise" (Phil 4:8), for all of these qualities, when they have lodged within the soul, are displayed in a pure life: they beautify the one that embraces them, and at the same time they themselves are beautified by the one that welcomes them.

Since, then, the Bride has dedicated herself to her kinsman and in her own form has taken on the beauty of her Beloved, let us, by attending to what follows next upon the passage just discussed, hear what she is judged worthy of by the one who glorifies those who glorify him. For the Word says to the Bride: *You are beautiful, my close one, like good pleasure, lovely, like Jerusalem, an object of terror, like serried ranks drawn up.*

Now "glory" is sent up to the "God" who is "in the highest" by "the heavenly host" because of his "goodwill toward his human creatures," and the shepherds, when they see that Peace has come to the earth, hear it (cf. Luke 2:13–14). | Furthermore, Jerusalem is called "city of the great King" by the Master of the entire creation (Matt 5:35). These two things are plain to anyone who is conversant with the language of the Gospels, and hence no one who takes account of them is unaware what sort of beauty it is that the Word attri-

τὴν Ἰερουσαλὴμ καὶ πρὸς τὴν εὐδοκίαν συγκρίσεως. δῆλον γὰρ ὅτι τοῦτο
περὶ αὐτῆς ὁ λόγος ἐνδείκνυται τὸ διὰ τῆς κατορθουμένης ἀνόδου μέχρις
ἐκείνου τὴν ψυχὴν ὑψωθῆναι, ὡς πρὸς τὰ τοῦ δεσπότου θαύματα ἑαυτὴν
ἐπεκτεῖναι· εἰ γὰρ ὁ ἐν ὑψίστοις θεός, Ὁ ὢν ἐν τοῖς κόλποις τοῦ πατρός, ὑπὲρ
5   τῆς ἐν ἀνθρώποις εὐδοκίας αἵματι καὶ σαρκὶ κατακίρναται, ἵνα γεννηθῇ ἐπὶ
τῆς γῆς εἰρήνη, δῆλον ὅτι ἡ πρὸς ταύτην τὴν εὐδοκίαν τὸ ἑαυτῆς ὁμοιώσασα
κάλλος τὸν Χριστὸν μιμεῖται τοῖς κατορθώμασιν, ἐκεῖνο γινομένη τοῖς ἄλλοις
ὅπερ ὁ Χριστὸς τῇ φύσει τῶν ἀνθρώπων ἐγένετο· καθάπερ καὶ ὁ μιμητὴς
τοῦ Χριστοῦ Παῦλος ἐποίει ἑαυτὸν τῆς ζωῆς ἀφορίζων, ἵνα τοῦ ἰδίου πάθους
10   τὴν σωτηρίαν τῷ Ἰσραὴλ ἀνταλλάξηται, λέγων· Ηὐχόμην ἀνάθεμα εἶναι
ἀπὸ τοῦ Χριστοῦ ὑπὲρ τῶν ἀδελφῶν μου, τῶν συγγενῶν μου κατὰ σάρκα.
πρὸς ὃν εἰκότως εἰπεῖν ἁρμόζει τὸ εἰρημένον τῇ νύμφῃ ὅτι· | τοιοῦτόν ἐστι   444
τῆς ψυχῆς σου τὸ κάλλος, οἵα ἡ τοῦ δεσπότου γέγονεν ὑπὲρ ἡμῶν εὐδοκία,
ὃς Ἑαυτὸν ἐκένωσε μορφὴν δούλου λαβών, καὶ ἔδωκεν ἑαυτὸν ἀντάλλαγμα
15   ὑπὲρ τῆς τοῦ κόσμου ζωῆς καὶ Δι' ἡμᾶς ἐπτώχευσε πλούσιος ὤν, ἵνα ἡμεῖς ἐν
τῷ θανάτῳ αὐτοῦ ζήσωμεν καὶ ἐν τῇ πτωχείᾳ αὐτοῦ πλουτήσωμεν καὶ ἐν τῇ
τῆς δουλείας αὐτοῦ μορφῇ βασιλεύσωμεν.

τὸ δὲ αὐτὸ μέγεθος καὶ ἡ πρὸς Ἰερουσαλὴμ ὡραιότητος ὁμοιότης
ἐνδείκνυται, τὴν ἄνω δηλαδὴ Ἰερουσαλήμ, τὴν ἐλευθέραν, τὴν τῶν
20   ἐλευθέρων μητέρα, ἣν πόλιν τοῦ μεγάλου βασιλέως εἶναι παρὰ τῆς τοῦ
δεσπότου φωνῆς μεμαθήκαμεν· ἡ γὰρ χωρήσασα ἐν ἑαυτῇ τὸν ἀχώρητον,
ὥστε ἐνοικεῖν αὐτῇ καὶ ἐμπεριπατεῖν τὸν θεόν, τῇ ὡραιότητι τοῦ ἐν αὐτῇ
κατοικοῦντος καλλωπισθεῖσα Ἰερουσαλὴμ ἐπουράνιος γίνεται τὸ ἐκείνης
κάλλος ἐφ' ἑαυτῆς δεξαμένη. κάλλος δὲ τῆς πόλεως τοῦ βασιλέως καὶ
25   ὡραιότης, αὐτοῦ πάντως ἐστὶ τοῦ βασιλέως τὸ κάλλος· ἐκείνου γάρ ἐστι κατὰ
τὸν λόγον τῆς ψαλμῳδίας ἡ ὡραιότης καὶ τὸ κάλλος, πρὸς ὃν ἡ προφητεία
φησὶ Τῇ ὡραιότητί σου καὶ τῷ κάλλει σου καὶ ἔντεινον καὶ κατευοδοῦ καὶ
βασίλευε ἕνεκεν ἀληθείας καὶ πραότητος καὶ δικαιοσύνης· τούτοις γὰρ τὸ
θεῖον κάλλος χαρακτηρίζεται, τῇ ἀληθείᾳ λέγω καὶ τῇ δικαιοσύνῃ καὶ τῇ | 445
30   πραότητι. ἡ τοίνυν ἐν τοῖς τοιούτοις κάλλεσι μορφωθεῖσα ψυχὴ ὡραία γίνεται
ὡς Ἰερουσαλὴμ τῇ τοῦ βασιλέως ὥρᾳ καλλωπισθεῖσα.

Ἀλλὰ ταῦτα μὲν πρόδηλον ἔχει τοῦ τῆς νύμφης κάλλους τὸν ἔπαινον
τῇ πρὸς τὴν εὐδοκίαν τε καὶ τὴν Ἰερουσαλὴμ συγκρίσει πληρούμενον, τὸν
δὲ ἐφεξῆς λόγον ἐγκώμιον μὲν εἶναι τῆς νύμφης οὐκ ἀμφιβάλλομεν, τὴν
35   δὲ διάνοιαν, καθ' ἣν τῷ τοιούτῳ ἐπαίνῳ σεμνύνεται ἡ τῆς εὐφημίας ταύτης
ἀξιωθεῖσα, οὐκ ἔστιν ἐκ τοῦ προχείρου μαθεῖν. ἔχει γὰρ ἡ λέξις οὕτως· Θάμβος

butes to the Bride by his comparison of her with *Jerusalem* and with *goodwill*.
For it is obvious that where she is concerned the Word is pointing to this: that
the soul, through the upward journey she has completed, has been exalted
to the point where she is straining forward toward the wonders of the Lord
and Master. For if God "in the highest," the One who is "in the bosom of the
Father" (cf. John 1:18), has been mingled with flesh and blood because of his
"goodwill toward his human creatures," so that "Peace" has come to be "on
earth," then plainly the soul that has brought her own beauty into line with
this "goodwill" is imitating Christ by her righteous deeds; she is becoming
toward others what Christ became for the human race, just as Paul too, that
imitator of Christ, did by renouncing his life so as to exchange his own suffering for the salvation of Israel when he said, "I could wish that I myself were
accursed and cut off from Christ for the sake of my brethren, my kinsmen by
race" (Rom 9:3). It is surely fitting to say to him what was said to the Bride: |
"The beauty of your soul is of the same order as was the goodwill exercised
toward us by the Lord and Master, who 'emptied himself, taking the form of a
slave' (Phil 2:7), and gave himself in exchange for the life of the cosmos, and
'though he was rich, became poor for our sakes' (2 Cor 8:9), in order that in
his death we should live, and in his poverty grow rich, and in the form of the
slavery that was his should reign."

The very same quality of greatness is manifested by the likening of the
Bride's comeliness to Jerusalem—the Jerusalem that is above, to be sure, the
Jerusalem that is free and the mother of the free (cf. Gal 4:26), the city that
we have learned from the words of the Lord and Master to belong to the
Great King (cf. Matt 5:35); for the soul that contains the Uncontained, so that
God dwells and tarries within her, has been beautified by the comeliness of
the One who indwells her and becomes the heavenly Jerusalem because she
has taken its beauty to herself. The beauty and comeliness of the King's city,
though, are surely that of the King himself, for according to the language of
the psalm, the beauty and comeliness are his to whom the prophecy says, "By
your comeliness and by your beauty, gather yourself, and prosper, and reign,
for the sake of truth and gentleness and justice" (Ps 44:4–5). For it is by these
marks that the divine beauty is recognized—by truth, I mean, and justice
and | gentleness. Therefore the soul that is shaped by such marks of beauty
as these becomes comely like Jerusalem, rendered beautiful by the graceful
charm of the King.

These statements contain a palpable praise of the Bride's beauty, praise
that culminates in the comparison of her to goodwill and to Jerusalem. Where
the next expression is concerned, however, though we do not doubt that it is
a praise of the Bride, it is impossible to make out on the basis of its surface
meaning how she who has been counted worthy of this honor is magnified by

ὡς τεταγμέναι. τάχα δ᾽ ἄν τις τοῖς προθεωρηθεῖσιν ἑπόμενος εἴποι διὰ τῆς
πρὸς τὴν ὑπερκόσμιον φύσιν συγκρίσεως μεγαλύνεσθαι ὑπὸ τοῦ λόγου διὰ
τῶν ἐπαίνων τὴν νύμφην· ἐκεῖ γάρ εἰσιν αἱ τεταγμέναι [δυνάμεις] ὅπου αἱ μὲν
ἐξουσίαι διὰ παντὸς ἐν τῷ κυριεύειν εἰσί, κρατοῦσι δὲ διόλου αἱ κυριότητες,
5   βεβήκασι δὲ παγίως οἱ θρόνοι, ἀδούλωτοι δὲ μένουσιν αἱ ἀρχαί, εὐλογοῦσι δὲ
ἀδιαλείπτως τὸν θεὸν αἱ δυνάμεις, ἥ τε πτῆσις τῶν Σεραφὶμ οὐχ ἵσταται καὶ ἡ
στάσις οὐ μεταβαίνει καὶ τὰ Χερουβὶμ ἀνέχοντα τὸν ὑψηλόν τε καὶ ἐπηρμένον
θρόνον οὐκ ἀπολήγει, οἵ τε λειτουργοὶ ποιοῦντες τὸ ἔργον | καὶ ἀκούοντες   446
τῶν λόγων οὐ παύονται. ἐπεὶ οὖν αἱ ἐξουσίαι αὗται ὑπὸ τοῦ θεοῦ τεταγμέναι
10   εἰσὶ καὶ ἡ τάξις τῶν νοητῶν καὶ ὑπερκοσμίων δυνάμεων ἀσύγχυτος εἰς τὸ
διηνεκὲς μένει μηδεμιᾶς κακίας ἀνατρεπούσης τὴν εὐταξίαν, διὰ τοῦτο καὶ
ἡ πρὸς μίμησιν ἐκείνων [ψυχὴ] πάντα κατὰ τάξιν καὶ εὐσχημόνως ποιοῦσα
τοιοῦτον ἐφ᾽ ἑαυτῆς κινεῖ τὸ θαῦμα οἷον ἐν ταῖς δυνάμεσιν ἐκείναις ταῖς
τεταγμέναις ἐστίν· ἔκπληξιν γὰρ ἡ τοῦ θάμβους ἑρμηνεύει διάνοια, διὰ δὲ τῆς
15   ἐκπλήξεως τὸ θαῦμα νοοῦντες τῆς ἀληθείας οὐχ ἁμαρτάνομεν.

Ἡ δὲ τούτοις ἐκ τοῦ ἀκολούθου προσκειμένη ῥῆσις ἀμφίβολα ποιεῖ
τὰ πρόσωπα, παρ᾽ οὗ τε εἴρηται καὶ πρὸς ὃν εἶπε τὸ Ἀπόστρεψον τοὺς
ὀφθαλμούς σου ἀπεναντίον ἐμοῦ, ὅτι αὐτοὶ ἀνεπτέρωσάν με· τοῖς μὲν γὰρ
δοκεῖ παρὰ τοῦ δεσπότου πρὸς τὴν καθαρὰν εἰρῆσθαι ταῦτα ψυχήν, ἐγὼ
20   δὲ τῇ νύμφῃ πρέπειν ὑπονοῶ μᾶλλον τὸ ῥητὸν ἐφαρμόζεσθαι. | ταύτῃ γὰρ   447

a praise of this sort, for it runs like this: *an object of terror, like serried ranks drawn up.* It may be, though, that one could say—following up on the conclusions of earlier explorations—that in these praises the Word is magnifying the Bride by comparing her to the supracosmic species. For the *serried ranks drawn up*[16] are in that place where the Authorities[17] are ever engaged in governing, where the Dominions are always exercising power, the Thrones stand firmly, the Principalities remain unsubdued, the Powers bless God without pause (Ps 102:21), the flight of the seraphim ceases not and their fixed station does not change (cf. Isa 6:2), and the cherubim never stop upholding the high and exalted throne (cf. Ezek 10:1), and the ministering spirits do not stop doing their work | and hearing the words (cf. Ps 102:20–21). Since, then, the Authorities themselves are *drawn up* in their ranks by God, and since the array of the intelligible and supracosmic powers stands forever unconfused because no evil whatever disturbs their good order, for this reason, I say, the soul that imitates these beings by doing all things "decently and in order" (1 Cor 14:40) evokes for herself the very same sort of wonder as is found in those Powers drawn up in serried ranks. For in its deeper sense, *terror* means amazement, and if we think of wonder when we hear "amazement," we do not stray from from the truth.

The statement that follows immediately upon these words makes the question of the characters[18] involved doubtful—that is, the question by whom and to whom it is said: *Turn your eyes away from that which stands over against me, for they give me wings.*[19] To some interpreters it appears that the words are spoken by the Lord to the purified soul, but I suspect they are more properly assigned to the Bride. | For she is the one to whom I find the sense

---

16. Langerbeck (1960, 445) deletes the word δυνάμεις here (if it were retained the translation would read "the powers in their serried ranks"); he points out in his *apparatus criticus* that just a few lines later Gregory uses the word to name not the whole but a particular division of the "supracosmic species." I am inclined, as against Dünzl 1994b, 3:788 n. 31), to follow Langerbeck, especially since the deletion also leaves the words of the text under discussion to stand on their own.

17. Ἐξουσίαι; cf. Eph 3:10 (RSV: "powers"), Col 1:16 (RSV: "authorities"), and possibly Rom 13:1 (RSV: "powers"). The list that follows draws on various New Testament texts; for "Dominions" (κυριότητες), "Thrones" (θρόνοι), "Principalities" (ἀρχαί), and "Powers" (δυνάμεις), see Col 1:16; Rom 8:38; Eph 3:10; Tit 3:1.

18. In Greek τὰ πρόσωπα. The identification of the speaker and addressee(s) of a given passage or speech was a standard concern of ancient exegesis.

19. The verb translated as "give me wings again" (ἀναπτερόω, literally "re-wing") might more usefully be rendered as "excite" or even "turn [me] on," but Gregory's exegesis depends on it being constructed on the same root as the noun "wing."

κατάλληλον εὑρίσκω τὴν τῶν σημαινομένων ὑπὸ τοῦ λόγου διάνοιαν.

τὰ δέ μοι παραστάντα δι᾽ ὀλίγων ἐκθήσομαι· ἤκουσα πολλαχῇ τῆς θεοπνεύστου γραφῆς πτέρυγας εἶναι τῷ θεῷ διηγουμένης, νῦν μὲν τῆς προφητείας λεγούσης ὅτι Ἐν σκέπῃ τῶν πτερύγων σου σκεπάσεις με, καὶ ὅτι
5   Ὑπὸ τὰς πτέρυγας αὐτοῦ ἐλπιεῖς, πάλιν δὲ τοῦ Μωϋσέως ἐν τῇ μεγάλῃ ᾠδῇ τὸ αὐτὸ ὑπογράφοντος ἐν οἷς φησιν ὅτι Διεὶς τὰς πτέρυγας αὐτοῦ ἐδέξατο αὐτούς. καὶ τὸ παρὰ τοῦ κυρίου πρὸς τὴν Ἰερουσαλὴμ εἰρημένον, ὅτι Ποσάκις ἠθέλησα ἐπισυναγαγεῖν τὰ τέκνα σου ὃν τρόπον ὄρνις συνάγει τὰ νοσσία ὑπὸ τὰς πτέρυγας αὐτῆς, οὐκ ἔξω τοῦ προκειμένου νοήματος εἴποι τις ἂν εἶναι
10   πρὸς τὸ ἀκόλουθον βλέπων. εἰ τοίνυν κατά τινα λόγον ἀπόρρητον πτέρυγας εἶναι περὶ τὴν θείαν φύσιν ὁ θεόπνευστος διορίζεται λόγος, ἡ δὲ πρώτη τοῦ ἀνθρώπου Κατασκευὴ τὸ κατ᾽ εἰκόνα καὶ ὁμοίωσιν θεοῦ γεγενῆσθαι τὴν φύσιν ἡμῶν μαρτύρεται, | ὁρίζεται πάντως ὅτι διὰ πάντων εἶχεν ὁ κατ᾽ εἰκόνα   448 γενόμενος τὴν πρὸς τὸ ἀρχέτυπον ὁμοιότητα. ἀλλὰ μὴν ἐπτέρωται κατὰ
15   τὴν ἁγίαν γραφὴν τὸ πρωτότυπον. οὐκοῦν πτερόεσσα καὶ ἡ τοῦ ἀνθρώπου κατεσκευάσθη φύσις, ὡς ἂν καὶ ἐν ταῖς πτέρυξιν ἔχοι πρὸς τὸ θεῖον ὁμοίως.

δῆλον δὲ ὅτι τὸ τῶν πτερύγων ὄνομα διά τινος τροπικῆς θεωρίας εἴς τι θεοπρεπὲς μεταληφθήσεται νόημα, δυνάμεώς τε καὶ μακαριότητος καὶ ἀφθαρσίας καὶ τῶν τοιούτων διὰ τοῦ ὀνόματος τῶν πτερύγων σημαινομένων.
20   ἐπεὶ οὖν ταῦτα καὶ περὶ τὸν ἄνθρωπον ἦν, ἕως ὅτε τῷ θεῷ διὰ πάντων ὅμοιος ἦν, μετὰ ταῦτα δὲ ἡ πρὸς τὴν κακίαν ῥοπὴ τῶν τοιούτων πτερύγων ἡμᾶς ἀπεσύλησεν (ἔξω γὰρ τῆς σκέπης τῶν τοῦ θεοῦ πτερύγων γενόμενοι καὶ τῶν ἰδίων πτερύγων ἐγυμνώθημεν), διὰ τοῦτο ἐπεφάνη ἡ τοῦ θεοῦ χάρις φωτίζουσα ἡμᾶς, ἵνα ἀποθέμενοι τὴν ἀσέβειαν καὶ τὰς κοσμικὰς ἐπιθυμίας
25   πάλιν δι᾽ ὁσιότητός τε καὶ δικαιοσύνης πτεροφυήσωμεν. οὐκοῦν εἰ ταῦτα τῆς ἀληθείας οὐκ ἀπεσχοίνισται, πρέπει παρὰ τῆς νύμφης ὁμολογεῖσθαι τὴν ἐπ᾽ αὐτῆς γεγενημένην παρὰ | τῶν θείων ὀφθαλμῶν χάριν· ὁμοῦ τε γὰρ ἐπεῖδεν   449 ἡμᾶς τοῖς τῆς φιλανθρωπίας ὀφθαλμοῖς ὁ θεὸς καὶ ἡμεῖς κατὰ τὴν ἀρχαίαν χάριν ἀνεπτερώθημεν.

of what the text says appropriate. But I shall set out in brief compass what has come to my mind.

In many places I hear the divinely inspired Scripture relate that God possesses wings. To take an instance, the prophecy says, "You will shelter me under the cover of your wings" (Ps 16:8); and again, "Beneath his wings you will find hope" (Ps 90:4). Moses, moreover, in his great song describes the same thing when he says, "He has spread his wings and taken them" (Deut 32:11). Then too the words the Lord directed to Jerusalem, "How often have I wanted to gather your children, even as a hen gathers her chicks under her wings" (Matt 23:37), these words, one might venture, are not foreign to the idea we are considering if one attends to the logic of the context. If, then, the divinely inspired text declares that in some inexpressible way wings are associated with the divine Nature, and if the first account of the creation of humanity[20] attests that our nature came into existence as the creature made "after the image and likeness of God" (Gen 1:26), | it is at any rate determined and settled that the creature that came to be "after the image" was characterized by likeness to its original in every respect. But according to Holy Scripture, the original did indeed have wings. It follows that the human race was constituted with wings, so as to possess likeness to the divine in this regard also.

It is obvious, to be sure, that the word "wings" must, by some figural understanding, be transposed into a notion that can suitably be applied to the divine, one according to which the word "wings" refers to power and blessedness and incorruption and the like. Since, then, these qualities belonged to humanity also as long as it was in every way like God, but afterwards the downward impulse toward evil robbed us of such wings as these (for once we are removed from the cover of God's wings, we are stripped of our own wings too), for this reason, I say, the grace of God was manifested and illumined us, so that as we put away ungodliness and worldly desires we shall again, by holiness and justice, grow our wings again.[21] If, then, this line of interpretation does not stand outside the truth, it is proper for the Bride to confess the grace that has become hers | by the agency of the divine eyes. For as soon as God looks upon us with the eyes of his love, we regain our wings in accordance with the grace of old.

---

20. See the remarks of Langerbeck in his *apparatus criticus* (1960, 447): the isolated word κατασκευή is a reference to the *narrative* of the creation of the human being.

21. It is impossible not to see in this passage a reminiscence of Plato's myth of the fall of souls in *Phaedr.* 246ff. Langerbeck (1960, 448) in his note *ad loc.* refers to Methodius of Olympus, *Symp.* 8.1ff. (trans. Musurillo 1958, 109), as the possible source of the line Gregory takes in this passage.

ταὐτὰ οὖν οἶμαι διὰ τῶν εἰρημένων τὸν λόγον ἐνδείκνυσθαι, ἃ
προσευχόμενος ὁ Δαβὶδ ἐν ἑξκαιδεκάτῃ ψαλμῳδίᾳ φησὶ πρὸς τὸν κύριον ὅτι
Οἱ ὀφθαλμοί σου ἰδέτωσαν εὐθύτητας, τὰς ἐμὰς δηλονότι· Ἐδοκίμασας γάρ,
φησί, τὴν καρδίαν μου, ἐπεσκέψω νυκτός, ἐπύρωσάς με καὶ οὐχ εὑρέθη ἐν
5   ἐμοὶ ἀδικία. ἴσον οὖν ἐστιν εἰπεῖν ὅτι Οἱ ὀφθαλμοί σου ἰδέτωσαν εὐθύτητας,
καὶ ὅτι οἱ ὀφθαλμοί σου τὸ ἐναντίον μὴ θεασάσθωσαν· ὁ γὰρ τὸ εὐθὲς ἰδὼν
σκολιὸν οὐκ εἶδε καὶ ὁ σκολιὸν μὴ ἰδὼν τὸ εὐθὲς πάντως τεθέαται. οὐκοῦν διὰ
τῆς τοῦ ἐναντίου ὑπεξαιρέσεως τὸ ἀγαθὸν τοῖς θείοις ὀφθαλμοῖς ὑποδείκνυσι,
δι' ὧν ἀναπτεροῦται πάλιν ἡ ψυχή, ἡ διὰ τῆς παρακοῆς τῶν πρωτοπλάστων
10   πτερορρυήσασα. τοῦτο τοίνυν διὰ τῶν εἰρημένων κατενοήσαμεν ὅτι· οἱ
ὀφθαλμοί σου, ὅταν ἐπ' ἐμὲ ἐπιβλέπωσιν, ἀποστρέφονται ἀπὸ τοῦ ἐναντίου·
οὐ γὰρ ὄψονταί τι ἐν ἐμοὶ τῶν ἐναντιουμένων μοι. διὰ τοῦτο γίνεταί μοι ἀπὸ
τῶν ὀφθαλμῶν σου τὸ πάλιν πτερωθῆναι καὶ ἀναλαβεῖν διὰ τῶν ἀρετῶν
τὰς πτέρυγας τῆς ὡσπερεὶ περιστερᾶς, δι' ἧς γίνεταί μοι ἡ τῆς | πτήσεως   450
15   δύναμις, ὥστε πετασθῆναι καὶ καταπαῦσαι, ἐκείνην δηλαδὴ τὴν κατάπαυσιν
ἣν κατέπαυσεν ὁ θεὸς ἀπὸ τῶν ἔργων αὐτοῦ.

Πάλιν δὲ μετὰ τὰς φωνὰς ταύτας ἡ τοῦ κάλλους τῆς νύμφης ὑπογραφὴ
διαδέχεται τῶν εἰς τὴν ὥραν αὐτῆς συντελούντων ἕκαστον διά τινος
προσφυοῦς ὁμοιώσεως τοῦ λόγου σεμνύνοντος· ἐπαινεῖται γὰρ αὐτῆς τῶν
20   τε τριχῶν τὸ κάλλος καὶ τῶν ὀδόντων ἡ θέσις καὶ τὸ ἐπὶ τοῦ χείλους ἄνθος
καὶ τὸ ἡδὺ τῆς φωνῆς τῆς τε παρειᾶς τὸ ἐρύθημα. ὁ δὲ περὶ ἑκάστου τῶν
εἰρημένων ἔπαινος διά τινος καταλλήλου συγκρίσεώς τε καὶ παραθέσεως
πληροῦται τῇ νύμφῃ. αἱ μὲν γὰρ τρίχες ἀγέλαις αἰγῶν ταῖς ἀναφανείσαις ἀπὸ
τοῦ Γαλαὰδ ὡμοιώθησαν, αἱ δὲ τῶν κεκαρμένων ἀγέλαι αἱ διδύμοις τόκοις
25   ἐπαγαλλόμεναι τὸ τῶν ὀδόντων ἐγκώμιον πληροῦσι διὰ τῆς ὁμοιώσεως,
σπαρτίῳ δὲ κοκκοβαφεῖ τὸ χεῖλος εἰκάζεται καὶ τῷ λεπύρῳ τῆς ῥόας ἡ
παρειὰ καλλωπίζεται. ἔχει δὲ ἡ λέξις οὕτω· Τρίχωμά σου ὡς ἀγέλαι τῶν αἰγῶν
αἳ ἀνεφάνησαν ἀπὸ τοῦ Γαλαάδ, ὀδόντες σου ὡς ἀγέλαι τῶν κεκαρμένων
αἳ ἀνέβησαν ἀπὸ τοῦ λουτροῦ, αἱ πᾶσαι διδυμεύουσαι καὶ ἀτεκνοῦσα οὐκ
30   ἔστιν ἐν αὐταῖς, ὡς σπαρτίον κόκκινον χείλη σου καὶ ἡ λαλιά σου ὡραία, ὡς
λέπυρον ῥόας μῆλόν σου ἐκτὸς τῆς σιωπήσεώς σου.

ὧν ἁπάντων ἐν τοῖς φθάσασιν ἱκανῶς ἐξητασμένων περιττὸν ἂν εἴη διὰ
τῆς τῶν αὐτῶν θεωρημάτων παλιλλογίας ὄχλον | ἐπεισάγειν τῷ λόγῳ. εἰ δέ   451

Hence it seems to me that in these words our text says the same thing as David said in his prayer to the Lord in Psalm 16: "Let your eyes see things that are straight" (Ps 16:2)—and he obviously means "as belonging to me," for he says, "You have tried my heart, by night you have inspected it, you have tested me by fire, and no unrighteousness has been found in me" (Ps 16:3). It is the very same thing, then, to say, "Let your eyes see things that are straight," and to say, "Let your eyes not look upon that which is opposed," for one who sees what is straight does not see what is crooked, and one who does not see what is crooked surely looks upon what is straight. It follows that by its exclusion of that which is opposed, the text is intimating the presence, to the divine eyes, of what is good; and it is by means of those eyes that the soul, who lost her wings on account of the disobedience of the first human beings, once again receives wings. What we understand by the words of the text, therefore, is this: "Your eyes, when they look upon me, are turned away from what is opposed, for they see in me nothing of what is contrary to me. For that reason it comes about for me that by the agency of your eyes I am again accorded wings, and because of my virtues I receive the wings, as it were, of the dove,[22] through which I am given | the power of flight, so that my wings are spread and I come to a rest—that rest, to be sure, by which God 'rested ... from ... his works' (Gen 2:2)."

Once again, after these words, there follows the description of the Bride's beauty. The text extols each element that contributes to her attractiveness by an appropiate simile. The beauty of her hair is praised, as well as the placing of her teeth, and the bloom of her lips, and the sweetness of her voice, and the blush of her cheek. The praise accorded each of the things just mentioned is carried out for the Bride by way of comparison and juxtaposition. Her hair is likened to herds of goats that have appeared from the direction of Gilead. The flocks of shorn sheep who rejoice in twin offspring bring off, by way of simile, the praise of her teeth. Her lip is likened to a scarlet cord, and her cheek is adorned with the husk of a pomegranate. The text goes like this: *Your hair is like flocks of goats that have appeared from the direction of Gilead. Your teeth are like flocks of shorn sheep that have come up from the bath, all of them bearing twins and without a barren one among them. Your lips are like a scarlet cord, and your speech is seasonable. Your cheek is like the skin of a pomegranate outside your veil.*

Since this entire passage has been sufficiently investigated in an earlier homily, it would be superfluous to add to the difficulties of our discourse by

---

22. For Gregory, here as elsewhere in these homilies, the dove symbolizes the Holy Spirit, in accordance with the Gospel accounts of the baptism of Jesus.

τις καὶ νῦν τὸν περὶ τῶν αὐτῶν λόγον ἐπιζητοίη γενέσθαι διὰ τοὺς ἀνηκόους τῶν πρώην εἰς τὰ ῥητὰ ταῦτα θεωρηθέντων, δι' ὀλίγων τὴν διάνοιαν τῶν αἰνιγμάτων ἐπιδραμούμεθα·

5   αἱ τρίχες τοῦ σώματος ἰδιάζουσαν ἔχουσι παρὰ τὸ λοιπὸν σῶμα τὴν φύσιν· παντὸς γὰρ τοῦ σώματος αἰσθητικῇ δυνάμει διοικουμένου, ἧς ἄνευ ἐν τῷ ζῆν εἶναι φύσιν οὐκ ἔχει (ζωὴ γὰρ τοῦ σώματός ἐστιν ἡ αἴσθησις), μόνας ὁρῶμεν τὰς τρίχας καὶ μέρος οὔσας τοῦ σώματος καὶ ἀμοιρούσας αἰσθήσεως. δείκνυσι δὲ ταύτην ἐπὶ τοῦ μέρους τούτου τὴν ἰδιότητα τὸ μήτε διὰ καύσεως μήτε διὰ τομῆς καθ' ὁμοιότητα τοῦ ἄλλου σώματος καὶ ταύτας ἀλγύνεσθαι.

10   ἐπειδὴ τοίνυν κατὰ τὴν Παύλου φωνὴν δόξα τῆς γυναικός ἐστιν ἡ κόμη <ἡ> διὰ τῶν πλοκάμων τὴν κεφαλὴν ὡραΐζουσα, τοῦτο διὰ τοῦ ἐπαίνου τῶν τῆς νύμφης τριχῶν διδασκόμεθα ὅτι χρὴ τοὺς περὶ τὴν κεφαλὴν τῆς νύμφης θεωρουμένους, δι' ὧν ἡ ἐκκλησία δοξάζεται, κρείττους τῶν αἰσθήσεων εἶναι κρύπτοντας διὰ τῆς σοφίας τὴν αἴσθησιν, καθὼς ἡ Παροιμία φησὶν ὅτι Σοφοὶ

15   κρύψουσιν αἴσθησιν· οἷς οὐχ ὅρασις τοῦ καλοῦ κριτήριον γίνεται, οὐ τῇ γεύσει τὸ ἀγαθὸν δοκιμάζεται, οὐκ ὀσφρήσει τε καὶ ἁφῇ οὐδὲ ἄλλῳ τινὶ αἰσθητηρίῳ ἡ τοῦ καλοῦ ἐπιτρέπεται κρίσις, ἀλλὰ πάσης νεκρωθείσης αἰσθήσεως διὰ μόνης τῆς ψυχῆς τῶν | κατ' ἔννοιαν φαινομένων ἀγαθῶν ἐφάπτονταί τε καὶ   452 ἐπορέγονται καὶ οὕτω δοξάζουσι τὴν γυναῖκα, τὴν ἐκκλησίαν, οὔτε τιμαῖς

20   διογκούμενοι οὔτε μικροψυχίαις πρὸς τὰ λυπηρὰ συστελλόμενοι, ἀλλὰ κἂν τέμνεσθαι δέῃ διὰ τὴν εἰς Χριστὸν πίστιν, κἂν θηρίοις ἢ πυρὶ παραβάλλεσθαι, κἂν ἄλλο τι τῶν λυπηρῶν ὑπομένειν, τὴν τῶν τριχῶν ἀναισθησίαν ἐν τῇ πείρᾳ τῶν ἀλγεινῶν ὑποκρίνονται.

τοιοῦτος Ἠλίας ἦν ὁ ἐκ τοῦ Γαλαὰδ ἀνασχὼν ἐν δασεῖ καὶ αὐχμῶντι τῷ

25   σώματι, δέρμασιν αἰγὸς σκεπαζόμενος, πρὸς πᾶσαν ἀπειλὴν τοῦ τυράννου μένων ἀπτόητος. ὅσοι τοίνυν κατὰ μίμησιν τῆς τοῦ προφήτου μεγαλοφυΐας τοῦ κόσμου παντὸς ἑαυτοὺς ὑπεραίρουσιν, ὑστερούμενοι, θλιβόμενοι,

stating the very same ideas | all over again.[23] On the chance, however, that someone, being unaware[24] of our earlier interpretations of these words, may wish us to speak even now about the same matters, we will briefly summarize the sense of these enigmatic statements.

In contrast to the rest of the body, the body's hairs have a special character. For since the entire body is indwelt by a perceptive faculty, apart from which it is deprived of natural life (for sense perception is the life of the body), we observe that only the hair is both a part of the body and without a share in sense perception. It is an indication, where hair is concerned, of this special character that it suffers pain neither from burning nor from cutting as does the rest of the body. Since, then, according to what Paul says, the glory of a woman is the hair of her head (1 Cor 11:15), which adorns her head with its curls, we are taught the following by the praise of the Bride's hair, namely, that those who are seen about the head of the Bride, those who bring glory to the church, must be superior to sense perceptions, concealing sense perception by wisdom, just as the proverb says: "The wise will conceal sense perception" (Prov 10:14). Sight does not serve as their criterion of beauty, taste does not provide their assessment of goodness, their judgment of virtue does not depend on smell or touch or any other organ of perception; on the contrary, all sense perception is done to death, and it is through the agency of the soul alone that they touch the good things and yearn for them | as they are manifested in an intelligible form. In this manner they bring glory to the woman, the church, being neither puffed up by the honors accorded them nor shrunken down by pusillanimity in the face of pain. On the contrary, even if necessity require that they be cut[25] because of their faith in Christ, even if they be thrown to wild beasts or cast into fire, even if they endure some other form of pain, they assume the insensibility of hair in their experience of pain and suffering.

Such a one was Elijah, who appeared out of Gilead with a body hairy and unwashed, covered with the skins of goats, remaining undaunted in face of the tyrant's threats. Therefore all those who imitate the nobility of the prophet and raise themselves above the entire cosmos, being "destitute, afflicted, ill-

---

23. See homily 7, with Gregory's elaborate (and arguably overingenious) treatment of Song 4:1–4 (pp. 219–31 [Jaeger]), which is verbally identical with the passage summarized here.

24. It is entirely plausible that some persons in attendance at the present sermon should have missed the seventh of Gregory's homilies and that Gregory should be eager to fill them in on what he had said earlier. His remarks show, as Dünzl 1994b, 3:798 n. 43, observes, that the text of Gregory's commentary really was, in its original form, communicated orally.

25. The use of "cut" (τέμνειν) here echoes Gregory's reference above to the effects of the "cutting" (τομή) of hair and at the same time evokes, though with an unaccustomed word, the sufferings of the martyrs.

κακουχούμενοι, ἐν ὄρεσι καὶ σπηλαίοις καὶ ταῖς ὀπαῖς τῆς γῆς, ὧν οὐκ ἔστιν ἄξιος ὁ κόσμος, οὗτοι ἀγεληδὸν περὶ τὴν τοῦ παντὸς κεφαλὴν θεωρούμενοι δόξα γίνονται τῆς ἐκκλησίας ἐπὶ τὴν οὐράνιον χάριν τῷ Γαλααδίτῃ συναναβαίνοντες.

5   Τὸ δὲ τῆς αἰγὸς ζῷον εἰς τὸν τῶν τριχῶν ἔπαινον ἀνελήφθη τάχα μὲν ὅτι καὶ ἡ φύσις τοῦ τοιούτου ζῴου κατάλληλος πρὸς γένεσιν τριχῶν κατεσκεύασται, ὥστε αἴνιγμα τοῦ διὰ τῶν τριχῶν κόσμου γενέσθαι τὸ ζῷον τὸ ταῖς θριξὶ φυσικῶς δασυνόμενον, ἢ ὅτι διὰ τῶν πετρῶν ἀνολισθήτως | 453
βαίνει καὶ περὶ τὰς κορυφὰς τῶν ὀρῶν ἀναστρέφεται διὰ τῶν δυσπορεύτων
10   τε καὶ ἀποτόμων εὐθαρσῶς τὴν πορείαν ποιούμενον, ὅπερ τοῖς τὴν τραχεῖαν τῆς ἀρετῆς ὁδὸν κατορθοῦσι προσφυῶς ἁρμοσθήσεται· μᾶλλον δ᾽ ἄν τις εἴποι διὰ τὸ πρὸς πολλὰ τῆς νομικῆς ἱερουργίας ὑπὸ τοῦ νομοθέτου παρειλῆφθαι τὸ ζῷον συντελεῖν ταύτας τῇ κεφαλῇ πρὸς ἐγκώμιον. οἶδα δὲ καὶ ἐν τοῖς τῆς Παροιμίας αἰνίγμασιν ἐν τοῖς τέσσαρσι τοῖς εὐοδουμένοις ἓν καὶ τοῦτο
15   τῶν καλῶς διαβαινόντων ἀπηριθμῆσθαι τὸν τράγον τὸν ἡγούμενον τοῦ αἰπολίου.

ὃ δὲ περὶ τούτου στοχαστικῶς ὑπονοοῦμεν τοιοῦτόν ἐστι· πᾶν ἐπιτήδευμα δι᾽ ἑνὸς ἀρχόμενον εἰς πολλοὺς διαδίδοται· ὡς ἐπὶ τῆς χαλκευτικῆς ἡ γραφὴ τὸν Θόβελ εὑρετὴν τῆς τέχνης εἰποῦσα πάντων τῶν μετ᾽ αὐτὸν
20   μεταχειριζομένων τοῦ σιδήρου τὴν ἐργασίαν εἰς ἐκεῖνον ἀνάγει τὴν ἐπιστήμην. οὕτω καὶ τῆς ποιμαντικῆς ὁ Ἄβελ ἡγήσατο καὶ ὁ Κάϊν τῆς γεωργίας, καὶ τὸν Νεβρὼδ ἀρχηγὸν λέγει τῆς κυνηγετικῆς ἐπιστήμης καὶ τῆς ἀμπελουργίας τὸν Νῶε καὶ τῆς εἰς θεὸν ἐλπίδος τὸν Ἐνὼς φησιν ἄρξασθαι· καὶ πολλὰ τοιαῦτα παρὰ τῆς ἁγίας ἔστι διδαχθῆναι γραφῆς, ὅτι ἑνός τι ἐπιτηδεύσαντος
25   εἰσῆλθε κατὰ μίμησιν εἰς τὸν βίον τὸ ἐπιτήδευμα. ἐπειδὴ τοίνυν τοῦ θείου ζήλου διαφερόντως κατὰ πᾶσαν ἐξοχὴν ὁ Ἠλίου καθηγήσατο, ὅσοι μετ᾽ ἐκεῖνον τὸν ἐκείνου μιμησάμενοι ζῆλον τοῖς αὐτοῖς | ἴχνεσι τῆς τοῦ προφήτου   454
παρρησίας ἐπηκολούθησαν, αἰπόλιον γεγόνασι τοῦ ἡγησαμένου τῆς τοιαύτης ζωῆς· οἵτινες δόξα τῆς ἐκκλησίας καὶ ἔπαινος γίνονται εἰς τὸν τῶν τριχῶν
30   καταγέντες κόσμον, ὧν ἡ αἰσθητικὴ ζωὴ κεχώρισταί τε καὶ ἠλλοτρίωται.

διὰ τῶν ὁμοίων δὲ πληροῖ καὶ τοῖς ὀδοῦσι τὸν ἔπαινον. οὗτοι δ᾽ ἂν εἶεν οἱ τρέφοντες δι᾽ ἑαυτῶν τῆς ἐκκλησίας τὸ σῶμα, οὓς βούλεται πάντοτε μὲν ὡς ἀπὸ λουτροῦ καθαροὺς ὁρᾶσθαι, ἀπερίττους δὲ διὰ παντὸς ὡς ἀπὸ προσφάτου κουρᾶς, κατὰ δὲ τὸν τόκον τῶν ἀρετῶν διδυμεύοντας τῆς διπλῆς

treated," in "mountains and dens and caves of the earth," "of whom the world is not worthy" (Heb 11:37–38), these, I say, discerned in their herds around the head of the universe, become the glory of the church as they ascend to heavenly grace in the company of the Gileadite.

Why is that living creature the goat mentioned in the praise of the Bride's hair? Possibly because the nature of this animal is so constituted that it is suited to the growth of hair, and so the animal that is naturally covered with hair becomes an enigmatic figure for the adornment that hair provides; or else because the goat journeys over stony terrain | without slipping and, by moving boldly over narrow and precipitous ways, dwells about the crowns of the mountains—a description that quite naturally fits those who successfully complete their journey on the rugged road of virtue. Even better might one say that goats contribute to the praise of the head because the Lawgiver employs this animal for many purposes in the law's sacrificial rituals. I also know, however, that in the enigmas of Proverbs, among the four whose way prospers, the he-goat that leads the herd is counted as one of those that step out handsomely.

The meaning I discern in all this—conjecturally, to be sure—is as follows. Every kind of pursuit originates with one individual and is passed on to many. Thus in the case of the art of the smith, the Scripture calls Tubal its inventor and attributes to him the knowledge of all those after him who undertake to work iron by hand (Gen 4:22). In the same way it pronounces Abel the founder of the art of those who tend livestock, and Cain, of agriculture (cf. Gen 4:2); and it pronounces Nimrod the pioneer of the science of hunting (Gen 10:9), and Noah, of viniculture (cf. Gen 9:20), and it says that Enoch was the one who started to put hope in God. The Holy Scripture teaches us many things of this sort, namely, that when one individual has made something his business, that form of activity makes its way into the stream of our life by being imitated. Since, then, the outstanding and exemplary original of the life of devotion to the things of God was the practice of Elijah, all those who have stood in his wake and imitated his devotion, and so have followed | in the steps of the prophet's directness and candor, have become the herd of goats that belongs to the founder of that form of life. These, counted in with the adornment that the hair provides, become a glory and a subject of praise for the church, and for them the life of sense perception is put away and alien.

The Song carries through its praise of the Bride's teeth in similar terms. The teeth must surely signify the people who make it their business to nourish the body of the church. Further, the Song desires that they always be seen as clean and pure, straight out of the bath, as it were; and wholly without excess or extravagance, as if straight from a shearing; and where the breed-

καθαρότητος γινομένους πατέρας, τῆς τε κατὰ ψυχὴν καὶ τῆς κατὰ σῶμα
θεωρουμένης, ὡς ἐξόριστον εἶναι τῶν ὀδόντων τούτων πᾶν τὸ ἀγονοῦν ἐν
τῷ κρείττονι.

τὸ δὲ σπαρτίον ἐπὶ τοῦ χείλους τιθέμενον τὴν μεμετρημένην τοῦ
5   λόγου διακονίαν παραδηλοῖ τῷ αἰνίγματι, ὅπερ ὁ προφήτης φυλακήν τε καὶ
θύραν περιοχῆς κατωνόμασεν, ὅταν ἐν καιρῷ ἀνοίγηται τῷ λόγῳ τὸ στόμα
καὶ κατὰ καιρὸν ἐπικλείηται. μέτρου δὲ ὄνομα τὸ σπαρτίον εἶναι παρὰ τῆς
προφητείας Ζαχαρίου ἐμάθομεν, ὅτι σπαρτίον γεωμετρικὸν ἐν χερσὶν εἶχεν ὁ
ἐν αὐτῷ λαλῶν ἄγγελος. τότε δὲ μάλιστα τυγχάνει τοῦ μέτρου ὁ λόγος, ὅταν
10   περικεχρωσμένος | τύχῃ τῷ ἐρυθήματι, ὅπερ τοῦ αἵματος τοῦ λυτρωσαμένου   455
ἡμᾶς αἴνιγμα γίνεται. ἐὰν οὖν τις κατὰ τὸν Παῦλον λαλοῦντα ἔχῃ ἐν ἑαυτῷ τὸν
Χριστὸν τὸν τῷ ἰδίῳ αἵματι ἡμᾶς λυτρωσάμενον, οὗτος ἔχει τὸ γεωμετρικὸν
σπαρτίον ἐπὶ τοῦ στόματος τῇ βαφῇ τῇ αἱματώδει καλλωπιζόμενον.

ὁ δὲ ἐφεξῆς λόγος ἑρμηνεία ἐστὶ τοῦ αἰνίγματος· λαλιὰν γὰρ ὡραίαν
15   ὀνομάζει τὸ σπαρτίον τὸ κόκκινον, δι᾽ οὗ πάλιν σημαίνει τὸ κάθωρον
καὶ ἔμμετρον· τὸ γὰρ ἀκριβῶς ὡραῖον, ἐν τῷ ἰδίῳ τῆς ἀκμῆς καιρῷ
προφαινόμενον, οὔτε ἄωρόν ἐστιν οὔτε ἔξωρον.

τῷ δὲ λεπύρῳ τῆς ῥόας τὸ μῆλον τῆς παρειᾶς ὡραΐζων μεγάλην τινα
προσμαρτυρεῖ τῇ νύμφῃ τὴν ἐν τοῖς ἀγαθοῖς τελειότητα· σημαίνει γὰρ μὴ ἐν
20   ἄλλῳ τινὶ τὸν θησαυρὸν αὐτῇ παρεσκευάσθαι, ἀλλ᾽ αὐτὴν εἶναι θησαυρὸν
ἑαυτῆς παντὸς ἀγαθοῦ παρασκευὴν ἐν ἑαυτῇ περιέχουσαν. ὡς γὰρ τῷ
λεπύρῳ περιέχεται τῆς ῥόας τὸ ἐδώδιμον, οὕτως ἐνδείκνυται τῷ φαινομένῳ
κάλλει τοῦ βίου τὸν ἔνδον αὐτῆς θησαυρὸν περιέχεσθαι. οὗτος οὖν ἐστιν ὁ

ing of virtues is concerned, as twin-bearers, fathers of the twofold purity, namely, that discerned in the soul and that discerned in the body, so that any infertility in regard of higher and better things may be entirely banished from these teeth.

As to the cord that is placed upon the lips,[26] it refers enigmatically to the ministry of the word as properly measured out. This is what the prophet named "a guard" and "a door for shielding" (Ps 140:3), when the mouth is opened to speak at the appropriate time and at the appropriate time is closed. That "cord" is the name of a measure we learn from the prophecy of Zechariah, since the angel that was speaking in him[27] had a cord in his hands for measuring the earth (Zech 2:5). And the word comes closest to being rightly measured when its color happens | to be red, since red is an enigmatic figure for the blood that has redeemed us. If then, like Paul, a person has within him the Christ who redeemed us with his own blood, that person has on his mouth the earth-measuring cord that is embellished with the color of blood.

The next statement provides an interpretation of the enigma, for it refers to the scarlet cord as "seasonable[28] speech," an expression by which again it signifies that which is timely and duly measured, since speech that is in the proper sense seasonable, uttered at the crucial moment, is neither nontimely nor untimely.

When, further, the text beautifies the apple[29] of the Bride's cheek with the skin of the pomegranate, it attributes to her a certain high degree of perfection in goodness, for it indicates that her treasure house has not been made ready in some other place but that she is her own treasure house and contains a supply of every good thing within herself. Just as the edible fruit is contained by the skin of the pomegranate, so too it is shown that her interior treasure is contained by the manifest beauty of her life. This then is the hidden treasure

---

26. Here I agree with Dünzl 1994b, 3:805 n. 49, against Langerbeck 1960, 454, *ad* line 13, as to the interpretation of τιθέμενον. Gregory seems to understand the enigmatic "cord" as a measure, i.e., a criterion, of appropriate speech.

27. The LXX text of Zech 2:7 (English 2:3) has "the angel who was talking in me."

28. The word ὡραία, an adjective formed from the noun ὥρα (denoting any season or period of time; thus, e.g., the hours of the day), refers in its basic sense to things that are "of the season *or* time *or* period." Derivatively, however, it came to connote primarily that which belongs to the season of spring and therefore that which is youthful, graceful and lovely. The latter is plainly the sense it bears in the LXX text of Song 6:7b and, moreover, the sense that Gregory himself gave it in his somewhat different interpretation of the same words as they occur in Song 4:3b (see above, homily 7, p. 229 [Jaeger]). Here, however, Gregory takes it to connote timeliness and indeed enjoys himself by indulging in a minor wordplay involving words formed on the root ὡρ-.

29. See above, homily 7, pp. 229–30 (Jaeger), for the application of "apple" to the cheek.

κρυπτὸς θησαυρὸς τῶν ἐλπίδων, ὁ ἴδιος καρπὸς τῆς ψυχῆς ὁ τῷ ἐναρέτῳ βίῳ
| καθάπερ τινὶ ῥόας λεπύρῳ περικρατούμενος.   456
τὸ δὲ Ἐκτὸς τῆς σιωπήσεώς σου ταύτην οἶμαι τὴν διάνοιαν ἔχειν, ὅτι ὁ
ἔπαινος οὐκ ἐκ τῶν φαινομένων τοσοῦτόν ἐστιν ὅσα τῷ λόγῳ μηνύεται, ἀλλὰ
5   μᾶλλον <ἐκ τῶν> ὅσα τῇ σιωπῇ ὑποκέκρυπται τὴν τοῦ λόγου διαφεύγοντα
μήνυσιν· ὥσπερ γὰρ τὸ ἐκτὸς τοῦ λόγου ἡ σιωπὴ νοεῖται, οὕτω καὶ τὸ ἐκτὸς
τῆς σιωπῆς τὸν λόγον νοῶν τις οὐχ ἁμαρτήσεται. ἐκεῖνο γὰρ σιωπῶμεν ὃ
διὰ τῶν ῥημάτων ἐξαγγεῖλαι ἀδυνατοῦμεν. εἰ οὖν τὸ ἐκτὸς ἐκείνου ἡ σιωπὴ
νοεῖται, τὸ ἐκτὸς τῆς σιωπῆς ἀκόλουθόν ἐστι πάντως τὸν λόγον οἴεσθαι.
10   οὐκοῦν ὁ εἰπὼν τὸ Ἐκτὸς τῆς σιωπήσεως, τοῦτο σαφῶς τῷ λόγῳ παρίστησιν
ὅτι καλὰ μέν ἐστι καὶ μεγάλα τὰ τῷ λόγῳ φανῆναι δυνάμενα, ὅσα ἐκτός ἐστι
τῆς σιωπήσεως, τὰ δὲ τοῦ λόγου ἐκτός, τὰ τῇ σιωπῇ καλυπτόμενα, τὰ ἄρρητά
τε καὶ ἀνεκφώνητα, μείζω πάντως καὶ θαυμασιώτερα τῶν ἐκφωνουμένων
ἐστίν.
15   Ἀκούσωμεν δὲ καὶ τῶν ἐφεξῆς ἐπαίνων, ὧν ἡ διάνοια τῷ τῆς ἱστορίας
ἔοικε φρέατι οὗ βαρύς τις λίθος ἐπέχων τὸ στόμιον ἄπορον ἐποίει ταῖς
ποιμαινούσαις τὴν μετουσίαν τοῦ ὕδατος. ἀλλ᾽ ὁ Ἰακὼβ ἐπιστὰς ἀναμοχλίζει
τε τοῦ στομίου τὸν λίθον καὶ πλήρη τὰ ποτιστήρια ποιήσας | τοῦ ὕδατος   457
ἔδωκε τοῖς θρέμμασι κατ᾽ ἐξουσίαν ἐντρυφῆσαι τῷ νάματι. τίνα τοίνυν ἐστὶν ἃ
20   τῷ τοιούτῳ φρέατι προσεικάζομεν; Ἑξήκοντά εἰσι βασίλισσαι καὶ ὀγδοήκοντα
παλλακαὶ καὶ νεάνιδες ὧν οὐκ ἔστιν ἀριθμός. μία ἐστὶ περιστερά μου, τελεία
μου· μία ἐστὶ τῇ μητρὶ αὐτῆς, ἐκλεκτή ἐστι τῇ τεκούσῃ αὐτήν.
τίς οὖν ἡμῖν ἀποκυλίσει τῆς ἀσαφείας ταύτης τὸν λίθον; τίς ἐξαντλήσει
τῶν νοημάτων τὸ ὕδωρ οὕτως ἐν βάθει κείμενον, ὡς ἀνέφικτον εἶναι
25   τῷ ἡμετέρῳ λόγῳ; ἀλλά μοι καλῶς ἔχειν δοκεῖ τοῦτο ταῖς ἀκοαῖς ὑμῶν
διαμαρτύρασθαι ὅτι τὸ ταῦτα γνῶναι μόνων ἐκείνων ἐστὶν πρὸς οὓς φησιν
ὁ ἀπόστολος ὅτι Ἐν παντὶ ἐπλουτίσθητε, ἐν παντὶ λόγῳ καὶ πάσῃ γνώσει.
ἡ δὲ ἡμετέρα πενία τῶν προκειμένων τοῦ λόγου θησαυρῶν περιδράξασθαι
ἀδυνάτως ἔχει. πλὴν ὡς ἂν τοῦ τῆς ἀργίας κατακρίματος ἔξω γενοίμεθα, διὰ
30   τὸν ἐρευνᾶν τὰς γραφὰς ἡμῖν νομοθετήσαντα μικρόν τινα καὶ τούτοις ἱδρῶτα
προσθεῖναι οὐ κατοκνήσομεν.
φαμὲν τοίνυν δόγμα τι τῶν ἀστειοτέρων τὴν ἐν τοῖς ῥητοῖς τούτοις
φιλοσοφίαν διὰ τῶν ἐπαίνων τῆς νύμφης ἡμῖν παρατίθεσθαι. τὸ δὲ δόγμα

of hopes, the soul's proper fruit, firmly enclosed by the virtuous life | as if by a sort of pomegranate skin.

As to the words *outside your veil [of silence]*,[30] they mean, as I see it, that the praise is not as great as it is because of the sorts of perceptible things that speech refers to but on the contrary because of all the things that the veil of silence conceals and that escape what speech declares; for just as silence is understood to be that which stands outside of speech, so too you will make no mistake if you understand that what is outside of silence is speech, for we are silent regarding that which cannot be conveyed in words. If, then, silence is understood to be that which is outside our capacity for speech, it follows that that which is outside of silence must surely be thought of as speech. Hence one who says *outside your veil [of silence]* is clearly asserting that the things that can be expressed by speech are great and beauteous—those, namely, that are *outside* the *veil [of silence]*, but those that are outside of speech, those that are veiled in silence, unutterable and incapable of being articulated, are altogether greater and more wonderful than those that are spoken.

But let us attend to the praises that come next. Their meaning is like the well in the story, the well that had a heavy stone stopping its mouth and making it impossible for the women shepherds to get any of the water. Jacob, however, came up, lifted the stone from the well's mouth, filled the drinking troughs | with water, and enabled the animals to drink to their hearts' content (cf. Gen 29:2–10). What is it, then, that I am comparing to this well? *There are sixty queens and eighty concubines and young maidens without number. One is my dove, my perfect one, the only one that belongs to her mother, the elect of the the one who bore her.*

Who, then, will roll away for us the stone of this obscurity? Who will draw up the water, the thoughts, that is, that lie so hidden in its depths that our reason cannot attain them? For my part, however, I think I am bound to bear witness in your ears that knowledge of these things belongs only to those to whom the apostle says: "In every way you were enriched … with all speech and all knowledge" (1 Cor 1:5). Our poverty, though, has not the strength to lay hold on the treasures of the text. Yet to avoid the condemnation that befalls idleness, and for the sake of the one who commanded us to search the Scriptures (cf. John 5:39), we do not shrink from contributing a bit of our own sweat to this task.

We assert, then, that the philosophy contained in these words sets out, by way of the praises accorded to the Bride, an essential teaching of great sophis-

---

30. The Greek word here translated as "veil" has the root meaning of "keeping silence," and Gregory's exegesis, here as in homily 7 (see above, p. 231 [Jaeger]), makes use of this circumstance.

τοιοῦτόν ἐστιν· οὐ μετὰ τῆς αὐτῆς ἀκολουθίας καὶ τάξεως κτίζεται τὰ ὄντα
καὶ ἀνακτίζεται· ὅτε μὲν γὰρ κατ' ἀρχὰς διὰ τῆς θείας δυνάμεως ἡ τῆς
κτίσεως ὑφίσταται φύσις, ἐφ' ἑκάστου τῶν ὄντων | ἀδιαστάτως τῇ ἀρχῇ   458
συναπηρτίσθη τὸ πέρας πᾶσι τοῖς ἐκ τοῦ μὴ ὄντος εἰς τὸ εἶναι παραγομένοις
5   ὁμοῦ τῇ ἀρχῇ συνανασχούσης τῆς τελειότητος. ἐν δὲ τῶν κτισθέντων καὶ ἡ
ἀνθρωπίνη φύσις ἐστίν, οὐδὲ αὐτὴ καθ' ὁμοιότητα τῶν ἄλλων ἐκ προαγωγῆς
προελθοῦσα ἐπὶ τὸ τέλειον, ἀλλ' ἀπὸ τῆς πρώτης ὑπάρξεως συμπλασθεῖσα
τῇ τελειότητι· ἐγένετο γὰρ ὁ ἄνθρωπος, φησί, κατ' εἰκόνα θεοῦ καὶ ὁμοίωσιν.
ὅπερ ἐνδείκνυται τὸ τῶν ἀγαθῶν ἀκρότατόν τε καὶ τελειότατον. τί γὰρ ἂν
10   ὑπέρτερον εὑρεθείη τῆς πρὸς τὸν θεὸν ὁμοιώσεως;
     ἐπὶ μὲν οὖν τῆς πρώτης κτίσεως ἀδιαστάτως τῇ ἀρχῇ συνανεφάνη
τὸ πέρας καὶ ἀπὸ τῆς τελειότητος ἡ φύσις τοῦ εἶναι ἤρξατο. ἐπειδὴ δὲ τῷ
θανάτῳ διὰ τῆς πρὸς τὴν κακίαν σχέσεως οἰκειωθεῖσα τῆς ἐν τῷ ἀγαθῷ
διαμονῆς ἀπερρύη, οὐκ ἀθρόαν καθ' ὁμοιότητα τῆς πρώτης συστάσεως
15   ἐπαναλαμβάνει τὴν τελειότητα, ἀλλ' ὁδῷ τινι πρόεισιν ἐπὶ τὸ μεῖζον διὰ
τινος ἀκολουθίας καὶ τάξεως κατ' ὀλίγον ἀποσκευαζομένη τὴν πρὸς τὰ
ἐναντία προσπάθειαν· ἐπὶ μὲν γὰρ τῆς πρώτης κατασκευῆς οὐδὲν ἦν τὸ
κωλῦον συνδραμεῖν τῇ γενέσει τὸ τῆς φύσεως τέλειον κακίας οὐκ οὔσης,
ἐπὶ δὲ τῆς δευτέρας ἀναστοιχειώσεως ἀναγκαίως ἡ διαστηματικὴ παράτασις
20   συμπαρομαρτεῖ τοῖς πρὸς τὸ πρῶτον ἀγαθὸν | ἀνατρέχουσιν. διότι τῇ ὑλικῇ   459
προσπαθείᾳ συνδεθεῖσα διὰ κακίας ἡμῶν ἡ διάνοια κατ' ὀλίγον ὥσπερ φλοιοῦ
τινος τοῦ περιέχοντος διὰ τῆς ἀστειοτέρας ἀγωγῆς περιξύεται τὴν συμφυΐαν
τοῦ χείρονος.
     τούτου χάριν πολλὰς εἶναι παρὰ τῷ πατρὶ μονὰς μεμαθήκαμεν κατὰ
25   τὴν ἀναλογίαν τῆς ἐν ἑκάστῳ πρὸς τὸ καλὸν σχέσεως καὶ τῆς τοῦ χείρονος
ἀποστάσεως, ἑτοιμαζομένης πᾶσι τῆς ἀντιδόσεως· ὁ μὲν γάρ τις ἐν ἀρχῇ
τῆς τοῦ βελτίονός ἐστι κληρώσεως ἄρτι καθάπερ ἐκ βυθοῦ τινος τοῦ κατὰ
κακίαν βίου πρὸς τὴν μετουσίαν τῆς ἀληθείας ἀνανηξάμενος, τῷ δέ τις
γέγονεν ἤδη δι' ἐπιμελείας καὶ προσθήκῃ τοῦ κρείττονος, ἄλλος ἐπὶ πλεῖον
30   διὰ τῆς ἐπιθυμίας τῶν ἀγαθῶν ἐπηυξήθη, ὁ δὲ μέσως ἔχει τῆς τῶν ὑψηλῶν

tication. The teaching in question is the following. Members of the realm of Being are not re-created in the same sequence and order in which they were created. For when at the beginning the created order[31] came into existence by God's power, it was the case for each of these that its start and its full actualization were achieved together | without any interval, since for all that were brought from nonexistence to existence their perfection coincided with their beginning. Now the human race is one of the things that were created, and it did not, like the others, go forward to perfection by promotion, but from its first moment of existence it was formed simultaneously with its perfection, for humanity, it says, came to be "after the image and likeness of God" (Gen 1:26–27). And this is manifestly the highest and most perfect of goods, for what can be found that is nobler than being made like God?

In the case of the first creation, then, the final state appeared simultaneously with the beginning, and the race took the starting point of its existence in its perfection; but from the moment it acquired a kinship with death by its inclination toward evil and so ceased to abide in the good, it does not achieve its perfect state again all at once, as at its first creation. Rather does it advance toward the better along a road of sorts, in an orderly fashion, one step after another, and rids itself bit by bit of its susceptibility to that which opposes its fulfillment. For when it was first created, since evil did not exist, there was nothing to prevent the race's perfection from going hand in hand with its birth, but in the process of restoration, lapses of time[32] necessarily attend those who are retracing their way | toward the original good. Hence our mind, which because of its vice is locked into a passionate attachment to materiality, scrapes away, bit by bit, with the help of a cunning discipline, the wrong that has grown together with it like a tree bark that encloses it.

This explains why we have learned that with the Father there are "many places to stay" (John 14:2), corresponding to the degree of each individual's inclination to the good and withdrawal from the worse, since there is a reward prepared for all of them. One person, who is rising as it were from the depths of a life of vice toward participation in the truth, now stands at the threshold of the nobler inheritance. To another, who is earnest and zealous, there has already accrued a nobler good. Yet another, out of lust for good things, has grown even further than this. Here is one who is at the midpoint of an ascent of the heights, while another has passed the very midpoint, and there are

---

31. The Greek is ἡ τῆς κτίσεως … φύσις, which I take to mean something like "the realm of created things qua created." This is another instance of Gregory's use of φύσις as a collective noun.

32. In the Greek, διαστηματικὴ παράτασις: cf. just above, the adverb ἀδιαστάτως ("without any interval").

ἀναβάσεως, ἕτερος καὶ τὸ μέσον παρέδραμεν, εἰσὶ δέ τινες οἱ καὶ τούτων
ἑαυτοὺς ὑπεράραντες, ἄλλοι κἀκείνους παρήλασαν καὶ ὑπὲρ τούτους
ἕτεροι πρὸς τὸν ἄνω δρόμον συντείνονται. καὶ ὅλως κατὰ τὴν ποικίλην τῶν
προαιρέσεων διαφορὰν ἕκαστον ὁ θεὸς ἐν τῷ ἰδίῳ προσδέχεται τάγματι τὰ
5   πρὸς ἀξίαν ἀποκληρῶν | τοῖς πᾶσι, καὶ συνάγων τοῖς ὑψηλοτέροις τὰς τῶν   460
ἀγαθῶν ἀμοιβὰς καὶ συμμετρῶν τοῖς ἐλάττοσιν.

ταῦτα διὰ τῶν προκειμένων ῥητῶν φιλοσοφεῖν τὸν λόγον ὑπενοήσαμεν
τὴν διαφορὰν τῶν ψυχῶν, αἳ πρὸς τὸν νυμφίον ὁρῶσιν, ἐν τοῖς εἰρημένοις
ἡμῖν διαστείλαντα· τὰς μὲν γὰρ ὀνομάζει νεάνιδας τὴν τοῦ ἀριθμοῦ φύσιν διὰ
10   τοῦ πλήθους νικώσας, ἄλλας δὲ παλλακίδας καὶ ἄλλας βασιλίδας εἶναί φησιν,
ὀκτὼ δεκάσι τῶν παλλακίδων τὸν ἀριθμὸν περιγράψας, τὰς δὲ βασιλίδας
συντελεῖν εἰπὼν εἰς ἑξήκοντα, ὑπερτίθησι δὲ πασῶν τὴν ἐν τῇ μονάδι
θεωρουμένην τελείαν περιστεράν, ἣν καὶ μόνην τῇ μητρὶ καὶ ἐκλεκτὴν εἶναι
τῇ τεκούσῃ αὐτὴν ἀποφαίνεται.

15   ταῦτα οὖν διὰ τῶν θείων τούτων λογίων νοεῖν ἐναγόμεθα ὅτι οἱ μὲν
ἄρτι καθάπερ νηδύος τινὸς τῆς ἐν βάθει κειμένης ἀπάτης ἔξω γενόμενοι,
ἀρτιγενεῖς τινες ὄντες καὶ οὔπω διηρθρωμένον ἐν ἑαυτοῖς τὸν λόγον
χωρήσαντες τῇ ἀλογωτέρᾳ συγκαταθέσει τῆς πίστεως ἐν ἀπείρῳ θεωροῦνται
πλήθει, σωτήριον μὲν εἶναι πεπιστευκότες τοῦ μυστηρίου τὸν λόγον, οὐ μὴν
20   ἐν ἐπιστήμῃ τινὶ καὶ τῇ διὰ τοῦ λόγου πληροφορίᾳ καθιδρυμένην ἔχοντες
ἐν ἑαυτοῖς τὴν ἀλήθειαν. αὗται εἰσιν αἱ ὀνομασθεῖσαι νεάνιδες διὰ τὸ ἔτι
νέαν ἄγειν τὴν πνευματικὴν ἡλικίαν, αἳ γεννηθεῖσαι τῷ λόγῳ τῆς πίστεως
οὐδέπω διὰ τῆς καθηκούσης αὐξήσεως τοιαῦται γεγόνασιν ὡς ἐπὶ γάμου
ἀκμὴν προελθεῖν καὶ φθάσαι εἰς ἄνδρα τέλειον, εἰς μέτρον γαμικῆς ἡλικίας,
25   ὥστε τῷ φόβῳ | τοῦ κυρίου δύνασθαι κυοφορῆσαι καὶ πνεῦμα σωτηρίας   461
παιδοποιήσασθαι, ἀλλ' ἔτι τῷ νηπίῳ τε καὶ ἀτελεῖ τῆς διανοίας ἀλογωτέρᾳ
πως συζῶσι τῇ διαθέσει. πλὴν ἀλλὰ καὶ οὗτοι τῶν σῳζομένων εἰσί, καθὼς
φησιν ὁ προφήτης ὅτι Ἀνθρώπους καὶ κτήνη σώσεις, κύριε, κτήνη λέγων τὸ
ἀλογώτερον μέρος τῶν σῳζομένων.

30   Τῶν δὲ διὰ τῆς καθηκούσης ἐπιμελείας αὐξηθέντων τῇ διανοίᾳ καὶ
καταλελοιπότων ἤδη τὴν νηπιότητα διπλῆν ὑπὸ τοῦ λόγου τὴν διαφορὰν
διδασκόμεθα· γίνονται μὲν γὰρ αἱ ψυχαὶ σύσσωμοι τῷ λόγῳ καὶ αὗται κἀκεῖναι,

some who have surpassed even these, others who have overtaken the latter, and above these still others strain forward in their upward course. And, in short, God receives each individual into the proper rank, in accordance with the many different sorts of choices that are made, and allots to all severally what corresponds to their desert, | at once matching to the more advanced and measuring out to the less advanced the recompense of good things that is theirs.

It is this philosophy, we surmise, that the text is teaching in the passage now before us: with these words it is defining the difference between the souls that look upon the Bridegroom. For there are some whom it names *young maidens,* who because of their multitude have surpassed what can be numbered. Others it says are *concubines,* and yet others *queens,* specifying the number of concubines as eighty and asserting that the queens make up a total of sixty. Above them all, however, it locates the *perfect dove* that is discerned by reason of her being one alone and who is represented as the only one for her mother and a chosen one for the woman that bore her.

By these divine oracles we are brought to understand this, that some folk have just emerged from deep-set delusion as out of a kind of womb. Being like newborns who have not yet made room within themselves for the articulate Word because theirs is the less rational assent of faith, these are represented as an innumerable multitude. They have believed that the word of the mystery is saving, but they do not possess the truth within themselves as it is established firmly by a kind of certain knowledge and by the full assurance accorded through the Word. These are the ones who were called *young maidens* because they are still young in spiritual stature. Begotten by the word of faith, they have not yet undergone the growth that is requisite for them to advance to the pinnacle of marriage and to attain "to the perfect man" to "the measure of the age[33]" (cf. Eph 4:13) of marriage, so that they are able to become pregnant by the fear | of the Lord and bring forth the Spirit of salvation. Rather do they still, by reason of childishness and immaturity of mind, live in the companionship of a less rational bent of mind. For all that, these folk too are counted as those who are being saved, just as the prophet says: "You save men and beasts, O Lord" (Ps 35:7)—by "beasts" meaning the less rational portion of those who are being saved.

The text teaches us, however, that there is a twofold division of those who by taking the requisite pains have grown in mind and already left childishness behind. Both sets of souls become one body with the Word, but some of

---

33. The Greek term here is ἡλικία, which is normally rendered as "stature" but which Gregory here, as elsewhere, takes to mean an "age" or "stage of maturity," a legitimate sense of the word.

ἀλλ᾽ αἱ μὲν ἐρωτικῇ τινι διαθέσει προσκολλῶνται (οἵα ἦν ἡ τοῦ Δαβὶδ καὶ
ἡ τοῦ Παύλου ψυχή, ἡ μὲν λέγουσα τὸ Ἐμοὶ δὲ τὸ προσκολλᾶσθαι τῷ θεῷ
ἀγαθόν ἐστιν, ἡ δὲ τὸ Οὐδεὶς χωρίσει ἡμᾶς ἀπὸ τῆς ἀγάπης τοῦ θεοῦ τῆς ἐν
Χριστῷ Ἰησοῦ· οὐ ζωή, οὐ θάνατος, οὐ τὸ παρόν, οὐ τὸ μέλλον, οὐκ ἄλλο τι
5   τῶν ὄντων οὐδέν), αἱ δὲ φόβῳ κολάσεως τὰς μοιχικὰς ἀποφεύγουσι πείρας·
μένουσι γὰρ ἐν ἀφθαρσίᾳ καὶ ἁγιασμῷ καὶ αὗται, ἀλλὰ τῷ φόβῳ μᾶλλον ἢ
τῷ πόθῳ μόνῳ παιδαγωγούμεναι τὸ κακὸν οὐ προσδέχονται. αἱ μὲν οὖν | διὰ   462
τῆς τελειοτέρας διαθέσεως πόθῳ τῆς ἀφθαρσίας ἀνακραθεῖσαι τῇ τοῦ θεοῦ
καθαρότητι βασίλισσαι διὰ τὴν κοινωνίαν τῆς βασιλείας κατονομάζονται,
10 τὰς δὲ τῷ τῆς ἀπειλῆς φόβῳ τὴν ἀρετὴν ἐκπονούσας παλλακίδας ὀνομάζει ὁ
λόγος· οὔπω γάρ τις αὐτῶν μήτηρ βασιλέως καὶ κοινωνὸς τῆς ἀξίας γενέσθαι
δυνατῶς ἔχει. πῶς γὰρ ἂν δυνηθείη ἡ μηδέπω ἀναλαβοῦσα ἐν ἑαυτῇ τὸ
ἀδέσποτον καὶ αὐτοκρατὲς τοῦ ἐναρέτου φρονήματος, ἀλλὰ δουλικῷ φόβῳ
τῆς τῶν κακῶν κοινωνίας ἀφισταμένη;
15   ὑποδείγματα δὲ τῶν εἰρημένων ἐστὶν ἐπὶ μὲν τῶν βασιλίδων τὸ κατὰ
τοὺς τῆς δεξιᾶς στάσεως ἠξιωμένους, πρὸς οὓς ὁ βασιλεὺς λέγει· Δεῦτε,
οἱ εὐλογημένοι τοῦ πατρός μου, κληρονομήσατε τὴν ἡτοιμασμένην ὑμῖν
βασιλείαν· τοῦ δὲ δευτέρου καὶ ὑφειμένου τάγματος εἶεν ἂν ἐκεῖνοι, πρὸς οὓς
λέγει ὁ κύριος· Φοβήθητε τὸν μετὰ τὸ ἀποκτεῖναι ἔχοντα ἐξουσίαν ἐμβαλεῖν
20 εἰς τὴν γέενναν τοῦ πυρός.
       ταύτην δέ μοι δοκεῖ τὴν διαστολὴν τῶν δύο ταγμάτων ἡ κατὰ τοὺς
ἀριθμοὺς διαφορὰ παραδηλοῦν δι᾽ αἰνίγματος. πῶς τοῦτό φημι; ἓξ εἰσιν
ἐντολαὶ δι᾽ ὧν ἡ βασιλεία τοῖς δεξιοῖς ἑτοιμάζεται. λογισώμεθα τούτων
ἑκάστην τὸ δεσποτικὸν εἶναι τάλαντον, ὃ προσήκει παρὰ τοῦ ἀγαθοῦ καὶ
25 | πιστοῦ οἰκέτου δεκαπλασιασθῆναι διὰ τῆς ἐργασίας, ἵνα οὕτως εἰσέλθῃ   463
εἰς τὴν χαρὰν τοῦ κυρίου αὐτοῦ ἐν ὀλίγοις πιστὸς εὑρεθεὶς καὶ ἐπὶ πολλῶν
καθιστάμενος. εἰ τοίνυν διὰ τῶν ἓξ τούτων ἐντολῶν ἡ τῆς βασιλείας
γίνεται τῇ ψυχῇ κοινωνία, τὸ δὲ τέλειον τῆς ἐργασίας ἐφ᾽ ἑκάστης ἐστὶ τὸ
δεκαπλασιάσαι τὴν ἐντολήν, καθὼς ἔφη ὁ ἀγαθὸς δοῦλος ἐκεῖνος ὅτι Δέκα
30 τάλαντα τὸ ἕν σου τάλαντον κατειργάσατο, εὑρίσκομεν ἐκ τοῦ ἀκολούθου τὴν
μίαν βασίλισσαν εἰς ἑξήκοντα πλατυνομένην, τὴν διὰ τοῦ δεκαπλασιασμοῦ
τῶν ἓξ ἐντολῶν εἰς κοινωνίαν τῆς βασιλείας παραδεχθεῖσαν, ὡς πολλὰς εἶναι
τὴν μίαν τῷ πολυτρόπῳ χαρακτῆρι τῶν ἐντολῶν ἐμμερισθεῖσαν καὶ ἑκάστῳ

them are joined to him by a disposition shaped by erotic love[34] (such were the souls of David and of Paul, one of whom says, "But for me it is a good thing to cleave to God"; and the other, "None shall separate us from the love of God that is in Christ Jesus, not life or death or what is present or what is future, or anything else"). Others, however, avoid adulterous experiences from fear of punishment, for they too abide in incorruption and holiness, but it is as disciplined by fear rather than by desire alone that they refuse evil. Those, then, | who on account of a more perfect habit of mind have been joined together with God's purity by their desire for incorruption are called *queens* because they share in the divine kingship. But to those who work hard at virtue out of the fear generated by threats, the text puts the name *concubines,* for none of them has the ability to become mother of a king and a sharer in his dignity. What can she accomplish who has never received within herself the independence and self-rule that belong to the virtuous mind, but keeps aloof from partnership in vice out of servile fear?

An example of what I am saying in the case of the queens is their being reckoned with those counted worthy to stand at the right hand, those to whom the King says, "Come, you blessed of my Father, inherit the kingship prepared for you!" In the case of the second and lower order, an example would be those to whom the Lord says, "Fear the one who has the authority to kill you and to cast you into the Gehenna of fire."

To me it seems that the difference between the numbers clarifies, by way of an enigma, this difference between the two orders. How can I say such a thing? There are six commandments[35] whose observance readies kingship for those at the right hand. Now let us reckon that each of these is that talent of the owner's that the good | and faithful servant had to multiply ten times by his business activities, so that having been found "faithful" in small things and set "over much," he may "enter into the joy" of his Lord. Suppose, then, that a sharing in the kingship accrues to the soul by observance of these commandments and that in each case the completion of the enterprise consists in multiplying it by ten, as that good servant said, "Your one talent has produced ten." As a consequence of all this, we find that the one queen has been multiplied so as to become sixty; she who because of her tenfold multiplication of the six commandments has been accorded a participation in the kingship, so that the one is become many, because she has been apportioned

---

34. On this contrast between love and fear, see homily 1 above (pp. 15–16, 19, 22–23 [Jaeger]), with n. 1.

35. Cf. Matt 25:35–36: "I was hungry and you gave me food; I was thirsty and you gave me drink; I was a stranger and you welcomed me; I was naked and you clothed me; I was sick and you visited me; I was in prison and you came to me."

τῶν κατορθωμάτων ἰδιαζόντως ἐμμορφωθεῖσαν. οὕτως οὖν εἰς ἑξήκοντα βασιλίδας ἡ μία καταμερίζεται πρὸς τὰ εἴδη τῶν ἐντολῶν διαιρουμένη τε καὶ ἀριθμουμένη καὶ γίνεται κοινωνὸς τῆς τοῦ Χριστοῦ βασιλείας ἡ νύμφη, δῆμος βασιλίδων ἡ μία γεγενημένη ἡ διὰ τῶν τοσούτων, τῶν κατὰ τὰς ἐντολὰς
5   ἀξιωμάτων, ἀριθμηθεῖσα.

Εἰ δὲ τὴν ἑξάδα τῶν ἐντολῶν ἐν μιᾷ κατὰ τὸ δεκαπλάσιον γεωργηθεῖσαν ψυχῇ διὰ τῶν ἑξήκοντα βασιλίδων σημαίνεσθαι | δι᾽ αἰνίγματος οὐκ ἔξω   464 τοῦ εἰκότος ὑπενοήσαμεν, ἀκολούθως καὶ διὰ τῶν ὀγδοήκοντα τὸ τῆς ὀγδόης μυστήριον παραδηλοῦσθαί φαμεν διὰ τοῦ ὁμοίου αἰνίγματος, πρὸς
10   ἣν βλέποντες οἱ τῷ φόβῳ παιδαγωγούμενοι τῆς τῶν κακῶν κοινωνίας ἀπείργονται· οὕτω γὰρ ἐν ταῖς ψαλμῳδίαις ἐμάθομεν, ἐν αἷς προτέτακται μὲν διὰ τῆς ἐπιγραφῆς ἡ ὀγδόη, μαστιγουμένων δὲ ἄντικρύς εἰσιν αἱ φωναὶ τῷ φόβῳ τῶν ἐλπιζομένων εἰς ἔλεον τὴν ἀκοὴν ἐπικάμπτουσαι. φησὶ γὰρ πρὸς τὸν φοβερὸν κριτὴν ὁ πρὸς τὴν ὀγδόην βλέπων· Κύριε μὴ τῷ θυμῷ σου
15   ἐλέγξῃς με μηδὲ τῇ ὀργῇ σου παιδεύσῃς με. ἐλέησόν με, κύριε, ὅτι ἀσθενής εἰμι· ἴασαί με, κύριε, ὅτι ἐταράχθη τὰ ὀστᾶ μου, καὶ ὅσα ἐκ τοῦ ἀκολούθου τῷ ἀδεκάστῳ κριτῇ διὰ τῆς ἱκετηρίας προτείνεται, ἐν οἷς καὶ τὸ μὴ εἶναι θεοῦ μνήμην ἐν τῷ θανάτῳ ὀδύρεται (πῶς γὰρ ἂν εἴη δυνατὸν τοῖς κλαυθμῷ τε καὶ βρυγμῷ καταδεδικασμένοις τὴν ἐκ τῆς μνήμης τοῦ θεοῦ εὐφροσύνην
20   ἐγγίνεσθαι οὕτως εἰπόντος ἑτέρωθι τοῦ προφήτου ὅτι ἡ μνήμη τοῦ θεοῦ εὐφροσύνην ποιεῖ;), καὶ ἄλλα τοιαῦτά τινα προτεινάμενος ὁ δεδοικὼς τὴν ὀγδόην ἐν αἰσθήσει τῆς τοῦ ἐλέου γίνεται μετουσίας λέγων ὅτι Εἰσήκουσε κύριος τῆς φωνῆς τοῦ κλαυθμοῦ μου.

πολλῶν δὲ μακαρίων φόβων ὑπὸ τῆς ἁγίας δηλουμένων γραφῆς εἴη ἂν
25   καὶ ἐπὶ τούτων ἀναλόγως ταῖς | ἓξ ἐντολαῖς ἡ ἐπὶ τὸ δεκαπλάσιον αὔξησις,   465 ὥστε τὸν διδαχθέντα παρὰ τῆς ψαλμῳδίας, πῶς κατορθοῦται τοῦ κυρίου ὁ φόβος ἐκ τοῦ ἐκκλῖναι μὲν ἀπὸ τοῦ κακοῦ ποιεῖν δὲ τὸ ἀγαθόν, οἷόν τινα μνᾶν ἢ τάλαντον δεκαπλασιάσαι διὰ τῆς ἐργασίας τὸ χρῆμα τοῦ φόβου καὶ οὕτω τὴν δευτερεύουσαν μετὰ τὴν βασιλίδα ψυχήν, ἣ φόβῳ καὶ οὐκ ἀγάπῃ
30   τὸ καλὸν κατεργάζεται, πρὸς τὸν ἀριθμὸν τῶν ὀγδοήκοντα πλατυνθῆναι

in accordance with the manifold character of the commandments and has been shaped in a particular way in accordance with each of the righteous deeds. In this manner, then, the one queen is divided into sixty, differentiated and numbered in accordance with the forms of the commandments, and the Bride becomes a partner in Christ's kingship: the one queen becomes a populace of queens, and she is numbered in the plural because of the multiple dignities defined by the commandments.

Now if we suppose that the sixty queens, after the manner of an enigma, signify the sestet of these commandments as it is cultivated within a single soul to yield a tenfold increase, and if this supposition | is not wholly implausible, then following the same principle we assert that the number eighty intimates, by way of a similar enigma, the mystery of the eighth day—the day that, when contemplated by folk that are governed by fear, dissuades them from participation in evil.[36] For so we have learned in the psalms to which "eighth day" is prefixed as an inscription; the words are plainly those of persons who are afflicting themselves, inclining the hearer toward mercy by their fear in the face of the future they anticipate. For to the fearsome Judge the person who is contemplating the eighth day says: "O Lord, rebuke me not in your anger, neither chasten me in your wrath. Have mercy upon me, O Lord, for I languish; O Lord, heal me, for my bones are troubled"—and everything else he thereafter addresses by way of supplication to the impartial Judge, including dismay that in death there is no remembrance of God. (For how could it be possible for joy in the remembrance of God to awaken in people condemned to weeping and gnashing of teeth—even though the prophet elsewhere says that remembrance of God occasions joy?) Then, having set forth some other sentiments of this sort, the speaker who is anxious about the eighth day becomes aware of having a share in mercy, for he says, "The Lord has heard the voice of my weeping."

Now since the Holy Scriptures exhibit many types of fear that are blessed, it may be that in their case too there is a tenfold increase analogous to the one that occurs | in the case of the six commandments. Thus a person who has been taught by the psalm how fear of the Lord is established by disinclination to evil and positive doing of the good will put that fear to work and multiply it as if it were a talent or a hundred drachmae. In this way the soul that ranks behind the queenly soul—that is, the one that works the good out of fear and not out of love—will be increased in number until she achieves eighty, as she

---

36. For on the "eighth (day)" or "octave," see Gregory's *Inscr. Pss.* 2.5 (GNO 5:83–85; trans. Heine 1995, 136–37). The eighth day is the "next age," the age of resurrection, which succeeds the "week," the age "in which one thing comes to be and another dissolves" and which is therefore the realm of time and change. The image of the eighth day first appears in *Barn.* 15.8.9.

ἕκαστον εἶδος τῶν διὰ φόβου κατορθουμένων ἐπὶ τοῦ βίου ἑαυτῆς ἀσυγχύτως
τε καὶ διακεκριμένως δεικνύουσαν, ὡς καὶ ἐπὶ ταύτης τὸν τῆς ὀγδόης λόγον
τῇ πρὸς τὸ δεκαπλάσιον αὐξήσει συμπλατυνθῆναι καὶ οὕτω γενέσθαι ἐν
φόβῳ δουλικῷ καὶ οὐχὶ ἔρωτι νυμφικῷ τῷ ἀγαθῷ προσεγγίζουσαν παλλακὴν

5　ἀντὶ τῆς βασιλίδος διὰ τὸν τῆς ὀγδόης φόβον, ὃν δεκαπλασίως ἐν τοῖς
κατορθώμασιν ηὔξησεν, εἰς τὸν ἀριθμὸν συντελοῦσαν τῶν ὀγδοήκοντα. ἣν
κελεύει καὶ ὁ τῆς ἱστορίας λόγος νόθῳ πρὸς καιρὸν καὶ οὐκ εὐγενεῖ τόκῳ
ὑπηρετήσασαν μὴ συνοικεῖν εἰς τέλος τῇ βασιλίδι, ὡς οὐκ οὔσης ἐκ τοῦ ἴσου
τῆς βασιλικῆς κληρονομίας τῇ δουλικῇ γονῇ πρὸς τὸν ἐλεύθερον τόκον·

10　Ἔκβαλε γάρ, φησί, τὴν παιδίσκην καὶ τὸν υἱὸν αὐτῆς· οὐ γὰρ μὴ κληρονομήσῃ
ὁ υἱὸς τῆς παιδίσκης μετὰ τοῦ υἱοῦ τῆς ἐλευθέρας.

εἰ δέ τινι βιαιοτέρα φαίνεται ἡ εἰς τὸν προκείμενον τοῖς | ῥητοῖς　466
ἀριθμὸν θεωρία, ἀναμνησθήτω ὅτι καὶ κατ' ἀρχὰς τὸ μὴ δύνασθαι τυχεῖν
τῆς ἐν τούτοις ἀληθείας ἐμαρτυράμεθα τοσοῦτον μόνον ἁψάμενοι ὅσον μὴ

15　ἀγύμναστα καθόλου παραδραμεῖν τὰ αἰνίγματα.

Πλὴν εἰ ἔξω βάλοι τελείως ἡ ἀγάπη τὸν φόβον κατὰ τὸ γεγραμμένον καὶ
μεταποιηθεὶς ὁ φόβος ἀγάπη γένοιτο, τότε εὑρίσκεται μονὰς τὸ σῳζόμενον
ἐν τῇ πρὸς τὸ μόνον ἀγαθὸν συμφυΐᾳ πάντων ἀλλήλοις ἑνωθέντων διὰ τῆς
κατὰ τὴν περιστερὰν τελειότητος. τοιοῦτον γάρ τι νοοῦμεν ἐκ τοῦ ἐφεξῆς

20　λόγου ὅς φησιν ὅτι Μία ἐστὶ περιστερά μου, τελεία μου· μία ἐστὶ τῇ μητρὶ
αὐτῆς, ἐκλεκτή ἐστι τῇ τεκούσῃ αὐτήν.

ὅπερ ἐν τῷ εὐαγγελίῳ διὰ τῆς τοῦ κυρίου φωνῆς σαφέστερον ἡμῖν
ἑρμηνεύεται· πᾶσαν γὰρ τοῖς μαθηταῖς ἑαυτοῦ ἐναποτιθέμενος διὰ τῆς
εὐλογίας δύναμιν τά τε ἄλλα διὰ τῶν πρὸς τὸν πατέρα λόγων ἀγαθὰ τοῖς

25　ἁγίοις χαρίζεται καὶ προστίθησι τῶν ἀγαθῶν τὸ κεφάλαιον, τὸ μηκέτι
αὐτοὺς ἐν διαφορᾷ τινι προαιρέσεως ἐν τῇ περὶ τοῦ καλοῦ κρίσει πολλαχῇ
διασχίζεσθαι, ἀλλ' ἐν γενέσθαι τοὺς πάντας τῷ ἑνὶ καὶ μόνῳ ἀγαθῷ
συμφυέντας, ὥστε διὰ τῆς τοῦ πνεύματος τοῦ ἁγίου ἑνότητος, καθώς φησιν
ὁ ἀπόστολος, τῷ συνδέσμῳ τῆς εἰρήνης διασφιγχθέντας | ἓν σῶμα γενέσθαι　467

30　τοὺς πάντας καὶ ἓν πνεῦμα διὰ μιᾶς ἐλπίδος εἰς ἣν ἐκλήθησαν.

βέλτιον δ' ἂν εἴη αὐτὰς ἐπὶ λέξεως παραθέσθαι τὰς θείας τοῦ εὐαγγελίου
φωνάς· Ἵνα πάντες ἓν ὦσι καθὼς σύ, πάτερ, ἐν ἐμοὶ κἀγὼ ἐν σοί, ἵνα καὶ αὐτοὶ
ἐν ἡμῖν ἓν ὦσιν. τὸ δὲ συνδετικὸν τῆς ἑνότητος ταύτης ἡ δόξα ἐστίν· δόξαν

manifests in her own life, unconfusedly and distinctly, every single species of good thing that fear accomplishes. The result is that in the case of this soul too the number of the eighth day is multiplied in virtue of the soul's tenfold increase; and in this way—by drawing near to the good through servile fear rather than through a bride's love—she becomes a concubine rather than a queen because of her fear of the eighth day, a fear that she increases tenfold by her righteous deeds, attaining the number eighty. Furthermore, the words of scriptural narrative forbid her—because when the time came the help she gave took the form of an illegitimate and not a legitimate offspring—to dwell permanently together with the queen, since the the royal inheritance was not the same for the slave child as it was for the free. For it says: "Cast out the serving woman and her son, for the son of the serving woman shall not inherit with the son of the free woman."

If this interpretation of the number in our text seems a bit forced, | remember that at the start[37] we confessed that it is not possible to attain the truth that lies in these words. We have touched on them only to the extent that we have not left the enigmas entirely without treatment.

Nevertheless, should love cast out fear completely,[38] as it is written, and should fear transformed become love, at that point that which is saved is discovered to be a unity, since on the basis of a perfection like that of the Dove all are united to one another in being joined to the life of the one Good. It is in any case something of this sort that we understand by the next statement: *One is my dove, my perfect one, one is she for her mother, the chosen of the one who bore her.*

The meaning of this is made much clearer by what the Lord says in the Gospel. When by his blessing he conferred all power upon his disciples and also, by his address to the Father, endowed the saints with the other good things, he also added to all these the chiefest good of all: that in their judgment regarding the Beautiful they should never be split up by any difference in the choices they make. Instead, they would all become one by their growing together with the one and only Good, so that, as the apostle says, having been bound together in "the bond of peace," they might all become | "one body" and "one spirit" through the one hope into which they had been called (Eph 4:3–4).

But it would be better to set out the divine statements of the Gospel themselves, word for word: "That they may all be one, even as you, Father, are in me and I in you, that they also may be one in us." Now that which holds

---

37. See above, pp. 456–57 (Jaeger).
38. 1 John 4:18 says that "perfect love casts out fear." Gregory, perhaps unthinkingly, turns the adjective "perfect" into an adverb.

δὲ λέγεσθαι τὸ πνεῦμα τὸ ἅγιον οὐκ ἄν τις τῶν ἐπεσκεμμένων ἀντείποι πρὸς
αὐτὰς βλέπων τὰς τοῦ κυρίου φωνάς· Τὴν δόξαν γάρ, φησίν, ἣν ἔδωκάς μοι,
ἔδωκα αὐτοῖς. ἔδωκε γὰρ ὡς ἀληθῶς τοῖς μαθηταῖς τοιαύτην δόξαν ὁ εἰπὼν
πρὸς αὐτούς· Λάβετε πνεῦμα ἅγιον. ἔλαβε δὲ ταύτην τὴν δόξαν ἣν πάντοτε
5   εἶχε πρὸ τοῦ τὸν κόσμον εἶναι ὁ τὴν ἀνθρωπίνην φύσιν περιβαλόμενος,
ἧς δοξασθείσης διὰ τοῦ πνεύματος ἐπὶ πᾶν τὸ συγγενὲς ἡ τῆς δόξης τοῦ
πνεύματος διάδοσις γίνεται ἀπὸ τῶν μαθητῶν ἀρξαμένη. διὰ τοῦτό φησι· Τὴν
δόξαν, ἣν ἔδωκάς μοι, ἔδωκα αὐτοῖς, ἵνα ὦσιν ἕν, καθὼς ἡμεῖς ἕν ἐσμεν· ἐγὼ
ἐν αὐτοῖς καὶ σὺ ἐν ἐμοί, ἵνα ὦσι τετελειωμένοι εἰς τὸ ἕν. ὁ τοίνυν ἐκ μὲν
10 νηπίου πρὸς ἄνδρα τέλειον ἀναδραμὼν διὰ τῆς αὐξήσεως καὶ φθάσας εἰς τὸ
μέτρον τῆς νοητῆς ἡλικίας, ἐκ δὲ τῆς δούλης τε καὶ τῆς παλλακίδος τὴν τῆς
βασιλείας ἀξίαν μεταλαβών, δεκτικὸς δὲ τῆς τοῦ πνεύματος δόξης γενόμενος
| δι' ἀπαθείας καὶ καθαρότητος, οὗτός ἐστιν ἡ τελεία περιστερὰ πρὸς ἣν ὁ   468
νυμφίος ὁρᾷ λέγων ὅτι Μία ἐστὶ περιστερά μου, τελεία μου, μία ἐστὶ τῇ μητρὶ
15 αὐτῆς, ἐκλεκτή ἐστι τῇ τεκούσῃ αὐτήν.

ουκ ἀγνοοῦμεν δὲ πάντως τὴν μητέρα τῆς περιστερᾶς ἐκ τοῦ καρποῦ τὸ
δένδρον γνωρίσαντες· ὡς γὰρ ἄνθρωπον θεασάμενοι ἐξ ἀνθρώπου αὐτὸν
εἶναι οὐκ ἀμφιβάλλομεν, οὕτω καὶ τῆς ἐκλεκτῆς περιστερᾶς τὴν μητέρα
ζητοῦντες οὐκ ἄλλην τινὰ ἐκείνην ἢ περιστερὰν ἐννοήσομεν· τῷ γὰρ τέκνῳ
20 πάντως ἡ τοῦ γεγεννηκότος ἐπιθεωρεῖται φύσις. ἐπεὶ οὖν τὸ γεγεννημένον
ἐκ τοῦ πνεύματος πνεῦμά ἐστι, περιστερὰ δὲ τὸ τέκνον, περιστερὰ πάντως
καὶ ἡ τοῦ τέκνου μήτηρ ἐστίν, ἡ ἐπὶ τὸν Ἰορδάνην ἐξ οὐρανῶν καταπτᾶσα,
καθὼς Ἰωάννης μαρτύρεται.

ταύτην μακαρίζουσι νεάνιδες, ταύτην αἰνοῦσι παλλακαὶ καὶ βασίλισσαι·
κοινὸς γὰρ ἐκ παντὸς τάγματος πρόκειται πάσαις ταῖς ψυχαῖς δρόμος πρὸς τὴν
25 τοιαύτην μακαριότητα. διὸ φησιν· Εἴδοσαν αὐτὴν θυγατέρες καὶ μακαριοῦσιν
αὐτήν· βασίλισσαι καὶ παλλακαὶ αἰνέσουσιν αὐτήν. φύσις δὲ πᾶσίν ἐστι
πρὸς τὸ μακάριόν τε καὶ ἐπαινούμενον τῇ ἐπιθυμίᾳ συντείνεσθαι. ὥστε εἰ
μακαρίζουσι τὴν περιστερὰν αἱ θυγατέρες, ἐπιθυμοῦσι | πάντως γενέσθαι   469
περιστεραὶ καὶ αὐταί. καὶ τὸ αἰνεῖσθαι τὴν περιστερὰν παρὰ τῶν παλλακῶν
30 τε καὶ βασιλίδων τεκμήριόν ἐστι τοῦ καὶ ταύτας πρὸς τὸ ἐπαινούμενον τὴν
σπουδὴν ἔχειν, ἕως ἂν πάντων ἓν γενομένων τῶν πρὸς τὸν αὐτὸν σκοπὸν
τῆς ἐπιθυμίας βλεπόντων, μηδεμιᾶς ἐν μηδενὶ κακίας ὑπολειφθείσης, γένηται

this unity together is glory, and no one who looks into the matter will deny that "glory" means the Holy Spirit, if account is taken of the Lord's words; he says, after all, "The glory that you have given me, I have given to them." For the one who truly gave the disciples glory of this order was the one who said to them, "Receive the Holy Spirit." He who invested himself with humanity[39] received this glory before the cosmos existed, and when that humanity had been glorified by the Spirit, the further gift of the Spirit's glory was passed on to the entire heredity [of that humanity], beginning with the disciples. That is why he said, "The glory that you have given me, I have given to them, so that they may be one, even as we are one: I in them and you in me, that they may become perfectly one." Therefore the person who has left immaturity behind, and by growing attained to mature manhood, and achieved the measure of the intelligible stature, who from being a slave and a concubine has come to share the status of kingship and | by impassibility and purity has become a recipient of the Spirit's glory—this is that perfect dove upon whom the Bridegroom looks as he says: *One is my dove, my perfect one, one is she for her mother, the chosen of the one who bore her.*

Nor are we unacquainted with the dove's mother, recognizing as we do the tree from its fruit. For just as we are in no doubt whatever that a human person upon whom we gaze derives from another human person, so too, if we are inquiring after the mother of the chosen dove, we shall not think of her as anything other than a dove; for the nature of the one who begets it is always discerned in the child. Since, then, "that which is born of the Spirit is spirit" and the child is a dove, the child's mother must surely be a dove as well—the dove that flew down from heaven upon Jordan, as John bears witness.

Her the young maidens bless, her the concubines and the queens praise, for the course that leads to such blessedness is the same for all souls, no matter what status they start from. That is why it says: *The daughters saw her, and they bless her. The queens and concubines praise her.* For it is the nature common to all of them to press forward in desire toward that which is blessed and worthy of praise. So if the daughters | pronounce the dove blessed, they too are desiring to become doves; and if the concubines and queens praise the dove, this is a token that they too are eager for that which is worthy of praise—until that time when, since all have become one in desiring the same goal and there is no vice left in any, God may become all in all persons, in

---

39. Greek: τὴν ἀνθρωπίνην φύσιν, literally "the human nature." Of course Gregory means "human nature," but he means it collectively as well as abstractly.

ὁ θεὸς τὰ πάντα ἐν πᾶσι, τοῖς διὰ τῆς ἑνότητος ἀλλήλοις ἐν τῇ τοῦ ἀγαθοῦ κοινωνίᾳ συγκεκραμένοις ἐν Χριστῷ Ἰησοῦ τῷ κυρίῳ ἡμῶν,

ᾧ ἡ δόξα καὶ τὸ κράτος εἰς τοὺς αἰῶνας τῶν αἰώνων.

ἀμήν.

those who by their oneness are blended together with one another in the fellowship of the Good in our Lord Jesus Christ,

To whom be glory and power to the ages of ages.
Amen.

BIBLIOGRAPHY

Alexandre, M. 1971. "La théorie de l'exégèse dans le *De hominis opificio* et l'*In Hexaemeron*." Pages 87–111 in Harl 1971.

Amand, D. 1945. *Fatalisme et liberté dans l'antiquité grecque*. Recueil de travaux d'histoire et de philologie 3.19. Louvain: Bibliothèque de l'Université.

Aubineau, Michel, ed. and trans. 1966. Gregory of Nyssa, *Traité de la virginité*. SC 119. Paris: Cerf.

Baehrens, W. A., ed. 1925. Origen, *Homilien zu Samuel I, zum Hohelied und zu den Propheten*. GCS 33. Leipzig: Hinrichs.

Cahill, J. B. 1981. "The Date and Setting of Gregory of Nyssa's Commentary on the Song of Songs." *JTS* 32:447–60.

Colson, F. H., and G. H. Whitaker, trans. 1932. Philo, *On the Confusion of Tongues. On the Migration of Abraham. Who Is the Heir of Divine Things? On Mating with the Preliminary Studies*. LCL. Cambridge: Harvard University Press.

Coulter, James A. 1976. *The Literary Microcosm*. Columbia Studies in the Classical Tradition 2. Leiden: Brill.

Dalsgaard Larsen, Bent. 1972. *Jamblique de Chalcis: Exétète et philosophe, Thèse*. 2 vols. Aarhus: Universitetsforlaget i Aarhus.

Daniélou, Jean. 1954. *Platonisme et théologie mystique: Essai sur la doctrine spirituelle de saint Grégoire de Nysse*. 2nd ed. Paris: Aubier.

———. 1956. "Le mariage de Grégoire de Nysse et la chronologie de sa vie." *REAug* 2 (1956): 71–78.

———. 1966. "La chronologie des oeuvres de Grégoire de Nysse." Pages 156–69 in vol. 1 of *Papers Presented to the Fourth International Conference on Patristic Studies Held at Christ Church, Oxford, 1963*. Edited by F. L. Cross. 3 vols. StPatr 7–9. TU 92–94. Berlin: Akademie-Verlag.

———. 1970. *L' être et le temps chez Grégoire de Nysse*. Leiden: Brill.

Dörries, Hermann. 1963. "Griechentum und Christentum bei Gregor von Nyssa: Zu H. Langerbecks Edition des Hohelied-Kommentar in der Leidener Gregor-Ausgabe." *TLZ* 88:569–82.

Dünzl, Franz. 1994a. "Formen der Kirchenväter Rezeption am Beispiel der physischen Erlösung bei Gregor von Nyssa." *TP* 69:161–81.

————, ed. and trans. 1994b. Gregory of Nyssa, *Homilien zum Hohenlied*. 3 vols. Freiburg: Herder.

Graef, Hilda C., trans. 1954. Gregory of Nyssa, *The Lord's Prayer. The Beatitudes*. ACW 18. Westminster, Md.: Newman.

Harl, Marguerite, ed. 1971. *Écriture et culture philosophique dans la pensée de Grégoire de Nysse: Actes du colloque de Chevetogne (22–26 septembre 1969), Organisé par le Centre de recherche sur l'Hellénisme tardif de la Sorbonne*. Leiden: Brill.

Heine, Ronald E. 1984. "Gregory of Nyssa's Apology for Allegory." *VC* 38:360–70.

————, ed. and trans. 1995. *Gregory of Nyssa's Treatise on the Inscriptions of the Psalms*. Oxford: Clarendon.

Hennecke, Edgar, and Wilhelm Schneemelcher, eds. 1963–65. *New Testament Apocrypha*. Translated by A. J. B. Higgins et al. Edited by R. McL. Wilson. 2 vols. Philadelphia: Westminster.

Hill, Robert. C., trans. 2006. *Theodore of Mopsuestia: Commentary on Psalms 1–81*. SBLWGRW 5. Atlanta: Society of Biblical Literature.

Kelly, J. N. D. 1994. *Golden Mouth: The Story of John Chrysostom*. London: Duckworth.

Langerbeck, Hermann, ed. 1960. Gregory of Nyssa, *In Canticum canticorum*. GNO 6. Leiden: Brill.

Lattimore, Richmond, trans. 1962. Homer, *The Iliad*. Chicago: University of Chicago Press.

Lawson, R. P., trans. 1956. Origen, *The Song of Songs: Commentary and Homilies*. ACW 26. New York: Newman.

Malherbe, Abraham J., and Everett Ferguson, trans. 1978. Gregory of Nyssa, *The Life of Moses*. CWS. New York: Paulist.

Malingrey, Anne-Marie, ed and trans. 1968. Jean Chrysostome, *Lettres à Olympias*. 2nd ed. SC 13 bis. Paris: Cerf.

May, Gerhard. 1966. "Gregor von Nyssa in der Kirchenpolitik seiner Zeit." *Jahrbuch der Österreichischen Byzantinischen Gesellschaft* 15:105–32.

————. 1971: "Die Chronologie des Lebens und der Werke des Gregor von Nyssa." Pages 51–67 in Harl 1971.

Mühlenberg, Ekkehard. 1966. *Die Unendlichkeit Gottes bei Gregor von Nyssa: Gregors Kritik am Gottesbegriff der klassischen Metaphysik*. Göttingen: Vandenhoek & Ruprecht.

Musurillo, Herbert, trans. 1958. Methodius, *The Symposium. A Treatise on Chastity*. ACW 27. Westminster, Md.: Newman.

Norris, Richard A. 2002. " 'Two Trees in the Midst of the Garden': Gregory of Nyssa and the Puzzle of Human Evil." Pages 218–41 in *In Dominico elo-*

quio = *In Lordly Eloquence: Essays on Patristic Exegesis in Honor of Robert Louis Wilken*. Edited by Paul M. Blowers. Grand Rapids: Eerdmans.

Rondeau, Marie-Josèphe. 1974. "D'ou vient la technique exégétique utilisée par Grégoire de Nysse dans son traité 'Sur les titres des Psaumes'?" Pages 263–87 in *Mélanges d'histoire des religions offerts à Henri-Charles Puech*. Paris: Presses Universitaires de France.

Wagner, M. Monica, trans. 1950. Basil, *Ascetical Works*. FC 9. New York: Fathers of the Church.

Young, Frances M. 1997. *Biblical Exegesis and the Formation of Christian Culture*. Cambridge: Cambridge University Press.

INDEX OF BIBLICAL REFERENCES

OLD TESTAMENT

Genesis
1	xxxiii, xxxviii, xliv, xlv, xlvi, li
1:6	405
1:26	475
1:26–27	xxviii, 287, 487
1:31	9, 61, 269, 367
2:2	477
2:6	339
2:9	xlviii, 369
2:16–17	219
2:17	9
3:19	347
3:21	67, 347, 367, 371, 385
4:2	481
4:22	481
8:20	281
9:20	481
10:9	481
15:5	313
24:2–9	143
24:9	145
24:65	381
25:13	53
25:27	461
27:27	145
29:2–10	485
32:28	313

Exodus
2:11–12	375
3:1	375
3:2	375
3:4–6	375
3:5	349, 375
7:1	229
7:12	375
12:8	323
13:21	375
14	81
14:20	345
14:21	375
14:25	83
14:25–31	81
14:28	375
15:25	375
16:14–15	375
17:6	375
19:9	li
19:10	27
19:10–11	79
19:14	27
19:15	27
19:16	29, 375
19:18	375
19:19	29, 375
19:20	375
20:21	xxvi, li, liv, 193, 341
21:23	237
24:7	375
24:12	437
24:16–18	375
25–26	47

Exodus (cont.)

27	47
28:5	349
28:8	349
28:15	349
30:23	301
30:37	281
32:20	221
33:12	377
33:13	377
33:13–22	373
33:20	119
33:21–23	liv, 377
33:22	373
34:5	li
34:29–35	375
37:4	441
37–38	441

Leviticus

4:18	281
19:18	25

Numbers

9:11–12	xlvii, 205
12:8	33
17:1–11	207

Deuteronomy

6:5	25
19:15	7, 227
32:8	177
32:9	367
32:11	475
32:39	383
34:10	377

Joshua

4	207
5:2	207
5:2–9	207

Judges

13:18	379

1 Samuel/1 Kingdoms

9:9	417
9:11	229

2 Samuel/2 Kingdoms

1:9	233
11	7

1 Kings/3 Kingdoms

3:1	xxiv
3:4	17
10:1–13	217
11:1	xxiv
11:5	17
17:1	233

2 Kings/4 Kingdoms

2:11	311
2:12	83
12:3	xxxii

2 Chronicles

26:19	387
26:21	387
26:23	387

Job

40:18	177
41:7	177
42:14	303

Psalms

1	xxxii, xxxiv
1:1	133
1:3	169, 419
6:2	133
8:2	379
8:10	379

9:30	177	67:18	83, 249
9:30–31	265	67:23	11
15:2	131	67:30	11
16:2	477	67:34	163
16:3	477	68:15	425
16:8	475	72:1	281
17:2	xxvi, 193	73:17	159
17:2–3	145, 379	77:20	387
17:3	379	77:25	375
18:6	335	77:49	447
20:4	225	78:1	65
22:1	69	79:4	463, 465
22:5–6	383	79:14	129, 179, 289
23:7	343	79:14–20	465
23:8	179	83:2–3	449
23:9	343	83:6	259
28:5–6	11, 221, 449	83:6–8	297
31:9	87	83:8	191, 259
31:19	289	85:15	379
32:9	163	86:1	215
33:8	249, 385	86:3	53
33:9	261	86:5a LXX	53
35:7	489	88:21	385
35:9	325	88:22–24	385
39:3	351	89:17	469
44:4–5	471	90:4	475
45:2	379	90:13	155
45:3	155	91:9	259
45:4	155	91:13, 14	449
47:8	435	91:16	45
47:9	153	92:1	351
49:9	283	100:8	367
49:13	283	102:11	311
50:19	283	102:20–21	473
51:3–4	177	102:21	145, 473
51:8	289	103:15	37, 107, 151, 465
53:8	173	103:16–17	123
62:2	201	103:20	129
62:12	395, 397	103:20–21	209
67:16	11	103:24	215
67:17	11	113:16	159, 265

Psalms (*cont.*)		6:8	283, 285
114:3	383	6:22	23
115:2	325	8:17	23, 41
118:72	249	8:20	21
118:103	131	8:21	43
118:108	173	9:1	441
118:131	35	9:2	465
119:4	177	9:2–5	169
120:4–8	383	10:14	277, 479
120:6	57	10:20	97
120:8	373	16:24	451
123:7	123	23:13–14	381
126:1	383	23:21	349
127:3	179, 289	27:6	399
131:3–5	397	27:15	123
131:7	463	27:16	315
131:11	143	30:17	413
140:3	483		
144:16	319	Ecclesiastes	
145:3	259	1:2	145
145:5	259	10:18	123
146:4	407	11:8	23
146:6	321		
147:7	161, 319	Song of Songs	
		1:1	29
Proverbs		1:1–4	**15–45**
1:6	3	1:2	xlix, li, 25, 43
1:8	19	1:2–3	279
1:9	19, 93	1:5–8	**47–77**, 341
2:5	37	1:7	1
2:9	133	1:8	1
3:4	125	1:9	xlviii, 85
3:10	133	1:9–14	**79–109**
3:16	21, 141, 143	1:10–11	343
3:18	21	1:11	xxvi
3:19	21	1:14	445
4:6	23	1:15–2:7	**111–47**
4:6–9	23	1:16	57, 103, 121
5:3–4	371	2:3	li, 321, 449
5:15	309	2:7	395
5:17–18	291	2:8	397, 449

2:8–9	liii	Isaiah	
2:8–17	**149–81**	1:8	65, 67
2:9	157, 229	1:21	67
2:10	169	5:14	177
2:11–13	liii	6:1	447
3:1–4	xxiv, xxxvii	6:1–7	387
3:1–8	**183–211**	6:2	473
3:5	395	6:4	389
3:7	xlvii	8:3	5
3:9	219	10:13	177
3:9–4:7a	**213–55**	10:14	177
4:1–3	457	10:34	449, 451
4:1–4	479	11:1	11, 167, 449
4:3	457	11:6–8	451
4:5	249, 251	14:13–14	177, 447
4:6	251	40:4	45
4:8–9	**257–75**	40:9–12	425
4:10–15	**277–309**	49:2	141, 389
4:13	293	49:22	57
4:14b–15	305	53:9	413
4:15	319	55:13	289
4:16–5:2a	**311–31**	58:9	321
5:1	323	60:4	57
5:2	l, li, 333	63:2	133
5:2b–4	**333–59**	65:17	405
5:3	xxxvi	66:2	355
5:5	341	66:7	411
5:5–7	333, **361–89**	66:20	57, 59
5:7	385		
5:8–12	**391–421**	Jeremiah	
5:9	xlix, 391, 463	2:13	307, 419
5:10	409	4:19	439
5:11	393, 413	5:8	87
5:13	423, 465	31:33	441
5:13–16	405, **423–55**		
5:14	435	Lamentations	
5:15	445	1:1	67
6:1–9	**457–99**	4:1	67
6:7	457, 483		
6:8–9	69	Ezekiel	
6:9	459	1:16	435

Ezekiel (cont.)

3:3	439
3:17	229, 417
10:1	473
33:7	417

Daniel

12:42	xxxix

Hosea

1:2	5
11:10	43
13:7–8	281

Amos

6:4–7	307
7:12	229, 417

Jonah

1:3	435

Micah

4:1	11
4:4	289

Habakkuk

2:2	439
3:2	371
3:2c	371
3:3	39, 101
3:8	83, 93

Zechariah

1:8	83
1:10	83
2:5	483
2:7 lxx (2:3 Eng.)	483
5:1–2	391
6:12	315
9:17	323, 393

DEUTEROCANONICAL WORKS

Wisdom of Solomon

2:23–24	367
7:26	271

Susanna

42	xxxix

NEW TESTAMENT

Matthew

1:2–17	407
3:9	161
3:9–12	11
4:19	179
5:8	xxix, 209, 259
5:14	249, 407
5:16	125, 407
5:17	391
5:21–26	391
5:27–32	391
5:33–37	393
5:35	469, 471
5:37	393
6:9–10	321
6:21	105
6:24	209
7:14	373
7:16	251
7:24	173
7:25	121
8:9	313, 315
8:10	313
9:5–6	161
9:13	53
10:3	415
10:5	349
10:9	349
10:10	347
10:14	5
11:28	453

11:29	139	5:9	447
12:12	175	6:9	347
12:50	129	9:2–3	15
13:3–23	57	12:10	9
13:24	395	12:30	193
13:38	395	13:18	317
13:43	407	14:8	103
15:11	9	14:9	103
16:5–12	7		
16:13–15	31	Luke	
16:17	33	1:2	43
16:18–20	373	1:28	411
17:20	155	1:79	217, 463
22:10–13	15	2:13–14	469
22:27–39	25	2:14	447
22:30	147	2:29–30	177
22:40	443	3:8	161
23:37	475	3:8–9	11
24:20	317	5:32	53
24:28	9	6:45	105
24:32	9	6:48	173
24:35	355	7:8	313, 315
24:41	9	7:45	35
24:45	365	8:5–15	57
24:45–51	313	8:15	251
24:48–49	367	8:23–24	315
25:32–33	73	8:30	447
25:34–46	281	9:3	347
25:35	325	10:19	157
25:35–36	491	10:20	407
26:12	103	10:29	453
26:13	103	10:30	453, 465
26:26	325	11:7	211
26:53	447	12:34	105
27:37	215	12:35	335
27:48	323	12:36	335
		12:37	337
Mark		12:42	365
2:21	349	12:42–48	313
3:35	279, 289, 295, 327, 343	12:43	337
4:39	165	12:45	367

Luke (cont.)

12:49	311
15:4–7	383
15:8–10	383
16:13	209
17:34	9
23:38	215

John

1:1	97, 405, 407
1:3	61, 355
1:14	49, 119, 401
1:18	269, 471
1:23	451
1:29	253, 459
1:43	459
1:45	461
1:46	461, 463
2:19	9
3:5	411
3:8	251
3:14	7
3:29	27, 335
4:10	309
4:14	69
4:32	7
4:34	321
5:22	217
5:24	33
5:30	217
5:39	485
6:33	319
6:50–51	7
6:51–52	131
6:63	33
6:68	35, 177
7:37	35, 261
7:37–38	7, 309
7:38	439
8:18	7
8:42	309

8:44	177
10:9	9, 375
10:10	383
12:3	103
12:24	365
14:2	487
14:6	9, 375, 443
14:23	141
15:5	453
19:34	69
19:39	307
21:9–14	323

Acts

1:15	317
2:2	317
2:2–4	435
2:3	311
2:4	317
2:24	411
7:44	47
9:15	97, 247, 427, 447
10:10–16	327
20:22	367
20:24	367
26:24–25	325

Romans

1:3	17
1:20	405
1:25	55
1:30	61
2:15	441, 455
2:29	241
5:6–8	53
5:8	399
6	263, 363
6:4	263, 363
6:5	305
7	315
7:7–8	25

7:14	5, 175, 239	7:9	299
7:22	423	7:32	145
7:23	33, 63, 315, 423	8:2	339, 345, 373
8:6–7	33	8:6	61
8:7	205, 315	9:9–10	5, 237
8:13	117	10:4	173
8:15	129	10:6	283
8:23	43	10:11	5, 243, 283
8:29	411	11:1	51, 223
8:38	473	11:15	231, 479
9:3	471	11:29	327
9:22	447	12:3	117
9:33	173	12:7–11	223
11:1	325	12:12	449
11:16	413	12:12–26	227
11:33	293	12:12–27	403
11:36	319, 323	12:14–28	223
12:3–8	223	12:21	415, 431
12:6	35	12:28	223
12:11	299	13:9	343, 345, 355
13:1	473	13:12	xlvi, 3, 5, 157, 343
13:14	347	14:2	293
		14:40	125, 133, 135, 473
		15:24	447
1 Corinthians		15:28	407
1:5	485	15:31	323
1:9	433	15:53	287
1:24	145		
2:6	423	2 Corinthians	
2:6–8	285	1:9	323
2:9	259, 355	2:14–15	323
2:10	43, 293	2:15	101, 283, 319, 427
3:1–2	279	2:15–16	103
3:6	307	3:3	441
3:8	13	3:6	5
3:10–15	219	3:15	67
3:11	443	3:15–16	283
3:12	137, 219	3:16	5, 173, 363
3:18	267	3:16–17	381
6:11	39	3:18	xxviii, 199
6:15	121	4:2	427
6:17	25, 27, 33		

2 Corinthians (*cont.*)

4:6	463
4:10	367
4:18	xxv, 437
5:13	325
5:19	431
6:9	367
6:10	367
6:14	315
6:16	77
8:9	471
8:21	125
11:2	25, 121, 279
12:1–4	257
12:2	xxiv
12:2–4	43, 345
12:3	xxv
12:3–6	95
12:4	xxv
12:9	285
12:10	367
13:3	219, 247, 451

Galatians

1:16	427
2:7	57
2:9	223
2:20	219
3:27	xxxv, 15, 295
4:4	107
4:12	51, 223
4:20	5
4:21–31	5
4:22	237
4:22–24	xlix
4:24	5, 237
4:26	61, 219, 397, 471
5:6	399
5:22	287
5:25	117
6:14	429, 431

6:17	385

Ephesians

1:9	119
1:21	447
2:2	53
2:8	253
2:14	179
2:14–15	215
2:16	215
2:17	215
2:20	215
2:22	215
3:6	295
3:10	473
3:10–11	269
3:16	423
4:3	215
4:3–4	495
4:11–13	403
4:12	223
4:13	269, 489
4:14	41
4:15–16	245, 403
4:24	347
5:25	135
5:28	135
5:30–31	295
5:31	287
5:32	121
6:12	177, 447
6:14–15	315

Philippians

1:21	467
2:5–7	139
2:6	97
2:6–7	403
2:7	7, 39, 119, 471
2:8	139
2:15	407

3:5	325	3:15	441, 443
3:10	305	3:16	11, 403
3:13	43, 187, 259, 307, 345, 373, 385	4:13	xxxii, 9
		6:15	447
3:13–14	xxxiv	6:16	269
3:14	133		
3:21	305	**2 Timothy**	
4:7	33	2:21	221
4:8	467, 469	3:16	xxxii, 3

Colossians | | **Hebrews** | |
1:13	53, 225	1:1	153, 177
1:15	411	1:2	liii, 153
1:16	215, 473	1:3	95
1:18	411	1:4	179
2:5	405	1:14	27, 97, 383
2:9	413	2:9	307
2:14	215	2:14	177, 253
3:1–4	277	4:12	221
3:5	363	4:15	129, 413
3:9	15, 347	5:14	423
3:9–10	xxxv	6:7	405
3:10	407	6:16	395
		6:17	395

1 Thessalonians | | 7:14 | 463 |
2:7	253, 423	10:1	283
4:12	125	10:4	453
5:5	251, 305	11:24	375
		11:25	375

Titus | | 11:37–38 | 481 |
3:1	473		
3:5	53, 221	**1 Peter**	
		2:2	423
1 Timothy		2:3	261
1:13	53, 415	2:5	215
1:15	53	2:22	413, 431
1:19	445		
2:3–4	lii	**1 John**	
2:4	xxxvi, 17, 143, 227, 321	1:1	37, 405
2:9–10	231	3:2	xxviii, xxix
3:1	239	4:8	133, 141

1 John (*cont.*)
    4:16   133, 141
    4:18   495

Revelation
    3:12   223
    19:11–21   83

INDEX OF MODERN AUTHORS

Alexandre, M. xxxviii, xlviii, 501

Amand, D. 55, 501

Aubineau, M. xvi, 501

Baehrens, W. A. 11, 19, 25, 29, 35, 37, 39, 41, 43, 45, 49, 51, 53, 55, 57, 61, 63, 65, 67, 69, 71, 73, 83, 85, 89, 95, 99, 103, 105, 107, 117, 119, 121, 123, 125, 127, 133, 135, 137, 145, 153, 155, 157, 161, 163, 179, 501

Cahill, J. B. xx, xxi, xxiii, 501

Colson, F. H. 345, 501

Coulter, J. A. xxxn

Dalsgaard Larsen, B. xxx, 502

Daniélou, J. xv–xvii, xix, xx–xxi, xxxviii, 3, 15, 17, 21, 121, 271, 339, 343, 349, 363, 429, 501

Dörries, H. xxii, 501

Dünzl, F. xxii, 371, 373, 427, 461, 473, 479, 483, 501

Ferguson, E. xxvii, xxxiv, 113, 233, 299, 339, 401, 502

Graef, H. C. 101, 155, 365, 371, 502

Harl, M. 501–2

Heine, R. E. xvii, xxx, xxxi, xxxii, xlviii, 493, 502

Hennecke, E. 429, 502

Hill, R. C. xxxii, 502

Jaeger, W. vii, x, xix, xxii, *passim*

Kelly, J. N. D. xx, 502

Langerbeck, H. vii, xxii, 143, 201, 243, 249, 271, 305, 315, 391, 409, 461, 473, 475, 483, 501–2

Lattimore, R. 201, 502

Lawson, R. P. 11, 25, 29, 35, 37, 39, 41, 43, 45, 49, 57, 83, 85, 89, 95, 99, 103, 105, 117, 123, 127, 133, 135, 137, 145, 153, 155, 157, 163, 179, 399, 502

Malherbe, A. J. xxvii, xxxiv, 113, 233, 299, 339, 401, 502

Malingrey, A.-M. xx, 502

May, G. xv–xvi, xvii, xviii–xix, 502

Mühlenberg, E. xxvii, 502

Musurillo, H. 57, 107, 269, 271, 291, 319, 321, 361, 502

Norris, R. A. vii–viii, 369, 502

Rondeau, M.-J. xxx, 503

Schneemelcher, W. 429, 502

Wagner, M. M. 17, 503

Whitaker, G. H. 345, 501

Young, F. M. xxx, 503

INDEX OF MODERN AUTHORS

Alexandre, M. xxxviii, xlviii, 501

Amand, D. 55, 501

Aubineau, M. xvi, 501

Baehrens, W. A. 11, 19, 25, 29, 35, 37, 39, 41, 43, 45, 49, 51, 53, 55, 57, 61, 63, 65, 67, 69, 71, 73, 83, 85, 89, 95, 99, 103, 105, 107, 117, 119, 121, 123, 125, 127, 133, 135, 137, 145, 153, 155, 157, 161, 163, 179, 501

Cahill, J. B. xx, xxi, xxiii, 501

Colson, F. H. 345, 501

Coulter, J. A. xxx

Dalsgaard Larsen, B. xxx, 502

Daniélou, J. xv–xvii, xix–xxi, xxxviii, 3, 15, 17, 21, 121, 271, 339, 343, 349, 363, 429, 501

Dörries, H. xxii, 501

Dünzl, F. xxii, 371, 373, 427, 461, 473, 479, 483, 501

Ferguson, E. xxvii, xxxiv, 113, 233, 299, 339, 401, 502

Graef, H. C. 101, 155, 365, 371, 502

Harl, M. 501–2

Heine, R. E. xvii, xxx–xxxii, xlviii, 493, 502

Hennecke, E. 429, 502

Hill, R. C. xxxii, 502

Jaeger, W. vii, x, xix, xxii, *passim*

Kelly, J. N. D. xx, 502

Langerbeck, H. vii, xxii, 143, 201, 243, 249, 271, 305, 315, 391, 409, 461, 473, 475, 483, 501–2

Lattimore, R. 201, 502

Lawson, R. P. 11, 25, 29, 35, 37, 39, 41, 43, 45, 49, 57, 83, 85, 89, 95, 99, 103, 105, 117, 123, 127, 133, 135, 137, 145, 153, 155, 157, 163, 179, 399, 502

Malherbe, A. J. xxvii, xxxiv, 113, 233, 299, 339, 401, 502

Malingrey, A.-M. xx, 502

May, G. xv–xix, 502

Mühlenberg, E. xxvii, 502

Musurillo, H. 57, 107, 269, 271, 291, 319, 321, 361, 502

Norris, R. A. vii–viii, 369, 502

Rondeau, M.-J. xxx, 503

Schneemelcher, W. 429, 502

Wagner, M. M. 17, 503

Whitaker, G. H. 345, 501

Young, F. M. xxx, 503

CPSIA information can be obtained at www.ICGtesting.com
Printed in the USA
LVOW081951200613

339468LV00005B/356/P